RICH DEMOCRACIES

RICH DEMOCRACIES

Political Economy, Public Policy, and Performance

HAROLD L. WILENSKY

UNIVERSITY OF CALIFORNIA PRESS

Berkeley   Los Angeles   London

University of California Press
Berkeley and Los Angeles, California

University of California Press, Ltd.
London, England

© 2002 by the Regents of the University of California

Library of Congress Cataloging-in-Publication Data

Wilensky, Harold L.
    Rich Democracies : political economy, public policy, and
performance / Harold L. Wilensky.
        p.   cm.
    Includes bibliographical references and index.
    ISBN 0-520-23176-7(cloth : alk. paper).—ISBN 0-520-
23279-8 (pbk. : alk. paper)
    1. Welfare state—Case studies.   2. Comparative govern-
ment.   I. Title.
ClassifNumber   PubDate

JC479 .W55 2002
320.3—dc21   2001053048

Manufactured in the United States of America
10   09   08   07   06   05   04   03   02
10   9   8   7   6   5   4   3   2   1

For Mary

CONTENTS

Contents

FIGURES

TABLES

Tables

Tables

PREFACE AND ACKNOWLEDGMENTS

One should really never say "the state does this or that." It is always important to recognize who or whose interest it is that sets the machine of the state in motion and speaks through it.

Joseph Schumpeter (1918)

This book is about consensus and conflict, a central theoretical issue in the social sciences and a problem of mounting importance in all modern democracies. It deals with what governments do to bring together diverse interests and accommodate clashing values—the Madisonian problem of containing factional war, the Durkheimian problem of overcoming threats to social integration. Plainly the 19 rich democracies discussed here, as they cope with the problems of aggregating interests and resolving conflict, differ greatly in their labor relations and in the interplay of politics, markets, and the nonprofit sector. They differ in the shape of their welfare states, in their patterns of taxing and spending, in the clusters of public policies they pursue and their effectiveness in implementing policies. Most important, they differ greatly in system outputs—what all the taxing and spending, all the policy choices mean for the well-being of their people. Yet, despite the obvious differences among rich democracies in social structure, culture, politics, and policy, despite their separate paths of development in the 20th century, there are several areas of convergence.

My aim is to specify these differences and similarities and explore diverse national responses to common social and economic problems. I attempt to synthesize three complementary theories I have found useful in explaining convergence and divergence among the currently rich democracies. My strategy is to play convergence theory (modernization theory, theories of advanced industrialism)—the idea that as rich democracies became richer they became more alike in social structure, culture, and politics—against a theory of democratic corporatism and a theory of mass society, useful in explaining persistent differences. Part I, "Paths of Development of Rich Democracies," covers this ground and adds a critique of "postindustrialism," a perspective I find of limited use. Evidence for and against convergence theory is examined in chapter 1, which emphasizes nine areas: changes in family structure and function and associated political demands; the push for equality among minority groups; the rise of mass higher education; the increasing dominance of the media of mass communication and entertainment; the roles and influence of experts and intellectuals; the changing organization, schedules, and hours of work; changes in social stratification and mobility; the growth of the welfare state; and changes in political systems. These are what make modern society modern.

The second theory (chap. 2) specifies types of political economy—democratic corporatism, corporatism-without-labor, and decentralized and fragmented systems. Here the emphasis is on the structure and interaction of government, electoral systems, political parties, and major interest groups (especially labor, employers, professions, churches, farmers) and what they do to promote or diminish consensus. I generate these types by combining the cumulative power of mass-based parties, mainly left and Catholic, historically of great significance, with national bargaining arrangements. The scheme is spelled out in figure 2.1, with a list of policies and real welfare outputs it predicts.

The third theory, "mass society," is the inverse of theories of democratic corporatism. Instead of structures conducive to consensus, this theory accents the breakdown or erosion of these structures as threats to democracy, or social order, or both. From Tocqueville to Karl Mannheim (1940), Franz Neumann (1942), Hannah Arendt (1951), and other refugees from the Nazis, these scholars tackled two problems. The first is the debilitation of culture-bearing elites (and the core values they sustain)—lawyers who subvert the law, professors and media managers without standards, politicians with no constraint in their campaigns, business executives busy feathering their own nests. The second problem is the atrophy of such primary groups as the family and neighborhood, and the erosion of such self-governing associations as unions and churches, which result in the rising power of the mass media and the proliferation of political demagogues and extremist movements. From the 1960s to the 1980s theories of the mass society went out of fashion. In the past couple of decades, however, they have been revived in political science and sociology under different labels—party decomposition, the erosion of civil society or civic engagement, the proliferation of protest movements, overloaded government, crises of legitimacy, and of course, discussion of the impact of the mass media and the cult of celebrity in politics and culture. Chapter 3 covers this ground, assessing evidence on social participation rates and trends and the organization and effects of the media. Throughout the book, I show that the half-dozen most-fragmented and decentralized political economies are most vulnerable to mass-society tendencies but that the theory cannot be generalized; it applies least well to other types of political economy.

Because the welfare state is at the center of conflict about the proper role and size of government, the five chapters of Part II ("The Welfare State and Social Policy") explain the patterns of taxing and spending and social policies comprising the welfare state. It specifies the ways in which the rich democracies converge and analyzes the structural and ideological sources of differences among them. It shows how industrialization and its demographic and organizational correlates explain the universal increase and some convergence in the level of taxing and spending. It also shows that the types of political economy developed in chapter 2 account for remaining national differences in the current level of spending, sector-spending emphasis, tax structures, the size and efficiency of bureaucracies that deliver cash and services, and specific social policies (e.g., universalistic family policies vs. means-testing and a consequent welfare mess). Chapter 10 on tax-welfare backlash discusses the political effects of all these differences.

Part III ("System Performance") continues to play convergence theory against types of political economy. It is an analysis of system performance. It shows how variation in types of taxes, types of spending, and policy packages shape a large number of outcomes: economic performance, equality, poverty, job security, safety and risk, real health, the environment, the effectiveness and fairness of regulatory regimes, and political legitimacy. Some of these have conventional measures. I have developed my own where they do not. For instance, political legitimacy is measured by the vitality of political parties (chap. 11) and the capacity of government to collect taxes to pay for the demands of modern voters without triggering paralyzing protest (chap. 10). To show national differences in risk and safety I develop a measure of mayhem (chap. 14).

Chapter 17 addresses the objection that my emphasis on the similarities and differences among national institutions as sources of system performance is outdated because of "globalization," that all-purpose cause of all our ills and opportunities. Unpacking the concept, I discuss the flow of capital and labor across national boundaries, the rise of multinational corporations, the alleged deregulation of the labor market, and the role of central banks. I conclude that of these five dimensions of globalization, only the rapidly increasing autonomy and power of central banks is a major threat to labor standards, job security, stable economic performance, and the welfare state.

Any good theory of social change should address five questions. What is changing? How much? How fast? In what direction? What are the engines driving change? What is too often vague or absent in much discussion of change in modern society is answers to the first question: exactly what technologies, social structures, values and beliefs, and patterns of political behavior are changing? Just as sociology has neglected a basic task for students of group life—a taxonomy of types of social groups that is useful for explaining the behavior of groups (Wilensky, 1961b)—so political science needs a more effective mapping of types of interest groups, political parties, nation-states, and bureaucracies that comprise the polity. In the past 15 or 20 years, as they revive an older tradition in political science, students of comparative politics have made progress in tackling this challenging task of explaining *what* is changing; I hope that this book furthers that progress. Throughout I avoid vague discussion of "the state" or "society"; instead I examine the components of these grand abstractions that are relevant for our understanding of similarities or differences among the rich democracies. The entire book is an attempt to specify the institutions—executive, legislative, judicial, military—that comprise the state and the groups and relationships that comprise society. Although I try to answer all five of the social-change questions, my main effort is to delineate major structures that help enhance our understanding of social, economic, and political outcomes—system performance. When I hear about the internal strains within particular countries—"democratic corporatism in Sweden is collapsing," "American democracy is becoming polarized and paralyzed," "the Japanese model is no longer economically viable"—I ask, "system strain, erosion, collapse of what, compared to what, in what specific policy areas?" More often than not this focus leads me to observe much continuity between generations and to greet the word "new" with skepticism. Most of the structures this book delineates are highly institutionalized, that is, publicly recognized and sanctioned in contracts, law, and custom. They persist over successive generations, adapting to changing circumstances but retaining their essential character.

In choosing the 19 countries to be studied I decided on the universe of democracies that have three million or more population (hence some degree of complexity) and are in the upper sixth of countries ranked by per capita GNP in the mid-1960s (very rich). The rich, as they say, are very different from the poor; they have more money. Average income per capita in our rich democracies is about 30 times higher than the average in the poorest countries. The size criterion excludes tiny countries (Iceland, Luxembourg) but includes New Zealand with more than three million. In 1966, Israel and Ireland were the poorest of the 19 rich democracies. It is a common mistake in both the press and social-science research to lump Greece, Portugal, Spain, and Turkey together with these 19 as "OECD countries" and use averages that obscure the great range of development and behavior within the category. In 1990, even after much catch-up, all but Spain were much poorer and had a much larger percentage of the labor force in agriculture than any of the 19 modern affluent democracies. For studying similarities and differences among similarly rich democracies, the 19 are the most appropriate universe. And for analysis of system performance the universe yields much more valid generalizations than any subset. For instance, if you conclude that lavish spending on the welfare state is a drag on postwar economic performance on the basis of a comparison of Italy and Denmark with Japan and Switzerland, you have selected the four deviant cases: for most of the postwar period, Italy and Denmark are big spenders with poor performance, the other two are lean spenders with good performance. The subset thus obscures the central tendency, a positive correlation for all 19 rich democracies before 1974 and a mixed picture thereafter (big spenders after the two oil shocks retained an edge in growth and did no worse in controlling inflation and unemployment.) (See chap. 12.) Similarly, if you explore the impact of public-sector education and health spending per capita on real health outputs in 1980 by comparing Japan, a lean spender with excellent health, and West Germany, an above-average spender with poor health, you would conclude that spending is bad for your health. But these are the two most clearly deviant cases. Bringing all 19 rich democracies to view, we find that the opposite is true (see chap. 16, table 16.4). So the first advantage of the universe is that we know when we encounter an exceptional case and can explore its peculiarities.

A second great advantage of studying the universe of rich democracies is that we can uncover similarities among subgroups that are obscured by two-, three-, or four-country comparisons. In several parts of my analysis, I compare the USA and the UK and note many structural differences that account for some specific difference in policy or performance. Britain, unlike the U.S., has a parliamentary system with party discipline, a more-centralized government, and more influential cabinet ministers and higher civil servants. In chapter 16 on the environment these differences make a difference. Similarly, modest structural differences between Canada and the U.S. help us understand why Canada got national health insurance while the U.S., despite many tries, has failed (chap. 17). But these differences turn out to be less than meets the eye. Comparing all 19 countries and considering a wider range of issues and patterns of behavior, Canada, the USA, and the UK are much closer to one another than to the corporatist democracies of Europe or to the similar systems of Japan and France. In their structures, policies, and performance they are members of a class of the most-fragmented and decentralized political economies.

A third advantage of the 19-country analysis is close to my heart. I have spent half a century trying to overcome my American parochialism. Early in my teaching and research and as a guest abroad I became convinced that only through systematic comparison could I understand the United States. In my courses on modern society, comparative political economy, and comparative public policy I became a missionary for this idea—preaching to students of American government and politics that they cannot talk about American exceptionalism without making the necessary comparisons. The last chapter of this book attempts to summarize what is truly exceptional about the U.S., what it shares with Britain and Britain abroad (Canada, Australia, New Zealand), and what it shares with all or almost all rich democracies. This exercise also provides a guide specifying which successful social and labor policies are transferable across nations despite differences in social structure, culture, and politics, and which are not.

When I compare a big country, the United States, with equally rich little countries, such as the Netherlands or Sweden, and claim that the U.S. can learn something from them, a few of my colleagues complain that the contrast is unfair or irrelevant, that size of population is a major determinant of the structure, culture, and politics and policies of a nation and therefore hardly anything is transferable from a little to a big country. It is true that the U.S. is by far the largest of my 19, but several others are hardly small—Japan, France, Germany, the UK, Italy. More important, I am not impressed with mere numbers of people as a social-science variable. When scholars say big, they usually mean something else— complex (many specialized roles) or oligarchical, or hierarchical, or heterogeneous, or centralized, or decentralized, or hard to govern, and more. I prefer to speak of the structures that interest me, and these are only loosely related to population size. For instance, hierarchy, oligarchy, and ungovernability are often found in small as well as large systems. Many small groups are hierarchical (e.g., a family service agency with four levels of authority) or oligarchic (local unions in the Teamsters or in the building trades have sometimes been tiny tyrannies), and some American cities with less than a million or two are extremely hard to govern. There is also a misleading assumption not only that small is beautiful, but that a decentralized polity like that of the U.S. or Switzerland provides more channels for social and political participation than a centralized polity like that of the Netherlands or France. In cross-national perspective, however, chapter 3 shows that on average the more-centralized political economies have higher rates of social-political participation than the more-fragmented and decentralized democracies. Advocates of devolution further argue that local authority is closer to the people, more responsive, more informed, more efficient, more accountable. In the U.S., a glance at the record of accomplishment of the federal (i.e., central) government in coping with major social problems relative to the record of the states and localities suggests no great advantage for local authority. In fact the three most bungled problems of the U.S.—K–12 school performance (chap. 12), welfare reform (chap.8), criminal justice and policing (chaps. 14 and 18)—are largely under the control of states and local governments. Moreover, a partial list of the most successful large federal government programs of the recent past includes social security and Medicare, the GI bill, the racial integration of the armed forces, mortgage subsidies for homeowners, highway development, student college loans, rural electrification, public housing for the aged, the preservation of natural resources, cleanup of air and water, the control of local vigilantes.

There is no more complex problem in organizational theory than ideas about decentralization (Wilensky, 1967, pp. 58–62). If we go beyond the ideologies of populist right and left about the joys of decentralization and limited central government, we find that all rich democracies have large doses of both. They all have central financing of many programs; they all necessarily rely on regional or communal units for delivery of personal social services such as job training, education, and health care. The great variations are in exactly what is centralized or decentralized in what degree—functions, location, authority, financing, records, intelligence, loyalty—and with what effect on equity, equality, efficiency, service, citizen response, and degrees of corruption. Throughout the book I discuss these matters, emphasizing the differences between the moderately or highly centralized bargaining arrangements of corporatist democracies and the more-decentralized political economies.

I think of small democracies as laboratories for innovative public policies from which other democracies can learn, whatever their size. Examples are the family policies of Sweden and Belgium (chap. 7), the radical neoliberal economic experiment of New Zealand (chap. 11), the work-oriented rehabilitation programs for the handicapped in Sweden (chap. 15), the works councils of Norway, the Netherlands, and Belgium (chaps. 2 and 3). It is not at all obvious that the U.S. can learn more about the possible effects of legalizing marijuana by comparing its own distant past experience with alcohol prohibition than it could learn by comparing the contemporary experience of the Netherlands. In social-political-economic context the distance between the U.S. of the late 1920s and the U.S. of 2000 may be greater than the distance that separates contemporary Americans from the Dutch.

If we wish to argue that the only countries that combine the USA's geographical reach, large population, and social heterogeneity are India, Indonesia, Brazil, and Russia, that is true enough, but the only rich democracy on that list is the USA. If the remaining argument is that the U.S. is uniquely divided by race, religion, ethnicity, and linguistic cleavages, that is not true. Social cleavages based on descent are very powerful in Belgium, the Netherlands, Canada, Switzerland and Israel, and, as chapters 1 and 17 show, most of the other rich democracies, because of immigration patterns of recent decades, are converging in minority/majority conflict. Systematic comparison of the most and least socially heterogeneous democracies at the same level of affluence can tell us much about the management of nativist protest and the fate of minority groups.

The cost of studying the universe of rich democracies, of course, is time, money, and a bundle of headaches to gather comparable data, combine quantitative analysis with interviews, case studies, and comparative historical context, and then report the whole in reasonable space. Throughout my career I have avoided methodological ideologies—the misleading dichotomies of "quantitative" vs. "qualitative" and "positivist" vs. "humanist." They are an excuse for remaining ignorant of relevant research using methods different from your own. In this book the reader will find regression analysis and causal models where relevant, simple cross-tabulations when they tell more, and deviant-case analysis and historical context throughout. (Appendix A on methods explains why I avoided time series and settled for something less complex.)

This project started 30 years ago. From a base in Sweden, I began the fieldwork in 1970. Over the next three decades I assembled a database bearing on the three theories above. I completed interviews with over 400 politicians, government health and welfare officials, experts in budgeting and taxation, and labor and employer negotiators in 15 of the 19 countries, and met informants from the other four as I participated in international conferences. I used these interviews to make sense of the quantitative results. They were an irreplaceable part of my education.[1] I remain both amazed and deeply grateful for the hospitality and openness of the busy people who agreed to straighten me out about how things

---

1. I took extensive notes during and after each interview. When these were transcribed, I coded each part by the categories of the project to produce a file by subject matter to add to the name file. I used the same procedure for abstracts of articles, books, conferences, and the like. Thus when

work in their country—sometimes for many hours and repeated encounters. I hope that their briefings prevented too many foolish remarks about their countries in these pages. While I was in the field I also gathered documents covering the period 1950–90, with some historical data going further back and some analysis extending to the late 1990s. The project was near completion in late 1991 when my home was burned down in the Berkeley-Oakland firestorm. I lost most of the manuscript, my library, files, notes, and so on. It took another eight years to reconstruct what was lost and complete this book; not even that was enough to update all chapters equally well.

The book draws on my 50 years of teaching and research on the shape of modern society. It taps what I consider to be two powerful interdisciplinary perspectives in social science—political economy (the interplay of politics and markets) and political sociology (the social bases of politics). I hope that it will be useful to both scholars and practitioners. It should interest students of comparative political economy, comparative politics, public policy, political sociology, social problems, American government, political behavior, advanced industrial societies, industrial relations, and European politics. Just as I believe that affluent countries can learn from one another, I am convinced that the experience of market-oriented rich democracies can provide an important guide for less-developed nations. But unless we grasp the democratic experience in all its diversity, unless we understand the great variation in types of political economy among countries equally rich, equally democratic, the models before us will be useless if not destructive to the aspirations of newly democratizing, recently industrializing countries. When we hear that developing countries making the democratic transition must follow the liberal democratic model and quickly privatize, deregulate, open their economies, and accept the bracing experience of free markets and government austerity (with correlated disruptions of society, community, and political legitimacy), are we talking about the corporatist democracies of Sweden, Norway, Finland, Austria, and Germany; the state-led achievements of Japan and France; the decentralized and fragmented democracies of the Anglo-American countries; or the peculiarities of Switzerland? Just as the economic models of newly industrialized countries range from the successes of South Korea, Taiwan, and Spain in combining economic growth with reductions in poverty and inequality to the unstable growth and failure to reduce inequality in Mexico and pre-Cardozo Brazil, so, too, have the rich democracies followed quite different paths of development, with contrasting results for the standard of living and democratic participation of their citizens. All of our rich democracies have achieved a level of affluence and liberty never before seen in human history. But they vary in how they got there. By specifying the common and disparate features of rich democracies this book can underscore the likely choices facing the emerging democracies.

A word about the tone of this book. It is not the mission of the social scientist to be as innocuous as possible. In the period just after World War II there was much uncritical admiration of American society in the pages of both academic and popular social science—a celebratory literature revived in the late 1990s as Americans boasted about replacing

---

interpreting and writing I could retrieve what was said about my inquiries by both my informants and the literature. Quantitative treatment of the interviews made no sense; these were elite interviews ranging over many topics. They constitute background briefings from informants, not survey respondents.

Japan as "Number One" and advised the world to follow the path of the only great super-power. Neither is it the mission of the social scientist to trash his or her society. This was the favorite sport when the academic mood swung toward pessimism in the 1960s and 1970s. It was reflected in a declinist literature, some of it phrased in an apocalyptic tone, and all of it full of parochial complaints about the sickness and oppression of American society. These mood swings are reminiscent of the 19th-century indictment of the industrial revolution as a catastrophe and its defense as the triumph of capitalism and the machine (Wilensky and Lebeaux, 1958, pp. 27–48). If rejecting both uncritical acclaim and indiscriminate social criticism makes me a "moderate," I am a dedicated moderate. This book attempts to assess performance in a thoroughly comparative way while embracing the use of such terms as dignity, security, safety, justice, and equality. In other words, it aims to combine scholarly discipline and a concern with the human condition.

I have reluctantly used the phrase "democratic corporatism" to denote the bargaining arrangements among governments and major economic power blocs in several modern democracies, including Austria, Finland, Sweden, Norway, and Germany. "Corporatism" historically has a fascist connotation, which is why Margaret Thatcher used it pejoratively to complain of the policy preferences of her Labour Party opposition in Britain. The regimes of Mussolini and Peron acted out an ideology that emphasized the representation and state control of functional groups (labor, commerce, industry, agriculture, the professions) as opposed to what they attacked as decadent parliamentary systems based on elections. Obviously there is a democratic version of corporatist bargaining arrangements that provides channels for influence of functional groups but does not undermine parliamentary democracy and civil liberties. I would prefer a phrase like "negotiated economy," "consensual political economy," or "organized market economy." But because "corporatism" is firmly embedded in the social-science literature I am compelled to use it.

Rich Democracies reports the findings of 30 years of research. The colleagues and students at Berkeley and abroad who helped me during those years are too numerous to mention. (Those left out of this preface may forgive me when I cite their work. Further, the long bibliography doubtless excludes sources that should be there. Aware that nine-tenths of originality is bad memory, I can honestly say that the oversights are inadvertent.) Some 65 graduate students in political science, sociology, economics, history, library science, and public policy worked closely with me on this project; many have written books of their own. I thank them all. The graduate students in my comparative political economy course provided continual critical assessment of my views and kept me on my toes. Among the project assistants whose dedication, intelligence, and extraordinary detective work in the library and on computers were indispensable are the following: in the early stages there were Tom Janoski, Richard M. Coughlin, Susan Reed Hahn, Jim Jasper, Mina Silberberg, Howard D. White, Kathleen Gerson, Timothy L. McDaniel, Lowell Turner, Anne T. Lawrence, Jeffrey Haydu, and economists Harry C. Katz, Theodore M. Crone, and Brian Main. In the later period of postfire reconstruction, I could not have done without the dedication, high standards, and analytical skills of Frederic C. Schaffer and Karen Adelberger. Totally committed to getting the story straight, they saved me from many an error. Equally important was the assistance of John M. Talbot in all quantitative analysis. Drowning in regression equations, he periodically surfaced with clarity and economy. Other excellent Berkeley students who served in the 1990s for shorter periods include Daniel Ziblatt, Susan B. Martin, John

W. Cioffi, Martin Gillens, Marc Howard, Susan Siena, Linus Masouredis, and Brenda McLaughlin. Anne Clunan and Diahanna Lynch made order out of chaos in the production of the final manuscript. Librarian Terry Dean graciously tracked down many a fugitive source.

Four Berkeley research institutes were sources of aid and comfort: throughout most of the life of the project, the Institute of Industrial Relations (and especially two of its directors, Lloyd Ulman and George Strauss); during the initial fieldwork, the Institute of International Studies (and its then director, Carl Rosberg); in the 1990s, the Institute of Governmental Studies (and its longtime director, Nelson Polsby, and more recently Bruce Cain); and the Center for German and European Studies (and its director, Gerald D. Feldman). Successive small grants from the University of California, Berkeley Committee on Research also helped. Among the many Berkeley colleagues who not only sustained my morale and kept me alert, but also gave me crucial feedback on various sections of the manuscript, I am especially indebted to Nelson W. Polsby, Ray Wolfinger, Lloyd Ulman, Neil Smelser, and Martin Trow. Bent Hansen helped in my comparison of various measures of economic performance; by redoing some of the analysis his way he assured me that my minor mistakes made no difference. Jesse Choper provided a critical assessment of my account of law, lawyers, and economic performance in chapter 12 when we shared the beauties of Bellagio at the Rockefeller Center in October 1992. Other colleagues here and abroad who kindly offered their comments are acknowledged in the relevant sections of the book. None of these tough-minded scholars will be quite satisfied with the finished product. Sins of factual error, taste, or bias are therefore mine.

Generous support at various times in the 1970s and 1980s came from the National Science Foundation, the German Marshall Fund, and the Ford Foundation (specific grants and years are specified in earlier publications). I am still drawing on the intellectual capital built up during two stimulating years at the Center for Advanced Study in the Behavioral Sciences, 1956–57 and 1962–63; they were intellectual feasts.

Finally, my gratitude and love goes to Mary Sharman, who tolerated my obsession with this project. She shared all of its ups and downs with the same strength and rhythmic flow of her Chopin at the piano.

HAROLD L. WILENSKY
Berkeley, California
November 10, 2000

PART I
PATHS OF DEVELOPMENT
OF RICH DEMOCRACIES

I
CONVERGENCE THEORY

As we search for the shape of modern society, it helps to focus on these questions: As rich countries get richer do they become more alike in social structure, culture, and politics? Do the changes labeled industrialism overcome the differences among societies labeled authoritarian, totalitarian, and democratic? If there is convergence, what specific attributes of structure, culture, and politics are becoming more alike? If they are *not* converging, if rich countries are following different paths of development, what are the differences and do the differences remain stable or become larger? This chapter concentrates on evidence for convergence theory. Chapters 2, 3, and 4 cover diverse paths of development—theories that explain persistent differences among the rich democracies and even occasional divergent tendencies.

Convergence theory is the idea that as rich countries got richer, they developed similar economic, political, and social structures and to some extent common values and beliefs. The driving force that moves modern societies toward common structures and cultures is continuing industrialization. By industrialization I mean the increasing and widespread use of (1) tools that multiply the effects of their initial applications of energy and (2) inanimate sources of energy (Cottrell, 1955; Wilensky and Lebeaux, 1958, chaps. 1, 2, 3, 4, and p. 117).[1] Think of high-energy technology this way: a hoe increases the effects of the application of human energy to digging a hole for planting far more than the stick that preceded it; a horse-drawn plow continues to multiply the effects of the human hand; the tractor continues the escalation of effects; and an atomic bomb can move a mountain (or destroy a city) with a push of one finger. This idea can be applied to recent information technology. The same fingers that operated the keyboard for a statistical report using the IBM mainframe of the 1950s can with the same energy expenditure now process gargantuan amounts of information—a continuous process of making smaller microprocessors do ever more work. As for inanimate sources of energy, perhaps 80–90 percent of the total energy consumed at any one time before the early modern period was derived from plants, animals, and men—an intractable limit on their productivity (Cipolla and Birdsall, 1980, p. 86).

It is important to confine the concept of industrialization to this technological idea. If we encompass all the organizational and demographic correlates of industrialization in its definition, we cannot invoke it as a cause of the structures, cultures, and political patterns of interest, which is why so much of the early literature on industrialism, based on broader definitions, was tautological. For example, scholars have identified "industrialism" or "industrialization" as including one or more of the following: high degrees of specialization and the concomitant monetary system of exchange; complex organizations; mechanization; urbanization; extensive use of capital; frequent technological change; rational capital accounting; the emergence of a working class; a reasonably predictable political order; the demographic transition; and individualism and the work ethic. There is no way to relate the underlying increases in high-energy technology and inanimate sources of power to these variable structures and values if they are all included in the concept (Wilensky and Lebeaux, 1958, pp. 44–48, 341–351). Thus I shall use the narrow technological definition, roughly measured by economic level (GNP or GDP per capita).

The phrase "continuing industrialization" captures two essential facts about these technological-economic changes: They cover many centuries, and, despite recurrent spurts of growth, they are continuous. A gong did not ring when the industrial revolution began; it was a long and gradual process. As economic historians remind us (Ashton, 1954; Cipolla and Birdsall, 1980; Rosenberg and Birdzell, 1986), it had been going on long before the 19th century. The high Middle Ages (c. 1000–1350) saw substantial economic growth and much innovation (the inanimate power of windmills, invention in armaments, marine transportation and navigation, optics, the mechanical clock). During the early modern period (c. 1500–1800) imperial expansion and a global trade network, combined with the spread of literacy among craftsmen and the experimental method among the educated, increased standards of living in the West. Of course the pace of technological change picked up in the 18th and 19th centuries in the period we label "the industrial revolution" and accelerated markedly after about 1850 wherever science was put in the service of agriculture and industry.[2]

Finally, as we examine specific convergent tendencies we will encounter threshold effects. The process and effects of early industrialization are not the same as the process and effects of later and continuing industrialization (Wilensky and Lebeaux, 1958, chaps. 3 and 4). How high is the threshold for fully modern? About the level of economic development where roughly three-quarters of the modern labor force is no longer in agriculture (because of the extraordinary increases in agricultural productivity) and 40 or 50 percent of adult women are at work in nondomestic settings. In 1910, the United States still had almost a third of its labor force in farming. This is about where France was in 1946, Japan in the 1950s, and the USSR in the mid-1960s.

What is truly modern about modern (highly developed, "advanced industrial") society are nine major structural and demographic shifts rooted in industrialization, especially at a high level of development. With some variation in timing, the convergent tendencies among the currently rich democracies include the following:

1. Changes in the kinship system and household composition and associated political demands (see figure 1.1).

2. The push for equality among minority groups. Increasing openness to ethnic-religious-racial claims. Increasing gender equality. Government policy responses, including some form of "affirmative action."

3. The rise of mass higher education.

4. The increasing dominance of the media of mass communication and entertainment in politics and culture.

5. The increasing number of experts and intellectuals, and less uniformly, their influence.

6. Associated changes in social stratification and mobility. Expansion of upper-middle-class occupations to about one-fifth of the labor force, the growth of the upper-working class and lower-middle class and their increasing similarity in behavior and orientation. The decline of farmers and unskilled manual workers.

7. The changing organization, schedules, and hours of work.

8. The emergence and growth of the welfare state. Seven or eight similar program packages (discussed in chap. 5).

9. Changes in political systems. At first glance, this is an area of least convergence; a high level of economic development may not be a decisive determinant of political systems. But the areas of most convergence (1–8 above) may well foster some convergence in politics.

The rest of this chapter presents a description of each of these trends and a summary of the evidence bearing on each. I begin with the impact of advanced industrialization on changes in family structures because those changes have wide-ranging effects on the shape of modern society.

Family Structure and Political Demands[3]

The massive structural changes associated with industrialization have brought major changes in family size, composition, functions, and lifestyles. By separating work from residence and changing the occupational and educational structure (see later discussion), industrialization increases mobility opportunity for both men and women, inspires rising aspirations among parents for themselves and their children, reduces the economic value of children and increases their cost, giving women both motive and opportunity to enter the nonagricultural labor force, thereby reducing fertility rates. It also reduces the family's motivation and resources to care for aging parents and to meet the risks of invalidism, sickness, job injuries, and other shocks. The net effect: a dominant family type in industrial society—independent, nuclear (the household consists of husband, wife, and nonadult children), and neolocal (postmarital residence is not with the kin of either spouse), and a long-term weakening of extended kinship ties. All of these structural and demographic shifts, in turn, make women more independent and foster more gender equality and higher divorce rates. One form or another of women's liberation movements is a natural final outcome. These trends are evident in industrialized or industrializing countries as diverse in culture and politics as Sweden, Italy, Austria, the United States, the former USSR, and, more recently, Japan, Korea, and Brazil.

This convergence argument—based on theory and evidence from Goode (1963, 1982), Kingsley Davis (1984), Kirk (1960), Wilensky and Lebeaux (1958), Wilensky (1968,

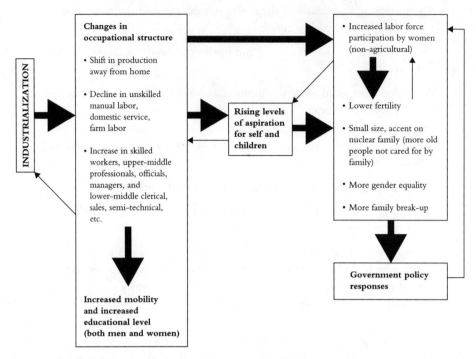

Figure 1.1. Impact of continuing industrialization on family structure*
*Specific links between variables are spelled out in text. Arrows indicate hypotheses about the direction and amount of influence. Thin lines = least influence.

1981b), Inkeles (1960, 1980, 1984), and Levy (1972)—is summarized in figure 1.1, where the arrows indicate the direction of causation.

The most serious critics of this scheme who present some counterevidence include Laslett (1972), Scott and Tilly (1975), and Goldthorpe (1987). A brief summary of the issues and an assessment of empirical data relevant to the industrialization theme will suggest that we can go quite far with a somewhat modified convergence theory.

Evidence of the relation of economic opportunity to family structure and family breakup in both the long run and the short is strong. Data on trends in female labor-force participation, fertility rates, household size, and divorce rates show a tight connection between economic development and family structure.

Female Labor-Force Participation Increased

The percentage of married women in the nonagricultural labor force has increased in all industrialized countries. The more highly developed the country, the higher the participation rate; this is generally true whether the national ideology favors gender equality or not. A systematic comparison of ideology, economic level, and women's work in 34 countries (Wilensky, 1968) confirms the point. This study classifies countries by elite values and official rhetoric favoring women's equality, quartile rank among 64 countries' per capita income, and two measures of women's participation rate in 1953 or nearest year. It shows that women's nonagricultural participation in the richest countries varied slightly by ideology, but the most-industrialized countries had the highest rates: for example, around 1953 egalitarian and rich Norway and Sweden as well as inegalitarian and rich Switzerland, the United Kingdom, and the United States all ranked high while egalitarian but nonrich Yugoslavia and India as well as inegalitarian but nonrich Japan, Brazil, Turkey, and Greece all ranked low. (Wilensky, 1968. Cf. Davis, 1984.)[4]

The partial exceptions to this rule were three Latin American countries (El Salvador, Ecuador, Chile) that had a heavy concentration of metropolitan women in domestic service; economic growth in such countries brings a shift *out* of such jobs. Eliminating this category—a product of "overurbanization"—these countries fall into place. Communist countries, especially Poland and the former USSR, also had rates of women working higher than their level of economic development in 1953 would suggest. On balance, Soviet culture (aggressive collectivism, including ideological indoctrination emphasizing gender equality and the strategic role of women in Communist economic life) and social organization (subsidies to encourage women to get out of the home into schools, factories, and street sweeping; severe overcrowding and a colossal housing shortage which offer added incentive for women to escape; a war-induced surplus of females; and a rapid rate of economic growth with concomitant shortages of workers)—gave the Soviet Union only about a 7 to 10 percent point edge over the United States in female labor-force participation and a preponderance of women in a few exceptional occupations (e.g., physician) still controlled by men. In general, however, a country's level of economic development is a crucial determinant of the place of women in the occupational structure; official ideology is a minor influence, unless, as we shall see in chapter 7, it is anchored in political parties with durable power and national structures of bargaining favorable to working women.

The greatest increases in women at work have been recent, that is, the last 100 years, and are concentrated among married women and especially wives with children. In this, the United States is about average among rich countries—a typical case. For instance, from a low level of 2 to 5 percent of married women working in 1890 (the first date for good data) "wives under age 60 have steadily increased their participation in the labor force, regardless of age, race, or parenthood" (Davis, 1984, p. 400). While the increase is steady, there is some indication of a recent slowdown in the rate of increase from an average annual increase of 2.8% for 1890–1950 and 2.7 percent for 1950–70 to 1.9% between 1970 and 1982, a time when economic growth also decelerated. The most recent, rapid, and significant increase in participation is among wives under 35 for whom the conflict between work and family is likely to be most intense. In the United States in 1960 16.6% of married women with children under six worked; by 1982 the fraction had increased to 48.7%. (Davis, 1984, p. 400).[5]

Fertility Rates and Household Size Declined and Divorce Rates Increased

These three aspects of the demographic revolution may or may not be products of industrialization, depending upon our concept and dating of "industrialization," how much attention we give to threshold effects and exceptional cases, and our concepts of "extended family" or "nuclear family" in the early modern period from the 16th to the 18th centuries.

In the long run of centuries and with few exceptions, economic growth and other measures of expanding opportunity increase marriage rates and divorce rates and decrease birthrates. In the short run, however, all three rates respond to the business cycle; they go up and down together, fluctuating around the long-term and recently accelerating trends toward the small nuclear family and single-parent households.

Long-run fertility declines linked to the increased practice of contraception and abortion began in France and the United States in the early 19th century, before the rapid acceleration of industrialization; almost everywhere in Europe, including Britain, the sharp declines began between 1880 and 1920 (Inkeles, 1984; Davis, 1984; Coale and Watkins, 1986; Goldthorpe, 1987, p. 38; Lesthaeghe and Wilson, 1986, p. 289).

Household size tracks birthrates; it is somewhat independent of fertility because it varies with the number of related adults living together, doubling up of families, and boarders and live-in servants. Americans moved slowly toward smaller units from 1790, when the average household had 5.79 persons, much faster after 1850, and still faster after 1890—again meshing with accelerating industrialization. By 1980 average household size had fallen to 2.86 persons (Inkeles, 1984, p. 14)—less than half of its early size.

Although the United States and the United Kingdom have recently led the pack in high and steadily rising divorce rates, the upward trend is evident in all industrialized countries, especially since 1900 (Davis, 1984, pp. 409–411; Inkeles, 1984, pp. 15–17; Goldthorpe, 1987, pp. 41–43, 216). For example, in the United States from 1870 to 1980 the divorce rate multiplied by 13, going from 1.6 to 21.9 divorces per 1,000 married women (Inkeles, 1984, p. 15). These trends are similar for all Western nations permitting divorce (Ogburn and Nimkoff, 1955, p. 219; United Nations Demographic Yearbook, various years). Nineteen seventy marks the beginning of purely no-fault divorce systems, a catch-up to reality in the legal codes of some rich democracies (Glendon, 1989, chap. 4).[6]

These correlations between the trend in expanding economic opportunity and the trend in fertility, household size, and divorce would be inconclusive if it were not for a few careful studies that link year-by-year changes in economic conditions and changes in family structure. Even in the short run these rates respond to the business cycle. For instance, Inkeles analyzes data from 1920 to 1980 relating changes in 11 measures of economic conditions to changes in marriage, birthrates, and divorce rates in the United States; these capture both the causal connection between economic opportunity and family structure as well as the short-term fluctuations obscured by the correlation of long-term trends. All three rates are positively related to indicators of economic improvement such as personal consumption and "negatively with indicators of bad times such as a rapid rise in business failures" (Inkeles, 1984, p. 29). The cumulative effect of the 11 economic change measures on family change was very powerful (p. 31)—consistent with the analysis by Kirk (1960) of the impact of changes in 3 measures of economic conditions on marriage and birthrates for the shorter period 1920–1957.

In a word, common sense holds true: When economic conditions are booming people go ahead with a previously planned marriage, a child, or see a lawyer about divorce; during a bust, they postpone marriage or having a child and stay away from the lawyer's office (Inkeles, 1984, p. 24). And, as we have seen, over the generations they respond to long-term increases in standards of living, especially at high levels of individual and collective aspirations and at high levels of individual or national affluence, by reducing both desired and actual family size.

Critics of convergence theory have made much of the cases of France and the United States (fertility declined too early to be attributed to the effects of urbanization and industrialization) and Britain (the "industrial revolution" was virtually complete before the big drop in fertility rates occurred). (Laslett, 1972, pp. 126, 139, 141–142; Goldthorpe, 1987, pp. 6–7.) They have also produced historical evidence that Western families have always been small—few children and few coresident kin. Laslett, analyzing English households between 1574 and 1821, emphasizes that the size of the average household remained fairly steady at 4.75 and did not decrease until very late in the industrialization process, perhaps until the end of the 19th century (Laslett, 1972, p. 126). The reduction in household size in Britain from large- to medium-sized families at the end of the 19th century was mainly due to a reduction in live-in servants (Goldthorpe, 1987, p. 34). Finally, critics sound a note of caution about the idea that increased labor-force participation by women produces a decline in fertility: again, the drop in fertility began in France when it was still agrarian and in the United States when nonagricultural labor-force participation was low among women. Regarding divorce, Inkeles notes that limited data on petitions for divorce submitted to the Massachusetts General Court from 1692 to 1786 suggest that these colonial citizens, at least after 1730, "did not wait for the stimulus of industrialization and urbanism to double the rate at which they sought divorce" (1984, p. 16).

To me the allegedly premature drop in fertility and small increases in a very low rate of family breakup, as well as precursor populations behaving in "modern" ways before full-scale modernization, do not contradict the convergence argument in my figure 1.1. Industrialization in the sense of the increasing use of high-energy technology and inanimate sources of energy was going on long before the 19th century.

What all this suggests is that we should not be surprised by the emergence, especially in urban areas, of precursor populations and patterns of behavior in the 17th, 18th, and early 19th centuries. Thus, the modest declines in fertility in France and the United States in the 18th and 19th centuries and the increases in divorce petitions in Massachusetts after 1730 may, indeed, be linked to expanding economic opportunity and rising aspirations.

Nor should we be surprised at lagging responses of national averages to long-term structural trends that vary by strata, region, and community. The most important exception to the convergence theme, medium-high fertility rates in Britain during the 19th century, could be a product of the stagnation or even deterioration of British living standards over several decades after 1810 among masses of unskilled workers—seasonally employed agricultural workers, hand-loom weavers, and similar groups. (Ashton, 1954, pp. 158–159, 133–136, dates this 1810–20, but Kuznets, 1955, p. 27, ventures the guess that income inequality widened in England during the entire first half of the 19th century.) Mass aspirations for mobility, security, and equality very likely remained realistically low for much of this period; if so, the "premodern" behavior of the British is not an anomaly. The need to relate particular economic circumstances to the behavior at issue is also illustrated by work on the decline of fertility in several hundred provinces of Europe (Coale and Watkins, 1986). Among the findings: vanguard groups such as Jews, "aristocracies" (high officers, ruling families, prominent members of the bourgeoisie), and some urban populations began the process of controlling fertility decades, even a century, before the widespread decline of fertility in Europe. Significantly, these social groups, although they differed in religion and culture, shared an above-average economic level and a strong urban connection or residence; the Jews and the aristocrats also shared lower mortality rates than the general population (less need to have large broods of children so that a few might survive)—a preview of later developments (Livi-Bacci, 1986, pp. 199–200).[7]

Whatever the regional, ethnic, and class differences, the evidence on nation-states suggests some powerful threshold effects. For instance, birthrates in the United States during 1800–40 declined at about one-half of 1% per year. But in the next period of rapid industrialization, 1840–90, the annual rate of decline increased to 0.96% and accelerated further to 1.14%, 1890–1940. After the brief baby boom of 1945–60 birthrates resumed their downward plunge at an even faster pace, declining 2.9% a year to 1970 and a bit less—2.6% a year—from 1970 to 1980, a decade of slower economic growth (Inkeles, 1984, p. 14).

Similarly, the interaction among women's nonagricultural labor-force participation rates, lower fertility rates, high divorce rates, and the political pressure for gender equality does not emerge full-scale until a high level of industrialization is achieved. We must remember that at early stages of industrialization most married women were still on farms or in unpaid family labor. Even as late as 1910 almost a third of the American labor force was in farming; numerous mom-and-pop stores using family labor formed an urban counterpart (Wilensky and Lebeaux, 1958, p. 92). Similarly, large proportions of the labor force were in agriculture or unpaid family labor at the same stage of industrialization in Britain in the mid–19th century and in Japan in the 1950s.[8]

Where agricultural labor is domestic there is no conflict between female labor and domesticity; the female farmer, the wife, and the mother are one and the economic value of children is high. When a working woman must move into contact with nonkin, when she can no longer walk out the back door and hoe the corn alongside her children, the modern tension between work and family emerges, with the consequences I have traced. In some places, notably Britain, early industrialization did not sharply separate work from family even in urban-industrial areas. As Smelser (1959) shows, in English cotton textile factories of the late 18th and early 19th centuries, whole families were employed together; parents trained and supervised their own children on factory premises—again a force for delay in the emergence of a modern family form. In these circumstances—families working together on farms and in factories—fertility remained stable or increased slightly.

Strong threshold effects with understandable delays are also apparent in the timing of female labor-force participation, divorce, and modern feminist movements. Like declines in fertility, married women's entry to the urban labor force and subsequent acceleration in divorce rates occurred only with gradual changes in educational and occupational opportunity, the rise in real wages, and the concomitant diffusion of mobility aspirations among married couples (see below). The "breadwinner pattern" with the father the "breadwinner" and the wife the "homemaker" was a product of early industrialization (Davis, 1984); it had to break up before these trends could accelerate. The likely sequence was rising educational and occupational opportunity and income, then the beginning of limitations on family size, then urban labor-force participation by women, then plunging birthrates, then the acceleration of divorce, and finally the widespread demand for autonomy and equality.[9]

In any case, in modern societies the breadwinner pattern (husband at work, wife at home) has all but disappeared. For instance, by 1992, it had declined to just 20% of white households in the United States and only 13% of black households—a decline of about 60% since 1963 in both populations.

The very last structural change is as yet embryonic. There is a slow shift away from patterns rooted in the family system of early industrialization—a division of household labor that minimizes men's duties and a "virilocal" family in which the couple locates where the husband's work demands. Studies of the division of household labor from the 1950s on suggest only slow change in releasing women from housewifery; although men are beginning to share these tasks a bit more, in the typical situation married women now simply add paid work to a 30- to 40-hour week in child care and housework (e.g., Wilensky, 1968, pp. 242–244 on time budgets in France and the United States; Szalai, 1972, pp. 584, 588, 599, 643 on the consistently meager help men give their working wives in household chores in 12 countries, communist and capitalist alike; the U.S. Time Use Survey for 1965–66 by Robinson and Converse analyzed by Vanek, 1973; and Pleck, 1985, pp. 30–31, 38, 41, 47 summarizing U.S. data from upstate New York in 1967–68, and from national samples taken in 1971, 1975–76, and 1977). There are only small national variations and hints of equally modest variations by educational level and number of children (the big jump in household labor among working women is from no children to one or more).

It is true that more-educated men of the baby-boom generation now share household tasks more than their less-educated counterparts of older generations; the big differences, however, are between couples where both have postgraduate degrees and those couples where both parents had eighth-grade education (Goldscheider and Waite, 1991, pp. 128–129). The trend toward household-labor sharing is up but it takes a long, expensive education to bring men around, and the vast majority of families—single parents, the unmarried, those without professional degrees—remain little affected, inching forward into the new world of gender equality.

These findings suggest that the transition to newer patterns of equality will often be painful; it may involve much bargaining over the division of household tasks and child care. We can expect much turmoil and tension among partners who are differentially "liberated" or come from different political generations. Among partners who are equally committed to careers—a small but growing avant-garde—we can anticipate sometimes unbearable conflict over whose work should determine the place of residence. (I would guess that as yet the proportion of couples who relocate where the wife's work demands is no more than 5% but rising.) Here is another reason to suppose that divorce rates will continue their climb in the decade ahead.

Although contemporary feminist movements are accelerating the shift toward equality in family life, it is apparent that the major liberating forces I have listed preceded such movements. Survey data in the United States, where "women's lib" has been most vocal and visible, confirm the point: the best predictors of the shift toward more egalitarian role definitions from 1964 to 1974, among high- and low-status women alike, were not their exposure to the women's movement but instead their level of education and whether they worked (Mason, Czajka, and Arber, 1976; for a subtle analysis of how these changes in social structure shape sex-role definitions and strategies of adjustment among women variously situated see Gerson, 1985).

That fertility rates and household size decline while divorce rates rise and that the very uneven hunger for gender equality is a new source of tension do not mean that the nuclear family is disintegrating. Marriage and remarriage remain popular. While there are some national variations, in countries both modern and premodern, East and West, somewhere between 85% and 99% of women are married at least once by the age of 50, and if we had data on stable partnerships not sanctioned by law it would be higher. (Inkeles calls being "ever married" a "pan-human need," 1980, p. 43.) We will not know whether very recent decreases in the remarriage rate will last, until the baby-boom cohort, where it is concentrated, moves through the life course, but so far there appear merely to be temporary delays in both marriage and remarriage. Young, urban, educated populations are rejecting their specific partners, not the institutions of partnership. Nor has having children gone out of fashion. Again we cannot yet know what today's childless young women will have done by the time they are in their mid-forties, but the expectation of childlessness in American survey interviews is uniformly low among all educational and income categories (Bane, 1976, p. 9). In fact there was a rise in the percentage of childless wives between 30 and 34 who said that they expected to have a child sometime—up from 34% in 1975 to 54% in 1988 (U.S. Bureau of the Census, Current Population Reports, Series P-20, No. 436, *Fertility of American Women: June 1988*, p. 12).

Regarding childlessness in Europe and America: While the desire for one or two children remains almost universal, the performance may fall short. Although the expectation of childlessness was uniformly low and stable at every educational and age level and showed little change in the 20th century (Hobcraft and Kiernan, 1995, pp. 26–27; Bane, 1976, p. 9), and although the performance was less than 1 in 10 (including childlessness caused by infertility), the rate may now be rising. Demographers estimate that 15 to 20 percent of women today will reach the end of their childbearing years never having given birth, not because they do not want children but mainly because they delay the attempt too long (Ryder, 1990; Bianchi, 1990; Hobcraft and Kiernan, 1995). Consider the national cohort of American women born 1944 to 1957 who had four years of college or more when surveyed in 1990: they are the vanguard group who are said to follow a strategy of "career then family" as shown by delays in marriage and childbearing; 29% had not had their first birth by 1991 when the group was 37 to 47 years old. (Goldin, 1995, pp. 3–4, 25–26.) By the time they are all past 44 years old and are surveyed again, we will know the performance of the whole cohort; it is likely that the childlessness rate among the "ever-married" would drop to 20% or less, even for this highly educated group (*ibid.*, p. 26). Because the childlessness rate among women who do not earn college degrees is much lower, the likely rate for the population as a whole is no more than 15 to 20 percent. And because many young college women of the 1990s, having achieved more gender equality in education and work than the previous cohort, are refusing to postpone marriage and family (they want it all), their childlessness rate may not exceed 15%. In other words, current evidence, both for the United States and Europe, suggests that 8 or 9 in 10 of those women in modern societies who can have children will give birth. (Chap. 7 analyzes national contrasts in both gender equality and family policies that ease the balance between parenting and work.)

Even in Sweden, which leads the world in these convergent trends—low marriage rate, a high cohabitation rate, a high rate of family breakup, small household size, high female labor-force participation, and gender equality—almost all Swedes, including young Swedes, still want to live as a couple sometime in their lives; they embrace the ideal of permanent monogamous relationships (Popenoe, 1987, p. 181). And there is no evidence that the desire for children is declining. As in the United States, Swedish fertility rates rose a bit in the late 1980s, putting them ahead of Germany and Denmark, and Swedish women of all ages overwhelmingly favor the two-child ideal (*ibid.*).[10] Even in this extreme case of modernization, the family, in modified form, is central. In short, the nuclear family, whatever its new instabilities, remains a central source of personal identity, loyalty, companionship, affection, and solidarity; in Mary Jo Bane's phrase, it is "Here to Stay" (1976).

What about the argument that an accent on the small neolocal nuclear family is not a modern development and that the shearing away of the extended family never happened because they were never part of the household? Both sides in this argument tend to exaggerate. If we ask, What was household size in the early modern period?, and answer, Households were not big and they included few coresident kin, that is accurate enough, but it misses crucial differences between modern and premodern families. From the 16th to the 18th centuries in Europe and North America, if there were two- rather than three-generation households, it was because of low longevity rooted in famine, malnutrition, and pestilence. Life was "nasty, brutish, and short." Many, perhaps most, grandparents and other relatives could not "live in" because they were dead. Others, the minority who reached old age, often formed three-generation households. If the aged parents survived the adult children, or if the latter moved far away, the aged would often make a contract with a younger friend or couple and their children to share a household under specified conditions of mutual care. While the nuclear family may have been the prevalent form in Western Europe (Scott and Tilly, 1975, pp. 36–64; Goldthorpe, 1987, pp. 9–35), compared with its modern counterpart it much more readily expanded to include other kin. In Natalie Davis's phrase, the early modern family "breathed" in a way the contemporary family does not (Davis, 1968, p. 88).[11]

In fact, there is no doubt that the percentage of old people who share bed and board with their adult children *has* declined. At every age level and marital status adults prefer an independent household, a trend apparent both in the United States at least since 1940 (Bane, 1976) and in other industrial societies at the same level of development; this is a force in the political demand for both the welfare state in general and a family policy in particular.

Japan provides a wonderful test of the proposition that the structural correlates of industrialization overcome cultural values and beliefs sustaining traditional family forms.[12] In religion and in politics, evidence of strong familial values abounds: ancestor worship and the Confucian *Book on Filial Piety,* to which all prewar Japanese children were exposed; surveys showing that in 1975 almost half of the people aged 30–54 believed that it is better to live with aging parents than live apart even when parents are healthy; the repeated concern expressed by politicians and bureaucrats that the welfare state might subvert Japan's family system (in 1980 Prime Minister Ohira advocated revitalizing the family as a means of reducing social expenditures). These affirmations of familial values are reflected in actual living arrangements of Japanese families. Although sources differ on this point, the best data suggest that in 1974 about three-quarters of Japanese older citizens (60–74) who had adult children were living with them, compared with no more than one-fourth in any rich country of Western Europe and North America (Lewis 1980; cf. Prime Minister's Office 1985, p. 44).

What is significant is that throughout the postwar period of rapid industrialization in Japan there has been a steady convergence in Japan toward the family patterns of other modern societies. The hold of the extended family in Japan is gradually eroding; household size is also decreasing. More and more old people prefer to live on their own if they have enough income. In such urban areas as Tokyo, the percentage of three-generation households is now approaching that of Europe and North America. Japan—like Korea, Hong Kong, Singapore, and Taiwan, all leaders in rapid economic growth—has also achieved swift and sustained drops in fertility rates in the postwar period. Indeed, Japan's drop in birthrates began in the 1920s. In Japan, as in the other Asian tigers, rates of non-agricultural female labor-force participation have climbed fast. Finally, in the first successful challenge to Liberal Democratic Party domination in the postwar period the woman leader of the opposition Socialists in Japan, Takako Doi, articulated the vanguard views of urban women on gender equality. Although kinship ties remain stronger in Japan than in most other rich countries, the convergent trends are striking.

Perhaps the most extreme test case for convergence theory is the traditional early marriage and female seclusion pattern among Muslim populations of the Middle East (e.g., Egypt, Iran, Pakistan), which in the 1950s had the lowest female labor-force participation rates among metropolitan areas of 38 countries studied (Collver and Langois, 1962). Even in these socially conservative countries, wherever they have imported modern technology and used their new oil wealth to modernize rapidly, deeply entrenched family structures begin slowly to erode. As Kingsley Davis indicates, the newly rich Arab oil states' first response to their dizzying pace of economic modernization is to bring in foreign workers while keeping married women home; but the political threat of so many foreigners has begun to overcome their attachment to female seclusion, and the women themselves are stirring. Muslim countries such as Jordan, Kuwait, Egypt, and Bahrain are beginning to employ their own women in urban areas. (Davis, 1984, p. 404.) In another sign of change, in 1999 Kuwait's Cabinet gave women the right to vote and run for Parliament. One or two generations from now we will know whether the demographic and structural changes other rich countries have experienced will shape family life and the place of women even in the modernizing sectors of the Middle East, assuming reversals in oil prices do not put their economies permanently in reverse and the armed truce of the 1990s does not give way to still larger wars.

In sum, until the household is no longer the prevalent center of production, until educational and occupational opportunities for married women expand and mass aspirations rise, we would not expect big declines in fertility and household size, accelerating increases in women working in nonagricultural, nondomestic jobs, big increases in divorce rates, and shifts toward gender equality. As I suggested at the outset, perhaps three-quarters of the labor force has to be off the farms, especially family farms, and one-third to one-half of adult women have to be at work in nondomestic settings before the full effects of continuing industrialization take hold.

THE PUSH FOR EQUALITY AMONG MINORITIES

A minority group may be defined as any collectivity that on the basis of shared social characteristics is discriminated against by a dominant group, comes to see itself as an object of discrimination, and organizes around this perception. This includes groups based on descent (racial, ethnic, religious, linguistic), age, gender, sexual preference, or physical disability. There is no doubt that minority groups so defined have moved from the periphery of modern societies toward the center, that discrimination against them in the long run has declined, that despite recurrent ethnic resurgence and sometimes militant political expression, the tendency in rich democracies is toward assimilation, and that the remaining minority-group grievances fuel divisive politics, especially among groups based on descent.[13] Finally, if one could argue that some rich democracies 40 or 50 years ago were relatively homogenous, with only tiny numbers identified as minorities, this is no longer so. With the revival of massive migrations of economic and political refugees from poor countries to rich after World War II, there has been a convergence in social heterogeneity by race, ethnicity, religion, and language, accelerating in recent years. (Chap. 17 traces the size and kinds of migration, and the political effects; chaps. 10 and 11 analyze the connections between minority-group protest movements and parties and tax-welfare backlash.)

The argument that modern society tends toward the structural and cultural integration of minority groups is both old and familiar and, for the long run, accurate (for detailed discussion see Linton, 1936; Schumpeter, 1942; Parsons, 1949, pp. 189ff.; Moore, 1951; Levy, 1949, 1952; Wilensky and Lawrence, 1979). For all minority groups, integration goes forward, with varying speed and amount and with some national variations and occasional reversals. It proceeds in the economy (occupational integration, income equality), polity (political organization and the franchise), kinship (intermarriage rates), and to a lesser extent the culture (values and beliefs, media habits, lifestyles). The reasons for economic integration apply to all dimensions of integration. A brief reminder will help.

1.   In modern society, unlike premodern society, work changes with changing technical and social organization and the pace of change accelerates; the division of labor is complex; and work is assigned more often on the basis of ability. Large portions of the population cannot "inherit" occupations because the occupations change too rapidly. Further, there are not enough age and sex differences to represent the vast number of specialized roles that need to be filled. Some of these roles are so complex that they cannot be left to the accidents of inheritance; modern society cannot afford too many idiots in high places. In fact, industrialization, by creating complex and important occupational roles, accents the importance of even *small* differences in ability. Compare, for example, the different amounts that can be accomplished by two machine-shovel operators of different degrees of skill and reliability, or by a good programmer and a mediocre one. In short, the number, complexity, importance, and frequency of change of occupational roles in industrial society have meant a shift in the basis of role assignment. "Who you are" becomes less important than "what you can do or learn to do."

2.   That work roles in modern society tend to be achieved, assigned to some extent on the basis of ability, intensifies competition for these roles. If few are excluded from consideration, then the number of potential competitors is vastly increased. This is why there is less chance for the development of a hereditary elite. This is, moreover, why modern industry is everywhere such a sifter, sorter, and above all a *mixer* of diverse racial, ethnic, and religious groups (chap. 3 and Hughes, 1943). It is a major reason, too, for the increased proportion of women who work outside the home, as we have already seen. Everywhere industrialization, by challenging the traditional criteria

of work assignment, by accenting ability instead of sex, invites women to participate as occupational equals.

3. If industrialization means increased competition for work roles and increased mobility opportunity, it also fosters a mobility ideology appropriate to the changing structure. Industrialization has everywhere been accompanied by agitation for equality of economic opportunity—movements for improving the life chances of women, minority groups, and lower classes. Thus, a system accent on achievement or "economic individualism" marks modern societies, whatever their political and cultural differences, and despite counteracting ideologies of "economic collectivism" (see chap. 4).

None of the scholars who make these arguments ignore discrimination or segregation; they merely assert that with continuing industrialization at a high level of development and in the long run, placement criteria relevant to role performance become more prominent; "ascriptive" criteria, less important.[14] By the long run I mean three or four generations. A sense of the integration of minorities into the mainstream of modern societies comes from trend data on each group or stratum. Because the United States is perhaps the most multiethnic of the rich democracies, I shall concentrate on the integration of ethnic, religious, and racial groups, women, and age groups in the United States, offering no more than a few illustrative studies from a vast literature. Cross-national variations are described and explained in several subsequent chapters, especially 10 (Backlash), 17 (Globalization), 5 (The Welfare State), 7 (Family Policy), and 14 (Mayhem), where the fate of minority groups is directly relevant.

From a review of evidence for the United States for the last half century or so and of more scarce cross-national data, I reach two conclusions. First, among our rich democracies, tendencies toward the Balkanization of society are offset by more powerful tendencies toward the integration of minority groups. Integration in the polity and economy increases intermarriage rates, a major source of assimilation. Second, in the United States, the extent and rapidity of occupational integration—which together with the franchise furthers other forms of integration—has been greatest for white ethnics and broad religious groups, more recently for women and Asian immigrants, much less for Mexicans, and least for blacks. The relative position of young people from lower-class backgrounds has improved only slightly, if at all, while job discrimination against the aged has actually increased, whatever their benefits from the welfare state.

Ethnicity and Religion

Structural assimilation has proceeded more rapidly for some white ethnic groups than for others, but by the second generation most white ethnics have achieved an occupational profile which closely matches that of the native white population. For instance, using a 1962 national survey, Duncan and Duncan (1968) found strong evidence of occupational integration, melting-pot style, among ethnic minorities. National origin had much greater influence on the occupational fate of fathers than of sons. When matched for education and social origin, respondents of different nationalities differed little in their occupational achievement, with the exception of the "overachievement" of Russians (mainly Jews) and

WASPs, and the "underachievement" of persons of Hispanic, Italian, Canadian, and Polish descent. Greeley's (1974) analysis of survey data for the 1960s demonstrates a continuation of the pattern documented by earlier researchers (e.g., Hutchinson, 1956), with Irish and German Catholics registering the largest gains. Thus, although the rate of absorption has varied, and is not simply a function of the time of arrival as ideas of ethnic succession suggest (cf. Wilensky and Ladinsky, 1967, p. 560), the occupational integration of most of America's ethnic-religious groups has been fairly complete. The election of President Kennedy in 1960 symbolized the integration of Catholics into American society.

What about the fate of more recent immigrants in the United States? A series of studies by the National Research Council suggests that even in the past 40 years of accelerated immigration, there is more assimilation than Balkanization. This is evident in the decline of residential, occupational, and educational segregation; the increase in intermarriage rates; and the consequent changed meaning of ethnicity (Smith and Edmonston, 1997, pp. 366–369, 209–219, 182–190, 369–372). These trends interact to make minority-group integration the main story of post–World War II America, even for racial minorities.

Leaving Mexican immigrants aside, children (0–17) of the foreign born in 1990—the second generation—are better off than their native-born counterparts. They score lower in the percentage on public assistance or having a single parent and higher in the percentage who live in a household where the head is a college graduate or is employed in an upper-white-collar occupation. The new immigrants, in fact, are more heterogeneous in socio-economic status upon arrival than were the immigrants of 1890–1920, who were more uniformly concentrated at the bottom. For instance, in 1990, a college degree was common among all immigrants (first generation) as among natives—one in five. The rate was 65% among Indian immigrants. First-generation Asian-American men (excluding refugees from Laos, Cambodia, and Vietnam) similarly match or exceed native-born white men in education and occupation. (Smith and Edmonston, 1997, pp. 185–187; Perlmann and Waldinger, 1997, pp. 899–901.)

The Mexican exception is big. About one in three of all immigrant children has at least one Mexican parent (Perlmann and Waldinger, 1997, p. 900). Their parents have the least skill and education and earn the lowest wages. They thus bring the averages for "immigrants" down in every dimension of welfare. This explains why the education and wage gap between foreign-born and native workers has recently widened. Even though recent arrivals are better educated than turn-of-the-century immigrants, the education and skills of the native born have improved even more than the average for all immigrants. And the poverty of the numerous Mexican immigrants is a handicap for the speedy integration of their children and even for their grandchildren (Perlmann and Waldinger, 1997, p. 901). However, because the Latino population is very young we cannot yet know the final fate of the second and third generations. Meanwhile we can conclude that, for whatever reasons, the gap in education, skills, and earnings over time closes significantly for immigrants from Asia and Europe, modestly for others, but so far not at all for those from Mexico (Smith and Edmonston, 1997, pp. 7–8, 177–181).

Since 1960 intermarriage rates have been climbing for both ethnic-religious and "racial" groups (Lieberson and Waters, 1988; Tucker and Mitchell-Kernan, 1990). If we want to use the label "assimilation," marriages across minority/majority group lines and between minority groups are its best indicators. By the third generation the levels of intermarriage among minorities of European origin became very high (Perlmann and Waldinger, 1997, p. 899). What about "race"? While over 93% of whites and of blacks still marry within their own categories, only 70% of Asians and of Hispanics and 33%of American Indians do (Waters, 2000, p. 28; Harrison and Bennett, 1995, p. 165). Assuming that intermarriage rates between "races" continue at current levels, the percentage of all Americans who report one or more races (or Hispanic origins) in addition to their primary race (or Hispanic identity) will climb from 7% in 1995 to 21% in 2050 (Smith and Edmonston, 1997, p. 119). The Asian rate will be 36%; the Hispanic rate, 45%. We can already see this trend in the actual intermarriage rate of younger native-born Asian and Hispanic men and women in 1990 (age 25 to 34): Asians, about 51%; Hispanics, 35% (based on *ibid.,* table 8.2, p. 371).

In short, if we combine rising intermarriage rates with blurred ethnic identity over two or three generations and the continued economic and political integration of all these "racial" groups, the story is unequivocally one of assimilation with a somewhat broadened and enriched American culture. Just as Italian, Irish, and Polish immigrants four generations ago were despised as inferior troublesome "races" and no longer suffer that stigma, so will the newer racial immigrants be redefined, both by themselves and society—quickly for Asians and Cubans, less quickly for other Hispanics (Alonso and Waters, 1993).

Two strong determinants of intermarriage have been identified in American studies: time of arrival and geographical dispersion. Those groups that arrived in North America first now have higher rates of intermarriage. And those groups that scatter are more likely to intermarry than are isolated or concentrated groups (Lieberson and Waters, 1988). Projections of mixed marriages are limited by the obvious blurring of boundaries and the changing meaning of ethnicity.[15] Think of a white Protestant married to a Catholic woman, both of whom watch *Seinfeld* as they eat takeout Chinese food.

Blacks versus Others

The pattern of structural assimilation over several generations experienced by many white ethnics—in jobs, residences, and intermarriage—has been replicated for black Americans in only small measure. Analysis of the jobs of blacks over the last 60 years reveals a pattern of slow occupational integration which is either speeded up or slowed down by the business cycle and by shifts in the political climate which favor or block antidiscrimination measures (Price, 1969, p. 131; Humphrey, 1977, p. 13). Although intermarriage rates have recently climbed, it is from a very low base. An analysis of census data by Price (1969) shows that blacks made significant occupational gains in the 1940s, largely because of labor shortages and economic growth associated with World War II (p. 131). Using an index of occupational change which compares shifts in the occupational distribution of blacks and whites between time periods, Price found that between 1940 and 1950 black men registered particular gains in clerical work, with black women gaining most in the clerical, sales, craft, and laborer categories (p. 116). In general, gains were greater for women than for men and were greater in the West than in other regions (pp. 115–130). The dozen years from 1949 to 1961, however, encompassed four recessions and a related slowdown in the gains of the war years—in some categories an actual reversal. Although blacks continued to gain in the clerical and craft sectors, in the defense industry, and in the West, their representation among managers and officials (except farm) declined and in most other sectors remained stagnant. Then, during the 1960s, the occupational position of blacks relative to whites advanced again, with the proportion of black workers represented in professional, technical, and managerial positions increasing from 9.4% to 12.6% compared with a shift from 24.7% to 26.0% for whites (Wilson, 1978, p. 131).[16]

It is likely that the occupational advance of blacks has been slowed by the recession of 1974–75, the subsequent slowdown in economic growth, and an erosion of support for strong forms of affirmative action. The previous convergence of black and white wages also slowed down during the late 1970s and the 1980s (Blau, 1998, p. 134; Wilson, 1978, p. 130). And by 1994 in every educational category, the income of black men as a percentage of non-Hispanic white income was still substantially unequal; it ranged between about 70% (high-school graduates or less) to 77% (college graduates) (Thernstrom and Thernstrom, 1997, p. 445).

There is a growing gap between educated, affluent blacks and poor blacks. The movement of blacks out of the least desirable jobs (low-paid service workers and laborers) is proceeding more slowly than their advance into the most-favored jobs (Wilson, 1978, p. 134). In fact, by 1990, 16% of black men and 23% of black women were in the categories "professional" and "technical and related support occupations" and "proprietors, managers, and officials" (Thernstrom and Thernstrom, 1997, p. 185), putting greater distance between themselves and the blacks below. Divergence in occupations is matched by divergence in family income: the average income of the top 5% of black families increased by $27,114 (in constant 1992 dollars) between 1975 and 1992; the average income of the lowest fifth decreased by $2,078 in the same time period (Wilson, 1996, pp. 195–196, table 7.1). These trends have contributed to a deepening economic schism in the black community.

Data on occupational attainment by education suggest that discrimination against blacks is more pronounced for those with less education. By the mid-1970s, black men appear even to have achieved parity at upper educational levels: 58% of black men with a college education were employed in professional and technical occupations, compared with 54% of college-educated white men. In 1978, black women college graduates scored an even more impressive concentration in this desired category: 65% of them were in professional and technical occupations, the identical percentage of their white counterparts.[17] For blacks with a high-school education, however, the situation is reversed: 30% of black men with only a high-school education were service workers or laborers, compared with 14% of white men (U.S. Bureau of Labor Statistics, 1975a, 1975b). Black women with only high school fared no better. Similarly, if we consider age and job experience, by 1972 the occupational status of black males who had recently entered the labor force approached that of equally experienced whites (Hall and Kasten, 1973, p. 790). The position of older, less-educated blacks had not improved comparably (Freeman, 1973, p. 118).

Residential segregation by race has been declining in the United States since about 1970 but the process is slow, especially among blacks (Massey and Denton, 1993, pp. 10, 49, 62, 64, 222).[18] Racial desegregation occurred most rapidly in young, Southern, and Western metropolitan areas with recent housing construction (Farley and Frey, 1994). The desegregation of Mexicans is faster and the desegregation of Asians and non-Mexican Hispanics is much faster than that of blacks (Smith and Edmonston, 1997, pp. 367–368; Massey, 1981; Myers, 1999). If we examine the fate of racial groups in racial enclaves, including the gateway communities of immigrants, we find that the second generation of both Asians and Hispanics does move up and out. The myth of downward mobility of these immigrants is much exaggerated.[19] For instance, a cohort analysis of Los Angeles and Santa Ana Latinos shows gains in white-collar jobs and reduced poverty. Dowell Myers (1999) found very strong intergenerational progress up and out of the gateway community.[20] Similarly, studies of Cuban workers in Florida suggest that even the first generation's employment in the enclave economy is not much of a drag on earnings. Enclave employment depresses male earnings and the return from education only marginally. Further, this does not hold for females. And a network of ethnic entrepreneurs often provides a foothold for ethnic employees—some jobs for recent immigrants who speak little English. Such a network also provides new entrepreneurial opportunities for both the newcomers and the second generation. These informal, self-help networks are highly developed among Asian immigrants as well as Hispanics and Iranians but are very scarce in black ghettos. Immigrants from China, Korea, and the West Indies have long ago established rotating savings and credit associations whose start-up capital is widely shared, a major base for mobility journeys for both first- and second-generation immigrants. (Light and Karageorgis, 1997, pp. 1–17.)

To say that recent racial immigrants move up and out of enclave economies, like the white ethnics of the past, is not to ignore their initial heavy overrepresentation among the low-skilled, low-wage, low-education poverty population. The very behavior that serves as a base for upward mobility in one or two generations is the hard work at low wages that their late-19th-century predecessors did. Nor does it ignore the depressing effects of such competitive behavior on the wages of native Americans, including earlier immigrants and blacks (see cross-national discussion in chap. 17). For example, Korean immigrants, who have a very high rate of self-employment, are willing to work long hours for little money in family businesses in inner-city neighborhoods where supermarkets fear to tread or in multiple entry-level jobs such as janitor, handyman, or maid. First-generation Latinos and Asians alike follow the formula "Sacrifice, save, pool resources, and borrow from family and friends."

If some minority groups are overrepresented among the poor, others are overrepresented among highly educated elites. For instance, the National Research Council found that in the mid-1990s, immigrants—including Jews, Japanese, Chinese, and those from Central and Southeast Europe—appear disproportionately as Nobel Prize winners, members of the National Academy of Sciences and the National Academy of Engineering, as business entrepreneurs, and as cultural and intellectual leaders in literature, music, film, and the top universities. Because almost all immigrants of the past 50 years arrived as minorities in a sociological sense, we can take the impressive showing of the foreign born as prize winners and intellectual stars as a rough guide to the accomplishments of minorities. The phrase that captures this is full integration. Finally, in the polity, the penetration of highly educated minorities and women into elite positions has been accelerating. Their participation in the Executive branch is obvious in Washington, D.C., as it is for racial minorities in the Pentagon. Locally, at the beginning of 1993, blacks were the mayors of 5 of the 20 biggest cities. Minority representation in Congress has lagged, especially in the Senate, but that trend, too, is up. In short, minorities, including today's immigrant population, are split between newcomers who are much better and much worse educated, and more economically depressed and more economically affluent, than the average native-born person. Further, when they have organized and formed political alliances with others, minority groups have increased their political power.

Why Variation in the Integration of Minorities?

This brief account of the structural integration of white ethnics and some racial minorities in the United States points to an explanation of variation in the rate of integration that can apply to minority groups in any rich democracy. Five factors shape the rate of integration of a minority group, including immigrants. First is the *resources* the group brings to the destination country or community—resources of urban or entrepreneurial experience; work-relevant skills, including work habits; and credit or money, as in the debt pools of Asians and West Indians. Second is whether the group has *exposure to public schools of reasonable quality* (segregated parochial schools until quite recently were inferior in both financing and quality). The third determinant of the rate of integration is *family structures and child-rearing philosophies and practices* favorable to their children's occupational mobility. Fourth is the *structure of economic opportunity* the group encounters upon its arrival. Finally, *public policies* shape the fate of minority groups, and these vary greatly across time and place. All these explain variation in the speed with which minorities achieve occupational parity with the nonminority population and ultimately full integration—political, economic, and cultural. Thus, among immigrant groups in America, Russians (including Jews), Scandinavians, Austrians, Romanians, Greeks, Northern Italians, and Northwestern European Protestants were occupationally advantaged and achieved occupational parity within one generation, while Italians from rural Sicily, Polish peasants, Yugoslavs, French Canadians, and some of the Irish were disadvantaged. The fast movers typically had urban experience, many as self-employed entrepreneurs. It was not a big leap for the impoverished Jews with previous entrepreneurial experience to work as peddlers, save a little capital, and in a few years open a small mom-and-pop grocery store. One such peddler, named Levi Strauss, built one of the world's most famous corporations, starting in the California Gold Rush years (Sowell, 1996, p. 294). Similarly, Greek restaurateurs and Armenian carpet importers used skills developed in the homeland. The contrast between the entering skills of Northern Italians from Milan or Turin and the lack of skills of their Southern Italian counterparts explains their later trajectories in America. Sicilian peasants manned the flaming forges of Pittsburgh steel mills or became construction laborers; their integration was slow. Urbanites from Northern Italy in short order went West, worked at whatever they could find, saved, bought land, and produced wine; within three or four generations they became leading executives and politicians (e.g., Mayor Alioto of San Francisco).[21]

Related to these patterns is the stance taken toward separate (and unequal) schools. The fast movers combined parochial schools with public schools (Jews, some upwardly mobile Italian Catholics) or took advantage of public schools and disciplined their children to pursue the academic track. Southern Italians and Polish peasants, in contrast, were encapsulated both in parochial schools of poor quality and ethnic neighborhoods where the ethnic language was the norm (e.g., the Polish enclave at the southeast tip of Chicago). This slowed up the first generation's rate of integration and their children's mobility. Although residential segregation was common for all entering ethnic and racial groups—and if complete, reduced their rate of intermarriage—it was not a barrier to economic integration for their children, unless it included the segregation of disadvantages (parochial schools of inferior quality, neighborhoods without social networks that provide entry to the job market and without strong families oriented toward education and better jobs).[22]

A little-studied force for second-generation achievement is the variation of minority groups in their family structures and child-rearing philosophies and practices. It has been shown that growing up in a single-parent impoverished family is a barrier to the educational and occupational achievement of sons and daughters (see chapters 8 [Welfare Mess], 14 [Mayhem], and 16 [Health Performance]). There are also strong hints of ethnic and racial variations in work-relevant values and beliefs shaping child-rearing practices even at the same socioeconomic status (SES). For instance, Fred Strodtbeck (1958) compared family interaction and child-rearing patterns in 24 Jewish families and 24 Italian families with third-generation 16-year-old sons in New Haven, Connecticut. Independence training and academic achievement values were much stronger among Jewish parents and their sons than among Italians; the sons evidenced equally sharp differences in autonomy, aspirations, and school performance, at each of three SES levels. Similar results come from a study of ethnic-group variations in the timing of mother's expectation for age of mastery. Early timing had a strong, positive effect on the achievements of their 8- to 10-year-olds. The indicators of making the child more independent of his family included what age should the child know his way around the city, try new things without depending on mother for help, try hard to come out on top in games and sports, and make his own friends among children his own age. The average age for expected mastery varied by ethnic group as expected: Jewish, 6.1; Irish Catholic, 7.1; Italian Catholic, 8.2, with achievement scores in that order. (*Ibid.*, pp. 144–146.) Finally, there are well-known differences in the accent on academic achievement between Jews, Chinese, and Japanese on the one hand, and blacks and Latinos on the other. That these differences in parental values and practices are distinctly ethnic or racial and have big effects on children's school achievement is shown by a recent study of adolescent development: Steinberg and his colleagues (1996; Steinberg et al., 1992a, 1992b) found that Asian-American students outperformed European-American students who, in turn, outperformed African-American and Latin American students by large margins that remained consistent and strong across nine high schools studied and even after controlling for social class, family structure, and place of birth of parents.[23]

In short, intact families with work-relevant values who accent independence training and public school achievement provide a favorable basis for their children's move out, up, and into the mainstream economy. The overseas Chinese as minority groups in places like Indonesia and the Japanese in Hawaii and Peru evidence the same entrepreneurial success based on the same pattern of behavior (Sowell, 1996, pp. 113–119, 200–206).

Resources of skill and urban experience, exposure to public schools (when they had higher standards than now), and favorable family structure and child-rearing practices by themselves will not suffice for speedy mobility and integration if the structure of economic opportunity is poor. Employers must be open to minority hiring and the economy must evidence steady growth. If we examine modern systems of job placement (Wilensky and Lawrence, 1979), we see that when work roles are more or less clearly defined and criteria can be specified which can be met by a wide range of people (semiskilled clerical or factory jobs), the satisficing manager assigns employees on a cheap ascriptive basis (white male, Italian Catholic, young female, or whatever established network of coworkers, relatives, and friends his employees connect with). When roles are vaguely defined (public relations manager, salesperson) or rapidly changing (middle manager)—perhaps this applies to most jobs in a modern labor force—room for ascription is even wider. However, four economic and political forces can shake managers up enough to change their natural job assignment strategies. First is a shortage of labor. There is nothing like a brisk labor market to make a high-school graduate look useful; an old man, strong; an inexperienced woman, skilled; a black, acceptable; and an "unemployable," a good bet for the next opening (Wilensky, 1965, p. xxxiii). A boom economy inspires managers to widen their search, launch more training, even restructure jobs to fit available applicants. In other words, in good times employees outside the usual ascriptive network get the glad hand; in bad times they get the brush-off. Shortages of labor in the period 1993–1998 helped to move the high unemployment rates of three groups to new lows by April 1999—teenagers to 14.1%, blacks to 7.7%, Hispanics to 6.9% (*New York Times,* May 8, 1999).

Beyond good times, a second impetus to changed hiring and promotion practices is government coercion via fair employment practice laws such as those of the 1940s and 1950s or affirmative action programs such as those of the 1960s and beyond. As I have shown, the occupational integration of blacks—their penetration of middle and upper-middle professional and technical jobs—proceeded faster in the prosperous periods of World War II and 1960 to 1973 than in the slumps of the 1950s or the slow growth period after 1974. But there was more than the business cycle at work. The armed forces during and after World War II led in occupational integration (Moskos, 1966). And most of the civilian gains since World War II have been in occupations in which a large portion of the nonwhites are hired by government. All of this suggests that vigorous antidiscrimination policies can make it too expensive for employers, public or private, to stick to the older combinations of ascriptive networks and merit.

A second cluster of policies that inspires employers to rely a bit less on cheap ascriptive networks is heavy government subsidy of an active labor-market policy designed to reach the hard-to-employ and to place everyone. Sweden, West Germany, and several Western European welfare-state leaders, in contrast to the United States, have developed strong labor-market boards and labor exchanges coupled with a great range of policies to match people and jobs and train everyone who does not fit the needs of a changing economy (see chap. 2, figure 2.2).

Government coercion and active labor-market policies interact with a third political pressure for change in employers' job placement strategies: social movements for equality, which are a product of industrialization everywhere. We must consider the push from below as it affects employer cost calculations. Social movements—whether based on minority-group interests or class—aim to introduce their own ascriptive criteria within a category of sufficiently qualified, just as employers in the absence of pressures for change had previously combined ascriptive and achievement criteria for their own convenience.

A related aspect of the managers' calculations goes beyond the cost of recruitment, training, and job evaluation. Where unions, workers' councils, or informal work groups press for seniority or other preferences in hiring and promotion, the manager who ignores their demands can provoke labor disputes, decrease morale, increase absenteeism and turnover, and lower product quality. At various times and places managers have confronted a wide variety of demands to modify placement practices. Consider this list for preferential treatment:

- seniority in promotions and layoffs (universal)

- superseniority for labor leaders and activists (USA) or war veterans (universal)

- preference for relatives (craftsmen in the USA; clientelismo in Italy)

- credit for "peasant" and "worker" parentage (university and hence job entry in Communist Poland)

- ethnic-linguistic background (Belgium, Canada) or race (USA)

- confessional-political affiliation (Holland)

- physical handicaps or sex (many countries)

- region (in Italian politics and the bureaucracy, preference for Sicilians has provoked the label, "the Southernization of Italy")

Most employers must make judgments, however imperfectly, about these costs. Since there is no predetermination of the outcome of struggles among minority groups and between minorities and majorities, the particular combination of ascription and achievement employers adopt will vary by country and region, and over time. Further, in some situations, employers see a cost advantage in playing one minority group against another. The point for me is that in no sense can we see the effort to substitute one ascriptive criterion for another—within the broad category of "adequately qualified"—as premodern. In fact, it is the universal correlates of industrialization—modern communication and transportation networks, mass education, urbanization, high rates of residential and occupational mobility—that have given force to the push for equality. The result is new self-consciousness, new aspirations, and new political and economic resources for minority groups.

In Norway, Sweden, Belgium, the Netherlands, and other countries with long periods of social democratic rule, the push for equality no longer comes mainly from below; those "below," now in control of the government, go to great lengths to ensure full employment of minorities and majorities alike. Norway, for instance, has written into its constitution the right to work, with the proviso that anyone "fit" to work may exercise that right. In such circumstances, the employer's cost calculations become even more complex because a large medical-psychiatric-administrative apparatus must certify everyone's "fitness" for the job entitlement. Even when full employment falters as in the 1990s these countries still maintained a relatively good standard of living for their least-privileged populations, including minorities (see tables 8.4 and 14.4).

Where does this leave the counteracting meritocratic thrust of modern society? Very much alive. Although equality of opportunity (a heavy accent on achievement criteria for job entry and placement) is at war with absolute equality or equality of results (a heavy accent on ascription), both principles have powerful roots in the structure of modern society (Wilensky, 1975, pp. 28–39 and chap. 4 in this text). The modern complex workplace mirrors this larger conflict. (That our rich democracies resolve this conflict in a variety of ways with a variety of backlash responses, especially in their immigration policies and politics, is discussed in chaps. 10 and 17.)

The contrasts between the speedy integration of white ethnics, West Indian blacks, and the similar mobility of recent Asian immigrants, on the one hand, and the slow integration of most blacks on the other, fit this scheme. In the United States, as Thomas Sowell (1978) has demonstrated, there were three black histories with contrasting urbanization, education, occupational fate, and to some extent family structures:[24] antebellum "free persons of color" (in the 1830s, 14% of American Negroes); black slaves emancipated by the Civil War and their descendants, the largest component; and later black immigrants (about 1% of the current population of the USA), mainly from other parts of the Western Hemisphere, especially the British West Indies, with substantial numbers arriving about the turn of the century. Then as now the West Indian immigrants were concentrated around New York City. What must be explained is the vastly different social and economic trajectories of the three black populations over several generations.

The free persons of color (FPCs) achieved freedom via manumissions, self-purchase, purchase of slaves by already free relatives or philanthropic whites, legislative reward for unusual service or Northern states' emancipation laws, or escape. Also, mulattos born to white women were by law declared free. Many additional blacks were semifree—slaves who "hired their own time," lived away from slave owners, paying them a share of their earnings. The family structures, the resources they brought to the economy and their achievement included the following:

- *Urban Experience.* Not only were they more urbanized than chattel slaves, they were more urbanized than the white population. They increasingly moved toward urban Northern and border states.

- *Family Structure.* Data from 1855 to 1880 show that their households were overwhelmingly male-headed, stable, two parent.

- *Literacy, Education-Mindedness.* Their literacy rates were 10 times higher than blacks in bondage, and this persisted for decades after emancipation. If not educated themselves, they were education-minded. Where their children were denied admission to public schools they established private schools of their own, sometimes aided by Quakers and Catholics.

- *Occupation and Income.* Their descendants were overrepresented among successful blacks well into the 20th century. With their cultural head starts, over half of the black professionals in Washington, D.C., in 1950 were descended from the small population of antebellum FPCs. Many of the descendants of FPCs became established Negro leaders of the post–Civil War and early 20th century—for example, as founders of the NAACP. Finally, the FPCs had much more entrepreneurial experience than field hands could have. They were disproportionately skilled—tailors, carpenters, masons—especially in New Orleans and Charleston, as early as 1860. In fact, in those years the freedmen of the Northeast faced competition from Irish immigrants of the 1840s and 1850s and won handily. Some advertisements in New York City were explicit: "A colored man preferred. No Irish need apply."

West Indian immigrants traced a later but similar trajectory, with even more success than the FPCs. West Indian slavery made escapes as well as slave uprisings more feasible because blacks were a vast majority of the West Indian population. Equally important, slaves were permitted to grow their own food and sell surpluses in off-plantation markets. The absence of a white working class created a wider occupational range for blacks, including self-employment. All this adds up to experience in self-management and entrepreneurship. Subjectively it fostered a sense of possibilities. The outcome over generations: Their mobility pattern resembled that of the fast-moving urban white immigrants from Europe (see the preceding) more than it resembled the limited mobility of native blacks. They had a lower rate of family breakup than that of emancipated slaves in the same areas. Either during their work lives or their children's, they moved up the ladder much faster than native blacks; they have long had much higher income, education, and occupational status than native blacks. A natural outcome: they are much overrepresented among prominent blacks, now and in the past—Marcus Garvey, James Weldon Johnson, Stokely Carmichael, Shirley Chisholm, Malcolm X, Kenneth Clark, James Farmer, Roy Innes, W. Arthur Lewis, Harry Belafonte, Sidney Poitier, and Godfrey Cambridge, among others.[25]

Emancipated slaves, in contrast, were handicapped in all dimensions I have outlined to explain the varied mobility patterns of white ethnics. Southern slavery was characterized by regimented dependence and repression unparalleled by any other slavery. There was a natural sense of the futility of resistance to white slave-owners. There was no self-employment, no market experience. Regimentation was carried to its extreme in the plantation-dominated "black belt" areas of the South. Plantation slavery was almost all rural (in the urban South almost a third of slaves were hired workers who frequently arranged their own daily lives). Escape possibilities were minimal. After Emancipation, peonage became common. Most of the few who had acquired skills could not find jobs. At the turn of the century, the pervasive pattern of discriminating segregation known as "Jim Crow" took hold across the South. The segregation of disadvantages perpetuated the economic deterioration of several decades after the Civil War. Again we see sharp contrasts to the two black histories outlined previously. There was almost total illiteracy; slave-owners forbade slaves to read or write. Meager education was the rule throughout the 19th century and into the early years of the 20th. The only pattern that does not fit my scheme is the family structure of plantation slaves. Because slave-owners viewed stable two-parent families as a barrier to escapes and a way of preventing chaos if men fought over women, most of these slave families were two parent. The broken families in today's trap ghettos are a new pattern developed after the massive migration of unskilled, uneducated blacks from South to North in the 20th century. Segregation then became more common and in the 1920s hardened. A final factor blocking the success of the later migrants was the changed structure of opportunity of the postwar period. The boom economies of World Wars I and II had provided semiskilled footholds in urban industry for blacks as well as Appalachian whites. Urban political machines had provided jobs and social services for white ethnics of an earlier migration (see chap. 11). By the 1950s both the semiskilled/unskilled job base and the political machines had eroded, drastically reducing opportunities for the least-skilled, late arrivers in the metropolitan areas.

In comparing the three black histories it is tempting to attribute their contrasting success rates to skin color. Lighter skin mulattos, it is said, experience less discrimination than blacks with darker skin. That might be a factor in the success of the FPCs, who were more often mulattos, but it certainly cannot explain the West Indian contrast; the latter were clearly more black than the average post–Civil War emancipated slave. Neither in comparing whites and blacks nor different populations of blacks can we explain much by skin color. Numerous sociological studies demonstrate that the disadvantage from growing up in an impoverished family much outweighs immigrant status or even racial status in predicting school and work achievement (see chaps. 8 [Welfare Mess], 14 [Mayhem], and 17 [Globalization]).

In sum: The main drift of rich democracies over the past century has been toward the structural integration of ethnic-linguistic, religious, and racial minorities. Multiethnic America, as the best test case, shows that within the general trend minority groups vary in their rate of integration. The speed and amount of educational and occupational integration is shaped by five interacting forces: (1) the resources of urban experience, education, and skills the group brings to the urban-industrial economy; (2) the quality of schools into which the group puts its children (segregation of disadvantages slows the rate of integration); (3) the family structure and child-rearing practices and values of the group; (4) the structure of opportunity the group encounters when it enters both the labor market and the political market (both vary by the business cycle); (5) public policies favorable or unfavorable to integration, which are a product of the strength of social-political movements for equality, government coercion to enforce antidiscrimination laws and force employers to open up to minorities and, of course, policies regarding the number, kind, and legality of immigrants and the naturalization rate. (National differences in immigration policies and politics are discussed in chap. 17 [Globalization].)

If, over two or three generations, family, relevant skills, education, job opportunity, and public policies are all favorable for economic and political integration, then increased intermarriage rates and, with them, cultural integration will follow. Intermarriage rates, as well as other indicators of integration, however, can be reduced wherever a minority population is residentially segregated or isolated and is new to the urban-industrial setting. Despite long-term gains for blacks and a marked improvement for employed, young, well-educated blacks in particular and for the black middle class in general, a significant gap remains between the occupational distribution of whites and that of blacks in the American economy, accounted for only partly by amount and quality of formal schooling. It is striking, however, that with all the barriers to full integration for blacks, evidence indicates a recent rise in intermarriages with whites or Hispanics, the most dramatic symbol of assimilation. In 1990, only 4% of blacks had contracted such marriages. But the rate for 25- to 34-year-old black men was 10%, most of them with white women. (Alba, 1995, pp. 16–17.) It is possible that this is a clue to coming attractions. The rate for Jews was only 11% in 1965; since 1985, 57% of Jews have married partners raised in other religions (ibid., p. 15). The concentration of postwar black migrants with least skills and education in central-city ghettos, however, is a major barrier to both their mobility and their social integration (see chap. 14 [Mayhem]).

Despite the long-term trend toward integration, modern democracies still experience episodes of ethnic resurgence. There is no shortage of political conflict based on race, ethnicity, language, and religion, as we can see from Ireland; the combat between Flemings and Walloons in Belgium; the role of race, religion, and language in the politics of the United

States, Israel, Canada, Switzerland, and the Netherlands; and nativist protests against immigrants everywhere (see chap. 17). That minority/majority conflict in many rich democracies has become or remains central to politics does not contradict the assimilation argument. First, it is the grievance about to be settled that is most poignant. Protest movements, like strikes and revolutions, are most successful on the upswing of the business cycle, not on the downswing. Militant black-power movements in the United States did not occur in depressed times and places; they occurred after much progress toward integration had been achieved and a political voice could be heard. In Europe, voting for xenophobic, nativist politicians is strongest in well-developed areas where economic readjustment is swift. And the anti-immigrant voters are far from marginal; they tend to be citizens of the middle mass with something to lose (see chap. 17). Second, side by side with structural integration, in every society segregated minorities are sharing a common fate. In the United States in 1998 first- and second-generation immigrants together comprise only about one-fifth of the total population, but they are highly concentrated in the metropolitan areas of six states—Florida, California, New York, New Jersey, Illinois, and Texas. They constitute 60% of the population of metropolitan Miami, over half of Los Angeles, 42% of New York City, and 40 % of the San Francisco Bay Area (Waters, Mollenkopf, and Kasinitz, 1999, pp. 5−6). Despite the trend toward desegregation, they still tend to be concentrated in the central cities of these metropolitan areas, giving them further political visibility. Where ethnic, racial, or religious groups are segregated residentially and at the same time experience economic reinforcement for minority identity and social solidarity, then a subculture with political potential flourishes. Neighborhoods composed of craft workers in the needle trades, truck farmers, and retail merchants, or intellectuals, artists, and entertainers, sometimes have an ethnic-religious or racial recruitment base. Their members derive job information or even entrepreneurial capital from propinquity, kinship, and friendship (cf. Wilensky, 1966c, p. 127; Light, 1972). The extreme case of persistent ethnic and tribal ties in the urban ghettos of South Africa is consistent. But overall segregation in rich democracies has declined; social, political, and economic integration proceeds, leaving large pockets of militancy behind, sometimes giving the impression of a Balkanization of society and politics.[26]

Gender Equality

Industrialization has everywhere been accompanied by a swift increase in female labor-force participation, a slower decline in sexual segregation in occupations, and a still slower increase in the relative and absolute occupational status of women. In the United States, the labor-force participation rate for women has climbed steadily from 20% in 1900 to more than 60% at latest count. During the same period, the occupational integration of women also advanced, but less rapidly. For instance, Oppenheimer (1970) found that sexual segregation in the United States (measured by the ratio of the number of women found in predominantly female occupations to that expected by chance) declined from 3.5 in 1900 to 2.1 in 1960 (p. 69). Using different indices, Gross (1968) and G. Williams (1975) also show a drop in differentiation during this period. Cross-national data by industry are consistent. In a rare, detailed study of trends in sex segregation by industry covering 10 European nations and the United States, Cooney (1978) found that from the early 1900s until about the 1960s sex segregation within broad industrial sectors declined in all countries examined, although rates of change varied by period and country. The same universal decline was uncovered in a study of sex segregation in 14 industrialized countries from 1960 to 1990 (Chang, 1999).

Whatever the pace of change and by any measure, the absolute amount of occupational differentiation in the United States remains high. In 1969, half of all male workers were concentrated in only 63 occupations, while half of all female workers were concentrated in only 17 occupations. And one-fourth of all women at work were concentrated in just five jobs: secretary, household worker, bookkeeper, elementary school teacher, and waitress (Hedges, 1970, p. 19). In other words, women in 1969 were occupationally segregated 3.7 times more than men. Although a similar measure as of 1984 shows some broadening of women's occupations, substantial differences in occupational concentration remain (Bergmann, 1986).

Sex segregation does not necessarily measure discrimination. Cooney shows that in all 11 countries she studied, sex desegregation proceeded faster than the pace of improvement in the absolute and relative work status of women (Cooney, 1978, pp. 70–71). Indeed, a more recent study of gender segregation by occupation in 9 countries (Australia, Austria, Germany, Hungary, Norway, Sweden, Switzerland, UK, and USA), circa mid-1980s, found that the countries least segregated by occupation are the United States and Switzerland; the most segregated country is Sweden, with Norway also ranking high (Blau and Kahn, 1996b, table 3). Yet, by better measures of gender equality, the pattern is reversed: Sweden and Norway lead in gender equality, the United States and Switzerland lag.[27] To measure discrimination more directly we must consider at least some indicator of relevant abilities.[28] Holding education constant, we find less discrimination: college-educated women in the United States are more likely than similarly educated men to be found in professional and technical jobs; 69.4% of women, compared with 54.1% of men, were in this favored category in 1975. However, college-educated women were less than a third as likely as men to become managers or proprietors (7.1% to the men's 24.1%). High-school-educated women are concentrated in clerical jobs; high-school-educated men in the "craftsmen and foremen" category (U.S. Bureau of Labor Statistics, 1975a, 1975b).

Of course, broad census categories obscure considerable variation within categories. For instance, Epstein (1970) showed that within the professional and technical category, women in the 1960s were concentrated in those sectors of the professions with the least pay, prestige, and opportunity for advancement. The past 30 or so years, however, saw an accelerated shift toward economic equality: The rising educational attainment of women led to accelerated labor-force participation and a rising expectation among both women and employers of continuous employment. In turn these trends led families, women, and employers alike to invest more in women's human capital. (See the preceding and chap. 7 [Family Policy]. Cf. Blau, 1998, p. 131.) The consequences include a decline in the earnings gap; women have fared better than men in real wage growth (*ibid.*). Women have clearly penetrated high-status occupations at a rapid rate. From 1970 to 1996 there was a large, steady rise in women's share of professional degrees: from well below 10% in 1970 to 44% of all law degrees, 41% of MDs, and 38% of MBAs (U.S. Department of Education, 1999, tables 259 and 280). In all three of these male domains women have now penetrated even the most powerful and lucrative specialties.[29]

The gender gap in earnings was dramatically reduced in the United States from 1979 to 1988 despite trends in overall wage structure that were increasingly unfavorable to low-wage workers, a trend that was reversed only in the six years from 1993 to 1998.

This puzzle—how the gender gap can close while low-wage workers were sinking—can be solved by noting three clear changes: (1) the improvement in women workers' relative qualifications (education, experience, commitment to work); (2) declining discrimination, as shown above; and (3) the larger negative effect of deunionization on male than female workers (women actually increased as a proportion of union members) (Blau and Kahn, 1997). These gender-specific trends occur within a larger trend toward wage and income inequality. As chapters 2 and 8 show, the integration of powerful labor movements into corporatist bargaining structures of most democracies in continental Europe and the consequent public policies explain why the U.S., despite improvements in gender equality, still remains at the bottom in cross-national comparisons. For instance, a study of earnings differentials in 10 rich democracies (Blau and Kahn, 1996b) shows that the U.S. has both the greatest concentration of very low wages at the bottom compared with the middle, and the greatest rewards to "skill" (i.e., education). The most powerful explanation of these country rankings is that the most egalitarian countries have national bargaining structures that result in wage compression and more income equality affecting both men and women. Blau and Kahn (1996b, pp. 535–538ff.) find that national differences in women's human capital or individual characteristics are far less important. In other words, while increases in gender equality in the U.S. are partly due to the rise in women's relative qualifications common to all countries, and while wage inequality for both men and women has been rising in most rich democracies, when we compare nations we must look to types of political economy and related policy differences to explain the U.S. lag in gender equality.[30]

National variations in the political power and representation of women match the differences in economic equality, as we shall see in chapter 8 (table 8.4). Here, too, within a general trend toward gender equality in politics over the past half century, substantial national differences remain, with the Anglo-American democracies, Japan, and France lagging. Applying the types of political economy discussed in chapter 2, the percentage of women in the lower house of national legislatures in the early 1980s shows a perfect gradation: The average for left-corporatist democracies was 22%; left-Catholic corporatist, 18%; Catholic corporatist, 8%; corporatist-without-labor, 6%; fragmented and decentralized democracies, 5%. The United States and Canada tied at 4%, the United Kingdom was at the bottom with 3%. (Data on our 19 countries are from Rule, 1987, table 2.) It is the interaction of left party power, proportional representation, and democratic corporatism that best explains the top scores for gender equality in politics (see my table 2.1). Even the laggards, however, evidence gains. A recent study of women in U.S. politics shows that if women run for office they win as often as men do and that women are running in steadily increasing numbers. The trend holds from 1972 to 1994 for state legislatures, governors, and the U.S. House and Senate alike. By 1995, women were 17% of state senators, 22% of state representatives, but only 11% of U.S. House members and 8% of U.S. senators (Seltzer, Newman, and Leighton, 1997, pp. 85, 87, 91–92).

In sum: Continuing industrialization has clearly improved job opportunities for women in all countries. The occupational and political integration of highly educated women has accelerated. Even so, most women still remain concentrated in nurturant, expressive, and subordinate roles such as nurses, preschool and elementary teachers and teachers aides, social workers, pediatricians, life scientists, dental hygienists, therapists, receptionists, models, secretaries and other administrative supporters, waitresses, workers in subordinate clerical and sales jobs, and workers in the arts, design, and personal care and services. Their economic position, however—their wages, poverty rates, cushions against shocks of family breakup—varies greatly across equally rich nations.

Age and Equality

Disadvantaged as they are in the labor market, minorities and women have generally enjoyed substantial labor-market gains with continued industrialization. Not so for the aged, many of whom are chronically unemployed or underemployed in modern economies. Older people who are employed evidence an occupational profile similar to that of other adults; they tend to be slightly overrepresented in managerial posts and in the farm sector and underrepresented in professional and technical jobs and in clerical work (Riley and Foner, 1968; U.S. Bureau of the Census, 1977, p. 406). However, employed or not, their skills are plainly underutilized. Although older workers are less likely to be laid off than their younger workmates, they are more likely to experience difficulty being rehired and this has intensified in recent years. Cross-national evidence shows that the duration of unemployment rises steadily with age in the United States, Canada, Belgium, and the Netherlands. (Riley and Foner, 1968, p. 47, cf. Kohli and Rein, 1991, pp. 11−17.) Job opportunities decline markedly with advancing years after the age of 45 (Wirtz, 1965, p. 4). For instance, a survey of employers conducted by the U.S. Bureau of Employment Security in the prosperous year 1965 found that only 9% of the previous year's new hires were over 45. Yet the percentage of unemployed workers in the older age group was much higher.[31] Three decades later, BLS data for 1995−96 showed that among displaced long-tenured workers, those aged 55 and over who were searching had a much harder time finding new jobs than did other workers.

Most important, there is no doubt that for many decades increasing numbers of talented older people have been forced to retire before they choose to. Since 1890, in almost all industrial countries, the labor-force participation rates of older men have steadily decreased. The main causes: the rise of compulsory retirement rules in legislation and in collective bargaining contracts, the preference of employers for younger men and women at cheaper wages, union preference for well-financed early retirement to make room for the young, and the growing occupational obsolescence of the aged. (Long, 1958; Riley and Foner, 1968; Fisher, 1978.) At the same time, increased longevity, improved health, and the increased educational level of successive cohorts of the aged have prolonged the years of productive life. The inevitable result of the intersection of these trends is a growing number of able older workers who are excluded from the labor market completely or are chronically unemployed or underemployed. Thus, discrimination against older workers accelerated as rich countries got richer; successive generations of men are less likely to be in work at age 65, 55, and even 45. And while older women (over 55) are now much more likely to have jobs than they used to, they have not shared in the recent general rise in female employment (N. Campbell, 1999).

It is fair to infer discrimination from these trends for two reasons: First, surveys show that voluntary decisions to retire early are not the major causes of the decline in work for older men. Most exit decisions are coerced; they are involuntary or at least heavily constrained by falling relative wages, restricted job opportunity, problems of health, especially chronic sickness, or the reluctant acceptance of an early retirement package when unemployment is anticipated (older workers are concentrated in declining industries). (*Ibid.*; Guillemard and Rein, 1993; Kohli and Rein, 1991, pp. 8ff.) The second reason for inferring discrimination against older workers is analyses of the impact of social-security legislation and private pensions on the timing and amount of labor-force participation of the middle-aged and aged. The consensus is that the effect of increased benefit levels, while statistically significant, is much smaller than the other forces already discussed. For instance, Leonesio (1993, p. 50) estimates that in the United States a 10 to 12% increase in benefit levels causes a decline in average retirement age by only "weeks or a few months." For similar cross-national findings see Kohli and Rein (1991) and Guillemard and Rein (1993). Generous benefits have the most effect where older workers are stuck in low-paid jobs or dangerous, heavy, hot, dirty jobs and are glad to get out.

Regarding age inequalities other than the age distribution of employment, the trend is more favorable. The expansion of the welfare state (chap. 5) has clearly reduced poverty among the aged everywhere. As with gender equality, however, national variations in the poverty rate of the aged are anchored more in general poverty rates of the population at large than in policies targeted to the aged. A study by Tim Smeeding (1993) of poverty among the aged in the mid-1980s in seven of our countries (Australia, Canada, Netherlands, Sweden, UK, USA, West Germany) showed that poverty varies more across countries than across age groups within countries. The core of the welfare state includes pensions, disability insurance, and health care, all three used disproportionately by the aged. Therefore, welfare-state expansion everywhere reduces poverty among the aged (chap. 5). In most age/country cells in the tables in the seven countries studied, poverty rates are actually lower for those with retirement income than are societal poverty rates. Yet in the United States double-digit poverty is commonplace among the aged and nonaged alike—this despite the fact that American social-security programs are the most modern part of its welfare state.

The most general conclusion from these findings is this: Common trends in social structure—increased technological and organizational change, increased structural unemployment since the early 1970s, common responses of management, unions, and governments to these changes, and the common trend toward early exit from work—cannot be explained by national contrasts in social and labor-market policies. As I show in later chapters public policies focused on the aged certainly improve their well-being and account for large national differences in their fate. But the convergent trend toward earlier exit from the labor force persists in the face of these policy differences.

Whether recent political pressure applied by the aged and their allies coupled with anti-discrimination laws will eventually reverse this trend is uncertain. Chapter 7 discusses the politics of aging, the alleged war between the generations, and country contrasts in responses to population aging.

Summary

With continuing industrialization modern society tends toward the structural and cultural integration of minority groups based on descent (racial, ethnic, religious, linguistic), gender, sexual preference, or physical disability. As integration proceeds in education, the economy, and polity, as residential desegregation progresses, intermarriage rates begin to climb, which in turn leads to some sharing of values, beliefs, and tastes. Rich democracies in particular are increasingly open to the minority-group thrust for equality. The reasons for variation in the pace and extent of integration among minority groups discovered in American studies apply quite well to all rich democracies. The rate is fastest where the minority group brings to the urban economy resources of urban or entrepreneurial experience, credit, money or occupational skill; sends their children to schools that do not segregate disadvantages; has family structures and child-rearing practices and values that facilitate school and job achievement; and enters the economy at a time of favorable opportunity. Public policies promoting integration are also important; these include the enforcement of antidiscrimination laws, immigration and naturalization policies, and the spread of the franchise. Finally, social-political movements from below pressure democratic governments to adopt and enforce integrative policies. These forces help explain the American immigrant experience: the quick integration of some ethnic and racial groups, the slow integration of others.

Although Britain and Britain abroad (USA, Canada, Australia, New Zealand), Switzerland, Netherlands, and Belgium rank high in social cleavages, other rich democracies are converging in the pattern of ethnic conflict and accommodation. The main reasons: a recent revival of massive migration from poor to rich countries and continuing industrialization. If there is convergence, it is toward the American multicultural model.

Increasing gender equality has been a long-term trend as all democracies got richer and opportunity in education and the labor force expanded. Occupational segregation by sex has everywhere declined faster than the absolute or relative status of working women has improved. Despite a rapid acceleration of equality in earnings and occupations, and a slow penetration of high positions in workplaces and politics in the past 30 or so years, most women, especially those with less than a college degree, remain concentrated in nurturant, expressive, and subordinate jobs. Nevertheless, rich democracies are moving toward the Swedish model—and they include even Japan and Switzerland, the countries most resistant to gender equality.

A strongly convergent tendency induced by industrialization is the steady long-term decline in age of exit from work. The gap between official retirement age of pension systems and actual retirement age is widening. Although welfare states have vastly improved the standard of living of the elderly, the pressure for retirement has mounted when most of them or at least a large minority would prefer to work. In fact, the healthy aged are the only minority group that has suffered an increase in occupational discrimination since World War II.

It is no paradox that while structural and cultural integration of minority groups is proceeding, ethnic resurgence, women's liberation movements, and gray power groups periodically burst forth. Not only are those grievances about to be settled the most poignant, but groups that have already entered the mainstream have more resources of skill, leadership, and funding for political action than groups on the margins of modern society.

THE RISE OF MASS HIGHER EDUCATION[32]

If the decrease in the age of exit from work is a major convergent trend in all modern societies, the extension of schooling at the lower end of life is an equally profound structural shift. There is little dispute about this trend, so I can be brief. In the course of their development, all modern societies first expanded primary and then secondary schools, gradually raising the level of compulsory attendance to 12 or 13 years. At the levels of development achieved by rich democracies by the mid–20th century, they began to converge toward mass higher education, with ever-larger portions of the college-age population going on to post-secondary education.[33] As we shall see in chapters 5 and 6 (tables 6.1 and 6.3), the welfare-state laggards lead in the move from elite higher education to mass higher education, with the United States, Canada, Israel, and Australia out in front in higher-education expenditures, enrollment ratios, and similar measures (see also Wilensky, 1975, pp. 3–7, 122).

The main reason for this trade-off is that modern education is overwhelmingly merito-cratic and vocational, a contribution to equality of opportunity, especially at the higher levels, while a nation's health and welfare effort is mainly egalitarian, a contribution to equality of results (*ibid.*; Wilensky and Lawrence, 1979). This trade-off varies by historical period and level of schooling. At early levels of their economic development the nations of Western Europe and North America did not trade off education for social security. In the period 1840 or 1850 to about 1910 in the 15 European countries studied by Kaelble (1981, pp. 241–256), there was no link between education expansion and welfare policy and private charity. National differences in secondary and postsecondary schooling in this early period were driven by differences in traditional markets for university graduates—the church, a few professions (including teaching in upper secondary schools), and public administration. A very small percentage of the relevant age cohorts got these opportunities. The period was characterized by small and stagnant enrollments. Essentially what there was of education was confined to upper-middle-class and elite demands for status maintenance and career advancement.

In the last decades before World War I in some countries and by World War I for all, the stagnation of postprimary education was ended and the link with economic growth was established (Kaelble, 1981, pp. 242–255). A slow expansion of opportunities in secondary school and university education began, both by simple enrollment growth and by slightly less unequal distribution by social origins of students. Two powerful forces drove this expansion: first, accelerating industrialization and its structural correlates, especially the demand for skilled, literate employees in both private industry and public bureaucracies; second, and later, an enfranchised mass organized in left political parties and labor movements that demanded equality of opportunity and to a lesser extent absolute equality. The timing of both advanced industrialization and left-labor power, of course, varied (see chap. 2). The full-blown demand for university graduates came quite late. Arnold Heidenheimer's analysis of policy thresholds for higher education and for social security shows that the year when university enrollment, both public and private, first comprised 10% of primary school enrollment was 1946 for the USA, 1968 for Sweden, 1973 for the UK, and 1975 for Germany (1981, pp. 294–299).

Just as there were variations in the timing of educational expansion, there were variations in the relationship between educational and social-security expansion. In the early period of industrialization in the United States, universal primary-school education was widespread before national social-security systems were invented and the acceleration of secondary school expansion was under way long before the New Deal. In contrast, Germany under Bismark put the welfare state into place a couple generations before substantial expansion of secondary schooling. Britain and Sweden broadened both secondary education and welfare-state entitlements much closer in time. (*Ibid.*, pp. 296–298.)

Why is the United States somewhat deviant in the timing and sequence of education expansion? In the 19th century, universal primary education for basic literacy and good citizenship was a demand of employers interested in a disciplined labor supply, Protestant sects and churches concerned that children be able to read the Bible, a labor movement interested in contradictory ideals of equality of opportunity and absolute equality, and a state concerned about political integration and social control. None of these concerns were unique to the U.S.: employers everywhere increasingly required literate employees, Protestant churches in Europe led in the desire for Bible-reading children, and left-labor movements were, in fact, stronger in Europe than they were in the U.S. But the U.S. was an early industrializer, and employer needs for a literate labor supply were early and urgent while problems of social-political integration in the context of a highly decentralized federal system and the absence of a feudal past and a state church were more intense. In fact, the founding fathers were keenly aware that they had to overcome the fragmentation and paralysis of the Articles of Confederation. Although they feared both a strong central authority and the tyranny of the majority and therefore set up a complex system of checks and balances in the Constitution, they also were alert to the dangers of social disintegration and the tendency of the states to fly apart. They explicitly advocated public education to create citizens with a national identity who would hold American society together and to foster the informed electorate they believed essential for democracy. Education to this day, at least in political rhetoric, is an American secular theology. While many European countries at equivalent levels of development adopted welfare-state programs to cope with their problems of social integration, political stability, and labor peace and delayed the acceleration of schooling, the United States reversed the sequence. What is important for convergence theory is that they all ended up roughly in the same place (see chap. 5). [34]

Throughout the 20th century in all currently rich democracies education has been the main channel for upward mobility. This function is clearest for the United States, but in recent decades other industrial societies have moved in the U.S. direction. A careful study by Donovan (1977) demonstrates the status protection and mobility functions of secondary schools at the turn of the century. She specifies the populations and times for which education did or did not function as a means of mobility. She regressed the proportion of 14- to 17-year-olds enrolled in all types of secondary education from 1870 to 1910 on the proportion of the economically active labor force in nonmanual jobs, taking account of variations by region, differential migration of educated labor, and race (white and nonwhite). Her main conclusion: Established elites (native-born whites) could rely on ascription (family origin and related advantages) for access to white-collar jobs, but less-favored groups—the foreign born and blacks—got access to such positions only by achievement through secondary schools. A century later, as we know, the same educational road is traveled by the least-privileged young people, including blacks and other minorities. Where it once took a high-school diploma, it now takes a college degree or graduate degree for such minorities to secure entry to upper-level occupations, again affirming the essentially meritocratic character of modern higher education for most of the population.

In modern society the trade-off argument applies only to postsecondary education: In my data for 19 rich democracies secondary-school enrollment ratios in the period 1965–1972 were not significantly correlated with either social-security spending as a share of GNP or per capita social-security spending (tables 6.1 and 6.3). The postsecondary enrollment ratios for these 19 countries, however, *are* negatively correlated with welfare effort, especially in the mid-1960s. In other words, the more meritocratic the education system, the more it provides channels for mobility, the more resistance to the rest of the welfare state (see chaps. 5 and 6 for an explanation).

As rich democracies moved from elite to mass higher education and then as they moved toward making it universal, they all developed a riotous diversity of function and quality among colleges and universities, although the education leaders are still much further along on this path than are the laggards. Adding to this diversity is the universal proliferation of nonuniversity forms of postsecondary education—vocational colleges, teacher training institutions, schools of music, art, drama, nursing, agriculture, management, and other vocations; continuing education for adults; and "open universities." The specialization and institutional stratification of modern education systems are necessary to meet the great variety of demands on the system and people to be accommodated, whose relevant abilities, cultural and genetic, vary (cf. Jencks and Riesman, 1968; Trow, 1972, 1974, 1991a, 1991b; Riesman, Gusfield, and Gamson, 1971; Wilensky and Lawrence, 1979). This combination of institutional diversity and increased mass opportunity is reflected in the finding that for 11 of 13 nations studied in Eastern and Western Europe, North America, and Asia, the effect of social class on educational attainment was remarkably stable during the 20th century. Educational expansion enabled more people to stay in school longer, but the underlying relation of social class and school completion did not change. Only Sweden and the Netherlands evidenced a decline in social inequality of educational attainment. (Blossfeld and Shavit, 1993, pp. 15–19.)

The question is whether the general push for equality and the specific demand for affirmative action for minorities will greatly weaken the meritocratic character of modern education. Although minority-group quotas for admission and curricula or schools segregated by ethnicity, language, race, or religion are most conspicuous in the United States, Canada, the Netherlands, and Belgium—countries with great social heterogeneity—other democracies are converging in the number and concentration of socially distant immigrants and are responding to the push for equality in similar ways (chap. 17 [Globalization] analyzes both similarities and differences). But I doubt that this will swiftly transform higher education. The intense resistance by higher-quality institutions in the most egalitarian countries indicates that meritocracy marches on. Consider the boldest attempts at affirmative action, those of Eastern Europe, based not on race or sex but on social class—attempts which have foundered. For instance, for university entry in Poland in the late 1960s and early 1970s you could get points for being the son or daughter of a worker or peasant. At its peak, affirmative class action could account for between 10% and 20% of the score for tough entry exams, both written and oral. However, before the collapse of the Soviet empire, the system withered away. The reasons include (a) a backlash from Communist party officials and bureaucrats who were old enough to have children entering college; (b) the trouble in securing sufficient resources for compensatory education for rural and lower-class students; and (c) the usual complexities of defining the preferred categories. Resistance was greatest at elite institutions with the highest academic standards (e.g., the University of Warsaw).

If you prefer an example of how a highly egalitarian democracy copes with the need to maintain meritocratic education standards while managing an expansive welfare state, consider recent reforms in Sweden. Although Sweden clearly reduced the relation of social origins and educational access between about 1930 and 1970, the trend leveled off between 1970 and 1990 (Erikson and Jonsson, 1996a, pp. 7–8; 1996b, pp. 82–90). In the 1980s Sweden gradually shifted toward more authority for local communities and more freedom for educational institutions to make choices about curriculum, definition of courses, number of places, and so on within centrally set targets. This educational reform movement culminated in the radical reforms of 1990–91 under the Social Democrats and continued under the new Conservative-led coalition. It was a shift in the role of the state from steering and direct supervision to monitoring and evaluation (Papadopoulos, 1993). But note that the central state remains active not only in financing education but also in ensuring equality of provision and the maintenance of national standards and a prescribed core curriculum, albeit with an increase in academic competition among institutions and individuals. The Swedish government is maintaining central control through block grants to municipalities; a national curriculum and minimum requirements for university degrees; and a central system to evaluate educational performance in municipalities, schools, and universities (*ibid.*, p. 26). The most radically egalitarian society in the world, having pushed education to embrace children and adults (via "folk high schools" and municipal adult education) with a pupil-centered approach, has had to back away and accent academic qualifications and training, making the schools somewhat more demanding and higher education a bit less egalitarian.

It is possible that in the enormous and diversified apparatus of higher education in the United States (California's postsecondary education for those who complete high school is almost universal), the common resistance to racial-ethnic preferences will erode and the traditional function of enhanced equality of opportunity will be replaced by a steady decline of standards in a drift toward equality of results. America's very diversity of curricula and opportunities, however, makes that prospect unlikely. For example, the elite institutions evidence substantial differences in response to the political demand for racial-ethnic preferences, both within and between universities. There is no evidence of an across-the-board collapse of standards. First, in the competition for the scarce pool of highly qualified high-school graduates from the least-privileged minorities, well-endowed private universities win out. For example, Harvard University, where in the late 1970s alumni children had a five times higher chance of admission than did other applicants (Heidenheimer and Layson, 1982, p. 160), affirmative action by race today skims off the most-qualified blacks and other minorities, most of whose test scores and typical preparation in upper-middle-class families and private academies are at least as good as those of nonminority applicants (Trow, 1999). Several other universities pursue similar policies and can make them effective by generous financial packages to preferred applicants.[35] The net effect is to leave the elite public universities (e.g., Berkeley, Michigan, UCLA, San Diego, Wisconsin)—less-affluent institutions more open to political pressure—with "affirmative action" programs that take the less qualified minority applicants from the least-privileged households and schools, and, in my opinion, they do suffer at least a minor erosion of standards. But here we encounter a second barrier to the spread of an antimeritocratic tendency: it varies by department and professional school. Clearly, at a place like Berkeley, while the Law School and the departments of sociology, anthropology, literature and English, and ethnic studies fully embrace the ideology of racial preferences and bend toward equality of results, most of the professional schools, including business, engineering, public health, public policy, and almost all departments in the physical and life sciences, as well as economics, statistics, computer science, and to some extent political science and history stand aside. They are far more resistant to racial-ethnic preferences in admissions, student evaluation, grading, placement, and faculty hiring and promotions. In other words, the closer we come to career paths that are clearly meritocratic, technical, or rigorous, the more departments and schools feed those paths with well-prepared graduates. Creating intellectual ghettos on campus based on skin color and devoted to ethnic-racial identity and solidarity will not change these necessities. A third counterforce to the demand for racial preferences is obvious: the new inequities thus introduced. Where "overqualified" Asians and Jews, as well as "white" ethnics must give way to less-qualified minority applicants at elite public institutions, their resentment is expressed in political backlash such as the successful ballot initiative in California to outlaw minority-group preferences. Chapters 10 and 17 discuss cross-national variations in the mobilization of such resentment in political campaigns. Chapters 12 (Economic Performance) and 18 (Policy Implications) discuss national differences in educational policy and performance, including the continued U.S. lead in the higher learning and its recent devastating lag in K–12.

A final convergent tendency of modern society is likely to retard any erosion of university standards due to minority preferences based on descent—climbing intermarriage rates, already discussed. This portends a time not far away where the already apparent confusion in minority-group labels will become impossible to administer. State classification by race, ethnicity, and religion and the official allocation of opportunities in education, jobs, and politics on that basis will erode. The extreme case of the Netherlands illustrates the point. In the Dutch system of separate-but-equal confessional-political blocs (Catholic, Protestant, secular-Socialist), everything from youth groups to schools to jobs to sports, television time, and travel agencies—not to mention political power—was divided up by religious/political orientation (Lorwin, 1971). These three subcultures consistently accounted for more than 85% of the vote until the 1970s; they became known as the pillars of Dutch society and government. As the intermarriage rate increased and residential segregation declined, however, the system could not be fully maintained; some "depillarization" has occurred, though much consensual bargaining persists (see chaps. 2 and 3). Joseph Houska (1985) developed a 25-year time series (from 1946 to 1972) covering these rates and their impact on all aspects of Dutch life. He found a steady erosion of subcultural segmentation and a decrease in the loyalty and voting consistency among members of each bloc. Its organizational expression in party politics has been the merger of the Catholic Party with several smaller Protestant parties in 1980. Its expression in industrial relations has been the merger of the Catholic and Socialist labor federations into the Federation of Dutch Trade Unions (FNV) in 1976. (Wolinetz, 1989, pp. 85, 87.) Intermarriage rates grew steadily from 1958 on—paralleling and perhaps causing this erosion (Houska, 1985, pp. 33–45). It is likely that the increase in intermarriage and the decrease in residential segregation and in-group friendships preceded the erosion of political loyalties, although Houska's data cannot pin this down.[36]

If assimilation and the breakdown of cultural segmentation gradually occur through intermarriage where, as in the Netherlands, social segregation was almost complete, it should occur faster in the more open and fluid system of the United States, thereby complicating the task of those authorities in government and universities who want to allocate rewards on the basis of descent. From the perspective of minority-group activists themselves, their ethnic-racial-religious colleagues will decreasingly follow their lead.

In sum: Despite remaining differences in the quality of education, in the organization and funding of higher education, and in the unionization and relative pay and prestige of teachers, the rich democracies show pervasive and deep convergence in their education systems. Everywhere education has become the main channel for social mobility. In the face of the pressure for absolute equality, higher education remains essentially meritocratic. Mass education at every level necessitates a high degree of specialization and institutional stratification; in modern society there is no alternative to the great diversity of curricula and standards that we see before us. The three-tier system of California—120 community colleges, 24 state university campuses, and the nine-campus University of California—is the epitome of this diversity and a great achievement in equality of opportunity. No rich democracy has yet reached California's postsecondary enrollment ratio, but the twin trends toward universality and specialization are unmistakable.

The Rise of the Media of Mass Communication and Entertainment

The media have become the victorious rival to education in hours of exposure and impact on cognitive and social development of the young. The broadcast media especially have become central to the leisure routines of everyone and central to election campaigns. Although large national differences in media dominance of culture and politics persist because of differences in the control, financing, and organization of the media, the differences have recently diminished.

The national differences include marked contrasts in the role of public broadcasting networks and their financial base (the license fee for a TV set in Japan and most of Europe buys a large public-interest presence) and related variation in cultural, educational, and news content of television and radio, in hours of broadcasting (nonstop in the U.S.), and in the amount and kind of advertising. Similar differences appear in restrictions on the media role in campaigns; almost all rich democracies prohibit or limit paid political advertising and have much shorter election campaigns than the U.S.; France even bans stage props and other gimmicks. However, the recent commercialization of large segments of broadcasting in several countries; the decline of license-fee revenue; the increase in cross-national access that comes with the new cable and satellite technology and multichannel expansion; the earlier development and technological edge of American producers of film, television, music, and press services (AP and UP)—all of these combine to reduce the national differences. The cultural mission, assurance, and pride of public broadcasting authorities in Europe are fading; the prestige newspapers are in some measure aping the tabloids. The media are indeed becoming American.

The convergence within types of media and among rich democracies is generally toward increasing media influence in culture and politics and in content, specifically toward the American talk-show model. This is an area where convergence was slow or nonexistent for most of the 20th century but has accelerated greatly in only the past generation or two. Most of chapter 3 (Mass Society) attempts to explain both similarities and differences in media content and impact. It relates media impact to national variations in social participation and civic engagement.

THE INCREASING NUMBER AND
PERHAPS INFLUENCE OF EXPERTS AND INTELLECTUALS

People of knowledge have always interacted with people of power, as Machiavelli's classic, *The Prince,* reminds us. But in modern society the demand for their services is more widespread and their impact more obvious. Chapter 2, however, shows that types of political economy powerfully shape the interplay of intellectuals and politicians. Corporatist democracies encourage stronger links between knowledge and power—a dialectic of expertise, a rational-responsible bias which itself is a force for accommodation among competing interest groups. It is ironic that a general theory of postindustrialism accenting the rise of experts in command of theoretical knowledge (Bell, 1973 and chap. 4), derived largely from U.S. data, applies least well to the United States and other decentralized and fragmented political economies (Australia, UK, Canada, New Zealand) and best to such corporatist democracies as Sweden, Norway, Austria, Belgium, the Netherlands, and Germany. In the latter, experts and intellectuals are located in national policy networks of centralized labor federations, employer federations, and at least moderately centralized governments with effective channels for steady policy deliberation and implementation. Japan accomplishes the same linkage of experts to policy without including labor. In contrast, while the United States has an abundance of experts and intellectuals, their voices are typically cast to the winds—or drowned out by the media noise; the relation of knowledge to power is erratic, a factor in the wilder swings of policy, as in the frequent reversals of tax policy and welfare policy in the U.S. and UK in recent decades.

Despite these differences, there is no doubt that rich countries have converged in the trend toward increasing numbers of highly specialized experts and to a lesser extent in the presence of many intellectuals. As Schumpeter foresaw, as modern societies expanded higher education and became richer, they would as a by-product produce a great many intellectuals who would become dedicated social critics of the very capitalist development that financed them (1942, pp. 145–55)—a noneconomic aspect of creative destruction. I shall return to the role of experts and intellectuals in chapters 2 and 4.

SOCIAL STRATIFICATION AND MOBILITY[37]

There is solid evidence of convergence in the occupational composition of the labor force. To a lesser extent some convergence occurs in industrial composition and even in some of the ways work is organized and work incentives are structured. Figure 1.2 tracks the major changes in the U.S. civilian labor force from 1910 (36 million at work or seeking work) to 1998 (130 million); it can be taken as typical of the trends in all very advanced industrial societies. (Table 4.1 traces shifts in employment by industry sector 1920 to 1992 for seven countries and is discussed in chapter 4's evaluation of ideas about "postindustrialism.") There are some cross-national variations, but the changes in gross categories are convergent.

As a first cut, consider these massive changes in jobs. There was a drastic decline in farm people and a steady increase of what used to be called the "new middle class" of

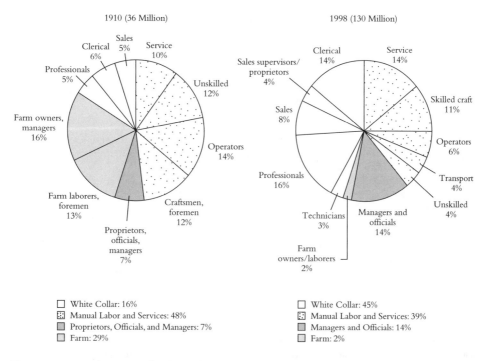

Figure 1.2. United States civilian labor force, 1910-98

Sources: Data for 1910 converted for comparability by Palmer and Miller (1954). Data for March 1998 from U.S. Department of Labor, Bureau of Labor Statistics. *Employment and Earnings,* April 1998, table 19. This analysis includes all those at work or seeking work, 16 years of age and over (14 years and over in 1910), and excludes the armed forces.

white-collar and professional and administrative employees (gains in clerical, sales, and professional occupations were most rapid). Within the "professional, technical, and kindred" category most of the growth came from newer professions (engineers, scientists, designers) and a host of semiprofessional, semitechnical occupations. The second major trend has been the growth in the proportion of "non-farm proprietors, managers, and officials," especially since 1940. The more specialization the more need for general coordination. An army of college-trained administrators, supervisors, troubleshooters and staff advisers emerges to meet this need.

A third major shift has occurred within the manual worker and service category.[38] The "working class" has declined only slightly (from 48% in 1910 to 42% in 1988). It was down to 39 percent in 1998. But there has been a dramatic shift in its occupational composition: Unskilled laborers and the semiskilled (generally machine operators) dropped sharply while skilled craft workers and repairmen grew slightly, then dropped slightly to 11% in 1998, about the same proportion as 1910.

The net effect has been a general upgrading of the whole population, reflecting both the average skill and educational level required. We can also say that in a gross sense there is a trend toward a service economy, whatever that means. (Chap. 4 shows that it does not mean much.)

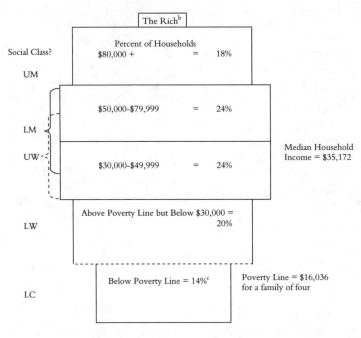

Figure 1.3. Social classes and household income before taxes, 1996[a]

[a]Source: U.S. Bureau of the Census, *Current Population Report 1996,* Series p-60, No. 197, table 3, Series p-60, No. 198, Figure 1. Households include all families and unrelated individuals living in one residence.

[b]The richest 1% of individuals have an annual income of over $229,000; they earn 16% of American income.

[c]For a family of four. The line is $12,980 for a family of three, $10,360 for a couple, $7,740 for a single without children (*Federal Register,* v. 61, n. 43, March 1996, pp. 8286-8288).

If we combine household income with these data on occupational status (the two tend to be correlated in the range of .4 or .5), again confining ourselves to the United States, we would arrive at a picture something like figure 1.3.

In this figure, the *upper-middle class* consists of people who exercise the authority of expertise or line authority or both. They have at least a college education, increasingly followed by postgraduate degrees. If they are executives or officials, they have many subordinates; if they own businesses, they have a large base of capital; if they are professionals, they are highly trained. Their income puts them in the upper fifth or sixth of the income distribution. Some of them become very rich. They experience little or no unemployment. The upper-middle class in the past century has grown rapidly and is now about a fifth of the household distribution.[39] The *lower-middle class* consists of a mass of semitechnical, semiprofessional occupations (e.g., X-ray technician, laboratory technician), small entrepreneurs, clerks, cashiers, salespeople, and nurses whose authority, if any, is limited; they generally provide the services in government, private corporations, and the medical-industrial complex required by the upper-middle class. School teachers' status and relative income vary substantially across countries; here they are at the top border of the lower-middle class. The *upper-working class* consists of "manual workers" in the building trades, manufacturing, trucking, the printing trades, and general maintenance and repair. In another phrasing they are craft workers, firstline supervisors, and high-paid operatives (formerly labeled "semiskilled"). The *lower class* includes the

working poor—laborers, farm workers, and other low-paid manual workers and service workers in every industry but especially in retail trades (e.g., food service workers, domestic workers, watchmen, janitors)—as well as the nonworking poor (mainly women heading broken
homes, youths out of work and out of school, recent immigrants and those least-privileged
minorities discussed previously). Rural and small-town populations tend to be overrepresented
among the poor. The education level and quality gradient follows the social-class gradient,
with the lower-middle class increasingly having two or three years of part-college or postsecondary vocational training; the upper-working class, high school plus apprentice training
or more recently part-college; and the lower class, as always, the least education.

The typical sociological layer cake in figure 1.3 captures common features of advanced
industrial societies for every stratum except the lower class; countries that have highly developed welfare states and well-financed social and labor policies (see Part II) have much
smaller poverty populations than the United States, and in income distribution, less distance
between rich and poor (see tables 8.4, 12.7, and 14.4). But there is no doubt that the
upper-middle class and lower-middle class have expanded greatly in all rich democracies
and that the upper-working class has at least held its own.

Research on stratification and mobility comprises about a third of published sociology.
From trends in occupation and income, social scientists have built elaborate theories of class
structure, class struggle, class consciousness, and class realignments. These ideas have shaped
the verbal environment of political leaders and rank-and-file alike. Think of the adoption of
social-class imagery in the recent rhetoric of political campaigns: from Richard Nixon's "silent
majority" in 1968–74 to Gary Hart's yuppies to everyone's favorite stratum today, the "middle class" (a term as vague in political debates as it was in the sociological debate). In many
a rich democracy in both academic journals and popular culture we hear discussions of the
affluent worker going middle class, with the result that the politics of moderation has seized
the minds of left and right alike; or conversely, the middle class is shrinking, the rich are getting richer and the poor poorer and therefore politics, like the class structure, will become
more polarized. Accompanying all this is much talk of the high-tech society.

"Class" and "class conflict" are among the vaguest and most misleading concepts in social science. Whether we analyze class in Marxian or non-Marxian terms, a clearly defined
"middle class" and "working class" in the United States and increasingly in other rich
democracies no longer exist, if they ever did. What I wrote three decades ago is even more
valid today: "Much behavior and many attitudes said to be rooted in class are instead a matter of race, religion, ethnic origin, education, age, and stage in the family life cycle. Indeed,
almost any of these traditional groupings of the population display more homogeneity of
behavior and belief than 'labor,' if by the latter term we mean all manual workers or even
all union members." (Wilensky, 1966a, pp. 12–13. Cf. 1961a, 1961b, 1961c, 1964c, and
1966b for elaboration and evidence. On family life cycle see chap. 4. For recent evidence
of the widespread reduction in the variance in party dealignment and political attitudes explained by "class," see the 16-country study by Franklin, Mackie, and Valen, 1992, covering the late 1950s through the 1980s; and chap. 11 [Party Decline].)

The chief limitations of a stratification model of modern society are three. First, there is increasing heterogeneity *within* each "class," not only by the forms of social differentiation already mentioned (minority-group origin, education level and quality, age and life-cycle stage)
but also by economic position. The persistence, importance, and discrete social-

political character of self-employment and its contrast with bureaucratic employment is a well-established feature of modern societies. It is true that industrialization brought a sharp drop in the self-employed, especially farmers. This continued throughout the 19th century (when the self-employed in the U.S., Germany, and France as a percentage of the employed ranged between 60% and 40%) through 1970 when the figures were about 10% in the United States, 12% in Germany, and 16% in France. (Steinmetz and Wright, 1989, pp. 984–985.) The share of both nonagricultural self-employment and total self-employment since the early seventies has, however, either increased or stabilized in almost all rich democracies (OECD, 1998; Steinmetz and Wright, 1989; Bechhofer and Elliot, 1981, pp. 201–202). The image of the small family business or the solo entrepreneur as a fading phenomenon is misleading. Neither small businesses (say, fewer than 20 employees) nor the self-employed are declining in modern societies; if anything they remain central to the politics and essential to the economies of rich democracies. (On small business and self-employed in Japan see Calder, 1988, pp. 184, 200, 333–348; on France see Berger, 1981a, pp. 90–92, 96–98 and Keeler, 1987, pp. 267–274, 284, 288. On Italy, see Berger 1981b, pp. 81–82, 86. On the sociopolitical role of small business see Berger and Piore, 1980, pp. 100–123. On Canada and the UK, see Bechhofer and Eliot, 1981.) The national differences in the small-business and self-employment share—with Italy, Belgium, New Zealand, Ireland, and France ranking high—can be explained not only by a larger farm sector (Italy, Ireland, New Zealand), which should decline with further economic growth, but also by policies favoring urban small businesses and self-employment: preferential credit, tax, trade and distribution policies; special social-security arrangements; strict limits on supermarket expansion, especially in Italy; the use of subsidies to encourage the unemployed to start businesses; and the calculations of conservative governments that small business, if favored, will act as a shock absorber in downturns and a political counterweight to wage-earner militancy. (*Ibid.*; and Meager, 1994.)

Because self-employment is spread throughout the system—for example, self-employed craft workers, truck drivers in the upper-working class; small business entrepreneurs in the lower-middle class; solo professionals, artists, and consultants in the upper-middle class; and even struggling low-income immigrant entrepreneurs and marginal farmers among the working poor—it is a major source of heterogeneity within each stratum. The self-employed and small business entrepreneurs live in a world of frequent ups and downs, a world of intense competition and unpredictability so extreme that it makes the rest of the population look secure.[40]

That social and political heterogeneity marks every social class and that the self-employed are part of this picture is illustrated by a detailed comparison of the work, leisure, and politics of two groups within the same profession, all white men of the upper-middle class, age 30 to 55, with at least an above-average income. As part of a larger study of the Detroit metropolitan area, we interviewed all 107 lawyers fitting that description in the 19 largest firms in the Detroit area (10 or more partners and associates) and compared them with a random sample of 100 solo lawyers. Table 1.1 shows some of the sharp differences we uncovered (Ladinsky, 1963a, 1963b; Wilensky and Ladinsky, 1967).

These lawyers of the upper-middle "class," the most homogeneous of the census occupational categories, lived in different worlds. Differences in parents' entrepreneurship and their religion and ethnicity are a clue to contrasting early socialization that led them to contrasting institutions for undergraduate education, future firm lawyers to selective liberal arts

TABLE 1.1 Big differences between two groups within one upper-middle class profession, lawyers*

Descent	Solo %	Firm %	% point difference
Religion			
Protestant	31	69	38
Catholic	34	26	8
Jewish	35	6	29
Generation American			
First or Second	89	10	79
Ethnic Origin			
Slavic, Medit.	68	28	43
W. Europe	32	75	
Father's occupation			
Entrepreneur	72	40	32
Education			
High Quality Law Sch. (Chicago, Harvard, Columbia, Michigan, Yale)	14	73	59
Low Quality (state, local)	36	2	
Part-time ed.	87	8	79
Worklife Mobility			
up	80	26	54
Politics	Liberal Dems.	Moderate Reps.	
Residence	Scattered	Grosse Point	
Work	Long hours. Family law, inj. and accid., immigration, repossession, criminal	Regular hours. Corporate, tax, marine, patent	
Leisure	bar, office, etc.	country club	

*Data from the Detroit Metropolitan area, 1960. See text.

colleges, their solo brothers to lesser places. The contrast in religion is not merely that 7 in 10 of the firm lawyers are WASP compared with 31% of solo lawyers; the former were almost all brought up in high-status Protestant churches—Episcopalian, Presbyterian, Congregational, Universalist-Unitarian; the latter were raised in lower-status Protestant churches or were Jews or Catholics. Socialization in family and undergraduate education led to contrasts in law-school quality and to the natural outcome—firm lawyers doing more lucrative corporate, tax, patent, and marine law; solo lawyers putting in long hours in the dirty work of the bar (family law, injury or accident, immigration, repossession, and criminal cases). These contrasts, in turn, spilled over into leisure and politics: the firm lawyers were concentrated in the posh suburb of Grosse Point where they hung out at the country club with notable executives, lawyers, and physicians and became moderate Republicans, almost to a man; the solo lawyers' homes were scattered about Detroit, they often had an ethnic clientele, and they hung out in local bars or their offices and became liberal Democrats. In short, "upper-middle class" captures very little of what was going on in the lives of these men. With rising integration, gender equality, and intermarriage since the 1960s, there are perhaps now fewer sharp contrasts in early socialization and a changed cast of characters. But from our discussion of the quality of education and the distinctive character of self-employment, it is likely that both men and women with different backgrounds and orientations are still channeled into different law schools that feed the different patterns of work of the bar.[41]

The second limitation of a stratification model is the emergence of a "middle mass" brought about by the increasing similarity of behavior, attitudes, and lifestyles of the lower-middle and upper-working classes and their increasing difference from college-educated upper-middle strata above and the poor below (Wilensky, 1961a; 1975, pp. 116–118). By the end of the 1980s, cross-national research on party decline and political behavior had abundantly confirmed the declining significance of social class. Scattered data on tax revolts and the rise of populist demagogues confirmed the idea of the revolt of the middle mass. For instance, Perot voters in the United States in 1992 were concentrated in the lower-middle and upper-working classes, as were voters for LePen in France, the Lega Lombarda in Italy, and the xenophobic anti-immigrant parties in Germany, who evidence similar anxieties and fears. While they share a common social base, such protest movements, of course, are channeled differently in different types of political economy. National differences in the mobilization of the middle mass in politics and culture will appear in several chapters, especially on tax-welfare backlash (chap. 10), party decline (chap. 11), protest movements against immigrants (chap. 18), mayhem (chap. 14), and the welfare mess (chap. 8).

The third limitation is that the stratification model is weakened by the extraordinary social mobility of modern populations and the multiple ladders for status attainment up which they can move or down which they can fall (Wilensky, 1966b). Sociologists have done much careful work on intergenerational (father-son) occupational mobility (e.g., Blau and Duncan, 1967; Featherman and Hauser, 1978) and similar research on worklife mobility, although complete work histories are hard to come by, longitudinal data are scarce,[42] and cross-national data are even more scarce. The results add up to the following:

• During the past 50 to 100 years, intergenerational mobility has likely increased because of the shifts in the occupational structure pictured in figure 1.2 (Gottschalk, McLanahan, and Sandefur, 1994, p. 101). The prestige and skill of the average occupation has gone up. Therefore the children of successive cohorts are doing work that in status exceeds that of their parents and, indeed, is somewhat more pleasant. This shift, however, is almost wholly due to the changes in occupations, not to any increased permeability of the class lines. (Rogoff, 1953, and subsequent studies controlling for shifts in structure demonstrate that although "classes" changed their relative size, they did not become especially open.)

- In the course of a 46-year worklife the average number of job changes may be as much as a dozen, over half of which cross broad occupational categories—for example, lower white collar to upper white collar, upper blue collar to lower white collar, low-skilled to semiskilled, skilled worker to small entrepreneur. Again, most of these job shifts are up, but a substantial percentage are down.[43]

- In distance moved, the typical change is short-step mobility: the carpenter's apprentice becomes the master carpenter, the semiskilled operative starts a small business or becomes a firstline supervisor, the first lieutenant becomes a captain, the nurse becomes a nurse-practitioner, the secretary becomes a paralegal or an office supervisor. And, of course, the stably employed middle-level, middle-aged executive is "downsized" and becomes an unstably employed salesperson or a self-employed consultant. And the skilled steelworker is laid off and remains intermittently unemployed in lower-paid jobs.

- The best predictors of upward moves are seniority and education (see chap. 4 on life cycle).

- When students of stratification have done multivariate studies of the effects of "social class" and have disaggregated income, occupational status, and education, they have generally found that education explains almost as much as the three variables combined. In other words, when we speak of "class" and talk about its impact on a wide range of behavior and attitudes, we might as well substitute the word *education* and concentrate on measuring its quality. And in defining the "middle mass" the most valid and most accurate measure is the level and kind of education—those with high school or one or two years of postsecondary education, usually vocational. Thus defined, the middle mass was about 60% of the U.S. electorate in 1996—high-school graduates were 30% of voters; "some college," 29% (U.S. Bureau of the Census, 1998a, p. 34). For reasons already discussed, the importance of education in defining "class" and in determining life chances is likely to be even more the case in the future.

The channels for mobility are multiplying as modernizing societies develop and as rich countries become richer. If we wish to deal with the individual's mobility experience as a source of personal and social organization and change, we must bring into view all the orderly ladders that integrate and all the discontinuities that disrupt. They have been listed repeatedly in introductory texts: stratification by descent (religious, ethnic, and racial origin); occupation; education; income; authority; residence, possessions, and leisure style. But systematic empirical studies of mobility give almost exclusive attention to "occupational mobility," including the shift from rural to urban economies and especially between the generations.

A discriminating analysis of mobility that fits the diversity of modern life and brings to view the multiple moves of each person leads to a "consolation prize" theory of mobility. For both society and the individual, the more education and income, the more urgent and widespread are great expectations; but the more social differentiation, the more consolation prizes for those who lose out. The ladders which a person can climb are sufficiently numerous that falling behind on one or falling off another may neither cause an irrevocable loss of social position nor yield much sense of deprivation. For instance, in my analysis of types of mobility experience and aspirations of 1,354 men aged 21–55 in the Detroit metropolitan area in 1960 (Wilensky, 1966b) I found that intergenerational skidders—men whose occupations rank below their fathers—tend to marry up. Men who achieve less education than their fathers or stay on the same level tend to marry women with superior education from families with occupational status higher than their own. Many skidders also marry up ethnically. Other studies have reported a low to moderate correlation between income and occupational prestige (about .4 in Duncan, Featherman, and Duncan, 1972, p. 38), reflecting such cases as the high income of unionized garbage collectors and miners or the low income of many unorganized teachers or child care workers—to which the brackets in figure 1.3 call attention. Many also note the high income of some minority groups already discussed.[44]

Why are modern societies able to contain the political effects of even high rates of downward mobility? In the typical case skidding is rationalized, often realistically, as a temporary setback; in American data we usually find that skidders and fluctuators are more like upwardly mobile than nonmobile men. Skidders tend to retain the values and practices of the class or occupational group from which they slipped and to which they expect to return.[45] Perhaps this is the single best explanation for "working-class Tories"—that third of manual workers in the United States who vote Republican, the similar proportion of the British working class who at times vote Conservative. Mobile workers moving in either direction, along with other workers who escape from what is left of working-class culture in spirit or practice, function to reduce working-class solidarity and social criticism from below—and thereby slow down the push toward equality.

This mobility out of the working class is impressive even if we switch from an occupational definition to an income definition and concentrate on the poor. Two cross-national studies are most relevant. The first, based on OECD data (OECD, 1996a, pp. 88–92), analyzed changes in individual earnings from 1986 to 1991 in eight of our countries. In all countries only a minority of those who were situated in the bottom earnings quintile were still there in 1991. Roughly 1 in 5 of these low-paid workers had moved up at least two quintiles, except for the United States where the figure is 1 in 10.[46] In these eight rich democracies, income mobility over five years was clearly substantial. The second study (Duncan et al., 1991, appendix and table 1) focused on economic mobility among low-income families with children in 7 of our 19 countries (circa mid-1980s)—Canada, France-Lorraine, Ireland, the Netherlands, Sweden, West Germany, and the United States. It shows that upward mobility was widespread and strikingly similar across countries. Using the bottom decile of families—easily recognized as relatively very poor—the percentage of poor becoming nonpoor ranged from about one in four to one in five. (The measure: of those in the bottom decile in the first year of longitudinal surveys covering from two to eight years, the percentage with incomes at least 20% above the bottom decile at the end of the period. Family income was size-adjusted, annual post-tax post-transfer family cash income, with minor exceptions.) Using the median size-adjusted income of the population, a looser definition of poor and a higher definition of nonpoor, substantial upward mobility is again evident, although here the Netherlands and Sweden were far ahead of the United States and Canada (44% and 37% vs. 12% and 14%) with France, West Germany, and Ireland about one in four. (The measure: of those with income less than 50% of the median, the percentage who achieved an income greater than or equal to 60% of the median.) None of this contradicts my previous picture of national and minority-group variation in economic ups and downs, cyclical variation, the incidence of poverty and near poverty, the duration of poverty, the plight of single mothers, or the variations by type of political economy and related public policies—to which the rest of this book attests. But if we want to get a grip on a significant feature of stratification systems of modern society, high rates of mobility cannot be ignored. It is one reason for the surprising political quiescence of lower strata in all rich democracies despite considerable insecurity if not chaos in their lives.

Although the prospects of individual mobility out of the working class and the experience of falling into it from above provide a powerful force for ideological heterogeneity within each social class, the movement of *groups* may have a reverse effect. If an entire stratum, craft, or profession is declining, there is more chance of unity in misery and a collective protest—scapegoating or lashing out against symbols of oppression. The tendency is evident in the populism of family farmers facing corporate competitors or of grain growers dependent on banks and railroads, in the anti-Semitism of obsolescent craftsmen, in the political extremism of small business entrepreneurs—the franchised dealer dependent on the big-business supplier, the small manufacturer dependent on one corporate customer, and the retail proprietor threatened by chain stores and discount houses.[47] Such responses are less likely and do not spread if they occur when the position of the group or stratum is stable but the individual is threatened.

The most important qualification to my consolation-prize hypothesis concerns education. If educational opportunity whets the appetite for a better life, but does not lead to job opportunity and income, it serves less as a compensatory reward than as a source of resentment. Thus, as their educational opportunities exceed their economic rewards and living standards, many minorities become more militant (see chaps. 4 and 17). Educated whites already receive roughly congruent rewards, and their political discontents are kept within manageable proportions; uneducated whites, if they are not lucky in the labor market, at least have a chance to shuck off lower ethnic or religious origins or marry up.

In measuring objective mobility as a source of social participation or civic engagement, some indicators of mobility that are typically lumped together are in reality discrete. For instance, direction and distance of movement in the worklife is not a good indicator of social discontinuity; some upward moves, like some horizontal moves, are orderly—involving gradual, predictable changes and anticipatory socialization—others are chaotic. "Instability" of job holding (generally based on number of jobs or employers) is also independent of orderliness in the job pattern. In analyzing types of mobility with an eye to their integrating or alienating effects, I compared men in the middle mass with two job patterns: the first, where jobs are hierarchically arranged and funtionally related in a more or less predictable pattern, as in the crafts, the established professions, the military, and the civil service; the second, where the job history evidenced much chaos, where mobility, whether up, down, or across, is chaotic in the sense that little can be predicted and jobs are unrelated in function and status (they are often punctuated by several episodes of unemployment).[48] These contrasting career patterns crosscut social classes; they are strongly related to the person's patterns of social participation and attachment to or alienation from community and society (see chap. 3 [Mass Society]), and consequently to the system outputs analyzed in Part III, especially chapter 11 (Party Decline), chapter 14 (Mayhem) and chapter 16 (Health Performance).

Summary

A stratification model of modern society is limited in four ways: First, the increasing heterogeneity of behavior and orientation within each "class" means that differences within classes are becoming greater than differences between them. Second, the emergence of the "middle mass," the blurring of class lines, makes such concepts as "working class" or "white collar" decreasingly useful. Third, the great and possibly increasing social mobility of modern populations—the multiple ladders up which they can climb or fall off—adds to the cultural heterogeneity of each stratum. Finally, the increasing importance of education as a determinant of life chances means that when we measure social class by occupation, income, and education and try to explain something by the combination "socioeconomic status," we might as well drop the (less reliable) indicators of income and occupational status and concentrate on the level and quality of education.

Insofar as class categories remain at all useful, the line that divides stably employed, well-educated, well-paid workers from the lower class is becoming more important than the split between upper-working class and lower-middle class. Whether we are witnessing the *embourgeoisement* of the workers or the sinking of the middle class into the proletariat, the top of one and the bottom of the other seem to form a new middle mass, a population that increasingly shares common values, beliefs, and tastes. While the lower-middle class and upper-working class merge, the growing upper-middle widens its distance from the poor and from the nonmobile parts of the middle mass. And the process goes on in every rich country. What varies among rich democracies is the size and character of the poor (chaps. 8 and 14), the degree of income inequality, and the extent to which the privileges, comfort, superior education, economic security, challenging work and challenging leisure of the college-educated upper-middle class have diffused downward to embrace substantial parts of the middle mass. Of most political significance are contrasting patterns of social mobilization and public policies that either exacerbate the restiveness of the middle mass or promote their solidarity with the poor (see chaps. 8 and 11).

To say "white collar" or "working class" or "middle class" is to obscure most of what is central to the experience of the person and the structure of modern society. "Lawyer" and "engineer" moves us closer to reality, for these workers develop quite different styles of life. To say "independent entrepreneur" is to capture even more. And finally, to particularize the matter with "solo lawyer" and "firm lawyer" is to take account of the sharp contrasts in recruitment base (social origin, especially ethnicity, religion and race, and the quality of education and professional training), type of work, career patterns, and rewards that divide the two. Thus even the fifth of the labor force that fits "upper-middle class" is highly heterogeneous. In general, age, gender, and especially "socioeconomic status" are becoming far weaker as predictors of social and political behavior, attitudes, and lifestyles than religion, ethnicity, and race, type of education, work, and career—variables that represent positions in established, organized groups.

I have underscored the wondrous variety of meanings encompassed by "mobility," both intergenerational and worklife. In the past hundred years, because of convergent shifts in technology and occupational structure and a concomitant net shift up in average occupational status, occupational mobility rates have probably increased in the currently rich countries. Because of the multiple ladders for mobility characteristic of modern society there are many possible consolation prizes for those who lose out on occupational or workplace ladders—higher income in a lower-status job, entrepreneurship, intermarriage, horizontal shifts to more pleasant work or work schedules, the cultivation of leisure. This helps to explain why modern society is able to contain the disruptive effects of even high rates of downward occupational mobility; it is a major source of the political quiescence of least-privileged workers. What increasingly sorts out modern populations is whether their job patterns fit the model of an orderly career or are chaotic. These patterns, which crosscut social classes, are powerful sources of alienation or attachment, isolation or social participation, apathy or civic engagement.

Hours, Schedules, and the Organization of Work

Both convergence and divergence are evident in the hours and schedules of work, the locus and incidence of industrial conflict, the spread of contingent labor, and the percentage of the labor force experiencing rising insecurity. Conclusions about trends depend upon the time period and the specific aspects of work we examine. This section also suggests that the attempt to capture very recent trends with such phrases as "post-Fordist" production, "flexible specialization," or the "high-tech society" are misleading: the variations in the organization of work and occupational profiles within these gross categories impose severe limits on their utility.

Hours of Work

There are many assertions that modern populations are withdrawing from work or abandoning the work ethic. In actual hours worked the picture is quite different. In an analysis of the impact of economic level on hours of leisure, using both our surveys of the Detroit area and archival data from Europe (Wilensky 1961c, 1966c), I showed that compared with their urban counterparts of the 13th century, modern populations increased their annual hours of work from the late Middle Ages until the mid–19th century; only in the next century did we return to the work schedules of medieval guildsmen. But work is today distributed very unevenly and perhaps increasingly unevenly as rich countries become richer. In contemporary America in recent decades there has been a slow increase in long-hours workers (percentage of workers working over 55 hours a week), an increase in moonlighting from 5.3% of the labor force in 1970 to 6.2% in 1989 and an even larger increase in the motive for it, and a soaring increase in work among women, both paid and household, while increasing proportions of the population are condemned to forced leisure (both unemployment and short hours among those who want to work more) (Wilensky, 1961c, 1963, 1966c and the preceding discussion of the aged and women). (For subsequent studies with similar conclusions see Scitovsky, 1992, and Schor 1991.) In the absence of good comparable data on the distribution of work and leisure by social class for our 19 rich democracies, we can only speculate about whether the intensification of labor we see for the American college-educated upper-middle class is a universal trend. Given some common trends in the occupational structures of rich countries, I think it is a likely convergent tendency, whatever their divergence in the average yearly total hours of work.

The return to 13th-century nonagricultural annual hours of work has been a common trend among the currently rich democracies from the late 19th century through 1960—in the U.S. from about 3,000 average hours per worker in all industries in 1870 to about 1,800 hours in 1960 (Fitzgerald, 1996, p. 14). The downward trend has slowed up in the United States while it continued in other countries. Are rich democracies converging in hours of work? Even though they all share the 20th-century decrease in hours, big differences remain and there is some sign of recent divergence. Ranking 11 countries for which we have OECD data (Fitzgerald, 1996, table 3) from highest to lowest in annual hours per worker in 1994 in manufacturing (where figures are a bit higher than hours for all industries), we find strong contrasts by type of political economy. The top six are the USA (1,994 annual hours), Japan (1,960 hours), Canada (1,898), the UK (1,824), Italy (1,804), and France (1,638). Except for Italy five of the six are decentralized, fragmented political economies with little left-labor power or they are corporatist-without-labor (France, Japan). The bottom five—least working hours per year—are democratic corporatist: Norway (1,549), Germany (1,541), Denmark (1,573), the Netherlands (1,599), and Sweden (1,627). But except for Canada and the United States, they evidence substantial declines in hours from 1960 to 1994—from Germany's drop of 27% to Italy's drop of 12%. Comparing starting points with the percentage declines 1960–1994 and leaving aside the North American exception (most hours of work, little or no decline in hours), we get a hint of divergence. The average drop in annual hours for the four hardest-working countries is 16.3%; the average drop for the leisured five is 21.5%.[49] In other words, the leisure-rich countries are becoming richer; the leisure-poor countries are becoming relatively poorer. As we shall see in the rest of the book, the best explanation for these national differences in labor-market policies is the power of labor unions and left parties to trade lower hours and other benefits for industrial peace, wage restraint, and pro-employer tax benefits through national corporatist bargaining arrangements.

A similar instance of divergence based on national differences in left-labor power is evident in patterns of industrial conflict, although we can find signs of convergence as well. Strike rates, for instance, vary greatly according to whether the locus of conflict is the local industrial level or national politics (Hibbs, 1978), as in the tripartite bargaining arrangements of corporatist democracies, which results in low strike rates (see chap. 12). Yet, even here, some patterns of behavior are convergent. For instance, a finding that has stood up is Kerr and Siegel's discovery in their 1954 cross-national comparison of the interindustry propensity to strike, that workers who are socially and geographically isolated from the containing society and given unpleasant work to do—miners, longshoremen, loggers, lumbermen, maritime workers—have relatively high strike rates whatever the political-cultural context. If by technological and social change they become less isolated and their work improves—the current case—their strike rates decline. In short, the total volume of strikes varies by type of political economy, but occupational rates vary by the nature of the work and hence the level of economic development. The impact of national variations in the interplay of labor, management, and the state will be analyzed throughout the book.

Flexible Specialization?

A brief skeptical comment on two convergent trends said to characterize modern economies—"flexible specialization" or "post-Fordist" methods of manufacturing (e.g., in Japan or Central and Northwestern Italy) and the celebration or explosion of "high-tech" jobs (e.g., in Silicon Valley)—can provide context for understanding what is new and what is not, what is dominant and what is not in the organization and character of work. These phrases capture something of modern life—that batch production and craft production are different from mass production; that worker involvement in production planning and process can pay off in increased flexibility and productivity; that collegial forms of organization blur the lines between management and the managed; that complex technologies are knowledge based. But these insights are not especially new; they have been embedded in industrial sociology for 50 years—in the accounts of craft and batch production and schemes for worker participation of the past, in both human-paced and machine-paced jobs (Stinchcombe, 1959; Wilensky, 1957, 1981b, pp. 246–255; Strauss, 1963, pp. 41–84; Strauss and Sayles, 1967, chaps. 2 and 3). Most workplaces during the past hundred years have been involved with batch production (which by its nature requires some flexible specialization), not mass production.

Since Piore and Sabel's *The Second Industrial Divide: Possibilities for Prosperity* (1984), the spread of theories and research regarding "flexible specialization" has been more rapid than the spread of its practices in modern political economies. Flexible specialization (FS) in Piore and Sabel's vision is a local development strategy of permanent innovation based on multi-use equipment (e.g., versatile machine tools coordinated through complex computerized controls); skilled adaptable workers; and the creation through politics of an industrial community devoted to innovations where networks of socially embedded small firms both compete and cooperate. They compete for contracts, but no one is left out completely. The industrial district and unions regulate competition so it does not result in a downward spiral of wages and working conditions. Through cooperative arrangements these small firms share the cost of purchasing materials, marketing regional products, and R&D; they secure credit on favorable terms for their members; they supply semifinished products whose manufacture permits economies of scale. Their culture of mutual trust is fostered by ethnic, political, or religious ties of family and community. The competitive position of the network is strengthened through infrastructure investments by regional and municipal governments, union-management cooperation, craft guilds and trade associations.

Beyond these regional conglomerates, FS occurs among groups of loosely federated, large enterprises with mutual stockholdings and interlocking boards of directors, especially enterprises with family ties, if not by blood then by corporate identity. A closely related form of FS is also found among "solar firms" that hold smaller firms in steady supplier orbit, as well as internally decentralized workshop factories. Toyota City is the epitome case of both. Such firms, as MacDuffie and Kochan (1995, p. 150) suggest, reduce the technical system's ability to cope with problem conditions by minimizing buffers of all kinds: they reduce slack, increase task interdependence through work teams, and raise the visibility of problems. The aim is continuous improvement in process and product; the means is an expansion of human capabilities at every level so people become involved in the work process and can deal with problem conditions. These solar firms typically treat external suppliers as collaborators instead of subordinates. They seek subcontractors' advice on design and production problems and develop long-term relationships with them. The most-celebrated cases labeled FS include the Uddevalla and Kalmar plants of Volvo; the Toyota-GM joint venture, the New United Motor Manufacturing, Inc. (NUMMI) in Fremont, California; the metalworking firms in industrial districts of Emilia-Romagna in Italy (Carpi, Modena, Bologna, Reggio-Emilia); Benetton in the Veneto region around Venice (Benetton manufactures brightly colored sweaters, T-shirts, and jeans with retail outlets in 79 countries); and Prato, an industrial district north of Florence (8,000 tiny producers of woolen textiles).

In contrast, "Fordist" or mass-production firms aim to achieve economies of scale through long runs of standardized products based on a mass of semiskilled workers whose involvement in the work process is minimal. To protect against potential disruptions such as sales fluctuations, supply interruptions, equipment breakdowns, and product defects, they rely on the technical system—extra inventories, repair space, big inspection departments at the end of the line—rather than human adaptability. In such cases the "just-in-time" inventory system and the quick model changes typical of Japanese large-scale industry would be difficult to implement both because the strong focus on quality and continuous improvement is absent and because suppliers dependent on the solar firms are treated like subordinates and sweated, with no long-term commitments to their survival.

Piore and Sabel (1984, pp. 251–265) argue that in the absence of a global Keynesianism that expands mass demand, rich countries cannot overcome the saturation of markets for standardized products. Nor can they compete with low-wage countries on labor costs using "Fordist" methods. So they must seek comparative advantage from product quality, flexibility, innovation, and product differentiation, all of which require heavy investment in a high-quality labor force and stable relationships with suppliers and sales people. In short, they must take what Bennett Harrison (1994) calls "the high road" (see chap. 17 [Globalization]).[50]

Because there are few clear applications of FS outside of the exemplar firms, and because Fordism itself is a stereotype, researchers who look for FS have been forced to invent new labels—"post-Fordism," "decentralized Fordism," "concentration of control without centralization," "lean production," "democratic Taylorism," "after lean production," "high-trust, high-skill" organization. Mario Regini (1995), comparing firms in France, Germany, Italy, and Spain, notes six types of competitive strategy and their associated human resource practices obscured by the labels "Fordist" versus "post-Fordist": "Fordist" and "neo-Fordist" (both common in Catalonia); traditional small firms (Catalonia); "diversified quality production" (predominant in Baden-Württemberg); "flexible mass production" (predominant in the Rhone-Alps, common in Lombardia); and "flexible specialization" (Lombardia). At various times during the 1970s and 1980s, all of these strategies have resulted in sustained periods of economic success, which suggests that there are many roads to high-performance workplaces.

Other researchers have noted great national contrasts between the Japanese model of "lean production" and the German/Scandinavian models, all labeled FS. For example, champions of the lean production model (Womack, Jones, and Roos, 1990) believe that organizational learning—and hence survival in a competitive world—is best served by a system of specialized tasks supplemented by modest doses of job rotation and great discipline in the definition and implementation of detailed work procedures (Adler and Cole, 1993, p. 85). This prevails in Toyota in Japan and its joint venture with GM, NUMMI in California. Champions of the German/Scandinavian work reform movement, in contrast, believe that organizational learning and adaptability are best served by a craftlike work process that gives work teams much autonomy in planning, organizing, and carrying out their tasks. The assembly line is abolished. Status barriers between managers and workers are reduced. The work cycle, which can be a few seconds in a Toyota plant (not much different from old-fashioned Fordist assembly lines) is greatly lengthened to as much as two hours. This human relations strategy was most evident in Volvo's Uddevalla plant and its famous Kalmar plant before they were shut down in the early 1990s. Such self-management cases are a bold attempt to democratize and humanize the workplace. (Cf. Adler and Cole, 1993; MacDuffie and Kochan, 1995; Kochan, Lansbury, and MacDuffie, 1997a, 1997b.)[51]

That these national differences in the technical and social organization of work extend widely is shown by comparisons of industrial strategies in OECD countries (Vickery and Wurzburg, 1996) and by a large-scale survey of management and labor strategies in the world auto industry that covers 90 assembly plants representing 24 producers in 16 countries (Kochan, Lansbury, and MacDuffie, 1997a, 1997b). They demonstrate that national political and economic contexts shape enterprise responses to technological change and intensified competition. OECD studies (Vickery and Wurzburg, 1996) suggest that three patterns have emerged. The first, market-driven, is typically found in firms of North America, Australia, and New Zealand—the least-corporatist democracies. These firms aim at short-run returns and adapt to change by shedding fixed assets through takeovers and divestments. Workforce adaptation is achieved by invoking the right to hire and fire at will, by reducing union and government barriers to managerial autonomy on labor issues, and by keeping labor costs down. They rely mainly on external labor markets and invest relatively little in employee training and career development. The second approach is typically found among corporatist democracies, especially in German industrial firms, in varying degrees in Nordic countries, Belgium, Netherlands, and perhaps France. This approach relies on negotiation with employees, various suppliers, customers, and the government to achieve consensus. More firms in these countries approximate the Swedish model of FS. The third approach is also consensual but is centered in the firm. Japan is the epitome case. Large business conglomerates focus on developing technology and market share rather than on short-term financial performance. Labor adaptability is achieved through heavy investment in a broad base of general abilities throughout society (e.g., a demanding K–12 curriculum), and through continual on-the-job training made possible by job security in large firms and reliance on internal labor markets. (Chapter 2 discusses types of political economy that parallel these three approaches.)

The comparison of managerial strategies in auto plants provides abundant empirical evidence confirming and elaborating these broad strategies within one highly studied sector (MacDuffie and Pil, 1997; Kochan, Lansbury, and MacDuffie, 1997b). This MIT study shows considerable national variation in measures of employment practices associated with lean production—measures of worker participation and involvement in the work process and of pay and job security. In 1993–94, auto producers in North America scored lowest on such practices as teamworking, job rotation, training, and pay for learning and/or performance. Japanese and Korean producers scored highest. Producers in Europe and to some extent Australia fell in between. The researchers conclude that among rich democracies the interaction of management and union strategies explains most of the national variation in lean production. Where labor is weak (Japan and Anglo-American countries, except Australia), management strategy is most important. Where labor is strong and has a history of involvement in work organization (e.g., Sweden, Germany), the negotiated adaptations to change are more democratic (e.g., the election of team leaders). (For further comparative evidence that national variations in labor policies and modes of interest representation are more important in shaping workplace practices and industrial relations than characteristics of industrial sectors, see Turner, 1991; and Keenoy, 1995, and citations therein.)

The closer we come to intensive case studies of workplaces, the more variation within each sector and each nation we uncover. For instance, within Sweden, even after the shutdown of Volvo's experimental plants in Kalmar and Uddevalla, there remain significant differences between Volvo plants and Saab plants; the latter look more like Japanese lean production than the former (Brulin and Nilsson, 1997). Adler and Cole (1993, pp. 92–93) similarly note substantial differences in the nature of lean production at Toyota City and that at Nissan's newer Kyushu production plant; the latter is a bit closer to the Swedish model, though these researchers argue that Volvo, Toyota, NUMMI, and Nissan are all moving closer together in their behavior.

With all this diversity in workplace organization, is there any sign of convergence as competitive pressures mount? Insofar as some version of FS exists, what is common to the firms that have successfully implemented it for substantial periods is a modified form of lean production—something between the Swedish experiments and Toyota City. Robert Cole (1996) provides a suggestive analysis of these common (and possibly convergent?) characteristics. He argues that despite some differences between the Japanese and the so-called Scandinavian/German models, the latter have absorbed from Japan or have arrived independently at the following interrelated features of Japanese lean production, features that simultaneously provide a performance advantage and enhance worker morale:

- A strong accent on an *integrated approach* to quality, cost, and delivery.

- A very strong focus on *quality.*

- A strategy for *rapid model introduction* or quick product modification in response to shifting demand.

- Implementation of *just-in-time inventory control*—the elimination of buffers of all kinds discussed earlier.

- *Supplier partnership* and adoption of a *tier system.* The core factories purchase supporting business services in transport, cleaning, and manufactures; they develop interfirm linkages by subcontracting parts, components, or services that are part of the final products. The first tier is a network of small to midsized firms that work closely with core factories at the top; the numerous lower-tier suppliers are typically small and highly specialized.[52]

- Dependence on *problem-solving teams* and their involvement in managerial and supervising decisions.

- A heavy *investment in human resources,* which is essential for the effective use of new technology—pay for individual worker skills, pay for learning new skills, job rotation for multiskill development, quality circles, an accent on continuing education, training, and career development. All this blurs horizontal and vertical differences in tasks and status.

- The application of *a philosophy of continuous improvement* of the work process. Incentives for product and process improvement (e.g., gains sharing). The system alternates between experiments with procedural change and careful standardization and wide diffusion of each improved method—yielding a steady stream of incremental advances.

This form of lean production appears most often in manufacturing—especially in auto assembly plants and electronics—and finance (banks, brokers, insurance companies). As I have suggested, strong union participation in continual negotiations makes it more effective and sustainable. Clearly, the success of NUMMI, the joint venture of GM and Toyota in Fremont, California, owes much to this union involvement. Regarding suppliers, the tier system can remain a stable network of mutual cooperation or degenerate into a subcontracting system of low-wage, part-time, no-benefits workers employed by subcontractors, themselves highly unstable, who are pressed to cheat on social security and other taxes and evade minimum-wage and safety laws. That low road is not prevalent in Toyota (Nishiguchi, 1994) but has developed in the celebrated flexible manufacturing district dominated by Benetton in Italy (Harrison, 1994, p. 89).

There is insufficient comparative evidence to know how widespread the modified form of lean production is and whether rich democracies are converging in this aspect of work organization. OECD (Vickery and Wurzburg, 1996, p. 17) estimates that an approximation to FS has been adopted by about a quarter of larger enterprises in the more-advanced industrial countries in sectors most exposed to heightened competition and in firms as diverse as Coca-Cola, Renault, Motorola, and the leading banks.

The Spread of Contingent Labor

If flexible specialization is not new, if it comes in many forms and covers only a small portion of the labor force, and if several of the celebrated cases have disappeared, there is one major shift that is new (at least in degree) and is very likely convergent—the spread of "contingent labor," part-time, temporary, or subcontracted workers in both services and manufacturing. The United States, Canada, and Australia lead the way in this high-turnover, low-training job creation, but other rich democracies are also moving in this direction (Wilensky, 1992b). The trend may reduce labor costs, enhance management flexibility, and increase choice for some workers. But at the same time it increases the risk of job and benefit losses and decreases investment in human capital. It is a new source of insecurity and instability—not confined to low-paid, low-skilled workers—that will play out in the politics of labor and public policy. Those countries that resist the trend will have an edge in both long-run productivity and social consensus. While downsizing, outsourcing, and workplace restructuring encourage this trend everywhere, the legal and industrial relations context varies among nations and creates different national responses. This may be a trend like total hours of work—moving in the same direction but because of labor-left resistance both to long hours and contingent labor, divergent in the speed of change and hence the portion of the labor force affected.

Is Modern Society "High-Tech"?

The current obsession with "high-tech" jobs and the image of the "high-tech society" run up against uncomfortable facts about where people work and what occupations are growing fastest. "High-tech jobs" generally connotes something new that requires substantial upgrading of knowledge and skills. The United States is said to be the leader in high-tech products and services—especially if we include military R&D—or it is at least one of the top three or four if we do not. This is symbolized by high-growth centers such as Silicon Valley (California), Route 128 (Boston-Cambridge), the Research Triangle Park (North Carolina), and federal facilities in space and defense around Cape Canaveral (Florida), Huntsville (Alabama), and Oak Ridge (Tennessee). Recent trends in occupational structure in the U.S., then, might be taken as a sign of things to come if the high-tech society is more than an illusion. But consider the 10 largest detailed job categories in 1983 that also grew substantially from 1983 to 1997. They are, in descending order of employment in 1983, sales supervisors and proprietors; truck drivers; janitors and cleaners; cashiers; cooks; sales representatives (commodities except retail);[53] registered nurses; elementary school teachers; nursing aides, orderlies, and attendants; and carpenters. Waiters and waitresses would make the top 10 list (about 1.4 million) but grew only 1%. Each of the 10 began the period with more than about 1.2 million employed. Not one is high-tech. Together these 10 categories added 6.49 million jobs 1983–1997 and employed 23,723,000 people by 1997. Or take another cut at reality: Of the 16 fastest-growing occupations for the same period only one—computer systems analysts and scientists—was unambiguously high-tech (960,000 jobs added). More ambiguously we might add "management analyst" (255,000 added), and even "securities and financial services sales" (217,000 added). These three added only 1,432,000 jobs over the 14 years, bringing their total 1997 employment to a mere 2,054,000, 1.59% of the total employed. (My calculations are from U.S. Department of Labor, January 1998, table 11; January 1984, table 22.) In short, statistically speaking, modern society remains "low-tech" or "no-tech" in the experience of vast majorities, whatever the privileged position and power of highly trained elites.[54]

No comparable detailed labor-force data are readily available for many rich democracies. If we examine gross categories such as those from OECD *Labor Force Statistics*, we find gross similarities in the percentage of employment in industry or services (with Germany, Austria, and Switzerland having an edge in "industry," North America in "services"). Comparing five of our rich democracies, John Myles (1991) found that the richest four (Canada, USA, Sweden, Norway) are similar in the proportion employed in goods production, distributive services, and public administration, but sharply different in business services (financial, legal, and clerical), where the USA and Canada have about twice the percentage of Sweden and Norway, and health, education, and welfare (where welfare-state leaders employ many more than the USA and Canada). Chapter 4 returns to these trends in industrial structure. Despite these data limitations, the likely convergent trends in general occupational structure and stratification, discussed earlier, suggest that the U.S. profile—excluding the very rich and the poor—is not exceptional. Whatever the impressive contribution of high-tech industries (computers, software, drugs, medical instruments, telecommunications, aerospace, etc.) to the GDP or productivity of rich democracies, the modern labor force as a whole remains low-tech or no-tech. Many high-tech consumer products are made with low-tech methods. And truck drivers, janitors, short-order cooks, or nursing aides in Silicon Valley are like their counterparts in central Chicago.

Are the Rise in Unconventional Schedules and Unstable Careers American Peculiarities?

A consequence of the changing occupational structure and the emergence of contingent labor is an increase in unconventional schedules of work. A thorough study of nonstandard days of work (e.g., Sunday, Saturday, variable) and nonstandard hours of work (evening, night, irregular) in the United States by Harriet Presser (1995, 1997) shows an extraordinary concentration in the fast-growing occupations discussed previously. She defines standard hours as working fixed-day schedules the week before the survey interview. All others—fixed evening, fixed night, irregular day, irregular evening or night, irregular (no hours given), and rotating shifts—are nonstandard. The percentage of employed adults with nonstandard work schedules in 1991 was a whopping 42.1. By 1997 the figure had risen to 44.6% (Presser, 1999, p. 1778). Such schedules are pervasive throughout the occupational structure but are concentrated in parts of the service sector, and especially in growing occupations. Consider the percentage of adults with nonstandard schedules who were employed in 1991 in the 10 occupations with the largest projected absolute job growth 1994–2005 (Presser and Cox, 1997, p. 33, table 5). Eight of the 10 are very high in nonstandard schedules. They range from about 9 in 10 of waiters and waitresses and home health aides to 6 in 10 of the janitors and cleaners, with cashiers, salespersons, registered nurses, guards, and nursing aides, orderlies and attendants in the middle of that range. The two exceptions in the top 10 big-growth categories are systems analysts (only 18% nonstandard) and general managers and top executives (41%). Who works in such schedules and why? Seven of the top 10 growth occupations are disproportionately female. Job characteristics (e.g., the evening and weekend hours required in retailing or 24-hour hospital and nursing care) are stronger determinants than are characteristics of the employee, although least-educated women, including single mothers, are disproportionately represented in occupations characterized by unconventional schedules. Presser shows that least-educated single mothers work such schedules much more for labor-market reasons—they have no other options—than for personal reasons such as a desire for flexible hours to care for parents or children (*ibid.*, p. 29). Among men, high rates appear in all the previously listed occupations, plus technical and related support occupations and, for nonday work only, operators, fabricators, and laborers—except those in construction where daylight is needed (Presser, 1995, p. 588, table 3). The health consequences of deviant schedules include sleep disturbances, gastrointestinal disorders, and chronic malaise; the social consequences include increased family breakups.[55]

These somewhat chaotic schedules are matched by the newer unstable careers of college-educated executives, engineers, and middle managers, which combine both unconventional schedules and contingent labor. In the United States, because of the increase in divestitures, mergers, acquisitions, joint ventures, joint research or marketing agreements, and a change in top managers' personnel policies, there has recently been an acceleration of corporate and even government downsizing, outsourcing, and subcontracting. Consequently, we see an increasing percentage of college graduates who are not employees of large, complex organizations; they are contractors, consultants, part-timers, and "temps," often constituting a service network of itinerant executives, engineers, and consultants. Corporations increasingly outsource information systems, maintenance, housekeeping, data processing, and even business management. Frequently they lay off in-house staff and executives who had expected lifetime careers and replace them with younger, cheaper workers or hire them back as temporary workers with no job security or benefits, and often at less pay. A joke in Silicon Valley regarding these high-tech nomads: "What does CIO (Chief Information Officer) stand for?" Answer: "Career Is Over." Peter Drucker notes that the number of temporary employment agencies in the United States doubled in only five years—from 3,500 in 1989 to

7,000 in 1994 (*Wall Street Journal,* March 29, 1995). Many of these "new-age nomads," especially specialists in computer software applications, make very big fees, at least for a time. But most, especially the older (40s, 50s) consultants, have joined the ranks of the downwardly mobile in a growing Darwinian market (*Wall Street Journal,* August 19, 1996).

Again no comparable data are available to test the idea that other rich democracies are moving toward the American pattern of work. However, we would expect countries with the largest service sectors (USA, UK, Canada) to have the highest rates of workers in nonstandard schedules. If there is convergence of other countries toward social, personal, and distributive services as a share of total employment, there will be convergence in both contingent labor and unconventional schedules—or at least parallel development. (See table 4.1 and discussion of industrial trends in chap. 4.) And if European business enterprises continue their trend toward downsizing and subcontracting, then their college-educated employees will increasingly join their American counterparts—a growing minority in unstable careers. But numerous counterpressures in Europe should at minimum slow down any trend in this direction: the much greater unionization of service occupations; labor laws restricting weekend work and even evening hours; restrictions on employers' autonomy to fire at will; the higher wages, restrictive entry rules, and subsidies of small retail businesses common in Japan, Italy, France, and Austria that block the low wages, frequent startups, and high bankruptcy rates of distributive services in the United States. Countries that avoid the high rates of solo-mother poverty characteristic of the USA, Australia, Canada, and Ireland (table 8.4) will also retard the trend. If there is movement in the Anglo-American direction, it will not be speedy.

Summary

With continuing industrialization, the aspects of work organization that are most convergent are hours and schedules of work and the spread of contingent labor. Total annual hours of work declined from the late 19th century until about 1960, a trend that has continued in all rich democracies since then. Diverse rates of decline, however, and an American exception, yield a hint of divergence since 1960: the leisure-rich countries, largely corporatist democracies, are becoming relatively richer; the leisure-poor countries are becoming poorer. Within countries, the uneven distribution of work is reflected in an intensification of labor among highly educated professionals and executives in great demand; they represent a slowly growing percentage of the labor force working at least 55 hours a week, putting distance between themselves and the rest of the population not only in income and knowledge but in amount of work.

High levels of economic development and related changes in the occupational and industrial composition of the labor force result in two areas of convergence: the gradual spread of nonstandard schedules of work, especially among women; and the substantial and rapid growth of contingent labor in both manufacturing and services and at every status level—part-time, temporary, or subcontracted work. While these trends are not a strictly new source of insecurity, they are now more widespread.

Within a context of convergence toward lower annual hours, unconventional schedules, intensification of work at the upper levels, and contingent labor at every level, the speed of change is shaped by left-labor power and public policies that flow from national bargaining arrangements discussed in chapter 2 (see figure 2.1). Remaining national differences are therefore substantial.

Regarding industrial conflict: There has been a postwar divergence in the total volume of strikes (e.g., in person-days lost). The more consensual democracies evidenced a rapid decline in strike rates, however measured. Among the decentralized and fragmented democracies these rates fluctuated around a high level or declined more slowly. The presence of a strong Communist party with a class-struggle ideology in Italy, France, and Finland fostered high strike rates for several decades, adding to cross-national divergence. What convergence we see is in the locus of intense industrial conflict within all democracies in occupations and industries where work is hot, heavy, dirty, or dangerous (or all of these) and workers are segregated socially and geographically, as in mining or longshoring. As changes in technologies, organizations, and labor laws both reduced the harshness of the work and desegregated the workers, those occupational strike rates everywhere declined.

Modern society is said to be a "high-tech society." Detailed analysis of recent trends in occupations in the United States, however, suggests caution. Plainly, for vast majorities work is low-tech or no-tech. If I am right about the common trends in occupational and industrial structure, the American trend is what we would find if we had comparable data for all 19 of our rich democracies, despite some differences in the international division of labor (e.g., Germany and Switzerland with larger manufacturing sectors than the U.S.).

Finally, the endless diversity in the technical and social organization of work, as well as managerial strategies and government regulations make it very difficult to uncover any general trends in workplace structures, convergent or not. Clearly such labels as "Fordist" and "post-Fordist" or "flexible specialization" obscure more than they reveal. Some clues point to a modest spread of various versions of Japanese "lean production" as a strategy to improve both productivity and worker morale in a few large, highly competitive manufacturing firms, especially in auto and electronics, and among some financial services providers. Whether that strategy takes the high road or degenerates into excessive stress for the bodies and minds of workers in the core workplaces and a bevy of dependent sweatshops among suppliers depends on managerial strategies and the strength of countervailing forces, principally labor federations, center-left parties, and government policies. (Chap. 17 returns to this issue.) And whether lean production is possible at all and how far it spreads depends on the general level of knowledge, discipline, and skill of management and the labor force necessary for its successful implementation. In any case, some version of lean production covers only a small percentage of any modern labor force.

THE WELFARE STATE

Convergence theory is a powerful explanation of levels of aggregate social expenditure on pensions, death benefits, and disability insurance; health insurance; education; family policies; job injury insurance; unemployment insurance and related labor-market policies; war victims benefits; and miscellaneous aid to the poor. Over the past century or so, as rich countries got richer they all instituted seven or eight clusters of social policies as a matter of social right, not charity. Regime type and social mobilization (e.g., the spread of the franchise and party politics) better explain the timing of initiation of welfare-state programs in industrial societies from Bismarck to World War I, but once in place these programs expand and converge. Remaining differences in program content, generosity, administration, and political and economic impact can be explained by the interaction of electoral systems, cumulative Catholic party power, and to a lesser extent, left party power, which are the main determinants of corporatist bargaining arrangements; in turn, type of political economy (corporatist, corporatist-without-labor, and fragmented and decentralized) explains policy and political responses and real welfare outputs, including national differences in the rate of poverty and inequality. Chapter 2 and Part II cover all of this in detail.

IS THERE ANY CONVERGENCE IN THE POLITY?

Given the contrast between authoritarian, totalitarian, and democratic regimes and the variety within each type, the polity at first glance may be the area of least convergence; a high level of economic development may not be a decisive determinant of political systems. But the areas of most convergence—increased family breakup and gender equality, the push for equality among minority groups, the rise of mass higher education, the increasing number of intellectuals and experts, changes in social stratification, mobility, and the organization of work, and rising social expenditures and taxes to finance them—may very well foster some convergence in politics.

What dimensions of political life converge with continuing industrialization? Several propositions can be supported, though they are quite general and it is easy to find exceptions: Economic development at high levels is correlated with a decline in collective political violence; a decline in coercion as a means of rule and an increase in persuasion and manipulation; an increase in pluralism, and, less surely, an increase in democracy. All democracies are market oriented, though all market-oriented political economies are not democracies.[56]

Decline in Collective Political Violence

It is well established that economic development at the level of our rich democracies brings a sharp decline in internal collective political violence, and even a decline in the intensity of peaceful demonstrations. The most extensive analysis of this relationship covers the extent and intensity of civil conflict at three levels of economic development in 87 countries (Gurr, 1979a, table 2.5, p. 62). Two dimensions of overt conflict were measured: "Protest" refers to conflicts over limited issues and usually takes the form of political strikes, demonstrations, and riots; "rebellion" refers to struggles over basic issues and typically takes the form of coups, plots, terrorism, and guerrilla and civil war (*ibid.*, pp. 50−51). A third measure is deaths from such conflicts. The findings: Conflict deaths per 10 million population in 1961−65 correlates −.55 with GNP per capita: the richest countries had a median death rate of 0.4; medium development, 31; low economic level, 400. The correlation of per capita GNP and person-days of civil conflicts is weaker, −.42: the richest countries exhibited a median person-days in protest and rebellion of 680 per 100,000 population; average development, a median of 2500; low development, 22,500. In short, the higher the standard of living, the less deadly and extensive is civil conflict.

If we examine a larger number of countries, take account of broad types of political regime, and confine the outcome to civil violence, we learn more about this relationship.

Table 1.2 shows the effect of four levels of industrialization and four types of political regime on civil violence. Total magnitude of civil violence (TMCV) is an aggregate measure of the pervasiveness, duration, and intensity of turmoil (e.g., violent demonstrations, riots); conspiracies (e.g., violent mutinous coups); and internal war (e.g., guerrilla

TABLE 1.2 Affluence and pluralism reduce civil violence, 119 countries, 1961–63.
Authoritarian regimes at low to medium economic levels have the highest rates of violence.

economic-technological development[b]	Political Regime Type[a]									
	Pluralist and/or democratic		Authoritarian "centrist," mainly communist		Authoritarian "elitist," mainly African		Authoritarian "personalist," mainly Latin		All regimes	
	TMCV[c]	N	TMCV	N	TMCV	N	TMCV	N	TMCV	N
High	12.6	21	8.0	7	na		55.5	1	13.0	29
Medium	24.5	15	33.3	11	na		29.9	4	28.4	30
Low	5.5	1	12.5	3	52.9	16	38.3	9	42.6	29
Very low	0.0	1	29.9	11	27.6	17	10.3	2	26.4	31
All levels	16.8	38	24.6	32	39.9	33	33.8	16	27.6	119

[a]From Gurr and Ruttenberg (1969), pp. 22, 202–207, whose label for democratic or pluralist is "polyarchic"; for authoritarian communist or Leninist is "centrist"; for authoritarian personalist (or patrimonial or clientelistic) is "personalist." Their "elitist" at the time meant oligarchical modernizing elites in Southeast Asia and all but a few new African states. Obviously these regime types are gross; but for the purpose at hand, adequate.

[b]A unidimensional "technological development" scale that corresponds roughly to per capita income in U.S. dollars for 1958 (Gurr and Ruttenberg, 1969), pp. 28, 154–55, 202–207.

[c]"Total Magnitude of Civil Violence" 1961–63 average (for countries in each cell of the table) calculated from Gurr and Ruttenberg (1969), pp. 38–42.

warfare, civil war, large-scale terrorism) in 119 countries during the three years 1961–63 (Gurr and Ruttenberg, 1969, pp. 30–34). Table 1.2 uncovers a curvilinear relationship between economic level and collective political violence, an inverted-U shape. The 29 most violent countries are poor but not the poorest; they have begun a process of industrialization. Somewhat less violent are countries at very low and medium levels of development. And, again the 29 richest countries are by far the least violent. The old idea that political violence and labor protest intensifies during the painful transformation of early industrialization from rural to urban, from peasant to dependent industrial or service worker (Wilensky and Lebeaux, 1958, pp. 49–89) is confirmed by this table. The second finding is that at low levels of development personal dictatorships and modernizing oligarchies alike provoke the most civil violence. In contrast, the 21 pluralist regimes and the 8 Communist regimes at relatively high levels of economic development yield the very least civil violence. Three forces are at work among the richer countries. Pluralist and democratic systems channel mass grievances and group protest into electoral politics while delivering abundant material benefits; Communist or other centrist authoritarian regimes could keep the lid on for decades by comprehensive agencies of political and social control, including one-party domination of secret police, armed forces, mass media, schools, and workplaces.[57]

However, modern populations cannot be governed mainly by coercion. At high levels of economic development, persuasion and manipulation become more prominent. Many writers, shocked by the barbarity of the Stalinist and Nazi regimes, have generalized a vocabulary appropriate to a single country or, as in the Nazi case, momentous but brief historical episodes and have thereby missed the main trend. As I suggested in 1964,

> The limits of terror have been encountered by every totalitarian elite committed to economic progress [and military power]. Even the most monolithic regimes are forced to supplement coercion with persuasion and manipulation, and to attend to problems of morale and motivation. This is especially true when they confront skilled workers at every level, including cultural elites, and is most evident when persons in these categories are in short supply. The argument is both familiar and accurate: some tasks cannot be mastered without the development of more-or-less autonomous groups— crafts, professions, scientific disciplines, and other private enclaves. Such groups cultivate technique and celebrate it, motivate disciplined work, provide stable careers and professional conviviality. The arts and sciences that flourished in the Soviet Union were not merely those which were politically safe; they were the ones which prior to the rise of Bolshevism were characterized by a high degree of skill and organization and either an aristocratic tradition (music, the ballet) or a tradition of intellectual achievement (mathematics, linguistics).[58] In short, the necessity of mobilizing social support for the performance of complex tasks sets practical limits on the baiting of intellectuals and professionals" and to the reliance on coercion. (Wilensky, 1964a, pp. 177–178)

Examining the same 1960s data on civil violence in 18 of our rich democracies varying from the least rich, Israel and Ireland, to the richest, the United States and Switzerland, I find no relationship between per capita GNP and Gurr's civil violence index (most of them score 0). Finally, collective political violence is unrelated to homicide rates and other indicators of mayhem analyzed in chapter 14, where we see big differences among equally rich democracies, explained by types of political economy.

Democracy and Markets

Students of comparative politics have established that all democracies have market economies. Historically, liberal constitutional systems—the United States, Britain, France— were established mainly to win and protect private property, free enterprise, free contract, and residential and occupational choice against government restrictions, not to achieve broad popular participation in governance. In the development of the older democracies this emphasis on liberty to engage in trade was more prominent than the idea of equality of participation in selecting leaders. (Lindblom, 1977, pp. 161–169; Dahl, 1989.) The expansion of civil liberties, the suffrage, and the rule of law in these countries was preceded or at least accompanied by the expansion of institutions supporting free markets. But while all democracies are market oriented, all market economies are not democracies. For instance, in periods following World War II, South Korea, Taiwan, Chile, Yugoslavia, Spain, Portugal, and Argentina were authoritarian and market oriented. However, because all our currently rich democracies have market economies and they did not all start that way a century or so ago, we can say that this is an area of convergence. That does not say much, though, because market-oriented democracies vary greatly in the institutions in which markets are embedded—in the legal, political, economic, and social context in which finance, industry, labor, the professions, agencies of the executive, the judiciary, and the legislative interact and shape market transactions. The rest of this book spells out these varied contexts for economic activity.

Economic Development and Democracy

The interplay between modernization, markets, and democracy is complex and clearly does not reflect any straight-line trend. Today if we take Freedom House's rating system for civil liberties and political rights, generally degrees of democracy (Gastil, 1989), there is a .8 probability that a randomly selected rich country is judged "free" (rather than "partly free" or "not free"). But historically, as Huntington (1991) notes, democracy advanced in waves from the early 19th century till now, each wave followed by reversals and new gains. Sometimes the reversals were drastic. Thus several of the worst cases of totalitarian or fascist rule emerged in relatively advanced industrializing societies—Hitler's Germany (12 years), Mussolini's Italy (22 years), Austria, Czechoslovakia, Hirohito's Japan. Happily, both for democratic values and convergence theory, each reversal did not undo all previous gains: the net number of democracies by Huntington's reckoning went from zero before 1828 to 59 in 1990. Are they all rich or near-rich? No, because that includes poor Bangladesh, India, Costa Rica, Uruguay, and Botswana. But clearly the central tendency is for successfully industrializing countries to become more pluralistic and even more democratic as they become wealthier—as we can see from the cases of South Korea, Taiwan, Chile, Mexico, and South Africa. These countries may represent the threshold beyond which changing social structures rooted in industrialization strongly favor pluralism. Among the relevant changes are those discussed throughout the chapter: growing middle and upper-middle strata, accommodation of the minority-group thrust for equality, mobility out of the working class, the rise of professionals and experts, the growth of the welfare state, and the spread of commerce and industry. Why commerce? An old idea with substantial truth is that business executives do not want to kill you; they extend not swords or guns but contracts. They want to do business, make a deal; and for that they need a rule of law, a requisite for both economic development and democracy.

Whatever the intermediate links between economic level and democracy, the two are strongly correlated. As of 1990 the number of countries with below-$2,000 per capita GNP (1987 figures) that had sustained democracy at least a few years was only 15. The number below $1,000 was only 10; the number under $500, only four (India, Pakistan, Nigeria, and Sudan)—and the last three had reverted to military rule. (Huntington, 1991, p. 272.) Put another way, why did some 30 countries in the 1970s and 1980s with authoritarian regimes—but not about 100 other authoritarian regimes—shift to democratic politics? Confining ourselves only to their levels of affluence in 1976 and tracing their trajectories up to 1989, the most frequent democratic transitions appear to be at an average to above-average per capita GNP of $1,000 to $3,000. Only about a third of the 97 countries classified as authoritarian in 1976 (Huntington, 1991, table 2.1, p. 62) had democratized and/or liberalized by 1989. But a breakdown by economic level excluding countries already democratic by 1974 shows that only 6% of those starting the period with a per capita income of less than $250 made the transition; 29%, between $250-$1,000; 76%, $1,000–$3,000. Thus, the authoritarian countries more or less successfully making the move to democracy were overwhelmingly middle income moving toward upper-middle. (A study of 131 nations based on annual observations, 1972–1989, using a pooled time-series analysis and 22 measures of degrees of democracy, pins down the strong causal relationship; it very likely runs from economic development to democracy, not the other way round. See Burkhart and Lewis-Beck, 1994; cf. Diamond, 1992, pp. 451–466.)

Level of economic development and its structural and demographic correlates help explain why democratic regimes in Greece, Portugal, and Spain by the 1980s and the Czech Republic, the former East Germany, and Hungary by the late 1990s successfully consolidated after their authoritarian regimes collapsed and why the transition to democracy has been so problematic in the less-developed countries of Central and Latin America (except for Uruguay) and even worse in the poorer countries of Eastern and Southeastern Europe, including Romania, Bulgaria, Albania, and Serbia.

Ethnic warfare can further complicate the democratic transition, as it has in the former states of the USSR and Yugoslavia, both of which also delivered drastic declines in standards of living. Consistent with convergence theory, however, it is the less-developed countries in which ethnic conflict is most virulent and violent. Such violence is most frequent and most destructive in nonrich regions of the world where feeble authoritarian regimes face ethnonational rebellions (Riggs, 1995; Gurr, 1993a). We have seen this manic nationalism in violent movements for self-determination in Bosnia, Georgia, Rwanda, and Haiti. In the postwar period we have seen also the slaughter of such minorities as the Ibo of Nigeria; the overseas Chinese of Indonesia, and, recently, the Kosovar Albanians in Yugoslavia. In the early 1990s there were about 120 shooting wars going on in the world, 90 of which involved states that were attempting to suppress ethnic minorities (Maybury-Lewis, 1993, p. 57). None were among our rich democracies. In fact, economic development at above-average levels and democratization together always channel such movements into nonviolent politics. One reason for this is that weak states at a low level of economic development find it difficult to redistribute resources to pacify potentially violent ethnic protesters. Rich democracies, in contrast, as the rest of this book shows, have both economic strength and a high degree of legitimacy—resources to use for any aspect of social peace. As Lijphart suggests (1984), dominant "majorities" in democracies do this by sharing power (coalitions), dispersing power (bicameralism, multiparty systems), distributing power more fairly (proportional representation in its various forms; see chap. 2), delegating power (federalism), and limiting power formally (minority veto). The mix of these electoral and constitutional arrangements varies, but all modern democracies have found ways toward minority/majority accommodation. Some form of affirmative action in assignment of jobs, political positions, or college admissions is also common, although specific government policies vary. Finally, an obvious and well-traveled road to social peace is expansion of the franchise and a well-developed, universalistic welfare state (see Part II).

Research on the breakdown or emergence or consolidation of democracy is beyond the scope of this book. Scholars analyzing lengthy lists of conditions favorable to the democratic transition include Huntington, who lists 27 economic, social, political, and cultural causes (1991, pp. 37–38); Diamandouros, Puhle, and Gunther (1995); Diamandouros and Gunther (1995); Lipset (1960, pp. 45–76; 1994); Przeworski (1991); Moore (1966a); Stephens (1989); Tarrow (1995); Weiner (1987); Di Palma (1990); O'Donnell and Schmitter (1986); O'Donnell, Schmitter, and Whitehead (1986); Diamond (1992); Linz and Stepan (1996); and a series of volumes on Asia, Latin America, and Africa edited by Diamond, Linz, and Lipset

(1988–1990). None of these scholars fail to note the crucial importance of economic level or material conditions for the emergence and the consolidation of democracy. However, they all offer a catalogue of noneconomic determinants. To explain 20th-century democratic transitions, this list includes the character of the prior regime, especially the following:

- The extent of liberalization. All four of the southern European countries that became democracies (Italy, Greece, Portugal, Spain) had parliamentary institutions during the mid to late 19th century and, except for Portugal, experimented with democracy in the early 20th century.

- The duration of the nondemocratic regime. Duration of the Colonels' regime in Greece was seven years versus almost half a century in Portugal. Democratic consolidation was fast for Greece, slow for Portugal.

- The penetration of the old regime into society, which is related to the degree of toleration of economic, social, and cultural pluralism. In the last 20 years of Franco's authoritarian rule, there was considerable pluralism. Even fascist Italy tolerated considerable institutional independence of the army, monarchy, and church. These cases experienced a smoother path to the consolidation of democracy. Contrast the totalitarian legacies of the USSR, Eastern Europe and the brutal personal dictatorship of Romania's Ceausescu, and some similar regimes of the Caribbean and Central America. They typically combined long duration, deep penetration of society, and lower degrees of pluralism. The result: a weak civil society that makes the democratic transition difficult and uncertain.[59]

- The role of the military. Important in the consolidation of democracy is whether the outgoing military has penetrated civilian leadership of the nondemocratic regime and, if so, it is induced through negotiations to stand aside during the democratic transition. The presence or absence of such negotiations is especially prominent in explaining outcomes in Latin America.

The comparative analysis of democratic breakdown and continuity during periods before World War II has shown that the structure and ideology of the main groups in the agricultural economy and the structure and ideology of the urban labor movement shape political coalitions that either subvert or strengthen democracy. From the last third of the 19th century to the Great Depression, as socioeconomic development proceeded and the franchise spread in Europe and North America, labor and agricultural interests organized politically. Land tenure arrangements appear to be crucial in the subsequent interaction between farmers and farm labor and urban labor—in whether the politics of extremism or of moderation prevailed. National differences in that interaction help to explain drastically different political responses in the interwar years and the Depression: the United States coped with crisis by choosing FDR and the New Deal while Scandinavia, Belgium, the Netherlands, and France responded with the ascendance of social democracy or alternating center-left and center-right governments for the rest of the century. In contrast, Germany reacted with Hitler's totalitarian regime and the Holocaust while others reacted with some form of authoritarianism (Italy, Portugal, Spain, Austria). Among the many historical-structural legacies that shaped these responses in the first group was the presence of numerous free farmers who owned and worked their own land—some poor, some not, but all independent. The agricultural sector in the countries where democracy collapsed was instead dominated by a politically powerful landed elite allied with independent farmers, urban entrepreneurs, and the state in combat with a peasant proletariat allied with a class-conscious, radical urban left. Agriculture was labor intensive and labor repressive. The crucial point is that in the continuously democratic countries when urban labor leaders and rising socialist parties confronted the need for allies to achieve a majority in competitive politics and when they reached out to the agricultural sector in which a majority worked, they encountered almost no powerful landlords with large estates but plenty of self-employed, independent farmers unresponsive to revolutionary appeals; they moved to the center-left, often forming farmer-labor coalitions. In the countries experiencing the breakdown of democracy, when labor leaders and socialist parties reached out for allies they found a large rural proletariat (migrant laborers, tenant farmers), many of whom were responsive to syndicalist or radical socialist ideas; they moved toward revolutionary rhetoric and militant action. The political extremism of a revolutionary left confronting a repressive right, scaring the "middle class," was antithetical to the accommodations and coalition-building that favor democratic continuity. However oversimplified this illustration may be, it gives a sense of the complex literature on how economic organization shapes democratic consolidation or breakdown among countries at similar levels of socioeconomic development (see especially Stephens, 1989; and Rueschemeyer, Stephens, and Stephens, 1992).

The safest conclusion supporting convergence theory is that economic development at fairly high levels and the related trends discussed in this chapter foster increased pluralism. With still further economic development pluralism facilitates the emergence and consolidation of democracy. But a host of other forces, of uncertain relative importance, determine the strength and composition of antidemocratic and prodemocratic coalitions and hence the specific trajectory and speed of the outcome.

A POSTSCRIPT ON ECONOMIC DEVELOPMENT AND INCOME INEQUALITY

Is there any sign of convergence either in world income distribution or in the distribution of income within rich countries? It depends on whether we deal with intercountry inequality or intracountry inequality and whether the period is 200 or 30 to 40 years. There is broad agreement that over the long haul—from the late 18th century through much of the 20th century—income disparities among nations greatly increased. Average incomes per capita at the beginning of that period in the richest nations were something like four times greater than those in the poorest nations; today that disparity is about 30 times the poor-country average—$18,000 versus $600 (Summers et al., 1994). In worldwide perspective the story is one of unequivocal divergence. The rich got richer; the poor relatively poorer.

There is much dispute about what has happened since World War II: Some studies conclude that in recent decades there has been a reversal in the trend toward either some convergence or parallel development; other studies say that national incomes continue to diverge (the latter include "dependency theorists"). The contradictory findings are mainly due to differences in measures of average per capita income and of inequality and in whether size of population is considered (Firebaugh, 1999). Continued divergence is typically found when per capita income is measured by constant U.S. dollars (market prices) and when tiny countries (Luxembourg, Iceland) are given the same weight as the United States, China, and India. When we compare 120 countries with huge disparities, however, we must recognize that official exchange-rate income distorts the real situation for a vast majority of them because little of what is produced in poor countries is traded internationally. Even among rich countries there can be short-run currency distortions.

As Firebaugh (1999) shows in a careful review of evidence, if instead we use estimates of per capita income based on purchasing-power parity (PPP) and control for population size, intercountry inequality (by four different measures) declined modestly from 1965 to 1989. Among 120 nations, the less-developed countries have been slowly catching up to the rich countries. Firebaugh shows that although both the faster economic growth rates of rich countries and the age structure of poor countries (the swelling of the nonworking young population) boosted inequality in recent decades, the slowdown in rich-country growth has offset the trend. And most important, he finds that the effect of differential rates of population growth overwhelms the effect of internal policies shaping economic growth: Examining the effect of big countries on world inequality and giving them proper weight reveals counteracting tendencies. Since 1960 "the inequality-enhancing effects of rapid growth in Japan and sluggish economic growth in India were blunted by the inequality-reducing effects of rapid economic growth in China and slower-than-world average population and economic growth in the United States . . . " (*ibid.*, p. 1623). In short, in recent decades a century of divergence has given way to a small convergence, if inequality among all the people of the world is at issue. When the dependency ratios of developing countries become more favorable (their baby boomers start working and their fertility rates decline) while the dependency ratios of rich countries deteriorate (as their population ages), the new trend toward income equality may continue or at least not reverse. Of course, much depends on the political stability of the developing nations, discussed earlier; and this, in turn, depends on what they do about their physical and social infrastructures and their labor markets to accommodate an abundance of urban workers.

If we concentrate on the currently rich democracies of my study, it is easy to show recent convergence in national per capita income. Whether we use market exchange rates or purchasing-power parities the distance between the least rich and the most rich has been declining at least since 1960. For instance, using real per capita income in 1990 U.S. dollars and price levels, the 1960 range among 18 rich democracies (data for Israel are missing) went from Switzerland's $23,250 to Ireland's $5,641; the average for the lowest four (Ireland, Japan, Italy, Austria) was $7,461; the 1960 average for the richest four (Switzerland, Sweden, USA, Denmark) was $17,058—a ratio of 2.29. The 1996 range went from Norway's $39,806 to New Zealand's $16,823. The 1996 average for the lowest four (New Zealand, UK, Ireland, Australia) was $20,848; the 1996 average for the richest four (Norway, Switzerland, Denmark, Sweden) was $35,931—a reduced ratio of 1.72. (Based on Mishel, Bernstein, and Schmitt, 1999, table 8.1 using OECD data.) The same trend toward convergence in standard of living is evident if we switch to per capita income using purchasing-power-parity exchange rates 1960–96 (1996 dollars) for the 13 of our rich democracies for which data are available. The 1960 range went from the USA's $13,797 to Japan's $4,508. The average for the bottom four (Japan, Italy, Austria, Norway) was $6,971; the average for the top four (USA, West Germany, UK, Canada) was

$10,814—a ratio of 1.55. The 1996 average for the lowest four (UK, Sweden, Italy, France) was $19,758; the 1996 average for the top four (USA, Norway, Japan, W. Germany) was $24,866—a reduced ratio of 1.26. (Based on *ibid.*, table 8.2, using BLS data.) In other words, no matter how we measure per capita GDP, the story is one of convergence in riches. As rich countries get richer, the distance between the most rich and least rich diminishes.

Convergence in affluence says nothing about the distribution of income and wealth within equally rich democracies or their poverty rates. Because inequalities of income and wealth are heavily shaped by type of political economy and because they are best considered in relation to system outcomes, they will be discussed in chapters 2 (Types of Political Economy), 8 (The Welfare Mess), 12 (Economic Performance), 14 (Mayhem), 16 (Health Performance), and 18 (Policy Implications). The story is one of recent trends toward inequality from a base of great disparity among rich democracies, contrasts rooted in different types of political economy (see tables 8.4, 10.4, and 14.4). After a long-run increase in income equality and a slight increase in wealth equality that accompanied continuing industrialization, the trend changed after the mid-1970s. In almost all of our cases for which data are available there has recently been increased inequality of income and great increases in inequality of wealth—again from a disparate base. So whether there is convergence on some dimensions of inequality or not, momentous national differences remain and they make a difference in system outputs.

Conclusion

Convergence theory has a lot going for it. As our 19 rich democracies got richer and passed the threshold of development they all reached by the mid-20th-century they developed several structural similarities. Ignoring differences in timing and occasional exceptions and short-cycle variations already discussed, and concentrating on the amount, pace, and direction of change, they all converged in nine dimensions of modern society:

1. Changes in kinship systems and household composition and associated political demands. Declining birthrates, increasing labor-force participation of women. Increased family breakup. Much change over two centuries, accelerating after about a third to a half of all women are in nondomestic work. (The causal sequence is summarized in figure 1.1.)

2. The push for equality among minority groups and the increasing openness of modern governments to minority-group claims and demands. Much change over at least a century, accelerating during and after World War II. Discrimination on the basis of race, ethnicity, religion, language, gender, sexual preference, and physical disability has everywhere declined. Despite the occasional resurgence of minority-group militancy—leaving the mistaken impression of the Balkanization of modern societies—the main story is the increasing structural and cultural integration of minority groups, even those based on race. The climb in intermarriage rates fosters some merger of values and tastes. A recent convergence in social heterogeneity rooted in a revival of massive migration of economic and political refugees moves all rich democracies toward the American multicultural model.

But as governments respond to the demand for gender equality, the rich democracies move toward the Swedish model, however varied their specific policies. The one exception to the rule of reduced discrimination is the aged. Although they have benefited greatly from the welfare state, the aged comprise the only minority group that has experienced an increase in job discrimination. This is reflected in a century-long decline in the age of exit from the labor force, most of it a matter of system pressure, not uncoerced choice.

3.   Facilitating the considerable achievement of minority-group equality and the great changes in women's roles and family structure is the increasing equality of educational opportunity, especially the spread of mass higher education. All industrial societies began a modest expansion of opportunities for secondary school and university education by World War I. With some variation in timing—the welfare-state leaders tend to lag in the expansion of higher education—they all increased postsecondary enrollment ratios at a fairly rapid rate since the early 1960s. As rich countries become richer and mass higher education spreads, however, quality variations within the same level of education become increasingly important. For mass education necessitates a huge diversity of schools, colleges, universities, and vocational training institutes to accommodate a great variety of people and meet the intensified demand for skilled labor. The resulting specialization and institutional stratification of modern educational systems means that the higher-quality, resource-rich schools and colleges recruit and graduate people whose abilities, motivation, and information give them a competitive advantage over people with identical formal levels of education. This growth in quality variation helps to explain why the basic relations of social origin (i.e., education of parents), school completion, and occupational fate did not change much in most of our rich democracies during the 20th century, despite expanded educational opportunities for vast majorities.

For more than a century education has been the main channel for upward mobility in occupation, income, and social status. The ambivalent mass demand for some combination of absolute equality and equality of opportunity—which often takes the form of demands for affirmative action or quotas for those groups presumed to be deprived—has had little effect on the essential character of higher education. Colleges and universities remain meritocratic, very much attuned to the demands of the economy, and quite vocational in emphasis. Education for alert citizenship and critical thought, for making moral judgments, for the pursuit of wisdom, for the enhancement of capacities of appreciation and performance in the arts, for broader understanding of the individual in society—all tend to take second place. The United States has no doubt established a long-term lead in postsecondary enrollment ratios, but all rich democracies now share the twin trends toward specialization and universality in higher education.

4.   The convergence of rich democracies toward the American model is evident not only in mass higher education but also in the increased influence of the media of mass communication and entertainment in politics and culture. Despite national differences in the control, financing, and organization of the media, which persisted for decades, there is an unmistakable, recent and swift convergence toward the commercialization and privatization of public broadcasting with a concomitant but somewhat slower shift toward

American style and content—increasingly competitive, frantic, sensational, negative, afactual, aggressively interpretive, and anti-institutional. This talk-show style has itself become dominant in American print and broadcasting media only in the last 30 or so years. In political campaigns, however, convergence toward the American model is quite slow; strong parties, government-assured access to television and radio for parties and candidates, restrictions on ads and the length of campaigns, as well as well-financed year-round public broadcasting news coverage are counterpressures. Chapters 3 and 11 explain these trends and the national similarities and differences in media behavior.

5.   Over the long run, modern societies converge in the increased number and labor-force percentage of experts and intellectuals. Their influence in public policy, however, varies by type of political economy in which they work.

6.   Continuing industrialization shapes social stratification (the "class" structure) and mobility in several ways: It blurs older class lines; it creates increasing social, cultural, and political heterogeneity within each social class such that internal differences within classes become greater than differences between them; and it fosters the emergence of a politically restive "middle mass" (upper-working class, lower-middle class) whose behavior, values, beliefs, and tastes increasingly differ from those of the privileged college-educated upper-middle class and the very rich above them and the poor below. Increasing mobility, both intergenerational and worklife (a product mainly of technological change and shifts in occupations), add to the heterogeneity of social classes. At every level the mobile population and those with mobility aspirations contrast sharply with the nonmobile population at the same SES. A little-studied but momentous difference even within the mobile population is the contrasting behavior and orientation of those with orderly careers and those with chaotic job patterns, a difference unrelated to SES. Finally the persistence and even slight growth in the urban self-employed portion of the labor force—people who live in a separate world—adds another source of heterogeneity within each "class."

In short, because of convergence in mass education and occupational structure and related increases in mobility among all rich democracies, because of multiple ladders for achieving income, status, or power, almost any major source of social differentiation—ethnicity, race, religion, the quality and type of education, work and career, stage in the family life cycle—explains more of the behavior of modern populations than social class, however measured.

7.   The organization of work, with all its variety within and across nations, is still an area of convergence. Continuing industrialization brought a steady decline in annual average hours of work from the late 19th century up to about 1960 with a divergence since then as the leisure-rich countries got richer and the leisure-poor became poorer. Within nations the uneven distribution of work increased in recent decades; the most-educated groups intensified their labor, the rest of the population typically continued to reduce average annual hours, or suffered forced leisure. There has recently been a gradual spread of nonstandard schedules of work, especially among women; and a sizable, rapid growth of contingent labor—part-time, temporary, or subcontracted work—a source of widespread insecurity.

As for modern society becoming a "high-tech" society, evaluation of occupational trends shows that the vast majority of modern populations work in low-tech or no-tech jobs and that almost all of the large and fastest-growing occupations are anything but high-tech. Similar skepticism is appropriate for the idea that modern societies are moving away from "Fordist" production toward "flexible specialization." Insofar as we have any comparative data, they suggest a great variety of organizational forms within each of these categories. There may be a modest trend among a few large manufacturing firms exposed to the most intense competition and some financial service providers toward a modified form of lean production epitomized by Toyota and its joint venture with GM, NUMMI. But as yet this covers only a small portion of any modern labor force.

8. For more than a century there has been gradual institutionalization of the social programs comprising the welfare state. Part II specifies exactly what has converged, what diverges, and what explains the remaining differences.

9. As a consequence of all of the preceding there are a few aspects of political systems that are common to all rich democracies. After a rise in civil violence at very early levels of economic development, there has been a steady decline. Rich democracies have a very low level of internal collective political violence. Although specific paths of development vary and reversals occur, we can say that economic development at a high level fosters pluralism, and at very high levels of development pluralism is typically transformed into democracy. All rich democracies are market oriented, whatever the causal order. All 19 of the rich countries in this study are market-oriented pluralist democracies with little civil violence.

Throughout this chapter I have noted substantial differences among equally rich democracies in the speed and amount of change, the limitations of cross-national data, and exceptions to convergence theory. The rest of Part I deals with theories that explain remaining differences among our 19 highly developed democracies, with special attention to types of political economy, mass-based political parties, electoral systems and constitutions, patterns of social participation and mass media behavior, and civic engagement.

Notes

1. Industrialization is not identical with urbanization; cities were known long before modern industry emerged. But every highly industrialized society is also highly urbanized. The widespread dominance of the metropolis would not be possible without the widespread use of high-energy technology. In this book, when I speak of "urban industrial society" or "modern society" I refer neither to a society that has only a few urban communities nor to cities at a low level of economic development. Nonindustrial cities like Peiping in China, Cairo in Egypt, Poona in India, and Rangoon in Burma, however large, do not make these nations "urban-industrial societies." The proportion of urbanites in these societies relative to the peasant population is still small, because of rural fertility rates and limited economic development (Dogan and Kasarda, 1988).

2. Students of modern society are often so impressed with the recent pace of change that they feel compelled to use such words as "unprecedented" and to search for new labels—"postindustrial," "postmaterialist," "postmodern." They should resist the compulsion. It is doubtful that the past 30 or 40 years evidence a greater pace of change than that of the late 19th century or periods of recurrent plagues and upheavals of still earlier centuries.

3. This section is based on a lecture presented at Oxford University, England, March, 1988; it elaborates and updates themes in Wilensky, 1981b. I am indebted to Eugene A. Hammel for critical comments.

4. In 1955 Japan, in the third quartile of affluence, ranked average among the 34 countries in percentage of women in the nonagricultural labor force (20%) (Wilensky, 1968, p. 237). As Davis indicates, Japan's early 1980s rate of participation of married women in the nonagricultural labor force was about where the U.S. rate was in the 1950s (1984, p. 404).

5. For a detailed discussion of the structural and cultural correlates of economic growth that foster urban labor-force participation by women, see Wilensky and Lebeaux, 1958, chapters 2–5, esp. pp. 63–74, 78–83.

6. A national household survey of divorce and cohabitation in the United States (Bumpass and Raley, 1992) indicates another reason for a continued climb in family breakup—the increase in multiple divorces. The researchers found that 37% of remarriages collapsed within 10 years compared with 30% of first marriages in the same period. Add the nearly one-third of American children born to unmarried mothers and a very large and increasing number of children will see their families split, reform, and split again. This is the center of the social problem posed by family transformation to which all modern governments have responded (see chap. 7).

7. The problem of specifying precise attributes of social structure and change that account for precise changes in behavior is illustrated by this pioneering database. Some researchers using the Coale and Watkins data argue that fertility decline occurred under a bewildering array of economic circumstances and therefore cultural factors common to regions or provinces are more important than economic development. However, their territorial units are so large, and therefore heterogeneous in economic level and types of industry and occupation as well as urban-rural composition, that they cannot provide a test of convergence theory. (See the review symposium by Tilly, Andorka, and Levine, 1986, pp. 323–340, especially Levine on social and economic context and Tilly on rural-urban variation.)

8. Consistent with this are the contrast in fertility rates among peasant populations versus the more modern urban sectors of Brazil and China. The Draconian "one-child" policy of the Chinese government has had much more effect in the urban sector where structural changes are consistent with government policy than in rural areas. Brazil, without such a coercive policy, also showed a decline in fertility rates during the economic boom of the 1960s and 1970s, which was accompanied by increased female labor-force participation (both in proletarianized farm labor and in urban areas) and increased consumption of durable goods (refrigerators and TVs). Similar trends are evident in the modernizing sectors of Mexico and Cuba, especially in the 1970s. (Potter, 1986, pp. 31–36.)

9. Precursors of modern feminist movements emerged in several countries at only moderate levels of industrialization: among early industrializers in the mid–19th century; among late industrializers in the late 19th century. For instance, in the United States, women's rights conventions were held yearly from 1840 to 1860 at Seneca Falls and Rochester, New York, and Worcester, Massachusetts, among other places; in the same period most state legislatures passed married women's property laws. No permanent organizations, however, were formed until after the Civil War (Evans, 1977, pp. 46–48). Organized feminism did not emerge in England until the 1850s, and demands for suffrage were first voiced clearly only in 1866 (pp. 63–65). Feminist movements in other countries appeared somewhat later: in Germany and France in the 1860s, in Sweden, the 1870s, Norway and Finland, the 1880s (p. 69). What is significant for my argument, however, is that all these movements were concentrated among the daughters and wives of urban, upper-middle-class men (pp. 31–32), the tiny fraction of the total population already exposed to the educational, economic, and demographic changes that would later shape the behavior of a growing majority of women.

10. Popenoe (1987) argues that although the divorce rates of the United States and Sweden are equally high, the Swedish rate of family dissolution is understated because the amount of nonmarital cohabitation in Sweden is so high relative to other rich countries. If a couple never marries, their breakup will not count in divorce statistics. This conclusion, however, may rest on a comparison of unusually well measured Swedish rates of cohabitation with poorly measured rates in other countries. The Swedes are champions in studying themselves.

11. There is even an argument that the extended family is alive and well today whatever its past—that the frequency of phone calls and visits with relatives not living in the household indicates the prevalence of a "modified extended family" (see Litwak, 1960a, 1960b; cf. Fischer, 1982). My discussion of social relations in the mass society (chap. 3) suggests that these assertions miss huge qualitative differences between modern and premodern (rural, peasant) communities: kin in agrarian societies of preindustrial periods, like the people in some tiny rural towns today, are linked by a complete and reciprocal set of obligations and rights as well as reciprocal knowledge of life histories and family genealogies—hardly typical of a modern mobile family.

12. The following two paragraphs are based on my "Preface" to the Japanese edition of *The Welfare State and Equality* (Tokyo: Bokutakusha Publishing Co., 1984, pp. 2–14).

13. For citations supporting these propositions for the United States up to 1979, see Wilensky and Lawrence (1979). For more recent evidence see the studies by the National Research Council; the summary volume is Smith and Edmonston (1997).

14. There are well-known ambiguities in the distinction between ascription and achievement. That *age* and its close correlate, *seniority,* are relevant to job performance is obvious for many complex jobs; accumulated work experience both in similar lines of work and similar workplaces is often indispensable, always helpful. "*Politicking*" and "*pull,*" if not "ascriptive" in the sense of inherited, are popularly viewed as irrelevant to performance. Yet upon close inspection their relevance is clear. Political judgment and loyalty are measures of ability in all organizations—ability to further the goals of the system through political or business connections, wisdom, and demonstrated loyalty; these "skills" typically require many years of cultivation and hence combine politics and age (Wilensky, 1967a, pp. 10–13). In these instances "Who you are" shapes "what you can do." These and other ambiguities are elaborated in Wilensky and Lawrence (1979, pp. 212–215), and Mayhew (1968). This chapter maintains the distinction of criteria relevant versus those irrelevant to role performance.

15. In 1980, when the Census for the first time asked a subjective identity question, "What is this person's ancestry?" only 8% of whites failed to mention a European country. Yet most of the adults from the largest European groups are not only native born but are the offspring of native-born parents. Further, some of the presumed ethnic identifiers are not reliable in their reports of their own nativity. (Waters, 1990.) Most important, nearly half of white Americans who identify with a European country name more than one (Farley, 1991). Second- and third-generation Americans, especially those of mixed heritage, evidence much free choice in defining their identity (Alba, 1990; Waters, 1990; cf. Hout and Goldstein, 1994), and much of it is superficial.

16. These figures are actually for "whites" and "blacks and other races." However, the latter category is approximately 90% black.

17. However, from 1940 to 1990, blacks made their biggest gains in the less well paid, largely female-dominated professions—social work, elementary and secondary school teachers , and nurses. In 1990, blacks were only 4.5% of physicians, 3.5% of attorneys and engineers. (Thernstrom and Thernstrom, 1997, p. 187, table 2.)

18. To make their comparisons, Massey and Denton (1993) use an "isolation index" which measures the extent to which blacks live within neighborhoods that are predominantly black. A value of 100% means that all blacks live in totally black areas; a value under 50% means that blacks are more likely to have whites than blacks as neighbors. They observe, "The highest isolation index ever

recorded for any ethnic group in any American city was 56% (for Milwaukee's Italians in 1910) but by 1970 the *lowest* level of spatial isolation observed for blacks anywhere, north or south, was 56% (in San Francisco)" (p. 49).

19. A good statement of the hypothesis of the downward mobility of second-generation immigrants is in Ruben Rumbaut's study of over 5,000 immigrant schoolchildren in the eighth and ninth grades of the San Diego and Miami/Ft. Lauderdale areas. Interviews were done in 1992 and covered 77 different nationalities; the children were either foreign born or born in the United States with at least one immigrant parent. Although his data do not bear directly on mobility, Rumbaut suggests that as the children of immigrants become more American they substitute television for homework and exhibit lower aspirations and lower achievement (1997, pp. 33, 37–39). And, if they live in neighborhoods with high rates of poverty and unemployment, they become entangled in the dangers of the street (cf. Zhou, 1997, pp. 76–79 on Haitian youth in Miami and West Indian youth in New York City). As Waters et al. (1999) suggest, however, there is little evidence of whether downward mobility of any kind—worklife or intergenerational—is a common pattern or whether it has long-term effects on social and economic integration. Studies of Asians, Latinos, and Cubans cited in the text give a different picture.

20. If you merely compared all averages for 1980 and 1990 you would conclude that the Hispanics were downwardly mobile. (See, for example, Zhou's 1997 review of literature comparing the poverty rates of first-, second-, and third-generation immigrants [1997, pp. 76–77].) Myers' (1999) more powerful cohort analysis shows the reverse for the Mexican-American second generation in Santa Ana and Los Angeles. Similarly, based on the 1990 Census comparing first- and second-generation immigrants in the greater Los Angeles area, Allen and Turner (1996) also found a near-universal pattern of upward mobility among 12 minority groups. The children of immigrants were higher in educational attainment, median income, and residential desegregation. The ups and downs of blacks variously situated is discussed below.

21. A comparison similar to my Italian example was the swift movement of German immigrants and the slow movement of the Irish. "Most Germans who worked in mid-nineteenth century New York, Boston, Detroit, St. Louis, or Milwaukee were either skilled manual workers or were in non-manual occupations, while the Irish . . . were in mostly unskilled occupations in the same cities at the same time" (Sowell, 1996, p. 294). The Germans brought more mobility-relevant resources to the urban economy.

22. With the decline of K–12 quality in most public schools in the United States since 1970, the average quality of parochial and public schools has converged (see chap. 12 for a comparison of the performance of public and private schools).

23. Based on a survey of nearly 20,000 students in Northern California and Wisconsin (response rate 80%), 1987–90, followed up by in-depth interviews with 600 students and some of their parents, selected for ethnic variation. Steinberg et al. argue that the big differences in achievement are attributable not to parents but to peer-group contrasts in the value attached to hard work and success and the perception that work leads to success (Steinberg with Brown and Dornbusch, 1996, pp. 134–137). "Good" parenting is scoring high on scales of "acceptance" (warmth), "behavioral control" (firmness), and the granting of "psychological autonomy" (democracy)—all inferred from student reports. Together, these scales constitute "authoritative parenting" (Steinberg et al. 1992b, pp. 1269–1271). By this measure the Asian-American students, outstanding performers, had parents who score least authoritative (and least involved in school affairs), while the poorer-performing black students had parents who score most authoritative and were most involved with schools. The authors say that the ethnic differences in "authoritative" parenting made little difference for school performance but that variation *within* each ethnic group did predict school achievement (*ibid.*). What is missing is any direct measure of ethnic variation in independence training and other performance-relevant practices. For instance, "good parenting" does not

include parental expectations of academic achievement. Insofar as the researchers get at this it is when they ask students such questions as whether their parents will be angry if they come home with less than an A-. The results closely match the ethnic variations at issue. Most important, Asian-American parents may score low on "authoritativeness" and "overt school engagement" (*ibid.*; Steinberg et al., 1992a, p. 726; and Steinberg, 1996, p. 134)—they may hesitate to confront teachers and school officials because of cultural traditions of deference and respect—while they closely supervise homework, the choice of school and curriculum, not to mention neighborhood, and while they make sure that their children head toward college by providing the necessary guidance and help. Black parents may behave "authoritatively," increase the self-esteem and assertiveness of their children, and pressure the school to treat their children right, but have low standards for academic achievement and offer little relevant academic guidance. If most parents in these ethnic groups vary in these ways, the respective peer groups will surely be different in their academic orientations, as they in fact are in this study as well as others.

24. The following account is based mainly on Sowell's essay (1978). For similar research with emphasis on the varieties of black (and immigrant) experience, see Lieberson (1980) and Waters (1996, 2000).

25. An account of the lives of teenage children of more recent black immigrants from the Caribbean similarly emphasizes marked variation in their prospects for integration depending upon family resources, school orientation, and job opportunities (Waters, 1996, pp. 19–23).

26. This analysis is confined to rich democracies as they got richer. Consistent with the thesis of convergence, it is the less-developed countries in which ethnic conflict is most virulent and violent. (See the "Polity" section.)

27. Part of the explanation is the high incidence of part-time work (less than 35 hours/week) among Scandinavian women (e.g., about 46% of Swedish and 53% of employed Norwegian women work part-time compared with only 24% of employed American women (Blau and Kahn, 1996b, table 2). Chapter 7 describes variations in family policy that make it easy for women in corporatist democracies to choose to combine part-time work and child rearing. In contrast, U.S. women, especially single parents, must work full-time to make ends meet. On national variations in poverty and income distribution, see tables 8.4 and 14.4.

28. The question of preferences and motives is discussed in the first section of this chapter. The rest of this paragraph refers to whites only. Black women with little education are still disproportionately clustered in private household and low-paid service jobs; they are a special case. Among women, black women experienced slower increases in labor-force participation than white women—in *all* education and headship categories. In the late 1970s and 1980s the previous convergence of black and white wages among men slowed down. (Blau, 1998, pp. 124–134.)

29. Gains at the very top, however, are slow. In the early 1990s women held only 5% of senior management positions in the largest companies, 11% of partnerships in law firms, and 15% of full professorships. The fuller pipeline at lower levels in all those fields, however, ensures a continuation of the trend toward gender equality. (Seltzer, Newman, and Leighton, 1997, pp. 85, 87, 91–92.)

30. A six-country study of female-male wage ratios in the mid- to late 1980s adjusted for measures of productivity (education, age, years at work) shows that earnings equality ranged from a high in Sweden to a low in the United Kingdom, with other countries (Ireland, Denmark, East Germany, and West Germany) in between. The extremes held no matter what controls were applied (Callan et al., 1996, table 3).

31. Although the Bureau of Employment Security survey did not directly collect data on the abilities of older workers, employer responses indicated widespread discrimination on the basis of age (Wirtz, 1965, pp. 5–10). A more recent meta-analysis of age differences in job performance—

restricted to a small number of U.S. studies that met the scientific requirements—showed a positive correlation between age and productivity measured by unit output over time (Waldmann and Avalio, 1986). Although older workers of the current generation may typically be less physically fit and less healthy than the young, successive cohorts will be healthier and will have been exposed to fewer hazards such as World War II or dangerous working conditions (Kohli, 1991, p. 6). Equally important as an offset to declining energy with age are job experience and disciplined work habits, always positive for productivity.

32. This section draws on my "Ideology, Education, and Social Security" (1982).

33. Inkeles and Sirowy (1983) systematically examine 30 dimensions of educational systems around the world, going beyond enrollment ratios and the duration of free public schooling to include the spread of the comprehensive school, levels of expenditure, school administration and financing, preparation and certification of teachers, standardization of curriculum, formal tests, and coeducation. They found a pervasive, deep tendency for national educational systems to converge on all the dimensions I listed. Only one dimension was clearly divergent (repetition rates or second chances). A few were variable or mixed (teacher-pupil ratios, who participated in policy, teacher power and autonomy, classroom dynamics, instructional styles, parental ideas about education, and the organization of higher education). My analysis is confined to currently rich democracies and their history.

34. U.S. higher education is still exceptional in its diversity of funding resources, the size of its private sector, its diversity of curricula, its elective system, its flat hierarchies (and its greater participation of lower-rank professors), and its openness to interest-group demands (Trow, 1991a, 1991b). U.S. elite colleges were also exceptional in their accent on general education and the liberal arts, but this is rapidly declining. On average formal postsecondary education not only sharpens cognitive abilities and develops disciplined work habits, it also enhances the capacity to learn new jobs quickly. That is one major reason that employers who recruit for job ladders or demanding jobs prefer college graduates.

35. Despite their effort to reach out to minorities, these selective private institutions have rapidly increased their tuition both in relative and absolute terms. In fact, they have increased their traditional bias toward high-income families, whatever their racial-ethnic composition. "The probability that a student from the highest income group (over $100,000 annually) attended a selective institution increased from one in five in 1981 to one in four in 1997" (Neely, 1999, p. 31).

36. How Dutch "consociational democracy" affects broadcasting networks is discussed in chapter 3.

37. This section draws on Wilensky, "Class, Class Consciousness, and American Workers," (1966a), "Measures and Effects of Social Mobility" (1966b), and "The Problems and Prospects of the Welfare State" (1965).

38. The "service occupations" are added to manual workers in Figure 1.2 because of similar types of work and occupational status. The largest occupations in this service category are in food preparation and services, cleaning and building services, personal services, and private household and protective services. For the most part the skill levels required match the skilled craft, operators, transport and unskilled of "manual labor."

39. In measuring class by occupational position it is still safe to use household head and, surprisingly, the occupations of male heads. A recent study of the relationship between husband's and wife's class position and identity in the United States, Sweden, Norway, and Australia (Baxter, 1994) showed that the husband's status is a crucial determinant of both the wife's objective class location and subjective class identity—a finding that holds for all four countries.

40. "To attempt entrepreneurship is to move in a very special labor market. The self-employment histories of men in the labor-leisure samples [1,354 men in the Detroit metropolitan area in 1960; see n. 41] show that most salaried and wage employees remain employees, while the self-employed

alternate between bosses and business: of all those self-employed now, a whopping 94% once worked for someone else, but of those not now self-employed only 19% were ever self-employed" (Wilensky, 1966b, pp. 113–114).

41. Samples of my labor-leisure study were dictated by my theoretical interest in (1) the effect of types of mobility on leisure style and the general problem of the content and implications of "blurring class lines" and (2) theories of the mass society. Long personal interviews were completed with 1,354 men in the Detroit metropolitan area in 1960, ranging from three samples of men aged 30–55 from the upper-middle class—184 engineers, 99 professors, and 207 lawyers, each in two contrasting work settings—to a cross section of the middle mass aged 21–55 ($N = 678$) down to two samples of underdogs long unemployed and on welfare, 81 blacks, 105 whites aged 21–55. Details are in Wilensky, 1961a, pp. 529–530; and 1964a, pp. 181–182. All were currently or previously married. Contrasts in the hours, schedules, and type of work and lifestyles were almost as sharp between lawyers, engineers, and professors as between solo lawyers and firm lawyers, again all upper-middle class.

42. But see the Michigan Panel Study of Income Dynamics (Blau and Kahn, 1997); the Swedish Level of Living Survey and the Swedish Household Market and Non-market Activities Survey (described in Edin and Holmlund, 1995, p. 313); and the National Longitudinal Surveys of four population cohorts (Center for Human Resource Research, 1999).

43. See work history evidence reviewed in Wilensky (1960, pp. 553ff. and listed in n. 2). Subsequent studies that attempt to elicit full work histories either retrospectively in surveys or through panel studies turn up similarly frequent worklife mobility. Because of shorter work lives—later entry and early retirements—current mobility patterns may turn up fewer worklife shifts; offsetting that, however, is the increase in mergers and downsizing and their displacement effects. A rare study based on the National Longitudinal Surveys, which has consistent questions about job changes and follows the same individuals from year to year over 20 years, found a substantial increase in involuntary turnover 1971–90, significant for all education groups but most pronounced for the less educated (Monks and Pizer, 1998). Many of the histories based on survey data underestimate the amount of mobility. For questionnaires that try to overcome this difficulty see Wilensky (1966b).

44. These phenomena are usually described, not in terms of mobility experience, but in terms of the strains generated by status inconsistency, incongruity, or low status crystallization (Lenski, 1954; Homans, 1953). Smelser and Lipset (1966b) formulate the general principle that highly differentiated systems foster individual mobility and status "disequilibrium," and Germani (1966) offers many propositions about the politically disruptive effects of such a condition. To view the matter in terms of status incongruity has the advantage of simplifying measurement, but it may not capture much of the experience of mobility implied by the observed incongruity. Most people may experience the shifts that produced the high-status portion of that "disequilibrium" as a compensatory reward— something instead of nothing in an imperfect world.

45. See Wilensky and Edwards (1959) and Blau (1956). I estimate that skidders are perhaps a fifth of the working class of urban background, a tenth of all urbanites in the labor force—in time of recession, more.

46. In Sweden, Denmark, Finland, and France roughly one in four moved out of full-time employment compared with two in five in Germany and the United States. Most of these workers exit the labor force entirely rather than moving into part-time jobs or self-employment. Data for the United Kingdom (13% leaving) and Italy (8% leaving) are not comparable; they exclude workers leaving wage and salary employment altogether.

47. In my Detroit area samples, as in many other studies, the "little man" who feels squeezed by both big business and big labor is more prone to both extremism and scapegoating than others in the same social class. For instance, among all the self-employed men of the middle mass, those who felt squeezed were nearly three times as likely as comparable entrepreneurs who did not feel squeezed to

remember Senator Joseph McCarthy with enthusiasm. (Cf. Trow, 1958; and Rogers, 1960.) On rural radicals, see Lipset (1950).

48. Only 30% of the middle mass can by any stretch be said to act out half or more of their work histories in an orderly career. I assumed that even a modest amount of job predictability can integrate people into the social system. The borderline cases in fact did occupy a middle ground regarding social participation, ties to community, and attachment to society. Degree of orderliness is unrelated to intergenerational or worklife mobility, religion, age, occupational stratum, income, education, or even percentage of worklife in self-employment.

49. Data on annual hours per worker for all industries 1960–94 for only eight of these countries show that the North American exception is really a U.S. exception. U.S. hours dropped only 2.9%; Canada joins the rest with a drop of 14.4% (Fitzgerald, 1996, table 2).

50. Both "Fordist" and "flexible specialization" are exaggerations of the work process they each designate. In the early intensive studies of auto assembly plants (e.g., Walker and Guest, 1952; Chinoy, 1955; Roy, 1952) researchers noted the very different jobs, attitudes, and behavior of men in these work situations. First, and most discontented, were men gripped bodily to the line whose work was repetitive, machine-paced, required only surface mental attention, and provided little discretion in choice of tools and techniques and little control over the pace and schedule of work. The second were men on subassembly lines (e.g., installing springs on auto seat frames) in a horseshoe arrangement where some sociability on the job and some discretion in pace was possible. They were higher in job satisfaction than men on the main moving conveyor belt. Finally, there were free-floating workers in maintenance and materials supply whose work stood in sharp contrast to that of the men on the main line in every way. They were quite happy with their work. To invoke images of Charlie Chaplin's "Modern Times" and cast them on the larger screen of all work in auto-assembly plants, let alone all work in manufacturing or the economy, is to miss the considerable variety of Fordist production. The variety of work situations under the label flexible specialization poses the same problem, discussed below. For example, machine pacing in the newer flexible plants is sometimes more programmed and rigid than in the old-fashioned main line.

51. These plants were not shut down because they were less productive than older Volvo plants, although they may have been less productive than Toyota or NUMMI (Adler and Cole, 1993; Berggren, 1992). The demand for Volvos fell and low-capacity utilization doomed them. Offsetting cost savings—mainly from high-quality work requiring little inspection and from a very small executive and support staff—were not enough. When I visited Kalmar in 1978, the only visibly harried people I encountered were the lone manager in his little cubicle and a few office staff in a pool. The rest was a workers' paradise. The LO (the dominant Swedish Labor Federation) had negotiated the plant location and participated in its design. Kalmar was chosen because shipbuilding yards were closing down and the Social Democratic government wanted to provide new jobs. Several planners believed the talk about the new alienated worker and employers faced high turnover and absenteeism; they all attempted to make the technology and the work attractive. Assembly work was organized around mobile docks or platforms. Teams of 8 or 10 workers rotated work so all could perform almost all tasks. When team work was completed in an ergonomically sound way (no bending or heavy lifting required), the platform moved automatically to another team. Two workers could do all the programming of supply, scheduling, and so on, in a highly automated system, but all members participated in planning and chose new members when vacancies occurred. Each team had very little supervision, some control over work pace, some variety in work, and a quiet, pleasantly lighted workspace, with music the group chose, topped off by a coffee bar and sauna of its own.

52. This tier system is an added reason that most people in modern economies work in small to medium-sized establishments. Large firms are a tiny percentage of all firms in the member states of the EU—only 0.1%—although they account for some 28% of total employment (Ferner and Hyman,

1992, p. xviii). Similarly, a survey of where adults in the United States worked in 1991 showed that 88% of establishments have only 1–9 employees, but the typical employee works in a fairly large one with 599 employees and 72 part-time workers. If we consider organizations, rather than establishments, the median size is 3,750. Well over half the establishments are dependent units of larger organizations. (Marsden, Cook, and Knoke, 1996, pp. 48–51.)

53. The U.S. Census Bureau creates 12 categories of retail sales people. If we aggregated them instead of sticking to the most detailed classifications, "retail sales" would be the largest fast-growing category in 1997, with 6,887,000 workers and a growth rate of 25% from 1983 to 1997.

54. If projected growth 1994–2005 is preferred, the picture is even more low-tech or no-tech. The 16 occupations with the greatest percentage increase (moderate estimates of 119% to 52% growth), in descending order of growth, are personal and home-care aides; home health aides; computer systems analysts, engineers and scientists; electronic pagination systems workers; physical and corrective therapy assistants and aides; occupational therapy assistants and aides; physical therapists; residential counselors; human service workers; occupational therapists; manicurists; medical assistants; paralegals; medical records technicians; teachers in special education; and amusement and recreation attendants. The list is dominated by the medical-industrial complex discussed in chapter 16. Again, only a couple of these can be seen as high-tech. If we instead examine occupations with the largest total job openings due to estimated growth and net replacement, the picture is the same. (Jacobs, 1997, pp. 166–174.)

55. Presser finds that "among couples with children, when men work nights (and are married less than 5 years) the likelihood of separation or divorce 5 years later is some six times that when men work days"; the odds for women in that situation are three times as high. And such schedules are the cause not the effect of family breakup; spouses in troubled marriages are *not* more likely to choose night work (1999, p. 1779). The gain, if we view fathers' involvement in child care as desirable, is that split-shift parenting among dual-earner couples increases fathers' caregiving—that is, if the marriage lasts.

56. Throughout this book, drawing on Robert Dahl (1989) and Joseph Schumpeter (1942, pp. 250–302), I maintain this distinction: "Pluralism" is a system in which many relatively autonomous groups representing a real division of values and interests compete for power within a nation-state. "Democracy" is a system in which the people choose leaders through competitive elections made possible by a rule of law and freedom of association and related civil liberties. All democracies are pluralist. But authoritarian regimes often have elements of pluralism; they tolerate a degree of autonomy for selected groups such as the church, the monarchy, the military, or industry—even some cultural diversity. They are different from totalitarian systems, which aim to eliminate all independent associations, all zones of privacy—Nazi Germany, Stalinist USSR (Linz, 1975). My distinction between persuasion and manipulation is that the latter is a means of control in which the subordinates (or target audiences) are unaware of the goals toward which their activity and sentiments are directed. Persuasion and coercion require no definition beyond customary usage.

57. The curvilinear pattern for degrees of both affluence and democracy is confirmed by a new study of civil wars from 1816 to 1992. Intermediate levels of both democratization and economic development are most prone to internal war (Hegre et al., 2001, pp. 39–44).

58. Within the general framework of a policy of strenuous intervention the Soviet regime alternated application and relaxation of controls over intellectual life (Bochenski, 1961). In the short run (e.g., during the period of maximum Stalinist terror) the regime did pretty much what it liked. But over the long pull, Soviet commitment to modernization forced some liberalization. The collapse of the Soviet regime as its economic performance deteriorated and as Gorbachev moved toward cultural pluralism is consistent with the idea that relatively autonomous groups move all nondemocratic regimes toward pluralism. (Cf. Moore, 1966b.)

59. This leaves aside the economic policies of the nation and of external lending agencies. There is much controversy about the political and economic effects of swift moves to "free" markets. Comparison of most and least successful cases suggest that the transition countries that put off drastic economic restructuring—closing or privatizing formerly subsidized "parasitic firms"—and postponed open trade until democracy took root are having most success (Spain, Greece, Portugal). Contrast the big bangs of Russia, Romania, and Bulgaria, where marketization and democratization were practically simultaneous. When that strategy was combined with a debt crisis, the IMF and to a lesser extent the World Bank imposed additional austerity. (Diamondouros, Puhle, and Gunther, 1995.) The net outcome: sharp increases in inequality, unemployment, and political polarization—mounting threats to democracy.

2

TYPES OF POLITICAL ECONOMY

To explain remaining differences among market-oriented rich democracies and the occasional areas of divergence mentioned in chapter 1, we must look to types of political economy. This chapter first delineates three types of national bargaining arrangements among major interest groups and government—democratic corporatism; corporatism-without-labor; and "least-corporatist," least-consensual democracies that are most fragmented and decentralized—and measures of the types. This scheme captures variations in the structure and interplay of government, labor, professions, farm organizations, employer and trade associations, other interest groups, and political parties. I then address the argument that in the last two decades democratic corporatism has collapsed or eroded, that globalization sounds its doom.

After discussing some ambiguities in theories of democratic corporatism, I present data that show the ideological and structural roots of these consensual political economies. By combining the cumulative power of mass-based parties—mainly Catholic and left—with corporatism, I generate the types of political economy used throughout this book to explain differences in public policies, taxes, spending, and the numerous system outputs in the causal model of figure 2.1.

My model of corporatist democracy (Wilensky, 1976a, 1983) accents four interrelated tendencies in several modern political economies: (1) Bargaining channels develop for the interplay of strongly organized, usually centralized economic blocs, especially labor, employer, and professional associations with a centralized or moderately centralized government. (2) The peak bargains struck by such federations reflect and further a blurring of old distinctions between the public and the private. (3) These quasi-public peak associations bargain in the broadest national context rather than focusing only on labor-market issues. (4) Consequently, social policy is absorbed into general economic policy, and chances for social consensus are enhanced. A variant is corporatism without full integration of labor—epitomized by Japan. And, of course, these types are sharply contrasted with the authoritarian corporatism of Mussolini, Franco, or Perón.

Much of the literature on democratic corporatism exhibits conceptual muddiness and too little effort to frame propositions for systematic tests.[1] First, in defining corporatism

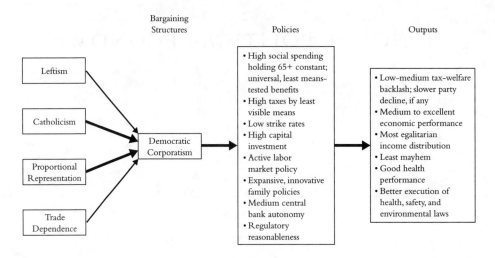

Figure 2.1. Model explaining performance among nineteen rich democracies, including economic performance

there is a strong tendency to mix up attributes of structures (e.g., degrees of centralization or bureaucratization or oligarchy); processes of policymaking (e.g., stages of decision making); the content of particular policies and programs (e.g., incomes policy); policy implementation (effective or ineffective implementation); or policy effects (good or poor economic performance, more or less equality). The result: It is impossible to relate corporatism as structural attributes of political economy to policy processes, content, implementation, and impact.

The second conceptual confusion is the recent tendency to counterpose democratic corporatism (or "liberal corporatism") and "pluralism," now lodged in the literature of comparative political economy. Students of American government and political behavior who developed theories of pluralism would hardly recognize their work as rendered by scholars who see pluralism and corporatism as polar opposites. Pluralism is a system in which many relatively autonomous groups representing a real division of values and interests compete for power within a nation-state. Democracy is a system in which the people choose leaders through competitive elections made possible by a rule of law and freedom of association and related civil liberties (see chap. 1). It follows that all democracies are pluralist, and democratic corporatism is a subclass of pluralist democracy. Comparativists could reread Robert Dahl and Stein Rokkan with profit. These conceptual confusions intensify the already severe difficulties of data collection and cross-national comparability familiar to everyone. They account for a few disagreements about which countries qualify as "corporatist," although there is agreement about most. In my scheme the 19 rich democracies are classified as follows: corporatist (Sweden, Norway, Austria, the Netherlands, Belgium, Finland, and, in lesser degree, Denmark, Italy, Israel, and, marginally, West Germany). A variant is corporatist without the full integration of labor (Japan, France, and, marginally, Switzerland). Least-corporatist democracies are the U.S., the UK, Canada, Australia, New Zealand, and Ireland.

DEMOCRATIC CORPORATISM

A word about the four attributes of structure comprising democratic corporatism:

1. *Channels for bargaining—a structure for consensus.* The structure provides for the interplay of *strongly organized interest groups,* especially labor, employer, and professional associations, with a *centralized or moderately centralized government* obliged by law or informal arrangement to consider their advice.

2. That structure leads to a second characteristic: *the peak bargains struck by such federations reflect a blurring of old distinctions between the public and the private.* Private bargaining and collective government decisions in corporatist democracies are difficult to separate. Holland's Foundation of Labor, a nonprofit institution for central deliberations of employer and labor federations, runs parallel to the powerful Social and Economic Council, a tripartite institution for collegial accommodations seldom ignored by the government. Norway's "voluntary" organizations on a national level have official status to negotiate with government or opposite parties; they receive subsidies for their activities as a political right. Sometimes these agreements are bilateral (e.g., the Ministry of Education negotiates with the authors' association about government grants and living stipends); sometimes they are trilateral, as in much of industrial relations and the administration of the labor market. These systems tend toward an interchangeability of personnel between public and private spheres. The career of a top official of the Investment Credit Department of the National Bank of Austria is typical. The bank is a national institution whose members are all the banks in Austria, including banks owned by labor unions. By its credit policies, this bank controls a large fraction of all industrial investments. The official has long experience in the unions, in the Chamber of Labor, and in politics. An ex-director of the Chamber of Labor, for five years he was a top man in wage-price agreements. For seven years he represented the Chamber of Labor on the Board of Directors at the National Bank, where he eventually became a vice general manager. Naturally he maintains close contact with Labor and the Socialist Party as he goes about making long-term investment credit decisions. They call it "social partnership," and it made Austria a model of economic performance for decades. In Israel, of course, one would be hard put to say whether the Kupat Holim, the medical arm of Histadrut, whose services are a major source of labor federation strength and whose deficits are covered by the government, is public or private.

3. *The scope of bargaining is wide; the trade-offs among bargaining parties encompass a wide range of national issues.* These quasi-public peak associations therefore have a chance to produce what eluded Prime Minister Wilson, what Prime Minister Callaghan officially pronounced dead, and what was alien to Prime Minister Thatcher: an effective social contract. Their struggle for consensus is not narrowly focused on the labor market—wages, hours, working conditions—as it has been in the UK, Canada, or the USA. The consensus may or may not involve a formal plan (as in French or Norwegian indicative planning). It may or may not involve high rates of membership in unions (the percentage is medium in Holland, low in France). It certainly does not require or result in "the detailed administra-

tive running of the economy" (G. K. Wilson, 1982, p. 232). *What counts are channels for influence for top leaders of economic interest groups meeting in the broadest national context.*

4. *Social policy is in some measure absorbed into general economic policy.* One reason for the relative effectiveness of this type of consensus is that the big issues are economic growth, prices, wages, taxes, unemployment, trade, and the balance of payments; welfare, housing, health care, and social security are absorbed into these broad discussions. Such an integration of economic and social policy tends toward an important result: At a time of slow growth (after the early 1970s) and rising aspirations, labor, interested in wages, job protection, and social security, is forced to take account of inflation, productivity, and the need for investment; employers, interested in profit, productivity, and investment are forced to take account of social policy; both labor and management are forced to take account of government concern with economic performance, tax revenues, and the balance of payments.

To illustrate the nature of trade-offs facilitated by such consensus-making machines, consider three cases (based on interviews with a few of the main actors). The first two illustrate typical trade-offs comprising an economic package. In Norway in the late 1970s labor, management, and government reached an agreement in which labor got a 3% increase in real wages (involving a realistic constraint on nominal wages), including government subsidies to fishermen and farmers, in return for a cut in profits taxes on industry. In Finland, September 1995, facing the collapse of its former USSR markets, a soaring unemployment rate, and a large public deficit, a broad-based coalition government reached an accord with labor, management, and government agencies. Negotiation took place in a negotiations office of government (the head of it is an ex-president of a technician's union). The budget was cut by 10% in real terms, an incomes policy restricted wages to 2.3% (with local adjustments it was about 3%) over two years. In return for its wage restraint, labor got small targeted tax cuts and an agreement to limit and negotiate the social policy cuts of the previous center-right government of 1991−94. All unions, even those in the paper industry where hi-tech processes were reducing the demand for labor while profits soared, joined the accord, which has persisted in subsequent years. Unemployment fell from 16.1% in 1996 to 14.3% in 1997 and was expected to fall to 10% in 1999. From the period 1995 to 1997 GDP growth accelerated from 2.5% in 1995−96 to 4.6% in 1996−97 to 5.0% in 1997−98. Net government deficit (% of GDP) dropped from 3.2% in 1994 to 1.9% in 1996. Export industries flourished, including telecommunications, electronics, metals, machinery, wood and paper products, and luxury liners. The third case suggests that corporatist bargaining arrangements do not depend on the continuity of left party power. In Sweden, from the early 1950s to the mid-1960s the top leaders of the Social Democrats, the labor federations, and the Federation of Swedish Industry met privately at the summer home of the prime minister to bargain out national economic and social policy. As the system became institutionalized and media coverage became more prominent, informal, private meetings continued, but agreements were ritually affirmed at a palace, Harpsund, donated to the state by a private industrialist. By the 1970s, these bargaining customs became known as "Harpsund democracy." When the "bourgeois bloc" took over in 1976, the system continued; only the faces changed. A 1978

Swedish bargain included a government-desired increase in the value-added tax (VAT) designed to dampen inflation and debt by cutting consumption; labor viewed it as regressive but accepted it in return for an increase in family allowances to offset the tax burden for large, relatively poor families. The defeat of Social Democrats did not change the essential machinery. Sections below suggest that even as Swedish corporatism weakened in the 1980s and 1990s, for reasons unique to Sweden, such trade-offs continued.

In short, democratic corporatism as a structure for bargaining does not predetermine either the issues to be joined or the content of agreements. Nothing in logic or practice blocks *any* issue from discussion and resolution. And with institutionalization, these systems can survive shifts in governing coalitions.

None of these corporatist bargaining processes requires a decrease in loyalties to subcultures of race, religion, or ethnicity as long as the representative groups have sufficient control over their members—that is, labor and employer federations are centralized. As I shall show, social cleavages can be dampened by centralized structures of autonomous groups meeting at the top. Thus Belgium and the Netherlands, with their complex social cleavages and profusion of political parties, can achieve much the same result as Austria, with its crisis-inspired harmony, limited cleavages, and simpler party structure. Neither does corporatist democracy require interlocking elites sharing a common socialization in family or school and university (apparently the English Oxbridge network does not help). Incidentally, corporatist democracy is compatible with either high levels of corruption as in Italy, Austria, France, and Belgium, or low levels, as in Sweden or the Netherlands.

In sum, the model emphasizes the capacity of strongly organized centralized economic interest groups interacting under government auspices within a quasi-public framework to produce peak bargains involving social policy, fiscal and monetary policy, trade policy, and incomes policy—the major interrelated issues of a modern political economy.

Measures

In devising a measure of the centralization of and the interplay between government and major private power blocs, as a clue to democratic corporatism, we used the appointment power of the central government weighted roughly equally with a measure of centralization of labor federations. Appointment power is straightforward: the Netherlands, where mayors are appointed in the Hague, ranks high; Sweden, medium; the U.S., low. (As a measure of the structure of government we eliminated the percentage of taxes collected by central vs. regional and local units as less stable and reliable, although central government tax take does correlate with appointment power.) Measures of the structure of industrial relations are more complex. We added four indicators of the centralization of labor federations—federation engages in collective bargaining, controls strike funds, has a large number of expert staff per 100,000 members, and collects big dues—and combined this score with the central government's appointment power. (See scores in Wilensky, 1976a and 1981c, p. 367.) We could not locate comparable data on employer federations. My measures capture neither ambiguities in two cases, Germany and Italy, nor shifts over time. Germany scores "low" because the Deutscher Gewerkschaftbund (DGB), the dominant labor federation, is relatively weak and there are important elements of decentralization in government. Yet functional equivalents of corporatism might justify a higher rank (Wilensky, 1976a, p. 51): industrywide bargaining by moderately centralized unions informally coordinating their strategy, the growing professionalization of union staffs, the wage leadership of the Metal Workers, the presence of a big employer association, and much centralized bargaining in the health industry (see chap. 16). During the decade of the "Konzertierte Aktion" especially, German unions traded off wage restraint for other nonwage gains (e.g., the growth of workers' councils). (Cf. Lehmbruch, 1979; and Streeck, 1978, 1983.) Even during the greater economic difficulties of the 1990s, however, Germany evidenced substantial continuity in bargaining among the social partners and great resistance to abandoning its social market economy (Turner, 1998, and chap. 17 below). The pattern of coordinated sectoral bargaining persists. A good case can be made that with the integration of East Germany, corporatist bargaining has been strengthened, at least up to the mid-1990s. Italy scores medium on my measures of corporatism, but its weak government and its system of clientelismo (Di Palma calls it "surviving without governing") makes it problematic. Although Italian corporatism has fluctuated in its strength since World War II, the medium score captures its central tendency (cf. Regini, 1987a, pp. 97−105). For instance, in the 1990s there was a series of tripartite agreements on incomes policy, collective bargaining rules, and job creation measures. The social partners also negotiated agreements on the reform of public employment and social security, which were then put into law (for details see chap. 5; and Regini, 1997, pp. 261ff.). Finally, nothing is static, and all rich democracies have experienced system strains since the early 1970s. There is no evidence, however, of a universal decline of corporatist bargaining arrangements. Later in this chapter I discuss sources of strain in democratic corporatism in particular cases, including Sweden and the Netherlands, countries whose consensus-making machinery has changed substantially.

Because there is usually an interaction between the centralization of unions and their federations and the centralization of employer federations, and because they try to match each other expert for expert, brief for brief (Wilensky, 1956b, 1967a), and therefore approach government experts with the same ammunition, we can interpret the government-labor combined index as a general clue to corporatist-technocratic linkages. I have elsewhere shown (*ibid.*) that such a process, once begun, tends to introduce a rational-responsible bias in bargaining. It is still combat, but the spirit is, "En garde! We'll meet you with our statistics at dawn."

This is the partial truth in the image of modern society as "postindustrial"—characterized by rising numbers and influence of experts and intellectuals in command of theoretical knowledge. But that image is most valid where experts attached to major power blocs have channels for bargaining and influence where their expertise is indispensable—that is, in corporatist democracies. While corporatist-technocratic linkages do *not* transform political decisions into technical decisions, they do provide a fuller integration of expert knowledge and insight into political deliberations; they foster more stable coalitions of experts and intellectuals, managers and politicians, each acquiring some of the skills of the other (Wilensky, 1967a, pp. 173ff.).

The scores used in quantitative analysis in Parts II and III—based solely on the degree of centralization of government and labor—cannot capture a subtype of corporatism in which business plays a more powerful role—corporatism-without-labor, exemplified by Japan, France, and Switzerland.

CORPORATISM-WITHOUT-LABOR

The second category useful for understanding variations in public policy and system performance is corporatism without full-scale participation by organized labor (cf. Pempel and Tsunekawa, 1979; Katzenstein, 1984). Japan, France, and perhaps Switzerland in varying ways have developed quasi-public bargaining structures for the interplay of industry, commerce, agriculture, professional groups, and government. These structures permit some coordination and planning of social and economic policies, but they have so far kept labor federations at a distance. In all three countries, despite obvious differences in the strength of the state bureaucracy, the business community enjoys a privileged position in the definition and implementation of public policy. These countries are thus in a position to achieve good economic performance without adopting many public policies explicitly designed to increase economic and social equality. In view of the urgency of mass demands and the severity of economic constraints, however, these three countries may one day be forced to move toward the full incorporation of labor into their bargaining arrangements, eventually joining the first group. The election of Mitterrand in France might have signaled a move in this direction, but the ideological and structural splits between Communist and non-Communist unions immensely complicated the process, and it never got off the ground. Indeed, with fewer local notables and businessmen in parliament; with the breakup of the three-way coalition of farmers (FNSEA), business (CNPF), and the bureaucratic-political elite; with the replacement of over half of the directors in the ministries, France was experiencing more erosion of corporatism-without-labor than integration of labor into the system. If these countries do not move toward inclusion of labor, they may swing toward the least-corporatist model, with more decentralized policymaking, less continuity of power and policy, and less capacity to implement national policy.

The strains within government/industry-style corporatism appear in variations in the effectiveness of conflict resolution by policy areas. In Japan, for instance, it is apparent that for several decades the machinery for consensus in economic and industrial policies (Johnson, 1982) worked far more effectively than it did for social and environmental policies, which are further from the central concerns of the bargaining parties. Thus the marks of Japanese corporatism so prominent in the interaction of MITI, the Finance Ministry, the ruling Liberal Democratic Party, and industry and trade associations in shaping economic policy—decision by consensus, bureaucratic dominance, long- or at least medium-range plans, assertion of national interests—are almost wholly absent in the history of pension development, especially from the 1959 National Pension System to today's pension crisis. Japan's pension system was conceived in acrimonious controversy that continues to this day, with labor unions, farmers, employers, the insurance industry, the finance ministry, the ministry of welfare, and political parties fighting it out, their positions very similar to those of their counterparts in the United States. (Wilensky, 1984.)

Similarly, Japanese corporatism was extraordinarily unresponsive to mounting environmental pollution and the mass protests that accompanied it. During the 1950s and the early 1960s the government ignored noxious air pollution over industrial cities as well as localized outbreaks of horrifying diseases rooted in pollution. For instance, in the celebrated case of deaths and disability from mercury poisoning in the fish eaten by residents of Minamata, the home of Japan Chisso (nitrogen) Company, it took 15 years before victims or their families received compensation. Intense public pressure, including a growing environmental movement, media coverage, lawsuits, and American-style mass protests and demonstrations, culminated in the 1970 "Pollution Diet," which passed more than a dozen laws. In 1971 the government set up an Environmental Agency. Between 1971 and 1973, four major court decisions imposed stiff fines and standards of negligence on industrial polluters. (McKean, 1980; Enloe, 1975.) It was only then that the usual machinery—the powerful ministries (MITI, the Finance Ministry, Ministry of Construction and Transport), the top leaders of the ruling party, with industry as a reluctant partner—swung into action. Government offered big depreciation allowances; government banks provided low-interest loans for pollution control; MITI helped finance research and development in pollution control technology; standards were high, penalties severe. In general, the action was quick and effective; the air in Tokyo, once the filthiest in the world, is today quite clean. Given the depth of risk (a densely settled industrial population), other environmental hazards have been impressively reduced. The lesson: Countries in this second category are slow to respond to mass pressures (from labor, environmental, and similar groups), but once they decide to respond, they can easily and swiftly implement the new policies. Compare Love Canal in the more open and fluid political economy of the USA: much agitation, saturation media coverage, resulting in quick state action to move residents out and quick compensation of victims, with no sustained national follow-through. (France and Japan display a similar lag in regulating tobacco use for the same structural reasons, but by the mid-1990s they had not yet taken decisions for bold action. Chap. 15 discusses regulatory regimes and the environment.)

If there is any common tendency toward change in this system, it is to move slowly and reluctantly toward accommodating a limited range of labor demands. Some specialists on Japan have recently argued that labor now has substantial and increasing national influence not captured by "corporatism without labor" (e.g., Garon, 1987, pp. 242–248; and Kume, 1998). They note that labor has been included in conferences with government and industry to discuss important social and economic problems (Taira and Levine, 1985). (Such bipartite and tripartite conferences and commissions are common in France, too.) Kume observes that rival federations have merged into one. Everyone notes that Japanese wages and working conditions have improved greatly throughout the postwar period, although this could reflect big increases in productivity, not union power.

Above all, researchers on Japanese labor point to some degree of informal wage coordination through the Annual Spring Labor Offensive (*Shunto*). Shunto's main characteristics: wide and intensive exchange of information among government agencies and labor and management federations; key settlements in a few sectors; and some pattern following based on advice from labor and management. Throughout the postwar period, however, the central labor federations had no strike authority and were not represented in negotiations with companies in most industries. In the late 1940s employers eliminated industrywide bargaining and broke the power of militant enterprise unions. The system of company-oriented local enterprise unions that emerged thereafter remains in place. Since the oil shocks of the 1970s Shunto has increasingly been dominated by large corporations (with market power over suppliers) in collaboration with government agencies (e.g., the government moved decisively to reduce the power of militant unions in the public sector). The tame union leaders now in office go along with the consensus. The main presence of labor is felt through enterprise unions. (See the analysis of industrial relations and wages in Brown et al., 1997, pp. 143, 148–188; and my account of joint consultation in the Japanese workplace in chap. 1). Regarding Japanese labor influence on national public policy, it may have increased but as yet remains narrow, confined to the jurisdiction of the labor ministry. In sum, the picture remains one of union weakness relative to management and relative to the corporatist democracies that fully integrate labor into national and industrywide bargaining. Shunto cannot match either the strong wage leadership of IG Metall in Germany or the much stronger, more-centralized bargaining patterns of corporatist democracies.

FRAGMENTED AND DECENTRALIZED POLITICAL ECONOMIES

The third category, an extreme contrast to the corporatist democracies, includes countries that are least corporatist in their bargaining structures—the fragmented and decentralized political economies of the USA, the UK, Canada, New Zealand, Australia, and Ireland. I use the label "least-corporatist" because these systems at times and in narrow sectors evidence at least an approach to corporatism. To vary the adjectival phrase, I use least-corporatist, fragmented and decentralized, least-consensual, and noncorporatist interchangeably. The idea can best be understood by considering contrasts in each of the structural attributes that define democratic corporatism. I concentrate on the U.S. as the strongest contrast; many examples of the structure, function, and behavior of other least-corporatist democracies appear throughout the book.

1. *Channels for centralized, tripartite, or bipartite bargaining are absent or weak.*

   • *Labor:* By 1980 only about one-fifth of the American labor force belonged to 168 national labor unions, of which 111 were affiliated with the AFL-CIO, a weak and decentralized federation, which does not bargain collectively. Several large unions were unaffiliated (Teamsters, Mine Workers, National Education Association). Contrast Sweden: 9 in 10 blue-collar workers and 75% of white-collar workers are organized in fewer, more-inclusive unions, whose interests are aggregated in three centralized labor federations, LO, TCO, and SACO with LO still dominant. (Recently, TCO, the main white-collar confederation, moved up in both influence and membership.) However, Japan (corporatism-without-labor) stands in sharp contrast to Sweden; in fact, its unions are even more fragmented than American unions. Although Japan's unionization rate in 1989 was 25% compared to the USA's 15%, its labor movement had 61,000 workplace-based unions, with little aggregation of interests; the weak national unions reflect intense ideological cleavages (similar to the French situation). (Levine, 1983; Golden, Wallerstein, and Lange, 1999.)[2]
   What about trends in the structure and functions of American unions? The tendencies are contradictory: there has been a long-run trend toward more-inclusive units—industrial, multi-industrial, and multiple-craft forms—and in response to the 45-year decline from the peak of almost a third of the labor force in 1954 to less than one-seventh now, a more recent trend toward mergers, again producing more-

inclusive units. There is even a tendency toward concentration of union membership in the larger internationals and in "catchall" unions. Further, a very determined
leadership that provides resources for organizing and political action and attempts to
coordinate separate unions at the state or metropolitan area level can increase the
labor vote, as in the 1998 and 2000 elections. These trends would suggest a mild
shift toward the Swedish model. But countertendencies are strong: power remains in
the international unions, not the Federation; and functions remain narrow, essentially
wage and job control in the workplace, craft, firm, or industry. Concession bargaining and falling membership density have accelerated the previous erosion of "pattern bargaining" in auto, steel, rubber, and meatpacking; smokestack industries with
more-centralized bargaining have declined. Growing "service" sectors and manufacturing firms are either nonunion or have small- to medium-sized workplaces that
are hard to organize (semiconductors, electrical equipment, biotechnology, real estate, parts of retailing); growing unions are either concentrated in local labor and
product markets (Teamsters, Retail Clerks, IBEW, and the United Food and Commercial Workers) or in public service (AFSCME, AFGE, and AFT) or both
(SEIU) and cannot set national bargaining patterns for private industry.

Another way to put this contradiction is that union structures are becoming
more inclusive but more local. In economic action that means more heterogeneity
of interests within each unit and looser nationwide ties; in political action it means
more difficulty in making members see their economic interests in national political terms. Contrast unions in auto and steel, whose educational tasks are a bit easier, but whose membership has declined the most.

• *Employer and trade associations.* The number and organizational structure of
American trade associations and employer associations do not permit them to
formulate policies that crosscut industries, functions, and areas. By 1980 the number of American trade associations had reached about 3,200—more numerous
and far more specialized than those in Western Europe and Japan. Although
there are some generalist forms (National Association of Manufacturers, Chambers of Commerce, Retail Merchants Associations), narrow product-oriented
associations dominate. They are voluntary, internally homogeneous, and specialize
in particular regions, product groups, or activities (technical research, lobbying).
Historically, generalist organizations have typically split up into a greater number
of specialist forms, following market segmentation. (Staber, 1982.)

Very few American trade associations spend much time on labor relations. Bargaining associations, like their union counterparts, tend to be regional or local. The
major multiemployer bargaining associations are in building construction, trucking,
hospitals, coal, and steel.

Only in brief periods of deep crisis—World War I and the Great Depression—
did the American government promote trade associations as an instrument of
national policy. From 1913 to 1919 and again during the National Recovery Administration period from 1933 to 1935, government-sponsored trade associations
proliferated, but most of them quickly disbanded. In general, coordinated action
among national trade associations is rare, and when it occurs it is an ad hoc
arrangement to cope with specific issues. In contrast to their counterparts in both

Japan and Sweden, American trade associations are so specialized in structure and function that they could not be used by the federal government to implement national policy (energy, occupational health and safety, social security, labor-market policy) even if the government were so inclined. They can be used only where policy is narrow (cigarette labeling, air traffic control, drug packaging). (Staber and Aldrich, 1982.) Thus, the enthusiasm for tripartite commissions or councils expressed in pronouncements about the need for an industrial policy (Felix Rohatyn, Lester Thurow, Robert Reich) may lead to meetings and dialogues among sophisticated business leaders, academics, and a few labor leaders, but the representational structure necessary for formulating and implementing such national responses is missing.

• *Government.* Among the universe of rich democracies, with the possible exception of Switzerland, there is no more fragmented and decentralized federalism, no greater division of powers, no weaker central government than that of the United States. The dogma of local self-government is enshrined in its constitution and laws; a federal system divides powers among the central government and 50 sovereign states, which, in turn, divide powers among thousands of counties, townships, municipalities, and other local units. Of course, these arbitrary geographical boundaries, drawn before the rise of industrialism and urbanism, have little relation to economic, demographic, cultural, and social realities, little connection with the loyalties, interests, and lifestyles of the people bound by them. To survive, the modern metropolis is therefore forced to create a staggering number of special district governments—school districts, water districts, fire districts, sanitation districts, park and port districts, rapid transit authorities—each concentrating on a limited areawide task; each competing for budget, tax base, or subsidy; all adding to the maze of overlapping and duplicating units. It is free enterprise in government—with every municipality, every district, every state for itself. If there is a constitutional explanation of why the United States finds it so difficult to come to grips with urban problems or to develop national social, labor, and industrial policies, it is here, in the tyranny of locality, made possible by federalism and the separation of powers. (Wilensky, 1965, pp. xviii–xix.)

Throughout this book, there is abundant evidence of the costs and gains of such decentralization. Consider the efforts of both federal and state governments to promote economic development via "industrial policies."[3] This area also illustrates the point that even the fragmented, decentralized political economies occasionally try corporatist solutions to their problems. To the extent that the U.S. government has had "industrial policies," they have been antitrust (to prevent major decreases in domestic competition), national security (defense spending, military and space R&D, including funding and guidance of R&D via direct procurement as in aviation, computers, and semiconductors), or reactive (trade restrictions such as tariffs, quotas, "Orderly Marketing Agreements," trigger prices for troubled sectors, occasional bailouts for troubled firms such as Chrysler and Lockheed and a massive rescue of banks in the savings and loan crisis of the 1980s).

Some states in the United States, especially in recent years, have adopted innovative policies that may have promoted new investment and, to some extent, the restructuring of industry. Typically, however, state policies are of the "beggar-thy-neighbor" variety, as when states compete for new plants with tax and land subsidies. Such policies are unlikely to increase the total GNP of the United States. This is evident in the area that tried hardest to develop manufacturing, the South. From the 1950s to the early 1970s, the South, both rural and urban, led in efforts to create a low-wage, low-value-added industrial policy. Southern states developed industrial recruitment to a fine art. They touted their right-to-work laws, probusiness attitudes, low taxes, and cheap energy; they boasted of their abundant workers hostile to unions and willing to work hard at low wages. Later they offered generous, specific tax breaks, infrastructure expenditures, and land donations. This attracted manufacturers of textile and apparel, shoes, simple appliances, wood products, and the like, often from neighboring states. By the late 1970s, as more and more states, North and South, entered the low-wage competition, as development departments boasted of "a rural Renaissance" in a resurgent South, a decline had begun. Suddenly the competitors were not just other states or regions but the developing nations of Latin America and Asia that could provide still cheaper labor, no less skilled.

It is significant that the plants that survived the 1980s and the counties that continued to increase their per capita income evidenced higher levels of education and literacy, good transportation and communication facilities, better race relations, and proximity to colleges, universities, and technical institutes (Rosenfeld, 1992, pp. 46–53)—attributes so prominent in the sustained high-tech growth centers of Silicon Valley (California), the Research Triangle Park (North Carolina), and federal facilities in space and defense around Cape Canaveral (Florida), Huntsville (Alabama), and Oak Ridge (Tennessee). The survivors in the rural South were plants that carved out special niche markets and achieved productivity growth by applying new process technologies.

As Paul Brace (1993) shows in his study of performance in 48 U.S. states from 1968 to 1989, the states are not well suited for the tasks of economic development because they are totally open economies; they have limited leverage on their economies and none on the national economy. State industrial policies have more than the usual self-canceling effects. If states are successful in stimulating income growth, they also retard job growth (*ibid.*, p. 115). If they use tax breaks and other industry incentives to sustain short-term growth, they are unable to promote development through heavy investment in public education and technical and physical infrastructure. Economists have shown that a dollar of expenditure stimulates more growth than the growth lost by a dollar of taxation (p. 114; see also chap. 12 in this book). Activist governments in "New York or Michigan [in the 1980s] may create conditions ripe for innovation and growth but technology and production practices developed at least partly under the auspices of these states can be transferred to Texas or Arizona" (p. 121). Brace shows that what success state-level industrial policies have (e.g., manufacturing and employment growth) is a product almost entirely of large national fluctuations. Arizona and Texas' probusiness, open-shop, anti-intervention strategies "worked" in the 1960s, 1970s, and early 1980s only because the national government directed funds and defense contracts to those states; when the national economy sputtered and defense spending sharply declined in the period 1989–92, state laissez-faire policies plus new state tax cuts could not prevent collapse.[4] Brace concludes that the real effect of state policy is limited to income growth (via taxing and spending and investment in institutions of learning and training); employment and manufacturing growth are generally beyond their reach (pp. 100–112, 115). National business cycles and national policies overwhelm state industrial policies.

In short, the working remnants of state industrial policies in the U.S. resemble the national industrial policies of Japan and Germany. But even the most innovative state policies do not form part of a coherent national industrial policy. Unconnected to national efforts and the programs of other states, frequently becoming part of a zero-sum game, state-level industrial policies highlight the structural barriers to policy success among fragmented and decentralized political economies.[5]

In historical perspective, this absence of a positive industrial policy since World War II is puzzling, for the United States pioneered one of the most successful coordinated government–civilian sector development policies in the history of modern nations—the promotion of agriculture in the 19th century. Aside from giving land grants to farmers, the federal government established a huge network of land-grant colleges and agricultural experiment stations, combining basic and applied research and teaching with outreach to farmers through agricultural extension services and widespread participation by farm organizations. As a result of more than a century of this sectoral industrial policy, about 3% of the labor force produces an agricultural surplus that by 1973 accounted for 25% of total American exports and even during the agricultural depression of the 1980s still accounted for about 18% (figures for 1982–84). Begun in the heyday of entrepreneurial capitalism, these productivity-enhancing programs have continued to expand in the age of the welfare state. Yet today, except for agriculture and defense, the United States has backed away from any attempt to manage structural change. From 1980 to 1992 it relied on two contradictory strategies: deregulation along with a loose fiscal policy in the hope of indirectly increasing investment, productivity, and growth; and continuing trade restrictions in the hope of slowing down the collapse of losing industries. President Clinton's fight in 1994 for NAFTA, GATT, and other trade agreements, however, moved the United States toward reductions of trade barriers; his 1993 budget moved toward a tighter fiscal policy (deficits were transformed into surpluses from 1993 to 1999).

2.   *The blurring of the division between public and private has accelerated in the U.S. but corporatist democracies have moved so far in this direction that it is a difference in kind.*[6] Recent public discussion of the relative effectiveness of markets, governments, and voluntary associations reflects a vast confusion in language and action. In the 1970s Governor Jerry Brown of California initially urged austerity in an era of limits. When confronted with dramatic erosion of the tax base for social services (Proposition 13), he invoked the spirit of good neighborliness as the solution: a collective volunteer effort would restore services lost by major cuts. At the same time, other enthusiasts for small government were saying that we must save the "nonprofit sector," revive voluntarism, and "do more with less" by

"getting public service into private hands." More recently a group of executives of foundations and national voluntary associations, including John Gardner of Common Cause, established a new association to promote the "Independent Sector," which by 1997 embraced 800 nonprofit groups.

Upon close inspection, the "voluntary," "private" sector turns out to be neither voluntary nor private. The growth of paid volunteers such as child minders and Peace Corps and Americorps members, and of the public funding of private agencies—long apparent in countries with substantial Catholic party power (Belgium, Italy, the Netherlands) but now spreading everywhere—underscores the obsolescence of older concepts. Although the precise magnitude and rate of growth of the "independent sector" in the U.S. and its public funding are unknown, one source (Weisbrod, 1997, p. 542) estimates that the total revenue of nonprofits, less than 6% of GNP in 1975, exceeded 10% in 1990 and that the paid employment of nonprofits grew at more than double the rate of growth of national employment. Excluding religious organizations the portion of nonprofits' revenue that came from direct government funding in 1996 was more than one-third (Salamon, 1999a). If we take account of federal block grant funds that went through a public agency subcontractor to end up with private service providers, both profit and nonprofit, the fraction of public funding of private activities would be much higher (cf. Smith and Lipsky, 1993, pp. 4–8, 53–57). As Sharkansky (1979, p. 5) suggests, the size of these activities on the margin of government activity may exceed that of the "core"; in the mid-1970s, for instance, the people working under contract to HEW at least part-time (750,000) outnumbered the regular employees of HEW (157,000) by four or five to one (cf. Milward and Provan, 1993, pp. 224–225 on the Hollow State; and Salamon, 1995, p. 61).

The need to disentangle various meanings of "voluntarism" is evident when we try to answer such questions as, Is voluntarism an obstacle to welfare-state development? Or, conversely, Does the expansion of the welfare state threaten the autonomy and functions of the voluntary agency? A sensible answer depends on distinctions among at least three concepts of "voluntarism."

- *Voluntarism as an ideology* justifying reliance on free markets. It is hostile to state intervention generally and to social policy in particular. It emphasizes the role of philanthropy and self-help in the solution of social problems. In this view government should deliver cash and services only when normal structures of supply, the family and the market, break down. The likely effect: to slow down welfare-state development, especially income maintenance programs. In recent years voluntarism as ideology has been increasingly resonant.

- *Voluntarism as voluntary associations* that extend, improve, complement, supplement, or sometimes substitute entirely for the delivery of social services by government. These services are typically labor-intensive; they require both local intelligence (knowledge of particular needs of specialized clientele) and local consensus (community support of the program). The main targets: the aged, the young, and the handicapped of any age. The likely impact: to make the welfare state more effective. The expansion of the welfare state has, in fact, everywhere meant the growth of voluntary agencies with increased reliance on government funding. In some countries, notably the Netherlands, voluntary agencies constitute the primary system of service delivery. The cost, of course, is huge government subsidies out of current operating budgets and compulsory insurance premiums funneled through voluntary agencies—money to finance all their staff, administration, and services. This has led to more than the usual fragmentation and duplication. In fact, the Netherlands has one of the costliest public sectors among modern democracies, although recent efforts to streamline the system may have cut costs a bit.

• *Voluntarism as volunteerism*—the mobilization and deployment of volunteers, paid or unpaid, in money-raising campaigns or direct service, in private or public agencies. Advocates of greater volunteer participation say that it humanizes the welfare state, revives the sense of community, combats big government, and even reduces inflation. But the realization of one or another of these benign effects depends on what kind of volunteers we are talking about: unpaid staff, unpaid fund-raisers, paid service volunteers, peer self-helpers, mutual aid associations, neighborhood service organizations, religious institutions, and more. The label "volunteers" obscures these differences. It also obscures variations over time and function in the number of hours volunteers give. If the trend toward intensification of paid work continues (chap. 1), especially among the educated who can offer most skills, the hours available for sustained volunteerism will decline.[7]

In its increasing reliance on voluntary agencies and government subsidies, the United States moves toward the Dutch model. In its emphasis on the profit-making sector and market competition to ensure the best quality at the lowest price, it is embracing theories of reprivatization. The first tendency is evident in increased government funding of voluntary agencies, many with mandated citizen participation. The second tendency is evident in the spread of service contracts and payments to private vendors (e.g., the Job Corps, Medicare, day care, nursing homes, dialysis centers). Unfortunately, there is no evidence that either trend has reduced the cost of delivering service, enhanced consumer choice, or even improved "accountability."

Apparently the U.S. is shooting for the Netherlands' level of dependence on voluntary agencies without the advantage of adequate, stable funding. The results: Service functions are overwhelmed by grantsmanship, budget-justification research, and accountability rituals. The agencies become "fund-raising instruments in search of a program"; agency volunteers are chiefly assigned to fund-raising; public relations and marketing techniques are prominent. In his four-country study of voluntary agencies serving the handicapped, Kramer (1981) concludes that in the U.S., and to a lesser extent, England, this arrangement diverts resources away from improved services, innovative programs, and leadership development, although it may increase citizen participation.

Consider the notion that small- to medium-sized private voluntary associations are pioneers in programs and service delivery, that they are dynamic innovators, lighting the way. If by "innovation" we merely mean expansion of or changes in existing programs, then the most vigorously innovative country is the United States. Because income from community campaigns is static, and because individual charitable private giving has declined since the 1960s both as a proportion of personal income and as a percentage of GNP, many voluntary agencies in the United States are engaged in a constant search for new funds, which not only increases their dependence on unstable government grants but puts them in competition with private enterprise.[8] When approaching funding sources, public and private alike, the symbols "innovation" and "demonstration project" are expedient; the assumption is that new is better. In practice, the proposals are typically a means of carrying out the agencies' existing function. In contrast, other countries place a higher value on government funding for implementation of existing programs. Perhaps this illustrates Wilensky's law: the more demonstration, the less follow-through; the more entrepreneurial spirit, the less service delivery. To the extent that funding bodies accent innovation, they may inhibit other aspects of social-service performance: access, continuity, choice, coherence, effectiveness, equity, and efficiency (Kramer, 1981, p. 190).

At first glance, it would appear that the United States shares the tendency of corporatist democracies to blur the lines between public and private. But what comparative data we have suggest that corporatist democracies subsidize many activities, both social and economic, at much higher levels. Consider agricultural policy, an area where the U.S. has had tight connections between producers, government agencies, congressional committees, and political parties, much like the corporatism of Japan. There are good reasons to suppose that all rich democracies would support farmers with tender loving care; in fact, from the Great Depression until the 1990s subsidies to agriculture everywhere increased even as farmers' share of both votes and the economy drastically diminished. Some reasons for this paradox: (1) Governments want to reduce imports, promote exports, and achieve stable prices; (2) food is critical in any economy and is seen as an issue of national security; (3) everywhere modern nations romanticize traditional rural values and the "Family Farm"; (4) farmers cannot control central aspects of their environment (the weather and swings in world commodity prices); (5) farm interests are well organized, focused, and in most countries have few interest-group competitors (e.g., the FNSEA, the National Federation of Farmers in France; the DBV, German Farmers' Union; and the NFU, National Farmers' Union in the UK have a near monopoly of representation); and, less universal, (6) wherever geographical units rather than population size are the basis of representation in legislatures, agriculture is greatly overrepresented (as in the U.S. Senate). Consequently, in modern society farmers are like veterans or war victims; as an interest group they are the object of generous, special treatment (cf. Wyn, 1995; and Keeler, 1987).

Despite these common grounds for the political power and influence of agricultural interests, the variations by type of political economy are impressive. Comparing the OECD's producer subsidy equivalent (PSE)—transfers paid either by consumers or by taxpayers in the form of market price support, direct payments, and other supports as a percentage of the value of production—for 10 democracies in 1991, we see that by far the highest subsidies appear in corporatist countries (Switzerland, 80%; Norway, 77%; Finland, 77%; Japan, 66%; Sweden, 59%; and Austria, 52%) while the lowest subsidies appear in noncorporatist countries (Canada, 45%; U.S., 30%; Australia, 15%; and New Zealand, 4%) (OECD, 1992a).[9] While farm supports fell everywhere throughout the 1990s, the PSE average for seven of our democracies by type of political economy widened: 66% for three corporatist countries, 10% for four noncorporatist countries (OECD, 1999, pp. 167–168).

Protection of farmers in corporatist democracies is matched by job protection for workers. The alleged deregulation of the labor market, as we shall see in chapter 17, proceeds, if at all, by very different rates and routes. For instance, with the exception of noncorporatist Ireland, corporatist democracies impose most obstacles to dismissals; they favor short-time work and similar measures advocated by works councils, unions, and left-leaning governments. Presenting the greatest obstacles (in a 1986 survey) are France, Germany, Italy, the Netherlands, Austria, Belgium, Norway, Sweden, and, the exception, Ireland. Denmark (a weak case of corporatism) and Finland had minor obstacles. Presenting the fewest obstacles, the least job protection, were the UK and (from other data) the U.S., Canada, New Zealand, and Australia. (Emerson, 1988, tables 6–8.)

Similarly, the subsidies for the nonprofit sector dealing with social policy in Catholic-corporatist democracies often exceed those of the least-corporatist democracies, while the advocacy groups in left-corporatist democracies enjoy greater recognition and support from government than the latter. Although the small number of countries compared and data difficulties limit generalizations, these differences do suggest that corporatist countries blur the lines between "public" and "private" much more than the more-decentralized, fragmented political economies do. For instance, the nonprofit sectors of both the Netherlands and Sweden are heavily funded by government. In 1979, 65% of Swedish nonprofit revenues came from the government (James, 1989b, p. 38). In 1973–74, 75% of voluntary agency income came from government in the Netherlands compared to 33% in the U.S. and 22% in England (Kramer, 1989, p. 235). France is apparently in the middle.[10] Among corporatist democracies the contrast between Sweden and the Netherlands in the delivery of services suggests that if we had comparable data on a large number of rich democracies, we would find that although all corporatist countries finance health, education, and cultural services through government, Catholic or Catholic-left corporatist countries such as the Netherlands rely most heavily on nonprofits, especially churches and faith-based institutions, for the delivery of those services while left-corporatist countries such as Sweden rely mainly on local government. Sweden does, however, promote nonprofits in the areas of culture, sports, and education. Even though its "independent sector" is small, Sweden encourages all nonprofits to play a large role of representation and advocacy in the policy process. (James, 1989b, pp. xix–xx, 32, 39, 53; and Badelt, 1989.) Table 16.3 in chapter 16 shows the strong effects of types of political economy on the private/public mix in health care for our 19 rich democracies.

In sum: The U.S. and other Anglo-American democracies share in the common tendency to blur the lines dividing public from private. But scattered comparative data suggest that the least-corporatist democracies have moved much slower down that path.

3. *The scope of bargaining on social, labor, and industrial issues in the U.S. is narrow: policy segmentation is extreme*—and so

4. *There is little integration of social and economic policy;* their interdependence is obscured not only among policymakers but among policy analysts who shape academic and public discussion of failures and successes.

The third and fourth attributes of democratic corporatism are almost wholly lacking in the U.S. The decentralized and fragmented structure of government, labor, and employer and trade associations and the weakness of broad-based associations and political parties that could aggregate interests and bring together groups with conflicting values means that interest groups are not constrained by the necessity of national bargaining and trade-offs typical of corporatist democracies. They can act out their most parochial strivings at every level of the system, often creating a mutual veto process (see chaps. 3, 11, and 18 for details).

The role of experts in noncorporatist democracies is severely limited or transformed into that of propagandist. The U.S. is loaded with well-trained experts and scholars, but their voices are typically cast to the winds. If they are isolated in universities or attached to adversarial interest groups and forensic think tanks, they add to polarization of debate rather than foster consensus. That is why extreme doctrines can penetrate high policy circles, prompting sudden swings in national policy, unconstrained by sober analysis. For instance, without grasping the erratic relationship of experts and intellectuals to policy in the U.S., we cannot understand how Reaganomics could overnight become public policy, so swiftly replacing a small, serious literature on both monetarism and supply-side economics, and thereby deepen and lengthen a worldwide recession, 1980–83, by 1992 tripling the national debt. Prominent in publicizing the supply-side component of Reaganomics and persuading the president of its efficacy were such "pop" economists as Jack Kemp, trained as an upstate New York football player; Jude Wanniski, trained as a *Wall Street Journal* editorial writer; and Arthur Laffer, an economist turned publicist. Herbert Stein, former chairman of the Council of Economic Advisers under Presidents Nixon and Ford, calls it "punk supplysidism," and gives this account of the issues:

> I borrow the term "punk" from Denis Healey, who characterized Mrs. Thatcher's economics as punk monetarism, meaning extreme to the point of being bizarre. . . . Until about 1979 or 1980 we were having a serious, active, professional discussion of the problems on the supply side of the American economy. A marked slowdown of the growth of total output and of productivity had been recognized. Work was going on to discover the causes of that slowdown—work associated with the names of Denison, Kendrick, Nosworthy, Jorgensen and others. This work had not yet led to final, agreed conclusions. At the same time it was pointing tentatively to partial solutions. Some policy steps, including limited tax reductions, were being proposed.
>
> Suddenly, all of that was swept to the sidelines—punk supply-side-ism took center stage. It offered a universal explanation for the slowdown: Tax rates (or government expenditures) were too high. It offered a universal solution: Cut tax rates (or government expenditures). This became the focus of discussion of the supply side of the economy.
>
> In its most extreme form supply-side-ism is no longer considered a serious contribution to policy. For example, in the recent budget crunch no one suggested that there should be another cut of rates in order to increase revenue. Nevertheless there is still considered to be a supply-side school of thought, which has superseded more conventional economics or at least deserves equal billing with it. (Stein, 1981)

I have elsewhere (1983, 1992a, 1997) shown that the character of policy research and its effect on public policy depend on the structure of the political economy in which it is financed and used. Fragmented and decentralized political economies foster isolated single-issue research, typically focused on short-run effects and used for political ammunition and ideological expression rather than policy planning; more corporatist systems foster research in which a wider range of issues are connected, longer-range effects are more often considered, and findings are more often used for policy planning and implementation as well as budget justification. *Larger contexts for bargaining mean larger contexts for policy deliberation and evaluation research.*

Paradoxically, the U.S. government combines a strong demand for rigorous cost-benefit analysis of social programs with an extreme degree of politicization of that research and distortion of its message.[11] For instance, American evaluation of programs of workfare (chap. 8) and job training is another illustration of Wilensky's law: the more evaluation, the less program development; the more demonstration projects, the less follow-through. Three problems are apparent: (1) The research itself is usually quite narrow, politically naive, and in design and execution often seriously flawed; (2) as Aaron (1978, pp. 155–157) suggests, research focused on a single program obscures the interaction and interdependence of many programs (e.g., job training may be pronounced a failure, but if combined with job creation and school reform, the same training could be judged a huge success); and (3) evaluated success has little to do with program funding.

There may be a corollary to Wilensky's law: not only does single-issue, short-term evaluation research subvert program development but evaluation research breeds more evaluation research. Once a culture of evaluation research is established with its supporting think tanks, agency research units, and training programs (e.g., schools of public administration or public policy), then the legislative committee, government agency, or interest group that does not have its own cost-benefit analysis will be defenseless in pursuit of its goals. Whether all this research functions only to legitimize established policy positions or actually adds an increment of rationality in policymaking depends, again, on the political context in which the research is done and used—the weight of adversarial vis à vis consensual structures for bargaining (Wilensky, 1983; Aberbach and Rockman, 1989). The U.S. is at the adversarial extreme.

At the other extreme are such corporatist democracies as Norway, Sweden, Austria, and the Netherlands. In these countries either American-style evaluation research is not done at all or, if done, it is more closely tied to policy deliberations and is used to foster consensus and implement policy (Wilensky, 1983, pp. 57–68; Levine et al., 1981, pp. 36–57; Richardson, 1982, pp. 169–177). In its politics and bargaining arrangements Germany is somewhere in the middle of these extremes, which may explain why its policymakers are both attracted and repelled by one-issue, short-term, forensic research and why much German evaluation research, in contrast to that in the U.S., is "softer," less rigorous, and more oriented toward facilitating political bargains (cf. Hellstern and Wollman in Levine et al., 1981, pp. 68–72, 80–86; Fitzsimmons in *ibid.*).

A brief examination of national contrasts in the capacity of elites to link industrial policies, incomes policy, active labor-market policy, and social policies can illustrate my point about the segmentation of policy in the U.S. It also shows how structures that facilitate policy linkages and a tighter integration of knowledge and power increase chances for the successful implementation of policy decisions.

DEMOCRATIC CORPORATISM AND POLICY LINKAGES

Industrial policy is defined in note 3 in discussion of development policies pursued by individual states in the U.S. By *active labor-market policy* (ALMP) I mean direct government

Figure 2.2. Twenty-one types of programs labeled "Active Labor-Market Policy"*

Government policies to create or maintain jobs (shape demand for labor)
A. Direct provision of work via
    1. sheltered workshops and other job creation measures for handicapped workers
    2. employment in regular public service
    3. public works projects—e.g., building and highway construction, conservation (e.g., Civilian Conservation Corps). Proposals for National Youth Service Corps fit items 2 and 3.
B. Subsidies to private business to
    4. hire new employees
    5. extend seasonal work year 'round—e.g., winter construction subsidies
?   6. locate or relocate workplaces in areas of high unemployment and create new jobs (e.g., area redevelopment).
C. Laws or subsidies to maintain demand for labor via
    7. short-time work (e.g., pay workers some of the difference between part-time pay and full-time pay to prevent layoffs)
    8. redundancy payment laws that increase the cost to employer of work force reductions (assumes employers will be shocked into better human resource planning).

Government policies to increase the labor supply and/or improve its quality by promoting or regulating
    9. apprenticeship training
   10. on-the-job training and retraining
   11. work-study programs to ease transition from school to work (e.g., part-time jobs while in school so student gains orientation to work, good work habits, job experience)
   12. job transition training for workers threatened with layoffs—training while still working for the same employer on the threatened job
   13. employability training—remedial programs to increase basic literacy and improve work habits and attitudes.

Government policies to decrease the labor supply by
?   14. lowering the retirement age
?   15. raising the age for compulsory schooling
?   16. shortening the work week or reducing overtime
?   17. reducing immigration of guest workers or encouraging their return (through subsidies or coercion).

Government policies to encourage labor mobility via
   18. placement services—labor exchanges providing job information to increase efficiency in matching job-seekers and job vacancies (can include compulsory notification of job vacancies or layoffs)
   19. vocational counseling in school and during the worklife
   20. mobility allowances and relocation advice for displaced workers; "starting allowance" if search is necessary
   21. relocation assistance via housing allowances or rent supplements tied to item 20 (includes government regulation of rules for apartment waiting lists).

*Based on Janoski (1990), Reubens (1970), and Lester (1966); question mark indicates a program marginal to the definition but included by some students.

action to shape the *demand* for labor by maintaining or creating jobs; to increase the *supply* and *quality* of labor via training and rehabilitation; and to encourage *labor mobility* via placement, counseling, and mobility incentives. ALMP is counterposed to such passive policies as unemployment insurance and public assistance. Of the 21 different programs that one can roughly fit into this definition of ALMP, 16 comprise the core, with 5 others somewhat marginal (see figure 2.2).

By *incomes policies* I mean government policies to hold down general wage levels by affecting directly the process by which wage levels are set. The purpose may vary: for example, to reduce the rate of inflation (when the labor market is tight), decrease unemployment (when the labor market is loose), or promote growth without increasing inflation or unemployment. The most common short-term goal is to reduce the rate of change of nominal wages. Included are government wage guidelines (whether legally enforceable or not), "jawboning," mandatory wage freezes and controls, and government involvement (either openly or behind the scene) in bipartite or tripartite wage bargaining. Excluded are policies designed to raise wages or to set minimum wage levels. Also excluded are policies which may indirectly affect wage levels, such as fiscal and monetary policies or legislation that weakens the power of labor unions.

Incomes policies are often counterposed to deflationary policies as an alternative method of achieving wage restraint. The former (it is claimed) can hold down inflation without increasing unemployment and reducing output; deflationary policies hold down inflation at the cost of unemployment and low growth. Closely associated with incomes policies are the trade-offs labor gets in return for lower wage increases. These include social transfers, tax changes, ALMP, employment security, institutional security for unions, and—most commonly—accompanying price controls or the promise of price restraint. Incomes policies did not emerge as a major instrument of macroeconomic policy until the 1960s. *Social policy* refers to all the programs comprising the welfare state (listed in Part II).[12]

In an eight-country study we explored the interdependence of each of these clusters of policies, their interaction, and reviewed literature on their implementation and effectiveness (Wilensky and Turner, 1987). The countries were chosen to represent contrasts in types of political economy: Austria, Sweden, the Netherlands, and West Germany (democratic corporatism), Japan and France (corporatism-without-labor), and the UK and USA (least corporatist).

The central theme is that the successful implementation of policies and programs in each policy area depends on *elite awareness* of the interdependence of public policies and *national bargaining structures* that permit top policymakers to act on this awareness. Unless elites in modern democracies grasp the interdependence of public policies and their multiple effects, they are unlikely to develop an effective policy mix to cope with the difficult constraints they have faced since the early 1970s. Even if administrative leaders and their expert advisers *are* aware of the contradictions and interacting effects of various social and economic policies, they cannot act effectively unless they are located in national bargaining structures where a wide range of issues are connected. For instance, the Austrians and West Germans could not have implemented their relatively successful incomes policies unless they had in place expansive social and labor-market policies that made wage restraint tolerable to union leaders and workers. And the Japanese could not have instituted a successful industrial policy without strong structures for national collaboration among industry, commerce, and government; local collaboration between management and labor, including bargaining about job security; and a quite active labor-market policy—in other words, structures and policies to cushion the shocks of industrial readjustment.

From a chronology of initiation and expansion of diverse policies in each domain since World War II and from qualitative and quantitative data on their success we tested two propositions:

1. The adoption and expansion of industrial and incomes policies as well as their successful implementation depend on the simultaneous or prior development of active labor-market and/or social policies.

2. In both elite perceptions and action, public-policy linkages are strongest where the structure of the political economy is corporatist. Specifically,

    (a) Corporatist democracies that fully include labor in their policymaking and implementation are most likely to evidence the interdependence of the four clusters of policies.

    (b) Corporatist democracies that keep labor at a distance from major policy decisions are most likely to adopt industrial and/or incomes policies before they expand ALMP and social policies, but if industrial and incomes policies are to be sustained and effective, they will sooner or later be accompanied by policy payoffs in these other areas.

    (c) Least-corporatist political economies are not likely to develop policy linkages that permit the mobilization of mass support through necessary trade-offs, nor will they develop the continuity of policy through different regimes that enhances program effectiveness. Fragmented and decentralized structures for bargaining among major economic power blocs produce extreme policy segmentation in which both policy deliberation and policy research are confined to separate compartments, a zero-sum mentality among competing interest groups is prominent, and continuity of policy is minimized.

Our reading of the record generally affirms these hypotheses and pinpoints partial exceptions.

Regarding the relation of corporatism to public-policy linkages (leaving aside the question of sequence), three of the four corporatist democracies—Austria, Sweden, and the FRG—show very strong interdependence of all four policy domains. The Netherlands appears to be a partial exception. It evidenced a tight integration of all areas beginning in the reconstruction period in 1945, with continuing linkage within a tripartite framework through the 1950s. After 1950 industrial policy receded, while incomes and labor-market policies continued. There was a turning point around 1962, when social policy showed a sharp expansion (e.g., social-security spending/GNP up from 12.8% in 1962 to 18.3% in 1966) while incomes policy weakened greatly, collapsing by the early 1970s, when unions and employers could no longer agree on a wide range of issues. Social policy, however, had a life of its own and continued its sharp expansion. As structures for big-bloc bargaining weakened, policy linkages weakened. In short, tight policy integration in the first half of the postwar period gave way to some policy segmentation in the last half. The rank for the whole period, medium, makes the Netherlands the exception that proves the rule. There was a resurgence of corporatist bargaining in the 1990s when labor accepted welfare-state reforms and wage restraint in return for slightly shorter hours, the creation of part-time jobs, expanded training opportunities, and the substitution of government subsidies for payroll taxes. This puts the Netherlands where it belongs in this scheme. (Change and adaptation in the Dutch case are discussed in the later section on Sweden and the Netherlands.)

The two cases of corporatism without labor fit the notion that such systems do not need as much policy linkage of deep interest to labor, especially dependence on social policy (Japan rates low; France, high). The least-corporatist countries, the United Kingdom and United States, fit the expected pattern; policy linkages, while apparent in some years of UK history, tend to be weak in both countries and policy continuity, limited.

Regarding hypothesis 1, about sequences of initiation and expansion, the record yields strong support. None of the eight countries either initiates or expands and sustains an *industrial policy* without (a) preceding or simultaneous initiation and expansion of *ALMP* (Japan, the Netherlands, Sweden, West Germany), and/or (b) preceding or simultaneous initiation and expansion of *social policy* (Austria, France, the Netherlands, Sweden, West Germany).

In a similar fashion, none of the eight countries either initiates or expands and sustains an *incomes policy* without (a) preceding or simultaneous initiation and expansion of *ALMP* (Japan, the Netherlands, Sweden, West Germany, United Kingdom), and/or (b) preceding or simultaneous expansion of *social policy* (Austria, the Netherlands, West Germany). Again the shape of the policies vary. In Japan de facto incomes policy is linked informally with other policies, while in Austria a formal incomes policy is a central component of government economic policy. Countries that do not fit the pattern—the United States and France—have had only limited and short-term success in the implementation of policies. In the United Kingdom major incomes policy efforts (with only short-term success) have risen and fallen with ALMP and industrial policy, as British governments alternate. Successful, sustained incomes policy, whether de facto or explicit appears to require the trade-off and cushioning effect of either ALMP, social policy, or both.

In the two corporatist political economies with little integration of labor into policy-making and implementation—France and Japan—industrial policy dominates the other three policy areas. Japan made use of limited ALMP (with an active placement service) during its industrial policy expansion in the 1950s and greatly increased its use of ALMP during the shift to readjustment in the 1970s. France expanded social policies after the war as indicative planning became a dominant strategy, and it later adopted ALMP as industrial planners encountered the need for readjustment in the 1970s. Although trade-offs between social and labor policies, on the one hand, and industrial and incomes policies, on the other hand, appear less necessary in these countries, the pattern remains.

The two least-corporatist countries show the most policy fragmentation and discontinuity. There is a consistency of failed interdependence in the United Kingdom's stop-and-go pattern. In 1948–50 a short-lived incomes policy was linked to the expansion of the welfare state; in 1961 short-lived attempts at incomes and industrial policies were linked; subsequent expansion and contraction in ALMP, incomes, and industrial policies were accompanied by a modest expansion in social policy. Although all four areas were cut back together in 1979–80, ALMP was again expanded after 1980 as the Thatcher government continued to cut education budgets but rediscovered vocational training (see McArthur and McGregor, 1986).

With its dominant free-market ideology and decentralized structure, the United States has made sustained use of neither industrial nor incomes policy. It is an extreme case which confirms my assumption that even where leaders are aware of the imperatives of policy linkages and try to act, implementation is unlikely without appropriate structures for bargaining and implementation. Consider a quarter-century effort to engineer the obvious trade-offs that would reduce dependence on tariffs as a means to resist import injury. In 1962 President John F. Kennedy proposed a program called Trade Adjustment Assistance (TAA), designed to give workers a way out of import-sensitive industries and reduce political opposition to free trade. As passed by Congress, TAA combined training to upgrade skills of workers threatened by foreign competition, relocation benefits, and income maintenance with a uniform national standard. President George Meany of the AFL-CIO, departing from the frequent protectionism of American labor, strongly supported the program.

The story of implementation is one of dashed hopes. For seven years not a single TAA petition was approved by the Tariff Commission. When during the next several years eligibility rules were relaxed, only about 35,000 workers received assistance, very few of whom received training. By 1973 the AFL-CIO complained of broken promises, and protectionism was on the rise again. Congress, against the wishes of the Nixon administration, improved the authorizing legislation. It set up a new trust fund which used tariff revenue to pay for the costs of worker adjustment, instituted a job-search benefit, increased adjustment assistance, and moved the certification process to a presumably more labor-oriented agency, the Department of Labor (DOL).

Again, implementation was slow, and violations of rules on timing and support were common. This time state employment agencies, responsible for outreach and delivery of benefits, failed to follow through. Both the DOL and the states lacked the funds, the database, and the competence necessary for implementation of the training, counseling, and relocation provisions. Further, while there may be a national interest in relocating workers, states charged with service delivery may doubt that depopulation is in their interest. At no point in this long history was there an effort to mobilize natural constituencies among unions, industries, and communities to make the program work. By 1976, when President Gerald Ford reduced tariffs in four "import-injured" industries and announced that he would expedite TAA petitions, both labor and industry had soured on the program and were looking out after their own protection, screaming for more trade barriers. The program had become a purely income-maintenance effort. Under President Jimmy Carter such income-assistance costs climbed sharply because of layoffs in the automobile industry; training continued to decline.

The inevitable cost-benefit analysts now closed in. In 1979 and 1980 evaluation researchers pronounced the TAA program ineffective: income maintenance was a disincentive to job search, recipients did not improve their labor-market position relative to the recipients of unemployment compensation, and so on. What the researchers ignored were the original purposes of TAA—to link training and mobility assistance to trade policy and thereby reduce political opposition to freer trade. They also ignored structural and budgetary barriers to implementation.

Under President Ronald Reagan, the TAA program was redesigned to cut costs; the legislative history of 1981 suggests that Congress was even unaware of the dormant training requirement in the 1962 law. By 1983 the administration was proposing to abolish the program. (For a detailed account, see Charnovitz, 1986.) In 1987, after six years of mounting protectionist sentiment and action, the Reagan administration finally endorsed an expanded but still modest worker assistance and training program; it proposed to abolish the TAA as a quid pro quo. Labor-left resistance came to fruition during the Clinton administration when it almost derailed NAFTA and in 1997 helped to defeat fast-track authority.

The structural barriers to effective policy linkage and implementation are plain: the division of powers between the executive branch and Congress; the incapacity of administrative agencies to link trade policy and ALMP; the complexities of federal-state relations; and the lack of institutionalized channels through which the main actors can resolve conflict, feed back intelligence, and participate in policy, implementation, and outreach. In short, even where the federal government has the awareness and the will, in the absence of appropriate bargaining structures, policy fails.

That policy linkage and continuity foster economic success in the four areas covered is generally confirmed for these eight countries. We found that if an industrial policy is to be made acceptable and effective in channeling labor and capital into areas of hope and out of areas of despair, it must be combined with social and labor policies that cushion the shock of change for workers and communities most affected—training and retraining, job creation, placement services, mobility allowances, rent subsidies for readjustment, preretirement pensions, and other income-maintenance or phased retirement for older workers stuck in declining areas; conversion allowances and research and development funds to encourage new products and industries, and more. Discussion of such issues in the United States, if they get on the agenda at all, is highly compartmentalized, as though they had nothing to do with one another; therefore policy debates result either in stalemate or policies that contradict one another.

Similarly we found that if an incomes policy—formal or de facto—is to restrain wages and reduce inflation or unemployment or both, it must be made palatable to labor leaders and workers by providing strong social policies and/or an ALMP, and/or job protection as in Austria, West Germany, Sweden, and the Netherlands. In contrast, among noncorporatist countries wages are held down (on the assumption that wage-push inflation is always imminent) by deflationary fiscal and monetary policies, high rates of unemployment, cutbacks in social transfers, and direct challenges to union power—policy combinations favored by the governments of Thatcher and Major in the UK and Reagan and Bush in the U.S. (Chaps. 12, 13, and 18 return to these issues and analyze policy and performance in the 1990s.)

If the postwar history of these economic and social policies and their implementation tells us anything, it tells us that types of political economy count. They predict the kinds of policies governments adopt; even more, how effectively and persistently policies are implemented. The linkage of major economic and political actors in corporatist bargaining systems facilitates policy linkages; it encourages those trade-offs that improve economic performance. It incorporates more reliable data and research into negotiations. Channels for talk become channels for consistent action. Thus, compared to the more-decentralized and fragmented political economies, where policies are segmented, the corporatist democracies on average and over long periods have an economic edge, even where they are more vulnerable to external shocks. (Chap. 12 on economic performance and chap. 17 on globalization present the data.) To link industrial or incomes policies to labor-market or social policies is to make the whole policy package more effective.

EROSION, TRANSFORMATION, OR PERSISTENCE OF CORPORATISM?

Some students of these national bargaining arrangements, concentrating on the economic constraints of the past two or three decades, have argued that democratic corporatism has collapsed or drastically eroded in recent years. They suggest that these negotiated economies suffer from bureaucratic rigidity and cannot adapt to changing economic circumstances, that if they are not collapsing, they are giving way to sectoral bargaining by industry or locality, that they face rank-and-file revolts as they fail to deliver benefits for labor, that they require left dominance for their persistence and are therefore unstable, that they bypass and thereby weaken parties and parliamentary democracy, and that globalization sounds their doom.

In my view these highly institutionalized bargaining arrangements—like the structures of labor, industry, political, and electoral systems and parties that created them—change only gradually, and that while some of them have eroded (Sweden, the Netherlands) others evidence little change (Austria, Norway, Denmark) or have been strengthened (Germany, Finland). This section provides reasons to doubt that the list above is fatal for democratic corporatism; instead, persistence with negotiated adjustment is the rule.

First, are national bargaining arrangements giving way to sectoral or "mesocorporatist" arrangements? This argument suggests that economic sectors such as auto, electronics, steel, chemicals, dairy, and the securities industry develop their own rules, networks, values, and interests, in short, their own system of governance (cf. Hollingsworth, Schmitter, and Streeck, 1994). As economists have noted since Adam Smith, there are, indeed, big differences in economic organization and performance by industrial sector. But whenever comparative analysts have tried to play economic sectors against national patterns of political economy as determinants of outcomes in politics, economics, and welfare, the latter typically win out.

The evidence includes the following: (1) A systematic comparison of industrial relations systems in two industries, auto and telecommunications, in the United States and Germany (Turner, 1991) concludes that national legal, social, and political contexts are far more important determinants than the technical and economic characteristics of diverse industries. (2) My data and other studies in chapters 14 (on mayhem), 15 (on the environment), and 16 (on health) show how national regulatory regimes differ as they confront very similar risks—health and safety, nuclear energy, smoking, and air pollution. Public policies and performance vary markedly by type of political economy. (3) Studies suggest that multinationals in particular industries adapt to host cultures as well as to the constraints of their home-based country; they are *not* aggressive change agents (chap. 17 on globalization). (4) Comparisons of regulatory reform in the 1980s and early 1990s in telecommunications, financial services, broadcasting, transport, and utilities in Britain, Japan, the United States, France, and Germany show that the common embrace of deregulation as a good idea belies the action. Ideology and practice were poles apart. What actually developed were contrasting mixes of *re*regulation and liberalization shaped by national institutions (Vogel, 1996). (5) Reviewing findings of the past decade regarding sectoral versus national differences, Hollingsworth and Streeck (1994) conclude that differences in performance and control in sectoral governance *within* nations are less than the differences *between* nations within the same economic sector. (Cf. Traxler and Unger, 1994, pp. 195–214.) In other words national institutional contexts overwhelm sectoral peculiarities. Of course, some sectors within consensual societies are full of conflict and some sectors within decentralized, fragmented, and polarized systems are consensual, but the central tendency, the major contrasts, are national, not sectoral.

Second, it is argued that corporatist democracies are rigid and bureaucratic and (a related argument) a technocratic threat to democratic accountability. Although corporatist bargaining processes have a technocratic cast, this does not transform political into technical decisions. A prime minister who walks into a room flanked by his or her staff experts to bargain with equally well staffed management and labor leaders does not forget his or her political base. Neither do the bargaining partners. As for bureaucratic rigidity, my findings in chapter 12 demonstrate that corporatist countries as they faced the two big oil shocks of 1974 and 1979–80 responded more flexibly and quickly with better performance than did the least-corporatist democracies.

Third, it is asserted that because of economic constraints since the early 1970s neither the government nor employers can deliver the continual harvest of benefits (wages, job security, social security, participation in policy decisions in workplace and community) that has sustained consensus and permitted labor leaders to embrace labor peace, wage restraint, and government tax policies and to cooperate on productivity, labor flexibility, and tax breaks for management—the trade-offs already discussed. This inspires rank-and-file protest against the unfavorable bargains their leaders obtain. Thus, it is alleged, worker disaffection is proliferating and corporatist democracy is fast disappearing. There are three answers to this dire picture: (1) Corporatist democracies provide stronger and more meaningful channels for participation of union members and the general citizenry than the least-corporatist democracies. Chapter 3 provides data on the amount and types of participation in most of our 19 countries. Lively participation in broad-based associations provides a prop for continuity; such participation patterns do not fall off because economic constraints appear. (2) The range of economic and noneconomic gains for labor is wide, the kinds of benefits numerous. Often low-cost gains (e.g., expanded participation in managerial decisions, pay-for-knowledge, flexible schedules) can be substituted for high-cost gains (big increases in wages or pensions).[13] (3) Habits of accommodation among the social partners are of long standing and have survived crises of the past. If we examine recent developments in the two cases that have evidenced most decline in the strength of bargaining arrangements—Sweden and the Netherlands—we can see that negotiated adaptation is a better concept than collapse or even erosion. They are discussed in the next section.

The fourth theme in the literature on the demise of corporatism suggests that when the bargaining partners interact with one another and the executive branch of government, they bypass and thus weaken political parties and parliamentary democracy. The mass base for the legitimacy of corporatist democracy therefore erodes. Chapter 11 shows the opposite: corporatism either strengthens party systems or retards their decline.

The fifth theme is that democratic corporatism requires left dominance and cannot survive the new weakness of left parties since the 1970s. Aside from the fact that in 12 of 15 governments of the European Union (EU) in early 1999 left parties either dominated or were part of center-left governments, a later section of this chapter shows that Catholic party power or alternating Catholic and left-dominated coalitions are stronger predictors of corporatist continuity than left power alone. And the Japanese style of corporatism flourished for decades with little labor-left power.

The final, most strongly argued, theme about threats to the survival of these consensus-making machines is that globalization undermines the economic base for the necessary trade-offs. This is a restatement of the third theme—economic constraints rooted in increased competition subvert the social partners' capacity to accommodate their conflicting interests. In chapter 17 I show that of several specific dimensions of globalization—recently increased immigration, the alleged deregulation of the labor market, the increased power of multinational corporations, capital flows across national boundaries, increased trade, and the internationalization of finance—only the increased autonomy of central banks is a serious threat to the welfare state, labor standards, and job security, because powerful monetary authorities subvert public policies that sustain negotiated economies.

One structural shift that adds strain to corporatist bargaining is the universal increase in the percentage of union members in white-collar unions, especially in public service. It is clear that the interests of government employees at times diverge from the interests of private-sector workers. Public employees, for instance, have a clear interest in raising taxes to finance expanding government programs; blue-collar workers in manufacturing do not always see it that way. But labor movements, like political parties, have always embraced groups of workers with diverse values and interests—high seniority workers vs. low, skilled vs. unskilled, immigrants vs. natives, minority groups vs. dominant groups, men vs. women, and so on—with fluctuating success in creating solidarity among them. The capacity of labor, management, and government to cope with internal cleavages as well as external shocks varies cross-nationally.

SWEDEN AND THE NETHERLANDS AS CASES OF MOST CHANGE

Students of industrial relations generally agree that among the strongly corporatist democracies only Sweden experienced a significant decentralization of bargaining in the past 20 or so years.[14] Central wage bargaining in Sweden was first discussed at the 1936 Congress of LO, the main labor federation, but it was promoted at the request of employers against the initial opposition of LO; labor, management, and the government, however, found this system mutually beneficial and it flourished for about four decades. In the early 1970s the two largest labor federations, LO and TCO, pressed for legal reforms to grant more autonomy to local unions; Parliament passed the Swedish Employment Protection Act giving unions more say in layoffs and downsizing. In 1983, in the first major break from centralized wage bargaining, the Engineering Employers Association (VF) and the Metal Workers Union struck a separate deal for pay higher than LO and SAF (the Swedish Employers' Confederation) could agree to.[15] While this did not block subsequent central agreements, formal or informal (e.g., central bargaining was reestablished in 1986–87), by the early 1990s wage bargaining had moved from stable tripartite and bipartite arrangements to less-stable industrywide and local bargaining, although intermittent revivals of central agreements have punctuated the slow erosion of the Swedish model. In 1991 the SAF dissolved its bargaining department. Yet one year later Swedish employers accepted the Rehnberg Commission's proposal for a central agreement banning local bargaining. In short, there has been fluctuation around a 20-year trend toward somewhat more decentralized bargaining—a move toward the German and Austrian systems.

Why has Swedish corporatism changed more than other corporatist democracies? We must first reject explanations that apply to similar systems of bargaining but did not bring about the same result. It was not due to universal changes in the organization of work (e.g., the alleged trend toward "flexible specialization" or "post-Fordism," ideas evaluated in chap. 1), or to the economic constraints facing all countries since the early 1970s, or to the integration within a single European market that is said to undermine the basis for centralized national bargaining, as Reder and Ulman (1993) suggest. If these were the main forces at work, there would be a universal collapse of corporatism, which, we have seen, is not happening. Instead, the erosion of centralized wage bargaining in the 1980s in Sweden was largely due to mistakes in macroeconomic policy decisions, especially during financial market liberalization and a recession, and to changes in LO's bargaining strategies that exacerbated employers' rising restiveness about the outcomes of central wage determination (cf. Huber and Stephens, 1996, 1999; Martin, 1996; and Wallerstein and Golden, 1997).

The economic crisis of the mid-1980s to mid-1990s, while not unique to Sweden, was deepened by fiscal and monetary policies pursued by both Social Democrats and the bourgeois bloc, with the latter making the most costly mistakes. From an economic performance that combined well above average growth, medium inflation, and full employment during the decades of strongest corporatism, which made Sweden one of the richest and most egalitarian countries in the world, Swedish performance moved to average after 1980 (see chap. 12, tables 12.4 and 12.6) when centralized wage bargaining and full employment unraveled. From 1984 to 1994 its GDP average annual growth in volume was 1.0%—at the very bottom of our 19 countries ("OECD in Figures," 1996 ed.). The post-oil-shock period was characterized by soaring debt and deficits; higher unemployment; lower levels of investment; and capital flight (e.g., between 1985 and 1990 under the Bildt coalition government, outward foreign direct investment from Sweden increased from 10.9 billion Skr to 69.6 billion Skr [Ingebritsen, 1996, p. 21]). As part of a plan to forge closer ties to the European Community (EC), the Bildt government adopted a fixed exchange rate policy, tying the krona to the ECU on May 17, 1991, with a narrow margin of fluctuation. In essence, Swedish currency was now at the mercy of the anti-inflationary zeal of the German Bundesbank (see chap. 17), which itself was intensified by the enormous burden of German reunification. The Bildt government stubbornly hung on to this rigid currency rate well after it was clear to everyone that its effects were devastating. Currency exodus soared within a week. On September 10, 1992, as the key lending rate reached 75%, Prime Minister Bildt said that past sins need not be eternal and that if necessary "the central bank is prepared to go even higher. The sky is the limit" (*Wall Street Journal*, Sept. 11, 1992). And it was: The overnight lending rate reached 500% before the policy was abandoned on November 19, 1992. By 1993 unemployment reached an annual average of 8.2%—for Sweden the worst rate since the 1930s. Subsequently the government and its Social Democratic successors returned to devaluation and a much less rigid currency regime.

Other policy mistakes by a series of center-right coalition governments of 1976–82 and 1991–94 included cutting taxes while increasing spending. The Fälldin government (1976–82) ran up unprecedented annual deficits that way.[16] When the Social Democrats returned to power in 1982, they aimed to reduce unemployment by increasing demand while decreasing budget deficits—what they called a "Third Way." That would be accomplished by changing the composition of demand: decrease the share of domestic consumption in GNP growth relative to the share of exports and industrial development, reform taxes, and institute modest welfare state cutbacks. To increase export-led growth, the government first adopted a big currency devaluation. This policy mix worked very well for a few years. Deficits declined, economic growth took off. However, the devaluation of 1982, based on an erroneous forecast of slow American and European recovery from the deep worldwide recession of 1980–82, proved to be excessive. (What economist could predict that the Reagan administration would adopt massive Keynesian deficit spending appropriate to the Great Depression?) Swedish unemployment dropped from 3.5% in 1983 to a low of 1.4% in 1989; labor markets became extremely tight. An out-of-control boom followed from 1983 to 1990. Compounding the effect of the oversized devaluation was a second policy mistake, a badly timed deregulation of the domestic credit market in 1985—badly timed because it came before the expansionary boom could be cooled down and, more important, before tax reform had completely eliminated the deductibility of interest on loans. This unleashed a speculative boom. Released from regulation, banks promoted loans to all comers; construction firms and speculators borrowed heavily. The typical loan financed projects that would succeed only if the boom was perpetual. The total volume of loans outstanding by all credit institutions more than doubled from 1985 to 1990. It was a classic speculative bubble. As in Japan, the bubble burst, leading to a collapse of asset prices and a severe and costly banking crisis.

Financial deregulation undermined the effectiveness of the 1982 devaluation. From 1985 to 1988 both exports and private consumption dropped sharply. Swedish inflation 1983–89 was about double that of the EC average; profits soared, but real income for most of the population declined. Wage restraint for labor unions became politically untenable, adding wage-push inflation to the mix.[17]

Finally, on the eve of another worldwide recession, in the two years leading to their defeat in 1991, the Social Democratic government increased household taxes (the VAT and, most unpopular, property tax revaluations). This at a time when consumer demand was falling and many small social-policy cutbacks that hit their electoral base were taking effect (see chap. 5, pp. 226–227 and 230–232, and chap. 10, p. 379ff.).

As causes of the erosion of corporatist bargaining arrangements in this period, these policy mistakes were perhaps less important than two basic shifts in labor strategies inspired by left factions of both the LO and the Social Democratic Party. The first was a ratcheting up of the traditional wage solidarity policy adopted in the 1950s—national agreements on general wage levels with larger portions going to low-wage workers than high-wage workers. Employers liked this policy because in practice it restrained wage increases and allowed flexibility through wage drift (paying more than the official wage where employers needed to recruit or retain skilled workers). Labor pushed for it because it achieved equal pay for equal work across the whole economy and furthered their egalitarian goals. As Hibbs and Locking (2000) show, from the mid-1950s to the late 1960s what they call "Wage Solidarity I" had benign economic effects—it helped to drive out marginal producers, increasing productivity, reducing unemployment, and restraining inflation. Substantial compression of wages occurred but, accordion-like, the wage structure quickly adjusted until the next agreement reduced the spread again. Hibbs' "Wage Solidarity II," however, pushed wage compression so far that it became a drag on the economy. Here the left demanded much greater emphasis on equal pay for all work within workplaces and within sectors. From the mid-1960s to the mid-1980s, the relative wage spread among blue-collar workers was reduced by about 80%. Further, employers found that sharp increases in the lowest wage became a floor from which the whole wage structure moved up. Labor costs sharply accelerated (in 1975–76 alone, wages, including wage drift, climbed 40%). Employers naturally rebelled.

The second radicalization of labor-left strategy was an even greater incentive for SAF to withdraw from centralized national bargaining—the adoption from 1971 to 1977 of legislation curtailing managerial prerogatives and then, the coup de grâce, the LO endorsement in 1976 of union-controlled "wage earner funds." These funds were designed to achieve eventual majority ownership by organized labor of all large companies. The vehemence of management and public opposition to this proposal was evident in one of the largest mass protests in the history of Stockholm. It was a parade of white-collar and professional people and executives, with banners held high condemning socialism. From SAF's viewpoint, "Wage Solidarity II" was bad enough, but the socialization of production was a clear break from the corporatist compromise, the postwar social contract. By a 1984 law, five regional funds were set up; money was actually collected from 1984 to 1992 from companies' net profits plus a fee based on payroll. Although the Social Democrats withdrew the original proposal and settled for a much watered-down version, and the wage earner funds were abandoned in 1992, the damage was done; the SAF formally quit the institution of national bargaining in 1990. Clearly, from the mid-1970s until 1990 the LO had overplayed its hand by going to the government to get what employers fiercely rejected at the collective bargaining table. (Cf. the SAF statement by Hans-Göran Myrdal, 1991.)

It is important to note that all of these centralized systems, in Sweden as well as other corporatist democracies, have large elements of decentralization in them. National wage and benefit agreements always leave room for adaptation to local and industry conditions. The percentage of the labor force working at the centrally negotiated wage is often small. Some of these systems depend on the wage leadership of the largest unions and employers, as in Austria and Germany. All of them evidence much informal consultation and coordination. Only by exaggerating the rigidity of central wage bargaining in the past can one see recent developments as a radical structural change. Even in Sweden during the crisis of the early 1990s, there was consensus among the major parties and bargaining partners regarding welfare-state reforms, including pensions, job-injury insurance, sick pay, and personal social services (see chap. 5). The reforms were designed to cut costs while maintaining Sweden's commitment to universalism and solidarity; the level of taxes needed to sustain this commitment was an area of compromise.

In my conversations with Swedish politicians, several leaders and staffers of the Social Democratic Party and the Liberal Party agreed with most of this account of uniquely Swedish developments that explain the erosion of Swedish corporatism, although their judgments about the relative importance of the causes differed. Indeed, even labor and management negotiators agreed with these broad outlines. But the party politicians of the center-left said I should add the subversive role of a new breed of model-building economists, theorists of unmodified free markets, some of them monetarist ideologues who gradually penetrated the finance ministry, business enterprises, and the SAF while converting journalists covering the economy. My informants railed against these expert right-wing ideologues, who claim that budget deficits and wage-push inflation are the root cause of sputtering economies, that the welfare state is the root of the deficits, and that a tight monetary regime, cuts in social spending and taxes (especially taxes on capital), restrictions on the power of unions and other interest groups combined with deregulation, privatization, and much more reliance on free markets are the solution (e.g., Lindbeck et al., 1994). These politicians claim that both the center-left and center-right are infected by these ideas. Although they support the welfare-state reforms described in chapter 5, the rest of this very American package, they say, is pure ideology, a formula for destroying Swedish institutions and polarizing Swedish society. My own view is that this combination of Reaganomics and Thatcherism in the heads of neoliberal economists was a major influence in New Zealand's recent shift toward neoliberal policies and the subsequent destabilization of economy and polity (details in chap. 11) but was only incidental in the Swedish story. In Sweden the countervailing power and ideology of the left and labor were and are much stronger and the pragmatism of the bargaining partners much more dominant.

Despite undergoing the most change of all the corporatist democracies, relative to the least-corporatist democracies Sweden's consensual style is still evident. Swedish corporatism is no dinosaur of merely historical interest.

The Netherlands is second only to Sweden in the degree of change in long-standing corporatist bargaining arrangements. Its centralized tripartite system of bargaining came under enormous strain in the last 30 years or so.[18] The postwar corporatist settlement was renegotiated and refined throughout this period. In the 1940s and 1950s labor unions exchanged wage restraint for full employment and the expansion of social programs. In the 1960s, some union leaders were confronted with rising worker militancy expressed in occasional wildcat strikes; they were forced to demand better wage increases than the national labor federations had agreed to. Governments responded by increasing the scope and generosity of social programs. The economy was booming throughout this period; among our 19 rich democracies the Netherlands ranked well above average from 1950 to 1974 (table 12.1). Generally incomes policies were very successful until 1963; then the pressures of full employment with its unofficial wage increases, worker dissatisfaction with wage restraint (especially in such profitable industries as natural gas), and increasing economic diversification and industrial restructuring as well as a gradual erosion of "pillarization" undermined social consensus and led to incomes policy failures in 1963–75 (Flanagan, Soskice, and Ulman, 1983; Houska, 1985).[19] Wages rose more than productivity and more than wages in other European countries. Party politics became more volatile, cabinet formation more difficult. In the severe recession of the early 1980s a center-right government pursued an uncompensated incomes policy, including deflation, high unemployment (up to 10.1% in 1980–1983), and cutbacks in social transfers (Visser and Hemerijck, 1997; Wolinetz, 1993, p. 24); the economy sputtered (table 12.4).

These and other economic problems cumulating since the early 1970s put further strain on the system: soaring public debt and deficits (up from 4.0% of GDP in 1961–73 to 5.9% in 1974–83 and 7.2% in 1980), rising unemployment (from 1.1% 1961–73 to 5.4% 1974–83 to 9.2% 1984–1991), and uniquely Dutch annual working hours per worker of only about 1,400, putting it at the lowest level of all our rich democracies, combined with gross inefficiencies in welfare-state design and administration. (See chaps. 5 and 15 and table 15.3 on the extraordinary cost of sickness pay and disability insurance and the very low rates of labor-force participation of middle-aged workers in the Netherlands.) Coping with all this obviously required substantial changes in social and economic policies.

Structural shifts since the early 1970s are often interpreted as the breakdown of democratic corporatism. Yet corporatist bargaining arrangements persist in modified form even to this day. The quasi-public Social and Economic Council (SER) now evidences more clashes of fixed positions, which decrease its moral authority. The Labor Foundation, officially bilateral, has taken over some of the functions of the SER. After the 1982 "Accord of Wassenaar," marking the return to wage moderation as the unions' dominant strategy for investment and job growth, what were formal consultations and negotiations gave way to informal discussions orchestrated by the Ministry of Social Affairs and Employment. These discussions led to central agreements between the social partners in 1984, 1986, and 1989. Instead of detailed pacts on wages and benefits to closely guide collective bargaining, these were shorter, nonbinding recommendations on specific issues—youth unemployment, or how to reduce long-term employment.[20] The government continued to consult with SER on a wide range of problems, but employers' associations that once went through SER now more often deal directly with unions. The government for its part draws on both SER and alternative sources of advice. In 1992 the cabinet requested advice from the SER on the consequences of the European monetary union and European integration. Tripartite consensus in its report was followed by agreement of labor, management, and government to meet two times a year under the auspices of the Foundation of Labor and the important November 1993 accord, "A New Course." In 1994, this time under the left-liberal coalition headed by the social democrat Wim Kok, the central federations of labor and employers recommended that unions and management coordinate sectoral bargaining to curb labor costs, an urgent management demand. In return, labor got a slightly shorter work week for full-time workers and an agreement to cut unemployment by the creation of part-time jobs, mainly through job-sharing, and especially for women. This was designed to overcome the handicap of extraordinarily low Dutch labor-force participation. In addition, employers promised to include local union representatives or works councils in negotiation over local issues. In the late 1990s unions traded continued wage restraint for expanded training opportunities and increased emphasis on paid and unpaid leave to care for children and the aged. Finally, recommendations of the Labor Foundation and labor-management agreement on "Flexibility and Security" led to new legislation in 1998–99. This provided temporary workers with more security and benefits in return for some loosening of tight dismissal rules that protected regular employees.

In short, meetings continue and bargains are struck. While the scope of issues covered has diminished and formal meetings are fewer, frequent informal consultations provide channels for solving problems. In an organized and controlled decentralization of industrial relations over the past two decades, consultation and coordination between the managers of major multinational firms, major central employers associations, and labor unions has been frequent and intense. (Visser and Hemerijck, 1997, pp. 111–112.) Further signs of continuing consensual bargaining are strike rates: they remained low throughout 1960–87, the period for data analyzed in chapter 12 and appendix G; among 19 countries the Netherlands ranked between 17th in 1960–72, and 14th in 1983–87 in man-days lost through strikes.

Despite some erosion of formal bargaining structures, as in Sweden, both informal and formal interaction among the social partners persists. The celebrated Dutch civility is very much alive; a high level of trust prevails; pragmatic accommodations are the continuing custom.

The outcome in the 1990s was a restoration of good economic performance—low inflation, low interest rates, lowered deficits, increased job creation, and declining unemployment—by 1997 down to 5.5%, half the EU average. All this with no significant increase in inequality.

One reason for the persistence of corporatist bargaining arrangements—even in the cases under most pressure—is that they have been institutionalized after a long period of development. This is clear from analysis of their causes.

STRUCTURAL AND IDEOLOGICAL SOURCES OF DEMOCRATIC CORPORATISM

Among the many forces scholars have listed as causes of democratic corporatism (or "negotiated economies"), four are most prominent, three of them national, one external: (1) the level, rate, and timing of industrialization (early, late, very late) as they shape the structure of industry and/or labor and/or agriculture (Gerschenkron, 1962; De Schweinitz, 1964; Ingham, 1974; Kurth, 1979; Lafferty, 1971); (2) the power and ideology of mass-based social and political movements and parties (Wilensky, 1981c); (3) electoral systems, especially various forms of proportional representation (Katzenstein, 1985a, pp. 150–157; Wilensky, 1976a, p. 37; cf. Lijphart, 1984); and (4) the openness of economies or trade dependence (Katzenstein, 1985a, 1985b; Abraham, 1981; Swenson, 1991; Lehmbruch, 1991, 1993; Wallerstein 1989).

Since the late 19th century these forces have interacted to produce fully developed corporatist bargaining structures, generally in place by the 1950s. I have tried to sort them out sequentially to uncover their causal order. Some quantitative tests can help to assess their relative importance. The following briefly summarizes the arguments.

Leftism, Catholicism, and Democratic Corporatism[21]

The last half of the 19th century saw the rise of mass-based left parties and movements (socialist, social democratic and labor parties with a labor movement base) and mass-based Catholic parties and movements (Christian Democratic, Christian Socialist, and Social Christian parties with a Catholic church base). What left parties of the past century or so have in common is an ideological commitment to use the apparatus of the state to redistribute income, power, and status toward lower strata or at least the lower half of the distribution. The ideological stance of Catholic parties is more difficult to delineate because of its greater diversity and the vagueness of party platforms and manifestos. But it emerges more clearly in what it opposes: it stands as an alternative to both 19th-century liberalism and socialism, its two major ideological enemies. In contrast to liberalism, Catholic parties generally favor an active role for the state. But as opposed to collectivism, they view such intervention only as a means of harmonizing the conflicting interests of rival groups, whose basic autonomy Catholics wish to safeguard. Within this framework there is room for both social Christian principles, which lean toward egalitarianism, and an emphasis on organic hierarchy. In short, my measures of Catholicism and leftism refer to a party's ideology, not to its electoral base or behavior in office. Thus Catholic parties carry into power an anti-collectivist, antiliberal theme laced with a concern for workers and the poor; left parties carry into power a persistent egalitarian ideology.

That Catholicism is conducive to corporatism, democratic or not, is not surprising. That left party dominance would have effects similar to those of Catholic party dominance is not so obvious.

116

Political history provides abundant illustration of the functional equivalence of Catholicism and leftism, including many episodes of ideological and structural convergence. Although Catholic parliamentary groups, drawing on medieval and romantic themes, have often been conservative or reactionary, the rise of Social Christian and particularly Catholic workers movements in Belgium, the Netherlands, Germany, Italy, and France pushed European Catholic politicians toward the left. For many decades they have increasingly emphasized support of free labor unions, labor legislation, social security, and an economic order based on industrial self-government and worker participation in management, ownership, and profits, with close collaboration between unions and employer associations. Opportunities for alliances with leftists opened up. For instance, in Germany during the 1920s a Catholic minister of labour, Father Heinrich Brauns, was responsible for vanguard progressive social legislation; the context was intermittent coalition between the SPD and the Center Party. Similarly, after World War I Belgium saw a variety of coalition governments: Catholic-Liberal-Socialist, Catholic-Liberal, Catholic-Socialist. But through them all, as Fogarty suggests, "the Catholic Party remained the pivot, and a steady stream of political and social reforms came forward" (1957, p. 299).

What contemporary socialists and Catholics have in common, aside from their desire to attain and maintain power, is a traditional humanistic concern with the lower strata, which has its roots in the early modern era. In the continental Catholic case, we find that Catholic humanists of the 16th century had considerable influence on the approach of urban businessmen and lawyers to their urban crisis and their poor, both "deserving" and "undeserving." Lyon provides one of the many examples of a religious coalition for welfare reform dominated by Catholics. In 1532, the French cleric and humanist Jean de Vauzelles urged the notables of Lyon to introduce sweeping new welfare measures including training and education for poor children, the recognition of the right of unemployables to support, a central treasury administered by laymen, and so on (Davis, 1968). The contemporary expression of this Christian concern is evident in passages on welfare, poverty, and labor in the "social" Encyclicals of Popes Leo XIII, Pius XI, and John XXIII, as well as in the activism of social-minded priests.

The affinity of Catholicism and leftism as sources of democratic corporatism is confirmed by empirical observation (Wilensky, 1981c, pp. 362 – 368). Data show that cumulative Catholic power and cumulative left power have similar effects on the direction of the political economies of rich democracies. Since World War I those countries with strong corporatist-technocratic linkages either have strong Catholic or left party power or both, except for France. Table 2.1 shows the interaction of party power and corporatism and presents cumulative scores for legislative and executive power combined. Appendix B discusses the measures of party power. Apparently their hierarchical structures, their support for progressive labor and social legislation, their advocacy of worker participation schemes, and their humanistic concern for the poor move these two mass-based parties toward the corporatist compromise when they achieve substantial power and can act out their ideologies.

At first glance the time order is a problem. Because one component of corporatism is centralization of government (which facilitates or necessitates the centralization of labor and employer federations), it could be argued that democratic corporatism is as old as Catholic party power. However, Catholic parties, once formed, can and do build upon the

TABLE 2.1 The interplay of left and Catholic party power, proportional representation, and trade dependence as sources of democratic corporatism

| Type of Political Economy[a] | Political Structures | | | | | Trade Dependence | | | |
| | Party Power 1920-76[b] | | | | Electoral System: Propor. Rep.[c] | Exports As A Percent of GNP[d] | | | |
	Left		Catholic			1880-1913[e]	1920-29[f]	1930-39[g]	1950-60
Left Corporatist									
Sweden	H	114	L	0	1.0	18.2 (5)	16.1 (10)	14.1 (9)	20.5 (8)
Norway	H	73	L	0	1.0	17.1 (6)	16.6 (9)	14.0 (10)	20.8 (7)
Finland	M	50	L	0	1.0	—	—	—	20.0 (9)
Israel	H	138	L	0	1.0	—	—	—	7.1 (18)
Denmark	H	87	L	0	1.0	22.0 (3)	27.2 (4)	21.8 (3)	26.8 (4)
Left-Cath. Corporatist									
Netherlands	ML	31	H	79	1.0	101.7 (1)	28.5 (3)	19.2 (4)	36.2 (1)
Belgium	M	42	H	105	1.0	—	49.9 (1)	34.0 (2)	31.7 (2)
Austria	M	39	H	88	1.0	—	18.6 (8)	10.9 (12)	17.8 (12)
Catholic Corporatist									
Italy	L	0	H	82	1.0	8.8 (11)	8.9 (14)	6.0 (15)	10.3 (16)
West Germany	ML	30	H	71	0.5	15.1 (9)	14.9 (12)	9.3 (13)	14.9 (14)
Corporatist w/o Labor									
France	L	7	LM	7	0.5	—	—	—	12.3 (15)
Japan	L	0	L	0	0.5	11.8 (10)	13.9 (13)	16.3 (7)	9.2 (17)
Switzerland	L	0	L	0	1.0	34.7 (2)	23.2 (5)	12.8 (11)	21.9 (6)

[a]See text for definitions and measures.

[b]Parties defined by their ideological stance, not by their social base or behavior in office. See text. The shorter period 1946–76 yields the same results.

[c]1 = presence of PR in national electoral system for first (lower) or only chamber 1945–80; 0.5 = mixed proportional-plurality; 0 = absence. The four parliamentary-plurality systems are Australia, Canada, New Zealand, and the UK; the ten parliamentary-PR systems are Sweden, Norway, Finland, Israel, Denmark, the Netherlands, Belgium, Austria, Italy, Germany. Ambiguities include West Germany: list PR; mixed PR and plurality but almost entirely proportional in allocation of seats; two votes per voter. Japan: single nontransferable vote in multimember district makes minority representation possible; it is semiproportional. France IV 1946–58 had list PR; France V 1958–on is mixed; national assembly is mixed majority-plurality with minimum of 12.5% for second ballot, where plurality rules; presidential majority by runoff if necessary. Ireland's system of a single transferable vote where voter ranks individual candidates makes it like PR. USA is the purest case (and among rich democracies the only case) of presidential-plurality. Sources: Lijphart (1984, 1990, 1991); Rokkan (1970); Bogdanor and Butler (1983); Grofman and Lijphart (1986).

[d]For 1880–1939, data for Europe are from B. R. Mitchell, *European Historical Statistics 1750–1970* (New York: Columbia University Press, 1975); data for USA, Canada, Australia and New Zealand are from B. R. Mitchell, *International Historical Statistics: The Americas and Australasia* (Detroit: Gale Research Co., 1983); data for Japan are from K. Ohkawa and H. Rosovky, *Japanese Economic Growth: Trend Acceleration in the Twentieth Century* (Stanford: Stanford University Press, 1973), Appendix tables. Figures for Sweden, Australia, and Norway are as a percent of GDP; for Switzerland, Germany, Belgium, Netherlands, and Ireland as a percent of Net National Product (= GNP minus maintenance and depreciation of capital stock); for New Zealand as a percent of Aggregate Personal Income. The figures for 1950–60 are averages of data for 1950, 1955, and 1960, all as a percent of GNP. The 1950 data are from *Yearbook of International Trade Statistics 1974* (New York: UN, 1975) and the 1955 and 1960 data are from *Yearbook of International Trade Statistics 1987* (New York: UN, 1989).

TABLE 2.1 *(continued)*

Type of Political Economy[a]	Political Structures			Trade Dependence			
	Party Power 1920-76[b]		Electoral System: Propor. Rep.[c]	Exports As A Percent of GNP[d]			
	Left	Catholic		1880-1913[e]	1920-29[f]	1930-39[g]	1950-60
Least Corporatist							
United States	H 98	L 0	0.0	6.7 (12)	5.8 (15)	3.4 (16)	4.2 (19)
United Kingdom	M 47	L 0	0.0	15.6 (7)	15.8 (11)	8.8 (14)	18.0 (10)
New Zealand	H 60	L 0	0.0	—	—	35.2 (1)	27.1 (3)
Australia	ML 35	L 0	0.0	21.8 (4)	19.1 (7)	16.5 (6)	16.6 (13)
Canada	L 0	L 0	0.0	15.1 (9)	22.4 (6)	16.2 (8)	17.9 (11)
Ireland	L 0	L 0	1.0	—	29.1 (2)	17.8 (5)	23.6 (5)

[e]Averages cover fewer years for some countries. For Japan, only 1905–13; for Switzerland, 1913 only; Canada 1880, 1890, 1900, 1910 only; and Netherlands 1900–13 only. The average for Netherlands is above 100% for two reasons: it may include the large amount of re-exports of primary products from the East Indies; and the denominator is Net National Product rather than GNP. In any case, monographic and historical literature confirms the early export dependence of the Netherlands.

[f]For Denmark, 1921–29; Belgium, 1924 and 1927; Austria, 1924–29; Germany, 1925–29; Switzerland, 1924 and 1929; Canada, 1920 and 1926–29; and Ireland, 1929 only.

[g]Belgium, 1930 and 1934–39; Austria, 1930–37; Germany, 1930–38; New Zealand, 1931–39; and Ireland, 1931, 1933, and 1936.

ancillary institutions of the Catholic Church, which are much older than the centralized state. Catholic party dominance thus taps an older social-political complex. Further, while highly centralized governments may precede the creation of both Catholic and left parties, the fully developed corporatist bargaining arrangements at issue here are a quite recent development. Although there are precursors of tripartite and bipartite labor-management structures under the formal or informal auspices of government (Hans Daalder [1974, p. 616] finds such accommodationist styles in cities and provinces of the Netherlands as early as the 16th century), not until the beginning of the 20th century and especially after World War I did the national systems in place today become institutionalized—that is, publicly recognized and sanctioned in contracts, custom, and law. For the 13 cases labeled corporatism in table 2.1 the corporatist threshold appears in the 1930s or later with the exception of Denmark (1899 marks the "September Agreement" between the DA, a private sector employer association and the LO, the labor confederation) and the Netherlands (1917 marks a grand compromise among competing political interests on religious schools, general suffrage, and PR that led gradually to the Social and Economic Council of 1950).

Electoral Systems as a Cause of Corporatism

Regarding proportional representation (PR), this electoral procedure clearly fosters the integration of labor movements and socialist movements as well as minority groups (based on ethnicity, religion, race, ethnic-linguistic identity) into the political center, ultimately promoting a corporatist compromise. Historically the PR compromise in 11 of our rich democracies preceded the corporatist compromise. Some form of PR appeared in these countries from 1855 to 1920, sometimes starting locally in cantons, provinces, or towns before spreading to parliamentary elections at a national level.

Most often PR was a response of dominant Conservative or Liberal parties facing the rise of mass-based Catholic or Socialist movements or parties, newly franchised, whose increasing electoral success threatened their dominance. For instance, in Sweden and Denmark from 1915 to 1920 it was a response of a dominant Conservative party to rising Liberal and Social Democratic parties; in Norway the dominant but declining Liberal party faced a rising Labor party; in Italy the declining liberals faced rising Socialist and Catholic parties; in Switzerland in 1919 the dominant liberals (mainly the Radical party) faced both rising socialist parties and a peasant party (especially in Bern and Zurich); in Austria bourgeois and Christian Socialist parties ceded to the demands of radical and Social Democratic parties. In three cases (Belgium, Netherlands, Austria), the adoption of PR was a response of dominant Catholic parties threatened by militant socialists. In several cases PR was also inspired by the interaction of dominant ethnic-religious groups and competing minorities as in the cases of Denmark's minority (in Schleswig-Holstein in 1855), or Ireland's minority Protestants. Less clearly, the extreme social heterogeneity of Israel and Switzerland was important in their adoption of PR.

Dominant groups in decline, anxious about their political future, facing gradual erosion if not ultimate extinction, saw PR as a means of ensuring their continued representation in government and as a way to tame the rising militants. In turn, the mass-based Catholic and left parties, unsure they would ever reach an electoral majority, also saw PR as their ticket to assured representation. In short, conditions for the PR compromise were ripe. And by 1920 all the countries that now use PR had adopted it.[22]

Why did PR foster democratic corporatism? The effect of PR on politics has been in dispute among students of electoral procedures. Anglo-American scholars for the most part argue that PR leads to a profusion of political parties (Finer, 1970, pp. 556–558; Hermens, 1941, pp. 15–19); and fosters political polarization and ideological extremes (Bagehot, 1928, pp. 137–138; Hermens, 1941, pp. 19–30; Finer, 1970, pp. 15–30). PR systems are even alleged to be a major cause of the rise of Hitler (Hermens, 1941, pp. 214–300) and Mussolini (*ibid.*, pp. 147–213).

Students of comparative politics, however, have presented much empirical evidence to suggest that, in fact, PR systems have almost all had a benign effect: they have fostered coalition building and a politics of moderation; and they are a major facilitating stimulus to consensual bargaining among interest groups, parties, and the state (Dahl, 1966; Bogdanor, 1983, pp. 248–253; Lijphart, 1984, 1990). The reasons are these: If a strong minority emerges and has no hope of parliamentary representation, it is likely to spend its time purifying its doctrine, finding extraparliamentary means of protest and training its cadres for militant action (political strikes, street demonstrations, riots). Under PR, small minorities stand a good chance of winning representation or, better, becoming a minority party in a governing coalition. This prospect entices them into accommodation to moderate agendas. Instead of pursuing maximal unnegotiable demands they spend their time bargaining with other parties about policies that might actually be enacted and implemented; they prepare for the moment of real power. Larger parties in decline, for their part, are open to coalition building because PR assures them of a soft landing on the way down. While they will never win an absolute majority of parliamentary seats, they will be assured of a substantial number and, better, can hope for possible dominance of centrist coalitions. By promoting the inclusion of labor, the left, and minority groups, by making government more representative of the preferences of the voting public, PR fosters the habit of consensual bargaining conducive to democratic corporatism.

Table 2.1 is unequivocal about this connection: All the clear cases of democratic corporatism have PR systems; one marginal case (West Germany) and two cases of corporatism-without-labor (France, Japan) have mixed systems; the fragmented, decentralized democracies, with the sole exception of Ireland, do not have PR.

A final reason that PR did not generally produce the dire effects predicted by its opponents is that the architects of PR in the late 19th century and the early 20th century modified it to keep extremes of left and right or militant minority splinter groups out of office: they set the seat-winning thresholds high; they kept district magnitudes within reason (so the number of seats per district would not be too high); and in other ways they discouraged extremes. Only 3 of the 13 countries in my study now using PR (Italy, Israel, and Denmark) have relatively pure forms of it, and all three display the pathologies critics complain about. For instance, the threshold for representation is 1% in Israel and 2% in Denmark; in Italy until the August 1993 electoral reforms, there was no legal threshold at all. PR is like patent medicine: a proper dose is good for you; an overdose can kill you.

The Timing and Nature of Industrialization as a Cause

Beyond the interaction of leftism, Catholicism, and proportional representaion there is a parallel process that plays its part in producing the inclusive, centralized economic organizations essential for corporatist bargaining arrangements—late industrialization and its structural effects. Theories of political development that accent the timing and nature of economic development emphasize variations in the structure and behavior of industry and/or labor unions and/or agriculture. Synthesizing their arguments in summary form:

- Late industrializers (Germany, Austria, Italy, Norway, Sweden, Denmark, Belgium, France, and Switzerland), facing already established developed countries with mass markets, must *target niche markets, concentrate capital, and coordinate government and business effort* (Ingham, 1974, pp. 38–44; Gerschenkron, 1962, pp. 16, 73, 353–355). Thus in capital formation the state either replaces commercial banks (mainly in late-late developers such as Russia) or guides investment banks closely (as in Germany, France, Italy, Switzerland, Belgium, and Austria) (Gerschenkron, 1962, pp. 14–15, 19, 354–355). That is why enterprises are on average larger than those of earlier developers such as the U.S. and Britain.

- Late industrializers evidence *highly developed product specialization and relatively simple technological and organizational structure;* they skip over earlier "craft" stages characteristic of Britain and the U.S. by applying already available mass production techniques to their leading industries. In Sweden it was the engineering industry, especially producers of turbines, internal-combustion engines, and ball bearings. In Norway it was the electro-chemical and electrometallurgical industries. In Denmark it was the producers of quality goods such as silverware, porcelain, marine engines, and beer (Ingham, 1974, pp. 41–42, 46, 61, 63–64).

- Industrial and financial concentration, specialized products, mass production technology, large enterprises, and strong government guidance combined to produce more or less centralized political economies. Because union structures tend to mirror industrial structures, unions among the late industrializers developed *fewer, more-inclusive structures (multi-industrial, multicraft) and more-centralized labor federations.* The structure of trade associations and employer associations, of course, reflect the same trends.[23] In contrast, the early developers with their many smaller, competing enterprises in each sector evidence more numerous, decentralized, narrowly based unions and similar, product-oriented trade associations and weaker employer associations.

It is possible that industrial concentration is a double-edged sword—facilitating corporatist bargaining structures until the 1980s or early 1990s but weakening them thereafter. Thus, it was Sweden, which leads in the percentage of its labor force in large firms, where management most strongly embraced labor in centralized bargaining. What centralized management gives, however, it can take away, if it feels strongly that the outcomes are bad. A unified, cohesive employer federation dominated by big industry, like the SAF, can in one stroke abandon consensual bargaining arrangements it earlier accepted. This may be one reason that Sweden, and, to a lesser extent, the Netherlands, suffered greater erosion in its bargaining arrangements since the 1980s than did Norway, Finland, Germany, or even Denmark (where corporatism never flourished anyway), as we have seen above. Several students of the Swedish political economy argue that one source of the erosion of democratic corporatism was Sweden's industrial concentration (Wallerstein and Golden, 1997; Huber and Stephens, 1998; Pontusson and Swenson, 1996).[24] My impression is that such concentration was a stronger source of the emergence and long persistence of democratic corporatism than it is now of its erosion.

Does Trade Dependence Matter?

If globalization is a driving force in shaping national institutions and public policies we should see its effect in the behavior of the most trade-dependent countries. Many scholars have recently argued that trade dependence and intensified international competition cloud the future of the welfare state and threaten high labor standards. Several students of the history of corporatist bargaining arrangements, in contrast, have argued that export dependence was a factor in the development of centralized industrial relations and, more broadly, tripartite bargaining between labor, management, and the state, which fosters high wages and expansion of the welfare state. Here is a brief summary of the argument that export dependence fosters corporatism and expansive social policies.

First, countries highly dependent on exports for their economic well-being could not rely on an unfettered free market. Their governments had to collaborate with industry to target foreign markets; they therefore drew on business associations as well as farm organizations and ultimately sought the collaboration of labor, encouraging the coordination and centralization of all three. Katzenstein (1985a, pp. 165–171) and Lehmbruch (1991, pp. 136–139; 1993, pp. 52–53) make somewhat similar arguments.

Second, industrial firms in the large export sectors are capital intensive; labor costs are a small percentage of total costs. This lessens the militant antilabor stance characteristic of labor-intensive industries aimed at the home market. The exporters can afford high wages, do not oppose the welfare state, and are willing to accommodate unions rather than try to break them. Labor, in turn, moderates its demands; unions and the political parties they support move from revolution to reform. The German case as analyzed by Abraham (1981, pp. 123, 143–151) epitomizes this point: in the late 19th and early 20th century an amalgam of old craft industries with the dynamic export sectors—especially chemicals, metal finishing, and machinery—was based on a shared antiprotectionist orientation that was mildly favorable to collective bargaining and social democracy. Kurth (1979, p. 23) points out that these same industries, especially chemical and electrical, had an added interest in promoting mass consumption and therefore supported parliamentary coalitions with social democrats who advocated expansion of the welfare state. Although the labor-export alliance of 1924 collapsed in 1930, its structural roots regenerated when democracy was restored after World War II under both Christian Democratic and Social Democratic regimes.

Third, in these export sectors, industry and labor alike become aware of what governments are already saying: economic welfare depends on productivity and labor peace. The bargaining parties are driven to corporatist accommodation not only by their structures but also because industrial conflict is far more costly to the national economy than it is in countries with large internal markets not so dependent on trade (cf. Katzenstein, 1985a, pp. 80, 86, 165–170; 1985b, p. 236; and Swenson, 1991, pp. 520–526).

Thus, late industrializers, it is argued, produce economic structures and political alliances in the expanding export sectors that are conducive to democratic corporatism. Their dependence on unpredictable external markets forces these countries to get their internal act together with government orchestrating cooperation among the social partners.

In sum: The sources of democratic corporatism in its various forms can be found in the interaction of rising mass-based political parties, notably Catholic and left, where incumbent regimes were moved to accept proportional representation. This electoral system, in turn, enhanced the power of leftism and Catholicism, ideologies sympathetic to both corporatism and the welfare state. We know that the PR compromise as well as left and Catholic party power preceded the corporatist compromise. A parallel process was the timing of industrialization as it shaped the structure of industry and agriculture, the size of enterprises, the concentration of capital, and above all, the centralization and inclusiveness of labor federations and employer federations and the role of the state. It is significant that all of these powerful forces are internal, institutional, and national.

We can now test their importance relative to trade dependence and use some quantitative tests. Just a glance at table 2.1 suggests that PR is by far the most important source of corporatism and that Catholic power is a close second. Left power is a less important explanation, largely because since World War I left parties are much more frequently thrown out than Catholic parties, and the duration of left power is rarely long. Further, substantial episodes of left power appear in the U.S., New Zealand, the U.K., and Australia where corporatism is notable by its absence. With rare exceptions, left power without PR has little lasting effect on anything. Regarding trade dependence, table 2.2 shows no clear picture, except perhaps at the extremes of the highly export dependent Netherlands, Belgium, and Switzerland.

A multiple regression analysis of the sources of democratic corporatism (not reported here) confirms the picture. Included are scores for corporatism based only on the centralization of labor federations and of government regressed on the following independent variables three at a time: left power, Catholic power, PR, and trade dependence for various periods (measured by either exports as a percentage of GNP or exports plus imports

TABLE 2.2 Zero-order correlations of trade dependence and corporatism

	Trade Dependence: Exports as % of GNP[a]			
	1880-1913	1920-29	1930-39	1950-60
1880-1913	—			
1920-29	.67**	—		
1930-39	.47•	.93**	—	
1950-60	.81**	.83**	.73**	—
Corpor. Score	−.02[b]	.14[c]	.12	.31•

	Trade Dependence: Exports as % of GNP[a]						
	1950	1955	1960	1965	1970	1974	1980
Corpor. Score	.19	.30	.40*	.45*	.44*	.46*	.42*

[a]See table 2.1 for sources and dates of trade dependence data.
[b]This correlation is .56* when the Netherlands, a clear outlier, is included.
[c]This correlation is .31 (n.s.) when Belgium, an extreme case, is included.

as a percentage of GNP). The results are unequivocal: export dependence fades as a source of corporatism when any two of the other variables are included. In fact, as we see from table 2.2, none of the correlations between trade dependence from 1880 to 1960 and corporatism are significant. If we delete the Netherlands as a clear outlier in both postwar corporatism and trade dependence in 1880–1913, the correlation is about zero; if we delete Belgium in trade dependence for 1920–29 as an extreme case, the correlation drops from .31 to .14. With these two cases excluded, the correlations of corporatism with trade dependence in five-year intervals from 1950 to 1980 increases over time. This suggests that if there is any causal relation, it is in the reverse direction: corporatism causes export success rather than the other way round (a finding somewhat at odds with the 12-country comparison of Peter Katzenstein, 1985a, pp. 81–87, 137, 165–173). In other words, the hypothesis that the external shock of heavy dependence on fluctuating world markets inspires consensual bargaining arrangements finds no support.[25]

Chapter 17 returns to the question of whether various aspects of globalization beyond trade dependence have already or will eventually undermine the institutions that sustain corporatist bargaining arrangements such as the bargaining power of labor federations—increased migration, increased international capital flows, the rise of multinational corporations, and the increasing autonomy of central banks. Only the power of central banks, I argue, is of great importance as a threat to the social contract, to the accommodations among labor, management, and the state that maintain labor standards and the welfare state.

Why No Corporatism in Ireland?

The Republic of Ireland has several attributes of polity and economy ordinarily favorable to the development of democratic corporatism. First, it has an electoral system equivalent to semi-PR—a single transferable vote where the voter ranks individual candidates. Indeed Ireland is the only exception to the rule that among 19 rich democracies PR has historically fostered some type of corporatism (see table 2.1). Second, although Ireland does not have distinctly Catholic parties in competition with left and other parties, its culture of Catholicism provides fallow ground for ideas about labor-management harmony and hierarchy as well as humanitarian approaches to reducing poverty and celebrating the place of labor. Further, by 1979 union density in Ireland reached about 57%, a bit more than the UK's. (In the 1980s, however, union membership dropped as fast as it did in the UK, by more than 11 percentage points. See Western, 1995, p. 181.)

But PR, Catholicism, and an above-average union density are not enough. As in Britain, efforts to develop corporatist bargaining arrangements ran up against unfavorable labor, industrial, and employer structures. Irish manufacturing industries have long been dominated by small- to medium-sized firms—even more so than Denmark; only 13% of Irish manufacturing workers are in companies employing more than 500 workers, compared to the also small 22% of Danish workers (OECD, 1993a).[26] The newer export industries developed since the 1970s—for example, engineering, information technology, medical equipment—are largely capital intensive and foreign owned, another barrier to inclusive unionism and national bargaining (Hardiman, 1988, pp. 30ff., 38–41; and OECD, 1993a, p. 77). Despite episodic attempts to link national collective bargaining agreements to government tax policies and to widen the scope of bargaining in the 1970s, despite many memos in government offices, especially from the tripartite National Industrial and Economic Council in the 1960s and the Department of Planning and Development in the late 1970s sketching the possibilities and advantages of social partnership (Roche, 1982, pp. 60–64; Hardiman, 1988, pp. 47–52; and personal interviews), centralized, tripartite bargaining failed to take hold. Ireland, like Britain, lacks the inclusive labor unions and centralized labor federations as well as matching industrial structures and employer associations to sustain such efforts (Hardiman, 1988, pp. 128–138, 161–165, 178–182, 243). Dispersed, decentralized, and fragmented union structures pursue straight trade union objectives. By 1983 in this small country there were still 78 unions, many of them competing for jurisdiction and membership. Labour federations, like their employer counterparts, remain weak. Irish employers are as likely to deal with shop stewards as with full-time union officers. Throughout the postwar years neither side of the industrial battlefield has displayed much solidarity.

Beyond the usual Anglo-American fragmentation by occupation and firm, the Irish labor movement was further divided by the national question and by competition between Irish-based and British-based unions. These divisions, especially important in the formative stages of electoral mobilization, kept the labor movement distant from the Labour Party (*ibid.*, pp. 124–125); to this day they give the party system a cross-class character (Farrell, 1992, p. 390), where loyalties rooted in the Civil War overcome union or Labour Party loyalties.

In short, the structure and interaction of labor, management, political parties, and the government puts Ireland much closer to the political economies of the UK and the U.S. than to the democratic corporatism of Austria, Belgium, and the Netherlands or to the weak corporatism of Denmark. Ireland's electoral system, Catholic culture, and union strength, however, may account for the incipient corporatism of the 1970s—the failed efforts to forge a social contract.

CONCLUSION

By combining our three types of bargaining arrangements with data on the cumulative power of two types of mass-based parties that have persisted at least since 1920, Catholic and left—parties that carry their ideologies into power—I generated the types of political economy and country classifications in table 2.1. The types will be used in Part II to explain national differences in the public policies rich democracies have pursued since World War II, their patterns of taxing and spending, and in Part III, nontrivial system outputs such as political legitimacy, economic performance, equality, poverty, health and safety, and environment protection.

Throughout I work with the causal model in figure 2.1. The inverse of the policies and performance of corporatist democracies are the policies and performance of fragmented, decentralized political economies. In analysis connecting these variables I predicted that the scores by type would rank from high to low in this order: left-corporatist, left-Catholic corporatist, Catholic corporatist, corporatist-without-labor, and, the lowest scores on policy and output, least corporatist. With exceptions to be noted, this scheme works very well across a broad range of issues.

So far I have said little about either patterns of social and political participation that divide rich democracies or the rising influence of the media of mass communication and entertainment in politics and culture. To explain momentous national differences in participation and the impact of the media, we must turn to a third useful perspective—theories of the mass society. Chapter 3 summarizes these ideas and their empirical support and underscores the point that least-corporatist countries are most vulnerable to mass-society tendencies; most-corporatist countries, least vulnerable.

NOTES

This chapter draws on my *The 'New Corporatism,' Centralization, and The Welfare State* (1976a); "Leftism, Catholicism, and Democratic Corporatism" (1981c); "Political Legitimacy and Consensus (1983); an unpublished paper, "Paths of Development of Rich Democracies," presented at the University of Chicago Nov. 1–3, 1984; and my interviews. I am grateful to Gerhard Lehmbruch for critical comments.

1. Exceptions include Schmidt (1982) Schmitter (1981), Kriesi (1982); Katzenstein (1985a), and more recently the research of Wallerstein (1989), Wallerstein and Golden (1997), Stephens (1989), Huber and Stephens (1998), and Lange, Wallerstein, and Golden (1995). Although theorists of corporatist democracy (Philippe Schmitter, Gerhard Lehmbruch, Peter Katzenstein) or more generally of various types of bargaining structures are not addressing a new problem, they have done much to revitalize an older tradition in political science—that is, the analysis of the interaction of parties, interest groups, public bureaucracies, and political elites (see Gabriel Almond, *A Discipline Divided,* 1990, chap. 7 on the work of Ehrmann, Dahl, Rokkan, and others). They have begun the difficult task of cross-national comparison of the structure, functions, and behavior of trade associations and employer associations, professional associations, farm organizations, and labor federations.

2. As Golden, Wallerstein, and Lange (1999) show in their study of union density in 12 of our 19 rich democracies from 1950 to 1989, the most decline has occurred in France (31% to 10%), Japan (36% to 25%)—both corporatist without labor—and the U.S. (28% to 15%). But these are exceptions; there is no uniform pattern of decline even in the period since 1980. Over the four decades, most of the 12 experienced increases, then declined in union density; 7 of the 12 ended with about the same density or higher density than in 1950. Substantial increases occurred in Denmark, Finland, Norway, and Sweden. In only five—Austria, France, Italy, Japan, and the U.S.—did density decline more than 10 percentage points and in three of those (Austria, France, and Italy) union contracts extend to a great majority of nonunion employees. In 1990, in 8 of the 12 countries coverage was greater than 70%. In coverage, the laggards are the U.S., Japan, Canada, and the UK. Finally, if the issue is not union membership or contract coverage but the alleged decentralization of bargaining, the data show a convergence toward greater concentration of authority *within* confederations, but divergence in concentration *among* confederations, that is, no sign of universal decentralization. What decline we do see in union strength in the 1980s, the authors conclude, is more a product of sustained unemployment and occasional political assault, as in the UK and USA, than any institutional decay. Both unemployment and right-wing antiunion politics are reversible.

3. There is a wide variety of definitions in the literature on industrial policy; the term is often used broadly to refer to any government policies that affect industry (see Adams and Klein, 1983, chaps. 1 and 2 for a useful overview). I shall adopt a more restricted definition. By industrial policy I mean an organized and coherent set of policies designed to affect directly the structure of industry and thereby shape production and investment decisions. Industrial policy is concerned with adjustment, most often and increasingly to promote international competitiveness in the face of changing patterns of supply and demand. Included in this definition are sectoral policies to promote growth industries, manage declining industries, encourage research and development and the spread of advanced technology in industry, and promote competitiveness by encouraging mergers and/or domestic competition. Excluded are broad fiscal and monetary policies; labor-market and wage policies; health, safety, and environmental policies; and other policies which affect industry in a nonselective way (such as general tax breaks and investment incentives—sometimes called "horizontal industrial policies"). (See Wilensky and Turner, 1987, for discussion of industrial policy, incomes policy, and active labor-market policy and analysis of their effects.)

4. In the case of Texas, the changing market for oil was an added external factor in its boom and bust cycle.

5. More recent state industrial policies in the United States may not be purely "beggar thy neighbor." The Southern states that once pursued corporations in the North are now vigorously pursuing foreign investors from Great Britain, Germany, Japan, and Canada.

6. This section draws on my "Foreword" to Kramer (Wilensky, 1981d, pp. xvii–xix).

7. The Independent Sector estimated that while the number of U.S. volunteers was growing from 1995 to 1998, the average volunteer was putting in fewer hours—down from 4.5 to 3.5 hours/week. The greatest shortage was apparent in those agencies that require training and long-term commitments—suicide hot lines, programs for battered women, abused children, literacy, education, youth mentoring, and the like. (Daspin, 1999.)

8. Even though the assets and income of the upper fifth exploded in the 1980s and 1990s the percentage of personal income of the U.S. population given to charity declined from 2.2% in the mid-1960s to 1.9% in 1998 (*New York Times,* Sept. 27, 1998) while corporate giving to charities and nonprofits, reaching a high of 2.36% of pretax income in 1986, dropped to 1.0% by 1998 (*Wall Street Journal,* Nov. 18, 1999). Support for social and health services—programs that benefit the poor—declined the most. If we include the market value of volunteer time, however, we find a slight increase in the nonprofits' share of national income and total employment 1977–1996 (Steuerle and Hodgkinson, 1999, p. 78; Hodgkinson and Weitzman, 1984, pp. 2–7). Whatever measures we use, *both America's reliance on the nonprofit sector and that sector's reliance on government have increased since 1960.* This blurring of

public and private spheres is matched by the blurring of the line between nonprofits and commerce (Weisbrod, 1997, pp. 543ff.; on commercialization in the USA and UK see Ware, 1989, pp. 85–92).

9. Farm households in 11 OECD countries studied in Europe plus Japan, the U.S., and Canada reach incomes that are close to or higher than those of other households (Moreddu, 1995). With agricultural households at 2% of all households, the U.S. Dept. of Agriculture accounts for about a fifth of federal employees—another measure of the power of the farm lobby.

10. In the early 1990s three-fifths of the French nonprofit sector's revenue came from the government (Archambault, 1997, p. 125). Salamon (1999b, p. 338) estimates the public sector share of total nonprofit revenue 1995 for 12 of our rich democracies. France and Austria are in the middle. The eight corporatist democracies average 70% reliance on government; the four noncorporatist countries average 47%. (Without the Irish exception, 78%, the average is a low 36%.)

11. In the month of February 1981 alone the General Accounting Office of the USA—which accounts for only a small share of the evaluation research industry—issued 41 evaluation reports. The 1975 congressional sourcebook on federal program evaluations cites 1,700 evaluation reports issued by 18 executive branch agencies and the GAO during 1973–75 (Nachmias, 1980, p. 1164).

12. Because almost all of these programs were in place before the other policies were initiated, we used major expansion in aggregate social spending as a proxy for this analysis.

13. Huber and Stephens (1999, pp. 18–21) outline a series of such trade-offs that are possible for corporatist democracies facing the financial turmoil and economic constraints of the late 1990s. These go beyond the standard trade-offs already prominent in the bargaining patterns of the past (discussed earlier and in chaps. 12 and 17): for example, wage moderation in return for commitments to invest capital domestically; lower payroll taxes in return for domestic investment commitments; a modest widening of skill differentials to overcome the economic drag of radical wage compression (especially prevalent in Sweden) in return for skills training, job security, and so on (see chaps. 1 and 12). The net effect of such trade-offs is to increase private and public savings and investment and hence real economic growth.

14. This account is based on Golden, Lange, and Wallerstein (1993), Huber and Stevens (1998, 1999), Wallerstein and Golden (1997), Lange, Wallerstein, and Golden (1995), Hibbs and Locking (2000), Kurzer (1996), Ingebritsen (1996), Pontusson and Swenson (1996), Soskice (1999), Petersson (1991), Traxler (1995), Hans-Göran Myrdal (1991), Heclo and Madsen 1987, and my interviews.

15. After the 1982 devaluation, Swedish exports surged. To meet the demand for skilled workers, employers and unions in these booming industries and localities wanted to enrich the pay package to attract needed workers. But employers wanted flexibility on the way down when demand slackened rather than ratcheting the entire wage level upward. Central bargaining tended to impose restraint on the way up and rigidity on the way down. This is one among many reasons that several large firms decided that they would have more flexibility if they abandoned central bargaining.

16. Throughout my analysis of economic performance of 19 countries, I find that on average and over long periods center-left governments behave with more fiscal responsibility than right-wing governments, partly because they educate their constituents to the idea that taxes buy benefits and there is no free lunch.

17. For detailed analysis of these policy mistakes and the "what if" argument that Swedish corporatism would have eroded much less if both the policies and their timing had been somewhat modified, see Andrew Martin (1996) and Evelyne Huber and John Stephens (1999).

18. This account is based on Keizer (1996), Wolinetz (1985, 1989, 1990, 1993, 2001), Visser and Hemerijck (1997), Houska (1985), Kriesi (1993), Carson (1987), Lijphart (1968), and my interviews. I am grateful to Martijn van Velzen and Steven Wolinetz for critical readings.

19. *Verzuiling,* literally "columnization" or "pillarization," refers to the separate pillars (*zuilen*) of Dutch society, each indispensable in supporting the national structure. They are the major confessional-

political blocs—Calvinist, Roman Catholic, "general," socialist, and at times a latitudinarian Protestant bloc. Each has encompassed a whole array of organizations, including political parties, labor unions, industry groups, schools and universities, health and welfare agencies, radio and television corporations, and sports and leisure associations. Segmented at the bottom, they have been integrated at the top through national accommodations. (Chap. 3 analyzes how Verzuiling shapes the organization and impact of broadcast media.) Although this complex cultural-political system still exists, especially in education, it was plainly in decline as a structural basis for consensus from the mid-1960s through the 1980s—partly because of the rising rate of intermarriages discussed in chapter 1. In my judgment, however, this very long structural change is less important as an explanation for changes in industrial relations than the scope and depth of the economic crises of the early 1970s and 1980s.

20. Broader agreements were not abandoned, however. When the center-right Lubbers cabinet, in an effort to restructure public finance, suspended the automatic indexing of public-sector wages and benefits, it got management and labor to restrain private-sector wages. In return, labor was assured that the money so saved would be used to reduce working hours and create new jobs. Management got a cut in corporate taxes.

21. I am grateful to the late Val R. Lorwin and Arnold J. Heidenheimer for critical readings of an earlier, longer version of this section and to Timothy L. McDaniel for his creative contribution to the coding. The concepts and measures of party power, duration, and continuity are elaborated in Wilensky 1981c and in figure 2B.1 in appendix B. We first measured left party dominance and then used the identical procedure for gauging Catholic party dominance, producing a month-by-month government-by-government score for every left and every Catholic party in the 19 countries from 1919 through 1976 whenever competitive politics prevailed. A long concept and coding memo is not included here, but the complexities are mentioned below and are further summarized in Appendix B. Michael Wallerstein (1989) replicated, validated, and updated to the mid-1980s my coding of cumulative left power. Comparing his independent coding and mine, the only notable discrepancies concern Israel and the U.S.: I place Israel higher on left power because I date the inception of the state earlier; and I count the Democratic Party as left while he scores it zero. Party dominance is defined as a large amount of party power continuously exercised over a substantial period of time. We focus on three dimensions of dominance: (1) degree of control or influence left or Catholic parties have had in their countries' governments; (2) the number of times such parties have been thrown out; and (3) the total number of years of left or Catholic power. By keeping amount and continuity of power separate, we leave open the question of what counts most: the possession of power, however brief, or the continuity in office that permits program planning. By distinguishing between continuity as long duration and continuity as few interruptions of tenure, we can determine whether the sheer number of years in office is more important than security of tenure.

22. There are two partial exceptions to this pattern and one deviant case. In Germany, PR was introduced by the Social Democrats in 1919 after the abdication of Kaiser Wilhelm II (Carstairs, 1980, p. 164); in France it was the Conservatives and Socialists who advocated PR as a compromise with the dominant (more-or-less center-left) Radicals (Carstairs, 1980 p. 178; Goldey and Williams, 1983, p. 69). Ireland is deviant: it adopted a system of PR in 1920 but as yet has not developed corporatist-style bargaining arrangements. Irish exceptionalism is discussed later.

23. For instance, we find that in 9 of 13 corporatist democracies, the formation of employer associations soon followed the founding of one or more centralized labor-union confederations. These are Germany, Switzerland, Austria, France, Sweden, Norway, Italy, Finland, and Japan. In Denmark and Israel, employer associations and labor federations were founded in the same year. Only in the Netherlands were employer associations founded before their opposites. Belgium is ambiguous: although an employers' association (CCT) was formed almost 20 years before the Trade Union Com-

mittee (a socialist confederation), it functioned primarily as a trade association before World War I. In any case, when rival organizations interact over long periods both their structures and functions become more alike.

24. By 1986, 61% of Swedish workers were employed in firms employing 500 or more employees, a very high percentage compared to other EC countries (Olsen, 1996, p. 13). The figures: Sweden, 61; Netherlands, 41; France, 40; Germany, 36; EC average, 30.4; UK, 30; Denmark, 18.

25. Incidentally, in the regression analysis if we substitute the broader measure of trade dependence, we get almost the same results. Further, if for PR we substitute an index of "unrepresentativeness" which measures the difference between the two largest parties' share of votes in each election 1945–80 and their share of seats (Lijphart, 1984, pp. 161–165) we get the same results. They are highly correlated ($r = -.92$).

26. In this paucity of large enterprises, Ireland as a late industrializer is an exception to the rule that late industrializers like Germany, Austria, and Sweden tend toward industrial concentration. Lars Mjøset (1992) attributes Irish exceptionalism to its unique demographic pattern: in contrast to all other modern societies Ireland has not completed the demographic transition; unlike other rich Catholic countries it still has a high fertility rate and a paternalistic family structure. Explaining Ireland's lagging socioeconomic development, Mjøset postulates a vicious circle: a weak national system of innovation and a minimal manufacturing sector leading to a slow rate of rural modernization and the persistence of live cattle as the dominant export (to Britain), slow change in family structure, the emigration of people in their most productive years, population decline, high rates of poverty that reinforce continuing emigration and the high fertility rate of nonemigrants, a sluggish growth of the home market, weak industry-agriculture linkages, and, more recently, technical progress confined to the export sector with its unusual dependence on direct foreign investment, all of which perpetuates a weak national system of technological and economic innovation, the slow completion of the demographic transition, and so on.

3
MASS SOCIETY, PARTICIPATION, AND THE MASS MEDIA

Individualism is "a mature and calm feeling which disposes each member of the community to sever himself from the mass of his fellows and to draw apart with his family and friends; so that, after he has thus formed a little circle of his own, he willingly leaves society at large to itself. . . . Individualism . . . saps the virtue of public life."

Tocqueville, 1835

So far this book has used the language of social structure—political, economic, and social organization—to describe relatively stable patterns of interaction that persist through generations. These patterns are highly institutionalized, that is, publicly recognized and sanctioned in contracts, law, and custom. This is one face of modern society—so structured that we hardly recognize the social controls that make us rise in the morning, commute to work (more or less on time), establish families, and act out the roles of worker, spouse, parent, sibling, son and daughter, neighbor, and sometimes citizen. In contrast is the other face of modern society where behavior is unstructured and fluid, where we are torn loose from kin, friend, workplace, church, union, and voluntary association and are susceptible to fashion and fads in culture and leisure and are vulnerable to manipulation by the media in consumption and mass politics. It is here that mass-society theory is most relevant.

Mass-society theory is a general theory of modern society inspired by a vision of the breakdown of social order or democracy or both. From Tocqueville to Mannheim (1940) and other refugees from the Nazis, traditional mass-society theorists have concentrated on two problems: (1) the debilitation of culture-bearing elites (and of the core values they sustain) brought on by their diminishing insulation from popular pressures; and (2) the rise of the masses, who, for various reasons, are increasingly susceptible to demagogues and extremist movements, the carriers of fanatical faiths of race, religion, nation, and class. Although these scholars varied in their depiction of the generating forces, they tended to accent either the atrophy of primary and informal relations or the atrophy of self-governing secondary groups and associations.[1] They generally invoked the mobility, heterogeneity, and centralization of modern society as root causes. They also believed that the mass society develops a mass culture in which cultural and political values and beliefs tend to be homogeneous and fluid. In the middle and at the bottom—in the atomized mass—people think and feel alike; but thoughts and feelings, not being firmly anchored anywhere, are susceptible to fads and fashions. At the top, poorly organized elites, themselves mass-oriented, become political and managerial manipulators responding to short-run pressures; they fail to maintain standards and thereby encourage the spread of populism in politics, mass tastes in culture—in short, a "sovereignty of the unqualified" (see Selznick, 1951; Kornhauser, 1959; Wilensky, 1964a).

Empirically minded critics—a later generation studying a more industrialized society—countered with these propositions: Primary groups survive, even flourish. Urban-industrial populations have not stopped participating in voluntary associations, which in the United States and other rich democracies, continue to multiply. Moreover, in every society, whether pluralist or totalitarian, there are potent limits to the powers of the mass media, the big organizations, and the centralized state.[2]

Although I have long had doubts about the generalizability of mass-society theory and have given some credence to some of the critics' assertions (Wilensky and Lebeaux, 1958, chap. 5), I think that the questions it poses are fundamental for our understanding of the direction of social change and for the explanation of differences among equally modern societies. Among the most important questions:

- What *are* the trends in the rates of participation in primary groups? In self-governing, secondary associations—church, union, political party, and voluntary associations?

- What are the trends in the density of such organizations (number of organizations in relation to the population)? In their goals and missions?

- In the relation of leader to follower in these organizations?

- In the power and influence of the mass media of communication and entertainment?

- How do national variations in the density of organization and the vitality of participation in them affect mass alienation from or attachment to major institutions? Do the media have an impact independent of patterns of social participation? How do all these variations shape the prospects for social order and political democracy? The real welfare of people or system outputs?

In other words, under what conditions do various types of social relations—primary, informal, or secondary—effectively mediate between the person and the larger community and society, between the person and the state?

Unfortunately, before a discriminating typology of social relations and organizations focused on their integrative or disintegrative potential was developed, interest in mass-society theory waned. Discussions of corporatism have revived these classic questions to good effect. Indeed, political science has recently resurrected the theory under the labels "party decomposition" and "party decline" and in discussions of "civil society," giving proper weight to the atrophy of mediating associations and the ascendance of the media.

Often the data brought to bear on these problems are irrelevant to the concerns of mass-society theorists. The critics and the theorists are talking past one another. The data are mainly American; cross-national studies of these issues are rare. And good data on trends in the U.S., let alone systematic cross-national comparisons of trends among many modern societies, are both rare and limited. The data, while better than nothing, are mainly self-reports of membership and meeting attendance in voluntary associations with little effort to assess the vitality of such participation or its meaning for the person's ties to the larger communal life or national politics.

In the rest of this chapter I briefly review what seem to me the general conclusions of research on social participation in the U.S. and the very limited cross-national data on participation. Then I discuss the need for more relevant research on membership and participation in various types of associations and present hypotheses and some data about how different patterns of participation shape consensus and conflict. Finally, I describe trends in media content and style, suggest three explanations of the impact of the mass media in culture and politics, and explore national variations in that impact.

PARTICIPATION IN THE UNITED STATES: AMOUNT, TRENDS, AND EFFECTS

Primary Relations[3]

It is true, as we have seen earlier, that the family survives in modern urban areas, that some neighborhoods, especially those with an ethnic-religious-linguistic social base, still have a lively social life, and that relatives or friends are often contacted by phone and even occasionally seen. For instance, a 1955 Detroit Area Study showed that 54% of a cross section of family units reported seeing relations (not living in the same household) once or twice a week; that 75% got together with neighbors (aside from relatives) a few times a month or more; and that 55% got together with "other" friends (other than neighbors or relatives) at least a few times a month (Wilensky and Lebeaux, 1958, p. 122. Cf. Smith, Form, and Stone, 1954; Greer, 1956; Bell and Boat, 1957). Later studies that capture the effects of the deconcentration of urban population in suburbs and outlying areas confirm this picture. For instance, Claude Fischer (1982, pp. 372–373), using more stringent measures of participation in California samples—the percentage of interaction in the last three weeks in one or another relationship—arrives at similar conclusions about the persistence of primary-group life, although the percentages are lower than the self-reports of average frequency in the Detroit area.

The increased mobility of modern society does not necessarily disrupt these ties to kin, friend, and neighbor; in time, newcomers to the metropolis fit in as participators in primary-group life, if not the wider community; most of them also maintain older ties despite new jobs and residences and increased geographical distance (Wilensky and Lebeaux, 1958, pp. 123; Fischer, 1982, p. 87–88). "Spatial mobility makes for city-wide ties; stability makes for local area ties" (Smith, Form, and Stone, 1954, p. 284).

All these researchers on American urban life conclude that primary groups not only survive in modern society, but the informal controls of family, friends, and neighbors are effective over wide segments of the population.

That primary groups endure in modern society is no contradiction to mass-society theory. For the evidence also shows a long-term decline in the intensity and scope of extended kinship ties, a rise in nuclear family breakup, and a decline in time spent with close friends. There is no doubt that the proportion of all relationships that are "primary" diminishes with continuing industrialization. We can infer this from evidence already reviewed on the changing structure of households and trends in family breakup over the past century or so (see chap. 1) and from contemporary comparisons of the most-urbanized areas with less-urbanized and rural areas—even within one modern society where we would expect these differences to gradually disappear. The combination of urbanization and industrialization weakens ties to extended families; rural households interact with their kin (both nuclear family and relatives) more often and they give and receive more services from kin than modern urbanites do (Winch and Greer, 1968, pp. 41–42; Tsai and Sigelman, 1982, p. 583), although urbanites shed extended kin at a much greater rate than they drop nuclear kin (Fischer, 1982, pp. 83–84). Similarly, an unusual time-budget survey of married men who were full-time workers in the Nashville area (Reiss, 1959, p. 186) found that urbanism was related to less contact with "close" intimate friends. Comparing rural, rural nonfarm, and urban residents, Reiss concludes that urbanites had the least contact (and least time) with intimate friends and most time with the mass media—even holding socioeconomic status constant.

More important for the theory is what is missing from these data on primary groups—evidence of the quality of relationships and their effect on ties to the larger community and society. There are hints of their irrelevance. For instance, a study of the effect of five types of social participation (voluntary association, church, community, interaction with friends, interaction with neighbors) on voting concludes that participation in voluntary associations, churches, and community events each independently increases participation in national elections but that high rates of informal interaction with friends and neighbors have no effect on turnout (Olsen, 1972; cf. Rogers, Bultena, and Barb, 1975; Verba and Nie, 1972). Another hint comes from a study of class structure and friendships in the U.S., Canada, Sweden, and Norway. Despite large differences in social structure and culture, the rate and types of cross-class friendships are very similar across these countries (Wright and Cho, 1992). We can infer that similar friendship patterns cannot account for national differences in the types of political economy, social consensus, and politics described in chapter 2.

In general, these studies together suggest that a pattern of family-neighborhood local-ism is prevalent among perhaps a majority of urban residents of the U.S., that it has little or no effect on community or political participation unless it is meshed with participation in churches, unions, or voluntary associations. And most modern Americans have little or no off-work contact outside the immediate family; most of their daily routine off-work is spent with kin or television or both.[4]

Finally, we know little about the effect of the types of mobility characteristic of modern society on either the quality of social relations or political participation. Clearly, residential mobility reduces voting rates as we shall see in chapter 11 on party decline. But this is peculiar to the U.S., where complex registration rules are a barrier to voting (chap. 11, p. 415ff.). Regarding the effect of occupational mobility on social participation and national solidarity, in an effort to test mass-society theory I contrasted two types of mobility: first, orderly careers where jobs are hierarchically arranged and functionally related, in a more or less predictable pattern, as in the crafts and established professions, the civil service and the military; and, second, chaotic job patterns characteristic of the rest of the labor force, where mobility, whether up, down, or across, is chaotic in the sense that little can be predicted and jobs are unrelated in status and function.[5] I then related mobility types to a variety of measures of the frequency, stability, and range of participation in primary groups, churches, unions, and voluntary associations as well as ties to the wider community and society

(Wilensky, 1961a).[6] I found that the life plan afforded by orderly careers, whatever the social class, resulted in wider, stronger ties to the larger communal and political life. Conversely, chaotic experience in the labor market fosters a retreat from work, politics, and society.

Even among people blessed with an orderly career whose social participation appears intense and wide-ranging, there may be an increase in lightly held attachments. We do not know what portion of the most-modern, most-mobile executives and professionals in national and international labor markets pick up and drop spouses and friends the way they buy and trade cars, speeding up the obsolescence of both. If it is a small minority, is it growing? Does it extend to their participation in the mediating associations that foster civic engagement?

The rest of the book introduces measures of mobility and meritocracy where they are relevant—as we play convergence theory against types of political economy in explaining similarities and differences in family policy (chap. 7), the welfare mess (chap. 8), tax-welfare backlash (chap. 10), party decline (chap. 11), and mayhem (chap. 14). We will have to settle for crude measures because no cross-national data are available that tap the types of mobility already discussed.

Mediating Associations and Civic Engagement

The critics of traditional theories of urbanism or mass society invoke American survey data showing that voluntary associations and corporate groups other than work establishments are numerous and reach a majority of the population. For instance, in some modern urban areas, a majority of adults are members of a church or union as well as a work establishment. For me, the relevant findings or missing data are these:

• By the 1980s, between a quarter and half of all American adults had no affiliation with anything—no church, no union, no voluntary association (based on national surveys by Baumgartner and Walker, 1988; Veroff, Douvan, and Kulka, 1981).

• During the period 1977–88 fewer than half of adult Americans belonged to a church-affiliated group and/or a union (calculated from General Social Survey—hereafter GSS—data reported by Davis and Smith, 1989a for 10 of the years from 1974 to 1988).

• Beyond church and/or a labor union, near-majorities belong to no voluntary associations. (Many of these surveys fail to separate unions from churches or both from voluntary associations; hence the "and/or." Ideally, churches and unions would be analyzed separately from "voluntary associations," for membership in each is in some measure compulsory.) Repeated surveys of national cross sections for the period 1974–88 report that more than two in five American adults (an average of 43%) belonged to no voluntary associations other than a church and/or a union and that two-thirds did not belong to two or more associations beyond a church and/or a union. (Calculated from GSS, Davis and Smith, 1989a and 1989b.)

• The trend of secondary-group membership is down. For instance, the percentage of respondents in GSS surveys who said they were members of a church-affiliated group or a union or both dropped from a high of 52% in 1974 to a little over 40% in the mid-

1980s. More important, when we make even minimal participation a criterion of membership—"active work" defined broadly as "been a leader, helped organize a meeting, been an officer, *or given time or money*" (Davis and Smith, 1989b, p. 375)—the rate drops sharply: in 1987, only 28% of respondents were minimally active in either a church-affiliated group or a union.[7] The same downward drift in the percentage of the U.S. electorate doing campaign or party work or contributing money to a party or candidate was evident from the 1960s to the late 1980s (see chap. 11, p. 405).

• The trend in weekly attendance at religious services is down. Here we can compare the results of direct interviewer-guided survey questions used by Gallup and GSS (e.g., "How often do you attend religious services?" or "Did you attend church or synagogue in the last seven days?" etc.) with results from self-administered questionnaires and time-use diaries or questions designed to overcome overreporting (e.g., Monday questions with a list of yesterday's activities). Examining trends from 1950 to 1984, direct questions show that weekly attendance declined among Catholics (up from 63% in 1950 to a peak of 72% in 1959 and decline to a low of 52% in 1984) and among Jews (from a high of 32% in 1950 to 13%), while Protestants remained steady at about 40% (Hout and Greeley, 1987, p. 326). In contrast, and I think more accurately, self-administered questions and time-use items reveal a drop in religious attendance of about one-third 1965–66 to 1975 and an additional five percentage-point drop 1975 to 1992–94 among adults (Presser and Stinson, 1998, p. 142). Whatever the survey method, researchers agree that Catholics evidence the greatest postwar drop in religious attendance.[8] By the mid-1990s the national rate of weekly attendance over three decades had continuously dropped to about 1 in 4 (as opposed to the exaggerated 4 in 10 of the direct interviewer questions). In other words, the most churched nation among our 19 rich democracies has followed the general pattern—reduced religious participation in established denominations.[9]

• Perhaps the best national trend study of both membership and informal activity (from informal visiting to meeting attendance) is by Veroff, Douvan, and Kulka (1981). Based on two interview surveys 19 years apart, one in 1957, the other a replication in 1976, the authors conclude, "The 1976 sample visits less with family and friends, they belong to fewer organizations, including church, and they are less likely to be married. All of the superstructures for easy social access have diminished" (p. 526).[10] More recently, Robert Putnam (1995a, 1995b) has made the same case, using data from the GSS.

• There are hints of much instability of membership in voluntary associations, but we lack any systematic studies of participation careers. To assess mass-society theory we would need data not only on density of organizations in society—their birth, growth, decline, and death—but also on the individual's biography of affiliations. If memberships are lightly held, and turnover frequent, if the typical citizen is moving often from one organization to another, the quality of his or her involvement is doubtless affected. One early panel study of this phenomenon, based on a representative cross section of adults living in a midwestern plains state who were interviewed in detail in 1961 and 1965 about their organizational affiliations, however, provides a clue. In four short years two-thirds "changed their membership profile in one way or another; 25 percent experienced an increase in number of affiliations, and 28 percent an over-all loss. The remaining 12 percent added and dropped memberships without changing the number . . . to which they belonged" (Babchuk and Booth, 1969, p. 36).

The decline of involvement in unions, churches, and voluntary associations is given sharper meaning because it has occurred while education levels—the best predictor of participation—have climbed. (Cf. discussions of this point in Putnam, 1995a; and Verba, Schlozman, and Brady, 1995, pp. 71–74.) Thus the trend should have been up, not down.

Finally, for the majority of Americans who report membership in something (a church or a union or a voluntary association), for the one in four who say they participate in the most minimal ways (e.g., give any amount of money or time), we cannot conclude that their affiliations mean much for the larger communal life. For that we must examine the integrative potential of various patterns of participation and, equally important, trends in the types of organizations available for participation.

The Significance of Types of Association and Participation

Plainly, at the level of individual behavior, not all organizations, not all "meaningful participations" have the same impact on social consensus, civic engagement, and political legitimacy. The mere number and frequency of contacts, so prominent in the literature on social and political participation, cannot give us the range of *values, interests,* and *status levels* represented by the roles the citizen plays. It is possible to have many social ties at work and off work, all of which reinforce one another (a narrow range of participation, e.g., all in the family or a working-class neighborhood). Coal miners, like residents of a black ghetto, reinforce their social alienation by a narrow range of contact.[11] Consistent with this idea is recent experimental and survey research showing that intense primary-group ties prevent trust from developing beyond the confines of the group (Yamagishi, Cook, and Watabe, 1998).

Equally obvious, at the level of the nation-state, all independent self-governing organizations—so central as mediating forces in mass-society theory—cannot function equally well either as buffers against state coercion and manipulation or as bases for aggregating and expressing interests and facilitating accommodation among warring parties. As a structural base for social consensus and democracy, major political parties, churches, and unions are crucial: they embrace broad masses; they are relatively stable because they represent enduring divisions of values and interests; and they are great mixers of age grades, genders, ethnic groups, and classes. They clearly have an integrative edge over single-issue groups such as bird-watchers societies or antipornography protesters, or local service associations such as the Rotary Club, whose membership is more homogeneous and goals are more limited. Even within heterogeneous, mass-based organizations there are significant variations. Although American unions everywhere move toward multi-industrial, multicraft models and are therefore mixers of classes and occupational groups, their civic engagement potential is limited. As we have seen in discussion of types of political economy in chapter 2, local and national unions of the United States and United Kingdom, even where they are strong and well organized, have less integrative potential than more inclusive unions with tighter ties to a central labor federation characteristic of corporatist democracies. Finally, the churches in decline are the large, established, integrative denominations. Although good national or cross-national data are lacking, it is likely that the churches and new religious groups that are growing are sects, cults, and televangelists that create internal solidarity while reinforcing alienation from society.[12] These religious sects typically adopt an oppositional stance toward all established institutions and minimize their contact with outsiders, except when proselytizing (e.g., when "pro-life" groups picket family planning clinics). They remain marginal. They seldom facilitate the integration of their members into the wider community and society. Politically, they further the balkanization of U.S. politics (chap. 7 on family policy discusses the role of evangelical voters in elections; chap. 11 on party decline analyzes the ambiguous role of protest movements and parties in decline).

Nothing here is entirely new and everything is a matter of degree. Single-issue groups have always been active in the United States, from the abolitionists and the Ku Klux Klan to the suffragettes, from the temperance movement and the gun lobby to antiabortionists and gay rights activists. But where parties could once protect their leaders and members from such groups and exert pressure on them to reach accommodation, political leaders now stand exposed (Fiorina, 1980, pp. 40–42). Add a fragmented, decentralized labor movement and similar employer and professional associations, themselves exacerbating the parochial pressures, and you end up with a fluid, massified polity incapable of achieving sustained consensus, community solidarity, or effective implementation of policy. A final American tendency is indeed new: the multiplication of movements-without-members made possible by the marriage of computerized, targeted mailing lists and the celebrity obsession of the media (Wilensky, 1983, p. 55). Examples on the left include Nader's Raiders; examples on the right include Pat Robertson's Moral Majority and other televangelist preachers—all heavily dependent on mass marketing for their messages and their funds.[13] The typical nexus between leader and "member" in these organizations is an occasional $10 check triggered by a television appeal or a letter listing the latest sins of enemies of the cause.

Two American studies shed some light on these issues. One is a longitudinal study of the changing number, types, and missions of associations in Seattle from 1929 to 1979 (Lee et al., 1984); the other is a cross-sectional study of the effects of types of participation on ties to community and society, based on long interviews of 1,354 men aged 21–55 in the Detroit metropolitan area in 1960 (Wilensky, 1960, 1961a, 1966b). The Seattle study captures much of what concerns scholars who claim a decline in civil society or community. It presents rare data on the changing character of neighborhood organizations and participation in them for an entire urban area over 50 years. The authors use as a base a detailed survey and historical account of neighborhood groups in metropolitan Seattle in 1929 based on interviews, documents (including minutes of meetings), and an officer questionnaire. Then they replicated the original study in 1979 in the central city areas they could match to the 1929 account. They make a good case for the comparability of both neighborhoods and data. Their main conclusions illuminate the theme of community decline. First, the 1929 neighborhood associations were both social and political, and these two functions reinforced one another. Although these associations were often founded to obtain improvements in municipal services by political pressure, they almost always added a lively sociability to sustain members' interest. They sponsored pageants, flower shows, street carnivals, parades, potlucks, baby clinics, talent shows, glee clubs, dances, card parties, bazaars, picnics, rummage sales, educational and philanthropic programs, and youth groups. About a third of them constructed community clubhouses. In contrast, by 1979, four in five of their successors considered themselves primarily political; there was, in fact, a drastic decline in social activities. They concentrated instead on a narrow range of issues, typically a fight against changing land use (commercial establishments, a new airport) or resistance to invasion by the wrong kind of people.

The second major finding is a trend toward reduced citywide contact. In 1929 about three-fourths of all organizations within the Seattle city limits belonged to one of three areawide federations of clubs. They combined their local interests with other multipurpose associations and engaged in communitywide or at least areawide coalition building to enhance their political influence. In contrast, by 1979, only a third of the associations reported affiliation with one of the four federations available. An obvious reason is the emergence of a zero-sum mentality: if a property-owners' association is devoted, say, to resisting low-income housing, its success creates losers in another neighborhood—not a good basis for coalition building.

The third finding is that resident involvement in neighborhood organizations was more frequent and extensive in 1929 than in 1979: there are now fewer opportunities for social participation outside the formal framework of a meeting; the number of meetings per year is sharply down; and the proportion participating has declined. In short, the structure for participation is now less favorable and the shift from social-political to purely political—with single issues dominating the agenda—reduces the integrative potential of today's associations.

The Detroit Area Study focused on work, social participation, social integration, and politics (Wilensky, 1960, 1961a, 1966b). My attempt to measure the range and functions of participation and the strength of ties to community and nation uncovered patterns extending from the most common, family-neighborhood localism (often meshed with church involvement), to the least common, most wide-ranging pattern that encompasses both a lively primary-group life and wide-ranging associational involvement. Wide-ranging patterns, in fact, do tie the person to community and nation. But I could never settle the ambiguities in my findings as they bear on mass-society theory:

> What takes place in the economy and locality—work, consumption, and participation in formal associations—forms coherent styles of life, one of which I have come to label "Happy Good Citizen-Consumer." The style includes these pluralist-industrial traits: strong attachment to the community (supporting increased school taxes, contributing generously to churches and charity, thinking of the neighborhood as one's "real home," voting in elections); consumer enthusiasm (planning to buy or to replace many luxury possessions); optimism about national crises; a strong belief that distributive justice prevails (feeling that jobs are distributed fairly). It also involves long hours at gratifying work, little or no leisure malaise; wide-ranging, stable secondary ties and, to some extent, wide-ranging, stable primary ties—the very model of a modern pluralist citizen. But this benign pattern of work, consumption, and participation is independent of participation in and feelings about mass culture. And both happy good citizenry and the uses of the mass media are more or less independent of approaches to national politics—or at least go together in ways not anticipated in received theory. Thus, the good citizen-consumers tend to be unusually prone to personality voting (party-switching, ticket-splitting), dependent on the media for opinions on issues, susceptible to advertising and to mass

behavior generally (e.g., they score high on a measure of susceptibility to manipulation by the media in politics and consumption). Men who have confidence in the major institutions of American society distrust "TV and radio networks;" men who trust the media distrust other institutions. Finally, men whose social relations are stable tend to have fluid party loyalties. *To be socially integrated in America is to accept propaganda, advertising, and speedy obsolescence in consumption.* The fact is that those who fit the image of pluralist man in the pluralist society also fit the image of mass man in the mass society. Any accurate picture of the shape of modern society must accommodate these ambiguities. (Wilensky, 1964a, pp. 195–196)

This book continues that exploration cross-nationally. Data on individuals in one metropolis—however one tries to situate them in the groups and organizations they belong to and however hard one tries to embed them in analysis of big social trends—cannot substitute for systematic cross-national comparison focused on the institutions and organizations themselves.

Obviously, we lack such studies for the U.S. as a whole, let alone comparable data for other rich democracies. From my previous discussion of types of political economy (chap. 2), however, we can infer that the model of mass society is the inverse of the model of corporatist democracy. The more corporatist, the less massified. This scheme enables us to pinpoint countries most and least vulnerable to tendencies predicted by mass-society theory. For instance, the decline of political parties as consensus builders is not yet a universal trend among modern democracies. In fact, corporatist bargaining structures may reduce the rate of decline of political parties or even reverse the trend, as we shall see in chapter 11. In corporatist countries the constituency base for major parties and coalitions includes strong and relatively disciplined, coordinated unions, employer federations, farm organizations, and churches, whose relations to parties are tight and whose consultation with government bureaucracies is frequent and easy. In turn, the quasi-public associations find parties helpful in mobilizing support for peak bargains. Together both parties and economic power blocs help governing parties or coalitions to control the policy agenda, framing media content and containing single-issue groups and other particularistic pressures. In contrast, the more numerous, fragmented, and decentralized interest groups of least-corporatist democracies open the way for dominance by the media in symbiotic relation to single-issue movements and political demagogues, thereby hastening the decline of parties and the development of a mass society (Wilensky, 1983). In the absence of alternative conflict resolution mechanisms, lawyers and judges—as they try to redress injustice and uphold the law—also enter the vacuum, creating a pattern of adversary legalism and adding to political polarization (chaps. 12 and 15 present comparative data on the number and impact of lawyers in 19 countries).

The phrase "fragmented and decentralized" acquires added meaning from the patterns of participation I have reviewed for the U.S. The most viable and vigorous are, on average, profoundly local and parochial, while participation in and the strength of the broadest-based organizations—employer associations that encompass many industries and occupations; established churches that embrace several ethnic groups, age grades, and even social classes; unions and labor federations that also bring together people of different ages, gender, ethnicity, race, religion, and occupation; and national political parties that aggregate conflicting interests and mediate conflicting values—these great mixers are in decline (for national variation in party decline, see chap. 11). And there is good evidence that decreasing involvement in voluntary associations in the U.S. is strongly related to decreasing involvement in politics (Rosenstone and Hansen, 1993, p. 126).

In short, analysis so far suggests that more or less centralized corporatist democracies that include labor and have strong political parties are more participatory than decentralized and fragmented democracies.

CROSS-NATIONAL EVIDENCE ON PARTICIPATION

Confirming these observations are cross-sectional, cross-national data on membership in voluntary associations and on worker participation systems. While membership is not the same as active participation, studies that compare the two cross-nationally (Curtis, Grabb, and Baer, 1992, table 1; Olsen, 1974) show that if there is a high rate of membership in associations, there tends to be a high rate of active participation in them. Olsen also shows that either rate clearly predicts political behavior and attitudes in the same way. In fact, even one inactive membership is related to a wide range of political activity in the U.S., although it takes multiple inactive memberships to produce the same effect in Sweden (Olsen, 1974, pp. 18, 25–26).[14] In short, "mere" membership is far from trivial.

Table 3.1 summarizes many national surveys 1959–72 and two studies of formal arrangements for worker and union participation (e.g., works councils, codetermination), one centered on 1976; the other, the late 1980s. Based on these studies, I have assigned a general rank of high, medium, and low for each measure. Note that while Germany, Austria, and the Netherlands are between medium and low in membership, they have strong systems of worker participation; their general participation rate is above average. Conversely, the United States scores medium (ranks 7th of 12) in membership but is very weak in its worker participation patterns; its general rate is below average.

Considering both organizational membership and worker participation schemes, the most participatory countries are democratic corporatist with strong labor federations and/or works councils—Sweden, West Germany, Denmark, Norway, Belgium, and to a lesser extent Finland, Austria, and the Netherlands. The least participatory are corporatist-without-labor (France, Switzerland) or least corporatist (e.g., UK, USA, Ireland). We have no comparable data on Japan, New Zealand, and Israel.

Italy, at the bottom by all criteria, is the deviant case—somewhat corporatist but low in participation. The Stephenses (1982) suggest that formal provisions obscure informal practice in both Italy and Britain, where worker mobilization on the shop floor has been intense; but in my view such militancy is ephemeral and has, in fact, led to less participation and less power in the long run from the Hot Autumn of 1969 to 1990. The formal provisions capture the reality of worker participation schemes. A better explanation of the Italian case is its extreme regional disparities in economic and political development. If we disaggregated Italian data by regions, we would find huge differences in organizational participation as in everything else (Putnam, 1993).[15]

Finally, a recent analysis of "membership" in "political organizations" in 13 of our rich democracies in 1990–91 (Morales, 1998) confirms my argument that participation varies by type of political economy in the expected ways. This study was based on the World Values Survey. The organizations covered the range from "new" movement organizations (peace, feminist, environmental) to unions and political parties—any formal association that

TABLE 3.1 Participation of adult population in voluntary associations, including churches and unions (circa 1968)[a] and in workplace-based organizations (circa 1976)[b]

Cross-sectional national samples of adult population in voluntary associations							Household samples			Strength of worker participation systems[b]	
One or more membership claimed				Multiple membership claimed			One or more membership				
Rank order	Country	%	Gen. rank	Rank order	%	Gen. rank	Rank order	%	Gen. rank	Rank order	Gen. rank
1	Sweden	79-80[c]	H	1	45-47[c]	H	1	87	H	1	H
2	Norway	67-72[c]	H	2	27-38[c]	H	2	77	H	6	HM
3	Denmark	71	H	4	36	H				4	HM
4	Canada	64	M	4	36	H					
5	Finland	62-62[c]	M	6	26-25[c]	M				9	M
6	Australia	60	M	8	24	M	3	69	M		
7	United States	58	M	5	33	M				14	L
9	Austria	51	ML	10	14	L	4	63	ML	4	HM
9	Netherlands	51	ML	7	24+	M	5	62	ML	7	HM
10	United Kingdom	48	LM	9	17	L				8	M
11	W. Germany	44	LM	11	12	L				2	H
12	Italy	29	L	12	5	L				13	L
	Belgium									6	HM
	Switzerland									11	L
	France									10	L
	Ireland									12	L

[a]Cross-sectional national samples 1959−72 (median year is 1968). Source: Pestoff (1977), p. 65.

[b]Extent of worker participation in 13 countries based on formal provisions of the law and collective bargaining agreements in 1976—a detailed code for *degree* of workers' control (varying from mere communication via joint consultation to majority control), *range* (the number and importance of areas of decision in which workers participate), and *direction* (from defensive challenge of management decisions to positive initiation of decisions), and the *coverage* of the schemes. The resulting rank order (1 = High) is quite strongly correlated with degree of labor organization and with left power (Stephens and Stephens, 1982). The rank of the U.S. is mine. A more recent analysis of legal participation rights in EC countries (Turner, 1991) yields about the same rank order except that Denmark and the Netherlands, like Germany, have both codetermination and works councils and would rank a bit higher than they do in this table.

[c]Two surveys, different years.

pursues collective goods and tries to influence government decisions. Churches were excluded. Membership was defined loosely to include any time or money contributed as well as dues-paying membership. The participation rate is the percentage of the total population reporting participation in one or more political organizations.

If we divide the 13 countries in three categories—high (50% or more of the total population are members), medium (30−39%), and low (below 30%)—and apply the types of political economy described in chapter 2, we see the following national variations (my interpretations, not the author's):

1. Five of the six countries that combine left party power with corporatist bargaining arrangements including labor (all four Nordic countries plus the Netherlands) score very high in participation (Belgium, the exception, scores medium-low).

2.   Countries that are Catholic corporatist with little cumulative left power are either medium-low (West Germany) or low (Italy).

3.   The rest are noncorporatist and score medium-low (USA, UK, Canada) or low (Ireland) or are corporatist-without-labor and score low (France). Data show some increase in participation from 1981 to 1991 in all these countries except the UK, which remained stable. The increase was most marked in the Netherlands and Finland. But the rankings by type of political economy have not changed.

In other words, the road to broad political participation runs through inclusive labor movements that are integrated with both left parties and corporatist bargaining institutions. (See discussion of the interaction of mass-based political parties and type of political economy in chapter 2.)

The Rising Influence of the Media of Mass Communication and Entertainment[16]

Of all the alarms sounded by theorists of mass society, their observations about the impact of the mass media in politics and culture have the most contemporary relevance. In the 1930s and 1940s, it seemed obvious that Hitler's use of radio and the Goebbel's propaganda machine helped to consolidate the Nazi regime and that, among democracies, FDR's radio fireside chats reinforced his popularity. Broadcast propaganda was seen as persuasive, subtle, and omnipotent. Since then there have been recurrent claims that the mass media have become a dominant force shaping voting behavior, political orientations, legislative agendas, consumer tastes, and popular culture, not to mention high culture. Media managers and owners, social critics say, are the new power elite. To test these claims is to tackle both major themes in mass-society theory: the subversion of representative democracy by the increasing vulnerability of the masses to manipulation; and the debilitation of culture-bearing elites whose standards and values erode as mass pressures mount. If this sounds a bit abstract, think of a modern president or prime minister preoccupied with polls and focus groups, with campaign consultants and television sound bites, who shapes policy to fit measurements of shifting public moods. Or think of publishers, editors, and journalists in the mainstream press who ape radio and television talk shows—poisonous in content, hysterical in style— and announce "What else can we do? This stuff is out there."[17]

Beginning in the late 1940s and 1950s, empirically minded critics—academic researchers as well as audience researchers working for the media—cast doubt on the argument of the rising influence of the media. They framed their field of inquiry as "Who says what to whom with what effect" and carried out studies of the technical and social *organization and control of the media* (who), *media content* (what), *audience* (to whom), and *impact* (effects on the values, beliefs, attitudes, and behavior of the audience). By the mid-1960s something of a consensus developed. It took the form of a central finding in audience research that emphasized limitations on media impact: There is a *self-selection of exposure to mass media content corresponding to predisposition or prior belief.* Bernard Berelson captured much of this research in a few sentences. The nature of the audience—its social position, education, interests, attitudes, beliefs—determines what is seen or heard and how it is perceived and interpreted. The more strongly the audience feels about an issue or candidate, the less likely they will see or hear uncongenial communication. If they *do* see or hear uncongenial communication, those with strong interest or feeling will discount opposed views. In other words, *those who read or listen cannot be swayed because of prior conviction; those who can be swayed cannot be reached because of a lack of interest.* (My paraphrase of Berelson, 1961, p. 4.) Republicans listen to Republican propaganda; Democrats, to Democratic propaganda. The media, in short, are mirrors; they reflect and perhaps reinforce popular concerns.

In this literature, especially from 1940 to the early 1960s, the idea was often put in the form of the "two-step flow hypothesis." Media messages flow from the producer (newspaper, broadcast networks, movies, advertising agencies) to informal group leaders (in neighborhood, workplace, community organizations) to the citizen, consumer, and voter (Lazarsfeld, Berelson, and Gaudet, 1948 and subsequent voting behavior studies described in chap. 11; and Katz and Lazarsfeld, 1955 and subsequent studies of politics and consumption). Thus, the media are absorbed into local cultures; the mediating leaders and groups reinterpret the message, discount it, elaborate it, reinforce it. Although some of these pioneers in audience research noted that the media might have both a narcotizing function (increasing passive absorption of television and radio, reducing reading and conversation) and an enlightenment function (bringing new worlds to view), they overwhelmingly emphasized the limitations imposed by self-selection and the two-step flow, as well as low interest, inattention, the discounting of opposed messages, and the prominence of superficial viewing measured by failure to recall what is seen or heard (cf. Sears and Kosterman, 1987; Lazarsfeld and Merton, 1971).

Empirical Limits

The limitations of these ideas are both empirical and theoretical. Empirical data on the "media-as-mirrors" theme encounter three limitations: substantial segments of the audience do not fit the theme; self-selection varies by subject matter; and when there is sustained saturation coverage of an alleged scandal, crisis, or crime, all signals are off—the media can reach large audiences heterogeneous in political orientation, social class, ethnicity, and social life, often with substantial impact. First, the numerous tables that demonstrate a tendency toward self-selection—smokers avoiding anticancer messages, Democrats avoiding Republican messages—also show substantial minorities or even majorities exposing themselves to uncongenial messages. The differences between the predisposed and the disposed are typically in the range of only 10 to 30 percentage points. For instance, poll data show that while 72% of Republicans tuned into some of the media coverage of the Republican presidential nominating convention in 1996, 58% of Democrats and 61% of Independents also watched—a maximum self-selection edge of about 14 percentage points (*New York Times,* Aug. 20, 1996; cf. Klapper, 1960, pp. 64–65).

Second, even these early studies showed that the two-step flow worked quite well for advertising and consumer product choices where local, informal "opinion leaders" in the neighborhood or workplace often interpreted media output and guided their friends' taste in dress, hairstyles, movies, or soap. But the two-step flow was much less apparent in politics (Katz and Lazarsfeld, 1955, pp. 154 ff., 273–274, 333).

Chapter 11 reviews recent evidence that campaigns are increasingly media-driven; that obscene amounts of money in politics in the United States are overwhelmingly devoted to buying broadcast time; that attack ads and media negativism deepen cynicism, reduce voter turnout, and in close elections help the attacker; and that the media—anchorpersons, reporters, and commentators—and "experts" certified by the media shape political attitudes far more than other influences such as real events, the opposition party, a popular president, interest groups, courts, and members of the president's party (Page, Shapiro, and Dempsey, 1987; Page and Shapiro, 1992; Brody, 1991; Zaller and Hunt, 1994, 1995; and chap. 11 in this text).

The third limitation of the media-as-mirrors idea is the great expansion of inadvertent viewers of two kinds: television or radio audiences with minimal interest in politics who stumble into political ads or political messages sandwiched between sports events, the news, or entertainment programs; or, more recently, viewers who cannot or do not escape from saturation coverage of scandals, real or imaginary—from Watergate, a real constitutional crisis, to relentless pursuit of alleged presidential crimes centered on "Whitewater" (six years of scandal while three independent prosecutors successively found that there was no presidential involvement), "Filegate," and "Travelgate" (four years of scandalmongering before reluctant exoneration), and the sex-and-lies business (a year plus an unprecedented partisan impeachment proceeding aborted in the U.S. Senate).[18] Research has established that the least-informed people are the most dependent on television for news, including political information. The main reason: They have lower cognitive skills (measured by tests) and prefer to obtain news from TV because they find it difficult to cope with newspapers (Neuman, Just, and Crigler, 1992, p. 98). There is also evidence that the weakly predisposed or the apathetic can be moved one way or another by one-sided saturation coverage—again the inadvertent viewer. When little is known about candidates in a congressional race or the race is confusing, campaign expenditures, largely on broadcast media and mass mailings, are strongly related to the vote (Grush, McKeough, and Ahlering, 1978). Moreover, agenda-setting research has shown that the public's priorities are rooted in intense media coverage over an extended period; MacKuen (1981) showed that such coverage precedes a rise in public concern about race, campus unrest, the Vietnam War, and energy policy (cf. Funkhauser, 1973 on crime, Vietnam, and other issues in the 1960s; and Protess et al., 1991 on six case studies where adversarial investigative reporting shaped the priority, pace, or particularity of agenda items). And media-shaped public priorities in some measure do shape public-policy agendas (Spitzer, 1993). Because sensational saturation coverage is increasing, as we shall see later, the direct media embrace of inadvertent viewers is also increasing.

Theoretical Limits

These are crucial qualifications to minimal effects theories. First, *if limits on media power are mediating groups and subcultures, then everything depends on the vitality of these groups and the nature of participation in them.* As we have seen, these patterns of social and political participation vary substantially over time and nation. With an increasing percentage of the U.S. population having few or no memberships and little involvement in wider associations that go beyond kin and friends, we would expect a concomitant increase in direct media effects, filling a vacuum left by the decline in civic engagement. Even within the family, there is some tendency to use TV as a baby-sitter and to substitute the media for ordinary conversation. For majorities, media content is *not* reinterpreted and absorbed by groups and associations articulating counterimages and values. In fact, increasing amounts of media exposure approximate the definition of mass behavior—direct response to remote symbols and events, outside the ken or the competence of local groups. In other words, millions have no firm place to anchor an opinion, no vital culture through which to filter the media impact.

Second, whatever the limitations of media impact shown by short-run stimulus-response studies using surveys and laboratory experiments, *the long-run, cumulative exposure to print, radio, television, and now the Internet, very likely has a large and increasing effect.* The sheer arithmetic of television exposure alone is striking. In the U.S., where the mass media are most ubiquitous, the average TV set is on seven hours a day. By the age of 65, the average male viewer will have spent about nine years of his life watching TV; by the age of 18 the average child has spent about 20,000 hours in front of the set—more time than is spent in classrooms, churches, and all other educational and cultural activities combined. The average senior in high school has already seen about 18,000 murders on television and 350,000 commercials. (Figures from Comstock et al., 1978, p. 89; Minow and LaMay, 1995, pp. 27–28; Dominick, 1987, p. 509; and Roberts and Maccoby, 1985, pp. 569ff.)[19] Beyond television there are added hours spent with radio, newspapers, and magazines. Total exposure has clearly increased in the past 50 years.

Of course, this does not say anything about whether viewers are paying attention or what the effects are. During some of the time a television set is on, no one is in the room; or if they are in the room, the "viewers" are reading, talking, dancing, cooking, eating, doing the laundry, playing games, or daydreaming. On the other hand, much of the inattentiveness is carefully timed: water utilities report great surges of use during scheduled station breaks on the half hour in prime time. The degree to which inattentiveness limits media impact for large populations is unknown; the evidence is anecdotal.

Regarding the net effects of this gargantuan exposure to the media we must be cautious. If our problem is the debilitation of taste, we can take Edward Shils' brilliant analysis of popular culture as an early warning: "Brutal culture," as he puts it, has *always* been aggressive and cynical, pious and sacrilegious, distrustful of authority, preoccupied with violence (Shils, 1960). Or, if one's time perspective is only a century or two, one can note with F. R. Dulles (1940) that Americans learned to be fans and spectators from variety shows and sporting spectacles that reached a truly mass audience as early as the 1820s. And one would be hard put to claim that the shift from bearbaiting and cockfighting to televised football, baseball, or ritual wrestling is a decline in mass culture.

Nevertheless, I believe that our condition, if not markedly worse, is very different from what it was 50 or 100 years ago. Only a view of the United States that assumes it is frozen solid would deny that something new can come from 35 or 45 hours of weekly experience with television, radio, and the press. The tantalizing questions concern the net effect over the long pull. Some hints come from history and literary criticism. A careful reading of F. R. Dulles, *America Learns to Play* (1940), and Richard Hoggart, *The Uses of Literacy* (1957)—both of which are sensitive to continuities in popular culture—points to the likelihood of subtle shifts that escape our sample surveys. While local groups select and reinterpret values and beliefs communicated by the media, cumulative exposure over a couple of generations or so can transform these preexisting local sentiments. Hoggart tells us that the printed media are received by industrial workers in England in the context of a strong oral tradition. But he also tells us of changes in values which can be traced to the cumulative impact of the media from the turn of the century to the mid–1950s. A native *skep-*

ticism ("You got to take it with a grain of salt") has become *cynicism* ("It's all baloney"); while *tolerance* ("Everyone's entitled to his own opinion") has become the *open mind* ("One man's opinion is as good as another's"). Historical research focused on the long-run absorption of media into changing local cultures—Hoggart applied more systematically to more populations—would fill a gap in our picture of reality.

In the analysis of mass culture, the functions of cultural elites are often underplayed. Here, too, precise historical comparisons are difficult. Shils argues that little of what is wrong with our intellectuals and our high culture can be attributed to the media or the mass society—that the belief that cultural standards are threatened rests on a romantic conception of intellectual life in past centuries. The unintellectual preoccupations of political, economic, and even educational and scientific elites, the dependence of the artist on the uninformed layperson, the scarcity of talent all around—these have *always* meant that refined culture would be in danger.

The argument is difficult to counter. When I assert that the greatly expanded opportunity for playing to a mass audience diverts intellectuals who in times past might have stuck to their mission, Shils can assert that if Raymond Aron writes for the *New York Times,* his thought is not thereby corrupted, that Walter Lippmann's *Public Opinion* is not markedly better than his later *The Public Philosophy,* that not all intellectuals waste their talents. Unfortunately, we cannot know what the quality of Aron's or Lippmann's thought would have been if as young men they had been watching "situation comedies" instead of reading books. Or what their output would have been if they were regular stars on American-style TV talk shows.

To invoke some standard of quality appropriate to each genre within television, radio, film, and print is *not* to express an elitist, snobbish contempt for popular culture. My bias is that of Gilbert Seldes' *Seven Lively Arts*—sympathetic to the media but concerned with quality. In my study of the interaction of high culture and mass culture (Wilensky, 1964a), I argued that the product does not have to be aggressively educative to get by as highbrow and that much of refined culture has, in fact, had mass appeal. But if it is drama, the contrast is *Playhouse 90* or *Upstairs, Downstairs* vs. the most stereotypical detective, western, and adventure shows. If it is investigative journalism, it is the *Washington Post* and *New York Times* of the Nixon conspiracies vs. the lazy, creative scandalmongering by the same prestigious newspapers during the Clinton administration. The most useful definition that distinguishes high culture from mass culture is one that emphasizes the social context of production, not the size of the audience. High culture is created by or under the supervision of a cultural elite operating within some aesthetic, literary, or scientific tradition; and critical standards independent of the consumption of the product are systematically applied to it. Mass culture refers to products manufactured solely for a mass market (Wilensky, 1964a, pp. 175–176). Clearly, high culture, whether it is confined to small audiences (avant-garde jazz) or embraces mass audiences (a Shakespeare play, a Chaplin film), is profoundly "elitist" in the sense that its practitioners, like those in professional sports, are judged by the merit of their performance.

If we concede that cultural elites everywhere are slowly losing their autonomy and their sense of intellectual community, and that we have come to a thorough interpenetration of highbrow, middlebrow, and lowbrow culture, unique to our time (*ibid.*, 1964a), then we must give attention to the structural facts that account for these trends. Shils lists some of them himself: for intellectuals and demi-intellectuals, *large numbers, spatial scattering, professional specialization;* for the general population, *mass media, mass literacy,* and long-run *income equalization.* These are all in some measure structural requisites or consequences of economic growth. They imply that opportunity in all advanced countries will continue to free up while colleges and secondary schools and, above all, the mainstream media will level down.

It is not so much that these trends debase the masses as it is that they make it more difficult to sustain the standards of cultural elites. If you want to argue the decline of civilization in rich democracies, do not invoke the middle three-fifths, the average citizen who has experienced an extraordinary post–World War II climb in her standard of living, her housing and health, her educational and occupational opportunities. Look instead to the privileged and powerful professionals, executives, civil servants, top officials, and top politicians and assess *their* behavior and values. The descent to the distant depths in culture and politics occurs only when these elites fail to articulate core values, only when they abandon their responsibilities to set high standards, to enlighten and lead. Such a descent occurs only when powerful politicians fail to observe decent restraints in their campaigns for office and when governing, fail to define and protect the public interest.

So far, I have suggested that where there is a decline in the vitality of social participation and civic involvement and where there is an increase in cumulative exposure over the long run, the media have a large and increasing impact on culture and politics; that the media contribute to subtle shifts in values and beliefs; and that cultural elites who could set high standards increasingly abandon the attempt. All these trends open the way for the direct reach of television, radio, film, and press.

Media impact varies in two additional ways that again suggest increasing influence. Media effects vary by (1) subject matter—the nature of the issue or the problem covered—and (2) type of medium and the quality of education of the audience. Assuming a lively local community life, when do groups and associations offer a stable guide and when do they not? Both logic and the literature suggest that media impact is limited on two types of issues: issues that are local, in the sense that almost everyone experiences the problem or knows someone who does, and issues that are concrete or nontechnical. Thus, for the political economy close to home—local unemployment, prices at the store, drug problems, access to health care—local experience provides a guide; and if media programming contradicts that experience, it is often discounted. For instance, an early study of media influences on public perceptions of social problems compared three versions of reality—a content analysis of media news accounts in newspapers and 501 half-hour broadcasts over an 18-month period; official agency records of the prevalence of 10 social problems; and a survey of the local population's perception of the prevalence of each problem (Hubbard, DeFleur, and DeFleur, 1975). The rank order of citizens' concerns (their idea of the relative importance of problems) and the rates computed by agency records yielded an almost identical rank order. But there was no relation of either community views or official records to the media emphasis on crime, transportation mishaps, and discrimination. The citizens instead accented unemployment, juvenile delinquency, and alcoholism (although they ranked crime fairly high). In other words, where they had local experience, they ignored the media. (Consistent results appear in Gamson, 1992; and Neuman, Just, and Crigler, 1992.) In contrast are more distant or abstract issues such as Star Wars or SDI, nuclear power, the Arab-Israeli conflict, or antiapartheid uprisings in Johannesburg. Here the media have maximum impact in constructing reality.[20]

Regarding technical issues: Media versions of reality strongly shape public images and even elite images of the size, trend, causes, and consequences of budget imbalances, unemployment, or economic growth, the economic and social effects of various health-care reforms, miscellaneous regulations and deregulations, environmental threats, the welfare state, and a host of other crucial issues of public policy—practically everything in this book (see Parts II and III). As the public sector grows, as the public agenda proliferates, these complex technical issues are frequently beyond the understanding of citizens, unless they are involved in broader associations that do a good job of issue interpretation. In fact, such issues are often beyond the grasp of all but the most conscientious investigative journalists whose editors give them months to work on a story. In short, on an increasing number of major issues neither local groups nor larger associations provide a buffer between the individual and the media.

Finally, media effects vary by medium—print vs. broadcast, major networks vs. cable, radio vs. television, the mainstream press vs. tabloids—and the education of the audience, although these differences are rapidly diminishing. There was a time when one could see sharp contrasts. The prestige newspapers reported news in the old-fashioned manner—accenting who, what, where, when, and why—while the tabloid press published gossip, rumor, paranoid plots. Television and to some extent radio were the media of intimacy, immediacy, and dramatic impact, bringing major world and national crises into your living room—from Vietnam to the Gulf War, from the civil rights movement to the Nixon impeachment proceedings to assorted terrorist bombings—while the print media, in contrast, could allocate time for checking facts and space for at least some thoughtful if not balanced interpretation. Radio could supply specialized music, classical and jazz as well as pop, brief newscasts, and local coverage while the television networks could concentrate on entertainment separate from national and international news, and both radio and television could cover sports and the weather and offer daytime soap operas. In the 1950s the networks also hired some of the best writers and producers in the country and gave mass audiences 90-minute televised dramas of high quality, comparable to those of the BBC. Finally, in the 1950s and early 1960s the celebrity cult had not yet come to dominate news organizations and the airwaves. By the 1970s, however, a shift toward a massive interpenetration of media content and style had begun. Local radio and television stations adopted a news format almost exclusively devoted to mayhem. National network news, too, moved toward more reports of violence-crime-sex-disasters. Within one generation, talk shows on both radio and television, national as well as local, became the medium of negative passion. There are now 8,000 such shows, most of them serving a steady diet of hatred for the government and other established institutions, with echoes on the Internet. Politicians, civil servants, judges, the professions, business executives—all are pictured as conspirators, corrupt to the core, either crafty manipulators or incompetent buffoons. Starting out as media of personal advice and entertainment, talk radio and television became political and ideological—celebrity journalists driving an agenda.

The interpenetration of the media at the production level has been paralleled by a half century of interpenetration of "brow" levels as the consumption habits of both mass audiences and educated elites moved away from print and toward electronic media and their program tastes converged. We can infer this trend from three types of evidence. First, scattered evidence indicates that the broadcast media in competition with print generally win out—in attraction, number of hours, perhaps persuasiveness, too. Reading of books, magazines, and newspapers declines. (Coffin, 1955, p. 633; Bogart, 1958, pp. 133ff.; Klapper, 1960, pp. 107ff.; Mosel, 1963; and J. P. Robinson, 1980.) Second, among the educated, total exposure to broadcast media has increased. Before television, radio listening among set owners averaged 4.9 hours daily; evening listening averaged 2.6 hours for all, 2.4 for college graduates. Program preferences did not vary much by education. Today, even excluding highbrow FM, radio listening has not declined to zero. (By the late 1950s the typical family that had acquired a television set cut radio listening from four or five hours to about two hours a day [Bogart, 1958, p. 114].) Meanwhile, television viewing for the average product of a graduate or professional school rose from zero to three hours daily (Steiner, 1963, p. 75). If we assume no major increase in the workweek of the educated, and no change in lifestyle that can remotely touch television in sheer hours, their exposure to undifferentiated broadcast media has risen as a portion of the daily round while their exposure to serious print has declined. Finally, direct evidence shows that the media habits of educated elites are not very different from those of the less educated (Wilensky, 1964a, pp. 190–194; Steiner, 1963, pp. 75, 161; Comstock et al., 1978, pp. 88–89, 94; and J. P. Robinson, 1977). In my study of the leisure styles of 1,354 men in the Detroit metropolitan area, ranging from professors, lawyers, and executives to unemployed underdogs, black and white, and covering the quality of books, magazines, newspapers, and TV to which they are exposed, I found that as early as 1960, the edge of the educated in cultivating high-quality material was amazingly slim. For instance,

> if we take interest in political news as a clue to wider perspectives, the most privileged, well educated firm lawyers have only a 10 percent edge over the middle mass and engineers are about the same as lower white-collar workers. In his interest in world news, the solo lawyer has only a 7 percent edge over the younger blue-collar worker. The differences in the proportion of diverse groups who rank local news as important to them in their daily reading are similarly small. Even more uniform from group to group are media habits tapped by more subtle measures of involvement with mass culture . . . being a loyal rooter for sports teams, rating comics as an important daily experience, becoming deeply involved with media heroes. And, when we come to television, at least in America, the constraint of structural differentiation seems doomed; uniformity of behavior and taste is the main story. Nowhere else has a "class" audience been so swiftly transformed into a "mass" audience. (Wilensky, 1964a, p. 191)

Education has a lot more to do with how people feel about TV than what they do with it. College graduates criticize TV programming, but they choose to watch extensively, and in doing so, find themselves in Mr. Minow's wasteland, unable, because of the limited highbrow fare available, to exert much more selectivity than the general population. They clearly display more signs of guilt and uneasiness at this state of affairs, but apparently it's not so punishing that it makes them flick the dial to "off" (*ibid.*, p. 193).

Perhaps the most telling demonstration of the interpenetration of brow levels, not merely in television viewing but also in reading, comes from these Detroit area samples. I found the following:

> Most of those who read at least one high-brow magazine, also read middle- or low-brow magazines. Only 3 percent of all these men read only high-brow magazines. How about books? Among college-educated professionals, only one in four claimed to have read a high-brow book in two months. Only about three in five of the professors and lawyers, the most highly educated, entirely avoid low-brow TV favorites. The typical professor crosses one or two levels of TV exposure. The engineers and executives, middle mass, and the underdogs on relief are quite similar in their TV-viewing habits. Television again, appears to be a powerful force for cultural standardization. (*ibid.*, pp. 193 – 194)

In short, the department chief at GM, the firstline supervisor, and the unemployed auto-worker on welfare are bound together in the common culture of Dan Rather, *60 Minutes*, The Pepsi Generation, and *Larry King Live*.[21]

There is every reason to suppose that this long-term trend toward cultural standardization on the level of mass culture has continued since the 1960s (Comstock et al., 1978, pp. 88 – 89). Again, those with privileged education were moving down while the masses were probably moving slightly up.[22]

News, Entertainment, and Politics

Recent studies of trends in media content confirm the theme of the interpenetration of the media, a gradual reduction of differences between television, radio, newspapers, and big circulation magazines, as they all drift toward talk-show style. Research also provides clues to the direction of media influence. Briefly, over time the media have become aggressively interpretive, negative, afactual, sensational, self-referential, and anti-institutional. Studies of media content unequivocally show a long-term trend toward the negative portrayal of politicians. For instance, in the early 1960s less than a third of the media evaluative references to political leaders were unfavorable (even during the Vietnam War). In the 1980s nearly two-thirds were (Patterson, 1993a, p. 20). Vietnam and Nixon's Watergate merely marked the beginning of this negativism; the escalation of media hostility continued into the 1980s and 1990s. (See Lichter and Amundson, 1994, pp. 137 – 139, on television networks; Parker, 1994, on broadcast vs. print; Zaller and Hunt, 1995, p. 104, on *Time* and *Newsweek;* and Hibbing and Theiss-Morse, 1996a and 1998, on styles of negativism of broadcast vs. print.) This negativism is indiscriminate; it is directed equally at Democrats and Republicans. Underdog candidates of a third party may receive a momentary buildup by television if they are sufficiently demagogic or entertaining—Ross Perot, David Duke, and Pat Buchanan—but they are typically brought down by the same media that gave them the underdog treatment with free time and space. Does this mean that there is no political bias of television, no political direction?

Inferring effects from trends in content is difficult. A subtle attempt by Michael J. Robinson (1977, 1976) underscores both the likely political direction of television and the different biases of "entertainment" and "information" from 1956 to 1976. During that transformative period the percentage of people relying solely on television for information about national campaigns doubled, and programs changed drastically. Combining mass attitude surveys with analysis of content of prime-time television, Robinson concludes that TV journalism generally increased its anti-institutional content and effect, while prime-time entertainment became politically "relevant" with a liberal-left impact. Under television's relentlessly negative portrayal of events, the civic culture of optimism, idealism, rationalism, and nationalism was gradually giving way to an anticivic culture of distrust, a sense of political inefficacy, "cynicism, pessimism, alienation . . . , the increasing concern with law and order and the 'social issue' and the growing fascination with 'backlash' politics"—as in the coverage of protest candidates such as George Wallace (1977, p. 27). Robinson makes a good case that the events at the root of this—the Vietnam War; the assassinations of President Kennedy, Martin Luther King, and Robert Kennedy; violence at the 1968 Democratic Convention; urban insurrection—cannot explain the strong connection between the political orientations of people and their reliance on television. Those relying only on television for their news embraced an anticivic culture much more than those who did not rely at all on television, while those with partial reliance on television were in between—even holding education constant.

While the news media were moving the civic culture toward indiscriminate negativism, television entertainment was moving in a different direction. Both the content and likely impact of prime-time entertainment was to raise the consciousness of the audience regarding war, racism, gender equality, and assorted social-moral issues—such as divorce, feminism, premarital sex, and gay rights. Liberals liked this; others sneered at "radical chic"; and evangelical citizens were deeply offended by it. By 1968, politically relevant variety shows (*Laugh-In, The Smothers Brothers*) had opened television to these themes, and the next year situation-comedy spin-offs with similar messages began their proliferation and climbed to top Nielson ratings (Norman Lear and his colleagues' *All in the Family, Maude,* and *The Jeffersons* as well as less political but more socially relevant programs with indirect effects such as *The Mary Tyler Moore Show,* and *Rhoda*).[23] By 1972, 5 of the top 10 programs could be labeled "establishment liberal" or "establishment swinger" (M. J. Robinson 1977, pp. 32–33). Later *Roseanne* (the new *All in the Family*) and *Murphy Brown* (a single woman "living in sin" and having a child) continued in this vein. (Chap. 7 analyzes the politics of family policy cross-nationally.)

In short, the network news programs were directly reinforcing the populist right view of government, politicians, and established authority, while entertainment television was indirectly legitimizing the liberal view of social-moral issues. The countermobilization of the Christian right in the 1980s and 1990s was partly a product of this media shift. This religious-political protest movement merged with the Republican Party; it took inspiration from the antigovernment din of the news media and found a voting base among evangelicals and fundamentalists enraged by what they saw as the spread of moral rot in TV entertainment (see chaps. 7 on family policy, 10 on backlash, and 11 on party decline).[24]

If there is any remaining difference between the negativism of the broadcast media and the negativism of the print media, it is this: the former has become the medium of poisonous politics while the latter has become the medium of disapproval politics. People who rely mainly on television or radio for their views about Congress say they are angry and disgusted with Congress; people who rely on print media say they disapprove of the job Congress is doing (Hibbing and Theiss-Morse, 1996b). The convergence toward broadcast content among the print media means that mere disapproval is giving way to belligerence. Both broadcast and print are moving toward the talk-show model. Within the print category, the prestige newspapers and mass circulation magazines are following close behind (Mann and Ornstein, 1994, p. 8; Fallows, 1996, passim.; Parker, 1994, p. 160 and passim.).[25]

The results of the media's pervasive negativism and aggressively interpretive "news" are evident in congressional and presidential elections. For at least two decades, the broadcast media and to a lesser extent print media have been downsizing political news and public-policy reporting. The networks have been less and less willing to cover statements and speeches by officials, from the president to cabinet secretaries to senators and representatives. If speeches are not ignored, they are clipped into progressively shorter sound bites. Driven by ratings and the bottom line, the TV networks have cut the number of Washington TV news correspondents, editors, and producers; they manage the evening news from New York by spicing it up with a heavy dose of conflict, gossip, and celebrity comments (Kimball, 1994). Further, where the networks once embraced gavel-to-gavel coverage of the quadrennial presidential nominating conventions, they now sharply reduce total time, and what time they allocate is increasingly devoted to their negative coverage of candidates (Jamieson, 1996). More important, during presidential primary campaigns, coverage has become not only negative, but increasingly self-referential. For instance, according to the Center for Media and Public Affairs, during the first three months of the 1996 Republican primary season, reporters in the evening network news shows had six times as much airtime as the candidates they were covering. Free time for the presidential nominees also dwindled. The average sound bite had already gone down from 42 seconds in 1968 to below 10 seconds in 1988 (Adatto, 1993, pp. 2, 177, n. 1); it compressed to 7 seconds in 1996 (Baum and Kernell, 1999, p. 99).[26] Talking candidates have been replaced by talking reporters and anchorpersons.

Faced with a virtual news blackout of their own voices and positions, and confronting a barrage of critical commentary passing as news, candidates are forced to buy time and frame their messages to get a little free time, hoping for echoes in newspapers and magazines. Campaigns are now almost totally driven by the goal of access to television. In addition to the escalating costs of television advertising there are related costs of tracking polls, focus groups, dial groups, "wave fronts," and digital-TV editing machines. (*Wall Street Journal,* Jan. 10, 1994.) Candidates must raise huge sums to pay for all this. Although longer in duration, campaigns are faster and meaner, a reflection of both rising partisanship and the negativism of the media. A study of 34 Senate campaigns in 1992 showed that over half the voting age population lived in states with negative campaigns (Ansolabehere and Iyengar, 1995, pp. 106–107). Ads that are confined to attacking opponents are now common; many of them either grossly distort the record of opponents or assassinate their character. Newspapers and television eagerly cover these ads as news, especially the more extreme ads, giving them even more visibility. Even when newspapers try to act as referees, suggesting the most and least accurate parts of the TV attack ads, viewers absorb not the journalists' skepticism but the very messages from which the reporters are trying to protect them (*ibid.,* pp. 133–142).

The effects of media domination of political campaigns are dramatically illustrated by the 1994 race for the U.S. Senate seat in California between the incumbent Dianne Feinstein, a moderate Democrat, and her challenger, Michael Huffington, an unknown about whom veteran observers of California politics said, "He gave empty suits a bad name."

Huffington, independently wealthy, amassed an all-time record senatorial campaign budget of $29 million, almost all spent on a barrage of television and radio attack ads. He drove Senator Feinstein's negative ratings from very low to over 50% and came within a hair of winning the seat. The campaign launched his wife, Ariana, as a favorite on TV-trash talk shows, a Beltway media star, a confidante of House Speaker Newt Gingrich, and a syndicated columnist.[27]

Some observers of the 1998 congressional election suggest that it showed that media manipulation and the politics of personal destruction had reached their limits, that "the 24-hour news cycle, instant Internet gossip, Beltway spin, saturation coverage of leaked raw testimony [as Imperial Prosecutor Starr exposed President Clinton's sex life], one-source journalism and weeks of nonstop attack ads did not breach the public's defenses against manipulation, whether by political consultants or Beltway commentators" (Popkin, 1998). This overlooks the cumulative effects: It has been well demonstrated, for instance, that attack ads in campaigns increase cynicism and lower turnout (Ansolabehere et al., 1994). And the 1998 election saw the lowest national off-year turnout since 1942—36%. It is not too great a leap to suggest that relentless scandalmongering by politicians interacting with attack-dog journalists, and the marketing of undifferentiated crises over decades, create propaganditis—the widespread and intense distrust of the media and eventually of all the institutions attacked. Propaganditis is not thoughtful propaganda analysis that insulates the citizen from political manipulation. In fact, mass cynicism and generalized distrust open the way for demagogues to use the distrust to direct voters toward ends of which they are unaware, the very definition of manipulation; propaganditis tears them loose from parties and other guiding institutions. The plebiscatory rampage of California in the past 20 years is the archetype of this development (see discussion of initiatives, referenda, and turnout in chap. 11).

The very people who tell survey interviewers that they hate the media for airing nonstop scandals account for sharp and sustained increases in television ratings whenever broadcasters market sensational "news" as entertainment. Ratings soared for saturation coverage of the O. J. Simpson murder trial and the Clinton-Lewinsky sex scandal alike—and in both cases long-hours viewers compulsively glued to the screen for many months told pollsters "Enough already."

EXPLAINING MEDIA CONTENT AND STYLE

Why do the media do what they do? Where do media managers get their predispositions? Each of three theories captures part of the explanation: an economic determinist theory accenting big business domination; a theory that emphasizes the organizational and occupational contingencies that shape media content; and a theory that accents country-specific regulations and financing. In my view the first explains less than the other two. What media content is consistent with each of these theories?

Big-Business Domination

Several analysts of modern media, including neo-Marxists such as Habermas and Gramsci and non-Marxists who merely accent economic-technological determinants (Lindblom, 1977; Bagdikian, 1997), emphasize that the media themselves are big business. In the United States they point to the increasing concentration of control evident in an increase in one-newspaper cities and interlocking corporate ownership (Disney owns Capital Cities/ABC, Westinghouse owns CBS, GE owns NBC, NBC owns a nonstop scandalmongering TV cable network MSNBC, the *Washington Post* owns *Newsweek,* Warner Communications owns *Time,* and the Gannet chain owns nearly two dozen TV and radio stations and 90-plus newspapers [Fallows, 1996, pp. 67–73; Bagdikian, 1997, pp. xv, 4, 18, 24].) They note that advertising is crucial to media survival and assume that business interests and values therefore dominate media content. The privileged position of business in government and politics, they say, means that business is not merely another interest group; it inevitably dominates modern political economies because of its unique indispensability, its control over technology, the organization of work, the location of industry, market structure, resource allocation, and what is to be produced in what quantities. Everyone's standard of living is in their hands. All of these business decisions are therefore strongly resistant to government control or to other countervailing democratic forces. Politicians are much more receptive to business pressure than to any other; the most powerful among them, left or right, always seek to gain the confidence of the business and financial communities. Consequently, business enjoys not only extraordinary sources of funds and organizations at the ready, but also special access to government. (Lindblom, 1977, pp. 170–188.)

Gramsci (1971, especially pp. 210–277), Habermas (1976), and Lindblom (1977) believe that these tendencies are common to all market-oriented ("capitalist") democracies. Reinforcing the inevitable economic domination of business, these scholars further argue, is the "cultural hegemony" of business—indirect control exerted through schools, colleges, and the mass media. By persuasion and manipulation, by identifying private enterprise with liberty and political democracy, business conditions the values and beliefs of the masses to serve business ends.

In short, from big business prestige and power these scholars infer the content of print media, broadcast media, and film alike, and from content they infer effects.

Leaving aside the obvious limitations of this view across time and space, to which the national variations in politics and public policy in this book will attest, we can surely find some media content that fits an economic determinist argument. But the commercial broadcast media evidence more direct influence than the print media. Newspapers have typically kept their advertising departments separate from their editorial departments, while advertising agencies hired by business choose and shape television, radio, and Internet programs directly. As broadcast media edged out print, there has been a major shift in power toward the electronic media, most vulnerable to business interests. Nevertheless, where there is an important local business or industry that dominates employment, the papers may pull their punches. When writing about government, no holds are barred; when writing about local industry, editors show caution (*Wall Street Journal,* Feb. 6, 1992). For example, editor John Perry of a suburban Seattle daily, the *Bellevue Journal-American,* fired his business editor in a dispute over how much coverage to give labor problems at Nordstrom, a big retailer that had recently sharply increased its advertising. Banking crises are widely known among editors during their long development, but because banks are central local institutions and bankers are typically friends of publishers, exposés are late bloomers. Similarly, coverage of auto issues is often subdued in Motor City Detroit, or, where auto dealers are numerous, consumer warnings about defects or price gouging are often censored.

But this is a small part of total print media coverage. In fact, there are probably more cases of big advertisers being attacked than protected from criticism. For instance in the

Nordstrom case, the *Seattle Times* published a string of articles about the retailer's labor problems despite blunt pressure, including a cutback in ads from Nordstrom. As we have seen, there is increasingly an adversarial stance toward all institutions. Publishers, editors, and reporters alike believe that circulation is aided by sensational exposés.

Similarly, where advertisers have direct influence on program content, as in the commercial broadcast media, their central interest is audience ratings, not probusiness, or prochurch, or pro-anything content. What they want is an increase in mass audience; whatever it takes is ok—violence, prurience, political pornography.[28] That GE owns NBC does not stop the network from trashing the Defense Department for cost overruns, $800 toilet seats, sexual harassment, and the like.[29] And advertisers are delighted with *60 Minutes,* CBS's top-rated longest-running "news magazine"—this despite its consistently prosecutorial interview style, its effort to entrap and wring damaging snippets from officials, CEOs, religious leaders, anyone in established authority. The targets have included numerous corporations as well as the military. For instance, *60 Minutes* broadcast a 17-minute piece "Out of Control," November 23, 1986, repeated it on September 13, 1987. It alleged that the Audi 5000, a German luxury sedan, had a dangerous defect, "sudden acceleration," which was supposedly responsible for hundreds of accidents and several deaths—5,000 incidents, claimed Ed Bradley. Audi sales dropped by more than two-thirds. But in 1987 the National Highway Traffic Safety Administration, after an exhaustive two-year study, concluded that there was no mechanical problem that caused sudden acceleration of the Audi or any other cars. All of the people featured on *60 Minutes* who sued Audi lost their cases; one woman featured in the opening scene was fined for filing a frivolous lawsuit (Farrell, 1998).

Thus, most media content and style cannot be explained by owner interests or big business dominance. The drift of the print media toward television and radio negativism, the drift of the electronic media toward the talk-show model, the convergence of news and entertainment, the marketing of undifferentiated crises, undifferentiated spectacles—all of this has little to do with the cultural hegemony of big business. It is more specific to the financing, control, and changing norms of the media.

Organizational and Occupational Contingencies

Content in this theory is rooted in the technical and organizational structure and aims of the medium. For explanation we look at what media managers, producers, and journalists must do to survive and grow, to the changing norms of the trade. First, the media are increasingly competitive and expensive. The broadcast networks compete intensely with one another and with cable. Newspapers and mass-circulation magazines compete with one another and with radio and TV. They all now compete with the Internet. The tabloidization of television and later of print "journalism" is a product of the loss of market share in this escalating competition. In 1961 TV viewers spent more than 90% of viewing time with three commercial networks; that figure went down to about 55 to 60% by 1997. When network news had almost all of the audience, CBS allowed its news department to lose money for many years while it fulfilled some of its public-interest obligations. When the audience, especially the young consumer audience, shifted to radio and television talk shows, to cable entertainment (and "infotainment") and to the Internet, the major networks abandoned their loss leader, the public-interest component of network news, and insisted that news departments make profits. Thus did the successful talk-show model spread.

Meanwhile, newspapers were losing their readers to the electronic media. Their typical response was to copy the content and style of the growth sectors. Because their aim is to build or maintain a mass audience, because cost escalates in what appears to them as a competitive struggle to the death, both television networks and print journalism must compress their stories and speed up their schedules. What was a one- or two-hour TV drama became a cheaper half-hour formula show, the sitcom. Print news began to resemble television sound bites. The need for compression and more urgent deadlines make for a work environment more frantic than that of the 1950s.

Because they want to win in competition or survive as their segment declines and because of their perceived need to speed up, compress, and capture attention, they accent the sensational in their programming.[30] As we have seen above, the producers of drama and film have increased the frequency and intensity of violence, sex, and mayhem, while news became even more negative and aggressively interpretive. One reason for the aggressively interpretive character of all "news" is that the editors of the print media—newspapers and magazines—no longer feel that they have to report "the facts"; TV does that. So at their best they try to provide analysis and context. Commercial TV, in turn, is so selective and so obsessed with the week's ratings and the need to be dramatic, that "the facts" (who, what, where, when, why) are overwhelmed by slogans, catch phrases, and scandals. That print media and broadcast news alike embrace gossip and rumor and report them as newsworthy facts—increasingly unchecked—is partly explained by this buck-passing habit. Print editors say that TV reports the timely facts; we do interpretation. But TV producers say the facts are boring; let's liven it up. They both end up with a similar antifactual product, featuring the reporter-celebrity as prophet and seer, and alternate between attack-dog barking and a chatty, gossipy tone.

The media formula in politics and political news reflects these occupational and organizational requirements. The formula consists of the well-known emphasis on the horse race in campaigns (Jerry Brown, coming up on the outside, gains on Clinton; Perot, the dark horse, moves up in the pack, becomes a miraculous second), the man-bites-dog theme, two politicians trading insults (Mondale to Hart, "Where's the beef?" Reagan to Bush, "This is my microphone"), the little guy slaying the big guy in the manner of Jimmy Stewart in *Mr. Smith Goes to Washington,* or David and Goliath (that's literally why the media for months loved Perot in 1992 and Carter in 1976). Alternative content and styles are, in the media managers' common view, BORING—and boredom is the great enemy of audience building.

The 1976 Democratic primary campaign is a dramatic illustration of how horse-race, scorecard journalism can shape a presidential election. Thomas Patterson (1980) carried out a panel survey of voters beginning in February 1976, before the primaries began, and ending in November after election day. The 1,200 respondents were interviewed as many as seven times each about their media use, impressions of the candidates and the campaign, their awareness of election issues, interest in the campaign, and more. Five of the waves involved hour-long personal interviews. In addition, Patterson did a content analysis of the news media's coverage of the 1976 presidential election—the entire year's reporting by ABC, CBS, and NBC; by four daily newspapers (*Los Angeles Times, Los Angeles Herald Examiner,* the *Erie*

(Pennsylvania) News, and the *Erie Times*); and by *Time* and *Newsweek* magazines. The high-lights of findings of this careful study follow:

- Media coverage was half or more devoted to the horse race—the strategy and tactics and style of the candidates—downplaying questions of national policy or leader-ship. "The candidates' policy positions, their personal and leadership characteristics, their private and public histories, background on . . . issues, and group commitments for and by the candidates accounted for only about 30 percent of election coverage" (Patterson, 1980, pp. 24–25). Comparing the 1940 election (Lazarsfeld, Berelson, and Gaudet, 1948), policy and leadership accounted for about 50% of coverage.

- Projecting a single state's results to the entire nation, the media used a "winner take all" rule and celebrated the underdog moving up, blotting out everyone else. Jimmy Carter received 28% of the New Hampshire primary vote. The remaining four candi-dates, all liberals, together received 60% of the vote; Morris Udall led with 23%, a close second. Yet the press termed Carter "the unqualified winner" and gave him prominent coverage until the next primary. *Time* and *Newsweek* put him on their front covers and gave his story 2,600 lines. Udall received 96 lines. Carter's television and newspaper cov-erage that week was four times the average amount given each of his major rivals. This pattern held throughout the Democratic primaries.[31]

- The media emphasis on the contest, winner's tactics, strategy, and style—a bit more extreme on television than print—strongly shaped voters' name recognition and percep-tion of the candidate and the election. For instance, matters of policy and leadership were at the top of voters' lists in interviews just before the campaign; they sank to the bottom during the campaign, replaced by a concern with who is up, who is down. All contenders in New Hampshire were largely unknown to the voters at the outset. The media obsession with Carter meant that he was the only Democrat to become dramati-cally more familiar to the voters; he gained many votes from this recognition edge.

In both the Perot and Carter candidacies, the media formula in campaigns—horse race, underdog moves up, the David and Goliath syndrome, exaggerated conflict themes—was reinforced by both candidates' antigovernment, anti-Beltway stance, dear to the hearts of the media at century's end.

Why do the media give prominence to so many scandals, always exaggerating and often inventing them? Why has the reporting of scandals, crises, and disasters in the mainstream press become so seamless, so casual? By all historical accounts, government is cleaner, freer of corruption, nepotism, and crime than it was a century ago (Ornstein, 1993/94). Teapot Dome and Nixon's Watergate were aberrations in a slow climb toward cleaner government (see chap. 11). The escalation of scandalmongering in the past 20 or 30 years, then, has an ever-looser connection to reality; it is increasingly devoid of the context and historical per-spective that give an event meaning. Three trends help to explain this disconnect: the changing character of investigative reporting since Watergate; the emergence of journalists as media celebrities on a gravy train and what that does to role models for younger journalists; and the impact of increasingly frantic deadlines on herd journalism—that is, the increasing self-absorption and isolation of working journalists as a group.

Regarding the first trend, many students of the mass media see Nixon's Watergate as a turning point—the time when the media's cynicism, already elevated in the Vietnam War, took off as a dominant feature of news reporting. And many journalists defend what I have called scandalmongering by the notion that reporters behaved like lapdogs during the early years of both Vietnam and the Nixon conspiracies, not to mention the decades before. Too often, they say, reporters wrote what an official handed them as a press release or what a celebrity staged for them as a media event. Too often, they ignored signs of corruption or wrongdoing in high places. In contrast, the great investigative reporters, Woodward and Bernstein of the *Washington Post*—played by Robert Redford and Dustin Hoffmann in *All the Presidents' Men* (who has not seen it?)—are the model for the journalists who came of age in the 1960s, who are now 40- to 50-year-olds who have moved up. Determined not to be led by the nose by those in authority, they adopt what they think is a perfectly justified adversarial stance; they are attuned to scandal and rumors of scandal and to a negative spin on the news. An ABC reporter expressed this norm in 1995: "You can be wrong as long as you're negative and skeptical. But if you're going to say something remotely positive, you'd better be 150 percent right or you're going to be accused of rolling over" (quoted in Fallows, 1996, p. 180).

There are two things wrong with this "let's-not-roll-over defense" of today's journalistic practice. First, it distorts the behavior of journalists' predecessors; and second, lapdog behavior of the press continues, but the handouts are taken uncritically not from officials but from pushers of scandal. Yes, an older press establishment refused to allow pictures of President Roosevelt in his wheelchair; yes, they refused to report President Kennedy's reckless sex life; and, yes, James Reston of the *New York Times,* on behalf of national security, kept the secret about the plan to invade Cuba in 1961. But this was far from a pattern of lapdog journalism. It is fair to say that among the mainstream media in the two decades following World War II, the competitive pressures were less intense, the time and space for a story were greater, and the standards for getting the story straight by using multiple sources and presenting it fairly were much higher. For these reasons, many journalists made a much greater effort to separate the important from the trivial, fact from fiction, real events from pseudoevents—events made to happen by journalists in order to satisfy the demands for sensational inside dope or by public relations agents in order to build up their clients or knock down their enemies. Although there was always some tendency to report undifferentiated crises and to build up minor scandals (Wilensky, 1967a, p. 149), this was not the main content of the mainstream press. Most stories in those years were far from an echo of some official line. And when there was a real crisis—Vietnam, Watergate—the prestige press evidenced investigative reporting of high quality, the kind that requires hard work, time, judgment, and a steady focus on evidence and the credibility of sources.

In fact, the main shift from the 30 years before the mid-1970s to the subsequent 30 years has been from occasional lapdog reporting combined with routine balance, accuracy, and hard work to attack-dog journalism aided by a new kind of lapdog journalism. Instead of giving officials space and airtime, editors, producers, and reporters now give space and time to politicians and activists engaged in the politics of personal destruction; the gift of access now goes to anyone promoting rumors of scandals—enemies of the accused or media favorites such as "experts" making the most extreme statements or dramatic television performances by witnesses and interrogators in congressional investigatory committees, which were metastasizing in the 1990s. Lapdog journalism was abundantly evident when journalists dutifully repeated press leaks by the staff of Kenneth Starr during his career as independent counsel investigating assorted allegations against President Clinton. Unsourced, unchecked stories of scandal multiplied in the media.

Related to changes in investigative reporting—the escape from fairness, fact, and balance—are two other trends: an acceleration of the long-standing cult of celebrities in politics and culture and the multiplication of journalist celebrities, who now find themselves on a gravy train, making more money and wielding more influence than some of the stars they interview.[32] Instead of an encounter between a reporter and a movie star, politician, or athlete, we see an interaction between two celebrities, feeding each other's fame. This is most highly developed in broadcast talk shows but, as we have seen, it has become the model for print media as well. Appearances as a regular on talk shows, often combined with a syndicated column, can create a demand for lucrative invitations on a speech circuit. The McLaughlin Group takes its show on the road and charges fees of $20,000 per appearance. By the 1990s, George Will's annual earnings from speeches climbed to over $1 million. In 1994, the glamorous team of Steve and Cokie Roberts were paid $45,000 for one joint speech to potential clients of a banking group in Chicago (Fallows, 1996, p. 111).

Celebrity journalists are now role models for aspiring young journalists. The shift from old-fashioned investigative reporting in Watergate to today's negative opinions tossed off the top of the heads of talk-show celebrities—this is a drastic change in only one generation. That the new role models shape recruitment to journalism is suggested by William Kovach, a former editor at the *Atlanta Constitution* and *New York Times*. He observed that after the movie *All the President's Men,* "A lot of people started showing up in newspaper offices because they saw journalism as a route toward celebrating themselves. It has greatly increased since then. More and more kids come out of journalism school wanting to be anchors. They are not interested in the work of reporting or finding information. They want to be known." (Quoted in *ibid.*, p. 160.)

The contrast between the Nixon conspiracies and coverage of the Clinton sex scandal could not be more revealing of the trends I have discussed. If anyone doubts that sloppy scandalmongering by celebrity journalists was a factor in the unprecedented partisan vote in the House of Representatives to impeach a twice-elected president in 1998, one should remember how it all started. "Whitewater" began with a string of rumors, gossip, innuendo, and tortured logic posing as investigative reporting by the *New York Times,* especially in a series of exposés of President Clinton and the First Lady's alleged criminal activity in connection with a 1978 real estate deal gone sour and with the 1989 collapse of the Madison Guaranty Savings and Loan in Little Rock, Arkansas.[33] (For an account of exactly how sloppy this reporting was, see the book by Gene Lyons, 1996.)

There followed a two-year $3.6 million investigation by an independent law firm hired by Independent Counsel Robert Fiske that found no wrongdoing by the Clintons; then six more years of investigations by Independent Counsel Kenneth Starr and his successor, several congressional committees, and an army of reporters. In each case—except for the media— the investigators reluctantly conceded that there was no evidence of Whitewater wrongdoing. Along the way, the press managed to parlay small errors of judgment into equally large "gates"—"Filegate," "Travelgate," even "Fostergate" (conspiracy theorists and gutter journalists' accusation that the suicide of White House Counsel Vincent Foster was a murder orchestrated by the president, quickly reported at length by the mainstream press). Each of these "scandals" was repeatedly investigated and found without substance—another spate of inventive journalism. Similarly, the year of impeachment began with media events, a high-stakes blockbuster publishing project. The principals in this drama were a New York City literary agent, Lucianne Goldberg, and Linda Tripp, who secretly taped Monica Lewinsky gossiping about her encounters with the president; they hoped for a lucrative "telltale" book deal, with possible movie rights and certain saturation coverage.

The chief marketers of these scandals, media celebrities interacting with political and cultural celebrities, displayed an odd combination of cynicism and sanctimony, of malice and moralism, devoid of solid substance but filled with rumor, gossip, out-of-context factoids, and their own instant opinions.[34] The "gotcha" mentality of today's media—their negativism, their tendency to magnify the slightest misstep or equivocation, and to treat all public figures as suspect—has persuaded the public that politicians are chronic liars or "wafflers" who break their promises (Shaw, 1996, Part A, pp. 1–2). This kind of coverage has the merit of being easy, cheap, and convenient. Yet in a study spanning seven presidencies, Thomas Patterson (1993a, p. 11) reports that by and large, "presidents keep the promises they made as candidates. . . . When they fail to deliver . . . it is usually because they cannot get Congress to agree; because the pledge conflicts with a higher priority commitment; or because conditions have changed." This is another major disconnect between simplistic media reporting and complex reality.

The media were not the only forces at work to create these multiple crises, multiple scandals, and public cynicism. There were also the 1978 independent counsel law, born of a serious constitutional crisis in 1974; the decline of political parties; the polarization of politics; the constitutional structure and electoral system of the United States (see chap. 11)—all of which helped to create the post-Vietnam, post-Watergate, post–cold war atmosphere. But without the transformation of journalists into celebrity attack dogs, it is doubtful that the Republican majority in the House could have escalated six years of scandalmongering into the only impeachment of an elected president in American history.

Because politicians pine for access to the media, if for no other reason than to defend themselves from the incessant attacks, their hopes and fears increasingly focus on the media gatekeepers, the most visible journalist celebrities. Two studies confirm this common observation. One analyzes changes in routine coverage of U.S. senators. It shows that network television increasingly reports the views and actions of a charmed few and regularly invites them for combat, ignoring everyone else (Kulinski and Sigelman, 1992). Because media coverage is now overwhelmingly focused on the continual race for the presidency and who is up or down in that race and why, access goes to those they judge to be presidential candidates or potential contenders. This makes the competition for space and time even more intense. The second study was based on interviews with legislators, government agency personnel, and interest-group leaders involved in federal and local policymaking and implementation in the Chicago area. It concludes that policymakers "respond to investigative reporters as if they *were* the public" (Protess et al., 1991, p. 248). There is no doubt that everyone from the president to the rank-and-file members of Congress and their staff spend increasing amounts of time monitoring what the media celebrities say, cultivating their own potential celebrity through television appearances (Sunday TV makes Monday-morning headlines), and devising daily strategies to counter media attacks. This, of course, leaves less time for policy planning and other aspects of governing. (Cf. Fallows, 1996, pp. 182ff, 235ff.)

The final reason for the spread of the talk-show model of journalism, especially its avoidance of policy issues and analysis of substance, is the speedup in the news cycle, the multiplication of deadline pressures. The new technology and new formats—C-SPAN, CNN, radio and TV talk shows, and on-line databases—have combined with the definition of news as conflict and scandal to create a cycle of nonstop "news." Today it is always deadline time, every minute, every hour (Fallows, 1996, p. 183). Although the media have always been in a hurry, the new technology and intensified competition have made the job more frantic. When you are in a hurry, continually frantic, you fall back on what you know (Wilensky, 1967a, pp. 75–77, 80–81). And what working journalists of the 1990s know is *not* the political, economic, and social context of the event or the substance of issues, but what happened this morning—the latest rumor or prediction on a talk show, the latest clever phrase by one of the contending politicians or celebrities, the latest tactic in the political game. One thing is clear: In a state of chronic crisis, under continual deadline pressure, journalists have neither time nor incentive to explore complex policy issues, new possibilities, alternative explanations, more evidence. Concretely, that means one source or no source instead of two or three. It means rushing into print or broadcast with undifferentiated crises and scandals derived from poorly evaluated sources.[35]

A good example of this hasty avoidance of substance in favor of horse-race journalism and the quick depiction of clashing personalities is the yearlong coverage of the Clinton administration's health-care proposal described in chapter 16, where I show how the media failed to help Americans to understand much of anything about the plan or the alternatives to it. One incident in this press coverage is emblematic. Conducting a study of media coverage, Kathleen Jamieson observed the behavior of reporters at a two-hour presentation of the plan by Hillary Clinton in 1994. Mrs. Clinton provided a lucid rationale for reform, and for the plan, including a detailed question-and-answer session, where she took on every argument against it.

> What was interesting to me was the physical sensation of being in the middle of the press corps during the different parts of the presentation. When she was talking about her plan, the reporters had clearly heard all of this before and found it completely uninteresting. They were talking to each other, passing notes around.
>
> But as soon as she made a brief attack on the Republicans, there was a physiological reaction, this surge of adrenaline, all around me. The pens moved. The reporters arched forward. They wrote everything down rapidly. As soon as this part was over, they clearly weren't paying attention any more. They were writing on their laptops as they began constructing the story of how the First Lady had attacked her opponents.
> (Jamieson quoted in Fallows, 1996, p. 224)

The speedup in reporting and the concentration on conflict reinforce the tendency toward pack journalism. If there is no time for adequate fact-checking, if reporters go out on a limb and are caught in a major error, they fear ridicule. But if they check with their colleagues in a similar situation to see what the collective spin of the hour is, they are safe. "Following the story" increasingly means talking to fellow journalists or fellow celebrities, with a side glance at the day's public opinion polls. This helps to explain the accelerated swings in press moods: the uniform fawning over rising underdogs (like Jerry Brown, Paul Tsongas, Ross Perot, Jimmy Carter, John McCain), followed quickly by the uniform feeding frenzy as the underdog becomes a top dog, bringing down the same candidates they raised up. What I have come to think of as "belly-button journalism" is part of this speedy, self-referential, pack journalism. It is as though each member of the press corps gazes at his or her navel and sees the world—and all the navels look alike.[36]

Country-Specific Regulation, Control, and Financing

So far I have concentrated on the United States as the case where the ascendance of the media in politics and culture is most extreme and where the countervailing forces are weakest. The third explanation of media content—as powerful as the occupational culture argument—focuses on national variations in public financing and regulation of the media. Here we find substantial variation with a recent shift toward the American model. By the time that all the American trends I have discussed were clearly evident, say the late 1970s, the U.S. stood alone in its intense degree of commercial competition, the long hours of broadcast time, its almost total dependence on advertising for revenue, the small budget and audience for public television and radio, the least educational-cultural content, the freedom of the media to deny access to the public airwaves, and the almost total lack of regulation of the media's role in election campaigns.[37] Those Americans who see every effort to control the media as a threat to the sacred First Amendment rights of the large corporate owners of the media and the preservation of democracy must confront the prevalence of strong regulations of the media in almost every lively democracy in the world. An overview of media regulation of 11 of our 19 democracies appears in table 3.2.

Regarding broadcast hours in this period, the national networks of Europe, both public and commercial, typically sign off at 11 or midnight; only the U.S. goes nonstop. Of 14 countries in a study of political advertising (Kaid and Holtz-Bacha, 1995), 10 either bar or strictly limit paid political commercials during election campaigns. The clear exception is the United States. The partial exceptions are Finland, which since 1990 has permitted paid ads but restricts their content—no attacks against individuals, no product ads in political ads; Italy, which since 1994 has banned paid ads in the month before elections; and the Netherlands, which does not prohibit paid political ads but publicly subsidizes them and gives parties free time for issue broadcasts year-round. Instead of being forced to buy access to the media, political parties in at least seven of these countries get free airtime from public funding for sustained presentation of their party platforms. There are minor variations in the formula for free broadcast time: Denmark and the Netherlands provide equal time for all parties; the UK provides equal time for two main parties and allocates time to minor parties according to other criteria; Germany, Israel, and France allocate free time according to the party's percentage of votes or seats.

Two countries with sharp contrasts in social-political context and very different broadcasting systems illustrate that a long history of public control shapes politics and culture in two ways that ensure access for diverse interests, even after substantial privatization. The Netherlands perhaps represents the extreme of a decentralized and wide-open system with the greatest cultural diversity; France is perhaps the extreme of central public control. They both evidence typical blends of centralization and decentralization.[38] Before 1984, French

TABLE 3.2 Funding and regulation of broadcast media, 1990s

	PUBLIC BROADCASTING PRESENCE, CIRCA 1994-1997[1]		REGULATION OF POLITICAL MESSAGE, CIRCA 1990[2]		
	Public television market as fraction of total national television audience	Advertising as fraction of total revenues for national public television	Restrictions on number of broadcasts during campaign?	Restrictions on content?	Media access for political candidates and parties during campaigns
U.S.	22%[3]	na	No Limit	No	No ad access guaranteed for candidates or parties
U.K.	44%	na	Limited; maximum of 5 blocks of free airtime per party	No	Free and equal ad access guaranteed for main two parties but limited for smaller parties on public tv; voluntary free access on commercial tv
Italy	49%	31%	No Limit; but since 1993, banned in last month of elections	No	
Germany	34%[4]	na	Limited; in 1990 main parties got 8 mins, 6 smaller parties got 4 mins each, 13 smallest got 2-3 mins	Yes; presentation of party views can't look like a bona fide news cast	Free and equal access for all parties on public tv; subsidized access for all parties on commercial tv
Belgium	25%	40%			
Neth	60%	36%	Limited; since 1989 each party gets 2 3-minute spots and 3 5-minute spots in three week period before elections	No	Free and equal ad access for all parties on public tv; paid access only on commercial tv
Norway	50%	0%			Free access but limited to main parties on public tv
Sweden	49%	0%			
Denmark	68%	66%	Limited; approval only for various panel discussion, interviews, and 10 min platform presentations	No	Free and equal access for all parties on public tv
Finland	65%	0%	No Limit	Yes; no attacks against individuals, no product advertising in political ads	Free access but limited to main parties on public tv
France	43%	54%	Limited;	Yes; detailed regulations for production and content	Free access for all candidates on public tv

[1]Source: Euromedia Research Group. 1997. *The Media in Western Europe* and citations in text.

[2]Source: Lynda Kaid and Christina Holtz-Bacha. 1995. *Political Advertising in Western Democracies: Parties and Candidates on Television* and citations in text.

[3]Estimates range from the Cable Advertising Bureau's 3% of total television viewing audience over a 24-hour period in 1996 (Cable Advertising Bureau, 1997) to the Euromedia Research Group's 22% share of the average weekly television audience.

[4]Source: Presse und Informationsamt der Bundesregierung. 1994. *Bericht der Bundesregierung über die Lage der Medien in der BRD.* Drucksache 12/8587 des Deutschen Bundestags, 12th legislative period, Bonn, October.

broadcasting was totally owned and programmed by government institutions. Tradition accented cultural and public-service content. This public-service model also reflected partisan politics. Incumbent governments tended to use broadcast power to enhance their own positions. The trade-off seemed to be cultural uplift at the cost of some politicization. In the 1970s, there was a small move toward privatization; two TV companies, TF1 and A2, brought in commercial advertising, no longer depending on license fees set by the government for most revenue. Government still made appointments to key posts in stations and companies. In the 1980s, the Mitterrand government attempted to deregulate and decentralize broadcasting but in a typically centralized, controlled way—with continued restrictions to promote French cultural and public-service programs. The government also retained power to regulate print communication and assure the equal treatment of candidates in elections through regulatory commissions. France not only bans paid political ads and gives parties much free time; it also regulates political spots (5 or 15 minutes each party, depending on number of candidates) and the content of political messages (no gimmicks—candidates cannot show films or conduct interviews in the street, candidate must speak without stage props). Guidelines for the 1988 election included a prohibition on using archival information in broadcasts without permission from the candidates involved—obviously a chill on negative, personal campaign talk; candidates could use allocated airtime any way they wished to discuss issues, but they could not introduce surprises just before elections. In short, despite the major shift toward commercialization, a heavy public-interest presence is maintained.

Reflecting Dutch *verzuilling,* centralized consensual bargaining among confessional-political blocs, the Netherlands' broadcasting system throughout its history has allocated radio and television time to voluntary associations with clear allegiance to one or another major bloc. At first there were four: the Catholic church, the established Protestant denomination, the Socialist Party, and nonideological (in practice politically liberal). Time is allocated on the basis of number of members in the associations. In addition, NOS, a public foundation with about 20% of airtime, serves needs not likely to be met by the other organizations, such as minority programming, almost all regular impartial news, and many documentaries. After the legislation of 1967–69 and 1987, the system was further opened up: three new bodies have entered since 1967—an Evangelical group, another general television provider, and one oriented to youth and popular culture. In the words of the 1987 law, broadcasting associations must represent "some clearly-stated societal, cultural, religious, or philosophical stream" and create programming that will both satisfy those special needs and increase diversity of the system. In the mid-1990s, nine main associations shared three channels. Each association was required to provide a full range of programming to ensure a balance in system content over the week or day. To add to diversity there is now access for about 30 small broadcasters' associations—religious, cultural, and humanistic—plus political parties.

The system is overwhelmingly noncommercial; since 1967 there has been an element of funding from strictly regulated advertising. Advertising accounts for more than a third of the public broadcasting budget and is administered by a public foundation. It is bunched at certain times, forbidden on Sundays, strictly controlled to protect consumers, and sharply separated from program content.[39] A broadcasting association must have broadcasting as its chief aim and is barred from making profits for third parties.

A large component of educational-cultural content in the public interest is assured in several ways by the requirement that every broadcaster give a significant share of its time to such programs, monitored by the NOS research department; by a separate educational broadcasting foundation which must devote at least 20% of its programming to culture; and by minimum percentage shares for information and education set by the Ministry of Health, Welfare, and Culture and applied to every broadcasting association.

Regarding politics, a total of 15% of all airtime is reserved for political parties, each of which receives an equal allocation of airtime in both election campaigns and between elections. Campaign advertising takes the form of regulated free time: for example, during the three to four weeks before the election of 1989, each party—and there are many—was allowed two minutes twice and five minutes three times.

In short, the broadcast system of the Netherlands combines extraordinary openness, diversity, and interest group autonomy (what one might label decentralization) with a centralized government and quasi-public social institutions to set the framework, monitor the whole, and assure equal access and public-interest content (what one might call centralization). When the Netherlands and France made a shift toward commercial broadcasting, they retained a substantial public-interest presence, each in its own way. Relative to their own public broadcasting past, the presence has diminished; compared to the United States, it is very heavy indeed.

The most important determinant of media content is the amount and kind of funding for public broadcast networks and the percentage of total audience these networks attract. For instance, in 1996 the BBC attracted 44% of the average weekly television audience (Tunstall, 1997, p. 258). In Japan, in November 1990, although all private channels together had more of the average weekday audience than the public network (each had 7–12% and together, 63%), no one channel exceeded the public network NHK (General and Educational), which had 37%.[40] Table 3.2 shows that in 1997, except for the U.S. and Belgium, the public television audience share ranged between one-third and two-thirds of the total television audience. In the 1990s Belgium joined the U.S. because of rapid privatization of public broadcasting.

Among our 19 rich democracies, the financing of public television broadcasting networks is typically from a license fee on TV sets—usually less than $100 per year—or some variation of it. In the mid-1980s, Japan, Belgium, the UK, Denmark, and Sweden relied exclusively on a license fee to fund public television. France, West Germany, Italy, and the Netherlands relied both on a license fee and advertising revenue; Australia on government general revenues. Only the U.S. starves its public broadcasting network and relies on periodic begging by the affiliated stations, yielding uncertain contributions. In fact, federal tax dollars in 1995 comprised only 14% of public broadcasting revenues in the United States, although that figure is more than 50% for a few smaller affiliates (*Wall Street Journal,* Feb. 22, 1995).[41] This small and unstable financial base makes public broadcasting vulnerable to big cuts. There were repeated efforts by the Republican Congresses of 1994–2000 to wipe it out entirely, on behalf of the free market. One charge is that it is elitist; House Speaker Gingrich called the Corporation for Public Broadcasting a "little sandbox for the rich." Although it is true that there is a modest income/education gradient in public TV viewership, the numbers by education are surprisingly similar to the educational distribution of U.S. households. For instance, in 1995, about a quarter of the public TV audience were college graduates; they were 22.3% of the U.S. population; high-school graduates were about one-third of both viewers and the population; those with less than high school were 20% of the viewers, 22% of the population. The biggest segment of the two million households that watched PBS's opera, Richard Strauss's "Elektra," December 1994, was those earning $20,000 to $40,000, making up 39% of the audience. (Nielson ratings reported by *ibid.*) As other democracies have discovered, with a little effort and sustained financing, modern citizens can be attracted to something better than formulaic sitcoms and attack-dog "news magazines."

Strong financing for public broadcasting combined with the typical media regulations of other advanced democracies (provision of free time for campaigns with prohibition or limits on political commercials, etc.), as well as shorter election campaigns, buys a large public-interest presence in the media. Comparison of programming in the United States and abroad suggests that this combination assures, first, more substantive content, more emphasis on parties and issues in politics, and certainly more room for candidates to speak for themselves; and, second, more educational-cultural content and a somewhat higher quality in drama, news, talk shows, even comedy.[42]

The history of BBC also suggests that when commercial competition comes into play, Gresham's law of media currency, the American media's race to the bottom, is not inevitable. A strong public network sets something of a standard—partly through the export of personnel possessing a public-interest outlook to the private sector and partly because of an audience trained to somewhat more sophisticated tastes. (Katz, 1977; Kuhn and Wheeler, 1994; Tusa, 1994; Garnham, 1994; Seaton, 1994; Wheldon, 1976; *The Economist,* July 9, 1994, pp. 14–15.) From the outset the BBC was headed by men of missionary zeal whose main aim was to lift the cultural-political level of Great Britain (Briggs, 1985). To this day that public-service ethos prevails, even though the technological, economic, and political pressures of the Thatcher years and after have been severe. Combine a large, steady license-fee income with a mission to set standards high, and programming will follow. Thus, in the U.S. there is a continual demand for material seven days a week, year-round. In contrast, the BBC takes a different approach to writing. It recruits top contemporary playwrights, historians, economists, scholars, and scientists and assumes that no one individual or team can churn out 52 to 365 episodes a year of anything without a great sacrifice in quality. Instead, the BBC gives its writers time and autonomy to write one or a few programs per year or so. The range of content on British television is therefore broader and the quality higher than the program content of American networks. This leaves aside the explicitly educational programs of public television, directed mainly but not exclusively to children and schools.[43]

In countries that shift substantial resources away from public broadcasting networks, however, commercialization, when combined with a vacuum of power created by dealignment of parties, can be filled by media-driven politics (see chap. 11). Italy provides an extreme example of exactly such a pattern. Italy also suggests that the emergence of broadcast media celebrities as politicians is not confined to the U.S.[44] In the national election of 1994, wealthy media magnate Silvio Berlusconi orchestrated an improvised political movement, *Forza Italia* ("Go Italy"), in which the broadcast media were dominant. Political observers said it came out of nowhere. Only two months after it was founded, *Forza Italia* scored first in the popular vote, with Berlusconi named prime minister. How did this happen? Berlusconi owned three national commercial networks as well as the leading soccer team (AC Milan) and an advertising agency that controls 60% of all TV commercials in Italy. Well before the election he had become a celebrity. His popularity increased when he loaded up his programming with housewives' favorite soap operas. In the election, he ran an American-style campaign, a media blitzkrieg guided by polls and consultants—ads, staged press conferences, media events, speeches—all shown at length on his television stations. (His campaign publicity manager formerly worked for Saatchi and Saatchi, famous for designing Mrs. Thatcher's image.) The campaign celebrated patriotism and the Italian nation, promised a new economic miracle, personalized politics, and attacked the Communist menace. Berlusconi also attacked the undue harshness and political bias of the prosecuting magistrates dealing with corruption. (Berlusconi himself managed to get a notorious law passed to allow his holding company, Finivest, to retain all three of his private channels.) One Italian observer, contemplating the power of media and money in this election, asked me, "If Clinton with his TV skills had also owned ABC, CBS, and NBC as well as the Dallas Cowboys . . . had long and favorable TV exposure, and incidentally had Perot's personal fortune to spend, wouldn't he have received more than 43 percent of the popular vote?" Berlusconi did not come out of nowhere; he came out of commercial television with no restriction on content and spending. By custom, the RAI, the public broadcast network, assured some pluralism by dividing time and control among the main political parties, although this partisanship declined in the 1990s. But there are virtually no controls on the more dominant commercial networks.

One could argue that in the Italian case a politicized public broadcasting system did not serve the public interest very well; it merely provided three versions of reality—Catholic, Socialist, and Communist. In this view, when in the late 1980s commercial competition was introduced, the network news departments were freer of party control and could therefore help to expose the political corruption and sweep away an entire political elite. The lesson for cross-national comparisons is that under conditions of party dealignment and deep system corruption (real as in Italy, not a product of creative journalism), commercial competition can counterbalance a party-controlled public network and expose politicians who abuse the public trust. But where corruption is minimal, as in almost all of our rich democracies, commercial media tend toward attack-dog journalism and indiscriminate scandalmongering.[45] In any case, even in Italy the move from the monopoly of RAI, with its diversified party-dominated news, to the dominance of Berlusconi, king of commercial television, is a mixed blessing.

Are the Media Becoming American?

The most popular show on television in many European and even African countries is *Dallas*. Although American public television is paltry, the one well-financed, high-quality children's series with substantial support and long life, *Sesame Street*, is the most watched program in the world. In coverage of readers, AP (Associated Press) and UPI (United Press International) lead all news services; Britain's Reuters Financial News and France's Agence France-Presse are third and fourth. Anglo-American pop music and CNN are everywhere. (CNN International is received in 150 million homes worldwide plus 80 million in the U.S.) In fact, American mass media products—film, television programs, news services, magazines, tapes, CDs—are a leading source of export surplus (exports minus imports), even exceeding agriculture (U.S. Department of Commerce, 1997, pp. 71–74). A major reason for U.S. success in selling media products abroad is that in technological innovation, commercial organization, and financing, the U.S. got there first—first in a mass radio audience, first in a mass television audience. Many decades of recruitment and training of writers, editors, producers, performers, and audience researchers gave the U.S. a competitive advantage in equipment, mass appeal, production technique, and promotion. With a heavy investment in industry infrastructure already accomplished, and a large, profitable domestic mass audience, American commercial media could sell their products cheaply as reruns abroad.

Similarly, what used to be a flourishing film industry in Europe with European directors and audiences has been replaced by American movies produced and distributed by Hollywood studios. This was facilitated not only by American economies of scale and financing, but by the construction of American-owned multiplex cinemas abroad. American films now dominate every hit list in almost every European country. Only France is the exception: domestically produced films, with large subsidies from the tax-financed Centre National de la Cinématographie, still account for more than a third of the French market (*The Economist,* Feb. 5, 1994, p. 89). Elsewhere, U.S. products are dominant, with 60% of world box office receipts.[46]

It is easy to exaggerate the penetration of American media abroad. Political and cultural elites of most modern democracies resist the onslaught of U.S. pop culture in all its forms. Led by the Minister of Canadian Heritage, an international conference met in 1997 in Ottawa. There, two dozen culture ministers from four continents pondered ways to offset what they view as American cultural degradation and to preserve their national cultures. Many countries try with modest success to require a portion of domestic content in the media; they have also increased funding for national cultural industries (*Wall Street Journal,* Sept. 24, 1998). They have been more successful in resisting American television and radio than Hollywood films. For instance, of TV programs from foreign commercial sources as a percentage of total program hours in the late 1980s the penetration was only 9% in France, 10% in Japan, 13% in Italy, 24% in Germany. (It was, however, 55% in Israel.) In fact, according to an *Economist* survey of television (Feb. 12, 1994, p. 12), "the biggest slice of European air-time ever filled by American [TV] programmes was 28 percent in 1987; it has been falling ever since." Further, in the Netherlands and Belgium, as we have seen, television hours are allocated according to the membership of confessional-political blocs; those groups are very resistant to imports from the U.S. Finally, television news, whether commercial or public, and even if it originates from an international news service, tends to be domesticated, with the national bias, if any, clearly evident (Cohen and Roeh, 1992, pp. 26–29).

The more significant penetration of the U.S. model is the shift in the past 10 or 20 years toward privatization. The recent commercialization of large segments of broadcasting in several countries, especially Belgium and France; the decline of license-fee revenue; the increase in cross-national access that comes with the new cable and satellite technology and multichannel expansion—all of these reduce national differences in content. The cultural mission, assurance, and pride of public broadcasting authorities in Europe are slowly fading; the prestige newspapers are in some measure aping the tabloids. The media are indeed becoming American. (Cf. Tunstall, 1977; Etzioni-Halevy, 1987; Blumler, 1992; and Patterson, 1998, pp. 62–65.)[47]

In sum: Despite a slow drift toward the American model, substantial national differences in media content and effects remain. If for no other reason, the variation in social and political structures I have described in this chapter ensure persistent variation in media influence in politics and culture. Yet the direction of change is no doubt toward the commercialization of parts of the broadcast spectrum and the concomitant development of American style and content, whatever the more tentative convergence in media impact.

Will New Information Technology Change Media Content and Impact?

Because this area is filled with pure speculation based on almost no systematic comparisons, I can be brief and offer my own speculations. The central notion is that the proliferation of electronic devices—"direct-broadcast satellites, personal computers, digital, high-definition, and interactive television, videotex, and teletext, electronic mail, and high-speed computer networks, as well as a variety of enhanced services for an expanding digital telephone network" (Neuman, 1991, pp. ix-x)—will enhance consumer choice, diversify media content, and somehow improve the quality of communication in politics and upgrade educational-cultural content. There is even a claim that "chatrooms," "newsgroups," and "message-board postings" on the Internet are generating a new community, as strangers with common specialized interests come together in cyberspace and acquire new attachments. Or that the new technology will facilitate electronic tabulation of the opinions of mass audiences, thereby restoring New England–style town meetings or producing a "global village." The new participatory patterns, it is said, will strengthen both democracy and community.

We should greet this dream of a technological utopia with intense skepticism. First, the history of the social impact of inventions almost always belies the predictions made when they were introduced. The telephone, said the prophets celebrating the new invention, would bring peace on Earth, eliminate Southern accents, break down class barriers, make Americans a truly united people. It would let people dial up symphonies; novels, orchestras, and movie theaters would vanish. H. G. Wells predicted that the telephone would help eliminate the (mild) traffic congestion of his day by pulling people out of cities. (Marvin, 1988, pp. 63–108; Fischer, 1992, pp. 60–72, 157–165.) Similarly, in the early days of the automobile—and even now, with the promotional celebration of autos on television—the car was seen as a revolutionary force for personal freedom and choice. Unanticipated was a two-hour commute in traffic jams, the enormous cost of the network of roads, highways, gas stations, and garages necessary to make autos useful, the eating up of urban land for parking space and roads, with the concomitant inflation of urban housing costs, and then the speedup in the deconcentration of population, leaving urban centers with a declining tax base, mounting needs for services, and deteriorating infrastructure (Wilensky, 1965, p. xxiii; Rochlin, 1997, p. 48). I leave aside the cost of slaughter on the highways. In the U.S., and to a much lesser extent elsewhere, the ascendance of the automobile in public policy and media imagery meant the diversion of funds away from efficient rapid transit and railway systems.

A second reason for skepticism about the claims of technological enthusiasts is that the culture and society within which new technology is embedded mightily shape its uses. Thus, we should expect strong trends already apparent in the countries I have discussed to continue or accelerate. In the U.S., there are several ways in which new information technology is likely to reinforce what I have outlined as changes in media content and effects over the past half century. Have the media come increasingly under concentrated commercial ownership and control? Expect more of the same. In theory, the Internet model was a free market in information, dominated by nobody. In fact, by 1999 America Online, a commercial gateway to the Internet with 15 million subscribers, had more subscribers than the next 15 largest Internet service providers combined (*New York Times,* Jan. 31, 1999). AOL was on the way to dominating its market the way Microsoft's system programmers dominated their market. Are FCC regulations of broadcasting in the public interest minimal or ineffective? The Telecommunications Act of 1996 grants on-line servers "common carrier" status, like that of a telephone company, with no responsibility for information itself, even if it is libelous—in other words, even less regulation than that for broadcasting. Have the separate media been merging not only in ownership but in content and style? Recent information technology will accelerate this trend. When print media are delivered to the home through broadcast, wire, or magnetic recording, the distinction among newspapers, magazines, newsletters, and even books, on the one hand, and broadcast programming and advertising, on the other, become blurred (Neuman, 1991, p. 72). Have the American media become increasingly competitive, frantic, negative, sensational, aggressively interpretive, afactual, and anti-institutional? The Internet speeds up the circulation of rumors, malicious gossip, and scandals as well as populist protest against authority. The broadcast and print journalists who attend to it, already in a state of information overload, find themselves drowning in bits of Internet information of indiscriminate origin and reliability. Although Walter Winchell was an attack dog on the radio of the 1930s, he could not come close to the negative influence of Matthew Drudge on the Internet today; mainstream newspapers pay attention to Drudge's allegations while their counterparts of the past ignored Winchell's gossip.

Is the speedy obsolescence of products characteristic of the affluent society? The new information technology is almost a parody of this trend. From international transfers to supermarket checkouts, from spacecraft controls to auto engines, from the home computer to the most powerful mainframe, we are as heavily dependent on the continued use of this technology as we are on the telephone and the automobile. That means dependence on hardware and software producers and their thrust for very speedy obsolescence. It means heavy service, administrative, and management costs to keep it going and changing. For the individual on-line it means mounting time absorbed by user-unfriendly devices and system incompatibilities, by hanging on the phone plowing through a maze of electronic menus that often lead nowhere, by the recurrent learning curves that in a more sensible environment would occur once in several years but now are demanded almost nonstop as new software comes bundled with every new PC, and as security problems multiply.

Then there is the question of what all this instant access to information means for the wisdom, judgment, and thought that foster good policy decisions in the economy and polity—or good reporting in the media. In his analysis of the unanticipated consequences of computerization, Gene Rochlin (1997) suggests the likely secondary effects of most significance, especially those rooted in the interactive reconstruction of organizational forms and social life and from changes in heavy users' mentality. "Decentralization," "empowerment," "choice," and "autonomy" are the catchphrases of the technological enthusiasts. And, indeed, among the most information-dependent sectors, what was once a hierarchical workplace governed by formal rules now looks flatter and appears to be more flexible and participatory. No doubt the professional model—where the authority of expertise is more important than rank, the model that spread to the more technology-based organizations during and after World War II—is enhanced by the new information technology (Wilensky 1964b, 1967a, pp. 173–191). Highly trained individuals in computerized workplaces are no doubt given a bit more flexibility and autonomy (and a lot more money). But as we have seen (chap. 1), these high-tech employees and entrepreneurs constitute a small percentage of the modern labor force. Further, as Rochlin shows (1997, pp. 8–9, 43, 47–48), behind all the decentralized empowerment is a new managerial elite with control of information and communication networks; they exercise authority as rigorous and demanding as executives in the traditional, more visible hierarchy. For these complex networks encourage top managers to try to monitor their subordinates' performance more frequently and closely. The new information managers constantly seek to tighten linkages between different parts of complex organizations (eliminate "loose coupling"), reduce slack, and cut response time. The reporting and maintenance requirements and the frequent changes of these systems often increase everyone's workload.

More important than these organizational and occupational shifts, which were evident before the rapid spread of computers, is the possible transformation of modes of thinking. As operations are increasingly computerized in networks of increasing complexity, there is a strong potential for the loss of experiential knowledge or common wisdom. As Rochlin suggests, "in personal life, in business, in markets, and the military"—and he might add, the media—there is "the substitution of data scanning for information-gathering, of rules and procedures for learning, and of models and calculation for judgment and expertise. In short, the replacement of art with artifice" (p. xiii; cf. Wilensky, 1967a, pp. 180–191). Proper respect for the GIGO principle (Garbage In, Garbage Out) is eroding.[48]

An example of this shift in styles of information gathering and processing is the modern university research library. Computerized catalogs and their associated powerful search and retrieval tools are supposed to be user-empowering. Indeed, for some of the material in this book, I have worked in my home office, linking up via the Internet with libraries and colleagues in Berkeley and abroad. Yet I frequently found that the standardization of process and procedure imposed by the library technologists was a frustrating barrier to the kind of scholarly work I did before computerization. (This is not a product of my Luddite prejudices, for I was blessed with excellent research assistants, some of whom had been computer literate since the age of six. I should also add that my personal library of about 5,000 books burned up in the Berkeley/Oakland firestorm of 1991 so I became especially dependent on the new computerized library.) The organization of the material on the Internet was often opaque, compared with the old card catalog. Most important, perhaps a third of the books I wanted had been the victims of a library computer program that automatically sends those books not recently checked out to storage in a remote warehouse, a decision rule that makes the library less and less useful for most scholars in the humanities and history. Academics are supposed to adapt their work to the possibilities of computer programs and their search rules.[49]

This development reinforces the long-standing cult of "the new" in the U.S.—especially prominent in the mass media but now spreading to college students and some faculty. This is the conviction that if an event did not happen yesterday or today, if a book or article was not written within the last 5 or 10 years, it is not worth attention. Now we are bombarded with propaganda about the latest software upgrade, the newest hardware, the newest way of interconnecting separate networks. And like the person who answers "It's there" when asked "Why do you want to climb that mountain?" journalists and academics alike tend to embrace the cult of the new because Lexis-Nexis or similar search engines are there. The self-referential journalism I described earlier has no doubt been reinforced by this marvelous new technology. Instantly searching through back issues of newspapers for what politicians are supposed to have said or journalists have written, searching the Internet for the very latest lead, reinforces editorial spin and helps perpetrate both plain errors and rumors of scandals. When Matt Drudge markets exclusive news stories on the Internet, many of them fabricated, many journalists will fail to access the Drudge Report at their peril.[50] The availability of these efficient search engines also encourages the endless repetition of the most damaging snippets in the biographies of celebrities. Think of the coverage of the "lies" of President Roosevelt versus the "lies" of President Bush. When FDR was running for office in 1932, he promised to balance the budget and attacked Hoover as a big spender. The promise quickly faded from press coverage and campaign memory. Nor was it aired in his 1936 reelection. When President Bush promised "no new taxes," a computer search through the film files could retrieve a sound bite for television, relentlessly replayed throughout the campaign of 1992.

Finally, there is reason to question claims that the new information technology will greatly enhance consumer choice, promote diversity of mass media content, restore community, and increase the vitality of participation, thereby strengthening pluralist democracy. The potential for "choice" and "diversity" of content is certainly remarkable. As W. Russell Neuman suggests, in theory we can have a "single, high capacity, digital network of networks that will bridge what we know as the separate domains of computing, telephony, broadcasting, motion pictures, and publishing" (1991, p. x). Sitting at a console at home, everyone, in theory, will tap into a worldwide cafeteria of products, services, programs in every genre, political information of every kind. Even now, on the Internet, the individual surfer can find people with common interests and beliefs—from creators of bombs to men with prostate cancer— and shop for all those highly advertised products. But the counterforces to this technological push for diversity are, I think, overwhelming, both in production of content and the consumer-audience absorption of content. And the national variations I have outlined will likely persist, at least in the medium term.

Regarding production, we see vertical integration of every form of mass communication and entertainment—global media mergers like Disney and ABC/Cap Cities in 1996 and joint ventures like AT&T and Time Warner in 1999, leading to the concentration of control (Rochlin, 1997; Neuman, 1991; Bagdikian, 1997). Media titans will continue to contest the territory. But insofar as there is no countervailing power to commercial promotion, including a strong public broadcasting network and regulatory regime, there will be little incentive for any of the big corporate actors to serve the public interest in diversified quality or equality of access, and even less incentive to upgrade the cultural-educational content. The political economy of commercial communication systems will prevail with their advertising agendas and economies of scale in print, in broadcast, and on the Internet and its cousins. So we are back to where we started in explaining media content: the occupational and organizational contingencies of commercial media and country-specific financing and regulation will shape performance of the new media as they have shaped the "old" of the past three decades.

Regarding consumption, it is clear from my discussion of the interpenetration of brow levels and the shift toward the talk-show model among broadcast media and print media alike, that the mass media, left to their own devices, move toward a standardization of content. Along with education systems, especially K–12, they train audiences toward homogeneous tastes, not at the *lowest* common denominator where illiteracy and low income prevents much consumption, but a little above that. Media audience researchers have shown that "subcultural programming" would embrace serious political analysis and high-quality cultural-educational material for large audiences only if the system as a whole—schools, the prestige newspapers and magazines, the large broadcast networks—exposed masses to such material over the long run of decades. The trend, as we have seen, is in the opposite direction.

Will the new technology serve as new channels for social and political participation? Taking the Internet as the epitome of the new possibilities, not much is known about who participates in what chatrooms, message boards, or newsgroups on the Internet with what effect on politics or culture. The hope of the revitalization of "community" and civic engagement, however, appears to be an illusion. There is the nontrivial matter of the unequal distribution of income, motivation, and the quality of education necessary to use the new technology, a barrier to mass use which is likely to persist for a long time. But suppose everyone goes down the Information Highway. If Internet users can narrowly tailor the information they receive and confine their cyberspace "conversations" only to those who share their interests and beliefs, it is hard to see how they can connect with the larger community and society. An already fragmented and decentralized political economy (see chap. 2) can with Internet use become still more balkanized. Further, if the issue is overcoming tendencies toward political polarization (chap. 11), it is unlikely that a medium without even the porous gatekeepers of print and broadcast media can restore civility in political discourse or promote accommodation of clashing interests and values. As David Shaw (1997) suggests, the Internet provides worldwide access to fringe groups who otherwise would reach only tiny audiences or be constrained in their invective; such groups can now make a larger public still more vulnerable to rumor, nonsense, and scandalmongering.[51]

Or, if the problem is party decline, none of the above would seem to reverse that trend. In fact, a study of U.S. Senate campaigning on the Web suggests that it will further strengthen the already well-developed trend toward individualized campaigns (see chap. 11). The party affiliation of candidates is seldom mentioned on their Web sites and sometimes is not mentioned at all. Candidate "issue platforms" are highly individualized (Klotz, 1997). Although there may be some gain in a more positive spin and a more equal playing field than that provided by media ads, the likely net effect is a further erosion of political parties.

Regarding the new media as new channels for meaningful participation, we have a hint of the real effects from the first systematic, longitudinal study of Internet users. The Carnegie Mellon study (Krauft et al., 1998) tracked 169 individuals in the Pittsburgh area selected from four schools and community groups. The participants kept a record of their time using the computer network at home. Half were followed for two years, the other half for one year. Most of their Internet use was interactive—e-mail exchanges, chatrooms, or bulletin board postings as compared with reading or videos. The study measured their interaction with kin and friends, and their psychological well-being according to two scales, one of depression, the other of lonely feelings. To examine possible self-selection effects, the researchers compared the nonusers, medium users, and high users. Subjects who were lonelier, less socially engaged, or more depressed at the start of the study were no more drawn to the Internet than the happier and more participating subjects. To the surprise of the researchers,[52] the more the respondents used the Internet—even a few hours a week on-line—the more they experienced high levels of depression and loneliness. An even stronger impact was evident in their social life; Internet use lessened their interaction with their families and friends. Even one hour a week led on average to a loss of 2.7 members of their social circle (which averaged 66 people). In other words, disembodied "relationships" in the vacuum of cyberspace were isolating and bad for one's mental health. Many hours of Internet use—the epitome of the new interactive technology—is no different in its effects from the absorption of large doses of commercial television. The only "social participation," the only "community" that comes from both is the pseudogemeinschaft of the mass society. Again, the new technology reinforces and perhaps accelerates the trends I have discussed in this chapter.

SUMMARY AND CONCLUSION

Mass-society theory is useful for describing social and political trends in the more-decentralized and fragmented political economies, the least-consensual democracies. Although there may be a slow convergence in mass media behavior and impact toward the American commercial model, national differences in the amount and kinds of social participation and the strength of civic engagement make a big difference in the power of the media. In assessing data on the nature of social participation—ties to kin, friend, and neighborhood, ties to mediating associations such as churches, unions, workers' councils, and political parties—I showed that for the questions posed by mass-society theorists, the *types* of associations are critical. Although there are indicators of a century's decline in the strength of ties to primary groups, they are least important as a structural base for social consensus and democracy. Most important are those relatively stable political parties, established churches, and unions with a broad, heterogeneous mass base; they are great mixers of age grades, genders, ethnic groups, occupations, and social classes. Cross-national comparison shows that corporatist democracies have an edge over the more-decentralized and fragmented democracies in the number, density, inclusiveness, and strength of such associations. It also shows that they function to bring people into the larger community and nation and foster meaningful participation in politics. The pattern characterizing the majority of U.S. households—family-neighborhood localism (often including some affiliation with local churches)—cannot serve as a source of civic engagement unless it is meshed with these broad-based mediating associations.

I have concentrated on the United States because it highlights both similarities and differences in the vulnerability of modern democracies to mass-society tendencies. Some kinds of social and political participation in the U.S. are quite lively, especially in local ethnic, religious, and racial groups and service clubs. However, with the decline of participation in political parties, unions, broad-based churches and communitywide neighborhood associations, with the increasingly superficial quality of such participation where it occurs, the pattern does not function to develop ties to community and society. Most important, the balkanization of much of American life creates a vacuum of power into which the mass media, in symbiotic relationship to the more parochial interest groups, pour.

Thus, in only a generation or two, the United States has become an extreme case of the rising influence of the media of mass communication and entertainment. Minimal effects theories that accent self-selection of exposure or predispositions formed in social groups that insulate individuals and their families from direct media influence miss the main story. Substantial segments of the audience in fact expose themselves to uncongenial communication. Where the issue is technical, abstract, or distant—an increasing proportion of the agenda—neither local groups nor larger associations provide a guide and people rely on the media. Where there is sustained saturation coverage of an alleged crisis, scandal, or crime, the media reach large heterogeneous audiences and have substantial impact, especially among the apathetic or inadvertent viewers or readers.

More important limitations on minimal effects theories are three themes in this chapter: First, if offsets to media power are mediating groups and subcultures, then we must attend to national variations in the vitality of these groups and the nature of participation in them; this chapter shows great variation over time and across countries in these receiving structures. Second, the long-run cumulative exposure to all the media has a large and increasing effect; the media contribute to subtle shifts in values and beliefs. Third, cultural elites who could set high standards for media content, increasingly abandon the attempt. These trends open the way for the direct reach of print and broadcast media.

Over the past 30 or so years, the American commercial media have become increasingly competitive, frantic, sensational, negative, afactual, aggressively interpretive, and anti-institutional. They have created or escalated continual scandals, undifferentiated crises, and public cynicism about politics. They are increasingly important in setting the public agenda.

There are some differences in the content and effect of different media. Which of the media are most negative, least substantive, and most heavily focused on scandals and crises? Radio and now the Internet top the list, television is a close second, with the print media (especially the prestige newspapers and magazines) pulling up last. These differences are diminishing, however, with the massive interpenetration of the media, and as broadcast talk shows—with their inflammatory rhetoric, their "gotcha" journalism—emerged as the dominant model for all. The tabloidization of the leading newspapers is the most dramatic illustration. This trend is paralleled by the interpenetration of "brow" levels as the consumption habits of both mass audiences and educated elites shifted from print toward electronic media, and their program tastes gradually converged. Both the ascendance of the broadcast media and the shift in style and content toward the talk-show model imply a less-informed electorate and a decline in high culture. The erosion of elite standards is at the root of these trends.

In explaining media content and style, I found one theory very limited and two persuasive. It is not big business domination of either society or the media that explains the shift toward negative, attack-dog, pack journalism, infotainment, and scandalmongering. It is instead the organizational and occupational requirements of commercial media and the absence of a strong, well-financed, standard-setting public broadcasting network.

Cross-national comparison pins this down. Democracies that combine strong financing for public broadcasting, usually from a tax on households using television sets, media regulations that prohibit or limit political commercials and assure free access for political parties and/or candidates during campaigns, and in other ways assure cultural and political diversity in broadcasting year-round—these public policies permit them to avoid the worst pathologies of American media. A strong public broadcasting presence means more substantive content, more emphasis on parties and policy issues in politics, more educational-cultural programs, and somewhat higher general quality. The United States is the only rich democracy that forces candidates and parties to spend huge sums of money for media access; all others make plenty of room for candidates to speak for themselves at public expense. Even Canada, which is closer to the U.S. in political and economic structures than any other democracy, has such public-interest offsets to the commercialization of the media. Although there are signs that European democracies and Japan are to some extent moving in the American direction, these differences in financing and regulation still make a difference in the quality of media and hence the quality of culture and politics.

The mass-society model I have outlined in this chapter is the inverse of corporatist democracy described in chapter 2. Thus, countries most vulnerable to mass-society tendencies should have policy profiles and system outputs opposite to those in figure 2.1. The rest of this book shows much support for almost all of the connections in that figure. The role of the media in particular policy areas and campaigns will appear again in relevant chapters, especially those on health care (16), the environment (15), family policy (7), backlash (10), economic performance (12), and party decline (11).

Before leaving these theories of modern society, we must dispose of the idea of "postindustrialism," which I find least useful. Readers who share this view could well skip to the substantive chapters in Parts II and III.

Notes

This chapter is in part a summary and update of Wilensky, "Social Structure, Popular Culture, and Mass Behavior" (1961d); "Mass Society and Mass Culture" (1964a); and "Political Legitimacy and Consensus" (1983). Fred Schaffer helped to update the social participation data.

1. Cooley, Mayo, and their students emphasize the functions of primary groups in the maintenance of social order and cite reasons for their declining functions and authority. Since the primary group is the training ground for good citizenship—for learning the norms of mutual trust, tolerance, honesty, duty—its decline, they felt, would produce mass men who would produce a "mass society," "anomie," or "social disorganization." (Cooley, 1927; Mayo, 1933, pp. 122ff.; 1945, chaps. 2 and 5.) Tocqueville, among other 19th-century observers, and Lederer, Neumann, and DeGré, among modern students of totalitarianism, tend to emphasize the functions of secondary associations in the maintenance of social order or democratic political systems, or both. Alienation from work, politics, and community, and a related susceptibility to mass movements, they argue, are mainly due to the weakness of independent organizations lying between the nuclear family and the state. (Tocqueville, 1963 [1835]; Lederer, 1940; Neumann, 1942; and DeGré, 1946. Cf. Nisbet, 1953.) Durkheim was aware of the possible links of both primary and secondary groups to the level of social integration. He tended to stress the atrophy of primary-group life as a source of anomie and expressed hope that larger secondary associations (especially the occupational group or workplace) could emerge as new bonds of

solidarity, new sources of civic virtue (Durkheim, 1960 [1893], pp. 1–31). (In later writings, Durkheim increasingly emphasized the second point.)

2. In evidence, the critics say, look at the following studies: Roethlisberger and Dickson (1939); Lazarsfeld, Berelson, and Gaudet (1948); Janowitz (1952); Greer (1956); Sussman (1953); Smith, Form, and Stone (1954); Wright and Hyman (1958); Miller and Swanson (1958); Katz and Lazarsfeld (1955); Klapper (1960); and so on.

3. "Primary" relations are those which are personal, intimate, and inclusive (involve the "whole person"), which seem to the participants to be voluntary and spontaneous, and which involve a complete and mutual identity of ends (including the relationship itself as an end). Examples are relations among kin, close friends, or lovers. "Secondary" relations are impersonal, segmental, calculated, and embrace only a partial identity of ends. An example is customer relations with car dealers. (Wilensky and Lebeaux, 1958, pp. 117–125.) I use "secondary associations" interchangeably with "mediating associations."

4. From a 1991 national survey, Robert Wuthnow (1994) estimates that 40% of U.S. adults participate in small "support groups" of which 54% are either Bible study groups or adult Sunday school classes; about 13% are self-help groups, especially those dealing with addiction; and 33% are special-interest groups focused on sports, hobbies, book discussion, or politics and current events (p. 76). These diverse informal, self-help groups function mainly to overcome feelings of isolation and nourish self-esteem. Except for the 10% of the groups that meet to discuss current events and politics and the groups fully meshed with a well-organized church, it is unlikely that they tie their members to the larger communal life, let alone activate civic engagement and political participation. They tend toward self-analysis and self-absorption, or in the case of church groups, toward already long-held sectarian beliefs. Members of church-based groups report that their support group did increase their involvement in their church (3 in 5 compared to 1 in 10 of the members of nonchurch groups); such involvement did develop interests extending beyond the group. The most active participants in church-based groups were most likely to volunteer time or money to organizations in education, social service, welfare, recreation, and so on (pp. 322–326). Early childhood attendance at religious services predicts this pattern of church-based volunteer work; the pattern is restricted largely to small-group members already actively involved with their churches (p. 331). It is concentrated among religious conservatives who embrace the Christian right agenda and lifestyle (pp. 333–335). It is this minority of the general population—deeply involved church members—that we can say are in small groups that activate civic engagement (.40 × .54 × .50, a generous estimate of the proportion of regular long-term participants in church-based support groups), no more than 10% of the adult population.

5. For discussion of types of mobility, see chapter 1 (section on stratification and mobility).

6. The sample for this part of the study was 678 urban white men of the middle mass (upper-working and lower-middle class), aged 21–55, in the Detroit metropolitan area. Median time they spent per month on all organizational activity in this relatively active sample was about two hours; median time watching TV in 1960 was 48 hours per month (no doubt up sharply by now). Measures of participation included: *number* of memberships; *frequency* of contact and *time* spent; *range* of secondary participation from community isolation through ever-widening circles and networks of involvement indicated by the *heterogeneity of membership* to which he is exposed (the degree to which the organizations he names provide opportunity for interacting with people who differ from him in important social characteristics); and the *number of institutional spheres covered* by his memberships (economic, political, military, educational, religious, public welfare, recreation-aesthetic). Similar concepts guided measures of primary relations. *Community attachment* was measured by voting to support schools in the most recent school election and size of contribution to church and charity. An index of attachment to and alienation from society was also used. (See chap. 1 [section on stratification and mobility].)

7. This question about "active work" was asked only in the 1987 survey. The GSS that year did not include the black oversample used in other years.

8. Studies contrasting these methods have been done in Canada, U.S., and Britain (Hadaway, Marler, and Chaves, 1998). Respondents in conventional direct question surveys substantially overreport their religious attendance for several likely reasons: the norm of social desirability in the face of an interviewer (lessened when the questions are self-administered or ask about time use over 24 hours); the respondent's broad interpretation of "Did you attend church?" as "Are you a good Christian?"; memory lapses and telescoping (lessened by focusing attention on specific events related to the last attendance); and the ease with which interviewers can reach women and the aged, thereby oversampling the high attendance population. (*Ibid.*; Smith, 1998; Presser and Stinson, 1998.) A question-wording effect appeared in Britain in 1993 where Gallup asked how respondents spent their time on the previous Sunday (going to church was only one of a list of options) and in 1996 asked the conventional question about church or synagogue attendance in the last seven days. The traditional question yielded a weekly self-reported attendance of 21%; the Sunday activities question, 14%. (Hadaway, Marler, and Chaves, 1998, pp. 127–128.)

9. In the World Values Survey of 1990–93, 44% of Americans said they attended a religious service at least once a week against 18% in West Germany, 14% in Britain, 10% in France, and 4% in Sweden (*The Economist,* July 8, 1995, p. 19).

10. A study reviewing various NORC, AIPO, and NES studies covering changes in voluntary association memberships suggests that the rates increased from the early 1950s to 1974—probably reflecting the spurt of protest movements of the 1960s and early 1970s—but leveled off and, by some measures, declined thereafter. The average number of memberships per person, for instance, rose steadily during the 1960s, peaked in the early 1970s, and has been declining ever since (Baumgartner and Walker, 1988, pp. 911–912).

11. For an attempt to use these concepts to explain attachment to and estrangement from nation and community, see Wilensky (1960, 1961a, 1961b, 1966b). No cross-national data focused on the integrative potential of types of participation are available. For measures of societal alienation and attachments, see the stratification and mobility section of chapter 1.

12. One limited clue to the increase in sects is the recent increase in percent of national Gallup samples answering "yes" to the question, "Would you describe yourself as a 'born again,' or evangelical, Christian?" from 33% in 1986 to 39% in 1995. (*Gallup Poll: Public Opinion,* 1991, p. 239; *Public Opinion 1996,* p. 232.)

13. Similarly, a massive study of private interests in national policymaking covering labor, health, energy, and agriculture found that the 100,000 or so Washington lobbyists are highly specialized and segmented (Heinz et al., 1993). There is no overarching power elite in any policy domain, no organization or coalition consistently in the center, and little contact with adversaries—a kind of balkanization of interest representation. The authors call the system a "Hollow Core." (See the discussion of types of political economy in chap. 2.)

14. Olsen's detailed comparison of Indianapolis, USA, and Gävle, Sweden (1974) required monthly attendance for "active" status; Verba and Nie's study of the USA (1972), which found that passive membership was irrelevant to political activity, used only a self-designated "active," a weaker measure. Burstein (1972), using data from Almond and Verba (1963) for five countries, relates nine variables to an index of political participation and finds that active involvement with nonpolitical organizations was second only to media use as a source of political participation in all countries. Finally, a study by Kees Aarts (1995, table 8.6) including 8 of our 19 rich democracies shows that in 6 of them (Germany, Netherlands, Italy, Britain, Ireland, France) union members are more likely to express a party preference than nonunion members, confirming the idea of reciprocal reinforcement of union strength and party strength.

15. Analysis of data from the World Values Survey of 1981–83 for 12 of the countries in table 3.1 plus Japan (Curtis, Grabb, and Baer, 1992) generally confirms this picture but puts the U.S. at the top and moves the Netherlands up. In rates of association membership (percentage of population having one or more memberships), three of the top four are corporatist democracies (Sweden, Norway, Netherlands); the bottom three are France, Japan, and Italy, two of them corporatist-without-labor. If church membership is excluded, the U.S. drops to fifth, below Sweden, Norway, the Netherlands, and Australia. This study, however, understates union membership; its self-reports of such affiliations are *much* lower than widely accepted union density figures. It may also underestimate membership and participation in such economic organizations as co-ops and tripartite committees shaping industrial relations and social policy and planning. For instance, Sweden, Denmark, Finland, and Belgium all have union-controlled unemployment insurance funds and/or local labor-management-government committees that administer active labor-market policies. In addition, two million Swedish consumers belong to the Retail Cooperative Society, and most farmers belong to the Swedish Federation of Farmers (Olsson, 1990, p. 279). Similarly, Japan—low by the Curtis, Grabb, and Baer measures (1992)—has numerous channels for worker participation at the firm, division, and plant levels (Cole, 1992). Such channels for participation may be more significant to the national economic and political life of a democracy than most of the memberships enumerated in the few cross-national surveys available. Thus, while cross-national studies of religious participation and religiosity (e.g., frequency of prayer, belief in God) all rank the U.S. far ahead of any other rich democracy, comparisons of participation in the workplace and economic organizations place the U.S. relatively low. The text above discusses the significance of types of associations for political consensus and social integration—from family-neighborhood localism to wider patterns of community participation.

16. The rest of this chapter benefited from comments by Jerry Lubinow, Danny Wilensky, and my interviews.

17. The theme of the debilitation of elites is not confined to media managers, although the tabloidization of prestige newspapers is its most radical manifestation. Add the politicization of academic life evident in campus intolerance of politically incorrect ideas; prosecutors and judges whose politics guide an increasing proportion of their cases; politicians who know that masses of voters are angry about immigrants or welfare mothers and use them as scapegoats to achieve power; or CEOs who spend increasing amounts of their time feathering their own nests. The argument is that every day, in every way, in the flow of daily decisions, elites in all institutional spheres—in politics, in religion, in industry, in the judiciary, in education, intellectual life, literature, and the arts—fail to uphold the standards and articulate the values of their professions or the organizations and institutions they lead.

18. On December 2, 1998, another of these numerous lengthy investigations of high officials, the core of the "news," sometimes initiated by gossip substituting for news, came to nothing. A federal jury acquitted Mike Espy, the former agriculture secretary, of corruption charges after an "independent" prosecutor's four-year $17 million investigation into 38 counts of alleged gifts of sports tickets and other small favors from companies the Department of Agriculture regulates. The media amplified those accusations, too, as they had in the similar prolonged prosecution of Labor Secretary Raymond J. Donavan, acquitted of fraud charges during the Reagan administration. Donavan's farewell question was "Where do I go to get back my reputation?" (*New York Times,* Dec. 3, 1998).

19. It is no answer to say that previous generations read Grimm's fairy tales, comic books, or similar material full of violence and little has changed. These previous generations—at least those parents who read to their children—did not use TV as a baby-sitter while their children racked up 30 or 40 hours a week, often without adult supervision to interpret media content. In any case, solid evidence shows that TV violence, indeed simply watching many hours, has negative effects on child

development—cognitive, emotional, and behavioral. For instance, four critical overviews of research show positive and significant associations between exposure to television and violence and aggressive attitudes and behavior, as well as fear of personal victimization. Much of this research deals successfully with the question of causation and shows that the aggression effect far outweighs the catharsis effect (harmlessly purging the viewer's own aggressive tendencies). (Paik and Comstock, 1994; Hogben, 1998; Gunter, 1994; and Roberts and Maccoby, 1985, pp. 573–583.) That these effects are long lasting is confirmed by longitudinal studies in the U.S., U.K., Canada, Finland, and Austria (Himmelweit, Oppenheim, and Vince, 1958; Williams, 1986; Gunter, 1994, pp. 174–79, 187ff.). Long-lasting effects are largest when television exposure occurs during a sensitive period, say up to the age of 10. Regarding advertising, research clearly shows that commercial ad campaigns influence children to want, request, and sometimes buy advertised products (Roberts and Maccoby, 1985, p. 571). Conversely, there is some evidence that watching specific educational or entertainment programs has prosocial effects and helps to develop cognitive skills. *Sesame Street,* for example, unequivocally promotes cognitive development (Lesser, 1974; Cook, et al., 1975; Wright and Huston, 1995). A variety of prosocial effects (helping behavior, cooperation, kindness, altruism, sharing, friendliness, empathy, tolerance, creativity, etc.) has been uncovered for such educational or entertainment programs as *Mr. Rogers' Neighborhood, Sesame Street,* and selected prosocial episodes of *Lassie, I Love Lucy,* and *The Brady Bunch.* In short, television can be put to any use, for good or bad. That public policy can shape these uses is shown in cross-national comparisons below.

20. For instance, Gamson (1992, pp. 13, 129–130) analyzes the transcripts of 37 group interviews among people heterogeneous in race, age, gender, and religion, most of whom had no college education—approximating my "middle mass." Each group discussed affirmative action, troubled industry, nuclear power, and the Arab-Israeli conflict. He found that 68% of the interview groups relied largely on media discourse to discuss the last two distant issues. But only 38% used media discourse to discuss local industry and affirmative action, where, again, experiential knowledge was prominent.

21. A similar interpenetration of brow levels is evident for musical tastes. Results of a national cross-sectional survey showed that differences in taste among these age-education subgroups had already diminished by the 1980s (Robinson and Fink, 1986, especially table 16.4).

22. The few studies that deal with media uses by education do not consider the quality of education, which may be increasingly important. In my study I found that for the number of media areas in which highbrow exposure is reported, the *amount* of education makes little difference from grade zero through "some college"; thereafter, both quality of education and sheer level count heavily. The biggest jump in mean scores is between baccalaureate level and graduate level (.462), but the difference between men with high- and men with low-quality undergraduate education (.318) is greater than the differences between less than high school vs. high school (an infinitesimal .025), high school vs. some college (.106) or even some college and low-quality baccalaureate degree (.313). Ultimately the mere rise in the average education level will do little for the cultivation of taste in reading and in broadcast media; what counts is the number who complete college, and especially the number fortunate enough to go through a few favored colleges, who are declining as a percentage of the educated.

23. From 1970 to 1974 Flip Wilson, a black comedian, made the first breakthrough to a network crossover program (a black performer with a mass audience of whites as well as blacks). One of his regular acts featured a cross-dressing prostitute.

24. It is by no means natural for evangelicals to buy Reaganomics—the free-marketeer, antitax, anti–social spending, antibureaucratic ideas of the post-Nixon Republican Party. Most of them are part of the middle mass and many are quite poor; they are not especially hostile to the welfare state, or the regulation of big business. I suggest that the rise of anti-institutional themes in the news media facilitated the uneasy marriage with Republican economic ideology while the liberal-left bent of en-

tertainment programs, offensive to evangelicals' religious values and beliefs, served as a focus for their anger.

25. If the issue is whether any public affairs information is absorbed from various types of media, research from the 1960s and 1970s shows that print use is positively related to the level of information about public affairs but that television use is unrelated to such information (Roberts and Maccoby, 1985, pp. 560–561). Thus, even if the content and style of the media were not shifting toward the talk-show model, the continued ascendance of broadcast media over print implies a less-informed electorate.

26. C-SPAN junkies, of course, can hear candidate speeches and policy conferences, but this is a tiny slice of the mass audience Only about 1 in 16 of adults in the U.S. are regular viewers of the Cable-Satellite Public Affairs Network (C-SPAN): 4–8% say they watch C-SPAN regularly, 13–20% view it "sometimes," and 53–58% "never" tune in. Older, more educated, and more affluent adults are the core of C-SPAN regulars. But the differences are not large: for instance, the percentage of adults who are regular viewers and are high-school graduates is 5%; college graduates, 8%; postgraduates, 11%. Because C-SPAN typically reports events fully and accents substance, context, and balance, its audience compared with the total population is less alienated from politics, less cynical, and more active; they believe that political campaigns and political debate are important and think that political action can lead toward positive change (Frantzich, 1999). Whether this is self-selection of the politically efficacious or the benign impact of C-SPAN is not known. Financed by the cable industry as a gesture toward the obligation to serve the public interest and as a way to fill the expanded news hole created by TV cameras in Congress, C-SPAN is an oasis of television quality in the broadcast desert.

27. Mr. Huffington dropped out of sight and, having campaigned on family values, resurfaced in 1998, confessing that he was gay and not quite sure that he belonged in the Republican party.

28. There are doubtless some instances in which a broadcast network engages in self-censorship in avoiding stories strongly injurious to their parent company. For example, ABC's *20/20* apparently killed a critical report that Disney hired convicted pedophiles at its theme parks and resorts (Stevens, 1998). In my view these are small eddies in the rushing stream of prosecutorial reporting by the networks' "news magazines."

29. Similarly, in 1998 CNN's *NewsStand* alleged that the United States military used nerve gas during the Vietnam War; the report was false and was later retracted.

30. In a study of editors, producers, and reporters of CBS and NBC evening news and *Newsweek* and *Time,* Gans (1980, pp. 146–181) found that the norms of journalism define a "good story" as one that has immediacy, drama, high stakes, and a colorful cast of characters. This is why an impeachment is considered the best imaginable political story—and why the media had a stake in blurring the difference between Nixon's crimes against the state and Clinton's sex-and-lies scandal. Dan Rather, CBS anchor, notes the effect of the recent intensification of the competition for survival: One fear, he says, is now common in all the newsrooms in the country—"the fear that if we don't do it somebody else will, and when they do it, they will get a few more readers, a few more listeners, a few more viewers than we do" (quoted in Brill, 1998, p. 117).

31. Similar underdog horse-race journalism catapulted Gary Hart into celebrity overnight in 1984. Based on a few thousand votes in the Democratic primary, the media declared him a leading contender for the presidency, a New Face with New Ideas. Of course after building him up, the investigator-prosecutor journalists were equally happy to bring Senator Hart down by exposing his sex life.

32. James Fallows (1996, chaps. 3 and 4) has chronicled this shift from a time when there were hundreds of working reporters plus a few media celebrities of limited income and modest influence (e.g., Ed Murrow, Eric Sevareid, and Walter Cronkite, who still retained the tradition of field reporting), to Barbara Walters (at least $10 million per year from ABC), Dan Rather ($7 million from

CBS), Tom Brokaw ($7 million from NBC), and Sam Donaldson (a modest $3 – 3.5 million from ABC). (Figures from a 1999 salary and bonus survey by *Brill's Content* 2, no. 4 [May 1999]: 84 – 95.) Fallows suggests that in their eagerness to get on one of the talk shows and join the lecture circuit, print reporters now bend their words to please talk-show hosts (1996, pp. 123 – 124). If sneering and succinct insults delivered in a condescending style is the talk-show norm, that's how they write. This is another illustration of the move of print media toward broadcast media and both toward the talk-show model, discussed previously. Incidentally the top media compensation paid in 1998 went to radio and television talk-show host Howard Stern ($17 million).

33. The savings and loan crisis was national. In the larger scheme of things, the Arkansas firm was a small matter and whatever white-collar crimes were uncovered were typical. The journalists' hoped-for connection to the White House was based on the Clintons' long-standing friendship with the owner of the S&L, and highly motivated allegations from Clinton's long-standing political enemies that money from Madison was illegally diverted to prop up Clinton's losing investment in real estate or to President Clinton's 1984 gubernatorial campaign in a Grand Conspiracy.

34. Less than two weeks after the new president was sworn in, Sam Donaldson of ABC asked on a weekend talk show, "Is the presidency over?" and "R.W. Apple, Washington Bureau Chief of the *New York Times*, wrote that the administration 'desperately' needed to recover from its 'politically devastating failure' in the Zoe Baird case" (where the media launched "Nannygate" to scandalize the failure of the nominee for attorney general to pay social security taxes for her baby-sitter). (Fallows, 1996, pp. 135 – 137.) Relentless reporting of alleged scandals is matched by relentless reporting of failures and/or false promises of officials. Almost immediately after Bill Clinton took office, Apple began declaring that the omens were bad for Clinton's success in office, and his prospects for a second term were poor. No event that could be fitted into this scenario of a failed presidency and pending defeat in 1996 was overlooked. Except for the months of the glow of the war against Iraq, President Bush suffered the same treatment, culminating in the constant replay of his broken promise, "Read my lips: No new taxes."

35. It is likely that there is an interaction between the journalist's increasingly frantic deadlines and her need for brevity and the public's increasingly short attention span. If the journalist assumes that the viewer is channel-surfing, she will try to capture the essence of a story in three or four catchwords.

36. Jerry Lubinow (conversation) suggests that there has been a change in the nature of pack journalism since the 1960s, that reporters do not now compare notes as much as they did then. There is still pack journalism in that they conform to the scandal-crisis-sensation definition of news. Because of increased competition, however, each reporter tries a different spin. The frequent result is to inflate trivial details simply because no one else has them.

37. Data limitations make systematic comparisons on each of these dimensions for our 19 countries impossible. I had to rely on a few cross-national studies, several single country studies, and my impressions from interviews and some firsthand television viewing in Europe. Rough comparisons from fewer than 19 democracies will have to suffice. The cross-national studies include, for example, Euromedia Research Group (1997); Kaid and Holtz-Bacha (1995); Robillard (1995); "The Overselling of Candidates on Television" (1984); "The Challenge to Public Broadcasting" (1987); Smith (1980, 1981); Noam (1991); Siune and Truetzschler (1992); Humphries (1996); and Blumler (1992, chaps. 1 – 3, 12 – 14). Single-country studies include Katz (1977); Humphries (1994); Blumler, McLeod, and Rosengren (1992); and Blumler (1992, Part II).

38. The following account of France relies largely on Johnston and Gerstlé (1995) and Wolton (1992). The account of the Netherlands draws on McQuail (1992), Brants and McQuail (1997), and my interviews.

39. "Behind the opposition to commerce," says Denis McQuail (1992, p. 102), "there are mixed elements of puritanism, high-mindedness, left-wing politics, conservatism, protectionism for the commercial press, and pragmatic assessment of the vulnerability of the whole regulatory structure if consumer market-forces were allowed free rein."

40. I am indebted to Steven Vogel for translations of regular Japanese surveys on TV viewing habits from which we calculated these figures.

41. The appropriation for the Corporation for Public Broadcasting in 1995 was only $300 million for 351 public TV stations and 629 radio stations. In 1998 it was down to $250 million.

42. For several years in the 1970s BBC television broadcast a sophisticated political satire, *That Was the Week That Was.* It pulled a mass audience out of the pubs and back home on Saturday night in prime time. This is another illustration that dumbing it down is not a mass demand but a judgment of media managers and governments. Mass tastes do not spring forth spontaneously; they are almost entirely shaped by family, school, and the media, with the latter, as we have seen, in ascendance.

43. BBC offers 840 hours of children's programming per year, more than 12% of its entire schedule. (American public broadcasting carries fewer than 200 hours a year and relies heavily on reruns while commercial networks dump a few hours into the Saturday morning ghetto of low-cost, low-quality cartoons, heavily interspersed with advertising.) Sweden also gives about 12% plus features for adults about children. Japan has a large public investment in children's television programs, using many of them to supplement classroom teaching. And since the 1970s Australia has had a nonprofit foundation to produce children's programs (Minow and LaMay, 1995, pp. 43–45ff.), making up for "market failures."

44. The following account is based on Adrian Lyttleton (1994), Pier Paolo Giglioli (1996) and my interviews.

45. There is no doubt some political corruption in a few developed democracies, especially France, Belgium, and Austria, but in scope and level it does not come close to Italy's.

46. Although India and Japan export the largest number of films, the U.S. has most box office impact. In late 1985, U.S. films accounted for 55% of the weekly box office in Paris and Rome, 65% in Copenhagen, and 70% in Helsinki (Dominick, 1987, p. 55).

47. By the mid-1990s, the BBC audience share among those with satellite and cable TV was down to 30%. Its income from set taxes was also down (*The Economist,* July 9, 1994, pp. 14–15).

48. For analysis of effects of electronic data processing on organizational structures and the quality of policy decisions see Wilensky (1967a, pp. 184–187).

49. For more detailed discussions of these subtle changes see the 1997 report of the Library Committee of the Berkeley Academic Senate by Leon Litwak, Chair; and Rochlin (1997, pp. 35ff.).

50. *Brill's Content* reviewed the 51 stories Drudge labeled "Exclusive" from January to September 1998. It found that of the 31 stories that actually were exclusive, 10 (32%) were untrue and/or never happened, 11 (36%) were true, and the accuracy of the remaining 10 (32%) was debatable or still unknown. Drudge, a high school graduate who got his inspiration watching the attack-dog talk show *Crossfire* as a teenager and became a regular on on-line chat shows, garnered nearly one million hits a month in late 1997 for his Drudge Report. This audience is growing apace (McClintick, 1998). While Drudge concentrated on alleged Clinton's scandals, another on-line magazine, *Salon,* was breaking the "news" that Henry Hyde, the lead accuser-prosecutor of Clinton in the Congress, had an extended extramarital affair in the 1960s. These are examples of gutter journalism with a high-tech flavor and an audience that embraces establishment journalists as well as those with no pretense to standards. In 1999 ABC Radio Networks hired Drudge to host a nationally syndicated talk show.

51. Experts from Klanwatch and the Militia Task Force, monitoring trends in hate groups such as the Ku Klux Klan, Neo-Nazis, Skinheads, white Christian fundamentalists, and black separatist organizations, observed the rise of a new subculture over the three years 1994 to 1997: 163 Web sites

popped up to preach hatred, and about 50,000 music CDs were sold by hard-rock groups urging violence. Teenagers are the main target (*San Francisco Chronicle,* March 4, 1998).

52. They began with positive views about the social impact of information technology. Financing came from companies with a stake in positive findings (IBM, Intel, Apple Computer, etc.) as well as NSF.

4
THEORIES OF THE POSTINDUSTRIAL SOCIETY

Among the widely accepted myths about the shape of modern society is the idea that a new "postindustrial" order is emerging in which intellectuals, scientists, managers, and experts in command of theoretical knowledge dominate the political system, while service occupations (the "tertiary sector") dominate employment and production, and "postmaterialist" values dominate the culture.[1] In other words, a vanguard of educated people, occupied in "health, education, research, and government" (Bell, 1973, p. 15), is already decisive in every modern political economy, and it is the carrier of the "cultural revolution." Older issues are giving way to newer issues, in a major shift in values—shift from the work ethic to freedom and expressiveness ("do your own thing"), from intellectual calculation to impulse and ecstasy (as in drugs and rock music), from hierarchy to equality and participatory democracy, from a competitive rat race to a quest for community, from economic growth and consumerism to environmentalism and a concern with the quality of life (cf. Davis, 1971; Turner, 1976), all with profound political effects (Huntington, 1974).

In this chapter I first evaluate evidence of the limits of the structural aspects of postindustrial theory and then deal with the even more limited cultural aspects. I argue that its account of industrial and occupational trends is too gross to be useful; its account of shifts in values and beliefs does not square with the evidence; and its view of the politics of modern democracies misses great variation among them. The major structural and cultural trends in rich countries are better captured by convergence theory with its accent on the universal and specific effects of continuing industrialization (chap. 1). Insofar as "postindustrial" means the rise to power of experts in command of theoretical knowledge, it is not a common feature of modern societies; it applies best to corporatist democracies and, as we have seen, misses the mark for the least-corporatist democracies such as the United States (chaps. 2 and 3).

Occupational and Industrial Trends

Using the U.S. as the most-advanced economy, we have already traced the well-established trends in the occupational composition of the labor force (see chap. 1 and figure 1.2): a

drastic decline in farm people; a steady increase of white-collar and professional and administrative employees; very fast growth in the newer professions and a host of semiprofessional, semitechnical occupations; growth in the proportion of "nonfarm proprietors,
managers, and officials," especially since 1940; a small decline in the "working class" from
1910 to 1988, accelerating since then but within it a sharp drop in laborers and the semiskilled, some growth in low-paid service workers, and stability in skilled craftsmen, repairmen, and foremen. The net effect has been a general upgrading of the whole population,
reflecting both the average skill and educational level required. All these trends were evident from 1910 (the earliest date for good data comparability) to 1950 (Wilensky and
Lebeaux, 1958, pp. 90–94); they cannot be called postindustrial. They are merely occupational changes induced by continuing industrialization.

But what about a postindustrial shift in the types of industries in which modern
populations work? Are these trends recent? At some threshold of development are they
universal?

Data available on the percentage distribution of employment for seven rich democracies
from 1920 to 1992 (table 4.1) cast doubt on the postindustrial thesis. I concentrate on three
categories that have shown substantial trends or notable national differences and are most
relevant to the theory of postindustrialism: "transformative industries," "producer services,"
and "social services."

1. *Transformative* (almost all of this is manufacturing). It includes machinery, construction, food, textiles, metals, chemicals, miscellaneous manufacturing, and utilities. The
pattern in table 4.1 is a rise in the percentage employed in these manufacturing industries from 1920 to 1970 in Japan, Germany, France, Italy, and stability in Anglo-Saxon
countries (UK, USA, Canada). (Was this the coming of postindustrial society?) Then,
after 1970, there was stability in Japan, and a decline in the rest ranging from small declines in Germany (47% to 40%) and Canada (27% to 22%) to large declines in the UK
(47% to 27%) and Italy (44% to 30%). What is significant is that the end point (circa
1990) for Canada, France, and Germany is about where they began in 1920, while Japan
and Italy *increased* the manufacturing share of employment. Only the UK and the USA
evidence a decline. Can increases in manufacturing jobs or a 1990s return to the manufacturing share of 1920 for five of these seven advanced industrial societies over 60 years
be called postindustrial?

2. *Producer Services.* Manufacturing versus services is a false dichotomy. Throughout
the history of industrialization, the two have been inextricably meshed. The section
"Producer Services" in table 4.1 includes insurance, banking, real estate, legal services,
accounting, engineering, and miscellaneous business services. Very few of these occupations are new to the post–World War II period, let alone to the 20th century. They
were essential to 19th-century industrialization and accelerated along with manufacturing. Lloyds of London did not spring forth in some postindustrial era. Its members were
covering risks of trade and manufacturing as early as 1734. And the Philadelphia gentlemen, educated as scientists and engineers, who gathered in the railroad shops of Pennsylvania as design consultants in close collaboration with skilled machinists and artisans to
forge the new steam locomotives of the 1830s, were hardly postindustrial (Green, 1972).

TABLE 4.1 The coming of postindustrial society? Percentage distribution of employment by relevant industrial sector, 1920–92, seven countries*

	Transformative (Manufacturing)			
Rank order circa 1990	1920	1940	1970	1990
(1) Germany	39	47	47	41
(2) Japan	20	25	34	34
(3) Italy	24	32	44	30
(4) France	30	30	37	30
(5) United Kingdom	42	44[a]	47	27
(6) United States	33	30	33	25
(7) Canada	26	28	27	22

	Producer Services			
Rank order circa 1992	1921	1941	1971	1992
(1) United States	3	5	8	14
(2) United Kingdom	3	3[a]	5	12
(3) Canada	4	3	7	11
(4) France	2	2	5	10
(5) Japan	1	1	5	10
(6) Germany	2	3	5	7
(7) Italy	1	2	2	nmf

	Social Services			
Rank order circa1992	1921	1941	1971	1992
(1) United Kingdom	9	12[a]	18	27
(2) United States	9	10	22	25
(3) Germany	6	11	16	24
(4) Canada	8	9	22	23
(5) France	5	7	15	20
(6) Italy	4	8	7	16
(7) Japan	5	6	10	14

*Source: Castells and Aoyama (1994), table 1, pp. 12–13, based on a classification by Singelmann (1978). Dates are approximate; Castells and Aoyama record slight variations in dates and discuss comparability of data. For detailed breakdowns on the U.S., see Castells (1984), table 13, p. 58. For definitions, see my text. The sector percentages for each country do not add up to 100 percent because I have eliminated sectors least relevant to the theory: extractive, distributive, and personal services, discussed in the text.

[a]1951, not 1940 or 1941.

Thus we would expect what we see in table 4.1: For as long as we can find data, manufacturing and producer services grew together, the latter faster than manufacturing, as specialized services grew to serve the needs of increasingly complex organizations. That Japan and Germany have a lower share of employment in this category than the USA, UK, and Canada may be a statistical illusion. These two high-productivity manufacturing leaders have internalized producer services in large companies and in integrated networks of suppliers rather than contracting them out, so they are not enumerated separately. I think Italy's very low figures also reflect difficulties in classification as well as its larger agricultural sector, its less-developed regions, and an abundance of small businesses. The celebrated flexible production networks of small producers pooling resources for expert help in finance, R&D, and marketing account for only a small portion of total Italian employment (see chap. 1). Similarly, where technology is truly new, the old ambiguity of the distinction between material goods and intangible services remains. Castells and Aoyama (1994) note this ambiguity for computer software, genetic engineering-based agriculture and many other modern products; they ask "Is a software programme sold as a disk a 'good' but, if sold on-line does it become a 'service'?" (p. 8).

3. *Social Services.* There is nothing new or uniformly postindustrial about the growth of social-services employment. As I show in our 19-country analysis in chapters 5 and 9, the welfare state, which generates such employment, is more than a century old; it accelerated after World War II; and its rate of growth slowed since the mid-1970s or early 1980s. However, both its efficiency and program emphasis, and hence public employment, vary across nations and time because of national differences in affluence, left power, types of political economy, minority-group cleavages, and rates of mobility. There is nothing in this picture of substantial variation among rich democracies to suggest a postindustrial trend, merely a continued universal growth of the welfare state. The remaining national variations in spending, finance, and program emphasis are rooted in politics as well as the level and timing of economic development and its demographic correlates. For an explanation of why the U.K. and the U.S. have an abundance of social-service employment despite their modest welfare states, see my treatment of the welfare mess (chap. 8) and of bureaucratic bloat (chap. 9).

I have excluded three categories from table 4.1: "extractive" industries, "distributive services," and "personal services." They either show no trend or are irrelevant to the concept postindustrial. (Wilensky and Lebeaux, 1958, pp. 93–94.) *Extractive industries,* or what Colin Clark called "primary," include agriculture and mining. These industries, with remarkable increases in efficiency, everywhere decline in employment as they increase in output. Figure 1.2 shows that in the U.S. the percentage in agriculture is down to 2.0%. In 1992, in the seven countries of table 4.1 all extractive industries' employment ranged from the UK's 3.3% to Italy's very high 9.5%. It is a universal, long-term trend of all rich countries, a product of continuing industrialization. "*Distributive services*" include transportation, communication, and wholesale and retail trade; with small variations, they account for a more or less stable percentage of employment from 1920 to 1992, ranging from a fifth to a quarter of all employment, again belying assertions about a postindustrial pattern. Finally, I have excluded "*personal services,*" which include domestic service, hotels, eating and drinking places, repair, laundry, barber and beauty, entertainment, and miscellaneous personal services. There is no pattern either in trend or cross-national comparisons. For instance, from about 1920 to 1992, personal services as a percentage of employment roughly doubled in Canada, France, and Japan; increased somewhat in the U.S. but was stable or dropped in Germany, Italy, and the UK. What can be said with certainty about this heterogeneous category is that domestic servants steadily decrease with industrialization; as mass standards of living climb, fewer people are willing to serve the persons or households of others. With mechanization, laundry services show a similar decline. These declines are offset by stability in the percentage employed in hotels, repair services, entertainment, and barber and beauty shops (beauty salons become innovative and mechanized and grow while barber shops stagnate and decline). The most important offset is the sharp climb of jobs in eating and drinking places—if we can take the U.S. experience as typical (Castells, 1984, table 13, p. 58).

A major problem with the idea of postindustrialism is the great heterogeneity of "services"—heterogeneity in income, status, power, freedom on the job, skill levels, and related political orientation and lifestyles. If the purpose of this theory is to connect changes in occupational structures with shifts in culture, politics, the nature of work experience, or anything important, "the service economy" is both vague and hopelessly heterogeneous. For instance, "retail services" include the big-ticket salesperson in a posh department store and the entrepreneur of the hot dog stand; the manager of a large auto repair shop and the owner of a mom-and-pop grocery store; the maître d' at New York City's Chanterelle and the hamburger flipper at McDonald's. "Services" embrace a computer scientist and an urban dog walker; the full-time, stably employed office supervisor in the headquarters of a drugstore chain and a part-time temporary worker at the check-out counter in the supermarket whose wages place him or her among the working poor; a high-tech consultant in a firm selling software for financial managers and a no-tech salesperson in a local dress shop; a corporate lawyer in a firm with 200 partners and associates and a solo lawyer with an ethnic clientele. In practically every routine of life that is important to people—the nature of their work and use of their skills; their income, status, security, and opportunities for upward mobility; their family life and leisure style—these pairs are in different worlds, as we have seen in my discussion of opposing trends in the organization of work and the limits of a stratification model of modern society (chap. 1).

Regarding the theme of technocratic dominance, my discussion of types of political economy above and elsewhere (1983, 1997) shows that while it is true that experts and intellectuals multiply with economic development, their influence—their integration with men and women of power—varies with the political and economic context within which they work. These differences in expert influence by type of political economy are elaborated in chapter 2 (on types of political economy). The role of economists is discussed in chapters 11 (on party decline, especially in the case of New Zealand) and 17 (on globalization, the section on central bank autonomy).

In short, if all the occupational and industrial shifts now labeled postindustrial amount to is a continuation of more than a century's rise in the level of education; an increase in the skill, discipline, and perhaps knowledge of the average worker; and the increased employment of experts, then we should talk about those long-term trends and not impose an elaborate superstructure of dubious claims about the revolutionary character of these gradual shifts.[2]

POSTINDUSTRIAL VALUES?

Postindustrial theorists argue that since the Great Depression there has been a major shift in values in all rich countries toward "postmaterialist," "postindustrial" values of self-expression, personal freedom, creativity, self-actualization, belonging, and participatory democracy. The acquisitive, materialistic values of the past, embraced by older populations who grew up in less affluent societies, they say, will fade away as younger political generations raised in the affluence of the postwar era come to power and dominate the culture.

Writers who see this vision of a postindustrial era vary in their depiction of the exact content of these values and the generating forces. But they usually mention the growth of service sectors, mass education, affluence (high levels of GDP per capita), and high rates of political participation as root causes. They all assert that postmaterialist values are especially strong and prevalent among vanguard groups—the educated, young, affluent, secure, and mobile—who are in a position to demand still more freedom, still more comfort, still more sense of community. With generational turnover, the postmaterialist consciousness of the possibilities of human liberation is presumably spreading to the masses of people in every rich democracy. The new values are said to be durable because they are learned early in childhood and teenage years and are little affected either by subsequent political or economic changes ("external" or "objective" events and situations) or by later socialization.

Such themes are familiar from a spate of countercultural books of the 1960s. Because Ronald Inglehart has attempted to trace these shifts empirically in two summary books, *The Silent Revolution* (1977) and *Culture Shift in Advanced Industrial Society* (1990), I concentrate on his formulations and subsequent comparative research using the same measures. Inglehart bases his conclusions on a series of surveys conducted between 1970 and 1973 in six West European countries and then for every year from 1976 to 1988 (1990, pp. 75, 84) for nine European countries and the U.S. He also analyzes data gathered by other researchers for up to 20 rich countries and occasional nonrich countries such as Mexico and Hungary. The measure of materialist and postmaterialist values is a pattern of answers when representative samples of citizens were asked to rank the following goals by their importance to them (an asterisk marks what Inglehart considers postmaterialist):

 A. Maintain order in the nation

 *B. Give people more say in the decisions of the government

 C. Fight rising prices

 *D. Protect freedom of speech

 E. Maintain a high rate of economic growth

 F. Make sure that this country has strong defense forces

 *G. Give people more say in how things are decided at work and in their community

 *H. Try to make our cities and countryside more beautiful

 I. Maintain a stable economy

J.   Fight against crime

★K. Move toward a friendlier, less impersonal society

★L. Move toward a society where ideas count more than money

For most of his analysis Inglehart uses the first four items as his value priority index. Respondents who chose both "more say" and "free speech" are termed postmaterial; those who chose both "maintaining order" and" fighting rising prices" are labeled materialist. Because that index is so often used in both Inglehart and subsequent studies of values and value change in contemporary democracies, I focus on it here, although my assessment holds true for the longer list of indicators as well.[3] Leaving aside almost-fatal weaknesses in these measures for later discussion, here are the main findings:

1.   *As a percentage of all those surveyed in Europe from 1970 to 1986 pure materialists (Ms) outnumber pure postmaterialists (PMs) in every one of 12 countries in every age cohort except for those born in 1956–1965 in the Netherlands (20% Ms to 27% PMs) and West Germany (22% Ms to 26% PMs).* In 1986–87, however, postmaterialists outnumbered materialists in the Netherlands and West Germany and among the young in Denmark and Great Britain (1990, p. 93). *Most respondents are mixed types:* In 1986–87, for instance, in the combined samples for 12 nations (EC and USA), 53.4% were neither postmaterialist nor materialist (calculated from 1990, p. 93). For Eurobarometer surveys of 1986–87, if we weigh the results by country populations, we get only 15% pure postmaterialists to 30% pure materialists (*ibid.*).

2.   *The locus of these pure postmaterialists is younger, more educated respondents, especially students* (1990, pp. 91, 93, 318–322).

3.   *Clearly, however, in the entire population, materialists outnumber the postmaterialists by hefty margins.* Much of Inglehart's case rests on trends in postmaterialist responses from 1970 to 1988. Based on the 12-item measure, materialists outnumbered postmaterialists three to one in 1973. By the late 1980s the ratio was two to one. (Using either the 4 items in 1986–87 calculated from table 2–4, p. 93, or the 12 items in 1988, pp. 97–98, the ratio is two materialists for every one postmaterialist.)

4.   Inglehart argues that the "Postmaterialists are no longer concentrated in student ghettos . . . they are as numerous as the Materialists (or even more numerous) among those in their 30s and well into their 40s. They have moved into positions of influence and authority throughout society" (1990, p. 319). The picture from the crude occupational breakdowns available (his table 9–10, p. 319), however, shows that the mass publics of the EC countries surveyed from 1980 to 1986 (9 countries, $N = 124,291$) are by his measure decidedly materialistic.[4] Only in the upper-middle class aged 15–49 ("top management and civil service" and "professional")—comprising only 3.25 % of the total sample—do the postmaterialists outnumber the materialists. Even the students under 35 (9.4% of the total) were split 24% PM to 20% M, hardly overwhelming. In all other categories (from white-collar and manual employees through the unemployed, retired, and housewives), the materialists outnumber the PMs by substantial margins even among the pre-

sumably countercultural cohort who entered the labor force from 1965 to 1974 (who when interviewed in 1980–86 were probably a majority of the "under 35" respondents).

Put another way, in this study the best case for postmaterialist penetration of vanguard elites is weak. If we assume that all "top management and civil service" and "professional" and student respondents from age 15 to 49 are "elites," and assume further that if they endorse "protect freedom of speech" and "give people more say" as important goals they are postmaterialist, then all we can claim is the following: *first, of the total sample only 0.79% are nonstudent elites under 50 with postmaterialist values; second, only 24% of the students are postmaterialist.* That leaves 76% of the students in these nine European countries who are classified by Inglehart's measure "materialist" or "mixed." That suggests special attention to what happens to the orientations of the (minority of) young people and especially college students who come on as postmaterialist now when they are 18 or so as they move to adulthood—as they enter the labor market, marry, and have children. Because this question goes beyond the issue of postindustrial value shifts, it will be saved for a later assessment of the relative effects of political generation (or period), age cohort, and family life cycle.

5. *Despite all these caveats, the finding (1990, p. 95) that during the 15 or so years of surveys postmaterialism increased in most rich democracies would be impressive if it were not for one serious flaw—the poor face validity of the measures of "values"* on which most of Inglehart's conclusions ride ("maintain order" and "fight rising prices" vs. "protect free speech" and "give people more say in government decisions"). First, it is not obvious why it is materialist to worry about rising prices and postmaterialist to worry about free speech, a concern of the American founding fathers. Surely some of the respondents might expect that their government could at once protect free speech and fight inflation, which may be one reason that for 1986–87 surveys, 53% of the sample are mixed types. Second, the general problem with asking people to rank their goals in surveys is that the respondents typically underrate the goals they have already achieved but still cherish: "money," says the high-wage worker earning the area or industry rate for his occupation, is "less important" than "intrinsic job satisfaction"; "income," says the high-paid professional who has a lot of it, is less important than "self-expression"; safety is not important to the already safe, and so on. Similarly, in the study of postmaterialism, upper-middle-class educated respondents living in safe neighborhoods will often say "maintaining order" is not one of the two "most important goals" while "giving people more say" is because they already have safety.

In other words, the social and economic context of the survey question mightily shapes the response. Consider the respondents who rank "protect free speech" as the "most important goal"; presumably a sign of their postmaterialist values. As McCloskey and Brill (1983, pp. 48–55) have conclusively shown, if one moves from such abstract questions about freedom of speech to questions about the exercise of speech in particular situations, the level of support drops off sharply among the same people who love free speech in the abstract.[5]

Finally, ranking the goal of "fighting rising prices" is peculiarly sensitive to two contexts: whether inflation is high or low, moving up or down; and whether the particular respondent is among the debtor majority who win from inflation or the creditor minority who lose. Dealing with changes in the inflation rate, Inglehart finds that the sharp price rise in the mid-1970s and 1979–80 brought an increase in materialism in the six West European countries he analyzed—a finding confirmed by subsequent studies using the same measures (Clarke and Dutt, 1991, p. 911; Duch and Taylor, 1994, pp. 816–817). Inglehart's data do not permit analysis of the second effect (winning debtors vs. losing creditors). Ardent consumers with heavy debt loads whose wages or social-security benefits are indexed will not worry much about inflation. Does that make them postmaterialists? This would be especially relevant in countries with easy credit and/or a history of moderate (not hyper-) inflation.

6. *In fact, as Inglehart's tables show (1977), the issues that excite Western publics are over-whelmingly economic performance and political and civic order, a pattern that has not changed since the early 1970s* (1990, p. 97). Asked in 1973 to choose the first and second most impor-tant of a list of 12 goals, the populations of these 11 nations ranked "fighting rising prices" as the leading goal, with "economic growth" and "economic stability" close by. "Fighting crime" and "maintaining order" were also typically near the top. In the aggre-gate, no postmaterial goal ranked higher than third in any of the 11 nations; the mean rating of "more say on the job," the most popular postindustrial goal, was only sixth; the mean ratings of "a less impersonal society" and "more say in government" were similarly low (1990, table 2–6, p. 98).

Slightly more recent data following the first big oil shock reveal that same pattern (1990, table 4–6, p. 149). In surveys conducted in nine rich democracies from 1974 to 1976 economic performance and political order were again the overwhelming preoccu-pation of mass publics, with the possible exception of Japan.

- "Maintaining a stable economy" was the leading goal for all but the popula-tions of the Netherlands and Italy; for the two deviant countries it was fighting crime.

- "Fighting crime" was at or near the top for all countries. In no country except the Netherlands, Finland, and Japan did postmaterialist goals rank above third. In the Netherlands "more say on the job" ranked a distant second to the fight against crime; in Finland and Japan "friendlier, less impersonal society" ranked a distant second to a stable economy; and in Japan "beautiful cities and countryside" ranked third.

- Averaging responses across the nine countries, no postmaterialist goal ranked higher than a distant third—far behind "maintaining a stable economy" and "fighting crime."[6]

Finally, as Inglehart notes, while the most recent European communitywide surveys of 1988 showed that compared to 1973 in the 12-item list of goals "fighting rising prices" fell from first in 1973 to sixth rank in 1988, "materialist" goals held five of the top six positions with roughly the same rank order. There were only minor changes: "economic growth" moved up from second to first place; "fighting crime" moved up from third to second, and so on (Inglehart, 1990, p. 97).

The realism in this pattern of responses is refreshing. Not only is the achievement of these top priorities a necessary condition for the fulfillment of all other goals, but even the national variations make sense. For instance, the percentage of the Italians who ranked "fighting crime" as the top priority in 1974–76 was 59%; the percentage of Japanese was only 20% (table 4–6, p. 149). Mass publics were reflecting real threats evidenced in high rates of crime in Italy (including a rising tide of Red Brigade kneecapping and murders) and low rates in Japan (see chap. 14); and when inflation was rampant, citizens expected their governments to fight it; when it was under control, they ranked some other basic goal higher.

Similarly, national differences in unemployment rates and their fluctuation over time shape these survey results. Although Inglehart does not include an item on anxiety about unemployment (an indicator of "materialism"?), it turns out in other studies using his measures that unemployment, like inflation, drastically shapes the scores on his 4-item "postmaterialist" index. The best of these (Clarke and Dutt 1991) covers the period 1976–86 using a pooled cross-sectional time-series regression analysis of eight countries (Belgium, Denmark, France, Great Britain, Ireland, Italy, the Netherlands, and West Germany). It shows that unemployment has a puzzling effect: increases in the jobless rate bring large increases in postmaterialist responses. The researchers explain that in the 1980s, as unemployment soared and inflation came down, these European respondents abandoned the item "fight rising prices" and sought something else on the list. In the absence of an item on "fighting unemployment" many of them chose "give people more say in government" to express their preference for government action to do something about the problem at hand. (In fact, increases in unemployment strongly increase the "more say" response.) Thus, it is not any rise in postindustrial values that explain this shift: it is instead "the changing salience of inflation and unemployment on the issue agenda" (*ibid.*, p. 913).

Clarke and Dutt (1991) also analyze stability in individual responses using more powerful panel data for Netherlands (1974–79), Germany (1974–80), and the U.S. (1974–81) and replicating both Inglehart's 4-item index and an 8-item measure of value priorities (E through L on the list above). Their conclusions: (1) There is "massive" response turnover among individuals (p. 915). Thirty-eight percent of the Dutch, 48% of the Germans, and 47% of the Americans change their value classification (materialist vs. nonmaterialist) across the two interviews. (2) The substantial country variation in their postmaterialist responses both in level and direction of change is explained by the sensitivity of these measures to short-term economic conditions and changing political agendas. Similar conclusions appear in Jackman and Miller (1996).

Inglehart recognizes both the phenomenon of low-rating goals you cherish and have secured, and the universal top ranking of old goals of economic well-being and safety—but he misses their meaning. If in attitude surveys vast majorities of modern populations (including the upper-middle-class vanguard groups labeled postindustrial) give top priority to economic security and growth, to civil order and the reduction of crime, if the upper-middle class is in a position to act out those values by successfully seeking more income, secure jobs, and safer neighborhoods, while one in four of them tell interviewers that they like self-expression or participation (p. 319), we are missing the main story when we infer that there is a great groundswell of postindustrial, postmaterialist values. Equally important, if modern citizens drastically change their answers to these "values" questions with short-term changes in economic and political contexts and agendas, it is doubtful that we are in the presence of a sea change in basic values.

The test for the existence of cherished basic values comes when they are threatened. It is when governments try cutbacks in universal welfare-state benefits to the majority or when a recession or industrial restructuring threatens the job security of the college-educated that we uncover basic values. Upper-middle-class citizens, presumably the vanguard of the postmaterial era, suddenly become terribly material, deeply concerned about earnings, security, dignity, and safety like everyone else. Thus, to say "they have it so they do not value it" is to obscure the meaning of basic values, which persist across generations through thick and thin.

Interlocking Cycles of Family, Work, and Social-Political Participation: A Comment on Age Cohort, Political Generation, and Life Cycle[7]

A key assumption of theories about a new political culture dominated by postindustrial values derives from the seminal work of Karl Mannheim (1952 [1928]) on political generations: historical conditions when one comes of age, say adolescence and early adulthood, have lasting effects on values, political orientations, and behavior. Thus the cohort that hit the labor market in the Great Depression will cherish job security for the rest of their lives; the 1960s countercultural generation who hit the college campuses during the Vietnam War will remain countercultural, postmaterialist, and antiwar. Early socialization casts the die for a lifetime.

Many scholars have tried to sort out the relative effects of birth or age cohort (the focus is on the size of the birth cohort and its common experience), political generation (the focus is on period effects or the unusual historical conditions present when a birth cohort came of age), and family life cycle (the focus is on universal changes during the life course—courtship, marriage, children, etc.). There is no consensus on their relative importance for a variety of outcomes that have been studied: life satisfaction, job satisfaction or alienation, political attitudes and behavior, social participation, fertility, crime, earnings, and more.

Struck with the lasting power of the experience of the children of the 1960s, whose children in turn are presumably being trained in postmaterial values in the affluent society, Inglehart has argued that cohort effects are far more important than life cycle effects. His data are age cohorts. He finds that successive age cohorts do not become more materialist for the 15 to 18 years for which data are available and concludes that life cycle effects are unimportant. He tries to test this by a multiple classification analysis of life cycle versus cohort effects on values in which marriage, having a job, within-nation quartile family income, and having one or more children are weighed one at a time against age cohort and again claims that age cohort overwhelms family life cycle.

Two things are wrong with this. First, subsequent research taking account of economic and political contexts in later life fails to show the importance of cohort effects. Second, in real life, these events in the family life cycle occur together in stages not captured by age brackets.

Cohort Effects?

Regarding adult contexts, three studies illustrate the weakness of cohort in explaining a wide range of value orientations and issue-specific opinions. Two are cross-national studies of postmaterialism. One is a study of opinion changes in the U.S. over three decades; it concludes that of all the theories to explain shifts in mass attitudes, the weakest are the ones accenting generational turnover and social and demographic shifts. The strongest hypothesis is that public opinion responds to external events in the worlds of government, public policy, politics, and the mass media.

In a multivariate analysis of postmaterialist values based on surveys carried out from 1973 to 1984 in eight West European societies, Duch and Taylor conclude that "once you control for education and inflation at the time of the survey the cohort effects become trivial" (1994, p. 819, and the exchange between Duch and Taylor and Inglehart and Abramson, 1994). A study of secondary-school students living in depressed and prosperous areas of the U.S. and Germany concludes that economic conditions during preadult years are poor predictors of postmaterialism—another indication that birth cohort contributes little to these value orientations (Trump, 1991). In a test of the theory that American public opinion changes because of population turnover—the entrance of new cohorts into the adult population and the gradual dying off of older cohorts—William Mayer (1992, pp. 156ff., 174ff.) found that from 1960 to 1988 generational replacement had little effect on attitudes toward foreign policy, the welfare state, economic affairs, or even crime and abortion. (It does explain some of the total change in attitudes about race, the role of women, and sexual mores, again reflecting values anchored in very long-term structural changes described in chapter 1.[8])

Life Cycle Squeeze and the Morale Curve

When family types are more precisely delineated, we find that family life cycle explains a wide range of attitudes and behavior, including variations in morale or life satisfaction, job satisfaction, and social and political participation. The outlook and morale of the vast majority of modern men and women is shaped by the normal strains of family transitions as they are intensified or lessened by variations in taxes, debt, and real income as these in turn affect the balance between aspirations and rewards. From a review of research using age or life cycle variables and from social-psychological theory about the effects of imbalance between aspirations and rewards, in an early paper (Wilensky, 1961b) I inferred a hypothetical morale curve for the general male population of modern society. I located stages of the life cycle where people experience least job satisfaction, lowest participation in community life, greatest financial and family burdens, and greatest psychological tension—a condition of "life cycle squeeze." The essence of my theory is that job satisfaction and, indeed, life satisfaction are

a function of disparity between rewards (what we get in income and job status) and aspirations and/or expectations (what we want in goods and services and job status); both pay-off and demand are likely to show a chronology linked to family life cycle and work history. Leaving aside the college crowd and the unusually ambitious, the young man fresh from high school, for a few years at least, finds himself with a happy combination of modest aspirations, limited responsibilities, and an income that seems large.

A sharp change occurs, however, when home and children come into focus. As family pressures mount, the demand for credit in the product market and income in the labor market begin their swift ascent. The appetite for consumer durables and the demand for money and job security reach a peak in the 30's among married men with children. . . .

But the peak in actual income and security is seldom reached in this critical period. . . . For the manual worker, who is most subject to instability of employment, seniority protection is as yet weak, and for all categories the period of maximum economic rewards comes later. A working wife is one solution, but the double-earner pattern is least frequent among the very families that feel squeezed—young couples with children at home. . . . The result: a morale trough which lasts until job aspirations and family pressures decline, rewards increase, or both. When children leave home and debts are paid off, job morale, indeed all satisfaction unconnected with child-rearing, should climb. Later, with retirement impending, the morale curve will vary, depending . . . upon type of career and strength of work commitment, but a final sag in morale seems most frequent. (Wilensky, 1961b, pp. 228–229)

The general hypothesis, pictured in figure 4.1, is that points of maximum "life cycle squeeze," and hence low morale, occur on average among couples with preschool children; older couples, especially those prematurely retired; and solitary survivors. Of course, with more women working now than at that time and the education level rising, the dual-earner family is today typical and high-school graduates have given way to those with less than a four-year college degree (Levy, 1987). But the life cycle squeeze appears with much the same timing and effect for vast majorities of Americans—all but the upper-middle class. It now takes two or three more years of education and two jobs to match the standard of living of the noncollege majority of the early 1960s.

The idea of interlocking cycles of family life, work, consumption, social participation, and morale is complex and yet parsimonious. It enabled me to reinterpret contradictory results of studies of job satisfaction—studies that ignored massive forces off the job that determined responses to work, whatever the alienating or nonalienating character of that work. It very likely can explain findings on age or life cycle differences in general life satisfaction, income dynamics, and cynicism about government. Campbell, Converse, and Rodgers (1976) investigated the general life satisfaction of a 1971 sample of more than 2,000 Americans aged 18 years and older. Their findings by stage in family life cycle match closely the morale curve of figure 4.1. The most satisfied are young married couples without children; the least satisfied are married couples with preschool children, the widowed, and the divorced or separated. Although women in these "happiness" studies are typically equally satisfied or more satisfied with the quality of their lives than men (see citations in Estes and Wilensky, 1978), in general they evidence the same life cycle curves as men. It can be argued that women more often than men say—and even feel—that they are "happy" at the same time as they admit to clinically suspect symptoms. But none of the studies which systematically compare men and women, controlling for life cycle stage (or even age), has so demonstrated.[9]

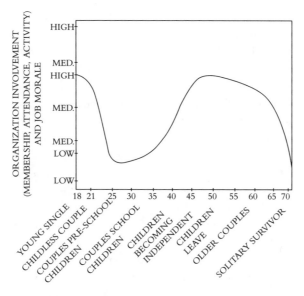

Figure 4.1. Morale and participation curve

Hypothetical picture of the participation and morale curve for the general population of an urban-industrial society. Inferred from existing data for the United States on variations by family life cycle and/or age in economic rewards and aspirations, consumer behaviour and aspirations, and participation in formal organizations. Sources cited in Wilensky, 1961b, ch. 8. Think of "high" as a man who loves his work, belongs to a union or professional association, a church, and three or four other organizations, is active in them and enjoys them. Think of "low" as a man who is unemployed, involuntarily retired, or work-alienated, and who belongs to nothing. Chart from Wilensky, 1981b, 257. See text for variations by education, career, and country.

If we concentrate on the income component of the interlocking cycles idea, we find further support in two detailed studies of income dynamics. A five-year panel study of some 5,000 American families (Morgan et al., 1974, pp. 37–79) shows that changes in a family's well-being are almost exclusively rooted in changes in family composition and labor-force participation; that young people starting new families typically become relatively worse off (compared with young singles or childless couples, they evidence slower rates of improvement in an "income/needs" ratio); that people moving into their prime earning years gain little because of increasing family financial pressures; but that, again, the economic base for improved morale is strongest for the middle-aged. After the age of 40 or so the head of a household starts to see more improvement in the family purse as children begin to leave the home and in many cases the spouse is freed of home responsibilities and gets a job. Retirement, the authors find, means a drop in income with no proportionate decrease in needs. Analyzing 1960 census data on earnings patterns by age and type of family separately, Oppenheimer (1974) adds an important elaboration: the imbalance between income and family needs varies only moderately by occupational group and category. For instance, "no matter how their economic fates subsequently diverge, low earnings were characteristic of most young men, whatever their occupational group" (p. 235). Only in very high-level professional, managerial, and sales occupations—a small minority of the labor force—do average earnings peak when family income needs are peaking.

A later simulation model of 4,000 representative British life histories gives a similar picture. It is based on data from the actual 1985 British population but is applied across complete lives to give a profile analogous to a complete longitudinal survey of incomes, taxes, and benefits for a single cohort (Hills, Glennerster, and Le Grand with others, 1993). It shows a peak in living standards in middle age (*ibid*., p. 27 and figure 7), around 50−55. Similarly, a thorough study of changes in American standards of living from 1949 to 1985 (Levy, 1987, pp. 199−206) found that the deterioration of real earnings and changes in family structure as well as changes in government transfers are root causes of the drift toward inequality since 1973. The breakdown by family types implies some slight shift in the morale curve: the position of younger couples since 1973 has remained unchanged (because the increase in double-earner families does not offset the deterioration in their earnings); the position of elderly families has improved (the sag in the morale curve is thereby delayed); and the position of female-headed families has worsened (intensifying their already strong life cycle squeeze). Since the late 1980s several rich countries have experienced a rising level of unemployment and underemployment among young people; this is now intensifying their normal economic squeeze and related discontent.

Research I reviewed on rates of social and political participation in the U.S. before 1961 showed a participation curve matching the morale curve of figure 4.1 (Wilensky, 1961b); this finding is affirmed in recent research. Leaving aside voting, people of middle age (30−55) have the highest rates of political participation—they are most likely to join a political party, work in a political campaign, attend a political meeting, and/or work in their community to influence politicians and solve common problems—while the oldest (56+) and the youngest (under 30) have the lowest participation rates. (See the five-nation study by Nie, Verba, and Kim, 1974, and the replication in another group of five countries by Marsh and Kaase, 1979, p. 111, table 4.4, and in Israel by Wolfsfeld, 1993, with the same curvilinear results. A 15-country study by Curtis, Grabb, and Baer, 1992, shows the same result for active participation in voluntary associations.)

Finally, if we consider political stance—an aspect of life more remote from the family and its earnings—we see a similar curve. There was a 34-year (1958−92) slide in confidence in government institutions among the general adult population of the U.S. with only a slight uptick from 1970 to 1972 and a brief surge from 1980 to 1984 (Citrin and Green, 1986, p. 435, updated by NES data from 1988 and 1992; cf. S. C. Craig, 1993, pp. 1−18). Within that context, "trust in government" has been least among American men and women over the age of 50; older persons have been the most cynical and estranged in every election since 1958, followed closely in 1964 and 1972 by the youngest age category studied (21−24 years). On the whole, people in their middle years have been and remain the most optimistic and trusting about Washington, D.C. (Miller, Brown, and Raine, 1973). Jennings and Niemi (1974, p. 278) reported almost identical findings for Americans with high-school education but variation for other educational categories.

This is a case where attitudes roughly match behavior. Voter turnout in the U.S. roughly follows the morale curve of figure 4.1: a low at 18 or so climbing to a peak in middle age, staying high or increasing after children leave, declining with retirement and especially after age 70 (Wolfinger and Highton, 1994, figure 2).[10] In early studies of voting turnout in the U.S. the turning point for a decline in voting among older citizens begins earlier than 70 (e.g., Hout and Knoke, 1975) and is still earlier for women than men (Wolfinger and Rosenstone 1980, p. 43). With the trend toward gender equality that gap may disappear. Consistent with the morale curve, the lowest voting rate by age and marital status is among those living alone—young singles or the divorced, separated, or widowed (*ibid.*, pp. 44–45; Converse and Niemi, 1971, p. 461). Just as higher education smoothes out the morale and participation curve, however, so does education reduce or even reverse the decline of voting for the aged and increase the (still low) rate for the young (Verba and Nie, 1972, p. 144; Wolfinger and Rosenstone, 1980, pp. 44–49). Maturity has a much greater impact in increasing voting among the least educated than among college graduates (*ibid.*, pp. 58–60). The resources for political participation—skills, information, knowledge, interest in complex political issues—are abundant for the college crowd, meager for the high-school graduate or dropout. But adult life experience—work, family—allows some later catch-up in political resources for those denied higher education (Converse and Niemi, 1971, p. 449).

In short, the life cycle squeeze hypothesis can embrace a wide range of behavior and attitudes, from the most personal satisfaction with the most local institutions (e.g., marriage and the family) to the most impersonal response to the most distant symbols (e.g., national politics).

Aware of possible "class" (i.e., education) differences, we applied this hypothesis to a sample of 73 employed and 157 unemployed professionals in the San Francisco Bay area (Estes and Wilensky, 1978). We excluded the divorced, the separated, and the singles over 30 who had never married. We interviewed them in 1971–73. Using an index of emotional stress (validated by independent clinical judgments) and an index of economic deprivation, we found that unemployed professionals experiencing high levels of financial stress fit the morale curve of the general population. Morale drops among couples with very young school-age children and among solitary survivors. These hard-pressed unemployed professionals display a sense of relief when children leave. For the continuously employed professionals, however, and, most surprising, even for unemployed professionals experiencing little or no financial stress, the morale curve is smoothed out; they show more balance between rewards and aspirations over the life cycle than most Americans; their morale stays high even after losing the spouse. The study suggests that the advantage of highly educated professionals in a solid economic position—having a professional identity embedded in a social network—functions as a buffer against social insecurity which, in turn, protects them from the intense psychological strains typical of the rest of the population. Employed or unemployed, they are cushioned against the standard shocks both by their privileged positions and by their anticipations for the future—in other words by the personal continuity afforded by a life plan.

To say that family life cycle explains a wide range of attitudes and behavior is not to deny that generational change (successive birth cohorts) explain large social-political trends. For example, while intact families in the middle years of life may be more participatory, trusting, and civically engaged, generation after generation, an entire society may simultaneously evidence a long-term decline in civic engagement, as chapter 3 and Robert Putnam's analysis of U.S. data suggest (1996, pp. 43–45). These are complementary theories.

Subjective and Objective Well-Being

We are now in a position to resolve the puzzle that appears in many of these studies—the recurrent finding in several countries that subjective life satisfaction or sense of well-being is more or less unrelated to objective conditions or the level of living (cf. Allardt, 1977; Inglehart, 1977; Argyle and Martin, 1991).

To deal with each major pattern of behavior—family, work, consumption, community participation, and political orientation—separately is to ignore their interaction over the life cycle. When we focus on these interlocking cycles of "career" (work and its rewards), consumption (and related debt), family life, and participation as they vary by group over time, we find that the objective conditions of living are closely connected with a variety of measures of life satisfaction and discontent. To understand the connections, however, we need a sense of the flow of time not only in the structure of societies but also in the biographies of persons variously located.

Subjective satisfactions and discontents are anchored in changes in family composition, consumption pressures, job patterns, income flows, and debt loads as they interact and vary over the life cycle. The imbalance between aspirations and rewards is most oppressive among displaced homemakers (divorced, separated, widowed), young couples with preschool children, and the aged, especially solitary survivors with limited income. However, as one would expect, the minority of more affluent, secure, and educated elites, blessed with challenging careers, evidence a higher level of morale over the life cycle and a somewhat different morale curve—less of a drop (and in some cases a boost) for couples with preschool children; hardly any drop for older couples and lone survivors. Elites and masses alike are thus responding to objective life circumstances most of the time.

Regarding public opinion and issue-specific attitudes, there are both stable structures of opinion and feeling common to all rich democracies and substantial national differences, both short term and long term. The similarities can be explained by the convergent tendencies mentioned at the outset in education, family structure, work and stratification, the welfare state, and the minority group thrust for equality. As we shall see in chapter 10 (on backlash), there is a fairly stable structure of issue-specific public opinion that varies little across nations—for example, the popularity of pensions and national health insurance, the unpopularity of public assistance to the nonaged poor, property taxes on households, and income taxes.

The national differences in short-run public opinion and fluctuations in "values" can be explained by short-run differences in economic performance and politics; the long-run differences by differences in types of political economy—national bargaining arrangements discussed in chapter 2—and related public policies. In fragmented and decentralized political economies most vulnerable to mass-society tendencies, there often appears to be no stable organization of attitudes for many issues other than the welfare state; modern masses in these countries increasingly respond to their perception of immediate economic circumstances and their leaders' shifting political agendas as amplified by the mass media.

Whatever the similarities of issue-specific opinions and whatever the short-run fluctuations, however, rich democracies display sharp differences in the way they channel public opinion and shape mass political behavior. Those differences in mobilizing structures—governments, political parties, interest groups, mass media—account for national differences in the volatility of politics, public policy, and public opinion (see chap. 11).[11]

If we had good cross-national data on family types and the life course, we would probably find substantial national differences in the amplitude and timing of the participation and morale curve. For public policies can ease the strains reflected in the morale curve. Investment in education, training, and job creation and placement can reduce unemployment and increase the productivity and incomes of young workers: chapter 2 notes national differences in active labor-market policies and unemployment; chapter 12 assesses the role of education and related policies in economic performance; chapter 13 reports data on job creation. Our 19 countries differ greatly in their family policies—for instance in public support for child care, parental leave, flexible retirement, and child allowances; chapter 7 analyzes their sources. Chapter 14 (on mayhem) analyzes their effects. Rich democracies also differ in the generosity and scope of policies focused on the aged; Part II on the welfare state and social policy deal with these. Obviously social security and related policies shape the degree to which the aged have sufficient income and opportunities to work at least part-time; and both an active labor-market policy and a family policy can ease the life cycle squeeze for young parents and make the morale curve and participation in community life look more like those of the upper-middle class. A final chapter gauges the degree to which any of these policies are transferable to the United States.

We lack the cross-national studies of life satisfaction necessary to link variations in public policies to life cycle stresses. The best comparative study of general life satisfaction shows substantial differences among cross-sectional samples in the nine EEC countries studied in 1976. On various measures, Denmark and the Netherlands led in average satisfaction while France and Italy were at the bottom.[12] Where life satisfaction was lowest, feelings of social injustice were strongest. Although Sweden was not included, its social policies and outcomes are closer to those of Denmark and Holland than to those of France and Italy. Crude age breakdowns, however, do not permit inferences about family life cycle variations (Commission of the European Communities, 1977, pp. 46–54).

A Postscript on Political Generations

In their accounts of the mid-1960s revolt, most American sociologists, anthropologists, and to a lesser extent political scientists were profoundly parochial. They attributed the outburst to the alienation of workers and students from a uniquely oppressive American political regime, the Vietnam War, or both. Even a little systematic comparison would tell them that American citizens were and are far less alienated from their society and political system than citizens of Italy or France (let alone those of the former Soviet empire); that the counterculture was bursting forth with varying amplitude during the same short period, 1965–71, in countries as diverse as Sweden, France, Belgium, Japan, Italy, Germany, and the U.S.; that it often took the form of ethnic, religious, linguistic, or racial militancy in movements dominated by teachers and college students (a good review of this part of the evidence is Allardt, 1979); that it varied in intensity by the size of the baby-boom cohort reaching college or the labor market (society was like the proverbial python that swallowed a pig and suffered indigestion); and that it was everywhere compressed into less than six or seven years. The counterculture cried out for an explanation rooted in cross-national observation rather than the navel-gazing sociology of the period.

For what was happening in all the rich countries having enough freedom of association to permit organized protest was a convergence of several powerful forces peaking in the 1960s:

- Mass education expanded apace, especially at the postsecondary level (a bit earlier and more vigorously in the U.S. but quickly followed by other modern societies).

- The expansion of education was a response to the postwar baby-boom cohort born 1946–60 and to the rising demand of their parents for more educational opportunity. Schools and then colleges became overloaded.

- Unusually swift economic growth 1950–65 enhanced mass appetites for a better life at the same time that social-political movements for minority rights gave urgency to the thrust for equality, for expanded opportunity. But, more important, just prior to the outbursts of the mid-1960s, college opportunities expanded at a rate much faster than opportunities for good jobs that could accommodate the baby-boom cohort, especially ethnic minorities among them, leaving many of the most ambitious and energetic with a sense of betrayal, ready to scream "discrimination" or "false promises."

The demonstration effect of U.S. student protests amplified by television may have reinforced these convergent structural shifts among other rich democracies.

At the time, I was amazed at the projection of this brief moment of history onto the large screen of "postindustrial society" and "postmaterialist values." This trendy social science led to an extraordinary overestimation of the power of the counterculture in American politics. Among Democratic politicians whose staff had read of this alienation and rising "postmaterialism," many believed that there was a huge pool of voters of countercultural persuasion that could be tapped to win the American presidency. Such political fantasies guided Democratic presidential nominee George McGovern (whose campaign manager was the yuppie philosopher of "new issues," Gary Hart) to the biggest defeat in post–World War II history. Among intellectuals, a stream of research from Samuel Huntington (1974) to Ronald Inglehart (1977, 1990), following leads in David Riesman's *The Lonely Crowd* (1950) and Daniel Bell's *The Coming of Post-Industrial Society* (1973), concluded that postindustrialism had spawned a shift in basic values (discussed above) leading to a new politics.

There may be some political generation effects that are long lasting. Efforts to locate them empirically, however, suggest that they are rare. Connections between political events in the coming-of-age years and present political and social orientations and behavior have been found for very small groups of activists or elites (Marwell, Aiken, and Demerath, 1987; Jennings, 1987). But they are generally both weak and limited in duration. For instance, analysis of college-educated Vietnam campus protesters and nonprotesters based on a national three-wave panel study of young adults surveyed in 1965, 1973, and 1982, showed that the activists mellowed during the period 1973–82, moving in a conservative direction (Jennings, 1987, pp. 380–381). More important, generational effects are typically absent for mass populations (Converse, 1976; and Converse's reply to Abramson, 1979). Where they are visible, they fade, sometimes quickly. For instance, a well-designed study based on national data gathered both before and after the war with Iraq provides a neat test of the enduring effects of youthful experience (Schuman and Rieger, 1992). The authors compared the attitudes toward the Gulf War of the Vietnam generation with attitudes of the World War II generation. As we might expect, the Americans who grew up during or in the aftermath of World War II found analogies to that war attractive when they were applied to Iraq's invasion of Kuwait, while those whose youth was influenced primarily by Vietnam found the Vietnam analogy more relevant. What is most important, however, is that within months the Vietnam generation swung over to support of the new war. Schuman and Rieger conclude, "Rather than past experience controlling the present, the present controlled the past, as most Americans of all generations came to accept the analogy to World War II—an analogy that justified massive military action against an enemy that was almost unknown a few months earlier" (*ibid.*, p. 325).

As Frederick Weil (1994, p. 415) suggests, for there to be political generation effects the events must be strong, compressed in time, and not overtaken by subsequent contrasting events; and what one predicts from the dramatic events of the cohort's youth must be relevant to those events. In a rare comparative study of political generations, Weil contrasts the post-1945 attitudes of cohorts socialized by the Nazi regime and the post-1989 attitudes of cohorts socialized by the East German communist regime. He found that the Nazi cohort lagged initially in embracing the new West German democracy after 1945 or 1949. But within 10 to 15 years their attitudes converged with the prodemocratic views of other cohorts as they observed the impressive performance of the new regime in both international and domestic economic affairs; the experience of the new overcame the memories of the old. Similarly, there were cohort effects in Eastern Germany in the three years studied after the fall of communism. But the effects are weaker. Weil explains: (1) "East German communism was a weaker generating event than Nazism, (2) it was more spread over time, (3) it is harder to ask interview questions about communism than the personalistic Nazi regime" (p. 415). Thus, even though East German attitudes were measured almost immediately after the fall of the regime, cohort effects were not as strong in post-1989 as they were in the West Germany of 1945–55.

In short, if they are to persist at all, the effects of a political generation must be very strong, rooted in a rare conjunction of political and economic circumstances, events that are dramatic, if not traumatic. Even then, as the cases of Nazism and the American countercultural Vietnam generation suggest, the effect fades with new experience, new events. Life cycle effects, however, are universal, are recapitulated in only slightly modified form by everyone, and are more predictable.

Conclusion: Let's Drop "Postindustrial Society" from Our Vocabulary

Relative to the older issues of "industrial society" (economic performance, equality, political order, and safety), postindustrial goals are not urgent mass demands. If after a quarter century of surveys since Daniel Bell announced *The Coming of the Post-Industrial Society* we still have to strain and stretch for evidence of these value shifts, if the *Silent Revolution* has not become more audible, perhaps we should abandon the phrase entirely. We should instead concentrate on changes in values and beliefs that can be more precisely anchored in major structural changes and for which the data are less ambiguous. Changing values anchored in real long-term shifts in social structures that have political import include the thrust for gender equality (a product of increasing rates of women's labor-force participation and declining fertility rates) and minority-group equality (a product of industrialization and democratization including the spread of the franchise and civil rights movements), and the continuing demand for security and welfare-state protections. The political restiveness of the middle mass is a product of changes in the occupational structure and the trend toward mass taxes; it varies in intensity with government policies on types of taxing and spending (see chap. 10) and labor-market policies (chaps. 2 and 18). The rise in environmental consciousness is perhaps another enduring change (a product of the interaction of education, science, population growth, and industrial pollution). And an ambivalent yearning for both community and individual freedom continues to provide cultural contradictions in modern societies. All of these shifts in structure and concomitant shifts in values have been in process for more than a century. There is nothing "postindustrial" about them.

Even the supposedly postindustrial environmentalism of Rachel Carson's *Silent Spring* is a continuous development from two strands of the "industrial" environmentalism of 100 to 120 years ago. Environmentalists such as John Muir, founder of the Sierra Club in 1892, the Pennsylvania reformer Gifford Pinchot, and President Theodore Roosevelt pushed reforms to preserve and conserve the land; they argued for sustainable development as well as the preservation of beauty. Urban environmentalists such as Jane Addams campaigned against the pollution and poisoning of workplaces and neighborhoods. Then as now upper-middle-class women were prominent in environmental movements. These were not mere precursors of postindustrial Greens; they led active movements that accomplished much. Like their successors they were responding to the effects of continuing industrialization. Perhaps the main difference between the "new" and the "old" environmentalism is that today's Greens are more ideological and attack pollution globally while yesterday's settlement-house workers were experiencing pollution firsthand in the factories and slums where they worked. (Cf. Gottlieb, 1993; Shabecoff, 1993.) One can argue that the environmentalists of today pay less attention to scientific knowledge than their predecessors did (Ames and Gold, 1995 and my chap. 15). A final sign that public concern about the environment may have little to do with affluence, let alone postindustrialism, comes from a recent ranking of 39 countries by scores on an environmental protection index (four survey questions about the urgency of environmental protection and the willingness to pay more taxes or sacrifice income to fight pollution). Six of the top 11 in environmental consciousness are nonrich countries (South Korea, Russia, Turkey, Czechoslovakia, China, Mexico); 14 of the top 22 are nonrich. Of the 17 countries showing the *least* mass support for environmental protection, 10 are rich democracies (Britain, Canada, West Germany, the U.S., Austria, Northern Ireland, Ireland, Belgium, Italy, France). (Inglehart, 1995, p. 61, table 4.) That less-developed countries have far more pollution than rich countries (Goklany, 1995) may account for their tendency toward environmental consciousness.

These weaknesses in the theory of postindustrial culture may explain why, when scholars have entered postmaterialist or similar values into mulivariate analyses of political behavior or economic performance, they find that such values are of little or no importance. For instance, in a 16-country study, Franklin, Mackie, and Valen (1992) show that postmaterialism predicts nothing of electoral volatility from the 1960s through the 1980s nor does it help explain left voting or voting for new parties. Jackman and Miller (1996) found that Inglehart's version of political culture had nothing to do with voter turnout from 1981 to 1990, political democracy, or economic growth rates. In 1975 (pp. 28–49) I showed why neither elite nor mass attitudes explain national variations in social spending (see also chap. 5 below), although if values are anchored in powerful mass-based political parties (e.g., Catholic or left), they have some influence. In following chapters I show why political culture and public opinion cannot explain national differences in tax-welfare backlash (chap. 10), party decline (chap. 11), or crime rates (chap. 14).

In sum: The theory of postindustrial society and postmaterialist culture can explain neither the structural uniformities of modern society captured by convergence theory nor the national differences captured by theories of democratic corporatism and the mass society. Its depiction of structural changes is superficial: the service sector is too heterogeneous to describe occupational and industrial trends; the idea of technocratic dominance is overblown and misses big national differences in the location and role of experts and intellectuals. As for postindustrial values, they apply to a small population, a minority even of college students. That these attitudes fluctuate so much with shifting economic conditions and political agendas casts doubt on the idea of a basic shift toward postmaterial values. The literature documenting such shifts is plagued with problems of survey validity. It goes up against a heavy weight of evidence showing that older issues of security, equality, civic order and crime, and economic growth and stability are dominant in the politics and mentality of modern populations; that cohort effects are weak to nonexistent; that political generational effects are rare and soon fade away; that family life cycle, if carefully delineated, has an impact across a wide range of attitudes and behavior. Most important, differences in national mobilizing structures shape both mass and elite responses to the dilemmas and problems of modern life.

Notes

This chapter is an elaboration and update of my critique of ideas about postindustrial structures and "postmaterialist" values in Wilensky (1981b, pp. 235–237, 255–262). I am grateful to Val Lorwin and Olaf Palme for critical comments on the first version.

1. Thus Bell (1973, 1976) and Galbraith (1967); their work draws on themes in Weber, Veblen, Schumpeter, and Burnham. For more empirically grounded arguments regarding such trends, see Inglehart (1977 and 1990 and citations therein).

2. The Dunlop Report (U.S. Commission on the Future of Worker-Management Relations, 1994, chap. 1) presents a useful summary of these trends and their policy implications.

3. Inglehart notes that he gets less stable results from his 4-item index than from the 12- or 8-item index (1990, pp. 127, 131; Inglehart and Abramson, 1994, p. 339) but uses the short index much more often and generally reports results as if there is no difference.

4. The countries are Great Britain, France, West Germany, Italy, the Netherlands, Belgium, Luxembourg, Denmark, and Ireland.

5. In the strange congressional debate of 1995 on the merits of enshrining an economic theory in the U.S. Constitution, the Balanced Budget Amendment, its advocates invoked a poll showing 79% support for the idea. However, when the same respondents were asked a second, more concrete (and realistic) question, "Do you favor a balanced budget amendment even if it means cuts in Social Security?" support dropped to 32% (*New York Times,* Feb. 28, 1995). Chapter 10 analyzes the difference between abstract ideology and issue-specific attitudes regarding the welfare state, taxes, and spending.

6. A similar conclusion comes from a review of many studies of American mass attitudes from the early 1950s through the early 1970s. Americans of every age cohort and every educational, occupational, and class level rank two goals at the top of their concerns, and the rankings show remarkable stability: first, family well-being and security; second, improving their standard of living—meaning their economic well-being (Hamilton and Wright, 1986, chap. 3).

7. This section summarizes and updates Wilensky, 1981b, pp. 255–262.

8. Mayer reports that where cohort has most effect (survey questions on premarital sex), it explains only about 25% of the change in U.S. attitudes (1992, p. 159).

9. A recent study of mental illness (Kessler et al., 1994) using a large national sample ($N = 8,098$) interviewed in 1990–92 is consistent with the morale curve: it shows a concentration of psychiatric disorders, broadly defined, among low-income persons age 25–34. But in this study women do have an edge but not in life satisfaction; they top men among the 14% of the sample showing severe pile-ups of mental disorders at age 25–34.

10. This study does not permit a test of whether a slump in voting rate occurs when noncollege couples have preschool children and a poor income/needs ratio. One would not expect there to be much of a slump, however, because young singles start from such a low base to begin with.

11. What issues parties and governments use to mobilize public opinion will also shape the "what's important" responses in surveys. Political context counts. For instance, there have been wild short-term swings in survey responses concerning "the #1 problem facing the nation" in the country with the biggest drug problem, the USA. In September of 1989, 43% of a U.S. cross section named drugs the nation's #1 problem; in July 1990 only 13% did (*Wall Street Journal*/NBC poll, *Wall Street Journal,* July 13, 1990). In those 10 months the problem of drugs and related violence did not change; the pollsters suggested that the shift "demonstrated people's despair." It more likely reflected the many TV docudramas and news "analyses" that exposed (or exaggerated) the problem and the success of political demagoguery surrounding it in 1988–89. The media and the Bush administration turned their rhetoric to other issues in 1990.

12. A recent 10-country study of life satisfaction, which did not include Denmark and France, similarly showed that the Netherlands led all countries in life satisfaction while Italy was at the bottom among the six rich democracies studied. Life satisfaction was closely associated with objective living conditions. That is why Slovenia, Russia, and Hungary rank very low. (Veenhoven and Saris, 1996.) A similar picture emerges from a single survey question asked by the International Social Survey Program in 1991 in 8 of our countries. "If you were to consider your life in general these days, how happy or unhappy would you say you are, on the whole—not at all, not very, fairly, very?" Twenty-two percent of both Italians and Israelis answered "not at all" or "not very happy," close to the unhappy responses of East Germans and the depressed responses of Slovenes and Hungarians. The least happy of respondents in all countries were the least attached—the unemployed, the divorced, widowed, or separated, and the least educated. (Blanchflower and Freeman, 1997.)

PART II

THE WELFARE STATE AND SOCIAL POLICY

The rest of this book applies the three theories I find most useful to a wide range of problems rich democracies confront and policies they pursue. Throughout I use convergence theory to locate and explain similarities among advanced industrial societies, pushing this idea as far as it can go. To explain remaining differences among our 19 rich democracies, I use types of political economy. These types are generated by combining cumulative power of mass-based political parties, mainly Catholic and left, with national bargaining arrangements—democratic corporatism, corporatism-without-labor, and the decentralized and fragmented systems most vulnerable to mass society tendencies (see chaps. 2 and 3). Throughout I attempt to synthesize the useful parts of the theories discussed in Part I.

The five chapters of Part II explain the development of the welfare state, patterns of spending, taxing, and social policy, with special attention to national differences in sector spending and program emphasis, family policy, bureaucratic efficiency and bloat, and means testing. The focus is on the specific ways in which rich democracies converge and the structural and ideological sources of differences among them. Part III analyzes system outputs—what all this spending and taxing means for human welfare.

5

THE WELFARE STATE
Convergence and Divergence

The essence of the welfare state is government-protected minimum standards of income, nutrition, health and safety, education, and housing assured to every citizen as a social right, not as charity (Wilensky, 1965, p. xii). In the abstract this is an ideal embraced by both political leaders and the mass of people in every affluent country, but in practice and at high levels of development it becomes expensive enough and evokes enough ambivalence to become the center of political combat about taxes, spending, and the proper role of government in the economy. In public expenditures, the welfare state is about two-thirds to three-quarters of what modern governments do. The core programs of the welfare state, often subsumed under the general heading of "social security," have taken the form of social insurance against the basic risks of modern life: job injury, sickness, unemployment, disability, old age, and income lost due to illness, shifts in family composition, or other random shocks (wars, depression, recessions). Because the welfare state is about shared risks cross-cutting generations, localities, classes, ethnic and racial groups, and educational levels, it is a major source of social integration in modern society. Because it lends a measure of stability to household income, it has also been an important stabilizer of the economy in the downswings of the business cycle especially since World War II.

The welfare state is at once one of the great structural uniformities of modern society and, paradoxically, one of its most striking diversities. In the past century the world's 22 richest countries (our 19 rich democracies and three countries that became communist, Czechoslovakia, East Germany, and Russia), although they vary greatly in civil liberties and civil rights, have varied little in their general strategy for constructing a floor below which no one sinks. The richer these countries became, the more likely they were to broaden the coverage of both population and risks. At the level of economic development they achieved in the past 30 years, however, we find sharp contrasts in spending, taxing, and the organization of the welfare state and, of course, in the politics of the welfare state.[1]

This chapter uses convergence theory to explain broad similarities in welfare-state development and corporatist theory—variations in types of political economy—to explain remaining differences among countries equally rich. (Chaps. 7, 8, 9, and 10 deal with the politics of the welfare state.) There has been much confusion in the welfare-state literature regarding economic vs. political vs. cultural (or ideological) determinants and effects of welfare-state development. Students who have done systematic cross-national studies of welfare-state development have used widely different samples (number of countries, range of development), different objects of explanation (aggregate social spending, sector spending, particular social and labor-market policies, program initiation, program expansion), and different measures of both independent and dependent variables; they have inevitably come to somewhat different conclusions about causation.[2] (For a review of these studies, see Wilensky et al., 1985; Hicks and Misra, 1993; and Huber, Ragin, and Stephens, 1993.) Then a secondary literature of criticism—sometimes called "theory"—proliferated, especially from the mid-1970s on. The critics tend to group and label the systematic studies in ways that ignore the differences in samples, variables, and measures and thereby distort findings; they exaggerate both theoretical and empirical differences among the more serious studies, picturing them as warring "camps"; they obscure convergent findings as well as complementary theories.[3]

Determinants of Welfare-State Development

In *The Welfare State and Equality* I suggested that convergence theory works well for the time span of a century and the range of development embraced by Sweden and Tunisia, Denmark and Bulgaria, the United States and India. But at the level of affluence of the richest 22 countries we find both convergence and divergence. Using social security as a test case, I showed that, on the one hand, whatever their political and economic systems or dominant ideologies, the rich countries converge in types of health and welfare programs, in increasingly comprehensive convergence, and to a much lesser extent in methods of financing. They all develop the same seven or eight programs. The fraction of national resources devoted to these programs climbs (eventually at a decelerating rate) and so do the taxes necessary to support them.

Whether we look at many countries at different levels of economic development at one cross-sectional moment or compare several countries over time, these trends toward increasing social expenditures are evident. For instance, comparing 64 nations in 1966, welfare effort (social security/GNP) varied consistently by economic level: average spending went up from 2.5% for the poorest quartile, to 4.0% for the next quartile, to 10.1 for the second quartile, to 13.8% for the richest quartile (Wilensky, 1975, p. 19). The correlation between economic level and social-security effort was .67.

Or if we concentrate on our 19 rich democracies from 1950 to 1986, we see that social spending as a percentage of GNP climbed in every country from 1950 to 1980, although the rate of growth varied (see table 5.1). After the mid-1970s in a few countries and after 1980 in all countries the rate of expansion of social programs slowed and in a few countries it has leveled off (e.g., Italy, Israel).[4] Whether researchers use the broad definition of aggregate "social security" (including health care) of ILO in table 5.1 or OECD data (which adds education and benefits in kind) or other sources (e.g., the Luxembourg Income Study), they have reached the same conclusions regarding trends (see appendix C, table 5C.1; Lindert, 1996a, 1996b; Alber, 1988; Brown, 1988; Hicks and Misra, 1993).

Because these trends are so similar—with every industrialized democracy showing rapid growth in aggregate social spending as a fraction of GNP or GDP from 1950 to 1980, then sooner or later slowing down or leveling off in the 1980s and beyond—the rank order of

TABLE 5.1 Social spending as a percentage of GNP for nineteen rich democracies, 1950–86[a]

	1950	1966	1971	1980	1986[b]
1966 Welfare State Leaders					
Austria	14.3 (2)	20.8 (1)	22.3 (3)	26.3 (7)	25.2 (7)
W. Germany	17.0 (1)	19.6 (2)	19.7 (7)	27.0 (6)	23.4 (8)
Belgium	12.8 (4)	18.6 (3)	20.6 (4)	29.8 (5)	25.9 (6)
France	13.2 (3)	18.3 (5)	17.5 (9)	30.4 (4)	28.5 (4)
Netherlands	9.1 (9)	18.3 (5)	23.6 (2)	31.3 (3)	28.6 (3)
Italy	9.6 (8)	17.5 (6)	20.5 (5)	19.6 (11)	n.a.
Sweden	10.0 (7)	16.5 (7)	23.8 (1)	33.1 (1)	31.3 (1)
1966 Middle Rank Spenders					
Denmark	8.6 (10)	13.9 (8)	20.2 (6)	32.8 (2)	26.1 (5)
United Kingdom	10.9 (5)	13.3 (9)	14.4 (12)	17.3 (12)	20.1 (11)
Finland	7.7 (12)	13.1 (10)	16.3 (10)	21.1 (10)	22.8 (10)
Norway	6.7 (14)	12.6 (11)	19.6 (8)	23.3 (9)	29.8 (2)
New Zealand	10.4 (6)	12.0 (12)	10.5 (16)	16.1 (13)	18.0 (12)
Ireland	8.0 (11)	11.2 (13)	12.7 (13)	23.3 (9)	23.2 (9)
1966 Welfare State Laggards					
Switzerland	6.3 (15)	9.5 (14)	11.4 (15)	16.0 (14)	14.7 (14)
Canada	6.8 (13)	9.4 (15)	15.8 (11)	15.1 (16)	15.2 (13)
Australia	5.1 (17)	9.2 (16)	9.3 (17)	15.7 (15)	9.7 (17)
United States	4.6 (18)	7.9 (17)	11.7 (14)	14.6 (17)	12.5 (15)
Israel	5.6 (16)	6.8 (18)	7.9 (18)	7.0 (19)	n.a.
Japan	3.8 (19)	5.1 (19)	5.5 (19)	11.0 (18)	12.2 (16)

[a]Social-security spending, broadly defined (but excluding education) as a percentage of GNP at factor cost. Based on ILO, *The Cost of Social Security*, various years. Different measures yield very similar rank orders and trends. See Appendix C for discussion and comparison of Luxembourg Income Study (LIS) Aggregate Statistics File, SS/GDP at market prices, and OECD Social Data Bank, SS/GDP.

[b]Based on LIS data for 1986, which are not comparable with other years, especially for Italy, and to a lesser extent, Australia and Norway. The rank order, however, is probably accurate. See appendix C.

welfare effort (SS/GNP or GDP) remains quite stable, with few exceptions.[5] Only 6 of the 19 countries in table 5.1 moved up or down more than three ranks from 1966 to 1986. Austria moved down from first in 1966 to seventh in 1986, West Germany moved down from second to eighth—although the burden of incorporating East Germany into the German welfare state since 1989 has moved Germany up again. Only Norway, Sweden, Denmark, and Ireland moved sharply up in the rank order of social spending. Norway, with uniquely abundant oil revenues, moved sharply up from twelfth to second (some of this is an artifact of changed definition, but there is no doubt that its spending moved from below average to much above average), the others less sharply—Sweden from seventh to first, Ireland from fourteenth to ninth. Clearly the universal effort to restrain social spending in the recent period of austerity was variably successful.

Finally, if we compare the four top welfare-state leaders (or, if you prefer, profligate spenders) with the four bottom welfare-state laggards (leanest spenders) in 1950, 1966, and 1980, we see substantial convergence in welfare effort (SS/GNP) from 1950 to 1966, but very little convergence thereafter. Ratios of the average social-spending share of the top four to the average of the bottom four in 1950 was 3.00; in 1966, 2.67; in 1980, 2.64. If, however, we use the European Community's broader estimate of "social protection" (including education, housing, or rent supplements, and some active labor-market policies) for its 12 member countries (including Portugal, Greece, and Spain), we find continued convergence in social spending as a GDP share or per capita. From 1980 to 1991, social spending grew in all 12 countries, but the differences between the less affluent countries and the most affluent declined. The coefficient of variation in the ratio of social protection expenditure to GDP, which measures divergence from the average, was 0.25 in 1980 but only 0.15 in 1991. Similarly the average benefit per head in constant prices increased by a range of 60% to 100% in Portugal, Italy, Greece and Spain; it grew by only 15% to 25% among several richer welfare-state leaders—Belgium, Germany, the Netherlands, and Denmark. (Eurostat, 1995, pp. 42–43.)

The root cause of the general trend is economic growth and its demographic and bureaucratic outcomes. Thus, economic growth has produced a large proportion of old people—at once a population in need and a political force for further social-security development. The main reason for this demographic trend is a marked decline in birthrates. Leaving migration aside and assuming that death rates do not increase, every day the birthrate declines, the proportion of people aged 65 and over creeps up. Big differences in past trends in birthrates have produced sharp contrasts in the present proportion of aged by level of economic development. As we have seen in chapter 1, other correlates of industrialization converge with demographic pressures to create both the political demand for social spending and the resources to finance it. By changing the occupational structure, economic development increases mobility opportunity, inspires rising aspirations for parents and their children, and invites women into the labor force, thereby reducing fertility rates while increasing family breakup rates. It also reduces the family's will and resources to care for aging parents and to meet the risks of invalidism, sickness, job injuries, and other shocks (see figure 1.1 in chap. 1 on convergence).

The second reason for the universal expansion of social-security spending is simply the age of the system—all systems mature and all government budgets are incremental, with only an occasional leap forward and still rarer reversals. "As the years roll by, more of the covered persons either reach retirement age or experience disability or the death of a working spouse; the mass of citizens press for higher benefits and expanded coverage for themselves and their dependent relatives; political elites see a greater need for programs; bureaucrats entrench and cultivate budget, personnel, and clientele; while politicians, bureaucrats, and the mass alike spread information about the programs, thereby encouraging claims and reinforcing the demand for more" (Wilensky, 1975, p. 25).[6]

In short, as economic level climbs, the percentage of aged climbs, which shapes spending *directly* since the aged use a disproportionate share of the most expensive programs—pensions, disability, and health insurance; with economic growth, the percentage of aged goes up, which *indirectly* makes for the spread of social-security programs through the complex bureaucratic-political process measured by "program aging" and this, in turn, is expressed in big spending. (Among subsequent studies confirming these findings on convergence see Lindert, 1996a; Williamson and Pampel, 1993; Overbye, 1995; Alestalo and

Uusitalo, 1992, pp. 44ff.; Huber, Ragin, and Stephens, 1993, pp. 742–744; and for 50 states of the USA, Dye and McGuire, 1992, pp. 319–322.)

On the other hand, at an advanced stage of affluence, we find momentous differences in welfare effort, in the timing and speed of program expansion, in program emphasis, in administrative style, and in the politics of welfare. By contrasting such "welfare-state leaders" (or profligate spenders) as Austria, Germany, Sweden, the Netherlands, Belgium, and France with such "welfare-state laggards" (or lean spenders) as Japan, the United States, Canada, Switzerland, and Australia, I arrived at hypotheses to explain differences (even some divergence) among nations once they have adopted the programs common to all. The welfare state is most developed and supporting ideologies most powerful, I suggested, when a moderately to highly centralized government is able to mobilize and must respond to strong, centralized labor federations and centralized employer federations, a population with only medium to low rates of social mobility, where the "middle mass" (upper-working class and lower-middle class) does not perceive its tax burden as grossly unfair relative to that of the rich and upper-middle class and does not feel great social distance from the poor, where the tax system has low visibility (e.g., least reliance on direct income or property taxes and most reliance on consumption taxes such as the VAT and social-security payroll taxes), the private welfare state is limited, and the military establishment, modest—for example, during the cold war not above 6 or 7% of GNP (Wilensky, 1975, chaps. 3, 4, and 5; 1976a; 1981c).

A complementary study not of aggregate social-security spending but of the timing of program initiation and amendment, using 12 West European countries—compared to the more diversified 19 of this study—was done by Flora and Alber (1981; cf. Flora et al., 1983). Analyzing an unusual 100-year time series, they discuss the interplay of socioeconomic development, regime type, and political mobilization. They find that dualist-constitutional monarchies (Austria, Denmark, Germany, and Sweden) initiated social insurance schemes earlier and at lower levels of socioeconomic development and political mobilization than did the parliamentary democracies (Belgium, France, Great Britain, Italy, the Netherlands, Norway, and Switzerland). Using a ratio of enacted to potential social-insurance legislation, Flora and Alber find that until 1901, dualistic-constitutional monarchies had a realization rate of 63% while parliamentary democracies had a ratio of 21%. *By 1914, however, the ratio of legislative realization for democracies had caught up with the ratio for dualist-constitutional monarchies,* an impressive convergence.

In short, if we combine my findings on spending with those of Flora et al. on program initiation, we come to this formulation: Where liberal democratic institutions developed early (Great Britain, the United States, Canada, France, Switzerland, Norway, Belgium, the Netherlands, and Italy) welfare-state development was somewhat retarded; parliamentary democracy and expansion of the franchise provided legitimation, but at the same time their liberal creed—with its emphasis on free markets, private property, minimum government—discouraged state intervention in the market. Monarchical regimes, lacking either the legitimation or the ideological constraint of liberal democracy, often facing militant labor movements, had a greater need for and bureaucratic ability to institute the programs of the welfare state. Thus Bismarck is counted as a pioneer of the welfare state. Once established, however, the social-security systems of the prewar monarchies (Germany, Austria, Sweden,

Denmark up to 1901) experienced the expansionary pressures of the system-aging process earlier than the liberal democracies. The early democratizers not only brought stronger anti-welfare-state ideologies and parties into mass democracy but also experienced the expansionary pressures of system aging later; they have remained welfare-state laggards (the United States, Canada, Australia, Switzerland), although some convergence has taken place in levels and types of spending. Among the early democratizers, the lag has been overcome only when a Catholic party or parties acquired substantial, persistent power as in the Netherlands, Belgium, and Italy (Wilensky, 1981c). The role of mass-based political parties in welfare-state development—both left and Catholic—is explored later as we deal with variations by type of political economy.

Because Flora and Alber did not include demographic data we cannot infer the relative importance of population aging and these other forces from their analysis. In fact, the median percentage of the population 65 and over for the four dualist constitutional monarchies in 1901 was 7.4%; the median for 10 early democratizers was 6.2%—more evidence that population aging must be added to regime type as a source not only of later social spending but also as a determinant of the timing of program initiation (based on B. R. Mitchell, 1981, tables B1 and B2; and 1993, pp. 1, 9; and U.S. Bureau of the Census, 1975, Part I, p. 10).[7]

One significant qualification: While pensions, health and disability insurance, family allowances and related family policies, job-injury insurance programs, and housing programs hang together as a welfare-state package, higher education, because of its stronger meritocratic component, is different; it is generally negatively correlated with spending as a percentage of GNP for pensions, health care, work injuries, war victims, and family allowances. Even per capita spending for postsecondary education shows no relationship to these other programs. (See appendix D, tables 6D.1 and 6D.2.) Means-tested public assistance is also inversely related to the welfare-state package, because the latter is universal and categorical, a matter of social right.[8] Thus, the welfare-state laggards lead both in higher educational effort (Wilensky, 1975, pp. 3–7; 1976a, 1982; Lindert, 1992, pp. 24–25) and in means testing for the poor (see chap. 8 and table 8.3). Chapter 6 explores reasons for variation in sector spending among the rich democracies. Table 5C.2 in appendix C shows that housing subsidies are positively correlated with aggregate social spending.

IDEOLOGY, POLITICAL SYSTEM, AND THE WELFARE STATE: THE CASE OF PENSIONS

Are ideology and political system major sources of the patterns of taxing and public spending we label "the welfare state"? In my earlier work (Wilensky, 1975, pp. 18–49) I showed that if we want to explain differences among nations around the world, we cannot go very far with gross categories of political system (liberal democratic, authoritarian populist, authoritarian oligarchic, or totalitarian) or with crude economic system (capitalist or market economies vs. communist or command economies). I also showed that elite ideologies measured by the belief in planning for equality and the belief in equality of opportunity consistently add nothing to an explanation of welfare-state development and practice. In fact, a veritable smorgasbord of values and beliefs have been invoked to justify welfare-state expansion—equality and solidarity (left parties), economic efficiency (efficiency socialists like the Fabians), family security (center-left and center-right parties), harmony, consensus, and community (Catholic parties and communitarians), social order, hierarchy, and the prevention of revolution (center-right parties and authoritarian regimes), and more. Such diverse values cannot explain a common outcome, the establishment of seven or eight similar programs. The role of ideology in welfare-state development is best expressed this way: In response to similar problems of providing economic and career incentives and maintaining political order under conditions of the general push for equality, security, and social justice and specific concerns about the aged, all rich countries develop a similar set of conflicting values and beliefs—welfare-state ideologies versus free mobility or success ideologies. In the short run, parties carry into power different blends of these ideological contradictions, emphasizing one side or another; but in the long run, the balance of these antinomies differs little among modern societies. The point is elaborated in chapter 10.

For the same reasons, there is a general convergence of social-security practice toward dual systems of income maintenance for the aged. One provides a minimum pension, which is egalitarian; the other, an earnings-related pension, which supplements the minimum and which is inegalitarian. If, as in Great Britain, one starts with a tax-financed, means-tested minimum pension providing flat benefits, one later adds either a contributory earnings-related supplement or an income-conditioned pension or both. If, like Switzerland, one starts with a pension providing an earnings-related benefit, one later constructs a better floor under it by adding an income-conditioned minimum pension guarantee, similar to the systems of France, Italy, and the Czech Republic. Subsequent research confirms this picture of convergence toward dual systems. For instance, Niemelä, Salminen, and Venamo (1996) show convergence of the Dutch social-security system toward the Nordic national insurance systems from 1945 to 1975 and then, as economic growth slowed, a move of all toward a continental European model—toward the integration of workers' insurance and national insurance. Convergence in earnings-replacement levels and in extension of coverage is more prominent than convergence in financing—for example, Denmark's pensions remain funded, Germany's and the USA's are mainly pay as you go (*ibid.*; cf. Palme, 1990, pp. 67–69). Similarly, Myles and Quadagno (1994) compared the policy trajectories of the United States and Canada as they expanded national coverage of the aged. They show that Canada started with a flat means-tested pension benefit in 1927, with uniform eligibility standards and benefits, accomplished universal coverage in 1951 (Old Age Security Act) by doing away with a means test for those over 70, but in 1965 added an earnings-related tier to the flat benefit. The United States, in contrast, started with an earnings-related pension in 1935 (Old Age Insurance), plus a means-tested social assistance program for the elderly poor under local control (the Old Age Assistance Act). But through major reforms in the late 1960s and early 1970s the United States not only enriched the earnings-related pension, it also added a national minimum benefit through the means-tested Supplementary Security Income (SSI) program. Although these two welfare-state laggards converged toward a dual system, the legacy of past timing in program design is still apparent: the Canadian income programs for the elderly, starting with the flat-rate concept, evolved into a system that provides a social safety net superior to America's but the United States, starting earlier with an earnings-related concept, now has a wage-related retirement pension superior to Canada's. Similar conclusions about institutional legacies appear in a broader study of 18 OECD countries (Palme, 1990, p. 150).

Again, program aging shows its effect: if you start down one of these two roads, its legacy will appear decades later even when you take a turn toward a dual strategy (Wilensky, 1975, pp. 105–107). Convergence is a slow process.

Finally, in the most thorough up-to-date test of the dual income-maintenance theme Einar Overbye (1994) shows that among 18 developed countries (including 16 of our 19 as well as Iceland and Spain), whenever they started their pension systems, and whatever their departure point, they have moved toward a common destination, with only two or three clear exceptions. Figure 5.1 specifies the policy trajectories of these countries since 1889 when Germany instituted its compulsory earnings-related scheme. Figure 5.2 traces the sequence of changes—a kind of natural history—that so far has brought almost all of them to today's dual strategy: they insure the working population through contribution-based earnings-related schemes designed to preserve among pensioners the income differentials of their working lives (the hierarchical-meritocratic impulse) while they ensure that marginal groups (nonworkers, low-income self-employed) receive an income-tested minimum (the egalitarian-universalistic-humanitarian impulse).

As figure 5.1 shows, the central tendency of the first strategy—secure a minimum standard for all the aged through a tax-financed income- or means-tested flat-rate pension—is toward the later addition of compulsory earnings-related supplements. This is the route followed by the Anglo-Saxon and Nordic democracies. The central tendency of the second strategy—provide income maintenance by either tax-subsidized voluntary pensions or compulsory earnings-related pensions—is toward the later addition of a universal flat-rate, tax-financed minimum pension. This is the route followed with minor variations by non-Nordic continental European democracies. The two points of departure are illustrated by two extreme and deviant cases: Denmark, which started early and stuck to minimum pensions, and Germany, which also started early and is the only clear case that stuck to compulsory earnings-related schemes without a flat-rate minimum supplement. Germany's 1889 insurance approach to social security at first targeted industrial workers with a pension benefit linked to earnings, financed by contributions from workers, employers, and the state. That system was gradually extended to other large occupational categories—white-collar workers, civil servants, and ultimately the self-employed. Most West European countries on the continent, like the old Soviet Union, are variations on the German theme. A few—Belgium, France, Italy, and Spain—started with state-subsidized voluntary insurance for industrial workers but later made them compulsory or replaced them with earnings-related public pensions for added occupational categories or both. All but Germany itself later converged toward a dual system by adding a flat-rate pension for old people with no employment record. (See figure 5.1.) Germany remains only a partial exception: it created a functional equivalent to a flat-rate universal pension by strengthening the legal entitlement to social assistance benefits (like SSI in the United States), and in 1972 it made it possible for housewives to voluntarily join the pension scheme (Alber, 1986, pp. 23, 43, 106–107). Today, most of the groups who tend to lose out in a contributory earnings-based system are, in fact, treated by the German state as if they had contributed—for example, students, registered unemployed, and parents who stay home and tend to small children. And pension rights are divided between spouses in case of divorce. It is de facto convergence.

In contrast, Denmark's old-age pension scheme in 1891 was purely tax financed and provided only a means-tested minimum pension; it was targeted to low-income people, in-

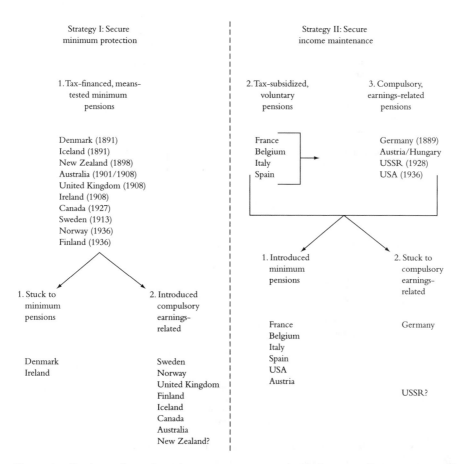

Figure 5.1. Pension policy trajectories: convergence toward a dual system of income security for the aged among eighteen countries

Source: Based on Overbye (1994). Cf. Wilensky (1975, pp. 40–42), Gordon (1988), Palme (1990), and Salminen (1993).

cluding the very large agrarian population. Agrarian interests generally push for extension of coverage rather than higher earnings-related pensions favored by urban Social Democrats (Salminen, 1993, pp. 366–371). That Denmark continued until 1990 to rely on flat-rate citizens' pension may be explained by the long-term political influence of self-employed farmers in a country with an unusual number of small- to medium-sized enterprises, a force against urban-oriented occupational or industrial pensions, German style; and by successive increases in the threshold for the minimum pension so that a majority of the aged qualify. Again, Denmark is the exception that proves the rule, because by the end of 1991 most workers had finally achieved collectively negotiated earnings-related pensions advocated by the unions, although they were not state guaranteed (Overbye, 1994, p. 164).

The two roads to convergence appear in figure 5.2. The countries that followed the 1889 German lead, with contribution-based earnings-related schemes for industrial workers, were pressured by uncovered groups for inclusion. Whatever their initial sentiments about state intervention, the middle class, the urban self-employed, and ultimately the farm-

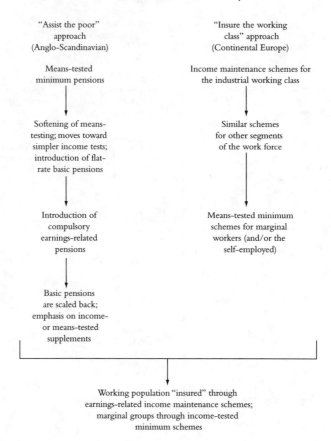

Figure 5.2. Typical stages in pension development: a natural history of convergence toward combinations of meritocratic and egalitarian-humanitarian principles
Source: Based on Overbye (1994). Cf. Wilensky (1975, pp. 40–42), Gordon (1988), Palme (1990), and Salminen (1993).

ers all came to view the partially state-financed workers' pensions as a special privilege; they insisted on parallel schemes for themselves. Governments responded by extending coverage or setting up parallel schemes for other occupational groups until vast majorities were covered. Pensioners and their families in the few countries that began with voluntary occupational pensions (figure 5.1) found them unreliable as the economy swung through cycles of inflation and depression; they demanded more secure compulsory insurance. Along the way the remaining groups left out, mainly the aged poor, were covered by tax-financed supplementary benefits. The political dynamics varied from country to country, but both center-left and center-right coalitions played their part in expanding coverage and increasing benefits. What began as a Bismarckian welfare counterpunch to the rising threat of labor movements and Socialist parties ended up as a near-universal coverage of all the aged, a welfare counterpunch to all politically restive groups.

Countries that followed the 1891 Danish lead, initially adopting a means-tested minimum pension, faced the same pressures from uncovered groups. They gradually softened or in some cases abolished means testing; they moved toward tax-financed, flat-rate, basic pensions, increasing their generosity; they then responded to the essentially meritocratic demand for income maintenance in the retirement years by adding an earnings-related scheme financed by contributions or earmarked revenues. Although data do not permit a precise analysis of means testing vs. income testing, the general tendency among all but the Anglo-American democracies is away from elaborate, stiff means tests, English Poor Law style, toward simple, less visible, less intrusive income tests (see chap. 8 on the welfare mess for the Anglo-American exception).

If the forces that drive convergence—increasing affluence as rich countries get richer, the concomitant changes in family structure and gender equality, the aging of both the population and social-security systems with their bureaucratic momentum, changes in social stratification and mobility—remain strong, the dual system will extend to the deviant cases of Denmark and Germany.[9] Denmark will extend and guarantee an earnings-related supplement and Germany will further strengthen its minimum floor. All rich democracies now have pension systems that reflect the never-ending tension between meritocratic-hierarchical principles and egalitarian-humanistic principles. Institutional legacies do leave their mark decades later but the convergence of all toward a dual pension system is the main story.

A Crisis of the Welfare State?[10]

Since the early 1970s there has been recurrent talk of a "crisis of the welfare state," mostly by politicians and finance ministers but also by some scholars. They complain that accelerating social spending accounts for a rising burden of debt and deficits; that public support for the welfare state has eroded, another reason for cutting it down; and that social spending is a drag on economic growth, is inflationary, or contributes to unemployment. We have already seen that among our 19 rich democracies and by any measure, social spending as a fraction of GDP has evidenced slower growth since 1975 or 1980, in some cases leveling off. Moreover, the burden of social spending in these countries varies both in level and trend. Thus, if by "crisis" we mean accelerating social spending, there is no crisis common to all.

If the welfare-state crisis means that the social budget is heavy and growing, that the welfare state is the root of public deficits, and that deficits are dangerous, then again there is no general crisis. Results are the same whether we consider total government spending or confine analysis to social spending. A thorough study of gross debt to GDP ratios from 1961 to 1990 among 12 EC countries shows that the ratio of government expenditures to GDP is unrelated to the gross debt ratio and that rising deficits are not the result of growing expenditures (Von Hagen, 1992, pp. 12–13; cf. Cameron, 1982). For instance during 1986–90 among welfare-state leaders, the average debt ratio ranged from 128% of GDP for Belgium and 110% for Italy to 44% for Germany and 35% for France, while among the welfare-state laggards the ratio ranged from 110% for Ireland to 50% for the United Kingdom (the U.S. ratio in 1994 was 70%). Similarly, the annual net government deficit 1993–94 among big spenders ranged from Sweden's 8.3% of GDP (down to 5.2% in 1996), to Belgium's 3.7%, Netherlands's 1.2%, and Norway's 2.4% surplus; among welfare-state laggards the annual deficits ranged from Japan's 6.0% and the USA's 4.1% to Ireland's 1.6% (OECD National Accounts). Debt ratios depend not on government spending but on what else these countries do—whether they tax enough to pay for the services their citizens demand, their economic performance, the structure of their government (e.g., the strategic dominance of the prime minister or finance or treasury minister over the spending ministers), and the structure of the budgetary process. For example, experience with budget norms in the United States shows that they are ineffective in the long run for two reasons: First, the decentralized and divided structure of government means that congressional spending committees and government agencies can maneuver to increase spending throughout the budgetary process by a principle of reciprocity; second, the states, whether they have spending and taxing limits or not, lavishly issue long-term bonds, resort to creative accounting tricks, and conduct onetime sales of assets to meet legal requirements for a balanced budget (Von Hagen, 1992, pp. 38ff.).[11]

In short, there is such great variation in the depth and duration of fiscal stress and debt and so much evidence that the welfare state is not the culprit causing changes in debt, that it makes no sense to talk about a general welfare-state crisis.

If the meaning of the welfare-state crisis is that there has been a withdrawal of mass support for social programs, there is no evidence of it. The most remarkable and solid finding of public opinion research on taxing and spending—both over time and across countries—is the stability of issue-specific opinion about social programs and the taxes to finance them. Since World War II pensions and national health insurance have remained overwhelmingly popular, and most family policies have retained a majority, while public assistance to the nonaged poor has remained stably unpopular. Similarly, consumption taxes and social-security payroll taxes evoke no sustained mass hostility, while property taxes and income taxes arouse the most persistent resentment. The rank order of enthusiasm regarding both spending and taxing is similar across countries and over time. Chapter 10 (on backlash, pp. 369ff., 380ff.) reviews the evidence and explains why the relative uniformity of public opinion about the welfare state cannot explain great national differences in the electoral success of tax-welfare backlash movements and parties like those of Mogens Glistrup in Denmark, Ronald Reagan in the United States, and Margaret Thatcher in the United Kingdom.

If the welfare-state crisis is not an inevitably accelerating rate of social spending, not the withdrawal of mass support for social spending, and not the inevitability and dangers of public debt, then surely it means that the burdens of the welfare state universally subvert good economic performance. Chapter 12 shows that the evidence is overwhelmingly to the contrary. Aggregate social spending up to 1973 was a positive contribution to the combination of low to moderate inflation, good real GDP growth per capita, and low unemployment; since the oil shocks of the 1970s it has been on average neutral. Much depends on the mix of social and labor market policies a nation adopts, how it finances and manages the welfare state, and, more important, what economic and industrial relations policies it pursues, as we shall see in the remaining chapters.

RETRENCHMENT OF THE WELFARE STATE?

If crisis talk, however misleading, is universal; if antitaxing, anti–social spending, antibureaucratic themes have helped candidates to win some elections (see chap. 10), has the action of governments matched the rhetoric of campaigns? What cutbacks have actually occurred in the period of austerity after 1975 or 1980 when economic growth and productivity growth slowed down? With some exceptions, the core programs of the welfare state—pensions, disability insurance, and national health insurance, programs that have generally outpaced GDP growth—have proved most resistant to real cuts in benefits per capita or even in their GDP shares (on disability insurance see chap. 15 [on the environment]). Most vulnerable to real cuts or at least spending restraint have been education, family allowances, social assistance, and unemployment compensation. For instance, in the period 1975−81, 10 of the 16 of our rich democracies studied by Jens Alber (1988, pp. 190−191) reduced the GDP share of education. Only Sweden, Italy, and Ireland increased as much as a point or more. In contrast, the GDP share of health spending increased almost everywhere (only Canada, Germany, Denmark, and Norway showed either a slowdown in growth or a stagnant share), and the share of pensions climbed everywhere but in Germany, where it leveled off at a high of 12.6%.

With few exceptions, there are five main reasons for this pattern of growth and restraint. First, demography, as usual, counts. Declines in education spending reflect declines in school-age populations. The "young" countries with a school-age bulge (measured by schoolagers per prime-age adult) cut education expenditures per child while still raising such spending as a share of GDP, but as the school population declined the GDP share leveled off or declined. The older countries spent more on pensions both per capita and in GDP share but at a diminishing rate, eventually leveling off (Lindert, 1996a, pp. 14−15). Aging, as we have seen, also increased health and disability spending, especially as the "old-old" increased their share of the population. Second, after universal coverage is achieved, various measures to control costs or restructure programs had some effect, especially in health care (as in recent German reforms). Third, programs where abuses were obvious and widespread (sick pay, disability insurance) have evoked substantial government reform efforts with varying success; disability cutbacks have encountered especially fierce resistance (see the five-country comparison in chap. 15 and table 15.3). Fourth, the rate of economic growth has an automatic effect on these numbers: below-average growth will automatically increase the expenditure ratio (SS/GDP) as the denominator levels off or decreases while social spending continues upward. Finally, the interaction of three forces—a very large clientele (all pensioners, all the health insured), strong political organization or influence, and great mass popularity—means that welfare-state leaders have already achieved generosity of benefits; their citizens now have entrenched interests and strong sentiments for maintaining the status quo. Conversely, if clientele is small, organization and influence is weak, and majority sentiment is hostile—as with means-tested benefits targeted to the nonaged, nondisabled poor and to a lesser extent unemployment compensation—real cutbacks are most likely.

To illustrate the patterns of retrenchment of the welfare state since the late 1970s, here are few examples drawn from a wide range of countries whose economies and polities differ substantially—UK, USA, the Netherlands, Germany, Italy, and Sweden.

• *USA and UK.* Comparing the United States and Britain, Paul Pierson (1994, pp. 142ff.) shows that aggregate real social spending by the national government on employment and training, housing, education, health care (in the U.S., Medicare), personal social services, and social security increased from 1978 to 1992 in both countries. There was, of course, some reallocation among types of spending. In both countries unemployment benefits and means-tested housing benefits were sharply cut back (*ibid.*, pp. 95−99,

127–128). In housing programs it was a shift from public-sector construction or producer subsidies to cheaper subsidies for housing consumption targeted to the poor, often cutting out the near-poor. Tax-subsidized housing for the middle classes and the affluent such as tax deductions for interest on mortgages remained sacrosanct. With the decline of union power in both countries, unemployment benefits were cut, especially for the better-off recipients.

Although President Reagan and Prime Minister Thatcher both launched verbal assaults on the welfare state, they were unable to make more than a marginal dent on aggregate social spending, mostly by expanding means testing and tightening eligibility rules for the most vulnerable populations—the poor.[12] By changing indexation (cost-of-living adjustments) of pensions, Thatcher was also able to reduce the rate of growth of this most popular program. In contrast, at the outset of his administration Reagan proposed to cut the minimum pension benefit for low-earnings workers and to delay a cost-of-living adjustment for three months; he immediately triggered a unanimous bipartisan advisory vote in the U.S. Senate against such a step and a big revival of an elderly lobby (the National Committee to Preserve Social Security and Medicare was formed in 1982). It is possible that Thatcher succeeded in this modest step where Reagan failed not only because a more-centralized parliamentary system with party discipline gave an ideologically committed prime minister more power than her counterpart in a divided presidential system, but also because of differences in the degree of consolidation of the pension system. As Pierson (1994, pp. 69–73) suggests, Britain's SERPS (State Earnings-Related Pension Scheme), the target of Thatcher's reform, was a young program first implemented by the Labour government in 1974; America's social-security law had four additional decades to become institutionalized and therefore more resistant to change. Again, system maturity counts.

The pension-reform recommendations of a bipartisan commission on social security were enacted in the United States in 1983. Rather than cutting benefits they raised payroll taxes slightly, taxed benefits for the first time, brought new federal employees into the system to broaden the payroll tax base, and trimmed future costs by slowly phasing in the higher retirement age from 65 to 67 by the year 2027—sensible steps, which "fixed" the system for 47 years, hardly a revolution.

Regarding cuts in health-care spending and benefits, Reagan, Thatcher, and their successors (Bush, Clinton, and Major) all attempted reforms designed to reduce the rate of growth of government health-care spending; Clinton in addition made a failed attempt to overcome American exceptionalism and establish national health insurance. It is a curious paradox that the United Kingdom, with by far one of the cheapest, most-accessible medical-care systems, made the most radical reforms while the United States, with by far the most expensive and least-accessible system, failed either to control spending or to increase access, while it succeeded in increasing the number of families with no medical insurance at all. It is another paradox, which runs through all policy areas (see chaps. 8 [the welfare mess], 15 [environment], and 16 [health]), that the most ideologically committed free marketeers, Prime Minister Thatcher and Presidents Reagan and Bush, created the most-intrusive regulatory regimes. In U.S. health-care reforms it was the Reagan-Bush regulations of hospital and physician payments—rate-setting, prospective payment plans based on diagnostic-related groups, and resource-based relative value scales

(Brown, 1991; Ruggie, 1992). These had little effect in controlling national health-care costs, although they made doctors unhappy. The payment reforms did modestly reduce Medicare costs through shifting the burden to private insurers, who then raised premiums and gave employers and providers strong motive to reduce coverage and services, a typical cost-shifting game in the U.S. nonsystem. Because the recent British restructuring of medical care is so sweeping, a brief account is relevant as we consider "cuts" in welfare-state spending.

A popular, universally accessible, tax-financed, already low-priced health-care system—the National Health Service (costing only 7.1% of GDP in 1992 compared to 8.7% for Germany and 13.6% for the United States)—was radically reformed in 1991 by Margaret Thatcher on both cost-containment and ideological grounds.[13] In 1989 she released *Working for Patients,* the product of a closely held review by her trusted lieutenants plus advisers from neoliberal think tanks—with no consultation with provider groups (the BMA, the Royal Colleges). Answering critics of her stewardship of the NHS who accused her of overzealous starving of health care through budget stringency, the report assumed that the NHS as structured subverts the free choice of individuals in the medical market; it claimed that doctors—so dominant in NHS policymaking and implementation—lack the incentives to respond to the patient-consumer; that doctors' monopolistic, self-aggrandizing behavior (e.g., restricting entry to the trade) increases rigidity and inefficiency (e.g., wide variation in patients treated and referrals per doctor) and accounts for long waiting lists for elective surgery and ward closures in hospitals that have used up their NHS budget; and that all of this is a drag on the economy. An underlying ideological theme of all of Thatcher's reforms was that the autonomy and monopoly power of professional groups, including doctors, must be checked by creating free markets. The power of physician groups, she felt, threatens not only the sovereignty of the consumer but the proper authority of the state. Although the Thatcher government did not dare to abandon the founding principle of the NHS—to provide a universal, comprehensive, tax-financed health-care service to the entire population—the reforms did introduce an "internal market" into the state system. Purchasers (District Health Authorities) were separated from providers (hospitals and their consultant-specialists); purchasers would no longer manage hospitals but instead buy services for their localities by contracting with NHS hospitals or private hospitals, hopefully the latter. Hospitals could choose to be self-governing trusts. By 1994 "more than 400 providers accounting for about 95 percent of the NHS's activities had become self-governing Trusts" (Klein, 1995, pp. 204–205). A new structure—General Practitioner Fundholders (GPFH) comprised of larger GP practices—was created as another group of presumably cost-conscious purchasers. Fundholders would negotiate contracts with providers to offer care more efficiently without massive extra funds. Instead of capitation payments (originally designed to overcome the overserving tendencies of fee-for-service medicine), fundholders will receive a fixed sum out of which they will buy hospital services; like the self-governing hospitals, they can retain surpluses but must balance deficits from their budgets (Döhler, 1991, pp. 264–265).

Finally, in this war on the autonomy of physicians, the Thatcher reforms increased the powers of managers of the NHS and governing ministers over practitioners: the trusts specify doctors' job contracts and review them annually; they have increased power to hire and fire hospital personnel. Both professionals and local governments are barred from serving on controlling boards. The Major government continued to implement these 1991–92 reforms.

Britain stands alone in the rapidity, depth, and implementation of reform, although New Zealand recently tried to match the pace of British change. It is too early to judge whether this combination of managerialism, statism, and market theory will either save money or improve access, innovation, equity, or quality of care, let alone real health (Klein, 1995, pp. 230–237). Because there was no consensus on reform or even what problem it was supposed to solve, there is no consensus on criteria of evaluation. There is consensus on four points, however:

1. Reform has not reduced costs. Spending on health care was 6% of GDP in 1989; in 1992, after reform, it had gone up to 7.1%, a more rapid growth than that of Germany and Netherlands while Sweden and Denmark actually cut the health-care share of GDP.

2. Reform inflated both the number and salaries of "bureaucrats." While 50,000 nursing jobs and 60,000 beds have disappeared since 1990, there has been an increase of 20,000 senior managers in the NHS (*New York Times,* August 6, 1996). There is dispute about how much of a managerial explosion exists, but no one doubts that there has been a large increase in administrative costs.

3. Reform has accelerated a 1980s trend toward copayments in dental, pharmaceutical, and ophthalmic services, with exceptions for the poor.

4. No great change has yet occurred in the behavior of physicians or of health authorities; for instance, they typically refuse to explicitly restrict the menu of services. But the reforms have reduced the power of hospital specialists and seconary-care providers while enhancing the power and status of general practitioners and primary-care providers, especially the "fundholders" who now have to pay the bills within a fixed budget. This may be the major achievement of reform. However, even with one of the lowest-cost systems among rich democracies and inthe face of increased demands, the Conservative government of the mid-1990s required annual cuts of 3% at every level. Continued budget stringency has put an already lean system under increased strain; many emergency rooms and intensive-care units must now impose long waits before any treatment. (New York Times, January 30, 1997.) Chapter 16 assesses the connection between the organization and financing of health-care systems and national health performance.

• *The Netherlands.* The Christian Democratic and Liberal cabinet of 1982 cut social benefits, education, and health care by 3% and froze a number of benefits at that level. In 1986 the link between wage increases in the private sector and social benefits changed so that the minister of social affairs could consider the ratio of workers to beneficiaries in determining benefits each year. Later the generous early retirement benefit was reduced. In 1991 and 1992 sickness and disability benefits were lowered. The social partners, however, rebelled by restoring the benefits through collective bargaining. Despite the unusual Dutch level of abuse of these generous programs (chap. 15) sickness benefits by 1995 were back to their former level at 80–100% of previous wages while most of the disability benefits were back to their former 80% level. An uphill effort to reexamine eligibility procedures was begun in 1995–96. The employer is now responsible for paying the first two to six weeks of sick leave before the sickness fund kicks in; employers also have more responsibility for disability benefits, a reform that gives them an incentive to get rid of less-than-healthy workers, thereby shifting costs to unemployment compensation or public assistance. (Keizer, 1996, pp. 4–5, 15–16.) However, the number on partial or full disability did drop from about 985,000 at the end of 1993 (14% of the labor force) to 735,000 at the end of 1996 (*Wall Street Journal,* Dec. 26, 1996). Recent governments have emphasized the need to increase the rate of Dutch labor-force participation and de-emphasize the replacement of income for the unemployed and disabled (chap. 15).

The Netherlands story is one of many small reductions in a wide array of social benefits that, over 10 or 15 years, add up. These cumulative adjustments and the effort to freeze some spending provoked older voters to form two new parties that won seven seats in May 1994.

- *Germany* was not only the pioneer of early welfare-state expansion but led in the late 1970s to mid-1990s effort to rein in its growth. Under center-right coalition rule, under the enormous fiscal burden of post-1989 unification (currently DM 170 billion per year), facing great demographic pressure (in 1992, 15% of the population was 65 or older, a high rate close to those of Belgium, Denmark, the United Kingdom, and Italy[14]), and in its role as dominant enthusiast for a strong EU and therefore having the most incentive to meet the Maastricht economic criteria, the German government has proposed many restraints on social spending and has enacted several. Given these pressures it is surprising how modest the reforms are. Efforts to trim social spending began in 1975 under the Social Democratic government and continued somewhat more intensely under center-right coalitions. Successive cuts have been concentrated on unemployment benefits, health insurance, and means-tested social assistance. Pensions so far have been little affected. Before 1984, successive limits were imposed on eligibility and duration of unemployment benefits; small copayments and some cost-containment measures were imposed for some health services and drugs; lengthy hospital stays for childbirth were shortened, sick pay was slightly reduced; social assistance to the poor was not increased at the rate of inflation; an increased proportion of college student allowances were transformed into loans; and child allowances were curbed for families above an income limit. (Alber, 1986, pp. 115–116.) Together these 1975–83 changes stabilized the social-spending share of GDP, making Germany an early exception to the rule of continued expansion among welfare-state leaders before the mid-1980s (Alber, 1988, p. 192; Brown, 1988, p. 10).

Since the mid-1980s there have been recurrent proposals to reduce pension benefits per recipient by changing the indexing basis, but so far they have come to nothing (Claus Offe, personal communication, July 20, 2000). Although in 1992 Germany increased social assistance benefits for single parents and pregnant women, in 1993 it capped annual increments and cracked down on abuses (Alber, 1996, table 2). In 1988 and 1992 two medical care cost-containment laws were passed with the help of the Social Democrats. They aimed to stabilize the insurance contributions by restructuring the corporatist bargaining process (Giaimo, 1995). They increased the power of the

Krankenkassen (sickness funds) vis à vis the doctors' associations in negotiating guidelines for practice and prescriptions, and they broke up the cozy relationship between doctors and pharmaceutical firms.[15] They capped health-care expenditures at the level of wages (and wage increases) of insured persons and froze them at the 1991 level. These reforms also introduced small copayments on some prescriptions, inpatient stays, and physical therapy and larger copayments for eyeglasses and dental care, with exceptions for low-income groups. A step in the opposite direction occurred in April 1994 in response to a growing "old-old" population: Germany introduced a new scheme of social insurance to pay for universal and long-term care. Finally, measures introduced by Chancellor Kohl and approved in June 1996 would reduce sick pay by one-fifth, to 80% of workers' salaries. Under the new regulations Germans will be entitled to only three weeks of state-subsidized health-spa vacations every four years compared with the present four weeks every three years. A Kohl proposal to increase by 75 cents the small copayment per prescription (previously about $1.50 to $5.00) was defeated by the Social Democrats along with bolder proposals for further cost control. While all this might not sound Draconian to American ears, it provoked demonstrations, processions of cars, and brief work stoppages all across Germany. A union-organized pro-welfare-state rally in Bonn in June of 1996 set a Federal Republic record, with 350,000 participants.

    • *Italy.* Cutbacks, begun in 1978 under the unity government with Communist support, accelerated from 1981 to 1983 (e.g., rules on public assistance were tightened, child allowances for children of high-income families were reduced). But Italy nevertheless joins Sweden, Denmark, Belgium, and France as the standout cases of welfare-state expansion that substantially exceeded their GDP growth from 1975 to the early 1980s (Alber, 1988, pp. 188–189). Major reforms, driven by cost considerations, were made in the 1980s and especially the early 1990s.[16] A major 1978 reform undertaken by the National Solidarity Coalition changed health-care entitlements from occupation-based funds to all citizens, modeled on the universalism of the British NHS—a principle of free and equal benefits to everyone. Severe problems of corruption (parties controlled every component of the system), concomitant cost explosions, and deterioration of services resulted in incremental revisions in the 1980s and 1990s. These reforms included gradual increases in the amount of copayments and their extension to new areas—for example, prescriptions, laboratory tests, and outpatient specialist care. A major structural reform was introduced in 1984, but it took 10 years to be fully implemented, at which point it provoked a storm of protest (Ferrera, 1994). For example, in December 1993 a three-tier system was introduced (users with no charge, users with limited copayments, and users with deductibles). Health-care entitlements for higher-income families were drastically cut back (the only "free" service remaining was hospitalization); for families earning less than the threshold, copayments were increased. While the poor elderly were exempt, a new voucher system put a ceiling on all services after which they would bear the full cost. The revolution lasted only a few months. The affluent were incensed at their exclusion; the poor and near-poor complained that the voucher system, like the means testing that preceded it, was cumbersome and humiliating; and everyone complained about increased out-of-pocket costs. Opposition parties and labor unions gave voice to these complaints. Income testing and means testing created a nightmare for administrators, exacerbated by the ineffectiveness of the tax system. Income testing encouraged even more tax evasion as benefit seekers just above the income threshold rearranged their official labor-force participation to avoid copayments.

It did not help public acceptance of the 1993 revolution that in the same year the head of pharmaceutical services was arrested for accepting huge bribes from drug companies and the minister of health and several of his associates were indicted on corruption charges. In 1994 the new system was abandoned. Income selectivity was replaced by risk selectivity: persons with one of a long list of illnesses (mostly chronic), pregnant women, the disabled, children up to the age of 10, and everyone older than 60 were exempted from cost sharing regardless of income. Reforms throughout the decade followed a stop-reverse-go pattern.

Italy has long had one of the most generous paid maternity leave policies. Even hints of possible cutbacks provoke a political uproar; the system remains intact.[17]

Meanwhile the efforts to restructure the state by decentralization of power also shaped the welfare state. New laws of 1991 regulated the financing of nonprofit and voluntary agencies in the social services. These reforms accented self-governing municipalities, the merging of small towns, and the setting up of consortia for the management and delivery of services; and the creation of metropolitan areas for big cities like Rome, Milan, Turin, and Naples (they are now accorded the powers of provinces). Municipalities are acknowledged as main actors in all areas of social services, except for the organization and planning of health services. Two laws of 1991 aimed to regulate and help finance voluntary associations and social cooperatives to which public administrators may contract out services. Relative to market actors, these cooperatives have a privileged position as contractees. As chapter 9 will show, none of this urge to decentralize reduced bureaucratic bloat or total spending, but it did enliven the blame game: the central government could point to regional and local governments as the source of trouble and vice versa. In general, however, the structural reforms were a laudable attempt to reduce political clientelism by strengthening the power and responsibilities of administrators and professionals within local agencies and especially within the National Health Service.

Italy is an extreme case both in acceleration of spending and repeated efforts to cut spending, only a few of which were successful. It uniquely combines political corruption and inefficiency in the administration of both taxation and social spending (even including pensions, health care, and disability insurance), strongly alienated voters, party realignment and dealignment, and very disorderly finances (a uniquely wide gap between revenues and expenditures over long periods). This helps to explain big swings in social policy and the limited modifications in the last 10 years—some shifts toward a more selective universalism in welfare-state design, some actual cuts in benefits, and ultimately a major brake on total social spending. After negotiations between unions and the Dini government, even a broad-pension reform was passed in August 1995. It begins a shift from the old very generous "defined benefit" formula to a new, somewhat less generous "defined contribution" formula to be phased in very gradually.

The vigor and breadth of demonstrations and strikes to protest cuts of benefits in the core programs of the welfare state are greater in France than Italy, largely because Italians are aware of the corruption of major programs and the need for reform. But Italian voters are moving in the direction of the French in their organized resistance to erosion of benefits. Welfare-state politics in Italy from 1965 to 1995 are described in chapter 10.

• *Sweden.*[18] Starting in 1980–82 under a "bourgeois" coalition government, there were minor cuts in already very generous health, housing, and even pension benefits (e.g., reducing compensation for part-time pensions) while unemployment benefits and child allowances were extended (see chap. 7). During subsequent years of return to Social Democratic rule, 1982–91, there were both incremental cutbacks and incremental expansions of social programs. The unprecedented annual deficits run up by a series of center-right coalitions from 1976 to 1982 (13% of GDP when the Social Democrats returned) were reduced not mainly by these 1980s spending changes but by currency devaluations, economic growth, and tax reforms.

On the eve of a recession, in the two years leading up to its defeat in the election of 1991, the Social Democratic government increased the VAT and, in its most unpopular move, changed property tax valuations (see chap. 10) while it made modest reforms to prevent waste and abuse in social programs, especially in the replacement rate of unemployment insurance and sick pay. For instance, sickness cash benefits were calibrated according to reduced capacity to work, with a doctor's certificate required after the eighth day. In 1992, the Bildt centrist government agreed with the Social Democratic opposition on a "crisis" package: the maximum sickness cash benefit was reduced to 90% of lost income. Only 65% is paid for the first three days; 80% from the 4th to 90th day. The cost for the first 14 days of claimed sickness was shifted to the employer instead of the government. Since 1993 no sickness cash benefit has been paid for the first day of illness (Denmark also introduced a waiting period recently), and other minor cuts were made. The result: a sharp decrease in the high rate of absenteeism; Swedes who used to report in sick because of a Monday-morning hangover now show up to work.

Similarly, in reforms of a second program most vulnerable to abuse, job-injury insurance, a stricter definition of job injury was adopted in the early 1990s and the insured were required to pay a larger portion of the cost themselves. Deficits in both these programs were turned into surpluses by 1994, although they remain costly. In addition, small downward adjustments were instituted in calculating pension benefits; and unemployment benefits were reduced to 80% of previous earnings (still high by any standard).

In January 1996 the Social Democratic government decided on a second round of austerity—a further tightening of sick pay, reduced child allowances, and a reform of family policy: the parental leave benefit was reduced from 90% of income loss to 80% (two months of the 12 to 18 months of parental leave will remain at 90%, one month for each parent, use it or lose it, then 80%); compulsory counseling will be required for the divorced or separated; and child care allowances were cut (in 1994 dollars, to a maximum of about $267 per month up to 3 years of age); families benefiting from municipal subsidies for a day care center get a reduced child allowance, depending on the hours.

Not all of the 1990s reforms involved reduced benefits and services. The Swedes have long led in rehabilitation programs to reintegrate the physically or mentally disabled into the labor force and promote independent living (for details see chap. 15, p. 554). In 1994 this effort to enable the handicapped to live an independent life was extended via a legal right to benefits, including counseling, support for individuals as well as parents with disabled children, escort services, housing with special service, support for minor handicaps, interpreter services for the deaf and blind, and more. At the same time, eligibility standards were tightened.

Finally, after 15 years of debate about pension reform, the 1996 proposals will result in real reductions, especially for middle- and upper-income earners—for example, in the pension benefit for married pensioners, and a gradual rise in the retirement age. The accrual rate at retirement will be indexed to the average life expectancy of the retiree's cohort, so more years in the labor force will be required to receive benefits equal to those of earlier cohorts. Two percentage points of the 18.5% contribution rate will be allocated to a fund "premium reserve" account to pay benefits on the basis of return on invested capital—a small step away from pay-as-you-go financing. Sweden leads in a continuing effort to make the pension system flexible by increasing a choice of various combinations of work and pensions. Sweden is also the world's "oldest" country; in 1995, 17.4% of its population was 65 or older compared to 12.7% for the United States.

What about health-care reform? In 1990 the Swedish health-care system spent 8.6% of GDP—less expensive than the United States and Canada (despite Sweden's much older population) but more costly than the rest of our 19 rich democracies. It delivers "care of high quality, equity in access and local accountability unrivaled in other countries" and a high level of patient satisfaction (Glennerster and Matsaganis, 1992, pp. 3, 5). (In a recent Swedish national survey 85% thought the quality of medical care in Sweden was either very good or good.)

One reason for Sweden's above-average cost of medical care—aside from the strong organizations of provider groups and the unusual percentage of the aged—is that the system is biased toward hospitals; there is no concept of the general practitioner (*ibid.*, p. 4). Primary care is organized around local health centers staffed with salaried doctors, nurses, and specialists acting as teams. There are significant user charges—copayments for prescriptions, visits to doctors, and other services (p. 5), with no exception but an upper limit of 1,600 SEK or $272 per year in 1990 dollars for all publicly provided health care.

In response to economic austerity and the need for increasing efficiency and consumer responsiveness, parties of left and right agreed in the mid-1980s to replace fee-for-service with capitation payments from the national insurance fund paid directly to counties, which would decide on reimbursement of practitioners. Most counties are led by Social Democrats. There are "almost as many reform programs as there are [county] councils" (p. 8). "Patients still have full freedom of self-referral" (p. 6). The net effect of these reforms is that waiting time and lists for nonemergency surgery and outpatient visits have been reduced, especially in the Stockholm district, and the GDP share is down from the 1980 peak of 9.4%. In fact, Sweden is the only country among our 19 rich democracies that reduced the share of total domestic expenditure devoted to health care from 1980 to 1991 (OECD, 1993f, vol. 1, table 1).

With all of these reforms, and despite levels of unemployment and annual deficits unprecedented for Sweden, the contours of the most generous welfare state in the world remain intact; the adjustments may actually make the social-spending share of GDP level off or even move slightly downward. In per capita benefits the Swedes moved in the 1990s from lavish to merely very generous social expenditures.

In short, the cutbacks among rich democracies are concentrated on either the greatest excesses and abuses of the welfare state (sick pay, disability), or on the least politically organized, marginal groups (single mothers, the unemployed, or the poor), or in sectors where the eligible population is declining (school-age children in the countries with older populations and a declining percentage of youngsters; decreasing unemployment on the upswing of the economy and hence decreasing expenditures on unemployment benefits and vice versa). Health-care reform is prominent everywhere. Benefit formulas for pensions are being modified in most countries; to account for increased longevity, "normal retirement age" is being raised in many. But nowhere have employment-based pension schemes been redesigned according to the American Concord Coalition recommendation for a tax/transfer, needs-based model (Myles and Quadagno, 1996, p. 20). Real cutbacks in benefits are typically small and incremental—trimming around the edges of the welfare state, sometimes making it more efficient. There is an increased use of income testing and the taxation of benefits. And while the GDP share of social spending is stabilizing, the recent growth of eligible aged, poor, and unemployed has meant some reduction of per-recipient benefits in several countries. But this is a slow process that encounters strong public resistance. Small, incremental reductions in many programs can add up over time; vast majorities of voters whose income and security are threatened sooner or later rebel. (We might call these prowelfare-state protests "frontlash." See chap. 10.)

Continuity at the Core: The Cases of Britain and Germany

Once the core universalistic programs of the welfare state are in place and mature, there is, in fact, a fierce resistance to real cutbacks among both masses and their allies within governing elites—parts of the state apparatus, churches, unions, centrist or leftist factions within major political parties, and advocacy groups. The welfare state persists through thick and thin, through prosperity and recession, through changes in party coalitions, even through shifts of regimes. The point is dramatically illustrated by Britain and Germany.

In 17 years of Margaret Thatcher and John Major's rule (1979–95)—prime ministers who articulated a strong 19th-century liberal ideology—no reduction in total government spending was achieved. Government spending in 1995 was 42% of GDP—just 0.25% less than it was when Labour was still in power 17 years before; real government spending rose an average of 1.9% a year (*The Economist*, Dec. 2, 1995, pp. 58–59). Despite sharp cuts in education and some means-tested social programs, especially those targeted to the sick and disabled, families with children, and the elderly (Evans, Piachaud, and Sutherland, 1994, pp. 90–92), aggregate social spending continued to increase. From 1978 to 1992 real social spending (including government outlays for housing, education, and training) climbed substantially; as a percentage of GDP, social spending fluctuated, with a slight upward bias from 24.1% in 1978 to 27% in 1992 (Pierson, 1994, pp. 143–144). The welfare state marches on even in the land of the boldest and most publicized right-wing democratic regime.

Germany from Bismarck to Kohl shows that pension and health insurance arrangements can persist through wars and violent changes of regime.[19] Scholars of the German welfare state agree that the basic system of social insurance established by Bismarck and built up through the Empire and the Weimar Republic remained essentially intact throughout the

Third Reich. This remarkable continuity of social policy was chiefly due to the continuity of specialists in the government bureaucracy, especially the Ministry of Labor. They were adept at deflecting any Nazi plan for sweeping reform (Heyde, 1966, p. 64; Syrup, 1957, p. 404); they were able to link their own traditional views of social policy to Nazi slogans so as to reform social insurance along their favored lines while seeming to implement Nazi concepts (Hentschel, 1978, p. 323). All this despite efforts of the Nazi Labor Front—created in May 1933 to discipline and indoctrinate labor and to fill the void left by the dissolution of the labor unions—first to bring social insurance programs under its direction (1933–37) and then to overhaul the entire system, making benefits depend on the will of the government rather than on social rights (1937–40) (Smelser, 1988, pp. 274ff.; Teppe, 1977, pp. 217–218, 238–247). The Ministry of Labor defeated these efforts, aided by industrialists and many health insurance carriers who wanted no major restructuring of the welfare state (*ibid.*, pp. 218–219). Even later when industry was subordinated to the Nazis and the Labor Front had acquired tens of thousands of employees and become powerful, the only changes to social insurance under the Nazis were efforts that any government might make to adapt to a changing economy and which were essentially drafted by the civil servants at the Ministry of Labor: a "Stabilization Law" of December 7, 1933, to maintain the solvency of the various pension insurance schemes; and the "Law of the Construction of Social Insurance" of July 5, 1934. These laws aimed to increase cooperation between different schemes by fusing the state institutions responsible for health insurance and pensions, by restricting the self-administration of the insurance carriers, and by increasing state supervision. The officials in the Labor Ministry found this a convenient means of achieving their own ends. There was almost no input from the Nazi party or any of its organizations. Hitler himself was reluctant to make bold shifts in these systems (pp. 220, 248–249). It is a lesson in both bureaucratic momentum and the integrative functions of the welfare state.

This is not to say that administrative practice did not change under the Nazis. For instance, health insurance rules became tougher (Syrup, 1957, p. 519) because many of the trade unionists and socialists who had staffed the sickness funds under the Weimar Republic were kicked out by the Nazis. Similarly, the Nazi mobilization drive to increase productivity for the war machine increased industrial accidents but decreased accident insurance benefits (pp. 371, 522). Average pension benefits, however, did not differ much from those under the Weimar Republic (pp. 368–369, 523).

Although the Nazis made few changes in the structure of social insurance, they, of course, made sweeping changes in industrial relations, wiping out free labor unions and collective bargaining; they created the notorious Labor Front (DAF) and a group of 12 "Trustees of Labor" to enforce the new labor laws; they eliminated self-administration of local and regional labor offices that had run both labor placement and unemployment insurance; and they kept unemployment insurance contributions high and the benefits low via means-testing, while diverting the surplus funds to the rearmament effort (Teppe, 1977, pp. 211–212, 236–237; Guillebaud, 1941, pp. 86–87; Syrup, 1957, p. 456).[20] The Nazis also made substantial changes in the funding and administration of public assistance; they reduced the number of private programs run by churches and eliminated programs run by unions, socialists, and political parties, while cracking down on benefits for the poor who were despised as physically or mentally unfit for the new master race (deWitt, 1978). In view of such drastic discontinuities of German political regimes over a century, however, the continuity of social insurance systems at the core of the welfare state is impressive.

In sum: Despite talk of "crisis" and "the end of the welfare state," despite various efforts to reduce spending in the past 20 years, despite some erosion of per-client benefits, the welfare state has become institutionalized and consolidated while social spending as a share of GDP continues to climb, or, if it flattens, it is at a high level. As I said in 1975, "in the end the welfare state in its wondrous diversity proves hard to shoot down" (Wilensky, 1975, p. xvii).

LEFTISM, CATHOLICISM, AND DEMOCRATIC CORPORATISM: EXPLAINING NATIONAL DIFFERENCES IN SOCIAL SPENDING

We can now play convergence theory (industrialization and its demographic, social structural, and political correlates) against types of political economy (the interaction of cumulative left party power, cumulative Catholic party power, and corporatist bargaining structures) to explain recent similarities and differences in taxing and social spending both as a fraction of GNP and per capita. Chapter 2 has described measures of leftism, Catholicism, and democratic corporatism. After reporting a few tests of types of political economy as a source of differences in spending, I shall describe measures in the industrialization model (GNP per capita, the percentage of total population 65 and older, an index of minority-group cleavages, and an index of mobility and meritocracy) and test that model. We can then bring the two theories together and suggest some likely outcomes as rich countries get richer and the least-rich countries catch up to the most affluent.[21]

I shall first present the bare findings concerning the effect of each type of mass-based political party, then integrate party dominance into my model of corporatism. As chapter 2 has shown, both Catholicism and leftism have encouraged the development of a corporatist political economy. We shall see here that, in turn, the trade-offs among labor, management, and the government characteristic of corporatist democracy lead to high taxing by least-visible means (great reliance on social-security taxes and consumption taxes), which facilitate high universalistic social spending. Finally there are clues in the data suggesting that under conditions of intense Catholic and left competition with accompanying discontinuities of left rule, social spending escalates, as in Belgium and the Netherlands.

Left Power and Spending

During the entire period since World War I or the shorter period after World War II, cumulative left power has had no effect on welfare effort or output. For instance, left party power from 1919 to 1976 has no significant correlation with SS/GNP in 1966 ($r = -.12$), SS/GNP in 1971 ($r = .04$), or SS per capita 1966 ($r = .22$) or 1971 ($r = .25$). In regression experiments including the major determinants of welfare effort—percentage of population aged 65 or more and corporatist-technocratic linkages—no measure of left power has any significant explanatory effect. Whatever influence left parties have is indirect and weak.

Left Power and Taxes

Left power does increase reliance on painfully visible taxes, that is, personal taxes on income, property, and capital gains; property taxes paid by households; individual net wealth taxes; and, the smallest fraction, net wealth, gift and inheritance taxes—all as a percentage of total tax revenues. These taxes, especially progressive income taxes, are favorites of left parties everywhere. From the 1950s to the 1970s, leftist governments suffered from the illusion that the road to equality runs through taxes on property and progressivity in the tax system. Thus, when played against two major determinants of tax visibility in the late 1960s—GNP per capita, which increases reliance on visible taxes, and corporatism, which decreases such tendencies—left power still inspires reliance on visible taxes.

Dependent Variable	Independent Variables	Beta	*p*
Tax visibility, average 1965 and 1971	Left party power, 1919–76	.47	.03
	Democratic corporatism score	−.42	.04
	GNP per capita, 1966 and 1971	.35	.08

Adj. R^2=.48

Later, as governments in which leftist parties were prominent needed much-increased revenues to finance their social-security and labor-market goals, they realized the political dangers of these most unpopular taxes and shifted toward other more tolerable mass taxes, social-security and consumption taxes. Left power alone, however—without structures for bargaining that foster trade-offs between tax structures, social policies, and labor policies—could not produce this shift away from painfully visible taxes toward a balanced tax system. This is evident in Australia, the United States, New Zealand, and Canada, and to a lesser extent the United Kingdom, noncorporatist democracies with extended periods of left party power that still rely heavily on visible taxes. Table 10.2 (backlash) shows types of taxes as a percentage of total taxation and total taxation as a percentage of GDP by country in 1971 and 1988; chapter 10 explains why tax visibility is a major proximate cause of tax-welfare backlash.

Catholic Power and Spending

In contrast to leftism, cumulative Catholic power since World War I increases welfare effort (for 1966, SS/GNP r = .74; for 1971, r = .60). Catholic power and social-security spending per capita, however, are unrelated (for 1966, r = .27; for 1971, r = .22). In both multiple regressions and cross-tabulations containing the most important sources of welfare effort—population 65 and over, corporatism, and avoidance of visible taxes—Catholic power holds up as a direct or indirect determinant of big spending. For instance, when they are in the same equation, Catholic power is about as important as the proportion of the aged as a predictor of welfare effort in 1966, although it becomes less important in subsequent years, while the beta weight for 65+ climbs.

Dependent Variable	Independent Variables	Beta	p
SS/GNP average, 1966 and 1971	Catholic party power, 1919–76	.34	.01
	Persons 65 and over as percent of total population, 1966 and 1970	.68	.01

Adj. R^2 = .79

And by 1980 the effect of Catholicism disappears when corporatism and population 65+ are in the same equation. The reason: Countries dominated by Catholic party power did not keep up with increases in social spending of such countries as Sweden, Denmark, and Norway.

Catholic Power and Taxes

In contrast to leftism, Catholic power decreases reliance on visible taxes ($r = -.50$ for 1965, $-.52$ for 1971, and $-.42$ for 1980). Catholic parties worried much less about progressivity in the tax system; they relied more heavily on less-visible taxes. In fact, no country scoring high on cumulative Catholic power scores high on tax visibility in any year (see tables 10.2 and 10.3, chap. 10 [backlash]). Neither leftism nor Catholicism increases per capita social-security spending. This is instead a product of affluence—GNP per capita with its demographic and bureaucratic correlates—and of corporatism.

In short, left party power alone is not directly related to welfare effort (SS/GNP). It is a poor second to Catholic power as an explanation of welfare effort. Left power, however, increases reliance on visible taxes, while Catholic power decreases such reliance.

Corporatism, Taxes, and Spending

Strong corporatist bargaining arrangements and low tax visibility go together with high taxes and strong welfare effort (SS/GNP), as well as generous per capita social spending. The trade-offs typical among the social partners—labor accepting nominal wage restraint, labor peace, high mass taxes, and low corporation taxes in return for management and government acceptance of generous social and labor-market policies (see chap. 2)—foster substantial consensus on a high level of social spending. In turn, expansive social spending requires a large tax base. Politically, this cannot be achieved with heavy reliance on the most painfully visible taxes, that is, property taxes on households and individual income taxes. (Chap. 10 explains why the Swedes are no longer an exception to that rule and traces the process by which corporatist democracies have moved toward the German balance among types of taxes since World War II.) Although in 1965 corporatism did not mean least reliance on visible taxes, by 1971, when taxing and spending had risen sharply in the corporatist democracies, they had reduced their reliance on such taxes. Table 5.2 relates corporatism to total tax burden, reliance on visible taxes, and welfare effort (SS/GNP) in 1971. Although we are forced to dichotomize our scores as either high or low, thereby obscuring marginal cases (such as Denmark's medium score on corporatism, Germany's low score but functional equivalents to corporatism), the table generally supports the theory. Specifically,

1. *Corporatism clearly fosters heavy taxes.* Of 10 corporatist countries that include labor in high policy, 8 are heavy taxers in 1971. (The figures on level and types of taxes by country are in chap. 10, table 10.2.) In contrast, all other countries—the more decentralized and fragmented democracies as well as corporatist countries that keep labor at a distance (Japan, France, Switzerland)—are light taxers.

2. *Corporatism leads toward low tax visibility.* Of all corporatist countries, only two (Denmark and Sweden) are high in visible taxes as a percentage of total tax take. Because tax visibility is a powerful proximate cause of tax-welfare backlash, these two deviant cases are discussed in chapter 10. Of nine least-corporatist countries, only two are low in tax visibility and they are corporatist-without-labor (France and Japan).

3. *The combination of corporatism and the avoidance of overreliance on visible taxes permits big social spending.* Of eight cases with strong to medium corporatist bargaining arrangements and low tax visibility, only Israel is a lean spender. At that extreme, a heavy military burden plainly retards welfare-state development (see chap. 12).

These conclusions stand up to multiple-regression experiments that include affluence (GNP per capita) and the age of the population (65+ percentage) which, as we have seen, are strongly related to welfare effort. No matter what we include in the regressions (affluence, 65+ percentage, Catholicism, leftism, tax visibility, or other tax variables), corporatism retains its positive, independent influence on both welfare effort (SS/GNP) and its even stronger effect on social spending per capita, a rough measure of cash and services delivered to individuals.

Like aging of the population, affluence is strongly related to social spending per capita (for 1966, $r = .57$; for 1971, .67; for 1980, .78). A very rich country like the United States can deliver quite a lot of cash to each person even though the percentage of its income devoted to the welfare state is modest; conversely a country that in 1971 was least rich, like Austria, delivers modest per capita spending even if its welfare effort is strong. Thus, it is impressive that controlling for both GNP per capita (ability to pay) and age of the population in the late 1960s (demand for social security), corporatism retained its independent influence. For instance,

Dependent Variable	Independent Variables	Beta	p
SS per capita average, 1966 and 1971	GNP per capita average, 1966 and 1971	.67	.00
	Persons 65 and over as percent of population, 1966 and 1970	.47	.00
	Corporatism score	.28	.03

Adj. $R^2 = .82$ ($N = 18$)

The results for 1980 regressions (not included here) show all three variables at work, explaining about the same variance but age structure is a bit less important and corporatism is more important.

In sum: Considering all regressions and multivariate tables, including those not reported here, the major consistent sources of strong welfare-state effort (SS/GNP) are democratic

TABLE 5.2 The interaction of democratic corporatism, tax load, tax visibility, and social spending in nineteen rich democracies, 1971[a]

Strong to Medium Corporatism				Weak or No Corporatism or Corporatism Without Labor			
High soc. spending Heavy taxes Low visibility	High soc. spending Heavy taxes High visibility	High soc. spending Low taxes Low visibility	Low soc. spending Low taxes Low visibility	Med. soc. spending Med. taxes High visibility	Med. soc. spending Med. taxes Low visibility	Low soc. spending Low taxes High visibility	Low soc. spending Low taxes Low visibility
Netherlands Norway Belgium Austria Finland[e]	Denmark[b] Sweden	Italy W. Germany[d]	Israel	United Kingdom	France[c]	New Zealand United States Australia Canada Switzerland[c] Ireland[d]	Japan[c]

[a]Figures, sources, and measures for spending in table 5.1; for taxes in table 10.2.
[b]Denmark scores medium on corporatism.
[c]Corporatism–without-labor.
[d]Germany and Ireland are medium in tax load.
[e]Finland is medium in both spending and taxing.

corporatism, Catholicism, and the percentage of the population 65+. By 1980 corporatism and an aged population remain significant, but the effect of Catholic party power disappears, mainly because the countries where Catholicism was powerful (e.g., Italy, Germany, Austria) did not match the accelerated spending of Sweden, Denmark, and Norway (see table 5.2). In explaining social spending per capita, corporatism, affluence, and the percentage of population 65+ are consistently the strongest predictors. Tax structures, when any two of these other variables are in the equation, are weaker sources of spending. Tax policies are instead a product of the interplay of bargaining arrangements and political party power.

We can now bring types of party power together with types of corporatism to generate five types of political economy and relate these to welfare-state development. Table 5.3 shows that any type of corporatist political economy that includes labor at the high table will exceed the average spending of the least-corporatist countries for all years from 1950 to 1986. Averages for each type show a descending order of spending from high to low as follows: (1) left-Catholic corporatist; (2) left corporatist (although in 1986, a noncomparable year, this category slightly edges out the first);[22] (3) Catholic corporatist; (4) corporatist-without-labor; (5) the most-fragmented and decentralized democracies. As chapter 2 has shown, Catholicism and leftism are in some ways functional equivalents: since World War I they have had similar effects on the direction of the political economy of rich democracies; they both foster corporatist bargaining; they both embrace a traditional humanistic concern with the lower strata. While left parties articulate a stronger, more consistent egalitarian ideology, both types of mass-based parties, when in power, have interacted with the social partners to promote welfare-state spending. (Types of spending and specific policies do vary, as subsequent chapters will show.)

The Effects of Party Continuity and Competition on Spending

That Catholic-left corporatist countries lead in average level of spending in table 5.3 suggests that the more intense the competition between Catholic and left parties, the more left parties in power will spend. It would be useful to consider the number of interruptions in either left or Catholic power as an indicator of Catholic-left competition. But because Catholic parties have remarkably stable tenure in office, we cannot make any inferences about the effect of competition on their spending policies.

Consider, for example, the cases of the Italian Christian Democrats, the Belgian Social Christians, and to a lesser extent the Austrian People's party—all of which, at least until the mid-1960s, dominated their country's postwar politics. With such stability among powerful Catholic parties, we must settle for interruptions of left rule as our measure.

There are three clues that the number of times the left was thrown out indicates Catholic-left competition and results in more spending. First, there is a significant correlation between interruptions of left party power and social welfare effort in 1966 (the same relationship approached significance in 1971, $r = .33$). Second, the country with the highest number of left party interruptions, Belgium with six such occasions, also has a stable Catholic party; even with its intense ethnic-linguistic divisions, the Social Christians have dominated except for the years 1954–58. The country tied for second place, Germany, with four left interruptions, has a similarly stable Catholic party, while France, with left parties thrown out three times, has a Catholic party which has at least held office. In these cases, interruptions of left party power appear to be good indicators of left-Catholic competition.

TABLE 5.3 Types of political economy and social spending as a percentage of GNP, 1950–86*

	1950		1966		1971		1980		1986	
Left Corporatist										
Sweden	10.0	(7)	16.5	(7)	23.8	(1)	33.1	(1)	31.3	(1)
Norway	6.7	(14)	12.6	(11)	19.6	(8)	23.3	(9)	29.8	(2)
Finland	7.7	(12)	13.1	(10)	16.3	(10)	21.1	(10)	22.8	(10)
Israel	5.6	(16)	6.8	(18)	7.9	(18)	7.0	(19)	n.a.	
Denmark	8.6	(10)	13.9	(8)	20.2	(6)	32.8	(2)	26.1	5)
cell avg.	7.7		12.6		17.6		23.5		27.5	
Left-Catholic Corporatist										
Netherlands	9.1	(9)	18.3	(5)	23.6	(2)	31.3	(3)	28.6	(3)
Belgium	12.8	(4)	18.6	(3)	20.6	(4)	29.8	(5)	25.9	(6)
Austria	14.3	(2)	20.8	(1)	22.3	(3)	26.3	(7)	25.2	(7)
cell avg.	12.1		19.2		22.2		29.1		26.6	
Catholic Corporatist										
Italy	9.6	(8)	17.5	(6)	20.5	(5)	19.6	(11)	n.a.	
West Germany	17.0	(1)	19.6	(2)	19.7	(7)	27.0	(6)	23.4	(8)
cell avg.	13.3		18.6		20.1		23.3		23.4	
Corporatist Without Labor										
France	13.2	(3)	18.3	(5)	17.5	(9)	30.4	(4)	28.5	(4)
Japan	3.8	(19)	5.1	(19)	5.5	(19)	11.0	(18)	12.2	(16)
Switzerland	6.3	(15)	9.5	(14)	11.4	(15)	16.0	(14)	14.7	(14)
cell avg.	7.8		11.0		11.5		19.1		18.5	
Least Corporatist										
United States	4.6	(18)	7.9	(17)	11.7	(14)	14.6	(17)	12.5	(15)
United Kingdom	10.9	(5)	13.3	(9)	14.4	(12)	17.3	(12)	20.1	(11)
New Zealand	10.4	(6)	12.0	(12)	10.5	(16)	16.1	(13)	18.0	(12)
Australia	5.1	(17)	9.2	(16)	9.3	(17)	15.7	(15)	9.7	(17)
Canada	6.8	(13)	9.4	(15)	15.8	(11)	15.1	(16)	15.2	(13)
Ireland	8.0	(11)	11.2	(13)	12.7	(13)	23.3	(9)	23.2	(9)
cell avg.	7.6		10.5		12.4		17.0		16.5	

*Sources and measures for spending in footnotes to table 5.1.

It is difficult to test directly the notion of competitive escalation of social spending because so few countries score high in both left and Catholic party power. For the entire period of democratic politics from 1919 to 1976, only Belgium scores high on both. In the post–World War II period, three countries (Belgium, Netherlands, and Austria) evidence strong Catholicism and leftism. Germany is a marginal case where Catholic power is high and left power medium. Since there are only six countries with positive Catholic party scores, it is impossible to sift out an independent interaction effect by means of regression analysis.

Although limited, the data in table 5.3 and the record of interruptions to party power 1919–76 (Wilensky, 1981c, p. 373) suggest first that long-term continuous rule by Catholic parties or Catholic domination of governing coalitions (West Germany, Italy) constrains the rate of increase of social spending; Catholic-corporatist countries consistently rank at the bottom in rate of increase among the five types, although their level of spending is typically above average. Second, frequent alternating victories and defeats of left parties with substantial mass base escalate their interest in spending their way to more stable power, whether from desire or necessity. (With Catholic power so continuous, we cannot know what effect their frequent defeat might have.) Thus, left-corporatist countries rank high in both spending and increases in spending, except in the rare cases of long-term continuous left rule (e.g., Austria).

These data also provide clues to the question of whether amount and number of years of power count more or less than the continuity in office that permits planning. Apparently for both Catholic and left parties, continuous power (few interruptions) generally permits the kind of planning that holds down spending (Catholic-corporatist Germany and Italy and Catholic-left corporatist Austria) while sheer amount of power and years exercised under intense competition has the reverse effect (Catholic-left corporatist Netherlands and Belgium). Austria fits the pattern of long periods of domination by left parties and slower growth in spending from a high base. Sweden is the deviant case: continuous left rule did not constrain Sweden's rate of growth of social spending.

In short, stable tenure and sheer amount of power without continuity may have opposite effects on social policy. It is the discontinuities of rule, under conditions of keen Catholic and left competition, that escalate spending most, although discontinuities in left dominance makes left-corporatist countries a close second.

These tests of my political economy model suggest two roads to a strong welfare effort: Catholic, corporatist, heavy taxers and spenders with balanced tax structures (avoiding over-reliance on painfully visible taxes); and leftist, corporatist, heavy taxers and spenders with balanced tax structures. The deviant cases that do not quite fit these patterns appear to be moving in the right direction. West Germany, counted as marginally corporatist, has probably become more corporatist in the past 30 or so years. Israel, a case of medium corporatism, is a high taxer but a low social spender; without its extraordinary military burden it would spend more on social programs (chap. 10 shows that military spending at the high level of the cold war subverts social spending). Finally, in 1971 Sweden and Denmark—left-corporatist countries that in 1971 were still relying on visible taxes—are with varying speed moving toward greater tax balance (chap. 10).

CONVERGENCE THEORY: ECONOMIC LEVEL, POPULATION AGING, MOBILITY-MERITOCRACY, AND MINORITY-GROUP CLEAVAGES

There are good reasons to suppose that at some high threshold of economic development very rich countries experience structural changes that decrease the appeal of heavy taxes to finance increased social spending from the high base already achieved by most of our rich democracies. At least there is mildly increased resistance to the pace of welfare-state expansion that prevailed from 1950 to 1975 or 1980, consistent with the data on the slower rate of growth in both economy and social spending discussed earlier.

First, as we have seen in chapter 1, at very high levels of development, postsecondary educational opportunities expand and the upper-middle class and the middle mass both grow. These educational-occupational shifts bring increased rates of occupational and residential mobility and more labor-force participation by women. Consequently, increasing fractions of modern populations can buy so much on the market or bargain for so much privately that they begin to resist the taxation necessary for the expanding welfare state they simultaneously demand (cf. Wilensky, 1965, p. x). Mobility is also a force for the development of meritocratic ideologies and the decrease of community solidarity (see chap. 14 on mayhem).

Second, the economic growth rate of the most-affluent democracies tends to be slower than the growth rate of the least rich. In fact, sheer level of affluence is negatively correlated with growth for all time periods up to 1974 when it fades to insignificance for subsequent periods up to 1990 (e.g., economic level is correlated only $-.28$ with real GDP growth per capita 1974–79). Among modern populations who are used to expanding standards of living for themselves and their children, slow or no economic growth exacerbates social cleavages, political conflict, and general discontent. Under modern conditions, the war of all against all, the zero-sum society, is held in check by decent growth; it may be released by fading growth. Equally important, growth provides the added resources to support growth in social spending; the less growth, the less leeway for social spending.

Third, the postwar period has seen increasing immigration, legal and illegal, to all the rich democracies, accelerating with the stream of refugees of recent years. Formerly more or less socially homogeneous nations such as Austria, Germany, Italy, France, Sweden, Norway, Finland, and Denmark are catching up in social cleavages with such countries as the United States, Canada, Australia, Switzerland, the United Kingdom, and Israel. In other words, the rich democracies are converging in their social heterogeneity, their cleavages of religion, ethnicity, race, and language (for details, see chap. 17 on globalization).

But social heterogeneity can cut both ways. In explaining the backwardness of the United States, Gunnar Myrdal (1960, pp. 54ff., 87, 100 passim.) invokes its deep social cleavages. In contrast, my argument (Wilensky, 1965, pp. xviii–xix) suggests that social heterogeneity and minority-group conflict slow down welfare-state development and create tax resistance only where they are given sharp expression by a decentralized if not fragmented polity. (Tables 10.4 and 10.5 on backlash support that argument.) Consider two countries at the extremes of social spending, both with strong social cleavages—the Netherlands at the top, the United States at the bottom. In the Netherlands one needs a special vocabulary (*verzuiling* or "pillarization," "view of life," "confessional-political blocs") to describe the diversity of religious and nonreligious groups which cut through all areas of Dutch life and are expressed in social issues. Even radio and television are organized by these blocs (see chap. 3). A strong central government, however, is able to channel their expression and dampen the cleavages. The provinces and municipalities are weak; their heads are appointed at the Hague; government integrates the confessional-political blocs at the top in a complex network of advisory bodies, public and semipublic (Goudsblom, 1967). The welfare state from 1950 to the 1980s flourished. A similar central containment of more bitter ethnic-linguistic struggles is evident in Belgium. The contrast of Holland and Belgium, egalitarian welfare-state leaders with low backlash, with the decentralized and fragmented federalism of the United States, Switzerland, or Canada—inegalitarian welfare-state laggards with high backlash—is obvious.[23]

Another aspect of minority-group conflict creates contradictory pressures. On the one hand, a wider civic virtue cannot fully flourish when ties to minority groups are strong, for racial, ethnic-linguistic, and religious cleavages block meaningful participation in less parochial voluntary associations and encourage separatist allegiances; furthermore, minority groups sometimes create welfare and education services of their own, thereby subverting public expenditures. And as we shall see in chapter 9 the minority-group thrust for equal opportunity increases mobility, which fosters backlash. On the other hand, minority groups create general pressure for equality and sometimes join coalitions in support of expanded state aid for education and welfare services. Insofar as that pressure reduces inequality, it reduces resistance to social spending and the taxes to support it. In other words, egalitarian corporatist democracies with the "right" taxing policies can offset the negative effects of increased social cleavages on social spending. Given these contradictory pressures of minority-group conflict, we would expect that their net average effect on welfare-state development for all 19 countries would be modest.

In short, structural changes characteristic of advanced industrialization—an expanded "middle mass," increased mobility and meritocracy, more minority-group cleavages, reduced rates of economic growth—should eventually slow down or even reverse welfare effort.

Offsetting these tendencies of very rich countries, however, are increased pressure from the demand side and, for some of our countries, corporatist bargaining arrangements. Continuing industrialization increases our old standby, the aging of the population, thereby increasing pressure for social spending both as a percentage of GNP and per capita. Continued growth provides the money to finance social spending. At the level most rich democracies had achieved by the late 1990s even slow growth brings amazing increments of cash; a meager one percentage point increase in real annual growth in the United States in a $9.25 trillion economy in 1999 yields an extra $92.5 billion for about the same number of people.

To test the industrialization model, we used measures of economic level, economic growth, and population aging and devised measures of mobility, meritocracy, and minority-group cleavages and explored their interaction. Because the distance between the GDP per capita of most-rich countries and that of least-rich countries is not great, we would not expect convergence theory to be as strong as our types of political economy in explaining national differences in welfare effort but to be better in explaining per capita spending.

We can now test these ideas by exploring the effect of industrialization and its structural correlates on social spending and then attempting to combine the results with types of political economy in a final causal model.

Measures for Testing Convergence Theory

We start with measures of affluence or levels of industrialism—per capita GNP in 1966, 1971, and 1980—which, as we have seen in chapter 1 and will see in chapters 8 and 9, leads to increased mobility and a societal emphasis on meritocracy. Mobility and meritocracy are here measured by intergenerational mobility (sons of working-class fathers moving up to nonmanual occupations; there are no data on daughters); the percentage of working-class sons and daughters in higher education (1965 and 1970); higher education enrollment ratio (average of 1965 and 1970); and higher education expenditures per capita averaged for 1965 and 1971. Each component was scored 0, 1, or 2, and equally weighted. Total scores range from 0 (Austria and Ireland) to 8 (USA, Canada).

Because we lack data for New Zealand on both mobility dimensions, we dropped it. Because of the positive correlation between occupational mobility and educational mobility, where we lacked data on one or the other variable we scored each case (H, M, L) according to the variable for which we had data. (See appendix I—for scores, details, and a comparison of residential mobility rates—closely related to the mobility rates we use here.)

All of the higher education enrollment and expenditure variables between 1965 and 1980 are highly intercorrelated so that any meritocracy measures we use to construct this index would yield the same results. In short, the index measures relatively stable structures of mobility and meritocracy.[24] We use higher education enrollment ratios and expenditures as indicators of a country's emphasis on meritocracy on the assumption that higher education still remains meritocratic. A society with a high enrollment ratio (e.g., a quarter to half of 20- to 24-year-olds were in postsecondary education as early as 1965–71) that also invests relatively large sums in higher education per capita is a society that acts out the value of equality of opportunity. Despite the egalitarian thrust of movements to increase access, reduce tracking and selection by ability, and relax requirements, modern universities, colleges, and technical institutes remain essentially meritocratic.

That investment in higher education is meritocratic is confirmed by its negative correlation with the rest of the welfare state (social security/GNP), which is more egalitarian and collectivistic (see chaps. 6 on sector spending and 8 on the welfare mess). Similarly, the correlation between the percentage of adults with postsecondary education circa 1989 (OECD, 1992b, p. 23) and social spending/GDP 1986 (table 5.1, footnote b) is −.69 ($p = .01$).

Minority-group cleavages in this model are a second source of mobility and meritocracy. As we shall see in chapter 9, democratic governments everywhere are responsive to the mobility aspirations of ethnic, racial, and religious groups. The public sector opens up first, the private sector follows. Whatever the ambivalence of minority groups about the conflict between equality of opportunity and equality of results, the net outcome is expanding opportunity for upward mobility, whose universal effects are to reinforce meritocratic values. Whether the upwardly mobile person who escapes from poverty, the working class, or an impoverished minority group extends a helping hand to those left behind depends on structures for cross-class solidarity—for instance, the strength of such broad-based associations as multi-industrial unions, political parties, and churches. But even where social solidarity is strong, the central tendency for ambitious mobile men and women is to distance themselves from their origins. The limited research on the political and ideological impact of mobility suggests that whether the mobility is up or down, it has similar effects: the upwardly mobile identify with the class of destination, while the downwardly mobile cling to the class from which they are falling, expecting or hoping to return (for a review of evidence, see Wilensky and Edwards, 1959; cf. Curtis and Jackson, 1977, pp. 145–146). The ultimate outcome is to reinforce a reciprocal alienation among the poor, the near-poor, and the comfortable majority. This can undermine the sense of shared risk that favors universalistic social spending.

Like mobility, meritocracy, and minority-group cleavages, persistent differences in the age structure of the population are rooted in differences in the past timing and rate of industrialization. But at very high levels of development, convergence takes place. This is evident in the rapid catch-up of Japan, a late industrializer with a young population that led all our democracies in rate of economic growth and the concomitant decline in fertility and thereby a most rapid increase in the percentage of population over 65 and a rapid increase in welfare effort since 1970. This, despite the weakness of labor-left pressure and a high (if declining) rate of traditional three-generation households (see chap. 1).

Results for Convergence Theory

Correlations between variables in the industrialization model are promising. In regression analysis, however, only affluence, aging, and minority-group cleavages survive as predictors of welfare effort. Economic growth and mobility-meritocracy drop out in all time periods. In predicting spending per capita, affluence becomes even stronger, aging remains a robust booster of benefits, minority-group cleavages are a weak drag on spending, while mobility-meritocracy drops out in all equations but one.

A word about the fate of each of these variables:

1. *Affluence and aging.* By changing family and demographic structure via increasing female labor participation, reducing fertility, and, later, increasing the health and longevity of the aged while reducing their opportunities to work, affluence increases the percentage of the dependent population over 65 and at a very high level of development, the percentage over 80, thereby driving the need for and political demand for social spending. This is confirmed by the path from GNP per capita to 65+ to welfare effort (figure 5.3). These relationships are even stronger for regressions explaining per capita social spending; the variance explained by affluence and aging increases from the mid-1960s to the mid-1970s to 1980.

2. *Minority-group cleavages* are strongly related to the index of mobility and meritocracy ($r = .73$), which in turn sets up increased resistance to social solidarity and social spending. Because of the offsets discussed earlier we would expect a negative but weak relationship. Minority-group cleavages are negatively correlated with the GNP share of social spending 1966 and 1971 ($-.46$; $p < .05$) and 1980 ($r = -.58$; $p < .01$). Cleavages have no relationship to per capita spending (except a marginal correlation of $-.41$ in 1980).

Regressions of SS/GNP 66–71 on affluence in 1966 and 1971, minority-group cleavages, and mobility-meritocracy, however, show no significant relationships for this part of the industrialization model, although the signs are in the right direction. Population aging, when in the presence of any two of the other industrialization variables, evidences a strong relationship to welfare effort. Using 1980 data, the results are better: affluence promotes spending while social cleavages are a drag on spending. (The correlations for mobility/meritocracy and spending are negative for all years but approach significance only in 1966 [$r = -.47$; $p < .10$]; so it drops out in all equations.)

Dependent Variable	Independent Variables	Beta	p
SS/GNP 1980	Minority-Group Cleavages Index	$-.58$	.06
	Mobility-Meritocracy Index	.04	n.s.
	GNP per capita 1980	.42	.05

Adj. $R^2 = .39$ ($N = 18$)

So far, we have a fairly weak confirmation of the convergence model.

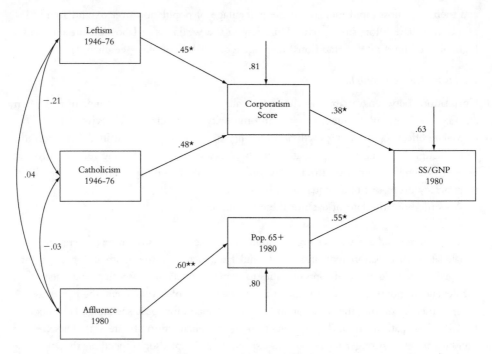

Figure 5.3. Combining the industrialization model with the political economy model: leftism and Catholicism foster corporatism thereby increasing social spending; affluence increases population aging thereby increasing social spending

N=19. ★ indicates path coefficient significant at $p < .05$; ★★ indicates path coefficient significant at $p < .01$. Adjusted R^2 for SS/GNP = .56; for Corporatism = .26; for Pop. 65+ = .32. Sources and measures for spending in footnotes to table 5.1.

3. *Economic growth in various periods does not stand up in this scheme as an independent predictor of SS/GNP, although the correlations are in the right direction* (positive). Real GDP growth per capita averaged for the whole period 1950–74 is correlated .45 ($p < .05$) with spending for that period, but it fades to insignificance for 1974–79 and subsequent periods.

Results for the Combined Models

To capture the causal order of the most consistently strong sources of welfare effort, we must combine the effects of industrialization with the effects of variation in types of political economy.

The path diagram, figure 5.3, shows two roads to lavish spending: the familiar path from leftism and Catholicism to democratic corporatism to welfare effort (SS/GNP 1980); and the second somewhat stronger path from affluence through population 65+ to welfare effort. This diagram, an adaptation of regression techniques to our causal models, shows that the only variables from convergence theory that still strongly shape both the level of welfare effort and per capita spending are affluence and population 65+. As we shall see in later chapters explaining tax-welfare backlash, mayhem, and bureaucratic bloat, however, the rest—especially minority-group conflict and mobility-meritocracy—also count heavily, sometimes more than types of political economy.

Figure 5.3 cannot capture the types of corporatism discussed earlier or the ambiguous role of minority-group cleavages as they interact with mobility and meritocracy. But together with the tables showing spending and taxing patterns by country over time and discussion of continuities and retrenchment in the welfare state, this combined path diagram is strong confirmation of my central theme: The structural correlates of industrialization push all rich democracies toward convergence at a high level of social spending; differences in the power of mass-based political parties as they interact with national bargaining patterns (especially the structure, functions, behavior, and interplay of labor, the professions, management and the government) explain the substantial differences in patterns of taxing and spending that remain among the countries equally rich. There is no uniform "crisis" of the welfare state, although there is much hysterical talk about it. Instead there is a slowdown in the rate of expansion and some reductions in benefits per person, with variation in the targets and the fairness of the cuts. Governing parties of every ideological persuasion have endorsed retrenchments in social spending, but center-left coalitions tend to impose more equality of sacrifice in the distribution of pain. The core programs of the welfare state remain immensely popular; efforts to reduce their cost encounter vigorous mass resistance everywhere.

The remaining chapters of Part II on the welfare state explore variations in sector spending and program emphasis; family policy and its opposite, the welfare mess; and bureaucratic bloat and efficiency.

NOTES

This chapter is a summary and updating with further tests of my conclusions in *Industrial Society and Social Welfare* (Wilensky and Lebeaux, 1958), *The Welfare State and Equality* (1975), *The 'New Corporatism,' Centralization, and the Welfare State* (1976a), "Leftism, Catholicism, and Democratic Corporatism" (1981c), "Ideology, Education, and Social Security" (1982), "Political Legitimacy and Consensus" (1983), *Comparative Social Policy: Theories, Methods, Findings* (with others, 1985) and an unpublished paper, "Paths of Development of Rich Democracies" presented at a conference at the University of Chicago, November 1–3, 1984. I will here cite only a few selected works that in my view have moved comparative analysis of the welfare state forward. For elaborate citation of the burgeoning postwar literature on the welfare state prior to 1985, see my earlier publications.

1. In 1966 East Germany and Czechoslovakia ranked 8th and 9th of these 22 in social-security spending while the USSR lagged at 16th. They fit a convergence theory because their estimated GNP per capita at factor cost puts the USSR quite a bit below the two more modern Communist regimes, both of which got into the welfare-state business earlier than the former USSR and have older populations (Wilensky, 1975, pp. 121–128). Because so many of the data on these three countries are of dubious comparability, we dropped them from further analysis.

2. For instance, inconsistencies in the findings about the importance of economic level in welfare-state development can be explained partly by the range of per capita GDP captured by a sample. The greater the range of riches brought to view for any one year, the more important economic level will be. Compare Cutright's 76-country sample (1965) and Wilensky's 64-country sample (1975) with Aaron's 22 (1967), Pryor's 14 (1968), and Wilensky's 22 richest countries (1975). A second source of discrepant findings is that time-series data such as those used by Pryor and Hage

and Hanneman (1977) capture shifts in demographic structure, ideology, technology, and social organization that can only be inferred from cross-sectional data, although both types of study typically yield very similar results in welfare-state research.

3. For example, such labels as "The Logic of Industrialism School" vs. the "Political Economy School" (Orloff and Skocpol, 1984) or "political explanations" vs. "economic explanations" (Castles, 1978), or "quantitative" vs. "historical" or "qualitative" (another misleading dichotomy) cannot adequately characterize either theory or findings in such work as Flora and Heidenheimer (1981), Flora et al. (1983) and the Historical Indicators of Western European Democracies group (comparative historical, quantitative); Wilensky (1975) and subsequent publications of the Berkeley Welfare State Project (comparative contemporary, both qualitative and quantitative); Pryor (1968) (comparative East and West and quantitative); Rimlinger (1971); Heclo (1974); Myles (1989) (comparative historical case studies) and Hicks, Misra, and Ng (1995) (comparative, historical, quantitative); or the Huber, Stephens, and Ragin Welfare State Project at North Carolina—for example, Huber, Ragin, and Stephens (1993) and Huber and Stephens (1996) (comparative quantitative and qualitative)—let alone such earlier work as Titmuss (1958); Wilensky and Lebeaux (1958); Briggs (1961); T. H. Marshall (1964); or Cutright (1965). All of these scholars attempt to unscramble both political and economic, as well as cultural and structural sources of welfare-state development; insofar as they are systematically cross-national they examine both divergence and convergence among the industrialized countries.

4. If we confine the measure to income transfers to the working population in OECD countries, the GDP share of unemployment or disability insurance, means-tested social assistance, and child allowances declined in the 1980s in additional countries—Belgium, Denmark, Luxembourg, and the Netherlands, largely because of tightening of eligibility rules (*OECD Observer*, 1996, p. 28).

5. Confirming my conclusions from comparing alternative measures of social spending in the pre-1975 period (Wilensky, 1975, pp. 125–128), Alestalo and Uusitalo (1992, pp. 40–41) compared social-spending measures for 18 rich democracies in 1980 and conclude that four different definitions of welfare effort (SS/GDP) yield a very similar rank order; table 5C.1 in appendix C compares the expenditure data used in this chapter (with GNP as denominator) with OECD data and LIS data (with GDP as denominator); it makes little difference for the comparisons I make. Other chapters deal with more specific types of taxation and spending and discuss particular economic, labor, and social policies and their effects.

6. The problem for research is to discover the relative weight of these different forces and processes in explaining particular outcomes. Incidentally, the three most careful multivariate studies that offer time-series analysis of both political and economic variables—Pryor (1968), Peters (1972), and Hage and Hanneman (1977)—consistently show that economic level (as a clue to available resources, demographic pressures, and the shape of social stratification) is a powerful determinant of social spending, either as a fraction of GNP or GDP or per capita, confirming cross-sectional analyses. The most thorough recent quantitative analysis of social transfers/GDP among 19 democracies (18 of ours plus Greece) from 1960 to 1981 (Lindert, 1996a, pp. 14–15, 30–31) shows that the percentage of the population 65+ is the leading cause of aggregate social spending with GDP per capita also important (more than inequality and deadweight costs as drags and voter turnout and turnover of the chief executive as stimuli to spending). But based on forecasts of age distribution and GDP per capita 1990–2020 and actual growth rates 1980–92, Lindert indicates that population aging has diminishing effects. His analysis suggests that "the threshold is crossed when there are 224 persons over 65 for every 1000 working-age adults. For 12 of the 19 countries that point came before 1976. Finland and Netherlands reached this threshold by 1980 while 5 others (Australia, Canada, Japan, New Zealand, and the United States) had not reached it as of 1981" (*ibid.*, p. 15). This is consistent with my 1965 suggestion of a threshold of

economic level beyond which the rate of growth in social spending will slow down or level off (Wilensky, 1965, p. x).

7. Peter Lindert (1992), using national statistics yearbooks and other data for 18 of our countries from 1880 to 1930, also concludes tentatively that even then the aging of the adult population was a major determinant of increase of government subsidies for the poor, the unemployed, the elderly, and the sick or disabled (pp. 15, 18, 26)—second only to democracy (measured by presence-absence of voter turnout and female suffrage) and well ahead of income per capita. Population aging, however, had a negative influence on enrollment ratios (Lindert's proxy for education spending). These findings confirm my argument about the early and continuing importance of aging in welfare-state development. In fact, as Estelle James (1995) suggests, developing countries today will have "old" demographic profiles at much lower levels of per capita income than the industrial nations: their fertility rates are declining faster and medical knowledge and care is diffusing more rapidly than before. Aging pressures on these incipient welfare states will likely accelerate faster than their ability to pay.

8. Theoretically, stiffly means-tested benefits targeted to the poor in some countries (including the United States before the welfare reform of 1996) are an entitlement. But there are typically so many eligibility rules and so much administrative discretion that these programs (such as AFDC in the United States) stand in sharp contrast to universal, categorical benefits such as pensions and health insurance, with uniform standards and predictable eligibility.

9. Ireland is an ambiguous exception. While it has gradually softened eligibility requirements for its original tax-financed means-tested pension, in 1961 it introduced a compulsory contribution-based, flat-rate pension for employees only; the original system is now mainly for the self-employed (Overbye, 1994, p. 151). Also, a large portion of Ireland's labor force are still self-employed farmers—a prop for a tax-financed minimum guarantee approach (Palme, 1990, p. 44); as industrialization continues and the farm population diminishes, pressure for an earnings-related addition should mount. The question mark for New Zealand in figure 5.1 indicates fluctuations in policy. In 1974 a Labour government introduced a contribution-based earnings-related scheme, as predicted by the convergence theory, but in 1976 a National (conservative) government repealed it, substituting a very generous flat-rate, tax-financed public pension (Overbye, 1996, p. 31). New Zealand's radical neoliberal experiment after 1985 again introduced more income testing in its welfare state, but a massive popular revolt, the formation of four new parties, and a unique shift from majoritarian winner-take-all electoral rules to a German-style proportional representation system makes further shifts all but inevitable (see discussion of dealignment in New Zealand, chap. 11).

10. This section is based partly on my remarks at an OECD Conference of Finance Ministers and Social Affairs Ministers (Wilensky, 1981c) and subsequent research. Among those who share my view of the alleged welfare-state "crisis" and provide empirical evidence casting doubt on the idea are Alber (1988), Klein and O'Higgins (1985), and Marmor and Mashaw (1988). Alber notes that crisis talk has been a feature of welfare-state politics for almost a century. In Germany, when Bismarck's social legislation reached a cost of 1.4% of GDP in 1905, it triggered heated debate over its backbreaking economic burden and threat to civic morals. In recent decades crisis-mongering has escalated, aided by the rise of the broadcast media, which amplify extreme views.

11. Because of variation in what is off budget, in onetime asset sales, and in other obscurities, measures of debt and deficits are not included in my analysis of economic performance, chapter 12.

12. Pierson concludes that Thatcher had more success than Reagan in increasing the share of total social expenditures that are means tested (1994, table 6.3, p. 145). But the comparison is misleading. He excludes U.S. state expenditures from the programs he covers (Medicaid, food stamps, public assistance, and SSI). Moreover, the aggregate figure lumps together visible, stigmatized benefits (AFDC and food stamps) with invisible programs targeted to the poor (EITC), which lack stigma and can

grow more easily (see chap. 8); SSI, where the aged population is the target and where stigma is less; and Medicaid, where provider and administrative costs soar and where much of the money comprises the only government support for long-term care for the aged, a program that enjoys broad popular support. Finally, the measure—percentage of total social spending—yields results different from those of GDP shares or per capita benefits. Cuts in real benefits in means-tested public assistance from 1980 to 1995 were substantial in both countries (see chap. 6; cf. Bawden and Palmer, 1984; and Alber, 1996).

13. This account of NHS reforms is based on Klein (1995), Giaimo (1995), and Döhler (1991).

14. One estimate suggests that by 2030, 38% of Germans will be over 60, 16% under 20 (*The Economist*, February 1994). Assuming no change in retirement age, a slightly different measure for 1995 and 2025—the ratio of retirement-age persons to 100 working-age adults—yields similar results: in 1995, 29.6; in 2025, 54.1. That is almost as burdensome as Austria's 36.7 and 61.4. Comparable figures for the United States, where the attack on "entitlements" is most hysterical, are only 22.3 and 35.1.

15. The long established system of tripartite self-governance involves government, patients, and providers, with some input from other groups. Nonprofit sickness funds based on occupation or region combine in national associations and must bargain with physicians' associations; they are governed by national framework legislation. Since 1977 they must take account of annual recommendations of the Concerted Action in Health Care, a roundtable which includes labor unions, employers, officials at various levels of government, and various provider groups. See chapter 16.

16. The following account of recent reforms of Italian social programs is based on Ferrera (1994), Saraceno and Negri (1994), MacFarlan and Oxley (1996), and my interviews.

17. At this writing, mothers are still required to take off two months before and three months after childbirth. For risky pregnancies, they can take off the entire period of pregnancy. (Many women claim "risky" pregnancies from day one, with the acquiescence of their physicians.) Most working women receive full salaries during leave, 80% covered by social security, 20% by employers. Chapter 7 compares an array of family policies in 19 countries, including parental leave. It shows that corporatist countries with the combination of strong Catholic and left parties score medium on an index of innovative and expansive family policies, reflecting the ambivalence of Catholic parties toward women's place and the offset of both corporatism and left power. But on maternal leave Italy ranks high and remains there.

18. Based on my interviews; publications of the Ministry of Health and Social Affairs and the Swedish National Insurance Board (various years), Niemelä and Salminen (1994), Huber and Stevens (1996), Kuhnle (1996) and Palme and Wennemo (1998).

19. This account has benefited from the research assistance of historian Craig Patton, who did a thorough review of German language sources, and discussions with Stefan Leibfried.

20. The paternalistic-authoritarian flavor of the Nazi doctrine of labor and the "plant community" is captured by Franz Neumann's account of the Charter of Labor, the Nazi Labor Courts, and the Labor Front (Neumann, 1942, pp. 413–439). Section 2 of the National Socialist Charter of Labor declares that, "The leader of the plant [the employer] decides as against the followers [employees] in all matters pertaining to the plant in so far as they are regulated by statute. He shall look after the well-being of the followers, while the latter shall keep faith with him, based on the plant community" (*ibid.*, p. 421; cf. Mason, 1976).

21. In the tests in this section, it would be desirable to go beyond 1980 and 1986 for the 19 countries. But later quantitative data are either noncomparable, less reliable, or became available after extensive analysis was completed. The post-1980 developments and literature discussed earlier do not contradict my conclusions in the rest of this chapter.

22. Even if we exclude Israel from this category as a deviant case, the average welfare effort of left-Catholic corporatist countries exceeds that of the left-corporatist countries for all years in table 5.3 from 1950 to 1980.

23. The above hypotheses refer only to that social heterogeneity based on descent (ethnicity, religion, race). Other sources of heterogeneity—education, occupation, income—are not considered here. Some observers of minority-group cleavages, including me, would rank the Netherlands and Belgium a bit higher than the scoring method in Appendix I ranks them (8th and 9th of our 19 countries). Chapter 2 explains why recent adjustments in Dutch bargaining arrangements and the erosion of *verzuiling* have not made a major difference in social policies, except to make them more efficient.

24. For instance, we constructed a new index of mobility-meritocracy using 1970–80 educational spending and educational mobility data; it is correlated .96 with the index using measures for 1965–70. Substituting this in regressions and path diagrams yields the same results.

6
SECTOR SPENDING AND PROGRAM EMPHASIS

Among the notable national differences in welfare-state development are variations in the priorities given to particular programs and spending packages. Data available to describe program emphases are limited. For instance, ILO measures of means-tested benefits are useless; active labor-market policies until recently were little studied and no comparable spending data are available for 19 countries; family policies, especially as they developed in recent decades, are not adequately captured by the "family or child allowances" category of sector spending in standard sources. Still, we can learn something from an overview of broad government spending categories for pensions and disability insurance, health care, work-injury insurance, war-victims benefits, family allowances, education, and higher education.[1]

This chapter specifies which of these spending packages hang together and shows how types of political economy (Catholicism, leftism, corporatism) and economic level (population 65+, affluence, mobility, and minority-group cleavages) shape patterns of spending. Chapter 8 presents our own estimate of means-tested public assistance (what Americans call "welfare"; the British, social assistance; and the Germans, social help) and puts the American welfare mess in comparative perspective. These data are added to tables in this chapter. Chapter 7 deals with a broad array of family policies and programs, including child care, maternity and parental leave, and flexible retirement, which are correlated both with one another and with family allowances. Governments that put money and effort into one family policy tend to evidence the same commitment to related policies. Chapter 2 deals with the trade-off between an active labor-market policy (training and retraining, job counseling and placement, and job creation coordinated by an effective labor-market board) and passive policies (unemployment compensation, public assistance).

SPENDING PACKAGES

Examining the correlations among different spending sectors as a percentage of GNP for 1966, 1971, 1974, and 1980 (table 6D.1 in appendix D), we see a clear pattern: spending for old-age pensions (including survivors and disability insurance) are significantly and consistently correlated with family allowances and work-injury spending and positively but not significantly correlated with health care. All four are positively related to aggregate social spending and to one another (except that work injury is unrelated to health care). Two areas stand aside. First, public-assistance effort (an accent on means testing) is unrelated to the core programs or social rights of the welfare state, although it shows a pattern of negative if insignificant correlations with universalistic pensions, family allowances, and health care. Second, aggregate education spending (all levels, kindergarten through college) has little consistent correlation with anything else (except a few negative correlations with spending on war victims and work-injury insurance and three positive correlations with means-tested benefits, diminishing to zero from 1966 to 1983). Higher-education effort, however, evidences a consistent pattern; it is positively and significantly correlated with means-tested benefits—reflecting what we have seen in chapter 5, their strongly meritocratic, antiegalitarian character.

What a nation does for war victims is unrelated to its effort in the areas of pensions, family allowances, public assistance, higher education, or even aggregate social spending. It is negatively correlated with health-care spending, and positively correlated with work-injury insurance. Benefits for war victims are instead a product of variable participation in wars. Thus, even such welfare-state laggards as the United States, Canada, and Australia or a middle-rank spender such as the United Kingdom—all major participants in World War II as well as subsequent small wars—typically developed a generous welfare state for veterans and their families. For instance, veterans' pensions, health care, and other benefits in the United States were a backdoor means of reducing poverty that never opened to anyone but veterans. Compared with ordinary public relief or old-age assistance, veterans' benefits pay better and come easier; the recipients are not badgered or made to feel they are a drag on society. These programs are, in fact, the very model of a modern humanistic socialism: they are characterized by federal standards and financing; a presumption of eligibility and of earned right; easy application and easy appeals; and a warmhearted collaboration of intercessor groups like the American Legion, who drum up claimants, and an administrative agency instructed by law to follow its natural sympathies in favor of claims (Steiner, 1971, pp. 239–242; and Wilensky, 1975, pp. 41–42). The symbol of the fighting man who was handicapped by his frontline injuries is steadily invoked to justify a straight welfare program to cover all veterans—battlefront or home front, disabled or not, those with service-connected disabilities, those whose deprivations developed long after or before brief periods of service, as well as those who suffered no deprivations at all. With cohorts of veterans much smaller than the passing bulge of World War II, the political strength of war victims has slowly declined, although their special place still persists in most countries.[2]

If we consider sector expenditures per capita, a measure of the output of cash and services delivered to individuals, we see a similar pattern (table 6D.2, appendix D). There is a tendency toward coherent, across-the-board generosity in pensions, family allowances, health care, work-injury insurance (except that work-injury insurance is unrelated to health-care spending per capita). The main difference here is that total education expenditures per capita are also positively related to aggregate social spending per capita. Public assistance and higher education, however, are still unrelated to the rest of the welfare state.

Sources of Variation in Sector Spending Patterns

Using the variables that capture both convergence theory and types of political economy we uncover contrasting sources of these spending patterns. I have come to think of them as cohesive and divisive clusters of social programs. Two patterns are apparent. In table 6.1 countries that in 1971 and 1980 put their money into the core programs of the welfare state—especially pensions and family allowances but also work-injury and health insurance—are characterized by Catholic party power, corporatist bargaining arrangements, an aging population, and low social mobility. In contrast, countries that accent aggressive means testing for the poor (public assistance) and higher education for middle and upper strata are characterized by minority-group cleavages, high mobility rates, left party power, and much public-sector employment and, at least in 1971, some affluence.[3] It is an ironic outcome of left party power that it successfully fosters public-sector employment, expands mobility opportunities for minorities and women in jobs and colleges, and thereby sets up a meritocratic thrust for means testing and for education spending at upper levels. In the absence of strong corporatist bargaining arrangements the pattern leads to a divisive politics of the welfare state, a finding that appears in many policy areas throughout this book, especially in the crafting of tax systems and strategies of poverty reduction. It is not that left parties are fond of means testing for the poor and near-poor; they in fact have typically advocated the denial of benefits to the affluent (see chap. 8). And it is not that they favor public financing of higher education for the sons and daughters of the elite. The pattern in table 6.1 instead reflects the unanticipated consequences of structural changes the left helped to achieve: expanded educational and career opportunities for workers, minorities, and women; and an expanded public sector (see chap. 7). The mobility consequences are a by-product both of affluence and the structural changes favored by labor and left parties. In other words, decades of center-left success in moving rich democracies toward equality and good economic performance set up a process by which further progress is more difficult. Success spoiled "the working class."

Figure 6.1 summarizes the strongest results so far of all these correlations, with both effort (spending/GNP) and output (spending per capita).

Personal Social Services versus Cash Transfers?

One of the choices governments make in crafting the welfare state is whether to emphasize cash benefits in the hands of its citizens or deliver services in the form of medical personnel, teachers, counselors, social workers, clinical psychologists, specialists in child care, job training and placement, learning disabilities, rehabilitation, recreation, home care, senior centers, and youth centers. When I started this study in 1970 I got the impression from interviews in Austria, Germany, and Scandinavia that the social democracies of Scandinavia had put into place a vast array of personal social services for the aged, children, disabled, poor, and immigrants, while the countries most influenced by Germany had a taste for cash transfers—for example, a pension check or child allowance triggered off by a low-cost computer. I attributed this to the left commitment to equality for minorities and working women and to Catholic parties' desire to keep mothers at home (where a family allowance, rather than child care for working mothers' children, might help). By the time I finished

TABLE 6.1 Cohesive spending patterns are linked to Catholicism, corporatism, and an aged population. Divisive spending patterns are linked to affluence, leftism, minority-group cleavages, social mobility, and much public-sector employment.

	CORRELATES OF COHESIVE SPENDING						CORRELATES OF DIVISIVE SPENDING					
	Catholic Party Power		Percent Population 65 and up		Corporatism Score		GNP per capita		Left Party Power		Minority Group Cleavages	
	1971	1980	1971	1980	1971	1980	1971	1980	1971	1980	1971	1980
COHESIVE SPENDING												
SS/GNP	.60**	.43•	.81**	.70**	.69**	.59**	.09	.46*	.04	–.00	–.47*	–.58**
Pensions[a]	.75**	.60**	.83**	.78**	.63**	.55*	–.05	.49*	–.06	–.07	–.48*	–.51*
Family Allowances[a]	.60**	.61**	.64**	.51**	.74**	.53*	–.19	.30	–.19	–.17	–.24	–.08
Work Injury[a]	.82**	.58*	.30	.26	.21	.24	–.03	.44•	–.42	–.34	.07	.17
Health[a]	.03	.04	.37	.42•	.52*	.43•	.13	.30	.08	–.01	–.30	–.64**
DIVISIVE SPENDING												
Public Assistance[a]	–.09	–.12	–.15	–.25	–.35	–.51*	.30	–.06	–.07	–.23	.67**	.58*
Higher Education[a]	–.24	–.07	–.41•	–.46•	–.05	–.05	.37	–.18	.47*	.29	.53*	.60**
MOBILITY INDICATORS												
Public Employees[b]	–.33	–.24	.06	.34	–.15	.06	.42•	.22	.43•	.49*	.15	–.18
Mobility Index	–.56	—	–.52•	–.55*	–.19	—	.17	–.43	.46•	—	.72**	—
Working Class Students in Higher Education[c]	–.22	—	–.34	–.03	–.20	—	.47•	.28	.19	—	.54*	—
Higher Education Enrollment Ratio	–.29	–.15	–.38	–.20	–.30	–.05	.52*	.15	.22	.40•	.38	.21

[a]Spending as a percentage of GNP.
[b]Public employees as a percentage of civilian labor force.
[c]Working-class students as a percentage of all students in higher education, 1965 or 1970.

the study and had talked to people in 19 countries, I was not so sure. More important, I had not located any data for the universe of rich democracies that could yield a clean comparison of public spending on services and public spending on cash benefits.

It is true, for example, that there were hardly any social workers in Austria in the mid-1970s while there was an abundance of them in Sweden, the United Kingdom, and the United States. One Austrian social agency executive expressed her great envy of the graduate schools of social work in America, with their clinical orientations, and wished that Austria could move in that direction. Further, Austria was indeed a specialist in cash flow; in 1971, it led all the leaders in the GNP share of pension spending (13.3%) well ahead of the Netherlands' 10.9%, Germany's 10.4%, Italy's 10.0% and Belgium's 9.5%, and was fourth among the leaders in the GNP share of family allowances (2.5%)—behind France's 3.3%, Belgium's 3.0%, and the Netherlands' 2.6%. In contrast, when I was living in Swe-

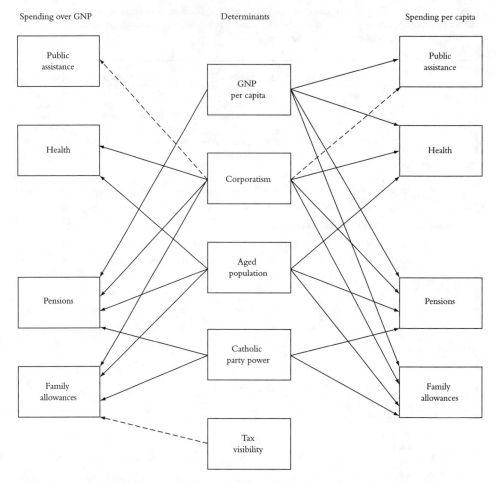

Figure 6.1. Structural determinants of sector spending as both effort (public spending/GNP) and output (per capita spending)★

★Spending data significantly related to structural causes for either 1971 or 1980 or both. Positive correlations indicated by solid lines; negative correlations by dashed lines.

den in 1970, I noted that its devotion to family allowances and pensions (spending/GNP) was modest while I could already see firsthand the extraordinary number of professional services delivered to anyone remotely in need of help.

My skepticism about the trade-off between services as a product of social democratic hegemony and cash transfers as a product of Catholic party power stems from three observations:

1.   By the early 1980s, countries that were leaders in their provision of child care for working parents—the epitome of personal social service—included in descending order France, Belgium, Sweden, Norway, Denmark, and Israel (see chap. 7 on family policy for details). The top two have had more Catholic than left power; three of the six are non-Scandinavian. West Germany and the Netherlands, however, were very limited in the availability and accessibility of public day-care programs; both have strong cumulative

Catholic power. Finland, a social democracy, is in the middle of the pack. In short, a mixed picture. As chapter 7 shows, there is in fact a positive correlation between spending on family allowances and spending on other aspects of family policy including services.

2. Considering spending on services in general, there is no "Scandinavian social democratic" pattern, even among the welfare-state leaders. For instance, "services for the aged account for more than one-fourth of all old-age and invalidity expenditure in Denmark" while in Sweden, Norway, and Finland (as well as Iceland) their share is only about one-tenth (Alestalo and Uusitalo, 1992, p. 50). In 1980 the Danes relied less on cash benefits to children than the others but spent as much as Sweden on family services (p. 55). Similarly, in unemployment expenditures there is no Scandinavian model: Sweden accents an active labor-market policy; Denmark, until very recently, passive-cash benefits to the unemployed. The only areas where there was a clear but slow process of convergence of the five Scandinavian nations from the early 1970s until 1987 were sickness and health expenditures and family policy (p. 61).

3. Several countries with strong Catholic party power, notably Italy and the Netherlands, lavishly subsidize "private" nonprofit associations as major suppliers of personal social services to children, the aged, and the handicapped. Unless we wish to argue that the nearly total government financing of these religious and other nonprofits is not public provision, we must be careful in the claim that Catholic power blocks public services in favor of cash transfers. Nor has anyone shown that these heavily subsidized quasi-public services are less effective in servicing their clientele than more direct government provision; they certainly are no less expensive (Wilensky, 1981d).

4. Table 6.2 shows pension spending—the epitome of big cash transfers—as a percentage of national income in 1971 and 1995; the generosity of pensions in 1995; and (for 8 countries for which we could use EC data) cash benefits as a share of total social spending in 1987.

This table once again reminds us that by 1971 the Catholic-left corporatist combination yielded the highest pattern of spending, with Catholic corporatist a close second, left-corporatist third, corporatist-without-labor fourth, with the Anglo-American fragmented and decentralized democracies dead last—as we saw in chapter 5 in the analysis of total social spending. By 1995, however, the Catholic corporatist countries moved to the top, with a pension share of GDP of 12.2%, while left-Catholic corporatist and left-corporatist categories averaged 8.4% and 8.5%. Because the Netherlands dropped in rank from 2nd in 1971 to 10th in 1995 and Austria from 1st to 7th, the left-Catholic group converged with the other corporatist countries, whether the latter integrated labor into high policy or not.

The big difference in the 1995 pension effort (GDP share of pensions) between corporatist democracies and the more-fragmented and decentralized political economies is matched by a big difference in pension generosity. By 1995, all of the corporatist countries achieved an earnings-replacement rate (ratio of average pension benefits to average wages) from 40% (Denmark, Austria) to 65% (Finland) compared to the least-corporatist average of 32%.

The only surprise in table 6.2 is the high replacement ratio of France and Japan, cases of corporatism-without-labor. Perhaps the elites in these countries, both of which faced

TABLE 6.2 Types of political economy, public pensions as share of national income 1971 and 1995, pension generosity 1995 and 1985, and reliance on cash benefits 1987

	Public pension spending as % GNP 1971[a]		Public pension spending as % GDP 1995[b]		Avg. earnings replacement rate 1995[b]		Minimum pension net replacement rate 1985[c]	Cash benefits as % of all benefits 1987[d]
Left Corporatist								
Sweden	8.5	(6)	11.8	(2)	54	(5)	H	n.a.
Norway	8.5	(6)	5.2	(13)	44	(9)	H	n.a.
Finland	7.3	(8)	10.1	(6)	65	(1)	H	n.a.
Israel	1.7	(17)	n.a.		n.a.		n.a.	n.a.
Denmark	7.3	(8)	6.8	(8)	40	(11)	n.a.	68
cell avg.	7.9[e]		8.5		50.8			
Left-Catholic Corporatist								
Netherlands	10.9	(2)	6.0	(10)	39	(12)	H	78
Belgium	9.5	(5)	10.4	(5)	63	(2)	M	77
Austria	13.3	(1)	8.8	(7)	40	(11)	H	n.a.
cell avg.	11.2		8.4		47.3			
Catholic Corporatist								
Italy	10.0	(4)	13.3	(1)	49	(7)	L	62
W. Germany	10.4	(3)	11.1	(3)	46	(8)	n.a.	70
cell avg.	10.2		12.2		47.5			
Corporatist Without Labor								
France	7.4	(7)	10.6	(4)	56	(3)	H	73
Japan	0.8	(18)	6.6	(9)	54	(5)	L	n.a.
Switzerland	5.6	(10)	n.a.		n.a.		L	n.a.
cell avg.	4.6[f]		8.6		55			
Least Corporatist								
United States	4.7	(12)	4.1	(15)	30	(14)	n.a.	n.a.
United Kingdom	5.1	(11)	4.5	(14)	23	(17)	L	66
New Zealand	4.1	(14)	5.9	(11)	51	(6)	HM	n.a.
Australia	3.3	(15)	2.6	(17)	30	(15)	L	n.a.
Canada	3.0	(16)	5.2	(13)	33	(13)	M	n.a.
Ireland	4.7	(12)	3.6	(16)	25	(16)	M	68
cell avg	4.2		4.3		32			

[a]Source: footnotes to table 6D.1 and appendix D.

[b]Ratio of average pension to average wages, "the retirement wage." OECD, *Economic Surveys: Canada* (November 1996), Table 15, p.114.

[c]Source: Palme (1990), pp. 28–29, 48–50. Minimum pension replacement rate for a single person after deducting direct income taxes and social security contributions from earnings and deducting taxes on benefits, where pension income is taxed. High, medium, low.

[d]Source: Eurostat, European Communities (1990). Cash benefits are transfers to households to cover social risks which entail financial costs or loss of income. They include benefits in kind which are earmarked goods and services—e.g., food, medicine, housing, child care, and other subsidies and cash refunds for which there must be proof of actual expenditure.

[e]Excluding Israel.

[f]Excluding Japan.

militant labor movements in the postwar period, shared the insight of Chancellor Bismarck: a generous pension at the end of a long, hardworking life would divert labor protest into calmer channels. They developed pensions as generous as Sweden's, even in the absence of labor-left participation in government.

New Zealand, with a replacement rate of 51%, is a deviant case among the low-ranking Anglo-American democracies. The New Zealand deviance may be explained by a legacy of universalistic social benefits dating back to 1935 when the New Zealand Labour Party began 14 years of uninterrupted rule—the longest among English-speaking democracies. Labour put into place a national health service, substantially free education, and universal child allowances while moving toward generous, universal flat-rate pensions (Castles and Shirley, 1996, pp. 92–99; Overbye, 1996, p. 31). Despite strong efforts by both major parties to constrain social spending and deregulate the economy after 1985 (see chap. 11) the generosity of pensions remained; table 6.2 shows New Zealand as ranking sixth of 17 countries in earnings-replacement rate in 1995 and well above average in the minimum pension.

If we use an alternative measure of generosity—the minimum earnings-replacement rate for a single person after taxes rather than the extent to which pension programs replace normal earnings—the 1995 picture more closely matches the findings for 1971. The Netherlands and Austria fall into place, moving left-Catholic corporatist countries higher toward the competitive escalation of spending as expected, while Switzerland and Japan, countries that keep labor at a distance, move down, where they belong. The New Zealand exception remains—too generous for the least-corporatist category.

Pensions became steadily more generous from 1930 to 1985. Joakim Palme's (1990, pp. 48–49) careful estimates of both minimum pensions and workers' pensions for 18 of our countries show that the all-country average of the minimum pension (net of taxes on earnings and benefits) for a single person climbed from 10% of earnings in 1930 to 19% in 1950, 25% in 1965 to 37% in 1985. The net earnings-replacement rate for workers' pensions quadrupled over the same period—from 14% in 1930 to 58% in 1985.

Finally for the eight countries, cash transfers dominate all social spending; they are two-thirds to three-quarters of the total. The difference between the most reliance on cash (the Netherlands' 78%) and the least reliance on cash (Italy's 62% and the UK's 66%) is small. This table confirms two themes in our previous analysis: there is a competitive escalation of spending where both Catholic and left parties alternate or form coalition governments; and their interaction with corporatist bargaining arrangements is an important source of welfare-state development.

5. While Austria led all 19 countries in its accent on cash for pensions and family allowances in 1971 and was above average in pensions/GDP in 1995 (table 6.2), it also tied for third place by a rough measure of expenditure on services; in 1987 it spent 31% of total social spending on civilian nontransfers (mostly health care and education)—behind only the standout leaders, Denmark at 39% and Sweden at 38% (Huber and Stephens, 1996, table 2). In other words, the king of cash transfers 25 years ago was moving toward personal social services by the end of the 20th century, largely through gradual expansion of home care and nursing homes for the aged, training, education, and job creation for workers, and spa vacations for substantial numbers.[4] Schools of social work offering three years of training were finally established and have recently expanded.

The tentative formulation I come to in view of our previous analysis of sector spending and case studies of service delivery is that the welfare-state leaders tend toward heavy

TABLE 6.3 Sources of the big trade-off: corporatism and Catholic power foster heavy spending on family allowances and pensions. Least-corporatist countries emphasize higher education and the military and have larger civilian bureaucracies and greater intergenerational mobility.

	Pensions + Fam. Allow. as % GNP[a]		Higher Education Exp. as % GNP[b]		Military Spending as % GNP[c]		Public Employees as % Civilian LF[d]		Mobility Score[e]
	1971	1980	1971	1980	1971	1980	1971	1980	(1960s)
Left Corporatist									
Sweden	9.8	14.4	0.8	0.8	4.2	3.3	20.2	28.6	.05
Norway	10.1	10.4	0.9	0.9	4.0	2.9	15.1	17.7	−.01
Finland	8.2	11.0	0.4	1.1	1.6	1.4	10.5	14.9	n.a.
Israel	2.5	2.6	1.7	1.8	28.8	30.2	10.5	12.1	.29
Denmark	8.8	11.9	1.5	1.3	3.0	2.5	15.5	24.9	.04
cell avg.	7.9	10.1	1.1	1.2	3.2[f]	2.5[f]	14.4	19.6	.03[f]
Left-Catholic Corporatist									
Netherlands	13.6	14.5	1.8	2.1	4.0	3.1	10.1	11.3	.04
Belgium	12.5	16.7	0.6	1.2	3.1	3.3	11.0	15.2	−.03
Austria	15.8	18.5	0.5	0.8	1.5	1.2	13.2	15.9	n.a.
cell avg.	14.0	16.6	1.0	1.4	2.9	2.5	11.4	14.1	.005
Catholic Corporatist									
Italy	11.8	9.8	0.4	0.3	3.0	2.4	8.9	12.9	−.08
W. Germany	11.2	15.4	0.5	0.7	3.9	3.3	9.8	12.8	−.07
cell avg	11.5	12.6	0.5	0.5	3.5	2.9	9.4	12.9	−.08
Corporatist without Labor									
France	10.7	16.5	0.5	0.7	4.6	4.0	10.0	11.8	.06
Japan	0.8	3.6	0.4	0.5	0.9	0.9	5.8	6.5	−.05
Switzerland	5.6[g]	8.8[g]	0.6	0.9	1.8	2.1	7.5	10.2	n.a.
cell avg.	5.7	9.6	0.5	0.7	2.4	2.3	7.8	9.5	.005
Least Corporatist									
United States	4.7	6.7	1.7	2.9	8.2	5.6	15.6	14.9	.11
United Kingdom	5.9	7.8	1.0	1.4	5.7	5.0	17.0	18.9	.10
New Zealand	5.3	8.3	1.0	1.5	1.9	1.8	16.6	18.0	n.a.
Australia	3.9	6.5	1.1	1.4	4.1	2.9	19.4	24.0	.14
Canada	4.0	4.6	1.8	2.1	2.8	1.8	18.9	18.0	.18
Ireland	5.7	8.8	0.7	1.1	1.2	1.9	10.1	12.4	n.a.
cell avg.	4.9	7.1	1.2	1.7	4.0	3.2	16.3	17.7	.13

[a]Source: ILO, *The Cost of Social Security*, 1976 and 1985.

[b]Source: *Educational Statistics in OECD Countries* (Paris, 1981), *Israeli Statistical Yearbook* 1974, and *UNESCO Statistical Yearbook*, 1977, 1978−79, and 1986.

[c]Source: International Institute of Strategic Studies, *The Military Balance* (London, 1973 and 1985).

[d]See appendix J for sources.

[e]Intergenerational occupational mobility. This is also correlated with residential mobility. See appendix I for source and measure.

[f]Without Israel.

[g]Pensions alone. Data for family allowances in Switzerland are missing.

spending on both cash transfers and personal social services while the welfare-state laggards do not deliver much of either—unless you can call the intrusive investigatory apparatus targeting the poor with the aim to cut costs and reduce welfare fraud and abuse, "personal social services." (For a 19-country ranking of means-tested public assistance by type of political economy, see table 8.3, chap. 8 on the welfare mess.)

The Big Trade-off: Pensions and Family Allowances versus Public Assistance, Higher Education, and the Military

Analysis of sector spending in the 19 rich democracies shows that the big trade-off between types of spending is not so much the left government subsidy of personal social services vs. the Catholic government enthusiasm for cash transfers, although left-corporatist political economies do a bit more with child care, occupational health and safety, and rehabilitation services for the handicapped. The big trade-off instead is suggested in table 6.3.

By 1971, corporatist countries with strong Catholic party power (sometimes interacting with left power) had already put great effort into family allowances and pensions while the least-corporatist countries were putting what effort they undertook into higher education and the military. Among the fragmented and decentralized democracies these two types of spending are both related to higher rates of intergenerational and residential mobility (table 6.3), minority-group cleavages, and the expansion of public-sector employment (see chap. 9). While the left-corporatist countries by 1980 had the most public-sector employment for obvious reasons, the least-corporatist countries are a very close second for less obvious reasons. Chapters 9 (on bureaucratic bloat) and 12 (on the economic and social effects of the military) explain why. As the military burden of the Anglo-American democracies declines, their populations age, and female labor-force participation increases, we can expect at least some convergence in sector spending patterns toward the continental European model.

Notes

1. Spending on unemployment compensation is eliminated from this analysis both because of data limitations and because such spending is mainly a product of national variations in the depth and duration of the business cycle. Policies to cope with unemployment and its effects are discussed in chapters 8, 12, 13, and 18. This chapter is confined to an overview of correlations among various spending sectors and their correlates with possible structural causes of national variations; other chapters sort out the sequence of causes for particular policies and programs and the relative importance of our causal models.

2. A sign of diminishing strength is that American veterans of the unpopular war in Vietnam are now prominent among the homeless. It is possible that the victors in wars treat their veterans as a special breed and create a benign welfare state for them, while the losers are less generous, viewing veterans as an embarrassing reminder. Comparing social and labor-market policies in Germany and the United States, Janoski (1990, pp. 34–35) notes that in two successive World War defeats Germany never accorded veterans radically separate treatment but, instead, folded them into their already well-developed active labor-market programs and welfare state, while the victorious American veterans had the opportunity to go their own way and embraced the veterans' own welfare state. Defeated German veterans were integrated with civilian victims of destruction into regular party politics, forming part of working-class coalitions; victorious American veterans could practice a separatist politics for a bigger payoff.

3. In this table 6.1, affluence, as we have seen in chapters 4 and 5, is correlated with mobility and minority-group cleavages and by itself fosters aggregate social spending by 1980. The correlate of GNP per capita that accounts for this is population aging.

4. Austria ranks fourth on its effort and implementation of an active labor-market policy of the eight countries covered in a mid-1980s evaluation (Wilensky and Turner 1987, table 2). Because of

the priority Austria gave to the creation and protection of employment through fiscal policy and its very low unemployment rate, its expenditure on either unemployment compensation or active labor-market policy was low. But in the 1980s expenditures on training and job creation and preservation climbed substantially (Schmid, Reissert, and Bruche, 1992, pp. 32ff., 184–186, and figure 12a). Regarding home care, despite some expansion, the service is still modest. For instance in Vienna, whose population above 60 is about 336,000 (21% of the total population), there are only 2,200 home helpers (in full-time equivalents), a ratio of 1 to 153, plus 120 home nurses. However, in 1993 a new "attendance allowance" increased cash payments for persons in need of care: About 300,000 Austrians receive cash benefits worth from $200 U.S. to $2,000 per month. Although a little of this money is spent for diet, heating, or other special household needs, most goes directly for caretakers and other personal home services, informal or professional—another case where a cash transfer becomes a service transfer. Regarding spa vacations, at the reduced 1996 rate of approved applications, within nine years over 1.64 million Austrians would have the pleasure of at least one social-insurance-subsidized spa vacation. That is more than the total number of Austrians above 60. (Data from Leichsenring, 1997.)

7

TYPES OF POLITICAL ECONOMY, PARTY IDEOLOGY, AND FAMILY POLICY
Contrasting Government Responses to a Common Problem

The changing structure and behavior of the modern family is a great subject for students of convergence theory. As we have seen in chapter 1, there have been very similar long-term changes in sex roles and family structure and functions as rich countries got richer. There is even a common political demand for a family policy to cope with the social problems posed by the transformation of the family. These similarities are rooted in continuing industrialization and its organizational and demographic correlates, especially increasing female labor-force participation, family breakup, and the aging of the population (see figure 1.1 for details on the causal sequence). But the public-policy responses have been very different.

This chapter shows that national differences in family policy and the politics of the family can be explained by types of political economy and the power and ideology of mass-based political parties. With continuing industrialization, however, these policy differences may be diminishing, as we shall see from recent developments in the two most deviant cases, Japan and the United States.

POLICIES AND POLITICS:
BIG DIFFERENCES AND MAYBE A LITTLE CONVERGENCE

Despite a recent, if slow, shift toward common government responses among our 19 rich democracies, there remain striking contrasts in the policies and politics of the family. Before we examine the 19-country differences, we can get a sense of both family politics and public policies by an intensive look at two extreme cases.

Comparing Sweden and the United States: Policy Contrasts

In the past 25 or 30 years the Swedes have quietly put into place scores of policies and programs aimed at increasing gender equality and family well-being. Sweden's income transfers to families include child allowances, housing allowances, and child support payments for single parents (known as the "Advanced Maintenance Payments") to supplement or replace the absent parent's contribution. With all those benefits the Swedes rely much less than other countries on means-tested "social assistance" for families in need. The child allowance is universal and tax-free; each Swedish household receives a basic benefit of about $500 per child under 16 (as of April 1978) (Kahn and Kamerman, 1983, pp. 15−67; Adams and Winston, 1980, p. 90). The housing allowance, instituted in 1969, was designed for low-income families; by 1975 it was going to about half of all Swedish families with minor children. In 1980 the full housing benefit was equal to about $300 per child per year plus 80% of rental costs up to a specified ceiling (Kamerman and Kahn, 1981, p. 50). Together the child allowance and housing allowance account for more than a third of the income of the single mother at home and more than a quarter of the working mother's income (Kamerman, 1984, p. 264−265, and my estimate). The Swedish policy regarding child support payments, adopted in its present form in 1964, aims to prevent dependent children from becoming poor as a result of family breakup (Kahn and Kamerman, 1983, p. 462). In 1979 about a quarter of all families were headed by a single mother; over half of the children in single-parent homes were receiving these support payments (Kamerman, 1984, p. 257, 267). In 1979 about 38% of the costs of the program were collected from the absent parent; it is now more.

Beyond these lush cash flows is an expensive apparatus of support for working parents with children—single, married, and unmarried partners alike. Included are parental leave, paid and unpaid; leave for parents when their children are sick; day-care centers, before-and-after-school leisure centers; and short workdays for parents. Consider this list of parental rights:

• In principle, every child has a right to a place in a day-care center *and* an after-school playground; and the government, national and local, has the duty to provide these facilities. While day-care centers charge fees scaled to parents' income, the fees for even the rich never cover more than a minor part of the real cost—even with the 1990s cutbacks. By 1980, about a third of all preschool children whose parents work or study had a place in a day-care center or municipally supported facilities. By 1984 the proportion of preschoolers in public day care had climbed to 42% (The Swedish Institute, 1987). By 1993 only 8% of the preschooler population still had no publicly provided child care (Fact Sheets on Sweden, June 1994).

• When parents have or adopt a child, they are entitled to a 12-month leave of absence between them with taxable benefits for nine months equivalent to at least 90% of the previous daily earnings of the parent taking the leave (public-sector employees get 100% earnings replacement); parents can save up to six months leave to use any time until the child is eight years old (Winstrand, 1981, p. 32). Retrenchments of the 1990s (see chap. 5) modified parental leave slightly: in 1995 earnings-replacement rates were dropped from 90% to 80% for 10 of the 12 months, with two months remaining at 90%, one for each parent, use it or lose it.

• Parents have a right to up to 120 days leave a year to take care of any sick child under age 12—or even to visit the child's preschool—also at nearly full pay. About half of parents need to use these rights; those who do take an average of only nine days a year looking after sick children (Fact Sheets on Sweden, June 1994).

• Anyone taking parental leave is guaranteed the same or a comparable job with no loss of seniority or pension rights.

- All parents with small children (up to eight years old) have the right to shorten their workday to six hours (with corresponding pay cut).

In addition to all of this, every woman has the right to an abortion, and health insurance pays for both hospital costs and lost wages. The school system works hard to encourage gender equality by teaching girls industrial arts and boys home economics. Equal pay for equal work is written into collective bargaining contracts, which cover more than 85% of the labor force. By 1978 there was only a 10% difference in the average wage of men and women for the same types of jobs in both the public and private sectors; today, although occupational segregation remains, the pay gap has been closed.[1] In legislation and in economic life there are not large differences in the way men and women are treated. Flexible work scheduling is so widespread that in 1980 half of the 75% of Swedish women who worked were part-timers—working less than 35 hours a week (Winstrand, 1981, pp. 50, 59). Plainly, the system provides a great range of choice in balancing family life and worklife while making vast efforts to ensure that children will not be neglected.

Now contrast the United States. It is the only country among our 19 with no family allowance. (Income tax deductions for dependents, also present in combination with family allowances in several countries, are regressive.) Except for pensions and Medicare for the aged, other income transfers are concentrated on the poor through an enormous and expensive apparatus of means testing, which has earned the label "the welfare mess." The essence of this mess is inadequate benefits for most of the poor; inequity in both cash flow and services; stigma and its two concomitants, low takeup rates and political uproar; and an unfortunate lack of fiscal and policy control (see chap. 8). This highly visible "welfare" system is what permitted President Reagan to bait mythical "welfare queens" and what inspired the welfare reform bill of 1996.

The main cash transfers are AFDC (Aid to Families of Dependent Children, after 1996 reforms, Temporary Assistance for Needy Families) and categorical aid for the blind, disabled, and destitute elderly (in 1974 these were combined in Supplementary Security Income [SSI] administered by the federal government). All means-tested cash and noncash income transfers, including those for veterans and the elderly, rose from 2.3% to 3.9% of GNP between 1965 and 1984. In real dollars, spending on cash benefits rose to a peak in 1976 and has fallen ever since. In contrast, real spending on means-tested in-kind programs has risen steadily since the mid-1960s (Burtless, 1986, pp. 22–23). In the early 1960s about 9 in 10 of these means-tested dollars were distributed as cash aid. By 1985, only about 3 in 10 of the means-tested dollars spent were in the form of cash; four dollars were provided in free medical care (Medicaid) and three in the form of subsidized food (food commodity distribution, school meals, and food stamps) and housing (public housing projects and other housing subsidies). Medicaid, the fastest-growing federal-state program, accounted for about 40% of all spending on means-tested programs in 1985. (*Ibid.*, pp. 21–24.) A small income-income tested benefit that entered the tax code in 1975, the "earned income tax credit" (EITC) for the working poor, is a contrast to the dominant means-tested system. The Clinton budgets greatly expanded the EITC in the 1990s. Except for the EITC, not much was changed in the American approach to the poor in the 1980s. Chapter 8 discusses the EITC, updates and assesses later trends in means-tested benefits, and puts the U.S. "welfare" system in cross-national perspective.

If the United States, in contrast to Sweden, has traditionally and increasingly relied on means-tested benefits in its attempt to reduce poverty among the nonaged poor, has the effort paid off? The most telling figures that capture the impact of these policy differences concern single-parent families (about 9 in 10 are single women with children). The comparison is fair because both Sweden and the United States have the same very high proportion of lone-parent families (families with dependent children headed by a lone parent as a percentage of all families with children). In a study of 14 rich democracies, both countries ranked first and second in the early 1980s, with a ratio of more than one in four families headed by a lone parent (Millar, 1987, p. 8). We can infer that Sweden and the United States are far ahead of the rest of the pack in their national risk of poverty from family breakup if neither did anything to cushion the shock. Data on income come from two careful studies of the economic situation of one-parent families. The first analyzes income from all sources, private (earnings, income from assets, private pensions, and private transfers) and public (government transfers such as public assistance, social security, and unemployment benefits) in three countries around 1970. If we describe poor as less than 50% of the median income for a standardized family size, the percentage of mother-only families who are poor based on *private* income is 40% in Sweden and 60% in the United States (Rainwater, Rein, and Schwartz, 1986, pp. 111, 32); the percentage of all solo-mother families receiving government transfers of any kind is 98% in Sweden and 57% in the United States (p. 109); and, most striking, the percentage moved beyond the poverty level by government transfers is 75% in Sweden, but only 25% in the United States (p. 111). The second study examines the position of one-parent families (living in their own households) relative to that of two-parent families in six countries around 1980, using average net income per adult equivalent unit (factor income plus employment-related pensions, plus public and private transfers, minus direct taxes and payroll taxes). It confirms the picture: Sweden has the least discrepancy between one-parent and two-parent families (13%) while the USA has the most (a 43% income discrepancy between lone-parent families and intact families).[2] (Hauser, 1987, p. 198.)

Plainly, it is not only the Swedes' greater generosity of benefits; their greater attention to training for work, job creation, placement, and employment; and their support network for all working parents that accounts for these differences but also the American emphasis on means-tested benefits, which maximizes administrative harassment and stigma and minimizes the payoff from what dollars we do spend (see chap. 8). In the Reagan years even this effort was reduced with stiffer eligibility rules and/or sharp cuts in such means-tested benefits as AFDC, housing assistance, child nutrition, food stamps, low-income energy assistance, and similar programs (Danziger, Haveman, and Plotnick, 1986, p. 52; Kamerman, 1985, pp. 12–14). And with the welfare reform bill of 1996, reductions in average aid to the nonaged poor are inevitable, although states will vary in their aggressiveness in cost cutting and the way they deal with the mandatory cutoff dates.

Regarding maternity leave or parental insurance, by 1984 the United States and Australia were the only two countries among our 19 with no *paid* leave provisions covering the majority of working women. Less than 40% of working women in the United States were entitled to a paid maternity leave at the time of childbirth; only five states had legislation mandating paid maternity leave (Kahn, Kamerman, and Kingston, 1983, pp. 4, 77, 97, 139); the United States was also among the six countries that provided no right to *un-*

paid leave—until President Clinton got Congress to pass his Family and Medical Leave Act of 1993.

Child-care provisions in the United States, including both childminding service *and* pre-school education, remain fairly weak despite accelerating talk about the desperate need for them. In 1984–85 in the United States less than 17% of all children under age 5 whose mothers worked received day care, public or private (including organized child-care facilities and group care); another 4% attended preschool (based on U.S. Bureau of the Census, 1987). The closest comparable figure from Sweden suggests that coverage of public day care excluding preschool is at least twice the U.S. figure for all care. In fact, using a much broader population base, by 1987 just over 45% of all children under age 7 receive public day care (licensed, supervised)—28% in a day-care center, 17% in family day care (The Swedish Institute, 1987). There are also sharp contrasts in quality of day care; the Swedes lead, the United States lags. The most thorough study of cost, quality, and child outcomes based on 400 randomly chosen child-care centers in California, Colorado, Connecticut, and North Carolina found that 40% of infants and toddlers were in conditions that threaten their health and safety and discourage learning; only 14% of centers—the well-funded centers with stable, well-educated, well-paid staff—offered high-quality care, including safe surroundings, adult warmth and support, and learning opportunities (*Wall Street Journal,* February 6, 1995; cf. similar conclusions in Scarr, 1996).

A "dependent care" tax credit became a significant benefit in the United States in 1976 and was increased in 1981. But the maximum benefit goes to parents who earn enough to pay taxes and spend a lot on child care (e.g., in 1983 the maximum benefit of $720 was paid on expenses of $2,400 for one child or $1,440 on expenses of $4,800 for two or more—heavily concentrated on upper-middle-income parents).[3] In 1982 between eight and nine million children were receiving some subsidies through this tax credit.

Since 1981 employers can also get a tax deduction (The Dependent Care Assistance Benefit) if they subsidize or sponsor child care for their employees. Most of the growth in child-care services is in the private sector, much of it profit making. Yet by 1988 only about 10% of U.S. firms with 10 or more employees offered *any* child-care benefit, and 84% of these employers provided only information, referral, or counselling. Put another way, less than 5% of American employers offered employer-sponsored day care or any help with child-care expenses (Bureau of Labor Statistics estimate, *Wall Street Journal,* April 4, 1988). Not an encouraging picture for those who believe that the private sector can meet working parents' need for child care.

Comparing Sweden with the United States in their policies for the aged, Sweden again comes out at the extreme, although in this instance the United States is not at the very bottom. Aside from paying generous pensions, Sweden has thought through the problem of maximizing choice for the aged:

• Eligibility requirements for early retirement for the partially disabled are loose (you can retire at age 60 with a full pension even if you are less than half disabled).

• Slack labor markets are defined as a disability. Because of problems of abuse of disability rules, eligibility standards were recently tightened, while rehabilitation programs were expanded (see chaps. 5 and 15).

• Unemployed older workers can retire with a full pension up to five years before normal retirement age.

• Most important, and most innovative, are the flexible retirement measures, a partial pension program adopted in 1976: workers aged 60–64 with 10 years of covered employment can choose a partial pension of up to 50% of the income lost if they shift to part-time work of at least 17 hours a week. This pension is added to part-time earnings; the combined total equals about 85–95% of previous income from full-time work. Rights to a normal pension at about 65–70% of former earnings are not affected (Tracy, 1979a, 1979b; Babic, 1984). By some criteria this scheme was a great success; about one in four eligible persons had taken advantage of it by 1980 (Rix and Fisher, 1982, p. 66).[4]

In comparison with its past, the United States has moved further toward generous public policy in this area than in any other; in comparison with Sweden, it is still a laggard. Pensions and Medicare are the two major reasons that the fraction of the poor among the aged in the United States is now a bit lower than the fraction of the poor among the population as a whole: about one-third of the aged were officially poor in the early 1960s; now it is about 12.2% and if adjusted for all in-kind benefits would be lower (Danziger, Haveman, and Plotnick, 1986). The United States also offers deferred retirement benefits and actuarially reduced benefits for early retirees. However, the rest of the package—universal flexible retirement via substantial partial pensions, and special measures for special populations—are absent. The policy contrasts are reflected in employment rates of the young-old: in 1989, 61.6% of Swedish males aged 60–64 were working compared to only 52.4% of same-age Americans (Guillemard and Rein, 1993, p. 475).

The Politics of Family Policy: More Sharp Contrasts

The politics of the family are as different as the policies. In the United States we find a strong accent on divisive social-moral issues, a sustained effort by mainstream candidates to claim family and women's issues as their own, and a delicate consensus in Congress and several states that child-care services for working parents and related supports are a good idea. The mix has not led to much policy development but has consumed an enormous fund of political energy and money.

In presidential and congressional campaigns of the 1980s and early 1990s, divisive issues such as abortion and gay rights became prominent as America's 16 million white evangelical voters were mobilized for political action.[5] For instance, in the 1988 presidential primary campaign, the candidate of the populist right in the Republican Party, televangelist Pat Robertson, complained that both mainstream Republicans and Democrats have lost their moorings in the Judeo-Christian heritage: that they have permitted mass murder of infants by legalizing abortion, allowed homosexuals freedom, permitted pornography and drugs to flourish, encouraged sexual license and easy divorce, and that all this is undermining the family and spiritual values, whose preservation is the #1 issue facing the nation. With some audiences he claimed that the plague of AIDS is no accident; it is God's punishment for our sins. That these family preservation themes have popular resonance is suggested by the following: (1) Robertson's success in the early Republican caucuses—Michigan, Hawaii, Iowa, and Minnesota; (2) presidential candidate Bush's adoption of an extreme position favoring a ban on federal funding of abortion in cases of rape or incest and his success in the South, where evangelical voters are concentrated and where he headed off Robertson partly by talking his language; (3) President Bush's continued adherence to this extreme position in 1988–92; and (4) the prime-time speech of Pat Buchanan at the 1992 Republican presidential nominating convention in which he declared a "cultural war" on anti-family Democratic enemies, themes echoed by many others, including Vice President Quayle. By 1989, the "pro-choice" forces, activated by a Supreme Court decision to give states new latitude to restrict abortions, had countermobilized and were counted as a major force in the victories of Democratic candidates for governor in New Jersey and Virginia (based on exit polls reported in the *New York Times,* November 8 and 9, 1989), in the 1992 election of President Clinton, and his reelection in 1996.

Pat Robertson's Christian Coalition, once confined to the Deep South, is now national, organized in 50 states and in control of Republican Party machinery in at least 18 states. By 1996 Robertson had become the most important person in the most powerful faction within the Republican Party.

Most of the mainstream candidates were also battling over the family. The leading candidates in both parties attended to polls showing that a majority of the voters feel their children are going to be worse off than they are.[6] They recognized the voters' deep anxiety over deteriorating schools, widespread drug use, violence, and AIDS. Who will capture the family issues is often at the center of discussion of campaign strategy among the consultants and pollsters who have come to dominate these marathon elections. In the 1992 election, some Democratic Party strategists saw "children's issues" as a way to make people think about the future and become serious after eight years of the Reagan lullaby. They wanted to reach the voters who think "Things are okay, Jack, I've got mine" and substitute the theme "Good times now but bad times ahead—and we're all in this together." In the 1996 and 2000 elections, when the economy was doing well, Democratic strategists accented education and training for the 21st century. Moreover, they saw children's issues as unifying, in contrast to divisive issues such as race and abortion; black voters do not resent a first home or college-loan program, and affluent white voters do not begrudge a poor black child a decent education.

Republicans and Democrats alike see children and education as the entree to the universal concern about the need to invest, train, work, sacrifice for the future, and improve American competitiveness. Although President Reagan's success with upbeat mood music has scared almost everyone away from mentioning the forbidden word, "taxes," the politicians talk much about saving the future for our children. Not all of this is cultural piety. Even Reagan in his last budget submission to Congress urged a sharp increase in federal aid to education. And George Bush endorsed a refundable tax credit to help low- and moderate-income families with child-care expenses and said he wanted to go down in history as "the education president." The 2000 campaign was filled with such talk.

Finally, the resonance of family issues was evident in the gradual emergence of an extraordinary bipartisan consensus, which although delicately balanced, actually resulted in legislative action: the Family Support Act of 1988, which became law, and the Act for Better Childcare Services ("ABC"), which died in a conference committee. By international standards, these are tiny steps toward a family policy but in view of the history of failure of welfare reform, from President Nixon's Family Assistance Plan through the 1990s, a political breakthrough.[7]

The story of the delicate bipartisan consensus of 1987 and its breakdown in welfare debates after the Republican congressional victory of 1994 shows a stop-and-go pattern that inches toward reality.

Drawing on models of "workfare" in California and Massachusetts, welfare reform combined absent parent child support with mandatory wage withholding, job training and education (including postsecondary) as an entitlement (learnfare vs. welfare, said the conservative governor of Missouri), and $3.3 billion in new federal spending. The political coalition that got it through in the last year of the Reagan administration, an election year, was similar to California's: over many years of tough talk from the right about welfare fraud and abuse, and a general baiting of welfare mothers as lazy luxury consumers, many conservative politicians changed their minds. They learned from lengthy hearings and overwhelming evidence that almost all of the welfare population was receiving meager support, public *or* private, and were mothers with multiple handicaps—poor job skills, poor education, health and housing; above all, the hardline politicians learned that punishing the poor meant punishing their children. The left learned that humanitarian aid to the poor was unsalable without tough absent-parent rules (in 1987, two-thirds of single mothers received no payments at all from absent fathers); that an emphasis on work and training could also attract conservative votes; that, in fact, the largest single category (about half) of AFDC recipients were not the separated or divorced but were younger mothers who were never married and could in time be expected to work; and, regarding levels of funding, that something was better than nothing. Thus, in Congress Republican Senators Dole and Packwood joined liberal Democratic Senator Moynihan in support of the package and many left liberals settled for the compromise. President Reagan and many populist conservatives liked the ring of "workfare," a California slogan originated by Reagan when he was governor, enacted federally in 1981, and preserved in the 1988 bill.

Similarly, the congressional coalition that led the fight for the child-care bill (ABC) included as sponsors Senator Orrin Hatch, a conservative Republican from the Mormon state of Utah, who had been converted by the evidence on child neglect and the feminization of poverty, and Senator Christopher Dodd, a liberal Democrat from Connecticut. Among other provisions, ABC combined a refundable earned income tax credit for working families, $1.75 billion in fiscal 1990 for child-care services for low-income families, and state standards for providers. It passed the Senate in 1989, 63 to 37, with 9 Republicans joining 54 Democrats in favor.

The House passed a different version. At the end of 1989 the conference committee remained deadlocked over the method of financing, the balance between tax credits and direct grants to the states tied to federally approved service standards and the separation of church and state. Opposition groups included not only President Bush and the vast majority of Republicans wedded to tax expenditures and hostile to government intervention generally but also the National Education Association, the largest union of teachers, which opposed a compromise provision permitting parents to use vouchers at religious day-care centers and wanted more control for Departments of Education and public schools. In the 1988 negotiations, the National Congress of Parents and Teachers and the American Jewish Committee also defected on similar grounds.

The delicate political consensus that accounts for the small reforms of 1988 and the Senate's child-care bill was broken when the Northern center-right Republicans were overwhelmed by the new majority and new leadership of 1994—the culmination of the Southern Republican ascendancy (see chap. 11). Once-moderate Republican positions on race, the economy, and moral-social issues were transformed as the centrists, under severe pressure from the Christian right and populist radicals, retired or drifted rightward.

Neither the welfare reform bill of 1988, the product of 20 years of effort, nor the welfare reform of 1996 can make much of a dent on the problems they address. As chapter 8 (on the welfare mess) shows, tough work requirements, while they can shove welfare mothers off the rolls, do little to move them into stable jobs and less to reduce their poverty. Their deficits in education, skill, health, housing, and transportation keep their wages low and job-holding unstable. In fact, the efficacy of all programs targeted to the poor via elaborate means tests is very limited.

The welfare reform of 1996 puts states under pressure to compete in cutting benefits, save money, and act tough on the undeserving poor. But even with this harsh law, a legacy from the 1988 consensus persists: the law allowed Medicaid and most of the food stamp program to stay intact, and, most importantly, provided a $4 billion increase over 1995 allocations in federal aid for child care to facilitate the shift from welfare to work.

In the most favorable interpretation, both welfare reforms and child-care bills can be seen as a backdoor entry typical of the history of American social legislation—a gingerly groping toward a family policy under another name. Just as Medicare targeted to the old may be the backdoor entry to "kiddiecare" and ultimately national health insurance (Wilensky, 1975, p. 42) so California welfare reform—with an elaborate set of options for child care, training, education, and job search—may be a backdoor entry to more universal family and labor-market policies, moving America from family piety to family policy. Chapter 18 describes the center-left political coalition that could create the necessary national standards, broad coverage, and funding.

What about the politics of policy toward the aged? From the scare talk of the 1970s about the pending "bankruptcy of the social-security system" (the headlines read: "The Pension Fiasco," "Catch 65," "The Social Security Ripoff") to 1980s' complaints about the burgeoning "surpluses" in the OASDI trust funds to the 1990s return to talk of impending bankruptcy, hysterical attacks on the social-security system and passionate defenses against any benefit cuts have permeated American debate.

A more-sophisticated attack accents alleged conflicts of interest between young and old, children and pensioners, workers and nonworkers. In the late 1980s Americans for Generational Equity (AGE) was formed with Senator Dave Durenberger as chairman. It describes itself as a nonprofit research and public education group "dedicated to forging a coalition among all generations to protect the future of young Americans—our most precious resource." The inaugural issue of its official publication, *The Generational Journal,* April 1988, features such articles as "Shadows in Time: The Perils of Intergenerational Transfers," "Social Security Actuaries Raise Doubts About the System's Solvency," "The Elderly Aren't Needy," "Do We Want Large Social Security Surpluses?"[8]

Regarding the twin "crises" of social-security bankruptcy and social-security surplus: Whether we hold the surpluses accumulated during 1990–2020 for drawdown in 2021–60 or gradually move to a pay-as-you-go system with a modest reserve ratio, there is no need for huge tax increases. In fact, an estimate from the 1994–96 Advisory Council on Social Security (1997, p. 77) says that a payroll tax rise of 2.2% alone (half from employers, half from employees), if adopted in 1997, would solve the entire long-range problem of social security for 75 years—even assuming no cuts in scheduled benefits, no adjustment in the cost-of-living measure, no acceleration in the scheduled increase in retirement age, no investment of trust funds in stocks, no extension of coverage to government workers not now in the system, no privatization. If this single 75-year fix through a tax increase were delayed until 2002, it would have to be 2.5% (*ibid.* vol., I, table III-I, p. 66. (Munnell, 1999, p. 804 puts it at 2.0%.)

In short, the politics of the aged in the United States is a politics of extremes—generally with little anchor in economic and social realities.[9]

To shift from the politics of family policy in the United States to the Swedish scene is like moving to another planet. By the mid-1970s, having put into place an enormous apparatus of support for children and working parents, having developed a generous and flexible retirement system for the aged, having achieved substantial gender equality, what did the Swedes have left to fight about? First, no political party, no major organized group dares to imply that women belong in the home; no one goes up against either family policy or gender equality. It would be political suicide to oppose these popular measures. Instead they argue about new inequities introduced by public subsidies to families. Since the ruling Social Democrats are responsible for almost all of these family programs, the "bourgeois" parties each stake out slightly different positions while the Social Democrats, as always, are restive about fiscal limits and the failure to achieve perfection in releasing women from the bondage of the home. Here is a sample of the issues they pose drawn from party positions and recent campaigns (Rollén, 1978; Eduards, 1980; Duval-Smith, 1986; and interviews in 1995):

- Because only about 1 in 10 Swedish men were using paid paternity leave— with 9 in 10 of the 12 months due being used by mothers—the Social Democrats in 1979 proposed that with few exceptions the mother and father should be compelled to share parental leave after the first six months in order to receive the full benefit (but this never became law). Although the percentage of men using paternity leave went from 0% in 1973 to 20% in 1983, the minister for equal opportunities, Mrs. Anita Gradin, felt compelled in 1983 to appoint a working party to study "the changing role of the male." Maybe this could speed up the process, she said, especially among the less educated who resist these newfangled ideas. More radical politicians like Stockholm councilwoman Agneta Dreber of the small "Stockholm Party" support a controversial amendment to the law compelling men to take their proper half-share of the leave or lose it. The mainstream parties range from advocating some limit on the parents' discretion to advocating completely free choice on how to divide the parental leave.

- Left-wing Social Democrats complain that too many women are choosing part-time jobs or are taking short workdays with corresponding pay cuts. They claim that employer's attitudes are hostile to men in responsible jobs taking parental leave. They advocate a full day's pay for short-days taking care of children and more aggressive steps to put more women in high posts.

• Hardly anyone resists the expansion of child-care places, staffing, and other child-care subsidies. But the nonsocialist parties (Conservative, Center, and Liberal Parties) at various times have complained that too much of the new money goes to large day-care centers rather than to family day care (childminders). They have mentioned the great inequities between families with two working parents and families with only one working parent where the wife stays home to take care of children (a small minority). Why should the traditional one-earner family with children who do *not* use public day-care centers pay thousands of tax dollars to subsidize an affluent working couple with two children who make lavish use of the full range of child-care services?

• Although they all favor more freedom of choice, the bourgeois parties differ on solutions: currently, the Conservatives want tax deductions for paying a childminder. Both the Conservatives and the Center Party want to pay women who choose to stay home with their children a "mother's wage" (without threatening anyone else's benefits it would begin after parental insurance was used up). The Liberal Party supports all of the above plus. The "plus" includes richer, tax-free child allowances, a six-hour day for parents of small children, flexible working hours, and so on. Such is the "conservative" viewpoint in Sweden.

It is apparent that the Swedes have passed a threshold of female labor-force participation where talk about cutting services or adding a mother's wage falls on deaf ears. By 1990, 85% of women aged 20–64 were working.

The Swedes do, of course, debate the costs of all this, and no doubt many childless couples see themselves as tax-overburdened because of the child-care benefits to working parents. The estimated average cost for one child in a day-care center in 1978 dollars was $8,000/year. It is considered the caviar of child-care facilities. The cost in 1995 is much higher. (Between 1968 and 1978 the inflation-adjusted price per place more than doubled.) (Jönsson and Paulsson, 1979, p. 28.) But these issues are endlessly reexamined without ever breaking the family-policy consensus. For instance, a Royal Commission on child care spent some three years in the early 1970s evaluating costs and benefits of day care for preschoolers in the broadest context, encompassing economic effects and effects on family welfare. Among the findings: In purely economic terms, the high cost of day care was more than offset by the tax-take from and productive output of working mothers who would otherwise (usually reluctantly) stay home. Parliament adopted the recommended laws, while evaluation researchers continued to monitor program effects. By 1980, the wages of nursery-school teachers had nearly reached the level of the average manufacturing wage and staffing ratios had improved—a cost greater than the tax-take by local and central governments (presumably from added working parents). The researchers concluded, however, that despite these escalating costs, the economic benefits to the economy as a whole—the positive effect of child care on female labor-force participation and the GNP, on taxpaying, and on women's education and productivity—still exceed the total day-care cost (Jönsson and Paulsson, 1979, pp. 28–29, 36–37, 42–47, 66–67, 71).[10] Obviously, we cannot know what the relevant rates (hours and numbers of working mothers, numbers of educated women, and productivity) would have been in the absence of child care. My impression is that the Swedes are not particularly excited about such analysis; elites and masses alike long ago decided that quality care of all kinds for children was an end in itself.

The 1990s did see retrenchment in the Swedish welfare state (see chap. 5), including modest reductions in parental-leave pay and child-care allowances, but the family-policy consensus is intact and the funding to back it up keeps Sweden at the top of service provision.

We cannot assume that these striking differences in politics and policies in the United States and Sweden are merely a matter of the homogeneity of Sweden and the heterogeneity of the United States or the presence of evangelical and Catholic voters in the United States and their absence in Sweden. First, the contrast between the historical legacy of religious traditions of Evangelical Lutheran Sweden and that of the Protestant fundamentalists of the American South are not so stark: Scandinavian teetotalist, antipornography, and religious education movements and party platforms recur over the past 150 years; they attest to the stern moralism of the Lutheran hierarchy and to the persistence of popular resentment against modernism (Elder, Thomas, and Arter, 1982, pp. 64–69; Scott, 1988, pp. 353–355, 412).[11] Teetotalism has been especially strong in Sweden; in 1967, 136 of the 383 representatives of the Swedish riksdag were teetotalers (Scott, 1988, p. 355).[12] Even in the aggressively secular social democracy of the 1960s when church attendance had dropped to today's low level of less than 1 in 10, two million Swedes signed a petition opposing a reduction in the levels of religious education in the schools; and most Swedes still connect with either the state church or dissenting free churches and evangelical churches at ritual occasions—birth, marriage, and death (Gustaffson, 1965, pp. 49–51). It appears that the tormented characters played by Max von Sydow in Ingmar Bergman's films are authentic reflections of a Swedish cultural heritage.

Second, the 3 in 10 American voters who are Catholics have become increasingly secular; their church attendance declined from 1960 to 1984; and their Catholicism does not prevent them from ignoring the pope's authority on a wide range of family issues from birth control to divorce (Hout and Greeley, 1987). Third, although the United States still has much deeper racial and religious cleavages than Sweden (see chap. 14, table 14.1 and appendix I), since World War II the homogeneity of Sweden has substantially lessened with the gradual influx of minority populations—Finns, Turks, Yugoslavs, Eastern European refugees. (By the early 1970s migrant workers were about 5.6% of the Swedish labor force compared with about 7.0% of the American labor force [see chap. 13 on migration and job creation]). Finally, as I show later, strong social cleavages under some circumstances are consistent with a consensual politics of the family: Belgium, a country whose ethnic-linguistic cleavages are even more intense than those of the USA, ranks with Sweden as a family-policy leader.

Going beyond these two extreme cases—the United States and Sweden—the next section compares family policies in all 19 countries as a first step in uncovering more general patterns and basic explanations for the differences.

Concepts and Measures of Family Policy: Patterns among the 19 Countries

Family policy refers to a wide umbrella of public policies providing shelter across the life span. Implicitly or explicitly, these policies aim to enhance family stability and well-being by direct government action. They are targeted mainly to the young and old, single parents (divorced, separated, or widowed), and women temporarily separated from the labor market due to maternity. Program benefits are timed to cushion the major strains of the family life cycle—for modern populations these are most evident in the early and late stages of life cycle, among families with preschool children and solitary survivors. Single parents and the young and old nonworking population are especially vulnerable to these pressures (Wilensky, 1981b).

Although the entire range of government action in some way or another impinges upon the family, programs comprising "family policy" function specifically and directly to replace or supplement household income (such as family allowances, pensions, and social assistance), offer services to families (such as family-planning services, family counseling, and child care), or serve in lieu of the family (such as home help for the aged and supplementary meals programs). In short, what justifies the label "family policy" is *sufficient unity of purpose* (enhancement of family stability and well-being with special attention to effects of poverty and/or family breakup on children), *similarity in target population* (old, young, low-income families with children), and *timing* (important transitions in the family life cycle). Even if "family policy" is not the most precise social-science category, politicians, social reformers, and social scientists alike have increasingly used it as a slogan in ideological combat.

Obviously, comparable cross-national data are not available for most of these programs. In chapter 6 (on sector spending), however, we saw that the three most-costly social-spending packages are strongly correlated: *pensions and disability insurance* (heavily oriented toward the aged), *health insurance* (both young and aged), and *child allowances.* This suggests some coherence among government decisions in the allocation of scarce resources that is consistent with the idea of family policy.

In this section I go beyond sector spending to examine three policy clusters which more precisely fit the idea of family policy, concentrating on the more innovative programs that have greatly expanded in recent decades and for which we were able to develop reasonably comparable data for all 19 rich democracies: *child care, maternity and parental leave and associated benefits,* and *flexible retirement provisions.*[13] We created a 5-point scale for each of the three, scoring each country 0–4, and then combined the three scores in an *index of innovative and expansive family policy.* The data are focused on the late 1970s and early 1980s (1976–82).

Two other research groups—for whom I made my measures available—have subsequently devised similar indices of family policy (Gornick, Meyers, and Ross, 1997, footnote 12; Siaroff, 1994). Despite their different methods and more-recent, more-detailed data on more policies, both produced a country rank order almost identical to our index. The first covers 18 family-policy variables for 14 of our countries from 1984 to 1987; the second applies my measures of child care and parental leave to 23 OECD countries and adds spending data and some more recent policies to arrive at a scale of "family welfare orientation." Both may be viewed as updated validation of our measures and another example of the persistence of national differences in the period 1976–82 into the late 1980s and early 1990s.

For each dimension we had to make compromises and sometimes settle for simple indicators of complex policy packages. A word follows about the final code and what noncomparable or unavailable measures were abandoned on the way to a score.

1. *Maternity and parental leave.* Provisions to aid working parents to care for their children take many forms. Nearly all of the 19 countries make some provision for *paid maternity leave* (only the United States, Australia and Switzerland lack federal provisions for paid maternity leave), and a few (the four Scandinavian countries and France) offer paid *paternity leave;* most permit women to take *unpaid job-protected leaves of absence;* and about half make provision for *paid breaks to allow women workers to nurse their infants.* All 19 offer some measure of job protection for women at childbirth: most guarantee women the right to return to the same or a comparable job and protect pension and seniority rights for the duration of the leave. We examined data on the *stiffness of eligibility criteria* and concluded that it was too difficult to code because some countries have more than one criterion. Sweden, for example, makes maternity leave benefits available to women who were employed 6 months prior to the pregnancy or 12 months in the past two years (ILO, 1984); the United Kingdom makes its flat-rate benefit available to women who worked at least 50 weeks prior to pregnancy, but to be eligible for the earnings-related benefit a woman must have worked for at least two years (Kamerman, 1980). We used *level of compensation* only as a secondary criterion to distinguish extreme cases; countries often have different provisions for different groups of workers, making systematic comparison difficult. *The final and overwhelmingly dominant criterion was sheer length of paid and unpaid leave.* The rationale: It is *simple,* evidences *wide variation* (paid leave varies from about three months in Israel, Japan, New Zealand to 290 days in Sweden, unpaid leave from three years in Belgium to none in seven countries), and, *most important,* the opportunity to combine paid and unpaid leaves gives most women maximum flexibility and allows them to balance work and family demands.

The code:

4. Very lengthy paid leaves and lengthy unpaid leaves: Sweden, Finland

3. Lengthy paid leaves only *or* average to lengthy paid leaves plus lengthy unpaid leaves: Italy, Norway, Austria, France, West Germany, Belgium

2. Average paid leaves plus short to average unpaid leaves *or* short paid leaves plus average unpaid leaves: Canada, United Kingdom, Denmark, New Zealand

1. Short paid leaves and nonexistent to very short unpaid leaves: Ireland, Switzerland, Israel, Japan, Netherlands

0. No legislation to cover majority of women workers: Australia, United States[14]

2. *Child-care benefits.* Here we measure public support for day care for small children. The major difficulties in measurement are these: no adequate data for 19 countries exist on *public expenditures* for preschool education or day care or both; support for *preschool education* is difficult to interpret (it may have little to do with efforts to encourage female labor-force participation or cope with its effects on children); *enrollment ratios* often do not distinguish between preschool and day-care programs and are based on noncomparable age grades (e.g., West Germany enrolls a large percentage of children age 3 and over in preschool programs with limited hours of operation but does little for children under 3; for France, one cannot separate day care from nursery school attendance, etc.) and are poor indicators of government support for child care (data, where available, do not sepa-

rate the various public/private mixes—private vs. public vs. publicly subsidized private facilities, public facilities that charge for their services); the *quality of public day care* and the groups using care facilities vary greatly and comparable data are not good; the *sheer number of places* may be a poor indicator of current policy effort; and, most serious, we cannot find systematic comparisons of *tax policies* toward child care. In the end we excluded tax provisions, assessments of program quality, and expenditure data. *We settled for a code combining judgments about the availability and accessibility of public day-care programs* (number of places, degrees of restriction or openness, whether there were provisions for children under three, and whether programs were full-day or not) *and policy effort* (evidence of active government efforts to expand day-care facilities and/or access to day care).

The code:

4. High levels of governmental support for public day-care programs that facilitate female labor-force participation: France, Belgium. (Although preschool programs are not systematically counted in this code, it happens that France and Belgium are quite strong not only in day care but also in preschool programs. There is some advantage in the French way of combining childminding services and preschool/nursery school programs: such a merger gives parents more scheduling flexibility, adds more educational content to day care, and gives diverse groups of parents common interests in program quality.)

3. Modest public day-care provisions and active attention to policy: Sweden, Norway, Denmark, Israel

2. Low to modest public day-care provisions and some attention to policy: Italy, Finland

1. Very limited public day-care provisions and little policy effort: USA, Austria, Switzerland, United Kingdom, Australia, West Germany, Netherlands. (Especially West Germany and Netherlands and to a lesser extent Switzerland, Austria, and the UK have fairly well developed nursery school or preschool programs but these are typically of limited use to working parents—they cover few hours and often do not accept very young children.)

0. Virtually no public day care and little or no attention to policy: Japan, New Zealand, Canada, Ireland

3. *Flexible retirement.* As with parental leave policies, we concentrate on those retirement provisions that maximize choice. Because data on level of compensation in various retirement schemes are unavailable or noncomparable, we settled for the sheer number of options that permit retirement before or after the *normal pensionable age.* Because we want a measure that accents flexible combinations of work and retirement, we weighed partial pensions heavier than other options. Because some options apply only to very limited groups we weighed these lighter than the rest.

The coding weighted three groups of programs as follows:

1. Early pensions for arduous occupations or long service. Justification is based on humanitarian and/or equity grounds and benefits are limited to spe-

cial groups—for example, mineworkers (arduous occupation); employees with more than 35 years of contributions to social insurance funds (long service). *Score 0.5 for either program* (arduous occupations or long service provisions).

2. Deferred retirement provisions; partial disability benefits; actuarily reduced benefits for early retirees; unemployment as a reason for early retirement. *Score 1.0 for any program* listed in this category.

3. Partial pension (designed for flexible work/retirement choices). *Score 1.5 for partial pension program.*

EXAMPLES: Sweden does not offer either arduous occupation or long-service pensions (score = 0) but offers each of the four programs listed in group #2 (score 1 for each = 4) and offers a partial pension scheme (score 1.5). Total score = 5.5.
The United States does not offer arduous occupation or long-service pensions (score = 0) but offers deferred retirement benefits and actuarily reduced pensions for early retirees (score 1 for each of these two programs = 2). No partial pension program exists (score = 0). Total score = 2.

Country scores follow:

4. Most flexible: Sweden, France

3. Above-average flexibility: Norway, Austria, West Germany, Belgium, Finland, Denmark

2. Average flexibility: Netherlands, United States, United Kingdom

1. Below-average flexibility: Italy, Japan[15]

0. Least flexible: Switzerland, Canada, Australia, Ireland, New Zealand

The three dimensions correlate strongly with one another, confirming our findings about sector spending: programs targeted on the well-being of the aged and the young cohere. Summary index scores (theoretically 0 – 12) range from a low of 1 (Australia and Ireland) to a high of 11 (Sweden and France).

Explaining the Similarities and Differences in Family Policy

Some of these contrasts can be explained by our industrialization/convergence theme: in the 1950s and early 1960s the United States had relatively low female labor-force participation rates while Sweden (like Switzerland, Japan, and Finland) had high female participation rates. One consequence was that the postwar baby boom in the United States was large while the baby boom in most of Europe and Japan was small. The greater rate of increase in women working in the United States in the 1970s and 1980s in part reflects a U.S. catch-up with general tendencies toward higher participation and lower fertility. Further, national differences in the fraction of aged is a product not mainly of increased longevity but of declining birthrates—again, a universal accompaniment of industrialization, forcing governments to respond one way or another.

If the convergence theory is right, national differences in the timing and rate of change in women working and the rate of population aging should explain some of the differences in government responses. As we shall see in a moment, public policies *do* differ by the rate of female labor-force participation. If a country has a big fraction of women working, it is likely to have expansive and innovative family policies. But whatever the modest differences in timing and rate of female labor-force participation, the baby boom in all rich countries was a blip on the long-term slide in fertility rates. And whatever the differences between countries with a small aged population and countries with a large aged population, the "young" countries are catching up. Convergence remains the main story. As rich countries become richer we can expect their family policies to converge in the long run in response to the continued rise in women at work and the continued aging of their population.

For an explanation of current contrasts in public-policy responses, however, we must look to our scheme for explaining national differences in taxing, social spending, economic performance, and tax revolts (figure 2.1): types of political economy and related contrasts in public policies (chap. 2; and Wilensky 1976a, 1981c, 1983). The theory suggests that democratic corporatism as a structure for creating consensus facilitates policy deliberation; the corporatist democracies more readily resolve conflicts about many issues, including family issues, more quickly respond to the universal troubles of the modern family, and more effectively implement a wide range of family policies. The second source of family-policy differences is the power and ideology of mass-based political parties, Catholic and left. Corporatism is itself partly rooted in these two types of parties. Because Catholic and left parties share a strong interest in family well-being but differ in their ideas about women's place, we would expect some differences among Catholic corporatist countries and left-corporatist countries. Because these parties dominate many governments, we can expect public policies targeted on the family to reflect their dominance.

And finally, because we know that the demographic structure of a society, rooted in industrialization, is a powerful force in welfare-state development and social policy (chap. 5), we must control for differences in the aged as a percentage of the population if we are to sift out the distinctive effect of parties and types of political economy.

In short, we would expect to find two roads to an expansive and innovative family policy: one through the effects of high and rising levels of women at work (matching figure 1.1), the other through the effects of political parties and types of political economies (chap. 2).

METHODS AND FINDINGS

First I conducted regression experiments to test the relative impact on family policy of female labor-force participation and the aging of the population (products of industrialization) and measures of the structure of political economy and party power and ideology—corporatism, cumulative left party power, and Catholic party power. The analysis used party power scores from 1946 to 1976, but the longer period from 1919 yields the same results.

These multiple regressions were run both with the combined family-policy index and then separately with each of the three components—child care, parental or maternal leave, and flexible retirement. Then a path diagram was designed to test a causal model combining the influence of both industrialization and politics (see figure 7.1).

To examine interaction effects, take account of types of corporatism (obscured by our quantitative measures), and locate deviant cases, I cross-tabulated trichotomized country scores on the policy index (high, medium, and low) with combinations of party dominance and corporatism (left-corporatist, Catholic and left-corporatist, Catholic corporatist,

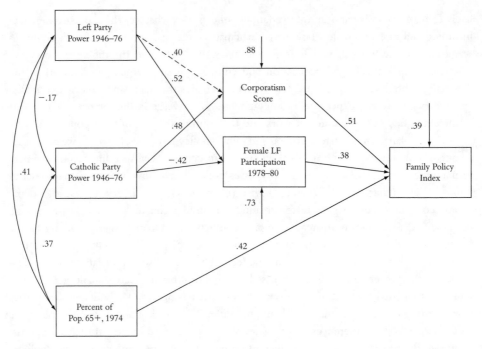

Figure 7.1. Left power encourages both corporatism and women at work and thereby expands family policy, 1976-82. Catholic power keeps women home but fosters corporatism, with mixed effects. Older populations independently encourage family policy★

★Eighteen countries (Israel missing). Solid arrows indicate path coefficients significant at $p < .05$; dashed arrow indicates significance at .10 level. Adjusted R^2 for Family Policy Index = .85.

corporatist-without-labor and least-corporatist). Finally, I explored the relation of parties, corporatism, and family policy to spending on family allowances.

The findings generally confirm the idea that there are two separate roads to an innovative and expansive family policy. The first leads from party power through women's work to family policy. The second leads from party power through corporatism to family policy. (See figure 7.1.)

Catholicism, Leftism, Corporatism, and Working Women

Female labor-force participation is directly related to family policy ($r = .49, p = .05$). In nine regressions controlling for all possible combinations of other variables in figure 7.1 it retains statistical significance at least at the .10 level, 6 times at the .01 level, all in the expected direction. And in the final path model $\beta = .38, p = .01$. The interpretation is straightforward: the more women at work, the more demand for government help in balancing the demands of family and work. The path diagram shows that left and Catholic parties, insofar as they shape labor-force participation, have opposite and indirect effects on family policy: leftism strongly fosters female labor-force participation which, in turn, expands family policy; Catholicism discourages female labor participation and thereby is a drag on family policy. However, when we examine the path from party power through corporatism we see that both Catholicism and leftism foster corporatist bargaining arrangements which, in turn, are strongly related to an innovative and expansive family policy ($r = .73$).[16] Thus, the ambivalence of Catholic parties is confirmed: they are not enthusiastic about releasing women from the home, but they also do not want old folks to be left stranded or single parents to neglect their children. And they are not, on principle, hostile to state intervention. Further, they are a major source of corporatism (as we have seen in chapter 2 when we examined the roots of corporatism and aggregate social spending). Once a bargaining structure includes labor, management and the state, the negative Catholic influence on women working is overcome by the consensus-making machinery that produces family policy. Governing left parties, in contrast to governing Catholic parties, are quite consistent in their effects: they accent equality, including gender equality, and they favor labor participation in big policy, which fosters tripartite bargaining. The combination of egalitarian ideologies in high places and democratic corporatism results in keen attention to family issues.

Demographic Pressures and Family Policy: Are the Young and Old at War?

Using demographic variables as controls in our analysis of the impact of industrialization vs. politics, we considered separately population aged 14 and under, population aged 65 and over, and the dependency ratio (young and old/population 15–64).

From the American debate about generational combat, one might think that parents with young children would be a political force for family policy while old folks in retirement might be a political force against government expenditures on the young. But the obvious is not true. The unexpected finding is that an aging population is a powerful source of family policy including the support of child care ($r = .63$) and parental leave ($r = .59$), not merely flexible retirement ($r = .73$). The percentage of population 65 and over is strongly and positively related to the family policy index ($r = .74$). Moreover, as figure 7.1 shows, the influence of the aged is direct—that is, independent of both corporatism and female labor-force participation.[17]

What about the effect of a young population? Contrary to the common sense that invokes the force of self-interest in politics, countries with a large percentage of population under 15 score low on family policy ($r = -.74$). But after controlling for female labor-force participation and corporatism, it has no significant effect on family policy.[18] In other words, population under 15 is negatively correlated with family policy only because countries with many young people tend to have lower female participation. (Dependency ratio is not related to any dependent variable because its two components pull in opposite directions.)

The significant independent impact of the aged on family policy, even programs favoring the young, might be explained in three ways. First, most of the older people are women, many with grandchildren whose parents work. An increasing number of their working daughters or daughters-in-law are single parents in need of special child-care help. Whether these daughters are single or not, they often ask their mothers (and where possible their fathers) for help in childminding. Because retirees increasingly prefer active and independent lives, and increasingly have the resources to support that style of life (adequate income and low taxes), they are attracted to all three programs for easing both the burden on their adult children and the pressure on themselves. In short, the aged, far from constituting a pressure group against a government apparatus to help working parents, become allies in the cause.

More speculatively, the aged in rich countries, having been through it themselves, may simply be more sensitive to the tensions of parents with young children, especially harried parents with preschoolers, and more open to legislative proposals to cushion the shocks of that stage of the life cycle. Conversely, young couples with preschool children and people undergoing divorce or separation—a substantial segment of parents of children under 15— are caught in a life-cycle squeeze where their aspirations are out of balance with their economic and occupational rewards (chap. 4; and Wilensky, 1961b, 1981b). They are not likely to want taxes increased for *any* purpose or any dependent population—and tend to be most apathetic about politics.

In short, that a young population is not a force for family policy and an old population is, might be explained by three forces: (1) Grandparents want to relieve pressures on both their working adult children and themselves; (2) wisdom about childrearing pressures, we hope, comes with experience; and (3) the numerous nonaffluent young parents with schoolchildren (especially preschool children) are at a stage in the family life cycle where they experience least job satisfaction, lower participation in community life, the greatest financial and family burdens, and the greatest psychological tension—a condition of life-cycle squeeze hardly conducive to intense political action, even on behalf of their own interests (chap. 4 and Wilensky, 1981b).

The model of figure 7.1 holds up when we decompose family policy into its three components—flexible retirement, child care, and parental leave policies—and repeat the path analysis. Everything said in the above analysis holds true for each policy cluster as well as the summary index. Slight differences do appear, however. The model is most successful in explaining flexible retirement policies and least successful in explaining parental leave policies. Old populations tend to support all three types of policy; corporatism is most strongly associated with child-care policies (perhaps the most expensive and cost-beneficial of the three); and female labor-force participation is most strongly associated with support for flexible retirement. Table 7E.1 in appendix E compares the regression coefficients for the family-policy index and its components.

Rather than reporting more path diagrams and regression results, I now turn to the cross-tabulations of table 7.1, which allow us to pinpoint the countries that account for the results so far and search for exceptions and interaction effects.

The Interaction of Types of Corporatism, Party Power, Women at Work, and the Aged: Consistent Patterns with a Belgian/French Exception

As expected, the combination of left party power and democratic corporatism yields the most innovative and expansive family policy (Sweden, Norway, and Finland with Denmark— medium on corporatism—scoring fourth highest; the average score is 9.3). In 1978–80 all four Scandinavian countries also had very high rates of female labor-force participation (62–73%), and in 1974 an abundance of old people (without Finland, which had only 10% aged, the Scandinavian average would be 13.7%; with Finland it is 12.8%). The second cluster reflects the ambivalence of Catholic parties toward women's place and the left offset: corporatist countries with the combination of Catholic and left parties—Austria, Italy, Netherlands, and if we can count it as corporatist, West Germany—score medium on family policy (4 to 7).

Belgium is the exception; it scores second only to Sweden and France on the family-policy index—mainly because it has the most generous provision for child care; leads in

TABLE 7.1 Interaction after World War II of types of political economy, party power and ideology, female labor-force participation, and the size of the aged population as sources of family policy**

Family Policy Score	Left Corporatist				Cath./Left Corporatist				Corporatist w/o Labor				Least Corporatist			
	Country	Policy Score	% Fem. in LF[a]	% Pop. 65+[b]	Country	Policy Score	% Fem. in LF	%Pop. 65+	Country	Policy Score	% Fem in LF	% Pop. 65+	Country	Policy Score	% Fem. in LF	% Pop. 65+
Most innovative (9-11)	Sweden	11	73	15	Belgium	10	47	14	France	11	54	14	UK	5	58	14
	Norway	9	62	13												
	Finland	9	69	10												
	Cell Avg.	9.7	68	13												
Average (4-8)	Denmark	8	68	13	W.Germany*	7	50	14								
					Austria	7	49	15								
					Italy*	6	39	12								
					Netherlands	4	34	11								
					Cell Avg.	6	43	13								
Least innovative (1-3)									Japan	2	55	8	USA	3	59	10
									Switzerland	2	49	12	Canada	2	56	8
													New Zealand	2	44	9
													Australia	1	51	9
													Ireland	1	35	11
									Cell Avg.	2	52	10	Cell Avg.	1.8	49	9
Col. Avg.		9.25	68	13		6.8	44	13		5	53	11		2.3	50	10

*Italy, Catholic power only; West Germany, ambiguously corporatist and marginally left.

**Israel missing.

[a]Percentage of females aged 15–64 in labor force, average 1978–80.

[b]Persons 65 and over as percentage of total population 1974.

unpaid maternal leave (three years), although it is only average in paid leaves (12 to 14 weeks); and is well above average in the number of options it provides in its retirement schemes. And yet it is only medium-low in labor-force participation (47%). Offsetting this is a quite high percentage of aged (65+/population = 13.8%, fourth among our 19 democracies). Two characteristics of Belgian politics might explain its top score in this group. First is the leftist character of its Catholic parties: Belgium has a long history of Catholic workers' movements; the Catholic Party after World War I was the pivot around which coalition governments formed; they often included socialists and produced a stream of social reforms (Fogarty, 1957, pp. 188, 296–299; Wilensky, 1981c, p. 364). The second reason for Belgium's strongly progressive family policy is the frequency with which left parties moved in and out of Catholic-dominated coalitions from 1919 to 1976; among my 19 rich democracies, only Belgium scores high in both cumulative Catholic and left power for the entire period (Wilensky, 1981c, p. 369). Thus, despite the sharing of power among left and Catholic parties, as well as liberal parties, the cumulative leftward tilt accounts for Belgium's higher than expected family-policy score.[19]

The third group—corporatist-without-labor—as predicted, has the third-highest family-policy score. But here France, like Belgium, is deviant, with a score of 11, tying that of Sweden. In this case both women workers and demography offset the weakness and exclusion of labor from top policymaking. France ranks medium-high in female labor-force participation (54%) and is among the top 6 of 19 countries in fraction of aged (65+/population = 14% in 1974). More important, as we have seen in chapter 2, there was a brief period of left-Catholic rule—Communist-Socialist-MRP tripartisme— at the beginning of the First Legislature of the Fourth Republic. Although in my scheme France is not counted as having either much left or Catholic party power, the Mouve-ment republicain populaire, a Catholic party, was the largest non-Communist group in the assembly in 1946; in coalition with the left it initiated much social legislation. The coalition increased coverage and benefit of family allowances established in the 1930s; it greatly enriched the "politique de la famille."[20] Once in place, those social policies tend to expand. So by 1980 France was second in paid parental leaves (15–18 weeks) in-cluding paternity leave, very high in unpaid leaves (two years), tops in child care, and sec-ond only to Sweden on flexible retirement. Like Belgium, France also led the league in spending on family allowances.

Again, the most-fragmented, decentralized political economies, with the United King-dom as a partial exception, have the lower scores. The UK's score of 5, a bit above the ex-pected, might be explained by its high fraction of aged (13.6%, fifth among the 19 coun-tries by 1974) and its quite high rate of female labor-force participation (57.6% puts it sixth among 18 countries). It also has experienced more than a touch of left power since World War II (eighth among 19 countries).

Tables for each of the components of the family-policy index show almost identical re-sults (see table 7E.1 in appendix E). If we substitute measures of cumulative party power for 1919–76 instead of 1946–76, we get virtually identical results.

In sum, whether we use correlational techniques or combine variables to generate more subtle types of political economy and examine cases in simple cross-tabulations, we see a consistent pattern: left-corporatist countries have developed the most innovative and ex-pansive family policy; least-corporatist countries are at the other extreme. Countries whose

TABLE 7.2 Family allowance expenditure as a percentage of GNP, 1980, and family policy index, late 1970s*

Family Policy Score	High F. A. Spenders (≥ 3.1%)	Med. High F. A. Spenders (1.5 - 2.3%)	Med. Low F. A. Spenders (0.8 - 1.2%)	Low F. A. Spenders (≤ 0.1%)
Most Innovative (9-11)	Belgium France	Sweden	Norway Finland	
Average (4-8)	Austria	Netherlands W.Germany UK	Italy Denmark	
Least Innovative (1-3)			New Zealand Ireland Canada Australia	USA Japan

*Israel and Switzerland missing.

left and Catholic parties both participate in governing tend to be second and cases of corporatism-without-labor, third; they present a mixed picture.

FAMILY ALLOWANCES AND THE FAMILY-POLICY INDEX

It is a common complaint about students of social spending (and the kind of analysis reported in chap. 6 on sector spending) that they obscure great variations in legislation, program structure, conditions of eligibility, administrative arrangements, and the like. It is therefore noteworthy that our index of innovative and expansive family policies, which captures these programmatic differences, is quite closely correlated with expenditures on family (or child) allowances both as a percentage of GNP in 1980 ($r = .54$) and per capita ($r = .66$). Moreover, as we have seen in chapter 6, the structural sources of family allowances are similar to those for family policies—Catholic party power, corporatism, and an aging population (although left party power is not correlated with family allowances while it is correlated positively with the family-policy index).

Table 7.2 cross-tabulates the family-policy index and family allowance spending as a percentage of GNP. Consistent with the previous analysis of the ambivalence of Catholic parties toward family policies that help working women, we see that corporatist countries with strong left *and* strong Catholic parties are big child-allowance spenders but only medium innovators in family policy (Austria, West Germany, the Netherlands). Belgium is the only exception; it scores high on both. Italy (strong Catholicism but no left power until very recently) scores medium on the family-policy index but medium-low on spending. The pattern is entirely consistent with the findings on the competitive escalation of social spending in chapter 5, where we saw that the number of times the left was thrown out indicates intense Catholic-left competition and results in more social spending. Belgium, the leader in left party interruptions (six occasions from 1946 to 1976), is also the top spender on family allowances and family policy in general. In contrast, corporatist countries with more continuous left rule—Sweden, Norway—are able to hold down family allowance spending but promote more innovative solutions. Italy, with continuous Catholic rule, is a relatively lean spender with an average score on innovation. The least-corporatist countries, along with Japan, again tend to cluster in the low side of spending with the least program expansiveness and innovation (the United States, Japan, New Zealand, Ireland, Canada, and Australia).

SUMMARY AND CONCLUSION

The story of changes in family structures, functions, and lifestyles, as well as government responses to those changes, is the story of divergent paths of development to a convergent outcome.

Convergence is driven by the demographic and organizational accompaniments of continuing industrialization—especially educational and occupational shifts that expand opportunity for intergenerational and worklife mobility in nonagricultural and nondomestic settings, thereby increasing mass aspirations. As a result of these shifts in social structure, in the past 100 years or so the currently rich modern countries, whatever their political systems or cultural traditions, have experienced very similar and accelerating trends in family life: increased participation by women in the nonagricultural labor force, declining fertility and an expanding percentage of the aged, reduced family and household size, an increasingly widespread push for gender equality, and rising divorce rates. Although these trends have not eliminated the independent, neolocal nuclear family as the center of daily life, they have increased its instability and in recent decades increased the population of lone parents and the threat of child poverty.

In timing and in policy packages, governments have diverged somewhat in their responses to the social problems posed by structural change. Empirical analysis of family policies and politics among our rich democracies explains the differences: countries with strong mass-based Catholic or left parties move toward corporatist patterns of interest-group bargaining which produce expansive and innovative family policies, with somewhat different policy mixes, depending on types of corporatism, and the relative strength of Catholicism and leftism. More-fragmented and decentralized political economies are slower to develop family policies, as we can see from striking contrasts in the politics and policies of extreme cases, Sweden and the United States.

If in this century divisive, moral-religious issues have not been absent among the family-policy leaders of Scandinavia (Sweden, Norway, Finland), why are there no Scandinavian equivalents to Pat Robertson, no power for evangelical voters? For the same reason that cross-national similarities in public opinion on the welfare state (chap. 10) do not lead to successful tax-welfare backlash movements in Sweden and Norway but do so in the United Kingdom and the United States. What counts is the kind of mobilizing structures that shape mass sentiments and channel social cleavages: the structure of interest groups, their relation to one another, political parties, and the state—again, the presence or absence of leftism,

Catholicism, and democratic corporatism. Neither a tax revolt nor a teetotalist, antimodernist movement that might have blocked a family policy is likely in Sweden, whereas such movements have had free play in the least-corporatist democracies.

Although contrasting political and economic structures explain current differences in family policies, there is much evidence to suggest some convergence even here, where moral-social agendas are most passionately pursued. Continuing industrialization means continued increases in both women at work and the aged, more family breakup, and stronger demands for gender equality. In some measure these universal forces may overcome the forces for divergence. Perhaps recent legislation and continuing family-policy debates in the United States are clues to the direction of change. Similarly, the rapid aging of Japan's population has in the past 15 years moved both government and employers toward much more flexibility in retirement rules. In fact, swift changes of recent years in aging, fertility, and women's work in both Japan and the United States have already changed the politics of gender equality, aging, and child care and triggered more serious policy debates in these two most deviant countries.

NOTES

This chapter is based on a lecture presented at Oxford University, March, 1988, and a paper presented at the International Political Science Association World Congress, July 21–25, 1991, Buenos Aires, Argentina. A short summary was published (Wilensky, 1990). I am indebted to Eugene A. Hammel for critical comments.

1. Do job interruptions—whether from parental leave, unemployment, or caretaking without pay—depress the earnings and job status of women? A comparison of the United States and Sweden shows no effect on Swedish women's earnings that can be attributed to parental leave; because almost all Swedish women take it, parental leave does not signal a lack of commitment to career. Studies in the United States, in contrast, do show a depressed earnings effect from women's time out of the labor market, an effect that goes beyond the lost job experience. (Albrecht et al., 1996.)

2. The six countries rank as follows from least discrepancy to most: Sweden (13%), Germany (22%), Israel (22%), United Kingdom (24%), Canada (34%), USA (43%). The excellent database is the Luxembourg Income Study (LIS).

3. In 1988, according to an estimate by economist Laurence Lindsey, roughly 43% of the credit was going to families making more than $50,000 with only 23% to families making less than $20,000 (*Wall Street Journal,* July 5, 1988). Single parents with less than $20,000 household income were receiving an average credit of only $361.

4. This system could not cope with the worldwide recession of the early 1980s as the need to restructure industry grew more urgent. Employers' renewed efforts to get rid of older workers were facilitated by the availability of generous full early-retirement pensions. Thus, from 1980 to 1985 the number of new entrants to partial retirement fell sharply after climbing steadily in the second half of the 1970s (Casey, 1987, pp. 355–358).

5. Evangelical Protestants emphasize direct experience of the Holy Spirit (being "born again") and a literal interpretation of the Bible. President Carter and about 23% of the adult population were evangelicals in 1979, 9 in 10 of them white. In 1984 about 16 million white evangelical citizens voted for president—about 17.2% of the total vote, three-quarters of them for President Reagan (my estimates from definitions by Reichly, 1985, p. 312; Hunter, 1983, pp. 50 and 141–142; and data from Gallup, 1985, p. 38, and the American National Election Study, 1984 Pre- and Post-Election Survey File). "Fundamentalism" is an extreme form of evangelicalism. By the 1994 congressional elections—because

of low total turnout and a surge in evangelical turnout, sparked by a massive mobilization effort by Christian-right organizations—the white evangelical share of the national vote was at least 26% of the electorate and at least 36% of the total GOP vote. Adding allied religious conservatives such as Mormons brings the pietist total to about 40% of the total 1994 Republican vote (Hertzke, 1995).

6. Even in 1994, the third year of recovery from the last recession, even as the recovery accelerated, the *Wall Street Journal*/NBC News poll found that less than half of all Americans said they expect their children's generation to enjoy a higher standard of living (down from 60% before the 1990–91 recession) (*Wall Street Journal,* October 10, 1994). One reason is that average weekly earnings rose 19% in the six years since 1988, while consumer prices rose 26.8%. Although President Clinton's first two years in office saw more than 4.5 million jobs created from 1992 to 1994, although the inflation rate remained at a mere 3% and in September 1994 the unemployment rate dropped below 6% for the first time since 1990, the voters remained convinced that it was not happening. The reality they grasped, which the media continually emphasized, was both the decline in their real wages and corporate layoffs, downsizing, and restructuring. Whatever the personal income, blue-collar workers and increasingly their white-collar brethren were anxious about their own job security, about future prospects for them and their children.

7. Prior to the Nixon administration the principle of a guaranteed annual family income had been discussed for more than 30 years—from FDR's failed public-assistance minimum proposal of 1935 (guarantee enough to assure "health and decency") to Nixon's FAP proposal of 1969 (sold to him by his domestic policy adviser, Daniel P. Moynihan). FAP proposed a minimum of $1,600 (1969 dollars) for every family, subject to loose work requirements, with a reduction of benefits by 50% of earned income until the breakeven point of $4,000. Nixon, the first Republican president to support the idea of a guaranteed income, backed FAP until early 1970. But realizing the cost and facing resistance from his conservative base, he deserted it in 1970–72. The interaction of extremes assured its demise: the right said it was too expensive, too much of a handout to the undeserving, and the problem should be left to the states or the private sector and charity; the left opposed work requirements and said the payout was too meager (the militant, highly visible National Welfare Rights Organization launched a "Zap FAP" campaign, condemned it as "disguised repression," and threatened violence). (Moynihan, 1973; Burke and Burke, 1974; Ribicoff, 1973; and Coyle and Wildavsky, 1987.)

8. Congressional and media accounts of public resentment of the old as takers and the nonold as overburdened givers are contradicted both by public opinion data that show little intergenerational conflict (Taylor, 1986; Minkler, 1986; Day, 1990) and data on family financial help patterns that show a big net flow from the elderly to their children and grandchildren (Butler, 1989, p. 144). Confirming these findings of intergenerational solidarity is a large-scale 16-year (annual or biannual) longitudinal survey of the Netherlands with some questions dating back to 1950. Although social spending and the percentage of the elderly are much higher in the Netherlands than in the United States, the Dutch show almost no generational or age differences in attitudes toward social security, income, and related issues (Dekker and Ester, 1993, Part 3). This popular support for the social contract between generations shows up in a Eurobarometer survey of and two surveys by the International Social Survey Program (ISSP). These show that popular support for current or increased spending on the aged is overwhelming and increased from 1985 to 1990 in four of the five countries with data on change (West Germany, Britain, Italy, and the United States) (Kohli, 1993).

9. For discussion of the steps the United States might take to dampen the mood swings and improve the system, see chapter 18 on policy implications.

10. I am grateful to Alison Woodward for a translation of the relevant parts of Jönsson and Paulsson's book, the most comprehensive of several studies of the 1970s and 1980s.

11. Only in Norway, however, where the Christian People's Party has occasionally been part of the postwar governing coalitions, has a moral regeneration party had much electoral success. Although

by 1970 similar parties were formed in Sweden, Denmark, and Finland—a backlash against secularization—they get tiny fractions of the vote, at best 2% in Sweden, 5% in Denmark (Berglund and Lindstrom, 1978, p. 61). The Swedish Christian Democrats entered Parliament for the first time in 1991.

12. My argument that, despite the huge political differences I have traced in this chapter, we should not exaggerate the religious-ethnic differences between the United States and Sweden gains further support from another surprising fact: from the 1830s to the 1960s American and Swedish preachers obsessed with the evils of alcohol were in close personal contact. For instance, the lodges of the International Order of Good Templars (IOGT), originating in the United States, were carried to Sweden by a Swedish Baptist preacher and immigrant agent active in the United States; by 1910 Sweden had 2,340 Good Templar lodges and 160,000 members devoted to both abstinence and democratization (Scott, 1988, pp. 354–355). Similar interchanges are frequent among Protestant pastors in both countries to this day.

13. I am indebted to Susan Reed Hahn for a creative coding effort that made this analysis possible.

14. The Clinton Family and Medical Leave Act of 1993 mandates up to 12 weeks of unpaid leave per year for family medical emergencies and childbirth or adoption. In 1995 it covered only about 5% of U.S. companies (those with more than 50 workers) and about 40% of the labor force (U.S. Department of Labor 1995). This still keeps the U.S. at the bottom of the list.

15. In the early 1980s, Japan, with one of the more-rigid retirement systems (out at 55), began to implement a positive policy of job maintenance and job creation for older people. Through the Ministry of Labor it required that companies raise the age of mandatory retirement and move toward a job quota for workers over 60; it offered a variety of subsidies to employers to keep, hire, and re-train older workers; and it targeted job-finding and counseling services to older workers (Campbell, 1992, pp. 254–281; Cole, 1992, p. 205; and conversation with John Campbell, February 25, 1997). Many firms today reemploy their own retirees or provide them with assistance in finding new jobs with their subsidiaries or client firms (Clark and Ogawa, 1997). In the fall of 1997 the parliament was expected to expand social insurance to government-paid institutional and community long-term care for the elderly. By 1997 the Japanese score, correct for 1978–82, would be closer to 3 than 1.

16. In nine regressions controlling for all possible combinations of other variables in the model, corporatism is always significant at the .01 level, always in the expected direction. $\beta = .51, p < .01$.

17. Once again, in nine regressions controlling for all combinations of other variables, 65+ is always significant at least at the .05 level, seven times at the .01 level. $\beta = .42, p < .01$.

18. An F-test tells the significance of the increase in R^2 which results from adding population <15 to a regression equation including women working and corporatism. The test shows that population <15 does not add significantly to explaining variations in family policy after the effects of women working and corporatism are taken into account. This is true for both the summary index and all three components.

19. Since 1973 Belgian politics has become more polarized. And since December 1981 under the Center-Right austerity governments of Christian Democrat Wilfried Martens, the left has not fared well. Perhaps Belgium will sink a notch into the proper middle cell in table 7.1, although once social rights are established they are hard to take away.

20. Much of this was inspired by a pronatalist ideology, the concern that the decline in birth rates would threaten French sovereignty against the German threat: no babies, no soldiers, no economic strength. Thus, voluntary levies on employers to finance family allowances had begun as early as 1918; an Act of March 11, 1932 made employer contributions compulsory. (Laroque, 1966, p. 439; Questiaux and Fournier, 1978, pp. 117–120.) The "politique de la famille" has been embraced by every regime since Daladier's decrees of 1939 (when the family code instituted a high premium for the first child and a bonus for more than three). (Laroque, 1966, p. 439; Stanley Hoffman in Hoffman et

al., 1963, p. 45; Saffran, 1985, pp. 8 – 10; Wilensky, 1981c, p. 352.) Even the Left, once in power, gave added force to this French preoccupation in both rhetoric and politics: President Mitterrand, declaring in January 1983 that the low birthrate was a major problem, proposed to pay families at the birth of a third child about $125 a month for two years; all families would receive $85 per month per child from the third month of pregnancy to age three. His minister of family affairs declared that dénatalité puts at risk France's place in Western civilization (*Wall Street Journal*, June 20, 1984).

8

THE AMERICAN WELFARE MESS
IN COMPARATIVE PERSPECTIVE

"There's no excuse for kicking someone unless he's up."

Murray Kempton

In 1976 I wrote an article entitled "The Welfare Mess: Is it American, Who Needs It, Will It Last?" (1976b). The answers then were yes and no; demagogic politicians who use the welfare poor as convenient scapegoats; and yes, it will last. Sadly, almost nothing had changed by the late 1990s.

In the intensity of political fuss about it, the welfare mess is peculiarly American, but in its broad outlines it is shared by several other countries that rely heavily on means-tested programs and have high rates of poverty (USA, UK, Canada, Ireland, and Switzerland).[1] The American welfare mess is perpetuated first by politicians who use welfare mothers (in the public image they are racial minorities) as convenient scapegoats who are somehow responsible for problems of racial conflict, crime, family breakup, illegitimacy, immigration, earnings deterioration, unemployment, budget deficits, fiscal strain and moral rot; and second, by the limited political capacity to reduce poverty by other more universal means—by education, by active labor-market and family policies, and by fiscal policy. It will last as long as the United States maintains a high rate of poverty and inequality and succumbs to polarized politics.

The American welfare mess consists of inadequate benefits and income for poor families; gross inequities in the flow of cash and services; an obsession with means testing and welfare fraud, which inspires an expensive, time-consuming, punitive apparatus of investigation and surveillance—a bewildering array of programs and agencies that recipients must negotiate when they need help. Although much exaggerated, some work disincentives are part of the welfare mess, especially America's peculiar avoidance of national health insurance (welfare recipients who receive Medicaid targeted to the poor eventually lose coverage if they go to work). Added to inadequacy, inequity, punitiveness, and inefficiency is an unfortunate lack of fiscal and policy control. Altogether the welfare mess makes the non-working, nonaged poor highly visible and unpopular, easy targets for scapegoating (see chap. 10). The mobilization of fear and hate, in turn, provokes mass backlash against welfare and recurrent attempts to reform welfare under such tough-sounding slogans as "workfare" and "end welfare as we know it." It also blocks the formation of a stable congressional coalition to fund the alternative policies most rich democracies have adopted.

American "Welfare" Programs

For several centuries of modernization every generation has discovered its own undeserving poor or "dangerous classes." And the current debate about the causes of poverty—personal moral failure or lack of opportunity—is as old as the English Poor Laws of the 16th century. The welfare reform bill of 1996 is merely one more episode in a long cycle of crackdowns on the poor followed by reforms to ease up a bit. Even the harshest of them all, the British Poor Law of 1834, was quickly followed by strong criticism. The critics noted that it did not distinguish between the nonworking poor who received poor relief and the more-deserving poor who did not; that it undermined incentives to obey the work ethic; and that it lumped together the worthy and unworthy in a miserable poorhouse, where criminals, alcoholics, women, mothers, children, infants, the aged, and the sick were jammed together and where brutality and corruption were common. Serving later as Conservative prime minister 1874–80, Benjamin Disraeli complained that the Poor Law Reform Bill of 1834 made it "a crime to be poor"—an idea echoed by today's liberals who are repelled by the "conservative" urge to punish the poor for their poverty. The principles of Elizabethan poor law—direct aid for the unemployed, work (or the workhouse or alms house, or prison) for the able-bodied, and local administration that would keep welfare benefits below the lowest wage and thus provide incentives to work—persist to this day in the U.S. (Handler, 1995, p. 12ff.).

This never-ending cycle is most prominent in the Anglo-American democracies, which rely most heavily on means-tested benefits targeted to the poor (see table 8.3). The cycle may occur around a long-term upward trend toward more cash and services for the poor as modern democracies became quite rich, but there is no doubt that the U.S. is now in a phase of getting tough on welfare.

In this century American welfare reform has gone through several phases that fit the cycle of punitiveness to lighter reform and back again.

1. *ADC 1911–25.* Before the "breadwinner" pattern broke down (see chap. 1)—when the typical urban family was still a male worker as household head and a wife as full-time homemaker and mother—the first Aid to Dependent Children (ADC) statute was enacted in Illinois in 1911. By 1925 similar statutes appeared in almost all other states (Bell, 1965). Previously, under child protection laws and the concept of "neglect," poor children had been removed from their single mothers and put into institutions or sent to farms. Now if the husband died or disappeared, they could perhaps stay at home. These new laws, sometimes mislabeled "mothers' pensions," were both heavily means tested and "morals tested." The single mother had to prove that she was destitute; in addition she had to be "fit and proper," a concept to be interpreted not by a welfare agency but typically by juvenile and county courts with power to give aid, declare children neglected or delinquent, break up homes, and place children in reformatories or state schools. As Joel Handler (1995, p. 25) and others have noted, few families were enrolled in these precursors to AFDC; recipients were almost all white widows; grants were small and even then typically had work requirements. The vast majority of poor mothers and their children were excluded. Yet it was a step ahead of previous practice; some poor but worthy mothers, if they maintained "suitable homes," could be morally

excused from work and receive aid. (*Ibid.*, 1995; Gordon, 1994, pp. 45–46, 298–299; Bell, 1965, pp. 5–13, 17–18; Handler and Hasenfeld, 1991, p. 24–26, 119–120.)

2. *AFDC as part of Franklin Roosevelt's Social Security Act of 1935.* Although in his first two years in office FDR spent $2 billion in cash relief (the "dole") administered by the states, by 1935, under prodding by Harry Hopkins and the academics who crafted Old Age, Survivors, and Disability Insurance (OASDI; Wilensky, 1997), he revived the work test for able-bodied men (the Works Project Administration) and made ADC a federal program. ADC (renamed AFDC) aimed to help families in which the breadwinner was "dead, disabled, or absent." This little-noticed part of the Social Security Act gradually developed into a program to support the children of divorce, desertion, and illegitimacy. Federal administrators were by now much more sympathetic to the poor; in the middle of the Great Depression it was easier to sell the idea that social structure, the fluctuations of markets, and fiscal policy shaped poverty. To project the blame on the poor, they argued, was both unrealistic and cruel. They saw "suitable home" policies as meddlesome and irrational, the denial of aid to out-of-wedlock children as punishment of innocent children for the sins of their parents. They prodded states to lighten up. (Kaus, 1992, p. 240; Bell, 1965, pp. 76–92.) By 1940, 30% of the ADC caseload consisted of families with absent father; by 1960 AFDC was 64%.

3. *The explosion of cost and the "casework" crackdown, 1960–68.* In the early 1960s, the welfare caseload climbed sharply and political resistance to welfare mothers mounted with it. From 1960 to 1974 AFDC rolls more than tripled from 3.1 million to about 11 million. States tried to reassert the "suitable home" restrictions of the early 20th century. This is the time of the infamous midnight raids to uncover boyfriends who were cohabiting with the welfare mother—taken as a sign of both immorality and the presence of a "substitute parent," both of which were grounds for cutting or eliminating AFDC aid. (Later I discuss this form of means testing and surveillance as we examine technical-administrative problems in heavily means-tested programs.) Repelled by this heavy-handed harassment of welfare mothers, civil-rights activists, welfare-rights activists, and the federal courts gradually shifted AFDC toward a "social right." I say "toward" because poor single mothers continued to be viewed as undeserving, agency approval of their claims was anything but automatic, and work requirements were widely applied.

Talk of crisis mounted along with the welfare rolls and the increasing numbers of blacks and never-married recipients. The response of President Kennedy's secretary of health, education and welfare, Abraham Ribicoff, was a massive dose of social work aimed at rehabilitation. The 1962 Public Welfare Amendments triggered a competitive state scramble for federal dollars for every variety of casework that might prevent the poor from sliding into welfare or move them up and out. The limited effectiveness of this solution in turn inspired a conservative reaction against what some called "poverty pimps," moralistic government caseworkers and welfare administrators who mediated between the poor and federal money. For a time, they and some liberal Democrats such as Daniel Patrick Moynihan and Sargent Shriver favored a guaranteed income and called for cash, not casework (cf. Kaus, 1992, pp. 112–113). We have seen in chapter 5 why such guaranteed minimum-income proposals as Nixon's Family Assistance Plan were killed in Congress and the White House. In only eight years the debate went from expanded casework and prevention to cash, with both fading away along with President Johnson's War on Poverty, while the AFDC caseload continued to climb from 7.4 million in 1970 to 10.5 million in 1980 (U.S. House of Representatives, *Green Book*, 1996, tables 8–25 and 8–27—hereafter cited as the Green Book).

4. *The revival of "workfare" 1980 to the present with fluctuations in punitiveness.* Regulatory work programs for welfare recipients were revived in the 1980s. There had been largely symbolic exercises earlier. For example, a Work Incentive Program (WIN) was enacted in 1967 and expanded and toughened in 1971; at its peak it had a budget of about $300 million. Only 2–3% of the eligible welfare recipients got jobs through the second, tougher WIN; of these, only 20% held their jobs for at least 3 months (Handler, 1995, p. 59).

For a brief period Democrats and Republicans came together on a welfare reform bill that was neither punitive nor utopian and took the challenge of welfare-to-work more seriously, the Family Support Act of 1988 (chap. 7 describes the struggle to achieve a coalition around this measure). It emphasized work and training and provided new federal spending, including money for a year of guaranteed transitional child care and Medicaid for women leaving AFDC. It also included substantial funding for research to evaluate its effects, which now permits us to show how limited the "workfare" solution is in reducing either poverty or welfare spending.

This lighter workfare reform lasted only about eight years; in 1996 the cycle moved toward a new, more radical crackdown, the Personal Responsibility and Work Opportunity Reconciliation Act of 1996. This law was driven by budget-balancing fervor combined with the usual hostility to the undeserving poor and the belief that coercion will make them work, marry, stop having illegitimate children, and become self-sufficient. (For good summaries of this law and the issues posed see Smolensky, Evenhouse, and Reilly, 1997; Bane, 1997; Waldfogel, 1996; and Super et al., 1996.) The law

- replaces Aid to Families with Dependent Children (AFDC), an entitlement, and the Jobs Opportunities and Basic Skills Training (JOBS) program with block grants to the states for Temporary Assistance for Needy Families (TANF). It abolishes any right to benefits and services.

- requires that state plans include a provision that at least one adult in a family that has been receiving aid for more than two years participate in work activities, as defined by the state. It imposes a five-year lifetime limit on the receipt of assistance. States can reduce these time limits. (The National Governors' Association reported that by June 30, 1997, 20 states had imposed shorter time limits.) Hardship exemptions may be made for up to 20% of families. The states have had increasing flexibility in administering welfare before this law; they now have free rein. They can spend money, set eligibility rules, and provide aid or not, as they wish; transfer funds to other more popular programs; and push the responsibility down to counties and cities or to for-profit companies (who are driven by cost-cutting considerations).

- requires states to reduce grants for those who refuse to engage in work (as defined by the state) and penalizes states for not meeting specified rates of participation by TANF recipients in work-related activities. The law contains a "caseload reduction credit" that allows states to count a reduction of 15% or more from 1995 to 1998 in their caseload toward "work activities" calculations—a perverse incentive to purge or churn the rolls.

- establishes a loose maintenance-of-effort requirement: States must maintain their spending at 80% of their 1994 level. That very likely means a cut in total spending on welfare and ultimately a cut in real welfare benefits per family.[2] But, more important, the bill makes across-the-board cuts in food stamp benefits, restricts these benefits to 3 months out of 36 for unemployed adults without disabilities or dependents, bans most legal immigrants from most federal benefit programs, and toughens benefit eligibility rules for disabled children under SSI. Cuts in food stamps and the denial of benefits to legal immigrants generate most of the $54 billion in savings in this law.[3]

- improves national child support enforcement. Calls for a National Directory of New Hires to catch deadbeat dads escaping across state borders. (Previous laws with nearly unanimous support also tried to make absent fathers pay child support.)

- authorizes more federal money for child care ($21 billion over seven years)—the one gesture in the 1996 bill toward the kind of support necessary for any move from welfare to work by able-bodied TANF mothers.

The scholarly critics of this bill include veteran students of the welfare mess such as Senator Pat Moynihan, Mary Jo Bane, and Wendell Primus. Bane, as assistant secretary for children and families in the Department of Health and Human Services, and Wendell Primus, who also held a top position in HHS, resigned their posts when it became clear that President Clinton would sign the bill. These critics argue that there will now be a competitive race to the bottom. In Bane's words, "All the political and financial incentives are for states to cut assistance, to impose time limits shorter than five years, to meet the work requirements without spending any money, to shift responsibilities to local government and private contractors, and to use the block grant funds for more politically popular programs. All of these tendencies were evident in waiver demonstrations proposed by states before enactment of the new law" (1997, p. 49).

Critics further claim the following: (1) The already large disparities between the states (see table 8.2) will be exacerbated by the funding formula, which locks in historical differences in spending per poor child. The richer, more-generous states tend to have stable or slowly rising populations and vice versa. Thus, disparities will increase. Because states will receive federal dollars based on the welfare populations of earlier years even as the rolls decline, there will be an initial windfall of almost $2 billion for 1997, permitting some lucky states to increase spending per recipient if they choose to do so (see note 2 above). (2) Vagaries of federal and state appropriation and economic cycles of states and regions assure disastrous cuts in child support when inevitable downswings come in either political mood or labor markets. (3) The law eliminates or sharply limits due-process protection; by repealing federal AFDC, Congress undermined 60 years of case law protecting recipients. (4) Analyses by both HHS and the Urban Institute predict that the new law will push at least 1 million children and 1.5 million adults into poverty and that 8 million families will lose income. (5) Without federal oversight and with unconstrained "flexibility" for the states, it will be virtually impossible to monitor outcomes in the way the 1988 Family Support Act required. What is sure is that welfare mothers, unlike the blind, the disabled, and the old, who have always been morally excused from work, will in theory be required to work. It is equally certain that these mothers will continue to be condemned for their failure to achieve self-sufficiency.[4]

There is a recurrent tension in the long history of attempts to combine welfare and work. Are the work requirements for poor families to be merely another prerequisite for continued eligibility, another set of rules for compliance, or is "workfare" to be a system that confronts the varied obstacles to work—child care, transportation, education, training, job search, and, need we say, job creation—and guides recipients from welfare to permanent work? (Bane and Ellwood, 1994.) Since 1980 especially but for many decades before, in theory workfare involves the necessary investment in human capital; in practice it is overwhelmingly intensified eligibility checking and cost cutting. That is why workfare as practiced by many states in the past 20 years or so has had little effect on setting the poor to work for more than temporary stints or imposing sanctions for failure to comply and has had only a marginal effect on moving AFDC clients from welfare to stable work. (See later discussion of why workfare on the cheap fails.)

MYTHS AND FACTS ABOUT THE AMERICAN WELFARE SYSTEM

The welfare system has been studied nearly to death. But social-science research has had little effect on the direction of welfare policy, a point explored comparatively and in detail in chapters 2 and 4. As we have seen, programs targeted to the poor have been repeatedly reformed in a long cycle of increasing and decreasing punitiveness. In my view, if the United States continues to insist on heavy means testing and does little to make low-wage work pay better, and health care universal, the welfare mess is intractable.

There is a consensus among scholars regarding the facts about welfare and considerable agreement on strategies for reducing poverty. The social-science consensus is often put in the form of myths vs. facts (Smolensky, Evenhouse, and Reilly, 1992, 1997; Handler, 1995; Jencks, 1992a, 1992b; Edin and Lein, 1997a). As an anthropological concept a myth is a story that is partially true, partially false, and validates a collective sentiment. In the case of the welfare poor, some widely held beliefs are real myths with a (usually small) component of truth; some are totally false. We consider first the false propositions that even a shaman in a primitive tribe would be ashamed to promulgate, then some common myths with a grain of truth. Misconceptions that are almost devoid of any truth include the following: American welfare is generous, many of its beneficiaries live like welfare queens; the welfare population is homogeneous and will respond to pressure to work via lower benefits and definite time limits; and welfare clients are minorities living in ghettos (a corollary to the myth of homogeneity).

First, welfare benefits are generous; many recipients are living in comfort. The main means-tested programs targeted to the poor are Aid to Families with Dependent Children (AFDC for poor children in single-parent families or families in which the principal earner is unemployed—after 1996 AFDC became TANF); *Supplementary Security Income* (SSI, for the poor disabled and their dependents, and for the poor elderly); *food stamps* (in 1995 about 9 in 10 of AFDC recipients received them); and *Medicaid* (virtually all AFDC families receive Medicaid coverage, although most of the total expenditure goes to the elderly poor). Several much smaller programs cover much smaller portions of the poor: the program for *Women, Infants, and Children* (WIC) gives nutritional screening and food assistance to children under six and food assistance to low-income women who are pregnant or have an infant (about half the eligible population and a quarter of the AFDC families receive WIC benefits); *Head Start* gives health and education and other services to poor children under six (about a quarter of poor three- to five-year-olds enroll); *miscellaneous housing assistance* (only about a quarter of AFDC families received any form of housing aid in the early 1990s); *Title XX social services block grant* to states for programs designed to prevent welfare dependency and homelessness, provide child care, and preserve intact families (capped at $2.8 billion since 1977, it has since declined by 59% in real funding); *federal outlays for job training for the disadvantaged* (cut from $3.1 billion in 1975 to $132 million in 1996 in constant 1990 dollars); *school lunch program* (slight decline since 1977) and *school breakfast program* (a large increase from a tiny base); *General Assistance* (a small benefit for the poorest of the poor who fall through the safety net above, a program most states scaled back or eliminated in recent years); and federal/state *Emergency Assistance Program* ($14 million in 1970 to $3.25 billion in 1995 in nonconstant dollars, a big increase as deep poverty increased; see table 8.4). The welfare reform bill of 1996 substituted block grants for Emergency Assistance as well as AFDC and JOBS.

In amount and eligibility all of these benefits vary greatly by state except food stamps, which, after the 1996 welfare reform also varied by state. The Earned Income Tax Credit, targeted to the working poor, is not like any of these means-tested programs; eligibility for EITC is determined by an invisible, simple income test. It will be discussed later in a comparative analysis of means testing, stigma, and takeup rates.

How generous is this patchwork system? Table 8.1 shows the average benefit per family or per beneficiary for the major programs and the trend since 1970.

Table 8.1 rather neatly confirms old themes in the politics of welfare: in congressional debate and political campaigns it is much easier to demonize welfare mothers targeted by AFDC (47% cut 1970–95 in real benefits) than it is to demonize poor disabled adults, disabled children, or the poor frail elderly targeted by SSI (only a 1% cut). And it is still more difficult to attack the working poor and near-poor targeted by the EITC (a 118% real increase in 20 years). Food stamps (a modest real increase of 34% in 25 years) are a special political case, peculiarly American. The food stamp program, enacted in 1964, was greatly expanded in 1970, after the well-publicized hearings of Senator George McGovern's Select Committee on Nutrition and Human Needs uncovered a shocking amount of malnutrition and even starvation in the United States (Melnick, 1994, pp. 187–188, 198–199). For a means-tested program embracing the nonworking poor, this alone would not carry the day. It was passed with the support of the farm lobby, greatly overrepresented in the U.S. Senate, who saw a new market for farm products and were willing to trade support for food stamps in return for urban liberals' support for farm subsidies; paternalistic conservatives who believed that cash grants to welfare mothers was being squandered on alcohol, drugs, and general dissipation and were attracted to food stamps that could only be spent on food; and liberals who felt that an affluent society could afford to eliminate starvation and malnutrition. In any case, the value of food stamps remained small—less than a fifth of 1995 AFDC grants.

Medicaid—the health-care entitlement for the poor—is the other large means-tested program in table 8.1. In contrast to AFDC, SSI, and food stamps, the estimated real cash value of Medicaid benefits has burgeoned (100% in 20 years). Is this an exception to the rule that it is easy to cut or constrain benefits to the undeserving poor? Not really. As a measure of the real welfare of the welfare poor, Medicaid increases are misleading. First, medical inflation much exceeds the inflation adjustments in table 8.1; providers, administrators, and insurance companies take much of the benefit. Second, an AFDC (now TANF) dollar or food stamp dollar that goes to a welfare mother clearly improves the family's well-being. In contrast, piling up medical bills under Medicaid is typically a sign of suffering and poor health; it is hardly an unambiguous measure of well-being. Finally, only 29% of total Medicaid spending goes to provide medical care for the welfare poor. The rest goes to indigents in nursing homes, SSI recipients, and low-income Medicare recipients—in other words to the frail elderly poor. A bizarre feature of Medicaid is its open invitation to fraud or at least behavior of dubious ethical standard: Medicaid is the only long-term care option available to the nonaffluent middle class—and even the upper-middle class—millions of whom spend down assets or reallocate assets so they can declare themselves paupers and meet the eligibility test for explosively expensive long-term institutional care. Frequently, well-off adult children of aging parents needing such care consult lawyers expert in asset-shifting strategies.

This is to say that Medicaid is prominent in the inequities and indignities of the welfare mess. It is, of course, better than nothing and is worth preserving to prevent the further immiseration of the poor pending the political moment when the United States joins the rest of the rich democracies by adopting universal national health insurance.

Perhaps the best conservative measure of generosity of aid to the undeserving poor is the maximum monthly potential benefit for a one-parent family of three persons as a percentage of the 1996 poverty line of $12,980 per year or $1,082 per month. Neither these figures nor those in table 8.1 suggest an overflow of humanitarian spirit. The median 1996 AFDC benefit is $389 per month or 36% of the poverty line; median food stamp benefits are $310 per month; and the value of the combined benefit is $699 or 65% of the poverty line. In fact, no state, even the most generous, has moved the welfare poor above the poverty line through the combination of AFDC and food stamps (1996 Green Book, table 8-12, p. 437). Similarly, the combined maximum benefit for SSI, social security, and food stamps for the poor elderly and disabled individuals in 1996 was $6,372 per year (87% of the poverty threshold) (1996 Green Book, table 4-9). For poor elderly, blind or disabled couples, the same combination yields $9,540, an inch above poverty—104% of the size-adjusted poverty threshhold (1996 Green Book, table 4-10, p. 290). Finally, because of the heavy debt run up from 1980 to 1992 and the political resistance to cutting support for social security, Medicare, and the military, the brunt of fiscal austerity was borne by the "discretionary" budgets of the 1990s, the home of all of the means-tested programs. Most dramatically, in two years of legislation enacted by the 104th Republican Congress from FY 1995 to FY 1997 the percentage change in appropriation levels for low-income discretionary programs adjusted for inflation was a cut of 10.2%; appropriations for other non-low income, nondefense discretionary programs shrank only 5.2%. More than 93% of the

TABLE 8.1 Average monthly benefit payments per family or per recipient for AFDC, food stamps, SSI, Medicaid, and the earned income tax credit, 1970–95 (in 1995 dollars)[1]

Year	Avg. AFDC benefit/month per family[2]	Avg. Food Stamps benefit/month per recipient[3]	Monthly fed. SSI benefits for singles and couples[4] singles	couples	Avg. Medicaid paymts./month per recipient[5]	Avg. earned inc. tax credit per recipient family[6]
1970	$713	$48[7]	NA	NA	NA	NA
1975	608	53	462	693	129	588
1980	509	59	450	676	171[8]	541
1985	467	64	461	693	203	399
1990	458	67	454	682	245	646
1993	394	72	458	689	259[9]	998
1995	377	71	458	687	257[10]	1278
% change	–47%	34%	–1%	–1%	100%	118%

[1]Figures given in constant 1995 dollars adjusted for inflation using the Consumer Price Index for urban Consumers (CPI-U) unless otherwise indicated.

[2]Source: Committee on Ways and Means, U.S. House of Representatives, 1996 Green Book: Background Material and Data on Programs within the Jurisdiction of the Committee on Ways and Means, table 8-1, pp. 386–87 (Washington, DC: US Government Printing Office, 1996). This is an average of the benefits paid out under both AFDC-Basic and AFDC-UP programs to families. Note that the average size of a family receiving AFDC shrank from 4.0 in 1970, to 3.2 in 1975, to 2.8 in 1993 (where it remained through 1995).

[3]Source: 1996 Green Book, table 16-11, p. 881.

[4]Source: 1996 Green Book, table 4-3, p. 274. The monthly figures were calculated from annual per capita benefit totals. All figures are for recipients living in their own households, not those living in another's household. This represents over 90% of all those receiving SSI. No figure is available for 1970 because the SSI (Supplemental Security Income) program began in 1974.

[5]Source: 1996 Green Book, table 16-19, pp. 906–907. Figures are in constant 1994 dollars, except for the 1985 figure which is in constant 1995 dollars. The bulk of Medicaid expenditures is paid out to aged recipients, along with disabled people. Medicaid is an anomaly; it is not targeted at the same population as the other programs in this table.

[6]Source: 1996 Green Book, table 14-14, p. 809. The figure for 1995 is a projection. Targeted to the working poor.

[7]This figure is for 1972, the first fiscal year in which food stamp benefits and eligibility rules became nationally uniform by law and were indexed for inflation.

[8]1981.

[9]1992.

[10]1994.

total net effects of reductions in entitlements came from programs for low-income people ($61 billion of the $65.6 billion cuts over 1996–2002). The food stamp program and the SSI program for the poor disabled and elderly bore the brunt of the cuts. This is true whether we adjust for inflation or not. (Greenstein, Kogan, and Nichols, 1996, using conservative estimates by the Congressional Budget Office.)

In short, the welfare system is anything but generous. Because the welfare poor are visible and unpopular, however, no amount of tough means testing will prevent political complaints about "welfare queens."

Decentralized federalism dominates the welfare system of the U.S. and accounts for striking differences among states in the fate of the poor. One puzzle in the system is why some states have cut back AFDC and associated benefits so much more than others. One might think that highly means-tested benefits would be most vulnerable to cuts where they are generous—where the cuts would do little harm. There was a hint of this in chapter 5 where we saw that big-spending Sweden, having achieved remarkable security for all its citizens, was able to make substantial cuts in social spending, even in health care, with very little loss in the standard of living of its citizens, including low-income families. But this is not true of the 51 states of the United States. Table 8.2 shows that starting from a low level of benefits for the poor does not insulate you from Draconian cuts.

The median maximum monthly benefits for a family of three for 51 states (including the District of Columbia) in 1995 was $404 ($4,848 a year). The median real cut in the maximum benefit from 1970 to 1996 was 46%, by any standard a punishing reduction. What is most striking about the state data on which table 8.2 is based is that even before the welfare reforms of 1996, there was a clear tendency for the states that are most generous in welfare benefits to avoid relatively severe cuts during this 26-year period while the already miserly states went at it with great vigor. Specifically:

• Of the eight states with the very fewest cutbacks (from California's 18% to Florida's 33%) four are the most generous in benefits (Alaska, Hawaii, California, Wisconsin) and two are close to the median (Maine, Nevada). Only two, Florida and Missouri, are well below the median. These eight states average $515 in the monthly maximum benefit for a family of three in January, 1996. Generous states tend to make the fewest cuts in benefits targeted to the poor.

• Of the eight states with the most drastic cutbacks (from Texas's 68% to Tennessee's 58%), seven are in the three lowest quintiles in generosity (Tennessee, Texas, Virginia, Idaho, Illinois, Pennsylvania, New Jersey). These eight states that made large cuts in AFDC average $323 in the monthly maximum benefit—at most a fulsom $3,876 a year in 1996 to support a single mother with two children or a couple with one. The already lean and mean are the states that tend to cut benefits the most.

Generosity, however, is unrelated to affluence: rich or booming states are among the most Draconian in cuts: Texas leads the 51 states at 68%; New Jersey is the runner up at 65%; Pennsylvania at 60% and Illinois at 59% are also in the top quintile in slashing spending for the welfare poor.

• Although lean spending on the poor is not confined to the South, the states in the bottom quintile of column one, table 8.2—states paying the very lowest benefits—are all Southern (ranging from Mississippi's $120 per month to North Carolina's $272).

Cost-of-living differences cannot explain such large cutback differences. The obvious candidates for further explanation of the patterns are the political complexion of these states and the occupational and residential mobility pattern in each (see chap. 5). Texas is the epitome instance. It is a boom state in most years, generating both great mobility in occupation and wealth; and it is Southern, with a resurgent Republican Party. The point remains hypothetical until the politics of welfare and mobility patterns are analyzed in each state; necessary data do not yet exist. There is one additional determinant of the politics of welfare in the U.S. states that deserves attention—variations in types of income inequality, which are probably related to the patterns of social mobility we found important in chapter 5. The

TABLE 8.2 Maximum AFDC grant and eligibility for a family of three, 1996, reductions in benefits from 1970 to 1996, and average grant per family 1994, by quintile averages of state generosity

State maximum benefit ranking[1]	Maximum monthly AFDC grant, family of three[2]	Maximum monthly income before losing AFDC eligibility[3]	Maximum monthly grant as % of 1995 per capita monthly income[4]	% Reduction in maximum monthly AFDC benefits 1970-1996[5]	Average monthly AFDC grant per family, 1994[6]
Quintile 1	$632	$1,138	30%	-38%	$558
Quintile 2	454	851	26	-45	383
Quintile 3	397	773	20	-45	321
Quintile 4	316	616	17	-40	284
Quintile 5	207	592	13	-50	209

[1]Quintile rankings for all columns based on ranking of maximum monthly state AFDC benefit as of January 1996. Source: 1996 Green Book, table 8-15.

[2]Source: 1996 Green Book, table 8-15. The maximum benefit for a family of three with no countable income. The figures for 1996 were derived from the Congressional Research Service survey data.

[3]Source: 1996 Green Book, table 8-17. This is the earnings level at which AFDC eligibility for a family of three ends, during the first four months of a job. The cutoff earnings limits are much lower after one year on the job.

[4]Source: Kilborn, Peter T., "Welfare All Over the Map," New York Times, December 8, 1996, Section E, p. 3. Checked against the Green Book and Commerce Department figures on per capita income.

[5]Source: 1996 Green Book, table 8-15 (real percentage change assuming a CPI-U value of 154.4 relative to a July 1970 value of 39.0).

[6]Source: Famighetti, Robert, ed., The World Almanac and Book of Facts, 1996, p. 395 (Table: "Aid to Families with Dependent Children, 1994") (Mahwah, NJ: Funk and Wagnalls, 1995).

resistance to redistribution of income via AFDC or General Assistance is directly related to the degree of inequality. A study of means-tested programs in the 50 states (Jacobs, 1980) concludes that the most politically significant inequality is the gap between low- and middle-income recipients, not the percentage of very rich. First, controlling for average state income, there is a strong negative association between the poverty rate (many very low-income families) and public assistance generosity (mean payments of AFDC 1962 and General Assistance payments per $100,000 in state personal income). Second, there is an equally strong negative association between that inequality resulting from differences between low- and middle-income families and public assistance generosity.[5] The greater the distance between the middle and the bottom, the more meager the public assistance benefits. This is consistent with my theme of a middle-mass revolt—the growing resistance to visibly redistributive policies for the poor among the upper-working class and lower-middle class in several countries (chap. 10, pp. 376ff.; and Wilensky, 1975, pp. 116–118).

A second stereotype devoid of truth is that welfare mothers have large families because welfare dependency stimulates fertility. In fact, AFDC families have 1.9 children; the national average is 1.8. Fertility rates of welfare mothers have fallen for several decades along with the fertility rates of other American women. Almost 9 in 10 of AFDC families have three or fewer children. (Handler, 1995, p. 106.) In other words, in size and trend welfare families are like nonwelfare families.

Does the level of welfare benefits or their rate of increase shape the size or fertility rate of welfare families? Careful studies of these relationships have failed to show any connection. Neither the level of a state's AFDC benefits nor its rate of change has any effect on fertility; and when real benefit levels were going up in the 1960s, fertility rates of welfare mothers were declining. (Jencks, 1992a, pp. 82–85; Bane and Ellwood, 1994, pp. 109–123; Handler, 1995, p. 106.)[6] There is even some evidence that AFDC mothers are less likely than non-AFDC mothers to have multiple pregnancies and more likely to use contraceptives (Williams, 1992, p. 740).

The third meritless myth: Welfare clients are racial minorities, trapped in ghettos; welfare pathologies are largely African-American pathologies. This myth validates the collective sentiment of whites that welfare poor are able-bodied but lazy blacks with large broods of illegitimate children, making a career of welfare at the expense of hardworking taxpayers.[7] In fact, less than 10% of welfare recipients live in ghettos—that is, areas of concentrated poverty in large cities (Bane and Ellwood, 1994, pp. 90, 118). And welfare families are racially heterogeneous: of all first-time AFDC recipients in 1994, 56% were white, 36% black, and 20% Hispanic, although minorities constitute a disproportionate proportion of the long-term welfare population and thus a larger percentage of recipients at any one moment. (1996 Green Book, table 8-48, p. 507. Note 10 below explains discrepancies between exit and entry data and cross-sectional data for one point in time.)

The final misconception is that the welfare population is homogeneous; they are able-bodied persons evading their responsibility to work and support their families like the rest of us. They will therefore respond to pressure to work via cuts in benefits and definite time limits. They need "tough love"—a phrase that resonated with the advocates of welfare reform bills passed by Congress in 1996. Congress members wanted to send a simple message: "Shape up. Get off your dead butt and get a job." Again the facts—especially about the social composition and history of exits and entries to welfare—belie the sentiments. First, the identity of AFDC recipients: Most welfare mothers have never married, less than a third are divorced or separated. Very few are teenagers. Almost half their children are younger than six; one-fourth are younger than three. At least half the mothers have not graduated from high school; fewer than 1 in 10 attended any postsecondary school. (1996 Green Book, tables 8-48 and 8-49, pp. 507 – 508; 1994 Green Book, pp. 401 – 402, table 10-27.) The typical long-term welfare mother has no high-school diploma, no significant job experience, and a very young child; she is single and receives no help from the absent father. These characteristics make her no more popular in the labor market than she is in the political market. Second, what do studies of entries to welfare and exits from welfare tell us about welfare recipients and their desire to work and support their families? Studies consistently show that welfare mothers typically move in and out of low-wage work, alternating it with welfare, and sometimes doing both. What needs to be explained is why so many entrants to welfare find work despite their great deficits in education, job experience, health, and self-confidence, and their need for child-care help. The answer seems to be that welfare mothers are typically struggling to make ends meet and take care of their children, and any kind of work, when they can get it, helps.

To understand patterns of work and welfare we must look to the structure of opportunity interacting with the limited personal resources of the poor. AFDC participation rates increase during periods of rising unemployment, as in the recession of the early 1990s; participation decreases in periods of declining unemployment when more welfare mothers can find some work, as in the Midwest in 1993 – 97 (Sandefur and Wells, 1996). Common jobs held by welfare mothers both before the welfare reform of 1996 and after, are maids, cashiers, nursing aides, child-care workers, and waitresses; whether part-time or full-time, these are low-wage jobs with few or no fringe benefits, high turnover, and few opportunities for advancement. Most welfare recipients work at official or unofficial jobs while on welfare and as a route off welfare (Harris, 1991, 1993). But nearly 60% of the women who work their way off welfare later return to welfare within a six-year observation period. The main reasons: They need to care for young children; and their deficits of education, experience, and social support prepare them only for low-paying, unstable jobs. These women earn an average hourly wage of under $6.50 (1988 dollars), which declines over two years of work and is the same after three years. Two-thirds are poor at the time of exit; more than half are still poor a year later. (Harris, 1996, pp. 413, 420.)

Even continuous work does not ensure that women remain off of welfare. Among the women who work continuously in every month following exit, nearly a third return to welfare even though they continue to work (Edin and Lein, 1997a).

The state of the labor market and the limited resources of the poor are half of the story of welfare exits and entries; the other half is family formation and breakup as they affect the poor. One analysis based on the 21-year Panel Study of Income Dynamics (Bane and Ellwood, 1994, pp. 53 – 60) shows that most entries to welfare (first spells only) are caused by family breakup (wife becomes female head) or family breakup followed by child birth (single, divorced, separated, widowed women who have a child), or never-married single women who have a child. And most exits from welfare are also unrelated to work: 29% became wives, 11% no longer had eligible children. "Only 25 percent of exits could be unambiguously traced to an earnings increase" (Bane and Ellwood, 1994, p. 56). Other studies based on different time frames or on monthly earnings data estimate that as many as

69% of exits were work-related (e.g., Harris's 1993 study of monthly data during the boom period of 1984–86). Bane and Ellwood (1994, p. 59) conclude that "If we had to pick a single number for the significance of work exits, we'd . . . pick one closer to the 40 percent who had moderate earnings in their first year off welfare than the 25 percent we find using our . . . classification system" allowing only one main reason per exit when an increase in earnings might occur the same time as a marriage. That still leaves a majority of exits that are nonwork.[8]

Exits from welfare that are unrelated to work include tougher eligibility rules (the periodic crackdowns endemic to the system), a move to another state, disability and a move to SSI or Social Security Disability, or, most important, marriage or cohabitation with someone who can help pay the rent. Studies uniformly suggest that marital status is related to entry to welfare, duration of welfare dependency, and exit from welfare, as well as to subsequent fate in the labor market. The marriage market is at the center of the problem. For instance, the percentage of all new entrants to welfare who were never married is 43, compared to 24 of the divorced, 23 of the separated, 7 of the married, and 4 of the widowed. The percentage of the new entrants who will have AFDC spells of 10 years or more is 32 for the never married, 22 for the separated, 13 for the divorced, 7 for the widowed, and 0.5 for the married. (Bane and Ellwood, 1994, table 2.5.) These figures tell us why black welfare mothers are much less likely to leave welfare to marry or remarry than white welfare mothers: the ratio of available and acceptable (e.g., employed, healthy) black men to poor black women is bleak—one factor in the overrepresentation of African-American women in the welfare population (*ibid.*, p. 60).

The importance of both work and the structure of the family as they interact is confirmed by studies of neighborhood effects on welfare dependency. For instance, in a multivariate study of female single-parent families in 17 Boston neighborhoods in 1988–89 (before the recession), Paul Osterman (1991) found only two robust predictors of neighborhood welfare use: the percentage of households with a working head and family structure (percentage of solo mothers, intact families, extended families). A neighborhood where few family heads work reduces job contacts, motivation, and opportunities for everyone; the isolation of solo mothers and their children from working heads as models and sources of job networks exacerbates the human capital deficits that bring these mothers to welfare in the first place.[9]

In sum, welfare recipients are heterogeneous in ways that count: They vary in marital status and prospects, in health, in race and ethnicity, in the number and ages of their children, in the ways they enter and exit from welfare, and in their job experience, literacy, and education (although the central tendency is toward heavy deficits in human capital). Considering that welfare can intimidate, isolate, and stigmatize and leave women feeling powerless and passive, it is remarkable how many welfare mothers attempt to obtain work and become self-reliant. Those who do not, generally cannot. When exits do occur they are almost entirely linked to characteristics that shape earnings capacity—education, job experience, and marriage. It is thus understandable that no policy shifts the United States has adopted, including workfare requirements that are the core of recent welfare reforms, have had a major effect on moving recipients to stable work, reducing child poverty, or, for those few states committed to these outcomes, cutting welfare spending (this evidence is summarized later). Welfare mothers are those among the poor who have the greatest deficits in education, job experience, physical and mental health, and self-confidence, as well as the poorest marriage chances. The labor market and wage structure of the United States are not hospitable to the least skilled whether they are the welfare poor or not. Even if the United States created an abundance of jobs for welfare mothers, the idea that they can become stably employed, self-supporting workers in low-wage jobs without added income, education, training, counseling, placement, child care, and other services is silly. The funding for all this, needless to say, does not typically accompany the crackdowns.

We can now turn to some welfare myths that contain a kernel of truth but are grossly misleading, though they serve as comfortable rationalization for cutting benefits, shifting money to more popular projects such as prisons and police, and calling it "tough love." They include: Welfare discourages work; welfare becomes permanent dependency, which is inherited by the children of welfare mothers; welfare subverts the family and family values, breeding divorce and illegitimacy; cracking down on deadbeat dads would clean up much of the welfare mess; and exploding welfare costs were breaking state and federal budgets.

1. *Myth: Welfare discourages work. Facts:* Neither in behavior nor in attitudes are welfare clients antiwork. But welfare programs combined with the wage structure of the U.S. do contain disincentives to work, which have a small effect in reducing hours of working. We have already seen that although women who end up on welfare are those among the poor with the fewest marketable skills who have never had jobs or had only part-time or minimum wage jobs, they nevertheless alternate work with welfare. Why do not more of them move out of welfare permanently? Human capital deficits aside, disincentives abound. Since 1967, when Congress decided to encourage work rather than keep welfare mothers home to care for their children, there have been efforts to provide financial incentives to work while reducing welfare costs. The famous "thirty-plus-a-third" rule allowed the AFDC recipient to keep the first $30 of monthly earnings plus one third of remaining earnings. It also allowed the deduction of work-related expenses including child care. After these deductions the benefit-reductions rate was still a high 67%. (Smolensky, Evenhouse, and Reilly, 1992, pp. 21–22.) This rule lasted until 1981 when President Reagan, noting that it made more families eligible for welfare, went back to the 100% reduction rate and capped the deduction for work expenses. Now, when a welfare mother works her way off AFDC, after one year full-time on the job her earnings will be below the poverty line (1996 Green Book, p. 450). Further, when she leaves AFDC because she has reached the cutoff earnings level (see table 8.2), she loses Medicaid—medical coverage for her family—and often loses child-care subsidies and other supports for working parents as well. A frequent response to this bizarre system among those able to find and hold a part-time or even full-time job is to try to combine welfare and work while hiding some earnings, a combination that may push their income slightly above the poverty line without losing Medicaid and food stamps.

Many students of the welfare mess, pondering the inadequacy of benefits, the disincentives to work, the administrative harassment of welfare mothers, and their deficits in experience and education, ask the question, "How on earth do they make ends meet on welfare benefits?" The answer is, "They don't." Suggestive insights come from an intensive study of 25 welfare families in a midwestern city in 1988 (Jencks and Edin, 1990, pp. 32–44). These families presumably lived on combined welfare and food-stamp benefits that were well below the basic costs of food and rent. In fact, "Not one of these welfare mothers was able to live on her welfare check. All 25 supplemented their checks with income from other sources. None reported all her extra income to the welfare department" (p. 32). Since food stamps and AFDC supplied an average of only 57% of their income, all of which went to survival, how did they pay their bills?

> Roughly half the rest came from work of various kinds. The remainder came from absent fathers, boyfriends, relatives, and student loans. The work these mothers did was extraordinarily diverse. Three held regular jobs under another name, earning an average of $5 an hour. Twelve worked part time at off-the-books jobs such as bartending, catering, baby-sitting, and sewing that paid an average of $3 an hour.
> The only well-paid work open to these women was prostitution, which paid something like $40 an hour. Four . . . supplemented their welfare checks this way. Four others sold drugs, but three of the four sold marijuana and earned only $3 to $5 an hour. They could presumably have earned more if they had sold crack on the street, but they sold only to acquaintances, which was much less risky. The fourth drug seller sold crack as well as marijuana and earned something like $10 an hour, but she was murdered soon after Edin interviewed her, apparently because she had not repaid her supplier. (pp. 33–34)

Even with their unofficial income these welfare mothers lived close to the bone with no or few amenities; less than 5% of their total expenditures went to little luxuries such as cigarettes, alcohol, eating out at McDonald's, or entertainment—renting an occasional videotape. Half lived in dirty, rundown, dangerous neighborhoods; the other half—whites, Hispanics, and some blacks—made enough income to pay $100 to $150 a month more in rent and escape to an average, somewhat safer neighborhood. Very similar findings come from multiple and intensive interviews with 379 AFDC recipients and low-wage working mothers in Boston, Chicago, Charleston, and San Antonio (Edin and Lein, 1997b). This study showed an average monthly deficit between welfare income and household expenses of $311. Among the welfare-dependent there was the usual struggle to make it up by work, most of it unreported, and extra income from networks made up of family, friends, boyfriends, or absent husbands. Both supplemental work and the cash from social networks are highly unstable; they fluctuate not only with the tolerance of relatives for taking in welfare families but with the state of the low-wage economy. Compared to the welfare mothers, the working mother had far more cash network support as well as noncash resources that lowered the cost of working (e.g., better child-care arrangements, health coverage, transportation).

Other detailed case studies picture an even more dreary life on welfare among mothers who live in areas of more limited job opportunity and who attempt to survive on the meager welfare benefits pictured in the bottom of table 8.2. Instead of working they spent their time and energy taking advantage of food pantries, school and camp feeding programs, lying to the soup kitchens about whether they received food stamps, asking their children to smuggle food home from the day camp lunch program (Edin and Lein,

1997a, chaps. 2 and 6). Low-level malnutrition was widespread among these families. (*Ibid.*, pp. 48–50.)

In attitudes, the welfare poor are almost as hostile to the welfare system as the rest of the population and are equally dedicated to the work ethic. For instance, in surveys large majorities agree with the idea that there are too many welfare cheats who should be working (Wilensky, 1975, p. 34), and in intensive interviews they feel the stigma of welfare, recognize the boost in self-esteem and status they gain from working, and express a strong desire to escape from welfare (Edin and Lein, 1997b, pp. 263–264). But when welfare mothers violate the rules of the system by not reporting earnings, they see themselves as adhering to a higher morality—supporting their children. They believe that when they work they ought to be better off; they reject rules that make them worse off. In this they are close to the core values of American society. Many welfare workers, the eligibility checkers themselves, share the same sentiments: A system that punishes hard work to provide for one's family is illegitimate. They often turn a blind eye to the unofficial economy of welfare mothers. The new welfare reform bill of 1996 will make it more difficult for eligibility checkers to ignore unofficial income, which will result in a declining income for those who have combined the two in the past.

In short, few welfare mothers have an aversion to work to support their children; most have multiple handicaps that prevent them from obtaining stable employment. That the system contains disincentives to work does not prevent most who can from doing it, officially or unofficially. Thus, studies of the impact of policy shifts such as benefit reduction formulas on hours of work of the welfare population conclude that the labor-supply effects are minimal (Smolensky, Evenhouse, and Reilly, 1992, p. 22; Harris, 1996, p. 419). If these studies were able to tap the unofficial economy they would show that policy changes have even less impact.

2. *Myth: Welfare is a drug; it becomes a way of life, a permanent lifestyle for welfare recipients, which is inherited by the children of welfare mothers in a never-ending cycle of dependency.* *Facts:* As we have seen, the typical welfare pattern is repeated spells of welfare, alternating with or concurrent with work. Monthly data on welfare departures show that half of welfare recipients exit within one year of their entry to welfare and three in four leave within two years. But if we look at multiple spells, the time lengthens, although we still do not uncover a majority making welfare a way of life: 30% are on welfare less than two years, 50% less than four years. Less than 15% stay on welfare continuously for five years. (Greenberg, 1992, p. 33; Handler, 1995, p. 49; Gottschalk, McLanahan, and Sandefur, 1994, p. 94.) However, all studies of exits and entries into welfare note a paradox: even though the typical user is a short-timer, at any one moment the longer-term recipients predominate; in fact, about two in three are in the midst of what in the long term will be a long period of welfare receipt. The short-termers enter and exit while the long-termers accumulate in the statistics. Considering the whole welfare population over time, those on welfare for 10 or more years are a small proportion; considering those on welfare at any one moment, they are numerous—up to a third.[10] (Bane and Ellwood, 1994, pp. 28, 37, 51; Handler, 1995, pp. 49–50.) As we might expect, the typical long-termer is a single mother who enters when she is young, has never married, is without a

high-school diploma and without significant job experience, and has a very young child—all good predictors of lengthy stays. (Bane and Ellwood, 1994, pp. 52–53; cf. Boisjoly, Harris, and Duncan, 1998, pp. 481, 486–489.)[11]

Regarding the *intergenerational transmission of welfare dependency,* the kernel of truth in this myth is the modest to strong correlation between the family of origin's welfare use and children's use. A typical study (Duncan, Hill, and Hoffman, 1988) shows that about 20% of girls who receive welfare continuously for three years ("heavy use") during their adolescence (13–15 years old) were themselves heavy users when they were 21–23 years old. One in five is much greater than the percentage of daughters from nonwelfare families who became highly dependent on welfare (Handler, 1995, p. 51; Gottschalk, 1992). When one controls for differences in the income and family structure of these individuals the correlation decreases but remains positive.

Little can be inferred from these studies. For daughters and welfare mothers share many characteristics that increase the probability that they will receive public assistance. What is passed on—that is, learned from parents, teachers, and peers—are the multiple deficits of poverty, not welfare status. After all, poverty is a condition of welfare receipt. For the entire society there is strong evidence of substantial persistence of occupational status and family income across generations. More than half a century of social stratification research has shown that father's occupation, family income, parents' education, whether parents remain married, and number of siblings all shape the educational achievement and occupational fate of children. (For summaries especially relevant to the understanding of poverty and welfare, see Gottschalk, McLanahan, and Sandefur, 1994; and Duncan et al., 1998.) The "inheritance" of socioeconomic status is most frequent at the extremes of rich and poor, where welfare recipients live. The well-established causal order is that parental background, especially parents' education, strongly predicts the educational level of their children which, in turn, predicts the occupational status and lifetime income of their children. Thus, "if both the mother and the daughter grow up in neighborhoods with poor-quality schools, both will be more likely to have lower earnings and, hence, a greater need for income assistance. In this case, taking the mother off of welfare will not lower the probability that the daughter will receive assistance. Changing the quality of the school the daughter attends, however, will raise her income and, in turn, lower the probability that she receives public assistance" (*ibid.*, p. 107).

The correlation between mothers on welfare and daughters subsequently on welfare may not be entirely spurious. But the message of research so far is that the intergenerational transmission of poverty is well established; the intergenerational transmission of welfare status is dubious (cf. Bane and Ellwood, 1994, pp. 92–94).

3. *Myth: Welfare subverts the family and family values—it breeds dependency, divorce, and illegitimacy.* Charles Murray (*Losing Ground,* 1984) made himself famous by claiming that there was one central problem and one simple solution: welfare made the poor worse off by making it profitable to have illegitimate babies and the obvious solution is to wipe out welfare. (With neoconservative foundation support, this well-written book was widely publicized and freely distributed—among others to members of Congress. That its elaborate statistics, charts, and footnotes are pseudoscientific has been established in careful assessments by Jencks, 1992a, pp. 70–91; Danziger and Gottschalk, 1985,

pp. 32 – 38, and S. M. Miller, 1985, pp. 684 – 687, among others.) The kernel of truth in this myth is that welfare does affect family arrangements. But not by inspiring divorce or illegitimate births. *Facts:* If there is any link at all between size of welfare benefits or receipt of any welfare benefits and divorce, separation, or illegitimacy, it is very weak. First, trend data contradict the idea. While real welfare benefits were declining dramatically—and there is no doubt that the disposable income available to welfare mothers was also declining from 1972 to 1997—the family breakup rates of welfare mothers were climbing. If it is lavish welfare checks that encourage easy divorce, the trend would be the reverse. Similarly while the value of welfare benefits went down, single motherhood, a major cause of entry to welfare, climbed. It is not generous welfare that caused single motherhood but the feminization of poverty combined with the long-term climb in societywide family breakup rates (see chaps. 1, 7, 13, and 14). Welfare mothers mirror the behavior of nonwelfare mothers. We have already seen that welfare mothers and nonwelfare mothers are alike in their fertility pattern. They are also alike in the long-term trend toward unmarried motherhood: From 1964 to 1987 fewer teenagers were having babies, both among blacks and whites (Smolensky, Evenhouse, and Reilly, 1992, p. 25). Since the 1940s, however, out-of-wedlock birth rates for the whole population moved up slowly and steadily. They accelerated sharply in the mid-1980s as welfare support diminished and leveled off in the early 1990s. The rates for all unmarried women and for unmarried adolescents track one another closely. (1996 Green Book, pp. 513 – 514.)[12] Unmarried adolescents, however, are overrepresented among welfare clients: 44% of AFDC mothers were adolescents at the time their first child was born compared with 17% of non-AFDC mothers (*ibid.*, p. 516). Again, as we have seen from entry/exit data, family composition and timing of first unmarried birth are good predictors of welfare dependency; they are not caused by the size of welfare checks.

Second, comparisons of states most and least generous in welfare benefits show that states with high benefits have less illegitimacy than states with low benefits, controlling for all the obvious differences that might explain this outcome—race, religion, region, education, income, urbanization, state political record, and the like (Jencks, 1992a, p. 82; Ellwood and Bane, 1985, p. 138, 179, 186 – 188). Neither is there the predicted relationship between increases in state welfare benefits and a rise in illegitimacy; the two are unrelated. (*Ibid.*, pp. 140 – 142.)[13]

Finally, the purest test of the proposition that generous welfare benefits for single mothers are the root of big families among the poor, illegitimacy, teenage pregnancy, and similar self-destructive behavior is the cross-national comparisons of these rates. Strong evidence shows that in modern industrial nations generous child allowances and other pronatalist policies (e.g., France, Italy) had no effect on fertility rates, which went down sharply as allowances went up and generous premiums for third and fourth children were paid.[14] Below we shall see that compared with the social policies of lean-spending democracies the lavish social spending of the corporatist welfare-state leaders, especially state-subsidized child care, is related to *lower* rates of teenage pregnancy, and is unrelated to abortion rates.

It is possible that some American welfare mothers under some circumstances are responding to bad incentives in the system, but both research and common sense suggest that in the usual case a momentous decision to have a child is unlikely to be heavily influenced by a welfare check. Major cuts or increases in welfare benefits do have some effect on living arrangements and maybe even a little effect on decisions to separate from a mate. Christopher Jencks captures the realities as he notes that in the early 1990s several million single mothers not on welfare got by on low-wage jobs that pay less than $15,000 a year.

> Why can't we just insist that welfare mothers do the same thing? The answer is that single mothers with low-wage jobs currently survive by making arrangements that not all mothers are willing or able to make. One lives with her mother. Another has a boyfriend who beats her up but whom she does not throw out because he also helps pay the rent. A third sometimes works as a prostitute at the hotel where she cleans. A fourth leaves her children home alone after school because she cannot afford paid child care. But we cannot create a system that assumes all single mothers will make such arrangements. If we try, a lot more single mothers will be unable to make ends meet, and we will end up with more families in shelters and more abandoned children in foster care.
>
> Yet as soon as we construct a system that allows a woman with a minimum-wage job to pay her bills without depending on anyone else, a lot more women will choose to exercise this option. The woman who now lives with her mother will move out, and the woman whose boyfriend beats her up will kick him out. The prostitute will turn fewer tricks, and the woman who works until five will get paid child care. Single mothers' lives will be a lot better, but there will probably be more of them, and taxes will certainly have to be slightly higher. (Jencks, 1992b, p. 39)

4. *Myth: Cracking down on deadbeat dads would solve much of the welfare mess.* If only absent fathers were located and made to pay child support, the poverty of lone mothers would greatly diminish. *Facts:* Everyone is for this, but past experience is discouraging. Such enforcement has had little effect in the past and there is no reason to suppose that stiffer enforcement would make much difference. The main reason: U.S. poverty rates are high and real wage rates have deteriorated since the mid-1970s, especially at the bottom (chaps. 5 and 12 and table 14.4). Thus, the earnings potential of these absent fathers, who, like their welfare partners, are only intermittently working, is fairly low. (Waldfogel, 1996, p. 10.) Many have started new families they are trying to support. A rising number are in jail or are drug addicted or in poor health or are homeless. Because of these realities, even perfect enforcement would make only a small dent in the poverty of welfare mothers. Despite more than 20 years of intensifying legislation aimed at "deadbeat dads," despite an increase in the number identified and ordered to pay, child support collections on average have shown little improvement (Garfinkel et al., 1998, pp. 3, 10). Some countries achieve a better payup rate from absent fathers than does the United States (chap. 5) not mainly because of better enforcement but because of more egalitarian wage structures, family policies that prevent the feminization of poverty, and, more generally, vigorous poverty-reduction policies; more of their absent fathers are in a position to pay, and more of their solo mothers are self-supporting.

5. *Myth: Welfare is a major cause of budget deficits. Facts:* As either a percentage of state and federal budgets or as a share of GNP, AFDC spending was always very small and is still

smaller after the 1996 welfare reforms, even if we add the cost of food stamps and 35 other programs more or less targeted to the poor. Combined state and federal spending on AFDC in 1990 was not quite equal to four-tenths of 1% of GNP (Smolensky, Evenhouse, and Reilly, 1992, p. 28). As Smolenksy et al. point out, "A conservative estimate of the cost of the Savings and Loan bailout ($300 billion, say) is the equivalent of 15 years of the entire AFDC program at 1990 benefit levels" (*ibid.*), which have since declined. State budgets yield the same picture. Consider California. It accounts for one in five of the nation's total welfare population, is one of the most generous states, had until 1997 a big deficit, and historically generates more political heat about welfare mothers than any other state. AFDC was only 5% of its total budget FY 1991–92 (it was 1.7% of the federal budget). Or if we go beyond welfare mothers and broaden the coverage to federal and state spending in fiscal year 1994 on the 37 programs comprising income- or means-tested cash to the poor and near-poor (and sometimes nonpoor), the total comes to only 2.1% of GDP and 10% of the federal budget (calculated from 1996 Greenbook, pp. 1322–1324).

If we are looking for a budget buster among the means-tested benefits for the poor, it would be Medicaid. In FY 1994 its costs were over five times what AFDC (now TANF) costs. Since 1968 most of the increase in social spending that is at all means tested or income tested is accounted for by Medicaid. By 1994 Medicaid and a few much smaller medical aid programs took more of the combined federal and state budgets than the total expenditure on all cash, food, and housing assistance—the 37 programs just mentioned—took together (calculated from *ibid.*, pp. 1322–1324).

In fact, we could eliminate the entire welfare system other than Medicaid and not make a significant dent on national and state budgets. These comparisons are a comment on the perverse politics of means-tested programs for the poor. Despite their limited cost, they frequently become the center of attention in budget battles and congressional elections.

In view of the complexities outlined above, it is no wonder that congressional debates and media coverage of welfare issues are dominated by myths and misconceptions. Listening to academic research or policy dialogue based on the facts, legislators' eyes glaze over. In action, they fall back on their favorite myths.

DOES WORKFARE WORK?

At a fund-raiser in St. Louis August 12, 1997, exhorting employers to hire welfare recipients, President Clinton boasted that 1.4 million people had left the public assistance rolls since he signed the welfare law in August 1996 and since he took office four years ago, the rolls had declined by 3.4 million or 24%, "the biggest decline in history." Eleven states saw caseloads drop by 40% or more in that four-year period. "The debate is over," the president said. "We know now that welfare reform works." (*New York Times,* August 13, 1997.) In this he echoed President Reagan's claim that his introduction of workfare in California in the 1960s cut the rolls and saved taxpayers money.

Because workfare—the core of 1996 welfare reform—has a long history and in one form or another has been evaluated systematically since the late 1970s (e.g., Friedlander and Gueron, 1992, table 4.1), it is possible to summarize what has become a consensus of the experts. By the single criterion mentioned by President Clinton, cutting the rolls, work-fare with strong sanctions—certain time limits for all welfare benefits if work is not ob-tained—can be effective. For instance, if you are solely concerned with removing people from the rolls under a deadline you will have considerable success with a week or two of "charm school"—quick exposure to want ads for job openings, instruction in the impor-tance of showing up on time, grooming for job interviews, and the like—followed by sanc-tions if any job at all is refused. A credible threat to cut off welfare will also encourage a substantial percentage of welfare recipients who already work off the books to disappear from the rolls. If at the same time you are blessed with an economy that is booming (1993–99), you will show a fine cost/benefit ratio for such tough workfare rules—so long as you do not follow the people who have moved from welfare to work too long or worry about how much they earn. But if your aim is to prepare the typical welfare family—a mother with young children, little education, little job experience, and all of the handicaps we have discussed in this chapter—for stable employment in the real world of work and not merely perpetuate the long-standing pattern of alternating or simultaneous low-wage temporary work and welfare, you will have to get serious about expensive education and training, placement, wage subsidies, job creation, counseling, child care, housing, trans-portation, rehabilitation of those on drugs or alcohol or who are mentally ill, and more.[15]

Almost all welfare-to-work programs in the past 20 or so years have had conflicting goals. It is misleading to declare victory when the welfare rolls have declined. Consider these obvious conflicts: You can reduce the number of families on welfare at the same time that you increase total welfare costs if the reduction is achieved by providing the necessary apparatus of support. You can reduce both the costs and the rolls by further impoverishing poor children and their parents while you increase the long-run costs of foster care, home-lessness, malnutrition, family violence, crime, the criminal-justice system, and prisons (see chap. 14 for evidence of these connections). You can force some women who have com-petitive advantages to take minimum-wage jobs without the necessary support and thereby increase child neglect. In short, the goals of reducing the rolls and cost cutting, now dom-inant in "welfare reform," conflict with the goals of reducing child poverty, moving wel-fare recipients into stable jobs with above-poverty earnings and prospects for advancement, and improving the economic base for stable family life and even marriage.

Research Findings on Workfare[16]

Some of the most-sophisticated evaluation research ever done has been focused on these programs. Using a variety of methods and research designs, mostly social experiments where a group exposed to a particular workfare program is compared with a randomly selected control group, an army of researchers has descended upon these welfare clients to assess outcomes. (See especially the reports, summaries, and critical assessments by the Manpower Demonstration Research Corporation [MDRC] and academic researchers: Gueron and Pauly, 1991; Miller et al., 1997; Friedlander and Gueron, 1992; Gueron, 1995; Riccio, Fried-lander, and Freedman, 1994; Greenberg and Wiseman, 1992a, 1992b; Nightingale and Haveman, 1995; Burghardt et al., 1992; Handler and Hasenfeld, 1991, chap. 5; Friedlander and Burtless, 1995; Harris, 1996; and Besharov, Germanis, and Rossi, 1997.)

Here is a brief summary of findings almost all researchers agree on:

1.   In implementing work-focused mandates, states show substantial variation in their degree and kind of success.

2.   If researchers compare welfare recipients who are subjected to (varied) welfare-to-work mandates with control groups who are not and measure the respective earnings gains over anywhere from a few months to five years, the workfare programs on average do show modest relative earnings gains for the workfare participants.

3.   Obviously, different program packages have different outcomes. Especially effective in decreasing welfare spending are short-term JOBS approaches. Job clubs, a week or two of charm school (how to dress, how to show deference and enthusiasm in an interview, etc.), a little help in job search—this approach can move many people into jobs quickly (on average it raises the percentage of people who find a job by a modest five percentage points); it can also save taxpayers money. But such quick solutions do not improve job quality, job stability, or succeed with the more disadvantaged. In varying amounts, some workfare programs add more-expensive skills training, basic education, counseling, job creation, and other work supports. These appear to produce better jobs for some people and probably make a greater long-term difference in earnings. A hint of this comes from a seven-county Minnesota experiment that combines work requirements with a variety of financial incentives. The Minnesota Family Investment Program (MFIP) officially permits welfare recipients to combine welfare and work. The MDRC observed welfare recipients in the programs and a control group operating under existing welfare rules for 18 months starting April 1, 1994 (Miller et al., 1997). The most favorable outcome appeared in three urban counties that provided very generous incentives and had unemployment rates as low as 3%. In these booming urban areas and in this generous state, some 52% of "long-term" cases (those who had received benefits for at least two of the previous three years) had jobs, and nearly 30% had incomes above the poverty line (*ibid.*, tables 4.3 and 4.4). The reason was that under the old system a welfare mother who got a job lost her welfare support when her paid earnings reached 85% of the poverty line, but under this new experiment support was not phased out until earnings reached $1,555 a month or 140% of the poverty level (p. 3).[17] The program also provides job counseling, training, and case workers; it continues food stamps, Medicaid, child care, and transportation subsidies (*ibid.*, p. 3 and table 1.1). These incentives and services of course increased the state's welfare costs. Minnesota-style workfare in other experimental groups exposed to weaker financial incentives and no requirement to participate in employment and training programs had little effect on jobs, earnings, or poverty (table 4.3, p. 94, table 4.6, p. 102). The weakest results were for rural areas and among single parents newly applying for welfare in urban counties, although, again, welfare costs for these populations also went up sharply (pp. 104–128). For taxpayers there is no free lunch.

4.   Mandatory work-for-benefits programs—the narrowest definition of workfare—do not save money, according to studies done in the 1980s. The reason is that they have been driven by cost-cutting fervor and could be applied only on a small scale. States have had trouble developing large numbers of work sites for "community service" let

alone private sector jobs for welfare mothers, and have, as always, rediscovered that large numbers of welfare recipients are unable to work. Without skill development and with few moves into unsubsidized employment, welfare rolls and spending did not drop.

As Gueron (1995, p. 5) suggests, enforcing participation in any kind of welfare-to-work program "requires an up-front investment in staff (to connect people to services, monitor their participation, review reasons for nonparticipation, and cut grants if people do not play by the rules); in providing activities (job clubs, training, work slots, etc.) that are sufficiently plentiful to give teeth to the mandate; and in childcare, transportation, and other support services so that AFDC mothers can participate."

5. Broader mandatory workfare programs with greater attention to job development have in many states decreased welfare caseloads, a short-run gain to taxpayers.

6. However, moving welfare recipients to jobs has rarely reduced their family poverty and in many cases has increased it. The Minnesota experiment is an exception but has been evaluated only for an 18-month period. Perhaps the best recent testimony to the limited effect of even the best-financed workfare programs is Milwaukee's New Hope experiment, which ran from August 1994 to May 1997. It aimed to move both welfare clients and working poor into more work and out of poverty. The MDRC evaluated the results, comparing 459 enrollees to 476 members of a control group. The context and program content could not have been more favorable: a very strong economy, volunteer clients who had more work experience and stronger motivation than the average welfare recipient, and generous benefits, including guaranteed jobs at a subsidized wage, health care, and child care. Yet 73% of the target group (vs. 81% of the control group) failed to work their way out of poverty without additional support from welfare checks or a second earner. In the second year the average participant worked 27.2 hours per week (vs. the control group's 24.8 hours). The evaluation uncovered a catalog of inner-city troubles that might explain these results: drug and alcohol abuse, violent or jealous husbands or boyfriends, conflicts with employers, unreliable cars, baby-sitter problems, low morale. Compared to the control group, the New Hope group after two years showed no decline in depression, no growth in self-esteem.

7. The net gain to both public and individuals on welfare is in doubt. At the extreme—the most-publicized Riverside County, California, GAIN program—there was a 49% increase in single-parent earnings and a 15% decline in welfare outlays. Over five years that returns about $3 for every $1 spent on the program. The average for two-parent households and for other California counties studied was about half that level. Riverside, says Judith Gueron, president of the dominant evaluation research corporation (MDRC), "was distinguished by its pervasive emphasis on getting a job quickly, its strong reliance on job clubs but substantial use of basic education, its tough enforcement of a participation requirement, its close links to the private sector, and its cost-conscious and outcome-focused management style" (1995, p. 1).

If we widen the analysis slightly to include more individual and social costs and gains, however, the success appears to be much more modest. For instance, consider this cost/benefit formula: for the welfare client, net gains from employment minus the loss in transfer payments; for the public, the value of work output of the workfare participant plus tax-transfer gains minus service-program costs. By that formula, Greenberg and

Wiseman (1992b, table 13) found that of 19 reported sets of cost-benefit estimates for both AFDC-R and AFDC-U in seven cities or states, 17 imply net gains for nonparticipants (e.g., taxpayers), but 9 show that workfare participants suffered net losses because employment gains, if any, were not enough to offset cuts in welfare and related benefits. In short, the net gains are generally very small and very often negative. A common pattern is budgetary savings at the expense of continued or worsening poverty of welfare mothers and their children.

8. As we have seen, the population targeted by welfare-to-work programs has many unfavorable characteristics for steady long-term employment. Nationally and for the past 20 or so years of study, most who get jobs do not keep them. Four major sources of this instability are these: (1) The job pays close to the minimum wage—and the former or current welfare recipient can't support a family on it; (2) jobs are dead-end because welfare recipients lack education, basic literacy and numeracy, and skill necessary for moving up;[18] (3) there are well-known disincentives built into the system—the welfare recipients typically lose Medicaid and related benefits when they leave welfare and their low-wage, high-turnover jobs seldom provide any or adequate benefits; and (4) labor markets turn down in an industry, area, or national slump. Workfare programs do almost nothing about (1), (2), and (4), and the resources are seldom available to do much about (3)— anything beyond limited assistance for child care and health care for a transition period only. Even in the most successful workfare program, Riverside, California, only 31% of those placed in jobs were working at the end of the third year (Riccio, Friedlander, and Freedman, 1994, table 4.1). And three years after enrolling in Riverside GAIN, 41% of participants were still receiving welfare benefits (Gueron, 1995, p. 8). Researchers agree that a substantial portion of the welfare populations are simply unemployable without very expensive, long-term help, if then.

If we examine the characteristics of the minority who exit from welfare, stay off welfare, and hold stable jobs for as long as a few years, we can see why it is so hard to break the revolving door pattern of welfare dependency. In these successful cases, the best evidence shows an interaction of education, marriage opportunity and stability, and stability of employment (Harris, 1996; Wilson, 1996). Even a modest amount of education improves the welfare mother's chances of securing stable work. Both education and work increase her chances of marrying or cohabiting with a partner who works. Education and partnering to a stable worker, in turn, improve the mother's chances to stay off welfare, gain additional education, and maintain employment. They also improve a family's chances of escaping poverty. Her working partner helps to overcome isolation; provides some mutual help in transportation, child care, household chores, and shopping; and widens her social contacts and job information network, thereby reinforcing stability of employment. The combined income under these unfortunately rare circumstances often moves the family above the poverty line. Such transitions from welfare to relatively stable work are rare because only a small minority of welfare recipients combine the necessary education, job opportunity, and the opportunity to marry a working partner (Harris, 1996, pp. 420–423).[19]

9. The final conclusion from the workfare evaluations is that staffing is weak for the purpose of training, job development, placement, and work support. (America's lack of an active labor-market policy is at the root of this problem. See Wilensky, 1992a.) Eligi-

bility checkers who devote themselves to rooting out fraud and abuse and avoiding errors in their paperwork for hundreds of cases are not trained to help people into jobs and often know nothing about labor markets. To rely on such overloaded staff for indepth job development and job counseling is foolish. They have neither the time nor the knowledge to facilitate transfers from welfare to work (the point is elaborated in the next section on means testing in cross-national perspective).

Among the limitations of these evaluation studies, three are most important: a limited time perspective; fairly narrow criteria of success; and the difficulty of generalizing the modestly favorable results to areas and times of weak job opportunity and weak networks of services. Few of the studies followed participants for more than three years, fewer still for as much as five years, which means that the long-run effects of more expensive investments in human capital cannot be uncovered. And the typical study defines success as sufficient increases in recipients' earnings to achieve a net reduction in welfare costs, thereby ignoring everything we have shown in this chapter about the history of exits and entries to welfare, the job instability and limited earning power of those who exit, the continuing poverty of vast majorities of both those who exit and those who stay, and the prominence of changes in marriage and family structure in both exits and entries. Finally, the authors of these studies themselves warn that there is no assurance that "Riverside's approach—including its focus on more rapid employment and job development—would work in other types of localities, particularly in inner-city areas such as those found in Los Angeles and Alameda, or whether they would succeed in more rural . . . areas with persistently high unemployment such as those found in Tulare" (Riccio, Friedlander and Freedman, 1994, p. 34). Yet, despite the limited impact of welfare-to-work programs, and the admirably cautious claims of the most-optimistic evaluators, Congress passed a welfare reform law that ignored most of what is known about workfare, poverty, and the welfare mess. Insofar as any theory underpinned this 1996 law, it was "work, not job training or education," essentially the notion that time-limited workfare could be implemented on the cheap. This idea not only rested on the myths that the welfare population was homogeneous and that cutting welfare rolls would help balance the budget; it was also based on a misinterpretation of the cost-benefit studies of workfare programs already in place—studies that raise numerous warning flags.

Barriers to Success: Policy Segmentation, Uncoordinated Programs, and Decentralized Federalism

One reason for the limited success of workfare and the repeated failures of welfare reform is the fragmentation and policy segmentation of the American system and the concomitant failure to connect what are clearly interdependent social problems. This is evident in the division of labor in Congress, in the cobweb of overlapping, competing, and uncoordinated programs comprising the welfare mess, and in the problems posed by a radically decentralized federalism. As R. Shep Melnick (1994, pp. 265–267) suggests in his comparison of AFDC, aid to education for the handicapped, especially children, and food stamps, the committee of jurisdiction is an important influence on legislative outcomes and program implementation. The Senate Labor and Public Welfare Committee and the House Education and Labor Committee are the authorizing committees for education for handicapped children. They are long known as liberal, policy oriented, and entrepreneurial. Both have been bipartisan in spirit and aggressive in support for education in general and assistance for the handicapped in particular (*ibid.*, pp. 150–151). The outcome was a liberal law, the Education for All Handicapped Children Act of 1975. It recognized and expanded the right to a "free appropriate public education." The outcome over the next decades was an equally benign administration—typically generous treatment of the disabled, including poor handicapped children. (Chap. 15 analyzes the broader topic of disability insurance cross-nationally, where the same pattern of generosity appears far more developed than it is in the United States and specifies the challenges this has posed for all countries.)

The authorizing committees for food stamps are the House and Senate Agriculture Committees. These are classic constituency committees that work closely with the U.S. Department of Agriculture; they have strong chairmen, weak subcommittees, and are accustomed to compromises and accommodation (Melnick, 1994, pp. 193–196). The result was a neat trade-off: Southern conservatives in both Houses and senators from rural states exchanged their support for food stamps for urban liberals' support for commodity price supports and farm subsidies. Especially since the mid-1960s farm representatives on those committees have depended on the food stamp advocates' votes to prevent the gutting of commodity bills. The result: The food stamp program is less harsh in its coverage and eligibility than AFDC (now TANF); the federal government foots the entire bill and imposes uniform standards and benefit levels. In contrast are the committees responsible for AFDC. Because this core welfare program was included in the Social Security Act of 1935, it fell within the jurisdiction of the House Ways and Means Committee and the Senate Finance Committee. These revenue committees, especially in the Senate, were typically conservative; they seldom attracted members committed to expanding welfare programs or antipoverty measures (*ibid.*, pp. 119–120). With a surfeit of members from southern and mountain states, they fought to force an AFDC focus on the old standby, "fraud and abuse." They emphasized short-run savings to taxpayers with little attention to the services that might promote jobs and self-sufficiency among welfare recipients.

Committee jurisdiction is not the only explanation for these outcomes. Because of the mass resentment of welfare mothers, these lawmakers in the revenue committees could accomplish their conservative aims more easily than their counterparts in food stamps and education for disabled children. Nevertheless we must count the committee structure of Congress as an added factor in the relative stiffness of means-tested programs.

The patchwork of policies and programs that focus on child poverty, each specializing in one aspect of the problem, illustrates the barriers to comprehensive planning or even mild efforts at coordination. At every level in the system we encounter separate agencies (sometimes multiple) to address public health, mental health, health care, developmental disabilities, school preparedness, child abuse and neglect, nutrition—not to mention various aspects of the welfare maze and the tax structure. (Cf. Golden, 1992.)

More important than the segmentation of congressional committees and uncoordinated programs is the decentralized federalism of the United States. We have seen that even with federal standards, mandates, and funding, state variations in spending and administration are huge (table 8.2). The effects of decentralization and fragmentation are also apparent in the "bloc grant" solution to the welfare mess that went into effect in 1997. This welfare reform bill, in a concession to opponents of its harshest provisions, gives the states authority to exempt 20% of welfare recipients from the two-year "work or out rule." State legislators now find themselves asking "which of the obviously hopeless cases shall receive these extensions"—the battered mother who might count counseling from a battered-women center in lieu of work or training, the woman who lacks both literacy and job experience and who cannot hack it in a hurry-up training program or minimum-wage job, the young mother with two children whose attendance at a mediocre high-school equivalency program is spotty because of the limited availability of child care and her own poor work habits, or the similar mother who has a handicapped child requiring her close attention. Liberals and conservatives alike found themselves orchestrating a war of all types of welfare poor against all others, as they tried to sort this out and realistically deal with the great diversity of the welfare poor. Meanwhile the added targeting and means testing continued to set up political resistance to adequate funding.

Decentralized federalism also fosters a race to the bottom in welfare policy. Without a national standard for eligibility and benefits, the great variation across states provides incentive for the welfare poor to migrate to areas of greater generosity. There is some evidence of a magnet effect; more generous states attract more welfare cases, especially after the Supreme Court struck down state residency requirements for eligibility (Peterson and Rom, 1990). The weight of evidence suggests that although welfare differentials have had a statistically significant effect on welfare migration, the magnitude is small. But even if the welfare poor do not migrate to places like New York, California, and Wisconsin, lawmakers think they do and feel compelled to get tough and restrict benefits.

Finally, the fragmentation and decentralization of the American political economy makes it extremely difficult to connect welfare reform with action on the closely connected problems of housing, transportation, education, job creation, and urban renewal. If Washington and the states do connect some of these problems—as in the provision in some states of child care, health care, education and/or training, and job-search services to supplement workfare or "learnfare" requirements—they refuse to fund such services at the level and over the time necessary for success. With rare exceptions, short-run cost cutting remains central. And almost no attention is given to long-neglected but tightly connected problems of poverty wages and benefits, transportation, and low-cost housing.

A striking illustration of the housing/transportation barrier to the employment of welfare recipients comes from research based on the experience of a cross section of the June 1995 adult caseload in Cuyahoga County (Cleveland), Ohio (Coulton, Verma, and Guo, 1996). The study examines both cross-sectional data at one time and 11 entry cohorts 1992–95; it also projects entry-level job openings for 1995–2000 in the Cleveland/Akron metropolitan area. Because Ohio was in a boom period in the years covered, the regional labor market provided some economic opportunity even for the low-skilled, least-educated population at issue. Moreover, the Ohio workfare program is more liberal than the 1996 reform bill. If there is any area where workfare should work, it is here. But job growth is overwhelmingly at the outskirts of the metropolis—in the suburbs and exurbs—while welfare clients cluster in five poor neighborhoods in inner-city Cleveland. In other words, there is a severe spatial mismatch. Most of these AFDC recipients do not own cars; those who do typically have autos in poor repair that often break down. The focus must therefore be on public transportation from where they live to where jobs are and will be. The study mapped the welfare homes in relation to potential jobs for a neighborhood of greatest AFDC client concentration, the home area within half a mile of East 116th and Kinsman, and then timed the bus routes (*ibid.*, appendix, Map C-1), using a best-case scenario (hours of peak frequency with buses on time).

The findings: The round-trip by bus, is, to say the least, discouraging. Only 19% of these 10,132 jobs projected over five years were accessible within a 1.5-hour round-trip bus ride; 28% would take 1.5 to 3 hours; 36% of these entry-level jobs require a 3 to 4 or more hour round-trip commute. And 17% of the job openings could not be reached by bus at all; no bus goes there.

In short, even if these welfare mothers and the welfare unemployed had no handicaps of poor literacy, education, training, and work habits, even if the government supplied all necessary child care and health care, even if the employers who had these job openings were eager to give priority to all the welfare cases in the area and once they were hired they were kept on in stable jobs—all of which is in the realm of fantasy—the spatial mismatch would block the steady employment of most AFDC recipients. Under time-limited workfare, welfare recipients living in the inner city who rely on public transportation will have four bad to impossible options: (1) They will not have access to most of the available job openings; (2) they will have commute times much exceeding those of most area workers (with fewer resources of social networks and money to ease the task); (3) they must displace existing workers in the city, or (4) they have to relocate to mostly white middle- and upper-income suburbs where rents are beyond their reach (*ibid.*, p. 28). Similar results come from a study of the effect of geographic access on actual welfare usage among people with a high-school education or less around 1990 in Los Angeles (Blumenberg and Ong, 1998). The measure of mismatch was the relative supply of low-wage jobs located within a three-mile radius of the person's census tract; more than three miles is a mismatch. Holding constant other characteristics predicting welfare dependency, increased access to jobs strongly decreased welfare use, a finding that holds among blacks, Hispanics, Asians, and whites alike.

The same Cleveland area study found five other effects of time-limited workfare policies that highlight the barriers to employment of welfare recipients and the negative side effects of welfare reform: (1) Assuming a three-year time limit rather than the more rigid two-year limit actually imposed by the welfare reform law of 1996 and assuming no exemptions, more than 60% of the Cleveland-area adults on welfare in 1995 would be at risk (20,000 individuals, affecting more than 40,000 children, most under six years old)—that is, they would have neither AFDC and related benefits nor a job. (2) Welfare money circulates in the form of rent payments and purchases at stores in the neighborhood. Because the caseload at risk is highly concentrated in a few neighborhoods, the income flow to both the housing market and business sectors that rely on welfare recipients' nonfood purchases will be sharply reduced (many welfare mothers will still receive food stamps so food stores suffer less). In such neighborhoods, a slash in tenant income usually has ripple effects—mass evictions, a rise in housing neglect or abandonment by landlords, and the decline or failure of local small businesses with concomitant erosion of the taxbase. (3) Labor demand cannot accommodate the number of welfare recipients. The researchers conclude, "If all of the long-term recipients sought to enter full-time employment to avoid impending time limits, there would be more than two applicants for every entry-level job opening in the region. Many recipients would either displace other workers or be unable to find work. The competition for scarce job openings in locations near recipient's homes would be even more intense." (*Ibid.*, p. vii).[20]

This threatens the working poor as much as the welfare poor. (4) Work-relevant services available are very limited. Very few welfare recipients in the Cleveland area have received subsidized day care. In their current welfare spell most long-term recipients have not received JOBS services (the workfare program of Ohio embraces basic education or training via job clubs or individual search, community work, or school). The half of the recipients who currently combined part-time work with welfare achieve little or no gain from working when they try full-time work, and the system does little to increase their earnings and benefits so they no longer need a welfare subsidy. Major deficiencies in basic education and skills are the rule. (5) Half of the new entrants to AFDC in the Cleveland area have been leaving the welfare rolls on their own within nine months; more than a third return soon after exiting. As we have seen nationally, the typical pattern has long been either alternating work and welfare or simultaneous work and welfare. Without providing stable jobs and ensuring earnings growth that moves welfare recipients away from poverty and toward self-sufficiency, workfare is an illusion. And the on-and-off pattern puts recipients at risk of reaching the lifetime limit of five years.

All of this assumes a continuation of the brisk Ohio labor market of the mid-1990s and further assumes that child care, health care, and other necessities will somehow be forthcoming. Any economic downturn would greatly worsen the prospect that workfare would work. The recession that began in early 2001, in fact, brought an increase in caseloads in 33 states at the very moment the time limit kicked in.

That the Cleveland study is quite representative of the situation in prosperous places and times is shown by a detailed study of the 1997 job mismatch in six midwestern states—Illinois, Indiana, Michigan, Minnesota, Ohio, and Wisconsin (Kleppner and Theodore, 1997). It again shows that despite recent robust growth and the lowest unemployment rates in 20 years, the Midwest economy is not generating near enough jobs to provide opportunities for welfare recipients and low-skilled workers currently unemployed. Using unemployment and welfare-recipient data for 1995 and projected openings for each occupation through the year 2000, the study estimates that there are between two and four workers (including welfare recipients) in need of low-skilled jobs for every low-skilled job opening in the region. The worker-job ratio is worse in major cities—7 to 1 in Chicago, 15 to 1 in Detroit, 7 to 1 in Milwaukee. If poverty reduction through work is the aim, the outlook is dismal: "There are between 55 and 97 low-skilled job seekers for every livable-wage low-skilled job opening in the Midwest" (*ibid.*, p. 8). The other barriers to employment uncovered in the Cleveland study—housing and transportation mismatches, child-care shortages—are evident for the entire region.

In sum: Workfare that is time-limited—the core of the 1996 welfare reform bill— cannot be judged successful if it merely reduces the welfare rolls. That was occurring with widespread crackdowns before 1996 under state waivers granted by the Department of Health and Human Services and by that criterion could be totally successful if the United States simply stopped sending any cash or service to anyone who is poor. It is reasonable to suggest that workfare must promote economic opportunity for adults without harming their children, devastating their neighborhoods, or displacing the already working poor. This chapter has shown that by these criteria workfare cannot be done on the cheap.

MEANS TESTING, STIGMA, AND TAKEUP RATES: A FEW COMPARISONS

There is much talk about the need for "means testing" the benefits of the welfare state. Conservatives typically want to tighten the flow of cash and services to the undeserving poor; some left politicians want to take benefits away from the affluent so there is more public money left for the poor and the "middle class." Both advocate means tests as a solution. The phrase obscures a plethora of meanings. Means tests vary in *range* of household members or relatives considered; *types of income and assets included; severity* (how low the poverty line is drawn, how detailed are the investigations of eligibility, whether there is concentration on possible fraud and abuse rather than help or service, and the severity of penalties for nonconformity to rules); and *implementation* (the efficiency of outreach if any, the percentage of targeted population reached, the efficiency of eligibility-checking or error rates) (cf. van Oorschot, 1991, p. 28).

For understanding national differences in poverty reduction and the politics of the welfare state I have found that a gross distinction between complex, most-visible means tests and simple, least-visible income tests is most useful. Table 8.3 applies this distinction to cross-national data based on a narrow definition of means testing: (1) noncategorical benefits targeted to the poor via a stiff income and/or assets test; (2) applied by welfare administrators with substantial discretion; (3) with a high probability of stigma (see appendix F for sources and discussion).[21]

Australia, for instance, ranks low to medium in means testing by this definition, although it has made extensive use of income tests, sometimes adding assets tests. These were applied largely to the top of the income and wealth distribution; vast majorities therefore received benefits from the (misnamed) "means-tested" programs. For instance, in 1986, 75% of all couples and 91% of single females were receiving such benefits (Myles and Quadagno, 1996, p. 11). If practically everyone receives the benefit, no stigma can be attached to it. Or consider means testing of Swedish pensions. In the early 1960s Sweden introduced what we might call transfer testing. Let's not worry about all this income from assets and investments, the egalitarian Social Democrats said. Instead, let's fix a minimum benefit below which no pensioner will fall. The ATP (the Swedish earnings-related pension) plus the supplement must meet that standard. If the earnings-related pension does not meet the minimum for a total transfer benefit because earnings are too low, then the pensioner receives the necessary supplement. As earnings rise, more and more pensioners get no supplement—a quiet sort of income test, administered cheaply and efficiently, with no stigma, and no administrative discretion.

Non-Takeup Rates

In magnitude and social consequences the problem of nonuse is far more important in modern welfare states than the problem of overuse (van Oorschot, 1991, p. 16). Although cross-national studies of these rates are rare, and the program structures are seldom comparable, single-country studies show that the nearer you get to means testing in the narrow sense, the higher the non-takeup rate. Illustrative evidence comes from four countries. In descending order of reliance on means testing, ranging from high to medium, they are the United States, Britain, the Netherlands, and West Germany. Although they differ greatly in

TABLE 8.3 Types of political economy and reliance on means testing

Type of Political Economy	Reliance on Means Testing[a]			
	Public Assistance/GNP		Public Assistance Per Capita	
	1966-71	1980	1966-71	1980
Left Corporatist				
Sweden	0.2 (18) L	0.0 (18) L	8 (15) L	6 (18) L
Norway	0.2 (18) L	0.2 (17) L	5 (18) L	23 (14) L
Finland	0.4 (14) L	0.2 (17) L	8 (15) L	20 (16) L
Israel	1.5 (4) H	0.5 (14) LM	23 (6) MH	18 (17) L
Denmark	0.3 (16) L	0.9 (11) LM	8 (15) L	99 (10) M
Left-Catholic Corporatist				
Netherlands	1.0 (7) M	2.1 (4) H	22 (7) MH	224 (4) H
Belgium	1.0 (7) M	0.9 (11) LM	23 (6) MH	99 (10) M
Austria	0.5 (13) LM	0.8 (12) LM	8 (15) L	68 (12) M
Catholic Corporatist				
Italy	0.9 (10) M	0.3 (15) L	12 (10) M	20 (16) L
W. Germany	0.5 (13) LM	1.1 (9) M	13 (9) M	132 (7) MH
Corporatist Without Labor				
France	0.9 (10) M	1.4 (7) HM	20 (8) MH	150 (6) MH
Japan	0.7 (11) ML	1.5 (6) HM	10 (12) M	124 (8) MH
Switzerland	1.0 (7) M	1.1 (9) M	29 (4) HM	171 (5) MH
Least Corporatist				
United States	1.8 (3) H	2.9 (1) H	78 (1) H	316 (1) H
United Kingdom	2.0 (1) H	2.8 (2) H	39 (3) H	229 (3) H
New Zealand	0.1 (19) L	NA	3 (19) L	NA
Australia	0.3 (16) L	0.5 (14) LM	7 (17) L	44 (13) ML
Canada	1.8 (3) H	2.6 (3) H	60 (2) H	250 (2) H
Ireland	1.0 (7) M	1.6 (5) HM	11 (11) M	79 (11) M

[a]Based on a narrow definition: (1) noncategorical benefits targeted to the poor via a stiff income and/or assets–test, (2) applied by welfare administrators with substantial discretion, (3) with a high probability of stigma. See text and appendix for measures. 1966–71 is an average of those two years, 1980 is a single year. Figures in columns 1 and 2 are public assistance spending as a percentage of GNP; figures in columns 3 and 4 are public assistance spending per capita in U.S. dollars. Appendix F describes how these figures were estimated.

their social expenditures, they all show very high to high non-takeup of means-tested benefits (van Oorschot, 1991, pp. 18–19). Here are some details on each:

1. *United States.* Estimates of the non-takeup rates of AFDC in the United States (which for claimants who pass its hurdles determines eligibility for food stamps and Medicaid) ranged from 45% to 30% in the mid-1980s. Each year from 1991 to 1994, about 40% of poor children were not receiving AFDC support (1996 Green Book, table 8-27). In 1992 the non-takeup rate for poor elderly persons categorically eligible for Medicaid was 41%; but a whopping 80–89% of the medically needy poor elderly did not participate (Ettner, 1997, p. 252). Haveman (1987, pp. 87–88) estimates that food stamp and SSI non-takeup rates were 40–50% in the late 1970s. Estimates for AFDC vary greatly by state, ranging from the District of Columbia's 5% to Arizona's 44% in the mid-1970s. National estimates put the AFDC non-takeup for 1986 and 1987 at 30–38% (Blank and Ruggles, 1993, p. 36).[22] In short, between a third and half of the people eligible for benefits of means-tested programs with low poverty thresholds do not claim them.

In contrast, the Earned Income Tax Credit (EITC), begun in 1975 and greatly expanded by legislation of 1990 and 1993, evidenced a non-takeup rate of 14–20% in 1990 (Scholz, 1994, p. 63) and, as information spreads, is probably lower now. Using an eligibility standard much like the simpler income tests of the corporatist welfare-state leaders, this program combines the principles of a tax-based cash transfer and an earnings subsidy. It respects privacy and is invisible (relies on the tax return), automatic, and cheaper in administration. It is aimed at the working poor and carries little stigma compared to traditional means-tested "welfare." The contrast in the non-takeup rate of AFDC (up to 45%) and EITC (no more than 20%) is a reasonable measure of different degrees of stigma.

Eligibility and the application process for EITC are relatively simple. In 1990 eligibility was determined mainly by (1) having at least one child in the house who is disabled *or* under 19 (or under 24 if a student) and who lives there more than half the year; (2) having less than $20,264 of adjusted gross income; and (3) having earned income between $1 and $20,264. There is no test for assets, interest income, or child support. The tax form is one or two pages long. About 10.7 million taxpayers were eligible for the credit in 1991. Because the IRS calculated and paid EITC to all taxpayers who appeared eligible on the basis of their tax form, whether they claimed the credit or not, the actual participation rate was 82–88% of the eligibles—and many of the nonparticipants are self-employed or household workers who are hiding off-the-books income (Scholz, 1994, pp. 63, 70–71, 75).

The simpler forms and the benign administration no doubt make the overpayment error rate for the EITC much higher than the overpayment rate for AFDC and similar stiffly, visibly means-tested programs. (*Ibid.*, pp. 66–67, 72.) But the public, unaware of who is receiving these earnings subsidies, does not get excited by it. And backlash politicians can make much more mileage by baiting the welfare poor than by attacking EITC, which was originated under Republican presidents, seriously expanded by President Clinton, and is not yet the focus of political campaigns (see chap. 10). Moreover, from a public-policy standpoint, the errors probably improve the lot of both the poor and the near-poor without the bureaucratic bloat, intrusiveness, stigma, and political fuss of the welfare alternatives in place. Indeed, by including the near-poor and focusing on the working poor EITC widens its political base, moving it a bit closer to the universalistic programs of welfare-state leaders. That the EITC is politically easier to expand than means-tested programs is evident in the 1993 Clinton budget: A Democratic Congress that invariably splits on the reform of means-tested welfare programs was unified on expansion of EITC in the 1993 budget, although it passed without a single Republican vote. That budget more than tripled the tax credit rate, more than doubled the maximum income for eligibility, and extended the credit to childless workers (Bird, 1996, p. 4). Meanwhile, when the 1993 changes are fully phased in, the credit will deliver benefits to more than six million working poor and close the poverty gap (the difference between total cash income and the poverty line) by $6.4 billion, while it moves over one million taxpayers up above the official poverty line (*ibid.,* p. 80). Limits on SSI and AFDC and related welfare reforms of 1996, however, will move at least that many people into poverty and many of the poor into deeper poverty (see above). The most recent and optimistic review of four years of experience under TANF (Besharov and Germanis, 2000) concludes that only about half of the mothers who have left welfare seem to be working more or less regularly. If to these contradictory trends we add the impact of increased minimum wages and the brisk labor market of the late 1990s, the net effect may be to reduce the number of working poor while increasing the number of nonworking poor.

There is an emerging consensus among students of American welfare that the Earned Income Tax Credit, if adequately expanded, would go far toward reducing poverty among the working poor, a substantial fraction of whom are intermittently on the welfare rolls. I share that view. But one cannot be very optimistic about any dramatic expansion. The politics of the welfare state in the United States are so resistant to explicitly downward redistribution of income that even incremental increases in the eligibility test for the EITC or the amount of rebate evoke controversy in congressional budget debates. From 1995 on, with the usual cries of fraud and abuse and complaints that some benefits go to people too high above the poverty line (the near-poor who are not near enough to the line to suit the critics), congressional efforts were launched to cut the program ultimately in half (*New York Times,* August 16, 1995). Ironically, conservatives who in welfare reform debates railed against the nonaged able-bodied poor for laziness but supported the EITC for the more worthy working poor in the late 1980s, by 1997 were attacking EITC in debates about tax cuts because its recipients were nontaxpayers. The latest issue was whether EITC recipients would be eligible for a $500 child tax credit that everyone else, except families with incomes over $110,000 and the nonworking poor, was to receive. Speaker Newt Gingrich charged that the Democrats' effort to give more to the working poor was a "welfare" sop (*Wall Street Journal,* June 26, 1997). While none of these proposals became law the 1997 budget agreement denied the child tax credit to the poor with annual incomes below $18,000, who might be receiving either the EITC or welfare. The prospects for the working poor, however, do remain better than the prospects for those who cannot work, are poorly prepared for work, or cannot find jobs. The latter will remain not only the target of increasingly hostile means tests but of continued political demagoguery.

2. *Britain* is the founder of means testing for the poor. Its Poor Law tradition, developed in the 16th century, culminated in the Poor Law of 1834, whose sponsors regarded poverty among the able-bodied as a moral failing, with employment in the workhouse of

Dickensian fame as the punishment. These old traditions die hard; they appear side by side with the modern welfare state. Thus, Britain joins the United States and Canada in greatest reliance on means testing today (see table 8.3). Non-takeup rates for its universalistic programs are close to zero. In contrast, in the late 1980s non-takeup rates for its means-tested programs were 24% for the Supplementary Benefit (the national social assistance scheme), 46% for the Family Income Supplement, 23% for the Housing Benefit, and 7% for the One Parent Benefit (van Oorschot, 1991, p. 19). Even a means-tested "Income Support" for the less-resented population of poor pensioners has a non-takeup rate among eligible pensioner units of 33% (1989 data reported by Atkinson, 1994, p.19). When "New Labour" took over, the new minister for welfare reform hoped to reverse the recent trend toward increased reliance on means testing by strengthening social insurance. He lost that battle and in 1998 resigned (Hills, 1998, pp. 18–20, 28–29).

3. *The Netherlands* evidences a similar reluctance among the poor to claim highly means-tested benefits. In the late 1980s, variations by program matched the degree of stigma attached to the target population: 49% of the social assistance claimants in the city of Tilburg did not claim at least one of five different local subsidies and rebates for the poor; 33% of the unemployed did not claim their right to a means-tested supplement; but only 11% of the disabled—the least-stigmatized of the three groups—failed to claim their right to a means-tested supplement (van Oorschot, 1991, p. 19).

4. A large national survey of 25,000 households in *West Germany* in 1981 uncovered a rate of non-takeup of *Sozialhilfe* (Social Help, the program closest to the American AFDC) of 48% of all eligible households (van Oorschot, 1991, p. 18). The non-takeup rate of means-tested German housing allowances in the early 1970s was more than 50% (van Oorschot, 1995, p. 20).

Reasons for High Non-Takeup Rates

We have already seen that stigma is a leading source of non-takeup. Other consequences flow from stigma. If both the public and program administrators are suspicious or hostile toward potential claimants, these means-tested programs will inevitably be complex. Thus, they typically have many complicated eligibility rules, often vague, inconsistent, and changing; programs often require client initiatives and are administered with an eye to cost cutting and fraud control rather than outreach and service; the process of claiming is typically long and frequently humiliating; the application forms are complex and opaque. The eligibility checkers often lack adequate training and have high rates of turnover. The clients typically lack education or are even functionally illiterate. If they are not totally ignorant of the program and their rights and therefore do not claim anything, they are confused and fearful of the process. They find it difficult to fill out the forms or to retrieve the necessary information. Observation of a New England welfare office in 1988 showed that applicants must furnish 15 to 20 verifications before they become eligible (Bane and Ellwood, 1994, p. 4). Federal rules require AFDC or food stamp recipients who have non-welfare sources of income to produce documentation of amounts earned and hours worked (wage stubs and letters from employers) every month (*ibid.*, p. 126). The applicants argue with administrators, who often view the client as morally unworthy, an irresponsible person trying to get away with something. Administrators themselves are running scared. However well intentioned they may be, they tend to overconform to the rules to avoid criticism by agency management and political critics.

In addition to the maze of mysterious and arbitrary rules, there is another well-established reason for low takeup rates of means-tested benefits—the problem of "poverty traps" or "savings traps." Low-paid workers lose much of the advantage from earning more because means-tested programs always take away an increasing proportion of the marginal benefit as earnings increase. There is also a "savings trap": where private savings or other assets exist, these programs reduce or eliminate benefits—a strong disincentive to savings among eligible persons who know about this in advance and a strong barrier to claiming a benefit for those who discover the rules too late. (Atkinson, 1994, pp. 19–20.)

Finally, takeup rates respond to the business cycle; a brisk labor market reduces welfare dependency. Thus the fraction of single-mother families receiving AFDC in the United States dropped from a high of 63% in 1973 to 42% in 1987, reflecting the economic recovery and expanding job opportunities for women after the 1981–82 recession (Smolensky, Evenhouse, and Reilly, 1992, p. 17).

Some evidence indicates that the problems of ignorant eligibles, stigma, work and savings disincentives, and administrative costs vary in severity with type of program (Atkinson, 1993). From most to least trouble are (1) intensively means-tested benefits; (2) income tests of a simpler sort based on last year's tax return or a simple declaration of income given to the appropriate agency; (3) categorical transfers conditioned on age, family status, or labor-market status—for example, education and training subsidies, family allowances; and (4) universal programs such as national pension rights or national health insurance.

No country has completely cleaned up its welfare mess. And when countries eliminate means tests they typically retain or introduce income tests. In fact, moderately stiff eligibility rules for means-tested or income-tested programs are present even in the more universalistic welfare states, reflecting popular views of the "undeserving poor" common to all modern democracies (see chap. 10). Consider the issue of the unit to which an income or means test is to be applied—the person, the household, or the extended family. Both France and Germany make claimants provide names and addresses of both ascendant and descendant relatives, and both countries hold relatives liable for sharing support of claimants (Atkinson, 1991, p. 18). A single mother would be liable to support her mother even if her mother lived in her own house. And the mother's income could be included with her daughter's in determining eligibility. Thus, although welfare-state leaders have greatly reduced poverty, they may treat the remaining nonaged poor with almost as much harshness as does the United States, at least in some rules of eligibility. The difference is that the welfare-state leaders have not only reduced poverty to a much smaller share of the population than countries relying heavily on means testing, but they have also put into place many non-means-tested programs such as family policies (chap. 7) and active labor-market policies (figure 2.2).

The remaining means testing is applied with more flexibility if not generosity. For example, although the proportion of the West German population receiving social help (5% in 1986) is a bit more than the comparable share of the U.S. population receiving AFDC (in the mid-1980s about 4.5%),[23] the administration of these means-tested programs stands in sharp contrast. A systematic comparison of the main American means-tested programs other than Medicaid (AFDC, SSI, food stamps, general assistance) with their German counterparts (Leibfried, 1979) concludes that German social assistance and related programs are national, have higher national standards (not generous but adequate), are financed by revenue sharing, and are more individualized, with less focus on routine fraud checking (investigation occurs only where there is clear sign of fraud or cheating in individual cases). Thus, the ratio of "welfare" population to total population may not be as important as the adequacy of benefits and the way they are administered. U.S. public assistance is less adequate and more visible; in administration, more fragmented, decentralized, and incoherent; and, in spirit, more hostile to the poor.

A similar updated comparison of means-tested public assistance in Germany and the United States by Jens Alber (1996) reaches the same conclusions about program structure and administration and analyzes the contrasting effects. From 1960 to 1994 the poor in the United States were big losers from "welfare" retrenchment; the German poor held their own. In fact, despite greater economic stress in Germany (the huge burden of unification, rising unemployment) German social assistance benefits increased in real terms and even kept pace with pensions and net wages (*ibid.*, p. 23). What political support there is for the poor in the United States is diffuse and scattered. It is more focused in Germany, where coalitions of unions, churches, and welfare associations successfully pushed for equality of sacrifice in the period of austerity. The social Catholicism of the CDU also helped. (Alber, 1996, pp. 24ff.; and my chaps. 2, 7, and 10.) Thus, even though Germany and the United States share the universal resentment of the undeserving poor (see chap. 10) and attach the same stigma to the programs targeted to them, the United States lacks Germany's organized counterweights to such mass sentiments and continues its welfare system's race to the bottom, while Germany avoids it.

In this comparison we cannot ignore differences in program growth rates and the interacting impact of other means-tested programs. If we confine analysis to AFDC compared to German social assistance, we ignore the great variety of other means-tested programs that account for the high figures for dependence on means testing for the United States and United Kingdom in table 8.3 compared to the medium figure for West Germany. Finally, the annual rate of growth of public assistance recipients is much greater in the United States and United Kingdom (9.2% from 1950 to 1980 and 8.3% from 1948 to 1988) than West Germany (5.2% from 1964 to 1986) (calculated from Atkinson, 1991, pp. 24–25).

In short, the remaining means testing and the wide use of simpler income tests among welfare-state leaders avoids the Anglo-American obsession with targeting the "truly needy" and its negative political and economic effects. (Chaps. 9 and 10 show that means testing is one source of bureaucratic bloat and tax-welfare backlash; chap. 12 shows that it is a drag on economic performance.)

TECHNICAL PROBLEMS, ERROR RATES, AND THE WELFARE MESS

The Anglo-American obsession with means testing also runs into practical, technical administrative problems that add to the welfare mess. The advocates of means testing for the poor or for pensioners think that it contributes to equity. Why should a well-off older citizen or a poor person with some assets like a house and car be treated the same as the "truly needy"? If you believe that this is a burning question, your next step is to measure "means." The U.S. government has created a relatively sophisticated measure for counting the poor and determining eligibility for benefits—the ratio of income to the specified level of poverty for a given household composition, roughly an income/needs ratio, widely used for determining eligibility for public assistance and similar targeted benefits, sometimes combined with an assets test. It has remained essentially unchanged for the past 30 years. It is less than meets the eye. As James Morgan (1993) has demonstrated, if you add disparities in wealth and disparities in leisure among households at the same level of "income/needs poverty," you get some wildly different results. That wealth—possessions, home ownership, income from investments converted to a lifetime annuity—can make a difference is obvious. Not so obvious is that leisure—time to shop, time to spend with children, time to do things for oneself, time to visit friends and relatives, time to enjoy even a meager income—is also a component of well-being. Using the 1984 interviews of the Panel Study of Income Dynamics (PSID), Morgan compares the efficiency of the three measures of means in targeting the poor at various age levels. For instance, what fraction of those in the *bottom tenth* of the income distribution by current measures are misclassified by (1) the full income/needs measure (money income less current income from marketable assets plus the value of food stamps plus an annuitized value of household convertible wealth such as house, stocks, bonds, real estate, business, cars, etc.); or by (2) a new measure of "well-being" (full income/needs times annual hours of leisure)?

Beyond the issues of disincentives to work, undermined dignity, and a terrible record of poverty reduction (see tables 8.4 and 14.4 and chaps. 7 and 12), there are big problems of equity—one stemming from these problems of measuring poverty; the other, from the interaction of separate programs comprising the welfare mess. The equity problem with means testing is, first, what Morgan demonstrates: the customary measure of income/needs qualifies people who are not really poor on a better measure or refuses benefits to people who are really at the bottom decile. For instance, the full income/needs measure shows that the customary measure misqualifies 43% of the lower tenth (20% qualify but are not poor, 23% are poor but not qualified). The "well-being" measure misqualifies even more. "Clearly," Morgan cautiously concludes, "the efficiency with which a means test promotes equity is low, and excruciatingly low among the oldest cohorts" (1993, p. 775). There is increasing evidence from poverty research of a weak association between income adjusted for need (the usual "poverty line") and direct measures of deprivation (Travers, 1996; Nolan and Whelan, 1996).

The second problem of inequity stems from multiple programs, all tightly targeted, that result in arbitrary disparities in benefits among equally hard-pressed families. If means-tested public assistance is linked to child care, medical care, and other benefits, as in the United States, these inequities can be glaring. A low-income AFDC single mother of two, with little education and less work experience, qualifies for AFDC (or today, TANF) and this in turn may bring food stamps, Medicaid, and child-care assistance to permit her to complete a high-school equivalency or training for a job. Next door a working couple with two children have an annual gross income of $20,000, which in almost all states disqualifies them for AFDC. Moreover, this working couple does not qualify for food stamps, Medicaid, or child care. Such inequities are legion. They set the working poor against the nonworking poor, the welfare mother who is skillful at working the system against the welfare mother who is not, and the public against everyone in or around the system. The EITC may reduce the inequity between the working poor and nonworking poor somewhat. By driving welfare mothers and their children into deeper poverty, recent welfare reforms achieve an equity based on increasing poverty for the welfare mother newly freed from AFDC and associated benefits by mandatory two-year workfare limits and five-year lifetime limits. If she is lucky enough to find and hold a minimum-wage job and in addition is lucky enough to marry another full-time, low-wage worker, she can join the working poor in a more equal struggle for survival.

Aware of both misclassifications and inequities, the means-obsessed welfare administrators often try to measure some assets. This daunting task results in rule books and eligibility forms stacked to the ceiling (or overloading the computer). With each revision of the law or administrative regulations designed to deny benefits to the undeserving or crack down on welfare cheats, these eligibility rules change, sometimes drastically, creating a demand for still more eligibility checkers or, under conditions of budgetary strain, an impossible work overload for existing personnel.

The number, complexity, and change of rules ensure a high error rate. In political debates about the welfare mess, these administrative errors are often lumped under "fraud and abuse" when most are clearly the inevitable result of an overloaded agency trying to conform to an overelaborate, sometimes ambiguous and contradictory set of laws and rules. There was a time—roughly from the late 1930s to the late 1960s—when American welfare agencies conducted surprise visits to the homes of single mothers: social workers looked for beer bottles on the kitchen table as a sign of the possible presence of a boyfriend. Under the legal interpretations of many states such a presence was a sign of cohabitation and hence "unsuitable" parenting; it was at the same time a sign of a "substitute parent" who could share household expenses. If further investigation sustained the suspicion, the AFDC grant could be denied or reduced on either ground (Melnick, 1994, pp. 83–90). Although these surprise visits generally ceased after a Supreme Court decision (*King v. Smith,* 392 U.S. 309, 1968) rejected the distinction between the "worthy" poor and the "undeserving poor," aggressive investigation and surveillance of the welfare poor continues. The Warren court's pro-poor reading of the law was under attack from the late 1960s on; by the mid-1980s the Burger court had moved back toward a more formal, less substantive, more restrictive understanding of welfare rights (*ibid.*, pp. 60, 102ff.), reflecting the changing legislative and executive climate and judicial appointments of the Reagan presidency, carried on by President Bush and the Rehnquist court. The extensive state and federal litigation around welfare issues for the past half century—whether the outcome was to expand welfare entitlement, restrict it, or merely confuse it—had the practical effect of severely straining state welfare-payment systems. Growing litigation and shifting court doctrines combined with recurrent congressional welfare reforms kept welfare systems in a constant state of flux—forcing much defensive data collection (with an eye to court cases) and frequent adaptation to new and everchanging agency rules.[24] In the late 1970s a large quality-control bureaucracy was created. Local caseworkers increasingly focused on cutting the welfare rolls and on possible fraud; welfare applicants had to prove their eligibility to increasingly suspicious eligibility checkers. Terminations of welfare cases and rejections of AFDC applications on procedural grounds increased apace. (Brodkin, 1986, pp. 39, 79, 86–92, 96–98.) In other words, what can no longer be tolerated as surveillance and home searches is accomplished today by tightening and complicating eligibility rules and reducing welfare grants. With the welfare reform of 1996—50 states aiming to meet new and ambitious workfare goals in a rapidly changing system—eligibility and behavioral rules will metastasize. There is already a General Accounting Office Report that in the first five months of Milwaukee's workfare program the error rate was astonishing: 44% of the penalties imposed were later overturned because of agency error (*New York Times,* June 30, 1997). If Wisconsin—with one of the more generous welfare budgets and one of the most efficient bureaucracies—encounters such trouble, error rates are likely to be worse in other states with fewer resources and less competence.

If we got serious about means tests, we would spend even more time and personnel devising ever-more sophisticated measures of income, wealth, and leisure and create an even more cumbersome, more intrusive apparatus of surveillance and investigation. The only side benefit I can see from such bureaucratic bloat is that many of the poor, especially welfare mothers, become smarter about maneuvering around the system as they struggle to survive. A small increment of bureaucratic skills among the poor is surely not worth the huge effort to target them.

For the purpose of crafting social policies, the technical problem of measuring "means" and targeting the poor is further complicated by the immensely varied situations of low-income populations. Poverty varies in duration, prevalence, repetition, and severity (Ashworth, Hill, and Walker, 1994). And the economic condition of the poor family when they are out of poverty also varies with most of them remaining near-poor or falling back, the rest, moving up. Finally, there are the variations by population type: the working poor, the unemployed poor, the depressed-region poor, the elderly poor, the teen-pregnant poor, the welfare mother, the homeless family, the homeless young single men who are alcoholic or drug-addicted, the physically or mentally disabled poor, the youth-gang poor, and more. If we tried to devise public policies that target each type of poverty—recurrent poverty, transient poverty, persistent poverty, occasional poverty, chronic poverty, and permanent poverty—and each population type, the fragmentation and complexity of the welfare mess would intensify. Chapters 1, 5, 7, and 14 and tables 8.4 and 14.4 discuss the incidence and variety of poverty and compare the United States with other rich democracies. The lesson of that comparison is that a better strategy for cleaning up the welfare mess and reducing poverty—one followed by countries with low rates of poverty—is the combination of four universalistic policy packages: education with high national standards (chaps. 12 and 18), an active labor-market policy (figure 2.2), national health insurance (chaps. 16 and 18), and perhaps most important, a family policy (chap. 7)—policies whose target is everyone sharing the demands of modern life.

EXPLAINING NATIONAL DIFFERENCES IN RELIANCE ON MEANS TESTS

Since the 1880s there has been a trend common to all rich countries away from general "Poor Law" legislation and administration—away from means testing toward more universalistic policies, as we have seen in chapter 5. For instance, Palme's study of worker pensions in 18 countries shows that in 1930 most of the countries with legislated old-age pensions relied on means testing. In the early postwar period about half still had means-tested pensions; in 1960, less than a third. By 1985, means-tested pensions remained only in Australia, where they had been wiped out but reintroduced in the 1980s (Palme, 1990, pp. 52, 69).

Within a long-term convergence, first away from means testing toward simpler income tests and then toward universality of social rights, there are both large remaining national differences and a recent but limited shift back toward income testing and even some expansion of means testing. For instance, in the late 1970s and early 1980s there was a move away from universality in family/child allowances. Italy introduced income tests for child allowances, Denmark and Germany subjected the maximum benefit to an income test, and France income-tested all new family allowances (Kamerman and Kahn, 1991a, p. 48). Other examples of the recent shift are above and in chapter 5 (section on retrenchment).

Large differences in reliance on means testing are evident in table 8.3 whether we measure it by the share of GNP going to tightly means-tested programs or per capita expenditures. And there is little change in the rankings from 1966–71 to 1980. (Only Israel and Japan changed more than four ranks in the 19-country ranking.)[25] We can go far in explaining the national differences by applying our types of political economy, familiar from tables in previous chapters.

The predictive power of types of political economy in table 8.3 is impressive. Of the nine countries that rely least on means testing in 1980 (public assistance/GNP), eight are corporatist democracies that integrate labor in their policy machinery. Of the nine most dedicated to means-tested programs, four are least corporatist and three are corporatist-without-labor. Very similar patterns appear for earlier dates and for public assistance spending per capita, although the 1974 per capita pattern is weak.

The sharpest contrast is between the avoidance of means testing by left-corporatist democracies and the penchant for means testing among the most-fragmented and decentralized democracies (United States, United Kingdom, Canada, Ireland). Why is there by 1980 almost a uniform avoidance of means testing among corporatist democracies with strong cumulative left party power? All left parties opposed needs testing from the 1930s on. They typically fought discretionary measures that would leave the lower classes at the mercy of hostile welfare bureaucrats. In time, of course, left power was sufficient to transform the political orientation of welfare bureaucracies and even their social composition; where means tests or income tests were still in place, their administration became more benign. While left parties with few exceptions were against means tests for the poor, they often advocated income tests and even assets tests applied to very high income groups; the idea was to free resources for the middle and the poor and take privileges away from the rich. (Baldwin, 1990; Davidson, 1989.)

The least-corporatist countries drew on the English Poor Law tradition; labor and left parties in the Anglo-American democracies were not enough of a countervailing force to fully overcome this legacy. Although Australia and New Zealand are exceptions to the hypothesis that the most-fragmented and decentralized political economies (the least-consensual democracies) rely most on means testing, developments since the mid-1980s put them closer to the leaders in means testing, the United States and the United Kingdom. In 1983, Australia reintroduced income testing for pensioners over the age of 70 and added assets tests in 1985. The result was a decline in percentage of the aged receiving benefits from 86% in 1983 to 76% in 1991. Australia also applied an income test to its only universal benefit, the child allowance, and tightened eligibility rules for a host of other benefits. (Castles and Shirley, 1996, p. 96.) Similarily, New Zealand, whose welfare state, like Australia's, has long made extensive use of income tests qualifying large majorities for benefits, has moved further toward means testing since the mid-1980s, to the accompaniment of sectarian economists' rhetoric about privatization, deregulation and the evils of taxing and spending. Chapter 11 provides details on the political and economic effects of New Zealand's neoliberal experiment. Thus, the two deviant cases appear to be falling in line, although neither has yet reached the harshness of the American welfare mess.

The Netherlands is an exceptional case. It is the only corporatist welfare-state leader with heavy reliance on means testing. The Tilburg picture of low takeup rates, if it is true nationally, requires special explanation. In my view, there are so many well-financed and overlapping programs for the poor and near-poor, and such lavish spending for the universal programs—Netherlands matches Sweden in aggregate social expenditures—that potential claimants do not need or want extra supplements that carry stigma. Uniquely among the heavy users of means tests, the Netherlands evidences high income equality and low poverty (tables 8.3, 8.4, and 14.4). Its low takeup rate in some measure may reflect the relative well-being of low-income Dutch citizens.

The rest of the table—16 of 19 cases—fits my scheme with the rank order of avoidance of means testing moving down from left corporatist, left-Catholic corporatist, Catholic corporatist to corporatism-without-labor and, with most reliance on means testing, the most-fragmented and decentralized political economies. Both left and Catholic parties are historically advocates of universalistic family policies, which as we have seen in chapter 7, are strongly negatively correlated with means-tested public assistance; they are alternative policy packages. Left parties are the most ardent opponents of stiff means testing for the poor. Catholic parties' strong support for family allowances and ambivalent support for other universal family policies (e.g., child care for working mothers) puts them in the middle of table 8.3. Thus left-corporatist democracies top all categories in avoiding means testing while left-Catholic and Catholic-corporatist democracies come next. Corporatist democracies that keep labor out of high policy—Japan, France, Switzerland—rank between medium and high in their reliance on means testing; they lack the left-labor offsets that facilitate more universalistic strategies. They are not as means-test prone as the United States, United Kingdom, and Canada but more so than corporatist democracies with either strong left party power or strong Catholic party power.[26]

TYPES OF POLITICAL ECONOMY, TEENAGE PREGNANCY, AND ABORTION[27]

In debates about the welfare mess in the United States, no perception provokes more passion than the claim that teenage pregnancies are soaring, that public assistance to single mothers fosters babies out of wedlock, that sex education and public support of contraception encourage sexual activity and teen births, and the entire syndrome reflects and furthers the moral decline of American society. While conservatives voice these concerns most stridently, moderates and liberals on the left also recognize the individual and public costs of teenage pregnancies, although they obviously advocate different policies to attack the problem.

Sometimes the debate about teen pregnancy is caught up in the even more passionate debate about abortion (see chap. 7). Here the political lines shift a bit. On the one hand, the Christian right is worried that supporting young single mothers might encourage out-of-wedlock pregnancies. On the other hand, cutting their welfare checks might encourage abortion as pregnant teenagers see the "end of welfare as we know it." Thus, in the 1996 welfare reform debate, both Catholic groups and the Christian right voiced concern over too drastic a reduction in support for children of single mothers. Together with the center-left and the Clinton administration they pushed for increased congressional funding for child care in the welfare bill.

What can cross-national comparison tell us about the problems of teenage pregnancy and abortion? Comparison tells us that the United States is extreme in its rate of teen pregnancy and birth as well as its rate of abortion. Teenage birthrates around 1980 were twice the average of other Anglo-American democracies, 10 times the rate of the Netherlands, 7 times that of Sweden and Switzerland, 4 or 5 times that of Belgium, Italy, Germany, or France. The United States is also the standout leader in abortions. (See table 8.4.) More recent data tell the same story: the United States is at the top of the teen-pregnancy list in the early 1990s (cf. Kiernan, 1995, p. 3) and except for Japan is still the star in abortions among 18 affluent democracies (Brooks, 1992, p. 348; Henshaw, 1992, table 2).

This section first examines the rates and trends, then attempts to explain national variations and the American deviance by analyzing the impact of my types of political economy and related social policies. Scholars agree on several trends common to all modern, affluent democracies:

1. Since the 1960s teenage birthrates have declined (United Nations, 1988, pp. 12–15). Despite some fluctuations, the rate continued to decline from 1980 to 1993 with the one exception of the United Kingdom (Kiernan, 1995, p. 3), where teen births moved up slightly.

2. Many more teenagers, especially younger teenagers and middle- or upper-middle class teenagers have become sexually active. At the same time they have become much more likely to use the pill, condoms, and other forms of birth control. (Mauldon and Luker, 1996, p. 82; Gustafsson, 1995, pp. 317–318; and C. A. Miller, 1991, p. 4). More activity, fewer births.

3. Long-standing educational differences in teen pregnancy have persisted or increased. Such pregnancy is a pattern of the poor. Girls who see themselves moving up in the education-occupational system postpone both pregnancy and marriage. Thus, countries that reduce poverty and expand educational and job opportunities for lower strata tend to have lower rates of teen births (see table 8.4). It is important to note that some sexual relations involving adolescent girls (and even boys) are anything but consensual; they involve rape and incest, with an unknown number resulting in pregnancy (Rosenheim, 1992, p. 226). This, too, is heavily concentrated among the least-educated, poorest populations, as is mayhem of all sorts (see chap. 14).

4. Beyond poverty reduction, the main reasons for the almost universal decline in teen birthrates is expanded sex education and AIDS education, public funding of contraception, and the expansion of family planning clinics and agencies. Countries that do most of this also tend to have lower teenage birthrates.

5. Teen pregnancy and births present a paradox: Compared with the 1960s the rates are down dramatically everywhere; but the subsequent costs to the teenager have climbed—poor housing, homelessness, unemployment, low income, and reliance on stigmatized public assistance. The increasing length of learning, training, and education required to enter decent jobs and at least moderately stable employment makes the handicaps of early motherhood much more severe and the long-run costs to society heavy. These are costs the United Kingdom, the United States, and other Anglo-American democracies have incurred as a by-product of their relatively high rates of poverty and inequality.

6. Insofar as trend data exist, abortion rates show no consistent pattern cross-nationally, although the central tendency in the late 1980s and early 1990s in 17 Western democracies was either steady or decreasing; only Sweden, Norway, Australia, Canada, and West Germany evidenced an increase during the four or five years at issue (Brooks, 1992, table 2, p. 348).

Applying my scheme to data on total teenage fertility rates in our 19 rich democracies, we find strong confirmation of the explanatory power of types of political economy and their social-policy outputs. Because most of teenage pregnancy is accounted for by 18- and 19-year-olds and the social problem posed is much more severe for younger cohorts who neither complete high school nor obtain any training or work experience, we used cumulative birthrates for women under 18. This is an estimate of how many births can be expected from 1,000 17-year-olds while they were between the ages of 12 and 17. It is based on actual births by single year of age of mother and corresponding estimates of the female population by single year of age, which are then summed to generate cumulative birth rates for 1979–80 (Jones et al., 1986, p. 3 and appendix 3, pp. 250–260). Comparing three other data sets—birthrates for women under 20, 15 to 19, or 18 and 19—we find a very similar rank order of countries with Japan, the Netherlands, and Switzerland comprising a very low category; Sweden, Denmark, Finland, and Israel (excluding Arab women) the next lowest category; West Germany, Ireland, France, Belgium, Italy, and Norway a medium category; while the UK, Australia, Canada, Austria, and New Zealand evidence high teenage birthrates and the United States is in a high class of its own, no matter what cohorts are examined.

Table 8.4 shows that democratic corporatism, whatever the type, keeps teen birthrates down. In contrast, the least-corporatist democracies, as predicted, have much the highest teen birthrates, except for Ireland's medium rate. The consensual democracies, whether they are left, Catholic, or keep labor at a distance, are able to produce patterns of spending and taxing and social policies that reduce both poverty and inequality. In turn, a low poverty rate and an egalitarian income distribution reduce teenage birthrates. Thus, excluding the United States as an extreme case, the strongest proximate cause of high teen birthrates is poverty by any measure: gross household income shares going to the lowest 20% of households ($r = -.56$), disposable income of the bottom tenth as a percent of the median ($r = -.51$), extreme poverty among two-parent families measured by an equivalent (family size-adjusted) income less than one-third of median equivalent income ($r = .61$), or extreme poverty of children under 18 in solo-mother families ($r = .64$). The ratio of gross household income shares of the top fifth to the shares of the bottom fifth—the distance between the affluent and the poor (see table 14.4)—is correlated .57 with teen birthrates. If the United States—an outlier in both its teen birthrate and in its poverty rate—is added to the analysis, all these correlations increase; for the two extreme poverty measures the correlations climb to .77 and .86.[28]

There is no direct correlation between birthrates and family policy (the family-policy index or any of its components) or family allowances or public assistance spending, but there are strong positive relationships between corporatism, family policy, family allowances, and equality and reduced poverty, as shown in chapters 7 and 14. In other words, equality

TABLE 8.4 Interaction of types of political economy, social policies, poverty and inequality as they shape teenage birthrates and societywide abortion rates

	Teen births 1979-80[a]	Abort. rate 1980[b]	Abort. rate 1987[c]	Deep child pov. solo mothers[d]	Deep child pov. two parents[e]	Inequal. ratio[f]	Family policy score[g]	Means-testing PA/GNP[h]
Left Corporatist								
Sweden	15	21	20	1.5 (14)	0.6 (10)	4.6 H	H	L
Norway	29	16	17	9.0 (6)	0.5 (12)	5.9 HM	H	L
Finland	18	14	12	2.7 (13)	0.5 (12)	6.0 HM	H	L
Israel	18[i]	na	16	8.3 (8)	1.2 (8)	6.6 ML	na	LM
Denmark	16	21	18	na	na	7.1 ML	MH	LM
cell avg	19.2	18	17	5.4	0.7	6.0		
Left-Cath. Corporatist								
Netherlands	10	6	5	2.8 (12)	1.1 (9)	5.6 HM	M	H
Belgium	26	na	8	4.6 (10)	0.6 (10)	4.6 H	H	LM
Austria	41	14	na	na	na	na	MH	LM
cell avg.	25.7	10	6.5	3.7	0.9	5.1		
Catholic Corporatist								
Italy	28	19	15	11.9 (5)	3.6 (3)	6.0 HM	M	L
W. Germany	21	11	7	8.4 (7)	0.3 (14)	5.7 HM	MH	M
cell avg.	24.5	15	11	10.2	2.0	5.9		
Corporatist w/o Labor								
France	25	22	13	6.8 (9)	1.7 (7)	6.5 ML	H	HM
Japan	2	84	84	na	na	4.3 H	L	HM
Switzerland	8	na	9	na	na	8.6 L	L	M
cell avg	11.7					6.5		
Least Corporatist								
United States	101	29	28	37.8 (1)	5.1 (1)	8.9 L	L	H
United Kingdom	42[j]	na	14[k]	3.4 (11)	3.7 (2)	6.8 ML	M	H
New Zealand	64	9	11	na	na	8.8 L	L	na
Australia	45	na	17	22.7 (2)	3.1 (5)	9.6 L	L	LM
Canada	46	13	12	20.3 (3)	2.3 (6)	7.1 ML	L	H
Ireland	23	na	5	18.1 (4)	3.2 (4)	na	L	HM
cell avg.	53.5	17	14.5	20.5	3.5	8.2		

[a]1979–80 cumulative birthrate for teenagers under 18, calculated from Jones et al. (1986, appendix 3, pp. 250–60).

[b]1980 abortions per 1,000 women aged 15–44. Source: fn. a.

[c]Circa 1987 abortions per 1,000 women aged 15–44. Source: Henshaw (1992, table 2).

[d]Extreme child poverty in solo mother families mid to late 1980s: equivalent (size-adjusted) income less one-third of median equivalent income. Although the UK has only about 4% of solo mother families in dire poverty, 60% are poor or near-poor. That puts the UK first in poor and near-poor, although the U.S. tops the UK in extreme poor, poor, and near-poor combined. Source: Rainwater, 1994, table 6.

[e]Extreme child poverty in two-parent families mid to late 1980s. *Ibid.*, table 5.

[f]Ratio of the highest to lowest quintiles in gross household income shares ranked from most to least egalitarian, early 1980s. See table 14.4, mayhem chapter. High numbers = most inequality.

[g]Rankings based on family policy score, text and tables, chapter 7.

[h]Reliance on means testing 1980 from table 8.3.

[i]Not counting Arab women in Israel. Including them, the rate is 32 (Jones, 1986, p. 243).

[j]England's rate is 41; UK other than England, 43.

[k]Residents only. Excludes Scotland (rate = 9.0).

and poverty reduction mediate the relation between corporatism and associated social policies, on the one hand, and teen birthrates, on the other.

Because of missing data on one or another of these variables, the number of countries drops to 12 to 15 when regression experiments are attempted, so I did not pursue correlational analysis beyond a few exploratory tests. However, these quantitative explorations did show that corporatism and the measures of extreme poverty explain substantial variance in teen birthrates, overcoming any other variable. This is consistent with the cross-tabulations of table 8.4.

Does the availability of generous state-subsidized child care encourage teen births? Just the reverse. Comparing left-corporatist and least-corporatist countries, there is a negative relationship between the child-care scores of chapter 7 and teen birthrates: all of the left-corporatist countries have high child-care scores and low to medium teen birthrates. All of the fragmented and decentralized political economies are below average to low in child care (scoring either 0 or 1 of a possible 3), and they have high teenage birthrates.

In short, if a rich democracy develops consensual bargaining arrangements; produces innovative and expansive family policies enabling working parents to better balance child care and work, if it opens up opportunity by an active labor-market policy linking education, training, and jobs, and through both family and labor-market policies reduces poverty and inequality, it will keep teen birthrates to a medium to low level. The big exception in table 8.4 is corporatist Austria, medium-high in its family-policy score, above average in poverty reduction and equality, and yet a teen birthrate of 41, close to that of the United Kingdom. A possible explanation is its very long tradition of marriage shortly *after* the birth of a child to a young mother, unique in Europe (Hobcraft and Kiernan, 1995, p. 47). Ireland, too, is out of line among the Anglo-American fragmented and decentralized democracies. It has a medium instead of a very high teen birthrate and yet is well above-average in poverty. We cannot say that the strong family orientation and restrictions of its Catholic Church and its low female labor-force rate account for Ireland's medium rate of 23. For Catholicism appears with rates above that of Ireland: Austria's high rate of 41, Italy's 28, Belgium's 26, France's 25 as well as with rates below Ireland's (the Netherlands and West Germany). In fact, the correlations of our party-power measures and teen pregnancy are close to zero. Similarly, the idea that teen pregnancy is caused by mothers who work and therefore fail to supervise their daughters is belied by the nearly zero correlation of female labor-force participation and teen birthrates.

What does table 8.4 tell us about abortions? It records the rates (abortions per 1,000 women between 15 and 44 years of age) for both 1980 for 13 countries for which estimates could be made (Jones et al., 1986, pp. 250–260) and for 1987 or closest year for all countries except Austria (Henshaw, 1992, table 2). Our usual pattern by type of political economy does not appear. Nor is there any obvious relationship of these rates to social policies or social spending. For instance, dividing the array in two we see that the top nine countries in abortion rates averaged 19.4% in 1980 social spending as a share of GNP; the bottom nine in abortion rates averaged a slightly higher 23.3. If we eliminate the extreme cases of Japan and the United States, the welfare effort of the top seven in abortions is close to that of the rest. In other words, there is no evidence that the welfare state, by undermining family values, encourages abortions.[29]

Another cross-national study of abortion policies and their consequences in the early 1990s among 17 Western democracies similarly finds no systematic relationship between a nation's abortion rate and the type of abortion law—criminalization, abortion for cause, or abortion on demand—and its rate of abortion; or Catholic culture; or the proportion of women in the legislature as an indication of feminist success (Brooks, 1992, pp. 351 – 356).

The only pattern by type of political economy that stands up to the data is Britain and Britain abroad vs. all other countries in the proportion of all abortions attributable to teenagers—paralleling the previous finding that these least-consensual democracies have high teen birthrates as well. Of 14 of our countries for which this age-specific figure is available, 5 of the top 6 in the percentage of teen abortions are Anglo-American (USA, England-Wales, Canada, New Zealand, Australia with Norway the one exception), with percentages from USA's 26.2 to Australia's 19.1. Finland, Sweden, Denmark, and the Netherlands are in the middle; France, Italy, West Germany, and Japan rank low. (Based on Henshaw, 1992, table 6, not reported in my table 8.4.)

While teen pregnancy rates can be substantially lowered by sex education and health services that promote contraception, the same policies appear to lower abortion rates only modestly. (J. Jacobson, 1990, pp. 34 – 35, 56 – 57.)

What we can tentatively conclude from all this is that whatever social policies or abortion laws a country adopts, and whatever its political complexion, and even after family planning services are expanded, women will go on seeking abortions for the urgent reasons they have in the past. Indeed, there is some evidence that as abortion laws liberalized, abortion rates trended downward from the early 1980s to the early 1990s—the reverse of the trend we would expect if restrictive laws reduce women's decisions to abort. Again, these decisions are universally viewed as so serious and so intimate that public policy has little effect on a woman's choice.

SUMMARY AND CONCLUSION

There is no support for the American stereotype of an epidemic of teenage sexuality, pregnancy, and parenthood—a picture of very young, black, never-married mothers, living in an inner-city ghetto, who are permanently welfare dependent and receive generous benefits, an incentive to have many children who will perpetuate welfare dependency across generations. This chapter has shown that welfare benefits in the United States are anything but generous; on average they have eroded while eligibility rules tightened. Neither the level nor the trend of welfare benefits has any relation to fertility rates. In fact, in size and fertility trend welfare families are like nonwelfare families. The welfare population is heterogeneous in race and ethnicity, physical and mental health, and the number and age of children. Most welfare mothers are white, about a third are black; a fifth, Hispanic. Very few are teenagers, though most are young. What are overrepresented among welfare recipients are very poor single mothers with enormous deficits in human capital. What welfare parents frequently pass on to their children is not welfare status but poverty and all its pathologies.

The American welfare system is a revolving door. The typical client alternates work and welfare or combines the two and, in attitude, embraces the work ethic as much as does the nonwelfare population. The key to more permanent exits from welfare to work is human capital investments.

Cross-national comparisons tell us that the most powerful proximate causes of teenage pregnancy and birthrates are poverty, especially deep poverty, and inequality, great distance between the rich and the poor. These in turn are rooted in types of political economy. The most-fragmented and decentralized systems have by far the highest rates. The epitome case is the United States: it has achieved the highest rate of deep poverty and inequality among the rich democracies for which data are available, and its rate of teen births tops all by a factor of 2.5. In contrast, corporatist democracies, because they tax and spend in more egalitarian ways, and on average invest much more in universalistic family policies that reduce poverty without provoking mass protest, have low to medium rates. Limited evidence on abortion rates, however, suggest no relationship to social policies or social spending, although again, the United States stands out as an extreme case.

The history of welfare reform in the United States since the 1960s has been one of increasingly macho talk about the evils of welfare dependency or the need to "make the tough decisions" to save money combined with strident demands that states and localities put huge numbers of welfare recipients to work. The talk is not accompanied by the upfront money and staff to make work mandates even modestly effective. Only in a few states with booming economies that have greatly increased spending and support services do we have hints of modest success in both reducing poverty and expanding job opportunity for welfare recipients. If we want to avoid punishing poor children for the sins or bad luck of their parents at the same time that we insist that parents work—both aims that reflect widely shared values—we must increase resources devoted to job development, education, training, counseling, and placement. And we must attempt to upgrade, stabilize, and expand low-wage jobs and benefits. Finally, we must avoid utopian aims. As one of the most thorough studies of welfare careers concludes, "Work exits are the least likely to end the pattern of revolving-door welfare dependency. For women who exit welfare through work and remain off welfare, wage rates do not increase over a three-year period . . . work among poor women should be viewed as the problem rather than the solution" (Harris, 1996, p. 424).

There are so many nasty aspects of the American welfare mess that it is tempting to say what many "conservatives" say, let's get rid of it by eliminating the safety net and starting over. That is essentially what the reform bill of 1996 tried to do. But if this chapter has shown anything, it is that repeated efforts to reform this system do not have their intended effects. In fact, reform efforts have generally decreased the adequacy of benefits and income for poor families, increased gross inequities in the flow of cash and services, and increased the cost of administering means tests, while creating a bewildering array of programs, agencies, and rules recipients must negotiate when they need help. Moreover, welfare reformers have been unable or unwilling to mobilize the resources to overcome work disincentives built into means-tested welfare programs (very limited earnings disregards, the removal of health care, the lack of adequate child care, the housing/transportation/job mismatch, etc.). A structural explanation of their incapacity to develop the necessary national standards and funding is America's decentralized federalism, which fosters a competitive race to the bottom. There is a little-noticed dilemma facing the more humanitarian reformers of these stiffly means-tested programs: If they *were* able to raise the funds to move the unpopular nonaged poor to decent jobs and out of poverty, they would set up even larger inequities between the welfare-working poor and the nonwelfare working poor who would receive none of these benefits. No political system could tolerate that for long—another reason that it will not happen.

Because the welfare mess is highly developed mainly in the Anglo-American democracies we can draw a lesson by comparing the policy profiles of countries that minimize it. Corporatist democracies produce patterns of spending and taxing and social and labor-market policies that reduce poverty and prevent the most extreme wage dispersion. They avoid overreliance on means tests and instead accent universalistic social policies and simpler income tests. They implement the two policy packages that are most effective in avoiding the welfare mess—family policies and active labor-market policies targeted to everyone. They have long maintained high standards for primary and secondary schools and have paid attention to the connections between education, work, low-income housing, transportation, and other infrastructure problems. They all have national health insurance. Almost all have family policies that help all working parents to balance the demands of the labor market and child care. In other words, these countries have recognized that the long list of measures needed to move people from welfare out of poverty, and, where possible, to work, is the same as the list of policies needed to improve the lives of the non-welfare population—the working poor and the celebrated "middle class." The benevolent side effect of universal social policies has been to prevent the political mobilization of the middle mass against the poor (see chap. 10).

The alternative, aggressively pursued by the United States, is to accent stiff means tests for scores of separate, uncoordinated programs; to develop a large, expensive, intrusive apparatus of surveillance and harassment of the poor; and to make the welfare poor dramatically visible, the target of mass resentment and political scapegoating, and thereby make certain that funding for welfare reform will be meager and the maze of programs, ineffective. Countries that combine all that with decades of neglect of urban problems—the deterioration of housing, neighborhoods, public transportation, and public safety—guarantee long life for the welfare mess.

NOTES

This chapter draws on Wilensky and Lebeaux, 1958, and Wilensky, 1965, 1976a, 1979, and 1982. I thank Eugene Smolensky for a critical reading.

1. The Netherlands is an exception; it scores high on means testing but low on poverty. See tables 8.3 and 14.4.

2. The National Conference of State Legislatures studied actual state behavior since the 1996 reform was implemented. It shows that 20 of the 44 states surveyed are spending 80% or less of the amount they previously spent on welfare; only five are spending at or above prior totals. Because the funding formula is based on welfare populations of previous years and the rolls have declined, per-family expenditures in 1997 climbed in most states even as they diverted federal welfare money away from welfare mothers—for tax cuts, prisons, education and other more popular causes. (*Wall Street Journal,* November 14, 1997.) These are onetime windfalls, however.

3. In the budget agreement of 1997 President Clinton traded massive tax cuts for wealthier Americans for some money targeted to the poor: $24 billion over five years to extend Medicaid to half the nation's 10 million children who lack health-care coverage; $3 billion over two years in job-hunting assistance and training; $1.5 billion (of the $4.8 he sought) for all food stamp spending; and a welfare-to-work tax credit for employers who hire welfare recipients. The agreement also restored program eligibility for legal immigrants who resided in the United States August 22, 1996, but it still

excludes legal immigrants arriving after that date. These changes, if implemented, will blunt a few of the law's harshest provisions.

4. After the passage of this law Senator Moynihan said, "The premise of this legislation is that the behavior of certain adults can be changed by making the lives of their children as wretched as possible. This is a fearsome assumption." And "In our haste to enact this bill—any bill—before the November elections, we have chosen to ignore what little we do know about the subject of poverty." The vote on the bill reflected the climate of hysteria about the undeserving poor of the mid-1990s. Of those senators up for reelection in 1996 only one, Paul Wellstone of Minnesota, voted against the welfare reform bill. (*New York Times,* August 2, 1996.)

5. Jacobs (1980) uses early 1960 data on the grounds that after that the federal government began mandating social policies and reduced state autonomy. The early 1960s provide maximum variability on the dependent variables.

6. Summarizing 10 studies of welfare and nonmarital childbearing, Gregory Acs (1995) confirms these conclusions, but he notes some findings that white women living in states with higher welfare benefits are a little more likely to have children out of wedlock than are white women living in lower-benefits states, while no such relationship appears for black and Hispanic women. None of the studies he reviews, however, controls either for differences in the young women's own characteristics or state differences in cost of living or for the benefit levels and economic circumstances at the time the childbearing decisions were being made. Considering all the evidence, Acs concludes that even if we eliminate welfare entirely, it would have no effect on nonmarital childbearing but would, of course, subject most of these children to lives of intensified poverty.

7. A national study by Martin Gilens (1996) presents strong confirmation of the race-coded nature of contemporary welfare politics. Basing his conclusions on both conventional survey modeling and a randomized survey experiment, Gilens shows that controlling for all the obvious influences (education, party identification, political ideology, income, individualism, etc.), racial attitudes are the single most powerful influence on white attitudes toward welfare spending and welfare recipients. An unspoken agenda of racial imagery is more important as a source of hostility to welfare mothers than any explicit debates over welfare reform cast in race-neutral language. This is consistent with my findings in chapter 10, a cross-national analysis of tax-welfare backlash: Nativism and ethnocentrism are always present in the most successful antitax, anti–social spending, antibureaucratic movements and parties.

8. All these studies may underestimate the importance of work as a supplement to welfare: they ignore an unknown number of welfare mothers who simply do not report work off the books and out of reach of the welfare office. Case studies uncover many women struggling to make ends meet by combining unofficial work and welfare checks.

9. William Julius Wilson (1996, pp. 51–110, 265) summarizes neighborhood studies that show such effects. See also my chapter 14.

10. This statistical paradox is frequently compared to the identical puzzle about hospital stays. If you focus only on people entering the hospital, you would find that vast majorities of those who ever enter stay less than a week. But if you go beyond the admitting room and walk around the hospital wards, you would find that a vast majority of the beds were occupied by patients with chronic conditions. (Making the hospital—read welfare—a way of life?)

11. From 1974 to 1987 "permanence" on welfare (the probability of receiving AFDC for the next three years for persons who had received AFDC for the previous three years), went down for whites and up for blacks (Gottschalk, McLanahan, and Sandefur, 1994, p. 97), reflecting the increasing concentration of poverty, family breakup, and single motherhood among central-city blacks (see chap. 14).

12. Births to adolescents are only 30% of the births to unmarried women but they comprise almost half of all first births to unmarried women (1996 Green Book, p. 514). If one wishes to accent

the explosion of births to unmarried women instead of the modest increase over 55 years shown by the trend of birthrates, one can divide all births out of wedlock by all births in wedlock. That ratio is exploding, because the married birthrate (the denominator) has greatly declined while the births out of wedlock (the numerator) have modestly increased.

13. One of the most comprehensive and systematic studies (Duncan and Hoffman, 1990) compares the effect of both generosity of welfare benefits and likely future career and marital opportunities on out-of-wedlock births using data from the Panel Study of Income Dynamics on nearly 900 black teenagers and more than 300 out-of-wedlock births, holding constant family background, sibling characteristics, and location. They conclude that the effects of welfare benefits are trivial while the effects of economic and marital opportunities are very strong. "Women with the least to lose are most likely to have children in their teen years" (*ibid.*, pp. 531–532).

14. For France, see chapter 7, note 24. Italy, despite its generous maternal leave and benefit policies (chap. 3, note 16) moved down to one of the lowest birthrates in the world and the lowest in Europe. For comparative evidence of negligible effects in rich Western nations, see Ekert (1986). For evidence of small fertility effects of family policies in less-developed countries of Eastern Europe, see Buttner and Lutz (1990).

15. It is common among workfare programs for even the most cost-conscious administrators to exempt up to half or more of the recipients from participation in state and local welfare-to-work programs. And typically at the end of three years, well over half of the participants remain without jobs. In one of the strongest get-to-work-now programs in Riverside, California, of the one-third who were exempt, 58% suffered from physical or mental health problems, 26% had a "family crisis," 7% had problems with child care or transportation, 7% had "legal" problems, and 2% were excused because they had only recently lost a job (Maynard, 1995, pp. 112–114). The 20% exemption limit imposed by the welfare reform of 1996 ignores these realities as well as labor-market realities.

16. I am grateful to Judith Gueron for helpful comments on this section.

17. By making part-time work pay even better than full-time work, the MFIP also recognizes the welfare mother's need and desire to take care of her children. Minnesota hopes that this combination of part-time work and welfare will be a stepping-stone to full-time employment.

18. Gary Burtless (1995, pp. 77–78) found that among 25-year-old respondents to the National Longitudinal Survey of Youth who had received welfare in all of the previous 12 months, 72% scored in the bottom quarter of the Armed Forces Qualification Test. Judith Gueron (1995, p. 5) notes that a survey of people who were targeted for the JOBS program " . . . shows that between a quarter and half lacked prior work experience, at least a third had extremely low literacy skills, and more than a quarter said they could not participate . . . because they or their child had a health or emotional problem." And the survey excludes AFDC recipients who were not currently subject to the JOBS work mandate because of still worse handicaps.

19. The accent is on *working* partner. A nonworking partner who shares the mother's handicaps cannot be of much help. Confirmation comes from the first-year record of the reform bill of 1996. On the assumption that two-parent families will be easy to force into low-wage work, the bill required work from 75% of them by October 1, 1997. States that fail to meet this goal (or the goal of 25% for single parents) can lose up to 5% of federal welfare money. About half the states failed to meet the 75% goal. California, which by the deadline had put only about 20% of the two-parent welfare cases into required work, reported that about half of these families are refugees with severe linguistic-cultural barriers. Once again the crackdown enthusiasts rediscovered that even the properly married poor are more disadvantaged than they had imagined; large numbers have physical or mental disabilities, language deficiencies, drug or alcohol problems, criminal records, or scant work histories. (*New York Times,* October 1, 1997.) While only 7% of the nation's caseload is two-parent families, they still provide a symbol in the politics of welfare. State workfare failures became an issue at

the end of 1997: should the sanctions be stiffer (welfare bums and their wives are slacking off, states are not trying), or should the federal government relax the rules (get real)?

20. For example, in a Columbia University study of 200 fast-food workers in central Harlem, a poor minority neighborhood, each opening for a fast-food job typically brings 14 applicants. The restaurants favor single or married men and women with some job experience and a high-school diploma but no children, who are referred by personal networks (e.g., legal immigrants) or commute from distant, less-disorganized neighborhoods. By all these criteria most welfare mothers cannot compete; under workfare deadlines they join the back of a very long employment line (Newman, 1995). If, as in this example of fast-food jobs, welfare mothers do not often displace the working poor, they may do so in still less attractive jobs such as cleaning lady, and, more important, they increase the supply of very cheap labor, which in the absence of unions is a drag on the wages of low-skilled workers. Consistent with this is a BLS report of a four-year reversal of the long-term decline in the wage gap between men and women (*New York Times,* September 15, 1997). It may be too early to tell how much of this is due to welfare mothers flooding the low-wage job markets, but the four years do parallel the acceleration of state-mandated workfare, 1993–97.

21. I view means-tested programs like AFDC as noncategorical, despite the notion that they are claimed by social right. In the United States the right to AFDC as well as the amount and duration of benefits are hugely variable — not only from state to state but also within states according to the discretion of administrators and welfare workers as they interpret and apply complex rules. That the welfare reform of 1996 took away this highly ambiguous right to AFDC and further increased state autonomy is not a great change from the previous situation. I prefer to reserve the term categorical for simpler statuses such as age (pensions), family size (family allowances), military service (veterans' benefits), taxable income, or even disabilities where the presumption of right is in favor of the client. If the presumption of social right is aggressively negative, it is a right in theory not practice.

22. Based on number of months in which single mothers were eligible. The non-takeup rate for eligibility spells was much higher: most women who ever become eligible do not claim either AFDC or food stamps (Blank and Ruggles, 1993, p. 36).

23. Figures calculated from Atkinson (1991, pp. 24–25) and the 1996 Green Book, tables 8-25 and 8-27.

24. The Supreme Court decided 12 statutory AFDC cases between 1968 and 1975 alone—and this is the tip of an iceberg composed of lower court decisions often at odds with one another and with the Supreme Court. And from 1967 to 1997 a large and increasing number of court rulings on means-tested programs have been overturned by Congress. (Melnick, 1994, pp. 253–255, 262–264.)

25. These figures are only roughly comparable. They are based on our own estimates from national statistical abstracts, government documents outlining eligibility and coverage, monographs, books, and other sources discussed in appendix F. They are expenditures, not a ranking of laws or administrative rules. Nevertheless, they match the country descriptions of means testing in the rest of this chapter. I am grateful to Susan Hahn and Mina Silberberg for their dedicated assistance in this arduous task.

26. A four-country comparison of long public assistance spells among single mothers provides confirmation (Gottschalk, McLanahan, and Sandefur, 1994, pp. 95–96).

27. I am grateful for Brenda McLaughlin's assistance in assessing and processing data for this section and for conversation with Stanley Henshaw clarifying methods used in Jones et al. (1986) to arrive at cumulative birthrates for teenagers.

28. The cross-national data on income distribution and poverty come from the Luxembourg Income Study (LIS): Rainwater (1994, tables 5 and 6); and Atkinson, Rainwater, and Smeeding (1995, table 2). Using the National Longitudinal Survey of Youth, 1979 to 1989, Lawrence Wu (1996) demonstrates that for the United States low income, declining income, and frequent changes in fam-

ily of origin structure are each associated with significantly increased risk of premarital births. Poverty and family instability are both powerful and independent predictors of a first birth out of wedlock.

29. Japan's abortion rate of 84 is extraordinary. In fact, Japanese women, especially older married women, have long used abortion as a major method of birth control; at the time of these measures, the pill had not been approved for contraception use and sterilization was rare; there were more abortions than live births, although this pattern is gradually declining with the continuing modernization of Japan. The abortion rate for Ireland is based only on Irish residents who obtained abortions in England and gave an Irish address—probably an understated figure.

9

BUREAUCRATIC
EFFICIENCY AND BLOAT

As we have seen, the expansion of the welfare state (especially the adoption of similar types of programs, rising levels of spending, increasingly comprehensive coverage, and even methods of financing) is strongly affected by continuing industrialization and its correlates—an aging population, expanding bureaucracies, changes in family structures, increased mobility and the push for equality, and the increased responsiveness of political elites to an enlarged and more vocal electorate. We have also seen that national differences in types of political economy (corporatist, corporatist-without-labor, and least corporatist), the power of mass-based political parties (Catholic and left), and the intensity of minority-group cleavages explain many of the remaining differences among countries equally rich—differences in aggregate spending, sector spending, program emphasis, family policy, the accent on universality or on targeting benefits to the poor (which in the few countries that accent heavy means testing in the end results in a welfare mess).

A final piece of the picture is national differences in the size and efficiency of public bureaucracies delivering the cash and services of the welfare state. The first puzzle we encounter is the very loose connection of government civilian employees and social spending. Table 9.1 ranks countries by welfare effort and shows nonmilitary public employees as a percentage of the civilian labor force. Five of the eight welfare-state laggards—United Kingdom, New Zealand, Australia, Canada, and the United States—have larger bureaucracies than their social spending would suggest. Conversely some of the big spenders, notably the Netherlands, France, and West Germany, have lean bureaucracies. The notion that continental Europe has a penchant for big government while the rest of us resist it does not stand up to data on the size of public bureaucracies.

ECONOMIES OF SCALE

One explanation might be that big spenders achieve economies of scale. To test that idea I devised two crude measures of efficiency and of bureaucratic bloat. If "efficiency" is indicated by how many employees it takes to deliver a given value of service and cash, then we can measure it by dividing the broadest comparable measure of social spending—social

TABLE 9.1 Although there is some correlation between social spending and government employees as a percentage of the civilian labor force in 1980 ($r = .34$), three of seven big spenders have few public employees, while five of eight lean spenders have many public employees

	High Government Employees (14.9% — 28.6% of CLF)			Low Government Employees (6.5% — 12.9% of CLF)		
	Country	*SS/GNP*	*Gov't. 'ees*	*Country*	*SS/GNP*	*Gov't. 'ees*
Welfare State Leaders (Soc. Sec. Spending 26.3% — 33.1% of GNP)	Sweden	33.1	28.6	Netherlands	31.3	11.3
	Denmark	32.8	24.9	France	30.4	11.8
	Belgium	29.8	15.2	W. Germany	27.0	12.8
	Austria	26.3	15.9			
	Cell avg.	30.5	21.2	Cell avg.	30.0	12.0
Middle-Rank Spenders (19.6% — 23.3% of GNP)	Norway	23.3	17.7	Ireland	23.3	12.4
	Finland	21.1	14.9	Italy	19.6	12.9
	Cell avg.	22.2	16.3	Cell avg.	21.5	12.7
Lean Social Spenders (7.0% — 17.3% of GNP)	United Kingdom	17.3	18.9	Switzerland	16.0	10.2
	New Zealand	16.1	18.0	Japan	11.0	6.5
	Australia	15.7	24.0	Israel	7.0	12.1
	Canada	15.1	18.0			
	United States	14.6	14.9			
	Cell avg.	15.8	18.8	Cell avg.	11.3	9.6

Sources: Social spending from ILO, *The Cost of Social Security, Eleventh International Inquiry, Basic Tables* (Geneva, 1985). For sources of data on nonmilitary government employees, see appendix J.

security plus education in constant 1974 U.S. dollars—by the number of government civilian employees.

The second measure, which I shall call "bureaucratic bloat," attempts to relate the size of the public bureaucracy to what people are getting from it in much the way citizens themselves might evaluate the size of government. Thus, we use the ratio of public-civilian employees as a percentage of the labor force to the per-head expenditure on social security and education in constant 1974 U.S. dollars—an indicator of what individuals receive from the welfare state. (See appendix J for measures.)

These measures of efficiency and bloat have two limitations. First, by using the dollar price of cash and services processed, they include differences in the pay of public employees; those countries that pay civil servants most, possibly because they have strong public-sector unions, may come out more efficient just because they pay higher salaries. Second, the big spenders may also spend more on health and education—the two most expansive and labor-intensive sectors of the welfare state (Wilensky, 1975, 1985; Rose, 1985b, pp. 8−13.) These limitations are not fatal, however. Differences in salaries are not a very large component of the very large differences among these 19 countries in aggregate spending. For instance, Japan spent only 11% of its GNP on social security in 1980 while Sweden spent over 33%; the per capita spread was about five to one. Both these measures show even higher spreads for earlier years. And we can deal with labor intensiveness separately; we shall see that although health and education spending has had an independent effect on the size of public bureaucracies in recent years, that impact is not as strong as the impact of types of bargaining arrangements and left political parties.

Table 9.2 shows the rank orders of efficiency and bureaucratic bloat for the three years for which the data are most complete and comparable. In brief we see that seven of the eight welfare-state leaders of 1966–74 (Sweden, Denmark, Netherlands, France, Belgium, Germany, Austria) tend to rank high to medium in efficiency (Italy is the one exception); and four of the eight big spenders are low in bureaucratic bloat (the exceptions are Austria and Italy, which were medium in bloat all along, and Sweden and Denmark, which rose to medium by 1974). Conversely, five of the nine welfare-state laggards are low in efficiency and high in bloat (United Kingdom, New Zealand, Australia, Ireland, Israel). Switzerland is a clear exception; it runs its lean welfare state as efficiently as it does its banks. And the ambiguous cases of Japan, Canada, and the United States are partial exceptions; they are low to medium in efficiency, as expected, but as their welfare states expanded they moved down to medium in bloat by 1974, a bit faster than expected. This table is strong confirmation of the hypothesis that at high levels of development the welfare state—like an insurance company with a broad base of clients—enjoys economies of scale.

Tables not reported here show that from 1966 to 1978 there was a general trend toward larger size, and from 1966 to 1974 greater efficiency and reduced bloat. They are consistent with my previous analysis of the almost universal expansion of the welfare state, more recently at a decelerating rate (chap. 5; Wilensky, 1965, p. x; and 1975). Here are the findings based on absolute scores, not on the relative rankings for each year reported in table 9.2:

- All 19 countries moved up in their public employees' fraction of the labor force except Canada, which moved slightly down from 18.9% in 1971 to 17.6% in 1978 and the United States, which had a similar move from 15.6% to 14.9%. If these small changes are not merely measurement error, they suggest a mild North American exception. In the 1980s, the growth in public employees' share continued in almost all countries but at a slower rate.[1]

- All 19 countries increased efficiency from 1966 to 1974. All increased efficiency from 1971 to 1974 except for Austria, Denmark, and Canada.

- All countries decreased in bureaucratic bloat from 1966 to 1974 except for Denmark and Austria.

EXPLAINING CONVERGENCE AND DIVERGENCE IN THE SIZE OF BUREAUCRACIES

Obvious economies of scale aside, let us now apply the general model I have used to explain national differences in social spending to the problem of differences in the size of public bureaucracies. Combining sources of convergence—industrialization (affluence measured by GNP per capita) and its structural correlates (measures of mobility and meritocracy)—with sources of divergence or differences—types of political economy (corporatism

TABLE 9.2 Rank orders of efficiency and bureaucratic bloat for ninteen countries

Country	Efficiency[a]			Bureaucratic Bloat[b]		
	1966	*1971*	*1974*	*1966*	*1971*	*1974*
Netherlands	(1) H	(1) H	(1) H	(17) L	(18) L	(18) L
W. Germany	(2) H	(2) H	(3) H	(18) L	(17) L	(17) L
Switzerland	(3) H	(3) H	(2) H	(19) L	(19) L	(19) L
Belgium	(4) H	(4) H	(4) H	(16) L	(16) L	(16) L
France	(5) H	(5) HM	(5) H	(15) L	(15) L	(16) L
Denmark	(6) M	(7) M	(10) M	(14) L	(14) L	(12) M
Sweden	(7) M	(8) M	(8) M	(13) L	(13) L	(14) M
Norway	(8) M	(6) HM	(6) HM	(10) M	(12) L	(13) M
Italy	(9) M	(11) M	(7) M	(9) M	(7) M	(9) M
Austria	(10) M	(10) M	(13) M	(11) M	(9) M	(7) M
Finland	(11) M	(12) M	(11) M	(12) ML	(11) LM	(11) M
United States	(12) ML	(13) M	(9) M	(8) MH	(10) M	(10) M
Canada	(13) ML	(9) M	(12) M	(7) MH	(8) M	(8) M
New Zealand	(14) L	(16) L	(16) L	(4) H	(3) H	(5) H
Israel	(15) L	(14) L	(15) L	(3) H	(5) H	(3) H
United Kingdom	(16) L	(19) L	(19) L	(6) H	(2) H	(1) H
Ireland	(17) L	(17) L	(17) L	(1) H	(1) H	(2) H
Australia	(18) L	(18) L	(18) L	(2) H	(4) H	(4) H
Japan	(19) L	(15) L	(14) L	(5) H	(6) MH	(6) M

[a]Total social security plus education delivered per civilian public employee, based on constant 1974 U.S. dollars. See appendices C and J. High rank = high efficiency.

[b]The ratio of the size of the civilian public bureaucracy to its social output, measured in constant 1974 U.S. dollars. See appendices C and J. High rank = much bloat.

and party power) and enduring social structures (minority-group cleavages)—we arrive at the causal model shown in figure 9.1.

The rationale in brief: The richer a rich democracy becomes, the greater the need and demand for public services and the larger the share of public employees in the labor force. Affluence (not only growth rates but sheer economic level) changes the occupational and industrial composition of the labor force, expands higher education, and thereby increases mobility opportunities for the less privileged (minorities, women, and working-class children). At the same time, by changing family structure and increasing female labor-force participation, continuing industrialization also reduces fertility, increases family instability, expands the aged population, and thereby creates pressure for expansion of the welfare state,

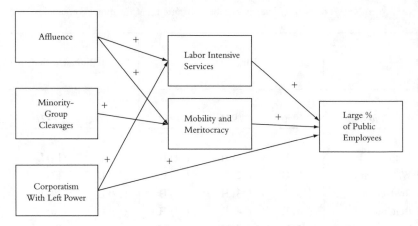

Figure 9.1. Industrialization and types of political economy as sources of bureaucratic bloat

including a self-expanding bureaucracy (see chaps. 5 and 7). As rich countries converge in their levels of affluence, continuing industrialization as a source of differences in the size of public bureaucracies should become less important than structural differences among nations, although past differences in timing and rate of industrialization should leave their legacy and retard convergence.[2]

Independent of affluence, in some countries, internal social cleavages based on descent (racial, religious, ethnic, linguistic) create a further demand for separate but equal government services (e.g., government-supported minority-based schools and curricula, cultural and recreational services) as well as conflict-resolution agencies (e.g., an equal opportunity, antidiscrimination apparatus). Even in the United States, the democracy with the strongest tradition of state-church separation where "separate but equal" has been declared unconstitutional, we see an increase in state support for religious and other "private" schools and social services.

Corporatist bargaining arrangements should have their own independent effect. The more corporatist, the less bureaucratic bloat because of (1) more centralized decision making and thus fewer local and regional government employees; (2) more reliance on cash transfers or universal categorical benefits, less on means-tested, heavily policed benefits; and (3) better human resource planning and lower public assistance costs (with their stigma, exaggerated abuse, and welfare bureaucracy). (For elaboration see chaps. 2 and 8.)

Offsetting the corporatist brake on public-sector expansion would be left power: clearly left parties are committed to government intervention to achieve equality; the more they participate in government, the more responsive those governments will be to demands for public-sector expansion. Thus left-corporatist countries should have more public employees than others; more-decentralized political economies with some left power should also score high.

Inspecting table 9.2 we see that the top eight in efficiency are all corporatist democracies, with or without the full inclusion of labor (Denmark, a minor exception, falls to 10th in 1974) while five of the bottom six in efficiency are decentralized, least-corporatist democracies. Conversely, five of the top six in bureaucratic bloat are all least corporatist while the seven least bloated are all corporatist. (Japan, with low efficiency and medium to high bloat, is the exception.)

Using multiple regression analysis and multivariate tables we can test hypotheses about the size of public bureaucracies. In general, we find that for the late 1960s both industrialization and its mobility correlates and types of corporatism and party power explain national differences in the public employees' share of the labor force. But by 1980, with the continued convergence of rich countries, with the growth rates of the least rich gradually closing the gap between themselves and the most rich, per capita GNP and some of the mobility variables lose their effect while left power, minority-group cleavages, corporatism, and, to a lesser extent, labor intensiveness retain their effect.

Table 9.3 shows the interaction in the late 1960s of all these variables except labor intensiveness, which I shall discuss later as we consider the late 1970s and early 1980s when it becomes more important. The strongest predictor of public employees as a fraction of the labor force in 1966 and 1971 is affluence ($r = .53$). Among the 10 countries with the highest GNP per capita in 1966, only 3 rank low in public employees; of the 9 least-rich countries, only 2 (United Kingdom and Austria) rank high in public employees. Three correlates of continuing industrialization that measure an emphasis on meritocracy are also significantly correlated with public employees—high mobility rates out of the working class ($r = .52$), higher education expenditures per capita 1965–71 (.50), and working-class sons and daughters as a percentage of higher education enrollments (.44)—and even more strongly correlated with one another, suggesting their coherence as a measure of a society's emphasis on mobility and equality of opportunity. Confirming the validity of these indicators of meritocracy is their positive correlation with means-tested public assistance expenditure per capita, a measure of a society's eagerness to stigmatize the poor. As I have noted elsewhere (Wilensky, 1975, pp. 54–57), the upwardly mobile workers or minority members of the middle mass look upward and across, not down, so they project their political resentments onto lower strata. As they scramble up the ladder, they are less inclined to extend a helping hand to those below than to give them the heel of a boot. The more mobility and meritocracy among the middle three-fifths of the population, the less their solidarity with the poor.

Although data on intergenerational mobility are limited to 14 countries, table 9.3 shows that 4 of the 5 countries with the *highest* mobility rates (Canada, Australia, United States, United Kingdom) all have high or medium-high minority-group cleavages *and* rank high in public employees as a percentage of the labor force. Of the 6 countries lowest in mobility rates (Denmark, Norway, Belgium, Japan, West Germany, and Italy) 5 rank low or medium-low in minority group cleavages (Belgium is the exception) and 4 rank low in public employees (Denmark and Norway are the exceptions). In other words, the public sector provides channels of mobility for minority groups who therefore fight for public sector expansion. The public sector everywhere accommodates the mobility aspirations of minority groups. There are no countries with high mobility and low cleavages; and only one with low mobility and strong cleavages (Belgium).

Once again we see that rich countries, as they get richer, expand the public sector, a product of continuing industrialization. But the centralized bargaining structures of corporatist democracies are a brake on public-sector expansion while minority-group cleavages foster such expansion. There is a Scandinavian exception: Sweden, Denmark, and Norway are deviant cases—low in ethnic cleavages, medium to low in mobility, but high in public employees. The explanation lies in the interaction between strong left parties and

TABLE 9.3 Affluence and decentralization create a need and political pressure for jobs in the public sector; more corporatist countries have fewer public employees as a percentage of the civilian labor force (1966 and 1971). At the extremes, the mobility aspirations of minority groups and left power add to pressures for public-sector jobs.

TEN RICHEST COUNTRIES (1966 GNP per capita $1793 - $3548)

	Least Corporatist		Corporatist With or without labor	
	Mobility rate[a]	Min. grp. cleavages[a]	Mobility rate	Min. grp. cleavages
High Public Employees 12.2—19.6% of CLF	United States .114 (4)	.55 (4)	Sweden(L)[b] .045 (7)	.04 (18)
	Canada .184 (2)	.71 (1)	Norway(L) −.008 (10)	.03 (19)
	Australia .141 (3)	.44 (6)	Denmark(L) .037 (9)	.05 (17)
	New Zealand —	.43 (7)		
Low Public Employees (5.9—10.4% of CLF)			Switzerland(W) —	.55 (4)
			France(W) .056 (6)	.28 (11)
			W. Germany(C) −.068 (13)	.28 (11)

NINE LEAST RICH COUNTRIES (1966 GNP per capita $878 - $1710)

	Least Corporatist		Corporatist With or without labor	
	Mobility rate	Min. grp. cleavages	Mobility rate	Min. grp. cleavages
High Public Employees	United Kingdom .102 (5)	.47 (5)	Austria(LC) —	.17 (13)
Low Public Employees	Ireland —	.08 (16)	Israel(L) .286 (1)	.58 (2)
			Belgium(LC) −.033 (11)	.34 (9)
			Netherlands(LC) .041 (8)	.37 (8)
			Finland(L) —	.12 (14)
			Italy(C) −.081 (14)	.10 (15)
			Japan(W) −.048 (12)	.19 (12)

[a] For definition of measures, see appendices C, I, and J.

[b] Types of corporatism: (L) = Left corporatist, (LC) = Left-Catholic corporatist, (C) = Catholic corporatist, (W) = Corporatist-without-labor.

corporatism. Among corporatist democracies, Sweden, Denmark, and Norway score among the top five in cumulative left power since World War II. For these countries, strong left power overcomes the constraint of centralized bargaining structures.[3] Israel is the extreme exception to all hypotheses but one: it is very high in ethnic cleavages and mobility and, before Menachem Begin, was high in left power; but it remains low in public employees. Its corporatist bargaining arrangements are not so strong that they could act as much of a brake on public-sector expansion. Instead Israel's extraordinary defense budget and its rank as one of the least rich of our rich democracies doubtless accounts for the starvation of its civilian public sector.

In sum, for the late 1960s we can interpret the interplay of affluence, decentralization, minority-group conflict, and mobility as a strong force for public-sector job creation; conversely, corporatism, social homogeneity, less affluence, and less mobility combine to reduce the rate of growth of public-sector employment. At the extreme, left power generates added pressure for public-sector expansion as it has in Scandinavia, and, in their intermittent periods of left rule, in the United Kingdom, New Zealand, and the United States, whether they have strong minority-group cleavages or not.

The likely causal process is this: By changing the occupational structure, continuing industrialization fosters high mobility rates both in the worklife and between generations (see chap. 1). Affluent countries with high mobility rates and strong minority-group cleavages also generate a need and political pressure for jobs in the public sector, which, in turn, provide further mobility chances for minorities, women, and working-class children, a force for still more public-sector expansion. Thus table 9.3 shows that all countries that combine affluence with high mobility rates *and* strong social cleavages (United States, Canada, Australia) rank high in public employees. Conversely, in the absence of both affluence and strong minority-group cleavages all countries but one rank low in public employees (Finland, Italy, Japan, Ireland). The exception is Austria: it is least rich and has low cleavages, but public employees are abundant.

There are mild surprises in these results. It is widely assumed that an accent on mobility, equality of opportunity, and meritocracy favors the expansion of the private sector and blocks the expansion of the public sector. That overlooks the political responsiveness of all modern democracies to pressure from minority-group movements and working-class families for both equality of opportunity *and* equality of results. The earliest and most effective antidiscrimination action is government action. The first means toward that end is the expansion of public-sector jobs for the less privileged, both in civilian agencies and the military. Similarly, it is often assumed that statist regimes expand the public sector. But our data show that while corporatist democracies, with their centralized bargaining structures and labor inclusion, may have a penchant for taxing and spending, many of them save on the personnel necessary to deliver the goods and hence cluster in the medium and medium-low levels of public employment. Corporatist countries that keep labor at a distance save the most on personnel; all three (Japan, France, and Switzerland) score low in public employment. We have earlier seen two reasons for the greater efficiency of corporatist democracies in general: they avoid the elaborate means-testing machinery of more-decentralized regimes in favor of universal, categorical benefits; and their very centralization slows the multiplication and growth of local and regional bureaucracies (see chaps. 2 and 8).

By the 1980s, as expected, the power of economic level and its mobility and merito-cratic correlates as an explanation for the multiplication of public employees faded away. The distance between the most-rich and least-rich countries diminished, so the effect of affluence lessened. Table 9.4 shows the interaction of the previous variables with one mea-sure of labor intensiveness, health and education spending per capita added and per capita GNP dropped.

Comparing tables 9.3 and 9.4, two countries, Belgium and Finland, change rank in em-ployees from low in the late 1960s to high in 1980; everything else stays the same. We see three major clusters: (1) the most-fragmented and decentralized democracies that have strong minority-group cleavages (upper left corner of the table) are high in public em-ployees (three have also experienced many years of left power); (2) of the eight corporatist democracies with strong left power, six rank high on public employees whether they have strong minority-group cleavages or not and five of the six are high to medium in labor-intensive services; (3) the three corporatist countries that keep both labor and left parties at a distance are all low in public employees (Japan, France, Switzerland). There remain five countries with low employees unaccounted for. Of these, three have weak cleavages (Italy, West Germany, and Ireland); three rank quite low in labor intensiveness (Ireland, Italy, Israel); only one, Israel, has strong cumulative left power not offset by stronger Cath-olic power (and since Prime Minister Begin came to power in 1977 and was succeeded by Prime Minister Netanyahu left power has eroded, bringing the exception into line).

Confirming these conclusions is a multiple regression analysis of the data on public em-ployees for 1966–71, 1974–78, and 1980. Because this method permits neither as good an examination of interaction effects as tables 9.3 and 9.4 do, nor any analysis of types of corporatism, and because of the concentration of high employees' ratios among countries with strong minority-group cleavages (Britain, Britain abroad, and Belgium) and coun-tries with weak cleavages (Scandinavia and Austria), regression analysis will understate the importance of corporatism and minority groups and should be seen only as complemen-tary to the tables above. The findings: Left power is significantly and positively related to the size of the public bureaucracy in all three periods; the corporatism score is negatively related (significant only for 1966–71). This confirms the finding that left-corporatist countries hire lots of public employees but, after controlling for this effect, corporatism is a constraint on that tendency. If we add each of the mobility and meritocracy variables one at a time to equations including left power and corporatism, none is significant. In-dependent of corporatism and left power, however, labor intensiveness does have a signi-ficant positive effect on public employees' share of employment. For instance, here is one result for 1980 for 19 countries.

Dependent Variable	Independent Variables	Beta	p
Public employees as % of civilian labor force	Corporatism score	−.34	.17
	Cumulative left power, 1946–76	.48	.04
	Education and health spending per capita, 1980	.48	.05

Adjusted $R^2 = .30$

TABLE 9.4 Interaction of types of political economy, minority-group cleavages, left and Catholic party power, and labor-intensive spending as a source of public-sector jobs (1980)

| | | Least Corporatist | | | | | | Democratic Corporatist | | | | | | Corporatist Without Labor | | | | | |
| | | Strong Cleavages | | | Weak Cleavages | | | Strong Cleavages | | | Weak Cleavages | | | Strong Cleavages | | | Weak Cleavages | | |
		Country[a]	Pub. 'ees as % CLF	Lab. Int. Spending[b]	Country	Pub. 'ees as % CLF	Lab. Int. Spending	Country	Pub. 'ees as % CLF	Lab. Int. Spending	Country	Pub. 'ees as % CLF	Lab. Int. Spending	Country	Pub. 'ees as % CLF	Lab. Int. Spending	Country	Pub. 'ees as % CLF	Lab. Int. Spending
High Public 'ees		Australia	24.0	(11) M				Belg.(L)(C)	15.2	(6) H	Sweden(L)	28.6	(1) H						
		UK(L)	18.9	(12) ML							Denmark(L)	24.9	(4) H						
		Canada	18.0	(10) M							Norway(L)	17.7	(2) H						
		N. Zeal.(L)	18.0	(18) L							Austria(L)(C)	15.9	(17) L						
		USA(L)	14.9	(13) ML							Finland(L)	14.9	(9) M						
	Cell avg.		18.8%	$954				Cell avg.	15.2%	$1550	Cell avg.	20.4	$1684						
Low Public 'ees					Ireland	12.4	(14) L	Israel(L)	12.1	(19) L	Italy(C)	12.9	(15) L	Switz.	10.2	(5) H	France	11.8	(8) H
								Neth.(L)(C)	11.3	(3) H	W. Germ.(C)	12.8	(7) H				Japan	6.5	(16) L
	Cell avg.				Cell avg.	12.4%	$847	Cell avg.	11.7%	$1166	Cell avg.	12.9%	$1162	Cell avg.	10.2%	$1557	Cell avg.	9.2%	$1143

[a](L) = Strong left party power 1946–76; (C) = Strong Catholic party power 1946–76.

[b]Labor-intensive spending measured by health and education spending per capita, in U.S. dollars, 1980.

The same equation without the deviant case of Israel increases the effect of left power and decreases the effect of labor-intensive spending; it explains 35% of the variance.

The hypothesis that the expansion of health, education, and other labor-intensive programs was the main driving force behind the growth in public-sector employment from 1951 to 1980 (Rose, 1984, pp. 137–138; 1985b, pp. 8–13) must be viewed with caution. First, the tables show that health and education spending per capita is a poor fourth as a cause; for all periods before 1980, despite its correlation with the public employees share, it washes out against the structural causes in all regression equations if we exclude Israel, and in the 1980 table it is not very impressive. Second, if we use other measures of labor intensiveness, we get mixed results. For instance, one can see a rationale for two alternative concepts and related measures of labor intensiveness. One is the *ratio of health and education to all other social spending* (including such heavy cash outlays as pensions). The idea is that elites, for whatever reason, are emphasizing these labor-intensive sectors and creating a demand for health and education personnel; and then the supply of college graduates, teachers, and medical specialists expands, creating its own demand. Unfortunately this measure is completely unrelated to the public employees' share of employment for any period. The other is a similar measure, *health and education spending as a fraction of GNP.* The idea behind this measure is that elites consider economic-growth and revenue projections, the state of the economy and other economic constraints, previous budgets, and current political demands and then they allocate scarce resources, creating a demand for personnel; the supply of personnel creates further demand. Here the results are similar to those for per capita expenditures on health and education; in all regression equations that eliminate Israel as an outlier these "effort" variables (social spending/GNP) have either no significant independent effect on the size of public bureaucracies or the effect is less than that of left power. In short, the hypothesis that an accent on labor-intensive services accounts for expansion of public employees is quite weak.

Instead, as our tables have shown, the interaction of three forces—types of political economy, political parties, and minority-group pressures—is the best explanation for the most recent data on national differences in nonmilitary public employees as a percentage of the civilian labor force for 19 rich democracies.

INSIGHTS FROM THE CASES OF THE UNITED STATES, CANADA, AND ITALY

The case of the United States illustrates how these conclusions play out in a decentralized system with great affluence, strong minority-group cleavages, high rates of occupational mobility, and, for some periods between 1946 and 1980, considerable left power in Congress or the White House or both, as well as in many states and metropolitan areas. Despite its late start in expansion of the civilian public bureaucracy, the United States had reached a medium level by 1980 (about 15% of the labor force, although some estimates put it a bit higher). As we have seen in chapter 1, the interplay of social movements for equality and government coercion is a powerful force for expanding opportunities for women and minority groups. Thus, fair employment practices commissions such as those of the 1940s and 1950s and affirmative action programs such as those of the 1960s on have clearly expanded minority representation in middle and upper-middle layers of the United

States; the civil rights movement and its institutionalization in such agencies as the Equal Employment Opportunities Commission (EEOC) accelerated the trend. The occupational integration of blacks—their penetration of middle and upper-middle professional and technical jobs—proceeded faster in the prosperous periods of World War II and 1960–73 than in the slumps of the 1950s, mid-1970s, or early 1980s. But there was more than the business cycle at work. The armed forces during and after World War II led in occupational integration (Moskos, 1966). And most of the civilian gains since World War II have been in occupations in which a large portion of the nonwhites are hired by government (Wilensky, 1965, pp. xxxvi–xxxvii; and Wilson, 1978, pp. 102–104). All of this suggests that vigorous antidiscrimination policies can make it too expensive for employers to stick to the older ascriptive networks (white ethnics, WASPs).

Public bureaucracies that are new or innovative are especially hospitable to minority-group ambitions—in the United States it is the Labor, Housing and Urban Development, and Health and Human Services departments, not State or Treasury, that led in expanding minority-group opportunities, as did the planning and welfare agencies in large urban areas, where minority politicians won office. Often city governments employ black and Hispanic professionals and skilled workers at double their fraction in the general labor force (Pascal and Menchik, 1980, p. 301).

Canada provides a similar case of interaction between social movements based on minority-group interests and government pressures. Before the rise of French nationalism, Anglophone employers typically preferred English-speaking Protestants to Francophones for supervisory and managerial positions (Hughes, 1943). After four decades of agitation for Francophone equality and the recent rise of separatist movements and politicians in Quebec, the tables have been turned: Anglophones in Quebec must now speak French in workplace and community; in Ottawa, French fluency gets you points for promotion. In a systematic study of men aged 25–45 at midcareer in five agencies of the Canadian federal administration, Beattie (1975) demonstrated the effect of this social movement on career development among Francophones. Although by 1965 older unilingual Francophones were still suffering disadvantages in both salary and career mobility in "English" organizations, young minority men were doing as well or better than their majority counterparts (holding constant level and type of education, linguistic skill, age, and seniority).[4] In private and public sectors alike the effects of political pressure on managers' cost calculations are plain.

Again, as in the United States, it was the newer, more innovative agencies of Canadian government that first opened up high-level positions to Francophones. In the 1960s while the routine agencies (State, Public Works, Taxation, Division of National Revenue) concentrated Francophones in routine jobs, the more "creative" agencies (Departments of Finance and Agriculture) opened the way for Francophone agricultural scientists, economists, lawyers, and administrators, most of them assimilation-prone *Quebecois* (Beattie, 1975, chap. 5).

The United States epitomizes the public employment expansion typical of a decentralized, fragmented political economy. Consider the trends in public-sector jobs by level of government. The historic growth in the federal share of both public spending and public civilian employment, up to 1949, has reversed with federal spending going down from 66% of total government spending in 1949 to 56% in 1979 while federal civilian employees as a fraction of total public employees declined from 34% in 1949 to 18% in 1977—a much swifter drop in federal share of employment than of spending. Conversely, the state share of spending increased from 13% in 1949 to 18% in 1979; while the local share increased from 21% to 26%.[5]

Again, the state and local share of public employees burgeoned—from 51% (3.1 million) *local* employees in 1949 to 59% (9.1 million) in 1977 (increasing by a factor of over 1.9) and from 16% (1.0 million) *state* employees in 1949 to 22% (3.5 million) in 1977 (increasing by a factor of 2.5). (Pascal and Menchik, 1980, pp. 293–294.)

As in our 19-country comparison, we encounter a disjunction of growth in spending and growth in employees, with the lean spenders less efficient and more bloated. This may be explained by the structures and functions of American state and local governments. The functions are far more labor intensive than the civilian functions of the federal government and represent much more of a bureaucratic maze: the lion's share of state and local spending is on education, welfare, health, and transportation with health and especially welfare (AFDC, now TANF) increasing disproportionately. The welfare mess discussed earlier requires a burgeoning bureaucracy as does the effort at welfare reform.

American local government presents another paradox for "Wagner's Law" which holds that as per capita income rises, the government share of that income rises: in fact, the multiplication of some kinds of bureaucracies restrains spending while the growth of other types increases it; yet almost all of them multiply personnel, more in keeping with Parkinson's law.[6] Our free-enterprising spirit in government has meant that local governmental units metastasize. In 1982, beyond the federal and state governments there were 82,290 government units below the state level—38,851 general-purpose governments (about 3,000 counties, 19,000 municipalities, 17,000 township and town governments), 43,439 single-function units (almost 15,000 school districts—with consolidation a sharp drop from over 50,000 in 1957), and 28,588 special districts (especially sanitary, drainage, transportation, environmental control, soil conservation districts—a sharp increase from only 14,405 in 1957). (Aronson and Hilley, 1986, p. 76.) The Chicago metropolitan area alone contains more than 250 municipalities, each duplicating or overlapping the services of the others. Overlapping these governments are 835 special districts, which typically have a monopoly over one function.

Insofar as government structure affects spending, the proliferation of special-purpose units accounts for most of the rapid rise in local expenditures (Eberts and Gronberg, 1988). They have a monopoly over the service they provide, and because they are on average larger than townships, municipalities, or counties, they can exercise this monopoly power effectively. Their competition is confined to a scramble for state, federal, and private budgets and grants, not for the cheapest service or lowest tax level. The overlapping labyrinth of special districts stimulates local spending. In contrast, the general-purpose governments within a county or metropolitan area reduce the share of personal income going to the local government; these central cities, suburbs, counties, and townships are in strong competition with other units providing similar services to the same market. For instance, adjacent counties or suburbs in a metropolitan area each subcontracts ambulance services or garbage collection; several townships do the same; they all require competitive bids, thereby keeping costs down.[7]

Thus, as Eberts and Gronberg demonstrate in a study of 218 U.S. metropolitan areas (1988, pp. 6–7), the competition among local general-purpose governments constrains local spending. From the data on public employees, however, I infer that although they differ in their effects on spending, both single- and general-purpose units in the United States have coped with their troubles by expanding personnel, especially administrators, planners, and coordinators.

We can expect that these trends in the structure and functions of state and local governments will move the United States and countries like it from medium to high levels of labor intensiveness in the provision of services.

In the United States, as elsewhere, affluence and left power count. The expansion of the public bureaucracy took place while the United States became the richest country in the world and despite an ideology allegedly hostile to big government. It was speeded up by Democratic Party regimes under FDR, Truman, Kennedy, Johnson, and to a lesser extent, Carter. Intense racial-ethnic-religious conflict hastened the growth, with the Democrats most responsive to minority-group pressures and mobility aspirations.

In the 1980s, paradoxically, these trends accelerated under the Reagan-Bush administration. Despite the skillful orchestration of President Reagan's antigovernment, antitaxing, anti–social spending ideology, his main impact on personnel was to continue the expansion of the bureaucracy at every level. In Washington he sharply increased the number of Defense Department employees and reduced employment in Health and Human Services, Housing and Urban Development, Transportation, Interior, and Commerce, and so on (for a net increase of about 7% in total federal civilian employees between 1981 and 1988) while dumping federal functions and the responsibility for paying for them onto state and local governments, thereby ensuring that the states, like the federal government, would eventually face a fiscal crisis. It was not until the election of President Clinton that the trend in federal government employment was reversed. His zeal for "reinventing government" resulted in a cut in total federal employees from 2,969,000 in 1992 to 2,870,000 in 1994. By another measure (federal executive branch civilian employment per 1,000 population including post office employees, part-time, full-time, and temporary workers) Clinton achieved a record low of 11.2 by 1994 compared to the high of 14.7 under President Nixon in 1969 (U.S. Office of Management and the Budget, 1996a, p. 245).

By the early 1990s many states were well along in the process of dumping *their* expanded responsibilities onto the counties and municipalities (Gold, 1995b, 1995c). This took the usual form of mandates without money: governors and state legislators, intoning the slogans about "decentralization," "local participation," and a level of "government closest to the people," were telling localities to do more to meet the needs of citizens, especially in health, welfare, and the environment. True, they simultaneously shared some state revenues, but in amounts that nowhere near offset the new local burdens and the rate of cost increases. The inevitable result: an early 1990s combination of local fiscal crises and bureaucratic expansion. Thus, even in the recession year of 1990–91—and despite workforce reductions in many northeastern states—overall state employment in the United States rose 1.3% while local government jobs jumped 2.1%. (*Wall Street Journal,* September 3, 1991.) Even after most states had gone into surplus and used it to cut taxes, sales taxes in cities and counties climbed to record levels in 1996 (*Wall Street Journal,* January 21, 1998).

The latest twist on this game of the downward shift of responsibility was the welfare reform law of 1996. The bill's advocates claim that it will pare welfare spending by $54 billion over five years. The bill replaces Aid to Families with Dependent Children (American "welfare")—a federal/state-funded entitlement program with federal standards—with block grants to 50 states frozen at minimum of 80% of fiscal 1994 levels, with wide state latitude in allocating the money.[8] It ends the categorical guarantee for all qualified poor families, and it places a five-year lifetime limit on benefits and a two-year deadline for participating in work activities before a welfare cutoff (see chap. 8 for other restrictive provisions).

Chapter 8 and chapter 7 discuss the social and political effects of these repeated campaigns to clean up the welfare mess; chapter 12 explains why they are a drag on economic performance. In the present context, the consequences of the welfare reform of 1996 for bureaucratic bloat are clear: more of it. Decentralizing welfare standards, giving almost complete discretion in allocating money to 50 states, and freezing the level of federal funding for welfare (whatever the increase in population; the cost-of-living, recession-induced poverty; or the severity of social problems) will have the usual effects: the multiplication of already large state bureaucracies. Frontline employees in each state and community will have discretion in allocating a dwindling supply of real cash and services to particular families, using their case-by-case judgment but trying to fit their decisions to state rulebooks whose eligibility and benefit criteria will metastasize. Added supervisory layers above the frontline will be necessary to control spending, prevent relaxation of the ever-changing rules, and minimize fraud and abuse. Because of the inevitable arbitrariness of the frontline decisions, which a recession would make more arbitrary by the intensified money squeeze, in many states there will be appeals procedures and administrative law judges (cf. Mashaw, 1988, pp. 153). Welfare-rights organizations will become more numerous so lawsuits challenging denial of benefits can be brought to court in the grand old American way.

Even if the states decide to cut welfare cases in half and reduce the number of welfare administrators and eligibility checkers, other parts of the local bureaucracy will grow—for example, personnel in homelessness programs, in emergency room medical care, in foster-care programs, in police departments, courts, and prisons—to cope with the pathologies of increased poverty, family disruption, and crime (see chap. 14 on mayhem). In the event that despite reduced funding some states choose to tackle the real problem of the highly visible, unpopular welfare population with education, training, job creation, "workfare," child care, nutrition, medical care, and the like, they will require more personnel than they now employ and much more money. This is already apparent in the cost of workfare programs in the few states making sustained efforts not only to cut the rolls but to reduce poverty (see chap. 8).

In short, decentralizing welfare planning and administration and cutting the resources going to the poor does not mean cutting the staff needed to process claims and monitor eligibility decisions. As in the past, the combination of more means testing and harsher eligibility criteria will bring an expansion of the local welfare bureaucracy. The economic growth and reduced unemployment of the few years after the welfare reform was passed have restored state budgets; any reversal will produce a budget squeeze, witness the year 2001.

To the extent that corporatist democracies decentralize their government structures, they, too, can join the leaders in bureaucratic bloat. The case of Italy since the early 1970s illustrates this effect of decentralization. In 1970 and then again in 1972, 1974, and 1977 the Italian government restructured its public sector by shifting major functions in health, social services, transportation, agriculture and forestry, and vocational education from the central government to 15 new regional governments with broad powers and substantial financing;

the regional governments then transferred health and social service functions to local governments. Although they differ greatly in their efficiency (Putnam, 1988), these decentralized units have had one clear effect: the growth of government accelerated rapidly. While the reform shifted expenditure responsibilities downward, it did not extend taxing powers downward. It established a system of revenue sharing similar to that in the United States.

With central financing and decentralized spending, and despite a freeze on hiring in the health sector after 1974, the result was predictable: both total spending and the public employees' share of employment grew rapidly. Starting in 1960 from a below-average 7.8% of total employment including the military and some public corporations, the Italian-public employees' share grew to 14.9% by 1982 (Fraschini, 1984, p. 404).[9] Just after the devolution, in the five years from 1976 to 1981, local public employment expanded by almost 20% (calculated from Cassese, 1983, p. 379). Adding impetus to this growth was a 1977 law giving regional governments subsidies to hire unemployed youths in public-sector jobs in six southern regions—in conception comparable to American affirmative action for minorities, and in result, a similar expansion of public employment.

Of course, what I have called "bureaucratic bloat" has its upside. To expand public employment via decentralization is to improve career chances for the least privileged—women, minorities, sons and daughters of poor parents. And to decentralize labor-intensive services is to facilitate flexible adaptation to local community needs. Moreover, an increased number of public employees may often enhance the quality of service: more workers at the Department of Motor Vehicles or the local social-security office reduce waiting lines; more fire stations and more police on the street may increase both safety and the public's sense of safety; more maintenance and repair personnel for sewers, roads, and electrical-power lines obviously can improve response time for those services; more workers in parks and recreation may improve the quality of leisure time in a society where one in five of those employed full- or part-time work odd hours (calculated from Mellor, 1986, pp. 17−18) and flexible schedules are increasing. On average and despite Parkinson's law, an understaffed local agency cannot deliver as high-quality service as can an overstaffed agency.

But as we have seen, government decentralization is decidedly no road to bureaucratic efficiency.

NOTES

1. A study of public employment in 13 of our 19 counties—all members of the European Community—appeared after I completed my analysis. It covers the 1980s and confirms this picture of continued growth. Using a different measure (public-sector employment as a share of total employment, including the military) and a French figure much larger than ours (appendix J discusses such discrepancies), Anthony Ferner (1994, p. 57) shows that the average annual growth rate of public employment slowed from 1979 to 1989, but the public share in employment climbed in all countries except Ireland and the UK, where it reversed slightly in the late 1980s. Sweden, the leader in the public share of employment, showed zero growth in that share in the period 1984−90.

2. Latecomers like Japan and Germany have some advantage beyond the privilege of losing World War II and hence avoiding the military featherbed. Actually, while all 19 countries were getting richer, the 6 countries that moved up fastest in GNP per capita from 1966 to 1980 (West Germany, Austria, Japan, Belgium, Norway, the Netherlands) were all either late industrializers, losers of

the war, or suffered great damage or all three, while the 4 countries moving down most in relative GNP per capita (USA, Canada, Australia, New Zealand) were winners in World War II and suffered minimal physical damage. That rich democracies are nevertheless converging in their riches is suggested by data comparing the distance in the average GNP per capita between the four richest countries and the average for four least-rich countries from 1950 to 1980. The ratio of the averages went down from 4.8 in 1950 to 3.5 in 1960, 2.7 in 1966, and 2.5 in 1980.

3. Confirmation of this part of my analysis comes from a study by Masters and Robertson (1988). They analyze public employment expansion in 20 rich democracies, excluding Israel and including Luxembourg and Iceland, and use average annual rates of change 1965–83 instead of the period averages and single years I have used; their estimates of public employment are similar but not identical to mine. They conclude that "tripartite coalitions" of state, labor, and capital labeled "institutionalized class relations" (similar to my measure of democratic corporatism) and "pro-labor political representation" (somewhat similar to my measure of leftism) are major sources of high rates of employment. However, Masters and Robertson do not deal either with affluence or with the interaction of types of corporatism, party power, and minority groups; and so they would miss the high public employment of decentralized, rich countries with some left power that provide expanding opportunity for minority groups in government. And their measure of left power is left representation in the lower chamber of the national legislature, which misses important differences between executive power and legislative power in Japan, Switzerland, the USA, France, and Italy (see chap. 2).

4. As a group, the older Francophones were handicapped by a higher and selective fallout rate (more ambitious Francophone civil servants left Ottawa for the action in Quebec in the 1960s) and by discrimination both on the job and in education before entry. The attraction of energetic, talented members of minority groups to social and political action (by criteria directly relevant to performance) is seldom considered in analysis of "discrimination" against those left behind in the sectors under study.

5. The state share of all taxes climbed from 15.9% in 1960 to 26.5% in 1988. Reagan era cutbacks in federal aid accelerated the trend. (*Wall Street Journal,* Aug. 15, 1990.) From 1960 to 1990 real state and local spending per capita grew from $1,153 to $2,376, driven largely by real income growth per capita and by federal spending mandates, especially for public assistance, health and hospitals, and corrections (Dye and McGuire, 1992, pp. 319–321, 325).

6. Parkinson (1957, p. 2) holds that "work expands so as to fill the time available for its completion" and adds two axioms: (1) "An official wants to multiply subordinates, not rivals" and (2) "Officials make work for each other" (p. 4). Thus, most organizations expand in size even if the number of tasks they perform does not increase (pp. 2–12).

7. Within the metropolitan area, the typical unit is large enough to avoid monopoly suppliers. In addition, these general-purpose governments receive tax subsidies from the federal government—another advantage in producing services at lower overt cost to the local taxpayer.

8. The bill ended the long-standing requirement for the states to spend their own money as a condition of getting federal money for assistance to poor people. In 1994 states had to put up $10 billion a year in order to get $12.5 billion from the federal government for AFDC (*New York Times,* March 28, 1995).

9. By 1990, according to a survey of Italy by *The Economist* (May 26, 1990, p. 20), "18% of the workforce [was] employed by the state." While public employment doubtless grew from 1982 to 1990, that figure may not be comparable to the Fraschini data.

PART III
SYSTEM PERFORMANCE

In recent decades social scientists have paid too little attention to national variations in the real welfare outputs from a nation's taxing, spending, and public policies. One reason is the difficulty of measuring cross-nationally such important system outputs as political legitimacy or "governability," social consensus or social integration, many aspects of economic performance, equality, health, security and safety, and a benign, clean environment. These are dimensions of societal welfare that matter in the daily routines of individuals and the vitality of democracies. Part III examines national variations among rich democracies in each of these system outputs. I shall continue my attempt to sort out the effects of continuing industrialization (convergence in the structure, culture, and politics of rich democracies as they get richer) from the effects of types of political economy and associated patterns of spending, taxing, and public policy.

Consider first the many meanings of political legitimacy, which is often used interchangeably with governability. When scholars have written about the increasing ungovernability of modern democracy (Huntington, 1974; Crozier, Huntington, and Watanuki, 1975; Brittan, 1975; O'Connor, 1973; Fiorina, 1980; Rose and Peters, 1978) or the erosion of political legitimacy (Schmitter, 1981; Wilensky, 1983; Dahl, 1994) they have invoked many indicators. Among the most prominent are the following:

- A polarized party system or the decline of party systems or of mainstream parties (dealignment and/or realignment)

- Fiscal crises or the increasing inability to collect taxes to pay for the services and benefits large majorities of voters expect

- The unconstrained, self-indulgent, disruptive pursuit of narrow self-interest

- Paralyzed policymaking machinery (the incapacity of governing elites to act when they believe action is urgent)

- Ineffective implementation of public policies (inefficiency)

- "Overloaded government," frequent reversals of important public policies or elite overresponsiveness to the fleeting moods of the public

- New protest parties and social movements
- A decline in public confidence in institutions of government

Chapters 10 and 11 single out two of these dimensions of "ungovernability" that are clearly defined, vary over time and space, and lend themselves to systematic cross-national analysis—"tax-welfare backlash" as an indicator of the inability to finance public services demanded by vast majorities; and "party decline" or dealignment. Chapters 12, 13, and 18 deal with various aspects of economic performance. These chapters show much variation in the duration and depth of "fiscal crises"; they attempt to sort out the structural, ideological, and public-policy roots of such variation.

Some dimensions of political legitimacy and social integration, while conceptually clear, are either less relevant to rich democracies than they are to authoritarian regimes and poor countries or are much harder to measure, or both: the breakdown of the social and normative order (the increasing refusal of a population to act out the central roles of a society—as family member, worker, citizen, political or religious leader—and the increasing refusal to accept common societal norms and values); the lack of accountability of leaders to citizens; the elite need to use increasing coercion. I deal with such matters only indirectly as we discuss crime, family breakup, and party dealignment. We shall see that, despite further evidence of convergence in many system outputs, modern democracies differ greatly in their capacity to govern and in the way they serve the general welfare of their citizens.

I O

TAX-WELFARE BACKLASH
How to Tax, Spend, and Yet Keep Cool

This chapter tries to solve the puzzle of why, under recent conditions of slow growth, unemployment, periodic external shocks (exchange rate swings, oil shocks), and rising aspirations for equality and security, countries that share similar levels of taxing and spending for the welfare state vary greatly in the political trouble they generate. The most striking impression I have from my interviews with politicians, health and welfare officials, and experts in spending and taxing in 15 of our 19 countries is that since the mid-1960s the level of spending and taxing does not explain the political uproar that has accompanied taxing and spending in a few countries—principally the United States, United Kingdom, Denmark, and, to a lesser extent, Switzerland. Denmark is a big taxer and spender, the UK ranks medium, while the USA and Switzerland are lean taxers and spenders; yet all four have led in "tax-welfare backlash" in the past 30 years or so. For our 19 countries, sheer level of spending has had no significant relationship to backlash (for 1966, $r = -.21$; for 1971, $r = .04$); nor is level of taxing related to backlash (for 1965, $r = .04$; for 1971, $r = .19$). And these patterns were stable up to the mid-1990s.

If we cannot explain tax revolts by big spending and taxing, what does cause them? After defining the phenomenon and discussing problems of classifying particular countries, I shall show that mass and even elite opinion about the welfare state cannot explain the success or failure of backlash movements and candidates; that mass protests about taxing and spending are almost always combined with the mobilization of nativist xenophobic sentiments; that it is the visibility of taxing and spending, not their level, that leads to backlash; and that different types of political economy differ not only in their structures of taxing and spending but in the policies that increase or decrease inequality. Democracies that increase inequality invite political disruption. A final section tests the idea that advanced industrialism and its structural and ideological correlates (especially increased mobility-meritocracy and social cleavages) may ultimately make all democracies more vulnerable to tax-welfare backlash.

CONCEPTS AND MEASURES OF BACKLASH

By tax-welfare backlash I mean strong social-political movements and/or parties that emphasize antitax, anti-social-spending, antibureaucratic ideological themes and achieve electoral

363

success for substantial periods. In independent coding we arrived at scores for each of 19 countries focused on intensity and duration for each of four expressions of backlash emphasizing the period 1965–75 when these movements and parties burst forth. Because of my interest in the direction of social and political change, the weighting favors social-political movements of reasonable duration (weight 3) which achieve recurrent electoral success and political influence (weight 4). Less important are other forms of collective behavior such as political strikes, demonstrations, and riots (weight 2). These may or may not constitute the seedbed for the eventual growth of social movements and party organization; more important, in most of our countries they are episodic, even ephemeral and often local, as are the Poujadistes in France. Least important are mass sentiments uncovered by sample surveys or close observers (weight 1); such opinions seldom come in unmixed or coherent form and even if predominantly antiwelfare state, can be channeled in diverse directions (see discussion of postindustrial values in chap. 4). In the end, if we eliminated mass sentiments from the index, it would make no change in the rank order of the 19 countries.

We were able to resolve all coding ambiguities by clarifying concepts and filling in gaps in evidence. The scores (intensity-duration + ideological theme × weight) ranged from 55 (Denmark) to 20 (Japan). That index was then reduced to the final six-point index of tax-welfare backlash (0 to 5). I think that this index avoids spurious precision and is both reliable and valid. Country scores appear in table 10.2. (Details on the coding scheme are in Wilensky, 1976a, pp. 14–18, 56–68.) I have not recoded tax-welfare backlash 1965–75 for subsequent years (although I discuss later developments) because the scheme turned out to be amazingly predictive. Countries that developed sustained and intense backlash resulting in electoral victories that ranked high then rank high now and vice versa. The United Kingdom, ranking high (scored 4) for 1965–75, would rank even higher from the mid-1970s to the mid-1990s (5) which would strengthen the causal analysis in this chapter. Finland, a corporatist democracy that scored a little above average in our scheme because of episodic protest parties would now score a bit lower, also strengthening my findings. (E.g., Veikko Vennamo's small antigovernment, antibureaucratic Farmers Party got 11% of the vote in 1968, accenting the traditional virtues of religion, isolationism, and populist localism, but it was not anti–welfare state. The Young Finnish Party, active before 1900, has been revived and articulates a Thatcherist line, but its vote is very small—only 1 MP elected in 1995.)

Not all protest parties and mass discontents fit the idea of tax-welfare backlash. While antitax, anti–social-spending, and antibureaucratic movements were emerging in the 1960s, the many environmental, peace, feminist, and civil rights movements were also emerging. Obviously some of these were quite antibureaucratic, accenting decentralization and local participation and expressing general hostility to authority, but they were typically not antitax or anti–welfare state. And the social composition of activists in these new movements has been quite different from that of tax-welfare backlash movements; the former are younger and more educated; the latter are heavily concentrated in the middle mass, as we shall see. More important for our purposes, there were several ambiguities in ranking countries by tax-welfare backlash. Consider the ambiguities of protest movements and parties in Italy, France, Sweden, and Ireland. I quote from coding instructions and coders' notes on these cases to convey a sense of how we resolved them. I add an account of 1975–96 developments for each case. None of the scores would change in ways that would weaken my explanation.

Italy: The presence of protest movements or factions seceding from established right or left parties do not in themselves merit high scores, unless the divisive issues are tax-welfare-bureaucracy issues. For instance, the Italian CP may be cutting into the self-employed and other parts of the middle mass at the risk of losing students, intellectuals, and maybe low-paid workers and high-paid bureaucrats who then go to extreme left (PDUP) or right (neo-Fascists). But the issues are not too much spending and taxing for social programs, but instead, inefficiency and corruption. The CP is cautious on taxes, the civil service, and even the corrupt welfare institutions (no frontal attacks); they need the votes. There are also media-covered intellectual debates re the "parasitic sector" but the guilty parties are seldom named (contrast Glistrup's assault on specific categories of civil service, Governors Reagan and Wallace's baiting of welfare bureaucrats, etc., which then encouraged Nixon and others to make this a major theme). So, despite Italian CP local election successes, and despite sporadic violence and large-scale mass protests, Italy receives a low score, "1", on "movements" because such phenomena are only in small measure tax-welfare backlash successes. The highest score for Italy is a "2" on the theme, "mass sentiments," because antibureaucratic themes are clearly present but antiwelfare themes are ambiguous. Final backlash score: 1. *Subsequent developments:* That low score fits Italy after 1965–75 until the early 1990s when the hegemony of the Christian Democrats was ended and a succession of trials of hundreds of leaders of the political and economic establishment for everything from bribery to murder accelerated. A major crisis of legitimacy spawned a succession of movement entrepreneurs—for example, Umberto Bossi of the Northern League and media-magnate Silvio Berlusconi of the Forza Italia ("Go, Italy"). The Lega, strong in the more modern regions of the North, achieved 8.4% of the national popular vote in the 1994 elections and joined the short-lived center-right coalition of Prime Minister Berlusconi of the Forza Italia and Gianfranco Fini of the Alleanza Nazionale (former neo-Fascists). The Northern League comes close to a pure backlash movement—antitax, anti–social spending, surely antibureaucratic (it equates the state with corruption and advocates federalism)—and adds as a secondary theme great hostility to the backward Mafia-infected South as well as all immigrants. After seven months, Bossi led his Lega out of the governing coalition, which collapsed. The Lega ran alone in the April 1996 election, winning 10.1% of the popular vote. The victors were the first center-left governing coalition since Italy was united in 1861. Under the label the Olive Tree, it was composed of former Communists, former Christian Democrats, Greens, and an array of academics and technocrats, including the new prime minister, economics professor Romano Prodi. They campaigned on a platform of maintaining social benefits but doing it with fiscal responsibility.

While it is true that the basic target of all recent protest parties has been the "parasitic state," much of the protest is not against the welfare state or even taxes, except as they are administered in clientelistic Italian style. And while the Northern League fits the idea of tax-welfare backlash, unless it persists and grows, Italy's score remains low. Nevertheless, in the 1990s Italy was moving in France's direction.

France: In contrast, ambiguities in the French case were resolved in favor of higher scores than those for Italy. *Regarding elections:* The Poujadistes in France reached their peak of 11.5% of the vote in 1956 and their successors continue to articulate antitax and antibureaucratic themes (not anti–welfare-state themes), but their electoral success has sharply declined. In the national election of 1974, the hero of the shopkeepers and artisans, Royer, received only 3.2% of the vote. Many of les indépendants, once hostile to the welfare state, were subsequently integrated into center and right parties, where they fight for more benefits and services although not for the privilege of paying their share. Score for 1965–75 intensity and duration, low; theme, medium. *Regarding movements:* There is much talk of the revolt of "les cadres" (ranging in meaning from the top 5% of business managers and engineers through all salaried college graduates down through technicians). But the action is confined largely to reasonably successful maintenance of the status quo—resistance to egalitarian reform of the tax system, especially of the "quotient familial" (a formula for greatly reducing income tax liabilities for large families, especially high-income large families), and to the raising of the ceiling on pension contributions. The Confédération Générale des Cadres (CGC), a union of white-collar strata, exerts diffuse pressure in these areas, sometimes blocking government planners' proposals for welfare reform and pressing for favorable pension arrangements. Similarly, the movements succeeding Poujadism, especially CID-UNATI, are ambiguous on welfare-state issues: They want benefits for themselves but are opposed to paying for them; and they are against benefits for foreign workers. The forces that have weakened backlash parties have weakened these movements. Intensity-duration, low; theme, medium. *Regarding other collective behavior:* Since 1965 there have been a number of strikes, demonstrations, and riots—usually intense, sometimes massive. For instance, raiding, occupying, and even burning tax offices continued to be a favorite tactic of shopkeepers and artisans. Farmers also continue violent protests, especially about taxes affecting wine production and alcoholic beverages. As for the great outburst of May 1968, one major effect was the transformation of segments of the system of higher education (excluded from this code); effects on tax-welfare issues are unclear. Two years later, the CGC organized a backlash demonstration to protest proposals in the Sixth Plan to narrow salary differentials, equalize health and welfare benefits, and make taxes more equitable. In general, although mass protest is frequent, it tends to be localized, episodic, staged by single-issue groups with at best modest impact on the direction of French politics, public administration, and social policy. Intensity-duration, medium; theme, medium. *Regarding public opinion, mass sentiments:* According to surveys we examined, there was a noticeable decrease in support for the administration of welfare policy in the early 1970s: Public opinion became much more divided after substantial approval in the mid-1960s. Intensity-duration, medium; theme, medium. *The final backlash score:* 3. *Subsequent developments:*[1] Although the emergence of LePen's Front National (FN) and the big national strikes of December 1995 are dramatic signs of the erosion of French statism, not much has changed in the ambiguous shape of tax-welfare backlash. These 1980s and 1990s developments continue the long-standing symbiotic relationship of the insular centralized French state and social movements that orchestrate massive street demonstrations (e.g., 1947, 1953, 1968, 1986). LePen also continues the old French tradition of right-wing populist extremism, a blend of "Bonapartism," xenophobia, and anti-Semitism. LePen ran as a mainstream conservative candidate in 1981, joined the FN in 1984, and has ever since spewed forth anti-Arab, anti-immigrant, anti-Semitic venom. He rails against the invasion of immigrants and bureaucrats in Brussels as a threat to French national identity, social order, and French jobs. In the 1988 presidential election he won almost 15% of the national vote and between 26% and 28% of the vote in areas of high-immigrant concentration in southwest France. In the by-election of 1992, support for the FN surged. In the 1995 presidential election, LePen again won 15% of the popular vote in the first round. It is true that the FN's message has become more general and its appeal broader (since 1983 the FN has advocated lower taxes, the dissolution of the bureaucracy, and deregulation), but it remains more interested in racial purity, cultural identity, and maternal salaries for French mothers than in cutting social spending. Indeed, the FN warns that the fiscal burden of immigration threatens to undermine cherished French pensions.

As for the late-1995 strike movement—three weeks that almost shut down the French economy—that was anything but tax-welfare backlash. It was triggered by the "plan Juppé" presented by the government with almost no consultation or participation as a nonnegotiable policy package to save the French welfare state, restore French competitiveness, and meet requirements for joining the European Monetary Union (EMU). The plan proposed to overhaul pensions for all public-sector employees by requiring longer service for benefits (from 37.5 years to 40 years) and reducing their generosity; to eliminate union seats on the boards of public-sector social-security funds; to control costs in the health insurance system by reducing union and employer influence in its governing bodies, capping expenditures, and instituting a new income tax targeted to health insurance and levied even on pensioners and the unemployed; and to speed up the effort begun by the Left government of 1983 to restructure and modernize the semicommercial public sector (urban transport, notably the Paris metro, electricity and gas, post, etc.). The changes were sudden and radical. In comparison to the events of 1968, the strikes of 1995 were less radical in both process and outcome. They had a narrower base of participation, confined largely to the public sector, although there was a much wider base of public sympathy; a secondary role for students (confined to such issues as a demand for more professors and smaller classes); and a less global set of political issues. Strikers concentrated on protecting pensions, health care, job security, traditional job rights, and working conditions. In the end the government gave little: it withdrew its proposal to reform public-sector pension schemes but insisted on the need for drastic reforms of the whole social-security system; suspended the reorganization of the rail system; and gave vague promises to create 25,000 jobs in 1996. In short, the events of 1995, while they perpetuate the chasm between technocratic elites and masses, are the reverse of a tax-welfare backlash movement. The medium score of 3 continues to capture the ambiguities of French social movements, elections, and collective behavior. Antistate, yes; antitax, sporadic episodes; anti–social spending, ambiguous at best.

Ireland: This case, with a 0 backlash score, illustrates what to do with moderate or conservative incumbent parties as targets of prowelfare, antitax movements and parties ("frontlash"). Recent developments illustrate. Ireland provides a contrast to Britain in the move toward the neoliberalism of the 1980s and early 1990s. When Fianna Fáil regained power in 1987, it announced retrenchments—some cutbacks in public expenditure and service, some privatization and tax reform—but only by agreement between labor, management, and the government. In January 1991 the unusual coalition government of the broad-based Fianna Fáil and the Progressive Democrats (a radical right party formed in the mid-1980s) continued negotiating on social and economic policies with the social partners, even including groups representing the unemployed. The extraordinarily high unemployment rate and other features of the Irish political economy, however, have limited the state's scope for drastic cutbacks. Finally, the Progressive Democrats, the closest we come to a backlash party, were in government for only a brief moment. The center-left coalition government formed by Fianna Fáil and the Labour Party in early 1993 is committed to defending the Irish welfare state; it raised taxes on incomes over £9000 and increased social expenditures. (McLaughlin, 1993, pp. 213–214, 222–225.) Thus, the Irish backlash score remains steadily low, making it a negative case for my hypothesis that decentralized and fragmented political economies and the policies they pursue invite backlash. Chapter 2 discusses Irish exceptionalism: despite its electoral system (proportional representation with a single transferable vote), Catholic culture, and above-average union density, Ireland did not produce democratic corporatism; but it does produce impressive resistance to tax-welfare backlash movements (see also Farrell, 1992).

Sweden: This case was originally used as a benchmark for low backlash, but ambiguities forced a final code of 2. Here are the coders' judgments: *Elections:* Electoral activity with backlash theme is confined to local protest parties (Småland, Sigtuna) and the rhetoric of the "Green Wave" movement, which peaked in the 1974 election. Their themes are not antiwelfare. And relative to the mobilization of hostility to guest workers in other countries, Sweden ranks low: the Swedes give them citizenship and then resent their slow assimilation. If there are antiwelfare themes in elections during this period, they are latent and subdued. Intensity-duration, low; theme, low. *Movements:* Like electoral activity, movements are confined to local action ("byalag" or community groups, etc.) and youth groups with ambiguous antiwelfare themes (Heimdal, Center Partiets Ungdomsförbundet). Intensity-duration, low; theme, medium. *Other collective behavior:* The SACO strike over income differentials in February 1971 represents the clearest marginal case of a strike articulating some backlash themes. SACO white-collar workers wanted to be excluded from the Swedish wage solidarity scheme. Thus, this one major strike can be interpreted as resistance to the egalitarian thrust of Social Democratic and LO policies. Intensity-duration (short but intense), medium; theme, medium. *Public opinion, mass sentiments:* Scored low for intensity partly on the basis of review of the *London Times* and the *New York Times* for the 10 years and partly on the evidence of opinion polls. For example, of the members of the Conservative Party, only 10% were unfavorable toward the supplementary pension scheme; 23% of the Center Party members were unfavorable (for 1964). Re theme: The evidence suggests that what discontent existed was antitax, antibureaucratic, anti-Stockholm (i.e., the anticentralization themes of the Green Wave), while antiwelfare sentiments were latent, if present at all. Intensity-duration, low; theme, low. *Final backlash score: 2. Subsequent developments:* As we have seen in our discussion of the alleged collapse of democratic corporatism (chap. 2), only Sweden among the Nordic countries evidences substantial erosion. The growing strength of "bourgeois" parties that ruled from 1976 to 1982 and again from the fall of 1991 to the fall of 1994, the political offensive of the SAF, which ended formal centralized bargaining in 1990 and culminated in the withdrawal of SAF from the tripartite boards of all state agencies in 1991 combined with severe economic troubles of the early 1990s (a deep recession, the run-up of interest rates, debt, and unemployment)—all this spelled big trouble for the Swedish Social Democratic model. It does not mean a rise of tax-welfare backlash, however, as we can see from the fate of protest parties and the targets of their protest. In the election of 1991, when the Social Democrats suffered their worst defeat since 1928, two new parties on the right emerged. New Democracy, with 6.7% of the vote and 25 seats, can be called populist; it mobilized discontent with all politicians and with taxes and bureaucrats and promised to reduce the price of alcohol and restrict immigration, but it did not complain about the welfare state.[2] The Christian Democrats, with 7.1% of the vote and 26 seats, appealed to voters concerned with moral values (e.g., abortions), not taxing and spending. By the next election both new parties faded: in 1994 New Democracy got 1.2% of the vote and no seats; the Christian Democrats, 4.1% of the votes and only 14 seats.

The four "bourgeois" parties that formed the government in 1991 campaigned against the Social Democrats for their economic mismanagement, promised tax cuts without pain, and said they would bring Sweden into the EC. The Social Democratic government's timing was bad: in the two years before the election, as a recession began and unemployment increased, they cut the top marginal income-tax rate from 72% to 50%, increased the VAT from 20% to 25% and, most important, made changes in property-tax valuations that hit renters and owner-occupiers in old houses, most of whom were Social Democratic voters; they also made small cuts in the welfare state, especially in the replacement rate of unemployment compensation. The net effect: If you were well-off, you got a tax cut; if not, you paid more and received less. The winning bourgeois coalition did not campaign against the welfare state; they were divided on the kind and amount of tax cuts and could agree only on small changes in social policies. In fact, in the next three years they ran up a huge debt, as they had in the late 1970s when it reached 13% of GDP, partly because they cut taxes without cutting social spending. (For other policy errors of both center-left and center-right governments, see chap. 2.) The Social Democrats returned to power in 1994 with 45.6% of the vote, up 8 points from 1991.

In short, neither in elections and collective behavior nor in the policies advocated can we see tax-welfare backlash beyond the score of 2 for the earlier period, although Sweden, like other very big spenders, has been forced into modest reforms of taxes and the welfare state to permit better balance (increases in social-security contributions and consumption taxes, cuts in income-tax rates) and to reduce spending excesses (modest cutbacks in benefits).

(For discussion of the resolution of all ambiguous cases and the method of scoring and its reliability, see Wilensky, 1976a, pp. 57–68.)

Why Public Opinion Cannot Explain Backlash Successes

That mass sentiments and public opinion are poor predictors of the electoral success of tax-welfare backlash movements and parties in our scheme requires explanation. The explanation is both theoretical and empirical. First, theory suggests that both elites and masses in all modern societies are ambivalent and contradictory in their values and beliefs. Second, survey data show that whatever national ideological differences appear in response to abstract questions, the issue-specific attitudes toward taxing, spending, and the welfare state are very similar across countries and over time. Cross-national uniformity of attitudes cannot explain great national contrasts in the fate of tax-welfare backlash movements.

The ideologies of all modern societies are a complex blend of contradictory themes, both meritocratic and egalitarian, individualistic and collectivistic or humanitarian.[3] For instance, every industrial society requires some competition for occupational position on the basis of criteria relevant to the performance of the role, as well as some system of special reward for the development of scarce talents and skills. It is plausible to assume that these universal structural features of modern economies foster similar mobility ideologies, that in the most diverse political and cultural contexts doctrines of economic individualism take root: increasing portions of the population in modernizing sectors believe that everyone has an equal opportunity to achieve a better job, that everyone has the moral duty to make the most of his or her talents, to try to get ahead, that if people fail it is at least partly their own fault, and so on. This success ideology is not uniquely American; it also appears in some measure in rich countries where the welfare state is more developed. In short, a universal elite requirement for incentives fosters mass adherence to a success ideology.

A similar elite demand for incentives underlies pro-welfare-state doctrines—not incentives to make the most talented use their talents, train for the most complex jobs, and so on, but incentives to keep the least successful in the race, or at least working. As Bismarck foresaw, a pension at the end of a life of hard work would be a powerful pacifier for workers confined to the least-attractive jobs (Briggs, 1961, pp. 247–249; Rimlinger, 1971, p. 121). This elite necessity for stable economic incentives combines with the also universal mass demand for family security and social justice to make it necessary that the shock of mobility failures be cushioned and the risks of modern life be tempered. So pro-welfare-state doctrines are as widely popular as the ideology of success.

The second explanation for the weakness of public opinion as a source of backlash successes is evidence from surveys, both American and cross-national. They confirm that modern populations in all the rich democracies surveyed display mass ambivalence on abstract questions that tap general ideology (with modest national differences), a cross-national uniformity in issue-specific opinion, and a strong pro–welfare-state majority. They also show that the structure of public opinion on taxing and social spending has remained quite stable since World War II.

Mass ambivalence is evident in our own data from 1975 and dozens of subsequent surveys, some extending into the 1990s. A staff member, Richard Coughlin (1980), did a secondary analysis of all of the more or less comparable surveys he could find over the postwar period up to the late 1970s and one we devised ourselves in 1975. The surveyed countries include welfare-state leaders (West Germany, Sweden, Denmark, France), middle-rank spenders (the UK and Canada), and two laggards (the USA and Australia). The surveys asked cross sections of these countries to choose between such alternatives as whether "government should see to it that everyone has a job and a good standard of living" or "government should let each person get ahead on his own." Hundreds of other questions, general and specific, subtle and simple, were analyzed.

Leaving aside Coughlin's careful qualifications and cautions, ignoring his meticulous attention to exceptions, we see the pattern of his results: on very broad ideological themes focused on government intervention and regulation of economic life, the mass of citizens express views that match their government's behavior. Although every country evidences a pro–welfare-state majority, in countries that spend and tax a lot to ensure a high minimum standard of living, that majority is largest. These big spenders also endorse the success ideology, although not as enthusiastically as Americans or Canadians do.

Among middle-rank spenders—Canada and the United Kingdom—the pro–welfare-state ideology scores medium in popularity, and the success ideology is a little stronger than it is in West Germany, France, and Sweden. Among lean spenders, the pro–welfare-state majority is still there, but the success ideology is a bit stronger.

In other words, in abstract ideological themes, a country's mix of economic collectivism and economic individualism matches its social spending and taxing and the actual amount of government intervention.

Although there is some congruence between broad ideology and levels of taxing and social spending, when we focus on specific issues—support for particular public policies—the structure of public opinion is strikingly similar across all these countries. Briefly, in the eight countries studied, people love pensions and are only a shade less enamored of national health insurance. Next most popular are family or child allowances; they are viewed with more favor than disfavor in four of five nations for which data are available. When we go beyond these three most expensive and popular programs, we find that the mass of citizens in Denmark, the United Kingdom, Canada, and the United States alike have serious reservations about unemployment compensation and are quite doubtful, if not downright hostile, to public assistance; they think the benefits too often go to the undeserving. These similarities in program-specific attitudes hold up in the face of variations in administrative structure, population coverage, and types and levels of benefits, despite even variations in economic performance in these countries. Nowhere do we uncover a mass defection from support of social security, especially pensions and health insurance.

Finally, when we anchor survey data in relevant groups and strata and link them to national variations in social policy, we see that although support for the welfare state everywhere is weak among the self-employed (rich or poor) and somewhat stronger among the least privileged—unemployed, poor, or minorities—the main story is the absence of internal cleavages. For instance, the widespread doubts about "welfare chiselers" are shared even among low-income populations who benefit most from public assistance. And all strata and groups evidence virtually the same enthusiasm about pensions and health insurance. The only sharp lines of cleavage are along party lines, with only modest differences by race and class.

Thus, comparing countries with different histories, cultural traditions, and political systems, we find only small differences in the answers to roughly comparable questions. In mass attitudes about specific social programs, capitalist America and social democratic Sweden are brothers (sisters?) under the ideological skin.

These cross-sectional findings have been abundantly confirmed in subsequent analysis of public opinion in the United States and many other countries. Surveys done by the International Social Survey Programme (ISSP)—one in 1985 on the role of government, the other in 1987 on inequality covering the United States, the United Kingdom, West Germany, Australia, the Netherlands, and Italy—show the usual mix of economic individualism and collectivism in all countries, with modest national differences that match levels of spending and taxing when the questions tap abstract ideology (e.g., orientations toward nationalization of industry, income equalization, government guarantees of jobs for all)

(Haller, Höllinger, and Raubal, 1990, pp. 55 – 57). At the same time, these countries all embrace the free-mobility ideology; indeed, their citizens have very similar "functional" beliefs and explanations of what it takes to "get ahead in life." Asked to rank the importance of 13 factors that determine achievement, people in all these rich democracies "tend to rank personal characteristics such as hard work, ambition, natural ability, and education as the most important" (T. W. Smith, 1990, p. 24); next was "knowing the right people" and last were ascribed characteristics such as race, sex, religion, region, and political connections and beliefs[4] (p. 24). Asked to explain income differences, the citizens of these six countries are even more alike in the distribution of answers: they all emphasize that large pay differences are needed to inspire people to work hard, take extra responsibility, acquire skills, and study for formal qualifications (p. 25). Many students of American values and beliefs have noted a similar ideological ambivalence and incoherence in U.S. surveys (Converse, 1964; Free and Cantril, 1967; Morone, 1990; Zaller, 1992), with most citizens simultaneously embracing the individualistic success ideology and humanitarian, "collectivistic," pro–welfare-state sentiments.

A comprehensive 1992 Eurobarometer survey of attitudes toward social protection in 12 EC countries (including 8 of our 19) confirms all the themes I have emphasized while adding data on more social programs. It shows nearly unanimous pro–welfare-state sentiments; a vast majority either wanting increases or a steady state in government spending for social security;[5] the rank order of enthusiasm for specific programs puts pensions and health care at the very top; universal child allowances elicit some ambivalence but support for single-parent families is endorsed by strong majorities; and there is very strong support for an active labor-market policy—for example, training the unemployed for new jobs. (Ferrera, 1993a.)

The general contours of public opinion on taxing, spending, and the welfare state have remained quite stable over time and across rich democracies ever since surveys asked about these issues: a pro–welfare-state majority with modest national differences in the size of majorities when the questions are abstract but a very similar rank order of enthusiasm for universal, categorical social protection (pensions, health insurance, education and training) but with less support for unemployment insurance and downright hostility to means-tested programs for the undeserving poor. (For American trend data see Sanders, 1988, p. 313; Page and Shapiro, 1992, pp. 129 – 132, 125; Mayer, 1992; and Cook and Barrett, 1992. For cross-national data over time see Shapiro and Turner, 1989; Taylor-Gooby, 1989; and Svallfors, 1995.) Although trend data from 1970 to the early 1990s did show some fluctuations, usually in response to political campaigns, this underlying structure of opinion remained either stable or became increasingly favorable to the core of welfare state, especially in the 1980s, as it did in the United States (Mayer, 1992; Shapiro and Turner, 1989, p. 66; J. Davis, 1992) and the United Kingdom.

It is striking that whatever their actual behavior in office, backlash politicians have been unable to change this structure of opinion, except for brief moments. For instance, in a Gallup poll that repeatedly presents a tax/spend trade-off question (see table 10.1), the percentage of British adults who opt for "tax cuts even if it means some reduction in government services such as health, education, and welfare" reached a peak of 37% during the month of Margaret Thatcher's victorious campaign of May 1979. But that minority quickly went down, and by September 1986 it was only 9%; in subsequent years it never went above 14%. (In March 1996 it was 10%.)

This kind of radical disjunction between elite rhetoric, public policies, and popular opinion appears in the United States 1980–96 as well.[6] The more that modern populations think that their welfare-state benefits are threatened, the more pro–welfare-state they become. Only in three of the more lavishly financed, inefficient welfare states—the Netherlands, Italy, and Denmark—is the overwhelming balance of enthusiasm over skepticism diminishing, although their governments find it extremely difficult to cut the most popular programs (Ferrera, 1993a, pp. 5–6).

Not all issue-specific attitudes are as stable as attitudes toward components of the welfare state. Students of public opinion have found that attitudes regarding non-welfare-state issues—for example, government action and spending to prevent crime, protect the environment or civil liberties, provide for defense—are either unrelated or negatively related to sentiments about welfare-state and equality issues, less related to party preferences, and much less stable (Page and Shapiro, 1992, pp. 50–60; Jacoby, 1994, pp. 344–349). The volatility of postindustrial values is covered in chapter 4; the special role of education both in public opinion and government behavior is discussed in chapter 6 (sector spending). The main point remains: Within a context of ideological contradictions and ambivalence, issue-specific attitudes toward the welfare state, in contrast to other attitudes, are very similar across nations and stable over time.

All of this implies that politicians in a position to mobilize public opinion can play it either way. If they are hostile to expansive and generous social policies, they can work the tax-welfare backlash; if they are friendly, they can mobilize majority sentiments. Because the structure of public opinion—the rank order of enthusiasm by program and group—is so similar across nations and so stable over time; because broad, abstract ideologies are partly self-canceling, with every country embracing both economic individualism and collectivism, we must look beyond public opinion for explanations of the success or failure of tax-welfare backlash movements and candidates, including such initiatives as California's Proposition 13 and the defeat of President Clinton's proposals for comprehensive health-care reform.

Nativism and Tax-Welfare Backlash Go Together

In analyzing tax-welfare backlash it proved impossible to separate antitax, anti–social-spending, antibureaucratic protest movements and parties from nativist, xenophobic, or racist protests; these two themes appear together in all the high-scoring countries except Denmark in the 1970s. (Even in Denmark the Progress Party began to complain about immigrants in the 1980s.) When Hollywood actor Ronald Reagan swept California in the 1966 gubernatorial election, he not only sounded the familiar antitax, anti–social-spending, antibureaucratic themes but also at the same time baited welfare mothers. He brought the house down when he asserted that welfare recipients (code words for black welfare poor) are on a "prepaid lifetime vacation plan." In 1970, after four years in office, with taxes rising, welfare costs soaring, and campus disruption recurring (all of which he vowed to stop), Governor Reagan ran and won on the same slogans: "We are fighting the big-spending politicians who advocate a welfare state, the welfare bureaucrats whose jobs depend on expanding the welfare system, and the cadres of professional poor who have adopted welfare as a way of life" (*Wall Street Journal,* October 9, 1970). That move-

TABLE 10.1 British Tory policies and campaign rhetoric 1979–96 strengthened an already large pro–welfare–state majority

	May 1979	Mar 1980	Mar 1981	Feb 1982	Feb 1983	Nov 1984	Feb 1985	Sept 1986	Oct 1988	Dec 1989	Aug 1990	May 1991	Mar 1992	July 1993	Feb 1995	Mar 1996
Question: People have different views about whether it is more important to reduce taxes or keep up government spending. How about you? Which of these statements comes nearest to your own view?																
Taxes being cut, even if it means some reduction in government services, such as health, education and welfare	37	25	22	22	24	13	17	9	10	14	14	11	10	8	9	10
Things should be left as they are	26	27	25	26	23	26	19	19	16	19	14	14	21	15	17	14
Government services such as health, education and welfare should be extended, even if it means some increases in taxes	37	47	53	52	52	62	63	72	74	67	72	75	69	77	74	76

Note: The small numbers of "don't know's," never more than 8%, have been eliminated.
Source: *Gallup Political and Economic Index*. British national sample.

ment culminated in eight years of the Reagan presidency, and ultimately a Republican takeover of Congress in 1994 with identical campaign themes—antitax, antispend, antibureaucracy—combined with the complaint that immigrants and other poor racial and linguistic minorities were creating immense burdens of welfare and crime. For backlash politicians the slogan "no welfare for immigrants" is a "two-fer": it encapsulates two unpopular targets, recipients of social assistance (the undeserving poor) and despised minority groups. As president, Reagan repeatedly referred to mythical "welfare queens" as symbols of welfare fraud and abuse.[7]

Similarly, in the early 1970s, Conservative Enoch Powell, the Cambridge-educated establishment version of George Wallace or Ronald Reagan, became the charismatic hero of the middle mass. He not only targeted social spending and taxing as a drag on the British economy; he also railed against the hordes of West Indian blacks and other immigrants who were un-English and would undermine the British way of life. Although Powell failed to become top man of the Tories—they were embarrassed by his racism—Margaret Thatcher managed to become their top person articulating all of Powell's arguments except the overt complaints about racial minorities. Switzerland, too, has blended tax-welfare backlash with nativism. James Schwarzenbach in 1970 reached his peak of 46% of the total vote in a national referendum which proposed to limit the admission of foreign workers, a measure that his party claimed essential not only to preserve the Swiss way of life but also to avoid an ultimately staggering burden of social services. In the late 1970s, a Schwarzenbach-type movement was still operating—various right-wing populist parties rose in votes in the late 1970s and early 1980s and remained strong in the 1991 election. They included the Swiss Democrats, especially strong in Berne, Zurich, and Graubünden; the Lega Ticinese (antitax, antispend, antibureaucratic, anticorruption) in Italian-speaking Ticino; and more recently the Motorist Party ("Parti des Automobilistes") who favor privatization of transportation and denial of social benefits to foreign workers and are generally antigovernment and anti-Green. In the 1990s, the populist, charismatic leader of the right, Christopher Blocher of Zurich, was orchestrating the themes of these disparate parties and groups. Although small right-wing parties lost votes in the 1995 election, Blocher's People's Party was a winner (up 3%); the total backlash vote remained steady. Finally, Canada, with an above-average backlash score (3) based largely on the populist tax revolts confined to Alberta and British Columbia, evidences the same merging of antitax, anti–social-spending, antibureaucratic sentiments with a rising Western resentment of the Francophones of Quebec and the politicians in Ottawa who coddle them. (The Social Credit Party, in office in Alberta from 1935 to 1971, also appealed to anti-Semites.) More recently, the Reform Party, emerging in Alberta, then BC, rose to third in popular vote nationally in 1993; it even more clearly combined tax-welfare backlash with hostility to Francophones and all foreigners.[8] And in June 1997 it became the official opposition to the ruling Liberals in Parliament.

In short, while nativism is widespread among all rich democracies (see chap. 17), only a few rank high on tax-welfare backlash; these few cases almost always combine hostility to taxing, spending, and government bureaucracy with hostility to socially distant minority groups.

A Revolt of the Middle Mass?

Backlash politicians are very different in style and training; they vary somewhat in the issues they emphasize. But they depend on the same underlying discontents and mobilize very similar constituencies. Their supporters invariably include a substantial segment of the upper-working class (the "hardhats" in Nixon's silent majority—a mass of craftsmen in the building, printing, and other trades, foremen, and high-paid operatives), and the lower-middle class (a mass of small farmers, small businessmen, clerks, salesmen, and semiprofessional and semitechnical people). The revolt of this middle mass everywhere cuts into the established parties' base, as in the defection of California Democrats to Governor Reagan in 1966 and 1970 and the defection of Democrats everywhere to Richard Nixon in 1968 and 1972; it drove Mayor John Lindsay out of office in New York City in 1973 as surely as it devastated the Socialist bloc and the bourgeois bloc in Denmark the same year.

In the countries where backlash politicians succeeded in riding the middle-mass revolt to power in this early period (1965–75), their rhetoric continues to dominate political campaigns, if not public policy. The line from Enoch Powell to Margaret Thatcher to John Major is quite direct as is the line from George Wallace and Richard Nixon to Ronald Reagan to Speaker Newt Gingrich and the freshmen members of Congress of 1995.

Studies of both the Perot voters in the 1992 and 1996 U.S. presidential elections and the Democratic defectors to the Republicans in the 1994 congressional elections show that they were overwhelmingly non-college-educated white men and women. Typically they had either high-school or part-college education and thought that the economy was getting worse or their personal financial situation had deteriorated (Teixeira and Rogers, 1995; Greenberg, 1993; and exit polls reported by the New York Times, November 10, 1996). Squeezed economically, ready for xenophobic appeals (minorities and aliens are taking away your jobs and undermining your way of life), these defectors in the middle mass are the most volatile and alienated voters in the United States. Between 1992 and 1994, Democratic support remained steady among college graduates and high-school dropouts but declined 20 points (to 37%) among white men with a high-school diploma and 15 points (to 31%) among white men with some college.[9] Fitting the same educational-occupational profile are Republican presidential primary voters for right-wing populist-nativist candidate Pat Buchanan in 1996 and Louisiana voters for David Duke, the former Ku Klux Klan grand wizard who won a seat in the state legislature in 1989 and a majority of all white voters in the U.S. Senate open-primary race in October 1990 by railing against "welfare," taxes, and affirmative action for blacks. (On Buchanan see Washington Post, March 3, 1996, and Frank Lutz, CNN Lexis transcript, March 10, 1996; on Duke see Powell, 1992, pp. 12, 18, 22–25, 33; Rose and Esolen, 1992, pp. 206, 209, 230–231.) Because high-school graduates comprise 30% of the electorate in 1994 and part college 29% (U.S. Bureau of the Census, 1998a, p. 34), this revolt of the middle mass is an important determinant of electoral outcomes, especially in countries where party systems are weak.

In sum: Tax-welfare backlash has flourished in assorted countries; it is unrelated to the level of taxing and spending. The modern tension between success ideologies and welfare-state ideologies, between economic individualism and collectivism, merely gives politicians an opportunity to come down on either side. What varies so much among rich democracies is not their national values regarding the work ethic or the welfare state but the political management and channeling of the anxieties of the middle mass and the number and degree of alienation of the poor. These things are wondrously varied. Spending that is profligate or lean, taxing that is heavy or light, treatment of the poor and weak that is generous or stingy have only a little to do with the political fallout.

The most dramatic illustration that big public spending does not explain the intensity of tax-welfare backlash is the contrast between Sweden and Denmark. The Swedish Social Democrats managed to govern with very little erosion of electoral strength for 44 years and since 1976 for most years (except 1976–82 and 1991–94) while they built an unparalleled range of humanely and efficiently administered social services, ran up one of the highest tax rates in the world (total tax revenue including social-security taxes as a percentage of GNP averaged 40% from 1965 to 1971 and about 50% in 1991 compared to the USA's 27–28%), and guaranteed a high minimum standard of living for everyone. Next door, in culturally similar Denmark, similar trends in spending, taxing, and social policy were evident; but in the 1970s the Danish political economy began to fall apart. On election day December 1973 the antitax, antiwelfare, antibureaucracy Progress Party led by Glistrup (who said his ideas germinated during his year in Berkeley in 1951–52) racked up 16% of the total vote. Each of the two traditional party blocs dropped from their 1971 level of about 46% to 32%, with the Social Democrats suffering the worst losses. The 11 remaining parties, including Glistrup's, increased their strength from 7% to almost 36%, with the Progress Party bursting forth as the second-largest parliamentary party. Glistrup could also honestly claim to represent the little man: Progress Party votes were concentrated in the middle mass (upper-working and lower-middle classes).

Consider the program Glistrup offered to the Danish voters:

- Abolish the income tax by 1980 and have a big ceremony burning all papers in the revenue office.

- Wipe out most of the self-expanding, self-aggrandizing government bureaucracy, especially useless paperpushers, diplomats, welfare bureaucrats, and leftist kindergarten and nursery school teachers.

- Abolish the welfare system and substitute "social guards" in each local community. The guards would be practical men such as doctors, businessmen, and engineers. Within a strict limit of expenditure, they would have complete initiative in judging citizens' claims on the state; they would say yes or no to welfare applicants with no red tape.

- Cut the pensions of remaining public employees but raise pensions for everyone else and spend a bit more on antipollution measures; and, adding the Dane's characteristic comic touch,

- Abolish all defense expenditures, substituting instead a few hundred kroner for one telephone call to Brezhnev to announce "We give up" (a slogan Glistrup later abandoned).

In an interview in 1974, Glistrup told me that these problems are not uniquely Danish: "We get the gold medal for high income taxes so we can start a movement here, but in ten years or so the Progress Party will spread to other countries."

When the premier of the Danish Liberal Party, Paul Hartling, called the parliamentary election of January 1975 over his proposal for a wage and price freeze, the Social Democrats and Liberals both made a modest comeback. The Social Democrats formed a government and imposed the freeze. Despite the effort of the established parties to adopt parts of Glistrup's program, however—especially proposals to cut income taxes—and despite his indictment on several counts of income tax evasion and fraud, Glistrup lost only 3 of his 28 seats and his Progress Party remains a not-so-comic power in Danish political life. Glistrup was put in jail in 1983, released in 1985, returning to Parliament. The Progress Party popular vote remained strong in the 1970s, plunged to 3.6% in 1984 but climbed to 9.0% in the 1988 election, then slid to 6.0% in 1993, when the Social Democrats returned to power. The Progress Party continued to express neoliberal themes (free market, deregulation, antitax, antibureaucratic, anti-intellectual) but increasingly added xenophobia. Its anti-immigrant rhetoric escalated in the 1980s as more immigrants and refugees entered Denmark; the Party argued that welfare-state benefits should be denied to these foreigners, as well as to welfare cheaters. Its electoral base remained the middle mass. The Progress Party was gradually integrated into the system. At various times from 1982 to 1992 it joined center-right coalitions to stop wage indexation of all cash transfers and public employee wages; to lower marginal income-tax rates; and to adopt an austere fiscal policy. Unemployment remained high. Especially on tax and social-spending issues the mainstream parties adopted some of the Progress Party's agenda. (Andersen and Bjørklund, 1990; and my interviews.)

If something is rotten in Denmark, it is what causes protest votes in several countries sharing similar problems. To put the American and Danish experience in perspective and gauge the consequences of increased social spending we can fruitfully look at the big spenders who seem to get away with it—that is, they continue to maintain a civilized welfare state with relatively little political uproar—countries as diverse as Sweden, Norway, Finland, Austria, the Netherlands, Belgium, and Germany.

THEORY AND HYPOTHESES: WHAT CAUSES BACKLASH?

To explain both national variations in tax-welfare backlash and some similarities among the richest democracies, I shall test two theories. The first, theories of democratic corporatism, accents the interplay of political parties, types of political economy, and their policy outputs to explain differences. The second, convergence theory, accents affluence and its ideological and structural correlates—especially mobility and meritocracy and social cleavages—to explain the importance of thresholds of economic development. The first shows the persistence of differences; the second hints that as rich democracies get richer they are prone to backlash. Both theories are helpful in explaining this aspect of political legitimacy, the capacity of governments to collect taxes to pay for social and labor-market policies modern populations demand.

To understand why lasting backlash successes in a few countries began in the 1960s and not in many others, we must look to types of political economy and related rates of tax increases, types of taxes, types of spending (especially means-tested benefits), and differences in income equality.

Tax Increases, Tax Strategies, Means Testing, and Income Inequality

The first lesson is that although all modern countries share the spending-taxing explosion, among the calmer welfare-state leaders the costs of health, welfare, and education rose more smoothly and less visibly and were not combined with disruptive rates of unemployment as they were in the United States, Denmark, and the United Kingdom. For instance, the OECD figures that show 1965–71 changes in the ratio of total tax revenues to GDP among 22 countries climb at different rates.

The Danish tax burden soared so fast compared to that of Sweden, France, and Germany, among the better-performing welfare states, that observers tagged it the "Glistrup curve" (see figure 10.1). Similarly, the public spending curves, while accelerating everywhere, especially in labor-intensive industries such as health, education, and social services for children and the aged, moved up more abruptly in Denmark. Contrast Sweden, which starts in 1965 as the top taxer and nearly the top spender but moved more steadily and deliberately, by 1971 falling behind Denmark and Holland. Regarding unemployment, there is no significant correlation of unemployment and backlash scores. Only at the extreme of Denmark, and then only if continuously high employment is combined with other forces and policy errors, is unemployment politically disruptive.

The second more important lesson is that the squeeze on real disposable income due to rising prices and government expenditures creates most tax resistance in countries foolish enough to rely too much on painfully visible taxes, especially on income taxes and property taxes on households. Included in the visible tax club during the 1960s and early 1970s were such welfare laggards as the United States, Canada, Switzerland, and such middle-rank spenders as the United Kingdom, Finland, and (in the 1960s) Denmark, countries where backlash voting has been prominent.

Table 10.2 relates the visibility of taxes to the intensity of tax-welfare backlash. It shows that all of the high backlash scores are in the high tax visibility columns. Reliance on visible taxes offers a powerful explanation of backlash. Sweden and New Zealand are at first glance strong exceptions that will be discussed later. A "country" not in the table, California, combined heavy reliance on both income taxes and property taxes and an exceptional rate of increase in these taxes. The landslide victory of the famous Proposition 13— California's 1978 property-tax limitation initiative—was preceded by months of rapid increases in property taxes including a beautifully timed, much-publicized doubling of property taxes in Los Angeles County one week before the election (Coughlin, 1980, pp. 148–150).

Although the arguments for income taxes in Denmark and the United States alike are egalitarian, the outcome is sure political trouble with no relationship to income redistribution: the United States achieved little equality because its spending has been at once lean and hostile to the nonaged poor; Denmark achieved somewhat more equality because its programs have been generous to all. Yet both managed to cultivate not only their income and property taxes but also successful protest candidates. If you want to enhance the power of Reagan, Wallace, Powell, Thatcher, Glistrup, and comparable champions of the middle mass, stick to dramatically visible taxes and call it equality.

With big inflation like that of the 1970s, these deluded countries invite another problem: the United States called it the notch problem, the United Kingdom called it the poverty trap, and by any name it plagued the Danes. If you combine slow growth, double-digit inflation, a large number of income-tested or means-tested benefits (targeted to the poor or near-poor), and heavy reliance on progressive income taxes, you will produce a large number of families whose real income deteriorates as they simultaneously move into

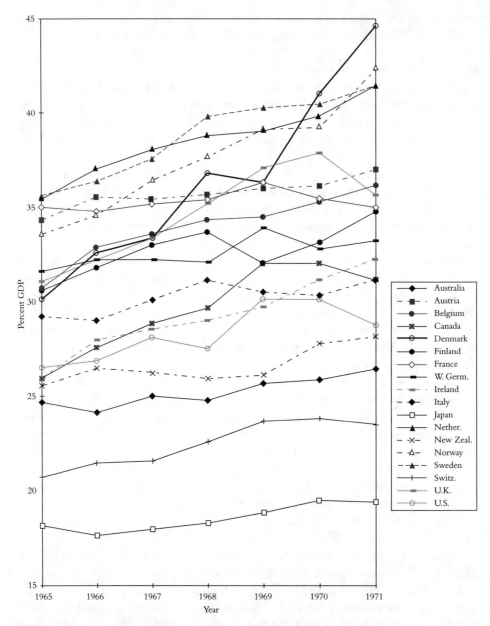

Figure 10.1. The Glistrup Curve: tax revenue as percentage of GDP at market prices, 1965–71
Source: Revenue Statistics of OECD Member Countries, 1965–76. Paris: OECD (1978), p. 82.

higher tax brackets and lose income-tested benefits (such as social assistance, Medicaid, or rent supplements). Hardly a formula for political calm.

Studies of public opinion are consistent with the finding that overreliance on visible taxes triggers tax revolts. They show that the most unpopular of all taxes are property taxes on households and income taxes—taxes that are paid once or twice a year with full awareness of the amount and ambiguity about what services they buy. Since 1972 American na-

TABLE 10.2 Tax visibility, tax load, and tax-welfare backlash in nineteen rich democracies[a]

Country	Backlash Score[b]	Type of Taxes as a Percentage of Total Taxation						Total Taxation as a Percentage of GDP	
		Visible Taxes[c]		Social Security Taxes[d]					
				1971		1988			
		1971	1988	Employee	Employer	Employee	Employer	1971	1988
Denmark	5	49.1 (1)[e]	54.8 (1)[e,f]	5.2	3.4	2.0	0.2	43.5 (1)	52.1 (2)
New Zealand	1	46.7 (2)	54.6 (2)[e,f]	0	0	0	0	27.5 (15)	37.9 (11)
Sweden	2	44.0 (3)	39.9 (6)	5.1	12.9	0.8	24.3	41.1 (3)	55.3 (1)
United States	5	43.6 (4)	39.7 (7)	9.2	11.4	12.7	17.0	27.8 (14)	29.8 (19)
Australia	2	42.5 (5)[e]	48.1 (3)[e]	0	0	0	0	24.7 (17)	30.8 (18)
United Kingdom	4	40.8 (6)	32.0 (12)	6.8	7.2	9.0	9.5	34.8 (8)	37.3 (13)
Canada	3	40.5 (7)[e]	41.6 (5)[e]	4.6	3.6	4.8	8.4	30.7 (13)	34.0 (15)
Switzerland	4	38.5 (8)	37.7 (8)	15.4	8.3	17.1	15.0	23.5 (18)	32.5 (16)
Finland	3	37.8 (9)	46.8 (4)	3.3	10.3	0	8.2	32.8 (11)	37.9 (11)
Ireland	0	30.2 (10)[e]	36.0 (9)[e]	3.8	4.5	5.5	8.4	32.3 (12)	41.5 (9)
Netherlands	2	29.0 (11)[e]	22.3 (18)[e]	19.2	16.5	25.6	16.9	39.4 (4)	48.2 (3)
W. Germany	0	28.4 (12)	29.9 (13)	13.5	20.3	18.4	19.1	33.4 (10)	37.4 (12)
Japan	0	27.8 (14)[e]	27.1 (15)[e]	9.7	10.3	14.6	14.4	20.0 (19)	31.3 (17)
Norway	3	27.8 (14)[e]	29.7 (14)	11.5	14.3	8.2	17.3	42.4 (2)	46.9 (4)
Belgium	2	26.5 (15)	32.6 (11)[e]	9.6	20.3	13.3	20.6	36.2 (7)	45.1 (5)
Israel	1	26.1 (16)	34.3 (10)	7.2	12.9	5.2	8.2	37.4 (5)	42.1 (7)
Austria	0	23.2 (17)[e]	23.3 (17)	8.9	17.3	16.5	16.1	36.4 (6)	41.9 (8)
Italy	1	12.9 (18)[e]	27.0 (16)[e]	7.3	30.6	9.9	23.4	29.6 (16)	37.1 (14)
France	3	10.8 (19)	14.5 (19)[f]	9.6	32.3	16.1	27.2	34.5 (9)	44.4 (6)

[a]Israeli tax data are from Israel Central Bureau of Statistics (1972a: table vi/8; 1972b: table i/16; 1973: tables vi/3 and vi/8; 1989: tables vi/1 and vi/13). Tax data for all other countries are from OECD (1973) and OECD (1991d).

[b]For measures, see Wilensky (1981c) and update in text.

[c]Visible taxes are personal taxes on income, property, and capital gains; property taxes paid by households; individual net wealth taxes; and gift and inheritance taxes. Note that net wealth, gift, and inheritance taxes comprise at most 4% of total tax revenues in both 1971 and 1988.

[d]Social-security taxes paid by the nonemployed and self-employed have been included in employee social-security taxes. For those countries which have social security taxes unallocable between employees, employers, and the nonemployed and self-employed, we have divided these equally between employees and employers.

[e]OECD figures on property tax revenues for these countries in these years do not include a breakdown into shares paid by households and shares paid by enterprises. I have assumed that each contributes half of total property tax revenues. This could lead to significant biases only for the following cases where property taxes comprise a large percentage of total revenues: Canada (11%) and Ireland (10%) in 1971, and Japan (11%), Australia (10%) and Canada (9%) in 1988.

[f]These countries have taxes in the OECD classification "income, profits, and capital gains taxes unallocable between individuals and corporations," which I have been unable to allocate between the visible and nonvisible categories of taxes. I have assumed a 50% share for each. Note that these taxes as a whole comprise 3.2% of total taxes for Denmark, and less than 1% of total taxes for France and New Zealand.

tional surveys consistently show that the federal income tax and the local property tax are ranked as the "least fair" of all taxes (MacManus, 1995, pp. 611, 616–617). Consumption taxes and social-security payroll taxes are viewed as most fair. Despite repeated increases in payroll taxes and the fact of their regressivity, a majority of Americans of all ages in surveys over the last several decades have never rated social security as the worst tax and, indeed, feel that the amount of the social-security tax is "about right," although repeated campaign declarations that the system is about to go bankrupt has shaken the faith of 18- to 34-year-old Americans that they will ever get what is due. (*Ibid.*, p. 612; Page and Shapiro, 1992, pp. 118–121, 161.) Despite their regressivity, sales taxes appear to be most popular. Economists' views of regressivity are not popular views. And the masses prefer to pay a little sales tax every day in every way than one big bite of an income or property tax.[10] As for social-security taxes, vast majorities understand that their taxes support the retirement of their older relatives as well as themselves (see chap. 7 on support for family policy), and they therefore resist cuts in spending even if it means cuts in taxes.

The rank order of dislike—from property taxes (most hated) to income taxes to consumption taxes (most acceptable)—was put to the test in a Michigan referendum of March 1994 on how to finance schools. The legislature, responding to popular pressure, eliminated property taxes as a primary source of school funding and asked the voters to choose between two alternatives: increasing sales taxes or increasing income taxes. An overwhelming majority of voters of all age groups chose the sales tax. (MacManus, 1995, p. 618.) A similar test came in a Swiss referendum of November 1993; Swiss voters, more addicted to direct democracy and even more resistant to taxes than California's voters, voted by a margin of two to one to introduce a value-added tax (VAT) of 6.5% to curb a rising government deficit (*Wall Street Journal,* November 29, 1993). Some observers believe that the resignation of Japanese Prime Minister Takeshita in April 1989 after he successfully steered a 3% broad-based VAT through the Diet demonstrates that the political costs of a consumption tax are as high as those of other taxes. But his defeat was perhaps more closely linked to his involvement in the Recruit scandal and his commitment to partially open the Japanese market to American agricultural products than to tax reform. Moreover, a recent intensive study of this episode of tax reform (Muramatsu and Mabuchi, 1991) shows that an elite strategy of negotiations with party leaders, parts of the opposition, the bureaucracy, and interest groups, especially business, the linking of the consumption tax proposal to the need for expanding social security coupled with an intensive media campaign to educate the public, overcame opposition (cf. Kato, 1994, p. 219). In the rare cases where a consumption tax has been politically costly, it appears that the cost is borne only at its first, sometimes inept, introduction, not at every subsequent increase; modern populations quickly become used to the VAT. At this writing Japan's VAT is scheduled to increase from 3% to 5% in 1997. It is a real case of American exceptionalism that the United States is the only one of our 19 rich democracies that is without such a broad-based national consumption tax.[11]

A final indication of the hostility to property taxes comes from the history of tax revolts in the United States. Throughout the 19th and 20th centuries, property-tax increases were the main source of tax resistance and tax revolts (Wallis, Grinath, and Sylla, 1994, especially pp. 2, 4, and 48–49; and Hartley, Sheffrin, and Vasché, 1996). For instance, one of several predecessors to California's 1978 property-tax-limiting Proposition 13 was the Riley-Stewart initiative of 1933. It emphasized property-tax relief through reduction in school expenditures by counties (shifting the burden to the state) and an increase in the property-tax base (utilities property would be returned to the local base), but left ambiguous the question of what new state taxes would support the schools and other popular causes. Then, as later, the voters wanted a free lunch—lower taxes and more services. (For evidence on 1933 see *ibid.*, p. 25; for evidence on Proposition 13 in 1978, see Sears and Citrin, 1985.) Because Republican Governors Rolph and Merriam in the 1930s were more responsible than their Republican successors of the 1980s and 1990s, what California got was the quick adoption of a sales tax, an income tax, and other taxes to finance the big increase in state aid to public schools and other social investments.

Not only are painfully visible taxes a source of tax-welfare backlash; painfully visible spending targeted to the "undeserving" poor is equally important: Backlash scores correlate .52 with visible taxes as a percentage of total revenue (1966–71) and .52 with means-tested stigmatized benefits. Chapter 8 (the welfare mess) analyzes national variations in reliance on means testing and explains why stigmatized benefits reinforce divisive politics. The heaviest users of means testing are the United Kingdom, the United States, Canada, and the Netherlands (see table 8.3).

The British Poll Tax: A Lesson in the Dangers of an Obsession with Tax Visibility

In April 1989 the Thatcher government first launched the ill-fated "poll tax" in Scotland; by April 1990 it was instituted in the rest of Britain. It was a substitute for the most painfully visible tax in the Western world, property taxes on households (the "rates"), but it was still more painfully visible.[12] Labeled the "Community Charge," the poll tax was a flat per capita levy on all adults, an average of £363 per adult (Butler, Adonis, and Travers, 1994, pp. 137–138). It was inspired by Prime Minister Thatcher's hostility to both local government (especially urban Labour councils) and progressive income taxes, and by the theories of her neoconservative advisers and consultants, especially members of the Adam Smith Institute and the Conservative Political Centre. The consultants popularized the idea in Tory circles, emphasizing tax transparency and the need to educate the population about the evils of government spending, thereby reducing both central-government grants to localities and the localities' capacity to tax and spend. The Tory justification for the shift: Under the property tax, lower-middle and lower-income people who paid less or none of it could outvote the more affluent homeowners; in contrast, the poll tax would hit all adults, be even more transparent, and make the local authorities more accountable. Some Tories thought it would also revitalize local government, forcing a more entrepreneurial management to reinvent government and live within its means. In theory, every voter would know exactly what he or she pays for what local services and whom to blame for the cost. A minimum of rebates, said the theorists, would ease the pain for the poor. In practice, "there were some 27 million people living in 'losing' households and just 8 million in households which gained," some at the top gaining large sums. "The heaviest losers were people living in small properties who were earning just enough to be disqualified from receiving a rebate," many of them pensioners, most of them citizens of the middle mass who had voted Tory in 1979, 1983, and 1987 (*ibid.*, p. 157). Not only were the poll-tax bills much higher than the Thatcher theorists had predicted, but they were patently unfair. A household with three adult wage earners paid three times more tax than a rich widow living by herself in a mansion.[13]

Within a year of implementation the outcomes became clear: The poll-tax cost twice as much as the rates (property tax) to collect (p. 291); levels of tax evasion approached 20% in inner cities; local government spending did not go down, but net tax collections did, while central government grants to offset the wilder inequities ballooned (p. 139); popular hostility reached fever pitch—expressed in the biggest mass agitation since World War II (p. 297). This tax produced the worst riots in London since the 1880s.

When the Tories removed Margaret Thatcher in favor of John Major, they simultaneously abandoned the poll tax to avoid defeat in the election of 1992. At least £1.5 billion had been wasted on setting up, administering, and replacing the tax. The capacity of local governments to collect taxes and deliver service was severely impaired. (p. 180.)

Like supply-side theorists of the Reaganomics era who in eight years added $1.78 trillion to the U.S. debt on the theory that sharp tax cuts would create such an economic boom that tax revenues would increase, the Thatcher ideologues remained impervious to experience; they now say that if the poll tax had only been done right, spending would have decreased and revenues would be up (*ibid.*, pp. 172–173, 183). Mrs. Thatcher, to this day, sings the praises of the poll tax, another testimony to the brittle resistance of ideology to fact. The rise and fall of the British poll tax of 1989–92 was both a remarkable exercise in self-delusion and a reminder of the power of painfully visible taxes to stimulate tax revolts.

Big Spenders, Low Backlash

Now contrast the countries that get away with expensive programs, however variable their efficiency: their financing of social programs rests heavily on indirect taxes such as the VAT or sales taxes, together with social-security contributions of employers and employees. My interviews with politicians and budget officers in Europe point to the process by which big spenders and taxers arrived at a balanced tax structure with great reliance on consumption taxes and social-security taxes. In France, it is clear that ingenious politicians and experts in the Finance Ministry (Direction Générale des Impôts and Ministère de l'Économie et des Finances) invented the VAT and increased social-security taxes because they could not collect the massive sums needed to finance the welfare state and the military from income taxes. They were attracted by the self-enforcing features of VAT and the efficiency of both VAT and payroll taxes compared with their corrupt and ineffective income-tax system. The French worker's payroll slip is like a telephone directory, there are so many contributions for one benefit or another. Workers view increased employer contributions as great victories, although they can readily be passed on in increased prices or lower wages. Note that France in table 10.2 is first in reliance on employer contributions. Employee contributions, although they should be visible, are earmarked and publicized in such ways that they create the delusion that workers will somehow eventually take out what they are paying in. In Sweden, as early as the early 1960s, the prime minister, the finance minister, and staff economists of the LO became aware of the political risks of continued reliance on a highly progressive income tax; they sent a team to investigate the French VAT and were convinced that if the French could collect such large sums from the VAT, the Swedes with their more virtuous tax behavior could collect even more. In other corporatist economies as well, it is clear that either by strategic design or by incremental steps, political elites, left and right alike, moved toward heavy consumption taxes and social-security taxes because of the rising resistance to income taxes and/or property taxes and the perception that more stable sources of revenue were required to meet mass demands.

How could politicians in these countries enact such taxes in the face of labor-left conviction that the VAT is regressive and social-security taxes are a burden on the great middle class? Because their centralized structure of bargaining permitted both labor and management to accept heavy mass tax burdens in return for other concessions and agreements on how the revenues would be spent. This process—broad elite and mass consensus on expanding the welfare state, increasing elite awareness of the political limits of painfully visible taxes, and the easy mass acceptance of consumption and payroll taxes—led to the tax balance pictured in table 10.2. By 1971, West Germany had achieved nearly even balance—about 30% of total taxation from consumption taxes, 34% from social-security taxes, and about 29% from "visible" taxes (mainly income taxes and property taxes). The Netherlands and Belgium had reached a similar distribution.

These contrasting patterns of taxation remained fairly stable from 1965–71 to 1988. For instance, the average reliance on visible taxes as a percentage of total tax take for the top five countries in table 10.2 is 45.2% in 1971 compared to 49.2% in 1988. Conversely, the bottom five in reliance on visible taxes averaged 19.9% in 1971 and 22.8% in 1988. The ratio of the averages for these extremes was 2.27 to 1 in 1971 and 2.16 to 1 in 1988—not much change. Only three countries in table 10.2 changed their relative reliance on visible taxes greatly: the United Kingdom moved from high to medium, the Netherlands from medium to low, Finland from medium to high.

Regarding the role of visible taxes in promoting backlash, two countries, Sweden and New Zealand, are at first glance exceptions—backlash low but heavy dependence on visible taxes. They are exceptions that prove the rule. Sweden went from third in reliance on visible taxes in 1971 to sixth in 1988 and continued that trend in the 1990s, moving gradually toward greater tax balance. Moreover, throughout those years, although the Swedish middle mass was taxed far more heavily than the comparable populations of the United States or Switzerland, as they looked up they knew the burden was still heavier on the more affluent; and, as they saw the flow of benefits and services, they did not scream for cuts. The revolt of the middle mass in the most-celebrated welfare state in the world has been contained, partly by modest steps toward diversified financing and by a fairer net outcome. The Swedish case suggests that reduction of income inequality reduces backlash, a theme explored later for all 19 countries. The second case, New Zealand, was able to move from a low reliance on visible taxes in 1965 (25%) to high in 1971 (46.7%) and stay second only to Denmark until 1988 (54%) with little overt backlash. It, too, is the exception that proves the rule, for New Zealand experienced dramatic shifts toward neoliberal spending, taxing, and deregulation policies in both major parties 1985–94 that destabilized both the economy and the polity and spawned four new populist parties of the right and left—a pattern similar to Denmark's, only delayed a decade. (That story is told in the next chapter on party decline.)

Evidence of a more recent convergence toward the German balance among types of mass taxes appeared in tax and pension reforms in Sweden and Finland in the 1990s, a shift from general income-tax revenues to social-security payroll taxes (Niemelä, Salminen, and Vanamo, 1993, pp. 32–33). And Denmark, number one in the visible tax club from 1965 to the 1990s, began to reduce the income tax in early 1993 when the center-left majority took over; further income tax cuts were planned for 1994–98—half the gap to be filled in 1995–96 by a big increase in social-security contributions (*The Economist,* November 5, 1994) as well as "green" taxes, much too late to avoid Glistrup and the Progress Party.

Testing Theories of Democratic Corporatism

We are now in a position to apply to all 19 countries a few systematic tests of my guiding hypothesis that types of political economy vary in their reliance on visible taxes, their preference for visible spending (stigmatized, means-tested benefits such as public assistance), and their degree of income inequality, and that these policies, in turn, determine variations in tax-welfare backlash. Again I focus on the critical period of roughly 1965–75 when these movements emerged fully blown, with the reminder that the rank order of backlash is still in place; only minor shifts occurred from the mid-1970s to the mid-1990s.[14] After exploring the role of types of political economy as sources of backlash, I test the convergence hypothesis that at very high levels of economic development rich democracies become increasingly vulnerable to populist backlash movements.

Applying the scheme of earlier chapters, table 10.3 relates cumulative left power, cumulative Catholic power, and corporatism to backlash scores using crude dichotomies (high versus low).

We see first that corporatism has no direct relation to backlash (r = .00). Leftism and Catholicism have opposite and indirect effects on backlash. Because left parties have a penchant for progressive income taxes, we find the highest scores among countries with strong left power that also rely heavily on visible taxes (columns 1 and 5); in fact, there is no country with strong left power that ranks low in tax visibility. In contrast, there is no country with strong Catholic party power that is high in reliance on visible taxes and the combination of Catholicism and low tax visibility yields the lowest backlash scores in table 10.3. If we take the viewpoint of a nonleft government facing strong left opposition (e.g., Belgium, Netherlands, Italy, Austria and to a lesser extent Germany) avoidance of visible taxes both permits and necessitates freer spending—a kind of welfare counterpunch to the left threat.

Left power is nowhere as continuous as it was in the 44 years of Social Democratic rule in Sweden. But even intermittent periods of left rule leave a legacy of tax visibility. Leftism, whether it appears with consensual bargaining structures or not, also encourages the sharper articulation of working-class interests, raises working-class hopes—along with income taxes—and thereby frightens the middle or upper class. Further, when upper-working-class citizens join the lower-middle class in property ownership and lifestyle, when they then see their income taxes and/or property taxes rising, many of them become available to backlash movements. This especially affects workers in the private sector who do not fully share public-sector employees' interest in expansion of the public sector and the taxes to support it. These interpretations are consistent with table 10.3 where we find such countries as Denmark, Norway, Finland, the United States, and the United Kingdom with strong cumulative left power from 1919 to 1976, high tax visibility in 1965, and medium to high backlash during 1965–75. (In that league, Sweden and New Zealand are the exceptions already discussed; subsequent developments moved Sweden to less tax visibility and still low backlash, New Zealand maintained its lead in tax visibility long enough for backlash candidates to burst forth in the 1990s.)

Table 10.4 permits a more subtle analysis of the role of democratic corporatism and related public policies. It enables us to examine the interaction of political party power, types of bargaining arrangements, and all three of the proximate causes of backlash—heavy reliance on visible taxes, the heavy use of means-tested, stigmatized benefits, and income inequality (great distance between the affluent and the poor).

1. The highest backlash scores (4–5) are in columns 1, 4, and 5: fragmented and decentralized political economies that fit all three policy patterns (the USA and the

TABLE 10.3 Left party power 1919–76 fosters visible taxes in 1965–71 and thereby increases tax-welfare backlash. Corporatism has no independent effect. Catholic power combined with weak left power and low tax visibility dampens backlash.

	Strong Corporatism				Weak Corporatism			
	Strong Left Power 1919–76[a]		Weak Left Power 1919–76		Strong Left Power 1919–76		Weak Left Power 1919–76	
	High Tax Visibility[b]	Low Tax Visibility	High Tax Visibility	Low Tax Visibility	High Tax Visibility	Low Tax Visibility	High Tax Visibility	Low Tax Visibility
	Denmark 5	Norway 3	No case	France 3	USA 5	No case	Switzerland 4	*Germany 0
	Finland 3	*Belgium 2		*Netherlands 2	UK 4		Canada 3	Japan 0
	Sweden 2	Israel 1		*Italy 1	New Zealand 1		Australia 2	Ireland 0
				*Austria 0				
Average Backlash	3.3	2.0		1.5	3.3		3.0	0.0

*Strong Catholic party power since WWI.

[a] If we substitute cumulative post–WWII left power for cumulative 1919–76 left power, the result is very similar. The correlation of left power in the longer period with the shorter is r = .97.

[b] Visible taxes as a percentage of total taxes, average of 1965 and 1971. Visible taxes are personal taxes on income, property, and capital gains; property taxes paid by households; individual net wealth taxes; and gift inheritance taxes. Note that net wealth, gift, and inheritance taxes comprise at most 4% of total tax revenues. See text and footnotes, table 10.2.

UK are both high in tax visibility and means testing and below average in equality); Switzerland, a case of corporatism-without-labor that ranks above average in tax visibility and means testing and low in income equality; and Denmark, which leads in tax visibility and is below average in equality, making it a deviant case in the left-corporatist column.[15]

2.   At the other extreme the lowest average backlash scores (1.3 and 0.5) appear among five corporatist democracies that evidence either strong cumulative Catholic party power (Germany, Italy) or strong competition between left and Catholic parties (Netherlands, Austria, and Belgium) *and* are below average in either tax visibility or means testing. All five rank substantially above average in income equality.

3.   The Nordic left-corporatist democracies have a high average backlash score (2.8) but vary greatly, depending on their policy patterns. We have already discussed how Denmark got into trouble while Sweden avoided it. Norway and Finland, slightly above average in backlash, present a mixed picture in policies—much above average in income equality, low in means testing, but medium or medium-high in tax visibility. Since the 1970s they have both moved toward less backlash (from 3 toward Sweden's 2) which would put them where they belong in table 10.4 in view of their achievements in equality, consensus, and avoidance of Denmark's extreme reliance on income taxes and property taxes. Israel is the exception among the left-corporatist countries. It is above average in means testing and below average in income equality and yet avoided backlash. While its unique defense burden subverts its social spending (see chap. 5), the same security concern—the well-founded perception that the nation is surrounded by enemies—may enhance social integration and constrain antistate political expression.

4.   There is a hint that corporatist countries that exclude labor from high policy foster above-average backlash (Switzerland, France) unless they avoid both visible taxes and means testing and achieve much income equality (Japan).

5.   The negative correlation of equality measured by the income share going to the lowest quintile (roughly, poverty reduction) and backlash is slightly higher ($r = -.54$) than the positive correlation of inequality measured by the distance between the top fifth and the bottom fifth and backlash ($r = .42$) used in table 8.4. In regressions, however, neither measure reaches significance, although the coefficients are always in the right direction (the more inequality, the less poverty reduction, the more backlash). We can see the central tendency from the broad rankings in table 10.4.

In sum: The consensus-making machine of corporatism has no direct effect on limiting tax-welfare backlash. But if a corporatist democracy adopts taxing and spending policies that move toward consumption taxes and social-security payroll taxes, lessening reliance on painfully visible taxes; if it reduces the distance between the rich and the poor; if it avoids means-tested benefits and relies on more universal, categorical social programs, then it will avoid the mass movements that paralyze government. In the absence of consensual bargaining structures, such benign policies are highly unlikely, as we can see from table 10.4. Because left parties in power foster reliance on the most-hated taxes (property taxes on households and progressive income taxes), the combination of left power and corporatism is not

TABLE 10.4 Types of political economy and backlash: Corporatist countries, especially those with Catholic power or left/Catholic competition, reduce inequality and avoid overreliance on visible taxes and stigmatized benefits, thereby reducing backlash

	Left Corporatist — Backlash Tax					Left/Catholic Corporatist — Backlash Tax					Catholic Corporatist — Backlash Tax					Corporatist without Labor — Backlash Tax					Least Corporatist — Backlash Tax				
	Country	Score	Vis[a]	PA[b]	Equal[c]	Country	Score	Vis[a]	PA[b]	Equal[c]	Country	Score	Vis[a]	PA[b]	Equal[c]	Country	Score	Vis[a]	PA[b]	Equal[c]	Country	Score	Vis[a]	PA[b]	Equal[c]
Most Backlash (4–5)	Denmark	5	H	L	ML											Switzer-land	4	HM	HM	L	USA	5	H	H	L
																					UK	4	H	H	ML
Med. Backlash (3)	Norway	3	M	L	HM											France	3	L	MH	ML	Canada	3	MH	H	ML
	Finland	3	MH	L	HM																				
Least Backlash (0–2)	Sweden	2	H	L	H	Nether-lands	2	M	MH	HM	Italy	1	L	M	HM	Japan	0	L	M	H	Australia	2	H	L	L
	Israel	1	ML	MH	ML	Belgium	2	L	MH	H	Germany	0	ML	M	HM						New Zealand	1	MH	L	L
						Austria	0	L	L	HM											Ireland	0	ML	M	L
Avg. score	2.8					1.3					0.5					2.3					2.5				

[a]Visible taxes as a percentage of total taxes, average of 1965 and 1971. Visible taxes are personal taxes on income, property, and capital gains; property taxes paid by households; individual net wealth taxes; and gift and inheritance taxes. Note that net wealth, gift, and inheritance taxes comprise at most 4% of total tax revenues. See text and footnotes to table 10.2.

[b]Public assistance spending per capita, average of 1966 and 1971. Based on a narrow definition: (1) noncategorical benefits targeted to the poor via a stiff income and/or assets-test, (2) applied by welfare administrators with substantial discretion, (3) with a high probability of stigma. See appendix and text for measures.

[c]Ratio of the percentage share of gross household income of the top fifth of the population to the share of the bottom fifth, ca. 1980, from World Bank, *World Development Report 1990*. Ranks for Austria and Ireland are based on table 2 of Atkinson, Rainwater, and Smeeding (1995), which gives the ratio of the relative income for individuals in the upper 10% of the population to that of the lowest 10%, measured as a percent of the national median for 16 of our countries in the mid-1980s. Austria ranked fifth; Ireland ranked fifteenth. See chapter 14 and table 14.4.

H = most equality. L = least equality. L = low ratio = high ratio = least equality.

a sure road to containment of backlash, whatever else these political economies do. It is only where corporatism and leftism are combined with Catholicism that backlash is reduced.

Testing Convergence Theory

As we have seen in chapter 5, there are several reasons to suppose that at some high threshold of development very rich democracies evidence structural changes that increase the appeal of tax-welfare backlash movements and candidates. They include the expansion of educational and occupational opportunities; increased occupational and residential mobility and more women working; slower economic growth and hence the exacerbation of social cleavages and less leeway for added social spending; and an increase in immigration, legal and illegal, hence intensified cleavages of religion, ethnicity, race, and language (for details see chap. 17 on globalization). Social cleavages are always fertile soil for xenophobic tax-welfare backlash movements while mobility and the growth of the privileged upper-middle class is a force for the development of meritocratic ideologies and the decrease of community solidarity (see chap. 14 on mayhem). Thus, while I have explained differences in backlash among the 19 rich democracies by contrasts in types of political economy and related social policies, it is also possible that as they all get richer these contrasts will diminish.

One additional trend that could make all rich democracies vulnerable to backlash is less certain. The income-tax-cutting mania of the 1980s and the 1990s, when many countries reduced both income-tax rates and the number of income brackets, had an unanticipated effect: the property-tax share of all government revenues climbed in most of our rich democracies. From 1985 to 1993, of 18 countries for which we have data, property taxes as a share of total revenue increased in 13 and stayed steady or decreased in only 5. If as rich countries become richer, the number of homeowners climbs, and the income-tax cuts are not replaced by consumption taxes and social-security taxes; if, in addition, central governments dump more functions on localities and reduce government subsidies to them (see chap. 9), the unfortunate effect will be an increased reliance on property taxes. While these trends still leave the decentralized, fragmented political economies far ahead of the corporatist democracies in their taste for property taxes, there are signs of increased home ownership, a move away from income taxes, and the decentralization of some functions even among corporatist democracies. If so, and they drift into increased reliance on property taxes, tax-welfare backlash might spread.[16]

If these convergent trends continue—if as rich democracies become richer they all experience more mobility and meritocracy, more minority-group cleavages as well as slower growth combined with higher mass aspirations—they will become more open to backlash movements and candidates, although the countervailing bargaining structures in place could maintain current national differences for some time.

We can test these hypotheses by noting the threshold of economic development of the late 1960s, when half of our rich democracies had become very rich and by comparing their backlash scores with the scores of the least rich. We can then relate our measures of mobility and meritocracy and minority-group cleavages to affluence, growth, and backlash. After a broad quantitative look, based on multiple regressions, we can examine some interaction effects.

Figure 10.2 is a path diagram testing the independent influence of each variable in this industrialism scheme. It shows rather neatly that affluence (GNP per capita averaged for

1966 and 1971) predicts mobility and meritocracy which, in turn, predicts backlash (1965–75).[17] Minority-group cleavages are strong predictors of mobility-meritocracy, again an indirect influence on backlash. Meanwhile, as anticipated, real GNP growth per capita has a direct effect: while very high levels of affluence foster backlash indirectly through mobility-meritocracy and by increasing minority-group conflict, economic growth tends to make backlash movements harder to mobilize. Growth is a salve for the political tensions of modern life.

Table 10.5 examines the interaction of affluence, mobility-meritocracy, and social cleavages as determinants of backlash. It shows that the highest average backlash scores appear among the richest democracies that are also strong in minority-group cleavages and are either high in mobility-meritocracy (the USA, Canada, the UK) or medium-low (Switzerland). The lowest average score (1.1) appears in the least-rich democracies (for the relevant period of 1966–71) with medium to weak cleavages and low mobility-meritocracy (Italy, the Netherlands, Belgium, Austria, Ireland, Japan).[18] Of course, to explain backlash differences among countries equally rich in the same column of table 10.5 (e.g., Sweden and Germany versus Denmark and France; or Israel versus the UK), we must look to types of political economy and their policy outputs, taxing and spending patterns, as we have seen in table 10.4.

In table 10.5 if we update the "most-rich" versus "least-rich" categories to 1993, only four cases change in their relative affluence. Japan and Austria, two corporatist democracies with zero backlash, moved up sharply in relative ranking, Japan to #1 in per capita GDP using current exchange rates, Austria to #6 (even using current purchasing power parities they rank 3rd and 9th); two move down, Australia to 16th (by PPPs, 13th) and Canada moves to about the average (#12 but by PPPs #7). The average backlash score for the most affluent, medium to weak cleavages, low to medium mobility column would be reduced from 2.6 to 1.9; the average for the least affluent comparable column would remain the same. The general conclusions are unaffected. Because there is considerable convergence in affluence among our 19 democracies, with the least rich coming closer to the very rich (see chap. 1), however, we would expect that as a predictor of backlash, affluence will gradually weaken relative to minority-group cleavages and mobility.[19]

A final word about the role of social cleavages in welfare-state development and the political responses I have labeled backlash. Social heterogeneity, as chapter 5 shows, can cut both ways. Although minority groups can be an obstacle to wider civic virtue, although their thrust for opportunity increases mobility, which fosters backlash, they also press for expanded state expenditures which reduce inequality, thereby reducing backlash. Further, deep social cleavages can create backlash, but only where they are given sharp expression by a decentralized if not fragmented political economy. Tables 10.4 and 10.5 support that argument. In short, egalitarian corporatist democracies with the "right" taxing and spending policies can contain the disruptive effects of advanced industrialization—minority-group cleavages and mobility—and at least limit backlash tendencies.

Summary and Interpretation

This chapter has shown that it is not the *level* of taxes that creates tax-welfare backlash but the *type* of taxes—property taxes and income taxes with their visibility and perceived pain. Conversely, consumption taxes and social-security payroll taxes keep things cool. Chapter

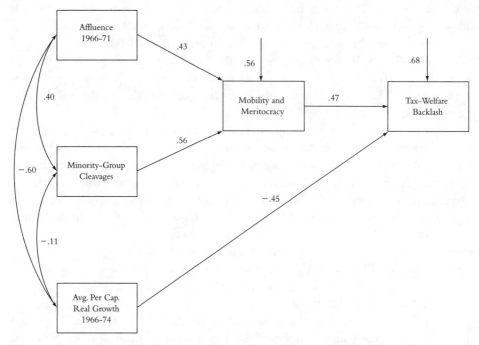

Figure 10.2. Industrialization and tax-welfare backlash: a causal model[a]

[a]N=18. New Zealand missing on Mobility-Meritocracy Index. All path coefficients are significant at $p < .05$. Adjusted R^2 for Backlash = 48. Adjusted R^2 for Mobility-Meritocracy = .65. For definitions and measures see footnotes to table 10.5.

12 shows the same for economic performance: the level of taxes is no problem but visible taxes, especially income taxes and property taxes, are a drag on economic growth from 1950 to 1979, neutral thereafter; while consumption taxes and payroll taxes are good for the economy in the long run because they foster savings and investment. In the words of the old pop tune, "It ain't what ya do but the way that ya do it."

Similarly, social spending creates backlash only if it is visibly targeted to the nonaged, nondisabled, "undeserving" poor via stigmatized, means-tested benefits. If social programs are universal and categorical, with everyone or at least large majorities sharing the benefits and the costs, as with pensions, health insurance, family policies, education and training, and similar broad-based programs, then the tendency of the middle mass toward backlash is reduced.

Less visible taxes and more universalistic spending make it possible to finance a generous welfare state whose benefits are substantial and widespread. Modern voters cannot be mobilized to resist gradual tax increases when the tax structure relies heavily on social-security taxes and consumption taxes and reduces reliance on income taxes and property taxes. Such a tax structure may be proportional or even regressive, but it raises enough revenue to increase social spending not only for the middle mass but also for the poor. The resulting increase in income equality reduces the politics of resentment.

What makes these egalitarian taxing and spending policies possible are types of political economies that permit trade-offs among the social partners—labor (including professions

TABLE 10.5 Industrialization as a source of tax-welfare backlash: The interaction of affluence, minority-group cleavages, mobility and meritocracy

Most rich[a]				Least rich			
Strong cleavages[b]		Medium to weak cleavages		Strong cleavages		Medium to weak cleavages	
High mobility and meritocracy[c]	Low to medium mobility and meritocracy	High mobility and meritocracy	Low to medium mobility and meritocracy	High mobility and meritocracy	Low to medium mobility and meritocracy	High mobility and meritocracy	Low to medium mobility and meritocracy
USA 5	Switzerland 4		Sweden 2	Israel 1			Finland 3
Canada 3			Norway 3	United Kingdom 4			Italy 1
Australia 2			Germany 0				Netherlands 2
			France 3				Belgium 2
			Denmark 5				Austria 0
							Ireland 0
							Japan 0
Avg. backlash 3.3	4.0		2.6	2.5			1.1

[a] Average GNP per capita 1966 and 1971.

[b] Measured by ethnic, religious, linguistic or racial cleavages. See appendix I and text, chapter 14. Netherlands, Belgium, Germany, and France score medium on cleavages.

[c] An index of mobility and meritocracy with four equally weighted components: intergenerational mobility out of the working class; percentage of working-class sons and daughters in higher education, 1965 or 1970; higher education enrollment ratios averaged for 1965 and 1971; and higher education expenditures per capita averaged for 1965 and 1971; New Zealand missing. See appendix I and text, chapter 14.

and farm organizations), management, and the state. The combination of leftism, Catholicism, and democratic corporatism fosters social consensus and a policy mix that reduces tax-welfare backlash. Left power alone cuts both ways: it leads to visible taxation, thereby increasing backlash; but it also typically fosters corporatist bargaining structures, less reliance on means testing, more income equality, and less poverty, dampening mass discontent. In the absence of strong corporatism and Catholicism, however, the net outcome is above-average backlash.[20] And if left parties as they attempt to achieve equality use race-ethnicity-religion as dominant criteria in allocating rewards (as in the racial quota systems for education and jobs embraced by the Democratic Party in the United States), the effect is similar to that of stigmatized public assistance—it provokes majority resentment and achieves little equality.

Crucial in explaining variations in the success of tax-welfare backlash candidates is the economic position and political tendency of the middle mass. In backlash-prone countries, when lower-white-collar workers and upper-blue-collar workers look up, they see an over-privileged, college-educated upper-middle class and the rich, who seem to evade taxes, live well, indulge their children who run wild at expensive colleges or worse, at state universities, at their expense. When they look down, they see the welfare poor and immigrants whose morals, lifestyle, and ethnic-racial origin repel them, whose children, they think, are at the root of crime and disorder. These citizens of the middle mass see themselves as working hard at disciplined jobs, living by the rules, struggling for a decent, safe home and more job security, fighting against the erosion of their earnings and standard of living. Obviously the structures and policies uncovered in this chapter that reduce the insecurities of the middle mass also reduce the success of demagogic appeals regarding taxes, social spending, bureaucracy, and socially distant minority groups. Insofar as taxes, spending, and social policies are perceived as fair by the middle mass they limit the politics of envy and hate while they keep a potentially large number of swing voters from losing their political moorings.

Convergence theory complements our findings regarding the political effects of types of corporatism and their public-policy correlates and provides a glimpse of the future. As the very richest democracies of the past 30 years got richer and as their least-rich counterparts converged in GDP per capita, there was at least some convergence in social and residential mobility and minority-group cleavages. Together affluence, racial-ethnic-linguistic conflict, and mobility as they interact foster backlash. If these convergent trends continue, it is possible that in a generation or two, the institutional differences that explain variation in backlash will decrease and intense tax-welfare backlash will spread beyond the United States, the United Kingdom, Denmark, and Switzerland. For the moment the story remains one of big national contrasts.

The next chapter turns to a second dimension of political legitimacy—national variation in party dealignment. At issue is the fate of a major force for social integration and political legitimacy, broad-based center-left and center-right parties that crosscut classes, minority groups, age grades, and gender.

NOTES

This chapter is a revision, update, and elaboration of Wilensky (1976c, 1981c). I am grateful to Richard Coughlin, Philip Armour, Kathleen Gerson, Paul M. Lewis, Harry Katz, Dan Finnegan, Timothy McDaniel, Jeffrey Haydu, Anne T. Lawrence, Alison E. Woodward, Theodore M. Crone, and

Brian Main—the interdisciplinary team that had command of five languages and did the early coding and qualitative analysis of tax revolts and their causes—and to Arnold J. Heidenheimer and (the late) Val Lorwin for critical readings of an early version. Karen Adelberger assisted in updating the chapter.

1. This account is based partly on Winock (1990), Mayer and Perrineau (1989), Kitschelt with McGann (1995, chap. 3), Bornstein and Tixier (1996), Barbier and Nadel (1996), Borrel (1996), and partly on interviews.

2. Protest parties in Sweden are not only of brief duration; their members fit the moderation and consensual style of Swedish politics. For instance, in one poll of New Democracy voters, 40% said they were neither left nor right.

3. This analysis of ambivalence and contradictions in modern ideologies among both elites and masses is based on Wilensky (1966b, p. 103; 1975, pp. 32–49; 1980; and Wilensky and Lebeaux, 1958, pp. 40–48).

4. Only the Italians ranked "connections" in general and "political connections" specifically anywhere near the top—reflecting Italy's extraordinary corruption in everyday life.

5. For example, the average percentage in the 8 of our 19 countries who "agreed strongly" (versus "agreed slightly") with the minimalist position ("the government should provide everyone with only a limited number of essential benefits and encourage people to provide for themselves in other respects") was 44.9%; the average percentage who "strongly agreed" with the maximalist position ("the government must continue to provide everyone with a broad range of social security benefits even if it means increasing taxes and contributions") was 62.4%—about a 6 to 4 edge for the maximalists (Ferrera, 1993a, pp. 5–6). When surveys add the option of keeping spending and taxing where they are now, we uncover vast majorities who reject any cuts (Kohli, 1993, pp. 7–10 and table 10.1 below [UK Gallup]; cf. Coughlin, 1980, pp. 131–150).

6. During the yearlong debate on President Clinton's complex health-care reform the disjunction between public responses to general slogans and to specific issues was evident. Despite the sharply partisan climate of 1993–94, despite fear-mongering slogans by the small business lobby and insurance companies (saturating television attack ads), issue-specific opinion remained friendly to the outlines of national health insurance. But the same respondents, asked whether they supported the "Clinton health-care proposal," gave their TV-driven negative response. Few, of course, knew what the proposals contained (Jamieson and Capella, 1994). Despite this cloud of confusion and hysteria, when confronted with the specifics of the Clinton plan, a majority showed support for the specific ingredients of reform. (Based on the *Gallup Poll Monthly* and the Roper Center reviews of diverse polls, *The Public Perspective*.)

7. Chapter 8 discusses why "welfare"—means-tested public assistance, a small fraction of public expenditures—became a political obsession in the United States.

8. A careful analysis of the 1993 election showed that the defectors from the Progressive Conservatives who went in droves to the Reform Party, while they shared the Reform Party's protest against taxing and spending, were virulently anti-immigrant and anti-Quebec—more xenophobic than other Tory voters (Nevitte et al., 1995). With the victory of the Conservative Party of Ontario in June 1995, a third provincial backlash movement with explicit inspiration from the campaigns of Ronald Reagan and Margaret Thatcher, came to power (*Wall Street Journal,* June 12, 1995, and October 3, 1995). Thus, developments in the 1990s might justify a score for Canada of 3.5 rather than 3, which would strengthen the results reported below. (Interviews with politicians and journalists confirm this.) I have already noted that recent developments in Norway and Finland would move their above-average scores of 3 toward Sweden's 2, strengthening the idea that corporatist consensus insulates a democracy against backlash. A study of the radical right in Europe similarly concludes that its greatest electoral successes occur when it couples a fierce commitment to free markets with equally fierce xenophobia or racism (Kitschelt, 1995).

9. Nonvoters in 1994—Democrats and Republicans who stayed home but who had voted for president in 1992—were also largely noncollege graduates under 50 years of age. Like the party switchers, these nonvoters were concentrated in the middle mass—white men without a college degree, full of anxieties about jobs, earnings, and declining morality. They were disproportionately Democratic voters in 1992 (Greenberg, 1995, pp. 67–68).

10. It is a comment on the disjunction between professional economists and the public that the tax least liked by taxpayers, the property tax that has long triggered tax revolts, is the one tax American economists have approved with a substantial stable majority—from a survey of senior finance professors in 1934 to a survey of professional economists in 1994 (Break, 1995).

11. By 1994, 17 of our 19 countries had a VAT and one more had a less-efficient equivalent—a wholesale sales tax in Australia. Because of a deepening recession, Japan lowered its VAT rate as part of an antirecession package in November 1998.

12. This account is based on Butler, Adonis, and Travers (1994, pp. 29–33, 46–50, 57–58, 71–72, 90–95, 171–177, 180–181, 183, 287, 289–296).

13. The inventors of this ingenious scheme figured that because the move would reduce the burden on *households* with one or two adults, and they are more numerous than households with three or more adults, a majority of households would gain. Apparently they ignored the number of voting *individuals* who would be losers. (Butler et al., 1994, pp. 128–129.) From 1986 to 1990, by creative use of statistics, they deluded both themselves and the public that this was a progressive tax. (*Ibid.*, p. 93.)

14. The minor shifts in backlash are *Italy* (despite the newly emerged Northern League, still low but perhaps moving toward medium low); *Finland* (scoring 3 moves to 2); the *United Kingdom* (already high at 4, now higher); *Canada* (moving a bit higher, up from 3.0); *Denmark* moving away from visible taxes in the mid-1990s—too late (Sweden began that shift in the 1960s) remains high; *New Zealand* (a deviant case with heavy reliance on visible taxes since 1971 but low backlash, falls into line with rising backlash from the mid-1980s on—like Denmark, moving away from income taxes too late). For discussion of a possible increase in backlash in *Austria* 1986–96, see note 19, p. 397. The *net effect* of these shifts is to strengthen hypotheses regarding corporatism as a dampener of backlash. Canada and New Zealand join the United Kingdom and the United States with higher scores; they more than offset Austria's possible increase; Finland's lower score offsets Italy's possible increase.

15. In table 14.4, Denmark ranks above average in income equality measured by the share of household income taken by the top fifth but medium-low by other measures (the share of the lowest fifth and the distance between top and bottom).

16. For data on property taxes 1965–87 by types of political economy, see table 12.13 (economic performance). Data from 1993 show that the property-tax share of total taxes in left-corporatist countries averaged 3.2%, in left-Catholic corporatist countries 3.0%, in Catholic corporatist countries 3.9%, in corporatist countries without labor, 7.9%, in least-corporatist countries (Britain and Britain abroad), 9.0%. (Based on OECD *Revenue Statistics of OECD Member Countries: 1965–1994* Paris: OECD, 1995, p. 83.)

17. Affluence and the index of mobility-meritocracy are highly correlated ($r = .65, p = .01$). They have a large joint effect on backlash which cannot be attributed uniquely to either GNP per capita or mobility-meritocracy. What happens in regressions when both are used as independent variables explaining backlash is that most of the joint effect is attributed to affluence because its correlation with backlash is slightly larger than that of mobility-meritocracy ($r = .59$). It is more appropriate theoretically to model this joint effect as an indirect effect of affluence operating through its impact on increased mobility and the increased use of meritocratic criteria than as a direct effect of affluence on backlash. As always it is the structural and ideological correlates of industrialization that are the proximate causes of system outputs (see chap. 1).

18. If we update Finland's score to 1 or 2 it would also fit the last column of table 10.5, bringing its average still lower.

19. It can be argued that political developments in Austria since 1986 suggest that Austria is converging with the richer backlash-prone countries. Until recently Austria's Freedom Party was a marginal part of national politics. It fluctuated between 4% and 7% of the national vote from 1954 to 1986, when it got 9.7% of vote in parliamentary election. It scored 16.6% in 1990 and almost 23% in 1994. Its leader since 1986, Jörg Haider, emphasizes three themes: (1) "Austria First"—end immigration, tighten laws against foreigners, repatriate those already in Austria, withdraw from the European Human Rights Convention; (2) populist attacks on beneficiaries of the Austrian welfare state—"social parasites" such as pensioners and government employees and cultural "swine" (*Schuft*) in Vienna who take subsidies from the state for musical, artistic, and theatrical productions and promote moral decadence; (3) pleasant talk about Austria's Nazi past and praise for the contribution of Waffen-SS veterans whose past sacrifices saved Western civilization and the Austrian homeland (Judt, 1996). Haider's showing in the 1999 election brought him into a rightwing coalition government. However, Vienna's voters in March 2001 reduced the FP share of the vote by almost a third.

On the basis of 1986–99 developments, Austria's low backlash score of 0 should perhaps be raised to 2 or 3. It is significant that Austria is one of the two countries that moved sharply upward since the late 1960s in relative rank of GDP per capita so if Haider does not fade away, Austria will fit the industrialization/backlash theme.

20. Slightly offsetting these tendencies among left-corporatist countries is a possible convergence in tax systems. Although we found only small signs of convergence toward tax balance from the late 1960s to 1988, some additional convergence—less reliance on visible taxes—occurred in the 1990s, especially among the Scandinavian countries.

ARE POLITICAL PARTIES DECLINING?
An Analysis of National Variation in Dealignment

Students of comparative politics often consider the United States as the standout case of party-system decline. Political parties in America are eroding in their strength and unity; their hold over both politicians and voters is ever weaker; and their capacity to create a public agenda, mobilize voters around it, and enact legislation is diminishing. These developments, if they are indeed in process, are critical for the vitality of democracy. Weak and declining parties, even in a nonparliamentary presidential system like that of the United States, are a major cause of ineffective governments and the related decline of public confidence and a rise in demagoguery and extremism. This chapter assesses the party-decline theme and asks whether this trend has occurred; if so, is it peculiarly American or a tendency common to all rich democracies? How can we explain national variation in both the presence or absence of system erosion and the rate of change?

Some analysts think that the tendency toward party decomposition is universal among modern democracies (Huntington, 1974; Brittan, 1975; Valen and Aardal, 1994). They attribute this to affluence and related changes in the social bases of politics: increases in education and a large, more-independent and critical upper-middle class; the decline of farmers and the "working class" who constituted the electoral base of agrarian parties and labor-left parties; mobility and the less-stable relationships and loyalties it brings; equality and the populist politics it fosters; the expanded role of government in the economy and the consequent disjunction between a rapid expansion of popular demands for government action and a slower increase in the capacity of governments to solve problems; the ascendance of the media in politics and culture, which subverts the capacity of parties and governments to set agendas and communicate with voters; and the decline of broad-based interest groups such as churches and unions that have served as major party supports in the past (see chap. 3 on mass-society theory). Some versions of this convergence theory suggest that we are entering a new stage of "postindustrial politics" (e.g., Dalton, 1988).

Other scholars believe that the United States is exceptional, if not unique, in the weakness of its political parties as well as the rapidity and extent of party decline (e.g., Crotty, 1984, p. 37; Ladd, 1982, pp. 77, 124; Dahl, 1994). As sources of long-standing weakness of parties they invoke America's divided government (the separation of powers), winner-take-all electoral system, bicameralism, a written constitution with its emphasis on rights enforceable by a strong judiciary, a weak national bureaucracy, and American individualism and populism. As sources of recent trends toward party decline even from this weak beginning, these scholars invoke an explosive growth in the number and variety of interest groups, many of them focused passionately on a single issue; peculiarly paralyzing Senate rules (e.g., the rising use of the filibuster in the 1980s and 1990s); an increase in the past four decades in the number of years when Congress and the White House were under control by different parties compared to previous eras where one party dominated for extended periods; a rise in populism of both the right and left; and, reinforcing all of the above, the unusual level of dominance of politics by commercial broadcast media that are increasingly preoccupied with undifferentiated scandals, exposés, rumor, and gossip.

The first problem we encounter in assessing the theme of decline is the distinction between party *re*alignment, where the vitality of one major party is sapped while that of another party surges, and *de*alignment, where the vitality of all major parties declines. Reduced vitality is indicated by a diminishing portion of the population identifying with or belonging to parties, a decline in party loyalty in voting among voters and legislators, and similar indicators (cf. Stanley, 1988, pp. 66–67). Few studies have tried to make a clear distinction between realignment and dealignment, and fewer have devised clean measures of dealignment. For cross-national comparisons we will have to settle for rough approximations. Also severe limitations of data do not permit the 19-country comparisons of previous chapters.

The second difficulty in assessing the party-decline theme is that a party system can evidence dealignment in several dimensions of party strength and the opposite in other dimensions. Students of party politics often distinguish between the party-in-the-electorate (party mobilization and cultivation of voters, voter identification with a party, and the effect of party identification on vote choice), party-in-government (the dominance of parties over individual legislative and executive officeholders, their ability to enact party programs), and party-as-organization—its structure and its resources of money, personnel, technology, and skill (Beck and Sorauf, 1992, pp. 11–13; Katz and Mair, 1992). An assessment of the American case can illustrate these ambiguities. Then we can deal with measures of dealignment in cross-national perspective.

THE UNITED STATES: IS IT THE TEXTBOOK CASE OF DEALIGNMENT?

There is much evidence for the idea of party dealignment in the United States, but the counterarguments and data suggest caution. I first summarize the case questioning the American-decline theme and then the case concluding that, on balance, the United States fits the dealignment theme.

Dimensions of American Party-System Vitality That Show No Decline or Increasing Strength

These include an increase in congressional party-line voting; greatly strengthened party leadership in both houses of Congress; some recent shift in money flow to parties, not candidates, and hence a slowing down of the long-term trend toward candidate-centered campaigns; a party realignment, not dealignment, in the South; and, finally, evidence that "independent" voters are *not* increasing as a percentage of all voters.

1. *Increased party discipline in House and Senate voting.* After declining from 1955 to 1970–72, party-line voting in the House increased through 1987 (Rohde, 1991, pp. 14–15 and Table 1.1; cf. Sinclair, 1995, pp. 93–95, 98–99). It reached a peak in the highly confrontational Congress of 1995–96. A congressional reform movement, spearheaded by the Democratic Study Group 1969–75, led to reforms on the selection of committee chairmen, strengthened the Speakership, revived the Democratic Caucus, created a Steering and Policy Committee, and somewhat reduced the weight of seniority in assigning committee chairmanships. Although these and other early 1970s reforms slowed down the legislative process in the House, they did not weaken the leadership; in fact, reform strengthened it. Neither did reforms fragment the parties any more than they already were. (Crook and Hibbing, 1985; Davidson, 1988, pp. 357–361; and Democratic Study Group, n.d.). The House Republicans, already more party disciplined than the Democrats, increased the concentration of power in the Speakership in the 104th Congress. In short, there has been a recent strengthening of party-line voting, a major indicator of the strength of the "party-in-government." If House Democrats find it more difficult to develop a unified position on tough issues such as trade, health-care reform, labor law, and taxes, it is because of other changes in the political environment: more demanding constituencies, the proliferation of better-financed and narrower pressure groups, the multiplication of issues, the rise of candidate-centered media-driven politics—trends that affect both Houses and both parties.

2. *Although entrepreneurial candidates* for Senate and House *raise huge amounts of their own money and run their own campaigns*—a force for distancing themselves from the parties—*the restrictions on money raising and campaign spending of 1974 and after somewhat increased party influence in the selection, training, and financing of candidates.* Under the post-Watergate reforms, candidates 1975–96 could not raise "soft" money while the parties could. Soft money going to parties therefore increased. It is used for party building (Cotter and Bibby, 1980). (Soft money is money outside the purview of federal election laws—contributions to parties that are neither limited nor disclosed. Much of it ends up in the national parties and is recycled in the form of services to state parties.) In the 1980s and 1990s the two parties at both national and state levels greatly increased their resources of money and staff, compared to the early 1970s, although the Republicans retain a big lead in this trend (Aldrich, 1995, pp. 253–260).

In the face of this increase in party resources, there has been at the same time a three- or four-decade increase in the independence of Senate and House candidates from the national and even state parties because of the explosion of money going directly or indirectly (via PACs) to candidates and because party leaders and party machines in most states no longer select candidates through their control of state primaries and conventions. What the soft-money rules have done is to constrain the increase in candidate-centered campaigns. Similarly, since the rise of presidential primaries dominated by sectarian advocacy groups rather than a few key party leaders, there has been a decline of party influence in the presidential nomination process (discussed later). But soft money going to the president's party gives him some leverage over congressional candidates. Here, again, the trend since the 1960s toward lone entrepreneurial candidates devoid of obligation to the party has been slowed down—that is, until Congress and the president go through their next round of campaign finance reform.

3.   *The party realignment in the South transformed a one-party system into a two-party com-*
petitive system, with the resurgence of the Republican Party. Since 1952, in both party identification and voting there has been a steady shift in the 11 states of the old Confederacy
from Democratic to Republican among whites; by 1994 the Democrats had become the
minority party. The number of Southern Democratic seats in both Senate and House
went from 121 of 128 (95%) in 1960 to 61 of 144 (42%) in 1996. Ideologically, the shift
was a steady decline in the power of the Dixiecrats who plagued every Democratic president from Roosevelt to Carter, the emergence of moderate to liberal Southern Democrats, a marked increase in turnout among black Democrats, and the ascendance of
Christian-right Republicans. In party identification " . . . native southern whites—both
young and old—have grown less Democratic, more independent, and more Republican"
(Stanley, 1988, p. 68). The election of 1996 marked an intensification of this regional
realignment (Meyerson, 1997, p. 63); so did the election of 2000. Party decline, party
dealignment, mostly no; realignment, yes.

4.   *Party identification and the alleged increase in "independents."* For many elections the
Gallup poll has asserted that upward of 30% of Americans are self-described "independents." Wolfinger and his colleagues, however, show that real independent voters remain
roughly stable at 1 in 12 or 1 in 10 voters since 1950 (Keith et al., 1992, p. 202). If we
measure independence not by self-identification in one question ("I think of myself not
as a Democrat or Republican but as an independent") but follow up with "Do you
think of yourself as closer to the Republican or Democratic Party?" we find that about
two-thirds of the respondents who initially call themselves "independent" say they are
closer to one or another party. This percentage remained stable from 1952 to 1994
(*ibid.,* table 1.1., p. 14 updated). Most important, these "leaners" vote overwhelmingly for
the party toward which they lean, especially in presidential elections. In voting, in their
choice of presidential primary elections, in the stability of their party identification, and
even in their attitudes toward the two parties, the Republican and Democratic leaners are
essentially partisan (*ibid.,* pp. 80–103).

When we eliminate the ersatz independents, what remains are "Pure Independents."
At their peak they were only 15% of the adult population and never exceeded 11% of
those who cast their ballots in national elections. As a percentage of voters these genuine
independents have not increased over the period 1956 to 1994. (*Ibid.,* table 1.1 updated.)

Wolfinger and his colleagues conclude that "the distribution of Democrats and Republicans is rather constant, the party system is stable, third parties do not prosper, and all
this has been true for many years" (Keith et al., 1986, p. 181). But caution is called for:
First, note the great fluctuation in voting not only among pure independents but among
the much larger number of leaners. In the 1968 and 1980 presidential elections, a high
percentage of democratic leaners defected to the Republican candidate or to Wallace and
Anderson; in 1964 a large percentage of Republican leaners defected to the Democrats,
in 1968, to Wallace (Keith et al., 1992, table 4.1); and in 1992, a large percentage of
both Republican leaners (28%) and Democratic leaners (26%) defected to Perot (update
of *ibid.*). There were similarly large defections in congressional elections, especially in
1966, 1968, and 1978 (*ibid.,* table 4.2). In fact, as Keith et al. note, data for House elections show a trend toward more defectors: they averaged 10% of all voters in the 1950s,
15% in the 1960s, 18% in the 1970s, and 21% in the 1980s. (*Ibid.,* p. 202.)

Second, although there has been no great change since the 1950s in the relationship of party identification to vote choice (p. 202; W. Miller, 1991; Miller and Shanks, 1996, pp. 149–150), party ID studies do show that *the strength of party ID has declined from 1960 to 1992.* If we ignore the 10% of voters who are African-American and whose strong partisanship increased, we find that strong party identifiers (strong Republicans plus strong Democrats) declined from about one in three in 1952–66 to about one in four in 1970–92 (Abramson, Aldrich, and Rohde, 1994, table 8.2). Even including blacks, strong party identifiers in preelection surveys in presidential years have gone down from an average of 36.5% in 1952–64 to 26.4% in 1966–80 and 29.6% in 1982–94 (based on Keith et al., 1992, table 1.1 with updates for 1992 and 1994). By this measure, party loyalties, such as they are, are more lightly held.

Third, for our purposes of cross-national comparison, party ID is of limited validity because of vastly different functions, strengths, and number of parties as well as doubts about the portability of American wording of relevant survey questions.[1] Although party ID means different things in different nations and the American concept of "Independent" is not universally understood, party ID may still have some uses. Where similar surveys of party ID are repeated over time in one country and show large shifts in the strength of partisanship, we can use them as indirect indicators of party decline.

Finally, party-line voting in Congress—an indicator of party strength for skeptics who doubt that party decline has occurred—can itself be interpreted as a source of party decline and related political paralysis. In the 1990s it meant sharply accelerating confrontational partisanship in Congress, culminating in shutdowns of the government and then the 1999 House vote to impeach the president. If party-line voting increases in a legislature we can say parties-in-government are becoming stronger. If at the same time, however, ideological extremes dominate the major parties and they are losing their mass base, we can reasonably label the combination system erosion. Political polarization—the inability to forge compromise and consensus—is subversive of the long-run viability of major political parties. Sustained confrontational partisanship in government contains the seeds of its own destruction. In cross-national comparisons below, we will encounter disciplined, united parties in contrasting contexts that produce more benign outcomes— corporatist democracies with different electoral systems where disciplined parties negotiate accommodations with other parties and interest groups, carry out party programs, and retain their mass base.

Beyond these caveats regarding the case against party decline, there are six dimensions of American-party decomposition that plainly fit the idea of dealignment or system erosion.

Dimensions of System Decline That Fit the Theme of American Party Decline

These are an increase in institutional estrangement and indifference; diminished partisanship among whites and the young; the long-term decline in urban political machines and patronage, and the more-recent decline of party influence in the presidential nominating process; decreasing turnout in elections and participation in political activity; more randomness in voting; increasing media dominance of campaigns with a concomitant accent on campaign tactics and personalities, especially alleged scandals, rather than issues or party.

1. *A decline in trust in politicians, government, and parties. Institutional estrangement and indifference.* As we saw in chapter 4, there was a 36-year (1958–94) slide in confidence in government institutions among the general adult population of the United States with only a slight uptick in 1970–72 and a brief surge in 1980–84 (Citrin and Green, 1986, p. 435, updated by NES data from 1988 and 1992 and poll data for 1994. Cf. Craig, 1993, pp. 1–18; Lipset and Schneider, 1983, pp. 14–29; and Lipset, 1996, pp. 281–284). Public cynicism about politics and politicians is now pervasive. Most relevant for the party dealignment theme are surveys that show an increase in mass indifference to political parties, a withdrawal of commitment to the system. For instance, the proportion of the National Election Study (NES) respondents who have neutral attitudes toward the two major parties rose from 13.0% in 1952 to 36.5% in 1980 (Wattenberg, 1990, p. 62). Other measures of attitudinal detachment and indifference yield similar results (*ibid.*, pp. 53, 60–62, 64–66, 30, 49, 155–156).

2. *Decline of party influence in the presidential nomination process* since the rise of primaries dominated by nonelected activists and sectarian advocacy groups. In the past century or so there have been successive waves of reform that have undermined the role of parties as mediators between citizen preferences, candidate selection, and public policies. In the late 19th century there was a norm of very strong party loyalty and high rates of participation in year-round activities of parties among white males (Marcus, 1971; Ware, 1996). Party involvement in the heyday of American party politics cut across the social spectrum. Funding and campaigns were party centered. Both supporters and candidates themselves were expected to give money and time to the party. Parties were important sources of identity, social life, and entertainment. (*Ibid.*, pp. 13ff., 36.)

The first wave of reform was the clean-government, progressive movement (roughly from 1910 to the 1950s) that led to numerous changes in electoral procedures and public administration. Reformers such as Hiram Johnson of California were successful in launching the initiative, so voters could put new laws on the ballot, and the referendum, so state legislators could get mass approval for laws they proposed. Primary elections gave states the right to set up an election outside the party and to choose the party's candidates. Primaries were open to all comers or to voters who declared that they were "members" of a party. Nonpartisan elections were a final reform that removed parties from a visible role. (Cf. Lawson, 1987; McCormick, 1986; and King, 1997, pp. 63ff.) Civil service reforms aimed to eliminate corruption and nepotism; they accented merit through testing. While this professionalized much of the civil service of federal and state government, it also drastically reduced patronage at the disposal of parties and the executive branch. The same clean-government movement subverted party machines that had created retail politics on a grand scale—precinct captains and ward bosses serving loyal party voters year-round, educating and mobilizing voters during campaigns, and turning them out for the party on election day. The heyday of urban machines run by Frank Hague of Jersey City, Big Ed Kelly of Chicago, and Boss Crump of Memphis ran roughly from the turn of the century to the "Last Hurrah" of Mayor James Michael Curly in 1955 or to the symbolic end of Chicago Mayor Richard Daley in the infamous 1968 Democratic National Convention and his death in 1976. Welfare-state expansion from the mid-1930s on also hastened the demise of the urban political machines, taking away most of their personalized casework functions. Of course, some party patronage remains; political appointees at high levels of the federal, state, and local civil service are still in evidence; and local parties still pass out contracts, arrange campaign events, and do favors for loyal constituents (cf. Wolfinger, 1972; Gibson et al., 1985). As Martin Shefter (1994) suggests, mayors at the top of urban machines such as Richard Lee in New Haven, Robert Wagner in New York, and Richard Daley in Chicago were able to carry stable winning coalitions into the 1950s and early 1960s by a partial accommodation of the liberal reformers' demands. They divided municipal government by islands of functional power, "granting the party organization access to the patronage of only certain municipal departments; at the same time, agencies . . . of greatest interest to would-be reformers (urban renewal, education, social welfare) were placed under the control of professionals, civil servants, civic leaders, and the downtown business community" (Shefter, 1994, pp. 85–86). But the trend is unmistakable; the argument is about how fast and far the machines declined in the 20th century.

The second wave of reform that weakened the party system came largely from the left activists who advocated changes in the presidential nomination process to make parties more responsive to popular will and more directly democratic. Chief among these are reforms crafted by successive reform commissions of the Democratic Party from 1969 to 1990, although these affected the Republican Party as well because state legislatures adopted some of them as they regulated elections (Polsby and Wildavsky, 1996, pp. 262–263). The most important were the McGovern-Fraser guidelines for selection of delegates, 1969–72. Quotas for blacks, women, and youths were established. Direct presidential primaries replaced many state conventions. The net result of these and other reforms was the virtual elimination of officeholders and party officials from the nominating process. For example, from 1956 to 1980 the percentage of Democratic members of Congress who were voting delegates or alternates at national conventions sharply declined—senators from 90% to 14%, representatives from 33% to 15% (Polsby, 1983, p. 114). The proverbial "smoke-filled rooms" were replaced by ideologically committed movement activists representing African-American caucuses, Hispanic-American caucuses, gay rights, civil rights, women's rights, and similar factions. They tend to be casual participants concerned with strong expression of their views and strong commitment to a particular primary contestant. They are less interested in winning elections through long-term coalition-building and governing through inevitable compromises. Primaries multiplied—from 13 states with one or more primaries in 1968 to 39 in 1992. Polsby and Wildavsky summarize the costs of giving up "peer review," otherwise known as "smoke-filled rooms." Widespread use of direct primaries, they conclude,

> encourages prospective candidates to bypass regular party organizations in favor of campaigns stressing personal publicity, and it provides for no peer review, that is, consideration of those aspects of fitness of candidates to hold office that can best be applied by politicians who actually know the candidates, who have themselves a heavy investment of time and energy in making the government work, and who know that they may have to live at close quarters with the results of their deliberations. (1996, p. 280)

The substitution of delegates with little stake in winning and governing for office-holders and party leaders opens the way for extremist candidates and demagogues in symbiotic relationship to the media, who emphasize the conflict of personalities and gravitate to strident advocates of nonnegotiable demands (see chap. 3). The decline of party influence in the long presidential nominating process is a force for erosion of the party system (Polsby, 1983). Whether we compare the turn of the century with today or the era of urban political machines with the last three decades, we can trace this decline.

3. *Diminished partisanship and party loyalty among whites and the young.* The strength of party ID among whites (a large majority of voters) declined from the period 1952–66 when strongly identified Republicans and strongly identified Democrats together comprised a range of 34% to 38% to the period 1970–92 when the strong party identifiers fluctuated between 23% and 30%; strong partisans were only 26% of the electorate in 1992 (Abramson, Aldrich, and Rohde, 1994, pp. 228–231 and table 8.2).[2] Regarding the young, shifts between the two major parties in both party identification and voting were most evident among young voters from 1972–76 to 1988–92 (Ladd, 1993, pp. 8–9; cf. P. A. Beck, 1984). And Perot got a whopping 26% of voters among young men (18–29) in 1992 (Ladd, 1993, p. 22). In short, the strength of party loyalty has diminished among the 85% of the electorate who are white as well as among the young.

4. *Decreasing turnout in voting, and a drop in percentage of adults doing campaign and party work or making campaign contributions.* The percentage of the electorate contributing money to a party or candidate dropped from 10.4 in the 1960s to 8.2 in the 1980s; the percentage of adults who worked for a party or candidate dropped from 5.5 in the 1960s to 3.7 in the 1980s (Rosenstone and Hansen, 1993, p. 211). From 1973 to 1990 citizen efforts to influence policy—writing a letter to a representative or senator, attending a local meeting on a town or school affair, or signing a petition—all declined, steeply for local politics, moderately for letters, and slightly for petitions (*ibid.*, p. 63). A large-scale study of civic volunteerism in the United States (Verba, Schlozman, and Brady, 1995) reports a decrease in the percentage of adults who mention membership in a political club—down by half from 1967 to 1987 (pp. 71–72).[3] Voter turnout has followed a similar downward path. Turnout of eligible Americans in presidential elections declined 24% from 1960 to 1996; turnout in midterm elections declined 21% from 1960 to 1994. In 1990 about a third of the electorate chose Congress. School bond elections attract even fewer eligibles—about a fifth. The 1996 presidential election saw the lowest presidential turnout since the 1920s. Finally, in midterm primaries in 1966, 33% of voting-age population cast ballots; that dropped to 24% in 1974 and 18% in 1994 (Lipset, 1996, p. 283)—a decline of 45%.

In explaining why eligible Americans increasingly shun elections, it is significant that turnout declined (1) during 1960 to 1996 when education levels rose and registration barriers at least did not increase and in some states were lowered (Brody, 1978; Rosenstone and Hansen, 1993, pp. 212, 214) and (2) after the national motor-voter law went into effect June 1, 1995 (turnout was lower in 1996 than 1992). Obviously, this is not yet a test of the efficacy of removing registration barriers, but it does suggest that such barriers, while important, are not the only major source of low turnout and perhaps not the most important. Rosenstone and Hansen (1993, pp. 217–218) show that the main causes center on declining electoral mobilization—parties gave up labor-intensive canvassing, electoral competition declined, social movement activity diminished, and demands on campaign resources intensified, spreading the supply of time and money thinner and thinner (the number of contested primaries nearly doubled from 1968 to 1980 and the cost of buying media time soared).[4] One additional factor in low and declining turnout is the *frequency and complexity of elections leading to voter fatigue.* Only Switzerland can match the United States on this score and it, too, is an extreme case of very frequent elections and an obsession with initiatives and referenda, with ballot explanations that look like telephone books (Jackman and Miller, 1995). The American voter makes as many choices on a single election day as a Canadian or British voter gets to make in a lifetime. I return later to the problem of voter fatigue in the analysis of cross-national variations in party decline.

5.   *More randomness in voting, an increase in ticket-splitting and party-switching.* Martin Wattenberg (1990, pp. 17–18, 20–23, 155, figures 1.1, 1.2 and table 9.5) shows that the proportion of split results—different outcomes for presidential and congressional races in each district—has risen sharply over the past 60 years. "Only about 10 to 15 percent of the 435 congressional districts had split results in the 1920–1944 period. In the twenty years between 1944 and 1964, however, this figure gradually rose to about 30 percent. And in 1972 one finds an all-time high of 44 percent" (p. 18). Individual-level survey data 1952–80 confirms the trend (*ibid.*, figure 1.2, p. 21). Although the 1980s saw some decline in split-voting from the 1980 peak (President vs. Congress, Senate vs. House), by historical standards it remained at quite high levels in 1984 and 1988 (pp. 164–165).[5] (The record high of 1980 was inflated by the abnormal number of Senate challengers and the Anderson vote of that year.) Similarly, "the number of divided state governments rose from eleven in 1946 to thirty-two in 1988; statistically, partisan control of the governorship and state legislature have been completely unrelated in recent years" (G. Jacobson, 1990, p. 14). A careful study of contests for five Ohio statewide offices in 1990 (Beck et al., 1992) points to the main sources of the increase in ticket-splitting. Ticket-splitters are weak in strength of partisanship and respond to the differential visibility of candidates—by far the prime determinants. Less important but still significant are higher levels of education and age. The attitude that government works better under divided control is unrelated to ticket-splitting as is interest in elections. These findings suggest a continued increase in split-ticket voting: strong partisanship is decreasing, education levels are increasing, and the population is aging.[6] Aging is another way of saying that the more party-loyal New Deal and World War II cohorts are dying off, to be replaced by less party-committed generations. Differential candidate visibility is a product not only of incumbency advantage but also famous names—for example, in Ohio, Republican challenger Robert Taft or, in national elections, various celebrities from sports, television, and Hollywood who have turned to politics since Ronald Reagan's success. And such visibility is itself increasingly a product of media marketing. Thus, media ascendance in politics should increase the differential visibility that leads to ticket-splitting.

Protest parties, as we shall see in cross-national comparison below, are an ambiguous indicator of dealignment. But billionaire Perot's vote of 19% in 1992 as a measure of alienation from government, politics, and parties is suggestive, taken with other indicators of decline. He epitomizes the new breed of antipolitics politicians who offer simplistic nostrums for everything that ails the body politic; they appeal especially to the middle mass (see chap. 10 on the social composition of the Wallace, Perot, and David Duke vote). Over the 100 years from 1864 to 1964 three third-party candidates got more than 6% of the vote; in just the last 30 years three third-party candidates got more than 6% in 4 elections (Wallace, Anderson, Perot). In other words, there has been a recent speedup in national third-party activity. Nevertheless, we cannot argue that third parties in recent decades have been more than a minor force for dealignment. The popular vote for Teddy Roosevelt was 27.4%; for LaFollette, 16.6%; Wallace, 13.5%; Perot, 18.9%—the only ones getting more than Anderson's 6.6% in 1976. Since the Civil War only five third parties have won any electoral votes at all; only two have made any difference to the outcome of the election—Teddy Roosevelt's Bull Moose Party in 1912 and the Prohibition Party in 1884. Comparative analysis below suggests that protest parties are only a secondary indicator of party decomposition, even in electoral systems more hospitable to their development than that of the United States.

6. *The media, especially broadcast media, increasingly dominate campaigns, reducing the voice of mainstream parties and politicians.* Chapter 3 reviews evidence on the impact of the mass media of communication and entertainment on politics and culture and the limited cross-national data on the effects of print media, television, and radio. It is clear that the United States is an extreme case of media domination of increasingly lengthy campaigns. American politicians and their consultants must spend increasing portions of their time raising money to buy commercial television, which itself escalates in cost. In 1972 candidates spent $25 million on political ads alone; in 1996, $400 million. The United States is unique in denying candidates free airtime. Where other democracies allow any paid political advertising, it is paid for by parties not candidates (Holtz-Bacha and Kaid, 1995, p. 11).

Because of the organization, financing, and content of the American commercial media, they amplify extremes, divert attention away from parties and issues, and exacerbate tendencies toward political polarization. After 1956 specific appeals to party loyalty in the media have been almost nonexistent; while negative advertising and negative media coverage have greatly increased (West, 1993; Lichter and Amundson, 1994; Patterson, 1996; Sabato, 1991; Lichter and Smith, 1993; Jamieson, 1992). Network television news—which still has well over half of the audience—now conveys a relentlessly negative image of candidates, governing politicians, and public officials; there is a steady tabloidization of the press, as prestige newspapers (e.g., the *New York Times,* the *Washington Post*) increasingly ape television and radio and both move toward the talk-show format (*Oprah, Donahue,* the McLaughlin Group, Rush Limbaugh, *Larry King Live*)—alternating between attack-dog "journalism" and sensational gossip and rumor. (There are now 8,000 talk shows in the United States.) Although print journalism, television network news, and talk radio are still different in many ways, they all converge toward talk-radio content, typically serving up a steady diet of hatred for the government, picturing politicians and civil servants as corrupt conspirators (Lichter and Amundson, 1994; Patterson, 1993a, 1993b, 1996; Sabato, 1991; Ornstein, 1993/94; Fallows, 1996). In other words, there is a Gresham's law of political discourse: bad talk drives out good talk. All this has had a significant impact on voter perceptions of the public agenda and their images of public officials (Iyengar and Kinder, 1987), deepening cynicism and discouraging turnout (Ansolabehere et al., 1994).

Two careful studies can illustrate the nature of evidence regarding media impact (chap. 3 reviews other studies). The first (Page, Shapiro, and Dempsey, 1987; Page and Shapiro, 1992) dissects the effect of TV news content on public opinion from 1970 to 1985. The researchers chose 80 pairs of policy questions on a great range of domestic, foreign, and defense issues that had been repeated over an average of three months in national survey samples. They then did a content analysis of news broadcasts aired in between and just before each pair of surveys. They focused on reported statements by a specified source, coding (1) its relevance to the policy question; (2) its salience in the broadcast; (3) "the pro-con *direction* of intended impact of the reported statement or action in relation to the most prominent policy alternative mentioned in the opinion item" (Page et al., 1987, p. 26). The results are unequivocal: of 10 sources in these broadcasts, the most dramatic impact on national attitudes came from news commentary by anchorpersons, reporters in the field, and special commentators; a close second influence was "experts"—themselves chosen and credentialed by the newscasters' networks. All other influences were very small: in descending order in regression equations, the trivial influences were events, unfriendly foreigners, the opposition party, a popular president, friendly or neutral foreigners. Groups with negative but still small influences were members of the president's party, "interest groups," and courts—sources that were most discounted by the public. In short, despite public complaints about the media, the network news and the experts they choose retain overwhelming credibility and shape public opinion far more than any other source, including the events themselves, presidents, and political parties. Richard Brody's (1991) study of presidential approval ratings also concludes that real events are much less important than the media selection of and spin about events. And opinion leaders' interpretation of events, while important, are filtered by the media (cf. Sahr, 1993).

The second study, by Zaller and Hunt (1994, 1995) focuses on the effects of news stories on vote outcomes rather than political attitudes. The researchers examined support for candidates Hart, Carter, and Perot over time and regressed candidate support on media content. They found that their overall measures of positive news coverage and negative news coverage for each candidate closely predicted shifts in voter preferences. Adding an analysis of *Time* and *Newsweek* coverage of 19 candidates for president from 1976 to 1992, they confirm the consensus of media researchers regarding the rise of competitive belligerence in the news media: "candidates running in more recent elections have had to endure far more press-initiated criticism than candidates running in 1976 or 1980" (Zaller and Hunt, 1995, p. 104).

Although the media are not the only factor shaping the public agenda and public images of the government and its leaders, they are now a leading factor. And, as we have seen in chapter 3, the United States is a leader in the degree of media dominance in campaigns. The effect is to diminish the voice of politicians who would accent substantive issues or party programs.

What is new in all of this? Popular distrust of politicians is not new; tabloid attack journalism is not new; populist attacks on authority are not new. What is new is the media amplification of previously scattered attacks; a sustained din about undifferentiated crises; and scandalmongering that is not only about current events but events of 10 or 20 years ago. In other words, the scope and depth of media penetration is new. Finally, and most important, the tabloidization of the respectable press is new; they, too, have become peddlers of gossip and venom. In the past there was offsetting serious discourse: the Federalist papers of Hamilton, Madison, and Jay were serialized in the major papers; the great presidential orators—Jackson, William Jennings Bryan, Wilson, Clay, FDR—drew large audiences. Some came from great distances and would be disappointed if a speech did not go on for at least two hours. Compare the bits of opinion in the op-ed page of the *New York Times* and the ever-briefer sound bites on TV.

In sum: Despite evidence of an increase in congressional party-line voting, a recent slowdown in the rate of increase in candidate-centered campaigns (soft money flowing to parties), more realignment than dealignment in the South, and a stable 10% of real "independent" voters, the countervailing evidence of party decline is the basic story. At the same time that parties-in-government (in Congress and many state legislatures) are becoming stronger, parties-in-the-electorate are weak and are becoming weaker. If masses of voters are withdrawing from the party system, if increased party discipline in Congress is accompanied by polarization, gridlock, and a rising tendency of politicians to trash the institutions of government, "parties-in-government" will follow their decline in the electorate. In my view, when it comes to the most important dimensions of party decomposition—those that shape the capacity to govern—the United States ranks very high: electoral volatility; ticket-splitting, and party-switching; low and declining voter participation that can be explained only partly by barriers to registration; the shift from party-centered and financed campaigns to candidate-financed and centered campaigns with a mass-media focus, from party and issue appeals to personalities and attack ads; increasing mass distrust of the system.

In comparative perspective, the case for ranking the United States as a model of party dealignment is even clearer.

TYPES OF POLITICAL ECONOMY AND PARTY DECLINE: CROSS-NATIONAL EVIDENCE

There was a time two or three decades ago when one could confidently speak of an American style of candidate-centered politics with weak parties and a European style of party-centered politics with strong parties. There is still much truth in the statement. Although American tendencies of recent years—the use of polls, surveys, specialized consultants, direct mailing technology, media mania—are beginning to infect the politics of all rich democracies, significant variations remain. Most important, outside of the Anglo-American democracies, and especially outside the United States, party-centered campaigns, not candidate-centered campaigns, remain the rule (Bowler and Farrell, 1992, pp. 1–23, 223–235.) Everything depends on where campaign resources—organization, money, and expertise—are located. Where parties are firmly established and campaigns are party-centered, modern political technology may facilitate centralized control by national parties and strengthen party systems. But where, as in the United States, polls, consultants, money, and the media are put at the service of individual candidates whose obligations to the party are minimal, then their use induces party decline.

(Soft-money rules shifted this pattern in the United States from overwhelming to merely highly developed.)

Party decomposition varies greatly by type of political economy and type of electoral system. Trends toward party dealignment are much more prominent among the least-corporatist, most-fragmented and decentralized political economies, largely but not exclusively Anglo-American. These countries are most vulnerable to mass-society tendencies discussed in chapter 3. In contrast, democratic corporatism reduces the rate of decline of political parties. In corporatist countries the constituency base for major parties and coalitions includes strong and relatively disciplined, coordinated unions, employer federations, farm organizations, and churches, whose relations to parties are tight and whose consultation with government bureaucracies is frequent and easy. In turn, the quasi-public associations find parties helpful in mobilizing support for peak bargains. Together both parties and economic power blocs help governing parties or coalitions control the policy agenda, framing media content and containing single-issue groups and other particularistic pressures.

Electoral systems also shape the vitality of parties and the prospect of party dealignment. Most important is the presence or absence of various forms of proportional representation (PR) and the initiative or referendum, types of direct democracy. Not only is PR the most important historical cause of corporatist bargaining arrangements, which, as we have seen throughout this book, foster societal consensus and industrial peace, but PR has a direct effect on politics: if properly modified, PR facilitates coalition politics, while plurality systems with first-past-the-post rules that result in grossly unrepresentative governments encourage polarized politics (see chap. 2 and table 2.1). However, pure PR—approximated in the electoral systems of Denmark, the Netherlands, and until 1993 Italy—may have the opposite effect; it may produce a very large number of contesting parties, a force for party decline. Evidence indicates that the higher the number of parties, the higher the electoral volatility, one measure of dealignment. Similarly, changes in the number of parties—either a decrease or increase—produce more electoral volatility. (Pedersen, 1979, p. 19, a study of 13 European party systems, 1948–77.) Denmark, a standout case of both pure PR and electoral volatility, has averaged 10 parties with seats in the Folketing in the period 1973–88 (Mackie and Rose, 1991, table 5.6c) and in the 1973 election doubled the number of parties. But Denmark is not typical. As we have seen in chapter 2, the architects of PR in 10 of the 13 rich democracies that now use it modified it to keep extremes of left and right or militant splinter groups out of office. They set seat-winning thresholds high (Sweden's is now 4%, Germany's is 5%); they kept district magnitudes within reason (not too many seats per district), and in other ways used PR to encourage a balance between moderation and representation.

In short, we can expect modified proportional representation as it interacts with leftism, Catholicism, and democratic corporatism to reduce the rate of party decline, if not prevent it entirely.

Measures of Party Decline and Tests of the Theory

Two cross-national studies that attempt to distinguish party dealignment from party realignment permit a preliminary judgment about the role of corporatism in slowing party decline: Howard Reiter's (1989) study using 10 to 12 measures of party dealignment applied systematically to six detailed country studies (measures are necessarily a bit different for each country) and Franklin, Mackie, and Valen's (1992) thorough study of 16 democ-racies 1960s–80s. They reach similar conclusions that are consistent with my theory.

A third study by Leithner and Vowles (1996) is a good introduction to the problems of measuring party decomposition. It develops an unusually rich database on voting, local polling-booth records for New Zealand; devises a measure of dealignment for each elec-tion to the New Zealand House of Representatives from 1908 to 1993; and compares three measures of voter volatility from 1963 to 1993.

Studies of electoral turbulence based on aggregate election returns must face the eco-logical fallacy—the difficulty of inferring patterns of individual behavior from aggregate data on a geopolitical unit such as a neighborhood, precinct, or community. For instance, Mogens Pedersen's (1979) widely used index of electoral volatility relies on changes in ag-gregate national-level party vote shares. Absolute differences between one election and the previous election are summed and then divided by two. An index so constructed cannot reliably tell us what individual voters are doing, and it cannot clearly distinguish between realignment and dealignment. If a third of Democrats in the United States vote Republi-can in the next election while a third of Republicans defect to the Democrats, the Peder-sen index would fail to detect the extent of individual shifts; for this unlikely case, the two-party vote shares would remain stable (zero volatility). Moreover, if a third of Southern Democrats defect to the Republican Party while the Republicans remain loyal, the Peder-sen index would detect the volatility; but, in this more realistic illustration, the numbers more likely reflect realignment than dealignment. Despite these difficulties, increases in ag-gregate vote fluctuations cannot be rejected as a clue to erosion of party loyalties. In fact, Leithner and Vowles (1996, pp. 2, 8, 19) find a positive correlation ($r = .42$) between the Pedersen index and survey data on individual voters 1963 to 1993. Thus, while weak, the Pedersen index is useful where no other measure is available. Noting the limitations, Lei-thner and Vowles devise a stronger alternative. They use Thomsen's logit method of eco-logical regression comparing aggregate electoral returns from pairs of successive elections, taking care to stay within the same electoral boundaries (1996, pp. 5–6). The correlation between these aggregate estimates of volatility and individual survey data 1963–93 is quite strong ($r = .74$) (*ibid.*, p. 7). And partisan dealignment by these measures of vote volatility are associated with declining turnout, as well as declining interest in politics, political effi-cacy, and party identification from 1963 to 1990 (Vowles, 1994). With these measures and other data on particular elections, Leithner and Vowles conclude that New Zealand, one of the oldest modern democracies, began a slow, steady slide toward dealignment in 1951, which, as I show later, accelerated after 1985.

Now we can consider some cross-national results where dealignment is distinguished from realignment and where many measures of dealignment can be combined to give us a general picture of relative party-system stability or decline. Reiter (1989) applies up to 12 measures of party decline to six case studies (USA, Britain, Sweden, Norway, France, West Germany)

1. Party identification (ID).

2. Time of vote decision (before campaign or convention = partisan).

3. Party loyalty. Of voters who identify, percentage that vote for that party (or presidential candidate).

411

4. Consistency in vote vs. switching from one election to another. Loyalty to prior vote.

5. Strength of party preference.

6. Parliamentary party unity in voting or congressional party loyalty (voting with your party).

7. Turnout.

8. Steadiness of vote intention throughout campaign.

9. Legislators or party leaders "interested in my views" (survey questions).

10. Names a party that "looks after my interests" (survey questions).

11. Parties in general "interested only in my vote, not my opinion" (survey questions).

12. Percentage of unspoiled ballots. Spoiled ballots are seen as an expression of alienation from all parties.

By these measures, most parties in the six nations have not experienced any increase in random volatility; there is no general pattern of decline.[7] For my theory the summary rank order of dealignment is most relevant. With only a little illustrative detail on each case, here is my interpretation of Reiter's data from most to least party decomposition:

1. *The United States 1952–84.* By far the leader in party dealignment. Decline beginning in the mid-1960s in strength of partisan identification and in percentage who said they identified with any party whether strongly or not and in party affect (percentage of respondents who give either positive or negative response at least once). All four measures of voter loyalty to party as well as turnout declined. These trends affect whites and young people most. For example, even though young American voters typically start from a lower base than their elders, they nevertheless declined in partisanship far more than older age groups. Only timing of voter decision, greatly influenced by the conditions of particular elections, showed no significant change. Party-line voting in Congress also declined in the period Reiter studies but increased thereafter.

2. *Britain.* The runner-up in party dealignment, with similar timing but conflicting trends. Large declines in self-reported partisanship, in early vote decisions, and a slight decline in proportion of voters who voted their party identification. Parliamentary party cohesion also has declined since the early 1970s. But on a range of other measures, little if any monotonic decline is evident. And there are mixed results on which social groups are most affected—no clear pattern. Some of the results regarding the dissatisfactions of Labour Party supporters with their party's policies and performance suggest a realignment coincident with the fairly strong signs of dealignment.

3. *Sweden 1956–85.* By some measures Swedish parties have very slowly lost some of their mass support since the early 1970s, especially among the "working class." But no decline appears for party membership, voter loyalty (percentage of party identifiers who voted for their party), turnout, and legislative behavior. Given the resurgence of the So-

cial Democrats in the 1994 election, we cannot even say that there is a major *realignment* going on.

4. *Norway 1957–85.* No clear pattern for the nine indicators available. Party ID by two measures declined after 1965, rebounded to previous levels in 1977 and thereafter. In fact, the percentage of strong identifiers was higher in 1985 than in any previous year. The proportion of early deciders did drop in 1977 and after. Turnout fluctuated. There was no long-term, dramatic drop in partisanship by any measure. Some realignment around new issues—membership in the EEC, abortion, and North Sea oil policy—is evident.

5. *France.* Parties have been reinvigorated since the Fifth Republic of 1958. There is an increase in the following indicators: the strength of party ID; turnout; attitudes toward the party system; party cohesion in the National Assembly; party membership; and the effect of partisanship on the vote. Rivals to the party system—interest groups and the media—remain weak. Two clues in the opposite direction—a decline in the proportion of voters who support the same party in two consecutive elections and a drop in the percentage of French citizens who say they feel close to a party—cannot offset the weight of evidence of system persistence if not party revitalization. France is a turbulent country in other respects (see chap. 10), but its party system shows little erosion.

6. *West Germany.* Very little sign of dealignment, many indicators of increasing system strength. Turnout and the percentage of unspoiled votes have risen since the Federal Republic began, with only a little drop in the 1980s. Party membership rose from 1960 to 1984 and leveled off recently. Some indicators of partisanship show a decrease, others an increase.[8]

This rank order is strong confirmation of the theory: the greatest party dealignment has occurred in the United States and Britain, noncorporatist political economies with plurality electoral systems and first-past-the-post rules and hence the most unrepresentative governments (cf. Lijphart, 1994, pp. 57ff.; 1984, pp. 161–165). The United States, the textbook case of party decline, adds other structural barriers to party discipline and a representative legislature (see above) and is more decentralized and fragmented than Britain; it therefore exceeds Britain in party decomposition. Very little erosion of party systems is evident in Norway and Sweden, left-corporatist democracies with electoral systems based on PR. Norway comes a bit closer to pure PR than Sweden: Norway has no legal threshold in its PR system, and its electoral formula is a little more favorable to small parties, although district magnitudes (number of seats per district) are similar to Sweden's. This may help to explain Norway's slightly higher electoral turbulence. Even less erosion is evident in France and Germany. France is a case of a highly centralized state, a corporatist political economy excluding labor, and from 1958 a mixed majority/plurality system: the national assembly is elected in two rounds with a minimum threshold of 12.5% for the second ballot, where plurality rules; the president is elected by majority, using a runoff between the top two candidates if necessary. (There was a moment of PR for one national election, 1986, and since then regional elections have been conducted by list PR, but in the larger picture this is insignificant, so France is a negative case for the theory; it should evidence more party decline than it does and some students of French politics believe it did in the 1990s.) Germany is a case of Catholic corporatism with some left party power and an electoral system mixing PR and plurality: list PR with two votes per voter but almost entirely proportional in the allocation of seats. Its political economy, while not corporatist by our quantitative measure, evidences strong functional equivalents to consensual bargaining arrangements (see chap. 2).

The main story so far is that by numerous measures there is great party dealignment in the two most-fragmented and decentralized political economies and little or no decline among corporatist democracies, with or without labor. Except for France, a modified PR system is an added barrier to party decline. Germany, with the most-modified PR system, has the least party decline.[9]

These conclusions find further support in studies that use different measures of dealignment emphasizing the crumbling of stable social cleavages that underpin party stability (cf. Lipset and Rokkan, 1967). The argument, in brief, is that changes in social structure lead to the erosion of old cleavages of class, religion, ethnicity, region, and residence (urban-rural) and the development of new ones—for example, public employees vs. private-sector employees, environmentalists vs. labor, the middle mass vs. the highly educated and the poor (see chap. 10)—or the exacerbation of the old ones (e.g., minority-group conflict). These changes in social structure undermine the social bases for system stability and party vitality. The argument resembles convergence theory and implies that all party systems among rich industrial democracies will erode as the older social cleavages give way to the newer, although the timing will vary by the timing and degree of structural change.

The most thorough recent study of electoral behavior and attitudes based on this type of analysis covers 16 countries, including 14 of our 19 rich democracies, from the late 1950s through the 1980s (Franklin et al., 1992) and can be used to test my theory about types of political economy and electoral systems.[10] For party decomposition Franklin et al. use the changes in the share of votes cast for the bloc of left parties identified in each country. The rationale: the left-right cleavage remains the defining and enduring division in these countries and left parties are more comparable cross-nationally than right parties (*ibid.*, p. 16; cf. Wilensky, 1981c, and chap. 2; and Valen and Aardal, 1994, p. 299). As proxies for the strength of traditional social cleavages they use numerous *social characteristics*—occupation, age, union membership, income, education, sex, rural-urban residence, and region in addition to language and race in countries where these are relevant—and *attitudes* (class self-identification and religiosity) (Franklin et al., 1992, pp. 17–21, 433). As proxies for new cleavages they use public vs. private employment, public vs. private consumption (specifically public or rental housing vs. private home ownership), gender issues, and "postbourgeois" vs. "materialist" values measured by Ingelhart (pp. 50–54).

The conclusions: First, while there has been a widespread reduction in the variance in party dealignment explained by traditional social structures (consistent with convergence theory), there are very large national differences in the timing, pace, and amount of party decline (pp. 385–393). Second, and most important for my theory, *corporatist political economies experienced later and less decline than the more-fragmented and decentralized political economies.* The countries that evidence the earliest decline (Canada, the United States, and Ireland, followed by Britain, Australia, New Zealand, and France) are all least corporatist, again with the exception of France. In the amount of decline, among democratic corporatist countries only two (Denmark and Belgium) have fallen to levels comparable to the least-corporatist countries.[11] Finally, reinforcing my conclusion in chapter 4 regarding the severe limits of "postindustrialism" theory, Franklin et al. found that the effects of "post-materialism" were negligible no matter what they try to explain—electoral choice or anything else. Such "values" added nothing even to the explanation of support for new parties to which the vanguard groups that comprise the postmaterialist generation are presumably attracted. Similarly, gender, consumption (e.g., home ownership), and public vs. private employment had only slight effects on electoral behavior in some countries, more in others (*ibid.*, chap. 20 and p. 414). "In no country," they conclude, "is the decline in the structuring properties of traditional cleavages balanced by increases in the structuring properties of new cleavages" (p. 386). Instead, the crucial sources of variation in party decline are the old standbys: structures of bargaining and electoral systems; and, in the Franklin et al. study, such social characteristics as education, age, occupation, and minority-group status and class. Leithner and Vowles' (1996) similar analysis of the impact of older and newer social cleavages on their party stability index reach similar conclusions for New Zealand.[12]

VOTER TURNOUT, ELECTION FREQUENCY, DIRECT DEMOCRACY, AND VOTER FATIGUE

Because low voter turnout is taken as a sign of a weak party system and declines in turnout are one measure of dealignment, we must give special attention to the radically deviant cases of the United States and Switzerland, two countries that share the distinction of having by far the lowest turnout in the democratic world. In a study of turnout in our 19 rich democracies plus Greece, Portugal, and Spain, Jackman and Miller (1995) examined average voter turnout 1981–90 as a percentage of the eligible population for the lower-house election (and average turnout in the United States and France for presidential elections). They found that turnout ranged from 41% to 93%. Without the two deviant cases (Switzerland at 41% and the United States at 51%), the average turnout was 80.3% with a low of 69% (Canada). Their multivariate analysis shows that three variables are most important in determining national variations in turnout: (1) *Mandatory voting laws.* This is consistent with the cross-national studies by Jackman (1987) and Wolfinger, Glass, and Squire (1990), who show that fines for not voting and the ease of registration are crucial predictors of high turnout. (2) *The structure of political competition,* that is, the extent to which electoral districts are nationally competitive. *Proportional representation with large district magnitudes* (large number of representatives to be elected from each district) fosters such competition; single-member districts where winner takes all discourages such competition (campaign managers write off losing districts). (3) *Multipartyism,* at least at the extreme of a *large number of effective parties,* discourages turnout. Jackman and Miller suggest that, in multiparty systems that produce coalitions, voters cannot predict the shape of the governing coalition so they are discouraged from voting. But in the United States and other majoritarian first-past-the-post systems, the voter knows with more certainty the shape of the government if one or another side wins; and yet turnout in these countries (the United States, United Kingdom, Canada) tends to be low. Instead, as we have seen earlier, it is the large number of parties in systems with nearly pure PR that dampens turnout (as in the Netherlands, Switzerland, and Denmark). In contrast, modified PR interacting with corporatist bargaining arrangements tends toward not only coalition politics but above-average turnout (as in

Sweden and Austria, 85%; Norway, 82%; Germany, 79%; and Belgium, 87%).[13] In the rank order of causes of turnout in the 1980s, unicameralism is a poor fourth and degree of disproportionality in the translation of votes into seats is a poor fifth. No cultural variable (e.g., life satisfaction, interpersonal trust, rates of political discussion) has any influence (*ibid.*, p. 481). This confirms Wolfinger et al. (1990) who found that national variation in political and social alienation had no effect on turnout; if anything, the more-alienated and distrustful populations (Italy, France) had quite high turnout relative to the less-alienated populations, again highlighting the overwhelming importance of electoral laws, ease of registration, and other political institutions and mobilizing structures.

Explaining the uniquely low turnout of voters in Switzerland and the United States—two countries so different in their size, culture, economy, and politics—is a challenge. As we have seen in previous chapters, they are both extreme cases of federal decentralization; they both have bicameral legislatures where the upper house has two members for each state (canton) whatever its size; both constitutions protect civil liberties and states' rights. But Switzerland, at least marginally, fits our category of corporatism-without-labor and has a consensual style of governing (the seven-member Federal Council that runs Switzerland—the grand coalition—has had the same party representation since 1959 (Klöti, 1991, pp. 2, 15–16). There is a sizable labor movement and industrial peace. The Swiss government bans political advertising on television and imposes universal military service. In sharp contrast, the United States has a confrontational governing style, a weak labor movement, above-average industrial conflict, unrestricted media dominance of politics, no large integrative national service, and more big swings in politics and policy. The differences in size of population are huge. These institutional differences explain why the Swiss can indulge direct democracy without subverting consensual democracy. The U.S.-Swiss similarities that explain their common low turnout are their extraordinary frequency of elections, their radical use of the initiative and referenda, and the voter fatigue that both of these create (cf. Crewe, 1981; Jackman and Miller, 1995).

If we combine the frequency of national initiatives and referenda, state (cantonal), and local (communal) initiatives and referenda, and elections of officials at every level, both countries are astounding in the voting demands they make on their citizens. And since 1970 both have increased the frequency of ballots and the choices they present. Switzerland is the star in initiatives and referenda; among democracies in the postwar period it accounts for two-thirds of the total (Kobach, 1994, p. 98). From 1972 to 1993 it averaged 8.4 qualified national ballot initiatives and referenda per year (up from 3.4 from 1945 to 1971) typically spread over two to four separate trips to the polls per year (*ibid.*, pp. 98–99, 141, and my calculations from table 4.1, pp. 117–129). While that high number of separate ballots per year has remained stable since World War II, the number of Swiss initiatives has become a deluge (based on pp. 116–129). While initiatives and referenda were accelerating in Switzerland, turnout was declining (Austen, Butler, and Ranney, 1987, p. 139), confirming the theme of voter fatigue.

There are no comparable figures for the United States because there are no national referenda or initiatives. But at the state level the number of initiatives on each ballot started to increase in the late 1970s. In vanguard California, initiatives exploded in the 1980s, reaching a peak of 28 or 29 in 1988 and 1990, then slacked off to a still-high level of about 15 per ballot in the early 1990s and back up to a combined total 27 in the March and November elections of 1996. Although California is the champion in the use of this direct-democracy device, other high-use states (Oregon, Washington) have also accelerated their use of the initiative, while states that have rarely used it in the past (South Dakota, Utah) are more recently voting on such measures more often (Magleby, 1994, p. 232). Beyond the rise of statewide initiatives are proliferating municipal and county initiatives.

Although Switzerland obviously leads in national ballot initiatives, it is likely that the United States leads in number of elections to choose officials. In any case the decentralization and populist character of both Switzerland and the United States ensure that ballots will be as abundant as berries. Crewe (1981, p. 232) describes the American peculiarity:

> No country can approach the United States in the frequency and variety of elections, and thus the amount of electoral participation to which its citizens have a right. No other country elects its lower house as often as every two years, or its president as frequently as every four years. No other country popularly elects its state governors and town mayors; no other has as wide a variety of nonrepresentative offices (judges, sheriffs, attorneys general, city treasurers, and so on) subject to election.

In addition, U.S. voters choose thousands of officials of school districts, water districts, tax districts, transportation districts, sanitation districts, and more. In referenda and initiatives in both the United States and Switzerland a single ballot typically includes multiple and disparate issues.

California is the scene of an entire industry devoted to qualifying initiatives on the ballot and selling them. Interest groups hire firms of specialized consultants who pay signature collectors 75¢ to several dollars a signature to reach the qualifying number. Advertising budgets on many issues are huge; the money is both raised and spent mainly in mass media buys and computerized mailing blitzes. Voters rely heavily on political ads to make up their minds on initiatives; they display great volatility in their vote intentions (Magleby, 1994, p. 249), which suggests both confusion and vulnerability to manipulation. That money talks is demonstrated by the pattern of winning and losing initiatives. Three careful studies converge in the conclusion that there is at least a modest impact of big one-sided spending in passing initiatives and an overwhelming impact of big one-sided spending in defeating initiatives (Owens and Wade, 1986; Magleby, 1994; and Banducci, 1998).[14] The ballots themselves and the explanatory material accompanying the ballot require a high level of reading comprehension (one California study claimed that a graduate degree was necessary). The legislature increasingly abdicates its deliberative role and turns over all manner of issues to "the people" in referenda. In fact, since 1978 when it passed Proposition 13, California has been on what Peter Schrag calls "a plebiscitary rampage . . . a continuous cycle of reform and political frustration, with initiative after initiative imposing state and local tax limitations, spending limits, term limits, a formula for school spending, three strikes [lifetime imprisonment for third-time offenders, a kind of pension for older criminals way past their prime], and prohibiting public education and other services for illegal immigrants . . . " (1996, p. 28). Students of California government agree that the net effects have been largely unintended: a shift in power from local government to a state government paralyzed by uncoordinated restrictions on its taxing and spending powers and its staffing; lengthy gridlock on annual state budgets; growing inequities in property taxes; excessive dependence on bond issues; an increasing difficulty for voters to comprehend the system and hold anyone accountable for the deterioration of services and the physical infrastructure; and a rise of populist demagoguery of every kind. Despite the obvious attractions of direct democracy, where it is most fully developed its practical results are an overload of voter decisions, voter disaffection and confusion, voter fatigue, and, finally, low and declining turnout, and party decline. Unless there are strong countervailing sources of consensus as there are in Switzerland, direct democracy also produces government paralysis.

THE PROTEST PARTY CHALLENGE

A final piece of the picture of party decline and party realignment is the new party challenge, the recent growth in the number of protest parties, most prominently the Greens and new ethnoregional and nativist parties. Are these signs of party dealignment? Three findings in the studies of these protest parties suggest that they are at best a supplement to better measures of party dealignment. First, while there has been growth in the number and electoral success of small parties since World War II, the growth is quite small. For instance, a study of 13 West European democracies (Mair, 1991) finds no substantial change in the balance between small parties and large, established parties. In the 1950s the major parties polled an average of 68.4% of the vote; that declined to 63.1% in the 1970s and then stabilized at 63.9% in the 1980s. The vote share of small parties—including Greens, regionalist-nationalists, extreme right parties, Communists, left-sectarian spin-offs from mainstream social democrats, as well as new Christian, Liberal, and Agrarian parties—rose from 30.3% in the 1950s to 34.5% in the 1970s, then fell to 32.0% in the 1980s—a rise of less than two percentage points in four decades (Mair, 1991, pp. 51–52).[15]

Second, these protest parties tend to be heterogeneous in ideology and even social composition and therefore are quite unstable; they lack the firm anchor provided by a distinctive and coherent ideology or a steady social base. The Green voters in Europe, for instance, range from older folks who are nostalgic about the destruction of the Black Forest where they hiked as teenagers to militant young radicals ("Fundis" or fundamentalists) who believe in direct and sometimes violent action against nuclear installations (see chap. 15) to conventional activists ("Reales") who advocate negotiation with industry and parliamentary participation on numerous issues. A study of Green politics in seven European democracies concludes "(a) Green voters are not sufficiently socially homogenous to lend support to theories linking Green voting with the interests of particular social groups, and (b) the variables measuring 'new politics' values [postmaterialism, left ideology, environmentalism] fail to a surprising extent to explain Green voting" (Franklin and Rüdig, 1995, p. 433). In fact, in some countries even environmental concern is not much more prominent among Green voters than among non-Green voters. What is most notable about this seven-country study is that all of the alleged causes of Green voting taken together—social structural (youth, high education levels, employment in the public sector) or ideological (left-wing values, postmaterialism, environmentalism)—explain no more than 8.8% of the variance in Green voting (p. 425). In short, neither social base nor ideology holds Greens together.

The lack of either a solid social base or a common ideology explains why the protest voters do not tend to shift their party identification. Scheuch and Scheuch (1997) estimate that at least two-thirds of voters for the new-left and new-right parties in Germany are neither rightist nor leftist in their orientation; they are pure protest voters.

The final reason for the limited use of protest parties as a sign of system erosion is that the dominant parties and governing coalitions have been quite flexible in responding to the new demands. They have incorporated much of environmentalism and feminism into their party programs and policies (Kitschelt, 1994, pp. 112–206); unhappily, they have also often accommodated the nativist and xenophobic sentiments of ethnoregional parties into their programs on trade and immigration (see chap. 17 on globalization).

There are, of course, variations in the success of protest parties across countries and over time. Some evidence indicates that the more decentralized and fragmented the political economy, the greater the success of protest parties. Thus, a study of 16 of the most threatening ethnoregional parties in five West European democracies (Britain, Italy, Spain, Belgium, Finland) shows that their electoral success from 1980 to 1992 is related to the degree of centralized corporatist bargaining. These parties had less success in corporatist Belgium and Finland, more where such structures are nonexistent (Britain) or weak (Italy) (Müller-Rommel, 1994, p. 194 and table 2;[16] and my discussion of nativist protest in chap. 17). Further, there are regional and local variations in protest-party success. In the relatively stable party system of Germany, for example, voters in the port city of Hamburg on September 19, 1993, massively defected from the established parties—from the Social Democrats, the Christian Democrats, and the Free Democrats. The Greens scored 13.5% of the vote; the neo-Nazi far right, 7.6%. Until this becomes national and persists over time, however, we cannot count it as a significant dealignment.

Both the Greens and the neo-Nazis have, in fact, shown no persistent uptrend in national support. The Republikaners and other radical-right splinter parties are fading; the Greens, like their counterparts in other countries, evidence a cyclical pattern with no clear trend but a likely decline. As a percentage of the Bundestag vote the extreme-right parties, the largest of which is now the Republican Party, rose from an average of 1.3% from 1949 to 1965 to a peak of 4.3% in 1969; fading to an average of 0.4% from 1972 to 1987. In 1990 the figure including both East and West was 1.8% (Dalton, 1993, p. 286). In 1994 the extreme right remained a small splinter of the electorate. Republikaner voters were a heterogeneous collection of the disaffected: conformist neo-Nazis; disappointed Christian Democrats; threatened old middle class, especially farmers; young workers with authoritarian values and poor economic prospects; and, more generally, the downwardly mobile (Jaschke, 1993). As for the Greens, their share of the vote climbed from 1.5% when they emerged in 1980 to a peak of 8.3 in 1987. They lost all their seats in 1990 but came back in 1994 as a moderate-left parliamentary party in coalition with the "Alliance 90" with 7.3% of the vote and 49 seats. Because of their social composition there is reason to believe that they will fade away, even though they are currently part of the ruling coalition, and even if the major parties do not do what they typically have done—accommodate widely shared environmental concerns. The Greens are often seen as a postindustrial vanguard movement of the young, the educated, and of women. Survey data from the mid-1980s, however, show that roughly one-third of Green voters are students; almost another third are unemployed or out of the labor force; many are young academics who are unemployed or disappointed with their career chances (Alber, 1989, p. 11). That this base will erode is suggested by evidence showing that the only variable that distinguishes Green voters from others is not education, not gender, not public-sector employment (60% of them are not in the labor force) but a specific age cohort. In 1987 it was 35- to 45-year-olds, the crowded baby-boom generation (see chap. 4 on life cycle, cohort, and postindustrial-ism). Neither the younger voters nor the older voters were overrepresented among the Greens. Because of the continued aging of the German population, the electoral weight of younger voters is rapidly declining. Equally important is the eventual emergence of a labor shortage, as the under-40 labor force shrinks. This should gradually open up economic op-portunities for the ever-scarcer young. In short, while the baby-boom cohort (now 45 – 55) marches on toward their pensions and the percentage of young or unemployed voters de-clines, the core constituency of the Greens will erode (ibid., pp. 12 – 13).

Finally, while these new protest parties were either fading or fluctuating in German na-tional elections, total party membership actually climbed (Selle and Svåsand, 1991)—anything but a sign of dealignment.

What all this suggests is that an increase in the number and electoral strength of protest parties whose grievances are directed against major governing parties is a measure of dealign-ment only where they (1) persist but neither replace major parties nor join in governing coalitions; (2) are national in scope, not merely local and episodic; and (3) combine with other dimensions of party decline such as voting volatility, voter alienation from the system, or a change in party affiliation and identity among the protest voters. Denmark, the United King-dom, the United States, and more recently Italy fit these three criteria. In short, the emer-gence of protest parties is a supplementary indicator of party decline in a few countries.

New Zealand 1984–93: A Cautionary Tale of Party Dealignment

Since 1984 New Zealand has been engaged in a neoliberal experiment launched with pas-sionate conviction and inspired by American-trained economists, one of the more suc-cessful exports of the United States. It is a case study in the vulnerability of decentralized, fragmented political economies to party decline, political polarization, and the erosion of political legitimacy. It also illustrates how sectarian economic ideologies can enter a polit-ical vacuum created by the combination of economic crises and the decline of broad-based political parties, unions, and churches that in the past have kept politics in the center. Al-though Britain and Britain abroad (the United States, Canada, Australia, New Zealand) are most vulnerable to these tendencies, we also see them in lesser degree for a brief period even in Sweden, where formerly pragmatic economists have swung to the right.

Under successive Labour (1984 – 90) and National (1990 – 96) governments those 10 years saw the gradual erosion of New Zealand's two major parties, the emergence of sev-eral radical parties of the right and left, a drastic decline in public confidence in all insti-tutions, and a massive popular revolt. It culminated in a referendum that shifted the elec-toral system from a simple plurality to PR, the only postwar shift of its kind among rich democracies. Both the economy and the polity were destabilized.

Several scholarly accounts explain this remarkable collapse of political legitimacy (e.g., Easton, 1988; Oliver, 1989; Miller and Catt, 1993; Chapman, 1992; Vowles and Aimer, 1993; Castles, Gerritsen, and Vowles, 1996; Castles and Shirley, 1996; Vowles and McAllister, 1996; and Vowles, 2000).[17] The context prior to 1984 was a half century of alternating domi-nance by the center-right National Party and the center-left Labour Party. There was much continuity of public policy. Both major parties, whatever their contrasting campaign rhet-oric, were committed to a comprehensive, universalistic, if modest welfare state (spending levels were like those of the United Kingdom and Canada); they advocated egalitarian ideas and a positive state with a mixed economy. A two-party system with a tradition of strong party discipline prevailed. Standards of living were high, politics were pragmatic.

Problems common to export-reliant countries in the mid-1970s hit New Zealand especially hard. Its exports of wool and lamb, lumber, and dairy products—most of them to the United Kingdom—gradually declined, as the United Kingdom's economy sputtered and the EC drove New Zealand out of its markets. Devaluations, wage and price controls, and high tariffs against imported manufactured goods did not stop a deterioration in both New Zealand's trade balance and growth rate and a rapid rise in its public debt. From an average performance among the 19 rich democracies, New Zealand slipped to below average in 1974–79, although 1980–84 was not bad.[18] By the early 1980s many business executives and several top leaders in both major political parties, facing a severe economic crisis, recognized the need for some economic restructuring.

The story of radical political change begins with the importation from America of one version of Reaganomics and a particularly doctrinaire form of monetarism carried by enthusiastic converts trained in the economics departments of Chicago, Rochester, and Duke who entered the Treasury and outmaneuvered their more pragmatic opposition. They guided the economy into 10 years of high unemployment, long and deep recessions and slow average growth. Beginning as a group of Treasury officials of neoliberal persuasion, civil servants who had refined their doctrines in 1981–84, they were ready with a detailed action program in 1984 (when the Labour government of Prime Minister Lange was elected) and one of them, Graham Scott (Duke, Economics), took over at Treasury. They sold an extreme version of the "Chicago-Rochester School" to Roger Douglas, the Labour minister of finance, already receptive to the message (he had written a book moving toward it in the early 1980s) and equally receptive to business pressure groups. They were determined to try the deregulation thrust of the Reagan and Thatcher experiments in a more thorough, more rational, and disciplined way. They were inspired by new-right theories of public choice, agency, and property rights.

On their left were the prime minister and most of the Labour Party leaders outside of Parliament. Among them were established labor leaders and intellectuals of both the party and the labor movement, including the young president of the Labour Party, Professor Margaret Wilson, a law lecturer at the time; Jim Anderton, former president of the Labour Party; and Helen Clark, the MP for Mount Albert who had done comparative research on Scandinavia, was a lecturer in politics, and is now the Labour Party leader. They advocated a corporatist solution to the developing crisis: start with an economic summit including government, labor, and industry to establish a structure for consultation and consensus, modeled after the similar effort by Prime Minister Bob Hawke of Australia.

After the 1984 election, an internal struggle in the Labour Party caucus began. Although there was some consensus about increasing the efficiency of government-owned enterprises, reducing the debt, and keeping New Zealand nuclear free, conflict over taxes, social spending, the forms of austerity and the role of government in the economy gradually intensified. The face-off was between a group who advocated tripartite discussion and bargaining about solutions (only later joined by Prime Minister Lange) versus a sectarian group with a coherent free-market theory and a long list of specific proposals for economic restructuring with cost-benefit analysis attached. The neoliberal ideologues in Treasury and

Finance won. Finance Minister Roger Douglas said an economic summit would be okay so long as it did not make policy; it could communicate the importance of austerity to the public and be good public relations. Prime Minister Lange called the summit in September 1984. Over 100 labor, management, and government representatives joined leaders of women's groups, Maoris, teachers, and so on in the Parliament building. The advocates of democratic corporatism believed that restructuring and tripartite bargaining were not incompatible but many doubted that a decentralized labor movement—with rivalry between occupation-based unions and a weak Federation of Labour—could deliver on centrally negotiated agreements. (For a detailed account of the Labour caucus debates between corporatism advocates and the free marketeers, see Oliver, 1989.)

In the end when budgets were adopted, a coherent theory with elaborate statistical support beat vague talk about consensus and consultation with the community. What came to be called "Rogernomics" began to be put in place. The idea that state-led restructuring could be combined with a universalistic welfare state was eventually abandoned. No more pandering to politics and the electorate, said the free marketeers. There would be targeted social assistance for the truly needy, but fiscal discipline would prevail.

Two waves of neoliberal reform of taxes, social spending, and the regulation and control of industry were carried out by the first and second Labour governments 1984–87 and 1987–90. The National Party massively defeated Labour in 1990; it then accelerated the reforms, extended them into the labor market, launching a full-scale attack on both unions and the welfare state. Neither party's manifesto mentioned the policies actually adopted, one explanation of the political uproar of 1984–93.

The measures adopted include the following:

- *Tax reform 1984–87:* lowered the top income tax rate from 66 to 48 %, reduced brackets from five to three; replaced the wholesale sales tax with a comprehensive single-rate goods and services tax (GST), like a VAT, including food. Targeted assistance to low-income families would partly offset the regressive impact. This was carefully explained to the public and, in itself, produced no tax revolt.

- *Tax reform 1987–90:* A single flat tax on incomes of 24% was proposed but later changed to two brackets—24% and 33%. GST was increased to 12.5%. New taxes included business taxes and a withholding tax on interest and dividends, a tax on fringe benefits, and other reforms. The net effects by 1988 were regressive (Stephens, 1993). The almost-flat tax and the general regressivity provoked a political uproar, the sacking of Minister of Finance Douglas (who accused the prime minister of losing his nerve) and the subsequent resignation of the prime minister (Chapman, 1992). While there was no major parliamentary rebellion, regional Labour conferences were the scene of fistfights, one of which was shown on prime-time national television.

- *Targeting of welfare-state benefits:* Means testing and income testing were increased. From 1986 on the government instituted a family support scheme based on tax credits for the poor with effective marginal tax rates of 46–48%. Estimates of the takeup rate vary from 30% to 70%. (As chap. 8 shows, Britain and Britain abroad are the countries that remain most obsessed with means testing. In all these Anglo-American democracies, the more targeted the benefits, the more visible the unpopular nonaged poor, the greater the stigma, the lower the takeup rate, the more hostility among the citizens not receiving the benefits, and the greater resistance to antipoverty programs.)

• *Surtax on pensions.* Introduced *student fees* for higher education.

• *Restructured the civil service* on the model of New Zealand business firms. Abandoned traditional pay-setting and grievance and arbitration procedures.

• *Cut tariffs and other trade restrictions.* Deregulated financial institutions, decontrolled foreign exchange, installed a free float of New Zealand currency.

• *"Corporatized" many public industries* including railroads, airlines, and public lands: the government retained ownership, removed all subsidies, and made them profit-making competitors. Many of these quasi-public enterprises were *later privatized.* Unprofitable post offices were closed.

• *Adopted a globally unique central bank statute in 1989.* Gave the Reserve Bank of New Zealand complete freedom to pursue a single goal, price stability, with a specified target (0 – 2%), and a link between the governor's tenure and inflation performance.

• In 1991 the National Party increased charges on prescription drugs and doctor visits and furthered the development of a *two-tier system of medical care:* Everyone has access to the public system and about three-quarters of medical expenditures remain public, but heavy targeting (income and means testing), copayments, and variable prices have inspired the spread of private insurance; about two in five families, mainly upper income, now use it to cover copayments or to jump the cue for more or better care. Structural reforms are similar to those in the National Health Service of Britain under Thatcher. The National government also moved toward *income testing of pensions,* but when 80 – 90 % of the public polled expressed disapproval they backed down.

• *The Employment Contracts Act of 1991 abolished government protection of unions,* banned the union shop, eliminated the arbitration system, allowed individuals and groups to choose alternative bargaining agents when all existing contracts expired, and curtailed the right to strike.

In the absence of the military Keynesianism of Reaganomics, the economic effects of these radical reforms were devastating: From 1984 to 1990 unemployment rose from 4.0% to 11%, inflation moved up from 12% to 18% in 1986, but, with a very tight monetary policy administered by the newly autonomous central bank, inflation came down to 3% and with the selling of public assets, the shift in taxes, and cuts in social spending, budgets deficits declined (Stephens, 1993, p. 46ff.). Bankruptcy rates and welfare dependency soared. Growth rates remained low at under 1% a year. This pattern of low or nearly zero inflation, low growth, and high unemployment continued through the early 1990s.[19] Because high interest rates attracted foreign capital and devaluation made exports cheap, however, the trade balance improved. Tax reforms gave Finance Minister Douglas a reputation in financial circles as a bold innovator. The London *Economist* and the economists of OECD praised the new tax structure as "the least distorting in the OECD." What was an efficiency economist's dream, however, was an egalitarian's nightmare. The combination of tax reform and spending cuts sharply increased inequality (Stephens, 1993, pp. 59 – 61).[20] Labor-market reforms exacerbated inequalities produced by changes in taxing and spending. Union membership plummeted; industrywide bargaining practically disappeared; firm-level bargaining became the norm. By 1999 New Zealand had become the least rich of our 19 rich democracies, measured by per capita GDP in either U.S. dollars or purchasing power parities.

The effects of 10 years of sectarian monetarism combined with Reaganomics (without Reagan's deficit spending) were devastating for political legitimacy. The three elections in this period (1984, 1987, and 1990) generated the highest voter volatility of the previous 30 years (Vowles and Aimer, 1993, p. 14); the flight of Labour voters to two new parties (New Labour and Green) in 1990 brought the Labour government down. In the election campaign the victorious National Party promised cautious pragmatism, decency, honesty, a balanced budget, and a 50% cut in unemployment; they said they would make Labour's reforms more fair and efficient. What they delivered were three more years of stubbornly doctrinaire economics. By 1991 the National Party and its leaders were the most unpopular in the history of polling. By 1993, the National Party exceeded the earlier Labour Party collapse in popularity. Surveys showed that trust in New Zealand institutions and occupational groups plunged; confidence in Parliament dropped from 33% in 1975 to single digits after 1988, down to 4% in February 1992 (Miller and Catt, 1993, p. 31). In a relatively clean society with practically no political corruption, a 1992 survey found that 81% of the public believed that there was "corruption" in New Zealand politics (by which many may have meant incompetence if not dishonesty) (National Business Review/Insight poll, 19 June 1992). In the 1990 election both major parties, rapidly losing support—even from their back-benchers—promised a referendum on electoral reform, thinking that it would mollify the defectors and result in the maintenance of the present system. A prestigious Royal Commission had recommended the adoption of a German-style PR system to restore more representative democracy.

The delegitimacy story ends with the voters vengeance: two referendums (1992 and 1993) on a sweeping change in the electoral system from first-past-the-post to mixed-member PR with a 5% threshold. The election of 1993 (the last under the old rules) saw four new parties and the further decline of the two major parties. The results of 1993: National won 50 seats with 35% of the votes; Labour, 45 seats with 34.7% of the votes; third parties won four seats with an unprecedented 30.3% of the votes (a left Alliance, 18.2%; a center party, New Zealand First, 8.4%; others, 3.4%). In November 1994 a new right party, ACT New Zealand, was founded by Roger Douglas and other true believers who created this 10-year experiment in pure theory as the sole guide to policy. The 1996 election saw additional right and left parties competing for the now thoroughly alienated New Zealand voters. Ironically, that may ultimately produce the very center-left coalition that the right-wing sectarians wiped out. In the 1996 election this did not happen but New Zealand First, the new minority party that negotiated with both Labour and the National Party to form a government, exacted a promise from the Nationals to spend more on health, education, and social programs; its leader became deputy prime minister as well as treasurer, a new post with responsibility for the budget. The net effect is a move away from the radical right. This tendency has been furthered by the result of a September 1997 referendum. In it the free marketeers in the new coalition government proposed to privatize the pension system. A resounding 92.4% of voters said "No." Finally, in 1999 the combination of mixed-member PR and a more representative Parliament gave expression to public hostility to the neoliberal agenda. It produced a center-left coalition of Labour and Alliance headed by Prime Minister Helen Clark (Vowles, 2000).

SUMMARY AND CONCLUSION

Just as tax-welfare backlash movements accelerated in the mid-1960s (chap. 10), so, too, party decline, although it is *not* universal, varies in rate, and began earlier in some countries, accelerated after the mid-1960s. Countries most vulnerable to mass-society tendencies—the United States and to a lesser extent the United Kingdom, Canada, New Zealand, Australia, and Denmark—evidence most erosion in their party systems. They either lack strong, broad-based mediating institutions—inclusive unions, labor federations, employer associations, and churches—to begin with or have experienced their diminishing vitality more than other, more-consensual democracies. With the exception of Denmark their plurality winner-take-all electoral systems, always more unrepresentative than systems with an element of proportional representation, reinforce tendencies toward mass disaffection from politicians and parties. These structural tendencies open the way for mass media ascendance in politics and culture. Interacting with a new breed of antipolitics politicians with little loyalty to party and little interest in governing, the media have become increasingly negative, strident, and anti-institutional, trashing government and its leaders.

These developments are writ large in the United States. Despite signs of increasing strength of parties-in-government—increasing party-line voting in Congress, stronger leaders with greater influence over committee chairmen—there is simultaneous growth of confrontational partisanship, as ideological extremes prevail in each party, and political polarization intensifies. The rise in congressional party strength is thus, at minimum, ambiguous in its consequences for the long-run fate of parties. Meanwhile multiple indicators show the United States as the textbook case of dealignment in the electorate: a decline in trust in politicians, government, and parties; a decline of party influence in the presidential nominating process; diminished strength of party ID among whites and the young; decreasing turnout in voting, and a drop in the percentage of adults doing campaign and party work or making campaign contributions; and an increase in random voting—ticket-splitting and to a lesser extent party-switching. The spread of the initiative and referendum adds to party decline by creating bewildering complexity and voter fatigue. Third-party activity in the United States, while an ambiguous indicator of dealignment, has speeded up in the last 30 years. As we have seen in chapter 3, the political vacuum created by the decline of broad-based mediating associations, including center-left and center-right parties, is filled by the mass media, single-issue interest groups, populist demagogues of the right and left, lawyers, and courts. (Chap. 12 presents data on the role of lawyers in countries that lack effective mechanisms of conflict resolution.) The New Zealand case, where parties have been declining since the 1950s, suggests an additional source of accelerating dealignment—the recently rising influence of doctrinaire economists who help to destabilize the economy and reinforce the power of ideological party leaders, promoting polarized politics.

In contrast, corporatist democracies evidence the least party decline. These negotiated political economies came into being because of inclusive, national unions and similar management counterparts, broad-based Catholic parties, and broad-based left parties. Their rise to power was facilitated by the PR compromise (see chap. 2). The interaction of PR, Catholicism, leftism, and democratic corporatism served as a check on mass-society tendencies, containing parochial interest-group pressures, countering media excess, and retaining effective government authority to set the public agenda. Thus, although data on party dealignment are limited in their comparability and unavailable for all 19 countries, it is clear that party decline is far from a general pattern. Relative to the Anglo-American democracies, such corporatist democracies as Germany, Sweden, Norway, Finland, and Austria evidence little or no erosion of their party systems.

The exceptions among the corporatist democracies are countries whose electoral systems approach pure PR, which results in very large numbers of parties, and more voting volatility—Denmark, which shows substantial dealignment, and, more recently, Italy where party breakup was apparent in 1992 under the old PR system (Woods, 1995). If we had party decline data on Israel and the Netherlands, they might fit this pattern of pure PR creating electoral turbulence. In all these cases, however, there are countervailing institutions and bargaining arrangements that slow down the process of dealignment.

Are modern democracies converging toward party-system erosion? If the social bases of the core support of mass parties in corporatist democracies—Catholic and left—are eroding, if unions and churches and other interest groups have reduced capacity to discipline their members, if major parties face unnegotiable demands from new social movements and single-issue groups, then the comfortable interplay of broad-based interest groups and broad-based parties will disintegrate and parties will no longer serve as effective mediators between citizen preferences and government policies. But, as I have shown in chapter 2, the large national differences in these tendencies are still in place.

Both tax-welfare backlash and party dealignment are indicators of a weakened capacity to govern, an erosion of political legitimacy. A third basic system output is economic performance. The next two chapters deal with this central concern of both elites and masses—and here data permit more systematic 19-country comparisons.

Notes

This chapter elaborates and tests themes in my "Political Legitimacy and Consensus" (1983) and an unpublished paper, "Paths of Development of Rich Democracies," presented at the University of Chicago, November 1–3, 1984. I am grateful to Ray Wolfinger, who, despite his strong disagreements with my interpretation of the American case, was generous with critical comments and helpful leads; to Nelson Polsby, Howard Reiter, and Jack Vowles for comments on a later draft.

1. David Butler and Donald Stokes' (1974) skepticism regarding the cross-national portability of U.S. wording of questions about party ID is supported in a survey experiment by Richard Johnston (1992b).

2. Data on voter defections in both presidential and congressional elections from 1956 to 1994 (Keith et al., 1992, table 10.1 updated to 1994 with NES data) confirms a quite strong trend toward less party loyalty in congressional elections and a milder trend in presidential elections. "Defectors" are strong, weak, and independent partisans (party leaners) who voted for another party's candidate. All partisans who voted for Wallace, Anderson, or Perot are defectors. My interpretation of that table is that from 1956 to 1964, i.e., until the escalation of the Vietnam War, there was a low average rate of defection in presidential elections (14.7%) and no significant third party. After the mid-1960s and until Ronald Reagan's election (1968–80), there was an increase in defectors as a proportion of voters to an average of 22.3% and two significant third parties (Wallace and Anderson). Eight years of Reagan saw a drop to low levels of defection (13% in 1984 and 12% in 1988); he polarized the electorate. But 1992 brought defection back to the post-Vietnam level of 23% and another third-party candidate (Perot). In House elections defection rates began at an average of 10.5% from 1956 to

1962, then climbed to an average of 17.4% from 1968 to 1976. From 1978 to 1994 the average defection rate climbed again to 20.8%, double the early period. Thus, measured by voter defections, party loyalty, while fluctuating with the circumstances of particular elections, is on a downward slide.

3. Data on trends in the percentage contributing money are contradictory, depending on phrasing. Verba, Schlozman, and Brady (1995) use the very broad question on the 1967 Verba-Nie study and the 1987 GSS: "In the past three or four years have you contributed money to a political party or candidate or to any other political cause?" They find that there has been nearly a doubling of the proportion who contribute any money. This might be explained by the increase in continual solicitation of money by interest groups and PACs. In contrast, Rosenstone and Hansen use American NES items confined to any money given to "an individual candidate" or "a political party" "during this election year" or "during the campaign." They show a drop of 21% from the 1960s to the 1980s. But Verba et al. do not exaggerate the meaning of their result: "nationalization and professionalization have redefined the role of citizen activist as, increasingly, a writer of checks and letters" (p. 73). Clearly, they add, "political activity has not grown at rates that we might have expected on the basis of the substantial increase in educational attainment within the public" (p. 74). The kind of ersatz gemeinschaft symbolized by contributions to mailing-list-based movements-without-members as compared to meeting attendance at a church or union is discussed in chapter 3.

4. Specifically, Rosenstone and Hansen (1993, pp. 214–219) find that weakened mobilization accounted for 54% of the variance in turnout between 1960 and 1990; a younger electorate, 17%; weakened social involvement, 9%; declining feelings of efficacy, 9%; and weakened attachments to and evaluations of the parties and their candidates, 11%. They estimate that removal of barriers to voting advanced turnout by 1.8 percentage points while the decline in mobilization lessened turnout by 8.7 percentage points.

5. For accounts of the norm of very strong party loyalty and high rates of party participation among white males of the late 19th century, see Marcus (1971) and Ware (1996). After 1984 when 74 Southern Democrats were elected in districts that voted for Reagan, split-ticket voting for House seats in the South sharply declined to a 1996 low of 14 Southern Democratic wins in districts where Dole won (Cook, 1997, p. 860). Aided by racial redistricting, this consolidated the realignment of the South. Yet the post-1984 decline in split-ticket voting for the House nationally left the rate at more than 1 in 4 (111 in 435 districts)—back to 1952 levels but high by any international standard. And, most important, this did not include substantial defections to third-party candidates, which made both 1992 and 1996 atypical. Voters for Perot who voted for Republican or Democratic candidates below the presidential line must be added to these split-ticket totals. Further, the split results are striking: 40% of the current House Republican majority represents districts that voted for President Clinton in 1996 (p. 860).

6. That the young in this study split tickets less often than older voters does not contradict the finding of diminished partisanship among the young (above). If it is peculiar to the 1990 election in Ohio, the young there may be expressing weak partisanship in other ways—party-switching, third-party voting, etc. In fact, a national study of generational effects shows that the younger the generation, the more the split-ticket voting (Brody, Brady, and Heitshusen, 1994, pp. 163–164; cf. Miller and Shanks, 1996, p. 41). Interpreting the national decline of party loyalty in the electorate, Gary Jacobson suggests two general sources of both split-ticket voting and "electoral disintegration" that complement the Ohio findings: the increased ability of candidates to bypass their parties via television (discussed above) and the diminished utility of party cues to voters—i.e., the decline of clear cut New Deal-Fair Deal issues and the rise of social issues (abortion rights, crime, etc.) that cross-cut parties (1990, p. 20).

7. Going beyond the six cases, Reiter uses a measure of "increasing unstructured volatility": if the standard deviation of a party's vote percentage over time increases and the absolute value of the correlation between that percentage and the election year declines, we can say this is not a linear trend

(realignment) but a more random pattern of change (party decline). Reiter concludes that only 16 of the 57 major parties in 20 nations experienced greater volatility over time. "Only in Denmark, Iceland and Switzerland did most of the major parties in the system undergo higher volatility" (*ibid.,* p. 328)—many fewer than the Pedersen index, which conflates dealignment and realignment, suggests.

8. Pedersen's index of the average volatility of party systems 1948–77 for 13 countries ranks France and Germany first and third (Pedersen, 1979, p. 9). The problem is that an unusual election can distort averages for the whole period (e.g., the EC membership issue in Norway) and, as we have seen, realignments appear as increased volatility. And a large number of parties moving to a small number (Germany) will appear as great volatility whether it is realignment, dealignment, or merely a merger of similar parties. Even the Pedersen index, however, shows that both France and Germany declined in volatility after 1960, Germany from 15.2% in 1948–59 to 4.9% in 1970–77, France from 21.8% to 10.6%. For another review of evidence demonstrating the stability of the German party system, see Alber (1989). Consistent with this theme of the strength and stability of the German system is a study comparing media content and voter perceptions of prominent politicians in Germany (Kaase, 1994). Personalization in politics (vs. party appeals) was absent in the 1990 German general election; and the accent on party has remained stable since 1972. In contrast, the United States evidences high and rising candidate-centered voter perceptions and media coverage of candidates.

9. For American scholars who believe that party strength can be measured by the capacity to raise money for campaigns, recent comparative data on such expenditures suggest the opposite: Farrell and Webb (2001, p. 8) and Farrell (1997, table 2) provide data from which I infer that the rate of increase in campaign expenditure is related to party dealignment. Countries with the greatest increases in campaign spending include the United Kingdom, the United States, Denmark, and Ireland; countries with the least increase in campaign spending include Sweden, Austria, Belgium, Finland, the Netherlands, and Norway. The first group are noncorporatist to weak corporatist with most dealignment. The second group are corporatist democracies with least dealignment except for Belgium, which by some measures evidences modest dealignment.

10. The 16 countries studied by Franklin et al. (1992) are Austria, Belgium, Britain, Canada, Denmark, France, West Germany, Greece, Ireland, Italy, the Netherlands, New Zealand, Norway, Spain, Sweden, and the United States. All but Greece and Spain are rich democracies in my study.

11. Individual country surveys reviewed by Franklin et al. (1992) confirm this picture. Two mid-1990s studies are consistent. Leithner and Vowles (1996) present a rich body of data tracing dealignment in New Zealand. Clarke and Kornberg (1996, pp. 470–473), analyzing Canadian panel data on partisan identification from 1974 to 1993 and a November 1994 survey show an increase in individual partisan instability: only 16% of Canadian voters switched federal party ID 1974–79; this increased to 21% in 1980–84 and 33% in 1988–93. Dealignment continued in 1994. The "critical" election of 1993 was not accompanied by national realignment.

12. For New Zealand, party-system stability is strongly and significantly correlated with class cleavage ($r = .68$), with the aged (60+) share of the population ($r = .81$), and the percentage below 40 years of age ($r = -.78$) but has no relationship to turnout, the number of effective parties (an indicator of new cleavages), or GDP growth (p. 14). Leithner and Vowles also show that crises or other rapid structural changes contribute to instability in partisan behavior (*ibid.,* pp. 10–12, 14–16).

13. Belgium's electoral formula for the decisive higher tier in two-tier districting is d'Hondt (like Germany's this is the least proportional and favors larger parties); its district magnitude is below the median for PR systems; and its effective threshold is above average—not quite as high as Germany's but somewhat higher than Sweden's or Norway's (Lijphart, 1994, tables 2.2 and 2.5).

14. Owens and Wade (1986, p. 688) show that in 85 cases of lopsided spending in California between 1924 and 1984, one-sided negative spending prevailed in 29 of 32 (a 91% defeat rate) while one-sided positive spending won in 29 of 53 (55%). Because on average only one-third of all these initiatives pass, while 66% of referenda pass, and because Owens and Wade include 68 initiatives and only

17 mandatory referenda—yielding a weighted average usual passage rate of 40%—the climb to a 55% success rate for disproportionate proponent spending is impressive (Magleby, 1994, p. 250). Similar findings appear in an econometric study of California initiatives from 1976 to 1990 and Oregon initiatives from 1970 to 1990 (Banducci, 1998). There is some indication that propositions on hot-button issues of the populist right (tax and spending limitations, abortion, death penalty, crime, term limits, immigration) and populist left (campaign reform, affirmative action, term limits, environmental cleanup) require less money than initiatives of central concern to industry (regulation of private insurance or health care). In 1988, five California insurance initiatives evoked more than $101 million in campaign spending, overwhelmingly insurance-company money (Magleby, 1994, p. 242). Movement-type initiatives, in contrast, can command free airtime and even some volunteers. Hence, their spending is not so obscene. Examples are anti–illegal immigrant Proposition 187 and the "Three Strikes" crime measure, where free national media coverage was prominent and total spending was well below the California average (Donovan et al., 1998, chap. 4).

15. There was, however, a substantial upward trend toward small parties, greater turnout, and more volatility in Denmark, Belgium, the United Kingdom, and Finland.

16. Müller-Rommel (1994) confines analysis to ethnoregional parties that contested at least two national and regional elections from 1980 to 1992, polled at least 3% of the regional vote, and actually gained seats in the national parliament—a fair test of serious challenges to established parties. In the United Kingdom these include separatists such as the Ulster Unionists and Loyalists and United Ireland/Sinn Fein, as well as the left-libertarian federalists, the Scottish National Party and the Social Democratic Labour Party. In Belgium, it includes parties that demand autonomy and language rights within the nation-state—the Christeijk Vlaame Volksunie and the Front Démocratique des Bruxellois Francophoners. In Finland, it includes the Svenska Folkpartiet, which aims to defend the interests of a linguistic community without secession or a major restructuring of the state. In Italy, the Union Valdotaine fought for linguistic rights and regional decentralization; today the Northern League advocates federalism, threatens secession, and expresses great hostility to the backward, corrupt South as well as all immigrants (see chap. 10). The secessionist Parti Québécois in Canada, like the Basques in Spain, would fit the more-militant secessionists in the Müller-Rommel study.

17. I am also indebted to Ray Miller and Michael Powell of the University of Auckland, Jack Vowles of the University of Waikato, and R. C. Mascarenhas of Victoria University of Wellington for background briefings on this episode in New Zealand politics. I thank Tony Dale, current Budget Manager in the New Zealand Treasury Ministry and Annette Dixon, Deputy Director-General, Strategic Planning and Policy, in the Ministry of Health, who generously corrected factual errors while they disagreed with some of my interpretations.

18. The measure is an index equally weighting good real GDP growth per capita, inflation control, and low unemployment. See chapter 12.

19. The latest data available at this writing shows that from 1985 to 1992 real GDP growth per capita averaged 0.06%, almost zero (OECD National Accounts, 1994b vol. 1, *Main Aggregates 1960–92*, p. 92). Treasury people argue that without their reforms the New Zealand economy would have been worse, that reforms take time to have an effect, and that in the years since 1992 the New Zealand economy has improved. The counterargument: If an economy performs badly for a decade and recessions are deep, any improvement will look good; the record of the first decade of the neoliberal experiment is clear; only another 10 years would test its merits for economic performance, equality, political legitimacy, and the real welfare of New Zealanders.

20. Peter Saunders (1994, pp. 19–20) shows a big acceleration of inequality in real disposable income from 1985–86 to 1989–90, mainly a redistribution from the middle to the top tenth of the distribution and then, with benefit cuts in the early 1990s, a sharp decrease in the real income of the poorest tenth.

12

TYPES OF POLITICAL ECONOMY, SPENDING, TAXING, AND ECONOMIC PERFORMANCE

Since the early 1970s there has been a spreading conviction among top policymakers in every rich democracy that we confront a crisis of the welfare state, an overload of social problems, and the rapid decline of the capacity to govern. Intellectuals, politicians, and bureaucrats alike have adopted the vocabulary of crisis. Only the phrasing differs, depending on their political mood, ideological persuasion, or disciplinary affiliation. In the 1990s, only in the U.S. did the declinists quiet down, to be replaced by equally strident triumphalists, as economic performance picked up.

If you go to a conference on public policy where economists dominate, you will hear that because of globalization and the acceleration of unit labor costs (especially fringe benefits), combined with an explosion of social-security costs (the heavy fiscal burdens of the welfare state), the industrialized countries' competitive position is deteriorating and their economies are stagnating. Urgent trade-offs and dilemmas common to every rich country are sharply posed: job protection and social security vs. economic growth; the protections of the welfare state vs. capital investment, economic performance, and the necessary structural adjustments.

Or if (before the collapse of the Soviet empire) you attended a conference of neo-Marxists who discussed "the fiscal crisis of the state" or "the political contradictions of capitalism" (O'Connor, 1973; Offe, 1972a, 1972b; Offe and Ronge, 1975; Habermas, 1975), you would have heard of the inevitable contradictions between the legitimacy of government bought through the welfare state and "the reproduction of capitalism" bought through state policies favoring private capital accumulation.

If they offer any prescriptions to cure the disease, conventional economists tend to favor cuts in social spending and job protection, reduction in taxes and benefits, the privatization of social services, "deregulation," and more means testing or income testing—the selective targeting of income transfers and services. The neo-Marxists tended to favor basic changes in the structures of domination—in what they called the distributional, repressive, or ideological apparatus of the modern capitalist state. Insofar as they offered concrete prescriptions, they emphasized the nationalization of industry or the collective control of capital; they viewed the expansion or reform of social policy as irrelevant or as merely another means of "capitalist hegemony." (Communitarian socialists, although they sometimes adopt neo-Marxist rhetoric, have favored formulas for decentralization and worker participation.) What they all have in common is the belief that the modern welfare state will overwhelm the capacity to manage a free-market economy.

In this odd convergence of ideologies, both conventional economists and neo-Marxists have been tackling recurrent issues in the history of social science: freedom and order, hierarchy and equality, the causes and consequences of the wealth of nations. But neither group was sufficiently comparative, neither was sufficiently systematic and empirical. Even now, economists dealing with social policy typically fail to take account of long-run effects of various policies on social consensus; they underestimate or ignore politics as a source of economic performance. And unless they are working for OECD or similar multinational organizations, they are seldom systematically cross-national. Neo-Marxists, on the other hand, typically failed to make the necessary comparisons to justify the adjective "capitalist" before their objects of attention—"crisis," "class relations," and so on. If they dealt with more than one market-oriented political economy, and needed to show its imminent collapse, they tended to concentrate on the UK, the USA, and Italy, countries whose troubles from the 1970s until 1992 were most obvious. And nowhere did we find systematic analysis of differences and similarities in problems of legitimacy and capital investment in "noncapitalist" countries at similar levels of development. With the demise of communism, only the free marketeers are left to sound the theme that the internal contradictions of capitalism—its crushing burden of the welfare state, its expanding entitlements—will doom it.

This chapter examines the question, Are the expanding welfare state and the continuing push for equality and job security barriers to good economic performance—a luxury we can no longer afford? My own view is that the trade-offs between job protection, social security, equality, and participatory democracy on the one hand, and worker productivity, economic growth, and other measures of economic performance, on the other hand, are not so stark as suggested in the burgeoning literature on policy analysis or in the media presentation of assorted economic crises. What is usually left out of the discussions of these big trade-offs are, first, empirical observations of the postwar economic performance of big spenders and lean spenders, and, second, analysis of the impact of various economic policies on consensus or political legitimacy, as these in turn shape economic performance. For instance, the tax-cutting mania in the United States ultimately paralyzed government at every level, reducing the capacity to use fiscal policy for any public purpose, alienating citizens who had been educated to believe in free lunches, and putting too great a burden on monetary policy.

Leaving aside the net contribution of the welfare state to such values as dignity, security, equality, family well-being, social integration, and political legitimacy, what are the net effects of social policies and the welfare state on productivity and economic performance? As we shall see, from 1950 to 1980 the economic effects of a high level of social spending and taxation were positive; since 1980 the effects have been either mildly negative or irrelevant. If variations in spending and taxation explain very little of national differences in economic performance, are there any components of the welfare state or any types of taxation that consistently help? Beyond taxing and spending, what are the main roots of relatively good economic performance?

THE WELFARE STATE AND ECONOMIC PERFORMANCE:
LESSONS FROM THE PAST

There is no uniform relationship between the costs of job protection, income transfers, and personal social services characteristic of advanced welfare states, on the one hand, and their economic performance on the other. Since World War II, by any major measure of economic performance, the heavy-spending corporatist democracies among our 19 have done as well as or better than the welfare-state laggards. So far, they have not been spending themselves into the grave.

To explore the interplay between types of political economies, social spending, and economic performance, we devised a general economic performance index which weighs three major measures roughly equally: average annual *real growth* of GDP per capita; *inflation* (average percentage increase in the GNP price deflator); and average annual *unemployment*. Rather than dividing the 19 countries arbitrarily by, say, quintiles (so that a one-tenth of 1% difference might separate excellent from good growth), we used natural break points and assigned ranks of 0, 1, or 2 for each of the measures, then added them up for a performance score ranging from 0 to 6 (poor to excellent). The commonsense labels I use reflect real differences.

For comparative analysis, this index has several advantages over the much abused "misery index" originated by Arthur Okun, which merely adds together the inflation and unemployment rate. First I include real GDP growth per capita: many scholars think of this as the best single clue to increased standards of living. Second, unemployment is doubtless understated more than inflation, especially where high rates of joblessness are tolerated for long periods as in the United States, Canada, Ireland, and the UK. By merely adding the two measures, the misery index gives the latter countries an edge they do not deserve. Third, there are typically more winners from increased inflation (debtors) than losers (creditors); it is hard to find many winners from increased unemployment. Finally and most important are arithmetical distortions: large inflation rates will almost always count more than large unemployment rates. For instance, the average inflation rate of our 19 countries 1974–79 was 12.0%; the average unemployment rate was 4.1% (see table 12.3). Thus, in the misery index, unemployment would count only about one-third as much as inflation. Even in 1980–84, when unemployment averaged 6.8%, average inflation was still higher at 8.2% (see table 12.4). So adding the two means that control of inflation will weigh much heavier than control of unemployment. Arguably a more valid measure would reverse that weighting because the costs of sustaining moderate unemployment are much higher than the costs of sustaining moderate inflation. (Long-term unemployment surely increases poverty, inequality, and demoralization; makes skills deteriorate; and decreases productivity.) My equal weighting of three clearly desired goals of high growth, low inflation, and low unemployment avoids arguments about the relative merits of the three. However, each component will be considered separately as well as together.

To explore the relative competence of types of political economies in coping with major economic crises and external shocks, we divided the analysis into four periods: (1) 1950–74, the 25 years beginning after reconstruction and ending with the first Arab oil shock of 1974; (2) the five postshock years 1975–79, which capture the effects of the first energy price explosion; (3) 1980–84, the five years after multiple and most severe shocks (the second oil shock, followed quickly by the Volcker tight-money interest-rate shock, roughly October 6, 1979, to September 15, 1980, an external shock for all countries but the United States, for which it was self-administered) and a deep worldwide recession and recovery; and finally, (4) 1985–89, a period of modest prosperity beginning with sharp declines in oil prices.

In measuring national differences in the vulnerability to external shocks, we used three indicators—two related measures of energy dependence comprising an index of energy dependence in 1970 and 1978, and changes in the terms of trade 1973–74 and 1978–79. The two components of the energy dependence index are (1) liquid fuels as a percentage of total energy consumption (mainly oil); and (2) energy production as a percentage of energy consumption. The idea is to measure big, sudden changes in economic resources beyond the reach of public policy. The two oil shocks clearly fit: what you have done or not done for many years to control inflation or improve productivity and trade balances cannot be changed overnight in the face of such energy price explosions. The same is true of sudden changes in the terms of trade—the ratio of export prices to import prices. Appendix G provides details about these measures, their interrelations, and their meaning.

If we are to rank 19 countries in their economic performance, we must consider their greatly varied vulnerability to external shocks. It is like a handicap race. For instance, at the beginning of the 1970s, Canada was least dependent on oil as a fraction of its total energy use and also produced more energy than it consumed. By the broader measure of changes in the terms of trade 1973–74, Canada was a great exporter of grain, energy, minerals, and lumber whose prices soared; its terms of trade improved (1.07). Contrast Sweden: it was highly oil-dependent and imported almost all of its energy. Further, its terms of trade deteriorated slightly 1973–74 (.98). That Sweden scores average in 1974–79 economic performance while Canada ranks fair to poor is all the more impressive; we should take credit away from Canada and give it to Sweden. Similarly, Japan, Italy, and Denmark begin the oil shock year with big handicaps; they are highly energy-dependent and produce the wrong tradable goods. Norway has an advantage on both counts. Thus, I report postshock performance in relation to these structural advantages and disadvantages. To specify the importance of internal social and economic structures and the public policies that flow from them, I control for vulnerability to external shocks.

After reporting the main findings by period with attention to specific countries, I search for explanations and subject the data to regression analysis.

Social Spending and Economic Performance 1950–74

Whatever the causal process, my findings about the direction of the relationship are unequivocal: the greater the average social-security spending, 1950–74, the better the economic performance score ($r = .48$; $p < .05$). Of the top 9 economic performers only 1 (Japan) is a lean spender; 3 (Switzerland, Norway, and Finland) spend close to the 25-year average (SS/GNP of 12.8%) while 5 (Germany, Sweden, Belgium, the Netherlands, and Austria) are big spenders. In contrast are 10 countries in the bottom half of the table on economic performance (table 12.1). Of the 5 very worst in postwar performance, none is a big spender (UK, with 12.7%, is an average spender; the USA, Canada, Israel, and Ireland are lean spenders). Of the 10 worst in economic performance, only 3 (France, Italy, and Denmark) rank higher than average in social spending.

TABLE 12.1 Corporatism, welfare effort, and economic performance, 1950–74

Countries ranked by economic performance	Corporatism score[a]	Average social security effort (SS/GNP)[b]	Economic Performance				
			Summary rating	Summary score[c]	Average annual real growth per capita[d]	Average inflation[e]	Average unemployment[f]
WEST GERMANY	1.00 (12)	18.9 (2)	E	5	4.7 (4) H	3.8 (17) L	2.2 (10) M
JAPAN	0.00 (17)	5.1 (19)	G	4	8.0 (1) H	5.7 (4) H	1.6 (15) L
AUSTRIA	7.00 (9)	19.3 (1)	G	4	4.6 (5) H	5.3 (8) M	2.1 (11) M
FINLAND	7.67 (7)	11.8 (11)	G	4	4.4 (6) H	6.8 (2) H	1.7 (14) L
NETHERLANDS	12.33 (1)	15.5 (6)	G	4	3.8 (8) M	5.0 (10) M	1.7 (14) L
BELGIUM	8.67 (4)	17.2 (4)	G	4	3.7 (9) M	3.5 (18) L	3.0 (6) M
NORWAY	8.67 (4)	12.3 (10)	G	4	3.4 (11) M	4.5 (14) M	1.5 (17) L
SWEDEN	8.67 (4)	15.5 (6)	G	4	3.2 (13) M	5.0 (10) M	1.8 (12) L
SWITZERLAND	1.00 (12)	11.6 (13)	G	4	2.9 (14) L	4.0 (15) L	0.2 (18) L
ITALY	8.00 (6)	15.0 (7)	F	3	4.7 (4) H	4.6 (12) M	5.2 (2) H
FRANCE	9.00 (2)	17.4 (3)	F	3	4.2 (7) H	5.8 (3) H	2.3 (9) M
DENMARK	5.67 (10)	13.8 (8)	F	3	3.4 (11) M	5.4 (7) M	2.7 (7) M
AUSTRALIA	1.00 (12)	8.6 (16)	F	3	2.1 (18) L	5.4 (7) M	1.5 (17) L
NEW ZEALAND	0.00 (17)	11.7 (12)	F	3	2.0 (19) L	4.5 (14) M	0.1 (19) L
ISRAEL	7.00 (9)	7.0 (18)	FP	2	5.2 (2) H	9.5 (1) H	8.2 (1) H
CANADA	0.00 (17)	10.3 (15)	FP	2	2.7 (15) L	3.8 (17) L	4.9 (5) H
UNITED STATES	0.00 (17)	7.9 (17)	FP	2	2.4 (16) L	3.2 (19) L	4.9 (5) H
UNITED KINGDOM	0.00 (17)	12.7 (9)	FP	2	2.3 (17) L	5.0 (10) M	2.6 (8) M
IRELAND	0.00 (17)	10.7 (14)	P	1	3.2 (13) M	5.6 (5) H	5.1 (3) H
Average:		12.8			3.7	5.1	2.8
Median:		12.3			3.4	5.0	2.2

[a]See text and chapter 2 for measures and discussion of marginal cases and subtypes.

[b]Average of social security expenditures divided by GNP at factor cost for each year 1950–74 inclusive.

[c]Strong annual real growth in GDP, good control of inflation, and low unemployment are each averaged for the period, ranked high (2), medium (1), and low (0)—using natural cutting points—and then added together to yield the index, with a possible range of 0 to 6. See text and appendix G.

[d]Average annual real growth of GDP per capita. Except for four countries the averages are for the 24 years 1951–74. For Belgium and Japan the averages cover 1954–74. For New Zealand and Finland the averages cover 1955–74. Sources: UN, *Yearbook of National Accounts Statistics* (Geneva, various years), "International Tables," table 4a, except for Australia and New Zealand, where data are from OECD, *National Accounts Statistics of OECD Countries* (Paris, various years).

[e]Average percentage increase in the GNP price deflator for the 24 years 1951–74. Source: UN, *Yearbook of National Accounts Statistics 1979,* vol. 2, table 10a.

[f]Three-year averages of the unemployment rate centered on the following years—1950, 1955, 1960, 1965, 1970, and 1973. Table reports the average of these six figures. Source for the unemployment rate for all countries except Israel: OECD, *Labour Force Statistics* (Paris, various years). Whenever possible these figures were adjusted to compensate for differing methods of measuring unemployment by reference to OECD, "Unemployment Rates Adjusted to International Concepts, 1950–74, Nine Countries," (unpublished mimeo). For Israel, the source is UN, *Yearbook of Labor Statistics* (New York, various years).

In short, if good economic performance is high annual real growth per capita, low inflation, and low unemployment, and we are willing to weigh the three measures as roughly equal, then the countries that invest heavily in social security have a substantial edge over the lean spenders during that quarter century. To pin the blame for poor performance on generous social spending is to distort the record. In fact, if there is any central tendency in these data, we would have to conclude that social spending is good for your economic health.

Corporatism and Economic Performance 1950–74

The correlation between corporatism scores (without regard to types of corporatism) and economic performance is .39 ($p < .05$). If we take account of types of corporatism and note ambiguous cases, the results are stronger: corporatist countries (with two notable exceptions) have an edge in economic performance. Of the top nine economic performers, six are clearly corporatist: Sweden, Norway, Belgium, the Netherlands, Finland, and Austria. One, Japan, can be classified as clearly corporatist-without-labor; another, Switzerland, is an ambiguous case. (But see Katzenstein, 1984.) Germany, although it scores low on our formal measure of corporatism, is perhaps marginally corporatist (see discussion in chap. 2). The box score for the nine strongest economies: seven clear cases of corporatism, two ambiguous cases.

Now contrast the 10 countries that lag in economic performance. Only 4 are either corporatist or marginally corporatist. Denmark, which is marginally corporatist (with a numerical score of medium), is average in economic growth, inflation, and unemployment, so it cannot count against the hypothesis that corporatism fosters effective economic management. France, with high per capita growth, high inflation, and medium unemployment, is a case of corporatism without labor, so it is a partial contradiction. There remain Italy and Israel, which are sufficiently corporatist to count partly against the hypotheses. "Partly," because they have both been strong in per capita growth, but weak in controlling inflation and unemployment. These two corporatist democracies are deviant in more ways than one. Italy is the 1 country among our 19 that appears to spend lavishly while its tax collection for much of that period has been only average. (Wilensky, 1976, pp. 11, 16.) Although there is generally no direct link between government deficits and inflation (cf. Cameron, 1982, pp. 54–55; Alber, 1982, p. 25), the frequency, size, and acceleration of Italy's deficits have perhaps been bad for both inflation and unemployment. And Israel's unique defense burden has clearly been a drag on those two aspects of performance. That leaves Britain and Britain abroad (Australia, New Zealand, USA, Canada, and Ireland) as least corporatist and least effective in managing their economies.

The Interaction of Types of Political Economy, Spending, and Economic Performance 1950–74

We already know that corporatist democracies tend toward big spending and taxing, even controlling for such powerful predictors of social-security spending as the fraction of population who are aged (chap. 5 and Wilensky, 1976). The correlation between corporatism scores and average social-security spending as a fraction of GNP 1950–74 is .51 ($p < .05$). If we now examine the economic performance of corporatist big spenders and taxers, taking account of types of political economy and ambiguous cases, we arrive at the picture in table 12.2.

Thus, the combination of corporatist bargaining arrangements and medium to heavy social spending has yielded good to excellent economic performance in Sweden, Norway,

TABLE 12.2 Interaction of types of political economy, welfare effort, and economic performance, 1950–74

Number	Interaction Pattern	Countries
(1)	Most corporatist Medium to big spenders Good economic performance	Sweden Norway Belgium Finland Netherlands Austria
(2)	Marginally corporatist Big Spenders Excellent economic performance	W Germany
(3)	Corporatist without labor Lean spenders Good economic performance	Switzerland Japan
(4)	Corporatist without labor Big spenders Fair economic performance	France
(5)	Corporatist Big spenders Fair or fair-to-poor economic performance	Denmark Italy
(6)	Least corporatist Lean-average spenders Fair, fair-to-poor to poor economic performance	U.K. Canada U.S.A. N Zealand Australia Ireland
(7)	Corporatist Lean spenders Fair to poor economic performance	Israel

Belgium, Finland, the Netherlands, Austria, and Germany. The least-corporatist, lean to average spenders, have, in contrast, not shaped up in economic performance: the UK, Canada, the USA, New Zealand, and Australia all had low growth per capita, and a mixed performance by other measures. Ireland had medium growth but high unemployment and high inflation. By the standards of rich democracies, their restraint in social-security spending and their greater reliance on an unfettered free market not only for competing firms but also for competing interest groups and localities has not paid off in economic well-being.

The countries that deviate from these two patterns (groups 3, 4, and 5) are corporatist-without-labor or during the period at issue had unstable or less fully developed corporatist bargaining arrangements. As I suggested above, political economies that exclude labor federations from full participation in social and economic policy decisions are in a position to achieve good economic performance without social spending responsive to labor demands—for example, Japan and Switzerland. Or, if like France and Italy, they spend a lot on social security but do not create the consensus necessary for labor peace, they suffer erratic economic performance, reflected in low averages. Denmark, as its marginal score for corporatism suggests, has not developed the relatively stable, centralized bargaining structures of its neighbors Norway and Sweden, where powerful employer federations and labor federations routinely make the trade-offs that enhance economic performance, a theme to which we return after reporting the postshock results.

Postshock Economic Performance 1974–79 and 1980–84

I have argued that corporatist democracies, compared to least-corporatist democracies, are more adaptable to crises, whether internally or externally generated (chap. 2, and Wilensky, 1976a, p. 8). Or, put another way, "the fiscal crisis of the state" or "the crisis of the welfare state" varies so much in its depth and duration that such phrases obscure major structural and cultural differences among "late capitalist" countries, differences that are fateful for both economic performance and the quality of life. The adaptability of our 19 rich democracies to the Arab oil shocks of 1973–74 and 1979 and the worldwide recessions of 1974–75 and 1980–82 varies greatly and can therefore provide a test of the theme that corporatism fosters flexibility.

The years 1974–80 saw the most massive shift of wealth in modern history from the oil-dependent industrial countries to OPEC countries, a shift which was exacerbated by the second and most severe oil shock of 1979–80. Because the 19 rich democracies vary greatly in their energy dependence—from Canada and Australia (which in 1970 produced more energy than they consumed and were also low in dependence on oil) to Sweden and Denmark (which are highly dependent on oil and import almost all of their energy supplies)—we must judge their flexibility in facing the energy crisis in light of their differences in vulnerability to OPEC action.

Thus, if Canada, Australia, the UK, and the USA with their lesser vulnerability to these shocks do not outperform the highly vulnerable economies of Denmark, Sweden, Finland, and Italy, we can say that these well-positioned countries failed to get their act together. Conversely, if the heavy users of oil who produce so little of the energy they consume are able to hold their own by sinking only slightly in relative economic performance, or even improving, we can sing their praises and search for an explanation in structures and policies that go beyond good luck.

Some countries are in the unhappy position of entering a world crisis when they must buy dear and sell cheap. Thus, to the external shocks of this period we can add sudden shifts in the terms of trade—a measure much broader than oil shocks.

Social Spending and Economic Performance 1974–79 and 1980–84

Consider the economic performance of big spenders in 1974–79 pictured in table 12.3. Of the 9 best performers, only 2 (Japan and Switzerland) are welfare-state laggards. Of the

10 worst performers (fair to poor, poor to fair), only 1 is high in social spending (Denmark), and only 2 are slightly above the average; 7 are lean spenders. In fact, the old correlation between spending and the economic performance index remains positive, if insignificant, even in this postshock period, mainly because the welfare-state leaders did significantly better in growth ($r = .34$; $p < .10$), and did no worse in controlling inflation and unemployment. Again, *all* of the top nine in economic performance are corporatist democracies, with or without labor, while 6 of the bottom 10 are fragmented and decentralized systems. Of the 4 poor-performing corporatist democracies, 3 (Italy, Denmark, and Finland) are highly energy dependent; and all 4 experienced some deterioration in their terms of trade, 3 of them serious deterioration.

Both table 12.4 and the correlations show that the second bigger shock reduced the edge of corporatist big spenders to insignificance (corporatism scores × economic performance 1980−84 = −.06; social spending × performance = −.22).

Again, as we found for the period 1950−74, poor economic performance after the two oil shocks cannot be blamed on generous social spending. To more fully grasp the postshock experience, we must examine the interplay of types of corporatism, social spending, and vulnerability to external shocks and attend to the cases that do not fit my scheme.

The Interaction of Types of Political Economy, Spending, Energy Dependence, and Economic Performance, 1974−79 and 1980−91

Table 12.3 gives details and table 12.5 a summary overview of this interaction. Appendix G provides detailed figures on vulnerability to external shocks. How well did corporatist democracies cope with the energy price explosion of 1974? The answer depends on the types of corporatism and the vulnerability to OPEC's lavish world income-transfer program. The only striking pattern from table 12.3 is that corporatist democracies with only limited labor participation fared very well, at least by the summary measure of economic performance. The top-ranked seven include Japan and France (clearly corporatist-without-labor) and Switzerland (ambiguous on this point). Three other stellar performers (Norway, Austria, and the Netherlands) are clear cases of corporatism with labor, and one (Germany) is ambiguously corporatist. The pattern becomes stronger after the second bigger shock. By then Sweden and Finland join the ranks of relatively good performers; the rest retain their top seven standing, except for Netherlands and France, which drop substantially (see table 12.4, col. 2). The only noncorporatist country that makes the top eight in 1980−84 is the United States.

What about energy price vulnerability? We must take credit away from Norway and the United States; the former, although average in both energy production and oil dependence, had abundant hydroelectric power and North Sea oil to top it off; the USA was both low in oil dependence and was producing over 90% of its needs at the beginning of the period. Thus, special credit must go to Japan and Switzerland for leaping the OPEC hurdles with such gusto when so heavily handicapped at the start, and to Austria and France, whose vulnerability was above average. Their corporatist bargaining arrangements, with or without labor, proved adaptable in a deep crisis.

Examining the rest of table 12.3 and column 4 of table 12.1, we see that after the first oil shock, one of the corporatist big spenders that had a good economic record during the

TABLE 12.3 Arab oil shock, energy dependence, and pre- and post-1974 economic performance

Countries ranked by economic performance 1974-79	Average economic performance rating and score 1965-74 [a]		Average economic performance rating and score 1974-79 [b]		Vulnerability to Shock		Average social security effort (SS/GNP) 1975-77 [e]	Economic Performance 1974-79		
					Energy dependence index 1970 [c]	Change in terms of trade 1973-4 [d]		Average annual real growth per capita [f]	Average annual inflation [g]	Average annual unemployment [h]
JAPAN	G	4	E	6	4 H	.77	8.4 L	2.5 (6) H	8.1 (14) L	1.9 (15) L
NORWAY	F	3	E	6	2 M	1.03	21.9 MH	4.4 (1) H	8.2 (12) L	1.8 (17) L
AUSTRIA	E	6	E	6	2 M	.98	24.5 H	3.0 (3) H	6.0 (17) L	1.8 (17) L
WEST GERMANY	G	4	E	5	2 M	.91	26.2 H	2.5 (6) H	4.8 (18) L	3.2 (13) M
NETHERLANDS	F	3	G	4	1 ML	.96	30.1 H	1.9 (11) M	7.4 (16) L	4.9 (9) M
FRANCE	E	5	G	4	2 M	.86	28.0 H	2.6 (4) H	10.5 (9) M	4.5 (10) M
SWITZERLAND	F	3	G	4	4 H	.95	16.0 L	-0.2 (18) L	3.7 (19) L	0.4 (18) L
SWEDEN	F	3	F	3	4 H	.98	30.6 H	1.5 (15) L	10.6 (8) M	1.9 (15) L
BELGIUM	E	5	F	3	3 MH	.96	27.1 H	2.0 (10) M	8.1 (14) L	6.3 (5) H
DENMARK	FP	2	FP	2	4 H	.87	25.0 H	1.6 (13) L	10.2 (10) M	5.3 (6) M
FINLAND	F	3	FP	2	4 H	.99	19.4 M	2.0 (10) M	12.5 (6) H	4.4 (11) M
UNITED STATES	FP	2	FP	2	0 L	.86	14.8 L	1.6 (13) L	7.6 (15) L	6.7 (3) H
CANADA	F	3	FP	2	1 ML	1.07	15.1 L	2.1 (8) M	10.1 (11) M	7.2 (1) H
NEW ZEALAND	F	3	FP	2	2 M	.77	14.6 L	-0.4 (19) L	13.3 (5) H	0.3 (19) L
IRELAND	PF	1	FP	2	2 M	.85	20.9 M	3.0 (3) H	14.4 (4) H	7.0 (2) H
ITALY	FP	3	PF	1	4 H	.82	22.7 MH	2.1 (8) M	17.1 (2) H	6.6 (4) H
ISRAEL	FP	2	PF	1	2 M	.85	9.7 L	0.9 (17) L	47.7 (1) H	3.4 (12) M
UNITED KINGDOM	PF	1	PF	1	1 ML	.87	15.8 L	1.5 (15) L	16.0 (3) H	5.0 (8) M
AUSTRALIA	F	3	PF	1	0 L	.84	14.3 L	1.4 (16) L	12.2 (7) H	5.0 (8) M
Average:						.90	20.3	1.9	12.0	4.1
Median:						.87	20.9	2.0	10.2	4.5

[a]See footnotes to table 12.1 and appendix G.

[b]See footnote c to table 12.1.

[c]The equally weighted components of this index are liquid fuels (almost all oil) as a percentage of total energy consumption, and energy production as a percentage of energy consumption in 1970. Source: UN Dept. of Economic and Social Affairs, *World Energy Supplies 1969–72*, UN Statistical Papers. Series J, vol. 17, table 2 (New York, 1974).

[d]Ratio of changes in export prices to changes in import prices. A figure below 1.00 indicates that the country's terms of trade deteriorated from 1973 to 1974. Source: see appendix G.

[e]An average of social-security spending as a percentage of GNP at factor cost for 1975, 1976, and 1977. Source: ILO, *Cost of Social Security: Tenth International Inquiry, 1975–77* (Geneva, ILO, 1981). See appendix C.

[f]Source: UN, *Yearbook of National Accounts Statistics 1979*, vol. II, table 6a (UN, New York, 1980). See appendix G for minor variations.

[g]Source: UN, *Yearbook of National Accounts Statistics 1979*, vol. II, table 10a (UN, New York, 1980). See appendix G for minor variations.

[h]All data are from OECD, *Labour Force Statistics 1968–79*, table II (OECD, Paris, 1981), with one exception. Israeli figure is from ILO, *Yearbook of Labor Statistics*, table 10 (ILO, Geneva, 1980).

preshock period 1950–74 slid substantially (Finland's score moved from good to below average, 4 to 2), and two (Belgium, Sweden) dropped from good to fair (4 to 3). The weak energy position of all but the Netherlands is part of the explanation.

Table 12.3 and appendix G show that both Belgium and Finland produced less than a fifth of their energy needs at the beginning of the period (ranking 13th and 18th) and ranked medium in their dependence on oil. Sweden, which scored average in economic performance, ranked near the bottom in domestic production of total energy consumption (17th) and near the top in dependence on oil. Thus, its postshock economic performance

TABLE 12.4 Vulnerability to energy shocks, welfare effort, and economic performance since 1980

Countries ranked by economic performance 1980-84	Average economic performance rating and score 1974-79[a]		Average economic performance rating and score 1980-84[a]		Vulnerability to Shock		Social security effort (SS/GNP) 1980[d]	Economic Performance 1980-84		
					Energy dependence index 1978[b]	Change in terms of trade 1978-9[c]		Average annual real growth per capita[e]	Average annual inflation[f]	Average annual unemployment[g]
JAPAN	E	6	E	6	4 H	.84	11.0 L	3.3 (1) H	2.0 (18) L	2.4 (17) L
SWITZERLAND	G	4	E	5	3 MH	.96	16.0 L	1.0 (11) M	4.6 (15) L	0.6 (18) L
AUSTRIA	E	6	E	5	2 M	.99	26.3 MH	1.6 (5) M	5.3 (14) L	3.2 (14) L
NORWAY	E	6	G	4	1 ML	1.08	23.3 M	2.3 (4) H	10.5 (5) H	2.5 (16) L
WEST GERMANY	E	5	G	4	2 M	.95	27.0 MH	1.0 (11) M	3.7 (17) L	5.7 (11) M
UNITED STATES	FP	2	G	4	0 L	.96	14.6 L	0.9 (14) M	6.7 (12) L	8.2 (8) M
FINLAND	FP	2	G	4	3 MH	.97	21.1 M	2.8 (2) H	9.5 (8) M	5.1 (12) M
SWEDEN	F	3	G	4	3 MH	1.00	33.1 H	1.4 (7) M	9.5 (8) M	2.9 (15) L
BELGIUM	F	3	F	3	3 MH	1.01	29.8 H	1.0 (11) M	5.5 (13) L	11.3 (2) H
AUSTRALIA	PF	1	F	3	0 L	1.00	15.7 L	1.2 (8) M	9.5 (8) M	7.5 (10) M
NEW ZEALAND	FP	2	F	3	2 M	1.07	16.1 L	2.4 (3) H	10.8 (3) H	4.3 (13) M
NETHERLANDS	G	4	FP	2	0 L	.97	31.3 H	-0.3 (18) L	4.3 (16) L	9.9 (4) H
DENMARK	FP	2	FP	2	4 H	.94	32.8 H	1.5 (6) M	8.7 (10) M	9.6 (6) H
ITALY	P	1	FP	2	3 MH	.98	19.6 M	0.9 (14) M	16.5 (1) H	8.6 (7) M
CANADA	FP	2	P	1	1 ML	1.06	15.1 L	0.6 (16) L	8.0 (11) M	9.8 (5) H
UNITED KINGDOM	P	1	P	1	0 L	1.04	17.3 L	0.5 (17) L	9.6 (6) M	10.3 (3) H
FRANCE	G	4	P	1	2 M	1.00	30.4 H	0.6 (16) L	10.7 (4) H	8.0 (9) M
IRELAND	FP	2	P	1	2 M	.96	23.3 M	1.1 (9) M	13.1 (2) H	11.6 (1) H
Average:						.99	22.4	1.3	8.2	6.8
Median:						.98	22.2	1.0	9.1	7.6

[a]See footnotes to table 12.3 and appendix G.

[b]See footnote c to table 12.3 and appendix G. Source: UN, *World Energy Supply, 1973–78* (UN, New York, 1980).

[c]Ratio of changes in export prices to changes in import prices 1978 to 1979. See footnote d to table 12.3 and appendix G.

[d]Social-security spending as a percentage of GNP at factor cost for 1980. Source: ILO, *Cost of Social Security, Eleventh International Inquiry, 1978–80* (Geneva, ILO, 1985). See Appendix C.

[e]Source: OECD, *National Accounts Statistics of OECD Countries 1960–84,* growth triangles (Paris, 1986).

[f]Average annual change in the GDP implicit price deflator 1980–84. Source: *Ibid.*

[g]Standardized unemployment rate from OECD, *Quarterly Labour Force Statistics,* 1989, No. 2, except for Switzerland, Denmark, New Zealand, Austria, and Ireland. For these countries, unemployment rates are unadjusted, from OECD *Labour Force Statistics 1964–84.*

relative to its position was not bad. The Netherlands, low in its oil dependence, was fifth in energy production (and, by rapid increase in natural gas production, arrived at surplus by 1972); its average economic performance was thus not as good as Sweden's.

In chapter 2, I discussed the structural changes in Dutch labor relations and social life that culminated in the unusual strikes of 1973 and subsequent erosion of the social partnership. We might interpret the somewhat less impressive economic performance of the Netherlands after 1980 as a reflection of a swifter decline in its long-standing corporatist consensus compared to other corporatist democracies experiencing similar strains, although the erosion is exaggerated and both the bargaining arrangements and economic performance were strengthened in the 1990s.

There remains the trio of partial exceptions to the rule of good economic performance of corporatist democracies during 1950–74—Denmark, Italy, and Israel (table 12.1). They dropped from mediocre to below average or poor (table 12.5), continuing their problematic general performance. But, again, all three at the outset were in a very poor energy position—almost completely dependent on oil, with Italy and Denmark producing only trivial amounts of their energy needs. (Israel, high in energy production in 1970, by 1976 had dropped to 1.6% of its 1975 production because it returned the Abu Rudeis and Sudir oil fields to Egypt in compliance with the interim agreement of September 1975. The oil fields were given up on November 30, 1975.) After the second shock, 1980–84, this trio stayed toward the bottom, now joined by France and the Netherlands.

In the more quiescent period of 1985–89, after energy prices collapsed, only one of the six least-corporatist lean spenders achieved more than average economic performance (USA), while three of the nine corporatist big spenders that included labor maintained their very good performance, and only three were below average (data on Israel are missing). Japan and Switzerland continued their winning ways. (See table 12.5.)[1]

Scores combining real growth, inflation, and unemployment, while useful for this quick overview, obscure some interesting patterns that divide corporatist democracies from the more-fragmented and decentralized political economies. During the post-1974 shock period (and before interest rates in the U.S. zoomed), the corporatist countries, including several welfare-state leaders, tend to have the best record on both inflation and unemployment; their real growth per capita, however, is either very good or very bad. For instance, in 1974–79,

1. *Of the eight countries with only single-digit inflation* (below the median case of Denmark, with an inflation rate of 10.2%) *seven are more or less corporatist* (Norway, Belgium, Netherlands, and Austria clearly corporatist with labor, Germany marginally so, plus Japan and Switzerland). Of these eight with relatively low inflation, five are corporatist big spenders. Of the seven *highest* in postshock inflation—from Israel's 47.7% to Australia's 12.2—only three are corporatist (Israel, Italy, and Finland).

2. *Of the six countries with very low unemployment* (New Zealand, Switzerland, Norway, Austria, Sweden, and Japan) *only one, New Zealand, is clearly noncorporatist.* All four of the next best users of human resources—Germany, Israel, Finland, France, ranging from 3.2% to 4.5% unemployment—are more or less corporatist. France, with 4.5%, is the median case. That leaves the worst nine, with unemployment ranging from the Netherlands' 4.9% to Canada's 7.2%; only four are corporatist (Belgium, Italy, Netherlands, Denmark).

3. *Although corporatism in the postshock crisis clearly fostered inflation control and good use of human resources, there was no consistent pattern for real growth per capita during those five years.* Of the six fastest growth countries (Norway, Japan, West Germany, France, Austria, Ireland), only Ireland is clearly not corporatist. But of the eight with the slowest growth, half are corporatist (Sweden, Denmark, Israel, Switzerland) and half are not (USA, UK, Australia, New Zealand).

The record of corporatist democracies in coping with the multiple shocks of the early 1980s is even more impressive than their record after the first oil shocks, suggesting that they learned more. Again, they kept unemployment and inflation under better control than

TABLE 12.5 The interaction of political economy, vulnerability to energy shocks, welfare effort, and economic performance, 1950–89

High vulnerability to energy shocks, 1970

Corporatist without labor; lean spenders

	Econ. perf. index				
	1950 -74	1965 -74	1974 -79	1980 -84	1985 -89
Japan	4	4	6	6	6
Switzerland	4	3	4	5	5
Averages	4.0	3.6	5.0	5.5	5.5

Corporatist big spenders

	Econ. perf. index				
	1950 -74	1965 -74	1974 -79	1980 -84	1985 -89
Sweden	4	3	3	4	3
Finland	4	3	2	4	3
Belgium	4	5	3	3	4
Denmark	3	2	2	2	2
Italy	3	2	1	1	2
Averages	3.6	3.0	2.2	2.8	2.8

Low to medium vulnerability to energy shocks, 1970

Corporatist without labor; big spender

	Econ. perf. index				
	1950 -74	1965 -74	1974 -79	1980 -84	1985 -89
France	3	5	4	1	2
Averages	3.0	5.0	4.0	1.0	2.0

Corporatist big spenders★★

	Econ. perf. index				
	1950 -74	1965 -74	1974 -79	1980 -84	1985 -89
W. Germany★	5	4	5	4	4
Norway★	4	3	6	5	3
Austria	4	6	6	5	5
Netherlands★	4	3	4	2	2
Israel	2	2	1	—	—
Averages	3.8	3.6	4.4	4.0	3.5

Least corporatist lean spenders

	Econ. perf. index				
	1950 -74	1965 -74	1974 -79	1980 -84	1985 -89
New Zealand	3	3	2	3	1
Australia★	3	3	1	3	2
United States★	2	2	2	4	4
Canada★	2	3	2	1	2
United Kingdom★	2	1	1	1	2
Ireland	1	1	2	1	3
Averages	2.2	2.2	1.7	2.2	2.3

★★Germany a marginal case of corporatism; Israel a lean spender.
★Least vulnerable to energy shocks.

did their least-corporatist brothers. As table 12.4 shows, six of the seven countries with the lowest inflation 1980–84 were corporatist (Japan, Switzerland, Austria, West Germany, Belgium, and the Netherlands); the United States was the lone exception. Similarly, all of the five lowest in unemployment were corporatist (Japan, Switzerland, Austria, Norway, Sweden). Again, there is no pattern for real growth. This picture is confirmed by our summary measure for this most difficult crisis period: of the eight countries that score above average or better (4, 5, or 6) on the economic performance index, seven are corporatist with or without labor.

Finally, the superior performance of corporatist democracies continued in the relatively good time of 1985–89 (see the overview in table 12.5 which presents summary scores for all countries and all periods and table 12.6, a summary of each component): five of the six countries that score above average or better (Belgium, Austria, West Germany, Japan, Switzerland) are corporatist, with or without labor.

The four problem cases (Italy, Denmark, France, the Netherlands), however, joined Britain and Britain abroad (New Zealand, Australia, Canada), continuing as poor performers; all four, as we have seen, have experienced some erosion of institutions supporting a social contract. By radically Keynesian deficit spending and consumption-led recovery without raising productivity to support it, the United States under Reagan became the 1980s great exception, with an above-average performance (see Friedman, 1989, pp. 109–162). As the world entered the recession of 1990–92, however, the United States returned to its pre-1980 performance, below average. Index scores combining three measures of economic performance for 1990–92 (table not reported) show that of the top 8 of 18 countries ranked, all but Ireland are corporatist democracies, 6 of them big spenders. Of the 10 worst performers (scoring 2 or 1), 5 are noncorporatist democracies (the USA, Australia, New Zealand, Canada, and the UK), whose social spending is below average.

In sum, if we bring the entire universe of rich democracies to view and examine their experience from 1950 to 1992, we find the following: (1) corporatist democracies—with a couple of possible exceptions (Japan and Switzerland, both with systems that do not fully integrate labor into social and economic policy making and implementation)—tend to devote more of their resources to the social-security package and related social spending (see chap. 5 and appendix C for measures and elaboration); (2) corporatist democracies pursue tax policies that strike a balance between painfully visible taxes (modest income taxes and property taxes on households), hefty social-security contributions, and heavy consumption taxes, thereby permitting high levels of taxation with minimal political uproar (Wilensky, 1976a, and chapter 10 above); (3) such social spending and taxing, far from constituting a brake on good economic performance, is a positive contribution; and (4) corporatist big spenders and taxers on average had an edge in economic performance, definitely before 1975, and if we take account of differences in their exposure to the oil shock of 1973–74 and the multiple shocks of 1979–82, even up to 1992, clearly in low inflation and low unemployment, less clearly in economic growth.

Prominent in the demonology of Reaganomics, even among some academic economists, is an imaginary vicious circle of confiscatory taxing, runaway social spending followed inevitably by inflation, declining capital investment, no growth, and unemployment, followed by more demands for welfare entitlements, and so on. In fact, what we see in the wondrous variety of real experience is a mildly benign circle: the consensus-making machinery

TABLE 12.6 Economic performance 1985−89 and 1990−96

Country	Economic Performance							
	1985-89				1990-96			
	Index	Growth	Inflation	Unempl.	Index	Growth	Inflation	Unempl.
Japan	6	H	L	L	6	H	L	L
Switzerland	5	M	L	L	3	L	M	L
Austria	5	M	L	L	3	M	H	L
United States	4	M	L	M	4	M	M	L
W. Germany[a]	4	M	L	M	2	M	H	M
Belgium	4	H	L	H	3	M	M	M
Sweden	3	M	H	L	2	L	H	L
Norway	3	L	M	L	5	H	M	L
Finland	3	H	H	M	2	L	L	H
Ireland	3	H	M	H	4	H	L	H
Canada	2	M	M	H	2	L	L	H
Denmark	2	L	M	M	4	H	M	M
Australia	2	M	H	M	4	H	L	H
France	2	M	M	H	1	L	M	H
United Kingdom	2	H	H	H	2	M	H	M
Netherlands	2	L	L	H	4	H	M	M
Italy	2	H	H	H	1	M	H	H
New Zealand	1	L	H	M	4	H	M	M

[a]1990−96 data are for unified Germany.

of corporatist democracies fostered fuller utilization of human resources and high levels of taxing and social spending, which together facilitate the kind of trade-offs between major economic actors that apparently result in better performance through thick and thin.

WHAT HAPPENED IN THE 1990S?

This picture changed in the 1990s. From 1990 through 1996, types of political economy were unrelated to average economic performance measured by my index; but corporatist democracies, with or without labor, continued to outperform noncorporatist democracies in holding down unemployment (average for corporatism-without-labor, 5.5% with Japan and Switzerland leading; average for democratic corporatist countries, 7.8%; for least-corporatist democracies, 9.3%). Least-corporatist democracies, however, had a slight edge in controlling inflation (2.6% vs. 2.9% for noncorporatist democracies, with the best performance again going to corporatism-without-labor). The real GDP per capita growth per year was 2.3% for least-corporatist, 2.0% for corporatist democracies; the worst performance goes to corporatism-without-labor, 0.4%, with Switzerland and France at the bottom and

Japan with an above-average 1.5%.

If we add figures available on labor-productivity growth in recent years (1979–96), real compensation growth per year (1989–96), and household income inequality about 1990, we find that by these measures of economic performance, our types of political economy predict the rank order in the usual way. Table 12.7 presents the scores and ranks by type of political economy.

By wide margins and for all three measures, corporatist democracies, especially those with strong left or competing left and Catholic parties, clearly outpace the more-fragmented and decentralized political economies as well as corporatist democracies that keep labor at a distance. They shine in labor productivity growth, real compensation growth, and the achievement of more household equality. In per capita income growth per year 1989–96 (using purchasing power parities for 12 countries available) the U.S., Canada, and France were the worst performers. Of seven corporatist democracies on that list, six had relatively high income growth. (BLS data analyzed by Mishel, Bernstein, and Schmitt, 1999, table 8.2.) Again we see that the greater earnings and income equality, job security, welfare-state protections, and poverty reductions of corporatist democracies have not retarded their productivity and income growth in the 1990s. And that the free marketeer United States falls at or near the bottom in these things.[2]

JAPAN VERSUS THE UNITED STATES: TRADING PLACES?

The elements of the Japanese model—union-management cooperation at the enterprise level, lean production methods (chap. 1), relationship banking, close business-industry-government ties, long-term employment security, low turnover, stable supplier networks, cheap capital, and massive savings—for decades pictured as secrets of Japan's success are now said to be the causes of its 1990s crisis. American triumphalists have pronounced the Japanese model dead and urged Japan to adopt American ways. There is no doubt that while the U.S. was moving to the top of the heap in economic performance in the mid to late 1990s, at least in GDP growth, job creation, declining unemployment and low inflation, Japan was mired in stagnation and recession. However, as we have seen, compared to the U.S., Japan's unemployment rate remained low (rising 50% from 2% to an unprecedented 3%), its productivity growth continued high, and its achievement of equality in workplace and society and its poverty reduction remained intact.

A careful analysis by Adam Posen (1998) shows that the model that brought sustained success cannot explain 1990s failures. Instead, the root of Japan's troubles is a series of major policy mistakes: it is a story of procyclical macroeconomic policies—fiscal austerity, mistimed shifts in taxing and spending, and lax supervision of banks followed by the wrong kind of reregulation. The proximate cause of the 1990s recession was a credit boom beginning in the mid-1980s, encouraged by the deregulation of banks and the easy monetary policy of the Finance Ministry and the Bank of Japan—the bubble in equity and property values that burst. Having allowed the expansion of shaky loans and speculative fever to go on too long, the central bank then responded by interest-rate hikes in 1989 that were similarly long-lasting, pushing Japan into a recession (*ibid.*, pp. 17–22). The government for its part prolonged the recession by tight fiscal policies. When confidence eroded, resulting

TABLE 12.7 Types of political economy, recent growth in labor productivity and real compensation, and household income inequality

	Labor productivity growth, 1979-96 (%)[b]		Real compensation growth / year, 1989-96 (%)[c]		Household disposable income inequality (90/10 ratio), circa 1990[d]	
Left Corporatist[a]						
Sweden	2.0	(8)	0.8	(8)	2.78	(17)
Norway	1.8	(10)	1.4	(4)	2.80	(15)
Finland	3.6	(2)	2.3	(1)	2.75	(18)
Denmark	2.1	(6)	1.6	(3)	2.86	(14)
cell avg.	2.4		1.5		2.80	
Left-Catholic Corporatist						
Netherlands	1.6	(12)	0.4	(15)	3.05	(13)
Belgium	2.0	(8)	1.7	(2)	2.79	(16)
Austria	2.3	(3)	1.3	(6)	3.34	(10)
cell avg.	2.0		1.1		3.06	
Catholic Corporatist						
Italy	2.1	(6)	0.7	(9)	3.14	(12)
(West) Germany	1.1	(15)	-0.1	(17)	3.21	(11)
cell avg.	1.6		0.3		3.18	
Corporatist Without Labor						
France	2.2	(4)	1.1	(7)	3.48	(7)
Japan	2.2	(4)	0.7	(9)	4.17	(5)
Switzerland	0.4	(18)	0.7	(9)	3.43	(9)
cell avg.	1.6		0.8		3.69	
Least Corporatist						
United States	0.8	(17)	0.1	(16)	5.78	(1)
United Kingdom	1.8	(10)	0.5	(13)	4.67	(2)
New Zealand	1.3	(13)	-0.8	(18)	3.46	(8)
Australia	1.3	(13)	0.6	(12)	4.30	(3)
Canada	1.0	(16)	0.5	(13)	3.90	(6)
Ireland	3.9	(1)	1.4	(4)	4.18	(4)
cell avg.	1.7		0.4		4.38	
18 country avg.	1.9		0.8		3.6	

[a]Israel missing.

[b]Business sector average percent increase per year. Source: OECD data in Mishel, Bernstein, and Schmitt (1999), table 8.4. The Irish exception is discussed in chapter 2.

[c]Compensation per employee in business sector. Growth rate for West Germany, 1979–91; unified Germany, 1992–96. Source: OECD data analyzed by *ibid.*, table 8.5.

[d]Source: Gottschalk and Smeeding (1997), figure 2. Post-tax and transfer income adjusted by household size based on real income (1991 U.S. dollars) as percentage of national median. The 10th percentile receives a higher income than 10% of the population.

in an investment bust, the government did not act. Industrial production declined sharply in 1992–93 and again in 1997–98 and did not return to 1991 levels for the rest of the 1990s. Consumer spending's contribution to GNP growth never regained its 1988–90 level. Real GDP annual growth 1992–97 was only 1.2%, worse than the USA's 2.8 and below that of most European countries. The boom and bust can be largely explained by major swings in nonresidential investment and private consumption (pp. 19, 23) leading to deflation in the mid-1990s and a classic Keynesian "liquidity trap," when expectations about the long-run return on capital drop so much that interest rates become insensitive to monetary policy and investment becomes insensitive to interest rates. The devastating 1995 Kobe earthquake was an added drag.

Confronted with the results of its lax regulation of banks, its encouragement of a speculative credit boom and bust, the Japanese government did briefly engage in a successful anticyclical policy. But it was a stop-go-stop policy that prolonged a poor performance for several years. The central bank cut its discount rate from 1.75 where it had been held since mid-1993 to 0.5 in September 1995, which had little effect, but the government coupled this with fiscal stimulus—actual public spending of more than 1.6% of GDP, mainly on public works, education, and science.[3] (A tax revenue decline due to the recession also helped.) This stimulus package led to economic growth of 3.6% in 1996. Far from crowding out private investment, it fostered a strong rise in nonresidential investment in 1995 and 1996, as well. (*Ibid.*, pp. 45–50.) But then the next series of policy mistakes led quickly to another contraction: a cut in public investment and a tax increase (a consumption tax increase from 3% to 5% in April 1997). Again growth was reduced and went negative in 1998. This contractionary policy was accompanied by repeated warnings from the Ministry of Finance that the aging of the population would soon bring a huge burden of social-security taxes. Such warnings naturally increased precautionary hoarding by millions of Japanese who already had an overdeveloped savings propensity. Finally, the deregulation of banks that got the financial system into deep trouble[4] was followed by reregulation of a perverse sort (pp. 127–132). The Finance Ministry pursued a "no failure" policy that hurt the banks that were most viable while continuing the cycle of bad lending by the others (the wildly undercapitalized banks had nothing to lose by making still more risky loans). Not until 1995 did this policy begin to reverse (e.g., some small banks were threatened with insolvency if they did not merge with sound institutions). By 1998 a little progress also was made in replenishing deposit insurance funds and recapitalizing banks. But the money is not targeted to viable banks; it goes to all of them indiscriminately.

As Posen shows, in view of these cumulating policy mistakes, it is misleading to attribute the depth and duration of Japan's recent business cycle to the alleged bureaucratic rigidity, inefficiency, and corruption of the "Japanese model." And "no wrenching transformation of [this model] beyond banking reform is required" (p. 114). One reason for believing that the 1990s did not reflect some systemic ailment is that the U.S. in the 1980s was a mirror image of Japan in the 1990s, except for its loose fiscal policy. Japan's cycle of financial boom and bust followed its last round of banking deregulation, exactly the path of unthinking deregulation of financial institutions that led to the U.S. savings and loan crisis. In the late 1980s the U.S. evidenced similar delays in recognizing the crisis; it was not until the passage of FIRREA in 1991 that action was taken, and its cost was colossal. In both cases it was the failure to regulate properly that encouraged grand-scale speculative loans and considerable corruption—casino capitalism style. Neither Japan nor the United States is in a position to lecture the other about its superior system.

During the years of Japan's troubles, especially 1993–99, the U.S. outpaced not only Japan but most European democracies in lowering unemployment while achieving moderate GDP per capita growth with low inflation. Can this be explained by a surge in productivity? Not if the productivity changes in table 12.7 (and the 1990–96 record) reported above are accurate. The U.S. performance of the past seven years can better be explained by a convergence of benign macroeconomic policies, the closer supervision of financial institutions (having got the S&L crisis behind it), and possibly (a trend affecting all rich democracies), the delayed effect of the spread of information technology. The taxing and spending policies of the Clinton administration beginning with the 1993 budget (including an increase in taxes on high-income groups) put the annual deficit on a downward path. This was designed to encourage the Federal Reserve Board to move from high real interest rates to medium real rates, thereby allowing increased GDP growth per capita and a decline in unemployment. Modest increases in the minimum wage and the Earned Income Tax Credit reduced poverty after 1995 and boosted the income and consumption of the working poor. More important, very high consumer debt added to consumption-led growth (the opposite of the explosion of savings and hoarding in Japan). Further impetus to growth was the continued willingness of foreign investors to finance the U.S. debt. Meanwhile the cumulative effects of a labor-crunch recovery and new technology began to pay off in the mid-1990s, reflected in growth with low inflation through 1999. Corporate America for 20 or so years has put unrelenting pressure on its employees. Their focus has been on cutting labor costs by downsizing, subcontracting, hiring more temporary and part-time workers at low pay and limited benefits, and making both part-timers and full-timers do more work for less pay while they bear more of the cost of benefits such as health care (see chaps. 1 and 16). After 1981, when President Reagan broke the PATCO strike, employer antiunion militancy intensified, hastening the earlier decline of the labor movement (chap. 18 discusses the sources of this decline). By maintaining annual hours of work at the highest level among rich democracies (chap. 1), the U.S. has become the leading enemy of leisure. The more hours of work, the more production, which contributes to the disparity between economic growth and lagging productivity growth. Americans work more and longer, not harder and smarter than other modern populations. With its hysteria about crime and its rigid long sentences in the 1990s (chaps. 14 and 18), the U.S. has reached the highest rate of incarceration. This accounts for 1.9 percentage points of measured unemployment—that is, with the low prison population of other democracies, the U.S. would record higher unemployment rates (Western and Beckett, 1999, table 4).[5] (These American peculiarities are discussed in chap. 18.)

As a result of the labor-crunch strategy, the intensification of work, decreased union strength, and lowered labor costs, the U.S. has been enormously successful in creating new low-wage jobs (see chap. 13), holding costs in check, and increasing the returns to the affluent educated. These trends together widened profit margins and accelerated the compensation of top executives and professionals while real wages either stagnated or declined since the early 1970s. This coincides with a massive upward redistribution of wealth and income in the 1980s and 1990s (see tables 12.7 and 14.4; Mishel et al., 1999; and Wolff, 1995). Corporate profit margins in 1996 reached 9.6% of GDP, the highest share in 28 years, while labor compensation declined below the 59% peak of the late 1980s. That the labor crunch was a major part of the economic performance of the 1990s rather than a surge in productivity is confirmed by Commerce Department studies (including its 1997 comprehensive revision of the national economic accounts) showing anemic productivity growth in the 1990s—a time of sustained recovery and unprecedented prosperity for Wall Street and the upper fifth of U.S. households. The average U.S. productivity gain in table 12.7 is below 1% per year, about the same as the 1980s and less than half the gain of the 1950s and 1960s.

This low-road performance does encounter the law of diminishing returns. Many rapidly downsizing labor-crunching corporations have discovered that their lack of loyalty to their employees and communities is reciprocated and that higher turnover has its own costs, including the loss of organizational memory, essential skills, and customer contacts. Evidence suggests that downsizing in recent years actually reduced productivity and profits (*Wall Street Journal*, Feb. 21, 2001). By the end of the 1990s some of these firms were cultivating employee commitment and even community goodwill and investing more in training in a sometimes radical change of course. Whether this will spread is an open question. The continued decline of American institutions that offset the political and economic power of business (chaps. 2 and 3) make it unlikely. (For a cross-national comparison of differences in the organization of work and worker participation, see chap. 1.)

In late 1995 U.S. productivity began to surge, averaging 2.6% annual growth for the next four years (although the government in August 2001 revised these figures downward for the entire 1990s to 2%). Technological enthusiasts, who had been saying that the new information technology would result in a major permanent rise in productivity increases, pointed to these increases as the long-delayed payoff. The increases were concentrated in "service" sectors such as transportation, public utilities, trade, finance, insurance, real estate, and professional and business services, and among the more-educated workers in those areas. Government statistics on hours report that the average workweek in the service sector in 1999 was 32.9—about five fewer hours than reported for 1964 when the revolution presumably had not yet occurred. Common observation of the workaholics in those industries as well as special surveys by the Department of Labor and polling groups, however, suggest that these hours figures cannot be taken seriously—and neither can productivity growth figures based on them (added value per unit of work time). Two difficulties: First, the laptops, cell phones, and computerized offices tie the so-called knowledge workers to their offices for unmeasured unofficial added work hours on trains, planes, homes, and vacations. As chapter 1 indicates, the fraction of the labor force working more than 55 hours per week has been climbing for some time. Second, there is little many of these workers can do to increase their productivity and less the statisticians can do to measure it. How do we measure the productivity of a string quartet? A technical sales executive playing customer golf? The professor training a future research professor by long hours of mentoring? The biotech researcher, very few of whose projects pay off? These well-known difficulties in measuring productivity led me to use other indicators of economic performance for most of my analysis.

Whatever happened in the 1990s, if we can sort out the structures and policies that account for the economic performance of all the rich democracies during the four preceding decades, we have accomplished a lot. The next section tackles that task.

Explaining National Differences in Economic Performance

If the welfare state as a whole is either a benign influence on competitiveness or irrelevant, if democratic corporatism is a clear advantage in achieving good long-run economic performance, what is the explanation? I first discuss some general hypotheses about the welfare-state impact and then apply systematic tests to sort out the most important specific causes of good economic performance especially characteristic of the most successful competitors among our 19 democracies.

Consider three sectors of social policy: *medical care and health; occupational health and safety;* and *active labor-market policy.* It seems reasonable to suppose that countries that increase dignified mass access to medical care and are aggressive in diffusing information about nutrition and other good health habits through schools, clinics, and child-care facilities will in the long run enhance the productivity of the labor force (see chap. 16). Similarly, insofar as the expense of job-injury insurance has inspired more preventative occupational health and safety programs in the workplace, it has enhanced productivity by reducing absenteeism and turnover and cutting costs. Although systematic comparisons of many countries have yet to be done, my comparison of Sweden and Germany vs. the United States in chapter 15 is suggestive. It shows that while all three increased both job-injury insurance spending and safety in the workplace, at least for the years data were available (1968 to 1976), the United States increased its accident-insurance spending more than Germany and Sweden, with less effect on safety, measured by trends in spending per capita and the decline in deaths from industrial accidents. The cost-benefit ratio for the Swedes was best, the Germans next, the Americans last, a rank order that fits the degree of industry-labor collaboration in implementing safety regulations and the commitment to prevention: the Swedes most, the Germans next, the Americans, least. Finally, there is strong evidence that those countries such as Sweden, Germany, and Japan that have invested in active labor-market policies (training and retraining, rehabilitation, job creation, placement, counseling, and mobility incentives, and a strong labor-market board), and have tried to reduce their reliance on passive unemployment insurance and social assistance, have a productivity edge over their competitors (Wilensky, 1985, 1992a; Wilensky and Turner, 1987, pp. 3–5, 25–31; and figure 2.2).

Beyond these still tentative generalizations, I can provide a general explanation for the economic advantages of corporatist bargaining arrangements and then more specific tests of hypotheses regarding the roots of growth, inflation control, and the reduction of unemployment, including further tests of the role of social spending. The general explanation is this: The centralization and broader bargaining focus of corporatist democracies make both elites and their staff experts aware of the interdependence of diverse public policies and the importance of medium-run, even long-run costs and gains (chap. 2 discusses the sources and effects of these policy linkages). Their concern with the "social contract" encourages at least some attention to hard-to-measure variables such as political legitimacy and social consensus, which, in turn, reduces uncertainty in industrial planning and investment. Finally, corporatism encourages stronger links between knowledge and power—a dialectic of expertise, a rational-responsible bias, which itself is a force for accommodation among competing interest groups, reflected in fruitful trade-offs (see chap. 2).

MEASURES OF TRADE-OFFS TYPICAL OF DEMOCRATIC CORPORATISM

The trade-offs that such structures facilitate are often directly relevant to productivity and macroeconomic performance. I here list these trade-offs and the measures available to assess them cross-nationally, then present data that show their relative importance in explaining the national variations previously examined. The corporatist trade-offs most positive for economic performance follow; details on measures and sources are in appendix G.

  1. *Labor restraint on nominal wages in return for social-security and related programs based on social rights and modest increases in real wages.*

Measures: OECD data for most of our countries 1965–73, 1974–79, 1980–84 do not distinguish between earnings (which take account of hours worked and overtime premiums) and wage rates (per unit of regular time like an hour). We used nominal hourly wages, filling in nominal earnings when nominal wages were not available; and real hourly earnings, filling in real wages when real earnings were not available.

A check on eight countries where either OECD or other researchers using different definitions have calculated both earnings and wage rates shows that while single years occasionally evidence large discrepancies, when we average them over the three periods used in the analysis the series are very close. (See appendix G.)

We computed three measures: *nominal wage changes, real earnings changes,* and *their relative acceleration* (the ratio of annual changes in one period divided by annual changes in the previous period, which takes account of a country's "normal" history of wage changes and also controls for built-in wage increases such as COLAs). Data are for manufacturing only.

It is clear from the strong correlation between nominal wage increases and inflation (.71 for 1965–74, .92 for 1974–79, .95 for 1980–84) that a large part of the story, especially 1974 on, was wage-push inflation. Hence, if some countries were constraining wages after the oil shocks, they were holding down inflation.

The payoff to labor—increases in the "social wage" by universal categorical benefits—is measured in five ways: social security as a percentage of GNP; social-security spending per capita; growth of SS/GNP; real growth of social security per capita; and the percentage of GNP spent for stigmatized means-tested benefits (vs. universal benefits).

  2. *Job protection in return for wage restraint, labor peace, and sometimes tax concessions* (lower taxes on corporations and capital gains).

Measures: For labor peace we use *strike rates* (average annual person-days lost to strikes or lockouts per 1,000 nonagricultural civilian employees 1960–72, 1973–77, 1978–82, 1983–87). A high strike rate is a proxy for poorly managed industrial relations systems. Strikes, both official and wildcat, are related to other, more continuous forms of industrial conflict at the workplace: sabotage, slowdowns, output restriction, as well as absenteeism, tardiness, playing dumb, quits, and grievance activity (see, e.g., Flaherty, 1987b, pp. 587–588, and Hodson, 1997). Both strike rates and associated job actions create bottlenecks and other inefficiencies, forestall managerial initiatives, and thereby increase unit costs and reduce economic performance. (Flaherty, 1987a; Norsworthy and Zabala, 1985, p. 557; and Hodson, 1997.)

In relating strikes to economic performance by period, we use both a one-year lag and no lag. The regression results are almost identical. In fact, the relative ranking of strikes in our countries remains similar for all of the period 1960–87.

We have no systematic comparative data for *job protection,* but there are numerous case studies of management concessions either coerced by labor movements and government or voluntarily given—ranging from accounts of lifetime employment in Japan to Western European laws and contracts that enhance job security (e.g., Emerson, 1988). My hypothesis: "While the employer may feel hemmed-in by laws and customs in hiring and firing, workers are likely to feel reasonably secure. . . . We must at least consider the possibility that job protection is a positive contribution to lowering unit costs by reducing worker sabotage, output restriction, slowdowns, strikes, and turnover" (Wilensky, 1981a, p.192; cf. ILO, 1995, pp. 156–157). It facilitates the rapid introduction and effectiveness of new technology by reducing labor resistance to change and tapping the know-how of workers; it reduces the costs of turnover and encourages management to invest in on-the-job training (*ibid.,* p. 180 and table 22). Further discussion is in chapters 1 and 18.

Regarding *tax concessions to employers,* the measure is *taxes on corporate income, profits, and capital gains* (1955–72, 1965–72, 1973–77, 1978–82, 1983–87). OECD data do not permit disaggregation of these taxes.[6] Again, a two-year lag is used. A leading student of this issue, Dale Jorgenson, using quarterly data for the United States found the greatest effect with a five- to eight-quarter lag between decreases in corporate taxes via accelerated depreciation, investment tax credits, and so on, and investment expenditure.[7] Sweden and the USA may be exceptions to this rule: the Swedes have used corporate taxes countercyclically, and American managers anticipated Ronald Reagan's corporate tax cuts even before they were enacted; in both cases, whatever effect there was would show up immediately. This would have very little effect on our 19-country, four-period analysis.

That corporatist democracies traditionally go light on such taxes is clear (the negative correlations range from −.45 to −.55 from 1955 to 1977 but fade to insignificance thereafter); the effect on economic performance, we shall see, is negligible.

3. *Participatory democracy in the workplace or community in return for labor peace and wage constraint.*

Measures: We have already seen that the density and scope of voluntary associations, especially economic organizations (unions, professional associations, employer and trade associations) and general levels of citizen participation are greater in corporatist democracies than in other democracies (see chap. 3 on mass society and chap. 11 on party decline). In Germany, for example, the local works councils and national codetermination machinery are combined with regional collective bargaining that is coordinated by centralized unions and employer associations to set a broad framework. Several countries provide channels for worker and union leader participation in tripartite boards administering parts of the welfare state—medical insurance, unemployment and accident insurance, and pensions (Wilensky, 1975, pp. 66–67).

Again, noneconomic payoffs to labor can yield productivity-enhancing industrial relations patterns with positive economic effects. Because the cross-national data on participation are so limited, however, we cannot include them in regression equations. But we can infer the process—worker participation ➤ labor peace ➤ wage restraint and better acceptance of change—from previous analysis.

Measures of strikes and wages are described above.

4. *In return for all of the above, the government improves its tax-extraction capacity and public acceptance of taxes on consumption* (the combination of value added taxes and social security taxes)—*not irrelevant to the control of inflation and to enhanced public and private resources for savings and investment and thereby better real GDP growth.* Chapter 10 has explained how big-spending corporatist democracies, either by strategic design or incremental steps, arrived at such a balanced tax structure despite labor and left resistance to regressivity in the tax system. Germany, for example, has long maintained about an even balance—almost a third of total taxation from consumption taxes, a third from payroll taxes, 29% from visible taxes (mainly income and property taxes).

There is a major counterargument to my hypothesis that consumption taxes and/or payroll taxes (which ultimately result in higher prices or lower wages, reducing consumption) foster economic growth and the control of inflation: When you increase VAT or sales taxes, the tax will appear as a onetime increase in your measure of inflation (by 1979 only the Netherlands, Denmark, Sweden, and Australia used an adjusted consumer price index to exclude the effect of consumption taxes) (OECD, 1976, pp. 45, 50; OECD, 1986b, pp. 71, 136). Further, as inflation rises, wages rise; in most of our countries, both wages and social-security benefits are indexed to inflation. Under some circumstances—for example, full use of industrial capacity, selected labor shortages—this can mean a wage-price spiral. Thus, while high taxes on consumption can reward savings, increase government revenue, and deflate demand, the larger effect, it is argued, is to increase prices and then increase demand (because wage increases will quickly follow).[8]

Finally, when Europeans shifted from turnover and sales taxes to the VAT, the move had little immediate effect because consumption taxes were already high, but later VAT increases did move the tax load up and in small measure, the price level (Aaron, 1981, p. 12). If consumption taxes increase inflation and the result is higher real interest rates, economic growth will suffer.

Social-security payroll taxes might have the same perverse effect: like consumption taxes, they raise government revenue and reduce consumer demand among the working population, but because the payout is a transfer from those who save to those who typically spend everything (pensioners), the increased demand could more than offset the anti-inflationary effect of the tax.

My test of these ideas below contradicts the negative view of these taxes on payroll and consumption; it shows that the VAT and social-security payroll taxes in the context of corporatist trade-offs enhance economic performance, especially before 1980. It suggests that the reduced demand effect and increased investment effect outweigh the inflationary effects. We used a one-year lag between these two taxes and economic performance.

5. *With the habit of making such trade-offs and faced with strong labor movements, management in the more corporatist democracies tends to join labor in the implementation of a wide range of policies.* The result: *less intrusive regulation* and more effective implementation of laws

and executive orders. Thus, the complaint that Western Europe is hyperregulated and hyperprotected—that it has the disease of "Eurosclerosis"—while America is flexible and its employers are free to adapt, ignores the evidence on types of regulation and regulatory styles. As Ronald Dore (1986) implies in his treatment of "flexible rigidity" in Japan, and as several researchers note in their treatment of American health-care regulations (Ruggie, 1992; Myles, 1993; Morone, 1992), an ideology of deregulation goes together with the most-intrusive and rigid kinds of regulation, while "statist" political economies may regulate more flexibly, as I have previously suggested (1983, pp. 58–59) and show below in chapters 15 (environment) and 16 (health care). (See also Kelman, 1981; Bardach and Kagan, 1982; and my discussion of adversary legalism in this chapter.) The paradox that the most-decentralized political economies with the most-liberal (free-market) ideologies have the most-rigid and intrusive regulations can be explained by the weakness of the structure and political power of labor and the absence of channels for collaboration among labor, management, and the state.

Measures. There are no measures of regulation, deregulation, and reregulation for our 19 countries, but several case studies are suggestive (they are reviewed in Vogel, 1996, a detailed examination of recent regulatory regimes in Japan, Britain, the United States, France, and Germany and in chap. 15 on the environment).

Total taxes: Total tax revenue at all levels of government as a percentage of GDP.

Consumption taxes: General taxes on goods and services (sales taxes and/or VAT).

Social-security taxes as a percentage of GDP: All social-security taxes paid by employees, employers, and self-employed.

Capital investment: Gross fixed capital formation as a percentage of GDP.

Sources: All data come from OECD. Taxes from *Revenue Statistics of OECD Member Countries* (OECD, various years). Gross fixed capital formation from *OECD Historical Statistics,* various years. See appendix G.

6.   *In return for all the above—for labor, the social wage, job protection, and worker participation, for the government, increased revenue especially from consumption and payroll taxes—both labor and the government tolerate low taxes on either capital gains or profits or both and avoid high property taxes.*

Measures: See above for taxes on corporation profits and capital gains. Property taxes are recurrent taxes on immovable property of households and businesses as a percentage of GDP, from *OECD Revenue Statistics,* various years.

In addition to these variables, designed to test theories of corporatism, I consider several possible causes of economic performance that economists and policy analysts have listed in the literature of the past 30 or so years—for example, Edward Denison (1967, 1974, 1979, 1985), J. R. Norsworthy et al. (1979), John Kendrick (1980), Robert Solow (1988), Dale Jorgenson and R. Landau (1988), Angus Maddison (1982), Robert Barro (1991), Robert Lucas (1988), Paul Romer (1986), Michael Bruno and Jeffrey Sachs (1985), and Benjamin Friedman (1989). These hypothetical causes include the age structure of the population, education and training, civilian research and development, military spending, and the size of the public bureaucracy. As a validation of the idea that corporatist democracies enjoy many effective mechanisms of conflict resolution and therefore need fewer costly lawyers and courts, I add the percentage of lawyers in the civilian labor force and data on recent expansion of law school enrollments and relate these to economic performance. Limited data on the interaction of inequality and economic growth are explored. I use measures of external shocks as a control in regression equations. The ambiguous meaning of job creation as a measure of economic success is analyzed separately in chapter 13.

Figure 12.1 provides a diagram of the causal model.

THE CAUSES OF ECONOMIC PERFORMANCE: FINDINGS FROM MULTIVARIATE ANALYSIS

In general, we see that corporatism ensures heavy social spending and heavy tax loads; the tax load is heavily weighted toward the least visible, least painful taxes (social-security taxes and consumption taxes); the spending avoids heavily stigmatized means-tested benefits. One consequence of this structure of taxes and spending is wage restraint by unions, low strike rates, and high capital investment. The pattern enhances economic performance, especially by increasing GDP growth and holding down inflation and unemployment and especially before 1980, and to some extent even in the 1980s. The rank order of 19 countries in these variables is quite stable over time for unemployment and inflation but less so for growth, especially after 1980. Specifically, cross-tabulations and regression analyses show the following:[9]

1. *There is a strong steady relationship between corporatism and social spending.* Correlations of corporatism scores and social security as a percentage of GNP range from .51 (1950–74) to .67 (1966–72 and 1975–77), all significant. The correlations using per capita spending are only slightly less strong. Corporatism is also associated with high rates of increases in social spending up to 1974 (but for 1974–80 the correlation becomes insignificant). As tables 12G.6 through 12G.10 show (appendix G), the pattern of big social spending (SS/GNP) is especially strong where corporatism is combined with Catholic party power, with or without left competition.

2. *The corporatist big spenders tend to avoid means testing* (noncategorical benefits targeted to the poor via a stiff income and/or assets test applied by welfare administrators with substantial discretion with a high probability of stigma). For instance, of 18 countries for which we developed a measure and had data on means-tested spending, the lowest reliance on means testing in 1980 appears for the 10 corporatist countries that include labor in their policy machinery with only two exceptions (the Netherlands scores high and West Germany scores medium). Six of the other 8 countries evidence a heavy reliance on means testing (they score high or high to medium); the exceptions are Australia (low to medium) and Switzerland (medium).[10] These intrusive systems are expensive and unproductive, one reason to suppose they are an economic drag. (The politics of "welfare" and "workfare" are discussed in chap. 8.)

Correlations show that public assistance spending as a percentage of GNP is more consistently related to measures of economic performance than public assistance per capita. When we control for our six basic variables, two at a time, using PA/GNP as a possible drag on the economy, we find that (1) it has an independent, significantly posi-

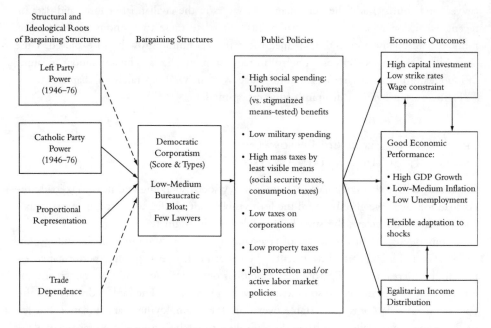

Figure 12.1. Causal model for regression analyses of the major sources of economic performance, nineteen rich democracies

tive effect on unemployment (i.e., increases unemployment) in all periods from 1950 to 1984; and (2) all other relationships (to growth or inflation) wash out in the presence of our most powerful sources of economic performance, except for one: public assistance spending/GNP is a significant drag on economic growth during the worst recession of our postwar analysis, 1980–84. With these limited data, there is no good way to sort out cause and effect (we do not have year-to-year data on changes in public assistance). For instance, the relationship could mean either that unemployment increases, then public assistance—the last resort social net—climbs; or that unproductive public-assistance spending increases, resources available for investment decline, productivity lags, then unemployment moves up. There is one hint, however, that the latter effect may outweigh the former: PA/GNP is consistently a drag on capital formation. That suggests the hypothesis of an indirect effect: that a heavy reliance on means-tested public assistance reduces investment, which in turn slows growth and increases unemployment.

A second complication in assessing the distinct economic effects of the welfare mess (symbolized by a heavy means-testing apparatus) is that in most countries (Germany is an exception) both unemployment and public assistance spending are highest among the young. The correlations between age 15–19 and unemployment are the strongest of the age grade correlations. Using that age control and relating PA/GNP, 1980 or 1974–79, to the relevant economic performance periods (1974–84) with one other variable at a time shows the following: (1) Age controls do not reduce the public assistance effect on unemployment before 1980 (i.e., from 1965 to 1980, the more a country relies on public assistance, the more unemployment it experiences). (2) But the age effect does reduce the public assistance effect on unemployment to insignificance for the multiple shock period of 1980–84, and it does the same for economic growth in that period. In other words, numerous teenagers, not public assistance, undermine both jobs and growth in 1980–84. (A later section deals with demographic structure.)

In sum: Stigmatized, means-tested benefits directly and independently increase unemployment except in one postshock period; they are indirectly a drag on economic growth because they consistently divert resources from capital investment and subvert human resource development.

3. *Corporatism and the level of taxes.* With one deviant case of Italy, whose spending for long periods exceeded its tax collection, taxes roughly match spending. Big spenders pay their way over the long run; or big taxers spend a lot; or both. *From 1965 to 1988, the correlation between the corporatism score and total taxes/GDP range from .60 (1974) to .72 (1980 and 1988).* The relationship is *especially strong for corporatist democracies with strong left party power in all periods (e.g., Denmark, Sweden, Norway are among the top four taxers in all periods; two countries, with both left and Catholic power, Netherlands and Austria, are among the top seven for all periods).*

4. *As a percentage of total taxes, the big taxers rely mainly on least visible and least painful taxes*—consumption taxes (e.g., sales or VAT) and social-security taxes (e.g., payroll taxes); they also *avoid heavy taxes on corporate income, profits, or capital gains,* although this relationship faded in the 1980s. Apparently, the trade-offs made when labor is at the high-policy table for many years favor management; in return for generous payoffs in the "social wage," labor supports tax breaks for management. In the absence of a steady labor influence (as in Japan, Australia, New Zealand, Canada, and the UK), the government turns to business as a source of revenue.[11]

5. *Least-corporatist democracies have a taste for property taxes: reliance on such taxes appears to be a drag on economic performance,* but it is so highly correlated with the rest of our variables that also predict poor performance that I leave it aside. A separate section later will attempt an explanation.

Wages, Capital Investment, Strikes, and Taxes

The level and structure of social spending and taxing above (1–5) leads to three major outcomes that favor good economic performance: labor constraint on increases in nominal wages; high or above-average capital investment; and low strike rates. The correlation of all the above variables—outcomes of corporatist bargaining arrangements—and the economic performance index appear in appendix G, tables 12G.1 through 12G.5. Tables 12G.6 through 12G.10 report results by country and types of political economy and party power.

A multiple regression analysis using three of the above variables at a time for each period demonstrates that each one has some independent effect on either the economic performance index or one or more of its components.

Wage Restraint While most corporatist democracies had higher wage increases before 1980 than their least-corporatist counterparts, *when the shocks of 1974 and 1979–82 hit, they resisted wage pressures.* The median nominal wage increase 1974–79 was 12.7% (between Belgium and Norway). Only 5 of the 12 countries with some form of corporatism (Israel missing) exceeded the median (Italy, France, Finland, Denmark, with Norway barely above), while only 2 of the 6 least-corporatist countries (USA and Canada) were below the median (see table 12G.8).

Similarly, the median nominal wage increase for 1980–84 was 8.8% (between Sweden and Canada). Among corporatist democracies, only Italy, France, Norway, and Finland exceeded this, with Sweden barely above, while four of the six least corporatist countries were above the median (the exceptions: Canada, 10th ranked, was close to the median; the USA was 13th)—a pattern that continues through the rest of the 1980s. (See table 12G.9.)

The wage acceleration measure strengthens the picture. For acceleration 1974–79 over 1965–73, only 3 of 12 corporatist countries are above the median (France, Norway, Italy), while all 6 least-corporatist countries are above the median. For wage acceleration 1980–84 over 1974–79, 5 of 12 corporatist countries score above the median (France, Switzerland, Sweden, Finland, and Italy); 4 of 6 least-corporatist countries score above (United States, Ireland, New Zealand, Canada). The case that centralized bargaining restrains nominal wages is stronger if we eliminate France and Switzerland, corporatist countries that keep labor at a distance. Again, the full inclusion of unions helps.

Regression analysis confirms the finding that restraint of nominal wages strongly reduces inflation in all periods but has no effects on unemployment or GDP growth and no effects on the general index for 1950–74. The control of wage-push inflation is plainly a feature of corporatist adjustment to inflationary shocks.[12]

Strike Rates, Capital Investment, and Social Spending   *The most consistently robust variables fostering good economic performance are strike rates* (low rates as a clue to effective industrial relations) *and capital formation* (indicated by gross fixed capital investment). One or the other of these two powerful variables consistently predicts more of the variance in the economy than corporatism, leftism, Catholicism, spending or taxing levels or types, or external shocks. The regressions (table 12.8) show that capital investment has a positive effect because it increases growth (1965–74, 1974–79, and 1980–84) and lowers unemployment (1965–74, 1974–79, and 1985–89 but not after the second oil shock 1980–84).[13] And high strike rates have a negative effect because they increase unemployment (1950–74, 1965–74, 1974–79, and 1980–84) and/or increase inflation (1974–79, 1980–84, 1985–89). Hundreds of regressions not reported here—using all relevant independent variables three at a time—confirm this pattern for the economic performance index and its components: either strike rates or capital investment or both have major effects no matter what is added to the equation. That often holds true for periods for which they are not significant in table 12.8 and for combinations of our main variables not shown in that table. On the basis of all the regressions aimed at testing the preceding hypothesis we can confidently say the following:

Social-security spending (SS/GNP) and, to a lesser degree, social security per capita are positive forces for GDP growth 1950–74 and the general index 1950–74. Holding constant strikes and capital formation, social spending *remains significant in some equations.* It is irrelevant to inflation and unemployment. The growth rate of social-security spending, either nominal or real, is not significant if Japan with very high growth in both social spending and its economy is excluded.

In no period and for no measure of performance is social-security spending a significant drag, controlling for leftism, Catholicism, corporatism, capital investment, and strikes, the major

TABLE 12.8 Best regressions of economic performance on strikes, capital investment, social spending, and type of political economy[†] (continues on p. 460)

Independent Variable	Performance Index	Average Growth	Average Inflation	Average Unemployment
Economic Performance 1950-74 as Dependent Variable				
Strikes	−.55**			.87**
Capital Investment	.34*	.29	.20	−.16
SS/GNP		.63*		
Corporatism Score			.40	
Catholic Party Power	.27*	.11	−.41	.37*
AR²(N)[a]	.83(16)	.62(16)	.12(16)	.72(16)
Economic Performance 1965-74 as Dependent Variable				
Strikes	−.11	.73**		.96**
Capital Investment	.25	.49*	.08	−.15
Corporatism Score		.75**	.21	.31*
Catholic Party Power	.57*		−.52•	
AR²(N)[a]	.42(16)	.57(16)	.06(16)	.82(16)
Economic Performance 1974-79 as Dependent Variable				
Strikes	−.63**	.25	.47•	.58**
Capital Investment	.57**	.63*		−.38•
SS/GNP		.52*	.23	
Corporatism Score				.09
Catholic Party Power	.38**		−.44	
AR²(N)[b]	.83(18)	.29(18)	.33(17)	.49(18)

sources of economic performance. In 1980−84, both strikes and SS/GNP appear to dampen economic performance, but that is due to Japan (very low in strikes, tops in capital investment, very low in social spending); eliminating Japan, social security is reduced to no significance or marginal significance in all but one of 20 equations (17 countries).

Where we eliminate both Japan and Switzerland (they have the same unique pattern), social security has no significant effect in any equation. This suggests two roads to good economic performance: corporatism-without-labor with lean social spending, high capital investment, and low strikes, *or* corporatism with full inclusion of labor with generous social spending, high capital investment, and, most important, low strikes.

TABLE 12.8 *(continued)*

Independent Variable	Performance Index	Average Growth	Average Inflation	Average Unemployment
Economic Performance 1980-84 as Dependent Variable				
Strikes	−.48*		.86**	.64**
Capital Investment	.39•	.66**		−.18
SS/GNP		−.30		.38
Corporatism Score			.47*	
Catholic Party Power			−.26	
Left Party Power	.18	.46*		
AR²(N)[c]	.36(18)	.44(18)	.61(18)	.38(18)
Economic Performance 1985-89 as Dependent Variable				
Strikes	−.68**	.30	.74**	.30
Capital Investment	.36*		.10	−.62**
SS/GNP		−.37		
Corporatism Score	−.32•			
Left Party Power		−.25	.23	−.50*
AR²(N)[d]	.56(17)	.29(16)	.47(17)	.53(17)

[†]See appendix G for definitions of, and sources for, independent variables; text for economic performance.

[a]Three cases deleted: Israel missing on capital investment; Italy an outlier on strikes; Japan an extreme case (high) on capital investment.

[b]Israel missing on capital investment; Italy an extreme case (high) on inflation.

[c]Israel missing on economic performance.

[d]Israel missing on economic performance; Belgium missing on strikes; New Zealand an extreme case (low) on growth.

During the period of recovery, 1985–89, strikes were consistently more of a drag than capital formation was a help. In almost every equation in which they were included, strikes were the strongest predictor of poor performance. In fact, as we see in tables 12G.9 and 12G.10 (appendix G), if a country has very high strike rates (Ireland in 1980–84, New Zealand in 1985–89), high capital investment will not prevent a slide into poor or nearly poor performance. Social-security spending was a modest negative in only 1 of 20 equations for that recent period, 1985–89. The only aspect of economic performance for which capital investment was more of a help than strikes were a hindrance was in reducing unemployment.

The only anomaly in 1980–84 is the USA: it failed to invest, suffered above-average losses from strikes, and still achieved above-average economic performance; it had low inflation (6.7%, ranked 12th), medium growth (0.9%, ranked 14th), and medium unemployment (8.2%, ranked 8th) (see table 12.4). That is because it ran a consumer-led recovery with heavy borrowing in public and private sectors alike, which continued through the 1980s, aided a bit by a slight drop in relative strike rates 1985–89 (from 7th to 10th). (See tables 12G.6–12G.10 in appendix G.) By 1990–92, the USA returned to its previous below-average performance (see table 12.9), but by most measures during the subsequent recovery outpaced Japan and most of Europe 1993–99 for reasons already discussed.

In a careful review of the mixed and weak findings of nine studies of the economic impact of social spending on economic performance—most authored by economists—Atkinson (1995) concludes that none of them shows that the welfare state is a drag on economic growth, employment, or productivity. Some of Atkinson's observations illustrate a complex argument. First, it may be poor economic performance that leads to increased social spending rather than the reverse; slow growth causes reduced employment and hence higher income transfers. Second, there is a phasing of growth rates and welfare-state development, two unconnected trends. Not only can rich countries afford more generous social security (a universal political demand) but they are past the period of early industrialization when economic growth was swift and their insurance systems were initiated. The two simultaneous trends are spuriously correlated: insurance systems mature and cost more at precisely the time (decades) when economic growth in all the advanced countries was approaching a steady-state value (the newly industrializing countries [NICs] almost always grow faster than the already rich). Third, as I have suggested (1983), the form of the benefit and the political context for its delivery mightily shape its economic impact (see later). Finally, when economic theory tells us that increased taxes to finance the welfare state cause a fall in measured output, we must ask whether GDP is the appropriate measure. "Along with the reduced labour supply," Atkinson observes, "comes increased home production. The Scandinavian economists who paint their own houses rather than write more books are still contributing to output" (1995, p. 21). An unfriendly critic might see this economic distortion as a positive benefit. All this is complementary to the arguments and data presented in this chapter.

A final set of studies of the interplay between social spending and economic performance using states within the United States, some with data extending to 1989, confirms my cross-national findings. Peter H. Lindert, reviewing these studies and adding his own current work, concludes that U.S. states, like nations, evidence either no significant relationship or a positive relationship between social transfers as a share of state product and either the level of product per capita or rates of economic growth and employment (Lindert, 1996a, p. 2; Lindert, 1996b, pp. 2–4). The most careful econometric study (Helms, 1985) shows that from 1965 to 1979 the drag on state personal income of extra tax-financed, means-tested public assistance that I found for 19 rich democracies was more than offset by the positive effects of tax-financed health and education expenditures. A follow-up by Helms, Eandi, and Lindert with U.S. state data from the 1980s found even more positive effects on state production and employment (Lindert, 1996b, p. 4). Again, these studies remind us of the need to focus on specific types of spending when we talk about the economic effects of the welfare state.

Taxes: Level and Type   Total tax levels (total taxes at every level of government divided by GDP), which are positively correlated with left power and corporatism in all periods, have *no* effects on economic performance, except in the period before 1974, when high taxes, because they permit generous social spending and lower strike rates, had a positive indirect effect, contrary to received wisdom. (See above and appendix G, tables 12G.6 – 12G.10 and 12G.1 – 12G.5. Regressions not reported.) As we found when we uncovered the roots of tax-welfare backlash (chap. 10), it is not the *level* of taxes that counts but the *type of taxes*.

Thus, regressions, controlling for all other variables, show that painfully visible taxes (income taxes on individuals and property taxes) were a drag on economic growth from 1950 to 1979 and reduced the broader economic performance index 1965 – 74. Conversely, *social-security taxes often enhanced economic performance. They constrained inflation 1965 – 74* and 1985 – 89, but had no effect just after the two oil shocks. These taxes also had a marginally significant positive effect on the general index, 1950 – 79. The only bad effect of social-security payroll taxes was that they lowered growth in 1980 – 84, the period of severe multiple shocks.

Sales and value-added taxes remained *significant and positive for economic growth* after controlling for other variables *for 1950 – 79,* with *positive impact on the index 1965 – 79.* These consumption taxes were consistently negatively related to strikes, while they were positively related to capital formation, which explains why they are good for growth.

There were no significant correlations between consumption taxes and inflation or unemployment, however, and no significant correlations with any performance measure in the 1980s.[14]

Corporate taxes had a negative effect on growth 1950 – 74, but no significant effects thereafter. There is a hint that such taxes marginally increased unemployment in only one period, 1985 – 89.

In short, relative to industrial relations systems and capital formation, the structure of taxes is only moderately or weakly related to economic performance, an effect that almost disappeared in the 1980s. If we are concerned only with economic impact, consumption taxes and social-security taxes were benign; income taxes, property taxes, and to a lesser extent, corporate taxes, were a drag. And the general level of taxes had no effect at all. The tax-cutting mania of Republican Presidents Reagan and Bush and the Republican Congress of 1994 – 2000 (and the echoes among conservatives in Europe) and the heated denials of their Democratic opponents that they were "tax and spend liberals" were, to say the least, misplaced.

OTHER FORCES: DO R&D AND EDUCATION AND TRAINING HELP? DO MILITARY SPENDING, YOUNG PEOPLE, BLOATED BUREAUCRACY, AND MANY LAWYERS HURT?

Several additional candidates for possibly important sources of good economic performance are discussed in the literature of economics and public policy. For some, there are no clean, comparable measures available for our 19 countries (e.g., investment in civilian research and development, education, and training). For others, we have approximate measures, but in regression equations they turn out to be of very limited importance or are so closely correlated with our strongest variables that their independent influence cannot be ascertained. A discussion of each follows with what data I could find.[15]

Civilian Research and Development

Data on total R&D spending as a percentage of GDP before 1980 are available only for a few countries. For 1981, OECD data cover all of our countries except Israel, but they do not separate military from civilian R&D. What emerges from an 18-country analysis of these very limited data is (1) a moderate correlation between R&D spending and military spending, which becomes strong if we eliminate Japan and Switzerland (high in R&D but well below average in military spending), and (2) correlations that suggest that total R&D spending in 1981 helped reduce inflation in 1985–89 but had no significant effect on growth or unemployment.

These data are misleading. Of the top seven in total R&D spending, three—the USA, the UK, and France—devote much of R&D to the military; Japan and West Germany in contrast devote almost all of it to civilian purposes. The evidence on the effects of military R&D suggests that it is a drain on the economy while civilian R&D is a positive force.

For instance, a study that attempts to divide military from civilian R&D and relate them to competitiveness (measured by the excess of output/domestic absorption) in six countries suggests that there may be a relationship between a country's effort in civilian R&D and its economic performance in the early 1980s. I add our figures on subsequent economic performance for 1980–84, 1985–89, and 1990–92.

What table 12.9 suggests is that military R&D, whatever the positive spin-offs from World War II (computer chips, jet engines, radar), has become a drag on economic growth and competitiveness, while civilian R&D has a positive effect on both; and, further, that the general economic performance of the three top spenders in civilian R&D (Japan, West Germany, and, to a lesser extent, the United States), had an edge in general economic performance in the 1980s. Adding to the advantage of Japan and Germany was a widening gap in civilian R&D investment. By 1987, they had increased their already strong effort while the United States retained its third place at 2.0% (table 12.9). In more commercially relevant R&D expenditures as a percentage of GNP, however, the United States had slipped to fourth behind Japan, West Germany, and France (National Science Board, 1989, p. 4); but in the mid-1990s, the U.S. began substantial increases in R&D spending. If we guess that the lag between R&D investment and economic payoff is 5, 10, or even 15 years, this trend should make itself felt well after the mid-1990s, other things being equal.[16] It is apparent that from the sputtering performance of Japan 1993–99 that a poorly regulated financial system combined with macroeconomic policy errors can offset R&D and productivity advantages, at least in the short run of a decade.

Why has military R&D become subversive of good economic performance? In theory, by generating a stream of new technologies, military R&D lowers the cost of overhead on civilian R&D projects. And by providing low-risk contracts with long production runs, military R&D helps all firms reap the benefits of economies of scale. In practice it does not work that way. There are four deficiencies of military R&D for the purposes of the civilian economy. First, the products developed are typically and increasingly highly specialized; esoteric metals and space technology have no earthly use. (Communication satellites are an exception.) Second, Schumpeter's "creative destruction"—new products driving out old ones—seldom applies; diverse military constituencies demand *both* the continued "improve-

TABLE 12.9 Research and development effort and economic performance, 1980s[a]

Country	R&D Expenditure Military R&D as % of GDP[a] 1982	Civilian R&D as % of GNP[b] 1982	1987	Competitiveness Indicator[a]	Economic Performance Growth of Real GDP per capita '80-84	'85-89	'90-92	Inflation — % Change GDP Implicit Price Defl. '80-84	'85-89	'90-92	Unemployment Standardized Rate '80-84	'85-89	'90-92	Economic Performance Index Score '80-84	'85-89	'90-92
UK	0.68	1.6[c]	1.7	94.3	0.5	3.6	-1.7	9.6	5.5	5.4	10.3	9.7	8.5	1	2	1
USA	0.72	1.9	2.0	99.7	0.9	2.0	-0.3	6.7	3.1	3.4	8.2	6.1	6.4	4	4	2
France	0.38	1.6	1.8	100.2	0.6	2.4	0.5	10.7	3.8	2.5	8.0	10.1	9.5	1	2	2
Sweden	0.24	1.7	—	117.2	1.4	2.0	-2.2	9.5	6.4	4.5	2.9	2.1	3.0	4	3	2
W. Germany	0.11	2.5	2.7	128.9	1.0	2.3	1.8	3.7	2.3	4.2	5.7	6.3	4.5	4	4	4
Japan	0.01[d]	2.5	2.8	138.3	3.3	3.9	2.3	2.0	0.9	1.9	2.4	2.6	2.1	6	6	6

[a]Source: Kaldor, Sharp, and Walker (1986), p. 32; and my appendix G. Kaldor defines competitiveness as the excess of output over domestic absorption measured by output divided by output minus exports plus imports.
[b]National Science Foundation (1990) pp. 14–15 and p. 59, table B-19.
[c]1983.
[d]1979.

ment" (endless increases in complexity) of old weapons *and* new miracle weapons, each modified for special services (air force, army, navy, etc.) resulting in the endless acceleration of unit costs (Kaldor et al., 1986, pp. 43–44). Third, tying up skilled scientists, engineers, and technicians in such technology diverts money and human resources away from the development of machinery and consumer products. (For evidence of this "crowding out" phenomenon, see Lichtenberg, 1988.) Finally, the "D" in R&D may be decisive for a nation's competitiveness in civilian manufacturing. The critical difference between the USA and UK vs. Japan is not in basic research; it is that the Japanese have an edge in management and engineering skill devoted to competitive civilian markets combined with worker flexibility in bringing innovations to market quickly.[17] When Japan gets its macroeconomic policies right (see above) these resources should once again pay off.

The loss of American preeminence in science as it serves technology is evident in the increased share of U.S. patents granted to foreigners from 27% in 1970 to 48% in 1988 (National Science Board, 1989, p. 356). Together with lean spending on civilian R&D, this trend was reflected in the dramatic decline in the U.S. trade balance in high-technology manufactures in the 1980s, from a surplus of $27.4 billion in 1981 to a surplus of only $8.1 billion by 1988, with 1986 actually showing a high-tech trade deficit. The trouble was concentrated in key product groups such as communication equipment and electronics components, where deficits worsened from about $3.4 billion in 1981 to about $19.8 billion in 1988. All this reflects in part the emergence of strong rivals with increasing investments in civilian R&D: for instance, Japan and the East Asian NICs in semiconductor products and manufacturing processes, Europe in pharmaceuticals, engines, scientific instruments, and aircraft. (U.S. Department of Commerce, 1989, pp. 87, 30–31, 54, 86, table B.5; and Ferguson, 1989, pp. 132–133.)

In sum: Although these data cover only six countries and a short period, they do suggest that civilian R&D improves economic performance, especially in enhancing growth without much inflation. More quantitative studies of single countries and longer time periods also conclude that R&D in general, including military, has a small but significant and positive effect on productivity (Griliches, 1980; Friedman, 1989, p. 193), perhaps explaining about a tenth of the variance, but that civilian R&D accounts for most of the benefits.

Education and Training

There is substantial evidence that a modern nation that gives careful attention to the literacy, numeracy, and analytic skills of its school children, especially from kindergarten through 12th grade or so, is in a position to train its average worker in flexible adaptation to modern industry and to achieve an edge in productivity improvements (see chap. 1; Schultz, 1971, and the citations there; and Mincer, 1974). If high-quality general education is combined with an active labor-market policy, including apprenticeships (see figure 2.2), fostering lifelong training and learning on and off the job, the competitive advantage of a good basic universal education will be multiplied. The countries that clearly fit this description include Germany, Japan, Sweden, Switzerland, and France, all of which had above-average or superior economic performance for long periods of post–World War II.

However, there are no really valid and reliable measures of differences among our 19 rich democracies in the level and quality of education and training and the linkages between the two. If we join the current sport of comparing national test scores of students at various grade levels as an indicator of school quality (the U.S. is scandalously low, the refrain goes), we ignore vast differences in the populations being tested; many European countries test only student elites, the United States and Japan test student masses. If we rely on levels of or trends in aggregate spending, we lump quite different types of education together—private and public, religious and secular, advanced and elementary. If we concentrate on the years from kindergarten through high school (K–12), arguably the most important period to prepare young people for learning at work, the national differences in aggregate spending are not large, and are diminishing. Such figures exclude everything that might be important for learning: teacher training, pay, status and autonomy; the uniformity and steadiness of funding and the quality of instructional materials and services; the content of the curriculum; standards of student achievement; school schedules; links between schools and labor markets (e.g., what employers are able to do with the average 12th-, 13th-, or 14th-grade product). If instead we concentrate on postsecondary education, we find larger differences in spending but economic relevance depends more on the mix of graduates and undergraduates, on the specialties most emphasized (e.g., lawyers vs. engineers), and on the strength of linkages between university research programs and industry R&D programs. In short, no matter what spending figures we use, as in the analysis of medical-care spending, the problems of the comparability and meaning of educational expenditures are daunting.

Regarding vocational training, apprenticeship systems, and labor-market programs generally, the problems of cross-national comparability are similarly difficult—for example, how to separate active from passive labor-market policies, how to compare the lengthy and intensive apprenticeship systems of Germany and Switzerland with more unified general education systems. (For comparative analysis of these issues, see Wilensky, 1992a.)

For our regression analysis of 19 countries the best we can do is use UNESCO data on gross educational expenditures and enrollment ratios for postsecondary education where national variation is substantial.[18] This yields very little of direct relevance to economic performance. After summarizing these results, I examine school funding, organization, and quality using more-intensive case studies of school systems in action, with special attention to two countries with mass education at every level, the United States and Japan. Because education spending is closely correlated with a young age structure, I then deal with the issue of whether a load of young people is a drag on the economy apart from what a nation does with its schools.

There appear to be many significant correlations between education variables and economic performance. Unfortunately, they are in the wrong direction.

Measures of education are confined to postsecondary enrollment ratios and expenditures as a fraction of GNP and per capita (for periods covering 1965 to 1988); expenditures and enrollment for primary and secondary schools do not vary enough among rich countries for this analysis (although school quality varies hugely and will be discussed later). The measures are described in appendix G. The results: For the 19 countries, one or more of these measures of investment in higher education is negatively correlated with the economic performance index in every period but 1985–89; one or more suggests a drag on growth in every period except 1974–79 and 1985–89; all measures show a positive correlation with unemployment for all periods before 1979 and that holds for higher education expenditure/GNP 1980−84. Further, education variables are negatively correlated with capital investment (for two of four periods) and positively correlated with strikes (for one of these periods)—our two most powerful sources of economic performance.

However, upon closer inspection, all this is either spurious or can be explained by two to six extreme cases, especially the United States and Canada. Generally poor economic performers, these two are highest in both higher education spending and enrollment ratios and are generally low on capital expenditures and high on strikes. Removing them reduces almost all correlations to insignificance. Removing one or another additional outlier further reduces these correlations.[19] No pattern of any kind remains.

Added spuriousness comes from the obvious relation of age structure to education enrollments and spending and the not-so-obvious relation of age structure to types of political economy and party power. For instance, left-corporatist countries happen to have older populations—fewer young people. But their egalitarian thrust nevertheless boosts their spending on education, especially in 1965−74. In contrast, the most-fragmented, decentralized democracies tend to have much younger populations, so they must spend more on education. The result: a statistical draw; no general pattern relating education and age to economic performance emerges because the commanding variables—types of corporatism and party power—are obscured.

In view of the severe limitations of these spending and enrollment figures, I now turn to more intensive examination of school performance with an eye to its impact on the economy. Two recent reports on American schooling frame the contemporary debate.

A National Commission on Excellence report, *A Nation at Risk* (1983), in a near-hysterical tone, reported that American school performance had declined drastically in relation to America's past and that it was weak in comparison to other nations. These conclusions were based largely, but not exclusively, on comparison of test scores. The report added that this "rising tide of mediocrity" in education was a major source of the decline in American competitiveness. In an effort to cast himself as the "education president," George Bush later issued a report called *America 2000* that echoed *A Nation at Risk* but claimed that the problem could be solved with virtually no added resources because total spending per pupil on elementary and secondary schools had increased about 33% in constant dollars during the 1980s without improving schools.

There are several things wrong with these statements. The test results are not comparable either across time or country; and the argument about funding is specious. The students taking the SAT exam in the early 1960s and the students taking it now are very different in their social origins and academic standing within their schools—that is, in their socialization in family and school. Similarly, students taking the standardized tests in many other countries are not comparable: age-matched test-takers in Europe (and, to a much lesser extent, in Japan) are higher status and are often selected for their previous academic achievements; they are being compared with U.S. students of whom a much greater proportion are not only from the bottom half of their schools but have been shunted out of the academic track (Berliner, 1993, p. 639). Further, wherever the comparative studies hold constant the relevant social or academic status, most of the American lag, at least in test scores, disappears. Even *A Nation at Risk* acknowledges this: when the international comparisons were made in the early 1970s by the International Association for the Evaluation of Educational Achievement (IEA), "The top 9 percent of American students compared favorably in achievement with their peers in other countries" (National Commission on Excellence, 1983, p. 34). Finally, during the 1980s, the period of increased spending to which the Bush report refers, SAT scores in the United States stopped their downward slide. In fact, minorities markedly improved their scores, albeit from a very low level: from 1975 to 1990, the mean SATs for most minority high-school students, including blacks and Hispanics, have gone up along with upper-middle-class test scores, while their completion rates increased faster than the rates of white students (Kirst and Kelley, 1993, pp. 5–6). After falling in the 1960s and early 1970s, scores on standardized tests such as the Iowa Tests of Basic Skills began rising in the mid-1970s and continued to climb through the 1980s (Bracey, 1991, p. 107). And in the 1980s, concurrent with the school reform movement, there was a significant jump in enrollment in serious academic courses at all levels (Kirst and Kelley, 1993, pp. 3–4).

The allegation about spending increases is deceptive, too. First, the 1980s increases reflect a partial recovery from cuts in teachers' real income from 1973 to 1982; the subsequent increase in teacher salaries is close to that for the cost-of-living (Bracey, 1991, p. 112). Second, the alleged 33% increase in per pupil expenditure in the 1980s reflects mainly the federally mandated expenditure on "special education" (mainly on physically or mentally disabled or otherwise handicapped children); excluding costs of special education at an average of $17,600 per pupil per year, we find very little rise in regular education cost (inflation-adjusted) from 1970 to 1988 when it stood at $2,500 (*ibid.*, p. 112).

The real problem obscured by the excitement over test scores is the trend toward dumping our social problems on the public schools—such problems as uncushioned family breakup, unsupervised children unprepared for learning or for orderly behavior, an increasing rate of poverty with concomitant deficiencies in child nutrition and health, and increasing racial tension and neighborhood violence spilling over into schools. After dumping these problems on the schools we self-righteously proclaim that our teachers are failing us, all the while decreasing both the moral and the financial support for instructional services. Among the most damning facts uncovered by *A Nation at Risk* (National Commission on Excellence, 1983) are these: the average teacher salary after 12 years of teaching was only $17,000, a subprofessional level that explains why increasing proportions of teachers are drawn from the bottom quarter of graduating high-school and college students—compared to the early 1960s, when almost half of graduating college seniors said they wanted to be teachers, and a third anticipated a career in elementary or secondary schools (Davis, 1964, table 1.4, p. 13). Their preparation is heavily weighted with courses in educational methods at the expense of courses in subjects to be taught; teachers have little influence in such critical professional decisions as textbook selection, and, in any case, expenditures for textbooks and other instructional materials declined by 50% from 1965 to 1982 (National Commission on Excellence, 1983, pp. 21–23).[20] Chapter 18 on public policy returns to possible educational reforms for the U.S.

Because of the noncomparability of test scores across time and space, because of very limited data on the allocation of educational budgets and the preparation and behavior of teachers and other indicators of school quality in our 19 countries, we cannot make definitive statements about education as it shapes the economy. Nevertheless, there are some relevant international comparisons based on more intensive case studies of curriculum content, hours of school and homework, academic standards, teacher pay and status, and what employers, in fact, are able to do with the average product of secondary schools in various countries differing in their economic prowess. Leaving aside questions of national differences in poverty, family instability, and television content and dominance—major sources of school children's motivation and capacity to learn—what can we say about national differences in the organization and funding of schools that might affect economic performance?

Consider two extreme cases, Japan and the United States (most European nations fall in between). Both countries have historically been committed to education as the main road to occupational success, social status, and income. They spend similar proportions of GDP on education, in the mid-1980s 6.5% for Japan, 6.8% for the United States; or if we include only public expenditures on public education at every level as a proportion of GDP 1985, 5.1% for Japan, 5.04% for the United States (OECD, 1989a, pp. 98–99). In both, education credentials are central to employment, although Japanese employers examine credentials more closely than do American employers. In both countries, education is nearly universal, and masses of voters aspire to make it more so. A larger proportion of Japanese (90%) finish the 12th grade than Americans (75%, but if we count later completion of a high-school equivalency, it is about 83%), and a greater proportion of Japanese males complete university degrees than in other countries, including the United States. So we are not comparing an elite system with a mass system. Another similarity makes the comparison reasonable: while almost all of the 19 rich democracies have a quite small proportion of private secondary schools, the standout exceptions are the United States and Japan (along with France and Britain), where the "private" sector is substantial (26% of total education expenditure in the U.S., 21% in Japan).

The remaining differences that have developed over the past 30 years in structure, finance, operation, and quality as well as outcomes are dramatic. Consider the following (based on studies by Rohlen, 1983 and 1985–86; Clark, 1985a, 1985b; Thomas, 1983; Hiroshi Kida et al., 1983; Cummings, 1980; and Heidenheimer et al., 1990, pp. 23–56), tracing the differences in K–12. Unless otherwise specified, figures in table 12.10 come from Rohlen.

These K–12 differences result in sharp contrasts in the mastery of academic subject matter, habits of discipline, and preparation for lifetime learning among the general population. It is clear that the average Japanese 18-year-old has an edge of about three years over his American age-mate in science and math; earlier in the elementary years, he has acquired an edge in languages, music, and art; and the Japanese gap between the well educated and the poorly educated is small compared to that in the United States. As Rohlen concludes, "In many respects the upper half of Japan's graduating high-school students possess a level of knowledge and analytical skills equivalent to the average American graduating from college" (Rohlen 1985–86 p. 30). It would be surprising if they did not: they have spent the equivalent of about three American years longer in school (more hours, more days) in which academic achievement is rewarded; they have spent more hours doing homework; they have been exposed to demanding teachers who are widely respected, well paid, use challenging teaching materials, have pedagogical autonomy as well as time to plan their work and consult with colleagues. The result: Japanese employers introducing new technology, say numerically controlled machine tools, can expect average high-school graduates to read instruction manuals comparable to American engineering textbooks and quickly master the new system. In Robert Cole's phrase, Japan has accomplished the "democratization of

TABLE 12.10 Comparing Japanese and American schools

	Japan	United States
Four-year olds attending school	63%	32%
Average daily hours of homework during high school	2 hrs.	0.5 hrs.
Daily absentee rate	negligible	9%
Years required of high school math	3 (typical)	1
Years required of foreign language (grades 7-12)	6	0-2
Days of school/year	240	180
Teacher pay: ratio of average secondary school teacher salary to per capita GNP 1987 (Heidenheimer *et al.*, 1990, p. 42)	2.03	1.44
Teacher status, other rewards	High status and pay; early tenure promotion by seniority	Low status; average pay low but big dispersion; later tenure; fluctuation in employment
Teacher unions (Shanker 1982)	Public schools almost 100% unionized, deeply entrenched, political	lower rate of unionization; rival organizations (AFT, NEA, state and non-union), weaker
Tutoring	Cram schools widespread; the *juku* enroll 1 in 3 middle school, 1 in 4 upper-elementary students	Rare
Equality of opportunity	Very meritocratic, with a high minimum achievement expected	Mildly meritocratic; heavily structured by social class and residence
Tracking	None until age 15 when students are sorted by ability for senior high schools of varied quality and status	Common at every level, but looser; no major sorting until academic vs. other in high school
Gifted student programs	None	Some
"Special education"	None	Much
Standards and curricula	Uniform and high (equivalent to those of elite education in Europe and America)	Greatly varied; locally controlled, with typically low expectations
University and college admissions	Highly competitive, universal standardized national entrance tests at age 18 for elite institutions	Greatly varied from open enrollment to highly competitive
University and college academic standards	Low, and increasingly class structured	Varied, but often high and quite meritocratic

statistical methods" (Cole, 1989, p. 278). No productivity mystery here: both managers and their workers have the trained cognitive skills and work habits for flexible adaptation to rapid technological change. Contrast the CEO of General Motors in Detroit. Not only is he handicapped by his own failure to plan, invest, and train (until he had lost most of his share of world markets); he cannot assume that Detroit workers have either the multiple skills or the work habits of workers of his competitors abroad. That is one reason he cannot successfully introduce the continuous improvement strategy so prominent in Japan and much of Europe (see chap. 1). Employers in South Korea and Taiwan, too, can now recruit and readily train skilled workers, building on the learning advantage of K–12 systems similar to Japan's (Postlethwaite and Thomas, 1983, pp. 308–342; Sah-Myung, 1983; Lin, 1983). Industrial firms everywhere adapt their technology and organization to the capacities of the average worker they can recruit (see chap. 13 on job creation).

Many observers who concede the existence of these differences say, "Ah, well, Japan is homogeneous—few minorities, few immigrants—and still has strong families; if Japan had America's racial and ethnic mix and divorce rates, it would have the same school problems." That ignores drastic differences in public policy that have nothing to do with America's social heterogeneity—practically everything on the list above. Neither social heterogeneity nor high rates of family breakup have prevented most of Europe from imposing high standards on K–12—not as high as Japan's, but much higher than those of the United States (Heidenheimer et al., 1990, chap. 2).[21] Nor have these problems prevented the United States from developing perhaps the most successful system of mass higher education in the world, with many of the demanding characteristics of Japan's K–12.

Going beyond the extremes of the United States and Japan, there appear to be three major differences between schools in some rich European democracies and American schools. First, the United States is unique in its automatic promotion of students from grade to grade whatever their school performance. The consequences include a large minority of American high-school graduates who still read at 8th-grade level or do math at the 6th-grade level (Clark, 1985a, p. 314). Undemanding programs, underperforming pupils. Second, American schoolteachers rank low in average status and income (compared to other college graduates or white-collar workers or average per capita income). This reflects three handicaps: huge district inequities; weaker teacher training; and a generally lower rate of teacher unionization than that of Europe or Japan. In Japan, teachers are almost totally organized in a deeply entrenched and politicized union; comparable American unions are less densely organized, more divided (AFT, NEA, separate state organizations, and a substantial nonunion sector). Regarding education, American secondary-school teachers are uniquely trained in Schools of Education with a focus on methods more than substance; in Europe and Japan alike, they are recruited mainly from higher-status university departments emphasizing subject matter. (Rohlen, 1985–86, pp. 38–39; Clark, 1985a, pp. 298–300, 269, 276–280.)

In addition to uniquely automatic student promotions and low teacher status and pay there is a third pattern: extreme decentralization resulting in huge inequities in funding from state to state, district to district, school to school (Howe, 1991, p. 200), in degree unique to the United States. Exacerbating this handicap in funding and performance is America's reliance on property taxes for school funding. Because this tax, the most unpopular of all, creates intense tax resistance (see chap. 10), it is a highly unreliable source of revenue. Thus, when California's Proposition 13 drastically cut property taxes—a 1978 ballot initiative enshrined in the Constitution, sold as "Something for Nothing" by demagogues, money, and the media—one of the best public school systems in the country moved from above average in per pupil current expenditure in 1977–78 to 36th in 1990–91 (Howe, 1991, p. 200; U.S. Dept. of Education, 1980, table 70; *San Francisco Chronicle,* November 16, 1992). At the same time, it moved up to become the system with the second-largest class size in the nation (Howe, 1991, p. 200). Other states, too, saw the revenue base for schools erode.

At first glance, Japanese schools are much more meritocratic than U.S. schools; European schools, too, typically have the edge in rewarding performance. This American disadvantage is no doubt true for the U.S. system on average. But there are large segments of the American system, both public and private, where upper-middle-class and upwardly mobile lower-middle-class parents send their children to quality schools practicing meritocratic values. And, of course, American colleges and universities are far more meritocratic and provide far more equality of opportunity than those in Japan or much of Europe, although these differences have slowly diminished as higher education has expanded everywhere (chap. 1; and Trow, 1988, 1991a, 1991b).

A final difference in table 12.10 is less than meets the eye—tracking. Japan keeps almost all students in school until the end of senior high. But it combines intense general education with tracking at age 15 into senior high schools of diverse entrance requirements and quality; students compete vigorously to get into the best. While the United States clings to the ideology of comprehensiveness, it indirectly accomplishes some of the Japanese-style tracking by the sharp differences in district funding I noted and by social-class segregation; for example, in 1982, 31% of families with incomes over $75,000 sent their children to private schools compared to only 3.3% of families with incomes below $7,500 and about 13% of those with incomes of $25,000 to $49,999 (Catterall, 1988, p. 59). Unfortunately, this road to tracking widens the gap between the well educated and the poorly educated, a factor among many in the lagging productivity increases of the average American worker since the early 1970s.[22]

That the upper-strata advantage in school performance in the United States is a class difference, not a private vs. public difference, is demonstrated by studies of school achievement that take the trouble to compare students in public and private secondary schools who have similar family background and have taken similar courses (e.g., algebra, history, literature). The alleged private school advantage trumpeted by enthusiasts for the all-purpose solution, school vouchers (e.g., Chubb and Moe, 1990), is entirely due to these differences in the social composition of the schools and the percentage of students in an academic track (Shanker and Rosenberg, 1992). A friendly critic of vouchers, in a careful review of recent empirical evidence comparing private and public schools (including the Milwaukee experiment with voucher subsidies for private nonsectarian schools) concludes that the costs of private schools are higher, "choice" increases system inequality, and per student achievement is about the same (Levin, 1998). Private schools have the added luxury of being able to select students by exam and throw them out if they are disruptive (the latter are typically dumped on the public schools). In view of these advantages it is a sad commentary that where similar students are compared, American private schools do not perform better than public schools and that by international standards both public and private schools perform badly despite recent improvements.

In sum: The gross measurements of investment in education used here have no consistent pattern of association with any of the economic performance measures nor with the structural and policy roots of economic performance. From our limited quantitative data we cannot specify the influence of education and training relative to type of political economy, industrial relations, and capital investment. However, more intensive examination of types and quality of education as they relate to active labor-market policy and the discussion of the United States and Japan above validate the theme that human capital investment pays off in good economic performance.

Demographic Structure

Some economists believe that this shapes economic performance. An economy burdened with a poor dependency ratio (many nonworking aged and young) or with many young and inexperienced workers, or with many inexperienced women, should be less robust than others. (Denison, 1979, pp. 1, 3, 34–36; 1974, pp. 33ff.) Using five indicators—dependency ratio, population aged 15–19, 20–24, 25–29, and 65+—we see many consistent correlations. At first glance, very young populations (aged 15–19) are negatively and significantly correlated with the economic performance index, mainly because teenagers increase unemployment in all periods and they increase inflation before 1974. But when we run regressions with two of our six main sources of economic performance at a time against any of the age brackets or dependency ratio (highly correlated with age 15–19), no age variable has any independent effect on any measure of economic performance, except one in one recent period. Age 15–19 significantly increases unemployment in 1985–89 even when we hold constant corporatism, leftism, Catholicism, capital investment, strikes, and social spending. In this broad overview of four decades and 19 countries, demographic structure rarely has any influence on the economy. And neither the level nor the rate of increase of women in the labor force has any effect on economic performance.

Data on the United States alone, however, are ambiguous. Benjamin Friedman argues that "the increase in the share of younger workers began in 1955, fully a decade before the productivity slowdown. And it was practically over by 1973, before the more serious phase of the productivity slowdown began" (1989, p. 192). But Edward Denison (1979, p. 106 and table 8–2), combining age and sex for an index of worker experience, shows that young populations are a small drag on growth for all periods from 1953 to 1976, including 1973–76. Relative to other causes of economic performance, age structure (and gender) may be minor, consistent with both our 19-country findings and those of Denison and Friedman.

In sum, age structure is strongly related to corporatism and welfare-state spending; older populations are found in corporatist democracies that include labor, which, for reasons discussed previously, are highly developed welfare states. But age structure and gender have little or no effect on economic performance.

There remain three variables that could have a negative effect on the economy: military spending, the size of the public bureaucracy, and the presence of many lawyers. The next sections deal with each.

Military Spending

In my previous analysis of the effects of military spending on social spending and economic performance (Wilensky, 1975, pp. 70–85), I found that while the destruction and total mobilization of World War II brought an ideology of shared sacrifice, the spread of social rights and benefits, and the reduction of unemployment, the cold war and small wars of 1951–73 subverted both the welfare state and economic progress. This was especially true of the welfare-state laggards or middling spenders that launched a military effort of well beyond 6% or 7% of their GNP in the early 1950s—United States, the UK, and Canada, countries located at or near the center of pacts and alliances. The effect was to retard both social spending and GDP growth and to increase unemployment in subsequent years (pp. 78, 84).

The political explanation: "A foreign policy accenting military spending [cold war, small wars] without total and sustained mobilization is expensive enough and inflationary enough to make the argument 'cut the domestic frills, balance the budget' seductive. But it is not so expensive as to put the middle majority in the mood for 'equality of sacrifice' " (pp. 79–80). So both social spending and taxing lag. The economic explanation: A heavy military burden diverts skilled workers and managers and scarce funds away from more productive investment and employment and thereby slows down economic growth and worsens unemployment. Budget deficits in the absence of productive uses of the borrowed money may be an additional drag. (pp. 74–85.)

In the context of a 19-country comparison covering the entire postwar period, does this conclusion stand up? Two findings emerge from our multivariate analysis. First, in regressions including corporatism, leftism, Catholicism, and military spending as independent variables, *the military effort (military spending/GNP) from 1960 to 1986 is consistently and strongly a drag on capital investment.* This relationship remains strong even when Israel and the United States and Japan are removed from the equation as extreme cases (Japan very high capital investment, very low military; United States second in military, very low capital investment; Israel first in military, missing data on capital investment). Second, that advantage in investment enjoyed by countries with a small military burden gives them a clear edge in economic performance, notably by increasing growth. The direct relationship between military spending and the index is negative but only marginally significant, except for the 1980s, when it was quite strong. There is little or no connection with inflation or unemployment. The military impact is entirely rooted in the negative correlation with economic growth. Using time series and comparing the multiplier effects of military and nonmilitary government spending, recent research on the United States also provides strong evidence that military spending has an indirect, delayed impact: by reducing investment it is a drag on economic growth (Mintz and Huang, 1991; Ward and Davis, 1992)—consistent with our 19-country analysis.

Bureaucratic Bloat

We have seen in chapter 9 that civilian bureaucracies in 1980 ranged from Japan's 6.5 as a percentage of the civilian labor force to Sweden's 28.6%. We also found that while corporatist democracies have a penchant for taxing and spending, many of them save on the personnel necessary to deliver the goods: they avoid the elaborate means-testing machinery of more decentralized regimes; and their very centralization slows the multiplication and growth of regional and local bureaucracies. So they cluster in the medium and medium-low levels of public employment. Regimes that keep labor at a distance are especially lean in their bureaucracies. This relative efficiency of corporatist democracies is one more reason for their advantage in economic performance.

Multiple regressions including corporatism, Catholicism, leftism, social spending, capital investment, and strikes (our six basic variables) show that big public bureaucracies were a drag on economic growth in the period 1951–74. This holds up even when we drop Japan, which has the leanest bureaucracy with the highest economic growth. The least-corporatist countries with large bureaucracies (USA, UK, Canada, Australia, New Zealand) had the lowest growth in 1951–74, while Italy, West Germany, and Israel with relatively small public bureaucracies had high growth. Big bureaucracies also increased inflation in one recent period, 1985–89. Although not as consistent or as strong as capital investment and low strike rates, lean bureaucracies do have a moderately favorable impact on economic growth at times.

Are Lawyers a Drag on the Economy?[23]

"The first thing we do, let's kill all the lawyers" (Dick to Jack Cade in Shakespeare, *Henry VI,* Part 2:73). In discussions of the decline in the rate of growth of American productivity after 1973, it is often said that the United States is plagued by a surfeit of lawyers who do unproductive tasks, divert talent and energy away from industrial progress, escalate conflict, and create an explosion in liability insurance and litigation (especially tort law) that imposes heavy costs on business and professional activity and restrains innovation, while our most serious competitors, free of such burdens, outpace us in economic performance. In the 1992 presidential campaign, President Bush and Vice President Quayle tried to make lawyers an issue. In many speeches, including their acceptance speeches, they both bashed rapacious trial lawyers and claimed that such lawyers had Bill Clinton in their pocket. Bush said that Americans need to care for one another more and sue each other less, and claimed that tort-law reform would restore economic growth. Quayle claimed that the litigation explosion is costing the United States $300 billion a year and has damaged its competitiveness. (*Los Angeles Times,* August 14, 21, and 28, 1992.)

In cross-national perspective it is certainly true that the United States is loaded with lawyers. Not only is the United States second only to Israel in lawyers as a percentage of the civilian labor force, but together these two countries are far ahead of the next most lawyer-loaded countries (Finland, Canada, New Zealand, Australia, UK, and Ireland). Further, with the exception of New Zealand and Finland, the same countries, with the UK in the lead, had the highest growth rate of law school graduates per 100,000 population from 1970 to 1979, suggesting the rule, "The more lawyers, the more lawyers." The leaders in lawyers now will be even further ahead by the year 2000.[24]

Finally, table 12.11 and multiple regressions show the following strong results:

- Lawyers and the recent acceleration of law school graduates are *concentrated in the least-corporatist countries* (especially USA, Canada, Australia, UK, and Ireland).

TABLE 12.11 Types of political economy, lawyers 1982, law school graduate growth rate 1970–79, and economic performance 1974–89[a]

	Lawyers as % of civilian labor force 1982		Growth rate of law school graduates 1970-79		Economic Performance											
					1974-79				1980-84				1985-89			
					Index	GR	IN	UN	Index	GR	IN	UN	Index	GR	IN	UN
Left Corpor.																
Sweden	.17[b]	(9)	6	(15)	3	L	M	L	4	M	M	L	3	M	H	L
Norway	.11	(14)	24	(11)	6	H	L	L	4	H	H	L	3	L	M	L
Finland	.35	(3)	3	(16)	2	M	H	M	4	H	M	M	3	H	H	M
Israel	.59	(1)	–23	(19)	1	L	H	M	NA				NA			
Denmark	.11	(14)	9	(14)	2	L	M	M	2	M	M	H	2	L	M	M
Left-Cath. Corp.																
Netherlands	.07	(17)	38	(8)	4	M	L	M	2	L	L	H	2	L	L	H
Belgium	.14[c]	(11)	47	(6)	3	M	L	H	3	M	L	H	4	H	L	H
Austria	.07	(17)	–15	(18)	6	H	L	L	5	M	L	L	5	M	L	L
Cath. Corpor.																
Italy	.11	(14)	23	(12)	1	M	H	H	2	M	H	M	2	H	H	H
W. Germany	.15	(10)	29	(9)	5	H	L	M	4	M	L	M	4	M	L	M
Corp. w/o Labor																
France	.07	(17)	–1	(17)	4	H	M	M	1	L	H	M	2	M	M	H
Japan	.03	(19)	14	(13)	6	H	L	L	6	H	L	L	6	H	L	L
Switzerland	.11	(14)	96	(2)	4	L	L	L	5	M	L	L	5	M	L	L
Least Corpor.																
USA	.51	(2)	89	(4)	2	L	L	H	4	M	L	M	4	M	L	M
UK	.20	(8)	105	(1)	1	L	H	M	1	L	M	H	2	H	H	H
New Zealand	.30	(5)	27	(10)	2	L	H	L	3	H	H	M	1	L	H	M
Australia	.27	(6)	92	(3)	1	L	H	M	3	M	M	M	2	M	H	M
Canada	.33	(4)	45	(7)	2	M	M	H	1	L	M	H	2	M	M	H
Ireland	.20	(8)	88	(5)	2	H	H	H	1	M	H	H	3	H	M	H

[a]Sources: Data on number of lawyers from American Bar Foundation, *International Directory of Bar Associations* (Chicago: American Bar Foundation, 1983, 4th ed.) refer to lawyers practicing or "members of the legal profession" except in six cases: "legally trained" (Sweden), admitted to the bar (Belgium), or to practice (the Netherlands) or licensed (Denmark). Ireland includes both barristers and solicitors. Data for the UK includes solicitors only. Adding barristers would move the UK up a bit to .28, closer to Australia. The Legal Services Act of 1990 began a merger of the functions of British barristers and solicitors *Economist* July 18, 1992, Survey p. 5. Civilian labor force data from OECD, *Labor Force Statistics 1983* (Paris: OECD, 1983) except those for Israel, from Central Bureau of Statistics, *Statistical Abstract of Israel 1985* No. 36 (Jerusalem: Central Bureau of Statistics, 1985), p. 314.

[b]Sweden based on extrapolation from number of lawyers 1972 and growth rate of 6% 1970–79 and inferred growth rate of 6.7% for 1972–82.

[c]Belgium based on extrapolation as for Sweden, with inferred growth rate of 52% for 1972–82.

• Lawyers are *strongly correlated with strikes in all periods.* (The U.S. is an outlier on lawyers. Israel is first in lawyers, last in lawyer growth. Eliminating either or both of these deviant or extreme cases strengthens the correlations.)

• Lawyers are *negatively correlated with capital investment* only in 1973–77.

• Lawyers are *negatively correlated with the economic performance index,* significantly in 1974–79 and 1985–89. The correlations with one or another component of the index are significant for one or both lawyer-density measures for all periods, including a negative correlation with growth in 1980–84.

• Because of strong negative associations of lawyers with corporatism and social spending and strong positive associations with strikes, it is difficult to sort out the distinctive economic effects of lawyers in regression analysis, controlling for the six basic variables. However, the most consistent pattern is that *lawyers increase unemployment rates* in all three periods, have a *negative effect on growth* in 1980–84, and *foster inflation* in 1985–89.

Quite an indictment. But we must try to sort out cause and effect. Applying theories of corporatism and mass society (chaps. 2 and 3), I suggest that an abundance of lawyers is more a consequence than a cause of the social and political vacuum created by mass-society tendencies. In the most-fragmented and decentralized political economies, mediating associations such as churches, unions, and other broad-based voluntary associations are losing their hold, political parties have declined, and the broadcast media are in ascendance. Lawyers appear where mechanisms of conflict resolution erode and where political polarization increases. In American labor relations, where management and unions engage in all-out war or armed truce, or where management tries to break unions, lawyers are used as weapons, especially by employers hiring outside firms that specialize in creating a "union-free environment," thereby further escalating conflict. Militant employers who succeed in eliminating unions increasingly find themselves in court defending against individual workers' charges of unjust dismissal—the Lord's revenge for their hostility to collective bargaining. In racial, religious, and ethnic conflict where political parties, unions, and legislatures lose their capacity to bring warring factions together, sectarian caucuses and splinter groups abound; maximum, unnegotiable demands become the custom. In such cases, confrontation is often followed by deadlock and a turn toward lawyers and courts. Thus, the proliferation of lawsuits charging discrimination by race, gender, age, handicap, or sexual orientation.

The judicialization of labor relations and minority relations has its counterpart in other areas of intense combat, such as environmental regulation, occupational health and safety, health care, and welfare; indeed, it is America's approach to all of its social problems. In the absence of strong mediating associations and political parties that can forge accommodation and cooperation, social problems are thrown into an often polarized legislature. There, laws are frequently changed and then challenged when executive agencies attempt to implement them with judicialized rules (see Shapiro, 1988, pp. 41–44, 73–75, 90–91). Often, the legislators' aim is to paper over conflicts with ambiguous language so they can dump unresolved problems on an administrative agency. The agency does its best to capture the intent of the law, but, anticipating legal challenges, issues labyrinthine regulations to cover all bases. Advocates opposed to the law, having lost in Congress, then launch constitutional challenges, pushing for substantive changes. Others aim to delay implementation by alleging that the agency is not obeying the law.

It does not help that 42% of the seats in the U.S. House of Representatives and 61% of seats in the Senate are held by lawyers. Legislator-lawyers both reflect and foster the American mass sentiment, "There oughta be a law to stop that." Their professional bias is to solve problems by prohibiting behavior with punitive sanctions; the typical results are elaborate, complex laws and regulations enforced by lawsuits and courts. As the Executive branch implements the laws every agency, every congressional committee, every interest group becomes a wary watchdog challenging every other, questioning conformity to the law. Thus, more than 50% of EPA's "major" regulations have been challenged in federal court (Coglianese, 1994, pp. 65–67). The EPA must also report to a labyrinth of legislative committees: 11 House and 9 Senate committees and at least 50 subcommittees. "During several years of the 1980s, EPA officials were called to Capitol Hill to testify more than 100 times—about every other working day" (Kagan, 1991a, p. 396). It is a wide-open system dominated by mutual veto groups equipped with a bevy of lawyers.

In short, although the availability of lawyers does not create the original demand for their services, once vacuums of power emerge, lawyers and judges along with single-issue groups and the media will fill them, reinforcing already well-developed adversarial, confrontational tendencies. Vacuums of power create the demand for lawyers; when lawyers appear, they create a demand for one another, exacerbating adversarial legalism and increasing the cost of doing business.

Obviously, the consensus-making machines I have labeled democratic corporatism—these negotiated economies—need and have fewer lawyers. And they need and have less civil litigation.[25] Consequently, they have an edge in the people, time, and the money devoted to productive activity. Hence the syndrome of decentralized, disorganized political economies, abundant lawyers, high strike rates, and lagging economic performance.[26]

In explaining the recent association of lawyers and poor economic performance, I have emphasized the diversion of talent, energy, and time from routine productive activity, the escalation of adversarial legalism, rather than the tort liability explosion in the United States because the facts about litigation trends and costs are in dispute.

Regarding trends, even before the recent expansion of lawyers and tort liability cases, the United States had long been a litigious nation, which did not prevent it from becoming the richest country in the world. In his sensitive portrait of *American Democracy* in the 1830s, Tocqueville observed that

> Scarcely any political question arises in the United States that is not resolved sooner
> or later into a judicial question . . . the spirit of the law, which is produced in the
> schools and courts of justice, gradually penetrates beyond their walls into the bosom
> of society where it descends to the lowest classes, so that at last the whole people
> contract the habits and tastes of the judicial magistrate. (1963, Vol. I, p. 280)

In fact, some scholars have suggested that the present level of civil litigation in either federal or district courts, while higher than in the past, is not an extreme departure from patterns of 100 to 150 years ago; the change is more incremental than explosive. Going further back, we find that in some jurisdictions colonial America was more litigious than contemporary America. In Accomack County, Virginia, 1639, the litigation rate of 240 per year per thousand population was more than four times that in any contemporary American county (Curtis, 1977, pp. 280–287; cf. Konig, 1979, for a similar picture of litigiousness in Essex County, Mass., 1672–1686).[27] The civil cases concern market transactions—contracts, property, and debt collection.

What is true about trends in the United States in the past 50 to 100 years is that doctrines of liability have changed, tort liability filings (like family-law cases) have soared, and the spirit of adversarial legalism has spread to new areas of American life. Since World War II, our period for the economic-performance analysis, doctrines of liability have become more hospitable to lawsuits: courts have removed the need to prove pain and suffering, introduced absolute liability rather than negligence as a criterion, expanded damages to encompass intangible damages, and abandoned the "no privity" doctrine so that anyone participating in the production or distribution of a product can be sued by an aggrieved purchaser. As Friedman (1985) suggests, these doctrines reflect a spreading demand for "total justice." Citizens, political activists, lawyers, and legislators alike generate this demand. There is also general agreement that whatever the long-term trend, litigation accelerated in the mid-1960s and exploded in the 1980s and 1990s, driven especially by business litigation (intellectual property, contracts, antitrust), as well as corporate mergers and takeovers.

Like the rate of litigation, the direct costs of litigation have accelerated in recent decades, although not as dramatically as some researchers (e.g., Sander and Williams, 1989, pp. 434–435) have claimed. Long-term shifts are difficult to assess because of changes in the definition of the "legal services" component of the GNP (1960 is not quite comparable to 1987). However, if we concentrate on a shorter period and confine ourselves to all private expenditures on lawyers (leaving out lawyers on payrolls of government bureaucracies and corporate legal departments), a good trend estimate can be made: in constant 1982 dollars, the total direct cost increased by almost 50% from $27 billion in 1977 to about $40 billion in 1988. As a percentage of GNP, however, the increase appears less explosive. In 1977, legal services were 0.9% of the GNP; by 1988, it rose to 1.0%—a jump of only about 11% (De Leeuw, Mohr, and Parker, 1991, pp. 34–35). If we include house counsel for government and business, the increase might be much higher. And we can only guess at the indirect costs (which is how tort-reform advocate Peter Huber, 1988, p. 4, arrived at the $300 billion figure Vice President Quayle used).

Regarding current costs of the overload of litigation, horror stories abound. My favorite is about the Chicago men, who, upon hearing a crash, poured out of a bar, climbed up to the elevated track, sprawled on the floor of the derailed train, and started to groan about their injured backs. But whether the Bush-Quayle assertion of $300 billion a year is about right or is wildly inflated, as the ABA and trial lawyers claim, the cost of litigation remains an open question. A more detached study of product liability by the Conference Board (Weber, 1987) suggests caution; except for a small number of specialized firms, the costs may be modest and the benefits, substantial. The Board polled 232 major U.S. corporations (annual sales of at least $100 million); manufacturing firms reported on product liability costs, service corporations on professional liability, utilities on general liability. What emerges is that two-thirds of the firms surveyed faced lawsuits within the past five years, most of them multiple lawsuits (14% were defendants in 101 to 500 suits per year). The economic impact these risk managers and other executives reported, however, was minor: two-thirds of the firms estimated that liability insurance accounted for less than 1% of the final price of the product, 11% of the companies said 2% to 3% of the final price.

Of course, for some segments of industry and for some professionals, the cost of tort liability and other litigation is much higher—ranging from the heavy awards and settlements paid by the producers of football helmets to the astronomical liability insurance premiums paid by obstetricians and other physicians who, in addition, practice defensive medicine— unnecessary lab tests and hospitalizations to ward off possible malpractice suits. "Malpractice insurance across Europe costs less than 10% of the $16,000 annual average in America (where some specialists . . . pay up to $250,000 a year in premiums)" (*The Economist,* July 18, 1992, p. 11). An insurance-industry consultant calculates that the liability-loss payment total in the United States in 1987 was $117 billion, about 2.5% of GNP, three times the proportion in any other rich democracy. About half goes not to the injured, but to lawyers' fees. In Superfund pollution cases, lawyers take about 80% of the money; only 20% goes to environmental cleanup (*ibid.*, pp. 12 – 13). Beyond large corporations and physicians, many other occupations and institutions are especially burdened by the prospects of legal review or tort liability. They include teachers, truckers, nursing-home operators, environmental engineers, architects and builders who all spend hours preparing defensive paperwork (Bardach, 1982, pp. 316 – 325). Hardly any profession is immune from liability, except judges and legislators. And finally, the Conference Board study excluded the small- and medium-sized firms for whom tort liability suits can sometimes be fatal.

When the Conference Board researchers note that lawsuits are overwhelmingly settled out of court, usually for very modest sums, they overlook the gobs of energy and time the paperwork and the confrontations in and out of court can consume. Whatever these costs, however, the Conference Board does point to some clear gains for both industry and society: "Where product liability has had a notable impact—where it has most significantly affected management decision-making—has been in the quality of the products themselves. Managers say products have become safer, manufacturing procedures have been improved, and labels and use instructions have become more explicit" (Weber, 1987, p. 2). And these are industry witnesses speaking, not Ralph Nader. Whether the cost is $117 billion or $300 billion—it is not all a loss to the economy.

What this discussion of the costs of the explosion of litigation in the United States suggests is this: while a few other nations have a high density of lawyers, the United States stands out in the proportion and power of lawyers; its adversary legalism is so widespread and so highly developed that some aspects of it are unique. As many students of American law and society have observed (Kagan, 1991a; Friedman, 1985; Bok, 1983; Langbein, 1985), the United States, compared to all other rich democracies, now has far more complex legal rules, more formal adversarial procedures for resolving political and scientific disputes, more punitive sanctions, more costly litigation, and, as we have seen in chapters 1 and 2, more unpredictability and reversibility in legislative, administrative, and judicial decisions alike. In frequency and strength of judicial review of its laws and intervention in executive branch decisions, the United States is also a leader, although France and Germany are close by (Shapiro and Stone, 1994).

The tort liability component of the lawyer drag on the economy, while it points to "American exceptionalism" may be a minor part of the total cost of economic activity. Without that cost—indeed if we simply eliminate the United States and Israel from the analysis as extreme cases—the pattern remains: an abundance of lawyers is a reflection of deeper problems of weak consensus among this largely Anglo-American group of democracies; weak consensus is bad for your economic health.

IS INEQUALITY HARMFUL TO ECONOMIC GROWTH?

Because of difficult problems of measurement and comparability, the answers to this old question seldom go beyond informed speculation.[28] The best we can do with our data set is to examine one cross-sectional moment. Using three measures of inequality for the year 1980 for 17 of our rich democracies and assuming that income distribution by quintiles did not change much in the short period 1974–84, we can relate inequality to our economic performance measures for the few years before and after 1980. The correlations appear in appendix G. Inequality is measured by the share of gross household income going to the richest fifth of households, the share going to the poorest fifth (a measure of relative poverty), and the ratio of the two (roughly, the distance between the well-off and the poor). Details and country ranks are in table 14.4 and chapter 14 on mayhem. All three measures of inequality are significantly related to the economic performance index and to average real GDP growth per capita in 1974–79—the more inequality, the less growth— but none of the correlations are significant for 1980–84 (see appendix table 12G.11). What this pattern suggests is that equality is a consequence, not a cause of economic growth and good general performance, at least for these two short post-oil-shock periods. A study using different measures and longer time periods, however, comes to the opposite conclusion. Persson and Tabellini (1991) use two samples: one of 9, the other of 67 countries. The first contains historical evidence from nine of our currently rich democracies (Austria, Denmark, Finland, Germany, the Netherlands, Norway, Sweden, the UK, and the USA) for 20-year periods from 1830–1970 and the 15-year period 1970–85. They regress average growth rate of GDP per capita for each country and each 20-year episode on income inequality (the share in personal income before tax of the top 20% of the population), schooling (as an indicator of average skills), level of development (level of per capita income at the start of the period), and political participation (extent of the franchise). In regression analysis, they find that inequality at the beginning of each period slows down economic growth; one standard deviation in the income share of the top 20% lowers the average annual growth rate almost half a percentage point. Differences in income distribution alone explain about a fifth of the variance in growth rates across countries and time (*ibid.*, pp. 17, 18, and table 3.2).

Examining less comparable data from a larger sample of 67 countries (covering 1950–85 for half of them, 1960–85 for the rest), and using the ratio of pretax income of the top 20% to that of the bottom 40%, Persson and Tabellini find a very similar negative effect of inequality on economic growth. When they analyze two types of regimes among their 67 separately for 1960–85—democratic and nondemocratic—and include controls for industrialization and urbanization, the relationship becomes insignificant for nondemocratic systems but remains strong for democracies. In other words, under democratic regimes, rich countries that achieve relative equality have a substantial edge in subsequent economic growth over all others. Cases in point include Japan, Israel, and Austria, industrializing democracies that strongly pursued income-equalizing and mass-education policies before their growth take-off in the late 1950s and early 1960s. Several "soft" authoritarian regimes among the NICs similarly initiated massive equalization before swift economic growth took place—for example, South Korea and Taiwan. (Adelman 1978; Persson and Tabellini 1991, p. 11.)[29]

A similar analysis by Alesina and Rodrik (1992) yields almost identical results: Using the average growth rate 1960–85 for 67 countries and controlling for school enrollment and initial level of per capita income, they find that increases in the income shares of poorer quintiles foster growth, while increases in the income shares of the richest quintile or the top 5% foster decreases in growth. When they analyze types of polities separately, the relationship for authoritarian regimes disappears but the positive effect of equality on growth for 24 democracies is very strong. Growth is particularly sensitive to the income share of the most politically active middle class and that of the top quintile. Advocates of growth should beware of too great a distance between the rich and the celebrated "middle class"— a finding that complements my analysis of the revolt of the middle mass (chap. 10 and Wilensky, 1975, pp. 116–118). More recent data for 1990 shows the same: inequality is bad for economic growth.

An intensive study by Hibbs and Locking (2000) of the impact of wage equalization on productivity in Sweden from 1956 to 1993 (an extreme case) suggests that the positive effect we find for income equality holds as well for wage equalization across industries and occupational groups (equal pay for equal work). In other words, the original policy of wage solidarity of the LO, the powerful blue-collar labor federation, enhanced productivity in Swedish private industry. Hibbs and Locking also find that if wage compression is too radical within plants and within industries, as it was during the 1970s up to 1983, it becomes a drag on productivity. There is something of an inverted U-curve in the relation of wage equality and efficiency: increase general equality, which handicaps the least productive firms, and you produce substantial economic gains; go too far within plants, ignoring skill differentials, and you lose the gains.[30]

The reverse causation inferred from my 17-country results for 1974–85 does not hold up in any of these three careful studies. So we cannot rule out the idea that equality is a source of economic growth, not the other way round. Although their models do not include the variables I have shown to be critical for good economic performance—types of corporatism and related policies regarding taxes, spending, training, labor, industry, and R&D—their findings are consistent with mine. Like most economists, Persson and Tabellini accent "the accumulation of knowledge usable in production" combined with incentives for individuals to acquire and use their skills (e.g., equality of opportunity in market-oriented economies); they add political institutions that diffuse both knowledge and economic incentives to masses of voters. In my version of the perverse effects of great economic inequality there is a vicious circle: inequality blocks the diffusion of knowledge and skills, intensifies industrial and political conflict, which further makes upper strata fight harder against equalization. For instance, if unions must struggle for equality by strikes and by driving up wages and hence inflation, if management provides little job security and opposes all taxes to pay for the welfare state or the "social wage," then growth will suffer.

Whatever further research shows about the direction of causation, we can conclude that there is a fairly strong interaction between economic growth and the reduction of the distance between rich and poor. Hence, the two-way arrow in my figure 12.1.

SUMMARY

From the analysis thus far we can see that the most important sources of good economic performance are corporatist bargaining arrangements (with or without the full integration of labor) and related public policies, specifically policies that foster low strike rates (a clue to effective industrial relations systems), high rates of capital investment, and worker participation in the community and workplace. Democratic corporatism also fosters restraint on nominal wages in the face of external inflationary shocks. In other words, a political economy that fosters labor peace has an edge in flexible adaptation to severe pressures.

Sheer *level* of taxes and social spending has no consistent effect, but the *structure* of taxes and social spending is often important. The positive impact of high social spending as a trade-off for labor peace and tax concessions to industry and thus enhanced growth and inflation control fades after 1973 and is nonexistent after 1979. *But in no period and for no measure of performance is social-security spending a significant drag.* Similarly, high total tax levels have a *positive* effect on economic performance before 1974 because they permit generous social spending and promote labor peace but have no effect thereafter. Thus the claim that the burden of high taxes and lavish social spending is the prime cause of our economic troubles misses the point. There are countries with low levels of taxing and spending that do well (Japan, Switzerland) and countries with high levels of taxing and spending that do well (Germany, Austria, Norway). And the poor performers include countries with lean taxes and spending and lavish taxes and spending. Insofar as taxes and spending shape the economy, it is their structure that counts, not their levels.

Contributing to the corporatist edge in economic performance is a tax structure emphasizing least visible taxes. Consumption taxes, because they are negatively related to strikes and positively related to capital formation, foster economic growth for almost all of the postwar period. Social-security taxes restrain inflation in normal times (1965–74, 1985–89) but have no effect just after the oil shocks; only in 1980–84, the period of severe multiple shocks, did these payroll taxes lower growth.

Regarding the structure of spending, the data generally show that an emphasis on means-tested, stigmatized benefits drains off investment, increases unemployment, and in 1980–84 was a drag on growth. The better-performing corporatist democracies, in contrast, emphasize universal categorical benefits and family policies.

Less complete data or data for fewer countries show that spending on civilian research and development and on education and training (with the accent on instructional services and high universally applied national standards) fosters good long-run economic performance. Avoiding high levels of military spending and bureaucratic bloat also helps. Avoiding lawyers and adversary legalism, which contribute to bureaucratic bloat, is also a good idea. But a surfeit of lawyers reflects the absence of strong institutions for conflict resolution (political parties, strong central governments, collective bargaining, inclusive unions, and other broad-based mediating groups); lawyers are more a symptom than a cause of polarized politics subversive of the economy. Finally, the less intrusive regulatory regimes of corporatist democracies are not only more effective than the confrontational styles of less consensual democracies but are also a factor in their long-term competitive edge, at least from 1950 to 1992.

Limited data suggest that income equalization, the reduction of great disparities between rich and poor, may enhance economic growth but it is also possible that prosperity is a source of equality. In any case, in the long run more successful economies are also more egalitarian societies.

It is a minor puzzle that corporatism-without-labor has an economic edge over corporatist political economies that include labor in high policy. Three explanations are consistent with my findings. First, Japan, Switzerland, and France, while they exclude labor federations from continuous sharing in national industrial and economic policies, do provide channels for local union participation; by law and collective bargaining they give close attention to job security, training, and employee motivation. All three join Germany and

Sweden as leaders in an active labor-market policy (see Wilensky, 1992a, and Schmid, Reissert, and Bruche, 1992, tables 18 and 20). Except for France, with its unruly and ideological labor movement and its poor economic performance in the 1980s, they have contained industrial conflict. Second, each in its own way achieves bureaucratic efficiency. In all three, labor pressures for a public-sector expansion are limited, so they score medium (Japan) or low (Switzerland and France) in bureaucratic bloat (see chap. 9). In France and Japan the key ministries recruit the very best university graduates who combine competence with esprit de corps (Ehrmann, 1976, p. 173; Suleiman, 1974, p. 247, 1984, p. 115; Johnson, 1982; Ridley and Blondel, 1969, pp. 36–41; Heady, 1979, p. 174; Fukai and Fukai, 1992, p. 31; Kim, 1988, p. 32; Pempel, 1992). In France, Switzerland and, to a lesser extent, in Japan, the careers of civil servants embrace both government and industry (Ridley and Blondel, 1969, pp. 42–43; Hughes, 1962, p. 34; and Smith, 1984, pp. 13–14); in Japan, this is accomplished by very early retirement with a move to politics and/or industry (Pempel, 1992). Third, because of their relatively comfortable interaction between government, commerce, and industry—and despite the limited inclusion of labor—these countries also avoid lawyers and adversarial legalism; they achieve economically useful consensus by other means. As I have suggested in chapter 2, however, the internal strains of this system—the tendency to ignore policy areas beyond the economic—make them unstable. They will either move toward fuller inclusion of labor, or experience increased industrial and social conflict. Japan especially has in recent years shown signs of greater labor integration. Both France and Japan seem to have undergone political realignments in the 1990s. And macroeconomic policy mistakes combined with lax regulation of banks stalled the Japanese economy for several years.

There remain two forces that I have not discussed in reporting the results of regression analysis. The first, external shocks, are often alleged to be increasingly important in a global economy, but, as we shall see, they are virtually irrelevant. The second, property taxes, are strongly associated with poor economic performance, but the meaning of that unanticipated correlation requires further discussion.

External Shocks Count Only at Extremes

As we earlier saw in tables 12.3 and 12.4, corporatist democracies, considering their greater vulnerability to energy price explosions and unfavorable shifts in their terms of trade, did quite well after 1973 compared to decentralized and fragmented political economies, especially in controlling inflation and holding down unemployment. At the extreme, energy shocks and trade vulnerability help to explain the lesser performance of the three exceptions, Denmark, Italy, and Israel. Each of these also had special internal weaknesses: Denmark an unusually sloppy welfare state and a marginal score on corporatism, Israel a uniquely heavy defense burden, Italy the worst strike record and budget deficits of our 19 countries.

Country ranks and scores for each component of energy dependence are in appendix table 12G.13; correlations with economic performance are in appendix table 12G.14. The multiple regression analysis plays each of our measures of external shocks—liquid fuels as a fraction of energy consumption, energy production as a fraction of energy consumption, and changes in terms of trade—against six basic sources of economic performance. The results (table 12.12) confirm my earlier country-by-country analysis: if energy dependence and the deterioration in the terms of trade have any effect—and it is very little—it is the reverse of what one would expect. There are only two marginally significant results: countries with poor terms of trade 1973–74 had *lower* inflation 1974–79, and countries with high energy dependence in 1978 had *higher* economic growth in 1980–84. Again, there are no significant effects on the performance index.

Regressing the components of the index on the three shock measures, we uncover only one statistically significant effect: deterioration of the terms of trade 1978–79 is linked to higher inflation in 1980–84 in equations that explain very little variance and do not include the robust causes, strike rates, and capital investment. (Regressions not reported here.) When these strong sources of economic performance are included, external shocks have no independent effect whatever (see table 12.12, which presents typical findings). If shocks have no direct effects on economic performance, perhaps they could have indirect effects on important sources of economic performance. When we use external shocks to explain strikes and capital formation, however, shocks again have no influence.

We can conclude that external shocks have little if any impact on economic performance; what counts are domestic policies that flow from political and economic institutions.

POSTSCRIPT: ARE PROPERTY TAXES A DRAG?

An unexpected finding is that high property taxes may create unemployment and retard economic growth. Appendix table 12G.12 shows quite strong negative correlations between property taxes and the economic performance index ranging from $-.87$ (1950–74) to $-.46$ (1985–89). Statistically speaking, property taxes are a drag on a major cause of good economic performance, capital investment (r for 1965–72, $-.68$; r for 1973–77, $-.45$; r for 1972–82, $-.40$; r for 1983–87, $-.38$) while such taxes are positively related to all the other sources of trouble: strikes (.79, .56, .40, .38), military spending/GNP (.39, .44, .48, .58), a large proportion of very young people (.48, .48, .27, .24), and most strongly, public assistance either as a percentage of GNP (.61, .68, .80, .79) or per capita (.61, .53, .70, .68), and lawyers as a percentage of the labor force (.63, .63, .57, .57). Multiple regression analysis suggests that the correlation of property taxes with everything else may not be entirely spurious. For instance, when strikes and capital investment—our two most powerful variables—are held constant, property taxes remain an independent dampener of economic performance until 1974 when the effect fades. Regressions for five periods are in table 12.13.

If property taxes are, indeed, a drag on economic performance, what is the explanation? First is the possible effect on housing costs. If, as in California in the mid-1970s, the average effective rate of property tax was about 2.5%, we can infer that the present value of the stream of tax payments and hence the cost of housing was at least 25% higher than it would be in the absence of property taxes—a nontrivial difference. That might be a major factor in a slowdown in construction and hence higher unemployment and slower economic growth. Another possible economic effect might be locational: with high property taxes, a nation's corporate offices and plants might be exported abroad or to an area or region where property taxes are lower. In a study of such location effects in the United States, Dick Netzer (1966, pp. 113–114) reports that even though property taxes are small frac-

TABLE 12.12 Typical regressions of economic performance on external shock measures, strikes, and capital investment[a]

Economic Performance 1974-79 as Dependent Variable								
Independent Variable	Performance Index		Average Growth		Average Inflation		Average Unemployment	
	(1)	(2)	(3)	(4)	(5)	(6)	(7)	(8)
Terms of Trade		.12		.27		−.38•		.14
Energy Dependence	.01		−.27		.00		−.23	
Strikes	−.61**	−.60**	.09	.10	.57*	.61*	.59**	.58**
Capital Investment	.47**	.46**	.54*	.41	−.03	.01	−.30	−.40*
AR²(N)	..66(18)	.68(18)	.09(18)	.11(18)	.37(17)[b]	.35(17)[b]	.53(18)	.50(18)

Economic Performance 1980-84 as Dependent Variable								
	(1)	(2)	(3)	(4)	(5)	(6)	(7)	(8)
Terms of Trade		−.20		.00		.28		−.14
Energy Dependence	.16		.39•		.13		−.15	
Strikes	−.52*	−.50*	−.09	−.16	.73**	.64**	.46*	.52*
Capital Investment	.29	.26	.49*	.57*	−.09	.02	−.29	−.36
AR²(N)	.37(18)	.38(18)	.41(18)	.24(18)	.43(18)	.49(18)	.27(18)	.27(18)

[a]Details on measures of external shocks and their meaning are in the text and appendix G.

[b]Israel is missing on capital formation in all equations; Italy is excluded from regressions of inflation 1974−79 as an extreme case.

tions of total business costs, they often reinforce other cost differentials such as those for labor, transportation, and corporate income taxes, especially in capital-intensive industries and in commercial real estate. For instance, he shows that in large American cities, effective property tax rates are much higher on large apartment buildings than on single-family dwellings (*ibid.*, p. 78; cf. O'Sullivan, Sexton, and Sheffrin, 1993, p. 54) and tend to be higher in central cities than in suburbs (Netzer, 1966, pp. 74−79, 83−85). He argues that heavy taxes on real property is a deterrent to rebuilding the big cities (p. 166). George Peterson shows that stiff property taxes are not only a deterrent to rebuilding but, more important, they fall most heavily on low-income urban neighborhoods, whose landlords respond by cutting repairs and maintenance costs while potential new buyers who might improve such properties withdraw (1973, pp. 110−124). The resulting deterioration of America's central cities has doubtless hastened the exodus of both population and industry already well under way from other causes. That reduces the urban tax base and, in the absence of any national urban policy, accelerates decay. Thus, despite economists' predisposition to the belief that property taxes are either neutral or trivial in their economic effects, we must at least entertain the notion that they make a difference for economic behavior independent of other sources of performance.

TABLE 12.13 Regressions testing economic effects of property taxes vs. strikes and capital investment[†]

Indep. Vars.	Dependent Variable = Economic Performance Index				
	1950-74	1965-74	1974-79	1980-84	1985-89
Strikes	−.37**	−.34	−.57**	−.47*	−.60*
Capital Investment	−.03	−.07	.37*	.25	.39
Property Taxes	−.75**	−.52•	−.25	−.22	−.01
Adj. R^2	.84	.33	.72	.38	.44
N	18	18	18	18	17

[†]Standardized regression coefficients (betas). • = $p < .10$, ★ = $p < .05$, ★★ = $p < .01$.

The correlations of property taxes with so many other sources of economic performance, however, may obscure the root cause: the interaction of types of political economy and party power, for which a case-by-case analysis is more appropriate. If we examine the countries with high property taxes over the four periods for which data are available (table 12.14), we see a striking pattern: all but one of the countries with a strong penchant for property taxes are least-corporatist countries whose economic performance for almost all of post–World War II has been mediocre to poor—United Kingdom, Ireland, United States, Canada, Australia, and New Zealand. In property taxes as a percentage of GDP, the median for all periods is above 2.4% (the UK reached 3.9% by the 1980s); the median for corporatist democracies is below 0.27%. Table 12.14 shows that corporatism-without-labor yields the lowest reliance on property taxes; the combination of leftism and corporatism yields the next lowest reliance on property taxes, the interplay of Catholic party power and corporatism yields only slightly more. The big contrast is between corporatist democracies and the fragmented and decentralized democracies. Denmark, the one exception, is a moderately corporatist country that ranks sixth or seventh in property taxes in every period (about 1.5% of GDP); it is also below average in economic performance and, like the UK and the USA, experienced one of the three strongest tax revolts in postwar history.

In short, while property taxes are clearly a source of political trouble (chap. 10), their economic impact remains ambiguous. There may be an interaction of a dozen variables disruptive to good steady economic growth and low unemployment of which property taxes are only one part: fragmented and decentralized democracies with high rates of mobility, strong minority-group cleavages, and many young people have high strike rates, spend a lot on the military and on means-tested public assistance, evidence bureaucratic bloat and intrusive styles of regulation, rely on visible taxes, including property taxes, have low capital investment, are overloaded with lawyers (lack other means of conflict resolution), and are vulnerable to tax-welfare backlash movements.

The whole syndrome of unfavorable structures, demographic forces, taxing and spending policies, and political responses makes it difficult to manage a modern economy. Countries that come close to fitting this description include the United States, the UK, Canada, New Zealand, Australia, and Ireland—least-corporatist countries with high property taxes.

TABLE 12.14 Property taxes[†] as a percentage of GDP, 1965–72, 1973–77, 1978–82, and 1983–87, by party power 1919–76 and types of political economy

Power and Types of Corporatism	Property Taxes as % of GDP							
	1965-72		1973-77		1978-82		1983-87	
Left Corporatist								
Sweden	0.01	(14)	0.00	(16)	0.01	(15)	0.36	(11)
Norway	0.21	(12)	0.19	(12)	0.16	(13)	0.22	(13)
Finland	0.00	(17)	0.00	(16)	0.03	(14)	0.10	(15)
Denmark	1.52	(7)	1.52	(6)	1.39	(6)	1.02	(6)
Left-Catholic Corporatist								
Netherlands	0.49	(9)	0.43	(9)	0.73	(8)	0.76	(9)
Belgium	0.00	(17)	0.00	(16)	0.00	(17)	0.00	(17)
Austria	0.36	(11)	0.29	(11)	0.29	(11)	0.30	(12)
Catholic Corporatist								
Italy	0.00	(17)	0.00	(16)	0.00	(17)	0.00	(17)
West Germany	0.41	(10)	0.39	(10)	0.40	(10)	0.40	(10)
Corporatist Without Labor								
France	0.60	(8)	0.55	(8)	0.70	(9)	0.94	(8)
Japan	0.00	(17)	0.00	(16)	0.00	(17)	0.00	(17)
Switzerland	0.13	(13)	0.17	(13)	0.18	(12)	0.10	(15)
Least Corporatist								
United States	3.62	(1)	3.49	(2)	2.80	(2)	2.72	(3)
United Kingdom	3.50	(2)	3.72	(1)	3.93	(1)	4.06	(1)
New Zealand	2.01	(5)	1.96	(5)	2.07	(4)	2.14	(4)
Australia	1.54	(6)	1.49	(7)	1.46	(5)	1.40	(5)
Canada	3.00	(4)	2.83	(3)	2.78	(3)	2.72	(3)
Ireland	3.20	(3)	2.45	(4)	1.15	(7)	0.98	(7)

[†]OECD Code 4100, Recurrent Taxes on Immovable Property, including both business and domestic property.

Notes

This chapter is a revision, elaboration, and update of themes and data summarized in a paper presented at the American Sociological Association meeting, San Francisco, September 8, 1982, and in Wilensky 1981a and 1983. I am grateful to William T. Dickens, Bent Hansen, and Jack Latiche for comments and advice.

1. A section below discusses the 1990s.

2. Regarding the myth that wealth was widely diffused in the U.S. in the 1990s: By 1997 the net worth of the top 1% of households was about $10 million, up 11.3% from 1989. Over the same period the net worth of the middle fifth of the wealth distribution fell by 2.9% and the percentage of households with net worth of $10,000 or less remained at about 32%. (Mishel, Bernstein, and Schmitt, 1999, tables 5.3 and 5.6 and figure 5c.) What about the stock market? In 1995 the bottom 90% of households, by wealth class, held only 11.6% of stocks and mutual funds (*ibid.*, table 5.4). In 1998 over half of all households owned no stock whatsoever, directly or indirectly (e.g., via pension funds); only 36% of households had more than $5,000 worth of stock (Wolff, forthcoming). Considering total compensation of executives over a longer period, in 1965 American CEOs made 20 times more than a typical worker; by 1997 that ratio reached 116 (Mishel et al., 1999, pp. 120, 212). Cross-nationally, "while U.S. workers earn less than workers in other advanced industrialized countries, U.S. CEOs make twice as much as their counterparts abroad" (p. 120). Of 12 rich democracies studied, the CEO/worker ratio in 1997 was largest in the U.S., Australia, and the UK; it was least (most egalitarian) in Japan, Switzerland, and Germany (p. 213, table 3.52).

3. "Actual" public spending because for this entire period, the government's frequent announcements of anticyclical spending goals, designed to restore consumer and business confidence, were nearly empty promises. The actual public spending in the 1990s ranged from zero to 56% of the announced figures. The only spending stimulus that exceeded half of its official annual level was the one that worked, September 1995. Among the devices to disguise the reality were front-loading of previously committed public works, land and other asset purchases, and direct funding of the financial system that ended with no net gain. In addition, local governments running deficits spent on average two-thirds of central government allocations—sometimes on wasteful projects (e.g., bridges with no traffic). (*Ibid.*, pp. 41–46.) The disjunction between pronouncements and reality likely accelerated the decline in confidence and a rise in precautionary savings.

4. Japan's bank supervisory staff for the entire country is under 300 total (Posen, 1998, p. 130).

5. Western and Beckett (1999) show that America's high incarceration rate combined with a high recidivism rate lowers the conventional unemployment rate by hiding joblessness. Using their measures for 1995 for 14 of our rich democracies, U.S. unemployment would increase by 1.9% while European unemployment would rise only infinitesimally. They argue that long prison terms, escalating violence, and overcrowdedness reduce the long-term employability of inmates. Thus the U.S. will have to continue to advance its incarceration rate if it is to sustain its 2% advantage (economic policies equal)—a bizarre road to good labor-market performance.

6. Taxes on capital gains of individuals may have little economic effect but OECD includes them under taxes on personal income, so we cannot test the effect.

7. The average lag between tax changes and investment in equipment is about two years for manufacturing and about 1.3 years for nonmanufacturing. The average lag for structures is longer. The peak impact is the year after the changes go into effect, but effects do not fully fade for many years. (Hall and Jorgenson, 1967, p. 401.)

8. There is some confusion in the label "consumption tax" for the VAT. The most common type of VAT falls on the difference between the value of output and the cost of goods and services purchased from other companies. In effect, it taxes the sum of labor income and all income earned by owners of capital of the taxed firm (Aaron, 1988). Thus it can be seen as a tax on income. There is

no doubt, however, that in both theory and practice the VAT reduces current consumption and increases savings. Therefore I follow convention and label the VAT a "consumption" tax.

9. Correlations among corporatist bargaining outcomes, taxing and spending policies, age structure, and economic performance by time period are in appendix G, tables 12G.1 through 12G.14.

10. For discussion of why I score Australia low to medium in stigma despite wide use of income testing, see chapter 8 on the welfare mess and appendix F on public assistance. This decision goes against my hypothesis.

11. Even after the recent wave of corporate tax reform this older pattern remains: corporatist democracies still go light on business; paradoxically, leftist regimes are most friendly to business. Thus, in 1989, of the top 7 in profits taxes as a percentage of total taxes, 5 are least corporatist (Japan and Italy are exceptions); of the bottom 11, all but Ireland are corporatist with or without labor (Germany, marginally corporatist, is near the median). Again this is a product of trade-offs discussed above, especially in left-corporatist regimes with a history of strong left power; among these 18 countries, Austria, Sweden, Denmark, Finland, and Norway have the least reliance on corporate taxes. Israel is excluded from this analysis. Source: Nørregaard, John and Jeffrey Owens, "Taxing Profits in a Global Economy," *The OECD Observer* 175 (April/May 1992): 35 – 38. The United States also fits this pattern: it was above average in its reliance on corporate taxes until 1983 – 87, when it dropped to 13th. Corporatist democracies in Europe go even lighter on such taxes than these data show, because unlike the United States they have moved toward integration of individual and corporate taxes by lowering taxes on income from dividends and capital gains of individuals. Thus, the total burden on European corporations is less than it appears while the burden on U.S. corporations is more than appears.

12. These findings are consistent with those of Cameron (1982) regarding inflation control and those of Flanagan, Soskice, and Ulman (1983), Garrett and Lange (1986), Bruno and Sachs (1985), and Crouch (1985) regarding nominal wage restraint. Using different measures and methods, these authors come to very similar conclusions. My finding that in the postshock periods corporatism restrains wages, hence inflation, but does not have much effect on unemployment and growth is consistent with Kenworthy (1990, pp. 118ff.), an analysis of 16 of our countries 1960 – 89; it concludes that strong centralized labor federations chose wage moderation whether the government policy was monetarist (e.g., Germany and the Netherlands in the 1980s) or Keynesian (Austria, Sweden, Norway). That successful implementation of an incomes policy over the long term requires simultaneous or prior development of generous social and/or active labor-market policies is shown in a comparison of policy linkages in eight countries (Wilensky and Turner, 1987) and chapter 2 above. In explaining wage restraint, the above authors variously emphasize left power, union density and/or centralization, and corporatism; they all leave out the role of Catholic party power as an alternative road to corporatism and wage moderation.

13. Economists studying the American slowdown in productivity experienced after 1973 attribute at least a fourth and as much as half of the slowdown to the lack of business investment (Friedman, 1989, pp. 196 and citations p. 310, fn. 11). However, they seldom consider industrial relations systems in a comparative context.

14. My finding that consumption taxes do not set off a wage-price spiral is supported by other studies showing that in 11 of 13 OECD countries surveyed, the introduction of the VAT "either had little effect on retail prices or simply resulted in a shift of the CPI trend line (one-time effect)" (Cnossen, 1991, pp. 634, 643). Cnossen also concludes that a VAT is superior to an income tax in promoting capital formation and economic growth, consistent with my findings. (*Ibid.*, pp. 633 – 634, 643 – 644.) See the similar finding for the United States 1955 – 80 in Jorgenson and Yun (1986), whose models show dramatic gains in potential economic welfare with a shift from direct taxation of income from capital to indirect taxation through a consumption-based tax.

15. Central bank autonomy (CBA) as a possible determinant of economic performance is not considered here because the measures of autonomy developed for 18 of our rich democracies are unrelated to the economic performance index. While CBA has a modest effect in constraining inflation (less than one would expect from the bankers' anti-inflation obsession), it has no effect or a negative effect on real GDP growth per capita and unemployment, depending on the period. Detailed discussion is in chapter 17 (globalization of finance section).

16. That the payoff in civilian R&D is much greater than the payoff in military R&D is confirmed by studies comparing the two by industry groups in the United States. Estimated rates of return or of productivity growth show huge differences in favor of civilian R&D. (Lichtenberg, 1988, pp. 13–14.)

17. Sheer numbers of engineers is not the issue. In fact, the claim that Japan, in sharp contrast to the U.S., is loaded with engineers is a myth—a statistical illusion based on different definitions of "engineer" (Kinmonth, 1991). The real differences are in the deployment, careers, and behavior of engineers. The U.S. has diverted far more of its engineers, especially in aerospace and electronics, to defense industries and the military; in Japan they are concentrated on civilian products. Further, U.S. engineers have a fast track to management; their interaction with workers and even technicians is minimal. Japanese engineers, in contrast, spend much time on the shop floor and belong to the same union as the operatives; in factories they have desks next to the foreman, not in a separate office building (*ibid.*, pp. 345–346)—a pattern conducive to steady, practical improvement of process and product. A final advantage: Like engineers, Japanese R&D is also distributed relatively evenly across all industry groups (Dobbeck and Woods, 1994).

18. The range of expenditures for primary and secondary schools—the ratio of the average expenditure of the top three to the average of the bottom three—was 2.2 in 1965–71 and only 1.7 in 1980. The same procedure yields a ratio of 4.5 for higher education expenditure in 1965–71, 3.6 for 1980. Enrollments are also more uniform for compulsory lower grades than for postsecondary education. Nevertheless, the pattern of correlations with economic performance is similar for both levels.

19. Specifically, Japan is an extreme case of growth before 1974; Israel had huge inflation before 1979 and unusual unemployment 1950–74. For 1980–84, Netherlands joins the USA and Canada in combining big education expenditures and poor growth for reasons, as we will see, having nothing to do with education. Ireland is a final deviant case: in 1985–89, it had very high unemployment and low education spending.

20. Repetition of the neoconservative mantra "money doesn't matter" obscures all these trends in the internal allocation of resources when money, rarely, *is* thrown at the problem. Does the money go to instructional purposes and teachers, or to bureaucratic bloat, busing, athletics, defensive record keeping, traffic monitors, school guards, and other noninstructional costs? That upper-middle-class schools continue to perform at a high and internationally competitive level reflects their greater capacity to pay and recruit good teachers, give them more professional autonomy (and safety) on the job, and provide instructional materials and parental support. It is the rest of the (non) system that stagnates or deteriorates. In a careful multiple regression analysis of 900 school districts in Texas, Ferguson (1991) shows that money matters: most of the effect of schooling on performance (measured by student scores in standardized reading exams over time) is due to teacher quality (measured by teacher performance on statewide recertification exams, experience, and the percentage of master's degrees) and good teachers are attracted to and stay in districts paying relatively high salaries. Money spent for instructional services and reducing class size to 18 also improves student test scores. All this is distinguishable from the direct effects of the social background and education of parents emphasized in the early studies (e.g., the famous Coleman Report); this parental determinant of student performance is no more important than teacher quality. The earlier studies, however, had no good measures of teacher quality (especially literacy); the Ferguson study corrects this data deficiency. Perhaps

you prefer purely economic criteria rather than academic performance in gauging the impact of spending. A study by Card and Kreuger (1992) shows that teacher salaries, class size, and length of school year significantly predict male earnings. Those U.S. states that had spent the most on their schools in the first half of the century had produced citizens with the highest incomes. Finally, a thorough review of evidence from 1990s British research on the determinants of educational attainment and subsequent achievement (Sparkes, 1999) concludes that independent of pupil intake characteristics, higher per pupil expenditure, teacher quality, and smaller class sizes all make a substantial difference in student performance at age 16, especially among disadvantaged pupils, and that test scores are strong predictors of adult outcomes.

21. In recent comparisons of achievement test scores of 14-year-olds in 32 countries in 1991 for reading and math, among countries with strong social cleavages, Switzerland scores about the same as the United States in reading (well below Finland, France, Sweden, New Zealand) but ranks near the top (after Korea and Taiwan) in math, while the United States ranked near the bottom (tied with Spain); also the Swiss low scorers were closer to the average than their American counterparts. (Elley, 1992, p. 24 on reading; data on math supplied by Arnold Heidenheimer, personal communication, August 20, 1993.) Israel is another heterogeneous country with high educational standards.

22. High standards for K–12 not only reduces the educational gap, it also reduces the earnings gap between experienced and inexperienced and between the college educated and high-school educated. A comparison of wage structures in Japan and the United States shows that these earnings differentials expanded dramatically from 1979 to 1987 in the United States while the college wage premium increased only slightly in Japan (Katz and Revenga, 1989); the distance between skilled and less skilled remains modest in Japan, huge in the United States.

23. I am grateful to Jesse C. Choper for stimulating conversations about this section.

24. The 1970s boom in U.S. production of lawyers was concentrated in the period 1970–77. Thereafter, production remained high. From 1970 to 1974, the number of law degrees conferred yearly almost doubles, from about 15,000 to about 29,000. From 1979 until 1990, the number hovered between 35,000 and 38,000 a year (U.S. Department of Education, 1992, table 244). Law school graduates reached a peak of 40,171 in June 1994, dropping slightly in 1995 and 1996 (*Wall Street Journal,* November 29, 1996). From 1960 to 1991, the number of lawyers in the United States nearly tripled, to 772,000 (The 1961 Lawyer Statistical Report, Statistical Abstract of the U.S. 1963, table 213, p. 162; and U.S. Department of Labor, 1992, pp. 185–186).

25. Of the 14 of our rich democracies for which Galanter (1983, pp. 52–54) estimated civil cases per 1,000 population in the period 1969–81, the least litigious were Netherlands, Italy, Japan, Norway, and West Germany (8.3 to 23.4)—all corporatist. The top four litigators were Australia (Western only), New Zealand, Canada, and the United States (62.1 to 44)—all noncorporatist. In the middle were England/Wales and Denmark (ranking 5th and 6th) and then Sweden, France, and Belgium (medium litigators scoring 41.1 to 28.2). Although Galanter warns that he has not solved all problems of comparability, the rough ranking of high, medium, and low probably captures reality; it is quite consistent with our data on lawyer density (table 12.11). The more lawyers, the more litigation; the more surgeons, the more surgery.

26. An overview of recent trends in lawyering around the world argues that the civil law systems of continental Europe (where judges rely on detailed codes, not judge-made laws, where judges, not lawyers, dominate the gathering and assessment of evidence, and where most disputes are negotiated without adversarial spirit and without lawyers) are becoming more like common-law systems (the costly adversary legalism of America and Britain), partly the result of the export of Anglo-American legal services to Brussels and to the former Eastern bloc countries (" . . . thick with yuppie lawyers as it once was with secret police"). ("The Legal Profession: The Rule of Lawyers," *The Economist,* July 18, 1992, especially pp. 6–8.) But the national institutions that sustain consensual bar-

gaining on the continent and in Japan will not fade away so readily. For a detailed account of the striking contrast between Anglo-American and continental civil procedure, see Langbein (1985).

27. Lawrence Friedman (1985, p. 36) warns that these figures are not strictly comparable because colonial courts did much work that now is done by local zoning, taxing, or probate authorities and notaries public and registrars. But he concedes that with comparable data "probably the seventeenth and eighteenth centuries still win, but by a reduced margin."

28. For some of the best general treatments of alleged conflicts between equality in its numerous meanings and efficiency, see Okun (1975), Rae (1981), Baumol (1986), and Schmid (1992).

29. Persson and Tabellini classify both South Korea and Taiwan as democracies but their results hold up with more stringent definitions of democracy (personal communication, July 17, 1993). The late 1930s and World War II saw substantial income equalization in Japan and Austria; postwar land reform accelerated this trend in Japan. Israel started out with an egalitarian land distribution, and both Israel and Japan put heavy accent on education. In further analysis, Persson and Tabellini (1992) show that concentration of land ownership is bad for economic growth in both democratic and non-democratic societies but an inegalitarian pretax income distribution of households is a drag only in democratic societies.

30. After 1983 the positive productivity effects of the restoration of reasonable wage differentials within Swedish plants were offset by the negative effects of increased interindustry wage differentials caused by the breakdown of centralized bargaining (see chap. 2).

13
THE GREAT AMERICAN
JOB CREATION MACHINE
IN COMPARATIVE PERSPECTIVE

In the ideological confrontation of the late 1970s and 1980s, "neoconservatives" and many mainstream economists asserted that the United States, despite its high rates of unemployment, had performed much better than the measures of unemployment, growth, and inflation used in chapter 12 suggested because it had created jobs at a faster rate. They said that America's job creation record should be at the center of our attention as we evaluate its economic performance. Certainly, American presidents have repeatedly boasted about employment gains—especially Ronald Reagan 1980–88 and Bill Clinton 1992–2000 (President Bush could not crow about it because few jobs were created during his tenure).

The two basic arguments of those who celebrate job creation are focused on *labor force pressure* and *total job opportunity*. Whatever the causes, they asserted, countries like the United States, which presumably have the fastest-growing labor-force participation rates, are under greater pressure to create jobs. If, like the United States, they have run 5–10% unemployment rates from the early 1970s to 1996 but created jobs fast for new entrants (illegal and legal immigrants, women, and a large, maturing baby-boom cohort), they should be rated high or medium on labor-market performance, not low. Regarding total job opportunity, the neoconservatives argued, even if most of the jobs created in the United States are low-paid service jobs, even if they are created as a product of weaker unions and lower real wages, they are real opportunities for those who take them—young people, minorities, women, immigrants. They make otherwise unmanageable social problems manageable; for example, it is better to keep teenagers working at McDonald's than pushing dope on the street.

Laissez-faire "job creationists" seldom confront the issues posed by close students of labor markets. The counterargument boils down to a judgment of: (1) what kind of comparisons are appropriate, and (2) what kind of a political economy is desirable.

Comparing the job creation record of 18 rich democratic countries[1] since 1968, this chapter elaborates these counterarguments and shows why some countries, including the United States, have created more jobs than other countries. My thesis is that current discussion of job creation in the United States versus Europe overemphasizes demand policies and (presumably European) barriers to labor mobility. There are more important reasons that explain national differences in employment gains. If job creation is a product of demand policies and is an end in itself, policy analysts should be concentrating their attention on an appropriate mix of fiscal and monetary policies. But if job creation is little affected by economic policy and comes at too high a cost (earnings deterioration, low investment in training, low-quality products and services, declines in union voice and worker participation, anemic long-term productivity gains and a concomitant stagnation in national standards of living), then a very different strategy for reshaping the supply and quality of labor is appropriate—an active labor-market policy (see figure 2.2), an education policy (chap. 12), a family policy (chap. 7), and labor-law reform (chap. 18). Of course it is likely that both economic and labor-market policies contribute to job creation; it is a matter of emphasis.

An initial caution about the database and an assumption underlying this argument: In every country where there is an expanding labor supply, it is possible that countercyclical demand policies help to turn the supply into jobs. Data on precise policy mixes for the 18 rich democracies over time are, however, skimpy. Yet it is very likely that when they are compared, their fiscal and monetary policies will not vary nearly as much as their employment growth rates. Similar economic policies cannot explain large differences in job creation.[2] In fact, it is variation in the growth and social composition of the labor supply that accounts for recent national differences in job creation.

RAPID JOB CREATORS VERSUS SLOW JOB CREATORS

Which countries are big job creators and which are not? And when did they create these new jobs? Here, I divide the years 1968–87 into four economically relevant job creation periods: first, 1968–74, before the first oil shock; 1975–79, the five years after the shock; 1980–84, the years after the second and most severe shock, which covers a deep worldwide recession and recovery; and 1985–87.[3] These are the major findings for the 18 rich democracies.

1.   *The top job creators (among the top six for the entire period) are Canada, Australia, the United States, and Norway. (New Zealand makes it to the top six from 1968 to 1979, but not in the 1980s.)*

2.   *Of the 18 countries, four are consistently below the median in job creation from 1968 to 1984: France, West Germany, Austria, and Great Britain. Belgium is similar: it ranks below the median for all periods except 1968–74 when it was at the median. The Netherlands is below the median until 1985–87 when it ranks 6th.*

3.   Except for 1980–84, job creation rates are statistically unrelated to unemployment rates ($r = .16$ for 1965–73, .27 for 1974–79, $-.44$ [$p = < .05$] for 1980–84, and $-.28$ for 1985–87) (see table 13.1). The great job creation machines are often the great unemployment machines. For example, three of the top four job creators rank quite high in average unemployment rates since 1950. Canada had high unemployment rates in all four periods; the United States was high in the pre-shock period and 1975–79, then medium; Australia fluctuated (low before the shock, high after 1974, medium in 1980–84 and 1985–87). Only Norway consistently kept unemployment low and job creation rates high. Conversely, among the poorest job creators, two are consistently

above average in unemployment—Great Britain and France—and two are consistently low—Austria and West Germany. The net effect: no consistent relationship between job creation and unemployment.

4. *Not only is job creation unconnected to unemployment, but it is unrelated to economic performance generally.* When we examine real GDP growth per capita for the 18 countries, we find:

- In the preshock period, the more job creation, the *less* growth, but the relationship is insignificant ($r = -.14$).

- In 1974–79, the relationship is positive but insignificant ($r = .33$).

- Only in 1980–84 is job creation significantly and positively related to real growth ($r = .57$): the more job creation the more growth. But in the three years after, the relationship disappears ($r = -.07$ for job creation in 1985–87 and growth in 1985–87).

Further evidence of the ambiguous meaning of job creation is the *absence of any relationship to inflation* ($r = -.23$ in the preshock period, .13 for 1975–79, .13 for 1980–84, and .13 for 1985–87).

In fact, if we use our broader index of economic performance (chap. 12), we see that in the entire postwar period from 1950 on, two of the six consistently poor job creators— West Germany and Austria—were excellent economic performers; that the Netherlands and France had sustained periods of good economic performance; that Belgium performed well before the first oil shock and was average to above average after. Only Great Britain had both consistently poor job creation and poor economic performance. Conversely, two of the top four consistent job creators—Canada and Australia—had consistently mediocre to poor economic performance.

The picture for the 18 countries from 1965 to 1988 is consistent: There are no statistically significant correlations between job creation and the index of economic performance for any period.[4] If job creation is not generally good for the measures of economic performance everyone agrees on (inflation, unemployment, and growth), if it has a life of its own, how can we explain the big national variations?

The major causes of job creation are beyond the reach of economic policy, although they can be affected by family and retirement policy. The major causes are *demographic* (the age structure of the population and migration rates) and *social structural* (the rate of family breakup as it relates to poverty and the history of female labor-force participation). Countries vary in their need for job creation, the pressure to create jobs.

Demographic Forces

If a country has a large and increasing percentage of persons of retirement age, it will not typically evidence a big growth in employment. In fact, *all four of the consistently "poor" job creators—France, Austria, West Germany, and Great Britain—have had large and increasing populations over 65.* Correlations for population 65+ and job creation for three of the four pe-

TABLE 13.1 Correlations of job creation by three measures of economic performance and the economic performance index[a]

	Unemploy-ment	Real GDP growth per capita	Inflation	Economic performance index
1965-73	.16	−.14	−.23	−.06
1974-79	.27	.33	.13	−.06
1980-84	−.44*	.57**	.13	.39
1985-87	−.28	−.07	.13	−.08

Sources: See chapter 12 and appendix G.

$*p < .05. **p < .01.$

[a]See appendix G for details regarding calculation of the economic performance index.

riods confirm this finding—*the more old people, the less job creation* (for 1968−74, $r = −.63$, for 1975−79, −.38 [$p < .10$], for 1980−84, −.42, and for 1985−87, −.04 [n.s.]).

The opposite is true for young people as a percentage of the population. If a country has a large fraction of late teenagers and young adults—a large pool of potential low-wage workers, as in Canada, Australia, and the United States—it can be expected to score high on job creation. The central tendency of the data is consistent: the percentage of 15- to 19-year-olds in 1968−79 and the percentage of 20- to 24-year-olds for all periods are positively correlated with job creation, especially during the years of stagnating or deteriorating real wages just after the first oil shock.[5]

Related to these demographic pressures for job creation are patterns of migration. The idea that the United States, because of its large wide-open borders, is uniquely exposed to migrant workers is incorrect (see chap. 17). If we calculate average annual net migration rates,[6] we find that since the early 1960s several European countries plus Australia and Canada have experienced more net migration than has the United States. In fact, most of the guest workers in Europe, despite pressures and bribes to leave, have stayed. Even during the crises since 1973−74, the size of the foreign workforce in some countries remained steady or actually increased (Casey and Bruche, 1985). It took strong coercive measures in West Germany and Switzerland to make significant reductions, and the potential for further cutbacks may now be exhausted. Once again, we have a structural force for job creation—a cheap supply of labor.

Of the four top job creators, three rank high in net migration (roughly immigrants minus emigrants) in all four periods.[7] Australia ranks first among 18 countries for 1963−74, 1975−79, and 1980−83; Canada moves from fourth to second and stays there; the United States moves from eighth to sixth to fourth. Even the exception, Norway, is only a partial exception, it moved from 13th to 7th to 6th. Conversely, there is a tendency for the lean job creators to have low or negative migration rates. Of the 24 entries in a table for six worst creators and four periods (not reported here), only six entries show rates of migration above the median.

Correlations for all the 18 rich democracies are consistent: job creation is significantly and positively related to average migration rates in all periods ($r = .61, .53,$ and $.58$; for job creation in 1985−87, the correlation goes up to .77). It is not surprising: increase net migration and you will use migrant workers.

Although some of the postwar migration from Southern Europe, North Africa, the Caribbean Basin, Latin America, and the area of greatest outmigration, Asia, include skilled workers and professionals, the great majority are unskilled. The most common destinations—readily visible in such global cites as New York, Los Angeles, London, and Paris—are low-wage jobs in restaurants, garment manufacture, electronics, production for specialty shops, building attendance, domestic service (dog walking, cleaning), and the entire informal economy (Sassen, 1988, p. 169; and my discussion of migration in chap. 17).

In short, age structure and the pressure of migrant workers—both clues to the availability of young, cheap labor—are the first explanation for national variations in job creation. Supply apparently creates its own demand.[8]

SOCIAL STRUCTURAL FORCES

Like age structure and migration rates, the changing structure of the family has little to do with economic policy. If a country has a relatively high rate of family breakup[9] and if it lacks a family policy to prevent the feminization of poverty,[10] there will be an acceleration of the rate of female labor-force participation. While much of the increase in working women is uncoerced—a product of changing sex roles and lower fertility—some of the increase is forced by family breakup, a major cause of pretransfer poverty. We cannot sort out the coercive versus voluntary percentage of female labor-force participation quantitatively and cross-nationally, but this situation obviously applies to the recent record of the United States.

Further, much of labor-market performance in the 1980s was a product of earlier performance. Thus, the low female labor-force participation rates in the United States of the 1950s and early 1960s were matched by high female participation rates among several smaller European democracies—Sweden, Switzerland, Finland—and Japan. Therefore, the greater increase in the United States of the 1970s and 1980s reflects, in part, a U.S. catch-up with general tendencies toward lower fertility and higher participation. Conversely, if a country starts high in women working, it has a slower rate of increase.

Data on rates of change in female labor-force participation in the 18 countries confirm this picture. In the years before 1980, the correlations between increases in women in the civilian labor force and job creation rates are strong and positive ($r = .63$ for 1963−74, .71 for 1975−79). By the early 1980s, as the 18 countries continued to converge in women's participation rates, the relationship between women's work and job creation faded ($r = .02$ for 1980−84, −.02 for 1985−87). Again, the extremes of job creation highlight the pattern: three of the top job creators—Canada, the United States, and Norway—ranked high in rates of increase in women at work or seeking work, whereas all four of the worst job creators—France, West Germany, Austria, and Great Britain—had small increases or actual decreases in women working in all periods.

As these countries got rich, they experienced declines in fertility rates, rising levels of mass aspirations, increasing fractions of urban women working, a push for gender equality, and increased family breakup (chap. 1). Family breakup rates are converging among rich countries, but they still vary substantially.

Job creation is partly the product of these variations in divorce rates, another source of a cheap labor supply. Data on divorce rates for five-year intervals from 1970 to 1985 show positive correlations in all periods, three of them significant: .38, .33, .29 (n.s.) and for 1985–87 job creation rates, .57.[11]

Although the rate of family breakup varies among the 18 countries, their governments' response varies even more. A good measure of coercive labor-force participation is the combination of a high divorce rate, little government action to deal with the problems of family breakup and working parents, and a high job creation rate.

Consider the seven countries with the highest divorce rates in 1980 (using the only available measure of family breakup for 19 countries) (see table 13.2). Three of these very high divorce rate countries (the United States, Australia, Canada) also have very high job creation rates and do very little to cushion the shock for children and working parents. New Zealand—seventh in divorce and medium in job creation—also scores low in family policy. Sweden, Denmark, and, to a lesser extent, Great Britain are below average in job creation, but they have a vast array of policies that help working parents to balance the demands of family and work and to avoid child neglect. The inference is clear: they do not coerce their numerous single parents into low-wage work quite as much as the top job creators do.

Consistent with these findings are microscopic analyses of job creation in U.S. establishments (Birch, 1981, 1987; Tietz, 1981; Birley, 1986) and one cross-national study (OECD, 1987a). There has been a major shift in the postwar period from job creation by large manufacturing firms to job creation by medium- and smaller-sized service firms using low-wage and temporary workers. Between 1954 and 1970, the USA's 500 largest industrial companies doubled their employment. By the early 1980s, however, they employed 1.2 million fewer U.S. workers than in 1970, although they expanded jobs overseas (Birch, 1987). The direct creation of new jobs in the United States is increasingly attributable to small establishments, overwhelmingly in the labor-intensive service sector, where low-wage women and migrants are prominent. That these smallish firms also destroy jobs at a higher rate than large firms does not change the net outcome, a positive contribution of volatile small firms to job creation.[12]

Establishment data for Pennsylvania (used in the OECD study as a surrogate for the United States) and Canada, France, West Germany, Sweden, and Japan demonstrate that it is the small service-providing firms that account for most of the job growth—Pennsylvania and Canada in the lead. The firms are concentrated in financial and business services and social and community services that employ increasing numbers of females and part-time or temporary workers (OECD, 1987a, tables 4.7, 4.8, 4.9, 4.11, and 4.12, and charts 4.3 and 4.4). By 1995 at least one of every five jobs in the United States was temporary or part-time or both; most of the workers who do not have an implicit or explicit contract for ongoing employment ("contingent workers") prefer permanent to temporary jobs (calculated from U.S. Department of Labor, 1995, Report 900, tables 1, 10, and 11). In Britain the part-timers had reached one in four; most are low-wage women. If we add temporary staff and the self-employed, two British workers in five are now outside permanent, full-time employment (*The Economist,* May 22, 1993, p. 61).

While contingent jobs in these small firms may reduce labor costs, enhance management flexibility, and increase choice for some workers, they also tend to pay low wages and benefits, evade legal obligations under labor and employment laws, and increase the risk of job and benefit losses for masses of workers, especially in the United States (Belous, 1989;

TABLE 13.2 Job creation and family policy among the seven countries with the highest divorce rates

Countries ranked by divorce rate, 1980 from high to low	Expansive and innovative family policy score from 11 (most) to 1 (least)[a]	Job creation rank, 1980-84 (18 countries)
United States	3 L	3 H
United Kingdom	5 M	17 L
Australia	1 L	3 H
Denmark	8 H	11 ML
Canada	2 L	4 H
Sweden	11 H	10 M
New Zealand	2 L	8 M

Source: Wilensky (1990). For further details on concepts and codes for the family-policy score, see chapter 7. The ranks (H, M, L) are relative to 19 countries for family policy and 18 countries for job creation.

[a]Based on a 5-point scale (0–4) for each of three policy clusters in place 1976–82: (1) the existence and length of maternity and paternal leave, paid and unpaid; (2) the availability and accessibility of public day-care programs and government effort to expand day care; and (3) the flexibility of retirement systems (number of options, with emphasis on partial pensions designed for flexible work/retirement choices). The three dimensions correlate strongly with one another (and with child allowances/GNP). See chapter 7.

U.S. Commission on the Future of Worker-Management Relations, 1995, pp. S-49 – 50). Finally, for the countries leading in this type of job creation, the trend may represent decreasing investment in human capital.

One little-noticed aspect of this emerging contingent economy among the leading job creators—beyond the low-wage, low-benefit, low-security, part-time, and temporary jobs— is the higher accident rate of subcontracted workers (versus stable, direct hires), especially in construction, maintenance, and repair. For instance, a detailed study of the petrochemical industry in the United States (Kochan et al., 1994) where safety mishaps can be catastrophic showed that subcontractors using temporary workers increased greatly in the 1970s; by the late 1980s they accounted for 32% of the normal hours worked in an average plant. The subcontractors were typically nonunion; their workers were lower paid, less educated, less trained, and less experienced than their regular counterparts in the contracting firm and had a much higher accident rate. One reason for the contrast in accident rates is that the host employer typically accepts no responsibility for the training and supervision of the contract workers and the subcontractors are indifferent to training. Equally important, experienced regular workers in the host plant are loath to share their know-how with temporary workers who threaten their jobs and wage standards. By their obsession with short-run savings in wage and training costs, petrochemical executives were incurring long-run costs in injuries, accidents, explosions, and shutdowns and concomitant lawyer costs, only some of which they could dump on the public.

MULTIPLE REGRESSION RESULTS AND THE QUESTION OF CAUSATION

The multiple regression analyses in table 13.3 confirm the cross-national findings of this chapter so far. The four major variables—net migration, percentage increase in women's labor-force participation, age structure, and divorce rates—in various combinations explain 57% to 85% of the variance in job creation for 1968–74, 1975–79, and 1985–87. The exception is the period of worldwide recession in the early 1980s, when, in the face of huge external shocks, only migration remained as a powerful predictor of job creation.[13]

Although I have shown that demographic and social structural changes are strongly related to job creation, I have not shown that demand policies (fiscal and monetary policies that expand the economy) are irrelevant to job creation. Additional findings, however, support my emphasis on the importance and perhaps dominance of an expanding supply of cheap labor and cast doubt on the importance of economic policy: data on real earnings changes and on capital investment and other causes of good economic performance that shape the demand for labor.

By relating my explanation of job creation to data changes in real earnings, we can test the inference that countries using many migrants and women, especially divorced women, will experience erosion of earnings or, in other words, that there is a trade-off between job creation and rising standards of living. Regressions of changes in real earnings on divorce rates, increases in migration, and increases in women working show that, statistically speaking, these variables were a moderate drag on real earnings increases for 1966–73 (28% of the variance), that female labor-force participation and divorce rates were a mild brake in 1980–84 (10% of the variance), but that only divorce rates were a strong barrier to earnings growth in 1974–79 (50% of the variance).

If we use a measure of acceleration of earnings growth over a base period of 1966–73 or 1974–79 (which takes account of a country's "normal" history of wage changes and also controls for built-in wage increases such as COLAs), we find that only divorces consistently depress real earnings (42% of the variance after the first oil shock, 29% in 1980–84). Regressions substituting the percentage of teenagers for divorce rates (not reported here) also show negative but weaker effects. The strongest predictor in four of the five regressions in table 13.4 is divorce rates, although the sign is in the right direction for all five.

Second, and more directly, there is a negative correlation between job creation and earnings growth: for the preshock period, the correlation is $-.41$ ($p < .05$); for the ratio of 1980–84 to 1975–79 earnings growth (acceleration), the correlation is $-.54$ ($p < .05$); the other correlations are negative but not significant. In other words, even if a demand curve shift is adding to employment growth, it is being overwhelmed by the shift in the labor supply curve.[14]

Third, the two major causes of good economic performance since World War II in our 19-country analysis (see chap. 12)—gross fixed capital investment and low strike rates (measured by person-days lost per 1,000 civilian nonagricultural employees)—are completely unrelated to job creation. In short, the structural and demographic causes of job creation are also sources of a slowdown in real wages, while the major sources of good economic performance are not connected to job creation.

TABLE 13.3 The best regressions of job creation on independent
variables for four periods since 1968, eighteen rich democracies

Dependent = Job Creation 1968-74		
Independent variable	(1)	(2)
Net migration 1963-74[a]	.42**	.32*
Female LF growth 1963-74[b]	.33**	.49**
% pop. age 65+, 1970		−.58**
% pop. age 15-19, 1970	.59**	
Adjusted R^2 (N)	.85 (17)[c]	.84 (17)a[c]

Dependent = Job Creation 1975-79		
Independent variables	(1)	(2)
Net migration 1975-79[a]	.32[•]	.38*
Female LF growth 1975-79[b]	.60**	.59**
% pop. age 20-24, 1977	.27[•]	
% pop. age 15-19, 1977		.33*
Adjusted R^2 (N)	.64 (17)[d]	.74 (16)[e]

Dependent = Job Creation 1980-84	
Independent variables	(1)
Net migration 1980-84[a]	.53*
Female LF growth 1980-84[b]	−.14*
% pop. age 65+, 1980	−.31
Adjusted R^2 (N)	.32 (18)

Dependent = Job Creation 1985-87	
Independent variables	(1)
Net migration 1985-87[a]	.65**
Female LF growth 1985-87[b]	.03
Divorce rate, 1985	.27
Adjusted R^2 (N)	.57 (17)[f]

[•] $p < .10.$ *$p < .05.$ **$p < .01.$
[a]Average annual net migration rates.
[b]Percent change in labor-force participation rates of females, 15−64.
[c]The Netherlands missing.
[d]Ireland missing.
[e]Ireland and the Netherlands missing.
[f]France missing.

TABLE 13.4 The best of regressions of real earnings growth on independent variables for three periods since 1966[a]

Independent Variable	Real Earnings Change as Dependent Variable		
	1966–73	1974–79	1980–84
Net migration, avg. ann. net			
mig. rates, 1963–74	−.26		
1975–79		.30	
1980–84			.23
Female labor force,			
avg. % ann. change, 1963–74	−.27		
1975–79		.29	
1980–84			−.47*
Divorce rates, 1970	−.33		
1975		−.75***	
1980			−.25
Adjusted R² (N)	.28 (17)	.50 (17)	.10 (18)

Independent Variable	Acceleration of Real Earnings as Dependent Variable[b]	
	1974–79/1966–73	1980–84/1974–79
Net migration, avg. ann.		
net mig. rates, 1975–79	.37	
1980–84		.14
Female labor force,		
avg. % ann. change, 1975–79	.16	
1980–84		−.14
Divorce rates, 1975	−.72***	
1980		−.67**
Adjusted R² (N)	.42 (17)	.29 (18)

*p < .10; **p < .05; ***p < .01.

Source: *OECD Historical Statistics* (various years) for real earnings.

[a]Because of missing data on earnings, 1985–87 was dropped from this analysis.

[b]Calculated as a ratio of the average change in real earnings during one period to the average for the previous period.

Thus, most of the sources of job creation—changes in family structure, age structure, and immigration—are beyond the reach of economic policy, except those policies that would directly discourage low-wage work, such as a strongly enforced high minimum wage and a Berlin Wall for every border. These findings raise questions both about what type of political economy is desirable and what public policies might help.

A DESIRABLE POLITICAL ECONOMY

There is consensus about the desirability of real growth, low inflation, and low unemployment. There is little consensus about the meaning of growth of labor-force participation or jobs added. The issue is not whether job creation is better than no job creation; it is what kinds of jobs to create with what long-run effect on living standards. If employment expands because of a rapid creation of low-paid service jobs, an increasing number of them part-time or temporary jobs taken by people looking for full-time work; because of stagnant or declining real wages; and because of increases in the rate of family breakup (forcing single parents to work with grossly inadequate child-care arrangements), while productivity increases fade and trade balances deteriorate, we can ask, is this progress? The better strategy—one clearly followed by such job creation laggards as West Germany and Austria—is to upgrade the labor force and improve the technical and social organization of work. These will increase productivity and product quality and thereby facilitate a move upscale in exports. Instead, the United States in a large and growing portion of its economy seems to be aping the once labor-intensive newly industrializing countries, such as South Korea and Hong Kong, even as they themselves move upscale in both wages and products.

Further, if real-wage decreases are achieved by labor crunching and union busting (the United States under Reagan, Great Britain under Thatcher), we incur the costs of mass insecurity, industrial conflict, ungovernability, and unproductive welfare spending (discussed in chaps. 5, 8, 10, 11, 12, 13, 15, and 18). If to this perverse combination we add a high level of family breakup and the feminization of poverty, should we label the brew "a superior record of job creation"?

Finally, no one has either firmly established or disproved a *long-term* U.S. trend toward low-wage jobs in or out of the service sector. The opposing views are familiar: there is an underlying structural trend toward low-wage jobs rooted either in deindustrialization, as Bluestone and Harrison (1986, pp. 5–7) claim, or in the growth of low-paid unstable nonunion jobs in several industry sectors (not mainly manufacturing) as my data suggest; or the deterioration of earnings is not structural but cyclical, as an early study by Wachter (1970) and the post-1996 pickup in real earnings suggest.

If there is a secular trend, fiscal and monetary policies will not stop it. What is required are structural changes that might be accomplished by radical reforms in education, training, and industrial relations systems; increased investment in physical infrastructure; and the adoption of family policies, higher minimum wages, and the like (see chap. 18's discussion of public policy). If in contrast, we adopt the view that all signs of this earnings deterioration in the United States since 1973 are not a trend but a cyclical pattern, reflecting the sharp increase in the percentage of low-wage workers in the recession years of 1975, 1981–82, and 1990–91, then fiscal and monetary measures are decisive. While economic policy has little to do with job creation rates, it *can* shape the depth and duration of recessions (Bean, Layard, and Nickell, 1986; and my discussion of central banks in chap. 17). Similarly, while an active labor-market policy may not greatly affect the rate of job creation, in combination with education and family policies it can affect the unemployment rate and, equally important, the long-run productivity of the labor force (Wilensky, 1985, 1992a, and chap. 12), resulting in a rise in real earnings. Whether the recent deterioration in earnings reflects a secular trend or cyclical fluctuations, there is a large role for government, although the appropriate policy mix depends on which analysis is most persuasive.

North Americans, Canadians, and Australians who congratulate themselves on their superior records of job creation might pause and ask themselves, how have such poor job creators as West Germany, Austria, and Sweden done so well from 1950 to 1990 with a smaller supply of young, cheap labor and a much larger burden of retirees? Could it be that fewer hours of work by better-educated and better-trained labor managed by more efficient firms with longer time perspectives and more active governments with similar time perspectives explain their competitive edge for four decades?

Notes

This is a slightly revised and expanded version of Wilensky (1992b). I am grateful to William T. Dickens and Jonathan Leonard for critical comments.

1. Israel is deleted from all tables except tables 13.1 and 13.2 because data for several variables are missing.

2. There is evidence of such similarities among 4–14 of the 18 countries: They typically prop up domestic demand by reduced taxes and/or increased spending and fight inflation by restrictive monetary policies (Heidenheimer, Heclo, and Adams, 1990, pp. 135–266).

3. The data are year-to-year employment growth rates calculated from OECD's *Economic Outlook* (1988a, p. 185). To smooth out short-term fluctuations, I averaged the annual rates for job creation and other economic variables; my focus is on long-term economic performance, with periods defined by major external shocks and subsequent years of recovery. I do not average annual rates or percentages for two types of variables—age structure and divorce rates—because the rank order of countries for these measures is quite stable during the five- to seven-year periods at issue.

4. Although consumer demand drives much of the economy, it is a relatively weak creator of good jobs or, for that matter, any jobs. A study of the job-creation effects of various types of spending by the public sector, firms, and individuals in the U.S. (Medoff, 1993) shows the following: for a given amount of spending the best generators of both the number of jobs and the quality of jobs (measured by wages and fringe benefits) are (1) state and local government expenditures, especially in public safety, education, health and hospitals, highways, transit, utilities, and construction in that order; then (2) private investment (durable equipment, construction); and then (3) federal expenditures (with non-defense spending edging out defense spending). The weakest force for job creation is personal consumption, which is a strong source of economic growth. For either sheer number of jobs or high-quality jobs, government expenditure gives the biggest bang for the buck. This is consistent with my finding that job creation and economic performance are unrelated in our 18 countries.

5. However, only three of the eight correlations between age grades and job creation are significant—all in 1968–74 or 1975–79, none in the 1980s.

6. January 1 to December 31 changes in total population minus natural population increase divided by average population for that year.

7. These average annual net migration rates are not the same as the *level* of migrant workers in the labor force. But the latter also show that the United States has plenty of company: Estimates of foreign workers as a percentage of the civilian labor force in 1988 suggest that levels in United States (8.1%) were less than half those in Switzerland (17.4%), and comparable to the rates of Germany (6.6%) and France (6.6%). Sweden scored about 5%. Data for Belgium, Netherlands, and the United Kingdom do not take into account unemployed foreign workers, which may explain why their rates are less than 5%. (Calculated from SOPEMI, 1992, p. 133; OECD, 1993b, table 5.0, pp. 30–31; and Borjas, Freeman, and Katz, 1992, p. 227.) Calculations for 1973 or nearest year for 16 of our rich democracies (based on *Migrant News* and other sources) suggest that the United States ranked sixth with about 7%, behind Switzerland (29%), West Germany (9.4%), France (9.0%), Austria (7.8%), and Great Britain (7.3%).

8. We do not know how much of migration is deliberate employer recruitment (demand first, supply follows) and how much is self-selection partly based on networks of friends and relatives who recruit their extended families (supply of cheap labor expands, employers create jobs).

9. In 1970, 1975, 1980, and 1985, the United States had the highest divorce rate among the 19 countries.

10. The United States stands almost alone in this lack, with women heading broken homes comprising almost half the poor households in 1998 (U.S. Census figures).

11. Complete cross-national data on divorces per 1,000 married couples (the preferred measure) are available only for 1970; I used divorces per 1,000 population for 1970–85. However, for 1970, the two measures are correlated .97; for our purposes they are interchangeable. Although some convergence is evident in these data (high divorce-rate countries such as Sweden and Finland declined somewhat in relative scores and ranks while low-divorce rate countries such as France, Belgium, and New Zealand increased a little), only two significant shifts occurred: Australia and the Netherlands moved from below average to above average. The correlation between crude rates for 1970–85 range from .89 (1970 × 1985) to .98 (1980 × 1985). That relative stability gives us a bit more confidence in the correlations reported above.

12. Although this varies over time and place, Birch (1981) found that two-thirds of the net new jobs in 1969–76 were created by firms with 20 or fewer employees (8 in 10 in firms with 100 or fewer). See similar findings using better data: Birley (1986) on St. Joseph County, Indiana, and Tietz (1981) on California. Leonard (1982) points to three limitations of studies that conclude that small firms outside of manufacturing account for so much of employment growth: (1) these firms typically both create and destroy jobs at a much higher rate than do manufacturing firms (cf. U.S. Commission on the Future of Worker-Management Relations, 1993, p. 9); (2) weaknesses in the use of Dun and Bradstreet data in the Birch (1981) study cast doubt on his conclusions; and (3) a cross-sectional picture of year-by-year net job creation obscures flows across size categories as small workplaces become big and big ones become small (Leonard, 1982, p. 152; cf. Birch, 1987, pp. 12–15). All researchers agree, however, that despite the volatility of the service sector—wide variation in annual job generation, a high death rate of firms—it shows the most net growth in jobs, most of them in small establishments and firms.

13. For each period, the same set of independent variables was tested for its relative importance in all possible combinations of three. While it would be desirable to include all six measures of the four independent variables in every equation, the N of 18 imposes the limit of three. See appendix A on methods.

14. Cross-national data on earnings are available only for manufacturing. It is reasonable to assume that countries with low earnings increases in manufacturing would also be low in general earnings growth for the labor force. In fact, in a study of inequality in the wage structure of the United States which ranks low in manufacturing earnings growth, Davidson and Reich (1988) show that the trend toward inequality since 1970 is accounted for in large measure by the growth in low-wage "secondary" labor markets, especially in retail service (low-unionized, weak internal labor markets where employment increased and already-low wages decreased). Similarly, in a comparative study of real wage growth and employment growth, Freeman (1988) concludes that "the United States paid for job creation with slow growth in real wages and productivity" (p. 298).

RISK AND SAFETY
American Mayhem in Comparative Perspective

"Law 'n Order" is a slogan that has had increasing resonance in American politics. In the 1988 election, the Bush campaign launched the infamous Willie Horton/prisoner furlough ads by mail and TV. In a 30-second spot we saw a line of evil, dark-looking prisoners going through a revolving door, while the voiceover explained that Bush's opponent, Governor Dukakis, had furloughed these rapists and murderers who naturally raped and murdered again. Mailed fliers attacking Dukakis pictured Willie Horton, a black in a Massachusetts prison for murder, who raped a woman and stabbed her fiancé while on furlough. By election day, the media had made Horton a celebrity. Crime was the text; race, the subtext.

From President Clinton's campaign of 1992 to his successful struggle to pass a $30.2 billion anticrime bill in August 1994, the Democrats sought to expropriate the law-'n-order slogan and neutralize the Republican's favorite attack theme, "Democrats are soft on crime," so effective in presidential races since Nixon in 1968. To attract six Senate Republicans, President Clinton had to cut down the crime-prevention money in the bill and devote 80% of the total to law enforcement and more jails.

One reason that American politicians of both parties make so many "tough on crime" speeches is that the United States had a high and increasing rate of violent crime from the early 1960s to the early 1990s and American voters approached a state of panic about it. But as we have seen in chapter 4, other countries share this concern. The mass publics of every democracy rank political and civil order (fighting crime) at or near the top of all goals they want government to pursue, a pattern of response that has not changed since the early 1970s.

This chapter explores three questions:

1. What explains the high crime rate in the United States, especially such violent crimes as murder?

2. To what extent do other rich democracies experience the same problem?

3. More broadly, how can we explain national differences and similarities in safety, security, and risk? If rich democracies vary in the risks faced by their citizens, how much can be attributed to differences in their degree of affluence? In other words, are rising

risks common to all of these countries as they become richer? Or can national differences be explained by contrasts in political and economic organization that result in
public-policy differences? Do public policies affect safety?

TRENDS IN VIOLENT CRIME

Crime statistics for any one year, let alone for two centuries, can be misleading: they reflect
the vagaries of reporting, changes over time in the type and efficacy of policing and criminal justice systems, as well as the changing ambiguities of definition (what is sexual harassment, what is rape?). These problems are intensified when we compare statistics across
nations. Yet there are some crime figures that probably reflect the real rate more than
changes in reporting. And historical accounts of daily life in earlier periods can provide a
reasonable guide for interpreting what historical statistics we have. Thus, the rate of inten-
tional homicide, scholars agree, is the most reliable of violent crime statistics; the victims of
murder are likely to be counted and recorded. Thus substantial differences in murder rates
over time or space very likely indicate real differences. Moreover, we cannot entirely discount serious efforts to estimate other crimes of violence, such as rape, assault, and robbery,
especially where the estimates correlate closely with variations in homicide rates and can
be traced to the same causes. Further, if we concentrate on the postwar period since 1950,
there are fewer shifts in policing and legal codes than in previous periods. In short, despite
the limitations of data, it is possible to analyze recent trends and roughly gauge long-term
trends in violent crime in the United States and abroad.

Perhaps the most careful effort to trace long-term trends is Gurr (1979), a history of violent crime in Europe and America, and Gurr (1977) on crime trends in 18 of our 19
rich democracies from 1945 to the late 1970s, based on country sources—for example, general or specialized yearbooks (cf. Graham and Gurr, 1979; Archer and Gartner, 1984). Gurr
(1977) compares trends within each country rather than using cross-sectional comparisons
and tries to adjust for national changes in crime reporting.

To assess the impact of industrialization and it correlates, here are the most relevant
findings:

- There has likely been a decline in homicide rates in Europe since the Middle
Ages. In England, there have been three peaks in violent crime—the mid-1700s, the
1830s and 1840s, and the 1970s (Gurr, 1979, p. 356); later studies suggest a leveling off of
the crime rate in Britain and the United States in the early 1980s (Wilson and Herrnstein, 1985, pp. 409–410), but the rate of violent crime in the United States increased
1985–91 and then leveled off before a recent decline.

- From 1950 to the early 1970s, among rich democracies (18 of our 19) there was
an almost universal increase not only in murder, manslaughter, and assault, but also in
property crime. The increase began in English-speaking countries earlier (1950s) than in
the rest (1960s). There are some exceptions: since 1955, Japan reduced almost all crime
(murder, assault, crimes against property, white collar crime, and common theft); Switzerland had stable property crime rates; and there was little change in crimes against persons
in Israel, the Netherlands, Italy, Austria, and Switzerland (Gurr, 1977, pp. 74, 83–84).

- In the postwar period, "sexual and moral offenses" (e.g., abortion, homosexual acts, prostitution, and the sale of pornographic literature) have increased in English-speaking countries, but because of the decriminalization of lesser moral-sexual offenses, these rates have declined in Scandinavia and continental Europe (*ibid.*, pp. 76–84).

- Crime rates in general decreased from the 1830s to the 1930s in London, Stockholm, and Sydney but started to rise again in the 1930s and rose sharply after 1950 (Gurr, 1977, p. 41) as they did in most of the rich democracies. The sharp rise is on the order of 300% to 500% (Gurr, 1979, p. 369).

These findings provide some support for the theme that advanced industrialism and its correlates—specifically the level of affluence reached by 1950 or 1960 by the United States, Canada, Sweden, New Zealand, Australia, the UK, West Germany, and France—fosters crimes of violence.[1] But why in the perspective of three centuries was there a *decline* in such crimes? Why the long-term decline from the early modern period, when life was "nasty, brutish, and short," to today; in the United States another decline after 1830; and in Britain a decline from the 1850s to the 1890s, with low crime rates from 1890 to 1935 relative to today (Davies, 1983)? One explanation is that in the early stages of industrialization, a vast majority of the population still reside in rural areas and small towns, and, although family breakup rates begin to increase, the big acceleration of divorces does not occur until much higher levels of development (see chap. 1). The family and other social networks remain intact. Thus the well-established differences in violent crime rates—rural less than urban, areas of greater social integration less than areas of social disorganization—would prevent an increase in violence while the decline in absolute poverty and its associated pathologies would foster a decrease in crime.

As later industrialization and urbanization proceeds, however, mobility rates, both residential and occupational, climb; mass aspirations soar (hence *relative* poverty becomes more painful, with a greater disjunction between rewards and aspirations); divorce rates accelerate; ties to extended kin, neighborhood, friends, and church atrophy. (See chap. 1 on the contrasting impact of early vs. later industrialization on family breakup and chap. 3 on mass society.) In short, social integration weakens and the crime rate climbs.

This classic argument, rooted in the theories of Emile Durkheim (1960 [1893]/1951 [1897]) also finds support in studies of internal variations by region, type of community, and social composition within the United States and Britain in the postwar period and in some recent cross-national studies. Because murder is both a dramatic symbol of all crimes of violence, and because the United States is a champion in murder rates, I concentrate on U.S. homicide rates in the postwar period of affluence. If we can uncover the causes of violent crime in an extreme case, and if we have a good general theory, we can assume that the same causes in lesser degree will yield similar results in lesser degree—that is, in other rich countries to be analyzed later.

Why Violent Crime in the United States, Especially Murder?

The most careful multivariate studies of homicide rates in the United States agree on the sources of homicide. Here is my summary of the findings in Land, McCall, and Cohen

(1990); Blau and Blau (1982); Greenberg, Carey, and Popper (1987); Currie (1985); and Allan and Steffensmeier (1989): *Across time and geographical areas and under modern conditions, the combination of poverty and inequality (i.e., great absolute and/or relative economic deprivation) and family breakup in the context of crowded urban living powerfully and consistently explain homicide rates.*

For instance, one of the most thorough studies, Land et al. (1990), analyzed homicide rates for all cities, metropolitan areas, and states in the United States. They found that areas with low median incomes, much absolute poverty, and great relative economic inequality in 1960, 1970, and 1980 have high homicide rates. Areas with large and/or more dense populations and a greater percentage of divorced men had higher homicide rates than those with smaller and/or less dense populations and lower male divorce rates. Resource deprivation, urbanism, and family breakup each have independent effects across all time periods and levels of analysis—a powerful result. The validity of divorce rates as an indicator of social disorganization is confirmed by its correlation with metropolitan net migration for the previous 10 years; both divorce rates and migration rates are clues to a general pattern of breakdown in family and social networks (*ibid.,* p. 945). Indeed, in a review of 21 American studies that use multiple regression analysis to explain interunit variation in homicide rates (by state, metropolitan area, city), the percentage of children under 18 not living with both parents is the only structural covariate that is always a statistically significant predictor (*ibid.* p. 931). Similarly, Blau and Blau (1982) compared the 125 largest metropolitan areas (SMSAs) and found that socioeconomic inequality (measured by the Gini index both within races and between races) and divorce rates strongly predict *all* forms of violent crime (murder, rape, robbery, and assault) (pp. 124–126).

A bit less strong and consistent as a source of homicide are unemployment rates and the presence of many teenagers and young adults (persons 18–29 years old as a percentage of total population) (Land et al., 1990, p. 953). There is no doubt that the consequences of unemployment are pathological and extraordinarily costly even when one disregards the direct economic costs: it is estimated that with every 1% increase in the American unemployment rate sustained over six years, 920 more people commit suicide, 648 more commit homicide, 495 more die from cirrhosis of the liver or heart and kidney disease, 4,000 more are admitted to state mental hospitals, and 3,300 more are sent to state prisons. (Based on regression analysis of national data 1940–73 by Brenner, 1976, pp. 88, 76–77.)[2]

Compared to continuously employed workers, unemployed workers are also more likely to experience headaches, stomachaches, high blood pressure, troubled sleep, ulcers, diabetes, and gout as well as feelings of anxiety and depression (Bluestone and Harrison, 1982, pp. 63–64). One of the most consistent findings is that people deprived of work are the most isolated socially and disturbed psychologically—in a word, demoralized (Wilensky, 1966c, p. 130).

If in the United States young people have the highest rates of both unemployment and violent crime and related pathologies, then the high homicide rate of the United States, a country loaded with young people, is not surprising. Yet the studies of the effects of unemployment and age structure in the literature on homicide rates are ambiguous and inconsistent. There are several reasons for this. First, there are the usual measurement problems: unemployment is a crude measure of economic deprivation—of the weak labor-market position of the least advantaged. The statistics do not adequately capture underemployment, the quality of employment, the effect of a high incarceration rate, and the discouraged worker phenomenon (workers not enumerated because they have given up the job search), all of which would make the labor-market position of the lower fifth of the income distribution and younger age groups look much worse than their official unemployment rate. One study relates both job quality (such as low hours and low wages) and mere job availability (unemployment) to arrest rates among young populations, controlling for indicators of the opportunity for crime, percent minority, residential mobility, and the deterrent effects of the justice system. It distinguishes between narrow age grades (males aged 13–17 and 18–24). It shows quite strong results: comparing state data from 1977 to 1980, the mere availability of employment strongly affects juvenile arrest rates for property crimes (robbery, burglary, larceny, and auto theft); full-time jobs mean low arrest rates, unemployment means high arrest rates. But low-*quality* employment is an even better predictor of high arrest rates for young adults. (Allan and Steffensmeier, 1989.)

The second cluster of reasons for the ambiguous findings about the impact of unemployment on crime is variation across studies in the level of analysis and the type of crime and the measure of unemployment. A national level of aggregation may be too large for this issue; more homogeneous subunits of neighborhood, city, county, metropolis, and state would be better. Furthermore, the causes of property crimes may be different from the causes of other crimes, and the rates of change in unemployment may have a different effect than sheer levels of unemployment. A careful review of 63 studies that use subnational units and were published since 1960, of which 40 use data from the 1970s when unemployment rose dramatically (Chiricos, 1987), shows that the frequency of positive and significant findings is highest for (1) property crimes, lowest for assault and murder; (2) 1970 data; (3) more homogeneous units. For the 1970s data, even the relation between unemployment and violent crime was overwhelmingly positive and often significant. A lower level but *increasing* rate of unemployment explains property crimes better than a higher level and decreasing rate, suggesting that some crime rates may be more responsive to changes in employment rates than to absolute levels (*ibid.*, p. 202).

A third reason for the ambiguous role of unemployment as a source of crime is that although unemployment increases the motivation for crime, it also decreases the opportunity. Reduced economic activity means fewer crime targets and better-protected property (more people at home, with alert owners aware that the risks may be rising). But unemployment, with all its tensions and pathological consequences, moves the unemployed to crime (*ibid.*, p. 201). From the evidence, the motivation effect overcomes the reduced opportunity but not enough to make for strong and consistent results.

Similarly, *poverty* is not a *direct* cause of crime, as we can easily see from the history of low crime rates among many poor immigrant minority groups—Jews, Chinese, Japanese, West Indian blacks. Most poor people, like most adolescents, do not become criminals. Indeed, in one well-designed study, less than 5% of the families accounted for almost half of the criminal convictions in a sample of 394 families in working-class areas of London in 1961–62 (West and Farrington, 1977, pp. 110–111). Poverty causes crime, including crimes of violence, only when it is associated with broken families, illegitimacy, low education and skills, poor jobs, unemployment, or a large number of children. In my theory about the long-range trends, relative poverty or, more generally, relative economic deprivation should explain violent crime better than the absolute levels of economic deprivation so common a century or two ago. But empirical findings for the United States suggest that today the two cannot be unscrambled: in the United States, levels of poverty and relative poverty are too closely correlated; both probably count (Land et al., 1990, p. 954).

What unemployment and poverty have in common as sources of violent crime is their effect on parents' capacity (little time and energy, few resources) and will (low morale, despair, pent-up frustration) to monitor children's or teenagers' behavior and punish them for deviance or reward them for good behavior (Hirschi, 1983). Such loss of authority is especially acute where the father is absent (family breakup) or loses his job (and appears to his children as a model of failure and weakness). In the tangle of pathologies that constitute American slums, the schools, too, have diminished capacity to monitor children's behavior. Conversely, social integration—the bonds of family, school, work, church, community—can in Durkheimian style protect the poor and/or the unemployed from the pathologies of crime and suicide (for a supporting study using state and county data on suicides from 1933 to 1980 see Breault, 1986). Confirming the theme that bonds of work and family prevent crime is a reanalysis and update by Robert Sampson and John Laub (1993) of the classic longitudinal study by Sheldon and Eleanor Glueck in the 1940s of 1,000 teenage white ethnic boys from impoverished areas of Boston. Half were juvenile delinquent and half had no criminal record but were matched case by case by age, IQ, and ethnicity. Both groups were followed up until they were age 45. The unsurprising conclusion: Two influences in the delinquent boys' lives between ages 17 and 25 turned them away from committing further crimes: getting a stable job that they cared about and where the employer valued them, or marrying a woman with whom they felt a strong tie, and supporting her and any children. Among delinquents who found a stable job only one in three went on to commit crimes compared to three in four of those who did not find stable employment. Similarly only one in three of the delinquents who committed to a marriage went into crime compared to three in four of those who did not. (*ibid.*, pp. 146, 161.) The effects of job stability and marital attachment in adulthood had large, significant, and enduring effects across both delinquent and nondelinquent groups (pp. 200–203).

The theory of violent crime implicit in this discussion accents the supervision of the young by parents, schools, and communities; it will be applied to cross-national data below.

How much of the U.S. violence I have discussed is explained not by economic inequality, poverty, divorce, and unemployment but by racial conflict? Perhaps there is a subculture of violence in the urban ghettos that explains violent crimes in the United States and we have another example of American exceptionalism. I think not. It is difficult to sort out the independent effect of race and economic deprivation in the United States, because blacks as a percentage of the population and the percentage of children not living with both parents are substantially correlated with measures of poverty and inequality. As William Wilson (1987) suggests, the social transformation of the inner city via racial segregation, discrimination, and the flight of the middle class, both black and white, has resulted in a criminogenic concentration of the disadvantaged. The high homicide areas tend to have large concentrations of blacks and children living in broken families; these concentration effects grew worse between 1970 and 1980 (Land et al., 1990, p. 945)—and in the 1980s as well when the net migration of poor blacks *into* these ghettos increased and escape from them became more difficult (Massey, Gross, and Shibuya, 1994, pp. 431–437).

But where researchers have tried to sift out the distinctive influence of race, they have found that economic deprivation is far more important than race. For instance, Blau and Blau (1982, pp. 125–126), comparing the 125 largest metropolitan areas, find that more than three-fifths of the variation in rates for all violent crime (murder, rape, robbery, assault) is accounted for by four factors: the percent divorced, the population size (log 10 transformation), the degree of inequality (Gini coefficient of total income inequality) and the degree of racial inequality. The addition of racial composition (percent blacks) explains only an additional 3% of the variation. If we consider murder only, racial composition explains only an additional 7% (*ibid.*, p. 125). An earlier study using different methods and measures comes to similar conclusions. Wolfgang, Figlio, and Sellin (1972) followed a large cohort of boys born in Philadelphia in 1945 and brought up in contrasting neighborhoods. By the time they were 18, boys living in low-income neighborhoods had been charged with almost twice as many criminal offenses as boys of the same race living in neighborhoods where the typical family had an income above the Philadelphia average, again demonstrating that the income position of the family and type of community shapes criminal behavior more than race.[3]

This is not to say that the black/white difference in crime is not large. Blacks are clearly more often both victims and criminals. A glimpse of the process by which rates of violent crime among poor blacks can become so much higher than the rates among their white counterparts can be had from the revival of the urban ethnography that produced *Tally's Corner* (Liebow, 1967), *Street Corner Society* (Whyte, 1943), and *Hard Living on Clay Street* (Howell, 1973). One of the more analytically powerful examples is a comparison of poor blacks, Hispanics, and white working-class criminal youths (Sullivan, 1989). All of these criminal cliques—white poor, black poor, and Hispanic poor in the inner city—have similar values and beliefs and teenage lifestyles: all three have low aspirations and little respect for education (indeed the whites have even more contempt for schooling than the others); all three have early training in street fighting and experiment with crime; as they grow older and need cash to "hang out," they look for jobs in both the conventional and the criminal sectors. What happens from there on depends on the structure of opportunity on their turf (Sullivan, 1989, pp. 118–122): the various neighborhoods channel white ethnics toward organized crime (pp. 178–192), black youths toward muggings (pp. 148–149), Hispanics toward burglary (pp. 123–124). In the conventional economy, however, the white ethnics have several advantages aside from their lower poverty rate. Practically all of them have family and neighborhood connections to obtain stable jobs with adequate pay as well as the benefits of neighborhood social controls that keep them in line. In contrast, the blacks living in projects lack relevant connections; the absence of stores around the projects means no local jobs; and there is almost a complete lack of family and neighborhood controls. While their white counterparts almost all move from petty hustling and drug experimentation to conventional jobs (sometimes supplemented by low-risk stealing from the workplace), many black youths move from the same to hard crime: they enter the crack trade and brandish machine guns; in their spare time they father crack or AIDS babies. Most, however, realize the risks of death or jail and leave muggings for the legal job market. Hispanic youths combine work and crime in a slightly different way: because their older relatives and neighbors have the worst-paid, least-skilled manual jobs—often seasonal, often requiring no English—these youths are the earliest of the three criminal groups to leave school and experience frequent unemployment. Undertaking crimes with less risk than the violent crimes of the blacks, their short-term careers in burglary last longer. When they eventually graduate to more risky street robberies, they are more often caught; the great majority, like the blacks, back away and turn to conventional jobs, however unstable.

Greater differences between black poor and Mexican immigrant poor were uncovered in a larger, more representative study in Chicago, based on face-to-face interviews with 1,186 blacks, 368 whites, 484 Mexicans, and 453 Puerto Ricans (Van Haitsma, 1991; and Wilson, 1991a), not confined to criminal gangs. Despite their lesser education level and poor language skills, Mexican immigrant men were 94% employed, while the black men were only 68% employed. Fully 34% of those black women living with their children have no other adults in the household, compared to only 6.2% of Mexican immigrant women. In other words, compared to inner-city blacks, the Mexicans have stable families, can more easily divide child care and housekeeping so that at least one adult can seek a job; they have more job information networks and a multiple earner system where unemployment for one member is not a catastrophe. They are also less likely to live in housing projects or areas of heavy poverty concentration (employers often use such addresses as signs of bad work habits). Although this study did not report rates of violent crime, based on my analysis we would predict a much higher rate for blacks, whose poverty is much more often combined with family breakup and isolation from conventional job networks.[4]

In short, what explains the patterns of violence uncovered in urban ethnography as well as the more abstract murder rates in statistical studies is not a racial subculture of violence. Instead, it is the interaction of poverty and inequality with family breakup (as a symbol of weak or nonexistent social networks), the lack of parental and school supervision, and the absence of conventional job opportunities.[5]

Similar findings come from a more systematic large-scale survey of black youths (age 16–24) in poverty areas in Boston, Chicago, and Philadelphia 1979–80 (Freeman and Holzer, 1986, especially chaps. 1, 2, and 9). Joblessness among the young blacks was tightly related to crime, drug and alcohol abuse, poor job performance (absenteeism), and some employer discrimination. The relevant findings are consistent with the insights of urban ethnography: (1) The bulk of the young black men are serious about seeking jobs and a significant portion were taking steps to escape from poverty (these have an edge in church attendance and occupational aspirations and have contact with other family members who work) (*ibid.* pp. 10, 13, 372–374). (2) Seven of 10 youths who are out of school and out of work think that they can get a minimum-wage job either very or somewhat easily (p. 16); most want to work but only at jobs and wages comparable to those of their white counterparts; when they do work, they are paid an average of $4/hour compared to $4.75 for the white youths (*ibid.,* pp. 34–35, 65). (3) Because their chances of finding any work in a two-week period is half that of whites and because they are generally unwilling to take jobs that are worse than those of whites, they are attracted to the other obvious alternatives—criminal careers. (Thirty-two percent of the youths said they could earn more from criminal street action than from legitimate work. *Ibid.,* p. 14.) Young blacks from welfare households in housing projects have the worst record in the job market and, as we have seen, are especially prone to violent criminal careers.

TABLE 14.1 Countries with very low minority-group cleavages tend to have below average homicide rates but three countries with strong cleavages also have low homicide rates (1998). The U.S. is in a class by itself.

Homicide Rates circa 1988**	Minority Group Cleavages*			
	High (.71-.55)	High-Med. (.47-.43)	Medium (.37-.28)	Low (.19-.03)
High (18.0)	United States 18.0			
Med-High (5.7-3.8)	Canada 3.8	Australia 4.8 New Zealand 4.0	Belgium 4.3	Finland 5.7
Med-Low (3.2-2.0)	Israel 2.7 Switzerland 2.6	United Kingdom 2.2	France 2.0 W. Germany 2.0	Italy 3.2 Norway 2.4 Sweden 2.4 Austria 2.3 Denmark 2.3
Low (1.8-1.3)			Netherlands 1.8	Ireland 1.6 Japan 1.3

*Measured by ethnic, religious, linguistic, or racial cleavages. See appendix I.

**Deaths from homicides per 100,000 population. Source: WHO, *World Health Statistics Annual 1989* (1990) and *1990* (1991). The rate for each country is listed to its right. All rates are for 1988 except Switzerland, UK, Austria, W. Germany, and Japan (all 1989); Israel, New Zealand, Sweden, and Italy (all 1987); and Belgium (1986).

Cross-national data can shed further light on the question of American exceptionalism and the theory of a racial subculture of violence. Table 14.1 relates minority-group cleavages to homicide rates in our 19 countries.

It casts doubt on the critical importance of race or the peculiarity of the United States. For none of the other high scorers on violence has America's history of slavery. And until recently countries with above-average homicide rates (Finland, Canada, Italy, Australia, Belgium) have had no substantial racial minorities. Moreover, if we consider the intensity of minority-group cleavages based on religion, ethnicity, and language as well as race, three countries with strong cleavages—Switzerland, Israel, and the UK—have low homicide rates. The cleavage scores (Appendix I) understate cleavages in a fourth exception, the Netherlands.

There is no reason to suppose that the historical hatreds, secession movements, or minority/majority political combat within other nations are much different from the conflict between blacks and whites in the United States. Consider the continuing social tensions and political conflict among Protestants, Catholics, and secular socialists in the Netherlands; or commonwealth blacks vs. Indians, and Pakistanis vs. the Irish Catholics vs. Protestant whites of the UK or the French-speaking Jura separatists vs. the German majority in Berne, Switzerland; or the Arab and Jewish minorities in France who are scapegoats of the party of LePen.

The main caution, however, is that the United States is in a class by itself in the murder rate: 18.0 deaths from homicides per 100,000 population in 1988 compared to the next highest-rate countries (Finland, 5.7; Australia, 4.8; Belgium, 4.3; New Zealand, 4.0; and Canada, 3.8). And the table does show a tendency for countries with low social cleavages to have below-average murder rates. But this does not prove that minority-group conflict is the main cause of crimes against persons. The few cross-national studies of this issue in fact confirm the same pattern uncovered in the U.S. studies: it is not the presence of minority populations but the degree of inequality (in the society as a whole, or between minority groups and dominant groups), poverty, family breakup, and unemployment that accounts for differences in violent crime. And the United States is extreme in these general sources of violence. Among the best recent studies is Gartner (1990). Analyzing sex- and age-specific victimization data on homicide in 18 developed nations from 1950 to 1980, she confirms the importance of economic deprivation, divorce, economic inequality, and cultural heterogeneity and adds the extent of official violence (measured by the number of wars 1900–80, the number of battle deaths, and the existence of the death penalty) as sources of homicide (and, incidentally, finds that increased female labor-force participation increases only the killing of women and children, not men). Similarly, Messner (1980) shows that in the early 1960s, income inequality (measured by the Gini coefficient) predicts murder rates in 56 countries, and (1989) confirms Blau and Blau's (1982) finding that economic discrimination against minority groups is an independent factor determining murder rates in 52 countries circa 1980, even more important than economic deprivation. (Messner, 1989, reached the same conclusion analyzing murder rates in 52 countries in the late 1970s and early 1980s.)

Before we move to a comparative analysis of risk and safety in our 19 rich democracies, a word about alternative explanations of violence in the United States: the "Southern (or Western) culture of violence" theme and the "soft-on-crime permissiveness" theme.

Students of Southern regionalism have observed that the deep South has markedly higher rates of gun ownership, suicide, assault, and homicide than the rest of the United States. From this they infer that the South has a subculture of violence, values variously labeled a romantic and hedonistic spirit, an intense egocentric individualism, pride of place and race, and most relevant, "a chip-on-the-shoulder swagger and brag"—the boast, voiced or not, on the part of every Southerner that he would "knock hell out of whoever dared to cross him" (Cash, 1941, p. 55). This appears in many studies of Southern politics and society (e.g., Hackney, 1969, and the subtle portrait of *The Mind of the South* by W. J. Cash, 1941). Then the subculture inferred from the violent behavior is used to explain the Southern pattern of violence.

We can overcome this problem of tautology, so typical of theories of cultural determinism, if we specify the values and attitudes comprising the subculture, locate them, and relate them to behavior. A study of American attitudes toward justifications for violence (Dixon and Lizotte, 1987) illustrates. What about punching or beating up a man who has committed a minor provocation? The percentage of Southerners who approve of items measuring that theme are a minority—about the same percentage as in other regions of the country. But when asked whether they approve of punching an adult male stranger who had broken into your house, or hit your child, or was "beating up a woman," far more Southerners approve than non-Southerners. Further, a "defensive attitude" scale (protect women, children, and home) *is* related to gun ownership while values justifying easy resort to physical force (measured by a violent attitudes scale) are no more widespread in the South than elsewhere and are not related to gun ownership. In other words, although a passionate commitment to protecting home and family may be Southern, attitudes justifying violence are not.

More fatal for the theory are multivariate analyses that compare the effects of Southern location or a scale of "Southernness" on homicide with the effects of the variables already discussed. Land et al. (1990, pp. 932, 953) uncover no Southern location effect that is not accounted for by urbanization (large dense populations), resource deprivation (poverty, inequality), and family breakup. (Only at the city level of analysis was there any Southern effect, and that was only for 1960; it faded to nothing in 1970 and 1980.) Blau and Blau (1982), analyzing 1970 data, similarly found no Southern effect.

But how about the Wild West—a subculture of violence in the Rockies, or in far-out California? Is there a Western ethos emphasizing "outdoor machismo, individualism, risk taking, conspicuous athleticism, danger seeking, and nature conquering" (Greenberg et al., 1987) which would explain crimes of violence? Again, at first glance we can find supporting evidence. The non-Mormon areas of Western states rank high in violent deaths. The six most dangerous Western states—Arizona, Idaho, Montana, Nevada, New Mexico, and Wyoming—have very high rates of death by violence (*ibid.*, pp. 40−41). And in an exception to the urbanism-crime connection, the rural Western areas show the highest violent death rate for youths, even higher than urban ghettos (p. 42)—figures that have been stable since 1949−51.

As in the case of a "Southern subculture of violence," however, when we examine variation in social structure and economic opportunity, the Western subculture is less than meets the eye. As Greenberg et al. (p. 44) note,

the divorce rate in the six most dangerous Western states has long been two to three times that of the four safest Northeast states. The rate of Roman Catholicism, a religion that forbids suicide, is twice as high in the four Northeast states (nearly half their population) as in the six Western ones. Almost two-thirds of the people living in the Northeast states were born in the state where they reside, compared with two-fifths of those living in the Western states. Less than half of Northeasterners moved at least once every five years, as compared to almost 60 percent of the Westerners. The Western unemployment rate averages about one-third higher than the northeast one.

Moreover, a closer look at violent deaths in the rural West shows that most of them are deaths from suicide, auto accidents, and dangerous trades (mining, quarrying, and agriculture where men die in violent industrial accidents). The homicide rate in these areas from 1939−41 to 1977−79, while about twice as high as those in the four safest states of the Northeast (Connecticut, Massachusetts, New Jersey, and Rhode Island), were above the national average in only three of five periods studied (Greenberg et al., 1987). Finally, when we look at cities, the leaders in violent crime rates are scattered and by no means confined either to the South or West: Dayton, St. Louis, and Washington, D.C., as well as Baltimore, Ft. Worth, and Atlanta.

Another alternative explanation of high American rates of violent crime is that the United States is uniquely "soft on crime" and is burdened with a permissive culture developed in the postwar era. The United States, the argument goes, gives too much protection to the accused, too little punishment, too late; is too tolerant of violence and deviance; suffers from a corrosive ethic of "socialist egalitarianism" (Davies, 1983) or from a welfare state that accents "entitlements" and "rights" without personal responsibilities (Murray, 1984). The evidence for any of this, to say the least, is ambiguous. Scholars of very different ideological persuasion who have examined the efficacy of wars on drugs and crackdowns on crime remain skeptical. They range between the view that the severity, frequency, and certainty of punishment are only marginally effective in deterring crime and the evidence is mixed (Wilson and Herrnstein, 1985, pp. 390, 392, 400, 403) and the more skeptical view that the wars on crime of the 1970s and 1980s were totally ineffective if not counterproductive (Currie, 1985, pp. 7, 11, 28, 61–63, 70–71).

In a book representative of hawkish scholars, Wilson and Herrnstein (1985) generally argue that any sanction that raises the costs of committing a crime should make crime less likely (p. 44); they point to evidence that "behavior changed when assaultive spouses were arrested, instead of merely counseled, when Chicago delinquents were placed in more rather than less restrictive institutions, and when the penalties for carrying guns or driving while drunk were made either more certain or more severe" (p. 403). But they hasten to add that if crime payoffs are high, and detection is difficult, crackdowns do not work. In more recent commentary James Q. Wilson (1994) emphasizes the diminishing marginal returns of imprisonment. He estimates that "doubling the prison population probably produces only a 10% to 20% reduction in the crime rate" for two reasons: first, judges already send the most serious offenders to prison (and always have done so); second, the most serious offenders typically get the longest sentences and "age slows us all down, mugger and victim alike" (p. 38), with the average violent criminal career lasting only about 10 years. Thus, if we continue to increase the rate of incarceration and the length of sentences of convicted offenders, we must "dip into the bucket of prisoners eligible for parole, dredging up offenders with shorter and shorter criminal records" (p. 38) and less and less potential for violence.

Currie (1985), representative of dovish scholars, argues that the weight of American and cross-national evidence is that neither general deterrence (high incarceration rates and strong punishments) nor specific deterrence (e.g., mandatory prison sentences and restrictions on parole) reduce crime. He suggests that tougher sanctions deter drunk driving and family violence because these are the only crimes the American criminal justice system has treated lightly in the past (Currie, 1985, pp. 68–69, 72–75, and 230–231). If police officers, prosecutors, and judges had been as remarkably lenient in dealing with murderers, rapists, and armed robbers as they were with drunk drivers and wife (or husband) beaters, a sudden crackdown would have similar effects. But, in fact, for almost all crime, punishments have been severe whenever convictions were obtained; making them still more severe has had no effect.[6]

Both Wilson and Herrnstein and Currie interpret the effect of the Bartley-Fox gun law of 1974 in Massachusetts, which said that anyone caught illegally carrying a gun would receive a minimum one-year prison term with no possibility of parole. Currie notes the unanticipated consequences: before the law was passed, about half of the gun-violation defendants were released without conviction; but two years after, four in five got off free. Apparently the tough penalty "spurred defendants to go to trial to seek acquittal" rather than plea bargain. "Accordingly, there were more verdicts of not guilty, more dismissals, more appeals, and more new trials" (p. 63). Although Wilson and Herrnstein, in contrast, point to "a reduction [after the gun law was passed] in the proportion of assaults, robberies, and homicides in which a handgun was used," they also note that the total number of such crimes either increased or stayed steady and that "calculating offenders" appeared unaffected (p. 400).

Beyond these ambiguities are some facts that justify caution in accepting the idea that the United States has a high crime rate because it is soft on crime:

1. *The prison boom in the United States coincided with a rise in the crime rate,* especially of violent crimes. Since the early 1970s incarceration rates have climbed fast; after 1985 they accelerated (U.S. Bureau of the Census, 1991, table 334). In the 1980s, the crackdown on crime took the form of mandatory minimum sentences, restrictive parole policies, and the increased use of the death penalty. The American prison population more than doubled in the 1980s; by 1988, we were spending $19 billion per year on prisoners (*ibid.,* table 318). By the end of the century, we achieved the highest known incarceration rate in the world, about 1 prisoner for every 163 persons, a rate six times the European average. The trend continued in the 1990s: the Justice Department reported that 1 out of every 167 Americans was in prison or jail at the end of 1995 (*Wall Street Journal,* August 19, 1996). Inevitably, the prison boom outpaced the public's willingness to pay for more judges and jails; conditions deteriorated. Thus, although the U.S. allocates an increasing percentage of its budget to penal institutions, they are increasingly overcrowded, and violence within them has escalated. Among rich democracies at the other extreme, the Netherlands imprisons only 1 in 2,500 of its population; Switzerland, 1 in 1,370; Japan, 1 in 2,200. With such low incarceration rates, these countries can afford realistic rehabilitation and more efficient separation of violent from nonviolent prisoners.

The percentage of young men (18–24) declined from 6.6 in 1980 to 5.4 in 1989, a sharp drop. Because young men commit most crimes, the crime rate should have gone down substantially during the 1980s. In fact, it dropped only 0.6% and, most striking, the rate of violent crime increased. The forcible rape rate climbed 14% from 1981 to 1990 while the rate of aggravated assault soared 46%; the murder rate dipped slightly in the early 1980s but increased 9% from 1986 to 1990 (Federal Bureau of Investigation, 1990, p. 50).[7] A major reason that the prison boom fails to deter crime, especially violent crime, is that American prisons are so efficient in socializing first-time offenders to a violent criminal subculture. The result: the more imprisonment without rehabilitation, the more recidivism.

2. *Repeated declarations of wars on drugs followed by boasts of near victory were accompanied by an increase in drug-related crime.* In 1973, President Nixon announced that the United States "has turned the corner on drug addition." When hard-liner William Bennett resigned as director of the Office of National Drug Control Policy in November 1990, he reported that casual consumption of cocaine and marijuana had declined, especially within the white middle class, as had emergency-room admissions and deaths from drug

overdoses. He proclaimed that success was in sight; President Bush echoed the sentiment. By fiscal year 1991, the U.S. was spending more than $10.4 billion for federal antidrug programs, up from $1.5 billion in 1981; 7 in 10 of these dollars went to enforcement, interdiction, and intelligence, only 3 in 10 dollars to prevention, treatment, education, and research (U.S. Office of Management and Budget, 1992, Part 2, p. 123). In 1997 Congress appropriated $16 billion for the drug war budget.

Scattered city reports (*Time,* Dec. 3, 1990, pp. 45–46) suggest that the tough drug laws, tough talk, and intensified policing have the following effects: while there are fewer deaths from overdoses, and may even be fewer customers, there are more drug-related shootings, stabbings, and assaults, as street dealers fight over the slightly reduced number of buyers. While the number of cocaine users has declined since the mid-1980s, total consumption remains steady because the number of heavy users has increased (Rydell and Everingham, 1994, pp. 1–2). An incidental effect of the criminalization of drug use and stiff penalties for peddlers is the spread of heroin and cocaine to high schools in the 1980s; traffickers hired kids to sell to kids because juveniles receive more lenient punishments. Regarding drug supplies, if the Columbian government disrupts the Medellin cocaine cartel's refining and transportation operations, dealers in Cali or Bolivia and Peru step in to fill the void and heroin traffic from Southeast Asia is revived. Heroic interdiction does seem to raise the price of drugs and increase profits for the cartels in the very short run. Unfortunately, supply remains abundant while desperate addicts escalate their robberies and violence to pay the price, and in the past 10 or 15 years the price of both cocaine and heroin collapsed, despite intensified efforts at interdiction and punishment.[8]

3. *Not only do American murder rates continue to climb in the face of all these crackdowns but the percentage of murderers apprehended has declined.* In the mid-1960s, the clearance rate for murder was over 90%; by 1990, murder cases solved dropped to 67% (Federal Bureau of Investigation, 1990, p. 14); in some metropolitan jurisdictions, below half.[9] One reason is the rising number of cases that are drug-related, where fear restrains witnesses from speaking or in which the killer and victim are strangers, which makes murder more random and fearsome and solving the crime more difficult. Random killing on the street with the body dumped in a back alley leaves few clues for detectives and spreads the fear that it can happen to anyone (Simon, 1991, pp. 72–75).

4. *Increasing the number of law enforcement personnel and increasing police efficiency may or may not reduce violent crime.* City studies by the Police Foundation show that increasing random preventative patrols did not deter crime and that reducing police response time to calls about specific incidents did not lead to more arrests (Sparrow, Moore, and Kennedy, 1990, pp. 45–46). Thus, increasing resources devoted to traditional policing would have little effect. However, there are hints in cross-national studies and in American experiments that transforming police missions and methods can contribute to crime reduction. Consider the contrasting role of the police in Tokyo, where violent crimes are few and gun control is strong and Oakland, where violent crimes are many and gun control is nonexistent. A systematic comparison of a downtown police station in a Japanese urban center and the Oakland, California, Police Department shows that the ratio of police to population is much greater in Tokyo—six police officers for every 1,000 population compared to Oakland's two.[10] Equally important is the relation of po-

lice to citizens. As in all of Japan, the police in Tokyo go so far beyond the traditional emergency responses of the police in Oakland that it is practically a different occupation. Tokyo police are scattered more evenly over the area in tiny stations containing two to eight officers in two or three rooms, one used for short naps and eating. From these *kobans,* they can fan out in all neighborhoods on foot. The purpose is not only law enforcement but also crime prevention. In addition to giving street directions and miscellaneous advice, they are responsible for two surveys of the population of their area per year. Although the patrol officers, especially the younger ones, resist this aspect of their work (reports vary about how much of it is done and most police stations have assigned "household visit specialists" to do it), it is clear that Japanese police officers know more about the social structure of neighborhoods and where the problem families are than do their American counterparts. They often confer with owners of boardinghouses and janitors of apartments about changes in the neighborhood and the behavior of residents. Because of this nonconfrontational interaction of police and community, citizens are said to be more willing to report problems and potential problems to police. Even discounting American criminologists' tendency to romanticize the Japanese case—Bayley (1991, pp. 97, 164) describes the Japanese police as a model of community policing—Japanese policing is clearly less dangerous, less confrontational, less emergency-driven, and more effective.

Where American police departments have moved in that direction it has paid off. There is some evidence that in high-crime areas of American cities crime is deterred by patrols—dozens of police officers on the street—combined with efforts at physical restoration of the neighborhood. Beyond instituting foot patrols and neighborhood police stations, the tactics include the following: interview residents door-to-door about their concerns; clean up littered lots; tear down abandoned houses; paint over graffiti; repair broken windows; install locks; blockade roads used by drive-by drug dealers; improve lighting; reorganize crime-ridden housing projects. All this frightens local drug dealers and their customers away or, at a minimum, weakens their criminal infrastructure, while neighborhood residents are given hope that order can be restored (Sparrow et al., 1990, pp. 3 – 29; and Wilson and Kelling, 1989, pp. 47 – 49).

Unfortunately, there are at least three barriers to an American transformation of police missions and methods: lack of police and other resources devoted to community problems, which reflects weak social consensus and weaker political will; a structure of government that makes coordination of police and other agencies difficult; and the limitations of community policing where there is no "community." American politicians prefer to demagogue the issue of crime rather than educate their constituents about the need to pay for public services to prevent and deter crime. For instance, in 1989, only eight officers were assigned to the problem-solving Community Mobilization Project in the Wilshire district of Los Angeles, a heterogeneous area of 300,000 residents (Wilson and Kelling, 1989, p. 51). In the Oakland/Tokyo comparison, Oakland police were wildly overworked and exposed to much more danger; the number of emergency calls per 1,000 population was 18 times greater in Oakland (Murayama, 1980, p. 24). To retrain police in new missions and methods in numbers adequate to the task requires not only a reorientation of police management but great increases in personnel and budget. A second barrier to community-oriented policing is the fragmentation and decentralization of American government, which makes concerted action on any urban problem difficult. It is what John Mudd in his book *Neighborhood Services* (1984) calls "the rat problem": "If a rat is found in an apartment, it is a housing inspection responsibility; if it runs into a restaurant, the health department has jurisdiction; if it goes outside and dies in an alley, public works takes over" (p. 8). To tell the police "Mobilize all relevant agencies to reduce visible signs of poverty and decay in high-crime areas" is to ask the impossible. Finally, while the evidence is far from conclusive, community-oriented policing apparently works best on issues that are minor and in neighborhoods that need it least. For instance, Neighborhood Watch programs, which encourage police-citizen collaboration, are an example of preventative community policing, but they are seldom found in high crime areas. As James Q. Wilson (1990, p. 60) suggests, an empathic partnership-oriented style of policing might be effective for removing graffiti but be ineffective with organized gang wars conducted with AK-47s.

In short, some reduction in some crimes is possible with a combination of community-oriented policing, increased numbers of personnel, and major improvements in the appearance of housing and neighborhood. But that brings us back to where we started: reduce poverty, inequality, and unemployment and cushion the shock of family breakup in crowded urban settings, and you will reduce violent crime. But more traditional policing alone or more community-oriented policing will have little effect where there is no community.

In sum: America's high rate of violent crime cannot be explained by a permissive culture that is soft on crime. For three decades, the United States has had increasingly tough laws on crime and drug use; its incarceration rates, already high, became the highest among industrial countries; the prison boom coincided with a rise in violent crime; wars on drugs—interdiction of supply, arrests of dealers and users—were accompanied by an increase in drug-related crime and a decreasing rate of apprehension of murderers; increasing efficiency of and resources for traditional policing has had little effect, although it is likely that increasing resources devoted to community-oriented policing *if* combined with an attack on the root causes of violent crime would have some effect. Of course we cannot know what the violent crime rate would have been if no crime crackdowns occurred. But the advocates of crackdown must accept a burden of proof that they have not yet met.

From 1993 through 1998 there was a substantial decline in the murder rate in several of the most violent American cities. It is too early to say that this is a trend or to know the importance of community policing relative to the structural shifts discussed above. Those years did see a shift in numbers and missions of police. In New York City, for instance, more officers patrolled the streets, more undercover agents bought drugs and guns and collected intelligence on gangs; there was more cooperation among city, state, and federal law enforcement agencies, more arrests for minor "quality-of-life crimes"—which provides search warrants and the seizure of guns and arrests for gun possession. Simultaneously, however, during the early and mid-1990s the percentage of violence-prone 15- to 24-year-olds was declining both in New York City and the country, unemployment rates were dropping, job creation accelerating, and even poverty and inequality were declining—the product of large 1993 increases in the Earned Income Tax Credit for the working poor and a steadily expanding economy in which the lowest wage began to increase in real terms. In short, the crackdown aspects may have played a role, especially since community policing did advance, but reductions in poverty, inequality, unemployment, and number of youths; improved gun control; and more job opportunities were also evident. A minor contribution came from trauma center improvements in the 1990s; such centers remove potential murder victims from the statistics; they appear as injuries. Some observers of the drug trade suggest a final structural shift in the 1990s that may have lowered murder rates in some urban centers: older drug kingpins, the big businessmen of the trade, have consolidated their power and suppressed the random violence of teenage gangs competing for status and territory so common in the 1980s; ironically, this more-efficient criminal organization for drug distribution reduces street warfare and hence murder rates (Skolnick, 1997).

Finally, as always, localized police crackdowns often shift the locus of violence. Because of the New York City gun-control campaign, gun traffickers have moved to the Carolinas and Florida. For the country as a whole, there has been little drop in violent crime. In 1994 Americans suffered 42.4 million crimes, 10.9 million of which were violent; the violent crime rate has been essentially unchanged since 1992, following a slight increase from a very high level between 1985 and 1991 (Dilulio, 1996).

A COMPARATIVE ANALYSIS OF MAYHEM

Murder rates, although they are a clue to broader patterns of violence affecting large populations, do not exhaust the threats to individual peace and stability. To broaden the discussion of risks and compare the performance of democratic governments in enhancing safety, I devised a measure of mayhem and applied it to our 19 rich democracies.

The Wilensky Mayhem Index

This is based on four external threats to the person from the social and physical environment for which reasonably reliable data are available in the 19 countries. These threats are usually unpredictable, often catastrophic, always momentous, and can be reduced by public policy. The four that fit that concept and cohere (are highly correlated with one another and through time) are *deaths from homicide; deaths from fire; unemployment rates;* and *divorce rates* that are unaccompanied by economic and social cushions against the shock of divorce.

Candidates we eliminated include deaths from any of the following: industrial accidents, auto accidents, diseases of the circulatory system, ulcers, cirrhosis of the liver, pregnancy and childbirth, and suicide. We also eliminated deaths from war or disruption of life from a military draft and several natural hazards. The rationale: Although deaths from industrial accidents fit the concept of unpredictable, momentous external threats (dangerous working environments), they are unrelated to our four indicators of mayhem. They are treated separately in chapter 15. We reluctantly eliminated deaths from auto accidents or, more broadly, transportation accidents (including auto, cycle, pedestrian) on three grounds:

1.   An unknown component of suicide is in these figures; anyone who has driven in Italy, France, or Texas can confirm this.

2.   We cannot sort out the thermal, mechanical, physical, and human causes of these accidents. Even the weather plays its part. Although public policy may have some effect (funding for rapid transit, taxes on gasoline), the effect may be minor.

3.   The rates appear to be related simply to whether the country has wide open spaces. Thus, Australia, Canada, and the United States lead in deaths from motor vehicle accidents per 100,000 population and are among the top six in deaths from all transport accidents, while the bottom seven in auto deaths and bottom six in transport deaths are small (e.g., Sweden, Denmark, Norway) or crowded countries (e.g., Netherlands, Japan) with good rapid transit systems (OECD, 1986a, pp. 156–158).

However, transportation accidents are the leading cause of violent deaths in 19 OECD countries. So, for those impressed by slaughter on the highway or who are intrigued by Jean-Luc Goddard's film "Weekend" (1967), a vision of the traffic jam as hell, here are figures to show that these deaths are related to our mayham scores:

Deaths from transport accidents per 100,000 people 1980 or most recent year		Mayhem Index *Score Average*	
		1980	1988
High	(25–27)	6.8	7.2
Medium	(18–22)	4.3	5.2
Low	(12–15)	3.8	4.7

With the above caveats, we can view transportation death rates as validation of the mayhem index as a broad, coherent measure of national performance in reducing risk.

We exclude suicide not only because of poor cross-national comparability (among other problems, Catholic countries probably undercount suicides) but also because it is an attack on the self, and the literature generally shows an ambiguous relationship between homicide and suicide (in our 19 countries the correlation for 1970 is only −.10). Durkheim's conclusion of 1897—"suicide sometimes coexists with homicide, sometimes they are mutually exclusive; sometimes they react under the same conditions in the same way, sometimes in opposite ways" (Durkheim, 1951 [1897], p. 355)—has stood the test of modern social research. Similarly, deaths from cirrhosis, ulcers, heart attacks, and strokes can be viewed as cumulative results of self-abuse and/or genetic factors. And pregnancy deaths are unrelated to our four indicators and in a basic sense are a chosen risk. Some of these health measures are analyzed in chapter 16 (on health performance).

We exclude rape, even though it fits my concept of mayhem very well, because no reliable, comparable cross-national data exist. The most thorough American study (Baron and Straus, 1989), using state-level data necessarily limited to official police reports, is suggestive, however. It shows that the same variables that explain homicide and related violence against the person also explain rape rates: urbanization, unemployment, and economic inequality lead to three proximate causes of rape, namely, gender inequality, pornography (an index of sex magazine circulation), and social disorganization (six indicators of weak social integration—geographic mobility, divorce, lack of religious affiliation, households headed by males with no females present, female-headed households with children, and the ratio of tourists to residents as an indicator of transients who undermine normative constraints). Approval of legitimate violence, a source of homicide in two other studies (Gartner, 1990; Archer and Gartner, 1984), had no effect on rape rates. Except for pornography and perhaps gender inequality, these causes of rape are the same as the main causes of homicide.[11]

Risks of disruption of life by military service or deaths and injuries from war are not rooted in national social or political structures or domestic policies; they are mainly a matter of types of wars, the alliance or pact position of the country, and its position in the postwar confrontations of the superpowers (Wilensky, 1975, chap. 4); it is hardly an indicator of social disorganization. Finally, although military effort (e.g., military spending/GNP averaged for 1966 and 1970) is moderately to weakly related to unemployment ($r = .44$), divorce rate ($r = .40$), and homicide ($r = .32$),[12] in the analysis that follows, when we add military spending in regression equations testing our two models, its effects on mayhem are insignificant.

Finally, we eliminate natural hazards that vary by region and country and have nothing to do with their social structure, culture, politics, policies, or economics—floods, tornadoes and severe windstorms, hurricanes and severe tropical storms, earthquakes and severe tremors.[13]

The four components of the mayhem index—divorce rate per 1,000 married couples (circa 1970, but for 1980 and 1988 only the rate per 1,000 population was available), homicide deaths per 100,000 population (various dates), fire deaths per 100,000 population (various dates), and unemployment rates averaged for appropriate periods—are equally weighted. Countries were arrayed from top to bottom on each dimension and natural cutting points were drawn (where meaningful jumps in the numbers were apparent) to arrive at a score of 0, 1, 2, or 3 for each component. Total mayhem scores can range from 0 to 12. Details and sources are in appendix I.

Because the meaning and coherence of this index are not obvious, here are a few comments about the connections among the four components, using illustrations from the most extreme case, the USA. Our discussion of homicide showed that family breakup and unemployment are closely linked to homicide, each having an independent effect. Hence it is understandable that we have strong correlations in our cross-national data among divorce, unemployment, and homicide (which itself is correlated with many forms of violence).

But why would these three indicators of mayhem be so closely correlated with the fourth, deaths from fire? Because they all reflect complex, long processes of neglect, which we can see most easily in the American case: neglect of housing stock, of urban infrastructure, of investment in human resources. At the extreme there are notorious sites of urban decay such as the South Bronx, Harlem, Bedford-Styvesant, and Brownsville sections of New York City, south central Los Angeles, much of Newark, parts of Chicago, Washington, D.C., and most other big American cities. As Mark Baldassare (1981a) observes, buildings are abandoned after long deterioration; the "middle class" (really the upper-working class and lower-middle class) flees, vacancy rates force lower rents, low-income replacements arrive—especially the unemployed poor, the single parents with large numbers of children, the old poor with no family roots. Owners disinvest by deferring maintenance, lenders refuse to finance mortgages or loan money for upkeep; services of heat and water collapse; renters and landlords alike fall behind in their payments (rent, mortgages, taxes); some of the landlords—one-building owners themselves squeezed—resort to arson and try to collect insurance, others abandon their buildings and the city assumes ownership.

The people living in such areas, in or around the abandoned or deteriorated buildings, face daily threats to their health, welfare, and safety: hallways become shooting galleries for junkies; vandalism and muggings abound. In these jungles of decrepit housing, populated by the isolated aged, by families without fathers, and by unsupervised youths (with unemployment rates of 40–50%), both murders and fires are common. In recent years, the situation in these areas has been exacerbated by the crack epidemic; it has brought brutal struggles among competing gangs for control of this lucrative drug of choice. And everyone involved is equipped with state-of-the-art firepower. Because schools and their playgrounds are everywhere, children are often caught in the crossfire.

All of this is not confined to the trap ghettos. A study of North Carolina and an incident in Oakland, California, illustrate my theme that fires belong in the mayhem index. In 1988, a crack house in a respectable, racially integrated, working-class neighborhood in East Oakland was the scene of two fires: in the first, the dealers torched a young woman after dousing her with gasoline for failure to pay a $50 drug debt. That was swiftly followed by a firebomb thrown into the dealers' apartment. Local homeowners, who had organized a neighborhood watch, assumed that the crack house was razed either by an irate relative of the severely burned user or one of the many frustrated neighbors who for two years had been pressuring the police, the landlord, and the city to bust the crack house. (The source is newspaper accounts and personal interviews with neighborhood organizers and a drug prevention official of Oakland.)

In North Carolina, it turns out that death from burns is common among young children. Analyzing the 191 fire deaths that occurred in the 13 months following January 1, 1989, and excluding arson, Gugelmann (1989) compared the 155 situations where fires were fatal with 284 nonfatal fires matched for type and time. He found that family structures and child-care arrangements were the main causes of fire deaths among children under five, the typical victims of residential fires. Single parents in poverty with poor child-care arrangements—the child who died was taken care of by no one or by a drunkard, a drug addict, or someone who is bedridden, deaf, or otherwise handicapped for the purpose of child care—evidenced a rate of death by fire seven times greater than two-parent families without gross pathology, parents who are not drunk, not absent, nor inattentive. Again, we see the correlation of poverty, family breakup, child neglect, and fires.[14]

Intercorrelation of the four components of the mayhem index for each year for which we have data—1970, 1980, and 1988—(4 × 4 matrices)—show that 15 of 18 correlations were positive, 9 of them significant; the other three had zero correlation. The correlations decline slightly from 1970 to 1988, with unemployment showing the most drop (near zero r's for unemployment averaged 1985–89). We therefore eliminated unemployment and redid the mayhem index with only three components (divorce, murder, fire). With that index, the results of the analysis below is slightly stronger. The correlations of the two indexes range from .88 to .95. We retained the four-component index because it is more theoretically apt.

Theory and Hypotheses: What Causes Mayhem?

Drawing on results from the analysis of homicide in the United States and applying my general scheme for analyzing both convergence (industrialization and its correlates) and divergence (types of political economy and their correlates), we can explore two causal models for explaining mayhem. The first starts with per capita GNP in 1966–71 as a measure of levels of industrialism (affluence), which, as we have seen in chapters 8 and 9, leads to increased mobility and a societal emphasis on meritocracy. Mobility and meritocracy are here measured by intergenerational mobility (sons of working-class fathers moving up to nonmanual occupations; there are no data on daughters); the percentage of working-class sons and daughters in higher education (1965 and 1970); higher education enrollment ratio (average of 1965 and 1970); and higher education expenditures per capita averaged for 1965 and 1971. Each component was scored 0, 1, or 2, and equally weighted (see appendix I for scores and details). Total scores range from 0 (Austria and Ireland) to 8 (USA, Canada).

Because we lack data for New Zealand on both mobility dimensions, we dropped it. Because of the positive correlation between occupational mobility and educational mobility, where we lacked data on one or the other variable we scored each case (H, M, L) according to the variable for which we had data. (See appendix I for details and a comparison of residential mobility rates, closely related to the mobility rates we use here.)

All of the higher education enrollment and expenditure variables between 1965 and 1980 are highly intercorrelated so that any meritocracy measures we use to construct this index would yield the same results. In short, the index measures relatively stable structures of mobility and meritocracy.

We use higher education enrollment ratios and expenditures as indicators of a country's emphasis on meritocracy on the assumption that higher education still remains meritocratic. A society with a high enrollment ratio (e.g., a quarter to half of 20- to 24-year-olds were in postsecondary education as early as 1965–71) that also invests relatively large sums in higher education per capita is a society that acts out the value of equality of opportunity. Despite the egalitarian thrust of movements to increase access and reduce tracking and selection by ability, modern universities, colleges, and technical institutes remain essentially meritocratic (see chap. 1). That investment in higher education is meritocratic is further confirmed by its negative correlation with the rest of the welfare state (social security/GNP), which is more egalitarian and collectivistic (chaps. 5 and 6).

Minority-group cleavages in this model is a second source of mobility and meritocracy; as we have seen in chapter 9, democratic governments everywhere are responsive to the mobility aspirations of ethnic, racial, and religious groups. The public sector opens up first, the private sector follows. Whatever the ambivalence of minority groups about the conflict between equality of opportunity and equality of results, the net outcome is expanding opportunity for upward mobility, whose universal effects are to reinforce meritocratic values. Whether the upwardly mobile person who escapes from poverty, the working class, or an impoverished minority group extends a helping hand to those left behind depends on structures for cross-class solidarity—for instance, the strength of such broad-based associations as multi-industrial unions and churches. But even where social solidarity is strong, the central tendency for ambitious mobile men and women is to distance themselves from their origins. The limited research on the political and ideological impact of mobility suggests that whether the mobility is up or down, it has similar effects: the upwardly mobile identify with the class of destination, while the downwardly mobile cling to the class from which they are falling, expecting or hoping to return (for a review of evidence, see chap. 1, p. 47ff.; Wilensky and Edwards, 1959; cf. Curtis and Jackson, 1977, pp. 145–146.) The ultimate outcome is to reinforce a reciprocal alienation among the poor, the near-poor, and the comfortable majority. This can take the form of group conflict as an upwardly mobile minority (e.g., Korean or other Asian immigrants in multiethnic neighborhoods) looks down the ladder they are climbing at a nonmobile minority (e.g., poor blacks) with resentment and contempt. That such hostility is reciprocated was evident in the Los Angeles race riots of May 1992 where about 8 in 10 of Korean stores were burned or looted by rampaging blacks, many of whom were shouting epithets at Koreans and Chinese (Hu, 1992). The interaction of mobile

TABLE 14.2 Means of mayhem variables and the index 1970–88

Year	Rate of death by fire (per 100,000)	Homicide rate (per 100,000)[a]	Divorce rate (per 1,000)	Unemployment rate[c]	Index of Mayhem (4-item)	Index of Mayhem (excl. unemp.)
1970	1.49	1.18	1.15[b]	2.66	4.6	3.2
1980	1.50	1.37	1.93	5.31	4.9	3.6
1988	2.25	2.86	2.08	6.90	5.6	3.9
(N)	(19)	(18)	(19)	(19)	(19)	(19)

[a]U.S. excluded as an extreme outlier. But including U.S., the results are similar: 1970—1.64; 1980—1.85; 1988—3.65.

[b]The mean of the crude divorce rate is shown here for comparability with later years.

[c]Average of 1960–75 for 1970; average of 1975–84 for 1980; average of 1985–89 for 1988.

and nonmobile minorities with one another and with dominant groups creates a climate ripe for mayhem.

In the first model, minority-group cleavages reinforce the relationship between affluence and mobility/meritocracy, thereby increasing mayhem.

I now turn to data testing this model for our 19 countries.

Trends in Mayhem 1970–88

For each component of the mayhem index, the trend since 1970 is up. Table 14.2 shows the mean rates for 1970, 1980, and 1988 for fire deaths, homicide deaths, divorce, and unemployment as well as the average scores for the four-component index of mayhem used in the analysis and the three-component index excluding unemployment.

Together with the results of my analysis of trends in murder rates in the United States, these cross-national comparisons of a broader measure of risk can be interpreted as confirmation of convergence toward high rates of mayhem as rich democracies become richer.

As a general tendency, this holds up even when we control for types of political economy, although now the pattern is not as strong.

Table 14.3 shows that within each of five types of political economy, the average mayhem score climbs over time. But it also shows that 8 of the 19 countries, whether they start high or low, evidence no substantial increase: 6 are roughly stable (Sweden, Finland, Israel, USA, Canada, Ireland); 2 actually decline (Austria down from 5 to 3, and Japan down from 3 to 1). The central tendency, however, is clear: the more affluent, the more mayhem-prone, confirming an advanced industrialism theme. Because the spread in the 1970 scores is greater than that in the 1988 scores, "convergence" is the right word to describe this pattern.

Note, however, that these mayhem scores for each date are relative, not absolute, and therefore are not strictly comparable over time. For example, when I say Japan's mayhem score declined from 3 in 1970 to 1 in 1988, those are scores reflecting the relative position of Japan for each year within a general trend upward, including the trend in Japan.

TABLE 14.3 Mayhem index for 1970, 1980, and 1988, by types of political economy

Left Corporatist	1970	1980	1988
Sweden	4	4	4
Norway	2	3	4
Finland	7	7	7
Israel	4	5	4
Denmark	6	6	7
Average	4.6	5.0	5.2

Left-Catholic Corporatist	1970	1980	1988
Netherlands	1.5	3	4
Belgium	4	7	7
Austria	5	3	3
Average	3.5	4.3	4.7

Catholic Corporatist	1970	1980	1988
Italy	3	5	5
W. Germany	3	3	5
Average	3.0	4.0	5.0

Corporatist Without Labor	1970	1980	1988
France	3	4	6
Japan	3	2	1
Switzerland	1	0	2
Average	2.3	2.0	3.0

Least Corporatist	1970	1980	1988
United States	12	11	11
United Kingdom	6	5	8
New Zealand	1	3	6
Australia	5	7	7
Canada	10	10	9
Ireland	6	6	6
Average	6.7	7.0	7.8

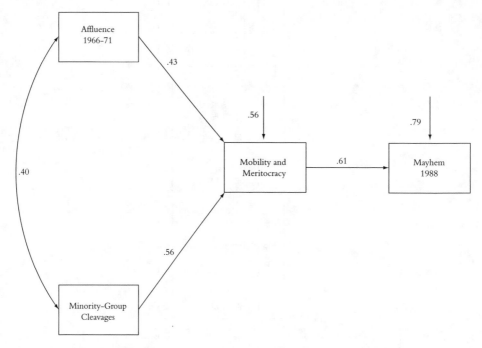

Figure 14.1. Affluence, minority-group cleavages, and mobility and meritocracy increase mayhem, 1988*

*$N=18$; New Zealand missing on Mobility-Meritocracy Index. All path coefficients significant at $p < .05$. Adjusted R^2 for Mayhem = .33; adjusted R^2 for Mobility-Meritocracy = .65. Variables defined in text.

Industrialization and Its Correlates

Fitting the language of interpretation above to a path diagram (figure 14.1)—a causal model of industrialism and minority cleavages as the roots of mayhem—we obtain some strong results.

If we ignore the constraining influence of those political economies that achieve above-average levels of social and political consensus, we have a simple finding: richer countries that have intense conflicts between ethnic, racial, religious, or linguistic groups provide high and often expanding mobility opportunities; in practice and doctrine, they emphasize meritocratic values. Mobility and meritocracy, in turn, foster mayhem. Neither affluence nor ethnic conflict has a significant direct effect on mayhem, after controlling for mobility and meritocracy. Because relative levels of mayhem are stable over time as are structures of mobility and meritocracy, using earlier dates for mayhem scores (1970, 1980) yields very similar results (e.g., correlations between mobility and meritocracy and mayhem are about .60 for all three dates).

Types of Political Economy: Explaining National Differences in Mayhem

The second model emphasizes types of political economy as they shape the welfare state and particular social policies as these, in turn, shape the income distribution, especially the poverty rate and the distance between the rich and the poor. Equality and poverty reduction then reduce mayhem. Thus, in the context of the trend imposed by industrialism and its correlates, what democracies do to arrange the interaction of interest groups, parties, and public bureaucracies, what taxing and spending they undertake, and what policies they implement, are important determinants of risk and safety for their citizens.

A first step in testing this scheme is to examine the interaction of social spending, equality, and mayhem. Table 14.4 presents three measures of income equality—in essence the share of gross household income going to the richest fifth of households, the share going to the poorest fifth (a measure of relative poverty), and the ratio of the two (roughly, the distance between the well-off and the poor). The table also presents the most general measure of aggregate social spending (social security/GNP or welfare effort) and the mayhem scores and ranks. The correlation between 1980 social spending and income equality (using the ratio measure, circa early 1980s) is .42 ($p < .05$).[15]

The average mayhem scores for each grouping of countries are shown in table 14.5.

The averages are consistent with the hypotheses: the more social spending, the more equality; the more equality, the less mayhem. But the averages of this ratio measure of equality may obscure deviations from the patterns as well as the effect of other measures of equality in table 14.4, that is, what kinds of equality count most and least.

From table 14.4 we can say the following, concentrating first on the pattern and the deviant cases, and then on two types of income equality.

- *Social spending and equality.* In the 1980s, of the six welfare-state leaders (highest percentage of GNP devoted to social spending 1980), four are most egalitarian (as measured by the distance between the rich and poor); in income equality, they are high (Sweden, Belgium) or high-medium (Netherlands, West Germany). In contrast, of the eight lowest in social spending, seven are least egalitarian; in income equality, they are low (New Zealand, Switzerland, Australia, USA) or medium-low (UK, Canada, Israel). Japan is the only egalitarian lean spender—and its social spending has been rising rapidly since the early 1970s (Shiratori, 1985, p. 210), while its already low mayhem scores have been dropping from 3 in 1970 to 1 in 1988.[16]

- *Equality and mayhem.* Of the eight most egalitarian countries (H or HM equality by the ratio measure), only two (Belgium and Finland) score above average in mayhem in 1988 (a score of 6 or more). Of the nine least egalitarian countries (ML or L), seven score above average in mayhem. The exceptions—inegalitarian but below average in mayhem—are Israel and Switzerland. What distinguishes these two is the central place of military service: in both countries, all men must serve long periods in the armed forces; Switzerland adds a volunteer contingent of women, Israel drafts women. In countries riven by social cleavages, a citizens' army is doubtless a strong source of social integration. It may offset the effects of a regressive income distribution.

- *Measures of equality and mayhem.* The correlation between the ratio measure (distance between rich and poor) and 1988 mayhem is .43. The correlation between the share of income received by the bottom fifth and mayhem is even stronger: −.52. However, the correlation between the share going to the well off and mayhem is near zero. Earlier years yield similar results. Put crudely, bashing the rich will not make you safer, but reducing the distance between the rich and poor or simply reducing poverty will help a lot.

TABLE 14.4 Percentage share of household income by percentile group of households (circa early 1980s), social-security spending, and mayhem, 1988

Countries ranked by ratio of top to bottom quintile household share of income[a]	Gross household income shares ranked from most to least egalitarian[b]			Social security in 1980		Mayhem score in 1988[c]
	Highest 20 percent	Lowest 20 percent	Ratio of highest to lowest 20 percent	Effort (SS/GNP)	Spending per capita in US$	
Japan	37.5 (4)	8.7 (1)	4.3 (1) H	11.0 (16)	923 (16)	1 (17) L
Belgium	36.0 (1)	7.9 (3)	4.6 (2) H	29.8 (5)	3204 (5)	7 (7) HM
Sweden	36.9 (3)	8.0 (2)	4.6 (2) H	33.1 (1)	4759 (1)	4 (15) L
Netherlands	38.3 (6)	6.9 (4)	5.6 (4) HM	31.3 (3)	3386 (3)	4 (15) L
West Germany	38.7 (8)	6.8 (5)	5.7 (5) HM	27.0 (6)	3186 (6)	5 (11) M
Norway	36.7 (2)	6.2 (9)	5.9 (6) HM	23.3 (7)	2847 (7)	4 (15) L
Finland	37.6 (5)	6.3 (7)	6.0 (7) HM	21.1 (8)	1943 (9)	7 (7) HM
Italy	41.0 (13)	6.8 (5)	6.0 (7) HM	19.6 (9)	1269 (14)	5 (11) M
France	40.8 (12)	6.3 (7)	6.5 (9) ML	30.4 (4)	3245 (4)	6 (9) M
Israel	39.6 (10)	6.0 (10)	6.6 (10) ML	7.0 (17)	265 (17)	4 (15) L
United Kingdom	39.5 (9)	5.8 (11)	6.8 (11) ML	17.3 (10)	1404 (12)	8 (3) H
Canada	40.2 (11)	5.7 (12)	7.1 (12) ML	15.1 (14)	1432 (11)	9 (2) H
Denmark	38.6 (7)	5.4 (13)	7.1 (12) ML	32.8 (2)	3482 (2)	7 (7) HM
Switzerland	44.6 (16)	5.2 (14)	8.6 (14) L	16.0 (12)	2511 (8)	2 (16) L
New Zealand	44.7 (17)	5.1 (15)	8.8 (15) L	16.1 (11)	1074 (15)	6 (9) M
United States	41.9 (14)	4.7 (16)	8.9 (16) L	14.6 (15)	1568 (10)	11 (1) H
Australia	42.2 (15)	4.4 (17)	9.6 (17) L	15.7 (13)	1370 (13)	7 (7) HM
Average:	39.7	6.2	6.6	21.2	2228	5.6
Median:	39.5	6.2	6.5	19.6	1943	6.0

[a]Income shares are from the World Bank, *World Development Report 1990* (Oxford University Press, 1990), p. 237, derived from surveys that estimate the percentage share of gross (rather than disposable) household income by percentile group of households. Although these data should be interpreted with caution, similar attempts yield roughly the same rank order among these countries. For example, Hannu Uusitalo (*Income Distribution in Finland: The Effects of the Welfare State and Structural Changes in Society on Income Distribution in Finland in 1966–1985,* Helsinki: Central Statistical Office of Finland, 1989, p. 80), estimates income distribution in seven of these countries (Canada, Finland, Israel, Norway, Sweden, United Kingdom, and the United States) based mainly on the Luxembourg Income Study. Computing the ratio of the highest to lowest quintile shares of gross income per household, only Israel and Norway change relative rank at all: Uusitalo ranks Norway more egalitarian by one rank and Israel by two. The results hold for both gross income per individual equivalent and disposable income per individual equivalent. Similarly, if we use his estimate of disposable income per household and compute the same ratio, we get a rank order identical to that of the World Bank quintile ratios in this table, except for Norway which moves up one rank in egalitarianism.

[b]Data for 1978–79 for Belgium; 1979 for Japan, Norway, France, Israel, and United Kingdom; 1981 for Sweden, Finland, and Denmark; 1981–82 for New Zealand; 1982 for Switzerland; 1983 for the Netherlands; 1984 for West Germany; 1985 for the United States and Australia; 1986 for Italy; 1987 for Canada.

[c]See text and appendix I. Scores of 8–11 = High mayhem; 7 = High-medium; 5–6 = Medium; 1–4 = Low.

TABLE 14.5 Welfare-state laggards have most inequality and mayhem

Social spending 1980	Income inequality 1980s ratio	Average mayhem score	
		1980	1988
Welfare-state leaders (High SS/GNP)	5.7	4.3	5.1
Middle-rank spenders (Medium SS/GNP)	6.0	5.3	5.5
Welfare-state laggards (Low SS/GNP)	7.6	5.5	6.0
Income equality 1980s ratio			
Most equality (H and HM, 8 cases)		4.3	4.6
Least equality (M and L, 9 cases)		5.7	6.7

We are now in a position to go beyond aggregate social spending and equality to search for the root causes of mayhem and learn whether public policies affect it.

Figure 14.2 further tests our second model to explain national differences.

Corporatist democracies pursue family policies that permit working parents to balance work and family demands and assure the care of children (see chap. 7). This is a powerful counterweight to modern tendencies toward mayhem. Whatever these policies do to lower tensions among hard-pressed family members (which could conceivably affect the divorce rate), they clearly prevent the feminization of poverty and improve the supervision of children (which, as we have seen, is essential for reducing violence and death by fire). Family policies also play an important part in reducing class warfare by reducing the distance between rich and poor.

Not only do corporatist democracies adopt a wide range of family policies with benign effects ($r = .72$), they also avoid heavy means testing—that is, stigmatized welfare systems ($r = -.51$). There is also a negative correlation between family policy and a reliance on means testing ($r = -.50$), suggesting that these are alternative policy paths. However, means testing (public assistance either as a percentage of GNP or as per capita spending 1980) has only an insignificant negative correlation with equality ($-.26$ or $-.33$) or poverty reduction ($-.24$ or $-.29$) and, contrary to my hypothesis, washes out completely in the path analysis whether the dependent variable is equality or poverty reduction. A possible explanation is that the cash flow indicated by high per capita spending targeted to the poor through tough means tests partially offsets the economic and political costs of an elaborate policing apparatus designed to limit the income of the "undeserving" poor. So the net negative effect of an obsession with means testing is not strong enough to increase poverty greatly.

As we have already seen in chapter 7, however, a family policy, rooted in corporatist bargaining arrangements, does help to prevent poverty and to reduce inequality. In turn, coun-

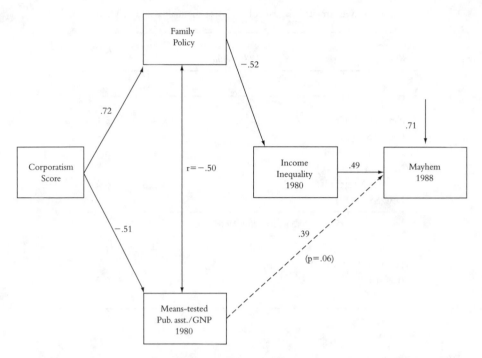

Figure 14.2. Corporatism, family policy, and equality reduce mayhem; means-testing increases it, 1988*

*N=18; Switzerland excluded as a distorting case. Adjusted R^2 for Mayhem = .43. Solid lines indicate path coefficients significant at $p < .05$; dashed line indicates path coefficient significant at $p < .10$. Inequality is the ratio of top fifth to bottom fifth. See text.

tries that aggressively pursue policies to reduce poverty and cushion the shock of family breakup also reduce risk and increase safety.

Why does means testing have a direct independent effect on mayhem?[17] Because it makes the poor visible, fosters a politics polarized around issues of income redistribution and, where the targeted poor differ from the majority in race, ethnicity, and/or religion, a politics of descent. The result is the alienation of the well-off majority from the poor and the poor from everyone else and a neglect of the problems of the poor. From the results of figure 14.1 we can infer that all of this increases mayhem. That targeting benefits to the "truly needy" either has no effect on poverty or slightly increases it, while it surely increases mayhem, should give pause to its advocates.

BRINGING THE TWO THEORIES TOGETHER:
INDUSTRIALIZATION VERSUS TYPES OF POLITICAL ECONOMY

We can now combine the models by examining specific countries and relating attributes of structure to policy patterns and outcomes. Table 14.6 permits us to uncover deviant cases, extreme outliers, and interaction effects obscured by the correlational analysis above.

First, the patterns at the extremes: The stars in mayhem, USA, Canada, and the UK, have fragmented and decentralized political economies, strong ethnic cleavages, and weak

TABLE 14.6 Interaction of industrialization and types of political economy as sources of mayhem

Mayhem score	Left corporatist						Left/Catholic corporatist						Catholic corporatist						Corporatist without labor						Least corporatist					
	Country	May'm score[a]	Cleav-ages[b]	FP[c]	PA[d]	Equal[e]	Country	May'm score[a]	Cleav-ages[b]	FP[c]	PA[d]	Equal[e]	Country	May'm score[a]	Cleav-ages[b]	FP[c]	PA[d]	Equal[e]	Country	May'm score[a]	Cleav-ages[b]	FP[c]	PA[d]	Equal[e]	Country	May'm score[a]	Cleav-ages[b]	FP[c]	PA[d]	Equal[e]
Most mayhem (8–11)																									USA*	11	H	L	L	ML
																									Canada*	9	H	L	H	ML
																									UK*	8	HM	M	H	ML
Medium mayhem (6–7)	Finland	7	ML	H	L	HM	Belgium	7	H	H	LM	H							France	6	M	H	HM	ML	Aust'l*	7	HM	L	LM	L
	Denmark	7	L	MH	LM	ML																			NZ	6	HM	L	—	L
																									Ireland†	6	L	L	HM	—
Low mayhem (1–5)	Sweden	4	L	H	L	H	Austria†	3	L	MH	LM	—	Italy†	5	L	M	L	HM	Switz	2	H	L	L	L						
	Norway	4	L	H	L	HM	Nether	4	H	M	H	HM	Germany†	5	ML	MH	M	HM	Japan†	1	L	L	HM	H						
	Israel*	4	H	—	LM	ML																								

*One of the five highest scores on a 4-component index of mobility and meritocracy: intergenerational mobility out of the working class; percentage of working-class sons and daughters in higher education, 1965 and 1971; higher education enrollment ratios averaged for 1965 and 1971; and higher education expenditures per capita averaged for 1965 and 1971; equally weighted (see appendix I).

†One of the five lowest scores on the index of mobility and meritocracy (see above).

aSee text and appendix I (on mayhem measures and scores). The mean score is 5.6.

bEthnic, religious, ethnic–linguistic, and racial cleavages–social heterogeneity based on descent. See chapter I and appendix I.

cIndex of family policy: existence and length of maternity and parental leave; availability and accessibility of public day-care programs and government efforts to expand day care; flexibility of retirement systems. See chapter 7.

dEmphasis on stigmatized means-testing measured by original estimates of public assistance spending as a percentage of GNP in 1980 (see chapter 6 and appendix F [measures of public assistance]).

eRatio of percentage shares of household income of the highest to the lowest quintiles see footnotes to table 14.4.

family polices; they strongly accent means testing and are mobile, meritocratic, and inegalitarian. Australia, with an above-average score of 7 on mayhem, fits the entire pattern except for public assistance. New Zealand fits, except for its medium score on mobility and meritocracy. Conversely, the nine countries with low mayhem—Sweden, Norway, Israel, Austria, the Netherlands, Italy, West Germany, Switzerland, and Japan—are all corporatist, with or without labor.

All of these "safe" countries vigorously pursue expansive family policies (high or medium-high) except for Switzerland and Japan; only the Netherlands and Japan accent means testing (H, HM). Six of the eight for which we have data are quite egalitarian (H or HM). I have already discussed the two deviant cases—Switzerland and Israel—whose citizen armies have an integrative effect offsetting inegalitarian tendencies.

We see the correlates of industrialization operating clearly at the extremes. Of the five countries scoring highest on mobility and meritocracy (USA, Canada, UK, Australia, and Israel), only Israel has a mayhem score below 7. Of the five countries scoring lowest on mobility and meritocracy (Austria, Italy, West Germany, Japan, and Ireland), only Ireland has a mayhem score above 5. The correlation of this index with industrialization (GNP per capita, 1966–71, not in the table) is quite strong: .69. Thus, because there is a convergence in riches, with the least-rich democracies among our 19 catching up to the most-rich (see chap. 1), we can perhaps expect a concomitant convergence in mobility and meritocracy. The correlation of this index with means testing is equally strong (.67), validating the idea that mobile populations embracing a meritocratic norm express it by hostility to the poor.

What about *minority-group cleavages,* said to be the root of the U.S.'s problem of crime, violence, and mayhem? As we have seen in our analysis of homicide rates, such cleavages alone may create trouble. But several countries with strong cleavages evidence a much calmer daily life. What table 14.6 suggests is that intense minority-group conflict without the constraining influence of consensual bargaining arrangements (some form of corporatism) results in medium to high mayhem. Thus the USA, Canada, the UK, Australia, and New Zealand all score at least an above-average 6 in mayhem. Strong cleavages combined with any form of corporatism, however—Israel, Netherlands, Switzerland—result in low mayhem (no score above 4).

Belgium is the exception—the purest deviant case in the entire table: although it is corporatist in its bargaining structure, avoids an emphasis on stigmatized public assistance, and scores high in social spending, family policy, and equality, it is an above-average 7 on mayhem. In 1970, however, it was a below-average 4. And the increase from 4 in 1970 to 7 in 1980 and 1988 is due almost entirely to high unemployment. Eliminating unemployment from the index—using a three-component index for all countries—Belgium falls to a mayhem score of 4, its "proper" place in the table.

In sum: Although mayhem has increased since 1970 in 11 of our 19 rich democracies and decreased only in low-scoring Austria and Japan, and although affluence and its correlates, mobility and meritocracy, explain much of the cross-national variation, types of political economy count. Democratic corporatism provides a general offset to modern tendencies toward mayhem because it opens up channels for shared power by economic interest groups. It fosters high rates of citizen participation through workplace participation schemes (see chap. 3) and through some form of proportional representation (chap. 2

shows that PR is a major source of corporatist bargaining systems). More directly, corporatist democracies tend toward high social spending, itself a powerful source of consensus (Wilensky, 1975), and they avoid divisive public policies such as welfare benefits that are heavily means-tested, stigmatized, and visibly targeted to the poor. Finally, they pursue both social and economic policies that increase equality and reduce poverty (e.g., fiscal policies that permit the funding and implementation of family policies and/or active labor-market policies)—the strongest proximate causes of reduced mayhem.

Consensual bargaining arrangements in the polity and economy and their policy outcomes not only offset general tendencies toward mayhem rooted in industrialization; they also offset the unhappy effects of strong minority-group cleavages, which otherwise create much mayhem, as we saw when we compared such unruly countries as the United States, Canada, and the UK with such calmer countries as Switzerland and the Netherlands.

NOTES

Revision and elaboration of a lecture to Harkness Fellows at the Institute of Governmental Studies, University of California at Berkeley (Spring 1991).

1. The eight richest of our rich countries are listed in descending order of GNP per capita in 1960. Switzerland, ranked sixth in affluence, is deleted as an exception; it has a low and stable rate of violent crime requiring separate explanation. Further, one country among the least-rich 10 also had a relatively high and increasing homicide and assault rate—Finland. (Gurr, 1979, pp. 363–364.)

2. Ralph Catalano (1991) provides a thorough assessment of the validity of research on the health effects of economic insecurity. He disentangles community-level indicators from individual experiences and is skeptical of Brenner's conclusions about mortality and his precise numbers of added disease cases but still concludes that economic deprivation fosters specific physical and psychological disorders as well as the increased use of mental health services.

3. Although at the same low socioeconomic level, blacks in this cohort study did have a higher delinquency rate than whites (53–36%) (Catalano, 1991, p. 54). A recent review of U.S. evidence on homicide victims by race and SES again shows that low-SES blacks are more likely to be victims than low-SES whites, but at higher levels these race differences are sharply reduced (Reiss and Roth, 1993, pp. 129–131).

4. Consistent with the point that poverty alone cannot explain homicide rates is a study of Latinos in 111 American cities. It shows that the Latino murder rate in 1980 was increased by population density and inequality (especially inequality of family income within Latino communities) and decreased by education, as expected. But absolute poverty rates did not predict homicide—in fact, the more Latino poverty in a city, the less Latino homicide (Martinez, 1996, p. 138). The stronger family networks and lesser isolation from job networks of Mexican immigrant poor described in the Chicago studies are the likely explanation; they are powerful offsets to the effects of poverty.

5. A complementary theory explaining American crime is cultural and social psychological. Robert Merton's classic essay on "Social Structure and Anomie" (1957) suggests that American crime is rooted in a disparity between the success ideology and institutionalized means for achieving success. Youths in poverty areas, he argues, internalize the American success ideology, but when they encounter barriers in the occupational structure, they become alienated and turn to crime; blocked mobility inspires criminal careers. Some of the data discussed above confirm this: there is an element of normality in these criminal careers, a sign of rational economic choice. But there is also evidence, especially from ethnographic accounts of both criminal gangs and lone criminals, of an aggressive nihilism that could hardly be called the internalization of the American Dream. (Cf. Howell, 1973, pp. 313–323; and Sullivan, 1989.)

6. Regarding the Chicago delinquents: Charles A. Murray and Louis A. Cox (1979) published an evaluation of the mid-1970s Unified Delinquency Intervention Services (UDIS), a project that offered hard-core delinquents a wide range of alternatives to imprisonment. Their study has been widely cited as proof that imprisonment reduced the number of arrests after "treatment" more than did the rehabilitation strategies. Currie (1985, pp. 72–75) shows that this claim is not supported by the data. E.g., while imprisonment in an Illinois Department of Corrections Institution "suppressed" delinquency by more than two-thirds, both the out-of-town camps and "intensive care" in group residential centers or psychiatric hospitals had even greater effects while at-home placements for a year had almost as much effect as imprisonment and were much cheaper.

7. An additional factor that should have pushed the homicide rate down is the spread of trauma centers, trauma teams in helicopters, and improvements in emergency room technology and procedures. Many gunshot and stabbing victims who would have bled to death before the 1980s were saved.

8. Rassmussen and Benson (1994) report that the real retail price per pure gram of cocaine is now about 15% of 1978 levels while the price of heroin per pure milligram is about 20% of early 1980s levels. They roughly estimate that between a quarter and a third of the 1.2 million persons in prison or jail in the U.S. in the early 1990s were doing time for violating drug laws. This diverts resources that could otherwise go to locating and isolating the most violent criminals, to the supervision and treatment of drug abusers, and to education for reduced demand.

9. These clearance rates are a product of gentle manipulation and are probably inflated. As David Simon observes in Baltimore (1991, pp. 186–187), a murder case in some places is reported as cleared as long as someone is locked up, whether for a week or a lifetime, and even if the case is later dismissed.

10. The following account is based on Ames (1981) and Bayley (1976, 1991) and an unpublished study by Masayuki Murayama (1980, 1989). The Tokyo district in Murayama's study had 101,067 population (1977), much more densely settled than Oakland's 328,000 (1978). The two areas had about the same number of policemen (600 Japanese, 608 Americans). They were similar in stratification (mixed blue collar and white collar, lower class and middle class, students and juveniles who gather for excitement). The Tokyo district was one of the major business, commercial, and entertainment centers in the prefecture. At its core was a railway hub; other neighborhoods in the area were dominated by bars, hotels, cabarets, etc. A great many commuters worked in the area. Its crime rate, for Japan, was high. In short, it was reasonably comparable to Oakland. Although this downtown Tokyo area is much smaller than the city of Oakland, the response time for calls was about the same: Japanese cars move through congestion at the pace of a bicycle.

11. In 1980, California, Colorado, Alaska, Arizona, and Nevada led in recorded rape. Four of the five were also among the top 20 states (of 50) in 1980 murder rates. Colorado was 30th.

12. Eliminating the United States and Israel, two outliers on military spending, the correlations are .27 with unemployment, .65 with divorce rates, and −.30 with homicide.

13. A study of such natural hazard victimization rates from 1970 to 1980, based on a household national telephone survey (Rossi et al., 1983), found that the four natural hazards I have listed were experienced by households more often than other "noxious events" such as drug and alcohol addiction, personal bankruptcy, or arrest but less frequently than unemployment, auto accidents, and marital dissolution. Few of the natural hazards involve personal injury, and the dollar costs to the individual are modest (the median is less than $100, although the median for property damage ranges from $800 for hurricanes to $3,000 for floods).

14. For the United States as a whole, deaths from house fires occur most often among young children (1–5 years old), the elderly, among blacks (three times as often as whites), and among the poor (nine times the rate of nonpoor). Social pathologies combine with dilapidated housing to produce this result and give America the lead in house fire deaths.

15. These measures of equality were available for only 10 of our countries for 1970. The correlation for that year between mayhem 1970 and income equality (ratio of the share of household income of the well-off to the share of the lowest quintile was −.48).

16. Despite lurid stories and films about the Japanese Mafia, the rates of violent crime in particular, and mayhem in general, remain quite low in Japan.

17. Relevant (and typical) regression results with mayhem as dependent variable (Austria, Ireland and New Zealand are missing data and are excluded):

$$\beta$$

Poverty reduction—1980	−.44 $(p < .10)$
Means testing (PA/GNP 1980)	.38 (n.s.)

$$AR^2 = .33 \ (16)$$

Excluding Switzerland and Japan as deviant cases, both betas are significant and the variance explained is 50%. These regressions use income share of the lowest quintile (poverty reduction), not the ratio measure in figure 14.2.

TYPES OF POLITICAL
ECONOMY, REGULATORY
REGIMES, AND THE ENVIRONMENT

To explain national differences in performance in reducing environmental threats for 19 countries would require data not now available. The available literature seldom tries to compare real outputs of environmental protection regimes. Almost all of the systematic comparative studies of two or more countries concentrate on differences and similarities in the policymaking or implementation process, not on success in improving the air, the water, or public health (e.g., Badaracco, 1985; Brickman, Jasanoff, and Ilgen, 1985; Heidenheimer, Heclo, and Adams, 1990; Lundqvist, 1980). Some suggestive data, however, are available for 14 of our countries in OECD studies of trends in air pollution from 1975 to the late 1980s, for three countries' performance in increasing occupational safety in the 1970s, for a few countries' policies and outcomes in coping with disabilities and nuclear energy risks, and for 13 countries' performance in reducing tobacco use in the 1980s. The data suggest that types of political economy and public policies are important in explaining national differences in air quality, occupational health and safety, nuclear energy development and safety, and rehabilitation of the handicapped but less important in explaining different rates of reduction in addiction to smoking.[1]

There is doubtless much exaggeration of environmental threats in modern societies. We have seen in chapter 4 that less-developed societies have far more pollution and environmental degradation than we have. As Joseph Gusfield (1981), Aaron Wildavsky (1988, 1995), and other students of culture and risk remind us, the scientific evidence of trends in a social problem, from pollution and disease to drunk driving and crime, may have little to do with the public attention given to it. The arts of media management and publicity, not science, are what define a high risk.

Critics who attack environmental activists for their excessive passion and ignorance are often themselves ideological. They tend to condemn regulatory regimes devoted to clean air and water or occupational health and safety that have a reasonable basis in science as much as they condemn dedicated fights against trivial or imaginary risks. In fact, the sectarian zeal of environmental activists appears much more often in such controversies as the cancer-causing effects of synthetic chemicals ingested in food grown with the help of pesticides than it does in controversies about clean air, clean water, or occupational health. A leading student of aging and cancer, Bruce N. Ames (Ames and Gold, 1995), summarizes the state of knowledge about cancer risks: about 35% of cancer deaths are attributable to tobacco; 20% to 40% to dietary factors (e.g., insufficient intake of fruits and vegetables that help reduce the risk of most types of cancer). Genetic inheritance, hormones, and chronic infections that cause oxidative damage to DNA are also important. Lesser causes include recreational sun exposure (a major factor only in skin cancers), medical interventions, obesity, and decreases in physical activity. Harmful intakes other than tobacco are minor: only 4% to 6% of cancer deaths for alcohol. Synthetic chemical intake is a trivial source. "For example, 99.99 percent of the pesticides we eat are naturally present in plants to ward off insects and other predators. Reducing exposure to the 0.01 percent that are synthetic will not reduce cancer rates" (*ibid.* p. 143). Because half of the chemicals that have been tested, natural or synthetic, are carcinogenic to rodents, extrapolations from the high doses tested in rodents to humans have led to grossly exaggerated mortality forecasts.

A bizarre side effect of the exaggerated attention to synthetic chemicals in food is that it diverts resources away from the two leading causes of a wide variety of deadly diseases—smoking and an imbalanced diet—while the regulatory and protectionist regimes for agriculture increase the price of food. For a low-income family, a small increase in the price of a food is enough to reduce consumption. The net effect: The poor and the near-poor of the world not only smoke a lot, they also fail to eat enough vegetables and fruit and therefore die early, while the more educated and affluent live on (Ames, Profet, and Gold, 1990). Egalitarians take note.[2]

No one can disagree with Ames's conclusion: public policy must distinguish between important risks and trivial risks. The work of such critics as Aaron Wildavsky (1995) is a needed corrective for the unfounded claims that an avalanche of synthetic chemicals in the air, the water, and our food is causing an epidemic of cancers. In the politics of social science, like the politics of environmental policy, however, the critics often make more general claims that the science base for all regulation is weak or nonexistent. An acrimonious standoff is the most common outcome of both research and public debate.

Let us turn to some nontrivial risks where data permit exploration of national political and policy differences that determine the effectiveness of government regulation.

Air Pollution

There is consensus that high sulfur-dioxide (SO_2) concentrations combined with particulate matter (PM) in the air in our urban areas are a bad thing, a threat to health and the quality of life. Before the Pollution Diet acted, many Tokyo citizens in the 1970s had to don surgical masks on days of high air pollution. Today Los Angeles citizens are urged to stay off the highways when smog alerts are declared. And China is notorious for its air pollution. It relies on coal for 76% of its primary energy (versus 17% in Japan); the air in its urban areas often has an acrid, sulfurous odor and the "Beijing cough" is heard everywhere. Current science (Goklany, 1995, p. 354; OECD, 1991b, p. 36) suggests that SO_2 aggravates respiratory and cardiovascular diseases, alters the body's defense systems against foreign materials, damages lung tissue, and in extreme cases (in Donora and London in the late 1940s and 1950s where both high PM and SO_2 levels were in the air) results in "excess" deaths. SO_2 also reduces plant growth, corrodes metal and stone in buildings and monuments, impairs visibility, and, through acidification of lakes and streams (acid rain, e.g.) injures aquatic life. In short, despite complaints that environmentalists exaggerate the threat of pollution (Douglas and Wildavsky, 1982, pp. 34–38, 50ff.), SO_2 and related pollutants are nontrivial in their effects. Happily, air pollution has diminished since 1970 in every industrial democracy, partly because of environmental protection regimes. Both absolute and per capita SO_2 emissions declined as did particulate matter except for the area of the former East Germany (Goklany, 1995, p. 364). However, mainly because of increased automobile traffic and mileage driven, nitrogen oxides (NO_x) which together with SO_2 contribute to the formation of acidic compounds that harm plants and animals, have not declined except in Japan (OECD, 1991b, p. 38).[3]

Table 15.1 shows that in the past two or three decades, while all rich democracies have reduced air pollution, there are large differences in the rate of reduction. Although these reductions of emissions of traditional air pollutants such as SO_2 and NO_x have been achieved since the early 1970s partly because of slower economic growth, no one denies the role of public policy: energy policies fostering more efficient use of energy, especially of fossil fuels (through energy conservation and greater use of nuclear energy), environmental protection policies (requiring cleaner fuels and emission control systems in power stations and automobiles, using "green" tax incentives), and transportation policies (funding more efficient, cleaner rapid-transit systems).

Of course, the data on SO_2 emission reduction in table 15.1 are merely suggestive: cities are not strictly comparable; their degree of initial pollution and measuring methods vary. But the differences are substantial and consistent with the idea that corporatist countries have an edge in adopting and implementing environmental protection policies.

If we average country performance by type of political economy for either all the cities in table 15.1 or for the largest cities only we find the following pattern:

	All cities: mean reduction of pollution	Big cities only
Corporatist including labor	−66%	−67%
Corporatist-without-labor	−60%	−65%
Noncorporatist	−43%	−43%

Countries that include labor in their national policymaking machinery have an edge in pollution reduction. With or without labor, corporatist countries clearly outperform the rest. The most prominent exception is the UK, the only noncorporatist country that scores high.[4]

The British exception underscores two general points. First, countries that differ in one or two policy areas (health care or environmental regulation in the U.S. versus the UK) may be very similar in most policy areas (e.g., fiscal and monetary policy, labor policy); even the least-corporatist countries may have area-specific structures that foster collaborative bargaining between government and industry in one policy domain, while in almost every other way they remain decentralized, fragmented, and polarized. Second, the British case may be the exception that proves the rule. David Vogel (1986), contrasting the styles of environmental regulation in the U.S. and the UK, argues that British law fosters decentralized, discretionary, flexible implementation of broadly worded statutes and comparatively few formal regulations, while American law fosters detailed statutes and regulations combined with frequent legislative oversight and judicial review, seeking to narrow

TABLE 15.1 Corporatist democracies are most effective in reducing air pollution 1975–late 1980s[a]

Country	Cities	% reduction in sulfur dioxide concentration	Average reduction by country	General rank
Finland**	Tampere	93	93	H
Italy**	Milan[b]	77	77	H
Norway**	Oslo	73	73	H
Sweden**	Stockholm	76		
	Gothenburg	68	72	H
Belgium**	Brussels	68	68	H
Japan*	Tokyo	67	67	H
United Kingdom	London	66		
	Newcastle	68	67	H
Canada	Montreal	60	60	M
Netherlands**	Amsterdam	59	59	M
France*	Paris	62		
	Rouen	44	53	M
Denmark**	Copenhagen	53	53	M
Germany	West Berlin	36	36	L
United States	New York	25	25	L
Australia	Sydney	19[c]	19	L

[a]From OECD, *The State of the Environment* (Paris: OECD, 1991b). Cities in which 5–10% of the population is concentrated; or industrial cities with high levels of pollutants in 1980.

[b]Because of large differences in regional governments, the performance of Milan may not be matched by the south. E.g., the earlier study (OECD, July 1985) covering only eight years shows Rome as a poor performer.

[c]Data only from 1975 to 1983. *OECD Observer* 135 (July 1985), pp. 12–26.

★★Corporatist. Germany a marginal case.

★Corporatist-without-labor.

administrative discretion. The regulatory process in Britain is secretive, informal, and non-confrontational and involves government regulators' consultations with business. The process in the United States is public, formal, and confrontational with participation by business and a wide range of other groups, depending on the current state of power struggles and media attention. The costs in lawyers and the inspectorate are larger in the United States (cf. Kagan, 1988; Wilensky, 1983; and chap. 12). Vogel attributes these differences to contrasts in the culture of the business community and the consequent pattern of public attitudes toward business and government-business relations. In the UK highly respected civil servants—products of the Oxbridge network—politely request compliance; respectful British industrialists defer, as gentlemen should. In the USA, in contrast, low-status civil servants and populist politicians confront business executives who regard them as their social and intellectual inferiors, leading to a highly politicized adversarial process.

Yet, if we put Britain and the United States in the context of our 19-country comparison, we find that they are brothers (sisters?) under the skin. They are members of a class of least-corporatist democracies, all of whose mechanisms of conflict resolution are weak. Adversarial legalism has taken up the slack in both countries. As chapter 12 shows, Britain joins the United States, Canada, Australia, Ireland, and New Zealand among the top eight in lawyer density—and Britain is first in the growth rate of lawyers. British consensual behavior and effectiveness in environmental matters is sector-specific. What looks like a major difference between the United States and the United Kingdom turns out to be small in cross-national perspective and smaller still when we consider other policy areas.[5]

Even if environmental regulation in the UK is an exception to the rule that fragmented and decentralized political economies with unruly or weak labor movements tend toward legalistic and intrusive regulation, it is an exception that is falling into line. During the Thatcher-Major years aggressive deregulation and liberalization in many areas was combined with equally aggressive reregulation. A study of the politics of regulatory reform in several countries in telecommunications, finance, transportation and public utilities, and broadcasting by Steven Vogel (1996) shows that the language and ideology of deregulation imported from America was neither the substance nor the outcome of deregulation. Vogel documents a 17-year trend in Britain toward reregulation that is infinitely more complete and comprehensive, more juridified and codified, more bureaucratic and confrontational and less consensual than it was before—all in the name of free and fair competition. For instance, the Thatcher government created 11 major new independent regulatory agencies (the Major government added one), some of them sharing power with the Ministries. In telecommunications a new agency, Oftel, was established just to handle all the new regulations and new agencies that "liberalization" would require. A natural accompaniment is the proliferation of rules and a boom in lawyers and accountants to keep track of it all. Such reregulation was needed not only to set rules governing market competition, but also to create competition (cultivate new entrants), to prevent or respond to financial scandals that frighten politicians, to raise revenue without increasing taxes, and even to protect consumers and workers when they scream too loudly about the dangers of free-swinging competition to quality, safety, health, employment, and job security (*ibid.*, especially chaps. 5 and 10).

Ironically, the free marketeers of Britain have fallen victim to the American disease: ever more complex and detailed rules created by ever more lawyers to protect both firms and citizens. Compared to its past, Britain is now less of an exception to the hypothesis that regulatory reasonableness flourishes in corporatist democracies.

It is a paradox that the ideology of minimum government, free markets, and private property—the market mania that seized Anglo-American elites in the past 15 years—results in bureaucratic bloat (see chap. 9) and full employment for lawyers. The Republican-dominated Congress of 1995 provides a splendid example. With government-bashing fervor (Congressman Tom DeLay, House Majority Whip, called the Environmental Protection Agency [EPA] "the Gestapo of government agencies"), intoning the slogans of free enterprise and commonsense government, they crafted a regulatory reform bill to reduce the intrusive apparatus of inspection and enforcement created by the EPA and other health and safety agencies. Because EPA and the associated legislation (the Clean Water Act of 1972, the Clean Air Act of 1970, the National Environmental Policy Act of 1970, the Safe Drinking Water Act of 1974) have been so successful in reducing pollution and are so popular with the voters, the reformers and business lobbyists had to attack them indirectly by concentrating on the rule-making process and by cutting appropriations for the offending agencies. Both critics and defenders of these regulations agreed that some aspects of the process are too rigid and cumbersome. The bill that was passed by the House in 1995, however, creates a mind-boggling, bureaucratic-judicial maze. It requires regulators to show that each proposed rule will generate more benefits (e.g., wetlands preserved, injuries avoided, lives saved) than costs (for any rule that would impose specified costs—costs of originally $100,000 or more, then upped to $50 million in the House version, more in the Senate bill). The cost-benefit analysis mandated for each rule must surmount numerous steps, each one of which is subject to judicial challenge by the regulated industry in court.[6] America's market mania fosters metastasizing rules. The British are not far behind. Predictably reregulation in the Anglo-American democracies will follow deregulation in a stop-and-go pattern. In comparative perspective the implementation of environmental laws will remain costly and the benefits, modest.

OCCUPATIONAL HEALTH AND SAFETY

In most developed welfare states the earliest social program, job-injury insurance, has become a more general program for safety and health in the work environment. Obviously, if such program expansion cuts absenteeism, sick leave, and job injuries, the program costs can be offset by increased productivity, lower training costs for replacements, and lower health-care and disability costs. Given the spreading ideology of participatory democracy, it can also provide a channel for worker participation that is at once meaningful to workers, helpful to management, and serves widely shared societal goals.

The limitations of data, however, preclude firm statements about relative national performance in occupational health and safety. For instance, the estimated number of occupational injuries and illnesses, available in a few countries, is not likely to be comparable across nations in either definitions or efficiency of data collection. Nor is there agreement on which workplace hazards have caused what incidence of illnesses or injuries, although there is consensus about the major hazards (Frankenhauser, 1981; Raffle et al., 1994). Job-related deaths are more likely to be counted with reasonable accuracy. Even here, the right phrase is "rough estimates." The U.S. Bureau of Labor Statistics, for instance, believes that its samples understate actual job-related deaths (personal conversations). Nevertheless, we can make a few inferences about costs and benefits from intensive study of three cases with contrasting political and economic structures—Sweden, the United States, and Germany. The state of scientific knowledge is the same in all three; benzene or asbestos pose the same risks to an American worker as to a Swede or German, and a poorly designed stamping machine can crush the hand in the same way, whatever the type of political economy. As usual, however, the regulatory regimes are different, with contrasting results. (Sources for the following account include Kelman, 1981; Wilensky, 1983, pp. 58–60; "Fact Sheets on Sweden," September, 1993 FS 85; and my interviews.)

The Swedish safety ombudsman and subsequent laws on the working environment are a model of innovative expansion and effective enforcement. Some excesses are also evident. Although Sweden's first occupational health and safety law was adopted in the late 19th century, the main administrative agency, the Worker Protection Board (*Arbetarskyddsverket*), and its guiding laws were adopted in 1949. Funding was greatly expanded in the late 1960s. The current Work Environment Act went into effect in 1978 and was subsequently amended to create the Working Life Fund to improve occupational safety and rehabilitation programs. More recently this act was broadened to include not only the traditional physical and technical environment as it shapes accidents and occupational diseases, but also the way work is organized, job content, working hours, career development, employee participation in decision making, and even the "psychosocial aspects of the workplace." Employers were given more responsibility for action in all these areas.

In the United States, similar concerns about occupational injury and illness led to the creation in 1970 of the Occupational Safety and Health Administration (OSHA) and subsequent amendments. In a study of the two systems, Steven Kelman (1981) observes that the two government agencies deal with the same issues, confront the same trade-offs between increased levels of protection and increased cost, the same problems of compliance, and make similar decisions regarding the content of regulations. Once again, the differences, fatal for the balance of costs and benefits, lie in the national bargaining machinery and related possibilities of consensus.

In the corporatist political economy of Sweden, regulations of the Worker Protection Board are accepted by unions and employers; the atmosphere is one of negotiation and cooperation. In the United States, OSHA's regulations are constantly challenged in courts; the atmosphere is confrontational. Unions complain of inadequate enforcement, employers denounce "overregulation." In an atrocity tale the opponents of OSHA are fond of citing, it is estimated that OSHA regulations to limit worker exposure to coke-oven emissions cost industry and consumers several million dollars a year for each life saved—about $9,000 a year for each coke-oven worker protected. These tales abound in the 1995 debate in Congress over the Republican deregulation agenda. (Of course, other regulations are more cost-effective, but the public debate centers on the dramatic case—whether fictional or true.)

Paradoxically, it is in allegedly individualistic, decentralized America that government inspectors are intrusive and routinely fine employers for noncompliance. In collectivistic, centralized Sweden, inspectors are loath to punish employers; instead, they rely on consultation with health and safety professionals and other representatives of LO (the largest labor federation) and SAF (the employer federation) and look to local control—the institution of the safety steward or workplace ombudsman—for enforcement. They also set up joint research and development projects to produce innovative solutions to difficult problems of the work environment.

The current Swedish system includes five main components. First, there are 330 employees of the National Board of Occupational Safety and Health (under the Ministry of Labor). Second is a Labor Inspectorate of 630 employees, 400 of whom visit workplaces, concentrating on the most severe hazards in workplaces with the worst records. About 40% of these visits result in written orders for changes. But only 3.4% of these cases (500 out of 37,000 annual visits) go on to the stage of injunctions or prohibition and only 20 cases (.001%) lead to proceedings in a court of law. Third are occupational health services that employ about 8,000 people at more than 800 centers in workplaces, industry sector locations, or regions. They concentrate on preventive measures and improvements in the working environment. More than 80% of the Swedish labor force have access to such services. Fourth is the Working Life Fund launched in 1989. It is financed by a special employer payroll tax for 1989–90. The Fund provides matching grants to employers who propose projects to reform the organization of work (half the Fund grants), improve the physical environment (24%), rehabilitation (2%), or new technology (3%). Finally, there are safety delegates (*skyddsombud*) in all workplaces with at least five employees. Labor unions choose them for three-year terms. As of 1993 there were 90,000 of these safety stewards, each empowered to suspend work involving immediate and serious danger to life or health. In the history of this institution, during the first startup year a number of shutdowns occur, but these quickly diminish as safety delegates jointly work out solutions with employers. Thereafter they almost never have to call in labor inspectors or even threaten a shutdown. Capping it all off, there is a small "Work Environment Fund" financed by a payroll fee devoted to research and development. For about 25 years Sweden has been a center for serious research on musculoskeletal injuries, ergonomics, chemical health hazards, stress, and the health impacts of work systems. Research is done by the government's National Institute of Occupational Health, the Swedish Center for Working Life, and universities. An aggressive education campaign to reach employees, employers' safety delegates, and professionals is an accompaniment.

The contrast in the operations of OSHA could not be sharper: adversary lawyers and environmental activists often perform in front of TV cameras in open hearings, make verbatim transcripts, and escalate conflict, thereby fostering deadlock, delay, and resistance to final decisions. Huge amounts of money and time are expended in diversions from problem solving. Employer backlash is then mobilized to weaken the law.

Safety rules in the United States could be more flexibly and sensibly enforced if the typical workplace had union-management committees. But with the decline of the American labor movement, such joint committees are a fading phenomenon. An equally important difficulty is the peculiarly American practice of separating the federal program for preventing workplace injuries and illnesses (OSHA) from state-administered programs for compensating injured workers (workers' compensation). Wherever prevention and compensation are organizationally linked and employers are responsible for at least some of the funding for safety, as in Sweden and in the Canadian provinces of British Columbia and Quebec (U.S. General Accounting Office, 1993, p. 11), there is a better chance to prevent job injuries, control costs, and persuade employers to cooperate with regulators. OSHA, in contrast, is congressionally funded, and prevention and compensation are kept in separate jurisdictions.

Similarly, the history of German industrial accident insurance suggests that program expansion and innovation, when combined with tripartite or bipartite administration and an accent on prevention, reduce costs in the long run (Alber, 1989, pp. 9–10). The prewar system was restored in 1949. The principle of self-administration was introduced in 1951, with worker and employer representation split evenly. The major reform came in 1963: benefits were indexed to wage levels, and several measures were introduced for the prevention of accidents. In 1971 the system was extended beyond workers to cover children in kindergartens and schools, and students. The law of 1973 further emphasized preventive measures, including the new position of "security engineer" for large workplaces. Despite the great expansion of industry, the number of industrial accidents, which had climbed from 1.3 million in 1950 to 2.7 million in 1960 before the reform, went down to 1.8 million by 1975. With the expansion of benefits and coverage, expenditures for accident insurance, however, went up sharply.

Aside from the limited resources devoted to prevention and rehabilitation (via counseling, training, and job placement, and the development of safety representation in the workplace), the administration of workers' compensation in the United States is marked by an adversarial, rule-bound, lawyer-ridden process of bureaucratic decision making and uneven representation by workers' advocates. The typical injured worker has neither union nor even passable legal representation (cf. Nonet, 1969). This combination of structural problems and political resistance means that both job-injury insurance and safety regulations remain costly, inefficient, and arbitrary.

The kind of comparative evaluation research necessary to assess these cases has not been done, but I can offer a few clues to suggest that a cost-benefit analysis taking account of long-run effects would show the largest net benefit for Sweden, next for Germany, and last for the United States. The lack of comparable data on deaths from industrial accidents precludes analysis after 1976.

Table 15.2 shows that job-injury expenditures as a percentage of GNP declined in Sweden from 1954 to 1974, stayed steady in West Germany, and increased in the United States. Although per capita job-injury spending increased sharply for all three countries, Sweden's expenditures remain low relative to those of Germany and the United States. What happened to the most dramatic and reliable measure of real welfare in this area—deaths from industrial accidents?[7] Comparable figures for the three countries are available only for 1968, 1971, 1975, and 1976. Sweden and Germany evidence a similar pattern of decline from about 2.5 deaths from industrial accidents per 100,000 population in 1968 to 1.5 deaths in 1976. The United States starts higher 3.0 in 1968 and declines less, to 2.4 in 1976. The safety performance of Germany and Sweden is all the more impressive in view of their industrial structure: the fraction of wage earners and salaried employees in the two most dangerous industries, mining and construction, is higher than that of the United States: In 1976 that of Germany was 9.6%, of Sweden, 7.6%, of the United States, 5.5% (OECD, 1979, pp. 78, 222, 376).[8]

In short, with far more direct regulation and intrusiveness, with far less participation by workers, the United States may spend more on accident insurance with less saving in safety and health than the big-spending, more-corporatist welfare-state leaders.

These systems have a tendency toward excess at the extremes. Just as the United States specializes in wasteful expenditures and unproductive conflict over goals and means, and undergoes periodic campaigns to paralyze or abandon all regulation, Sweden's social experimentation and commitment to safety and health sometimes gets out of hand. We can

TABLE 15.2 Work-injury expenditures and deaths from industrial accidents for three countries

	Spending on work injury insurance[a]					Deaths from industrial accidents per 100,000 pop.[b]	
	% of GDP		per capita in US $				
	1954	1974	1960	1971	1974	1968	1976
Sweden	.24	.13	2.35	5.02	9.90	2.5	1.5
West Germany	.52	.58	7.47	21.89	40.18[c]	2.5	1.5
United States	.29	.38	8.98	20.92	31.08	3.0	2.4

[a]From ILO, *The Cost of Social Security* (1958 and 1979). Figures for Sweden and West Germany represent expenditures on "employment injuries." To make figures for the United States more comparable, expenditures on "workers' compensation" were added to "temporary disability insurance" (the latter category comprises about 20% of the total work injury expenditure for the entire period 1954–74). GDP figures from OECD, *National Accounts 1952–1981,* volume 1, Main Aggregates.

[b]From UN World Health Organization, *Statistics Annual,* various years. The series on deaths from industrial accidents was discontinued after the 1970s with the changes in classification from ICD-8 to ICD-9.

[c]Much of this doubling of per capita dollar expenditure from 1971 to 1974 is due to the sharply increased strength of the German mark against the dollar. The correct figure would likely be less than $30.

see signs of excess in the 1990s when changes had to be made in occupational health services, the largest and most expensive program, in sickness pay, and in the operation of job-injury insurance and disability insurance. Until 1991 affiliation with occupational health services was regulated in labor-management contracts. The SAF, however, abandoned that practice for its portion of the private sector and Parliament eliminated the state grant to occupational health services starting in 1993. New labor-management negotiations are under way; they are likely to rein in costs more than in the past.

The excesses of job-injury insurance, which in many countries is coordinated with sickness pay, are even more apparent. Swedish sickness allowances normally run out after 180 days, after which the occupational insurance system provides full compensation for lost income due to injury. Under the Work Injury Insurance Act, decisions as to what constitutes a "harmful effect of work" and whether those work factors are connected to some physical or mental damage to the individual have traditionally rested on the principle of "reverse proof"—that is, a harmful effect is presumed to exist unless there are persuasive reasons against this. When insurance claims and awards soared from 1985 to 1990—because of new medical knowledge, more generous insurance rules, and new guidelines regarding musculo-skeletal injuries—tighter controls were adopted. In January 1993 the reverse evidence principle was abandoned. Highly probable connections between the harmful effect and individual injury must be proved. Total claims have declined. (Unlike the United States, there never was any compensation for "pain and suffering," instead a collective agreement provides no-fault employer liability insurance for this purpose.) The Work Environment Act has been tightened. More money is going for prevention—to improve working conditions, to expand rehabilitation, and to reduce absenteeism and increase productivity. As elsewhere, sickness pay—an area of clear abuse—has been reformed. Wherever sick pay begins on the first day of illness, the absenteeism rate for Friday and Monday soars; a yearning for a long weekend inspires a sick call and the Monday morning hangover becomes a sickness. This is more easily changed than disability pensions—by instituting a waiting period of a day or two, and reducing the portion of earnings replaced. Sweden took both steps in 1993.

Disability and Sickness as Slippery and Expansive Categories: Is There a Tendency Toward Excess?

Aside from job-injury insurance, every rich democracy provides disability insurance with medical/clinical certification as its main administrative mechanism. This is a component of social security that covers most workers; it is supplemented by a series of occupational schemes for historically well-organized workers—miners, farmers, civil servants, railroad workers, and others. All rich democracies except the United States also provide cash benefits to the temporally ill or disabled (sickness pay) in lieu of wages, as part of national health insurance. These temporary sickness benefits last anywhere from a few months to one or two years; if the disability persists, the beneficiary is switched to a permanently disabled status. The status of "disabled" typically brings privileges beyond cash and special medical assistance: draft exemption, special education and training, easier access to housing subsidies, a moratorium on debts or extension of credit.

Next to public assistance targeted to the poor, disability insurance is the most difficult social program to administer. And it is the most resistant to cost containment. Medical or clinical judgments on which eligibility is based are notoriously unreliable: How to distinguish those who cannot work from those who will not, those with small impairments from those with large or total impairments, those with disabling pain from those with discomforting pain or faked pain—these are a few of the questions about which the clinical gatekeepers for disability benefits disagree.[9]

Researchers who have done comparative studies (Haveman, Halberstadt, and Burkhauser, 1984; Stone, 1985; Aarts and De Jong, 1992, 1995) document six common trends in the area of disability benefits:

1. These programs have proliferated in all countries studied; both beneficiaries and the level of expenditure have climbed rapidly since the late 1960s—even controlling for the age composition of the population (see table 15.3).

2. The rate of growth in beneficiaries slowed in the mid-1970s, but the percentage of "disabled" remained high. After 1990, as debate about the "disability crisis" mounted and fiscal constraints grew stronger, the rate of growth again slowed. The United States, starting from a low base, may be an exception in the 1990s and the disability rate in the Netherlands continued its rapid growth until 1980, slowing from a very high base after then.

3. A growing percentage of all disability awards are granted for mental (versus physical) conditions and for musculoskeletal disorders (e.g., lower back pain)—in other words, ailments most difficult to diagnose. Although no other country matches the United States in litigation and awards for sometimes obscure pain and suffering (see chap. 12 on tort law and lawyers), all countries share the trend toward inclusion of ever-broader disabilities.

TABLE 15.3 Disability recipients per 1,000 active labor-force participants by age and older male labor-force participation rates*

	1970	1975	1980	1985	1990	1992	1993
Disability recip. per 1000 active LF 15-64 years							
Netherlands	55	84	138	142	152	152[a]	155
West Germany	51	54	59	72	55		54
Sweden	49	67	68	74	78		97[a]
United Kingdom	29[b]	28	31	56	68[c]		
United States	27[b]	42	41	41	43	53	53
60-64 years							
Netherlands	299	437	1033	1283	1987		2273
West Germany	419	688	1348	1291	1109		1064
Sweden	229	382	382	512	577		658[a]
United Kingdom	na	na	na	na	na		na
United States	154	265	285	254	250		na
Labor force participation rates per 100 males, 55-64							
Netherlands	81	72	63	47	46	43	
West Germany	80	70	67	60	58	na	
Sweden	85	82	79	76	75	73	
United Kingdom	88	88	82	69	68	66	
United States	81	76	72	68	68	67	

*Source: Leo J. M. Aarts and Philip R. De Jong (1995). 1993 figures from Aarts, Burkhauser, and De Jong (1995). "Active labor force" excludes the unemployed. Workers' compensation recipients are included only for the Netherlands, where the distinction between *risque social* and *risque professional* was abolished in 1967. Even if job-injury insurance recipients were included for all cases, the Dutch figure would remain at the top.

[a]Figure refers to 1994.
[b]Figure refers to 1971.
[c]Figure refers to 1991.

4. The growth in generosity toward the handicapped exceeds the expansion of the value of other benefits of the welfare state, even exceeding earnings in some cases. In the 1970s all countries increased this generosity; in the 1980s that increase slowed somewhat.

5. There has been an increase in the permanence of permanent disability—a decrease in the percentage leaving the rolls.

6. There is a steady expansion of the definition of "disabled" to give weight to the availability of suitable jobs or the state of the labor market. In the late 1970s, a Dutch Cabinet minister told me that when the labor market is slack for a long time many unemployed Dutch workers of middle age go to their doctors and get certified as perma-

nently disabled so that they can receive a generous permanent disability pension. Their doctors typically certify them as mentally and/or physically impaired. He added that many are, in fact, so discouraged in the futile search for work or by the condition of extended unemployment that their demoralization makes the certification plausible even for men in their 40s or 50s.

Dutch informants in the 1970s were anticipating a spreading phenomenon that the Netherlands brought to its most extreme form in the 1980s—the increasing use of permanent disability insurance as an early, generous retirement pension and as a cash substitute for long-term unemployment insurance and an active labor-market policy. More specifically, the reasons for the universal, rapid expansion of disability recipients, benefits, and services are these:

1. *Slack labor markets and the increase in structural unemployment.* Thus, one of the most consistent findings in this area is a strong correlation between increasing or high levels of unemployment and disability claims and awards since 1968 (e.g., Haveman, Halberstadt, and Burkhauser, 1984, pp. 102–114; Stone, 1985, pp. 166–168); the more unemployment, the more disability claims.[10]

2. *Management and union desires to ease out older workers.* Managers prefer younger, cheaper men and women and middle-aged women and if the state can pick up the tab, they will help older workers into an early retirement; unions go along because they want to reduce unemployment and make way for younger members. (See chap. 1.)

3. *Government responses to the organized aged and especially to the legitimacy of the claims of the disabled of any age.* As Deborah Stone shows (1985, pp. 144, 166), the popular conception of disability is broader than the legal-clinical judgments of disability. There is wide consensus in every modern country that people who suffer handicaps of one kind or another are, like the aged or veterans, morally worthy, deserving of special support. The average citizen can say, "There but for the grace of God go I." Of course, there is some stigma attached to the status of "disabled" but with rising levels of education, most modern citizens have learned not to despise the handicapped. And the handicapped themselves have become politically organized. The stigma of disability, if any, is nowhere near that of the nonworking poor.[11]

4. Reinforcing government receptivity is *a medicalization of social problems driven by compassionate humanitarian concerns coupled with a naive faith in the scientific basis of clinical judgments* (Stone, 1985, pp. 87–139). If Americans encounter an education problem, they label it a "learning disability"; if they encounter group conflict over scarce jobs, they say racism is a pathology of a sick society and launch compulsory seminars in "cultural diversity" to purge whites of their unconscious prejudices. Other countries share this tendency toward medicalization, if in lesser degree. Because doctors everywhere tend to be advocates of their patients and command great respect, they reinforce the medicalization of social problems and the belief in a scientific approach to classification of disabilities. Administrators of disability programs who need some decision rules in a situation of great ambiguity are only too happy to collaborate with the doctors' bias.

In short, structural unemployment, management and union preferences for state-financed early retirement, government and popular receptivity to the legitimacy of disability claims, faith in the validity of doctors' clinical judgments—all these interact to make permanent disability an instrument of personnel policy and a substitute for unemployment compensation and retirement pensions. Together with the natural tendency for bureaucratic agencies to expand personnel, clientele, and budgets (Wilensky, 1975, pp. 9ff. and chapter 9 above), these developments explain the recent, rapid, universal growth of disability programs and claims.

It is unlikely that the growth in these programs is a product of increases in the incidence of real disabilities; rich countries are countries with healthier populations (see chap. 16 on health). In fact, a quantitative study of factors explaining changes in the percentage of disability recipients in the Netherlands from 1980 to 1985 concludes that no more than one-third of the variance in the rate of entry into disability status is explained by medical factors. Two-thirds is explained by nonmedical factors: the two incentives of overwhelming importance were the generosity of benefits and the hazards of unemployment. (Aarts and De Jong, 1992, pp. 282, 298–303; Aarts and De Jong, 1993, p. 40. For similar conclusions for Germany, see Phaff and Huber, 1984, pp. 225–235; for Sweden, see Wadensjö, 1984, pp. 490–499.)

While all rich democracies share disability expansion, there are notable national differences comparing the five countries in table 15.3. The Netherlands is the standout case—number one in disability recipients per 1,000 in the labor force for every year, though it leveled off at 152 between 1990 and 1994. For those under 60 (rate not reported here) Dutch disability prevalence rates are more than triple those of other countries (Aarts and De Jong, 1995, p. 3). The German rate, starting in 1970 a close second to the Netherlands, grew only modestly to 72 and then was actually brought down to 55 in 1990, a fourth-place finish. The Swedes, starting as number three with 49 recipients/1,000, moved to second place in 1990, with a rate of 78. The UK, ranking fourth in 1971 with a rate of 29, moved to third place in 1991 with 68. The United States, starting in 1970 at a low rate of 27, moved to 42 by 1974, stayed steady through the 1980s as President Reagan tried to pare the disability rolls, and then climbed to a rate of 53 in 1992, remaining in last place.

Table 15.4 contains some clues to these different rates and trajectories.

For the cost-conscious, the *Netherlands* has become the symbol of what not to do. The Dutch are tops in total disability expenditures (5.24% of GDP) and have the lowest age of first-time claimants (42 years old). Among the reasons are a wildly loose definition of disability, unusually liberal cash benefits, and avoidance of serious efforts at rehabilitation. It did not help that the Netherlands' unemployment rate climbed after 1974 and accelerated to a very high level in the 1980s—10.6% in 1985, with a drop to our 19-country average of about 7% in the early 1990s (see chap. 12). Until the reforms of 1993, when the Dutch reached the limits of fiscal and political tolerance, any chronic ailment, whether caused by physical or mental impairment, whether work-related or not, might lead to disability benefit eligibility, provided it had reduced earnings in the current job for one year and was expected to continue to reduce earnings capacity to some measurable extent (Aarts and De Jong, 1995, p. 8–9, 13). Seven disability categories were specified ranging from less than 15% disabled to 80–100%; these wage-related benefits were supplemented by disability pensions covering anyone aged 18–64. Until 1987 the law also explicitly stated that ben-

TABLE 15.4 Public expenditure on labor-market measures and on cash benefits as a percentage of GDP 1991*

	Vocational rehabilitation	Work for the disabled	Disability benefits	Total % of GDP	Avg. age of new disability beneficiary, 1992
Netherlands	–	0.64	4.60	5.24	42
Sweden	0.10	0.68	3.30	4.08	57
West Germany	0.13	0.09	2.00	2.22	55(1990)
United Kingdom	0.01	0.02	1.90	1.93	na
United States	0.05	–	0.70	0.75	na

*Source: Aarts and De Jong (1995). – means less than 0.01 percent.

efit adjudicators should take account of poor labor market conditions. The combination of broad definitions of disability, indulgent administration, and the almost exclusive focus on cash benefits assured an expensive outcome: three in four of all Dutch disability claimants are classified as fully disabled; and the Dutch have by far the lowest labor-force participation rate of males aged 55–64 in table 15.3.

Sweden as usual does everything at once, although it does not run up the total bill for disability as much as the Netherlands. Because of their commitment to work—evident in an active labor-market policy, a family policy designed to facilitate work (chap. 7), and the highest rate of labor-force participation for adults, including women and older workers—the Swedes have devoted more of their disability budget to rehabilitation and the creation of public-sector jobs to accommodate the disabled than other countries. In 1992 about 90% of disability beneficiaries receive both a basic disability pension and a supplement for working.[12] Among the policy instruments that emphasize the integration of the handicapped into the mainstream economy are wage subsidies to employers (highest for the younger disabled), subsidized public-sector jobs for the disabled, and, in recent years, a major reallocation of resources toward medical rehabilitation (especially of those complaining of musculoskeletal disorders) and early intervention for those receiving sickness benefits—intervention to coordinate medical professionals, employers, unions, and occupational trainers and counselors in the Labour Market Board. Cost-reduction targets for both sickness and disability payments have recently been adopted. While none of this is cheap, it does result in a sharp contrast to the Netherlands' incentives for an early, easy, full retirement on disability pensions. The Swedes instead provide a package of incentives for the disabled to work; almost everyone in the system bends his efforts toward this end. This is evident in Swedish labor-force participation rates: among men aged 60–64 two-thirds work—three times the Dutch rate (Aarts and De Jong, 1995, p. 11).

If we are looking for a model that combines the Swedish accent on rehabilitation for work with cost control, *Germany* is it. Income-replacement rates are lower than those of either Netherlands or Sweden; entitlement for even partial disability requires a loss of earning capacity of at least half. Beyond these and other cost-containment measures is a strong emphasis on training and employment of the disabled below the age of 60. Experience rating (lowering payroll taxes for employers with a good safety record) gives employers motive for prevention of accidents and disability; expenditures on vocational rehabilitation is high; workers severely disabled are protected against dismissal and the employer receives a state subsidy to create jobs or adjust jobs for them. Further, the Handicapped Act requires both public and private employers to hire one disabled person for every 16 job slots or pay DM 200 ($130) per month for each unfilled quota position. Compliance with these quotas is far from perfect but as Aarts and De Jong (1995, p. 11) show, the German employment rate of disabled workers is high by international standards.

Offsetting these incentives for work and rehabilitation Germany encourages early retirement by giving unemployed workers over 60 years old full disability pensions. That explains why in table 15.3 recipients per 1,000 workers aged 60−64 in 1990 numbered 1,109, almost twice the Swedish rate for that age group. The net effect of all these policies for total labor-force participation in 1990 among the broader age group of males 55−64 is that Germany has a 12-percentage point lead over the Netherlands but is 17 points behind the Swedes.

Both the United Kingdom and the United States are less generous in disability benefits, do much less in rehabilitation, and show much more fluctuation in program design than the three corporatist democracies we have discussed. Their general disinterest in social policy, especially in the past quarter century, their tough talk about waste, fraud, and abuse—and some tough action—gives them one advantage: low costs. At the logical extreme, pressing the disabled to the wall, leaving them to the tender mercies of the market, might save 1% or 2% of GDP. Of course a cost-benefit analysis that took account of shifting costs from disability benefits to unemployment, public assistance, and health benefits as well as the social costs of increased poverty and the waste of human resources when rehabilitation funds are cut might show little if any net gain. But these are the long-run consequences of fiscal crackdowns seldom assessed in evaluation research (see chaps. 2, pp. 100ff., and 8).

In the *United Kingdom* in 1991 294,000 people were entitled to a Severe Disablement allowance and 375,000 people received means-tested Income Support benefits with a disability premium, while 192,000 workers received Disablement Benefits under the work injury scheme. The relatively high figure of 78 for adult recipients per 1,000 workers is partly a statistical artifact: in Britain, workers with prolonged sickness spells are transferred to invalidity schemes after only 28 weeks versus the Dutch 52 weeks. Aarts and De Jong estimate that from 1971 to 1990 disability benefit dependency as a proportion of the employed climbed, especially after 1980. The absolute number of Invalidity Benefit recipients, those incapable of any work who have exhausted sickness benefits, tripled—not from any increase in new entitlements but from a decline in the annual number of people coming off the benefit (Aarts and De Jong, 1995, p. 16; and Aarts, Burkhauser, and De Jong, 1995, chap. 5). There is no partial disability benefit.

British effort to promote reentry into the labor market takes three main forms: quotas, sheltered workshops, and a work assessment and placement service. The quotas are almost never enforced by fines; they depend on voluntary codes. The sheltered workshops are little more than welfare provision; as a fraction of GDP this category takes less than any of the five countries (table 15.4). The number of disabled actually reached is trivial. The British effort at rehabilitation (table 15.4) is nearly nonexistent, below that of the United States. There has recently been a move to privatize the Employment Rehabilitation Service. After 1992, the British also introduced a bonus for finding a job. Of the 20,000 claims within six months of its introduction, 90% were denied the benefit (too many assets un-covered by means testing or the job was not yet in hand).

In short, modest benefits, the avoidance of expensive rehabilitation, and tough adminis-tration are the main reason for the low cost of British disability programs, although the total costs exceed those of the United States and are a close fourth behind Germany in table 15.4, 1.93% of GDP. All this has not prevented a climb in the disability rate, partly because of Britain's high level of unemployment from 1980 to 1992 (see chap. 12).

Disability programs in the *United States* have followed a cycle of expansion-retrenchment-expansion. Although the social-security experts and advocates in the Roosevelt administra-tion repeatedly proposed the adoption of disability insurance (as well as national health in-surance) it was not until 1954 that a "backdoor" form of disability insurance was enacted.[13] A disability pension amendment of 1956 for the first time established the principle of cash replacement for lost income; it passed the Senate by only a one-vote margin. (Derthick, 1979, pp. 304–309.) By international standards this was both lean and late—a major reason that the United States in 1990 remained last in both benefit expenditures and recipient rates in tables 15.3 and 15.4. Tough eligibility criteria were prominent in the 1956 Act: cash be-nefits were available only to workers over 50 with a six-month waiting period; disability had to be medically determined as leading to death or indefinite duration; the worker had to have recent experience of work; the Social Security Administration (SSA) had the power to veto any award by a state agency that it saw as too generous (Derthick, 1979, pp. 308–309; Mashaw, 1988, p. 155).

From 1956 to about 1975, a series of amendments, a congressional investigation, ad-ministrative decisions, and judicial rulings resulted in rapid expansion of expenditures and disability rolls. Three components of the American political economy account for much of this expansion and increased generosity, although they still left the United States much behind the Netherlands, Sweden, and Germany in the recipient rate (table 15.3 for 1970–75). These structural forces also explain why the retrenchment efforts of 1975–83 met with such storms of protest and were stymied.

1. *Federalism.* Fifty states and their governors knew that they were spending federal dollars for a disability program that would keep claimants who might otherwise be a burden on the state budget for public assistance. The governors and everyone associated with state budget-making did not want disability cases dumped on their welfare rolls (Mashaw, 1988, p. 168). Many governors refused to apply more stringent SSA rules on eligibility from 1975 to 1980.

2. *Judicial review and appeals.* As with so much of American social policy, disability decisions were subject to a system of appeals from denials at the state level, initially to administrative law judges, ultimately to the federal judiciary.[14] These judges were increas-ingly willing to reverse denials of benefits by administrators. As Mashaw suggests, in the process of enforcing individual rights, these judges "constrain attempts to tilt disability administration toward cost containment, serve as focal points for public and congressional interest in the program, and provide avenues for interest group formation, mobilization, and action, which spill over into the broader policy process" (Mashaw, 1988, p. 153). Their bias is toward expansion. Thus, "administrative law judges who had granted only

about 20 percent of the claims presented to them in the early years of the program, were by 1973 granting nearly 50 percent of the appeals that went to hearing" (*ibid.*, p. 160). Federal judges joined in this tendency.

3. *The localism and "casework" function of Congress.* As many students have noted, every congressional office is a casework agency, where the constituents bring all manner of grievances and troubles to their representative for action. This was increasingly evident in the United Kingdom as well (Cain, Ferejohn, and Fiorina, 1987). When in the mid-1970s—with rising unemployment and fiscal crunch, as well as rising disability claims—the SSA began a crackdown on "lax management" of the state agencies awarding disability pensions, members of Congress were inundated by constituents who thought that their claims were lost by "faceless bureaucrats." The media, as always, amplified stories of bureaucratic inefficiencies and lack of compassion. Senators and representatives then attacked the SSA for overstrict interpretations and demanded a speedup in adjudication. Speed, as Mashaw argues, means generosity (*ibid.*, p. 162). An administrative law judge who grants awards to marginal cases not only bends the system toward more approvals but increases his recorded productivity (the successful claimants will not appeal the result).

The interaction of federalism, judicial review, and congressional responsiveness to constituent complaints explains why the retrenchment of 1975–83 was so brief and failed to reduce the rolls. The 1980 disability amendments capped the earnings-replacement rate of benefits, reduced the replacement rate for younger workers, and in other ways tried to increase the incentives for the disabled to work. The amendments also ordered the SSA to step up federal review of state awards and conduct periodic reviews of the permanently disabled. When President Reagan, after an abortive effort to cut the minimum old-age pension, decided to pare the rolls and budgets for disability, announcing that fraud and abuse were rampant, he set off a firestorm of protest—from the same Congress that passed the 1980 restrictions, from state agencies and governors, from the judiciary, from the increasingly organized disabled. The U.S. district courts faced mounting appeals. While they had reversed SSA denials of benefits in only 19% of the cases filed in 1975, they were either reversing them or sending them back a whopping 62% of the time in 1994 (*ibid.*, pp. 166–167). An acrimonious standoff in the politics of disability 1980–83 gave way to new amendments in 1983 and 1984, marking the return to expansion, a broader definition of disability, and easier eligibility standards. Table 15.3 reflects this shift: from a nearly steady rate from 1975 to 1985 of 41 or 42 recipients per 1,000 workers, the American rate climbed to 53 by 1992, nearly the German level, but, of course without the German level of funding for rehabilitation. The passage of the 1990 Americans with Disability Act has expanded these programs further.

If it were not for the similarities between Britain and the United States, we could peg this story as a case of American exceptionalism. Surely, at least in degree, the openness of the system to litigation, to countervailing pressures, and to occasional deadlock makes the United States unique. And this populist-judicial openness has increased substantially in recent decades. For instance, the debate about disability was historically confined largely to SSA administrators and experts, the American Medical Association, the Chamber of Com-

557

merce, the insurance industry, and the AFL-CIO (Derthick, 1979, p. 303). The 1970s and 1980s brought much more participation by claimants' advocacy groups, as well as organizations representing the interests of the Division of Disability Services personnel and administrative law judges. "Save Our Security" is an umbrella group representing over 200 grassroots organizations devoted to protecting social-security benefits, including disability benefits. There is even a specialized lawyers association, the National Association of Disability Claims Representatives, "a small army of disability specialists who both litigate disability test cases and participate in state and federal policy processes" (Mashaw, 1988, p. 172). They tend to transform policy debates into intense discussion about due process and the rule of law, thereby reinforcing the conflict among claimants, Congress, administrative agencies, the states, and the courts. They are a force for both bureaucratization of programs and their expansion. As Mashaw suggests, in times of fiscal strain the juridification of American disability programs moves policy talk to rights talk *(ibid.,* p. 174).

If there is a theme to this U.S. cluster of programs coping with disability and the data in the tables, it is this: we keep marginally productive workers, including the disabled, at low wages in a market-driven system. There is little connection between clinical disability evaluation (of "residual working ability") and job-finding services, a reflection of America's meager effort at an active labor-market policy (see figure 2.2). Thus, cost-conscious administrators can "find" a person able to work but not "find" a job for her (Stone, 1985, p. 180). Although periodic efforts to crack down on rising costs of disability bring loud protests, much judicial action, and even a rise in expenditures, it results in very little attention to rehabilitation and job creation, German or Swedish style.

If we want to balance the generosity of benefits that make life better for the handicapped with the goal of cost containment, the middle way between the Netherlands and the United States makes sense. Avoid the USA's low, litigious, and erratic benefits and Britain's limited commitment to rehabilitation; adopt the Swedes' commitment to an active labor-market policy, but avoid what they are gradually abandoning—overgenerous sick pay and a disability design that has promoted disability as an answer to unemployment. Adopt German quotas with fines, but avoid their strong incentives for an early retirement. Finally, retain the German and Swedish commitment to tripartite consultation and administration. When union, management, and public input is built into the system at every level, there is a greater chance of adequate representation of laymen's interests vis à vis agency or lawyers' interests or professionals' (doctors, social workers) interests—and substantive justice is a more likely outcome.

NUCLEAR ENERGY DEVELOPMENT AND SAFETY

The national differences in environmental policy, action, and impact in air-pollution reduction, in a three-country comparison of occupational health and safety, and in the five-country comparison of disability, are also evident in an intensive study of nuclear energy policies and regulatory regimes in France, Sweden, and the United States conducted by a member of our project, James M. Jasper (1990; cf. Joppke, 1993; and Campbell, 1988). Again it is the story of shared knowledge and similar problems followed by contrasting government responses. In all cases the powerful actors were insiders—top politicians and bureaucrats constrained only a little by protest movements and public attitudes, which they shaped by their policies, successes, and failures.

Within a decade after World War II, the three countries had command of the same science and shared the same enthusiasm about the potential for the peacetime uses of atomic energy. All three initially linked nuclear energy development to weapons programs. They all had domestic uranium supplies; each developed an industry for reactors with high ambitions to export them. By the early 1970s they had adopted the same American light-water technology and similar regulatory structures designed to encourage the construction of new reactors. All three depended on the competence and collaboration of public utility firms. In the early and mid-1970s they faced similar public debate and rising antinuclear movements, all visible and vocal. After the Arab oil shock of late 1973, however, the three countries diverged sharply in their policy trajectories, administrative styles, and production and safety outcomes. France pursued its nuclear development plans until it was producing about 80% of its electricity from 51 nuclear power plants by the early 1990s. The United States did not even complete all the reactors that were ordered or under way in 1973. No new orders were placed; over a hundred were canceled. At its peak in the early 1990s less than 20% of American electricity came from nuclear generation. Sweden, the most dependent of the three on energy imports (see chap. 12), falls between the extremes: it added 10 reactors to the two operating in 1973; by the early 1990s these produced about half of Swedish electricity. But the Swedes in 1980 more or less committed themselves to phasing out all 12 reactors by 2010.

The familiar differences in types of political economy go a long way toward explaining these divergent paths. A brief sketch of program structure and development in each country can illustrate.

The *French* case is characterized by elite and expert dominance, the exclusion of all countervailing forces, and centralized decision making by a small group of top bureaucrats belonging mainly to the Corps des Mines and the Corps des Ponts et Chausées. These technocrats are scattered among the main managing and operating company, Electricité de France (EDF) and the planning agency, Commissariat à l'Énergie Atomique (CEA), the Ministry of Industry, and other government agencies as well as nuclear manufacturers. The prestigious Corps des Mines, which dominates CEA, and the Corps des Ponts at Chausées, dominant at EDF, recruit the "best and brightest" from the grands écoles. The top 5 or 10 graduates of École Polytechnique go to the most prestigious technical corps, Corps des Mines; next in line for top recruits is the Corps des Ponts et Chausées.

Nuclear energy, emblem of the large-scale technological fix, held a special fascination for these polytechniciens, who are typically committed to technological prowess as the key to national economic progress. Their nationalist technological enthusiasm for big, bold projects has been labeled the "Concorde syndrome." They articulated a vision of a France awash in cheap energy, independent of any other nation. Polytechniciens are a tight-knit group. As their careers develop, they fan out about evenly in the state apparatus, nationalized industry, and private business. Of 28 "nucleocrats" identified as top managers of public or private organizations involved in nuclear energy 20 are graduates of École Polytechnique (9 in Mines, 7 in Ponts) (Simonnot, 1978, pp. 24–25). As one of them told Jasper (1990, p. 85), polytechniciens "speak only to Mines, and Mines speak only to God."

EDF, which produces and distributes electricity, is one of the world's best-run companies. It is autonomous, state-owned, and (after 1970) profitmaking. Its combination of service, autonomy, prestige, and competence attracts able managers, who recruit and train skilled workers. Although EDF has a governing board with representatives from the state ministries, labor unions, consumers, and others, there is no doubt that members of Corps des Mines and Corps des Ponts were in effective control of EDF, and indeed of the whole nuclear energy program. In time, EDF came to dominate the state nuclear advisory committee, Production d'Electricité d'Origine Nucléaire (PEON), which had representatives from the CEA, the EDF, the state, and industry. French nuclear policy may be "statist"; but it was EDF, a semiprivate "state within a state" that was the dominant force.

In the politics of the French nuclear bureaucracy, the technological enthusiasts of EDF orchestrated a strong, pronuclear coalition and outmaneuvered and outargued the cost-benefiteers of the powerful Ministry of Finance. This Ministry controls government grants and loans, necessary for nuclear development; it was the only ministry that resisted the big nuclear expansion plan of the early 1970s. In contrast to the Corps des Mines, Finance is dominated by graduates of École Nationale d'Administration (ENA) trained in economics. They combine a concern about costs with the polytechniciens' sense of the laws of broad technical systems. But neither their small numbers nor somewhat lesser prestige nor cost-benefit perspective could do more than slow down EDF's broad pronuclear coalition; they merely restricted the rate of growth of nuclear energy in the early 1970s. When the oil crisis struck, the technological enthusiasts forced the Finance Ministry to buy its optimistic assumptions about cheap nuclear energy—an optimism that was partly justified as it turned out. Finance could not overcome the EDF, the Ministry of Industry, the CEA, and other parts of the industry-government coalition. Furthering the ascendance of this coalition were the pronuclear views of successive presidents and prime ministers under the Fifth Republic who saw nuclear power as enhancing French competitiveness.

In the late 1970s, after a brief upsurge of national protest including violence and bombing (1975–77), the French anti-nuclear movement—defeated in elections and beaten by police in site occupations—was marginalized.[15] French public opinion in 1978 was actually more antinuclear than American opinion (Jasper, 1990, p. 241); this had no discernible effect on French nuclear policy.

France is a case of the triumph of technological enthusiasm. The combination of centralized decision making by a cohesive group of strategically placed, elite technocrats in both government and industry resulted in standardized construction processes, plant layouts, and control rooms. The state underwrote many costs. Large economies of scale were achieved. As one might expect from the recruitment pattern, levels of competence were high throughout nuclear-energy planning and operation. Because the French polytechniciens, unlike most American nuclear enthusiasts, admitted that error and even accidents were inevitable, they carried out more preventive maintenance, more careful design, and established strong safety teams at each plant.[16] The CEA perfected those aspects of safety that had been swept under the rug in the United States (Jasper, 1990, p. 86). The key to both safety and cost control appears to be the training and competence of managers and workers, as much as the technology (ibid., p. 253). By the mid-1980s, French electricity costs were 20% cheaper than German costs, 30% cheaper than British, 40% cheaper than the Dutch; they were competitive with coal. In short, although the French may have ended up with too many reactors and less flexibility in the use of alternative sources of energy, the outcome so far has been a cheaper, more efficient, and probably safer nuclear program than those of its competitors, except for Sweden.

At the other extreme, nuclear energy development in the *United States* was characterized by dispersed authority, the premature deployment of plants, lax supervision of operators, sloppy management, followed by cost escalation and safety problems that ultimately stopped further expansion. The dominant actors were private utility companies, reactor manufacturers such as GE and Westinghouse, banks and the federal government, especially the Atomic Energy Commission (AEC, later the NRC) and, at times, the Bureau of the Budget (later OMB).

The federal government combined a determination to make nuclear energy succeed no matter what with a faith that the utilities and the reactor manufacturers knew what they were doing. After the initial wave of commercialization of the 1960s, government regulation of the nuclear program was, to say the least, casual. There was no central control of siting decisions, no intervention in the process of construction and financing, no effort to improve utility management, no mechanism for screening out utilities that clearly should not have had plants. There was a good deal of indiscriminate technological enthusiasm in both government agencies and the Senate-House Joint Committee on Atomic Energy (JCAE), as well as among reactor manufacturers and, to a lesser extent, utilities. The regulatory regime was at once legalistic and indulgent. The AEC issued lengthy specifications and lists of procedures and was strict about conforming to the letter of the law in licensing but careless regarding the actual operation of the plants. Hands-off private enterprise was the main theme.

Matching the casual commitment of the government was the casual attitude of the utility companies ("nuclear reactors are just another way to boil water"). As the commercialization of the light-water reactor proceeded apace after 1963, inept management and the poor training and supervision of operators led to much greater costs than anyone expected.

In its structure and mission the AEC embodied fatal contradictions: it was simultaneously to promote new nuclear technologies but not interfere with private companies running existing reactors; it was to promote the commercialization of nuclear energy and at the same time regulate and protect public safety. Promotion without close supervision was the continual resolution of these dilemmas. The small safety-oriented Advisory Committee on Reactor Safeguards within the AEC remained isolated; its concerns were seldom incorporated in policy. Until the 1970s the "iron triangle" of AEC, the JCAE, and large corporations dominated nuclear policy.

The casual commitment of the federal government and the weak performance of the utilities throughout the history of the program allowed costs to escalate, alternative energy alternatives to be considered, and the public to become antinuclear. After the oil shock of 1973–74 utility managers themselves began to harbor doubts about the future demand for electricity. They experienced mounting difficulties in financing new construction and in meeting cost overruns for ongoing construction. Financial markets abandoned nuclear energy. Starting out as nuclear enthusiasts believing in rosy scenarios, the cost-benefit economists in the Council of Economic Advisers, Treasury, OMB, and AEC also began to question the chronically optimistic engineering assumptions and cost projections. A key figure here was James Schlesinger, an economist with experience in the Office of Management and Budget (OMB) who was appointed head of AEC by President Nixon in 1971 and later became energy czar under President Carter in 1976. He told the nuclear industry to fight its own battles as early as 1971, favored energy conservation as an alternative, and opposed further development—all on economic grounds.

Reinforcing the newfound skepticism of the alleged cost advantages of nuclear energy was a further decentralization and fragmentation of regulatory authority, from the mid-1970s on. The JCAE gave way to a dozen congressional committees. State public utility commissions (PUCs) became involved in nuclear regulation because the costs of nuclear construction skyrocketed and they had to decide who would pay (the utilities or the ratepayers). They increasingly squeezed the utilities by refusing to grant electrical rate increases. Regarding plant location, localities increasingly organized around the NIMBY syndrome ("Not in my backyard").

If any further impetus was needed to stop the expansion of nuclear energy development, the 1979 accident at Three Mile Island, a nuclear plant near Harrisburg, Pennsylvania, was the coup de grâce. TMI dramatized the mismanagement that had been hidden in the 1960s and became evident in the rising costs and safety complaints of scientists in the 1970s (some were "whistle-blowers"). The same year as the TMI accident the popular movie, *The China Syndrome*, starring Jane Fonda and Jack Lemmon, encapsulated rising antinuclear sentiments and protests; a spate of nuclear conspiracy movie scripts and books followed. For the first time American public opinion turned antinuclear. The further fragmentation of federal authority and the spreading alliances of local citizen groups and cost-conscious PUCs deepened the fiscal squeeze on utilities and prevented their recovery. By 1984, 11 states had followed California's lead in restricting nuclear energy (4 by referenda, 1 in a PUC, the rest in legislatures). These actions were somewhat moot because economics had already buried the prospects of the industry. Cost explosions and denial of risks coupled with well-publicized surprise accidents was a poor formula for inspiring confidence of investors or the public.

With the benefit of hindsight and comparative analysis we can conclude that the American nuclear energy program was relatively costly, amazingly sloppy in management, poorly regulated, and unsafe.

With respect to nuclear energy development, *Sweden* is truly the "middle way." As in France, there was state bureaucratic dominance, highly competent utility managers, and highly trained workers. In contrast to France, the system was more open and participatory. Swedish planners and regulators, as we have seen in the area of occupational health and safety, rely on continuous, informal communication and persuasion with government agencies, the Riksdag (Parliament), political parties, industry, labor, and professional groups. They use Royal Commissions to help forge consensus. In contrast to the American AEC, Swedish nuclear regulators and inspectors work closely with owners and operators in studying the technicalities of operations and safety; they are therefore both more trusted and effective.

Throughout its early development and the building of several reactors the nuclear energy program was marked by the typical Swedish consensus—until the mid-1970s. In 1973 the Center Party, at the time the largest of the three parties in opposition to the continuously ruling Social Democrats, became antinuclear. The Social Democrats and their labor base adopted a delay-oriented, cost-benefit strategy to defuse the developing antinuclear movement. "Wait till it cools down." Again in typical fashion, in a slow search for consensus they created several commissions to study the hazards of nuclear energy and launched an education campaign for citizens to discuss the pros and cons of various energy alternatives; about 1% of the population actually participated in these discussion groups in 1974–75 (Jasper, 1990, p. 140)—a U.S. equivalent would be over two million discussants.

The oil crisis of late 1973 lifted nuclear energy to a key source of party conflict. A compromise Energy Bill of 1975 called for a small increase in nuclear energy and a large reduction in the growth of energy demand—consolidating short-run measures adopted in 1974. However, when the Center Party and its coalition partners narrowly won the Parliament in 1976 and Thorbjörn Fälldin became prime minister, antinuclear forces had their first opponent of the nuclear program in a high position. The Center Party's women's and youth groups had developed close ties to environmental groups; they expressed moral outrage against what they saw as the blind faith of the Social Democrats in technology and economic growth. Now was their time.

Fälldin, the antinuclear moralist, was a product of the convergence of chance events: a very slight shift to the right in voting upset the balance between left and right; the Center Party had just become officially antinuclear; it won in 1976 by a hair; and it was able to put the bourgeois coalition together for a brief moment in history. The parties agreed on a two-year pause in new orders. Right after the 1976 election, however, Fälldin's coalition partners argued that it would be irresponsible to abandon nuclear plants already well along. In a series of compromises the antinuclear position gradually eroded. Further reactors were built and came on line. Fälldin resigned. Subsequently the Social Democrats and Liberals agreed to stop construction after 12 reactors and launch research on renewable resources and energy conservation.

The Three Mile Island accident of 1979 produced contrasting responses in the three countries. The French claimed it meant nothing; they accelerated their construction program. The United States, with great media fanfare, drifted into further delays, instituted a few safety precautions, and discouraged future construction (new investment had already ceased, anyway) but adopted no alternative energy policy. Swedish political elites, facing continuing conflicts about the program within and between parties, abandoned the compromise that was emerging in the late 1970s. In 1980 the Social Democrats, back in power, launched a rare referendum—surely one of the largest-scale national issue debates in the history of postwar democratic politics (if the measure is expenditure per voter and voter participation in political discussion). In contrast to the American advocates of nuclear energy, who dismissed the antinuclear activists as ignorant, irrational, and hopelessly romantic, their counterparts in the top layers of Swedish society tried to educate their opponents and the public by including them in policy deliberations. Although Swedes consider it bad form for their leaders to bow to public opinion, the referendum itself was an occasion for serious education. There were four months of intensive Parliament- and party-financed reading, talking, and campaigning. To assure total penetration, materials were distributed in all the languages of immigrants. Antinuclear activists saw to it that Swedes would watch antinuclear films in theaters and would hear members of the Union of Concerned Scientists and other antinuclear activists imported from the United States. This flood of campaigning surely aired any argument that could be marshaled against (or for) the program; for instance, volunteers on the "kill atomic energy" side visited 1 in 5 homes in big cities, 1 in 10 elsewhere (Jasper, 1990, p. 229). What could be the most-informed electorate on earth about this technical-political issue divided on the three ballot choices as follows:

Line 1, supported by the Conservatives. Use the 12 plants now   18.9%
    operating, completed, or under construction. Close them down
    at a rate consistent with the need for electricity to maintain
    employment and welfare. Safety considerations will determine
    the order in which reactors are removed from service. Etc.

Line 2, supported by the Social Democrats and Liberals   39.1%
    and touted as the middle way. The above "Conservative"
    statement with several additions: promote energy
    conservation, protect the weakest groups, expand research
    and development on renewable energy resources, improve
    safety and environmental rules, put the main responsibility
    for production and distribution in public hands. Etc.

Line 3, supported by the Center Party and the Communists.   38.7%
    "No" to continued expansion of nuclear power, shut down
    existing plants immediately if safety analysis shows them to
    be unsafe. Phase out the six reactors currently in operation
    within at most 10 years. Etc.

It appears that about three in five voters were saying "We have some doubts but let's not rush"—no radical change. Even Line 3 advocates were not urging a blanket shutdown. The major parties soon agreed to phase out nuclear energy by 2010—30 years away from the referendum. In 1983 they increased the liability for nuclear accidents. Few Swedish leaders with whom I talked believe that a complete phaseout will occur by then if Sweden's energy needs are not met with feasible alternatives. The accident at Chernobyl in 1986 when the wind blew fallout over Sweden, however, strengthened the Social Democrats' public commitment to phase out this controversial fuel and with it the most divisive issue that has hit consensual Sweden in recent history.

In sum: Types of political economy account for contrasts in both policy processes and output of nuclear energy programs. Our comparison suggests a clear rank order: In controlling the costs of nuclear reactors, the French and Swedes are far ahead of the United States with the French perhaps having an edge over the Swedes; Jasper (*ibid.*, p. 234) concludes that the first 10 Swedish reactors were as cheap as the French but that the last two—because of interest rate increases, delays, and added safety measures—were more expensive.[17] In production of cheap electricity the French rank first, the Swedes second, the Americans last. In the flexible use of alternative energy sources and conservation the French are locked into the nuclear option; the Swedes can move gradually in multiple directions and, in fact, have done much with conservation and alternative sources; the United States shows little capacity to frame an energy policy and is stuck with the 108 (now aging) nuclear plants it has.[18] Regarding safety, Jasper summarizes the weight of evidence: the high level of management competence and worker training combined with close and cooperative interaction between industry, science, and government make the Swedes first and the French a close second in operational safety; the United States, lacking these characteristics, remains relatively risky. Regarding nuclear waste disposal, I am skeptical about any country solving this problem in the near future, if ever, but the best study that compares national efforts to do so concludes that the cautious Swedish approach to waste disposal is better designed and executed than that of any other country (Carter, 1987; cf. Cook, Emel, and Kasperson, 1991/1992, p. 106).[19]

A final note on Germany's nuclear energy program highlights the structural differences that make a difference. As we might expect from its marginally corporatist classification, Germany lies somewhere between Sweden and the United States but closer to Sweden's consensual bargaining habits.[20] Its federalism and divided powers give state and local social movements a chance for expression, as in the United States. Its modified proportional representation system (see chap. 2) helped to turn the sometimes violent antinuclear, antistate movement into a more effective institutionalized, national Green Party, with parliamentary representation and strategies. In contrast, the majoritarian, winner-take-all electoral system of the United States fosters "public interest," single-issue group lobbying and litigation, not party-parliamentary participation.

Germany's stronger executive branch and its corporatist tendencies and highly trained workers give it an administrative capability far beyond that of the United States. Thus, compared to the United States, Germany's utility regulation was stronger and steadier, its quasi-public ownership, like Sweden's, assured a more supportive state, and its management and workers were more efficient, as in Sweden. By 1989, Germany was producing just over a third of its electricity from nuclear plants.

As in the United States, however, and in contrast to France, cost-benefit analysts within the German bureaucracy and in independent, economic research institutes (see chap. 17, pp. 662, 673 note 26) successfully debunked the industry's claims to cost advantage and, after the Chernobyl disaster, gained more credence. As sources of the nuclear slowdown of the 1980s these analysts, operating within a political regime strongly committed to economic growth, were much more effective than the confrontational protest movements.

In other words, compared to the United States the German polity was less open to antinuclear arguments and movements and more capable of planning and implementing a nuclear development policy. Conflict-averse elites, similar to Sweden's, were able to maintain consensus regarding both the initial development and the reduced pace of the 1980s. There has been no new construction since 1982 and plans for expansion have been put on hold.

That German policy and performance in this area locates it between the United States and Sweden makes sense; its political economy has structural attributes of each.

The Regulation of Tobacco Use

The tentative findings of this chapter on environmental risks and the firmer findings in chapter 14 on mayhem—that national differences in risk, safety, and security are rooted in differences in types of political economy and related public policies—are less true of efforts to regulate tobacco, one of many addicting drugs and the leading cause of death from cancers. Although the data, again, do not cover many of our countries, the scattered data available reveal sharp national contrasts in rates of smoking, rates of decline in smoking, and regulatory policies, including taxes on tobacco. But there is little evidence that either types of political economy or regulatory policies shape smoking behavior in any consistent pattern. Some insights can be achieved, however, from a four-country comparison of the policies and politics of tobacco, and from some measures of taxing and smoking for anywhere from 13 to 18 countries.

I begin with a brief summary of inferences from many tables (not reported) on tobacco use, tobacco taxes and prices, and trends in smoking; report three tables that illustrate the

TABLE 15.5 Smoking prevalence and reduction of smoking among men and women aged 15 and over in thirteen countries, 1980–90

Country	% reduction in prevalence of male smokers 1980-1990[a]		Male smokers as % of male pop. 15+[b]		% reduction in prevalence of female smokers 1980-1990[c]		Female smokers as % of female pop. 15+[d]	
			1980	1990			1980	1990
Sweden	29	(1)	36 (12)	26 (13)	10	(4)	29 (8)	26 (8)
United Kingdom	26	(2)	42 (7)	31 (8)	12	(3)	33 (3)	29 (4)
Australia	25	(4)	40 (8)	30 (9)	14	(2)	31 (4)	27 (6)
Netherlands	25	(4)	52 (3)	39 (3)	9	(5)	34 (2)	31 (3)
United States	24	(6)	38 (10)	28 (11)	24	(1)	30 (6)	23 (9)
Canada	24	(6)	39 (9)	30 (10)	7	(7)	29 (8)	27 (6)
France	19	(7)	46 (4)	38 (4)	+17	(12)	16 (11)	19 (12)
New Zealand	18	(8)	34 (13)	28 (12)	4	(8)	29 (8)	28 (5)
Denmark	17	(9)	57 (2)	47 (2)	8	(6)	44 (1)	40 (1)
Germany	16	(10)	43 (5)	36 (6)	+9	(10)	19 (10)	21 (10)
Japan	14	(11)	70 (1)	61 (1)	+1	(9)	14 (13)	14 (13)
Norway	12	(12)	42 (7)	37 (5)	+13	(11)	30 (6)	34 (2)
Finland	3	(13)	37 (11)	36 (7)	+31	(13)	16 (11)	21 (10)

[a]Percent reduction in the percentage of male population aged 15 and over who smoked from 1980 to 1990. Calculated from "OECD Health Systems Volume I, Facts and Trends 1960–1991." *Health Policy Studies* 3 (Paris: OECD, 1993f): 91. Australia figures are 1980–89; U.S. 1979–90; New Zealand 1981–90; Germany 1978–89; Canada 1979–90.

[b]*Ibid.*

[c]*Ibid.*, p. 90, for females same age. Australia figures are 1980–89; U.S. 1979–90; Canada 1981–90; New Zealand 1981–90; Germany 1978–89.

[d]*Ibid.*

differences; and then discuss the policy differences among France, Japan, the United States, and Canada. It is safe to conclude the following:

1.   All rich democracies have responded to scientific evidence that tobacco is harmful to health. They have all attempted to reduce or restrict cigarette consumption by one or more of these measures: provide warning labels on cigarette packages, limit advertising of tobacco products, increase tobacco taxes, limit smoking areas and places of sale.

2.   From 1980 to 1990, male smokers as a percentage of total male population age 15 and above have declined in the 13 countries for which we have data: reductions range from the very low 3% of Finland to the very high 29% of Sweden. Except for Finland they all dropped at least 12%. See table 15.5.

3.   The prevalence of smoking among the female population age 15 and above in the same countries starts in 1980 at a lower level and declines much less than the decline among men. Reductions range from the very low 0.7% in Japan to the very high reduction of 24% in the United States. In fact, 5 of these 13 nations show an *increase* in female smokers: Finland up 31%, France up 17%, Norway up 13%, Germany up 9%, Japan up

TABLE 15.6 Reliance on tobacco taxes 1980, tobacco tax increases 1985–90, and smoking reduction 1980–90

Country	Taxes on tobacco products as % of total tax rev. 1980[a]		Relative price increases for tobacco products 1985-1990[b]		% reduction in prevalence of male smokers 1980-1990[c]		%reduction in prevalence of female smokers 1980-1990[d]	
Ireland	4.6	(1)	6.7	(12)	—		—	
Australia	3.5	(2)	18.6	(3)	25	(4)	14	(2)
United Kingdom	3.3	(3)	0.7	(14)	26	(2)	12	(3)
Sweden	2.8	(5)	12.6	(6)	29	(1)	10	(4)
Denmark	2.8	(5)	–4.2	(16)	17	(9)	8	(6)
Germany	2.0	(6)	6.8	(11)	16	(10)	+9	(10)
Finland	1.9	(7)	18.2	(4)	3	(13)	+31	(13)
Austria	1.7	(8)	0.1	(15)	—		—	
Belgium	1.3	(10)	16.2	(5)	—		—	
New Zealand	1.3	(10)	—		18	(8)	4	(8)
Switzerland	1.2	(12)	—		—		—	
Netherlands	1.2	(12)	3.0	(13)	25	(4)	9	(5)
Japan	1.0	(13)	11.1	(8)	14	(11)	1	(9)
Norway	0.8	(15)	9.7	(9)	12	(12)	+13	(11)
United States	0.8	(15)	22.0	(2)[e]	24	(6)	24	(1)
Canada	0.8	(15)	44.1	(1)	24	(6)	7	(7)
France	0.7	(17)	11.1	(8)	19	(7)	+17	(12)
Italy	0.3	(18)	8.9	(10)	—		—	

[a]From "OECD Health Systems Volume I, Facts and Trends 1960–1991." *Health Policy Studies* 3 (Paris: OECD, 1993f): 89. The *r* of tobacco tax and reduction of male smoking is .09 (n.s.).

[b]Tobacco product price indices divided by the price indices for total private consumption, 1985 = 100. From *ibid.*, p. 88. The *r* of price increases and reduction of male smoking is .28 (n.s.).

[c]Percent reduction in the percentage of male population aged 15 and over who smoked from 1980 to 1990. Calculated from *ibid.*, p. 91. Australia figures are for 1980–89; U.S., 1979–90; New Zealand, 1981–90; Germany, 1978–89; Canada, 1979–90.

[d]*Ibid.*, p. 90, for females same age. Australia figures are for 1980–1989; U.S., 1979–90; Canada, 1981–90; New Zealand, 1981–90; Germany, 1978–89.

[e]U.S. figure for 1985–89 only.

less than 1%. It is perhaps an ironic by-product of gender equality—the manly right to die early.

4. The rank order of countries in the share of smokers remains almost identical for the decade of smoking decline. There is no regression to the mean—no greater reduction if a country starts with a high rate, no lesser reduction if it starts low.

5. Taxes on tobacco by any measure vary greatly by country but the country rank order remains remarkably stable (as seen in our discussion of other types of taxation). Data are for 18 of our countries from 1980 to 1990. The tax measures themselves show a very similar rank order: it does not matter whether we use tobacco taxes as a percentage of total revenue or as a percentage of GDP, even if we go back to 1970.

We can see from table 15.6 that the reluctant taxers and spenders are drawn to tobacco taxes. The top four in tobacco taxes as a percentage of total revenue in 1980 are

Ireland, the United Kingdom, Australia, and Sweden. (Among these least-corporatist countries only the United States shies away from tobacco taxes; it ranks 14th in table 15.6; even Switzerland scores above the United States.) A possible explanation for this minipattern is that all four tend to be low- to medium-tax states that have relied heavily on painfully visible taxes (property taxes and individual income taxes); they are therefore more attracted to "sin" taxes as an easier revenue source than countries that have relied more on social-security and consumption taxes to finance expanding government transfers and services. (See chap. 10, table 10.2.) A second pattern is that all three cases of corporatism-without-labor are low on tobacco taxes, confirming a friendly attitude toward their tobacco industries. The clearest cases, France and Japan, rank toward the bottom and also are below average in smoking decline. Switzerland ranks 11th in taxes (no data on smoking declines).

6.   Scattered data suggest little or no relation between reliance on tobacco taxes, or tax per pack of cigarettes, or the retail price of cigarettes, on the one hand, and smoking behavior on the other. For instance, table 15.6 aligns tobacco taxes as a percentage of total revenue in 1980 for 18 countries and price increases in tobacco products relative to other private consumption price increases from 1985 to 1990 for 16 countries with reduction in the prevalence of smoking among men and women in 11 countries from 1980 to 1990. Of the three highest in reliance on tobacco taxes, two show the very highest rate of reduction in male smoking: Sweden first with a drop of 29%; the United Kingdom second with a drop of 26% (no data on smoking trends for Ireland). But Denmark, a high taxer by any measure, ranks only ninth in rate of reduction, a low 17%. Of the five lowest in reliance on tobacco taxes, there is little pattern in reduced smoking.

But tobacco taxes in general are not taxes smokers feel when they buy cigarettes. And taxes on the products are not their prices. For the four countries where both the 1986 tax per pack of 20 cigarettes (in ECUs) and the reduction in prevalence of smoking are available, there is no connection (see table 15.7). In the same countries the relative retail price per pack is unrelated to behavior. For instance, while Denmark has the highest price, it ranks well below the median in male smoking reduction among the 13 countries in table 15.6. The United Kingdom, with the second highest price, is far above the median reduction in smoking; while the Netherlands, with a below-average price, has almost the same reduction. France, with a pack price about one-fifth that of Denmark, had a similar reduction in smoking.

7.   Regarding the issue of tobacco use, there is a reversal in the usual ranking of system outputs, a hint that the Anglo-American democracies outperformed the more consensual democracies in smoking reduction in the 1980s. Of 13 countries permitting calculation of decline in male smokers as a percentage of the total male 15 and over population, 4 of the 6 best reducers are Anglo-American: the United Kingdom, 26%; Australia, 25%; the United States and Canada, 24%. Conversely the 5 least successful are corporatist, with or without labor (from Denmark's 17% to Finland's 3). I explore this below.

Why is our scheme for understanding the effects of policy so limited when it comes to reduction of smoking? A first answer is that tobacco products, like other addicting drugs, have a low price elasticity of demand (the percentage decrease in demand for a 1% per-

TABLE 15.7 Cigarette taxes and prices in 1986 and smoking reduction
1980–90 in five countries

Country	Tax per pack of 20 cigarettes (ECUs)[a]	Retail price per pack 1986 (ECUs)[a]	% Reduction in smoking 1980-1990 Male[b]	Female[c]
Denmark	2.76	3.16	17	8
Ireland	1.88	2.54	—	—
United Kingdom	1.76	2.35	26	12
Germany	1.30	1.77	16	9
Netherlands	0.97	1.36	25	9
Belgium	0.87	1.24	—	—
Italy	0.73	1.02	—	—
France	0.51	0.68	19	17

[a]From O'Hagan and Carey (1988). The median retail price for eight countries is 1.57.

[b]Percent reduction in the percentage of male population aged 15 and over who smoked from 1980 to 1990. Calculated from "OECD Health Systems Volume I, Facts and Trends 1960–1991." *Health Policy Studies* 3 (Paris: OECD, 1993f): 91. German figures are for 1978–89.

[c]*Ibid.*, p. 90, for females the same age. German figures are for 1978–89.

cent increase in price), especially for experienced users. Estimates cluster around −0.4 for cigarettes and −0.7 for alcoholic beverages compared to −3.5 for movies (MacCoun, 1993, p. 503). That does not mean that taxes and price have no effect. For less affluent countries and for less affluent people in either rich or poor countries, price matters (Roemer, 1993, p. 89). Increases in tobacco taxes, for instance, appear to reduce consumption of tobacco among the young. While among rich countries a 10% price increase tends to reduce consumption only by about 4% in the general population, it decreases consumption by about 13% among adolescents, who not only have meager resources but have not been smoking long enough to be fully addicted (World Bank, 1993, p. 88). Similarly, smokers in poor countries evidence greater sensitivity to price: in India a doubling of the excise tax on most of the popular cigarette brands brought a 15% decline in cigarette sales; in Papua, New Guinea, a 10% increase in tobacco tax reduced consumption by 7% (*ibid.*). In short, tobacco taxes insofar as they increase retail prices have only a modest effect in reducing smoking in the rich democracies, although they have a stronger effect among the young and among less-developed countries, both not covered by the rough comparisons above.

The reason that all rich democracies have reduced smoking, at least among men, is that tax and real price increases, when combined with a wide array of aggressive regulatory and educational measures, can reduce tobacco use substantially. That countries vary so much in the recent rate of reduction in smoking reduction is explained by country variation in policy aggressiveness and choice of policy packages. This is evident from a four-country study of the politics of smoking regulation in France, Japan, Canada, and the United States (Vogel, Kagan, and Kessler, 1993). All four have attempted to reduce or restrict cigarette consumption by providing warning labels on cigarette packages, restricting advertising, increasing tobacco taxes, and limiting smoking areas. The initial efforts of all four were met with strong and effective resistance from their domestic tobacco-related industries, resistance that in some measure they overcame.

These common responses are matched by large national differences in the type, speed, and effectiveness of regulation. As we might expect from our discussion of types of political economy, in both France and Japan (cases of corporatism-without-labor) the process of tobacco regulation was more centralized than in Canada or the United States, more dominated by elite bargaining among top bureaucrats in finance, health, and other ministries as well as the leaders of the medical and public health communities. Regulation in both countries started late and did not go nearly as far as it did in North America in education campaigns, in enforcing advertising bans, in strong warnings on cigarette packages, nor in regulating smokers' behavior via restrictions in workplaces and public places.

In France a structure of corporatist bargaining shaped the regulatory regime. A small number of big tobacco firms are organized into 12 regional marketing boards whose interests are aggregated in a powerful tobacco trade association with strong ties to SEITA (Société d'Exploitation Industrielle des Tabacs et Allumettes), a state monopoly from Napoleon to the 1970s, now a quasi-public profit-making corporation. Thirty-nine thousand tobacconist shops are monopoly distributors with tight relations with SEITA. The powerful Finance Ministry regulates prices. The key actors in this negotiated tobacco economy were not inclined to curtail ads and restrict use, nor did they have the will to tax heavily; by 1986 France had the lowest tax per pack of cigarettes among eight European countries compared (see table 15.7). Instead of a bevy of outside single-issue groups agitating for nonsmokers' rights and smoking bans and baiting tobacco firms as murderous, as in North America, the French produced only a loose organization of doctors and professors—the "Smoking or Health Medical Association"—who accented public health themes and personal contacts with top bureaucrats rather than individual rights and public protest. The battles were fought among competing interests within the French ministries—the Health Ministry in collaboration with the medical elite advocating more taxes and bans on advertising and use, the Finance Ministry worried about revenue effects of reduced sales and possible inflation, Communications about the legalities of an ad ban, Sports and Culture about the loss of tobacco company sponsorship of events such as the Grand Prix. By the simple device of removing tobacco from the consumer price index used in measuring inflation and calculating wage increases, the French cabinet was able to agree in March 1990 on an all-media ban on tobacco ads and on tobacco sponsorship of public events; they also banned smoking in public transportation and government facilities and raised the price of tobacco products 15%. The Parliament approved. (*Ibid.*, p. 321.)

This picture of a centralized system of bargaining that excludes not only labor but other mass-based protest groups is even more evident in the Japanese response to tobacco interests. As in the matter of urban air pollution and the mercury-poisoning incident in Minamata (see chap. 2), Japanese government and business ignored the evidence on smoking and health—because of their overwhelming preoccupation with national economic performance. Cigarette sales in 1982 produced $6 billion for the Treasury. In response to American pressure, the Japan Tobacco and Salt Public Corporation (JTS), a highly protected, state-owned monopoly from 1905 to 1985, was split into two semi-"private" firms in 1985, Japan Tobacco, Inc. and Japan Tobacco International. But the powerful Ministry of Finance still owns two-thirds of the shares (Blum, 1985). Thus, in the early 1980s the minister of finance boasted to the Diet that he was a heavy drinker and smoker; the minister of health and welfare, in a bizarre statement, attributed his good health to smoking (Kagan and Vogel, 1993b, p. 61). With an opening to foreign cigarette imports TV cigarette commercials doubled from 1983 to 1987 (*ibid.*, pp. 70–71).

Again, issues distant from the central concerns of the Japanese bargaining partners—the key ministries, farmers, industry, small business, commerce, and until 1993, the Liberal Democratic Party—do not readily move to the national political agenda. Instead the government saw tobacco as an industry to be protected (leaf tobacco is Japan's second largest crop, after rice). The restrictions that were observed were self-imposed by the manufacturers comprising the Tobacco Institute of Japan: for instance, the 1985 voluntary agreement not to advertise on television at certain hours and the later extension of those hours; and some voluntary workplace restrictions on smoking.

In contrast to Minamata and air pollution, where Japan delayed for decades but eventually took broad, bold action to clean up its air and water (see chap. 2), its action on tobacco is still in the stalling stage. If and when the business and government partners decide to do something, they will likely exceed the rest of our rich democracies in effectiveness. For the moment Japan tops every other modern country in per capita cigarette consumption; by design it remains a smoker's paradise. In view of Japan's very good health performance in other areas, its tobacco use is an aberration.

Although France and Japan differ in the extent of restrictions and the rate of reduction of smoking, with France ahead of Japan, they share a late beginning in regulation, a reluctance to create and enforce no-smoking zones, an initial reluctance to tax tobacco products, a centralized, closed policymaking process, and a capacity to bring industry in line, whenever they wish, including the acceptance of restrictions on advertising.

Similarly, while Canada and the United States differ in extent of restrictions—Canada taxes a pack of cigarettes much more than the United States, and it went further and faster than the United States in restricting smoking in stores and workplaces—they both exceed France and Japan in all policy areas; more important, they both achieved an above-average rate of reduction in smoking. The explanation for both differences and similarities lies in the structure of the political economy. Both evidence a decentralized federalism, strong internal social cleavages, and fluid party politics; both are far more open to protest politics and have numerous well-organized activists that pressured the government to act early on a broad front.

The United States–Canadian differences, too, are important as a sign of American exceptionalism. The unique fragmentation of authority in the United States—its division of powers, its greater decentralization (50 states versus 11 provinces; a presidential system versus a parliamentary system), its greater profusion of lobbyists and single-issue groups, its lesser party discipline, its greater vulnerability to media agenda-setting—all this means that the United States was on the cutting edge of antismoking propaganda and moral fervor from the beginning, engaged in more action to bar smoking at a local level, with greater accent on nonsmokers' rights, and less of a sustained national follow-through on advertising bans and far less on taxes. Canada's greater party discipline and elite coherence meant that antismoking activists could focus on the federal government, with its greater capacity to act. Yet, in the perspective of the broader comparison, Canada and the United States are closer to each other than they are to France and Japan.

That an early start and comprehensive, aggressive antismoking legislation and education are effective in reducing smoking is evident in the Swedish case, the leader in 1980s reduction. Here is a chronology of antismoking activity in Sweden before 1982:[21]

1963	The first national funds are provided for antismoking activities.
1964	Adoption of an intraindustry agreement to reduce the impact of cigarette advertising on youth.
1965	The Tobacco Teaching Set, developed by the National Smoking and Health Association, is distributed to all schools.
1971–73	Government commission is formed to develop a long-range action plan; report outlining a comprehensive 25-year antismoking campaign is delivered in 1973, endorsed by the government, and begins.
1975	The 1964 intraindustry advertising agreement becomes a government-industry agreement, monitored by the National Board of Consumer Affairs.
Dec. 1975	The Tobacco Labeling Act is passed. Regulations implementing the Act, issued by National Board of Health and Welfare, become effective in January 1, 1977. The Act requires manufacturers to print 1 of 16 warning messages on each packet of cigarettes. Both the text and graphic presentation of the 16 rotating messages are to be changed every two to three years. Tar, nicotine, and carbon monoxide yield per cigarette must be listed on the packet, along with the industry averages for tar, nicotine, and carbon monoxide yields.
1976	The "Smoke-free Start to Life" program begins. The state provides midwiveswith training in one-on-one counseling, materials to be disseminated to expectant mothers, and antismoking posters.
1978	The "Campaign for a Smoke-free Generation" begins.
July 1978	World Tobacco reports that Sweden imposed a "heavy" tax increase on cigarettes.
Nov. 1978	The Riksdag passes legislation on advertising. The Act says that tobacco advertising should not be "intrusive or proselytizing," nor should it "seek out customers or encourage the use of tobacco product." The Act bans free samples, trading stamp schemes, and promotions which offer cigarettes at a lower rate when bought with another product.
	The Act prohibits outdoor advertisements, including those on stadiums and athletic fields, as well as advertising in the sports pages of daily newspaper,sports newspapers, or any publication targeting an audience under 20 years old. Any magazine or newspaper ad must meet severe space limits, factual review, and display specified health warnings.
	Violations of the Act are treated as violations of the Marketing Practices Act. If a vendor does not comply with the Act, the Marketing Court can order his ad campaign to stop and fine him.
1980	A course on the effects of smoking becomes part of the health education curriculum.
1981	The National Board of Education begins to provide teachers with training and materials for teaching the effects of smoking. The comprehensive school curriculum is revised to include information on smoking in traditional classes.

Since 1981 Sweden has banned smoking in public places as well as anywhere near the young or infirm and has expanded preventive measures. For the structural reasons discussed above, the implementation of educational, counseling, and health programs in schools and medical clinics, and the enforcement of advertising and smoking restrictions have, by international standards, been quite effective. In short, aggressive, coordinated action on all fronts over many years reduces male, teenage, and female smoking substantially.

It is possible that culture as it interacts with political structure has a greater influence in this policy area than in others. The recent reduction in smoking is greatest among the fragmented, decentralized Anglo-American democracies—United Kingdom, United States, Canada, Australia, and to a lesser extent, New Zealand. Perhaps their moralistic populism not only is more evident but also finds local and regional expression more easily than it can in more centralized systems with less Protestant righteousness (France, Japan). Thus the guerrilla wars waged by animal rights groups against women wearing fur coats and by grassroots nonsmokers' groups against smokers have been more successful than their counterparts in continental Europe or Japan. The politics of California, with its addiction to media and money-driven initiatives and referenda, are conducive to much moral agitation about nonsmokers' rights. Thus, such groups, having already achieved hundreds of no-smoking zones by pressure on city councils and county boards, sponsored successful voter initiatives to add 25 cents per pack to the state's cigarette tax in 1988 and 50 cents in 1999 with most of the money earmarked for an antismoking advertising campaign.

To stand up to the suggestive data in table 15.6 this cultural hypothesis would have to hold that Sweden (ranked first in reduction) and the Netherlands (ranked third) are also populist-moralist in political style, a dubious proposition, although Protestant righteousness is part of the culture of both nations. It would also have to account for Norway's, Denmark's, and Finland's lower rates of reduction, despite many values they share with Sweden, the leader in smoking reduction. Whatever the influence of cultural values, the surer conclusion is that the decentralized structures of the Anglo-American democracies facilitate local protest movements of all kinds, including antismoking groups.

Summary

For all five areas of environmental threat and policy response—air pollution, occupational safety and health, physical and mental disabilities, nuclear energy and safety, smoking and the regulation of tobacco—the story since the early 1970s is the same. Rich democracies have responded to the same scientific evidence (sometimes exaggerated); they have adopted similar statutes and roughly the same standards for pollutants and workplace hazards; and they have all achieved some success. After policies are adopted, however, institutional differences prevail. We see sharply different structures that determine timing, policy priorities, and effectiveness. Types of political economy—national variations in bargaining structures among labor, industry, commerce, farming, political parties, government agencies, and the judiciary—shape both policy priorities and their impact on human welfare.

Clearly, contrasts in the implementation of similar policies are critical in explaining variations in success. It is also clear that greater public participation—for instance, the disorderly openness of the United States—does not improve relative national performance in either environmental protection or occupational health and safety, although the protests of local antismoking activists in the United States may account for the numerous local zones of restriction and an above-average decline in the rate of male smoking. In fact, on average, countries with more-centralized, "elitist" bargaining arrangements achieve a higher level of compliance with emissions standards and workplace safety rules. This does not mean that citizens and activists are excluded from environmental decision making in corporatist democracies. As we have seen in the superior performance of Norway, Finland, Sweden, and Belgium in cleaning up the air or the German and Swedish edge in occupational safety and rehabilitation, or the Swedish advantage in nuclear safety, participation by labor, industry, and other economic interest groups through conventional party and government channels is a big plus. What is at issue here is not the mere fact of participation by environmental activists and their opponents but instead how that participation is channeled, conflicting interests aggregated, and consensus achieved. The mutual veto patterns of fragmented and decentralized political economies foster protracted conflict, slow progress, and, on occasion, paralysis; the net effect, a poor cost-benefit ratio over the long pull.

NOTES

1. Lack of comparative data or space precludes analysis of many other environmental problems and policies such as controversies over global warming; water pollution; the management of forests, land, wildlife, and solid wastes and hazardous wastes. For guiding me through the science relevant to environmental policy controversies I thank Bruce N. Ames, molecular biologist, and Allan H. Smith, epidemiologist.

2. In 1993 about one in four Americans still smoked, but 36% of those who failed to complete high-school smoke while only about 16% of those with graduate or professional degrees smoke, according to the National Household Survey on Drug Abuse. (*Wall Street Journal,* July 26, 1995.) Regarding synthetic chemicals, to say that synthetic chemicals in food intake are a trivial cancer risk is not to say that the runoff from the overuse of pesticides, fertilizers, and water in agriculture is not dangerous. An ecological chain reaction is set in motion by all the fertilizers, sewage, and runoff that end up in our river systems. For instance, nutrients dumped into the Mississippi stimulate an accelerating growth of algae and rising temperatures with consequent growth of phytoplankton. As they decompose they deplete the water of oxygen. Any fish or shrimp that cannot escape quickly suffocate. More efficient use of pesticides, fertilizer, and water would reduce this threat to aquatic life and still enhance the food supply.

3. Whenever NO_x and volatile organic compounds are present in the lower atmosphere, they form ozone, the main component of photochemical smog. Worldwide, indoor pollution may be more harmful than outdoor pollution. Very high levels of indoor air pollution are common among rural people in poor countries whose dwellings are smoky from burning coal or other fossil fuels. They account for as much as two-thirds of the global exposure to particulates. Such indoor air pollution contributes to acute respiratory infections in young children, chronic lung disease, and cancer in adults (World Bank, 1993, p. 91).

4. CO_2 emissions in tons per head among 11 rich democracies in 1989 (or nearest year) evidence a similar pattern: By this measure the three most polluting are the most-decentralized and fragmented democracies, the United States, Canada, and Australia (19.7 to 15.5 tons per capita); the least polluting are corporatist democracies—Switzerland, France, Italy, Israel (5.9 to 7.3 tons). In the middle are Germany, Britain, Japan, and New Zealand (10.5 to 7.8 tons). (*The Economist,* December 25, 1993 –January 7, 1994, p. 39.) CO_2 emission reduction in the 1990s continued the pattern. The top nine in percentage reduction are all corporatist democracies except for Britain. Of six poorest performers only one

(Finland) is corporatist. Except for Britain, the five English-speaking, most-fragmented and decentralized democracies all had substantial increases in CO_2 emissions. (*The Economist,* June 28, 1997, p. 41.)

5. Robert Kagan (1988, p. 732) observes that environmental regulatory regimes in the U.S. vary by region and type of industry and are sometimes quite "British" in style. For instance, federal officials are confrontational when enforcing strip-mine restoration laws in Appalachia but are cooperative mediators when doing the same on the Western plains. The difference is not cultural but structural: Western enforcers regulate a small number of large corporations, visit them regularly, and learn about their problems and trustworthiness. In turn, the large corporations hire environmental specialists to help smooth the agency-business interaction. Conversely, where regulators have infrequent contact with many small firms, legalistic, confrontational prosecution is common.

6. At this writing, Republican congressional leaders were belatedly recognizing that Republican activists in environmentally conscious states, towns, and affluent suburbs were upset at their attack on environmental protection. They were modifying the bill but still trying to surround the agencies with paralyzing rules (*Wall Street Journal,* March 6, 1996).

7. I concentrate on deaths because the reporting of injuries, especially of sprains and strains, are highly unreliable. In fact, of 16 studies of the relation between workers' compensation benefit levels and reported injury rates, most found that as benefits rise, reported injuries rise. Injured workers apparently report more injuries when benefits are generous, at least in the United States (Boden, 1995, pp. 284–285).

8. The German figures on work-injury expenditure since 1974 from ILO (1992), *Cost of Social Security 1984–1986,* are distorted by the accelerating strength of the Deutschmark from 1974 to 1979 and again after 1985. But figures on these expenditures for the United States and Sweden, both as a percentage of GDP and per capita, are roughly comparable. They show a continuation of the same pattern. By 1986 Sweden was spending 0.27% of GDP in work-injury insurance, the United States, 0.57. Per capita, the United States was spending $159, Sweden, $44 (taking account of Swedish devaluations of 1981 and 1982, this would be about $55). Regarding deaths from industrial accidents, the ILO (1985) *Yearbook of Labour Statistics,* table 28, and *ibid.* (1994), table 29, with measures not comparable to the WHO figures in table 15.2, permits comparison of all occupational deaths, all industries 1980–90 for the United States and Sweden but not Germany (whose figures include deaths from auto accidents while commuting). They show a continued decline for both countries: By 1986 Sweden was down to 1.3 deaths/100,000 population, the United States was down to 1.5 deaths, while spending 3.6 times what the Swedes spent on job-injury insurance per capita and more than twice what they spent as a percentage of GDP.

9. In a book emphasizing the changing conceptions of "disability," Deborah Stone (1985, p. 133) shows how unreliable clinical judgments are. She cites comprehensive research on the accuracy and consistency of disability determinations in the United States: in one study clinical teams and agency teams independently came to opposite conclusions on more than one-third of a sample of 1,500 cases. In another study comparing different state agencies using the same criteria there was complete agreement on disposition in only 22% percent of the cases. The limits of diagnostic procedures combined with the biases of doctors, administrators, courts, public opinion, and the uneven political pressures of applicants themselves assure very limited reliability and equity of decisions regarding disability benefits.

10. An exception to this rule: If older "disabled" workers stay on the job because disability benefits are reduced and the incentive to claim benefits is thereby lessened, unemployment rates and the duration of unemployment for the young may increase while the inflow into disability programs stabilizes. This was the case in 1985–90 when the correlation between unemployment rates and disability rates turned negative in the United States, Sweden, and the Netherlands but not in Germany (Aarts and De Jong, 1993, p. 23).

11. There is perhaps a hierarchy of sympathy for various types of disability. When I was at Michigan in the late 1950s a blind colleague briefed me on the amazing array of benefits the state supplied to the blind, even the partially blind. I then inquired into state benefits for the deaf, for paraplegics, and other groups. They were nowhere near what had already been achieved by organizations of and for the blind, with the possible exception of polio victims, whose plight had been dramatized by FDR and the immensely successful National Polio Foundation (Sills, 1957). One would be hard put to say that a partially blind person is worse off than a paraplegic. A psycho-political explanation for the differences in state largesse might go like this: A well-dressed blind person with a tapping cane and a handsome guide dog is as appealing on the street as the picture of the smiling child on crutches in the Polio Foundation posters. But a paraplegic in a wheelchair is less mobile. If she appears in public, she makes the passerby uneasy. And unlike the blind, the paraplegic cannot readily make her way up the Capitol steps or to the state Capitol offices to lobby for her particular group as the blind person and his dog can. All this began to change in the 1960s as other groups became more militant and better organized (e.g., in Centers for Independent Living), began to coordinate political action across types of disability, and acquired better technology and support.

12. Short-term or work-related sickness or injuries are covered under work-injury insurance; temporary loss of earning capacity is covered by sickness insurance. Because of abuse of sickness pay—workers calling in sick on Friday and Monday or prolonged episodes of illness—the Swedes, like the Germans and others, have reduced income replacement rates, adopted waiting periods, set lower income-replacement rates for the first two or three months' absence, and increased employers' share of costs for sickness insurance.

13. "Backdoor" because it merely froze the level of the social-security pension benefit that had been earned up until the time of disablement and stated that the totally disabled pensioners would not lose their pensions by subsequent failure to work and contribute payroll taxes.

14. In a case study of the Social Security Disability program administered by the SSA, Jerry Mashaw notes that in the early 1980s the SSA operated "the largest system of administrative adjudication in the world" (1983, p. 18). At that time, each year about 5,600 examiners reviewed 1,250,000 initial disability claims and 250,000 previously denied applications; about 150,000 subsequent appeals were taken to 625 administrative law judges.

15. Local protesters in France have been gassed and beaten, and in 1977 one was killed by police (Cook, Emel, and Kasperson, 1991/1992, p. 110).

16. Some of Jasper's informants mused that a small nuclear accident might be desirable so that the public would stop thinking that nuclear plants are completely safe (1990, p. 260).

17. This cost advantage of Sweden and France is partly based on their borrowing of American technology. But the differences are so large that the variables I have listed probably explain more.

18. As early as 1976, Sweden was using only about 60% as much energy to produce roughly the same per capita income as the United States.

19. For analysis of similarities and differences in radioactive waste-management strategies (including transport systems, repository operations, and engineered and geologic barriers) for the two leaders in this area, Sweden and France, see Cook, Emel, and Kasperson (1991/92). For comparisons with the United States see Cook, Emel, and Kasperson (1990) and Flynn (1995). For skeptical analysis of the prospects for designing complex, tightly coupled, technical systems that will never have accidents, see Charles Perrow's *Normal Accidents* (1984).

20. This account is my interpretation based on Joppke (1993).

21. A project staff member, Brenda McLaughlin, developed this list.

HEALTH PERFORMANCE
Affluence, Political Economy, and
Public Policy as Sources of Real Health

According to the Great Equation, Medical Care Equals Health. But the Great Equation is wrong. More available medical care does not equal better health. The best estimates are that the medical system (doctors, drugs, hospitals) affects about 10% of the usual indices for measuring health: whether you live at all (infant mortality), how well you live (days lost due to sickness), how long you live (adult mortality). The remaining 90 percent are determined by factors over which doctors have little or no control, from individual life style (smoking, exercise, worry), to social conditions (income, eating habits, physiological inheritance), to the physical environment (air and water quality). Most of the bad things that happen to people are at present beyond the reach of medicine. . . . No one is saying that medicine is good for nothing, only that it is not good for everything. Thus the marginal value of one—or one billion—dollars spent on medical care will be close to zero in improving health.

Aaron Wildavsky, "Doing Better and Feeling Worse" (1977)

A nation's health performance is difficult to measure and even more difficult to link to policy. In one of the earliest and most thorough cross-national evaluations of the effect of "health-care systems" in the literature, Odin Anderson (1972) compares the United States, Sweden, and England. He concludes that system contrasts in "input" are not connected in any direct way to any measurable output. Indeed, he abandons the attempt to link attributes of the system of medical care to customary indices of health and, in the end, argues that the main thing we can say with assurance is that Sweden is much superior to the United States in *equality of access* to doctors, dentists, drugs, and other medical facilities and personnel—whatever such equal access may mean for health—and that illness is more of a threat to family solvency in the United States. The British appear to be like the Swedes in equality of dignified access to physicians.

Leaving aside the question of whether equal access is a worthy goal in itself, what such studies and assertions overlook is the interdependence of all social policies. Sweden, like the Netherlands and similar big-spending corporatist democracies, not only distributes medical care more aggressively and fairly but also invests heavily in health-relevant programs of housing, safety, nutrition, health education, and child care, as well as environmental control, and draws the income floor for everyone higher and more uniformly; in short, it assures the least privileged of its population a higher standard of living. It is likely that the entire package—the interaction of all of these programs—is a major source of Sweden's superior health performance (Wilensky, 1975, pp. 98–104). (Evans and Stoddart, 1994, list five clusters of causes of health status that are difficult to sort out—lifestyle, environment, human biology, socioeconomic class, and health-care organization.)

A second problem is the definition of real health. If we use, say, such criteria as reduction in mortality rates of those over 75, we would put much effort and money into high-tech medicine and hospitals focused on prolonging the last years and months of life. Similarly, if we concentrate on morbidity and disability rates, we discover that they are inversely related to mortality rates; "strenuous efforts to save babies born with serious congenital defects will decrease the infant mortality rate while at the same time increasing the morbidity and disability rates for young children" (Anderson, 1972, p. 147). One indicator of health performance often cancels out another—a barrier to analysis which we can only partially surmount by striking a net balance of effects. If instead we adopt the broadest definition of health—well-being from the patient's perspective as "the absence of illness or injury, of distressing symptoms or impaired capacity" (Evans and Stoddart, 1994, p. 28)—we would turn our attention not only to medicine and illness but to the entire physical and social environment shaping human development. In this spirit, Patrick and Erickson (1993, pp. 5–6) devise a measure they call "health-related quality of life" defined as "the value assigned to the duration of life as modified by impairments, functional states, perceptions, and social opportunities that are influenced by disease, injury, treatment or policy" (p. viii). Their measure addresses the trade-off between how long people live and how well they live. There is a growing consensus among critics of modern medicine that the quality of health systems must be judged not only by the ability to provide life-extending treatments but by the capacity to promote health, reduce disability, and enhance the quality of life (Mechanic, 1994; Hadley, 1982; Patrick and Erickson, 1993). Obviously, even if we were precise about "quality of life," the database necessary to apply such ideas over time and across nations does not yet exist.

Beyond the problems of multiple causation of any measurable output and contrasting concepts of "health," there is a problem of short-run vs. long-run effects. Consider the outcome of a large-scale national health service like that of Britain. There is some direct evidence that the National Health Service is used most intensively by the least well off—the old, the young, the poor, the single (Rein, 1969)—although they do not tend to receive the highest quality service (Collins and Klein, 1985; Goddard and Smith, 1998). If, however, every other force making for the superior health of the upper half of the education and income distribution is not simultaneously equalized, the long-run effect of public health expenditures may be highly regressive. The poor die young—before they can contract the chronic diseases that dearly cost national health schemes. The more affluent citizens live to a riper age, chronically collecting health services paid for by the lifelong taxes of the deceased poor. A program that is highly progressive at a cross-sectional moment may be highly regressive in the lifetime of particular generations. (Wilensky, 1975, pp. 95–96.)

In view of these complexities, critics of modern medical-care systems argue that we can spend so much on medical care that we "cannot or will not spend adequately on other health enhancing activities" (Evans and Stoddart, 1994, p. 32). Critics sounding this theme see a choice between (1) the relative ineffectiveness of medical care and (2) the relative effectiveness of known environmental and personal hygiene risk factors for major cancers and other diseases—such measures as public health screening, early detection and treatment, and economic disincentives to young people's smoking, for example, tobacco taxes (McKinlay, McKinlay, and Beaglehole, 1989, pp. 193ff; Syme, 1986).

Some polemicists go further to argue not only that there is no evidence of any direct relationship between the cure of sickness and the progress of medicine, but also that organized medicine itself is iatrogenic (disease causing) (e.g., Illich, 1976, pp. 13 – 15, 26). They note negative side effects such as those associated with chemotherapy or the interaction of drugs; the high chances of becoming sick in a hospital, especially from the dangers of an intensive-care unit (Jennet, 1986, pp. 77, 88 – 89); and superinfections that result from the excessive use of antibiotics. They claim that the disabling treatment of nonexistent diseases is on the increase, for instance in unnecessary surgery. They complain that medical technology gets in the way of "care," the true calling of medicine.

Since the mid-1970s when fiscal constraints became central, there has been a tendency to individualize the health problem. Lifestyles chosen by individuals are the root of their poor health, so the solution is not to increase costly access to health care but to exhort individuals to do right by themselves—eat better, drink less, exercise more, keep clean, drive carefully, stop dissipating, and of course, stop smoking. As Wildavsky put it, do what your mother told you (1977, p. 122). In another of those strange convergences of ideology of the left and right, fiscal conservatives claim that cutting patient subsidies as a cost restraint will sacrifice mostly inefficient and inappropriate care while the radical advocates of alternative medicine and health-care strategies agree with the budget cutters that most of the health-care money spent on conventional medicine is wasted, although they see a role for government other than the provision of traditional medical care. They both seem to agree that an overload of health-care providers subverts economic and social well-being.

A more balanced view is that genetic inheritance aside, real health, however defined, is a product of economic development and its correlates—two of which are increased spending on medical care and more healthy lifestyles—and the organization of medical care. A review of the evidence follows. Then we can subject these observations to an empirical test on our 19 rich democracies.

AFFLUENCE VERSUS MEDICAL CARE

It is true that among modern countries many big advances in reducing mortality and overcoming disease occurred before the great expansion of expenditure on and access to doctors, drugs, and modern medical technology and hospitals. The control of epidemic diseases through sanitation, safe water, improved nutrition, and rising living standards led to reduced mortality, much of it before 1900 (Eisenberg and Kleinman, 1981; Powles, 1973; Dubos, 1959; McKeown, 1979; Fuchs, 1974; McKinlay and McKinlay, 1977; McKinlay et al., 1989; and McKeown, 1997). Even in the recent period of the ascendance of modern medical knowledge and technology, many diseases have not been cured or even influenced by medical intervention; they include the number two of the top killers, cancer, especially a few of the most important types (Jennett, 1986, p. 121; McKinlay et al., 1989, pp. 190 – 194), arthritis, advanced cirrhosis, and genital herpes, not to mention the common cold. In a study of the impact of medical measures on 10 major infectious diseases that account for nearly 40% of the total decline in the mortality rate from 1900 to 1973, McKinlay and McKinlay (1977) conclude that 6 of them—tuberculosis, scarlet fever, pneumonia, diphtheria, measles, and typhoid—showed negligible declines in their mortality rates subsequent to the date of medical intervention. This outcome cannot entirely be explained by already low rates when medical intervention began. For instance, even though medical measures against pneumonia, influenza, whooping cough, and diphtheria were introduced when the death rates were substantial, those mortality trends were unaffected by medical intervention. The researchers estimate that 3.5% is the reasonable upper limit of the total contribution of medical measures to the decline in total infectious-disease mortality in the United States since 1900.

At first glance, then, economic development and its health-inducing correlates are the main explanation for improved health before modern medicine expanded. Even after the medical complex greatly expanded, most of the decline in mortality and much of the gain in age-specific morbidity (especially among the nonaged) remained beyond the reach of medicine. An increased food supply meant improved nutrition and thus increased resistance to infectious diseases; improved hygiene and safer food and water also reduced exposure to infection; declining birthrates and the increase in child spacing (chap. 1) contributed mightily to those aspects of the standard of living that improve health; and finally the spread of mass education diffused health information.

But a first glance is not sufficient, for it is also true that medical intervention has substantial effects in preventing, alleviating, managing, or slowing the progress of many problems. Both preventive and therapeutic measures have been successful. Examples of useful preventive measures include vaccines for polio, rubella, measles, pertussis, mumps, and tetanus (Egbuonu and Starfield, 1985b, p. 48; Eisenberg and Kleinman, 1981, p. 1). Prenatal care and diagnosis can be used to assure a normal birth and reduce rates of neonatal death (Eisenberg and Kleinman, 1981, p. 1; Hollingsworth, 1986, pp. 213–214). Mortality resulting from circulatory diseases has been reduced by the use of diagnostic procedures, such as angiograms, ultrasound imaging, nuclear scanning, and positron-emission tomography (Hollingsworth, Hage, and Hanneman, 1990, p. 105).

Successful therapeutic measures include antibiotic treatment of diseases, such as pneumonia and meningitis, syphilis and gonorrhea, malaria, yaws, typhoid, and acute rheumatic fever (Eisenberg and Kleinman, 1981, p. 1; Starfield et al., 1985, p. 58); diuretics and alpha blockers to control hypertension (Eisenberg and Kleinman, 1981, p. 1); drug treatments for tuberculosis, tetanus, diphtheria, and scarlet fever (Illich, 1976, p. 23); various treatments for asthma (Wissow and Starfield, 1985a, 130–133); open heart surgery to correct valvular defects (Eisenberg and Kleinman, 1981, p. 1; Jennet, 1986, p. 115); balloon angioplasty, bypass and vascular surgery, defibrillator implantation, clot-dissolving streptokinase, and calcium blockers for various types of circulatory diseases (Hollingsworth et al., 1990, p. 105); iron supplements for iron deficiency anemia (Hutton and Starfield, 1985, p. 87); chemotherapy for childhood leukemia (Eisenberg and Kleinman, 1981, p. 1; Jennet, 1986, p. 121); drugs that abort acute psychotic episodes and minimize their occurrence (Eisenberg and Kleinman, 1981, p. 1); and renal dialysis (Siegler and Sheldon, 1987, p. 1; Jennett, 1986, p. 36). We might also add to the list of successful therapies efforts to prevent child abuse by fostering better parent-child relations in the prenatal or early postnatal period (Wissow and Starfield, 1985b, p. 66). More recently, beta-blocking agents have been shown to be unequivocally beneficial in postmyocardial infarction patients (McKinlay et al., 1989, p. 190) and improved medical management of hypertension explains perhaps one-sixth to two-fifths of the 1970–80 decline in stroke mortality (*ibid.*, p. 194).

Even the most prominent and critical medical researchers concede something to the medical complex. For instance, Thomas McKeown (1997) notes, "Medical intervention was valuable before sulfa drugs and antibiotics became available. Immunization protected people against smallpox and tetanus; antitoxin treatment limited deaths from diphtheria; appendicitis, peritonitis, and ear infection responded to surgery; Salvarsan was a long-sought 'magic bullet' against syphilis; intravenous therapy saved people with severe diarrheas; and improved obstetric care prevented childbed fever" (p. 12). But he estimates that all these medical measures account for only a small part of the decrease in deaths attributed to all infectious diseases before 1935. Similarly, McKinlay et al. (1989, p. 202), using their index of "a life expectancy free of disability" (estimated for 1964, 1974, and 1985), conclude that "although overall life expectancy has increased over the two decades, most of this increase was in years of disability" (p. 181; cf. Powles, 1973). But they also report an increase in life expectancy free of disability for 65-year-old males of 3.9 years and an increase for 65-year-old females of 3.2 years (table 3), far from trivial.

Regarding mortality and longevity, the more specific we are about what types of spending and what types of medical services have an effect, the more positive results we obtain. For example, the greater the proportion of total health spending coming from government (a clue to equality of access), the stronger the effect in reducing mortality. For older groups this makes sense: government-insured access to medical intervention reduces potentially lethal illnesses not only for the well-off but for everyone, improving the country averages. Why more "nationalized" systems should reduce mortality for young adults is less obvious: it probably reflects a more efficient and widespread trauma service, something private medicine has no incentive to provide. (Cochrane, St. Leger, and Moore, 1978, p. 204.) And, although this has not been a strong point for medicine in the United States, there may be a modest preventive medicine component, largest in countries that aggressively supply health information to the young through medical clinics, schools, and family policies.

Finally, new knowledge in biology and biomedical techniques such as genetic recombinations and imaging together with information systems have begun to reshape all health disciplines. Their great potential for specifying causal processes and improving public health is outlined by Susser and Susser (1996, pp. 671–672). On the horizon are such interventions as skin replacement, new uses for lasers, blood substitutes, new vaccines, disc transplantations, and cancer-susceptibility testing (Mechanic and Rochefort, 1996, p. 243) and, more generally, gene therapy.

Three additional caveats must be added to the idea that economic development and its correlates are the main story of improved health to which conventional medical intervention is a minor theme. First, some diseases have increased with rising affluence. As Hollingsworth notes, ischemic heart disease rates rise with increasing economic development, after controls for age: "While heart disease is associated with genetic predisposition, sex [i.e., gender], inactivity, smoking, hypertension, and stress . . . many epidemiological studies have found a link between a high incidence of heart disease and high annual consumption of calories, protein, saturated fat, cholesterol, and sugar"—eating habits associated with a high GDP per capita (1986, pp. 269–270). The incidence of cancer of the colon and rectum among adult males also increased with economic development, probably because affluent societies have, at least in the recent past, increased the intake of refined carbohydrates and removed dietary fiber.

The second problem with any assertion that economic level explains the lion's share of good health is that public spending on health care rises markedly at high levels of affluence. In my 19-country comparison below, the correlation is so strong that no regression equation can sort out the separate influence of GNP per capita and that of public spending per capita (as a clue to equal access to heath care) (Burkitt, 1971; Lancaster, 1990, p. 504). The third qualification is the presence even before 1900 of many scientists and practitioners within the medical establishment who developed and disseminated biomedical knowledge. They shaped public health measures against infectious diseases, environmental health measures such as sewage treatment, water purification, safe food processing, and factory safety; and they encouraged health education and healthful behavior. In short, the health effects of a rising standard of living are mediated by medical-care delivery systems; most public health officials responsible for sanitation, disease control, and immunization in this early period were physicians (Hollingsworth et al., 1990, pp. 88–89, 111).

Finally, even if the medical establishment had little or no effect on mortality, morbidity, or other major indicators of health, access to medical care improves the quality of life by decreasing pain, restoring the human machine to normal functioning, curing some diseases and easing the effects of others. It is the garage repair function of modern medicine. Like efficient auto mechanics, medical personnel fix broken bones, cuts, and bruises, replace parts, stitch you back together, and make you comfortable when you are sick. Students of medical care label this "the medical engineering model." (Hollingsworth, 1986, pp. 268–269. Cf. Mechanic, 1994.) It may be a peculiarly Anglo-American metaphor— viewing human health in mechanistic terms—but these functions remain the same everywhere, with generally benign effects.

Thus, despite healthy skepticism about the efficacy of medicine, it is clear that access to drugs, hospitals, doctors and other service providers alleviates suffering and has substantial benefits for longevity, mortality, and even for real health. Of course, affluence—whether it is the riches of a nation or of subgroups within the nation—is a major determinant of health outputs. But so is organized medicine.

The Organization and Delivery of Medical Care[1]

Beyond affluence and equal access to medical care, some aspects of the organization and delivery of care are important in a nation's health performance. Among the most significant national variations in organizational arrangements are the degree of centralization; the degree of state control over financing, prices, and personnel; the presence or absence of global budgeting; the amount of public spending per capita; the total number of physicians and the ratio of specialists to primary-care physicians, nurses, and midwives; effort devoted to preventive care; administrative costs and waste, which are related to the private/public mix; and dependence on hospitals vs. outpatient and/or home care. Some aspects of the organization of society, especially the amount of poverty and inequality and economic insecurity, also shape health outcomes.

Centralization, State Control, and Global Budgeting

All rich democracies other than the United States embrace universal coverage for medical care, based on principles of social right and shared risk; central control of budgets; and financing from compulsory individual and employer contributions and/or government general revenues to fund national health insurance or a national health service like that of the United Kingdom (the contributions are everywhere related to income). All permit the insured to supplement the universally assured standard of medical care with extra care—for example, private rooms or private doctors and nurses privately paid for. All, including the United States, rely to some extent on state coordination of health-care services; all ration health care. They ration explicitly through legislation and administrative decisions (the Oregon scheme is an extreme example[2]); or implicitly through general constraints on expenditures, entitlements, and expensive technologies while the actual allocation of services is determined within doctor/patient transactions (Mechanic, 1995, p. 1659; 1992, p. 1719); or through ability to pay (by cost sharing via deductibles, premiums, coinsurance, and payments at point of service)—or all three. The specific forms of coverage, finance, and budgeting, the balance between public and private provision, and the balance among forms of rationing vary greatly. And these national variations, by determining what care is distributed to whom, do shape national health outcomes.

Since Odin Anderson's three-country study of 1972 there have been several systematic cross-national studies that successfully link organizational features of medical systems to national health performance. (Blomquist, 1979; Hollingsworth, 1986; and various OECD health care monographs, 1985a, 1987b, 1993f, 1994, 1996b). One of the most thorough, systematic, intensive, and extensive is a study of the effects of state intervention in medical care in Britain, France, Sweden, and the United States from 1890 to 1970 with some updating to the late 1980s (Hollingsworth et al., 1990 and Hollingsworth, Hanneman, and Hage, 1992). Using causal modeling, making both historical and cross-national comparisons, these researchers demonstrate that centralized control of funding, prices, and personnel under state auspices is a powerful predictor of a democratic nation's health performance.[3] They measure system performance by the multiple and sometimes conflicting goals of *levels of health* (mainly measured by age-sex standardized death rates); *innovativeness* (the speed with which the system adopts and diffuses new technologies, services, or programs—whether they are low-cost and highly efficient, or complex and reach only a few patients); *social efficiency* ("how much output is achieved relative to cost—that is, the attainment of a certain level of health at some per capita cost" [p. 13]); and *equality* (how equitably access to medical resources is distributed by region, social class, and income and how much variation there is in levels of health by class and income).

Their index of centralization of state control over revenues is based on year-by-year data for each nation on proportions of medical system revenues contributed by central government and social insurance revenues, by local and regional government authorities, and by private-sector actors. Their index of centralization of state control over prices and personnel, again by nation-year, is based on (1) data on the proportion of physicians employed by each of the above levels (including self-employment with the private sector) and (2) weighted equally, and similarly constructed, data on proportions of all medical expenditures that occurred at prices regulated by each level (central, local, and private sector).

These attributes of organization, of course, can vary independently: a central government can increase funding for medical care and subsidize high-tech innovations in a system with a large "private" sector without controlling prices and personnel—with the sure outcome of a cost explosion, social inefficiency, and inequality in access and level of health (*ibid.*,

p. 11; Maxwell, 1981). This is a description of trends in the health-care (non-) system of the United States. In all their analysis, Hollingsworth et al. (1990) control for socioeconomic development, including education, communication, age structure, and real GNP per capita, so they can determine the distinct effects of organizational arrangements. The main findings, consistent with other cross-national research, follow:

1. Central state funding and control over prices and personnel (via direct employment, capitation payments, and/or government bargaining with providers) reduces inequality in access to health care by class and region, increases the volume of services available, and improves the national level of health (*ibid.*, chaps. 4 and 8).

2. There is a natural history of health policy in which state funding leads to increased control over prices and personnel. State funding by itself improves access to care and to some extent reduces national mortality rates. At first, expanded access through state funding increases costs and thereby decreases social efficiency, but in time state funding leads to state involvement in many other aspects of medical-care delivery not only because of concern about cost but also because governments are advocates of broader public interests (vs. interests of commercial insurers, pharmaceutical firms, and providers). Eventually that involvement leads to greater control over prices and personnel (including the supply of doctors, and limits on specialization) which in turn brings an increment of mortality reduction greater than that attributed to state funding alone. Together, the three forms of state intervention—control over funding, prices, and personnel—improve the trade-off between mortality reduction and cost escalation, that is, the combination increases social efficiency (*ibid.*, pp. 150–151, 180–181).

3. In the rare periods and cases where the state funds care but has very little control over prices and personnel (as in the U.S. Medicaid and Medicare programs) medical costs are relatively high and increase faster, access is less equal, and national health outputs are somewhat worse than at times and places where public funding is combined with regulation of prices and personnel—even if the private sector provides the best (or at least the most expensive) care in the world to affluent citizens (*ibid.*, pp. 91–92, 150–152).

4. Centralized state intervention redirects expenditures. It inspires efforts to reduce costs and search for more effective services. It results in more primary care, less duplication of expensive equipment and more restraint in its use (*ibid.*, pp. 70–72, 81–85, 114–116, 181–182, 186–190). As I suggest below, it also results in more effective preventive care.

5. The effect of centralized state intervention on rates of technical scientific innovation is mixed. On the one hand, it fosters a faster diffusion of vaccines and more effective screening programs (*ibid.*, pp. 179–182).[4] Using U.S. experience where federal intervention and funding has fluctuated, Egbuonu and Starfield (1985a, 1985b) report that both immunization and screening have been more effective when they have been centralized and that these public health measures when properly organized drastically reduce disease morbidity and mortality. On the other hand, centralized state intervention slows down the adoption of expensive technology demanded by small, educated high-income groups. Again, the net result is greater social efficiency—a bigger health bang for the buck. (Hollingsworth et al., 1990, pp. 135, 186–190.)

6. Privatized systems with low degrees of state intervention lead to a higher quality of care for upper-income groups—in many cases excess care; social and geographical inequalities of access; an accent on crisis cures rather than prevention; a cost explosion; and lower levels of national health. At least initially, privatization also results in more power and income for providers (*ibid*, p. 205) but this appears to be politically unstable, as I suggest in a discussion of the private/public mix below.

7. Controlling patient demand by cost-sharing (copayments, deductibles, coinsurance) increases inequality of access, especially for the chronically ill, the aged, and the poor. It is limited in restraining cost growth because it does not control the supply of services, many of them wasteful and inappropriate.

8. The case of Britain suggests some upper limit to the advantages of strong state intervention. The United Kingdom's National Health Service (NHS) is centralized, comprehensive, universal, tax-financed, and globally budgeted. It has achieved one of the lowest-cost health service among all modern nations (7.1% of GDP in 1992 compared to 8.7% in Germany and 13.6% in the United States); a high degree of equality of access; a reduction in inequality of health outcomes by class and to a lesser extent by regions; a good fit between need and utilization; a high degree of social efficiency (*ibid.* pp. 146–148, 166–167, 201–202); and extraordinary and persistent popular support. But its health status in my 19-country analysis is below average. And in recent years doctors, although long dominant in policymaking and implementation, have become restive with the stringent cost controls, the long queues for elective surgery, an inadequate supply of doctors, specialists, hospital beds, and some high-cost technologies, and a generally low level of innovation and high level of bureaucratic rigidity. Upper-income patients are as restive as the doctors. Chapter 5 describes Prime Minister Thatcher's radical reform of 1989–90 which was designed to cut costs even further in this already cheap system. The reforms so far have neither cut costs nor substantially changed the behavior of physicians and health authorities, though they did increase the power and status of general practitioners and primary-care providers. Instead they inflated the number and salaries of "bureaucrats," increased administrative costs, and accelerated copayments. In short, an efficiency-focused centralized system that is underfunded will tend toward excessive bureaucratic controls. In an attempt to improve service and reduce administrative excess, Labour Prime Minister Tony Blair has increased NHS funding (an extra $2.4 billion in the 1997–98 budget) and reversed some of Thatcher's reforms, especially her "internal market system."

These findings, however solid, are rather general, and the output measures are limited to mortality reduction. The rest of this section elaborates them by examining more specific dimensions of organization that have been linked to one or another health output.

An Index of Real Health

To arrive at an index of real health as part of our analysis of system outputs, I asked, "What health indicators could we expect to be affected by intervention of the medical community, indicators that could also be measured cross-nationally in all 19 countries?" We rejected numerous indicators for which knowledge about the effect of medical care is limited or dubious and cross-national comparability is insufficient (e.g., mental illness, peptic ulcers, cirrhosis of the liver, and other ailments listed at the beginning of this chapter). We used homicide rates, divorce, death by fire, auto accidents, and similar health risks in a separate analysis of the sources of mayhem in chapter 14. We ended up with five dimensions of real health that themselves are intercorrelated: infant mortality rate per 1,000 live births; life expectancy at age one for males; the same for females; circulatory system disease deaths per 100,000 males aged 65–74; and deaths from pregnancy and childbirth complications per 100,000 females aged 25–34. Countries were ranked on each health indicator, using natural cutting points for a four-point scale (0–3) and they were equally weighted. For the pregnancy and childbirth component we used a three-year average to avoid large year-to-year variations in these very low rates.[5] The summary scores ranged from Sweden's 14.0 to Austria's 3.0. We did extensive correlational analysis including multiple regression experiments using data from the mid-1960s, early 1970s, and 1980. We found nothing important that cannot be seen in the cross-tabulations and rankings of tables 16.1, 16.2, 16.3, and 16.4. The following sections relate this index to the density of doctors, the ratio of specialists to primary-care physicians, the density of nurses and midwives, and then the private/public mix and types of political economy.

Doctor Density and Real Health

The density of physicians (number per 100,000 population) everywhere went up with economic growth. Both variables—affluence and the supply of doctors—are strongly correlated with one another and with reduced mortality and other health indicators. But in cross-national perspective and at the level of socioeconomic development achieved by our rich democracies, it is not clear that by itself doctor density makes much difference in health outputs. In their four-country study of trend data over an 80-year time span, Hollingsworth et al. (1990) conclude that increases in physician density, net of other factors, does reduce age-gender specific mortality (pp. 108–109, 187). In contrast, a cross-sectional study of 1970 data on age-specific mortality rates up to age 64 in 17 of our 19 rich democracies using similar multiple regression methods (Cochrane, St. Leger, and Moore, 1978) finds a *positive* correlation between the prevalence of doctors and mortality rates, especially in younger age groups. No controls they could introduce—five other health-service indicators (including the percentage of obstetricians and pediatricians), health-care spending, dietary indicators, and several economic and demographic factors—none of these made the anomaly go away. Similar findings appear in other studies (Fuchs, 1974, pp. 31–39).

Using a wider range of health indicators in 1980 for our 19 rich democracies, I find little or no relationship between doctor density and health outputs. Table 16.1 aligns the index scores and ranks with doctor density data. There is no apparent association.

In tables incorporating type of political economy, not reported here, a close match between ranking on doctor density and health performance appears only in eight countries at the extremes: three left-corporatist democracies score quite high in both (Sweden, Norway, and Denmark) while four decentralized and fragmented democracies score below average in both (United Kingdom, Ireland, New Zealand, United States). Among corporatist democracies, Finland is an exception (below average in both); among least-corporatist democracies, Australia is an exception (average in both). The other 10 countries, whatever

TABLE 16.1 Density of physicians (circa 1984) and real health (circa 1980)

Doctor density (rate per 10,000 population)[a]	Real Health Index[b]		
	Good to excellent health performance	Average health performance	Poor to fair health performance
High (29-43)		Italy 8.5 France 10.0 Belgium 8.0	Israel 5.0
Medium (22-26)	Sweden 14.0 Denmark 11.0 Netherlands 12.5 Norway 12.0	Australia 8.0 Finland 6.0	Austria 3.0 W. Germany 4.0
Low (14-21)	Canada 12.0 Japan 12.0 Switzerland 13.5	United States 8.0	New Zealand 4.0 United Kingdom 6.0 Ireland 5.0

[a]World Health Organization, *World Health Statistics Annual, 1988* (Geneva: World Health Organization, 1988), pp. 43–70.

[b]See footnotes to table 16.4 and text. Health score is next to country.

their national bargaining arrangements, evidence large discrepancies in their rank in doctor density and their rank in health performance. This is reflected in the lack of any 19-country correlation between an abundance of doctors and good national health performance ($r = .02$) Much more important are the types of health-care providers and the organizational contexts in which they practice.

Ratio of Specialists to Primary-Care Physicians, Nurses, and Midwives

As the density of physicians everywhere climbed with economic growth, the proportion of all physicians who are specialists also climbed—in recent decades at an accelerating rate. By 1970, the proportion of specialists had risen from a trivial figure at the turn of the century to 34% in Britain, 42% in France, 56% in Sweden, and 77% in the United States (Hollingsworth et al., 1992, p. 14 and table 1). Recent figures show that the specialist share of all doctors in Canada and Germany is a bit less than half while the United States may be headed for a specialist share of 86%, a figure based on the choices of all 1992 graduates of medical schools (Koop, 1995, p. 44).[6]

In the absence of state control, more privatized, commercialized systems accelerate the trend toward increasing medical specialization. A high proportion of specialists with little constraint on their high-tech services has several effects: it speeds the diffusion of innovation, especially very expensive technologies (Hollingsworth et al., 1990, pp. 186–190); it means more expensive services in hospitals and more staff; it reduces age-sex standardized mortality rates but at ever-increasing cost (pp. 30–31). Thus, a high ratio of specialists reduces social efficiency. In fact, both the trend toward doctor density and a rising ratio of specialists boost medical expenditures more than they reduce mortality (p. 151). In other words, there is a diminishing return from increases in this most-expensive, labor-intensive service.

That government policy shapes the specialist ratio in all systems—the most-privatized as well as the most-nationalized and centralized—is illustrated by the United States, the extreme case of specialization with the largest "private" sector. Since World War II, beginning with the Hospital Construction Act of 1946 (popularly named the Hill-Burton Act), government policy has favored the expansion of the supply and diffusion of hospital-based care, biomedical research, and innovations in medical technology, as well as the training of specialists who further the demand for such sophisticated care (Jacobs, 1995, pp. 144–146). Under Hill-Burton, the government dramatically increased the number and geographical dispersion of hospital beds, not just in metropolitan areas but in smaller cities and rural areas. Then it actively promoted the training of specialists who would practice in these hospitals, providing acute care rather than primary or preventive care. Finally, it generously funded medical research and development through the National Institutes of Health (whose inflation-adjusted budget escalated from $26 million in 1945 to $7 billion in 1990) and to a lesser extent through the Departments of Defense and Energy (*ibid.*, pp. 144–145). In 1998, Congress doubled the NIH budget to $15.6 billion. The financing and diffusion of hospitals, especially acute care personnel, and the growth of a large market for innovative medical technology and drugs are major causes of the extraordinary specialist ratio and cost explosion of the U.S. medical-care system. As Lawrence Jacobs suggests,

> While other countries also have encouraged the development of medical technology, the U.S. government's unprecedented degree of involvement has contributed to the far greater availability of magnetic resonance imaging (MRI), radiation therapy units, organ transplantation, and other innovations than is the case in Canada, Germany, and other countries. The expansion of supply has been financed by direct government subsidies as well as by insurance companies and Medicare, which reimburse hospitals for capital expenditures. (p. 145)

In short, U.S. public policy gave priority to increasing the supply of specialized, technologically intensive health care; widening access took a back seat. This locked the United States into a payment system—procedure-based, fee-for-service—that discouraged primary care, preventive care, and low-tech solutions. The resulting institutionalization of expensive care made it more difficult to reverse course and embrace universal coverage, quite apart from the political-system barriers discussed in every chapter in this book. In contrast, all other modern democracies began with equality of access as their primary goal, which forced them to concentrate hospital care in fewer places, multiply and disperse primary-care clinics, increase the supply of GPs or family practitioners, and discourage overspecialization. Where they established universal coverage but still centered their care in hospitals as in Sweden and Germany, their costs did rise beyond the norm (see table 16.4), but they were in a position to consolidate the high-tech care and ration it more fairly according to need rather than income.

Everywhere specialists take enormous pride in their work and demand munificent reward for their prolonged training and scarce skills. If there is little countervailing power, their income skyrockets. For instance, the 1994 median income of the seven highest paid specialists in the United States (income derived only from practice) ranged from $279,060 (neurosurgeon) to $209,490 (gastroenterologist). GPs earned a median of only $100,240 (*Wall Street Journal,* December 21, 1995).

How difficult it is to dampen the enthusiasm of highly trained specialists for expensive procedures that only they have mastered or hope to master is illustrated by Norway's attempt to rein in heart transplants. In rationalizing health-care priorities the health planners were able to lengthen waiting lists for least-urgent surgeries and limit severe burn cases and liver transplants to one hospital to avoid duplicate facilities and personnel and gain the benefit of more intensive specialization. But later when they tried to limit heart transplants, they failed. First they decided that Norway would do none, that it is cost-beneficial to fly these patients to the United Kingdom or United States at much lower cost than the cost of training and paying Norwegian doctors to do such transplants. Norwegian heart surgeons, however, like their colleagues everywhere, love high-tech medicine; they think it is glamorous, exciting, not to mention a matter of national pride. So an Oslo hospital, on the sly, built up heart transplant skills (practicing on pigs) and called a press conference after their first attempt on humans. The headline: "Successful Heart Transplant in Norway." The politicians and health planners were both surprised and defeated by the publicity. Now Norway does heart transplants and is second only to the United States in the percentage of the population having transplants. (Personal interviews; see also Hollingsworth et al., 1992, pp. 32 – 33.) If Norway has trouble controlling specialist enthusiasms, the United States, with its much higher specialist ratio should have much greater difficulty.

It is a great irony that the United States has become a cash cow supporting both publicly and privately funded medical research, which is then diffused worldwide (Aaron, 1996, p. 55). If the United States ever got control over its profligate spending, most other rich democracies might have to increase their medical research and development budgets or suffer the loss of virtually free science and technology.

After decades of specialist expansion and cost escalation, most rich democracies are now attempting to increase the role of primary-care physicians (Eurostat, 1995, p. 116). Clearly, total costs are lower where primary-care doctors function as gatekeepers for specialists and hospital services (*OECD Observer,* February/March, 1995, p. 25; Glaser, 1991, p. 411). Whether an abundance of general practitioners (e.g., family practitioners, pediatricians, and general internists) yields better health performance is another matter. The British NHS— a high ratio of primary-care physicians but a below-average national health record (see my table 16.4)—suggests caution. Because we have data on the ratio of specialist to primary-care physicians for only a few of our 19 countries, we cannot systematically assess the effect on health indicators beyond what we have seen in four- or five-country comparisons (e.g., Hollingsworth et al., 1990; Weiner, 1987) or the 10-country exploration of primary care by Starfield (1992). In assessing the relative impact, we have to rely on leads from more intensive accounts. They suggest these questions: (1) Do specialists have a greater impact in widely diffusing biomedical knowledge to the population than GPs? (2) Which type provides most continuity of treatment? (3) Which pays most attention to the multiple problems that shape an illness (the "whole patient")? (4) Which gives most time and effective advice aimed at prevention? (5) Which has most effect on measurable indicators? Can we connect any of the above to health outcomes?

Most physicians are ambiguous disseminators of biomedical knowledge. The clinical mentality that accents the value of the patient's individual experience and the physician's personal, intuitive judgment (Wilensky, 1964b, pp. 148–150; Freidson, 1970) often results in antiscientific, anti-intellectual prejudices. This is evident in a reluctance to pay attention to systematic research that might show little benefit from new technology, new drugs, or surgical intervention (Payer, 1988, pp. 36, 51–53, 125–126). It is also evident in the great lag between scientific consensus about diet and prescription habits of physicians. It is not clear whether specialists or GPs are most resistant to scientific evidence. Much depends on their degree of interaction with knowledgeable persons. The early studies of the diffusion of innovative techniques and drugs show that the early adopters of scientific innovations were sociometric stars, physicians at the center of professional networks. They also read the medical journals more frequently and thoroughly. In contrast, the more socially isolated or peripheral physicians, typically solo practitioners, were slow to learn of these techniques, and incidentally, avoided risk (Coleman, Katz, and Menzel, 1966, pp. 79–93, 106–111). That suggests the hypothesis that specialists in research hospitals or large clinics would be more receptive to science than GPs unless the latter were also practicing in hospitals and interacting with them.

Beyond the possible edge of specialists as disseminators of medical knowledge and hence improved population health, they clearly do much to improve the quality of life. For instance, the great advances in surgical procedures combined with skilled physical therapy have restored increasing numbers of patients to normal functioning after severe trauma (as we have seen in earlier discussion of the garage-repair function of modern medicine).

On the other hand, the clinical mentality with its focus on the individual patient, perhaps most developed among GPs, is indispensable for maintaining the trust at the heart of doctor-patient relations and ultimately effective health care (Mechanic, 1992, 1995, p. 1658). Trust in turn is rooted in the degree to which the relationship is continuous. Continuity is much less likely in systems with high degrees of specialization and complexity. The continuity of care provided by a family doctor or pediatrician not only gives the patient a sense that she has an advocate vis-à-vis the bureaucratic and commercial pressures on medical care, but also gives the doctor a much better base of knowledge to guide her diagnosis and treatment. Physicians who know their patients and give them the time to learn more of their condition can avoid the single-disease error, the failure to uncover the relevant history or multiple conditions or multiple causes of a condition—in other words the incapacity to place the patient's ailment in larger contexts. Without continuous oversight by a primary-care physician, medical care is often fragmented, uncoordinated, and ineffective, if not dangerous.

A hint that societies with a medium or medium-high ratio of GPs to specialists have better health performance comes from the four-country study by Hollingsworth et al. (1992). They found that although increases in total number of physicians and the number of specialists both reduce mortality, the sheer number of doctors has a bigger effect than the percentage of specialists. Based on regression analysis the study concludes, "Net of other factors more state control over prices and personnel, interacting with more investment in the number of doctors, has a beta of −0.78 with age-sex-standardized mortality rates; state control over prices and personnel interacting with the level of specialization has a beta of −0.48" (*ibid.*, p. 25). They suggest that both types of practitioners have a good effect in all countries, partly because of the marked increase in this century in the number of visits to doctors. As doctor density increased and access to care widened, doctor-patient interaction increased. The findings on physician density and mortality are consistent with the argument that GPs, compared to specialists, disseminate a broader array of biomedical knowledge throughout society. Specialists may "keep up" better and be a bit more open to scientific evidence and innovation, but they speak to a narrower range of issues and treat only part of the organic whole. Continuity of primary care in which the whole patient can be assessed and managed apparently has a greater effect in reducing population mortality than the uncoordinated care of specialists, however dramatic the latter's impact on the smaller number of intensive-care patients. What is needed, however, is studies of these two broad types of care on a broader range of health indicators and a broader range of countries.

If an abundance of GPs, say about 50%, can favorably shape health outcomes, what about an abundance of nurses, nurse-practitioners, and midwives? Relating our real health index (described above and in footnote "a" in table 16.4) to data on the number of nurses and midwives per 10,000 population for all of our countries but Israel, we see that the cadres of nurses and similar staff do contribute to good health performance.

Table 16.2 shows that a high nurse-midwife density is associated with good to excellent health performance. Of the seven countries ranked highest in health outputs, five have the highest density of nurses and midwives. And of the eleven countries ranked average to poor in health performance, only two (Australia and the United Kingdom) are high in this staff category. The truly deviant cases in that table are the Netherlands (ranked 15th in nurse-midwife density but 3rd in health performance) and the United Kingdom (2nd in nurse-midwife ratio but 13th in health performance). It is possible that staffing figures for these two countries are not comparable (see footnotes b and c), but if they are roughly accurate, here is a possible explanation. The United Kingdom exceeds every other country in its GP to specialist ratio. If it also ranks so high in the nurse ratio we might infer that the specialist/hospital sector is underfunded and understaffed, as is the whole system (see chap. 5). Perhaps Britain's NHS represents the extreme beyond which the benign effects of GPs and nurses diminish. The Netherlands exception (low nurse/midwife density, excellent health performance) may be explained by the exclusion of midwives from the figure. (I could not confirm this.) For, in fact, Holland evidences a strong preference for midwife-attended home births. Public insurance pays for midwife and GP fees for a normal home birth and will reimburse for childbirths in a hospital only with a diagnosis of complications. Thus, it has the highest rate of home deliveries in Europe. (Glaser, 1991, pp. 250.) Consistent with my hypothesis, its infant mortality rate puts the Netherlands in the best-performing 2 to 6 of our 19 rich democracies from 1960 to 1990 (Scheiber, Poullier, and Greenwald, 1992, table 25).

Although I could not find data for many countries on the midwife ratio alone, there is good evidence that they, like nurses, nurse practitioners, and similar physician assistants, presumably less skilled than physicians, can do much of the traditional more routine work of the physician, such as immunization, distributing birth control devices, treating common infections, and educating patients in good health habits—sometimes with better effect

TABLE 16.2 Density of nurses and midwives and real health (circa 1980)[a]

Nurses and mid-wives per 10,000 population 1981	Real Health Index		
	Good to excellent health performance	Average health performance	Poor to fair health performance
High (68-85)	Sweden 14.0 Norway 12.0 Denmark 11.0 Switzerland 13.5 Canada 12.0	Australia 8.0	United Kingdom 6.0[b]
Medium (47-62)	Japan 12.0	Finland 6.0 United States 8.0 France 10.0	New Zealand 4.0 Ireland 5.0 Austria 3.0
Low (10-39)	Netherlands 12.5[c]	Italy 8.5 Belgium 8.0[b]	W. Germany 4.0

[a]Source for number of nurses and midwives per 10,000 population: OECD, *Measuring Health Care 1960–1983: Expenditure, Costs, and Performance* (Paris: OECD, 1985a), p. 115. For real health index, see footnotes to my table 16.4 and text.

[b]There is a large discrepancy with figures published by the German Association of Hospitals (Alber, 1988), which puts the Belgium nurse-midwife ratio much higher (about 77) and the UK ratio much lower (about 45).

[c]German Hospital Association data (Alber, 1988, p. 260).

(Ford, 1992; Mechanic and Rochefort, 1996, p. 259). A multiple regression study of prefecture reductions in infant mortality in Japan (whose rate of improvement was the best of our 19 countries, 1960–80) found that public health nurses per 100,000 population was the only significant medical intervention that is strongly correlated with reduced infant mortality. The nonmedical variables that were robust were economic development (per capita income and urban occupation) and low population density. (Morio, 1985.) The place we might expect midwives to be on average as good as or better than physicians is in reducing the neonatal mortality rate. Levy, Wilkinson, and Marine (1971) report a clinical trial in Madera County, California in which delivery of prenatal care by nurse midwives resulted in significant reductions in the neonatal mortality rate in the county; subsequent reversion to care by physicians resulted in an increase in the neonatal mortality rate. These are at least clues to the results in table 16.3. In the absence of good cross-national data we can speculate that countries that do best in universal access, in assuring equality of care, and in reducing inequalities of outcomes, as well as cost control probably approach 50% in their reliance on GPs, and are well staffed with nurses and midwives.

In sum: Although data are generally limited to fewer than our 19 countries, my analysis suggests that a balance between specialization and primary care, perhaps 50/50, results in wider diffusion of biomedical knowledge, more continuity of treatment, better diagnosis of "the whole patient," and more time and money for prevention. Further, if primary-care physicians and their assistants serve as gatekeepers to specialists and their activities are coordinated, better cost control is likely. Clinics that combine specialists and generalists where they interact freely—and are not hostages to insurance companies and other managers preoccupied with cost cutting—may be ideal for this balance (cf. Mechanic, 1992, p. 1723). Sweden and Norway approximate this picture. There is some evidence that all of the above improves a nation's health performance. In contrast, systems with a sharp separation between hospital-based specialists and GPs, such as Germany's and Britain's, are below average in real health performance (table 16.4). Finally, the case of the United Kingdom suggests that a willingness to pay more than 7% of GDP and a specialist ratio higher than 25% is necessary for good health performance.

Preventive Care and Health Performance

As we have seen, strong state intervention (financing, prices, personnel) boosts the ratio of GPs and nurses to specialists, which, in turn, leads to a broader dissemination of biomedical knowledge and an emphasis on disease prevention and health promotion services—a reallocation of medical budgets. Among the cost-beneficial preventive services are immunization, blood pressure screening, mammograms, and Pap smears (Mechanic, 1996, p. 155), as well as screening for some other cancers, cholesterol testing, and diet therapy (Glennerster and Matsaganis, 1992, p. 38). Regarding health promotion, the authoritative word of a physician about good health habits at a time when the patient is anxious and vulnerable is doubtless more persuasive than the same messages from a nagging mother. And, as chapter 15 has shown, a wide array of aggressive regulatory and educational measures can reduce tobacco use substantially.

But preventive medicine is no panacea and at its best—comprehensive education and health promotion as an integral part of health care for the entire population at risk—it hardly saves money; it is expensive. First, many preventive measures are of dubious value in prolonging life or improving the quality of life—for instance PSA screening for prostate cancer among men under 50, surgery for an enlarged prostate, drugs to remove cholesterol, annual Pap smears vs. one every three years (Russell, 1986, 1994, pp. 6–44). Second, a preventive approach to medical care takes time, one reason that increasing the percentage of GPs and nurses has a better effect on national health performance than increasing the percentage of less accessible specialists. As David Mechanic suggests, if the physician is to have an effect on a patient's eating habits, diet, smoking, and substance abuse, he must have sufficient time to communicate clearly, to elicit questions, and to provide appropriate feedback (1993, pp. 14–15)—time to develop a reasonably stable, trusting relationship. Again, time is of the essence, and time is money. The final and most important reason that preventive care at its best is expensive brings us back to the theme at the opening of this chapter: countries that have reallocated their spending toward family physicians and physician assistants, including public health nurses, and have constrained the overuse of high-cost technology and specialist services also tend to spend increasing amounts on health-related social policies that reduce the population at risk. They have reduced large inequalities in access and in levels of health. They have invested in public health. They have combined this with programs of subsidized housing, home care for the aged, poverty prevention, and health education in clinics and schools. They have developed family policies accenting prenatal and infant care, parental leave, and child care at every level of child development (chap. 7). They have crafted policies and programs that reduce teenage pregnancy and drug abuse (chap. 8). They have been effective in cleaning up the air and water (chap. 15). In short, the effectiveness of preventive medicine is greatly increased where it is integrated with broader health-relevant programs for the most vulnerable populations at risk and where cost pressures do not subvert the physician's clinical time and practice.

The United States is deviant in almost all of these measures. Although lifestyle risk factors (e.g., smoking, poor diet, drugs and alcohol abuse, firearms, sexual behavior, and auto accidents) accounted for about half of premature deaths in the United States in 1990, the United States spends less than an estimated 10% of its health-care dollars on disease prevention and helping people to adopt healthy habits (Bodenhorn and Kemper, 1997, pp. iii, 2). That includes all funding for personal preventive health and community health services. Whether in comparative perspective 10% is high or low is not known because no good comparable definition or data are available. But there is reason to believe that the preventive percentage is relatively low and, more important, that the money the United States devotes to prevention is less effective than it is in many European countries, especially for younger populations. First, the United States has not achieved the near-universal coverage that is the norm in all other rich democracies. And young adults who can benefit most from preventive strategies are also the age group that is disproportionately uninsured (*ibid.* p. 34). Second, the uninsured in rich California comprise nearly one in four of the population; they have the poorest health status, highest health risks, and least access to clinical preventive services such as blood-pressure screening, mammograms, and pap smears (*ibid.*, pp. vii). Third, although such "managed-care" providers as HMOs cover an increasing fraction of the medically insured and sell themselves as accenting prevention, this is more commercial propaganda than substance, more marketing than actual disease detection or early intervention. As David Mechanic suggests (1996, p. 156), HMOs have joined insurance companies as skillful risk avoiders; their wellness programs are designed to recruit young, healthy enrollees, who are at once the most attracted to this rhetoric and the least at risk of contracting expensive illnesses.

Finally, the U.S. deviance is pinned down in two studies: one of primary care in the United States, the United Kingdom, Denmark, Finland, and Sweden (Weiner, 1987); the other of preventive care in 10 European countries (Williams and Miller, 1991). Although Weiner argues that the United States is converging toward European patterns of increased centralization of management and integration of providers and a de-emphasis of retrospective and fee-for-service payment, and although he sees U.S. health maintenance organizations (HMOs) and preferred provider organizations (PPOs) as similar to European trends, he finds striking differences. As we have seen, the European countries closely control the distribution of physicians so that general practitioners and family practitioners are much more widely available than in the United States. Equally important for prevention, the four European countries are superior in having organized proactive programs of prevention (e.g., immunization uptake rates) and in preventive care to children (Weiner, 1987, p. 442). The more extensive Williams and Miller assessment shows that most preventive care is delivered outside physicians' offices in 8 of the 10 European countries studied. Six of them have separate, dedicated systems of community clinics to provide most preventive and well-child care (*ibid.*, p. 26). By age three or four nearly all European children are enrolled in public preschools that incorporate or are closely linked with programs of health care (p. 39) or have other relevant linkages (pp. 35–39). The general picture is one of national preventive standards and organized community services with decentralized administration (Miller, C. A. 1991, p. 4). As in the Japanese case—where huge gains in reduction of infant mortality occurred in prefects with an abundance of public health nurses (Morio, 1985)—and in contrast to the United States, these European countries coordinate the primary care of physicians with a great range of ancillary services such as nurses, midwives, personal social-service providers, and teachers. As we shall see in table 16.4 this is one reason for their better performance in such output indicators as infant mortality and pregnancy and childbirth deaths.

The Private/Public Mix and the Myth of the Market

No rich democracy has acted out the ideology of privatization of health care, although the political rhetoric in a few favors market solutions to the problems of cost, "free patient choice," quality, innovation, and access. At first glance, the United States is an exception. Table 16.3 shows that the private share of total health-care spending in the United States in 1990 was about three-fifths. That greatly exceeds the next highest private share: just under a third in Austria, Switzerland, and Australia; and typically less than a quarter elsewhere.

What table 16.3 shows is the following:

1. The central tendency is an increase from 1960 to 1990 in the public share of total health-care expenditures. Of 18 rich democracies, only Denmark and Austria show slight declines.

2. In 1960, types of political economy counted as a source of reliance on the public sector. The averages for left-corporatist or left-Catholic corporatist democracies are high, ranging from the left-corporatist 74% to the left-Catholic corporatist 66% public share (excluding the deviant case of the Netherlands). Corporatist countries that keep labor at a distance and the fragmented, decentralized political economies are at the bottom. But the main story is the very low reliance on public health-care spending of Australia, Canada, and the United States.

3. By 1990, however, there was considerable convergence. The average for each category went up except for Catholic corporatism, which remained stable at a high level. The main story in 1990 is the United States exception—only 42% public (largely Medicare and Medicaid) and the rest private. Even the Netherlands, Australia, and Canada moved sharply up toward the rest of the pack, with overwhelmingly public finance. The United States remained odd man out in its continued reliance on individually purchased or collectively bargained medical care and in the large number of its people with no insurance coverage or inadequate coverage.

4. In 1980 there is no clear relation between reliance on the public share and our health performance index. The top five in reliance on public spending averaged 9.4 on the health index; the bottom five averaged 8.9 on the index (table not reported). What counts as a source of performance is not this measure of public effort but the cash delivered per person—the public health spending per capita in table 16.4. A very rich country with moderate effort (public share of total health-care spending) can deliver more

TABLE 16.3 Types of political economy, public share of total health spending, and real health

	Public share of total healthcare spending (%)[a]			Real health index 1980[b]	
	1960	1990	1980		
Left Corporatist					
Sweden	73	80	93	14.0	(1)
Norway	78	95	98	12.0	(5)
Finland	54	81	79	6.0	(13)
Israel	na	na	na	5.0	(15)
Denmark	89	83	85	11.0	(7)
Avg.	74	85	89		
Left-Catholic Corp.					
Netherlands	33	71	75	12.5	(3)
Belgium	62	89	83	8.0	(11)
Austria	69	67	69	3.0	(19)
Avg.	66[c]	76	76		
Catholic Corporatist					
Italy	83	78	81	8.5	(9)
W. Germany	66	72	75	4.0	(17)
Avg.	75	75	78		
Corporatist w/o Labor					
France	58	75	80	10.0	(8)
Japan	60	72	71	12.0	(5)
Switzerland	61	68	68	13.5	(2)
Avg.	60	72	73		
Least Corporatist					
United States	25	42	42	8.0	(11)
UnIted Kngdom	84	84	90	6.0	(13)
New Zealand	81	82	84	4.0	(17)
Australia	48	68	63	8.0	(11)
Canada	43	72	75	12.0	(5)
Ireland	76	75	82	5.0	(15)
Avg.	60	71	73		

[a]OECD (1993f), table 7.1.1, p. 252.
[b]See footnote "a" to table 16.4.
[c]Excluding the Netherlands as a deviant case.

money per person than a less rich country with larger effort. For instance, in 1980 the USA with about half of Ireland's public share spent $363 per capita in public provision while Ireland with half of the U.S. GDP per capita but a public share of 82%, spent only $308 per capita in public provision.

Later, we shall see that types of political economy as they interact with affluence and both public health and education spending do have strong effects on health performance—effects obscured by table 16.3.

The U.S. exception is misleading anyway. First, government subsidies abound: at least 8 in 10 Americans receive health care that is federally subsidized. Beyond those on Medicare and Medicaid, this includes all people who receive income in the form of employer-provided health insurance not subject to income tax. It includes the self-employed who can exclude part of their medical expenses from taxable income. It includes veterans. Second, everywhere there is a blurring of public/private lines of distinction. In fact there is some evidence that countries whose elites articulate the most strident free-market ideologies—the United States, the United Kingdom, New Zealand—develop the most intrusive government regulations. We have encountered this combination of free-market rhetoric and intrusive regulatory regimes in the Thatcher-Major health-care reforms of 1991–96 (chap. 5); in the immense apparatus of investigation and surveillance of the poor among countries fond of means-tested benefits targeted to the poor (chap. 8); and in comparison of regulatory regimes for the environment and occupational health and safety (chap. 15). It was the antiregulation, promarket Reagan and Bush administrations that adopted intrusive regulations of hospital and physician payments (rate setting, prospective payment plans based on diagnostic-related groups and resource-based relative value scales) (Brown, 1991; Ruggie, 1992).

The concept of the market applied to health care borders on the absurd. It is only because medical economists have dominated debates about health-care reform, especially in the United States, Britain, and New Zealand, that it is taken seriously in the media and public discourse (Wilensky, 1997). The guiding concepts of these economists include willing buyers and willing sellers contracting for services in a more or less competitive market where the buyer (patient) compares alternative sellers (doctors); is adequately if not fully informed about the nature of the product, its price, and its quality; and makes a rational choice. The seller as he views his competition must provide either higher quality or lower price or both or he will go out of business. The system as a whole will thus tend toward a match between price and quality and a nice equilibrium between demand and supply. Further, under market discipline, as the price-conscious buyer constrains his appetite for service and the seller is constrained to be more efficient, cost containment will be the happy result. Many medical economists know that when applied to health care, these ideas must be modified; they speak of imperfect competition, managed competition, market failures, and so on.

As every observer of the institutions providing care knows, the health-care "market" is wildly different from the market in economic theory. The buyer at the peak of expense may not even be conscious, let alone adequately informed; if conscious, he is anxious, maybe in pain, full of fear and ignorant of the purchases before him. His demand for the service is sometimes urgent, even desperate. Whether the private share of spending is high as in the United States or low as everywhere else, the typical patient is not even spending his own money and no one in the system can accurately gauge the unit cost. The seller-provider in turn, is a licensed professional monopolist who creates demand by authoritative statements of what the purchaser should want and the buyer-patient has neither the competence nor the wish to second-guess the monopolist. Is this a market?

In a commercialized system with benefits voluntarily provided by employers to the stably employed it can be argued that the customer is not the patient; it is instead the employer or an insurance carrier. In that case, the competition is among HMOs and other corporate providers in relation to corporate purchasers and is based almost entirely on price rather than quality or convenience. Both patient and physician become pawns in that competition with decreasing autonomy of doctors, greater restrictions on their clinical judgments, less service, and increasing out-of-pocket costs to the patient, as the "customer" mounts pressure for reduced prices. This unique medical-industrial complex of the United States is discussed below.

During the yearlong debate about President Clinton's proposal for health-care reform in 1993–94, 500-plus economists wrote the *Wall Street Journal*: "Price controls," they said, "never work." As we have seen, however, all health-care systems that successfully combine equality of access, cost constraint, comprehensive preventive programs, adequate quality care, and a moderate to slow adoption of high-cost high-tech innovations rely heavily on public funding and government control over prices and personnel through bargaining with providers.[7]

If the health-care system is a market, it is a market in which supply creates its own demand, not one in which increased supply drives prices down. In the late 1950s, Milton Roemer examined the relation between the supply of hospital beds and occupancy rates. He found that availability alone promotes use (Roemer and Shain, 1959, pp. 12–16). Similarly, as medicine became more accessible and physicians found new technologies and methods of treatment and formed new specialties, demand rose along with price. The more surgeons, the more expensive surgery (Fuchs, 1986b, p. 144–147).

Beyond these obvious limitations of a market model applied to health care are more subtle effects of efforts first to devise private/public systems short of national health insurance, and, second, to increase commercial competition among providers. It is always wise to ask "What will any reform do to the patient's interaction with and trust in the physician?" Recent developments in the United States illustrate the consequences of the commercialization of medicine.

The Medical-Industrial Complex of the United States

Although the United States shares general long-term tendencies in modern health-care systems—increased public funding, a blurring of private/public distinctions, increased reliance on state coordination of health-care services, a combination of explicit, implicit, and ability-to-pay rationing, and increased use of specialized high-tech medicine—it is unique in many ways. The United States is the only rich democracy without national health insurance. It has a much higher specialist ratio than other countries and has fewer primary-care physicians and a much higher use of expensive technology and procedures. Its total costs, private and public, far exceed all others (at 14.2% of GDP in 1995 it was almost 4 percentage points above the runner up, Germany at 10.4%). Its "private"-sector share at 58% in 1990 was far larger than all others (table 16.3). In rationing medical care it relies much more than other countries do on ability to pay and on explicit commands from both private commercial firms and public authorities. A strong case can be made that the United States has developed a system with the lowest social efficiency, the most unequal distribution of health-care services, and, increasingly, the least room for the clinical judgments of physicians and other professional caregivers. With its astronomical costs, the United States achieves only a below-average health performance.

Efforts to reform this system almost always result in increased costs or poorer health-care services or both. The root of the problem is the rapid development of a "medical-industrial complex," the commercialization of American medical care. The label comes from an analysis by Arnold S. Relman, for many years editor in chief of *The New England Journal of Medicine* (Relman, 1992, 1997).

If it were not for the ascendance in rhetoric and practice of commercial medicine in the past 20 or so years, it would be unnecessary to repeat the obvious: medicine is not merely another commodity like food, clothing, or used cars. And patients (consumers) cannot fend for themselves, applying the rule of "caveat emptor." Nor in his daily practice is the physician a seller mainly concerned with profit. The social contract that governs physician-patient relationships, embedded in law, custom, and ethical codes, includes a state-licensed monopoly to practice medicine, heavy subsidies for training, autonomy in setting professional standards and working conditions, public support for the R&D and tools and techniques necessary for practice, as well as hospitals directly or indirectly funded by taxes. These hospitals provide the physician with the capital equipment and overhead costs that ordinary businesspeople must themselves pay. In return for the high status, income, and authority all this brings, the physician is expected to protect the patient's interests by acting as advocate and counselor. He is expected to adhere to the norm of selflessness—devotion to the patient's interests more than personal or commercial profit should guide decisions when the two are in conflict.

Because American medicine has always had a dominant "private" component (Starr, 1982), strains on this social contract have long been evident. When most physicians were paid on a fee-for-service basis, there were incentives to violate professional norms. The more consultations, tests, and operations doctors performed, the more they earned. No doubt that led to an unknown number of unnecessary tests, excess drug prescriptions, unnecessary surgery, some of it actually harming patients. However, as Relman suggests, the average encounter of patient and doctor was still one of trust, the tradition of professionalism was strong (1992, p. 101), and the number of GPs with more or less stable patient relationships was substantial.

In the 1980s a trend toward the full-scale commercialization of the delivery of health care began; it accelerated in the 1990s. There has been a massive shift in the ownership and control of medical-care provider organizations from public to private and from nonprofit to profit. It has taken the form of a large, fast-growing industry of "managed care" that in 1998 covered roughly 160 million people. The speed of this growth is indicated by the fact that as recently as 1990 over 90% of Americans whose employers (voluntarily) provided some kind of health coverage still received traditional, fee-for-service insurance (*The Economist,* March 7, 1998, p. 23). By 1995, that figure had fallen to 27% (Jensen et al., 1997, p. 126). With rare exceptions these commercial chains are investor-owned. More and more of them are regional or national in scope, as the industry consolidates and vertically integrates. These new businesses have bought or built and operated chains of hospitals, clinics, nursing homes, and diagnostic laboratories. As the government tried to control hospital costs, especially for acute care, they expanded their holdings in ambulatory and home services and in more specialized services that are harder to regulate. Relman estimates that by 1992, a third of all nonpublic health-care facilities were operated by investor-owned businesses. The main story of recent years is the consolidation and management of physician practices by these investor-owned corporations.[8]

As the for-profit corporate sector grew, new financial opportunities for physicians expanded: a growing number have invested in health-care facilities to which they then refer their patients. They

> become limited partners in for-profit diagnostic laboratories and MRI centers to which they refer their patients but over which they can exercise no professional supervision. Surgeons invest in ambulatory-surgery facilities . . . owned and managed by businesses or hospitals, and in which they perform surgery on their patients. . . . A recent study in Florida revealed that approximately 40 percent of all physicians practicing in that state had financial interests in facilities to which they referred patients. (Relman, 1992, p. 102)

Similar entrepreneurial medicine is practiced by office-based doctors who make deals with wholesalers of prescription drugs and sell those drugs to their patients at a profit. Or they buy prostheses from manufacturers at a reduced rate and sell them at a profit. Some university-based research physicians, perhaps a small but growing minority, also have become commercial hustlers. They make financial arrangements to test products, buy equity in the firms making the products, and serve as paid scientific advisers and consultants, all the while promoting the products made by their corporate paymasters for use with their patients or university clinics and laboratories.

Obviously all these illustrations of the trend involve clear conflicts of interest and violations of ethical codes going far beyond the fee-for-service temptations of 20 to 30 years ago. Equally obvious, they subvert both the trust and stability of patient-doctor relationships. The government, insurance companies, and employers alike have supported this trend in the belief that commercial competition and a market model of medical care would contain costs and improve efficiency. It is a great irony that this effort to preserve or increase health-care competition necessitates a complex apparatus of intrusive regulation. For instance, a Prospective Payment System (PPS) based on Diagnosis-Related Groups (DRG) was adopted in 1983 for Medicare payments to hospitals. Providers responded by raising prices to privately insured patients to recoup shortfalls. Employers who provided some coverage for their employees saw their insurance costs triple from 1980 to 1991. They responded by demanding that insurance companies crack down on high-cost providers. (Many small- and medium-sized firms simply dropped coverage for their employees.[9]) Insurers responded with a variety of managed-care schemes that micromanaged physicians and hospitals or tried an arm's-length adversarial utilization review. They dropped coverage or increased prices for poor health risks. (Brown, 1994, pp. 199–200; Morone, 1992, pp. 44–45.) The managed-care managers (HMOs, PPOs), under pressure from government, employers, and insurance companies, then began to reduce both the pay of physicians and the services to patients. HMOs, too, have become adept at risk selection.

Meanwhile, the community-oriented, nonprofit, nonpublic hospitals were forced to compete with investor-owned hospitals and outpatient facilities. Their response has been threefold: consolidate into large nonprofit chains such as Sutter Hospitals and Catholic Healthcare West; give up by selling out to corporate chains (some of their trustees and managers became executives or board members in the medical-industrial complex); or try to compete by avoiding or limiting their customary services to the poor while actively promoting their profitable services to insured patients—a formula that at once shifts costs to the public sector and increases the overuse of high-priced services. The pattern is for the payers (government, insurance companies, and employers) to push down on hospitals, many of which are half empty. The hospitals then push down on employees (from doctors to nurses aides), who then, with increased workload, must reduce contact with patients.[10] More work for the same or less pay fosters demoralization among workers in this managed-care industry; they come to believe that patient care is secondary to the bottom line. Finally, some of the managed-care firms have now shifted the risk of handling prospective reimbursements to groups of doctors, some of them quite small, who, preferring autonomy and thinking they could make as much or more money on their own, accept a per capita rate and contract to cover all medical needs of each patient on a list. These physicians then find themselves denying appropriate care—or, worse, doing work that should be referred out—on behalf of their own bottom line, with no HMO manager or insurance company to blame it on. By 1997 about one in four of the 483,000 physicians in the United States had at least one capitation contract (*New York Times,* May 30, 1998); the tendency was for the small independent practice groups to merge with larger ones (Robinson and Casalino, 1996).

All this, in turn, fostered a congressional consensus, first to regulate insurance companies—legislation to stop them from skimming off healthier patients and shifting costs to the public sector—and, second, to prevent them from denying insurance to those who lose coverage when they lose their jobs or retire early. In the late 1990s both Congress and state legislatures were also crafting codes of behavior for HMOs, some quite specific and detailed; 43 of the 50 states had already passed laws expanding patient rights in HMOs. And in 1998 President Clinton proposed a national "Patient's Bill of Rights." Politicians were responding to a groundswell of patient complaints about refusal of care, delays in care, violations of confidentiality of medical records, gag rules that bar HMO physicians from informing patients of alternative expensive treatments, and premature hospital discharge. "HMO," said the critics when HMOs discharged mothers within 24 hours of giving birth, stands for "Heaving Moms Out."

In the end, by 1998 the United States had developed a chaos of public and private regulation, all under the slogan "managed competition" while the totally uninsured continued to climb, from 38.3 million of the population under 65 in 1992 to 41.4 million in 1996 (*New York Times,* March 22, 1998). There was also an unknown increase in the number of those inadequately covered, surely tens of millions who could no longer afford the growing number of deductibles, copayments, and other out-of-pocket expenses. Even Medicare beneficiaries found their out-of-pocket expenses climbing.[11] In 1997 the average Medicare beneficiary was paying about $2,600 a year—21% of the typical recipient's annual income

(*Wall Street Journal,* June 23, 1997). Medicare was the last bastion of fee-for-service medicine; now these patients are gradually being channeled into the managed-care industry.

What is the impact of the shift to "managed care" or "managed competition" on the cost-effectiveness of health care? First, there is some consensus that it cuts costs, at least initially—or, more precisely, it saves money by moving toward increased copayments and by reducing coverage via queues, exclusions, and barriers to hospitalization and costly procedures. For instance, during the years 1993–96 total health-care spending as a share of GDP actually leveled off at about 14.2%, although per capita expenditures continued to climb.[12] Advocates of managed care saw this as proof of efficiencies achieved. But the GDP fraction resumed its double-digit growth rate after 1997. Moreover, many of the efficiencies claimed by the private HMOs and managed-care firms come from adverse selection. The sick stay in high-cost plans if they can afford to, while the more healthy either join the ranks of the uncovered or gravitate to low-cost plans with proliferating exclusions, copayments, and deductibles (Oberlander, 1998). The best way to make money in this business is to sell insurance or medical services to healthy people. State-administered Medicaid, which is America's only long-term care program as well as the means-tested safety net for the poor (see chap. 8), has run into the same problem of adverse selection. In 1998 in New York, Connecticut, Ohio, Missouri, and Florida, HMOs that had sought Medicaid patients in the early 1990s as a lucrative market were pulling out. One reason: During 1995–97 state legislatures, under cost pressures from welfare, education, escalating prison expenditures, and deteriorating infrastructure, had reduced the monthly rates they pay HMOs per Medicaid member by 10% to 20% or so. The HMO chains then passed on the pressure by shutting down nursing homes or evicting their patients. Vencor, Inc., the fourth-largest chain of nursing homes in the United States, explained that it wants to attract wealthier patients who can afford the higher levels of medical care it plans to provide. It also fears that growing litigation against nursing-home owners will impose higher standards of care than Vencor can profitably provide at Medicaid rates. Florida's attorney general was, in fact, launching a sweeping Medicaid fraud and abuse case against the entire industry. (*Wall Street Journal,* April 7, 1998.)[13] Florida health regulators have already fined Vencor $260,000 for evicting Medicaid residents from a Tampa nursing home (*Wall Street Journal,* April 13, 1998).

A major rationale offered by enthusiasts for commercialized managed care and its intrusion into the clinical encounter is that it not only cuts costs but improves quality. It does so by squeezing out unnecessary and dangerous procedures and encouraging the use of more effective treatments; the growth of "evidence-based" medicine, they say, will be cost-effective. Aside from lack of good evidence that this has taken place, this assertion ignores the typical case: the biomedical "evidence" is frequently ambiguous or weak; and whether data are good or bad, it is interpreted by management personnel overwhelmingly guided by cost-cutting fervor. This chapter so far suggests that the clinical judgments of professionals within very broad cost constraints are better than the talk about "evidence-based medicine."

"Managed care" comes in many forms. Any assertions about its efficiency must take account of a veritable smorgasbord of managed-care enterprises. When unmanaged indemnity insurance dominated the medical insurance market in the 1970s, the form of payment was fee-for-service and there was no control over provider treatment choices and no control over the patient's choice of provider other than ability to pay. By 1987 the share of unmanaged indemnity insurance declined to 41%; by 1991 it collapsed to 5%. Taking its place were a variety of group-health insurance plans (Robinson, 1993). In 1990, in descending order of importance, were four main types. First were *managed indemnity plans* (57% of the group health-insurance market). To commercial insurance these add an arm's-length adversarial utilization review but do not contract selectively with providers. Second, and at the opposite extreme, are *prepaid group-practice HMOs* (14%).[14] They combine exclusive contracting between the insurers and providers with a cooperative approach to utilization and control, including physician peer review. The best few of these, like Kaiser-Permanente, are held up as models of efficiency and good care expected from the managed-care revolution. Third are *preferred provider organizations (PPOs)*. By 1990 they achieved a 13% share. PPOs contract with a moderate number of providers but offer partial coverage for patients who use nonpreferred providers. The fourth major form of managed care is *independent practice associations (IPAs)*, which had an 11% share in 1990. These limit choices to a closed, usually broad-based panel of physicians. Unlike many prepaid group-practice HMOs, they do not require doctors to restrict their practices to those enrolled in the plan. Like PPOs, the IPAs contract with independent doctors with office-based practices. Both types are subject only to arm's-length, adversarial utilization review and control.

In short, Robinson's 1990 figures show that the prepaid cooperative group-practice HMOs had only about one-seventh of the national market, although they had a much larger share in California where they got started early. Dominant were managed-indemnity, preferred-provider, and independent-practice arrangements, together accounting for 81% of the group health-insurance market. In the past decade of rapid change the fastest-growing type was the PPO, but the various types of managed care have interpenetrated as insurance companies and HMOs contracted with various types of provider associations and groups. The main form is now a hybrid.[15] Only a few managed-care arrangements now resemble the Kaiser-Permanente HMOs—cooperative prepaid plans that have indeed reined in costs in the 1990s without sacrificing much care.[16] These HMOs are older and more established; they have large memberships (Kaiser serves more than 5.5 million people in California alone); they have paid for much of their capital equipment and buildings, although with expansion this cost advantage has diminished. Most important for health outputs, until recently these Kaiser-type HMOs respected the professional autonomy of their physicians and clinical staff. Their cost-savings measures did not typically subvert clinical judgments.

It is likely that what cost cutting managed care had achieved by 1997 had already reached its limits. By then many were losing money—even Kaiser, the deviant case held up as a model of cost-effectiveness. And by then even Kaiser had hired management consultants skilled in public relations and labor shedding, in the end accelerating pressures on its staff to see more patients for less pay, thereby reducing both morale and care. One consequence was an increase in labor strife. Over a year, 1997–98, the 7,500 members of the California Nurses Association who work in Kaiser's Northern California region called six strikes of one or two days to protest what they called "hit-and-run" nursing and the speedup in their work.[17] Despite its cost-cutting efforts, Kaiser as a whole incurred operating losses of $881 million and a cumulative net loss of $544 million for two years (1997 and 1998); in January 1999 it announced rate increases from 8% to 12% for most groups (*Wall Street Journal*, May 3, 1999).[18]

Finally, none of these arrangements attack the overhead problem. Paperwork will continue to metastasize unless the United States cuts down the power of the 1,500 insurance companies generating paper and instructions for the hospitals, the HMOs, doctors, and patients. The medical-industrial complex is one source of the uniquely high administrative costs of the U.S. system, discussed below.

There is controversy about the real health effects of the shift to managed care. The change is too recent to assess 10- to 20-year effects, which would be ideal, given the nature of the population at risk with chronic diseases, ailments difficult to diagnose, or treatments and advice that require time to take effect. And as we have seen, the facilities labeled managed care are heterogeneous in size, structure, control, payment systems, and professional autonomy. With so many types of managed care and little agreement on which types are best for health care, research linking these variations to health outcomes is limited. The impact studies available are most often one- or two-year follow-ups or literature reviews that do not adequately assess the quality of data or of research designs (e.g., Miller and Luft, 1994), and they typically tell little about changes in health among the elderly and the poor, who if covered are likely to be in fee-for-service systems. Two systematic studies, however, are especially relevant to my analysis of how organizational arrangements affect patient-doctor relationships and trust, as well as health outcomes. The first is a four-year observational study of physical and mental health outcomes among chronically ill adults treated in health maintenance organizations (HMOs) and fee-for-service (FFS) systems 1986–90 (Ware et al., 1996, hereafter the "Ware study"). The second is a study of the causes of voluntary disenrollment rates among Medicare enrollees in HMOs across the United States, state by state (Families USA Foundation, 1997). Both studies have the merit of dealing with patients most at risk.

The Ware study is comprehensive, longitudinal, and careful. It observed changes in a wide range of health indicators[19] among 2,235 patients (18 to 97 years of age) in Boston, Chicago, and Los Angeles and separately analyzed those 65 years and older and low-income patients. It compared a wide range of organizational types within each service area: both prepaid group HMOs (72% of patients) and independent practice associations (28%); HMOs vs. FFS care in large multispeciality groups as well as solo or small single-specialty practices. Because there were no significant differences in outcomes between staff-model HMOs and IPA network models, they were combined under the HMO category. Multivariate analysis with all the relevant controls was carried out. The conclusions most relevant to my analysis of the medical-industrial complex are these: (1) As many well-designed studies have shown and the Ware study confirms, *HMOs reduce health-care utilization;* they "achieve lower hospital admission rates, shorter hospital stays, rely on fewer subspecialists, and make less use of expensive technologies" (*ibid.,* p. 1045) than fee-for-service systems do. (2) *While HMO and FFS systems did not differ in health outcomes for the average patient, there were sharp differences for the elderly and the poor.* Elderly HMO patients were twice as likely to decline in physical health than patients in FFS systems (54% vs. 28%). The physical health of poor patients who were ill at the start of the study improved by only 22% in HMOs; their health improved by 57% in FFS systems. These results held across the three major metropolitan areas. (3) *Organizational arrangements made little or no difference for mental health performance.* In short, up until 1991, HMOs achieved substantial cost savings at the expense of the population most at risk—the elderly and the poor, especially the poor who were most physically limited.

The second study provides a clue to the differences between profit and nonprofit HMOs. Families USA analyzed 1996 voluntary dropout rates for the 158 HMOs in the

United States with at least 1,000 Medicare enrollees. The survey was based on data from the federal Health Care Financing Administration. The study reports disenrollment rates per year (all of 1995, all of 1996, and the first four months of 1997) and for three months (rapid disenrollment) in 31 states and the District of Columbia. Nationwide one of seven Medicare beneficiaries are enrolled in HMOs, but this will increase as 1997 legislation encouraging HMO enrollment takes effect. California already has 38% of Medicare beneficiaries in HMOs. The relevant findings: (1) *Disenrollment rates (dropouts as a percentage of average monthly membership) were increasing* during the study period. (2) *Disenrollment rates vary dramatically by state.* The national rate is 13%, but states range from a low of 2.7% in Hawaii and 4.2% in Minnesota to a high of 31.6% in D.C., 25.3% in Florida, 21.8% in Kentucky and 19.4% in Texas. In 1996, 6 of the 10 Medicare HMOs with the highest disenrollment rates were in Florida, 3 were in Texas, and 1 was in California (Health-Net Central Valley). Among states with more than two Medicare HMOs in 1995 and 1996, Florida and Texas had the highest disenrollment rates. For assessing the impact of the medical-industrial complex, it may be significant that HMOs in these two rapid-turnover states are numerous; they also remain profitable despite heavy turnover and they rank high in the proportion of physicians who have financial interests in health-care facilities to which they refer patients.[20] (3) Where there is a large choice of HMOs, *Medicare beneficiaries who drop out of one HMO tend to join another HMO.* (4) Most important for assessing the impact of the commercialization of medicine, *disenrollment rates are highest among profit-making plans.* Seven of the 10 plans with the highest disenrollment rates were for-profit while 9 of the 10 plans with the very lowest disenrollment rates were nonprofit.[21]

The authors of this study point out that high disenrollment rates are not a perfect guide to either low-quality care or patient dissatisfaction. Enrollees might leave if their doctor left; or where there are many options, they might change HMOs because of small differences in cost or coverage (e.g., copayments for drugs). There are also peculiarities in particular markets. For instance, "one insurer significantly raised its premiums to encourage members to disenroll and reenroll in the insurer's other, and less generous, HMO product" (*ibid.,* p. 14). Finally, small and new HMOs have higher quit rates than large and established HMOs. The beneficiaries in some states have little or no experience with HMOs. They face bewildering choices of new and ever-changing types of insurance and managed-care plans. Examining the very large differences between HMOs of equal size and age, however, the researchers conclude that the main reasons for high quit rates are misleading marketing, poor service, and patient confusion and dissatisfaction.

> Serious marketing fraud in the Medicare HMO program has been well documented. Marketing agents have lied about the "advantage" of Medicare HMO enrollment compared to the "disadvantages" of fee-for-service Medicare, obtained beneficiary enrollment signatures under false pretenses ("just sign here to show that I have visited"), forged signatures, and in other ways misled beneficiaries into joining their HMO. (Families USA Foundation, 1997, p. 15)

In contrast, HMOs with very low disenrollment rates tend to rate high in quality of service. Many of these low-quit rate plans receive top grades in a number of HMO report cards. For instance, in October 1997, the Pacific Business Group on health, a coalition of

33 large California employers, gave Kaiser Permanente Health Plan in Oakland its "blue ribbon" award as the best-rated plan, based on enrollee satisfaction, quality of care, cost, and leadership in improving standards (*ibid.*, p. 15). Kaiser, one of the few large nonprofit HMOs left, was also rated near the top of the more than 1,000 HMOs in quality of care by the National Committee on Quality Assurance (*New York Times,* April 9, 1998).

We can infer from these two studies and others cited above that HMOs compared to the U.S. alternatives, including fee-for-service arrangements, are worse for the elderly, the chronically ill, and the poor. Managed care in general reduces unnecessary care; but it also reduces necessary and beneficial care.[22] Conclusions about variations in disenrollment rates among Medicare HMOs support my earlier discussion of threats to the professional autonomy of the physician and the subversion of stability and trust in physician-patient relationships. The low patient turnover of nonprofit HMOs and the very high turnover of for-profit HMOs in Florida and Texas, where marketing fraud and poor-quality service abound, suggest that it is the commercialization of the medical-industrial complex, not the form of managed care, that subverts good health performance. But careful assessments of health outcomes linked to organizational forms are rare and the duration of most studies is too short to make more than tentative judgments.

The advocates of managed competition thought that private health plans and insurance companies would compete to enroll large regional pools of workers and other groups. Vigorous competition to win contracts with cost-conscious employers would drive down the cost of care; the savings would be used to extend care to the uninsured and improve the cost-benefit ratio. It is not only this chapter that suggests that the argument was flawed. Dr. Paul M. Ellwood, one of the architects of managed competition, looking back at Jackson Hole where he and health-economist Alain Enthoven organized a famous series of conferences to promote the idea, said "the real weakness of the system now is that nobody trusts anybody. Health plans are on the defensive, doctors are on the defensive and patients are skeptical" (quoted in *New York Times,* March 22, 1998). Well, yes.

Why Health-Care Reform in the United States Fails

A side effect of the medical-industrial complex is to increase the political barriers to a comprehensive reform of the U.S. system. I once thought that incremental reform—piggybacking "kiddie care" onto OASDHI, and gradually adding other categories in the good old American way of backdoor entry—was the best feasible option (Wilensky, 1975, pp. 41–42). Twenty or 30 years ago that was a reasonable position. But with the rapid commercialization of medical care, such incremental reforms are ineffective. For instance, a 1996 reform, the Kennedy-Kassebaum law, in theory guarantees that people losing group health insurance will have access to coverage in the individual insurance market regardless of pre-existing medical problems—a typical pinpointed, incremental reform to expand coverage. The General Accounting Office in March 1998 found the following: (1) Some states did not cooperate; they refused to subsidize or spread the costs of individual insurance, say through pools for high-risk people, and the federal government had not allocated money or personnel to fill the gap. (2) Consumers lose most of their rights if they do not buy a policy within 63 days of losing group coverage and are usually unaware of that. (3) Some insurers redesign benefits to exclude coverage of particular illnesses or costly procedures for a specified period. (4) Some companies deny commissions to their insurance agents if they sell policies to people with medical problems. (5) Most important, insurers typically price the target population out of the market. The GAO found that "premiums range from 140 percent to 600 percent of the standard rates." That means an outlay of at least $10,000 to $15,000 a year. (*New York Times,* March 17, 1998.) Another notable failure of incremental reform was the enactment in 1988 of a law to protect Medicare beneficiaries against the costs of catastrophic illness—and its quick repeal before any of its major benefits took effect.

Without a dominant public share of total spending, without universal coverage under national health insurance, without a global budget, the game of risk selection and cost shifting is the main game in town. Managers in the private sector devote themselves to shifting costs to the public sector and avoiding sicker patients and less affluent populations. Controls over one part of this fragmented system inspire rising prices in other parts and reduced service in the area controlled. This is the record of commercialized "managed care." The political effects are to invite closer regulation by government, still more ineffective incremental steps, more intrusive regulation, and so on.

Recurrent efforts to achieve national health insurance from Teddy Roosevelt through Truman to Clinton have failed. In debates about health-care reform it is invariably said that the United States cannot achieve European or even Canadian and Australian health-care coverage because of the American culture of economic individualism—the accent on minimum government, private property, and the free market. So the United States must settle for "market" solutions and incremental reforms that have given us the new medical-industrial complex. But we have seen in chapters 4 and 10 that mass sentiments and public opinion are poor predictors of the electoral and legislative success of antitax, antispending, antibureaucratic movements and parties—Reagan in the United States, Thatcher in the United Kingdom. They are equally poor explanations of the defeat or victory of advocates of national health insurance. Both elites and masses in all rich democracies are ambivalent and contradictory in their values and beliefs. The survey data presented in chapter 10 show that whatever national ideological differences appear in responses to abstract questions—and these differences are not large—the issue-specific attitudes toward taxing, spending, and the welfare state are very similar across countries and over time: modern populations everywhere love publicly financed pensions, disability insurance, national health insurance, and, increasingly, family policies. Moreover, the contours of public opinion have remained quite stable since World War II. The universal popularity of national health insurance remains intact. Whatever their rhetoric or whatever their behavior in office, backlash politicians such as Reagan and Thatcher or the Republican leadership of Congress 1994–2000 have been unable to change this basic structure of opinion except for brief moments (see table 10.1).

This kind of radical disjunction between elite rhetoric, public policies, and popular opinion was evident during the yearlong debate over health-care reform in 1993–94. Striking contrasts appeared between political rhetoric in Washington and public opinion, between responses to general slogans and to specific issues. Despite the sharply partisan climate, despite fear-mongering slogans by the small business lobby and insurance companies (including the Harry and Louise commercials that pictured a nice couple over a kitchen table bashing the Clinton plan as a threat to everything they cherish), despite all that, issue-specific opinion remained friendly to the outlines of national health insurance. Cross sections of the American population that were polled about issues remained enthusiastic about universal and government-guaranteed coverage via an employer mandate; portability of all medical insurance, and prohibition against insurance companies' refusal to cover preexisting conditions—in short, the content of the administration bill. But the same respondents, asked whether they support the "Clinton health-care proposal," gave their TV-driven negative response. Few, of course, knew what the proposal contained (Jamieson and Capella, 1994). The media, especially television but also the prestige press, concentrated on politicians shouting at one another in 20-second sound bites, the style and content of the advertising war, and the details of the political process, accenting extremes (Fallows, 1996, pp. 222–229; Johnson and Broder, 1996, pp. 628–635; Hamburger, Marmor, and Meacham, 1994). Despite this cloud of confusion and hysteria, a majority of the public showed support for the specific ingredients of reform (as reported in the *Gallup Poll Monthly*, and in the Roper Center reviews of diverse polls in *The Public Perspective*). My favorite example of media-filtered "information" that is fed back to pollsters as public opinion is from a focus-group survey on the proper role of government, done at the height of the balanced budget debate of 1994–95. One older citizen on social security who was a heavy user of government-provided Medicare explained that "I want the government off my back . . . I don't want the government messing around with my Medicare."

Because the structure of public opinion—the rank order of enthusiasm by program and group—is so similar across nations and over time; because broad, abstract ideologies are partly self-canceling, with every country embracing both economic individualism and collectivism, we must look beyond public opinion for explanations of the American peculiarity, the repeated defeat of national health insurance. Instead we must look to the structural differences discussed in every chapter of this book: electoral systems and the structure of government; the strength and character of political parties; the structure and function of major interest groups, including labor, the professions, employers, and their bargaining arrangements with one another and with government.

The mystery is why the United States is unique in its resistance to national health insurance while it shares so many common features of other public policies with the United Kingdom, Canada, Australia, New Zealand, and Switzerland. A brief comparison of the United States and Canada may shed some light on this puzzle.

The United States and Canada share their origins in the British empire but lack a feudal past. As I have shown in other chapters, they are both characterized by a decentralized federalism with continual battles over "states (provincial) rights"; alternating major party control of government; majoritarian electoral systems with the rule of "first-past-the-post"; and fairly rapid erosion of political parties. Both countries are well below average in their social spending and were late in developing the welfare state. There is even a parallel in the regionalism of the two countries: from President Johnson on, federal largesse has flowed disproportionately to the South and Southwest just as federal funds in Canada went disproportionately to Quebec (militants, who win attention and cash transfers by threats to secede, derisively call this "fédéralisme de portefeuille"). Among our rich democracies, all this makes Canada and the U.S. most-similar systems. Until 1980 they also shared relatively poor economic performance, including high unemployment (tables 12.1 and 12.3). Thereafter the U.S. economy outperformed Canada's (table 12.6), which should have made it easier for the United States to enlarge health-insurance coverage and quality. Yet in 1972 Canada adopted a national health-insurance plan, while the United States avoided it and eventually moved toward decreasing coverage and greater inequality of access in a burgeoning medical-industrial complex. The outcome has been well above average health performance in Canada, below average in the United States (see table 16.4).

If the two countries had begun with different medical-care systems, their contrasting paths of development might be more easily explained. But that is not the case. Before Canada adopted comprehensive reform in the early 1970s, the medical care systems of the two countries were much alike. In 1971 their health-care spending as a percentage of GNP was nearly the same (Canada, 7.4%; the United States, 7.6%). Hospitals were a mix of non-profit and commercial. Most medical insurance was private. In both countries physicians were paid by fee-for-service, and their training and outlook were alike (Kudrle and Marmor, 1981, p. 104). Finally, the politics of medical care had strong family resemblances. Just after World War II, while President Truman's proposal for national health insurance was being defeated in Congress by a coalition of conservative Republicans and Southern Democrats open to medical, hospital, and insurance-company interests, a similar proposal by Canadian provincial and federal governments was going down at the hands of a similar coalition.[23] For instance, the ideological position of the American Medical Association to what they called "socialized medicine" had its counterpart in the Canadian Medical Association and provincial associations, although Canadians were somewhat more open to government-financed, income-tested medical care for the poor where the market could not do the job. In fact, in 1962 when health-care reform was again in the air and when the CCF/NDP government of Saskatchewan actually adopted comprehensive medical-care insurance, doctors responded with a 23-day strike. Later, when comprehensive national reform was in place and the government prohibited extra billing—billing on top of the generous ceilings authorized by the state—doctors staged another strike in Ontario.

Explanations of the different outcomes despite these similarities emphasize differences in the politics of reform that on most issues made little difference but on issues of medical care were crucial.[24] Five are most relevant. First, while decentralized federalism prevails in both countries, the 10 provinces of Canada have more explicitly reserved powers than the 50 states of the United States. The fewer, larger, more powerful provinces of Canada facilitated innovation in medical care that could serve as a model for federal social policy much more than, say, social reforms in Minnesota or New York could spread to Washington. Second, electoral laws shape the prospects of social-democratic parties that advocate national health insurance. State laws in the United States are serious barriers to the appearance of third parties on the ballot. In contrast, a substantial social democratic party in Canada provided the impetus for national health insurance. More generally, its credible electoral threat to the two major parties pushed the entire political spectrum somewhat to the left. The Cooperative Commonwealth Federation (CCF)—later renamed the New Democratic Party (NDP)—came to power in Saskatchewan in 1944, placing health care firmly on the political agenda. They adopted a provincial hospital plan in 1947; British Columbia followed in 1948, and Alberta in 1950. By 1957, again against the opposition of providers and insurance companies, the central government adopted national hospital insurance with cost sharing between Ottawa and the provinces. The biggest breakthrough occurred in 1962 when the prairie populists of Saskatchewan adopted a comprehensive public medical-care insurance program with generous terms for doctors, including the option to bill the patient directly above the fee covered by the government. Saskatchewan was following UK's minister of health, Aneurin Bevin, who said of the opposition to the NHS, "I stuffed their mouths with gold." As their income became steadier and higher, doctors became less militant in their opposition to national health insurance. By the early 1960s Ontario had developed mandated hospital and medical insurance for the employees of medium- and large-size enterprises.

In the end, the demonstration effect of the western provinces and Ontario eased the passage of the Medical Care Act of 1966, which was fully implemented by 1972, and strengthened in 1984 by banning extra billing by physicians. It required public, nonprofit administration, comprehensiveness of service, universality of coverage, portability if the person moves or changes jobs, and equal accessibility. The system is "centralized" in the sense that the provincial governments are single payers with costs shared by the federal government, combined with "decentralized" decisions about the pattern and volume of health care delivered. Delivery of services is based on privately organized practices and hospitals governed by community boards, with global budgeting. (Tuohy, 1992, p. 112.) Regulations are much less intrusive than they are in the United States. Financing is from general revenues with very little from payroll taxes. As costs accelerated, the federal government in 1977 capped the open end of its commitment; it limited the rate of increase of its contribution to provincial costs to the rate of increase of population and GNP. By 1988, the feds paid 30% of total medical-care costs, the provinces 42%, the private sector 25% (Adams, 1993, p. 125).

Both cause and consequence of laws that create opportunities for social democratic parties are labor laws facilitating unionization. While the U.S. labor movement was declining from 29% of the labor force in 1960 (its peak was 36%) to 15% in 1988, Canadian union membership climbed over the same period from 28% to 33%.[25] This no doubt strengthened labor-left political influence and the coalition for health care.

Beyond differences in the political potential for demonstration effects by provinces vs. states and the presence in Canada of a social democratic party with national impact, there is a third difference that helps to explain the contrasting outcomes of political battles over health care—the great difference in the size and influence of the insurance industry. The insurance company lobby in the United States has long been much stronger than its Canadian counterpart. The medical-industrial complex in the United States is dominated by some 1,500 insurance companies. They were a major force in the defeat of national health insurance in 1993–94. Haynes Johnson and David Broder (1996, pp. 198–224) report that the Health Insurance Association of America (HIAA) spent almost $50 million to defeat the Clinton plan. If we add other interests arrayed against it, total spending reached at least $100 million. If we include the costs of polling and advertising and the "grassroots" campaigns waged separately by many companies and other interest groups, the total may have been as high as $300 million. HIAA alone mobilized almost a thousand phone calls to every member of the House and Senate.[26] Nothing like this occurs in Canada, both because of limitations on the time and money spent on campaigns and the relative weakness of the insurance industry at the time of health-care reform. Thus, Canada was able to prohibit insurance companies from selling insurance for services covered by the national plans.

A fourth reason for the different outcomes of health-care reform is the difference in Canadian party discipline in a parliamentary system vs. the entrepreneurial politics that have developed in the United States Congress (see chap. 11). When the governing Liberal Party, facing left pressure from the CCF/NDP, pushed national health insurance, it could count on its parliamentary support, as could the other party leaders who joined the reform. Congressional Democrats, however, can go against a Democratic president on health care with impunity.

A final explanation of the U.S. paralysis on this issue is Senate rules as they have come to be (ab)used in the 1990s. The lavish use of the Senate filibuster or the equally effective threat of its use makes it certain that any major controversial proposal can be stopped by a minority of 41 out of 100 senators. The Republican leadership used the filibuster more times from 1990 to 1994 than in the previous 150 years of Senate history. This American peculiarity is a major block to comprehensive reform. Academics who explain the demise of national health insurance in the 1990s by invoking President Clinton's political ineptitude or the complexity of his proposal should do some counting: FDR ranged between a two to one and a four to one margin in the United States Senate when he signed New Deal social legislation (and even he backed off from national health insurance); Lyndon Johnson had a two to one margin when he launched partial coverage for the aged and the poor, limited steps toward universal comprehensive health insurance that remain just that, limited. No president since Johnson has approached such a majority.

In sum: Five contrasts in the politics of health-care reform explain the Canadian success and the U.S. failure to achieve comprehensive national health insurance—modest differences that on this issue interact to make a big difference. Favoring Canada is a federalism that facilitates the wider spread of demonstration effects in fewer, larger, and more-powerful provinces that have national impact; electoral laws and customs that facilitate the national presence of a third left party; smaller size and weaker influence of the insurance industry; party discipline in a parliamentary system; and no counterpart to the minority capacity to paralyze reform in the United States Senate. We have seen throughout this book that the two countries share abundant structural similarities that account for many similar policy outcomes: low levels of social spending; an accent on means testing and the concomitant achievement of a welfare mess; similarly low family-policy scores; high poverty and inequality; mass disaffection from politicians and a relatively rapid decline of established parties; a below-average economic performance until 1980; heavy reliance on painfully visible taxes; and, more recently, similar intensity of tax-welfare backlash. Despite all these shared policies and outputs, the modest differences I have discussed probably explain the striking difference in the development of health-care systems and health performance since the early 1960s.

ADMINISTRATIVE COSTS, WASTE, AND CORRUPTION

As chapter 9 on bureaucratic bloat demonstrates, the most-decentralized and fragmented political economies are least efficient and rank high in public employees as a portion of the labor force. In health care, decentralization of financing and fragmentation of service delivery result in even more bureaucratic bloat, in both private and public sectors.

Administrative Costs and Waste

In the most careful comparative study available, Jean-Pierre Poullier (1992, table 2, column 4) takes account of substantial variations in the definition of health expenditures attributable to paperwork, management, monitoring, and regulation for seven of our rich democracies (Australia, Canada, France, Germany, Netherlands, Sweden, and the United States). In view of the character of the medical-industrial complex, it is not surprising that the United States is the leader in administrative costs. Per capita costs in the U.S. in 1990 far exceed those of West Germany and the Netherlands (countries that are the highest in Europe) and top the other countries by factors of 6.5 (Canada), 6.2 (France), 3.9 (Australia), and 3.8 (Sweden). And these other countries deliver health care to virtually all of their population. By Poullier's measure, Canada's recorded administrative outlay is only about 15% of the U.S. level. As one comparative study concluded, "The United States shuffles paper; Canada delivers health care" (Evans, Barer, and Hertzman, 1991, p. 501). It is likely that Poullier's estimate for the United States is low. He could not include the opportunity costs of paperwork for consumers or the administrative costs and profits of providers such as insurance companies, private hospitals, and HMOs, which in the United States constitute the lion's share of administrative costs. That is why Poullier's estimate of the 1990 U.S. per capita figure is $149 while another, more-intensive study of the total per capita costs of the U.S. health-care bureaucracy, public and private, puts it at between $637 and $769 per capita, using two different methods of estimation (Woolhandler and Himmelstein, 1991; Hellander, Himmelstein, and Wolfe, 1991). This includes insurance overhead, hospital administration, nursing-home administration, and physicians' billing and overhead. This study also compares 1987 administrative costs in Canada and the United States (Woolhandler and Himmelstein, 1991, table 1, p. 1253). The results suggest that in 1987 while total administrative costs in the United States exceeded those of Canada by about 3.3 to 1.1, the most astonishing differences were in insurance administration and hospital administration.[27] These researchers note that Blue Cross/Blue Shield of Massachusetts insures 2.7 million subscribers and employs 6,682 people, more than is employed by the entire Canadian national health program to cover 26 million Canadians. They estimate that in the United States the paperwork for each insurance claim consumes six minutes of the doctor's time and one hour of secretarial work in the doctor's office. The time spent on each claim in Canadian doctors' offices can be counted in seconds.

As I have shown above, the commercialization of the U.S. system decreases social efficiency. From this study (Woolhandler and Himmelstein, 1991) it appears that it also decreases administrative efficiency. Private health insurers have almost three times more overhead costs in the United States (12% of premiums in 1987) than public programs such as Medicare and Medicaid (3.2%); Canada's provincial insurance plans run an overhead of 0.9% (*ibid.*, p. 1254). Again, the U.S. estimates may be low; this study omits the administrative costs of union and employer benefit programs as well as the administrative work of hospital nurses and other nonphysician clinical personnel, probably greater in the United States than Canada.

Hundreds of competing insurance companies each generates its own insurance packages and claim forms with varying and voluminous regulations on coverage, eligibility, documentation, referrals, and utilization. United States hospitals, doctors, and other medical-care personnel waste prodigious amounts of time just keeping track of bills. They must develop an extensive internal accounting apparatus to accommodate both private insurers' and the government's demands for billing on a per patient basis. Insurers and managed-care firms alike employ an army of clerks and bureaucrats to scrutinize the clinical encounter in a massive effort to eliminate what is in their judgment unnecessary care. This leaves out what employers and government agencies, the purchasers of this care, must do to keep track of the insurers and providers. Patients, too, must play their part to cope with the paper flow—reading the fine print, locating the clever loopholes, protesting plain errors, appealing denials of their claims, hanging on the phone.

HMOs were supposed to be the great cost-containing solution to the U.S. cost explosion. We have seen that they do cut costs by risk selection, reducing care, and cutting caregivers' income. But there is no reason to believe that this can long continue. The limits to cost savings limits have already been reached as shown by steep increases in premiums in 1998 and patient revolts expressed in congressional support for a patient's bill of rights. Further, it is doubtful that commercial HMOs save on administration. A California survey by the California Medical Association based on self-reports by managed-care companies in 1996 shows that on average the 15 largest HMOs spend 16.4% of each health-care dollar on administration, including advertising and profits. The range was from 27.7% (Chinese Community Health Plan) to 3.5% (Kaiser Foundation Plan). Smaller HMOs, without economies of scale, reach as high as 50% or so in per patient administrative costs.

In short, the United States has a plethora of insurers and purchasers micromanaging the delivery of health care. That the most rapidly growing component of U.S. health-care expenditures in the 1980s was "administration" is understandable. Single-payer systems with global budgets, of course, eliminate almost all of this.

Commerce and Corruption

An inevitable consequence of this cobweb of commercial complexity is what is loosely called "corruption" or in congressional attacks on big government, "waste, fraud, and abuse." Evidence regarding the scale of this behavior remains shaky, mostly anecdotal, and certainly not comparable across nations. In the United States by the mid-1990s the federal government as well as many state governments were launching investigations into alleged corruption in the medical-industrial complex.

Some of this is raw fraud—billing for services not provided, providing expensive services that are not medically appropriate, kickbacks and payments for patient referrals, bribing administrators who run hospitals that a corporate chain is trying to acquire. Much of it, however, is the structured evasion of laws, regulations, and ethical norms. "Structured" because of the conflicts of interest discussed above: Doctors who face managed-care pressure on their income become investors in medical facilities to which they can refer their patients, or they develop cozy relations with drug firms. Insurers facing tough competition find ways to discourage sales to eligible but undesirable groups and individuals—for instance, by charging very high premiums or penalizing insurance agents who sell policies to high-risk patients. HMOs and hospitals hire consultants expert in "revenue maximization" who earn contingency fees based on a percentage of any increased reimbursements they bring in from hospital Medicare checks—typically 25% to 40%. When the government tried to crack down on the abuses that consultants' zeal produced, the consultants changed their brochures to "coding compliance services"; they promised to ensure "optimal DRG reimbursement" (Diagnosis Related Group, industry shorthand for the reimbursement codes at the core of the Medicare billing system). (*Wall Street Journal*, February 10, 1998.)[28]

There is something of a Gresham's law of medical purchases at work here. Employers choose plans that are bigger and cheaper. Medicare and Medicaid program administrators facing budget pressures pass them on to providers of care. In this situation, one strategy for competitive victory for a managed-care firm is not only to cut service, reduce medical personnel's income, and increase premiums, but also to pad the bills. Companies that play by the rules or give too much attention to the quality of service get more than their share of high-risk business, forcing them to increase prices for all of their customers. The net effect is competitive reductions in health care on behalf of the bottom line.

Finally, beyond raw fraud and beyond structured evasion of the rules, there is a large gray area where complexity fosters error in the service of cost cutting. As in the case of the apparatus for means testing in the welfare mess (chap. 8), much of "corruption" is simply the difficulty of applying ever-changing rules imposed by multiple authorities, private and public—errors, not always deliberate abuse. For example where big money turns on how a patient's illness is classified, there can be good faith disagreements over interpretations of clinical evidence. Where rules are complex and numerous there are also inadvertent mistakes. Regulators and prosecutors, aware of these ambiguities, engage in selective enforcement. James Blumstein likens the American health-care industry to a "speakeasy, with wholesale illegal conduct taking place but being winked at by prosecutors who say they will move only against the loud and obnoxious drunks" (*Wall Street Journal,* December 8, 1997), like Vencor, Inc. and Columbia/HCA Healthcare Corporation described above.

Do other countries evidence the level of fraud and abuse of the United States? Where the public sector is reasonably clean and the public share of health-care expenditures is well above three-quarters (e.g., Sweden, Norway, Denmark, and the UK), it is likely that "corruption" is far below the level in the United States. Where the public sector itself is ridden with corruption (Italy), the health-care sector, public or private, will not be immune to corruption. Also, methods of compensation can have specific effects in narrow areas. For instance, Japan ranks high in prescription drug consumption because drugs are sold by doctors themselves. Patients in Austria and Germany stay in hospitals a very long time because hospital funding is based on payments per occupied bed. And before its massive reform of bargaining arrangements in the health sector (see chap. 5), German physicians had quite close alliances with pharmaceutical firms. In general, however, the United States has gone much further than other countries in commercializing health care. Because of this extreme commercialization and concomitant decentralization and fragmentation, the U.S. health-care system has very likely achieved the highest administrative costs and has perhaps invited the highest corruption quotient.

AFFLUENCE, SPENDING, TYPES OF POLITICAL ECONOMY, AND HEALTH PERFORMANCE: AN EMPIRICAL TEST[29]

Turning from the more intensive studies of the impact of the organization of health care on real health, this section explores the interaction of government spending, level of economic development, and types of political economy as determinants of health outputs in all 19 rich democracies. Regarding spending, I assumed (and the evidence is overwhelming) that spending through the public sector has benign effects on a nation's health performance because it indicates improved equality of access to doctors, drugs, hospitals, and public health services. Second, I reasoned that it was not the effort a government makes that enhances health (measured by the percentage of GDP spent on health care) but the cash and services it delivers to its population (measured by per capita health expenditures).[30] Third, in view of our discussion of the importance of the wide diffusion of biomedical knowledge about health, I added education spending per capita at all levels to the spending package that might have health effects. It is well known that education is related to a wide range of health indicators; a more-educated population not only learns more health-relevant information and deals with the medical community more effectively but it also develops healthier lifestyles than less-educated populations. This applies both to countries at different average education levels and to educational strata within countries. Fourth, because we have found above that economic level is a strong predictor of good health, although the intervention of the medical community also plays its part, I added per capita GDP to the equation.

The first complication is that these spending variables are so strongly correlated with one another and with affluence that regression analysis cannot help to sort out their independent effects on health performance. In other words, richer countries spend more per capita on both public health and education—even where the spread of GDP per capita is only from most rich to least rich. Further, these three sources of health performance are almost as strongly related to the health index as they are to one another—whether we measure them in U.S. dollar exchange rates or purchasing power parities.[31] What we can say with assurance from table 16.4 is that both health spending and education spending are each strongly related to a high score on the real health index. Affluence appears to be equally important. Corporatist bargaining arrangements alone do not have much effect, but the interaction of all four variables—health spending and education spending per capita, affluence, and any type of corporatism results in by far the best health performance in the universe of rich democracies. Thus six of the seven countries with the top health scores (upper left on the table) are corporatist. They are also big spenders and quite affluent. Canada, the exception in its bargaining structure, still fits: its health and education spending is well above average and as we have seen above, its national health-insurance program is highly cost-effective.[32]

The notable deviant cases in table 16.4 are Japan and Germany. For my hypothesis, Japan spends too little and in 1980 was still no richer than the United Kingdom; but its health score, 12.0, was a very good fifth among our 19. Germany, on the other hand, spent far too much on health care (more than four of the very best performers—Denmark, Netherlands, Switzerland, and Canada) and was too affluent for its poor health score of 4.0 and its rank (17th among our 19).[33]

If we use purchasing power parities in the analysis (table not reported), the only major changes are that Finland sinks to the bottom right cell where it belongs and the United States becomes even more deviant than it is in table 16.4. By PPS measures the United States is #1 in affluence and is above average in education spending (average in government health spending) and yet ranks only 11th in its health score of 8.0. We have already seen why the health-care system of the United States evidences poor social efficiency: its performance is below average in infant mortality (15th) and male life expectancy at age 1 (13th); average in female life expectancy (9th); and average in circulatory disease deaths among males aged 65−74 (10th) and a little above average in keeping down pregnancy and childbirth deaths (8th). Despite its lavish health-care spending, largely through the private sector, despite its great wealth, the United States produces a relatively poor outcome.

TABLE 16.4 Interaction of government health and education spending per capita (1975 and 1980), corporatism, and affluence fosters good health performance (circa 1980). Public spending and affluence each enhances health performance. Corporatism alone has little effect

	Seven countries with good to excellent health performance					Five countries with average health performance					Seven countries with poor to fair health performance				
	Health Index[a]	Health per cap.[b]	Educ. per cap.	Health and educ. per cap.[c]	GDP per cap.[d]	Health index	Health per cap.	Educ. per cap.	Health and educ. per cap.	GDP per cap.	Health index	Health per cap.	Educ. per cap.	Health and educ. per cap.	GDP per cap.
Big health and educ. spenders ($1109 and over per cap. average)															
Sweden**	14.0 (1)	$974	$865	$1839	$11,963										
Norway**	12.0 (5)	$703	$608	$1311	$10,607										
Denmark**	11.0 (7)	$595	$635	$1230	$10,182										
Netherlands**	12.5 (3)	$574	$625	$1199	$9,382										
Switzerland*	13.5 (2)	$574	$551	$1125	$12,180										
Canada	12.0 (5)	$497	$612	$1109	$9,133										
cell avg.	12.5	$653	$649	$1302	$10,575										
Med. health and educ. spenders ($844 to $1064 per cap. avg.)															
Belgium**						8.0 (11)	$467	$541	$1008	$9,145					
France*						10.0 (8)	$551	$437	$988	$9,426					
USA						8.0 (11)	$363	$562	$925	$9,621					
Australia						8.0 (11)	$430	$444	$874	$9,051					
Germany**											4.0 (17)	$654	$410	$1064	$9,944
Finland**											6.0 (13)	$414	$430	$844	$8,409
cell avg.						8.5	$453	$496	$949	$9311	5.0	$534	$420	$954	$9,177
Lean health and educ. spenders ($725 and below per cap. avg.)															
Japan*	12.0 (5)	$296	$266	$562	$6,775										
Italy**						8.5 (9)	$311	$196	$507	$5,927					
UK**											6.0 (13)	$351	$374	$725	$6,863
Israel**											5.0 (15)	$388	$313	$701	$4,745
Austria**											3.0 (19)	$334	$354	$688	$7,626
New Zealand											4.0 (17)	$279	$281	$560	$5,771
Ireland											5.0 (15)	$308	$224	$532	$4,135
cell avg.											4.6	$332	$309	$641	$5,828

** Corporatist. Germany a marginal case. * Corporatist without labor. Switzerland perhaps marginal.

[a] Combines infant mortality, life expectancy at one for females, the same for males, circulatory disease deaths, and pregnancy and childbirth deaths, equally weighted. See text.

[b] Total government health expenditure per capita, average of 1975 and 1980 using U.S. dollar exchange rates. Source: OECD, 1985a, 19–20 and table A2.

[c] Current public education expenditure per capita, average of 1975 and 1980, U.S. dollar exchange rates. Figure for Japan excludes public subsidies to private education. Source: UNESCO, 1986, tables 4.1 and 4.2.

[d] Average of 1975 and 1980 GDP per capita in dollars (OECD, 1993d). Data for Israel from World Bank (1989).

Disaggregating the health index components sheds some light on other deviant cases. Germany's very low rank in 1980 (17th) reflects below-average scores for infant mortality, life expectancy for both male and females, as well as circulatory disease deaths, and very poor performance for pregnancy and childbirth deaths. Several features of health-care organization might account for these results: Germany ranks very low in the density of nurses and midwives (table 16.2). Starfield's comparison of 10 of our countries, rates Germany as "poor" in coordination between specialists and primary-care physicians, in "family centeredness" and in "community orientation." Before major reforms of the 1980s and early 1990s, Germany evidenced an unusually sharp separation of hospital physicians, most of whom are salaried, and fee-for-service physicians in offices. This had the effect of reducing the rate of medically appropriate referrals while increasing unnecessary treatment and costs. Expensive and excessive services were also assured by the system of reimbursement: retrospective per diem payments for hospital operating costs, which encourage long stays; and no effective ceiling on aggregate outlays for fee-for-service, office-based practitioners (Alber, 1989, pp. 5–6).

Germany assures comprehensive near-universal coverage through a complex array of 768 nonprofit Krankenkassen (sickness funds based on occupation or region that mediate between the consumer and providers); in 1996 there were 571 in West Germany, 197 in East Germany. The federal government administers health insurance plans for the uninsured poor, supervises private insurance for the affluent who use it, and coordinates a system of negotiations between labor, management, providers, and the Krankenkassen (see chap. 5). Obviously, multiple sickness funds in a complex system of bargaining generate substantial administrative expense; Poullier's conservative estimates (1992) show that Germany's per capita expenditures for health administration were second only to the USA's ($102 vs. $149). More important in the cost escalation of the 1970s was the power of providers and pharmaceutical firms. From 1970 until major reforms in the period from 1981 to 1992 (chap. 5) contribution rates for statutory health insurance moved up an average of more than 4.0% a year (Bundesministerium für Gesundheit, 1996, table 10.11). Most of the fee negotiations took place between single sickness funds and doctors organized in regional associations with public law status. When in the late 1970s I asked the chief national negotiator and strategist of the physicians association whether the Krankenkassen functioned as a countervailing power to his organization, he scoffed. He told me that the sickness funds could easily be outmaneuvered by regional KVen (doctors associations) that were much better equipped with personnel and resources than their bargaining partners. He also observed that competition between different types of sickness funds was not for cost control but for better service ("the region next door has the latest hospital technology, why can't we have the best?"). For the same reasons, physicians' income also climbed to new heights. In short, all these characteristics of the German system help to explain its low social efficiency as of 1980.

In the 1980s and early 1990s, however, the federal government realigned the association bargaining structure. It increased the power of the Krankenkassen by centralizing them and enhancing their coordinating capacity (an incremental process from 1981 on); by upgrading the hospital association and allowing salaried hospital doctors to do some of the outpatient work previously monopolized by office-based fee-for-service physicians; and by excluding the pharmaceutical industry from participating in a drug-pricing plan of 1988 that reduced reimbursements by sickness funds and gave physicians incentives to prescribe generics. Reform and cost control were accomplished by a combination of budget pressures (mounting when massive finance transfers into the former GDR began), an SPD majority in the Bundesrat in 1992 that outmaneuvered the provider-oriented FDP, as well as skillful handling of reform by Health Minister Seehofer, who among other moves created divisions among provider organizations (specialists vs. GPs, big drug firms vs. smaller generic drug firms).[34] Since the early 1980s corporatist bargaining in the health-care sector has been strengthened, costs have come under some control; and by the late 1990s Germany had moved up in its relative health performance. Increases in social efficiency by now have made Germany less of a deviant case. (Bundesministerium für Gesundheit, 1996, tables 2.4, 5.3, 5.4; cf., Reinhardt, 1997, pp. 176–178.)

Japan, the other clearly deviant country in table 16.4, presents a paradox. Its total health-care spending, whether measured by share of GDP or per capita, is low; its organization of health care, modeled on the German system without recent German reforms, is hardly ideal; and yet its health performance is excellent. It is tempting to conclude that fish, rice, soybeans, and the rest of the traditionally good Japanese diet is everything while the intervention of the medical community is nothing. That is not the main story, however.[35]

Regarding 1980 spending, in table 16.4 Japan's public-sector per capita outlays put it second to last, edging out only New Zealand. Spending per capita on education puts it third to last, above only Ireland and Italy. (Using purchasing power parities does not change the picture.) In density of doctors (not related to health performance) it ranks a low 16th (table 16.1); in density of nurses and midwives (strongly related to good health performance) it is not much better, ranking 14th.

At first glance, lean spending and low personnel/population ratios cannot be explained by an efficient organization of health care. For some of the most cost-explosive features of the most expensive health-care systems are prominent in Japan:

- Lavish use of prescription drugs. In 1980, drug costs averaged just over 38% of national medical expenditures. Doctors dispense drugs directly; money from this trade is a large part of their income, accounting for the dominance of prescription drugs over non-prescription drugs.

- Care is hospital centered. Japan's inpatient beds per 10,000 population in 1995 made it #1 (16.2 beds). Although all 19 countries reduced average length of stay in hospitals from 1985 to 1995, Japan remained in a class of its own: its average was 45.5 days with the next nearest a high 32.8 for the Netherlands, while every other country ranged from Australia's 14-day average to Denmark's 7.5. ("OECD in Figures," 1997 ed., pp. 48–49.) One reason for long hospital stays, especially for older populations, is that Japan has a weak infrastructure to which patients might be discharged: the three-generation household is eroding as female caregivers go to work outside the home (chaps. 1 and 5); there is a severe shortage of nursing homes and severely cramped housing.

- Hospitals and "clinics" (which are really small hospitals) compete intensely for patients. "A closed staff system means that every clinic and hospital is exclusive with regard to patients and tries to offer 'all-in-one' medical services" (Steslicke, 1987, p. 45), which means covering too much too thinly. Physicians also strive to make maximum use of high-technology equipment, especially for diagnostic tests—for example, CT scanners. Much of this equipment is owned by physicians, another incentive for their (over-)use. The net effect: much overlap, redundancy, and excess capacity.

- There is very uneven training for physicians even within one hospital or clinic. The competition among hospitals for patients is therefore not mainly on quality.

- Coordination and continuity of service from primary-care physician to specialist to rehabilitation and prevention is poor. Like Germany, Japan achieves universal coverage and equality of access by aggregating many separate employment-based insurance schemes with the government setting ground rules and filling in gaps. There are also about 40 national associations active in medical policymaking; they represent providers, insurers, business, and labor—all bargaining with one another and with political parties and the government. Such a system presents formidable problems of coordination.

All of this should result in poor social efficiency. But there are many counteracting forces at work to keep costs down, most of which, we have seen above, enhance national health performance.

- In 1980—the date of the health index scores in table 16.4—a majority of Japanese doctors were salaried employees working in hospitals, clinics, and other institutions, both public and private.

- Although almost all Japanese physicians are officially specialists, most are actually fully engaged in general practice, doing the work of primary care. This may result in an optimum balance between generalists and specialists discussed above.

- Cost containment is achieved not only by low density of doctors and nurses but by tight government controls over reimbursement, especially for expensive treatment. In 1987 the incomes of private practitioners were 8.2 times average wages; salaried physicians had incomes only 2.4 times the average wage. In addition, there is patient cost-sharing for some high-cost medical care.

- Regarding nurses: Families still do much of the nursing. Professional nurses, many of them public health nurses, are concentrated in a well-developed system of maternal and child care. Universal health insurance covers maternity and infant care services. All pregnant women, infants, and young children receive free and unlimited medical exams. Medical clinics run classes for pregnant women. Midwives and nurses make regular visits to the homes of pregnant women and women with infants. Family planning services are widely available. (Marmor, 1992, p. 13.) Shinsuke Morio (1985) demonstrates that the more public health nurses in a Japanese prefect, the better its health performance.

- Health programs in the schools are extensive. But even without their emphasis on prevention and promotion of good health habits, Japan's very high standards of literacy and numeracy in its universal basic curriculum K–12 (see chap. 12), would have a positive health effect by diffusing biomedical knowledge throughout the entire population.

- In 1980, Japan's percentage of population over 64 was very small—another reason for low health-care costs.

In addition to these cost-effective forces in the health-care system, several attributes of Japanese society are known to enhance health performance: rising standards of living, low unemployment and relatively high job security, low rates of poverty, an egalitarian income distribution, a consensual system of decision making, and a strong sense of solidarity and community. Their health effects will be discussed in the final section of this chapter.

These features of the organization of both health care and society probably explain Japan's excellent score of 12 on our health index. Its performance places it at or near the top of all 19 countries in all but one indicator: #1 in male life expectancy, #2 in infant mortality and in circulatory disease deaths, and #4 in female life expectancy. It falls short only in pregnancy and childbirth deaths, ranking at the bottom (highest death rate). In 1980 that might be due to the wide use of abortion as a major method of birth control; at that time there were more abortions each year than live births.

Observers of health-care systems sometimes point to Japan as proof that the lowest input of money can bring the best output, repeating the mantra, "throwing money at the problem won't solve it." Table 16.4 says that public money is almost a necessary condition for good national health performance. Moreover, like the German deviance in table 16.4, the Japanese peculiarities are becoming less peculiar. Cost pressures are now acute. If one combines a fee-for-service, hospital-centered system with comprehensive, universal health insurance (in place since 1961), free choice of providers, and a rising penchant for high-tech medicine with the most rapidly rising population over 64 among all rich democracies, there is bound to be increased costs for the same good health outputs. In fact, by 1995 Japan had tied Sweden for 13th place in total health-care spending as a share of GDP, 7.2%; and was 12th in spending per capita, $1,581, ahead of Sweden's $1,360 and ahead of five other countries—Italy, Finland, Denmark, Norway, and New Zealand. ("OECD in Figures," 1997 ed., pp. 48–49.) Its convergence with the rest of the pack is apparent.

In sum: This section has shown that if a country has developed a system of consensual bargaining among labor, management, the professions, and government, if it delivers a large amount of cash and services in health care and education at every level, and if it is relatively affluent, it will score high on our health performance index. No one of these forces alone suffices; it is the interaction of types of spending, types of political economy, and level of riches that determines good health.

Mass Society, Poverty, Inequality, Insecurity, and Health Performance

It is not only the organization of medical care that shapes health outputs; it is also the organization of society. There is increasing evidence that if a society tolerates a high rate of poverty, inequality, or unemployment; if it organizes its economy to maximize job insecurity and stress; if it fails to develop social policies that assure the care of children and ease the task of balancing work and family demands—it will foster poor health for large segments of its population. Here cross-national evidence is very limited, but several studies of single countries or communities are suggestive. A few careful, cross-national studies are available; they confirm findings from single cases. The studies cited below are systematically comparative and use appropriate controls for variables known to affect health outcomes, such as access to medical care, age, sex, level of affluence, and health habits (or lifestyles). Some use individuals as the focus of study, others nations or subgroups within nations. Individual-level studies and population studies that emphasize the socioeconomic and cultural contexts of disease rates are complementary. As Neil Pearce (1996, p. 681) suggests, "just as a variety of health effects in various organ systems (e.g., various types of cancer) may have a common contributing cause (e.g., tobacco smoking) at the level of the individual, a variety of individual exposures (e.g., smoking, diet) may have common socioeconomic causes at the population level (e.g., poverty rates or inequality)."

Moving down the gradient from high socioeconomic status (SES) to low SES, or more generally, increasing economic deprivation, increases mortality, disability, and morbidity (Dutton, 1986; Bunker, Gomby, and Kehrer, 1989; Chandra, 1991; Mechanic, 1993; Feinstein, 1993; Wennemo, 1994; Pearce, 1996; Duleep, 1995). Why this is so will be discussed below.

Aside from the inequalities of status and income tapped by these studies of social class and health, poverty has an independent effect in increasing health risks—for instance the poor, even in an egalitarian society, may be at greater risk than the nonpoor. A few studies have attempted to sort out the distinctive impact of poverty from the effects of SES gradients, inequality, and affluence, either for individuals or nations. For instance, a cross-national study of infant mortality in 18 industrial democracies by Irene Wennemo (1994, pp. 114–183) found that income equality has a more positive effect in reducing infant mortality than does the level of economic development (GDP per capita). As rich countries converged in per capita GDP from 1950 to 1985, however, level of economic development had a decreasing effect on infant mortality rates. In fact, as a source of variation in these rates, affluence is now not as strong as income equalization or poverty reduction. Other important sources of infant mortality in this study are family policies; high levels of family benefits relate to low mortality rates. While high unemployment and low unemployment insurance by themselves are not important, the combination of high unemployment rates and low unemployment benefits—because it increases the population with poor living conditions—is associated with particularly high infant mortality rates. (Cf. Marmot et al., 1994, and similar findings reviewed by Pearce, 1996.) Just as economic deprivation interacting with family breakup in the absence of a generous universal family policy is a major source of mayhem (chap. 14), the same combination results in many babies dying before the age of one (cf. Liu et al., 1992).

Inequality—the distance between the rich and poor—as distinct from relative poverty also shapes health outcomes. Using 1980 LIS data on inequality and poverty for 9 to 11 of our countries, Wennemo (1994, pp. 126–129) finds that affluence has only a weak effect on infant mortality while inequality (Gini coefficient) has a strong effect and the relative poverty rate a medium effect. Germany, as I have shown above, is an outlier with a much higher infant mortality rate than predicted by its low relative poverty rate. Eliminating Germany from the analysis strengthens the effect of poverty.

In my 19-country analysis, using different measures of poverty and inequality (the measures in table 14.4), I find a weaker association with health indicators. The pattern of correlations with the components of the health index (table 16.4) is in the right direction, but the correlations are at best of marginal significance. However, country scatter-plots and cross-tabulations (not reported here) do show interesting results for infant mortality: the higher the share of income taken by the lowest fifth of households (a rough indicator of a low poverty rate), the lower the rate of infant mortality. Conversely, the higher the share of income taken by the top quintile, the higher the rate of infant mortality. For instance, if we divide the 17 countries for which we have all relevant data into high and low poverty rates, we find that 6 of the 9 least poverty-ridden (all 9 are corporatist) have the lowest infant mortality rates, while 6 of the 8 countries with the highest poverty have the highest infant mortality rates. Out of line are Italy, Belgium, and West Germany (too low in poverty for their above-average mortality rates), and Denmark and Switzerland (both too high in poverty for their good performance on infant mortality). Offsetting their deviance on this measure of poverty are social policies that tend to reduce deep poverty: all but Switzerland are welfare-state leaders that also score quite high on our broad measure of innovative and expansive family policies (chap. 7).[36]

Similarly, large income shares to the rich and the upper-middle class are associated with high rates of infant mortality. The same dichotomy yields almost identical results. The United Kingdom, whose upper fifth takes the median income share, has almost a median mortality rate. Of the eight egalitarian cases above the United Kingdom, all corporatist democracies, six have low mortality; of the eight least-egalitarian countries where the upper fifth takes from 40% to 45% of the household income, six have high infant mortality rates. Here we see the same deviant cases, except that Italy falls into the proper place (low equality, high mortality).

A more direct approach to this problem is to examine the interplay of types of political economy, deep child poverty for solo mothers, deep poverty for two-parent families (the country scores appear in table 8.4), and infant mortality. Comparing the averages for 13 countries (table not reported), there is a clear relationship: corporatist democracies with considerable left power achieve the lowest rates of deep poverty and by far the lowest rate of infant mortality; France, with a medium rate of deep poverty, has a medium rate of mortality; Catholic corporatist countries (Italy and West Germany) rank above average in deep poverty and are highest in infant mortality; and finally, the most-fragmented, decentralized political economies have by far the deepest poverty and are above average in infant mortality.

In short, on the basis of these studies it is definite that corporatist democracies decrease both poverty and inequality, and it is likely that such an outcome in turn reduces infant mortality.

The explanation for the impact of poverty and, more generally, relative economic deprivation on infant mortality is straightforward. And the same explanation holds for a great range of health indicators, including disability and morbidity. The poor everywhere but especially in those countries whose taxing, spending, and social policies have fostered a high rate of deep poverty are exposed to higher and more numerous risk factors: when exposed they have fewer resources to cope with harmful situations; and in the less-egalitarian countries, they have much less access to prenatal, neonatal, and child care and to preventive services. At the extreme, the poor and least educated in the United States, especially poor blacks and Hispanics in large urban areas but also the old-old poor and the rural elderly poor receive only inferior, episodic medical care. (Ory, Abeles, and Lipman, 1992, p. 6–7; Mechanic, 1993, pp. 20–22.) Mechanic (p. 21) notes that because much of this occasional care is in emergency rooms and hospital outpatient clinics and involves limited or no insurance coverage, it lacks continuity, preventive appraisals, proper referral to specialists, and any pretense of health maintenance.

Regarding risk factors among the uneducated poor in every country, there is good evidence that the relatively poor health of this population is rooted in chronically poor or inadequate nutrition from conception to maturity, which leads to short height (height at maturity is inversely associated with risk of chronic diseases and dying in the later stages of adult life) as well as overcrowded housing and in some countries dangerous neighborhoods. That stunted development in early life as a result of poor nutrition leads to poor adult health and an early death (Fogel, 1991, pp. 47–61) is not due to any specific disease; it is related to the development of the immune system and other organ systems (Barker, 1992). Finally, two other clusters of risk factors are prevalent among the poor: destructive personal habits and child-spacing patterns. The poor use more tobacco and have higher rates of drug abuse than the nonpoor (see chaps. 14 and 15 on mayhem and the environment). The poor tend to have more children, tightly spaced; countries that reduce poverty and provide wide access to family planning services also reduce class differences in fertility, nutrition, and height, thereby improving national health performance (Frank and Mustard, 1994, pp. 5–7).

Not so obvious is the explanation for the health effects of inequality—whether we examine the income and health gaps between the rich and the poor, whatever the rate of poverty, or the gradation in health status throughout the educational and income distribution. Consider my finding that infant mortality is affected by the share of household income taken by the upper fifth. The causal chain separating those two variables is long. The rich getting very rich and the upper-middle class distancing itself from the rest of the population initiates a political process in which downward redistribution of any kind, including delivery of services and cash to the poor, is less likely. If at the same time large groups in the middle mass think they are getting squeezed between the educated affluent and the nonworking poor, they will succumb to demagogic appeals of race, ethnicity, religion, and language (see chap. 10). However, the revolt of the middle mass is not universal. It is only in the absence of strong center-left parties and corporatist bargaining arrangements that this angry resistance to redistributive policies prevails. Thus, Canada, the United States, Australia, and New Zealand, least-corporatist countries with weak center-left parties, lead in both the highest shares of income taken by the top quintile and the highest infant mortality rates. Italy, medium in corporatism, is a partial exception. It fits this category of high mortality and high top quintile share, but its divided left parties were kept out of governing coalitions for most of the postwar period, and its politics are not strongly consensual. In contrast, Norway, Sweden, Finland, Netherlands, and Denmark—corporatist democracies with strong center-left coalitions—lead in both the lowest shares of income taken by the top quintile and the very lowest infant mortality rates. They have managed to create a stronger sense of national community and a sense of solidarity between the middle mass and the poor. Egalitarian Japan and Belgium are clear exceptions, explained above.

Similarly, there are well-established SES gradients in height and health (Evans and Stoddart, 1994, p. 27; Frank and Mustard, 1994, p. 7; Pearce, 1996, p. 679; Kawachi et al., 1997; Wilkinson, 1992, p. 1082; Sen, 1980). These cannot be readily explained by sheer differences in "class." As I have suggested in chapter 1, the concept of social class—and typical measures of it such as income, occupational status, and level of education—obscure more than they reveal. They are only very rough guides to more specific patterns of behavior and life conditions that directly shape health outcomes. Nutrition as it affects early development and adult stature is one. Other health-relevant correlates of SES, especially of the level and quality of education, include patterns of social participation—the number and vitality of ties to kin, friends, and neighbors, the same for churches, unions, and voluntary associations; the duration and intensity of economic insecurity; and tensions at work as they spill over in leisure. My discussion of mass society (chap. 3) suggests that these often vary among groups at the same SES level and they certainly vary across nations. With rare exceptions the connections of health status to social networks/isolation, to job insecurity, and to work situation are little studied and no systematic cross-national comparisons are available. The exceptions are worth noting.

Regarding social cohesion, a comprehensive nine-year longitudinal study of Alameda County, California, from 1965 to 1974 demonstrated that adults with few social ties were two or three times more likely to die of all causes than those most strongly attached to the community, holding constant age and health practices (smoking, drinking, exercise, and the actual use of medical services). Social support networks—marital status, ties to kin and friends, church membership, and organizational affiliations—plainly act to reduce the risk of mortality and morbidity (Berkman and Syme, 1979; Syme, 1986). Consistent with the Alameda findings are several less comprehensive studies of the negative impact of family breakup on health and well-being. Divorced, separated, and widowed adults, especially those living alone, suffer more physical illness and psychological distress than adults with partners (Seeman et al., 1987; Estes and Wilensky, 1978). Similarly, "happiness" studies find that the least happy of survey respondents in all countries are the least attached—the unemployed, the divorced, widowed, or separated, and the least educated (chap. 4, note 12).

A second comprehensive ecological study of inequality, social cohesion, and health (Kawachi et al., 1997) used a broad range of indicators (all-cause mortality, infant mortality, plus age-adjusted mortality from heart disease, malignant neoplasms, cerebrovascular disease, and unintentional injuries). It compared 39 U.S. states on measures of inequality (estimated from shares of household income arrayed by decile groups), controlling for poverty (in 1990 an income of less than $13,359 for four-person households). It measured social or civic mistrust and perceived lack of fairness by the proportion of survey respondents who agreed with the distrust alternative in two questions: Do you think most people would try to take advantage of you if they got the chance, or would they try to be fair? and Generally speaking, would you say that most people can be trusted or that you can't be too careful in dealing with people? Level of civic engagement or social participation was measured by the per capita number of groups and associations (e.g., church groups, labor unions, sports groups, professional or academic societies, school groups, and fraternal organizations) to which residents in each state belonged. Their conclusions, based on regression and path analysis: As income inequality increases, civic engagement decreases and the level of social mistrust climbs. These, in turn, significantly and strongly determine state health performance. The findings are consistent with my discussion of mass-society theory in chapter 1 and with Emile Durkheim's classic cross-national analysis of suicide rates, which he showed are anchored in the lack of social cohesion. Unrelieved anxiety among people without social support not only triggers suicide; it is bad for health among the living. See similar findings in Frank (1995, p. 162) on heart disease; Marmot et al. (1991) and Marmot et al. (1994, p. 37) on numerous health indicators.

Related to the vitality of social participation is economic security. Both have been found to relate to one another and to shape health performance. For instance, in my study of work, careers, and social integration among white men of the middle mass aged 21–55 in the Detroit metropolitan area in 1960 (Wilensky, 1961a), I compared those with more or less orderly careers and those whose job histories evidenced much chaos—whose jobs were numerous, unrelated in function and status, and punctuated by many episodes of unemployment. Holding age constant, an orderly career, another way of saying a predictable worklife, was strongly related to a wide range of strong social ties, both primary and secondary, and frequent participation in community life; the inverse was true of men whose experience in the labor market was chaotic. Many measures of economic insecurity have subsequently been connected to physical and mental illness. Ralph Catalano (1991) carefully reviews 68 studies in several countries that meet minimum standards of internal and external validity and that use time series or argue plausibly against the possibility that a biological or psychological predisposition to illness caused both the health outcome and the economic insecurity (job loss, substantial loss of income, being unable to pay one's bills, etc.). By these stringent criteria, there is strong evidence of the effect of economic insecurity on suicide or on reporting symptoms of psychological disorder or on seeking help for such disorder. Evidence of the impact of economic deprivation on nonspecific physiological illness controlling for age, sex, SES, and other stressors is based on surveys or small samples and is counted as weak or moderate. However, evidence for the effects of loss of jobs or income on myocardial infarction is strong. It is plain from many of these studies that the health effects of economic insecurity are not confined to the lower class; insecurity may be more frequent among lower strata, but it is a cross-class phenomena, as are well-measured patterns of social participation.

As in much social research, the closer we get to organizations and groups rather than broad "social classes" or "socioeconomic factors," the more powerful effects we find (chap. 1). An impressive example of this is the comprehensive, intensive study of health inequalities in the British civil service. This "Whitehall" study was longitudinal; it followed about 18,000 men for the 10 years beginning in 1967 when they were 40 to 64 years old (Whitehall I) and then established a new cohort of 10,314 civil servants from 1985 to 1988—both men and women aged 35–55 working in the London offices of 20 departments (Whitehall II). (Marmot, 1986, 1994; Marmot et al., 1991; and Chandra, 1991.) It permits analysis of specific features of the immediate work situation and career prospects and position in a well-defined hierarchy of six grades, as well as variations in social support. Both medical exams and self-administered questionnaires were used. These were all office workers in stable employment with quite equal access to medical care (the NHS). The researchers found a steep gradient of morbidity and mortality from a wide range of diseases as one moves down each step in the hierarchy. They summarize:

> In the 20 years separating the two studies there has been no diminution in social class difference in morbidity: we found an inverse association between employment grade and prevalence of angina, electrocardiogram evidence of ischaemia, and symptoms of chronic bronchitis. Self perceived health status and symptoms were worse in subjects in lower status jobs. There were clear employment-grade differences in health-risk

behaviors including smoking, diet, and exercise; in economic circumstances; in possible effects of early-life environment as reflected by height; in social circumstances at work (e.g. monotonous work characterized by low control and low satisfaction); and in social supports. . . . Among men there was an inverse association between job status and number of symptoms reported in the last 14 days, likelihood of rating health as average or poor as opposed to good or very good, and a prior diagnosis of hypertension or diabetes. In general, women reported greater morbidity than men. . . . Obesity . . . was more prevalent in lower status jobs, especially in the clerical grade. As in Whitehall I, height correlated with job status. (Marmot et al., 1994, pp. 34, 36, 37)

We may think that top leaders are as likely to be as short as Napoleon or as tall as De-Gaulle, but this study makes it plain that both average height and good health increase as we move up the hierarchy. These differences in height by grade in Whitehall indicate differences in early environment, especially nutrition, that persist in adult life and that appear in broader population studies. Even controlling for conventional risk factors, civil service status was a powerful prediction of health outcomes. For instance, less than half of the excess risk of a fatal heart attack could be explained by higher cholesterol, blood pressure, smoking, or other relevant factors.

There are clear differences in patterns of social participation by civil service grade, with less, and less satisfactory, social support among those with lower-status jobs (*ibid.*, p. 39). The study also found that civil servants in lower-status jobs—even in this secure, white-collar "middle-class" environment—think that they have little control over their work, that their jobs provide little variety and make little use of their skills, and offer little chance to learn and develop new skills (*ibid.*, p. 39). As we have seen above, stimulating, challenging work spills over into stimulating, challenging leisure and increases the vitality of social participation; together, favorable work situations and strong social support enhance health. This was especially true of the risk of cardiovascular disease among these civil servants. Contrary to the myth of the workaholic working herself into an early grave (or the hostile "Type A" personality getting sick) the Whitehall data show that hostility is more prevalent among those in lower ranks and that they report fewer pressures to work fast. Workers in the top grades had to work harder and faster, but they were gratified by the challenge and were able to find release in a more active, yet relaxing leisure style (cf. Frank, 1995; Wilensky, 1964a, pp. 182ff. and table 2).

In these studies of the health impact of inequality, poverty, economic deprivation, and weak social cohesion, there is a difficult problem of causal order, especially when comparing individuals. Poor health could be the cause of a person's low income, unemployment, poor work environments, and social isolation rather than the other way round. The problem of reverse causality is not a major problem in comparisons across countries, states, or provinces, but it plagues the estimation of relationships across individuals. Almost all the studies I have cited, however, deal with this problem and confirm that it is the social and economic experience of individuals and the structure of nations that cause poor health performance, whatever the subsequent interaction of individual experience, social structures, and health outcomes. For instance, in the United Kingdom, health-related downward mobility does not account for large differences in mortality by social class (Marmot et al., 1994, p. 38). Similarly, Duleep (1995) estimated the effect of five income classes in the

United States on the probability of death for men aged 35–64, for 1975–77 and 1988–90. To cope with the problem of causality she examined disability records prior to or concurrent with the year of income used in the analysis. She employed the same procedure for survey data where individuals reported that health problems concurrent with the relevant year prohibited or limited work. Controlling for disabling illness, the income differences in premature mortality remain very strong. The effect of income distribution increased from 1974 to 1990. Duleep also compared the average income of the lowest decile in 37 countries (all 19 of ours plus a variety of other somewhat-developed countries) and other income classes. She found that differences in poverty as well as inequality have large health effects, decreasing with age.[37] Finally, the numerous studies of economic deprivation and health outcomes evaluated by Catalano (1991) either sort out the sequence of events by time series or make a persuasive case that deprivation leads to poor health.

In short, poverty, inequality (in both society and workplace), impoverished social relations, and generalized distrust (low social cohesion in society or community) each results in high rates of morbidity, disability, and mortality. Because these patterns of economic and social life are interrelated, we may never sort out their relative effects. We can, however, speculate about the causal process. Poverty and inequality weaken social cohesion. Together these three variables stiffen the political resistance of the well-off to those universal social policies, labor-market policies, and patterns of taxing and spending that reduce poverty and inequality and increase social integration. The social impact of such political resistance reduces national health performance. In full circle, the poor health of the most vulnerable population then plays its part in further increasing poverty, inequality, and social fragmentation. Large cross-national differences in this process help account for large national differences in health performance among countries equally rich. In other words, an inegalitarian mass society is bad for your health.

SUMMARY AND CONCLUSION

Although there is much healthy skepticism regarding the effectiveness of the medical community in improving health and well-being relative to the influence of improved living standards rooted in economic growth, this chapter shows that both are important. In fact, counterposing affluence to the distribution of medical care ignores their universal interaction: both health spending per capita and health-relevant education spending per capita grow along with the standard of living; therefore, it is difficult to sort out the effects of increased access to medical care and a society's level of affluence. Further, even before the rise of the medical complex, biomedical knowledge with good health effects was diffused mainly through public-health doctors, again confounding the health impact of economic development as distinct from that of the medical community. Most public health officials responsible for sanitation, disease control, and immunization in this early period were physicians.

Anyway, medical intervention has had substantial effects in both preventing and managing many diseases; it clearly has extended life expectancy free of disability for elderly men and women by several years and has helped to reduce rates of infant mortality. This leaves aside the essential garage mechanic functions of doctors, nurses, and related service providers. Access to the medical establishment everywhere clearly improves the quality of life by decreasing pain, restoring the human machine to normal functioning, curing some diseases, and easing the effects of others. It is no irrational passion for useless medical treatment that makes the mass of voters in every rich democracy put government-guaranteed health care at the top of their priorities. Mass attitudes and voting behavior testify to strong, stable, sensible support for that component of the welfare state.

With the cost-cutting, "privatizing" fervor of the past 20 or so years—universal in the doctrines of medical economists, repeated in the rhetoric of politicians in a few countries— we hear such slogans as "Stop throwing government money at the problem," "We need market competition among the providers," "True competition has not yet been tried," "Tell people to take responsibility for their own health, make them cost-conscious so they choose less-costly care." The evidence of this chapter is not only that the market model of health care borders on the absurd, but that spending per capita through the public sector strongly improves a broad range of health indicators and moves the system toward prevention.

Although the types of political economy that explain so much throughout this book do not work as well in predicting health outputs, the scheme does work at the extremes. Leftism, corporatism, and affluence interact to produce the best health performance among our 19 countries, while least-rich political economies that are also fragmented and decentralized have the poorest health performance. Four notable exceptions in table 16.4—the United States, Canada, Germany, and Japan—are explained by additional structures and demographic facts that shape types of spending and the organization of their health-care systems. In all cases but the United States they have become less exceptional in recent years.

In the past hundred years, the currently rich democracies have converged in the broad outlines of health care. Except for the United States, they all developed universal and comprehensive coverage for medical care, based on principles of social right and shared risk. They all developed central control of budgets with financing from compulsory individual and employer contributions and/or government revenues. All permit the insured to supplement government services with additional care, privately purchased. All including the United States ration health care. All have experienced a growth in doctor density and the ratio of specialists to primary-care personnel. All evidence a trend toward public funding.

Centralized state funding, by itself, expands access to care and to some extent reduces national mortality rates and improves health. In a natural process, state funding eventually leads to increased control over prices and personnel via direct employment, capitation payments, and/or government bargaining with providers. This combination yields better national health performance because it reduces inequalities in access to care by class and region, increases the volume of services available, and limits the degree of specialization (and the concomitant duplication and lavish use of expensive high-tech machines and procedures). In general, the assertion of public interests over the interests of insurance companies, pharmaceutical firms, hospitals, physicians, and other providers results in a gradual reallocation of budgets toward primary care and preventive community care. There is some evidence that centralized control of funding, prices, and personnel under state auspices compared to the alternatives yields greater social efficiency—an improved trade-off between mortality reduction and cost escalation—as well as a better balance between equality of access and levels of health (both improve) and innovation (a mixed effect). The effect on innovation is to speed up the adoption and diffusion of vaccines and effective screening programs while slowing down the use or overuse of expensive high-tech medical practice—basing it on medical need rather than ability to pay.

The U.S. medical-industrial complex, its uniquely extreme commercialization, is not matched by any other rich democracy, although some of its manifestations (corruption, doctor-drug firm collusion) appear in some degree elsewhere. In fact, unlike the welfare mess or lag in family policy, active-labor market policy, and social spending in general, where the United States has plenty of company, health care is one policy area where the United States is, indeed, exceptional: no national health insurance; a private sector that greatly exceeds that of every other country; a very high ratio of specialists to primary-care physicians; and much higher use of expensive technologies. Limited data on preventive care suggest that the United States is at the bottom in both effort and efficacy. Finally, incremental reforms of this system without powerful offsets to the medical-industrial complex have typically been ineffective.

In the United States the dominance of insurance companies may be the most important political barrier to the adoption of the universal, comprehensive health care of every other rich democracy. All other countries have either had smaller private insurance sectors or have contained the power of insurance companies and confined their reach. Of course, other structural barriers to the adoption of national health insurance in the United States play their part, too. My comparison of Canada and the United States, similar in so many ways, points to a more paralyzing decentralized federalism, weaker demonstration effects by the states, an electoral system unfavorable to a left third party, the increased use of the Senate filibuster, and weaker party discipline. Public opinion, and the alleged peculiarities of American culture, cannot explain the USA's failure to adopt national health insurance; these structural differences can.

Regarding administrative costs and waste, the cross-national evidence, while uneven and covering only from 4 to 10 of our 19 countries, does suggest that system organization explains variations in administrative costs. Such costs are related to the private share of total expenditures. The larger the private share, the more decentralized and diffuse the financing, and consequently the greater the administrative costs and waste. Thus, insurance-based private systems with partial public funding tend toward most bureaucratic bloat (the USA), insurance-based public systems with health care usually delivered by private doctors and community or private hospitals are medium (Germany, France, the Netherlands), while direct government delivery systems with capitation payments (Sweden, the United Kingdom) save most on administrative costs and maximize the service component of the health-care dollar.[38] The difficulty of cross-national comparison of these costs, however, makes these conclusions tentative.

Because of its extreme commercialization and concomitant decentralization and fragmentation, the U.S. health-care system has very likely achieved the highest administrative costs. It has perhaps invited the highest corruption quotient. Finally, the USA's percentage of GDP spent on health care puts it in a big-spending class of its own. However, this chapter also shows that health spending per capita through the public sector, with few exceptions, is good for your health.

If U.S. experience of the 1990s is any guide, it is an illusion that privatizing health services increases choice, reduces government interference in the market, and cuts costs without drastically reducing appropriate services, thereby freeing money for expanded coverage of the uninsured. To the contrary, the "managed-care" revolution, although it comes in many forms, has in the national aggregate given us a brief moment of restrained cost increases (1993–96).

It has saved money largely by risk selection, reducing care (including hospital care) and cutting caregivers' income. Both economic and political limits to this commercial strategy may have been reached. Regarding "choice," by the mid-1990s well over half of employees of firms providing some health insurance were offered no choice of managed-care plans; 17% of employees were offered no health benefits at all. As for reducing government interference in the market, this chapter repeats a paradox running through the book: the more commercial privatization, the more intrusive and complex the government regulations.

All of the above is not intrinsic to "managed care," for several exceptional nonprofit HMOs such as Kaiser-Permanente in Northern California, at least until very recently, have a strong record of cost-beneficial care. Unfortunately, they are anything but typical. Careful assessments of the real health effects of the shift to commercial managed care are too few and the change is too recent to say how nonprofits compare with profits, let alone how various types of managed care stack up. But two unusual impact studies that included patients most at risk suggest two hypotheses: (1) fee-for-service systems are superior to HMOs for the health of the elderly and the poor, though they are about the same for the more healthy adults in the middle; and (2) nonprofit HMOs are much better than for-profit HMOs in retention of patients and hence the stability of doctor-patient relationships; high quit rates among the for-profits are due to misleading marketing, poor service, and patient confusion and dissatisfaction.

The history of the rapid shift from fee-for-service to commercial managed care in the United States has been a shift from overuse and overtreatment to cutting care, both inappropriate and appropriate. What were conflicts of interest and occasional lapses of medical ethics in the old system have become entrepreneurial medicine in the new, marked by a grand-scale obsession with the bottom line. The choice for the United States is a rationed, government-financed, government-regulated health-care system like that of every other rich democracy where clinical decisions are typically left to doctors within global budgets; *versus* a rationed, corporate-run system, partly government-financed, with increasingly explicit rationing and subversion of clinical judgment. Our choice for the latter type has given us corporate cost-slashing crusades, the highest administrative and total costs of any country, substantial corruption, decreasing coverage and care, and decreasing patient satisfaction, large numbers of families uncovered or inadequately covered—and last but not least—below-average health performance.

Entitlement to health care must be distinguished from the way priorities are set and care delivered. If we leave the United States aside as a unique case, we still find that organizational differences shape health outputs by determining who delivers what care to whom. Although doctor density makes little or no difference for national health performance, an abundance of nurses and midwives is associated with good to excellent performance. And data from only a few countries suggest that an abundance of GPs, say about 50%, not only constrains costs but also improves health outcomes, especially if they are in easy interaction with specialists, as in clinics or well-organized hospitals. Regarding the organization of society, it is clear from many studies, both of individuals and nations, that high rates of inequality, poverty, economic deprivation, and social disorganization undermine national health performance. Within the United States, which has become the champion of economic inequality and deep poverty among our 19 rich democracies, the spread of life span by education and SES is greater than we see within all of Europe; its life-span spread is like that between affluent Japan and poor Bangladesh. That it is poverty and inequality, not ethnic-racial-religious cleavages, that are a drag on U.S. health performance is suggested by the excellent performance of Switzerland, the Netherlands, and Canada, similarly ridden with majority/minority conflict.

The next chapter explores the question of whether globalization will undermine the national differences in patterns of spending and taxing, public policy, and system outputs that I have emphasized.

NOTES

Parts of this chapter were presented at the 1998 Peder Sather Symposium IV, "The Impact of New Technology on Health and Health-Care Systems," University of California at Berkeley, March 5–6, 1998. I am grateful to Dr. Arnold S. Relman for stimulating discussion of these issues and to Rudolf Klein and Joseph Houska for critical readings.

1. For country-by-country descriptions of variations in the structure of health-care systems, see Glaser (1991, especially chap. 4 and appendix A); Mechanic and Rochefort (1996); Heidenheimer, Heclo, and Adams (1990, chap. 3); Immergut (1992); Roemer (1991); Anderson (1989); Craig (1991); Rosenthal and Frenkel (1992); and Starfield (1992, chap. 15).

2. In 1989 Oregon extended means-tested Medicaid to a larger population while restricting benefits to 588 of 709 specific illness categories—triage by explicit cost-benefit analysis. Initially, capping a tooth was given a slightly higher priority than surgery for an appendectomy; a political uproar ensued. (Mechanic, 1992, p. 1744.) New Zealand recently moved toward explicit rationing of surgery: "patients get points for such things as their operation's chance of success, the number of dependents affected by the patient's illness, and the time they have already waited. Those with the most points are operated on first." (*The Economist,* July 4, 1998, p. 57.)

3. Heidenheimer, Heclo, and Adams (1990, chap. 3), comparing between 9 and 12 of our rich democracies, reach similar conclusions.

4. The Federal Drug Administration (FDA) of the United States may be an exception to the rule that centralized government control speeds up the adoption and diffusion of medical technology. After the Thalidomide debacle and because of its unusually bureaucratic character, the FDA became more centralized but imposed a more cumbersome process of approval.

5. All data are centered on the year 1980 because the structural and ideological sources of system outcomes were available up to that time period. There has since been some convergence in health performance, but the country ranks remain quite stable. Updates for several countries appear below.

6. If we count family physicians, general internists, and general pediatricians as primary-care doctors and all others as specialists, the percentage of specialists in the United States climbed from 13 in 1931 to 55 in 1965 to 62 in 1970, leveled off in the 1980s at about two-thirds, peaking at 68% in 1995 (Council on Graduate Medical Education, 1998, p. 14). A study of primary care in 10 of our rich democracies (Starfield, 1992, table 15.2) shows a similar ranking of countries in the proportion of specialists in the 1980s with the United States at one extreme and the United Kingdom at the other. The percentages: United States, 87 (66% if general internists and pediatricians are included as primary-care physicians); Sweden, 77 (but an abundance of nurses and social-service workers strengthens primary care and there is good coordination of primary/specialist care for the long term, as well as community-oriented preventive care); Netherlands and Denmark, 65; Finland, 63; Australia, 56; Canada, 48; Belgium, 47; West Germany, 46; UK, 37. Starfield finds that her index of "primary careness," which goes beyond the specialist ratio, relates positively to a variety of health indicators as well as patient satisfaction (pp. 219–231).

7. Joseph White (1995) notes that even in the five fee-for-service countries that come a bit closer to a market model—Australia, Canada, France, Germany, and Japan—price controls and fee schedules under national health insurance work: Fees have been and remain lower than fees for comparable services in the United States. For instance, a chest X ray with two views costs $45 in the United States, $24.60 in Canada, and $19.00 in Germany.

8. In the 1990s, the interests of two types of organizations diverged: first were closed-panel, group or staff HMOs, primarily nonprofit, built on a tradition of community service, and dominated by physicians and hospital managers. Second were the new "Physician Practice Management Companies" (PPMCs), generally for-profit, built on the model of the physician-entrepreneur, and dominated by corporate management. The latter aim to increase efficiency and to grow "in physician affiliations, patient enrollment and capitation revenues to sustain the confidence of investors and the value of their equity" (Robinson, 1998, p. 149; Health Care Advisory Board, 1995, p. 29). Robinson describes the growing tendency from 1994 to 1996 of medical groups and independent practice associations in California and New Jersey to consolidate and contract with either hospital-based HMOs or the burgeoning for-profit nonhospital PPMCs.

9. Brooks Pierce of the Bureau of Labor Statistics reports shrinking health insurance coverage by employers from 1982 to 1996; the percentage of employees with any kind of coverage declined at every level of compensation. The portion of the lowest tenth of employees covered dropped drastically from 49% to 26%; the portion covered in the middle 50% of earners dropped from 90% to 84%; even the coverage of the highest tenth of earners dropped from 98% to 90%. The net effect was to widen the gap between the well-off and the working poor. (*New York Times,* June 14, 1998.)

10. Because two-thirds of the total costs of hospitals are labor costs, cost-cutting means shedding labor while reducing the income of the employees kept on.

11. Direct out-of-pocket expenses by households headed by someone age 65 or older plus their private insurance premiums plus their Medicare premiums climbed from 10.6% of their after-tax income in 1972 to 17.1% in 1991 (Oliver, 1993, p. 123). The trend continued in the 1990s. A similar trend affected the covered working population. A UCLA study of out-of-pocket costs found that just between 1989 and 1996, the dollar amount of HMO family premiums paid for by employees in firms with 25 or more employees rose 90% to $1,778 (*San Francisco Chronicle,* June 17, 1998).

12. Per capita expenditures on health care were $2,867 in 1991, $3,299 in 1993, $3,498 in 1994, and $3,701 in 1995. OECD Health Data, various years. In PPPs for our 19 countries, the next highest figure for 1995 was Switzerland's $2,412, only 65% of the U.S. per capita spending despite Switzerland's much older population (15.7% aged 65 and over vs. 12.7%) and its near complete coverage of its population. That Switzerland comes in a high second might be explained by what it shares with the United States: a similarly decentralized and fragmented medical-care system, similarly populist politics and parochial interest-group power (doctors, small businesses, private insurers, and farmers). (See chap. 11. Cf. Immergut, 1992.) [The source for figures: "The OECD in Figures," 1997, 1996, 1995, 1994.]

13. In the late 1990s Medicare fraud was also spreading. The CEOs caught violating the law seldom experienced economic losses. Amid a large-scale investigation of its Medicare fraud, Columbia/HCA Healthcare Corp. paid Chief Executive Richard Scott almost $10 million after ousting him in June 1997. That payoff included a five-year consulting contract costing the hospital chain $950,000 a year—an increase in his salary. (Lublin, 1998, p. 4.) Columbia/HCA is the largest managed-care corporation in the United States.

14. This includes "group," "staff," and "network" model HMOs and their point-of-service options.

15. This is one reason that there is no agreed-on map of the managed-care market and the number and kinds of organizations in it. But there is agreement that the nonprofits, especially the staff-

model HMOs, a small minority, were fading fast in their market share (Hoechst Marion Roussel, Inc., 1997, p. 5; Health Care Advisory Board, 1995, p. 29). And not all of the remaining prepaid nonprofit group HMOs approach physicians in a cooperative, accommodative spirit. Some cooperative HMOs such as Harvard Community Health plan and FHP in Southern California have severed ties with their medical groups so they could broaden their physician base and contract at adversarial arm's length.

16. Other deviant cases held up by managed-care advocates as models typical of the great gains to be expected from managed care are the Harvard Community Health Plan and a small, well-managed HMO in Seattle, Group Health Cooperative of Puget Sound, studied by the RAND Corporation. On the cost-beneficial performance of Kaiser in Northern California in the mid-1990s, see California Cooperative Healthcare Reporting Initiative (1996).

17. In March 1998, faced with a seventh strike, Kaiser agreed to let the union select 18 members to serve as "quality liaisons" who would investigate accusations of poor care and to force a management response. This makes Kaiser even more deviant among HMOs as does its break with the HMO industry when it supported White House proposals to institute patient protection laws. (*New York Times,* April 9, 1998).

18. In a 1997 comparison of 19 HMOs in the San Francisco Bay Area, using both patient ratings and doctor ratings, Kaiser Northern California got high to above-average marks for 23 of 28 criteria: it was near the bottom in "Time with doctors and staff," below average for "How long you wait to get appointment when sick," and only average for "Attention to what you say," "Personal interest in you," and "Members rating for overall quality of care and services." In this most cost-effective, most ballyhooed HMO, the increasing patient load per doctor was taking its toll.

19. Hypertension, non-insulin-dependent diabetes mellitus, recent acute myocardial infarction, congestive heart failure, and depressive disorder. In addition, two 36-item health scales were used, one for physical health, the other for mental health. Mortality rates were included in the physical health scale. (Ware et al., 1996, pp. 1040–1041.)

20. In Texas, each of the five plans with disenrollment rates of over 20% gained both members and market share. They ran a revolving-door show—enrolling new members at a pace faster than they lost members. In other words, insofar as disenrollees are voting with their feet, the market does not weed out plans that perform poorly.

21. The distinction between profit and non-profit plans is rough and, with the rapidly-increasing commercialization of medicine, is becoming blurred. Howard Tuckman (1998, pp. 187–192) describes several mixed forms: (1) *holding companies* where a nonprofit parent hospital creates for-profit ambulatory surgery centers and diagnostic laboratories or a nonprofit nursing home acquires a for-profit home health agency or a nonprofit hospital uses its administration staff to run a for-profit sports-medicine clinic; (2) *joint ventures* where nonprofit hospitals partner with for-profit medical groups or physician investors (to bind doctors and staff to the nonprofit entity, provide new services, secure referral sources, or diversify); and (3) *coevolutionary arrangements* between two or more nonprofits or between nonprofits and for-profits where the combination can end up mixed or totally commercial. From 1981 to 1995, the percentage of HMOs classified as nonprofits fell from 82% to 29% (Goddeeris and Weisbrod, 1998, p. 216). The tendency to merge profit and nonprofit sectors makes nonprofits look increasingly like business-oriented firms; their social-charitable-community missions tend to be compromised by their commercial missions. At minimum, when they restructure, the semicommercial nonprofits tend to locate or relocate in areas where consumers have the ability to pay for care (Sloan, 1998, p. 243).

22. Managed-care plans vary in payment mechanisms, in their pressure to undertreat, and in the size of patient copayments. There is some evidence that substantial cost-sharing does not reduce inappropriate use of hospitals (Siu et al., 1991); but it does indiscriminately reduce all kinds of use, including visits to doctors and episodes of hospitalization, appropriate or not. In one study 3,958 peo-

ple aged 14 to 61 free of disability were randomly assigned to a set of insurance plans: one provided free care; the others required enrollees to pay a share of their medical bills. For persons with poor vision and for low-income persons with high blood pressure free care brought substantial improvement and reduced the risk of early death (Brook et al., 1983). But HMOs and substantial copayments combined discourage quality care and in serious cases, for example, cancer, delay prompt exams and treatment (Greenwald, 1987). Small copayments do not affect appropriate treatment.

23. Tuohy (1992, p. 110) suggests that in Canada there was a momentary consensus among doctors, hospitals, and insurance companies for acceptance of some sort of national plan in principle on the assumption that it was inevitable and therefore it was politically wise to join the train and shape its route before it left the station. When the plan was chewed up in conflicts about financing between provinces and the federal government, private insurance developed apace and comprehensive reform was delayed until the early 1960s.

24. This section draws on Kudrle and Marmor (1981), Lipset (1950, 1990), Tuohy (1992, chap. 3), Taylor (1978, 1990), Beatty (1993), Adams (1993), Pollack (1993), Leman (1980), and my interviews.

25. S. M. Lipset (1990, 1998) argues that these union density figures and other differences between Canada and the United States can be explained by cultural differences: "Europe and Canada are more Tory/social democratic, noblesse oblige, statist, and group oriented, whereas the United States is more competitive, laissez faire, antistatist, and individualistic" (1998, p. 123) and further, the former have hierarchical values while the U.S. is egalitarian. We have seen that these ideas do not stand up to cross-national survey data in chapters 1, 3, 8, and 10 above. Regarding union density, a careful review of Canadian and U.S. poll data by Peter Bruce (1989, pp. 116–119) shows that on questions measuring general approval of unions, Canadians have been slightly but consistently *less* favorable than people in the U.S. and the percentage favorable has declined similarly in both nations. Similar popular opinions cannot explain drastically different trajectories of union density. Finally, it is fatal for the cultural argument that the same "individualistic" U.S. value system produced the New Deal and the Wagner Act in the 1930s while Canada resisted such prounion laws for many years. And it is unclear how the same U.S. values could produce union density a bit higher than Canada's in the mid-1950s and half of Canada's union density in the 1990s. Contrasting labor laws, union structures, and resources devoted to organizing are the main explanation of post-1960 trends. For example, if a majority of Canadian workers in a workplace say they want a union, the union is quickly certified as the exclusive bargaining agent; in the U.S., the process stretches out while the employer is free to conduct lengthy antiunion campaigns. Why the difference in labor laws? The same modest structural differences that created national health insurance in Canada facilitated friendly labor laws.

26. Equally important and closely allied with the insurance lobby was the National Federation of Independent Business (NFIB), which was adamantly opposed to any employer mandates. The annual budget of the NFIB was $60 million. It alone had six full-time people assigned to political liaison in the House of Representatives; the White House had four. In the successful effort to kill the bill the NFIB sent more than two million pieces of mail to small business owners and flooded the talk shows and local media with attacks on "Clintoncare." Partly though their efforts to recruit and train candidates, more than half the new members of Congress in 1994 came out of a small business background.

27. Here are the United States vs. Canada per capita figures: insurance administration $106 vs. $17; hospital administration $162 vs. $50; nursing home administration $26 vs. $9; physicians professional expenses and billing, expense-based estimate $203 vs. $80; physicians expenses and billing,

personnel-based estimate $106 vs. $41. Total: high estimate, $497 vs. $156; low estimate $400 vs. $117 (Woolhandler and Himmelstein, 1991, pp. 1255–1256).

28. These provider reimbursement consultants are experts in "upcoding," the practice of getting larger reimbursements by inflating the severity of the patient's illnesses. Taking advantage of the complexity of regulation, a patient who has a fever and a bad cough is assigned a DRG code based on the severity of the illness. A diagnosis of pneumonia earns more than a common cold. Pressing the system too much might bring an investigation of fraud and abuse. But where there is any ambiguity, the consultants earn their money by "upcoding."

29. I am grateful to Susan Hahn, Tom Janoski, John Talbot, Karen Adelberger, Fred Schaffer, and Susan Martin for creative contributions to this section.

30. These spending measures are crude indicators of access to health care, but as this chapter has shown, more subtle measures cannot usually be made comparable for more than a few countries. Health spending measures reflect national differences in provider compensation, medical inflation, and unionization. Counteracting this possible source of error is unmeasured variation in the kind and quality of medical care delivered. Thus, some of the lean-spending countries with less equal access buy expensive equipment and more specialists who might improve the health of some subpopulations, principally affluent citizens. So if these lean spenders have below-average health performance despite their private and public investment in expensive medicine, the better performance of the big public spenders is even more impressive.

31. Correlations between the spending measures computed using U.S. dollar exchange rates and purchasing power parities (not reported in table 16.4) are all over .90. The correlation between GDP per capita measures computed in these two different ways is .83. Consequently, the correlations of all spending measures and affluence measures with the health performance index are nearly identical— between .59 and .67. The correlations of corporatism with all these variables are positive but insignificant.

32. We did a separate analysis of decreases in infant mortality (relative improvements) from 1960 to 1974, using databases different from the 1980 cross-sectional analysis, with much the same results. We divided the 19 countries by low vs. high starting points (22.6 deaths per 1,000 or fewer vs. 26 deaths or more), then examined real GDP per capita increases, increases in per capita health-care spending (cash and services), and improvement of infant mortality rates. We found that as a source of mortality improvement, increases in health spending count more than increases in GDP when initial rates of infant mortality are low (the rapid-spending increase, big-improvement cases are Sweden, Norway, Finland, Switzerland, and Denmark). But when initial rates of infant mortality are high, increases in GDP per capita are more important than increases in health spending per capita (the high-growth and high-improvement cases are Japan, France, Belgium, Italy, and Canada). Both spending increases and standard-of-living increases, however, are powerful sources of this health outcome. These relationships are strengthened if we eliminate two deviant cases: Israel was second only to Japan in economic growth but only 16th in infant mortality improvement (its defense spending was a drag on civilian standards of living); while the Netherlands increased its health spending 15-fold (the mean is 690%) but ranked a low average in mortality improvement (14th of 19), again reflecting its relatively inefficient welfare state (see chaps. 5, on the welfare state, and 15, on the environment, the section on disability).

33. Finland is not much of a deviant case because its below-average health score (6.0, ranking 13th) matches its below-average GDP per capita and below-average spending and health performance. Italy is a marginal case—it gets slightly better health for its well below average GDP per capita and its lean spending in 1980.

34. For detailed accounts of both the development of the German health-care system and the politics of recent reform see Alber (1986), Döhler (1995), and Giaimo (1995).

35. For overviews of the organization and performance of Japan's health-care system and elaboration of these themes, see Powell and Anesaki (1990), Steslicke (1987), Marmor (1992), Morio (1985), and OECD (1990a).

36. Family-policy scores closely match the real health index for two types of political economy: left-corporatist democracies (Sweden, Norway, Denmark, Finland) all rank very high in family policy (data missing for Israel), and all but Finland rank very high in health performance. At the other extreme, the more-fragmented and decentralized democracies (United States, United Kingdom, New Zealand, Australia, Canada, and Ireland) rank low in family policy, and all but Canada rank well below average in health performance. The averages by type including the deviant cases: for family policy, 9.3 vs. 2.3; for health scores, 18.8 vs. 7.2.

37. Duleep suggests that several cross-national studies that did not find a relationship between age-specific mortality and average income are misleading because the relationship is nonlinear: "the effect of income on a nation's mortality will depend upon how income is distributed" (1995, p. 38). Her analysis of the United States shows that income has little effect beyond an average level of income. The more pinpointed data from the Whitehall civil service study, however, show a rather even gradient in health and well-being from top to bottom, where the bottom is far from poor.

38. The National Health Service reforms under Thatcher and Major, however, increased administrative costs somewhat. See chapter 5 (the section on retrenchment).

GLOBALIZATION
Does It Subvert Job Security,
Labor Standards, and the Welfare State?

Among the basic questions about the impact of "globalization" on public policy and human welfare, three are of great interest to both scholars and policymakers:

1. Is the nation-state eroding as a unit of social-science analysis and as the center of political action?

2. Do capital and labor flows across national boundaries threaten the social policies of the rich democracies—especially job protection and good earnings and welfare-state benefits?

Because these questions assume that globalization gives countries with low labor costs and lean social policies a competitive advantage over their rivals, we must give an estimate regarding a third question:

3. Leaving aside the net contribution of the welfare state to such values as dignity, security, equality, family well-being, social integration, and political legitimacy, what are the net effects of social policies and the welfare state on productivity and economic performance?

THE NATION-STATE IS ALIVE AND WELL

In recent decades one group of social scientists have argued that the nation-state is eroding in its political capability and analytical utility. They include Immanuel Wallerstein's analysis of the relations of core, semiperiphery, and periphery in the modern "world system" (1974), Peter Evans's treatment of "dependent development" in Latin America (1979) and such students of international relations as Robert Keohane and Joseph Nye (1971, 1977) who emphasize the increasing power of transnational and international actors (multinational corporations, international organizations) and the global forces of technology, communication, and trade. Peter Gourevitch (1978, 1986) articulates these views in a more cautious and balanced way in his analysis of the international sources of domestic politics. When these scholars analyze national

TABLE 17.1 Migration rates 1900 to 1980 in four European countries*

	Year		
Country	1900	1970	1980
UK	.83	.90	.79
Belgium	.81	1.12	.95
Netherlands	1.00	1.13	1.22
Sweden	.56	1.31	.83

*Immigration plus emigration as a percentage of the total population. Dates vary slightly: UK 1901, 1971, and 1981; Belgium 1981; the Netherlands 1899. Source: calculated from B. R. Mitchell, *International Historical Statistics: Europe, 1750–1988,* 3rd ed. (New York: Stockton Press, 1992).

differences in public policy, they generally argue that a nation's position in the world economy determines its institutions and policies more than anything else or at least is becoming a prime determinant.

A second group of scholars, which includes myself (1975, 1976a, 1981a, 1981c, 1983, and with Turner, 1987), Peter Katzenstein (1985a), Peter Flora (1986 and Flora and Heidenheimer, 1981), David Cameron (1982, 1984), Hugh Heclo (1974), Gosta Esping-Andersen (1985), Walter Korpi (1978), and most students of the welfare state, are much more impressed with the importance of national differences in social, political, and economic organization as sources of variations in public policy and performance.

In all the talk about the fiscal crisis of the state or the crisis of the welfare state, we often attribute changes in national policies and patterns of behavior to globalization, international competition, or external shocks rather than to these internal structural differences. There are two things wrong with this. First, it ignores the previous history of diverse national responses to cross-national capital and labor flows and external shocks. Second, it ignores evidence of the internal causes of labor policies and welfare-state development and their economic effects.

Capital flows and mass migrations across national boundaries are hardly new. It is not even clear what the trend is. We must remember that all the great empires since the 16th century were built upon the flow of capital from creditor nations to debtors.[1] It appears that since the late 19th century net foreign lending of creditor nations as a percentage of GNP declined to a low in the 1950s and then rose again in recent decades (Edelstein, 1982, p. 3; and calculations from OECD, 1974 and 1992b National Accounts). It does not yet quite match the earlier rate. But if we go back more than a century, sovereign debt as a proportion of creditor-country GNP shows a steady decline since the early 1800s (Eichengreen and Lindert, 1989, pp. 2–3).[2] In short, compared to the mid-20th century capital has become somewhat more mobile; compared to previous 50-year periods capital has become less mobile.

Whatever the trend in capital flows, the assertion that we now live in a new world with a single capital market in which funds flow freely to the investments with the highest rate of return is simply wrong. As Martin Feldstein observes in an analysis of global savings and

TABLE 17.2 Immigration as a percentage of population
1901 – 88 for three destination leaders*

Country	Year				
	1901	1911	1971	1981	1988
Canada	1.04	4.59	.69	.53	.63
New Zealand	3.06	3.88	1.57	1.44	1.46
United States	.59	1.13	.18	.23	.22

*Figures for 1901 to 1981 calculated from data in Mitchell (1992,
pp. 1, 4, 93). 1988 calculated from UN, *Demographic Yearbook 1989, 1991.*
pp. 142 – 43, 145, 624 – 25, 644.

investment, "The patient money that will support sustained cross-border capital flows is surprisingly scarce. . . . Only 10 percent of the value of the assets in the 500 largest institutional portfolios in the world is invested in foreign securities." (*The Economist,* June 24, 1995, pp. 72 – 73.) In other words, even today there is a strong home-country bias among managers of big money.

Like the trend of capital flows, labor may or may not be more mobile than in the past. For the European countries where data are available, migration rates (immigration plus emigration as a percentage of the total population) were at about the same levels in the early 1980s as they were at the turn of the century (see table 17.1).[3]

For the United States, Canada, and New Zealand—countries of popular destination—there was less immigration in the 1980s than there was before World War I.

Immigration as a percentage of population plainly dropped sharply from the early 1900s to 1988 in all three countries (see tables 17.2 and 17.3). Although in recent years mass migrations have again picked up they do not yet match the historical patterns.[4]

Of course, in some cases the sending and receiving countries have switched places. The main point, however, holds: mass migrations are an endemic feature of industrialism, nothing new either in degree or kind. Similarly, external shocks—wars, energy-price fluctuations, and quick changes in trade patterns—are not new. Neither are the concomitant dislocations of employment. Industrialization for two centuries has meant the continual dilution and obsolescence of old skills and occupations and the creation of new ones (Wilensky and Lebeaux, 1958, pp. 59 – 65, 90 – 94). I doubt that the rate of change since 1960 is greater than the rate for previous 35-year periods. That is why the early retirement schemes so prominent among rich countries are not a response to the economic effects of globalization but a continuation of previous responses to a 100-year trend toward lower labor-force participation among older men (chap. 1 explains the trend). The more important new social fact is the rapidly increasing percentage of healthy older workers; the policy challenge is to devise flexible retirement systems, which the Swedes and French have tried to do.

Most of the variations in the welfare state we see throughout this book are a product of (1) the timing, rate, and level of industrialization and its demographic and organizational correlates and (2) the character of national bargaining arrangements between major blocs of economic power—the number, structure, and degree of centralization and inclusiveness

TABLE 17.3 Gross number of immigrants (1000s) for three
destination leaders 1901 to 1988 by ten-year periods

| | Country of Destination | | |
Period	Canada[a]	USA[a]	New Zealand[b]
1901-1911	1975	9675	388
1912-1922	1538	5972	294
1923-1933	1138	3148	97
1934-1944	134	506	31
1945-1955	1244	1990	188
1956-1966	1498	3201	323
1967-1977	1815	4345	404[c]
1978-1988	1365	6304	NA

[a]B. R. Mitchell, *International Historical Statistics: The Americas,
1750–1988*, 2nd ed. (New York: Stockton Press, 1993), pp. 92, 93.
[b]Total arrivals. From Mitchell, 1983, pp. 145–146.
[c]1967–75.

of labor unions and labor federations, of trade associations and employer federations; the degree of centralization and bureaucratic competence of governments; the character of other interest groups (churches, voluntary associations), their relation to one another and to political parties. From those long-standing national differences flow the public policies on taxing, spending, social issues, how well they are implemented, and their effects on economic performance, political legitimacy, and human welfare. (See figure 2.1.)

The power of these internal structural variations has been demonstrated in every chapter of this book. I have repeatedly found that the external pressures that are labeled "globalization" have little or no effect in explaining social policies or system outputs—such nontrivial outcomes as economic performance, political legitimacy, equality, poverty reduction, safety, and real health. What counts are national differences in political, economic, demographic, and social structures. Although these structures are converging with continuing industrialization, the national differences remain large.

This is demonstrated in three parts of my analysis where one might expect external forces to have some influence: findings regarding (1) the causes of types of bargaining arrangements—especially democratic corporatism vs. others (in chap. 2); (2) the effects of the welfare state on economic performance (chaps. 12 and 13); and (3) the effects of the two oil shocks in 1974 and 1979 and sudden shifts in the terms of trade on subsequent economic performance (chap. 12). In each area the domestic structures overwhelm the external pressures and shocks as sources of national policies and performance. After a brief reminder of these findings, we can consider more recent global developments that are alleged to undermine national sovereignty, national institutions, and related social and labor policies—the deregulation of labor markets, increased immigration, the spread of multinational corporations (MNCs), and the globalization of finance, especially the increased autonomy of central banks.

Analysis in chapter 2 of the structural and ideological sources of democratic corporatism (or "negotiated economies" in their various forms) showed that since the late 19th century four have interacted to produce fully developed corporatist bargaining structures, generally in place by the 1950s. Three of them are national and strong, one external and weak: (1) the level, rate, and timing of industrialization (early, late, very late) as they shape the structure of industry and/or labor and/or agriculture; (2) the power and ideology of social and political movements and parties; (3) electoral systems, especially various forms of proportional representation; and (4) the openness of economies or trade dependence, always cited as an attribute of globalization that will allegedly undermine labor standards and the welfare state.

Historical analysis shows the sequence: rising mass-based political parties, notably Catholic and left, moved incumbent regimes to accept proportional representation, typically modified to exclude extremes of left and right or militant minority splinter groups. This electoral system, in turn, enhanced the power of leftism and Catholicism, ideologies sympathetic to both corporatism and the welfare state. We know that the PR compromise as well as left and Catholic party power preceded the corporatist compromise. A parallel process was the timing of industrialization as it shaped the structure of industry and agriculture, the size of enterprises, the concentration of capital, and above all, the centralization and inclusiveness of labor federations and employer federations and the role of the state. It is significant that all of these powerful forces are internal, institutional, and national. Tests of their relative importance show that PR is by far the most important source of corporatism; Catholic power is a close second. Left power is a less important explanation, largely because since World War I, left parties are much more frequently thrown out than Catholic parties and the duration of left power is rarely long. With rare exceptions, left power without PR has little lasting effect on anything. Regarding trade dependence, the results are unequivocal: if we delete the Netherlands and Belgium as extreme cases, export dependence fades as a source of corporatism when any two of the other variables are included. In other words, the hypothesis that the external shock of heavy dependence on fluctuating world markets inspires consensual bargaining arrangements finds no support.

We have seen that all external pressures and shocks are filtered through and greatly modified by the domestic structures I have discussed. But maybe increased global competition will have a stronger impact on the welfare state and labor-market policies in the future, whatever the limited impact of trade dependence since 1880. Because so many politicians and scholars believe that the welfare state is a drag on economic performance, we must first know precisely what social programs reduce productivity, what social programs increase it, and which are simply neutral.

Analysis of the economic performance of 19 rich democracies from 1950 to 1989 as well as the 1990s (chap. 12) casts doubt on assertions that aggregate social spending is a threat to economic growth, inflation control, or low unemployment or that the lean welfare states of Japan and the United States give them a competitive advantage over welfare-state leaders saddled with huge social budgets.

In fact, the comparative evidence shows that over long periods big spending has either made a positive contribution to economic performance or is unrelated to economic performance, depending on the period considered. The correlations between an index of economic performance combining good real growth in GDP per capita, low inflation, and low unemployment and a broad measure of social spending (SS/GNP) are positive before the oil shocks of 1973–74 and 1979 (for 1950–74, $r = .48$; the after-shock correlations are insignificant—for 1974–79, $r = .26$; for 1980–84, $r = -.22$; for 1985–89, $r = -.17$). In multiple regression analysis, neither welfare effort (SS/GNP) nor its rate of growth nor the rate of growth of social spending per capita stand up against the robust causes of economic performance (the structure of the political economy, capital investment, and industrial relations systems).

Why is the welfare state as a whole either a benign influence on competitiveness or irrelevant? First, some major sectors of social policy are plainly productivity-enhancing: mass access to medical care and health education via schools, clinics, and child-care facilities (chaps. 5, 7, and 16) reduces long-term medical costs and in some measure enhances real health and lifetime productivity; preventative occupational health and safety programs in the workplace reduce absenteeism and turnover and other labor costs (chaps. 12 and 15); active labor-market policies reduce reliance on passive unemployment insurance and public assistance (chaps. 12 and 13) and improve the quality of labor; innovative family policies reduce the cost of both mayhem and poverty (chap. 14), they also reduce income and gender inequality, which are a drag on economic growth (chap. 12). These are substantial offsets for the cost of welfare-state benefits to the nonworking poor, handicapped, and the aged. The net economic effect of all the programs labeled the "welfare state" is therefore either positive (before 1974) or neutral (since 1974).

Beyond these economic benefits of social spending is the evidence that countries with strong corporatist bargaining arrangements more flexibly adapt to external shocks and more effectively implement productivity-enhancing social and labor policies. Corporatist democracies provide channels for the interplay of management, labor, and the state. The trade-offs that such a structure facilitates are often directly relevant to productivity and macroeconomic performance (chaps. 2 and 12; Wilensky, 1981a, p. 192; Wilensky et al., 1985, pp. 43–47). As a reminder, the corporatist trade-offs most positive for economic performance follow:

1. *Labor constraint on nominal wages in return for social security and related programs and modest increases in real wages.* While most corporatist democracies had higher wage increases before 1980 than their noncorporatist counterparts, when the shocks of 1974 and 1979–82 hit, they resisted wage pressures and did better controlling inflation in the five years after each shock.[5]

2. *Job protection in return for wage constraint, labor peace, and sometimes tax concessions* (lower taxes on corporations and capital gains). There is some evidence that job security is a positive contribution to lowering unit costs; it reduces worker sabotage, output restriction, slowdown, strikes, and turnover. One of the two most robust sources of good economic performance in all periods (chap. 12) is low strike rates—a clue to effective industrial relations systems characteristic of corporatist democracies.

3. *Participatory democracy in the workplace or community in return for labor peace and wage constraint.* A case in point: The German local works councils and national codetermination combined with regional collective bargaining that is coordinated by centralized unions and employer associations setting a broad framework. Several countries provide

channels for worker and union leader participation in tripartite boards administering parts of the welfare state—medical insurance, unemployment and accident insurance, and pensions (chaps. 2 and 5). Such union participation in unemployment insurance and related labor-market policies is especially strong in Belgium, Sweden, Denmark, and Finland.

4. *In return for all of the above, the government improves its tax-extraction capacity and public acceptance of taxes on consumption*—not irrelevant to reduction of inflation and budget deficits. Thus, the combination of high VAT and social-security taxes is a moderately positive contribution to high scores on my economic performance index before 1974 (although it is insignificant after).

5. *In return for all the above, both labor and the government tolerate low taxes on either capital gains or profits and avoid high property taxes.* Although my study shows that taxes on capital gains, corporate income, and profits have only moderately negative effects on capital investment and little effect on economic performance, property taxes may be a drag in all periods. Reliance on property taxes is characteristic of the more-fragmented and decentralized democracies.

6. *With the habit of making such trade-offs and faced with strong labor movements, management in the more corporatist democracies tends to join labor in the implementation of a wide range of policies.* The result: *less intrusive regulation* and more effective implementation of laws and executive orders. Thus, the complaint that Western Europe is hyperregulated and hyperprotected—that it has the disease of "Eurosclerosis"—while America has an excellent ability to adapt ignores the evidence on types of regulation and regulatory styles. The paradox that the most-decentralized political economies with the most liberal (free-market) ideologies—for example, the U.S.—have the most rigid and intrusive regulations can be explained by the weakness of the structure and political power of labor and the absence of channels for collaboration among labor, management, and the state.

A final bit of evidence that corporatist democracies with big welfare-state burdens nevertheless adapt flexibly to external shocks is the record of responses to two Arab oil shocks 1974 and 1979 (see tables 12.3 and 12.5). One would think that a country that produces little energy and is highly dependent on oil would be handicapped in adjusting to those shocks. Yet in chapter 12 neither energy dependence nor sudden deterioration in the terms of trade were related to economic performance in each of two five-year postshock periods. This again underscores the overwhelming importance of structures of bargaining and their policy consequences (corporatism as it relates to strikes, capital formation, tax structures, as well as social, industrial, and labor-market policies). Such domestic structures and policies explain great national differences in the capacity to adapt to external shocks—so much so that by 1979, with few exceptions, the countries most exposed (Japan, Switzerland, Sweden, Finland, Belgium) were able to adapt more quickly and effectively to the next big shock than countries well situated (Canada, United Kingdom, Ireland). It is striking that all five of the most-energy-dependent, quickest-adjusting good performers are corporatist with or without labor, and three of them are big spenders. In contrast, three of the poorest performers after both shocks—Canada, UK, Ireland—were medium to low in social spending *and* much less energy-dependent.[6] Of course there are exceptions to these general patterns. A series of policy mistakes in Japan in the 1990s and Sweden in the mid-1980s to mid-1990s including a classic burst of a speculative bubble (combined with the erosion of centralized bargaining in Sweden) accounts for periods of poor performance. In both cases, policies exacerbated and deepened the bust (chap. 2 discusses Sweden, chap. 12, Japan).

CONVERGENCE DOWNWARD, UPWARD, OR JUST PERSISTENT DIFFERENCES?

What is the lesson for the present context? Will the shock of increased globalization inspire a move of the most successful rich democracies downward toward Portugal, Greece, and Spain? That is very unlikely. If the structures and policies now in place have enabled Germany, Switzerland, Norway, Austria, Finland, and Japan to outperform the rest through thick and thin for four decades of the postwar period, why should they now move toward low wages, weak job protection, low social spending, less investment in education, training, and job placement, low productivity, and low value-added products? Why should they copy Margaret Thatcher and Ronald Reagan in bashing unions? Even if they wanted to imitate the U.S. and the UK—which I do not think they do—their governments would encounter mass resistance as well as strong labor protest. To turn quiescent unions or reformist unions into radical confrontationist unions is not what most political and industrial elites desire.

To better grasp whether there are convergent tendencies of globalization that undermine labor standards and the welfare state, the next sections analyze national variations in job security, immigrant policies and politics, the role of multinational corporations, and the rising autonomy of central banks.

DEREGULATION OF THE LABOR MARKET?

Some recent evidence from Germany suggests that industrial managers themselves do not want what orthodox economists and center-right politicians say they want—deregulation of the labor market—and for good reasons.

The 1980s saw accelerated rhetoric regarding the evils of job protection in law and collective bargaining contracts; there was even some shift in public policy. A number of countries, especially the UK, Germany, France, Italy, and Spain, relaxed legal restrictions on layoffs and dismissals and widened existing loopholes in established systems of job protection. For instance, they encouraged fixed-term vs. permanent contracts or reduced barriers to hiring temporary labor (OECD, 1989; Auer and Buechtemann, 1990). The aim: reduce institutional rigidities, increase the efficiency of labor markets, and decrease labor costs and thereby increase employment, speed up innovation and industrial readjustment—all the goodies in the promised land of the free marketeers.

If we examine employer behavior, however, we discover a radical disjunction between political rhetoric and industrial practice. Germany is a good case for examining the validity of the attack on the allegedly detrimental effects of job-security regulations on the firm and, more generally, "Eurosclerosis" in the economy. It has long had an elaborate system of job protection, a model followed by other countries in the 1960s and early 1970s, and in 1985 was the European leader in job stability; in continuous job-tenure rates Germany was second only to Japan (Buechtemann and Meager, 1991, p. 10).[7] To the tune of the ideological music of the 1980s Germany passed a new "Employment Promotion Act" (EPA) in 1985. Among other legal changes, it relaxed job protection rules for new enterprises, extended maximum periods for the use of temporary workers hired from agencies, and, most important, made it easy for employers to hire workers on fixed-term contracts and fire them at the end without "just cause" or consultation. The law was pushed mainly by the Free Democrats (FDP), the free-marketeer wing of Chancellor Kohl's coalition government.

In a careful evaluation of the employment impact of the law, based on a review of subsequent studies, including a representative sample survey of 2,392 establishments, using ingenious measures of changes in hiring-and-firing practices that could be attributed to the law, as well as in-depth case studies of the motives of employers who did and did not use the new law, Buechtemann (1989) and Buechtemann and Meager (1991) found that the employment effects of the EPA were negligible; employers were overwhelmingly uninterested in using the law. Here are the relevant findings:

- Despite strong job protection, the annual labor turnover and job separation rates of Germany both *before* and *after* the EPA of 1985 are quite high (more than one in four). (Buechtemann and Meager, 1991, p. 10).

- In the two years after the law, worker turnover was highly concentrated in small and medium-sized firms in construction, food processing, and low-skill personal services (hotel and catering, transportation, body care and cleaning). One-half of all terminations and new hires were accounted for by only 19% of all firms. These are firms with low-skill, high-labor costs as a fraction of total costs, and big fluctuations in demand. Their massive labor turnover, however, does not reflect superior adjustment efficiency. Both before and after the law these high-turnover firms pursued this "hiring-and-firing" strategy (*ibid.*, pp. 11−15).

- Before and after the law, dismissals have played only a minor role in total turnover; German employers tend to avoid layoffs as long as possible by attrition, adjusting hours, early retirement schemes, and so on. Most turnover is from voluntary quits, expired apprenticeship contracts, or early retirements. In downturns employers hoard labor to avoid high search, recruitment, and training costs on the upswing.

- Before the EPA, a comprehensive study of dismissals in private industry in the late 1970s found that neither unions and works councils nor job protection laws strongly impede employers from firing workers they wanted to fire. That is why 85% of personnel managers interviewed at the time said that their firms had been able to fire and lay off close to all the workers they wanted to without any major financial and/or legal difficulty. Personnel managers in the post-EPA period reported the same judgment: employment protection legislation both before and after the reforms was no major obstacle to dismissals and necessary workforce reductions.[8]

- Actual use of the options offered to employers by EPA for temporary hires was confined to a small minority (4%) of all private-sector firms and to a tiny number of cases (2% of all new hires) (*ibid.*, p. 22). Only 0.6% of all firms in the private sector used the new fixed-term contracts created by the EPA in order to adjust their workforces more flexibly to external demand.

- Far from expanding employment, deregulation had negligible net effects. If anything, it had slightly negative effects. It increased the layoff risks for fixed-contract workers in a downturn but increased hiring only slightly in expanding firms (*ibid.*, p. 24).

Most damaging for the advocates of labor-market deregulation, the German employers in the most dynamic sectors, the expanding engineering and higher-skill service industries—the drivers of the economic machine that conquered world markets—said that they do not take advantage of the law because they do not want to incur the costs of a hire-and-fire strategy: transactional costs and productivity losses, training costs, loss of loyal workers motivated by job security and good wages and benefits.[9] German employers, unlike the ideologues who inspire the laws, know that investment in human capital pays off in the superior productivity and flexibility of a stable workforce.

In short, whatever the political rhetoric of deregulation and the free market, German employers in the late 1980s were pursuing the same labor policies that had brought them success since 1960 (Turner, 1998).

Finally, in assessing the idea that globalization subverts job security it is important to distinguish among types of industries. In the high-wage export sectors of Japan, Germany and several smaller European democracies, job security has been high because labor costs as a percentage of total costs are low (as in pharmaceuticals, chemicals, mainframe computers, or oil refining), or because productivity in export sectors is high and exports are growing, or where worldwide investments have long been the core of profits (insurance and banking). It is the nonexport service industries and trades that evidence most fluctuation in employment and minimum job security. These "domestic" sectors are much less affected by globalization; they continue to fluctuate according to business cycles and local markets. The export sectors, however, remain much the same as they were before all the talk about globalization: they were and are dominated by productive, high-wage firms with continued growth.[10] It is hard to see how migration and capital flows will change this established pattern very much.

If there is convergence in the programs and expenditures comprising the welfare state and job protection, it is not the convergence downward imposed by greater ease of mobility of labor and capital across national boundaries. It is instead the convergence rooted in continuing industrialization and the trends all rich democracies share: the continued aging of the population, now accelerating in Japan and North America, the upgrading of skills and job demands, and the convergence in female labor-force participation (see chap. 1). These common trends will most affect family policy, active labor-market policy, and pension expenditures, all of which I believe will become more, not less, alike.

CONVERGENCE IN IMMIGRATION,
DIFFERENCES IN POLICIES AND POLITICS

Perhaps an increase of net migration to the successful political economies of Europe will make them look a bit more like Canada, the United States, and Australia in their cultural and social diversity and minority-group conflict. But it is not clear that this will mean a dualism in jobs, wages, and living standards as radical as the dualism of North America and Australia, countries that have developed a large "underclass." Those latter countries were among the leading job creators from 1968 through the 1980s while France, West Germany, Austria, and the UK were below the median in job creation. The top job creators, as I have shown in chapter 13, were responding to demographic changes (high net migration rates and high rates of 15- to 24-year-olds entering the labor force) and changes in social structure (the combination of high rates of female labor-force participation, high rates of family breakup, and the feminization of poverty). The jobs they created were mainly low-paid, low-skill service jobs using migrants, young people, and divorced women pressed to the wall, many of them part-time or temporary workers looking for full-time work. The net outcome over long periods has been anemic productivity increases, high job turnover, lowered investment in training, deterioration in real wages, and an increase in unproductive welfare spending—all of which puts them in competition with the newly industrializing countries, for example, South Korea and Taiwan, themselves moving in the opposite direction toward high wages and high value-added products. There is no reason that Germany, Japan, and the Scandinavian countries would now want to go down that road.

Some of these nations are able to regulate immigration from outside the EC a bit better than the North Americans can. For instance, Switzerland has long practice in controlling its borders; Germany levies stiff fines and penalties on employers who hire illegal workers and enforces these regulations, more or less, by identity cards and inspectors visiting work sites (e.g., building construction). Historically, both countries were able to incorporate immigrant labor into the secondary sector: a few years after foreign workers were stabilized, 73% of West German immigrants (1975) and 67% of immigrants to Switzerland (1972) were in manufacturing and related jobs, not in agriculture, construction, and service (Sassen, 1988, pp. 44–45). The Mediterranean countries—Italy, France—as well as the United States may have a harder time regulating and integrating foreign labor because of long unfenced coast lines and easier access.

Whatever these differences, liberal democracies evidence convergent trends in immigration experience (cf. Freeman, 1994, pp. 17–30; Collinson, 1993, pp. 57–59; and Hollifield, 1992, pp. 32–33, 84–85, 204–213):

- Increasing effort and capacity to regulate migration flows, especially absolute numbers.

- The increased moral resonance of family unification as a major criterion for admission, accounting for an increasing percentage of total immigration and decreasing state control of the social characteristics (education, skills) of the immigrants.

- An hourglass shape of the education and skills of the recent immigration population. Although there are some national differences here, the central tendency is toward some overrepresentation of college graduates and a very big overrepresentation of the least educated and least skilled. Philip Martin (1992, p. 14) estimates that American immigrants are 30% highly skilled, 20% in the middle, and 50% unskilled.

• The transformation of temporary work programs into permanent immigration. (Like The Man Who Came to Dinner and stayed for several months, the guest workers of Europe increasingly settled down in the host countries for long periods, even their whole working lives.) Movements for expanding immigrant rights were a natural outcome.

• The uneven spread of migrants in Western Europe 1950–93. The explanation: variation in (1) the demand for and recruitment of "temporary" labor; (2) the openness to the rising tide of political refugees, East to West and increasingly South to North.[11]

• As legal entry routes are restricted in response to xenophobic political pressure, illegal entrants and visa overstayers have increased, although as we have seen above, nations vary in their capacity to police their borders and control illegal immigration.[12]

Because unskilled jobs are a declining portion of the labor force in all these countries, however, they all confront a choice between burgeoning welfare costs for their least-educated new immigrants, women heading broken homes, and young people, on the one hand, or the more productivity-enhancing strategies they have already pursued, on the other. The German-Swedish-Japanese model (cultivate labor relations, invest heavily in human resources, maintain high rates of capital investment, etc.) or the North American model (maintain confrontational labor relations and adapt the technical and social organization of work to a large, cheap labor supply)—these are the real choices. Happily the demographics of the next decade are favorable in many countries: the lower rate of entry of native young people will create labor shortages that immigrants, if trained, can fill. That window of opportunity in the U.S., however, will close shortly after 2000 when the bulge now in secondary school reaches college and/or the labor market. Because the marked acceleration of American retirees will not take hold until 2020 or 2030, American reliance on immigrant labor will be about 20 years behind Europe's: from about 2000 to 2020 we can expect increased tension between natives and immigrants in the United States—even beyond what we already see in California.

The economic impact of immigration, considering all costs and benefits over the long run, is very likely positive. This reality, however, is not what plays out in politics, where immigrants are used as scapegoats for a wide range of troubles. Complicating any assessment, the real economic effects vary over time and place.

Studies of the U.S. using data from before 1980 (Borjas, 1990, chap. 5; Abowd and Freeman, 1991a; Muller, 1993) show that " . . . immigrants have been absorbed into the American labor market with little adverse effect on natives" (Abowd and Freeman, 1991b, p. 22). In fact, in areas of greatest immigrant concentration—for example, Miami, Los Angeles, New York, San Francisco—employment of natives increased with rising immigration, except for New York (*ibid.*, p. 24). The reasons: immigrants purchase goods and services where they work, thereby raising demand for labor; immigrant skills complement the skills of many native workers, raising demand for them; even with their concentration in gateway cities, if immigrants had not taken the low-skilled jobs there, similarly young, uneducated Americans would have filled the gap via migration from other areas (Abowd and Freeman, 1991b, pp. 22–24); and natives attenuate the negative earnings effects of recent immigration by moving to other localities (Borjas and Freeman, 1992, p. 11) while at least 20% to 30% of the foreign born in the U.S., probably the least self-supporting, return to their birthplace or migrate elsewhere within a decade or two, thereby relieving pressure on the labor market (Borjas, 1992, p. 18).

But as the percentage of uneducated, unskilled immigrant labor rose in the 1980s when the U.S. job market for the least educated was deteriorating, studies of that decade concluded that immigration was depressing the earnings of natives, especially the relative earnings of high-school dropouts, including young blacks and earlier-arriving Hispanics (Borjas, Freeman, and Katz, 1992, pp. 238–242; see also chap. 13 above on job creation and Wilensky, 1992b). An oversupply of cheap immigrant labor was competing with an oversupply of cheap native labor.

Are immigrants a disproportionate burden on the welfare state? This myth was given credence by Donald Huddle's flawed research (1993) claiming that the 19.3 million immigrants entering the U.S. from 1970 to 1992 were in 1992 a net burden on native taxpayers of $42.5 billion, projected at $67 billion a year from 1993 to 2002. On the contrary, immigrants—even those arriving since 1980—are probably being ripped off by American taxpayers. The reasons: First, they are overwhelmingly young workers who pay social-security and Medicare taxes (not the native aged who use most of the expensive pension, disability, and health-care services) whose fertility rates are as low as the comparable young natives (no disproportionate use of schools). The very youth of the immigrant population is a boon for the U.S.; the immigrants will help pay for the baby boomers' retirement and medical care, partially offsetting the looming mismatch of pensioners and workers. Second, they pay state sales taxes, local property taxes, and gasoline taxes; their employers pay unemployment insurance and worker's compensation taxes. Third, if they are legal, their use of social welfare benefits in earlier decades was less than that of natives. Although such use is now slightly above the natives' (because of higher unemployment rates of the young and because the aged among them use means-tested SSI), these are the smallest parts of welfare-state burdens and have deteriorated in real value.[13] Finally, if they are illegals, they are by law denied almost all welfare benefits and are afraid to use *any* services for fear of being deported.

All this leaves aside the long-run assimilation of immigrants and the economic recovery since 1992 as well as the contribution of their work to GNP. Thus cross-sectional estimates (e.g., 1990–92) capture neither business-cycle variations nor variations over the life cycle that show more long run payoff and less cost. Today's cross-sectional picture overrepresents new arrivals who earn less and use more state services; later, like their predecessors, they earn more, pay more taxes, and use fewer public services. Even those initially in an enclave economy (e.g., Asian immigrants in ethnic neighborhoods in Los Angeles whose job histories were analyzed in the early 1990s) typically transcend the ethnic economy and enter the mainstream metropolitan economy as they gain local work experience and increase their human capital (Nee, Sanders, and Sernau, 1994). As Fix and Passel (1994) show in their careful review of studies emphasizing the immigrant burden, all of them understate the revenue stream from immigrants and overstate the cost to government.[14]

Again national experiences differ depending on institutions and policies. In Germany, for instance, although foreigners are increasingly overrepresented among the recipients of social assistance (which is only 5% of the Federal Republic's social expenditures), the aggregate impact of foreigners on the entire German system of taxes and transfers is positive—for example, a fiscal gain of about 14 billion DM in 1991 (a 1992 study by Barabas et al. from a leading economic research institute cited by Alber, 1994, p. 5). A similar finding of net gain is reported from studies of France (Hollifield, 1992, pp. 85–86). Regarding the labor market, both Australia and Germany evidence much less negative earnings impact than the U.S. because their occupational wage differentials are smaller than those of the U.S. and their unionization rates are much higher. Germany also invests more in training, job creation, and job placement. And Australia from the 1970s through the early 1980s used education and skills as criteria for admission so the differences between natives and immigrants did not grow so much (Abowd and Freeman, 1991b, p. 23). On the other hand, countries that match Sweden's generosity in social programs for immigrants may find that the costs exceed the benefits even in the long run.

Whatever the European political economies do about the welfare state and labor-market and social policies, and whatever the real economic effects of immigration, I suspect that they will all experience a moderate increase in ethnic-racial-religious conflict, hardly unknown to the continent in the past, only this time without major war.

Insofar as rich democracies converge in the number of immigrants as a fraction of the labor force, they are likely to experience cycles of nativist, xenophobic protest, some of it parliamentary, some violent, as in the history of the older immigrant nations, the U.S., Australia, and Canada. The cycles of protest are driven by the convergence of economic downturns (unemployment, downward mobility, declines in income), immigrant population numbers and concentration, and the social distance between immigrants and natives.[15] How anti-immigrant sentiments are channeled, however, is another matter. National and local mobilizing structures—political parties, legislatures, prime ministers, interest groups—can either legitimize or oppose xenophobic expression, exploit mass fears and prejudices in a search for scapegoats, or try to contain those fears.

We can see the interaction of strong economic deprivation, much immigrant concentration, big social distance, and nativist political mobilization at work in the U.S. and Germany in the early 1990s. In the Los Angeles riots of 1992 much of the violence of blacks was targeted at Koreans and Chinese; the locations were areas of high unemployment of young males. In the 1994 election in California and in most closely contested congressional districts in many states, the Republicans used the problems of crime, welfare mothers, and illegal Mexican or Caribbean immigrants as negative symbols in a successful campaign to direct a frenzy of anger at their Democratic opponents. Media "talk shows" poured oil on that fire. White men of the middle mass (high school or part-college educated) from the West and South who said their family's economic situation had worsened in the last four years were especially attracted to those appeals (based on exit polls, *New York Times,* November 13, 1994). (See chap. 10 on the revolt of the middle mass.)

That increased minority-group numbers and concentration can produce intensified resistance from native populations is evident from an earlier time in U.S. history. Lieberson (1980, pp. 284–291) shows that in the early 20th century, major increases in both the residential segregation of blacks and their percentage of the population brought on an escalation of violent protest by whites, most of them earlier-arriving immigrants who felt threatened by black encroachment.

Anti-immigrant violence and voting in Germany has similar roots. From 1961 to the mid-1990s, the percentage of foreigners in the German population rose from 1.2% to over 8% (Alber, 1994, p. 5)—about the same as the 8.7% of the United States in 1994. As Alber shows (graph 7 and table 1) bursts of nativist violence (acts/1000 asylum seekers) occurred in 1983–84, a time of accelerating unemployment, and 1991–93 (combining recession, the economic strain of reunification, and rising immigration). He reports an average of nearly 6 violent acts per 1,000 asylum seekers every day, including several arson fires during 1991–93. Regarding social distance, although Germany's proportion of resident foreigners is not as large as Belgium's its percentage of immigrants from non-European countries (6%) puts it first among countries of the European Union. Regarding mobilization, in the 1990 election male East German voters below the age of 25, whose unemployment was greatest, gave the extreme right nativist Republican Party its best election result of 7% (*ibid.,* p. 8). The party broke through first in Bremen, a port city with a declining industrial center, a high rate of unemployment and a heavy concentration of Turks, Poles, and other immigrants. The combination of youth unemployment and social distance is also captured in Solingen, where the killers of a Turkish girl in May 1993 were members of a youth gang who had been kicked out of a Turkish restaurant (*ibid.,* p. 11); five other Turkish females, long-term residents, were killed in a single gruesome arson fire in the same city that month.

That public policies toward immigration shape the intensity of anti-immigrant violence and voting is suggested by a comparison of two countries with substantial recent immigration, generous social policies, and low rates of poverty and inequality, but contrasting immigration policies: Germany, where the principle of *jus sanguinis* is dominant and nationality is conferred mainly by blood ties, and Sweden, where the principle of *jus soli* is dominant and nationality is conferred mainly by place of birth. In 1992 Germany accepted 5.3 times as many asylum seekers as Sweden but experienced 29 times as many acts of antiforeign arson or bombing attacks (*ibid.,* p. 3). In a rough comparison of nativist violence in the early 1990s in five European countries (France, Britain, Switzerland, Sweden, and Germany), Alber suggests that while Britain, Switzerland, Sweden, and Germany all experienced an increase in violent incidents, the number and intensity of antiforeign violence is highest in Germany (*ibid.,* p. 3). An explanation of Sweden's much lower rate of violence is its policy of assimilating immigrants by aggressive education, training, and integrative social programs and by giving immigrants the right to vote and run for office in community and regional elections after three years of residence. Sweden is also first among 12 European countries in its naturalization rate.[16]

Comparing Germany and France yields a hint of an inverse relationship between anti-immigration voting and anti-immigrant violence.[17] It also validates the idea that integration policies reduce the rate of violence even where perceived economic deprivation and social distance are similar.

First, the similarities. The supporters of anti-immigrant, populist-right groups and parties in both countries are concentrated in areas of exceptional immigrant concentration and economic instability or at least perceived instability. These groups draw support from both the losers and winners of structural readjustment. It is not only economic deterioration alone that provokes protest; it is any major economic change, up or down, that heightens the sense of insecurity. For instance, among the German winners are Baden-Württemberg and Bavaria; among the French winners are Paris and the Ile-de France and Alsace. German losers include Schleswig-Holstein and Bremen; French losers include Marseille and Bouche du Rhône. All of these areas are either strongholds of protest voting or evidence above-average support for anti-immigrant politicians.

The core supporters of Le Pen in France and the Republikaner in Germany are not especially marginal. They are citizens of the middle mass (lower white collar, upper-working class, self-employed). In both countries, most are males with vocational training or high school but no higher education. Whether they are employed or not they have a strong sense of insecurity—economic and physical—that is much more intense and widespread than among voters for other more established parties. They rank insecurity, law and order, and crime at the top of their concerns. Even the lawless skinheads in Germany identify their biggest worry as Zukunftssicherheit or "future security." Responding to political demagogues, they blame their job insecurities and other troubles on immigrants.

In both countries the targets of protest voters and violent gangs are distant in language and appearance; they are typically Islamic—for example, "guestworker" Turks and Balkan refugees in Germany, Arabs from North Africa and the Sub-Sahara in France. In both countries ethnic segregation in substandard housing and poor neighborhoods is common. Both include immigrants in universal welfare-state benefits, whose alleged drain on the taxpayer-citizen is a centerpiece of political propaganda (see chap. 10). All this should sound familiar to television viewers in the United States who were exposed to saturation advertising on crime, immigrants, and welfare during the poisonous congressional campaign of 1994.

With all these French-German similarities it is striking that Germany has much more anti-immigrant violence than France while France has much higher populist-right anti-immigrant voting than Germany. For instance, per capita acts of extreme right xenophobic violence in Germany after 1990 were at least 2.5 times higher than in France. But electoral support shows the reverse pattern: Le Pen's *Front National* received between 26% and 28% of the vote in 1988 presidential elections in areas of high immigrant concentration in Southwest France—Marseille, Toulon, and Nice (Frears, 1991, p. 116); in February 1997, the *Front National* won its first absolute majority of the vote in a municipal election in the Marseille suburb of Vitrolles. In contrast, from 1973 to 1989 German support for similar extreme right-wing parties at its peak in the 1989 Euro-elections was only 7.1% (excluding Bavaria and Baden-Württemberg the other Länder ranged between 4% and 6% of the vote going to the REPs). At its peak in national elections since unification that vote was less than 5%. In fact, in the 1994 national election the Republikaner got only 1.9% of the vote.

Contrasts in public policy and politics as well as rates of immigration provide a reasonable explanation. The German policy of ethnic exclusion based on descent and combined with wide open access to refugees up to 1993 (perhaps driven by historical guilt) makes the cultural and social integration of minorities difficult, no matter how long they stay (some of the Turks are third-generation workers).[18] Sheer numbers add to nativist resentment and violence.[19] In contrast, French policy, while not as assimilative as that of the U.S.

or Canada, is inclusive (Esman, 1992, pp. 3–4, 36, 39). French official administrative classifications from the first have been socioprofessional or "national"; from the Third Republic on, the French forbade all Census questions about ethnic, religious, and linguistic origins. The French version of the melting pot myth is that the fusion of peoples came to an end with the Revolution and no redefinition of "French" can come from subsequent waves of immigration (Noiriel, 1992, pp. 72–73; and Brubaker 1992, pp. 104–110). French universalism has had a paradoxical result: it exaggerates the social distance between nation-conscious French citizens and foreigners; at the same time it shapes the law of immigration in more liberal directions. Encouragement of assimilation may reduce violence but still permit political expression of nativist sentiments. As an added explanation of LePen's strength, France has run a much higher rate of unemployment than Germany for many years. Vitrolles, where LePen's party reached its first majority, has not only a large concentration of North African immigrants; it also has an abundance of alienated French workers hard hit by 19% unemployment (*New York Times,* February 10, 1997).

A final piece of this puzzle is the role of electoral laws as they shape protest voting. Both France and Germany have mixed proportional-plurality electoral systems with two-stage voting (see chap. 2). But the two ballots in the French case are cast a week or two apart; only the second is decisive. The two ballots of the Germans—one for the candidate, one for the party—are simultaneous, and both ballots shape the final political composition of the government. French voters can therefore indulge their xenophobic sentiments in a first-ballot protest against the political establishment with little consequence in most cases; German voters are denied any second thoughts. In short, the German combination of much higher numbers of socially distant strangers, an exclusionary naturalization policy, and an electoral system that discourages pure protest voting (and incidentally makes neo-Nazi parties illegal) encourages violence; the French combination of lower numbers of immigrants, universalistic ideology and assimilative policies, and greater unemployment but electoral laws and traditions favorable to protest voting minimizes violence and provides xenophobic movements with an abundance of voters.

In sum: Migration from poor areas to rich is new neither in its rate nor in its consequences. Rich democracies are now converging in their cultural and social diversity and in their conflict focused on immigration. They differ, however, in their openness to political and economic refugees, their policies toward immigrant integration, and the intensity of anti-immigrant mobilization. Anti-immigrant sentiments are most intense where the number and concentration of immigrants are heavy, the social distance between natives and strangers (in education, religion, language, ethnicity, and race) is great, and the economic instability of industrial readjustment is most widely experienced. Most important, industrial democracies differ in their ways of channeling mass prejudices and populist-right movements. A country that makes a serious effort to minimize illegal immigration, and to assimilate immigrants via inclusionary naturalization policies; job creation, training, and placement; and language and citizenship education will minimize nativist violence. It may ultimately reduce the electoral appeal of political demagogues who intensify mass fears and hatreds to achieve power.

Finally, I doubt that European democracies and Japan, as they experience increased immigration, must necessarily produce an alienated underclass, the target of a middle-mass revolt, American style. Only if they abandon the public policies that encouraged labor peace and kept their poverty rates low—family policies, an active labor-market policy, an accommodative framework for industrial relations, a universalistic welfare state—will they drift into the Anglo-American pattern. Some may choose that road; but the choice is there.

There is no tidal wave of immigrants to the affluent democracies. In relation to world population international migration is a rare event. In general, the negative economic effects of increased migration are exaggerated and the political effects can be contained.

As they argue that globalization undermines national institutions and policies, many scholars go beyond international capital flows and migration to two other supposedly eroding forces: the growth of multinational corporations and the increasing autonomy of central banks. The next two sections discuss these trends.

THE ROLE OF MULTINATIONAL CORPORATIONS

There is no doubt that multinational corporations (MNCs), using economies of scale and scope, have dispersed all their activities across the globe, accelerating the flow of goods, services, investment, technology, and people. They are increasingly important in employment, sales, and investment, especially in the already rich countries.[20] It is not obvious, however, that the MNCs have negative effects on unions, industrial relations, earnings, income distribution, economic performance, and political legitimacy of nations, or that they subvert national cultures, social structures, or politics—the subject of this book. In fact, some recent research suggests that the MNCs typically adapt to national patterns; they are not aggressive change agents. The evidence comes from studies of the behavior of foreign firms in the U.S. and Europe, especially Germany, and from analysis of the growing importance of various forms of interfirm networking, overwhelmingly driven by large multinational firms.

As Abowd and Freeman show (1991b, pp. 2, 22–23), foreign-owned firms in the U.S. employ only 3% of American workers. The bulk of direct foreign enterprises in the U.S. are European; they use more highly educated labor, more R&D personnel, and, compared to domestic producers, are more concentrated in traded goods sectors (exports) (*ibid.*). Despite popular complaints about their subversive effect on labor standards, the wages of production workers in fact are higher in foreign-owned firms and the rate of unionization is the same as those in domestic-owned companies.

That the MNCs adapt to local and national laws and customs rather than changing them is shown by a detailed study of 34 Japanese production systems in the U.S. and Canada 1989–94, which also compared eight U.S.-owned and Korean-owned plants in the U.S. and seven Japanese-owned plants in Mexico. Plants from four industries were included: auto assembly, auto parts, consumer electronics, and semiconductors. The case studies were supplemented by a questionnaire sent to 450 manufacturing companies fully or partly owned by Japanese in North America (with a response rate of only one in five) (Abo, 1994). The conclusion: Japanese transplants did not significantly change the industrial landscape of the countries in which they operate. In the U.S., for example, they either adapted to existing practices (unions, wage structures) or they brought in from Japan those people and machines essential to production that they could not find in the U.S. (trainers, managers, equipment, high-quality suppliers). Japanese firms adopted the American wage system with its big differentials; they embraced American job classification schemes and promotion criteria (compensation based on job grades rather than seniority and merit and very little mobility between blue-collar and white-collar jobs). If unions already existed (about one in five cases), they included unions; where workers were not organized, they followed American managerial practices (no union) (*ibid.*, chap. 4). If the industry practice was easy firing and hiring, as with the least-skilled workers in electronics, Japanese transplants conformed; if the industry required high skill, they kept to the Japanese practice of low turnover. They did emphasize training and teamwork more than their American counterparts: two-thirds sent Japanese trainers to the U.S. for training sessions followed by on-the-job training; most sent either engineers or workers or both to Japan for study. And where they felt American parts suppliers and equipment were inferior they either procured them from Japanese parts plants (highly sophisticated parts) or Japanese plants in Southeast Asia or Mexico (less-sophisticated parts), or they established local suppliers in the U.S. to avoid friction with local managers (*ibid.*, chap. 3, pp. 78 – 79; and Encarnation, 1993, p. 21). Similar conclusions were reached in an intensive study of 8 of the 11 Japanese auto assembly transplants in the United States (Pil and MacDuffie, 1996) and a broader survey of industrial relations in foreign-owned subsidiaries in Europe (Schulten, 1996, pp. 306 – 307).

There is nothing here to support the idea that the transplants are subverting labor standards or collective bargaining. Indeed the net effect may be a slight upgrading of training and labor-management relations. What the Japanese leave at home is their more-organized enterprise unions, their flat hierarchies, and their more egalitarian wage and income distribution. They are not bringing Japan to the U.S.

The necessary adaptation of MNCs to national customs and laws is also evident in Germany. Foreign firms get the German benefits of long-term financing, technology, information sharing, and the apprenticeship system only if they adopt German employment practices—pay high wages to highly skilled workers, observe rules on job security, safety, and worker participation (cf. Harrison, 1994, pp. 213 – 214, 165; and Lincoln, Kerbo, and Wittenhagan, 1995, pp. 433ff.).[21] Perhaps this explains why when Germans buy an Opel (made by GM in German plants) they do not think of it as an "American" car.

The same picture emerges if we examine U.S. foreign investments by industry and world region. The complaint that U.S. MNCs are merely escaping high union wages and benefits in the U.S. by moving to places with very low labor costs—America's average compensation for production workers is five times higher than Taiwan's, nine times higher than Brazil's—has no empirical foundation. A study of 32 manufacturing industries in 10 geographical regions found that U.S. foreign investments were "no more likely to originate in heavily unionized industries than in lightly unionized ones," a finding that holds even in developing countries where corporate flight from union strongholds should be most apparent (Karier, 1995, p. 117). This study confirms what many others have concluded: American MNCs, like the foreign transplants in the U.S., are involved in foreign production mainly to avoid trade barriers, to use their concentrated capital in areas with educated workers and R&D advantages, and to seek new lucrative markets close to home. The search for low wages or nonunion localities, if not completely absent, is low on their list. (Cf. Woodward and Glickman, 1991; Wasylenko and McGuire, 1985; Davidson, 1980; Ajami and Ricks, 1981; Dunning, 1977, 1988; Cooke and Noble, 1998.)[22]

Reinforcing and reflecting the MNCs' bias toward national cultures and policies were two trends in the concentration of corporate investment from 1970 to 1992. First, capital flows become increasingly concentrated on the richest parts of the world; direct foreign investment in developing countries was only about 25% in the 1970s; it is now below 20%. Modern countries are less risky than the rest.[23] Second, the MNCs, except for oil companies and similar natural resource firms, are not typically global, they are regional: European firms invest mainly inside Western Europe; American firms in the U.S., Canada, Mexico, and South America; Japanese firms principally in Japan, South Korea, greater China, and Southeast Asia. In short, MNCs take the line of least resistance, moving along geographical and cultural lines—areas close to customers, where recruiting and managing is easiest, and where familiarity with national customs is greatest (*The Economist,* "A Survey of Multinationals," March 27, 1993, p. 12; Davidson, 1980; Hirst and Thompson, 1996, pp. 58ff.).

It is possible that one characteristic of big MNCs—their effort to orchestrate various forms of interfirm networking or partnering—will increase the death rate of small to medium-sized firms dependent on them and thereby increase job insecurity and earnings inequality. Bennett Harrison (1994) argues that the suppliers and decentralized producers who face powerful MNCs that centralize finance, control, and distribution will promote the growth of a contingent workforce. All networked firms rely on a core labor force of high-paid, highly trained, secure workers in whom the firm heavily invests and a large number of contingent workers employed by small subcontractors as needed and replaced at will. Outsourcing and downsizing are the watchwords. "Lean and mean" is the slogan. The core remains small, the periphery grows, subcontracting spreads. The subcontractors are played against one another by the MNC. This "dark side" of "alliance capitalism," Harrison argues, means wage stagnation and rising earnings inequality—most obvious in microelectronics and computers, but spreading to other industries where MNCs are prominent.

I am not convinced that these trends originated with MNCs or that the MNCs greatly accelerate them; they have been long evident in the USA and UK. First, the contingent labor force of temporary and part-time workers is more prominent among non-MNCs in domestic sectors—the service industries such as retail trade, hotels and restaurants, and the building trades—than in the export sectors. Second, subcontracting and downsizing have a long history, preceding the rise of MNCs as in the old days of the "putting out" system—sweatshops in the needle trades turning out clothing and textiles—a system still alive in American central cities. Third, Japan and Germany have had such networks for many decades without much increase in earnings inequality or job instability. Japan, in particular, has had a dual labor force of core workers (about one-fourth to one-third of the economy) and layers of dependent firms that do not provide its famed lifetime employment. As we have seen, much depends on the countervailing power and policies of governments, parties, and unions as they shape managerial behavior.

Observers of transnational corporations contend that even though on average they adapt to national laws and customs, their immense resources and strategic alliances permit them to shift operations across national boundaries in a continual search for new markets and friendly environments. The global network model is therefore a threat to corporatist bargaining and more generally to the national institutions through which labor has demanded job security, good earnings, and participation in both business and government policies. Consistent with this idea is the fact that some MNCs in recent years have relocated production at the site of the most "flexible" labor and the union response—international labor collaboration—has been weak. For instance, Hoover, the vacuum cleaner company owned by Maytag, eliminated 600 jobs in Dijon while adding 400 at its plant near Glasgow, partly because the engineering union in Scotland offered it more concessions than the French unions would give (Turner, 1993b, pp. 7–8). Such whipsawing provides a strong incentive to unions to collaborate across national boundaries. But strong incentives are not enough, and the prospects for Europeanwide collective bargaining, like the promise of an effective European social charter, are to say the least, uncertain.

Embryonic structures for Europeanwide collective bargaining already exist—the European Trade Union Confederation (ETUC) with its staff of 45, many sectoral European industry committees, a few European works councils at large MNCs, and many informal networks of union leaders, as well as their employer counterparts, the European Confederation of Employer Associations for private industry (UNICE) and the parallel confederation of employers in the public sector (CEEP) (Turner, 1993b, 1996). Of course, several of the member confederations (including the German DGB and the British TUC) do not themselves possess bargaining power; they have no mandate to negotiate substantive agreements on most issues. And the employer federations are in Brussels to prevent the passage of any binding laws or directives that would restrict employer discretion. Further, the variations in structure, interest, and ideology among these national labor movements and employer associations are substantial (Streeck, 1991a; Timmersfeld, 1992; Lange, 1992; Turner, 1993a, 1993b; Martin and Ross, 2000). These are powerful barriers to cross-national collective bargaining. Exacerbating the situation is the extraordinary cost of German reunification: inflationary pressures meant high interest rates (at least in the early years) and unemployment while German union leaders, who are at the center of ETUC and other cross-national networks, are preoccupied with the incorporation of East German workers—diverted from the tasks of European integration.

For all these reasons the protracted union campaign for EC-wide collective bargaining and worker participation rights has been largely unsuccessful. The exceptions—glimmers of possible progress—are instructive in assessing the role of MNCs. So far, union progress has been confined to a few French- and German-based multinational corporations. They have agreed to a limited arrangement for cross-national consultation and information sharing, not negotiation (Turner, 1993a, pp. 61–63; 1996), but it is a union foot in the door. Another foot in the door is the coordinating role of the European Federation of Building and Woodworkers (EFBWW), closest to becoming a Europeanwide labor union. It has a long history of "sectoral social dialogue" with its employer counterparts, for example, the European Construction Industry Confederation. It has achieved agreements on health and safety and training and, while it has little hope of establishing international contracts setting wages and labor standards, it is becoming increasingly important as a means by which unions can coordinate disparate strategies in relation to MNCs.[24] In other words, if there is any relaxation of employer resistance to multinational works councils and community-wide collective bargaining, it is found among MNCs in particular industry sectors (e.g., VW in auto, EFBWW in construction), not in the European Community (cf. Schulten, 1996). This is not a case for arguing the negative impact of MNCs on labor.

The picture is one of strong union motives for cross-national collaboration meeting equally strong institutional barriers. The outcome is unclear. With the shift from unanimity voting to qualified (weighted) majority voting, the European Community in 1994 adopted a new directive on European works councils mainly devoted to information sharing, so long vetoed by the British and opposed by employers. The EU mandate applies to all firms with 1,000 or more employees doing business in two or more countries (about 1,200 – 1,300 companies). This may be a precursor for more significant rights of consultation and power sharing. The most likely progress in multinational bargaining, however, is likely to be made at the MNC level. This is where some works councils were earlier established by the European Metalworkers Federation using funds provided by the European Commission (Turner, 1993b, p. 27) and where most of the cross-national labor-leader contacts and activist networks are growing (Martin and Ross, 2000).

In sum: The argument that multinational corporations undermine labor standards and collective bargaining finds no support when we compare nationals with multinationals and trace recent trends in the MNCs' investment targets, ready adaptation to national laws and practices, and policies on wages, union recognition, and consultation.

The Globalization of Finance: Are Strong Central Banks a Drag?

If the emergence of MNCs, the flow of migrants across national boundaries, and even the international flow of capital are only a moderate influence on consensual bargaining, domestic politics, and public policies, perhaps another global trend will be a stronger threat— the spread of independent central banks and the increase in their autonomy and power. Recent cross-national research on financial markets and central banks suggests that, although there is still much variation among nations, there is a general trend toward the increased power of central banks.

As Sylvia Maxfield (1997) and Alesina and Summers (1993, p. 153) show, central banks with strong formal-legal and informal independence, Bundesbank style, are spreading among both developed and developing countries. Where once the German Bundesbank and the American Federal Reserve Bank were the standard cases of powerful central banks, in the five years from 1989 to 1993 at least 27 countries, most of them in Europe and Latin America, created or increased the independence of central banks (including Japan, New Zealand, Italy, France, and Belgium) (Maxfield, 1997, table 4.1). And the Maastricht Treaty stipulated that by 1997 the central banks of all participating member states must be independent.

If we can locate the sources of the national differences in the independence of central banks, we can better understand the recent general trend toward increased autonomy. From recent research we can infer that four structural differences among developed or developing nations explain national differences: (1) the size and internationalization of credit markets; (2) the relation of industry to government, especially the degree to which industry relies on government for credit; (3) the presence or absence of a corporatist bargaining structure that permits either labor and the left or industry or both to shape economic policy; and (4) the role of key currencies when countries increase their trade dependence. Let us first briefly examine each of these interacting forces. Then we can look at the rank order of our rich democracies in central bank autonomy, assess whether central bankers know what they are doing, and gauge the economic and political consequences if their power continues to increase.

Strong, autonomous central banks emerge where the size and internationalization of financial markets (especially robust bond markets), and the perception of the need for capital these markets create, induce politicians to cede authority to central banks (Maxfield, 1997, pp. 4, 35–49; Cukierman, 1992, pp. 449–450). Financial communities want price stability, stable currencies, guaranteed bank transactions, and restriction of "excess" competition among private banks. If they get into trouble, bankers and investors want central banks that will bail them out as in the October crash of 1987 when Federal Reserve Chairman Greenspan ran the Fed's printing press overtime or when his predecessor, Paul Volker, earlier bailed out Continental Illinois. Almost all the time, however, the financial community believes that restrictive monetary policies serve their interests (Maxfield, 1997, p. 22) and that central banks independent of elected officials can administer the necessary strong medicine, that is, vigorous anti-inflation measures. Among developing countries, where hyperinflation has often emerged, the same beliefs, institutionalized in such creditor agencies as the IMF, the World Bank, and money-center banks, have even more force. The fear of creating an excuse for foreign intervention or the need to establish or reestablish international creditworthiness inspires government reform of public finance and a move toward strong central banking (Mexico and Thailand in the late 19th century and early 20th). More recently, the growth of international financial markets, and the incentives for cross-national capital mobility it creates, has again forced the leaders of NICs to cede more authority to central banks because they think such a move helps to attract or reassure creditors and investors (Maxfield, 1997, chap. 3). In the rare case where a developed country experiences hyperinflation and successfully stabilizes its currency (Israel in the late 1970s, Germany after the 1920s), it too, will cede more authority to its central bank. Cukierman (1992, p. 455) suggests that the crisis of hyperinflation makes competing interest groups aware of their shared interest in preventing chaos.

If, in contrast, financial markets and private banks are weak and industrialists must rely on government credit, industry and government alike will have a stake in the subordination of central banks to government mandates. If in addition industry and government have achieved a corporatist compromise—without labor (Japan, France) or a collaboration with labor (Austria, Sweden, Norway, Belgium)—the countervailing power to the financial community will be enhanced. Finally, state-led industrialization as it interacts with trade dependence limits the power of central banks. If initially a government, motivated by its own financial needs, collaborates with credit-hungry exporters and industrialists to set up a central bank, that bank will be weak (e.g., South Korea and Brazil) and may remain so for generations. The enthusiasm for tight monetary policies will be minimal (Maxfield 1997).

Reinforcing this tendency is export dependence in the early stages of industrialization. Where a large portion of state revenue comes from international trade, fluctuations in export earnings will provide an incentive for the state to create suppliant central banking institutions that finance industrial and growth policies of government. Cases that fit include Japan and Korea in recent decades and New Zealand, Belgium, the Netherlands, and Denmark in an earlier period, 1880–1934. (On trade dependence see table 2.1.) Again a more accommodative, flexible monetary policy is likely to be institutionalized and to persist. Some of these banks virtually print money on government demand. In contrast are Germany and the United States: after World War II they have both been below average in trade dependence and remain at the top in bank autonomy and monetary conservatism.

In sum: Where industry relies on government for credit and stock and bond markets are small, where labor or industry or both act as countervailing powers in the context of

TABLE 17.4 Measures of central bank autonomy before 1990

	Combined Autonomy Scores Political and Economic[a]		Political Autonomy 1955-88 (Alesina)[b]		Autonomy Increased 1989-93?[c]	
Switzerland*	4.0	H	4.0	H		
W. Germany**	4.0	H	4.0	H		
United States	3.5	HM	3.5	HM		
Canada	2.5	MH	2.0	M		
Ireland[d]	2.5	MH	—			
Denmark**	2.5	MH	2.0	M		
Netherlands**	2.5	MH	2.0	M		
Austria**	2.0	M	—			
United Kingdom	2.0	M	2.0	M		
Australia	2.0	M	1.0	L		
Sweden**	2.0	M	2.0	M		
Finland**, [d]	2.0	M	—			
Norway**	2.0	M	2.0	M		
Belgium**	2.0	M	2.0	M	yes	1993
France*	2.0	M	2.0	M	yes	1993
Italy**	1.75	LM	1.5	L	yes	1992
Japan*, [e]	1-1.5	L	—		yes	1990
New Zealand	1.0	L	1.0	L	yes	1990s

**Corporatist. Germany a marginal case.

*Corporatist-without-labor. Switzerland marginal.

[a]Average score for legal autonomy using comparable metrics from Bade and Parkin (1987) as extended by Alesina (1988) and the sum of political and economic independence computed by Grilli, Maciandaro, and Tabellini (1991). Austria is ranked medium by Burdekin and Willet (1991). See text and appendix H, which compares these scores with Cukierman's (1992) survey data for validation.

[b]Index developed by Bade and Parkin (1987) and extended by Alesina (1988).

[c]Source: Maxfield (1997).

[d]A score translating Cukierman's formal-legal score (1992, p. 382, table 19.4) into an equivalent metric for column 1.

[e]My judgment of the autonomy of the Bank of Japan in relation to major ministries and the government. Bade and Parkin rank it high, Grilli et al. rank it medium, and Epstein and Shor (1986) rank it low.

increasing trade dependence, central banks remain weak; their autonomy is limited. Where credit markets are large and internationalized and key currencies (the U.S. dollar, the Japanese yen, the German mark) dominate, and where the countervailing power of industry and labor is weak or absent, central banks acquire increasing power.

Data tend to support both this picture of national differences and the idea that some convergence is taking place. Although it is very difficult to measure the autonomy of central banks cross-nationally, several students of the political economy of banking have produced estimates of reasonable quality. Their rankings of our rich democracies tend to agree. Table 17.4 summarizes their findings and appendix H discusses the measures.

At first glance, there is no clear pattern of relationship between type of political economy and central bank autonomy for the postwar period 1955 – 88. The least-corporatist countries appear at every level of central bank autonomy (U.S., high; UK and Canada, medium; New Zealand and Australia, low) as do the more-negotiated economies (Germany and Switzerland, high; Italy, France, and Japan, low). However, there is a tendency for corporatist countries that also have strong left parties to cluster in the medium autonomy category (Austria, the Netherlands, Denmark, Sweden, Norway, Belgium). That may reflect the countervailing power of labor movements and left parties that participate in high policy. In these countries tight money that restricts growth and employment are not popular. The idea that all groups gain from growth and job expansion takes hold; central banks are constrained.

In the cases of France (medium central bank autonomy) and Japan (weak autonomy) the constraints on bank autonomy come not from labor and left power but from centralized governments and key ministries. Japanese elites—at least during their period of greatest economic success (up until 1992)—have clearly been less enthralled by an ideology of monetarism, less obsessed with the dangers of even moderate inflation than has the Federal Reserve Board in the U.S. The tight connections between industry and government and industry and finance are celebrated in every description of Japanese economic prowess (see e.g., chaps. 1, 2, and 12; Johnson, 1982; Dore, 1986; Zysman, 1983). The recent increase in the independence of the Bank of Japan is quite modest and entirely informal (Maxfield, 1997, p. 20; Deane and Pringle, 1994, p. 259). Japanese industrialists, like MITI and the Finance Ministry, are seldom interested in a contractionary economy; they like a monetary policy that accommodates the expansion of markets, prices, profits, and credit.[25] Thus, when industry-finance relations are cooperative and close, industry can counteract the central bankers' phobia about inflation. At the extreme, bankers and industrialists see themselves as part of the same industrial group; credit relations focus on bank financing of industry. Epstein (1992, p. 14) notes, as one indicator of this relationship, that in 1970 – 84 Japan, like France, Germany, and Italy, had a large share of nonfinancial assets held by banks, a pattern he calls "enterprise finance," while the UK, USA, and Canada did not, a pattern of "speculative finance." (Because of Japan's policy errors in the 1990s, however, it traded places with the U.S. in economic performance. See chap. 12.)

In contrast, where financial systems have large stock and bond markets dominated by large private banks and other large investors oriented toward global exchange, industry and finance, as Thorstein Veblen (1921) foresaw, are in conflict over monetary policy. For instance, in September 1994, after the U.S. Fed had raised interest rates five times, the National Association of Manufacturers reported that its members were deeply anxious and suggested that the Fed constrain its enthusiasm and stop killing the recovery. Credit relations in these systems tend to be more speculative, unstable, and short-term.

There remain the anomalies of Germany and Switzerland, the two highest scorers on bank autonomy. Although I have scored them as only marginally corporatist (see chap. 2), it is clear that both countries evidence substantial institutional offsets to the ideology and power of their independent central banks. In Germany the major counter influence is left and labor strength; in Switzerland it is more the tight connection between industry and finance than it is labor-left politics. The Swiss central bank, which began operations in 1907, by a 1978 revised law aims at "a balanced positive growth, especially . . . protection against and prevention of unemployment and inflation"(Schweizerische Nationalbank, 1993, pp. 26–27). Although it is more autonomous than the Bank of Japan, it fits the Japanese pattern of enterprise finance. Swiss bankers not only work closely together in and around the central bank but they also work in intimate association with industrialists and entrepreneurs. In his analysis of the Swiss international multifunction bank W. Blackman (1989, pp. 241ff.) notes that Swiss bankers early on adopted the slogan "It was not industry which was short of capital but capital which was short of industry." Bankers often serve as board members of the corporations in which they invest; their interest in industrial growth balances their interest in fighting inflation. In Germany, too, banks and industry have long had a close relationship, although this has diminished since Shonfield's (1965) account of that interplay (Soskice and Schettkat, 1993, pp. 106–108).

The German labor movement remains a major countervailing force to the Bundesbank. Although the German labor federation, the DGB (Deutscher Gewerkschaftsbund), has little control over the 17 unions in the system, there is, as we have seen in chapter 2, much coordination of union policies because of the dominance of IG Metall and quite strong employer associations. As Carlin and Soskice (1990) have shown in a study of 17 of our countries from 1965 to 1985, Germany therefore ranks above average in coordinated wage bargaining despite its low degree of centralization. Thus the postwar record of low inflation with only medium unemployment is a product not only of the Bundesbank's autonomy but of a labor movement that has traded off wage restraint and industrial peace for social benefits and worker participation (see the detailed analysis in chap. 12; and Soskice and Schettkat, 1993). The consensual bargaining between labor, government, and industry eases the Bundesbank's task of controlling inflation without greatly reducing employment (chap. 12, pp. 451ff., 457–458; cf. Hall, 1994). Even the institutional transfer of unions and collective bargaining from Western to Eastern Germany, while criticized for initially raising wages above productivity increases, may in the long run help to control wage-push inflation as the Eastern economy recovers (Soskice and Schettkat, 1993, pp. 121–122).

Adding to Bundesbank accountability and moderation is the presence of six prominent, independent economic research institutes whose concerns transcend inflation and whose orientations differ.[26] They present their economic forecasts every spring and fall. The institute in Berlin is viewed as more "left" than the others, but together they constitute another countervailing source of data and interpretation. Even so, the power of the Bundesbank occasionally overwhelms the opposing interests. For instance when the huge costs of reunification mounted after 1989, and especially in 1992, the Bundesbank insisted on maintaining high interest rates, refusing to accommodate the demands of either the German government or its opposition and driving unemployment up to 8.2% in 1993 (9.7% by the first quarter of 1994), forcing its European neighbors into devaluation and/or recession.[27]

Beyond these national differences is a second message from table 17.4 (column 3): rich democracies are converging toward more central bank independence, often because of what they think is the success of the Bundesbank and always because of the weight of the German economy in determining exchange rates. From 1990 to 1993 at least six of the countries ranked low or medium in central bank autonomy have increased the independence of their central banks. And in Britain, already medium in bank autonomy, the victorious Labour government of May 1997 in a surprise first step gave the Bank of England "operational independence"—the right to set interest rates, formerly in the hands of the Treasury.

It is a shift in power to increasingly insulated bankers and economists, technocrats hostile to the welfare state and the taxes to finance it, enthralled by an ideology of monetarism, obsessed with the dangers of even moderate inflation, ignoring cross-national evidence that there is no link between such inflation and economic growth. They are champions of bond traders. In essence, a small elite of central bankers acts as agents for big international investors in bonds with, at best, only incidental concern with unemployment or even steady growth.

The evidence that they know what they are doing is, to say the least, slim. A major study of the effects of the monetary policy of the Federal Reserve Board (FRB) on economic performance in the postwar period (Romer and Romer, 1989) shows that in the six episodes when the FRB attempted to contract the economy to fight what it said was "excessive" inflation (October 1947, September 1955, December 1968, April 1974, August 1978, and October 1979) it precipitated and then prolonged and deepened recessions (beyond what would have occurred for other reasons), although it also prolonged recoveries. Updating that study to 1950–90 and concentrating on the effects of the Fed on the pace of recovery (from the depths they often caused), the Romers conclude that Fed policy "has made recessions more severe, and recoveries more rapid, than they otherwise would have been" (Romer and Romer, 1994, p. 51). For instance, without Fed action, the 1953, 1960, and 1969 recessions would not have occurred at all and the output declines in the 1973 and 1981 recessions would have been half as deep as they were. Monetary policy "helped to both start and stop postwar recessions" (*ibid.,* p. 52). In other words the Fed's penchant for tight money when growth rears its ugly head triggers and deepens recessions but when the governors decide to loosen up, their reductions in interest rates are crucial to recovery. The Romers also find that Fed policy, whether contractionary or expansionary, has long-lasting effects. Fiscal policies—both automatic changes in taxes and spending and discretionary changes—also aid recovery, but their effects are not as strong as the effects of monetary policy.[28]

What we can infer from this careful study, which adds the Federal Reserve Board's contemporaneous records to its quantitative narrative, is that the U.S. central bank in its zeal to fight inflation and its limited concern for unemployment, has destabilized the American economy, creating more and bigger booms and busts. Because their mission in the words of the Federal Reserve Reform Act of 1977 is "to promote the goals of maximum employment, stable prices, and moderate long-term interest rates," and because Fed chairmen often announce that they aim at "stable prices and sustainable growth," we can conclude either that they lack the knowledge to carry out their mission or, as the Romers' seem to imply, they deliberately create recessions to avoid inflation, whatever the social costs. I prefer the hypothesis that they are guided by a combination of ignorance and ideology. For many years the Fed believed that manipulation of their measures of the money supply (M1, M2, M3) would bring low (or even zero) inflation with steady growth; then in the early 1990s, as evidence mounted that these were poor measures and/or that the underlying theory was weak, they shifted their attention to commodity prices as harbingers of inflation and justified their preemptive strikes (interest rate hikes, tighter money) on those grounds (Greenspan in testimony and answers to questions before congressional committees in July 1994). To many observers and investors, the game was not to assess the real economy but to assess what the prevailing ideology of the Fed would make them do and when, an even more difficult task. Don't worry about your country's economy; worry about what the Fed thinks about the economy. So investors dump bonds and buy commodities in anticipation of hard-line preemptive action by the Fed. Then the Fed interprets the bond traders' fear of the Fed as a sign of an inflation threat. It is a model of the self-fulfilling prophecy.[29]

My skeptical observations about the limits of Federal Reserve Board knowledge are reinforced by cross-national research on the relationship between central bank autonomy (CBA) and economic growth, unemployment, and inflation. Regarding growth, where researchers have controlled for initial GDP they find that CBA has a positive effect on growth in the NICs (newly industrializing countries) but no effect in the rich countries I am discussing (e.g., Alesina and Summers, 1993, p. 151; Cukierman et al., 1993, pp. 110–112, 136; and Grilli, Masciandaro, and Tabellini, 1991).

Using the economic performance index of chapter 12 (equally weighting low inflation, good growth, and low unemployment) for four postwar periods and averaging those scores for four degrees of central bank autonomy (CBA high, medium-high, medium, and low) among the 18 rich democracies in table 17.5, we can see that central bank autonomy is unrelated to economic performance.

In 1965–74 the three countries with the strongest CBA tied the three countries with the weakest CBA, and the best performers were those with only moderate bank autonomy. In all periods after the first oil shock, the top economic performers were countries with the strongest banks (Germany and Switzerland taking the lead), but the worst economic performers were the countries with medium-high CBA (Canada, Netherlands, and Denmark) while the close second in performance 1974–79 was the medium CBA and the close second in 1980–84 was the low CBA. (For details on economic performance see chap. 12 and appendix G.)

Decomposing the economic performance index and correlating each of its three components with central bank autonomy among the same 18 rich democracies, again we find only weak relationships. What other researchers who include less-than-rich countries in their studies conclude—CBA dampens inflation—is evident for our countries, too. But the correlations are strong only for 1974–79 ($r = -.60$). For other periods CBA has only a marginal or moderate negative correlation with inflation: $r = -.42$ (n.s.) for 1965–74; $-.40$ ($p = .10$) for 1980–84; $-.47$ ($p = .05$) for 1985–89. More important, if we exclude Japan as an outlier (low bank autonomy, very high growth), CBA has a negative or no effect on real GDP growth per capita ($-.11$, $-.09$, $-.42$, and $-.29$) and no effect on unemployment. Of course, these averages obscure the more interesting results at the ex-

TABLE 17.5   Central bank autonomy (CBA) and economic performance by periods, 1965–89

CBA Average Score by Group[a]		Average Score for Economic Performance Index[b]			
		1965-74	1974-79	1980-84	1985-89
High autonomy	3.8	3.0	3.7	4.3	4.3
Medium-High	2.5	2.3	2.5	1.5	2.3
Medium	2.0	3.6	3.3	3.1	3.0
Low and L-M	1.4	3.0	3.0	3.7	3.0

[a]See footnotes to table 17.4.

[b]See chapter 12 and appendix G on index of economic performance which equally weights unemployment, real GDP growth per capita, and inflation. The range is 0 (poor) to 6 (excellent).

tremes and the much more important institutional sources of economic performance discussed above and in chapter 12. The averages for growth and unemployment also obscure the destabilizing effects of some powerful central banks as they initiate and exacerbate slumps and accelerate recoveries (net average effect may be zero). If the more independent central bankers knew what they were doing, we would surely get stronger results on inflation and some positive results on growth.[30]

That several of the countries whose central banks had limited autonomy before 1990 (Japan, Austria, Norway, or Belgium 1965–74, 1985–89) outperformed countries with more independent central banks (Canada, the Netherlands, Denmark, or the U.S. before 1980) should give pause to those who have adopted the "Bundesbank model" for the European Central Bank without the German labor, management, state, political, education and training, and other institutions that make it work. Unfortunately, the European Union has neither the offsetting institutions to constrain such a bank's behavior nor the European-wide welfare state and job creation antidotes to its strong deflationary medicine.

I do not deny the need for a relatively stable currency, the avoidance of huge price fluctuations, and a "lender of last resort" to supply emergency cash reserves to faltering banks and to avoid financial panics.[31] The trouble comes with the radical shift in power away from elected politicians to a group of bankers and economists with a highly specialized ideology who are only remotely accountable. The ideology in most cases goes beyond monetarism to Reaganomics: deregulate, reduce taxes (especially on upper-income groups and corporations), cut social spending—these are the cure-alls typically advocated by authoritative central bankers. Like the doctors of the 18th century who bled their patients to cure them, many central bankers also regard recessions as a necessary purge to restore labor discipline as well as confidence in the currency. (Michael Kreile, 1978, p. 209 cites former Bundesbank President Emminger to this effect.) And if the political class does not shape up, these ideologues, given enough autonomy, can administer shocks that will threaten politicians' survival. As I have shown in this book, this ideology is contradicted by empirical evidence on variation in the economic performance of rich democracies from 1950 to 1992. Sheer level of taxes and social spending has no consistent effect on economic performance; before 1974 the impact of aggregate social spending was actually positive as a trade-off for labor peace and tax concessions to industry; it fades after 1973 and is neutral after 1979 (pp. 451, 458ff.). Indeed some components of the welfare state continue to be productivity-enhancing—for example, health-care access, occupational health and safety, active labor-market policy (chaps. 2, 12, 15, 16, and 18). Tax structures have a modest effect: consumption taxes, because they are negatively related to strikes and positively related to capital formation, foster economic growth; social-security payroll taxes (used to finance health care, pensions, etc.) actually restrain inflation in normal times; they rarely lower growth (only in the brief period of multiple shocks, 1980–84). Property taxes, however, may be a drag on the economy (chap. 12, pp. 485–488). Intrusive regulations in a context of combat between labor, management, and the government are indeed a drag on the economy. But it is the least-corporatist countries with the most free-enterprise ideology that evidence ineffective intrusive regulatory styles (as in the controls over medical professionals introduced by President Reagan and Prime Minister Thatcher); corporatist democracies, in contrast, arrive at consensual rules that can be better implemented (chaps. 12, pp. 453–454, and 15).

There are already enough elected politicians who ignore such evidence and pin economic troubles on the welfare state, high taxes, and government regulations. Why enhance the power of ideologues in central banks who share their views and cannot be removed when the limits of their revelations become apparent?

Even if the effects of central bank independence and ideology on employment and growth were not on balance negative, their effects on political legitimacy would be worrisome. The extreme case of New Zealand may be a sign of things to come; it recently concocted a brew of radical and sudden shifts in fiscal, monetary, and social policies and simultaneously created the most powerful independent central bank in the world. A blend of full-blooded monetarism and Reaganomics from 1984 to 1993 resulted in high unemployment, reaching 11% by 1991 and remaining at about 10% in 1992–93, anemic growth (real GDP growth per capita averaged 0.5% from 1985 to 1992), with inflation increasing to 18% by 1986 but trending toward zero when the central bank got going. Within 10 years this combination of sectarian economics, indiscriminate deregulation, means testing, cuts in social spending, shifts in tax burdens to the middle and bottom, and union bashing brought about the near-collapse of the major political parties, the emergence of several radical parties of the right and left, a drastic decline in public confidence in all institutions, and a massive popular revolt. It culminated in a referendum marking the first and only postwar shift among rich democracies away from a simple plurality electoral system to a mixed-member proportional representation system. Ironically that seems to have revived the very center-left coalition that the right-wing sectarians wiped out. The full story of New Zealand's neoliberal experiment appears in chapter 11 on party decline.

In short, strong central bank independence without the corporatist institutions of Germany and Switzerland can destabilize both the economy and the political system and increase the potential for polarized politics.

Large national differences in bargaining structures and public policies described in this book remain; they are associated with differences in central bank autonomy and behavior. That is the main story. Yet increasing trade dependence, while it so far has little effect on national institutions, policies, and politics, when it is combined with the growth of international financial markets may foster some convergence in monetary policies. Insofar as center-left political pressure and labor movements in Japan, Germany, and the U.S. decline, insofar as the relations between industry and finance weaken, the central banks in these three countries will become still more independent. As trade dependence increases among all our rich democracies, these banks—whose comparative advantage will increasingly rest on maintaining a stable value for their key currencies—will become more preoccupied with fighting domestic inflation and less concerned with either domestic or world economic growth and oblivious to unemployment. The rest of the democracies—increasingly dependent on trade and international financial markets with their central banks forced to follow the lead of the big three—will be constrained in their economic policies. The option of moderate global reflation and growth to resolve the conflict between central bank restrictive monetary policies and proemployment, progrowth fiscal policies will be foreclosed. The flexibility and benign effects of taxing and spending would be reduced. Remember that Bretton Woods, aiming to support expansionary national macroeconomic policies, explicitly limited the role of central banks. The reverse may now be occurring—a convergence in the independence of central banks with a bias toward restrictive monetary policies. Speculative international financial markets dominated by ideologically driven private bankers oriented toward like-minded central bankers could threaten the state-labor-industry collaboration that has been so productive since World War II. In other words, if there is any one force that can in the long run undermine democratic corporatism, the spread of autonomous central banks is it.

SUMMARY AND INTERPRETATION

The nation-state may no longer be a viable unit of security; collective security and regional alliances are necessary; the UN may occasionally contribute something. Modern economies are no longer independent, if they ever were; economies are becoming more open. Problems of the environment, of human rights, and of terrorism transcend national boundaries as do the solutions to such problems. Yet the nation-state remains the center of political action, social solidarity, and personal identity. Indeed, in recent decades globalization has proceeded in tandem with the proliferation of nation-states. It is a paradox: the more globalization, the more national fragmentation.

This chapter has shown that neither the flow of capital and labor across national boundaries nor the increasing prominence of multinational corporations are major threats to the social and labor-market policies of rich democracies. Because social spending has both positive and negative effects on productivity, and net effects since 1974 are nil, the welfare state is not the culprit that explains the lagging economic performance of some nations. Because national responses to similar external shocks are so varied, we must look to national institutions—to variations in political, economic, and social organization—for an explanation.

Are job protection and labor standards threatened by the international mobility of labor and capital or by countries with very low labor costs? Again the answer depends on the institutions and policies in place. Job security and low labor turnover combined with worker participation in workplace and community greatly enhance enterprise productivity and flexibility, as we have seen in our discussion of Germany and Japan and in chapter 12. In contrast are countries and industries producing low value-added products whose workers are hired and fired frequently, have low job security, little union voice, declining real wages, and increasing poverty rates (to these costs the U.S. adds the costs of litigation about safety, labor standards, unfair labor practices, etc.). Such countries and industries are no major threat to countries and industries with more collaborative industrial relations and efficient employers. The threat of the great economic shifts of recent decades (see chap. 1) is to the least-skilled, least-educated, least-trained workers, who in any case are a declining breed, with or without globalization. And modern democracies that attend to education, training, job creation, labor standards, and poverty prevention can reduce the pain of their transition to other, often better jobs.

Migration from areas of economic despair and repression to areas of opportunity and hope is as old as poverty and persecution. Current rates of immigration into rich democracies have not even reached the level of a century ago. In recent decades industrial societies have been converging in the ratio of foreigners to natives and hence in their social diversity and in their conflict about immigration. What is most striking is a radical disjunction between the economic and employment effects of immigrants, which on balance are positive, and the political effects, which on balance vary from mild animosity to intense nativist voting and violence. Intensity of such protest varies with the number and concentration of immigrants, the degree of mass insecurity, and the social distance between immigrant groups and natives. Most important is the political structure that mobilizes or dampens these common xenophobic sentiments. If political elites adopt liberal naturalization policies, if they combine efforts at border control with programs for cultural and economic integration, they can reduce the electoral appeal of anti-immigrant demagogues who inflame mass fears and hatreds. Comparison of Sweden, Germany, and France affirms the importance of such policies.

What about the impact of multinational corporations and "alliance capitalism"? Analysis suggests that if a country or industry has high labor standards and accommodative labor relations, the MNC adopts the high road; if a country or industry has low labor standards and confrontational labor relations, the MNC tends toward the low road. Multinationals are anything but aggressive change agents. Regarding their decisions to relocate plants from rich democracies to the NICs or poor countries, such moves are infrequent, except for industries with low skill and low value-added products that are labor intensive. Studies of location decisions of both MNCs and national corporations both within nations and among nations generally show that they are determined less by labor costs than by infrastructure (transportation, communication, housing, and other urban amenities), worker quality (including education, training, and development of executives, technicians, and workers), access to universities and research laboratories, and access to markets.[32] That is why despite their increasing interest in new markets in Asia and Latin America, the multinationals' capital investments are still overwhelmingly targeted to rich, stable democracies. If labor costs were at the center of corporate location decisions, the rich democracies would have emptied out long ago. Finally, there is evidence that MNCs, compared to national domestic industries in local labor and product markets, pay better wages and benefits.

Perhaps one recent trend does undermine the capacity of modern democracies to shape their economic destinies: the increasing independence of central banks, a clear threat to collaborative relations among labor, industry, and the state and to the flexible use of fiscal policy (taxes and spending). Reinforcing this trend is not any unprecedented flow of capital and labor across national boundaries but the flow of peculiarly American economic doctrines across those boundaries. What is new is a breed of model-building economists, theorists of unmodified free markets, sectarian in style, less knowledgeable about political and economic institutions than their predecessors. Some of them, marketing a blend of Reaganomics and monetarist ideology, have penetrated finance ministries and financial communities, on the way converting journalists who cover economic issues. This recent tendency was apparent in the 1990s in New Zealand, France, and for a brief moment (1989–94) even in Sweden.

Even here, however, even with the rise of central bank autonomy and the export of American-trained doctrinaire economists, national differences in the strength of countervailing powers are substantial: a Bundesbank in the German sociopolitical context is not the same as a Federal Reserve Board in the American context, let alone a bank in a Japanese or Swedish context.

The nation-state remains the ultimate object of allegiance; national institutions and policies continue to make a big difference for real welfare.

Notes

This is a greatly revised and extended version of a paper presented to the Conference on "Globalization and Welfare Systems," Torino, September 20–21, 1990, and published in *Globalizzazione e sistemi di welfare,* M. Ferrara (a curadi), Torino, Italy, Edzioni della Fondazione G. Agnelli, 1993, pp. 41–63. Short versions were presented at the International Sociological Association XIII World Congress, Bielefeld, Germany, July 18–23, 1994, and the International Political Science Association World Congress, Quèbec, Canada, August 6, 2000.

1. Spain achieved dominance in the 16th and 17th centuries by relending money gained from silver taken out of Mexico and Peru; Holland's strength in the 17th century rested on profits from its colonial empire and from lending to Britain, Austria, and the Baltic countries. Pax Britannia in the 19th century rested not only on the Royal Navy but also on a flow of development capital to other countries; from 1870 to World War I Britain's net foreign investment averaged 5% of income. Later Germany and France deployed large amounts of capital while during and after World War II, the U.S. became a dominant lender through Lend-Lease, the Marshall Plan, the IMF, and the World Bank. Japan's net foreign investment in 1981 as a fraction of national income at 4%, had not yet reached Britain's 5% in its heyday. (Friedman, 1989, pp. 77–78, 81; and Edelstein 1982, chap. 2.)

2. There is a difference, however, in the national response to defaults. In earlier periods international loans were sold to a wide range of bondholders while now they are concentrated in the hands of top money-center banks, which makes defaults more visible and provokes more intervention by banks and governments (Eichengreen and Lindert, 1989, pp. 2–3).

3. For example, table 17.1 shows that total migration in the UK as a proportion of population decreased slightly from .83% in 1901 to .79% in 1981. Belgium and the Netherlands saw modest increases; only Sweden had a large increase in total migration. Much of the mass migration in 16th- and 17th-century Europe was triggered by the push of war and religious intolerance but some migration was the pull of economic opportunity. For instance, by the late 1680s over a quarter of the burghers of Amsterdam were German (Moch, 1992, p. 54).

4. Philip Martin points out that industrial democracies are not being overrun by a tidal wave of immigrants. There are only about 40 million of them in all the industrial countries: 15 to 20 million in North America, 15 to 20 million in Western Europe, and 2 to 3 million in industrial Asian countries (Martin, 1992, pp. 11–12). "International migration remains an extraordinary event despite the

evolution of demand, supply, and network factors that encourage migration . . . 60 percent of the world's migrants move from one developing nation to another. One unlikely country, Iran, includes almost one-fourth of the world's 19 million refugees" (Martin, 1993, p. 6). The main source of refugee flow is the combination of deep poverty and repressive regimes: almost all of the most serious refugee-generating countries fall below $400 per capita GNP and are ruled by military governments—e.g., Vietnam, Haiti, Uganda, Ethiopia, Chad, Mali, Zaire, Laos, Afghanistan, Burundi, Rwanda, Sudan, etc. Since the early 1980s the "Third World" share of the world's refugees (both sending and receiving countries) is about 80% to 90% (Hakovirta, 1993, pp. 37, 40–44).

5. See note 12 in chapter 12 for six other studies consistent with my findings.

6. Chapter 12 reports a multiple regression analysis of the causes of good economic performance—capital investment, labor peace, corporatism, tax structures, party power—played against our measures of vulnerability to external shocks (liquid fuels as a fraction of energy consumption, energy production as a percentage of energy consumption, and sudden changes in the terms of trade). It shows that external shocks have no independent effect on economic performance whatever. Nor do they have any effect on the most important proximate sources of good performance—low strike rates and high capital investment. Only at the extreme, as table 12.5 suggests, do energy shocks and trade vulnerability help to explain the lesser postshock performance of the three exceptions—Denmark, Italy, and Israel. Each of these also had special internal weaknesses: Denmark an unusually sloppy welfare state and a marginal score on corporatism, Israel a uniquely heavy defense burden, Italy the worst strike record and budget deficits of our 19 countries.

7. "In 1985 almost two thirds of all workers in Germany had been continuously employed in their current job for more than five years (U.S.: 45%; France: 58%; U.K.: 52%)," most of them for more than 10 years (Buechtemann and Meager, 1991, p. 10). General restrictions on layoffs and individual dismissals imposed by collective bargaining and labor law are complemented by special job protections for vulnerable groups (e.g., pregnant women, the handicapped, draftees, older workers). If we add tenured public servants, about 20% of the total "dependent" workforce are totally protected against ordinary dismissal.

8. Reviewing cross-national studies of Europe and North America on this point, ILO (1995) concludes that in terms of gross job destruction and creation, the most regulated European political economies are as flexible as the least regulated (e.g., the United States).

9. This empirical finding is consistent with older industrial relations research and with recent economic theories of "efficiency wages": firms may pay a premium over market-clearing wages because they want to retain worker loyalty and encourage hard work (Weiss, 1990). Many opponents of job protection by government and by high-performance firms argue that while this may be good for a minority of workers it is bad for job creation in the economy as a whole. Cross-national evidence reviewed in an ILO report on the creation of stable long-term jobs, however, shows that labor-market regulations (including rules on hiring and firing, levels of unemployment benefits) are not responsible for a nation's unemployment, job insecurity, or poor job creation. The trouble lies in the combination of technological change, weakened unions, poor industrial relations, and reduced demand with slow growth (ILO, 1995, pp. 155–157), as well as demographic shifts (see chap. 13 on job creation).

10. A recent careful analysis of four decades of German export expansion 1953 to 1994 (Holtfrerich and Lindlar, 1995) confirms this observation. It concludes that even in the turbulent times of 1975–89 German exports grew (in real terms) at an average yearly rate of 4.0%, an excellent record compared to other countries and the long-run past. From 1985 to 1990 Germany's trade surplus on the current account climbed to a remarkable 6% of GDP (p. 4). Even during the peak of the unification burden and a deep recession, 1990–94, exports grew at an average yearly rate of 6.3% including trade with East Germany (p. 5). The composition of these exports also remained exception-

ally stable for the four decades: machinery, chemicals, automobiles, and transportation equipment—despite increased competition from low-cost producers using cheap labor (p. 18). Germany continues to excel in medium-tech products (as a percentage of value added to the entire economy) while matching Japan and the United States in high-tech production (pp. 20–23). In short, the German model, contrary to pronouncements of its death, held up well through thick and thin. The dark spot is the very recent climb in unemployment, reflecting the rigidity of the Bundesbank in the early 1990s, when it engaged in a war against the inflation phantom. (See below, "Are Strong Central Banks a Drag?").

11. According to Heinz Fassman and Rainer Münz (1994), of an estimated 14,160,000 migrants from East to West (including those from the GDR, ex-Yugoslavia, Poland, Soviet Union and the Balkans) from 1950 to 1993, 68.1% landed in Germany, 8.1% in Israel, 6.6% in Turkey, 4.8% in the U.S. and 12.8% in other countries (Austria, Scandinavia, France, UK, Canada, etc.).

12. Employer sanctions, used by almost all our 19 countries (Britain is an exception) vary in their effectiveness: vital to their success are adequate resources for enforcement, a secure identification system, links to broader strategies for controlling illegal migration and enforcing labor standards, and steps to prevent employer discrimination. The U.S. fails on all counts. Several European countries—Germany, France, Switzerland—approximate them. (M. J. Miller, 1987.)

Openness to refugees also varies. In 1992 Germany took in two-thirds of the 572,000 asylum seekers entering Europe as it struggled to get other countries to share the burden. On July 1, 1993, it changed its open asylum policy to accept refugees only from regimes that were persecuting them. It made it difficult for persons who passed through "presumably safe countries"—including Romania, Bulgaria, Gambia, Ghana, and Poland—to apply for asylum. Germany worked out arrangements with each adjacent country to help police its borders, giving money to Czechoslovakia and Poland for that purpose. All this sharply cut the number of applicants. The German Bundestag later approved an expansion of the number and power of the border police and raised penalties on illegal alien smugglers. Again, it is far from impossible to regulate immigration. (*Migration News*, vol. 1, #7). Of course it is a beggar-thy-neighbor policy—one country's successful border control is often another country's headache, a powerful reason for international agreements on burden-sharing.

13. Further, even before the welfare reform of 1996 (chap. 8), permanent legal residents were effectively barred from receiving AFDC for three years following admission, and the three-year waiting period for legal immigrants' claims to SSI (Supplementary Security Income for poor retirees) was raised to five years in 1993. Legal permanent residents can be deported if they become public charges within five years of admission. Using welfare at any time increases the difficulty of later bringing relatives in. Thus, the image of recent immigrants as a welfare burden is misleading, although if we compare the percentage of households in which the head receives public assistance without controlling for age or condition, the immigrant percentage in 1990 was somewhat higher that the natives: Fix and Passel (1994, pp. 63–67) calculate that 4.9% of pre-1980 entrants age 15 and over received some form of welfare in 1990 (SSI, AFDC, or other), vs. 4.2% of natives. But examining only working-age (15- to 64-year-old) naturalized and nonnaturalized immigrants from nonrefugee countries (Mexico, Philippines, India, etc.), they find that the 1980–90 entrants are much less likely to be on the dole (2.8%) than comparable natives, 4.2% of whom receive "welfare." Refugees are typically in worse shape and take longer to adjust.

14. Huddle's (1993) is the worst: he not only fails to take account of any positive economic impact of immigrant businesses or consumer spending; he also massively understates revenue collected (e.g., he ignores about $50 billion of taxes immigrants paid in 1992) and omits the necessary comparisons with natives that show that they, too, receive more in services than they pay in taxes (Passel, 1994; Clark and Passel, 1993).

15. These three forces that encourage nativist protest action—economic deprivation, large numbers and concentration of immigrants, and great social distance between immigrants and natives—are the same as the forces that foster prejudice and the perception of group threat. See Lincoln Quillian (1995), an analysis of Eurobarometer Survey #30 results on attitudes toward immigrants and racial minorities in 12 EEC countries, Fall 1988. Individual characteristics had little impact on prejudice and explained none of the country differences. Economic conditions of the country, the size of the minority group, and its social composition (e.g., non-EEC immigration) are the important variables shaping both levels of prejudice and the militancy of protest movements discussed above.

16. In the most recent year available (circa 1991) naturalizations as a percentage of the stock of foreign population in the year before was 5.4% in Sweden, 2.7% in Germany (Guimezanes, 1994, p. 25).

17. The next six paragraphs draw on data developed in a 1993 term paper by my assistant, Karen Adelberger, from French and German surveys and recent literature. See also Wilensky (1975, pp. 57−59; 1976a, pp. 12−34).

18. For an account of recent German immigration debates, policies, and administrative practices, see Halfmann, 1995. Brubaker (1992) describes the evolution of French and German citizenship policies.

19. Alber (1994), using Eurobarometer surveys and data from Wiegand and Fuchs, Gerhards and Roller, devises an index of "rejection of foreigners" (respondents who say that there are too many foreigners in their country, that the presence of foreigners is disturbing, that the rights of foreigners should be restricted, and that asylum seekers should no longer be accepted). For 11 EC countries this index of xenophobia correlates .82 with the percentage of foreigners from non-EC countries in each nation, underscoring the importance of numbers.

20. By 1992 the 36,000 multinationals with over 170,000 affiliates abroad (only about 70,000 of which are in less-developed countries) had reached a *stock* of foreign direct investment of about $1.9 trillion. By 1990 worldwide *sales* by foreign affiliates had reached $5.5 trillion; they became more important than the worldwide sum of exports (3.3 trillion in 1990). (Sauvant, Mallampally, and Economou, 1993, p. 37; Gold, 1993; Encarnation, 1993, p. 25). Regarding *employment,* most overseas employment by MNCs is in other industrialized countries, except for Japanese MNCs whose expansion into Asia is concentrated in developing countries. In the early 1990s, however, with rapid growth and fewer restrictions, MNCs in Europe and North America and Japan alike expanded faster in Asia, Latin America, and the Caribbean. Although an estimate of worldwide employment by MNCs in parent firms and foreign affiliates was only 65 million (ILO, 1992, p. 49), up from about 40 million in the mid-1970s (Parisotto, 1993, p. 34), the jobs are concentrated in rich countries. More than 9 in 10 of the MNCs are headquartered in industrialized countries—most of the biggest are in Japan, Germany, and the U.S. (Gold, 1993, p. 100)—and about 7 in 10 of the jobs created by their affiliates abroad are concentrated in the same affluent countries (ILO, 1992, p. 49). Still these figures suggest that multinationals account for only a very small portion of employment in rich countries and a tiny fraction of employment in less-developed countries—less than 1% (Sauvant et al., 1993, p. 37)—whose *un*employed number is in the hundreds of millions.

21. Bennett Harrison (1994, p. 165) describes another motive for adaptation—expand markets by strategic alliances—in his account of the 1990 Daimler-Benz/Mitsubishi agreement to engage in "intensive cooperation": "Daimler gains access to Mitsubishi's prodigious knowledge of mechatronics (the wedding of mechanical and electrical engineering). What Mitsubishi gets from the alliance is Daimler's aid in blocking French and Italian resistance to letting Japanese car makers into post-1992 Europe, and a connection to Europe's single largest and most commercially successful public-private partnership: the Airbus Industrie consortium that has made itself one of the world's three largest producers of civilian aircraft and a leader in airframe technology" (p. 165).

22. That foreign transplants are not looking for cheap, nonunion labor is confirmed in a study comparing changes in foreign and domestic manufacturing investment across the 48 contiguous states

for 1978–85 (Grant and Hutchinson, 1996). Highly unionized states such as Pennsylvania and Ohio were more successful in attracting foreign firms than in preventing American firms from moving out to the South or abroad. Union avoidance was a much more frequent motive for American managers than among their European and Japanese counterparts, who were used to unions, investment in training, and worker participation. Even for Americans, however, union avoidance was less important in plant location than market demand (and the absence of recessions), tax policies, and federal revenue transfers (permitting states to invest in physical and human infrastructure).

23. A *Wall Street Journal* survey of capital flows based on World Bank data concludes that 10 of the 12 countries that receive the lion's share of foreign capital directed to the developing world are nonpoor; most are "upper-middle" in GNP per capita (*Wall Street Journal,* September 18, 1997).

24. Personal communication from Andrew Martin, September 2, 1997.

25. The Finance Ministry's restrictive stance during the 1990s crisis was an aberration. In 1997, the law changed to give the BOJ primacy in monetary policy and reduce the coordinating role of Finance. In the face of recurrent recession, the Bank continued to fight inflation, worsening the situation described in chapter 12.

26. They are the HWWA-Institute for Economic Research in Hamburg; Ifo-Institute for Economic Research in Munich; Institute for the World Economy in Kiel; Institute for Economic Research in Halle; the Rhine-Westphalian Institute for Economic Research (RWI) in Essen; and the German Institute for Economic Research (DIW) in Berlin. A seventh more prominent source of independent analysis and forecasting is a group of professors on the Council of Economic Advisers completely independent of the government, located in Wissbaden.

27. If we exclude the former East Germany from these figures the unemployment rate for West Germany is lower by just under one percentage point. The Bundesbank in late 1992 aimed to reduce inflation from 3.7% to 2%, while Germany was itself slipping into recession. Hans Tietmeyer, president of the Bundesbank since 1993, rails against the welfare state; an anti-inflation hawk, he favors a European Central Bank, if it is a carbon copy of the Bundesbank (*Wall Street Journal,* January 17, 1996).

28. Because stimulative fiscal policy in the U.S., although rapid in its impact, must be approved by a slow-moving Congress it is less effective in shaping recoveries than monetary policy (Romer and Romer, 1994, pp. 37–38, 55). Anticyclical increases in spending within the discretion of the executive (e.g., accelerating planned spending or tax refunds) are always small and so are their effects; the big changes plowing their way through Congress are typically mistimed or defeated (except for the popular extension of unemployment benefits). This may be an American peculiarity, however; in less-paralyzed political economies, fiscal policy may have greater, speedier impact.

29. James K. Galbraith's caustic analysis of Fed behavior as self-fulfilling prophecy based on incoherent theories concludes that Fed policy reduces to a syllogism: "good times are followed by bad times; therefore good times must be prevented" (1994, p. 36). The syllogism in action has meant that since 1951, when the Fed was freed to conduct an independent monetary policy, all of our recessions, without exception, were preceded by a shift to a tight monetary policy (Friedman, 1989, p. 104).

30. Deane and Pringle (1994, pp. 309–310, 324–325) point to an irony: at the very time the central banks' autonomy is increasing, their effectiveness in controlling inflation is being undermined by the large number of big private speculators in currency and arcane derivatives over which the central bankers have no control. Thus, central bankers' anti-inflation measures are likely to be even more exaggerated because moderate interest-rate increases are less and less effective. The authors also note that while New Zealand, with its strongly autonomous central bank (after 1989) achieved a low inflation rate by 1992–93, Australia, with a controlled central bank, did just as well (*ibid.,* pp. 339–340).

31. The lack of global exchange-rate discipline fuels currency speculation, creates uncertainty for business firms, reduces economic growth, and encourages protectionism (as we saw in the passion-

ate debates over NAFTA and GATT in 1994, the Mexican crisis of January 1995, and the WTO meeting in Seattle, 1999). Some cross-national regime to prevent extreme volatility and misalignments among key currencies may be desirable—a more flexible successor to Bretton Woods.

32. MNCs evidence an additional nonlabor cost motive for direct foreign investment: an American multinational like Intel enters an EC country to preempt potential trade barriers (to be in a position to cope if the community raises barriers against imported chips) and to counter competitors' moves (distract the rival, lower his profits, learn about his tactics and technology) (*The Economist,* "A Survey of Multinationals" March 27, 1993, p. 10).

AMERICAN EXCEPTIONALISM
AND POLICY IMPLICATIONS

My conclusions about specific similarities and differences among the universe of rich democracies can shed light on the theory of "American exceptionalism"—the idea developed by many political philosophers (e.g., Alexis de Tocqueville, 1963 [1835]; Louis Hartz, 1955) and social scientists (e.g., Werner Sombart, 1976 [1906]; Seymour Lipset, 1996; Byron Shafer, 1999) that the U.S. because of its unique culture, society, or polity is simply so different from other highly industrialized societies that it cannot borrow policies or patterns of behavior, however benign, from abroad. If, however, as I have shown, the U.S. in fact shares many aspects of culture, society, and politics with all, most, or a few of these countries, then we can surely learn from their experience as they have learned from ours. So this chapter asks, "What has this book shown about American peculiarities, if any?" and "What are the policy implications?" Both of these questions are answered at length in previous chapters, but the answers are scattered; it will be useful to briefly bring them together. I shall mention the relevant chapters in the hope that the reader will glance at them as well as the overview of chapter 17 to reprise the evidence.

How Different Is the United States?

What is said to be different about the U.S. is almost always a difference of degree, diminishing as the U.S. moves toward other countries or as they move toward America. This is true of technology, culture, society, and politics.

Culture

According to theorists of American exceptionalism the American Creed of liberty, equality, individualism, laissez-faire, and populism defines American culture and culture shapes the peculiar institutions of the United States. (The most forceful recent argument on this line is Lipset, 1996.) The point is often elaborated by invoking a series of opposites: the U.S., compared to other rich democracies, is individualistic vs. collectivistic; egalitarian and populist vs. hierarchical; laissez-faire vs. statist; and social Darwinist vs. humanitarian.

As this book has shown, cultural explanations of the paths of development of rich democracies since World War II are weak once we examine empirical evidence of national variations in values, beliefs, ideologies, or mentalities and try to anchor them in social, economic, and political structures. In fact, all modern populations embrace both of the contradictory values in each pair I have listed. The theory of the ambivalent modern citizen is spelled out in chapters 1 and 4, and is applied in chapters 5, 10, and 15.

Theories of cultural determinism tend to fall apart when one employs three essential tests: (1) specify precisely the values or beliefs said to determine some specific outcome; (2) avoid the common trap of tautology (e.g., observe a pattern of behavior such as long hours at hard work, infer the values, "the work ethic," from the behavior, then postulate the values as a cause of the behavior); (3) make relevant comparisons (e.g., if mass sentiments in systematic surveys show, as they do, that workers in Japanese, Swedish, and American auto plants articulate very similar views about work but patterns of behavior—hours of work, productivity, and the behavior of workers and managers—vary greatly, the work ethic cannot explain the variations).

Where data passed those tests and we played various aspects of culture against the structural differences outlined throughout this book, culture plays a minor part in explaining either public policies or system outputs. Thus, political culture and public opinion cannot explain national differences in tax-welfare backlash (chap. 10), party decline (chap. 11), or mayhem (chap. 14). In dealing with welfare-state development, chapter 5 shows that if the ideology of economic individualism—the accent on free markets, private property, and minimum government—had any effect, it was only in relation to early democratization and the timing of initiation of programs. Thus where liberal democratic institutions developed early (Great Britain, the United States, Canada, France, Norway, and Switzerland) welfare-state development was somewhat retarded; parliamentary democracy and expansion of the franchise provided legitimation for government, but at the same time the liberal creed discouraged state intervention in the market. Constitutional monarchies (Austria, Denmark, Germany, and Sweden), lacking either the legitimation or the ideological constraint of liberal democracy, often facing militant labor movements, had a greater need for and bureaucratic ability to institute programs of the welfare state. Yet by 1914, in types of social legislation initiated, European democracies had caught up with the constitutional monarchies. The subsequent speed of development, however, was affected by the timing of first initiation. Thus, the early democracies not only brought stronger anti-welfare-state ideologies into mass democracy but also experienced the expansionary pressures of system aging later than the constitutional monarchies did. They have remained welfare-state laggards (U.S., Canada, Australia, Switzerland), although considerable convergence has taken place in levels and types of social spending. Contributing to the lag of early democratizers is the fact that even 100 years ago they had relatively young populations. As chapter 5 shows, the lag has been completely overcome only when Catholic parties acquired substantial persistent power as in the Netherlands, Belgium, and Italy and the population of the elderly accelerated.

The cultural ambivalence of all modern democracies is evident in their century-long convergence toward dual systems of income maintenance for the aged. Wherever they start, they end up in the same place: they insure the working population through contribution-based earnings-related schemes designed to preserve among pensioners the income differentials of their working lives (the hierarchical-meritocratic impulse) while they ensure that other groups (nonworkers, low-income self-employed) receive an income-tested minimum (the egalitarian-universalistic-humanitarian impulse).

Not only do the same populations embrace contradictory values, but the same patterns of behavior are defended by a vast array of ideologies. For instance, consider the list of values justifying welfare-state expansion—equality, solidarity, and social justice (left parties), economic efficiency (efficiency socialists like the Fabians), family security (center-left and center-right parties), harmony, consensus, and community (Catholic parties and communitarians), social order, hierarchy, and the prevention of revolution (center-right parties and authoritarian regimes), and more. Such diverse values cannot explain a common outcome, the establishment of seven or eight similar programs and increased taxes to fund them. The role of ideology in welfare-state development is best expressed this way: in response to similar problems of providing economic and career incentives and maintaining political order under conditions of the general push for equality, security, and social justice and specific concerns about the aged, all rich countries develop a similar set of conflicting values and beliefs—welfare-state ideologies versus economic individualism or free-mobility ideologies. In the short run parties carry into power different blends of these ideological contradictions, emphasizing one side or another, but in the long run the balance of these antinomies differs little among modern societies. If we go beyond abstract ideologies ("Do you think the government should see to it that everyone has a job and a good standard of living" or "government should let each person get ahead on his own?") and consider issue-specific opinion, even these modest national differences disappear, as we have seen in the uniform popularity of pensions, national health insurance, disability insurance, and family policies, and the equally uniform suspicion of public assistance targeted to the nonworking, nonaged poor (chaps. 5, 8, 10, and 17). Such a common structure of public opinion among nations cannot explain substantial differences in social policies and system performance.

I do not argue that values and beliefs are irrelevant to policies and outcomes. I merely make three claims. First, modern populations, including vast majorities in the United States, embrace contradictory values; they are simultaneously collectivistic and individualistic, humanitarian and social Darwinist, statist and laissez-faire, populist and meritocratic, believers in both individual liberty and community as well as equality of opportunity and (to a lesser extent) absolute equality. Second, the balance of these values in national politics is shaped by the structures this book has emphasized. The great ambivalence of mass publics permits politicians to play it either way. If they are hostile to expansive and generous social policies, they can work the tax-welfare backlash; if they are friendly, they can mobilize majority sentiments. To understand diverse political outcomes, we must look to our types of political economy, mass-based political parties, electoral systems, and the structure and interaction of major interest groups and government. Unless particular clusters of values are carried into power, as they have been in corporatist democracies with strong left and Catholic parties, they remain dormant, shaping the verbal environment but little else. Third, if there are any strongly held, widely shared, persistent values that appear in the recent history of all rich democracies, they are anything but "postmaterialist" or "postindustrial." Chapter 4 shows that the older issues of family security, civic order and safety, equality of opportunity (with an occasional bow to equality of results), and economic growth and stability remain dominant in the politics and mentality of modern populations. That is one explanation for the pro-welfare-state majority in all rich democracies and the intense mass

resistance to cutbacks, the resonance of law-and-order appeals in politics, and the continued demand for job security.

In short, in the ideational realm we call culture and at the level of development of our
rich democracies there is little support for the theory of American exceptionalism. But
surely there are patterns of behavior—social, political, or economic structures—that are
uniquely American?

Structure

In social, political, and economic organization the United States shares much with Britain
and Britain abroad (the UK, Canada, Australia, New Zealand, Ireland) and even Switzerland; and it shares many convergent tendencies with all 19 rich democracies. It is unique
in only a few aspects of structure and related public policies and these are matters of degree, diminishing as the rich countries become richer. Among the convergent tendencies
the U.S. shares with all 19 market-oriented rich democracies are these:

- *A level of living that is so different from that of the rest of the world,* that even anemic
growth brings extraordinary dividends. In 1999 in the U.S. a 1% increase in GDP means
$92.5 billion extra. Is the U.S. the richest country in the world? By market-price GNP
per capita, no; by purchasing power parities GNP per capita (if you can accept the complexity of comparisons), yes. But in any case the per capita differences among our 19
countries are diminishing as the least rich catch up (chap. 1).

- *A long-term increase in family instability and the percentage of solo mothers.* The demographic and organizational accompaniments of continuing industrialization—especially
educational and occupational shifts that expand opportunity for mobility in nonagricultural and nondomestic settings, thereby increasing mass aspirations—account for very
similar and accelerating trends in family life. Whatever their political systems or cultural
traditions, the currently rich democracies have experienced increased participation by
women in the nonagricultural labor force, declining fertility and an expanding percentage of the aged (both young-old and old-old), reduced household size, an increasingly
widespread and effective push for gender equality, and rising divorce rates (figure 1.1.).
In recent decades family instability has increased the population of lone parents and the
threat of child poverty (chaps. 1 and 7). In none of this is the U.S. unique. What differs
is political responses to this common social problem. As chapter 7 shows, countries with
strong mass-based Catholic or left parties move toward corporatist patterns of interest-
group bargaining; these produce expansive and innovative family policies, with somewhat
different policy mixes, depending on types of political economy, including the relative
strength of Catholicism and leftism. Least-corporatist countries, including the U.S., while
slower to develop family policies, do move in that direction. In short, the family-policy
laggards such as Japan, Switzerland, USA, Canada, New Zealand, Australia, and Ireland
are slowly converging toward family-policy leaders such as Sweden, France, Belgium,
Norway, and Finland—even in the politics of family policy, where moral-social agendas
are most passionately pursued.

- *A push for equality among minority groups and the increasing openness of modern governments to minority-group claims*—not confined to the United States. Among rich democra-

cies there has been a century-long trend toward structural and cultural integration of minority groups, accelerating during and after World War II (chap. 1). Discrimination on the basis of descent (race, ethnicity, religion, language), gender, sexual preference, and physical disability has everywhere declined. As integration proceeds in education, the economy, and polity, as residential desegregation progresses, intermarriage rates begin to climb, which in turn, leads to some sharing of values, beliefs, and tastes. Chapter 1 explains different rates of integration of different minority groups. Although the USA, Canada, Australia, New Zealand, Switzerland, the Netherlands, and Belgium have strong minority-group cleavages and have experienced these trends early, the rest of the rich democracies now share in the pattern of ethnic-racial conflict, accommodation, and integration. The reasons: a four-decade revival of massive migration from poor to rich countries and continuing industrialization. The convergence is toward the American multicultural model. The convergence in gender equality, however, is toward the Swedish model, even in Japan and Switzerland, countries most resistant (chap. 7). Gender equality is speeded up in democracies that have proportional representation, left power, high rates of women working, and corporatist bargaining arrangements.

The only minority group that has suffered increasing job discrimination over the past half century is the healthy aged. Everywhere there has been a steady long-term decline in the age of exit from work. Although welfare states have vastly improved the standards of living of the elderly (chaps. 5 and 7), the pressure for retirement has mounted when most of them or at least a large minority would prefer to work (chap. 1).

It is no paradox that while structural and cultural integration proceeds, ethnic resurgence, women's liberation movements, and gray-power groups periodically burst forth. Chapters 1, 10, and 17 explain variations in the militancy and timing of such cycles of protest and why demagogues in some countries are able to mobilize nativist backlash while they fail in others.

• *A common shape of social stratification and an increase in social mobility.* There is little that is unique about the U.S. in its "class structure." Trends in occupational distribution of the labor force are common to all (chap. 1); the industrial composition is similar among subgroups of countries (chap. 4). Continuing industrialization shapes stratification and mobility in several ways: it blurs older class lines, creates increasing social, cultural, and political heterogeneity within each social class such that internal differences within classes become greater than differences between them; and it fosters the emergence of a politically restive "middle mass" (upper-working class, lower-middle class) whose behavior, values, beliefs, and tastes increasingly differ from those of the privileged college-educated upper-middle class and the very rich above them and the poor below. Increasing mobility, intergenerational and worklife, and multiple ladders for achieving income, status, and power (a product mainly of technological and occupational change) add to the heterogeneity of social classes. While there are some national differences in mobility rates (see table 9.3 and appendix I), these are likely to diminish, as most countries move toward the high rates of the U.S.

The middle mass (people with high-school or part-college or vocational school education) constitute about 60% of the electorate (chap. 1 on stratification); there is no reason to suppose that this is unique to the U.S., although higher voting rates of the lower fifth in other democracies would reduce the 60% figure for the middle electorate. Even the political mobilization of the middle mass—as in the campaigns of Governor Jesse "The Body" Ventura, Richard Nixon (his "silent majority"), Ronald Reagan and George Wallace (gaining votes among white ethnic Democrats)—is evident in the antitax, anti-social-spending, antibureaucratic movements and parties of the UK, USA, Switzerland, Denmark, and Canada. And in both the U.S. and these other democracies, nativist protest movements tend to merge with the antitax parties. National differences in how the resentments of the middle mass are channeled appear in chapters 10 on backlash, 11 on party decline, 17 on protest movements against immigrants, 8 on the welfare mess and scapegoating the poor, and 14 on mayhem.

 •   Also rooted in the universal effects of continuing industrialization—and another area where America is not exceptional—are *a few common trends in the organization of work*. A steady decline in yearly average hours of work from the late 19th century to about 1960 has been followed by divergence as the leisure-rich countries got richer and the leisure-poor got poorer. The bottom five in working hours (leisure-rich) are democratic corporatist—Norway, Germany, Denmark, the Netherlands, and Sweden. The hardest-working six (leisure-poor) in descending order are the USA, Japan, Canada, the UK, Italy, and France; except for Italy they are either least corporatist or corporatist-without-labor—in other words they lack the bargaining arrangements that foster left-labor power. Only in recent trends in hours of work is the U.S. a genuine exception. From 1960 to 1994 all countries for which we have data evidence substantial declines in annual hours, except for the U.S., which starts at the top and declines only 2.9% (chap. 1, p. 52 and note 49).

Analysis of detailed occupational trends in chapter 1 (organization of work section) casts doubt on the idea of modern society as "high-tech." Whatever the contribution of sophisticated technology to the GNP, and whatever the privileged position of highly trained elites, the vast majority of modern populations work in low-tech or no-tech jobs. Almost all the large and fastest-growing occupations are anything but high-tech—truck drivers, salespeople, janitors, cashiers, cooks, schoolteachers, nurses, nursing aides, orderlies, carpenters, and so on. Similar skepticism is appropriate for the notion that modern societies are moving away from "Fordist" production toward "flexible specialization." Limited comparative data suggest a great variety of organizational forms within each of these categories. There may be a modest trend in all our countries among a few large manufacturing firms and some financial service providers toward a modified form of lean production epitomized by Japan's Toyota and its joint venture with GM, NUMMI in California. But as yet this covers only a small portion of any modern labor force. The more common and likely convergent trend is the spread of unconventional schedules and "contingent" labor—with lean benefits and little job security—part-time, temporary, or subcontracted workers in both services and manufacturing (chap. 1). The U.S., Canada, and Australia lead the way in this high-turnover, low-training job creation (chap. 13). But insofar as other rich democracies converge toward social, personal, and distributive services as a share of total employment, there will be convergence in both contingent labor and unconventional schedules, or at least parallel development. A common trend toward downsizing and subcontracting adds to the growing minority in unstable careers at every status level. Counterpressures of labor law, social policy, left power, and unionization, however, will retard the growth of contingent labor among corporatist democracies. But it is likely that even they will move slowly toward the American model, modified to ensure better wages, benefits, and a modicum of job security.

• *The spread of universal, compulsory schooling and the rise of mass higher education.* The United States led in both developments, which are a convergent tendency in all rich democracies. In the past three or four decades, however, the U.S. has become exceptional in its neglect of K– 12 and the consequent terrible performance of most of its secondary schools. At the other end it remains exceptional in the size and excellence of its higher education and related basic research. In medical innovation the U.S. has become a cash cow supporting both publicly and privately funded medical research which is then diffused worldwide as virtually free science and technology (chap. 16). Further, American higher education is still unique in its diversity of funding, size of the private sector, elective system, diversity of curricula, and openness to interest-group demands. Other countries, however slowly, are converging toward the American model of higher education; two long-term shifts especially are common to all—the twin trends toward specialization and universality of access. Also common to all is the central function of education as a channel for upward mobility that remains more or less meritocratic (chaps. 1 and 12). There are signs of American convergence toward other democracies' higher standards for K– 12, although this is still more talk than action. The USA's enrollment ratio in postsecondary institutions is high, but in this it has the company of other welfare-state laggards. (Chap. 1 explains why historically there has been a trade-off between the essentially egalitarian accent on the welfare state and the essentially meritocratic accent on higher education.)

When we go beyond what the United States shares with other rich democracies, we find that it either shares attributes of structure with five or six others or is unique only in degree—that is, extreme within the category. In its political economy the U.S. is fragmented and decentralized. I hope that this book has given meaning to those two labels. In its polity what is often described as uniquely American are a decentralized federalism, separation of powers, a weak central government, an independent judiciary with strong powers of judicial review, a bill of rights, a populist cast to its politics, and a proliferation of parochial interest groups, themselves fragmented and decentralized (as is evident in the structure and functions of labor, management, and the professions). In its economy, the United States is supposed to be uniquely rich, entrepreneurial, competitive, laissez-faire, and open to big business domination. In its social structure, America is said to be unique in its social heterogeneity—its intense conflict among racial, ethnic, and religious minorities, and between minorities and dominant groups. As Part I shows, however, in varying ways and degrees the Anglo-American democracies share these structural attributes. Even in the combination of decentralized federalism and populist politics expressed in frequent elections, direct democracy, and voter fatigue—Switzerland joins the U.S. Both countries have bicameral legislatures, where the upper house has two members for each state (canton) whatever its size; both constitutions protect civil liberties and states' rights; both evidence strong social cleavages. California's plebicatory rampage since 1978, which has slowly spread to other states, is matched by Switzerland's long-standing reliance on the initiative and referendum. And both countries have low and declining voter turnout (chap. 11). Swiss-American exceptionalism?

What this book shows is that the U.S. is one of six countries that are least corporatist, least consensual, and that the common consequences in policies and system performance are captured by the inverse of figure 2.1. These decentralized, fragmented political economies are most vulnerable to the mass-society tendencies described in chapter 3—a decline in the strength of broad-based integrative political parties, churches, unions, and communitywide neighborhood associations and the vitality of participation in them. That creates a vacuum of power into which the mass media in symbiotic relationship to the more parochial interest groups and sectarian religious and political groups pour. So despite differences that look large when we compare two or three countries within this category—presidential vs. parliamentary systems, a well-trained, well-paid, efficient civil service vs. its opposite—the more important differences that hold the six together fit the label, least corporatist (chap. 2).

Among the attributes of structure the United States shares with other decentralized and fragmented political economies are the following. (I leave aside the occasional deviant case explained throughout the book.)

• *Confrontational industrial relations and a weak labor movement.* This book shows that corporatist democracies reduce strike rates and related labor protest by transferring the locus of conflict to national politics and accommodative tripartite or bipartite bargaining arrangements, widening the scope of bargaining and integrating labor into the machinery for policymaking and implementation. In contrast, the least-consensual democracies keep labor-management relations at the local or firm level where it is every employee for himself or every union for itself and where national solidarity is limited on both sides of the industrial battlefield. Businesses in these circumstances have more power to block social and labor policies favored by unions.

Even here, however, there is some convergence: strike rates in the more militant occupations and industries (e.g., mining, longshoring), high in all industrial societies, decline with new technology that reduces both unpleasant work and the social isolation of workers. Finally, there appear to be two roads to a common outcome, that is, reduced economywide strike rates: integrate the labor movement into the system or break its power (U.S., UK, Japan, New Zealand).

• *Poverty, inequality, means testing, and the welfare mess.* The U.S. joins the least-corporatist democracies in very high rates of poverty and inequality and in heavy reliance on means testing (table 8.3). Means tests refer to noncategorical benefits targeted to the poor via stiff income and assets tests applied by welfare administrators with substantial discretion with a high probability of stigma. Income tests, in contrast, are simple, private, and in administration, low cost. Means testing creates a welfare mess (chap. 8) and is both cause and consequence of poverty (table 8.4). These high rates of poverty are a prime cause of high teenage birthrates (table 8.4). Cross-national comparison also shows that this group of countries has achieved the highest rates of deep poverty among both solo mothers and two-parent families (table 8.4). The UK and the USA vie with one another for the role of champion of poverty—near-poverty, poverty, and deep poverty alike—

although the U.S. tops the UK in inequality (ratio of highest to lowest quintiles in gross household income shares) while Australia is even more inegalitarian than the U.S. (table 14.4). Chapter 12 suggests further that devoting a large expensive and intrusive apparatus to means testing is a drag on economic performance. Both poverty and inequality also foster mayhem (chapter 14 and tables 14.4 and 14.6) and to some extent subvert good economic performance (chapter 12 and table 12G.11 in appendix G).

- A consequence of the trend toward universal higher education is *an increase in the number of experts and intellectuals.* As we have seen in chapters 1 (on convergence), and 4 (on postindustrialism), however, *their influence varies by type of political economy.* If they are attached to the top of powerful inclusive interest groups that interact with a more or less centralized government in bipartite or tripartite bargaining arrangements, their influence is strong and they lend a rational-responsible bias to the policy process. In least-corporatist political economies their influence is limited and erratic. The United States, for instance, is loaded with experts and intellectuals, but their voices are cast to the winds. Moreover, there is no shortage of single-issue evaluation research and demonstration projects. But research focused on a single program obscures the interaction and interdependence of many programs (e.g., education in schools, job training programs, and job creation) and, in any case, evaluated success has little to do with program funding. Wilensky's law applies to the least-corporatist democracies: the more evaluation, the less program development; the more demonstration projects, the less follow-through (chap. 2, pp. 100ff. and chap. 14).

Although it can be argued that the U.S. is extreme in the politicization of research and the disjunction of knowledge and power, ideas do make their way in the long run, even in cultures that are most populist and anti-intellectual. This is evident in the 30-year intellectual ferment regarding social security and labor legislation preceding FDR's New Deal, and a similar 30-year lag between comparative research on health-care delivery systems and President Johnson's Medicare and Medicaid (Wilensky, 1997; cf. Polsby, 1984).

- *Great difficulty in linking national policies that belong together.* Chapter 2 reports results of our eight-country study of the interdependence of industrial, incomes, active labor-market, and social policies. I show that a decentralized and fragmented government cannot use equally fragmented and uncoordinated labor unions, employer associations, and trade associations to formulate and implement policies that crosscut industries, functions, and policy domains (social security, health care, industrial policy, or incomes policy). They can be used only where policy is narrow and disconnected from broader concerns (cigarette labeling, air traffic control, drug packaging). When such a system confronts a major problem, its fragmentation is a formidable block to effective action. For example, many politicians, labor leaders, academics, and advocacy groups have argued that industrial restructuring and freer trade require that the workers, firms, and communities bearing the burden of change must be compensated by programs of retraining, job counseling, relocation, and targeted public investment. In the U.S. and the UK these debates have led to many meetings among sophisticated business leaders, academics, and a few labor leaders. But the representational structures necessary for formulating and implementing a national response is missing; little action occurs. Even where incumbent leaders—not merely outside intellectuals and elder statesmen, but men and women of power—are aware of the imperatives of policy linkage and try to act, implementation falters, as we have seen in the sorry tale of the Trade Adjustment Assistance Act of 1962 and in President Clinton's failed effort to pass a comprehensive health-care reform bill in 1993.[1]

In contrast, we found that the linkage of major economic and political actors in corporatist bargaining systems facilitates policy linkages; it encourages those tradeoffs that improve economic performance in the long run.

- *Economic organization and performance. Is the U.S. uniquely laissez-faire?* Again the United States has the company of least-consensual democracies. Chapter 12 explores the ranks of our 19 countries in real GDP growth per capita, inflation, and unemployment, equally weighing the three measures. The most important sources of good economic performance are corporatist bargaining arrangements (with or without the full integration of labor), high rates of capital investment, labor peace, and worker participation in the community and workplace. Democratic corporatism also fosters restraint on nominal wages in the face of external inflationary shocks. A political economy that fosters labor peace has an edge in adaptation to severe pressures.

Sheer *level* of taxes and social spending has no consistent economic effect, but the *structure* of taxes and social spending is often important. The positive impact of high social spending as a trade-off for labor peace and tax concessions to industry and thus enhanced growth and inflation control fades after 1973 and is nonexistent after 1979. *But in no period and for no measure of performance is social spending a significant drag.* Similarly, high total tax levels have a *positive* effect on economic performance before 1974 because they permit generous social spending and promote labor peace but have no effect thereafter. Thus the claim that the burden of high taxes and lavish social spending is the prime cause of economic troubles misses the point. There are countries with low levels of taxing and spending that have done well (Japan, Switzerland) and countries with high levels of taxing and spending that have done well (Germany, Austria, Norway). And the poor performers include countries with lean taxes and spending and lavish taxes and spending. Insofar as taxes and spending shape the economy, it is their structure that counts, not their levels.

Contributing to the corporatist edge in economic performance for most of the postwar period is a tax structure emphasizing least-visible taxes. Consumption taxes, because they are negatively related to strikes and positively related to capital formation, foster economic growth for almost all of the postwar period. Social-security taxes restrain inflation in normal times (1965–74, 1985–89) but have no effect just after the oil shocks; only in 1980–84, the period of severe multiple shocks, did these payroll taxes lower growth.

Regarding the structure of spending, the data generally show that an emphasis on means-tested, stigmatized benefits drains off investment, increases unemployment, and in 1980–84 was a drag on growth. The better-performing corporatist democracies, in contrast, emphasize universal categorical benefits and family policies.

Less complete data or data for fewer countries show that spending on civilian research and development and on education and training (with the accent on instructional services and high universally applied national standards) fosters good long-run economic performance. Avoiding high levels of military spending and bureaucratic bloat also helps. Avoiding lawyers and adversary legalism, which contribute to bureaucratic bloat, is also a good idea. But a surfeit of lawyers reflects the absence of strong institutions for conflict resolution; lawyers are more a symptom than a cause of polarized politics subversive of the economy. Finally, the less intrusive regulatory regimes of corporatist democracies are not only more effective than the confrontational styles of less consensual democracies but are also a factor in their long-term competitive edge.

Limited data suggest that income equalization, the reduction of great disparities between rich and poor, may enhance economic growth, but it is also possible that prosperity is a source of equality. In any case, in the long run more successful economies are also more egalitarian societies.

In short, if economic performance is at issue, the U.S. generally shares the below-average record of the least-consensual democracies from 1950 to 1974 and a mixed performance from 1974 to the early 1990s. Only in 1993–99 did the U.S. by some measures lead the pack. There may be an interaction of a dozen variables disruptive to good steady economic performance: fragmented and decentralized democracies with high rates of mobility, strong minority-group cleavages, and many young people (who are not working or have little work experience) exhibit high strike rates, spend a lot on the military and on means-tested public assistance, evidence bureaucratic bloat and intrusive styles of regulation, rely on visible taxes, including property taxes, have low capital investment, are overloaded with lawyers (lack other means of conflict resolution), and are vulnerable to tax-welfare backlash movements.

The whole syndrome of unfavorable structures, demographic forces, taxing and spending policies, and political responses makes it difficult to manage a modern economy. Countries that come close to fitting this description include the United States, UK, Canada, New Zealand, Australia, and Ireland.

Since the early 1970s the Anglo-American democracies have increasingly chosen the low road to economic growth and job creation (chaps. 7, 13, and 17): low and stagnant or declining wages; intensive use of low-skilled, least-educated workers in large, expanding sectors (e.g., retail trades); a widening spread between high-wage, high-skill workers and the least-educated; emphasizing low value-added products and services for much of the economy while upgrading processes and products in the most-sophisticated sectors that employ a minority of the workforce; meager investment in both physical and human capital; increasing reliance on subcontracting, a system of low-wage, no-benefit workers concentrated in small firms, themselves highly unstable, who are pressed to cheat on payroll and other taxes and evade minimum wage and safety laws; the rapid spread of contingent labor and unconventional schedules; decreasing job security for most of the workforce; greater concentration of wealth; increasing poverty and inequality, and associated mayhem. The corporatist democracies of continental Europe and Japan followed various versions of the high road: greater participation of unions in workplace and community and in national policymaking; relatively high wages, greater job security; labor and social policies that retard the growth of the contingent economy; heavy investment in human capital; more stable relations between large corporations and their subcontracted suppliers and salespeople; high productivity (working smarter, fewer hours); a lesser spread between high- and low-wage workers; much lower poverty and inequality; and a concentration on high value-added products and processes, with R&D that accents the D. And they avoid the worst pathologies of poverty. While the increasing autonomy of central bankers obsessed with inflation, suspicious of growth, and unconcerned about unemployment contributed to the high unemployment rates of the 1990s (chap. 17), the high-wage short-hours strategy at its extreme may also have played its part in the 1990s rise in unemployment in some of the corporatist democracies.

Chapter 12 explains why Japan and the USA by some criteria traded places in the 1990s as "Number One." In both cases it was an unusual convergence of circumstances with little structural change. Further, in 1990s productivity the U.S. is far from #1; and in productivity growth it is still a laggard (see pp. 445–449). We certainly cannot attribute U.S. 1990s success in job creation and reduced unemployment to unfettered free markets. No market is without its regulatory guidance. In fact, all rich democracies evidence heavy state intervention. All of them expand similar programs comprising the welfare state and in 1995 ranged between 33% and 63% of GDP moving through the public sector; all adopt various mixes of regulation of economic transactions; when they try deregulation, they soon reregulate. In fact, the regulatory machinery of the U.S. is more intrusive (and inefficient) than that of most rich democracies, as we have seen in chapters on the environment and occupational health and safety (15) and health care (16). Although the mix of public and private shares of total health-care spending varies, no country has a public share less than 42% (table 16.3). In size of government measured by public employees as a percentage of the labor force, the U.S. joins the two highest categories—noncorporatist democracies with strong minority-group cleavages and left-corporatist countries with weak minority-group cleavages. In bureaucratic bloat the U.S. has plenty of company (chap. 9, tables 9.1, 9.2, 9.3). Similarly, the private/public mix in the financing of "private," "voluntary," nonprofit organizations varies cross-nationally but the very least reliance on government is almost a third (chap. 2, note 10).

The notion of the U.S. as a uniquely high-risk-taking, entrepreneurial country with heavy reliance on free markets is, to say the least, exaggerated. From the savings and loan bailout of the 1980s to the 1998 Federal Reserve rescue of the Long-Term Capital Management hedge fund, or the Fed and Treasury arranging measures with banks and host countries to make whole most of the speculative high-risk, high-reward U.S. lenders to Latin America, the wealthiest investors have achieved a New Deal for entrepreneurs. If by the impersonal workings of the market—that is, their greed and foolish mistakes— these high rollers are threatened with big losses, the government steps in to assure their security and continuity. In essence they share risks by shifting their losses to society, taxpayers, and employees (the S & L bailout cost at least $300 billion).[2] More significant and more expensive cumulatively is the great range and depth of routine government subsidies to business and industry, some serving the public interest, many not. This is not to say that no entrepreneur goes bankrupt. Nor does it mean that Silicon Valley is not filled with innovative firms. It is to suggest that the image of risk-taking entrepreneurs is misleading not only in the financial and other areas discussed above but in places like Silicon Valley, in view of the pay packages, stock options, golden parachutes, and government infrastructure and tax subsidies typical of both big and little businesses in these growth centers. When things go wrong for a firm in Silicon Valley its executives and engineers have little trouble moving sideways or up. It is not only the American masses who seek security and predictability against the vagaries of the market; it is the American corporate elite as well. It is ironic that these government-protected risk-averse corporate operators, all recipients of corporate welfare as well as lavish private benefits, rail against government intervention in the market and know so little about the other side of the digital divide. They are in a comfortable cocoon so insulated from the majority of the population that they cannot imagine people who are nonaffluent for reasons beyond their control.

In comparative perspective is there anything left that we can call truly exceptional about the U.S.? If we are willing to see the U.S. as an extreme case within the noncorporatist fraternity and call that exceptional, then there are at least eight patterns of behavior where differences in degree are perhaps differences in kind: the size, excellence, and diversity of higher education; the dealignment of parties; the swift rise of the commercial media in politics and culture; the polarization of congressional politics; arcane Senate rules that thwart the will of even substantial majorities; the criminalization of politics; the heavy weight of lawyers and judges in shaping public policy and the related pattern of adversarial legalism; and a score for murder, mayhem, and imprisonment that puts the U.S. in a class of its own. All of the above sometimes results in lengthy public-policy paralysis, which I shall discuss in the final section.

- *Almost universal postsecondary education.* As we have seen in chapters 1 and 12, despite a long-term convergence toward universal compulsory schooling and mass higher education, the U.S. is still unique in the diversity, openness, and excellence of its higher education institutions and in its extraordinary neglect of K–12, evident in a poor performance compared to other countries.

- *Party decline.* There is no universal dealignment of parties or decline of party systems. And the U.S., the textbook case of party decline, shares this trend with those democracies that have plurality, winner-take-all electoral systems, and an absence or erosion of strong, broad-based mediating associations—inclusive unions, labor federations, employer federations, and churches (e.g., the UK, Canada, New Zealand, Australia). Yet *compared to these other countries vulnerable to mass-society tendencies, the U.S. is extreme in party dealignment* (chap. 11). Since the mid-1960s the U.S. has experienced a rise in confrontational partisanship, as ideological positions hardened in each party and political polarization intensified. Indicators of dealignment in the electorate put the U.S. at the top of the countries for which reasonably comparable data are available: a decline in trust in politicians, government, and parties; a decline of party influence in the presidential nominating process; diminished strength of party identification among whites and the young; decreasing turnout in voting, and a drop in the percentage of adults doing campaign and party work or making campaign contributions; and an increase in random voting—ticket-splitting and to a lesser extent party-switching. The spread of the initiative and referendum adds to party decline by creating bewildering complexity and voter fatigue. Third-party activity in the United States, while an ambiguous indicator of dealignment, has

speeded up in the last 30 years. As we have seen in chapter 3, the political vacuum created by the decline of broad-based mediating associations, including center-left and
center-right parties, is filled by the mass media, single-issue interest groups, populist demagogues of the right and left, lawyers, and courts.

• *Commercial media dominance.* In only a generation or two the United States has
become an extreme case of the rising influence of the media of mass communication
and entertainment. Minimal effects theories that accent self-selection of exposure or
predispositions formed in social groups that insulate individuals and their families from
direct media influence miss the main story. Substantial segments of the audience in fact
expose themselves to uncongenial communication. Where the issue is technical, abstract,
or distant—an increasing proportion of the agenda—neither local groups nor larger associations provide a guide, and people rely on the media. Where there is sustained saturation coverage of an alleged crisis, scandal, or crime, the media reach large heterogeneous
audiences and have substantial impact, especially among the apathetic or inadvertent
viewers or readers.

More important limitations on minimal effects theories are three themes in chapter 3.
First, if offsets to media power are mediating groups and subcultures, then we must attend to national variations in the vitality of these groups and the nature of participation
in them; the U.S. shows most erosion of the types of associations that encourage wider
civic attachment. Second, the long-run cumulative exposure to all the media has a large
and increasing effect; the media contribute to subtle shifts in values and beliefs. Third,
cultural elites who could set high standards for media content increasingly abandon the
attempt. These trends open the way for the direct reach of print and broadcast media.

Over the past 30 or so years, the American commercial media have become increasingly competitive, frantic, sensational, negative, afactual, aggressively interpretive, and anti-
institutional. They have created or escalated continual scandals, undifferentiated crises,
and public cynicism about politics. They are increasingly important in setting the public
agenda. With the massive interpenetration of the print and broadcast media, broadcast
talk shows—with their inflammatory rhetoric, their "gotcha" journalism—emerged as
the dominant model for all. The tabloidization of the leading newspapers is the most
dramatic illustration. Both the ascendance of the broadcast media and the shift in style
and content toward the talk-show model imply a less-informed electorate and a decline
in high culture. The erosion of elite standards is at the root of these trends.

Changes in elite standards are themselves largely a product of the structure and
financing of the American media—the organizational and occupational requirements of
commerce and competition and the absence of a strong, well-financed, standard-setting
public broadcasting network. Cross-national comparison pins this down. Democracies
that combine strong financing for public broadcasting, usually from a tax on households
using television sets; media regulations that prohibit or limit political commercials, and
assure free access for political parties and/or candidates during campaigns, and in other
ways ensure cultural and political diversity in broadcasting year-round—these public
policies permit them to avoid the worst pathologies of American media. A strong public
broadcasting presence means more substantive content, more emphasis on parties and
policy issues in politics, more educational-cultural programs, and arguably, somewhat

higher general quality. The United States is the only rich democracy that forces candidates and parties to spend huge sums of money for media access; all other rich democracies make plenty of room for candidates to speak for themselves at public expense. Although there are signs that European democracies and Japan are to some extent moving toward the American commercial model, these differences in financing and regulation still make a difference in the quality of media and hence the quality of culture and politics. And the even larger national differences in the amount and kinds of social participation and the strength of civic engagement make a big difference in the capacity of elected officials to offset the power of the media in setting the agenda. In short, while the media may become American in the long run, for the moment the U.S. is extreme in the lack of regulation of the broadcast media and the weakness of organizational offsets to media influence; it is unique in the limited access of politicians to free media, hence the extraordinary and exploding cost of campaigns.

 • *A load of lawyers.* Chapter 12 (on economic performance, table 12.11) shows that in lawyers as a percentage of the labor force, the U.S. and Israel are most lawyer-loaded, far ahead of other lawyer-rich democracies—Finland, Canada, New Zealand, Australia, UK, and Ireland. (And Israel, while first in lawyer density, is last in lawyer growth.) Except for Finland and Israel, all corporatist democracies are very low in lawyer density. The main reasons: An abundance of lawyers and judges appears only where alternative mechanisms of conflict resolution erode and where political polarization increases.

The U.S. is an extreme case in the judicialization of major public issues. In the past half century, doctrines of liability have become more hospitable to lawsuits; tort filings, like family law cases, have soared. Since the mid-1960s the spirit of adversarial legalism, the demand for "total justice," has spread to new areas of American life—to labor relations, minority/majority conflict, environmental regulation, occupational health and safety, health care, and welfare. Litigation has accelerated as have the direct and indirect costs. While a few other countries have an abundance of lawyers, the U.S. stands out in the density and power of its lawyers. Adversarial legalism is so widespread and so highly developed that some aspects are, indeed, unique: compared to other rich democracies the U.S. now has far more complex legal rules, more formal adversarial procedures for resolving political and even scientific disputes, more punitive sanctions, more costly litigation and more unpredictability and reversibility in legislative, administrative, and judicial decisions alike. In the frequency and strength of judicial review of its laws and intervention in executive branch decisions, the U.S. also leads, although France and Germany are close by.

An abundance of lawyers is more a consequence than a cause of mass-society tendencies in the United States. The likely sequence is this: the numerous fragmented and decentralized interest groups; a fragmented, decentralized government structure; and the dealignment of parties together open the way for dominance of the media in symbiotic relation to single-issue movements and political demagogues. Under these circumstances, the president, executive agencies, Congress, and state legislatures have increasing difficulty resolving conflicts over major public policies. They often dump such problems on the courts. Lawyers and judges enter the fray, reinforcing already well developed confrontational tendencies. Vacuums of power create the demand for lawyers; when lawyers appear, they create a demand for one another, exacerbating adversarial legalism and increasing the cost of doing business in the economy and polity. These tendencies, while not unique to the U.S., have been most fully developed in the U.S.

Lawyers and judges are ill-equipped to run prisons and schools, integrate neighborhoods or universities, or manage similar problems. In decisions that at least appear reasonable, in cases of overcrowded and abusive prisons or segregated schools, they end up supervising and second-guessing wardens and guards, school boards, principals, and teachers who know the complexities firsthand and often lack the resources to carry out court commands. Not all decisions have even a superficial appearance of common sense. For instance, in 1997 the Supreme Court faced a suit that charged the president with an incident of sexual harassment several years earlier. In *Clinton v. Jones* the Court told us that a sitting president may be sued in civil court during his tenure because this will *not* create a media circus and distract him from his duties, the District courts being perfectly capable of conducting quiet, proper proceedings. Such decisions betray the Justices' insulation from life. In the most favorable interpretation, lawyers and judges are merely applying the law and pursuing justice in areas beyond their grasp, beyond their competence.

• *Polarization of congressional politics and Senate rules that thwart the will of even substantial majorities.* Despite signs of increasing strength of parties-in-government—increasing party-line voting in Congress, an occasional strong leader with greater influence over committee chairs—there is simultaneous growth of confrontational partisanship, as ideological extremes prevail in each party and political polarization intensifies (see chap. 11). Like the checks and balances of the U.S. Constitution, Senate rules were designed to make policy change difficult. But with rising polarization in the past 20 years, there has been a dramatic rise in abuse of the rules. We see this in the extraordinary lengthening of time between the president's naming an appointee and Senate action on confirmation. JFK averaged two months from naming to confirmation; both Bush and Clinton averaged eight months with some recent appointees for judgeships cooling their heels for four years, unable to get a vote. Worse, the process of investigation and evaluation became poisonous, marked by invasions of privacy, personal attacks on appointees and their families, and the demolition of reputations. In addition, the process now involves a maelstrom of complexity—an enormous number and length of forms to fill out that serve no proper function. Naturally, the process has become a barrier to recruitment of talented people. An epidemic of Senate filibusters or threats of filibusters is at the root of much of this paralysis. It takes a supermajority of 60 votes (out of 100) for cloture to halt a filibuster. From 1990 through 1996 there have been 155 attempts to end filibusters, an average of 22 per year, compared to fewer than one per year 1917–67 and just over 10 per year 1968–89 (*Congressional Quarterly*, 1998, pp. 1102–1105).

• *The criminalization of politics.* Related to the polarization of politics, the tabloidization of the media, the proliferation of lawyers, and increasing deadlock in Congress is the criminalization of politics. There is an increasing tendency to search the financial records and private lives of political opponents not merely for signs of poor judgment or wrongdoing but for opportunities to accuse them of criminal behavior. As American politics grew cleaner, accusations of corruption climbed. In the past eight years Congress has conducted multiple, overlapping investigations of scores of civil servants and White House officials, including four cabinet officers.

The use of public institutions—the judiciary, the congressional oversight function—to conduct relentless personal investigations designed to destroy political enemies is described in chapter 3. Of course other countries have had their scandals in high places. And scandalmongering and real corruption have a long history in American politics— Senator Joseph McCarthy's crusade against the alleged treason of Communists and assorted leftists and the web of corruption in the administrations of Ulysses S. Grant, Warren Harding, and Richard Nixon. But except for Italy, and until recently in the U.S., the scandal machine never had such resonance, scope, and duration. Since the Nixon conspiracies and the Independent Counsel Act of 1978, a new growth industry has emerged; it consists of ethics police, watchdog groups, congressional investigators cum prosecutors, and journalist celebrities posing as investigative reporters. No gossip is too trivial, no source too questionable, to feed this machine. Imperial prosecutor Kenneth Starr, unconstrained by the normal standards of criminal prosecution, driven by puritanical zealotry, was able to parlay his five-year investigation into a yearlong media circus culminating in a partisan impeachment of President Clinton for a sex-and-lies scandal. An epidemic of high-cost negative campaigning accelerates the trend (chap. 3 analyzes the impact on politics and culture).

• *Murder, mayhem, and incarceration.* Again there are both common trends among all our rich democracies, substantial differences by types of political economy, and an American extreme. Since 1970 murder rates and related crimes of violence have increased in most rich democracies. To broaden the discussion of risks and compare the performance of governments in enhancing safety, I devised a measure of mayhem— external threats to the person from the social and physical environment, threats that are usually unpredictable, often catastrophic, always momentous, and can be reduced by public policy. The four for which cross-national data are available and which are highly correlated with one another over time (deaths from homicide, deaths from fire, unemployment rates, and divorce rates) constitute my mayhem index (chap. 14). (Public policy cannot much affect divorce rates, but it can mightily reduce the shock to the families and children involved.)

Affluence and its correlates, especially mobility and meritocracy, explain some of the common trends and the national differences in both murder and mayhem. Democratic corporatism, however, provides a general offset to modern tendencies toward mayhem because it opens up channels for shared power by economic interest groups. It fosters high rates of citizen participation through workplace participation schemes (see chap. 1) and through some form of proportional representation (chap. 2 shows that PR is a major source of corporatist bargaining systems). More directly, corporatist democracies tend toward high social spending, itself a powerful source of consensus (chap. 5), and they avoid divisive public policies such as welfare benefits that are heavily means-tested, stigmatized, and visibly targeted to the poor (chap. 8). Finally, they pursue both social and economic policies that reduce inequality and poverty—the strongest proximate causes of mayhem.

Consensual bargaining arrangements in the polity and economy and their policy outcomes not only offset general tendencies toward mayhem rooted in industrialization; they also offset the unhappy effects of strong minority-group cleavages, which otherwise create much mayhem, as we saw when we compared such unruly countries as the United States, Canada, and the UK with such calmer countries as Switzerland and the Netherlands.

What is unique about the United States is that it is extreme in both murder rates and the broader mayhem index and their causes. Comparing either 19 countries or the 50 states of the U.S., what accounts for high rates of murder is the interaction of poverty, inequality, family breakup, and dense urban living. What accounts for high scores of mayhem are means testing, inequality, and poverty, the absence of a family policy, and the correlates of industrialization (mobility and meritocracy, and minority-group cleavages). No one of these alone predicts either murder or mayhem; all together give the U.S. its extreme position. The decline in murder rates and related violence in the most violent U.S. cities after 1993 is partly explained by reductions in poverty, inequality, unemployment, and number of youths, improved gun control and job opportunities, and less surely, an increase in tough community policing. But compared to other rich democracies the U.S. is still tops in violent crime and mayhem.

Also unique to the U.S. is the response of politicians and the criminal justice system to crime, the rise in a crackdown mentality that has led to a prison boom—the highest incarceration rate in the civilized, democratic world. By applying long, fixed prison terms to drug users and hardened criminals, nonviolent and violent criminals, to criminals way past their prime and young thugs alike; by removing judges' discretion in sentencing; by neglecting forms of parole, prevention, and rehabilitation that have had demonstrated success, we have managed to create a federal and state prison population of about 2.1 million. If we combine adults on probation, in jail or prison, or on parole in 1997, the figure rises to 5.7 million at an annual "corrections" cost of $37.5 billion in 1996 dollars (U.S. Bureau of the Census, 1999b, tables 385 and 504).

The crackdown mentality also increased police and prosecutorial misconduct and incompetence, as suggested by the 1999 revelation by the Los Angeles police chief that dozens of people are known to have been framed by the police and by police confessions that at least two unarmed gang members were shot. Similar incidents of police abuse occurred across the country, most dramatically in New York, New Jersey, and Washington, D.C. Excessive zeal in pursuit of the bad guys is not typically corruption, where police join thieves, deal dope, or take bribes. Instead the police, operating in a dangerous environment, are responding to the sometimes-hysterical but always-consistent demand of the public, politicians, and prosecutors and their supervisors that they apprehend and help convict criminals. Stretching the truth to put a known bad actor away comes to be seen as righteous protection of the community. When the police and prosecutors cross that line, as they have in Los Angeles, they may start down a slippery slope that ends with framing a suspect for murder.

POLICY AND POLITICS3

The Idea of Policy Paralysis

All rich democracies must cope with similar social and economic problems. Many students of American politics suggest that the U.S. is paralyzed in dealing effectively with those

problems. They often list their favorite policies and call it paralysis when these are not enacted. A more precise definition is needed. Clearly where (1) both elites and masses favor
a policy or program, and (2) other countries have acted successfully, and (3) there is no action in the U.S. for long periods, say 25 to 50 years, we can call it paralysis. Examples that
approximate this idea include national health insurance, effective gun control (domestic disarmament), family policy (including long-term care for the frail elderly), serious investment
in raising standards for K–12, policies to reduce violence in the media and to increase party
and candidate access to the media in election campaigns.

This disjunction between public policy and public opinion as well as elite inclinations
is evident in chapter 5 on the welfare state, 10 on tax-welfare backlash, 11 on party decline, 4 on postindustrialism, and 16 on health care. I believe that there is an agenda around
which a political coalition could be built to reduce paralysis. But to identify it we must first
cut through the vast confusion of language reflected in media diffusion of slogans about
"moderation" or "centrist politics." Then we must ask, What potential progressive coalition could be created and persist long enough to break deadlocks on these issues, where in
the political spectrum does it lie, and what election reforms and results are required?

The Myth of Moderation and the Rightward Shift

In the mandate mongering that follows every election, the media pundits of the 1990s told
us that the victories of the Republican right (e.g., in 1994) signified the electorate's dislike
of "big government" and that the elections of Bill Clinton and Tony Blair were the triumph
of centrist politics, by which they meant "fiscal responsibility," "balanced budgets," and
"control over entitlements," as well as the neutralization of right-wing claims that Democrats
in the United States and Labourites in the United Kingdom were soft on crime and welfare cheats. Joined by many academics, the pundits now see a major shift toward the "vital
center" (what Europeans call the Third Way and what left critics call the "dead center").
According to this vision of voters' motives, the Clinton-Blair victories were possible because
"New Democrats" and "New Labour" appealed to moderate, affluent voters searching for
financially prudent government that would be more market-friendly. There is some truth
to the claim that many voters were attracted to the left articulation of values of work and
family security; this tapped into widely shared sentiments (including the idea that government must ensure public safety)—sentiments that are long-standing and more universal than
"moderate." But this vision of centrism misses both the social composition of the center-left
vote and the themes that, in fact, appealed to Clinton-Blair voters. In both countries, victory was based on the return of the middle mass—the Reagan Democrats, the Tory lower-
middle and working-class voters—and the candidates' pledges about jobs, education, medical care, and tax fairness. These are rather old populist-left concerns. The only pollster who
served both Clinton and Blair, Stanley Greenberg (1997), is adamant that the main reason
voters gave for voting for Clinton in 1996 was his defense of Medicare, social security, and
expansion of educational opportunity. In 1992 it was Clinton's pledge to create eight million jobs, expand public investment, and guarantee health-insurance coverage for everyone.
Equally important, he promised to raise taxes on the wealthy, move people from welfare to
work, and get tough on crime. Similarly, the Blair voters in 1997 wanted "a government
that would slow privatization and diminish inequality" (p. 44) while it saved the National
Health Service (Blair promised to increase NHS spending each year, to cut the waiting list,

to increase the number of nurses and abolish Thatcher's "internal market" for health care). British voters also responded to Labour's pledge to increase the percentage of GDP going to education, shift state subsidies from private to public schools, institute a minimum wage, stop the privatization of pensions, sign the European Social Charter, and tax excess profits of utilities to finance 250,000 government-created jobs for the long-term unemployed. In the 1990s, Greenberg concludes, "both countries voted for reformed center-left parties that would fight the extension of Reaganism and Thatcherism and that would strive to make government work for ordinary citizens" (*ibid.*). Data in chapters 5 and 10 on welfare-state retrenchment and backlash show that mass opinion everywhere continues overwhelmingly to favor the core programs of the welfare state. And, when pollsters offer questions that connect program support with willingness to raise taxes to pay for favored programs, the support remains strong—in the United Kingdom, steadily increasing in the 16 years leading up to Blair's huge victory (table 10.1). More significant is the fierce mass resistance to government efforts to cut universalistic social programs in all countries, evident in chapters 5, 10, 11, and 16.

In short, nothing in the voting and opinion record of the 1990s in these two presumably most free-marketeer democracies shows a shift toward the centrist politics of media invention, let alone a shift to the right. In the sense that large majorities of voters reject extremes of the sectarian right and left, "centrist" politics is here to stay. But beyond that vague idea is a host of mass preferences, voting patterns, and party appeals that point to a left-of-center majority in the United States, as elsewhere.

The Social Composition of a Center-Left Coalition

The components of a progressive coalition that reflects mass preferences include six groupings of voters: (1) *Most of the middle mass,* provided tax fairness, education, family policies, job security, crime control, and the protection of universalistic programs of the welfare state are central in party appeals, offsetting racist and nativist appeals. (2) *Women,* including single women and single mothers, who everywhere are attracted to left parties that support family policies, educational reform, expanded health care, active labor-market policies, and environmental protection, and avoid government intrusion into their private decisions about birth and abortion. It is the development of the gender gap and the image of homogeneous affluent suburbs that account for the myth of moderation as applied to women. "Soccer moms" are a small minority of women voters: suburbs come in all shapes at every level of education and income, and it is nonaffluent women trying to balance work and family who respond most to progressive politics. (3) *Labor unions*—everywhere still the core of a center-left coalition. Even with its declining membership base, the American labor movement in many recent elections has offset the decline in Democratic Party loyalty by its vigorous fieldwork, doing the job political machines once did; the labor vote, the core of FDR's coalition, is still alive, if we measure it by comparing union and nonunion turnout and voting preferences, holding socioeconomic status constant. To say that union members are only 16.5 million (not a trivial figure in itself) is to overlook not only this recent record of voter education and mobilization, but to ignore the network effect. Union members have families; union contracts cover another million and a half nonmembers; union leaders are coalition players. Union political influence is not only stable, organized, and concentrated in strategic states; it goes beyond the number of members. (4) *Racial-ethnic-linguistic-religious minorities and immigrants,* who respond to left parties where they defend their civil rights, promote their social and economic integration into national life, and extend universal welfare-state benefits to minorities. Where left candidates accent race preferences in education and jobs in their campaigns, however, they lose majority voters. (5) *Public-sector employees* who, for obvious reasons, favor an activist government. Women and minorities are prominent among them (see chaps. 7 and 9). (6) *Sophisticated business leaders,* especially those in export industries or high-tech firms who strongly support government-imposed education standards, government support for research and development and infrastructure investment, and who often favor family policies and active labor-market policies. Many would be glad to have the government take over the burden of financing health care. While not numerous, they help to neutralize strident business opposition to center-left causes. More generally, graduate-degree holders disproportionately vote center-left. Of course these categories overlap. A black single mother who is a government secretary and a union member covers five of six. But she is not the typical case. There is plenty of evidence in surveys of voting behavior and political orientation that the six groupings constitute a majority of voters and respond to a center-left agenda.

Policy Implications: A Center-Left Agenda

It is highly unlikely that the United States will in the near future cut new channels for centralized bargaining that facilitate the adoption and implementation of public policies widely supported by mass publics and most elites. It lacks the structural and ideological sources of corporatism discussed in this book. The U.S. is not about to adopt a modified form of proportional representation, create mass-based Catholic or left political parties, or launch a serious left challenge to the two major parties, abandon its decentralized federalism, or transform its numerous, narrowly focused interest groups—labor, industry, commerce, professions—into a more coherent, inclusive, and centralized system of representation. In the absence of such consensus-making machinery, what shifts in structure are possible? What public policies can realistically be adopted under what political conditions? How can political polarization and deadlock be reduced?

There are some modifications of law and structure that might reduce the disjunction between stable popular demands (of which most elites approve) and policy responses. Three of these would require major shifts in the political landscape: national health insurance, labor law reform, and improvements in the representative and deliberative aspects of American democracy. Such policy changes would require a rejuvenated Democratic Party, at least a little revival of "moderate" Republicans in Congress (most likely through a rebellion against the dominance of the South and the Christian right in the Republican Party), a substantial Democratic majority in the Senate—perhaps not the two to one margin President Johnson had when Medicare and Medicaid became law, but close to it—and an activist president with a substantial popular majority of the same party.[4]

• *National health insurance.* Chapter 16's analysis of why health care reform fails makes the case against small incremental reforms to solve this uniquely American social problem—a health-care system that costs more than that of any other democracy with below-average results in health performance. I have recounted numerous incremental reforms that failed to achieve their aims, as the portion of the population with poor coverage or no coverage increased. Without a dominant public share of total spending, without universal coverage, without a global budget, the game of risk selection and cost shifting is the main game in town. The uniquely extreme commercialization of the medical-industrial complex with its high administrative costs, a private sector that greatly exceeds that of every other country, a chaos of private and public regulation, a very high ratio of specialists to primary-care physicians, a shortage of nurses, and much higher use of expensive technologies account for the poor cost-benefit ratio; they make change difficult. The most important political barrier to the adoption of national health insurance is the dominance of insurance companies. All other countries have contained their power and confined their reach.

In view of these structural barriers, it is understandable that the center-left and even parts of the center-right who favor national health insurance have shied away from it. Reform efforts from Teddy Roosevelt through Truman to Clinton have failed. FDR's two-to-one to four-to-one margin in the U.S. Senate when he signed New Deal social legislation did not bring national health insurance; and Johnson, with his big margin, had to settle for Medicare for the aged and Medicaid for the poor and handicapped. That Canada, similar to the U.S. in so many ways, including similar medical-care systems in the early 1960s, was able to achieve national health insurance at less cost and better outcomes is explained by many small structural contrasts that in this one policy area added up to a near-insurmountable obstacle for the U.S. My comparison of the two countries points to a somewhat more paralyzing decentralized federalism in the U.S., weaker demonstration effects by the states, an electoral system more unfavorable to a left third party, the increasing use of the Senate filibuster, and weaker party discipline, differences that do not make a difference for a great range of other policies and outcomes.

Yet the popular demand for national health insurance in the U.S. remains strong and steady; politicians of every persuasion give lip service to the idea of universal coverage. Given the change in the political landscape described above, which could offset the power of insurance companies, the U.S. will likely join the rest of our rich democracies in comprehensive, universal health insurance.

• *Labor law reform.* If this book shows nothing else, it demonstrates the key role of inclusive, coordinated unions and strong labor federations in moving politics to the center-left. It also shows that accommodative industrial relations that integrate workers and unions into managerial decision making enhance productivity and economic performance (chaps. 1 and 12). Finally, as one of the largest broad-based mediating associations, the labor movement is essential to the vitality of democracy—a force that counters mass-society tendencies (chap. 3).

Students of industrial relations have shown that a substantial portion if not most of the decline in U.S. union density in recent decades is explained by rising management antiunion militancy reinforced by state laws hostile to unions and collective bargaining and the promanagement bias of the White House in the 1970s and 1980s. A full range of union-busting devices, legal and illegal, came into play. Law firms devoted to a "union-free environment" devised sequences of actions to defeat union organizing. Some are legal under "free speech" doctrines: order supervisors to tell their immediate subordinates about the dangers of unionism and strikes, accuse union leaders of corruption, deny union organizers access to the workplace, challenge the "election district" and in other ways prolong the election campaign. Some are illegal: threaten to move the plant if the union wins, fire union activists, threaten reprisals for workers who vote union.[5] Finally, if after a several-month campaign of intimidation, workers vote for a union, employers increasingly refuse to agree to a first contract; they stall and stonewall. This rising employer militancy and the hostile political-legal climate that gave it expression is not the only force accounting for American labor's decline. Equally important is the failure of labor to devote resources of money and personnel to the tasks of organizing. Counterintuitively, the studies suggest that changes in the occupational and industrial composition of the labor force, in the increase of women and minorities at work, in regional population shifts, and even business cycles are of minor significance relative to the growth in management opposition, the bias of public policy, and the weak organizing effort of unions (e.g., Freeman and Medoff, 1984, pp. 221 – 245; Dickens and Leonard, 1985; and Rogers, 1990). In comparative perspective, a similar and familiar message is that since 1970 corporatist democracies with centralized labor movements (except for Austria and the Netherlands) have experienced growth or little or no decline in union density, especially if they administer unemployment benefits, while fragmented and decentralized democracies (except for Ireland) and countries whose corporatist bargaining excludes labor (except for Switzerland) have labor movements in decline (Blanchflower and Freeman, 1992, table 1; Western, 1993, 1995, table 1; Visser, 1992).

As with health insurance, a major shift in the political landscape would be necessary to improve the fairness of American labor law. Again a U.S./Canadian comparison is suggestive. As chapter 16 has shown (note 25 and Bruce, 1989), neither differences in political culture nor contrasts in public attitudes toward unions can explain why Canada and the U.S., starting from nearly identical low union densities 1945 – 65, subsequently followed contrasting trajectories. U.S. union density declined from about a third to the current 14% while Canadian unions—in the face of public attitudes *less* favorable to unions than those of the U.S.—climbed to over a third. Canadian labor law, almost the antithesis of U.S. law, provides the lion's share of the explanation. In brief, and most important, union certification procedures are automatic and quick in Quebec and among federal employees if the union gives evidence of over 50% signed cards; in British Columbia, Manitoba, and New Brunswick 55% must sign the card. If only a minority sign, an election is held promptly after a petition is filed. There is no chance for a long employer intimidation campaign. Canadian law also prohibits the use of permanent striker replacements, although Ontario has modified this. Provinces covering 80% of the labor force provide for "interest arbitration" of first contracts to prevent bad-faith bargaining. Finally, labor boards are more powerful in Canada and hear more cases more quickly than in the U.S. (Abraham and Voos, 1996.)

It is obvious that Canadian-style labor-law reform would make a difference for labor prospects in the U.S. The Dunlop Commission (U.S. Commission on the Future of Worker-Management Relations, 1994), representing government, management, and academia, spells out the minimum steps needed to restore fairness: update and expand the coverage of labor relations statutes; strengthen protection for workers' right to organize; speed up certification elections; give workers the same access to union spokespersons as they have to management spokespersons during certification campaigns; issue prompt injunctions to remedy discrimination against employees during organizing campaigns or first-contract negotiations; assist employers and newly certified unions to achieve first contracts through an upgraded dispute-resolution system. The Commission stopped short of endorsing an outright ban on employers' practice of hiring permanent replacements for strikers, which most students of labor relations consider essential to preserve a balance of power in collective bargaining. Combined with new resources labor is already committing to organizing, which in 1998–2000 slowed the slide in union density and increased membership, this agenda would go far toward revitalizing the labor movement.[6] Like national health insurance, however, a substantial shift in the political terrain is a prerequisite.

• *Reform the appointment process and Senate rules. Reduce reliance on initiatives and referenda. Reduce the number and duration of elections.* As Robert Dahl suggests, "the *plebiscitory* aspect of American political life has grown . . . without a corresponding improvement in its *representative* and *deliberative* aspects" (1994, p. 2). I have traced the poisoning of the process of investigation of presidential appointees, the extraordinary lengthening of time between the president's naming of an appointee and Senate votes on confirmation; an epidemic of filibusters or the threat of filibusters, especially since 1990; more generally the rise of populist politics, epitomized in California's plebiscitory rampage, now spreading to Oregon, Washington, South Dakota, and Utah. The behavior of Congress reflects and reinforces political polarization and policy paralysis. Chapter 11 shows that political dealignment of the electorate and dependence on the initiative and referendum together open the way for the dominance of money and the media; they foster the rise of demagogues of every persuasion, and the subversion of the deliberative and representative functions of Congress and state legislatures. The frequency and complexity of ballots foster voter fatigue and reduce turnout, as they have in the only two countries with an extraordinary number of elective offices and great reliance on initiatives and referenda, Switzerland and the USA. Finally, populist politics interacting with weak parties result in a profusion of policies judged by almost all scholars as bad for the vitality of democracy. Examples include indiscriminate, uncoordinated, unworkable taxing and spending limitations; arbitrary restrictions on staffing; gridlock on annual budgets; deterioration of services; and undemocratic term limits for legislators. Term limits, a favorite item on the populist agenda, squeeze out wisdom, experience, and organizational memory, while they increase the power of the continuous bureaucracy and permanent lobbyists and block expression of voters' strong preferences for popular, even outstanding incumbents. (See chap. 11.)

None of these trends can be reversed without the election of many more politicians who respect politics and political institutions and believe in governing—the shift in the political landscape I outlined above. When and if that occurs, modest improvements in political processes would be possible. If the Senate voted to end filibusters with 55 votes instead of 60, this would hardly result in a tyranny of the majority. It might, however, reduce the tyranny of the minority that now routinely prevents major issues from coming to a vote. If Congress has a substantial majority who want to overcome paralysis and who respect the Senate as an institution, appointments would not be indefinitely bottled up by a committee chairman or be destroyed by lengthy character assassination. Individual senators could not stall action by privately asking the majority leader to put a "hold" on the item. We could also go back to the two-month lag between presidential nomination and Senate action that prevailed in the early 1960s. Appointee forms could be simplified, the investigation made more professional. The number of congressional investigations that have no legislative purpose other than destroying political enemies could be reduced. Many other minor modifications of congressional rules to facilitate deliberation, fairness, and accommodation in the legislative process would be possible.

Even more difficult is the reduction of the politics of simplification, the populist politics of manipulation and total victory. When legislatures abdicate their responsibilities and pass the buck to "the people" through initiatives and referenda, the "people" in practice turn out to be single-issue groups interacting with a growing industry of paid "volunteers" to gather signatures and money to buy media for distorted messages that elicit more money, and a fading electorate utterly confused about the ballot. To reduce reliance on initiatives (many are in the form of constitutional amendments) would again require a major shift in the political landscape. There is no shortage of proposals on how to do this. Academics produce them by the barrel. There is impressive consensus among experts on American politics that the initiative and referendum subvert representative democracy. Many commissions and conferences have been convened to consider the content and prospects of reform. But politicians in the current climate lack the structural props for their courage to do the right thing. An instructive example is the California Constitution Revision Commission appointed in 1995 by Governor Wilson of California, the Speaker of the Assembly, and the Senate Rules Committee. In 1996 they recommended changes in the political system that would restrict the initiative process, lengthen the limit on legislative terms, and restructure local government and the budgetary process. The proposals died upon arrival. The governor dropped it. Republican leaders feared attacks from the populist left (you are denying the people their voice) and opposed many of the recommendations. A profusion of interest groups, left and right, each attacked parts of the reform agenda: teachers did not want to abolish the post of superintendent of schools; tax reformers and antigovernment groups and campaign reformers love the initiative as it is, by which they have thrived. Finally, legislators do not relish having to confront hot-button issues that they can offload to "the people." This is another case of a coalition of minorities with strong views overcoming a majority worried about the main drift of politics and mildly favoring reform.

As for eliminating a few hundred of the tens of thousands of elective offices in the U.S., or lengthening the terms of representatives in the House to reduce voter fatigue and increase turnout, these would require a sea change in politicians' outlook and are highly unlikely, even more difficult than national health insurance and labor-law reform. A more likely step forward is campaign reforms that expand media access for parties and candidates and other modest changes that would strengthen parties and give Congress and the Executive branch more time for governing instead of money-raising. Although everyone in the current system finds it enervating, these changes would still require a major shift in the political landscape described above.

• *What should be done about money and the media in politics?* Current debate about money in politics and the evil influence of "special interests" exemplifies a solution in search of a problem. The *New York Times* labels "soft money" "sewer money"; Common Cause advocates still more limits on campaign contributions and, like politicians of every persuasion, rails against the "special interests." What is wrong with money in politics is not that there is too much of it; in view of the costs of media access, there is too little of it, it is not visible enough, and it is not as widely distributed as it should be. (Ornstein, 1992; Jacobson, 1993.) And what is wrong with ritual complaints about special interests is that groups vary hugely in their specialness; some foster wider civic attachments, others do not. Special or nonspecial, their capacity to influence government is indispensable to the vitality of democracy (chaps. 3 and 11).

If the problem to be solved is to restore the representative and deliberative aspects of American politics, to raise the quality of campaign discourse, and to involve more voters in the process, we must focus first on politicians' access to the mass media and other increasingly costly means of communication with voters, both during election campaigns and year-round. Second, we must think of ways to strengthen political parties. Regarding money: To reach voters in large political units such as congressional districts and most states, let alone the whole country, politicians must have very large sums. That is why, when confronted with limitations on spending, they invent "soft money" and political action committees (PACs) that can buy media messages on issues. Soft money is individual and group contributions to state and local parties that are neither limited nor disclosed. The money moves between states and the national parties, too. It is usually spent on voter registration and get-out-the vote drives, polling, and party ads coordinated with national campaigns. It is the only money that gives both national and state parties leverage over candidate selection. A mounting problem for party viability is the proliferation of self-selected entrepreneurial candidates (often weak or incompetent candidates) with their own money-machines and separate campaigns. When and if these folks reach the Senate or House, they owe little to the national or state parties. This intensifies the already big problem of aggregating interests and accommodating clashing ideologies in order to govern.

Eliminating PACs and soft money without finding other means of campaign finance would not only further weaken political parties but would make political action difficult both for narrowly focused interest groups (corporations with a product focus, the gun lobby) and for broadly based interest groups such as labor, churches, and many multi-issue voluntary associations. Efforts to remove money from the system have, in fact, resulted in elaborate and opaque rules that are unenforceable, coupled with the inevitable phony charges of "corruption"; they do nothing to increase access to the media, increase the competitiveness of elections, cut the time politicians devote to money-raising, or strengthen parties.

Among the small steps that might help (these are adapted from Norman Ornstein, who has long and persuasively advocated such reforms): Enact a tax credit for small in-state individual contributions to candidates and parties, say up to $250/year. Create incentives for candidates to raise this "good," "rank-and-file" money by federal matching funds for all such money raised over a threshold of $30,000. The tax credit for small contributions could be financed at least in part by a 10% fee for contributions over $1,000—another incentive to broaden the campaign base. If these two reforms were enacted, accountability could be enhanced by timely (48-hour) mandatory disclosure of the source of all contributions over $1,000, including PAC money. A robust system of disclosure using the Internet would require funding a strengthened enforcement and disclosure arm of the Federal Election Commission. Finally, to enable challengers to surmount the campaign-finance barrier that now discourages many good candidates, double individual contribution limits from the present $25,000 per year to $50,000 for federal candidates but add another $50,000 to political parties. Incidentally, indexing these ceilings to inflation would prevent the erosion that would trigger repeated combat over the same issue.

Of all the political reforms that would strengthen democracy, the most difficult to achieve is political party and candidate access to the broadcast media (chaps. 3 and 11 describe the ways other democracies have achieved this goal). The U.S. is unique in forcing its politicians into a continuous scramble for money to buy media access; all other rich democracies make plenty of room for party leaders and candidates to speak for themselves at public expense. It is significant that whenever a campaign finance reform bill reaches bipartisan sponsorship in Congress, it has already been stripped of provisions to provide free TV time for federal candidates. For obvious reasons Congress is supersensitive to broadcast industry opposition (see chap. 3).

When Commerce Secretary Herbert Hoover addressed one of a series of national radio conferences leading to the Radio Act of 1927 and to the predecessor to the FCC, the Federal Radio Commission, he put the issue plainly: "It is unthinkable that we should allow so great a possibility for service to be drowned in advertising chatter. . . . There is in all of this the necessity to establish public rights over the ether roads. . . . There must be no national regret that we have parted with a great national asset" (Hoover, 1952, pp. 140–141). Similarly the Communications Act of 1934 granted broadcasters free and exclusive use of the public airwaves in return for a pledge to serve the "public interest, convenience, and necessity." Yet industry has been very successful not only in escaping from public-interest obligations but in obtaining subsidy for commercial needs. In 1997 the government doubled the amount of spectrum space it licensed to broadcasters; estimates of the value go as high as $70 billion, all for free—a generous dose of corporate welfare. Throughout, the powers of the FCC to regulate broadcasters in the public interest have been severely limited. (For detailed enumeration see Hilliard, 1991, pp. 29–41, 66ff.) It has the power to lift the license of a broadcaster who fails to fulfill public-interest obligations, but its admonitions and fines are largely ineffective.

Even assuming an administration that wants to assert the public interest, expand access, and offset media power, it is not easy to craft regulatory regimes that would do the job. Those who favor free airtime and/or format requirements to improve the discourse in campaigns, redress the imbalance between incumbents and challengers, and overcome the necessity of endless money-chasing to buy sound bites (mostly attack ads) must solve several difficult problems: How many candidates get how much time? How should it be divided among candidates and parties? If the government requires all stations to give minimum time to parties and to thousands of candidates in hundreds of districts, what formula can account for the wide differences in media costs, market reach, and political realities in different electoral jurisdictions? Do the reforms apply to radio, as well as television? What about cable, which is not licensed by the federal government? If the loss of audience is substantial when candidates use the time, if all that happens is an increase in Blockbuster's movie rental profits, what has been accomplished? Will format requirements violate constitutional free speech provisions? Political scientists have offered practical proposals that answer these questions. For instance:

1. *Mandate free prime time for qualified parties* in the two months preceding presidential and congressional elections and/or provide *public subsidies to buy that time.* Let parties choose what to air, as is done in most other democracies. The party allocations could reflect the share of seats in the House or, if minor parties are to be accommodated, the percentage of popular vote in presidential elections above a nontrivial threshold. This would strengthen parties and reduce the exclusively candidate-centered elections. Format requirements: Time minimums (to overcome the sound bite/attack ad pathology) and personal appearance by the candidates (to promote accountability for the tone of the message). In the short run, this is less politically feasible than the following.

2. *Create a "broadcast bank" or national political time bank* consisting of minutes of television and radio time on all broadcast outlets.[7] At the beginning of each election cycle every station must contribute two hours of prime advertising time to the bank. The Federal Election Commission (FEC) will disperse vouchers from the bank to candidates to purchase political ads. Half the vouchers go directly to general election candidates for the U.S. House and Senate who have raised over a threshold amount from small donors in their district or state. The other half goes to major (and qualifying minor) parties, which are free to distribute vouchers to candidates of their choice for any office. Candidates who do not use their vouchers can trade them in to their party for other resources such as phone banks or direct mail. *The format requirements* (like those in several sister democracies): No message can be less than 60 seconds; the candidate must appear on screen for the duration and for radio use his or her own voice. The aim, again, is to overcome the worst excesses of nearly anonymous attack ads. *Financing:* The two hours each station contributes are assigned a monetary value based on market rates where it originated; the vouchers are denominated in dollars, not time. Candidates and parties can use vouchers at any station they wish. After the election, the bank reimburses stations that redeemed more than two hours worth of free time with proceeds it collects from stations that redeemed fewer. This ensures that all stations bear an equitable burden and maximizes user flexibility. A ceiling of $500 million per two-year election cycle—the estimated value of the political time sold in 1995–96—should be indexed for inflation.

All of the political reforms above could be financed in two ways, each contributing to an upgrading of campaigns, without utopian spending limits that do not work, without deadening the participation of mediating associations so essential to the democratic process: (1) a tax on PAC contributions to candidates and parties; and (2) a tax on television and radio advertising revenues. The fastest-rising cost of campaigning is those ads, which are increasingly profitable for the stations. The tens of millions of dollars so raised could be put into a trust fund to help pay for the tax credit for small contributions. The rationale is straightforward: Those who benefit from the current system should pay a reasonable price to improve it.

A More Feasible Part of the Agenda

I see eight public-policy shifts that can be accomplished without a huge Senate Democratic majority or a resurgence of Republican moderates in the Congress. They would, however, likely require Democratic control of both houses of Congress and the presidency. Coalitions favoring most of these policies are already evident in the behavior of past presidents or one or the other branch of past Congresses or reforms adopted by some states. Most have been successfully implemented by all, most, or a few of the 19 rich democracies. They are the policies that, if adapted to American circumstances, are transferable from abroad. Together these policies and programs would reduce poverty and inequality and their associated pathologies; they would lessen political polarization, making it difficult to mobilize the middle mass against the poor. Much of this agenda is a restatement of the obvious, but reminders are often useful.

- *Family policy and social security*. Chapters 5 and 7 give a detailed account of what other rich democracies have done to enhance family stability and well-being through direct government action. "Family policy" embraces a wide range of programs designed to assure the care of children, increase gender equality, and maximize choices in balancing the demands of work and family for everyone. It functions to (1) *replace or supplement household income* (e.g., family or child allowances, rent supplements and housing assistance, and pensions with flexible retirement), (2) *offer services to families* (e.g., family-planning services, family counseling, child care, including preschools, day-care centers, before-school and after-school leisure centers, short workdays for parents, parental leave, paid and unpaid, leave for parents when their children are sick) or (3) *serve in lieu of the family* (e.g., home help or long-term care for the frail elderly and supplementary meals programs).

Three findings are especially relevant for the U.S. as it moves toward a sensible family policy. First these are universal, categorical programs that avoid heavy means testing or targeting to "the truly needy." If the benefits are income-related, the income tests are simple—a declaration at point of service or a tax return. Also they do not kick in at very low levels; benefits are typically reduced gradually as income brackets climb. For instance day-care places are free or almost free for a substantial portion of the population and copayments increase with increasing income, but no one pays the full cost. Second, countries that have innovative and expansive policies spend very little on means-tested public assistance; there is a strong inverse relationship between scores on my family-policy index and spending on means-tested programs. The reasons: A family policy reduces poverty without an intrusive, expensive apparatus of harassment of the poor; and because its benefits are widely shared it is easier to fund. In contrast, public assistance targeted to the nonworking nonaged poor facilitates the mobilization of the middle mass against such symbolic targets as "welfare cheats." Further evidence of this trade-off is the finding in chapter 6 that public spending on pensions (including survivors' and disability insurance), family allowances, work injury, and, to a lesser extent, health care comprises a package that is inversely related to spending on public assistance and higher education. The third finding is that in no rich democracy is there a war between the generations about any of this. Two of the strongest predictors of an expansive, innovative family policy are the percentage over 65 and women working. In the U.S. as elsewhere, the aged make common cause with their adult children, not merely about pensions and flexible retirement but also about paid parental leave and public day care. The politics of these family policies are integrative.

Needless to say, the lush cash transfers and services delivered by the family-policy leaders—Sweden, France, Belgium, Norway, and Finland (chap. 7)—are expensive. But they are so popular that funding for them is politically feasible. And the alternatives—social problems that come from family breakup and population aging without a family policy—are both costly and severe. Family policy pays off in the long run in poverty reduction, productivity increases of working parents, a better life for the aged, and the improved supervision, education, and cognitive development of children. That coalitions for family policy already exist in the U.S. is evident in small steps already taken in recent Congresses and proposals made by recent presidents. Most notable are the Family and Medical Leave Act and successive increases in the Earned Income Tax Credit (EITC), which uses a simple, confidential income- and family-composition test administered by the IRS (chap. 8). The EITC has reduced the rate of poverty among working families; if expanded greatly, it would have a major impact. Other steps were blocked. For instance, proposals for publicly subsidized child care have passed one or the other branch of Congress or have appeared in presidential State of the Union addresses. Chapter 7 recounts the coalition politics that brought politicians of opposing persuasion together on this issue. Nine Republican senators joined Democrats to pass a child-care bill with modest funding, the ABC Bill of 1989. It died in a conference committee. Until we are willing to produce serious and sustained funding for training and paying child-minders, nursery school teachers, and other educators and spread the benefit well beyond the poor, the child care that has become routine in most other rich democracies will elude us. Child-care provisions in the U.S. remain weak despite accelerating talk about the desperate need for them. For those who believe that the private sector can provide such services the record described in chapter 7 (pp. 267, 276–277) is poor. For instance, a large-scale study of cost, quality, and child outcomes in 400 randomly chosen child-care centers found that 40% of infants and toddlers were in conditions that threaten their health and safety and discourage learning. With extremely low pay and high turnover of typical child-care workers we can expect no better. Doing the job through the tax system is also a delusion; the money moves toward the affluent (chap. 7, p. 267 and note 3).

Public pensions is an area where in 1995 the U.S. was second to last in the GDP share of spending and ranked 14th of 17 countries in average earnings-replacement rate (table

6.2) but has much improved over its past and ranks average on our index of flexible retirement (chap. 7, pp. 277ff.). The main American peculiarity is the intensity of periodic hysteria orchestrated by politicians and the media over the alleged crisis of social security (the system is bankrupt, "catch-65," "the young will never see a dime of it"). Chapter 5 has shown the absurdity of these successive crises, alternating between claims of the social-security trust fund's imminent bankruptcy to the complaint that it is overfunded, both labeled a "crisis." We have thus far reluctantly begun to do what other rich democracies have done to cope with the growing percentage of the aged. What other countries do is to increase funding either through incremental payroll-tax increases or general revenues and to trim future costs by increasing the official retirement age and by making small technical adjustments in the basis for indexing. In this way the U.S. negotiated a settlement of the alleged crisis of the early 1980s; this was accomplished by a bipartisan commission, a group of congressional and administration leaders and interest groups. In 1983 the U.S. raised payroll taxes slightly, taxed benefits, brought new federal employees into the system, and very slowly phased in a higher retirement age from 65 to 67 by the year 2027. With very little fuss this "fixed" the system for 47 years, said the actuaries. Recently we have undergone another cycle where both parties claim that there is a deep crisis and promise to "Save Social Security," this time by an accounting device that promises to allocate budget surpluses to the cause for decades ahead. In view of the dismal record of economic and social forecasting, a touch of humility when making such forecasts is appropriate. To know with any reasonable precision what the cost of a national pension scheme will be even 10 or 20 years from now, let alone 30 or 50 years ahead, we need to forecast not only the age and sex composition of the eligible population, but also the rates of inflation, unemployment, and growth as they shape the size of the tax base and benefit levels. It would also be necessary to predict the policies of unions and employers and the changing character of work as they affect the taste and pressure for retirement, the party composition of the government as it shapes tax policy, pension reform, and immigration, and more. (Wilensky, 1997.) With all the ambiguity, the most prudent approach is small increases in payroll taxes, phased increases in retirement age, and phased extension of coverage of state and local workers, as well as taxing benefits of the more affluent pensioners and removing the ceiling on payroll taxes. In other words, do what all rich democracies facing more serious burdens of population aging than the U.S. are doing—make incremental changes.

The most difficult problem posed by social-security systems everywhere is how to craft flexible retirement systems to reverse the long-term slide in the age of exit from work. Here we can learn from the very modest success of Swedish reforms that together with an active labor-market policy accounts for the high rate of labor-force participation of Swedes over 55 (see chap. 7 and table 15.3). It is surely good public policy to transform the healthy aged who want to work into taxpayers, part-time workers and partial pensioners rather than pressuring them to retire fully. The trick is to find the balance between reductions in benefits for very early retirement and generous partial pensions for continued part-time work for workers aged say 60–64 while avoiding pressure on worn-out workers in the least-attractive jobs to postpone retirement, which necessitates adequate income and medical support. It is a formidable challenge for system design. (For a discussion of rising job discrimination against the aged see chap. 1.)

For the reasons listed in chapter 16, health care is a more serious fiscal problem for the U.S., and even less predictable than pension costs. Short of comprehensive, universal national health insurance with global budgets and cost controls, or politically unacceptable cuts in needed services, this problem cannot be solved. Unlike pensions, the problems of adequate health-care financing and delivery do not yield to small incremental changes and cannot wait decades before major system reforms are made.

There is much casual comment that the existing social security and Medicare systems have done little to reduce poverty. In fact the universalistic programs targeted to the aged and sick have been the most successful poverty-reduction programs of the past half century. In 1965, 30% of the officially defined poor were over 65. By 2000, that figure had fallen to one in eight. The main cause: expanded coverage and benefits for social security and Medicare. Pension checks obviously reduce the number of "pretransfer poor." But half of Medicare and 70% of Medicaid also go to those who would have been poor without these programs. (Glennerster, 2000, p. 16.) Any policy that protects these programs prevents their recipients from sinking into poverty.

• *An active labor-market policy (ALMP).* ALMP refers to direct government action to shape the *demand* for labor by maintaining or creating jobs; to increase the *supply* and *quality* of labor via training and rehabilitation; and to encourage *labor mobility* via placement, counseling, and mobility incentives. Chapter 2 (figure 2.2) lists 16 types of programs that fit this idea (plus 5 that are marginal); I have reviewed evidence on their effectiveness elsewhere (1985, 1992a). They are substitutes for such passive policies as unemployment insurance and public assistance that make little or no contribution to human resource use. The U.S. has adopted many active programs, from the Job Corps to wage and training subsidies. But the funding is too meager and their average quality too limited to have much national impact; the effort moved from less than one-tenth of 1% of GNP 1950–64 to a peak of 0.52% in the late 1970s and back down to 0.18% by 1983, then up a little in the 1990s. To get an idea of what adequate funding would be, consider that Sweden, the leader in this area, spends on average at least 2.5% of GDP on its ALMP. That is equivalent to more than $231 billion in U.S. 1999 GNP—near Pentagon budget size. Even if we add the armed forces' excellent training effort to the current U.S. civilian effort, it would still be feeble.

Like family policy, the cross-national transferability of ALMP is easier than most policy areas for the same reason: coalitions of the center-right and center-left have often formed around the evidence of the effectiveness of these programs or at least around their general appeal as a way to expand equality of opportunity and productivity. Because these programs are not exclusively targeted to the "undeserving poor" but to many groups— displaced workers in their prime, entire distressed communities, as well as hard-to-employ young, minorities, handicapped, single mothers, displaced homemakers, and older men— they do not set up a backlash against funding. Because they ease the shock of industrial readjustment, they can dampen labor's opposition to free trade. Because the training components of ALMP have been most successful with women, they supplement a family policy in reducing the feminization of poverty, so prominent in American society.

In short, an ALMP for the U.S. that is serious and feasible would combine job creation; apprenticeship training; incentives for on-the-job training and retraining; work-study programs to ease the transition from school to work; much better vocational counseling in high schools with continuous follow-up for two or three years; remedial programs to increase basic literacy and improve work habits and attitudes; a much strengthened placement service to increase efficiency in matching job seekers and job vacancies for everyone, including compulsory notification of job vacancies or layoffs; mobility allowances, relocation assistance, and rent supplements tied to mobility for workers trapped in depressed areas and industries.

- *Upgrade K–12.* It is no mystery why the primary and secondary schools of other democracies perform at a much higher level than ours. They pay their teachers more and respect them more. They spend more of their budgets on academic resources. They insist on national standards for performance, they train and educate their teachers in subjects to be taught, and they give them more autonomy in the classroom. Both principals and teachers expect a higher level of performance from students and comprehensive tests measure that performance. Teachers are given time to confer with one another and plan their work; professional development is valued. The school year and school day tend to be longer among the better performers. This picture of our sister democracies' K–12 equivalents is approximated in upper-middle-class public and private schools in the U.S. The U.S. problem is that the other four-fifths suffer from mediocre to disgraceful schools. When discussing this problem, many politicians and some academics argue that no big change is possible without privatizing the system and/or breaking the power of teachers' unions. Chapter 12 shows that if we compare the performance of private and public schools of similar social composition, privatizing is no solution to the problem of upgrading standards even if it did not drain funds from public schools. Regarding unions, cross-national comparison shows that in countries with superior K–12 performance teachers are more highly unionized, one reason for the higher relative income and respect they have achieved. And in fact, there is no unified teachers' union resistance to the performance pay and the school accountability proposals necessary to upgrade standards; the American Federation of Teachers supports both. In debates about reform it has become a popular sport not only to blame unions but to bash teachers for not shaping up, when, in fact, we have dumped our unsolved social problems on them—uncushioned family breakup, unsupervised children unprepared for learning or orderly behavior, rising poverty rates with related deficiencies in child nutrition and health, increasing racial tensions and neighborhood violence spilling over into schools. Then, while we self-righteously proclaim that our teachers are failing us, we decrease both the moral and financial support for instructional services and let the buildings in which they work deteriorate (chap. 12).

The main barriers to a passable national K–12 performance are, first, the extraordinary decentralization of the system, the tyranny of locality; second, the grip of low-standard Schools of Education on teacher training and certification, which diverts attention from academic content to dubious lists of methods of teaching and stages of child development and aimless statistics while it turns off bright students who would otherwise enter teaching; and, finally, inadequate funding for both preschool and primary and secondary education. Today, after increases by the Clinton administration, the federal share of K–12 finance is only 6.6%, lower than it was before the Great Society. If we are to overcome local resistance to raising standards, expand the supply of competent teachers, reverse the deterioration of the physical plant, and make funds available for upgrading teacher education, this federal support will have to be doubled or tripled. That these measures are possible with a popular center-left leader and a legislature of the same party is suggested by the large increase of 16% in the first two budgets of Governor Gray Davis of California, 1999–2001. Included are incentives for professional development and tested school performance, incentives for teachers who agree to teach in hard-to-staff schools (it should be called hazard pay), and monitoring of student progress via a mandatory new Standardized Testing and Reporting (STAR) program. All the components of the center-left coalition combined to give Davis his big victory. His campaign centered on K–12 reform. Business leaders added their voices in support.

To address the shortage of teachers and their poor preparation, we need to bypass or offset the influence of Schools of Education. One way is to follow Massachusetts' lead: change teacher certification standards to require substantial hours of credit in an academic subject taught in high schools. Another way is to create numerous in-service training opportunities and teaching jobs for well-educated professionals in such fields as science, math, languages, music, and literature from the private or nonprofit sectors. These include retirees who want part-time jobs, career changers who would like to switch to K–12 teaching, and other outsiders who know their subjects. (All this is already part of Governor Davis' school reform program.) A small Teacher Corps has been federally funded, but unless it is linked to competence testing and in-depth training it cannot do much to upgrade standards. Some of these recruits could be tested for competency and certified via Internet courses. Of course, increasing starting pay and enhancing opportunities for performance-based promotion and professional development would increase the supply of above-average college graduates entering teaching.

In all the effort to upgrade K–12, reformers need to keep the interdependence of policies in mind. It does no good to say, "End social promotion, set high standards for student performance" (typical of congressional amendments to appropriation bills), unless at the same time you fund remedial education for those held back, enrich instructional materials, reduce class size, expand early childhood education, train qualified teachers, pay them a professional salary, and hold principals and teachers accountable for student achievement. A useful device would be tuition subsidies and loans for the top 20% of college students followed by loan forgiveness if they go into teaching for five years, a kind of GI bill for talented prospects.

Although we can learn from other countries whose preschool and K–12 performance is better than ours, they can learn from the U.S. about how to run a system of mass higher education. As we have seen, the U.S. is as yet unmatched in equality of postsecondary opportunity, diversity of curricula, and continuing adult education. Its numerous junior colleges and adult-education programs provide expanding opportunity for lifetime learning, although this remains an unlikely prospect for those with very poor K–12 schooling. One reason for the outstanding performance of elite research universities in the U.S. is diversified funding, including extensive federal and state support. For instance, the University of California's 1999 operating budget of $13.7 billion, including research but excluding capital improvements, is 25% from the state, 33% from the federal government, 12% from the teaching hospitals, 7% from student tuition and fees, 5% from private gifts, and 17% from "other" (University of California, 1999).

• *Kiddiecare and women's health.* Only the U.S. stands aside in the universal assertion of public over private interests in the delivery of health care. Only the U.S. leaves between a quarter and a third of its population with no health insurance or clearly inadequate insurance coverage (J. Campbell, 1999, p.1; Bennefield, 1998, p.1). Without the great political shifts described above, the U.S. is destined to take small steps toward comprehensive national health insurance despite evidence that incremental changes tend to have perverse effects because they fail to prevent cost shifting, risk selection, and commercial interference in the clinical encounter between doctors and patients. In other countries the countervailing power of government—assertion of national interests over the interests of insurance companies, pharmaceutical firms, hospitals, physicians and other providers—brings both full coverage and a gradual reallocation of budgets toward primary care and preventive community care, which pay off in improved national health performance (chap. 16).

Nevertheless, if we are to take another step short of national health insurance, the most cost-beneficial approach would be to open medical care to all women of childbearing age with graduated copayments, and with benefits applied universally. The reasons: The U.S. now has about one in five of its children in poverty; 57% of the poor are women; maternal health even before birth has strong effects on child outcomes; and because about half of all births are to first-time mothers, targeting health care only to women who already have children misses half those who would most benefit from this incremental reform. (Chap. 16 analyzes the health effects. Cf. Danziger and Waldfogel, 2000.) The combination of a family policy and providing health care to all women of childbearing age is a major component in the interrelated policies by which most rich democracies have reduced poverty and inequality and their unhealthy consequences. (Chap. 16 shows why reducing poverty and inequality each independently improves a nation's health performance and how the financing and organizing of medical care shapes real health.) To combine "kiddiecare" (health insurance for all dependent children added to OASDHI and, like Medicare, financed by a payroll tax) with income-tested women's care is a cost-effective way to improve the health and productivity of the next generation nationwide. The United States could remove itself from the honor of champion of deep poverty (table 8.4) by linking this incremental health-insurance reform with investments in a family policy, including measures to raise the quality of and access to child care, preschool education, and after-school programs; an active labor-market policy; and programs to raise not only the standard in K–12 but also to raise the level of college attendance among high-ability youth from low-income families (one step in that direction would be a national service corps discussed below). If only one of the two steps—kiddiecare vs. all women of childbearing age—is politically feasible, targeting all children would be best.

• *A higher minimum wage and an expanded Earned Income Tax Credit.* In the interim before much of the above is done and the welfare mess continues, it is important to make work pay, so those who can work, can escape from poverty. As chapters 1 and 8 show, the U.S. remains #1 not only in household income inequality but also in earnings inequality. Of 10 rich democracies compared in the mid-1990s, the U.S. had both the greatest concentration of very low wages at the bottom compared to the middle and the greatest and increasing rewards to education, which moves earnings of the upper-middle class and rich ever more distant from the rest (Blau and Kahn, 1996b). Of 17 of our countries, the U.S. in 1996 ranked #12 in relative hourly total compensation—wages plus fringe benefits—of production workers in manufacturing, using market exchange rates. (If we use purchasing power parities, the U.S. was still behind Germany, Belgium, Austria, Netherlands, Canada, and Finland). (Mishel, Bernstein, and Schmitt, 1999, tables 8.6 and 8.7.) In real growth rates of total compensation of all employees in the private sector from 1989 to 1996 the U.S. was almost stagnant at 0.1% per year, ranking 15th of 17 rich democracies. For all employees in the same period the U.S. turned in the worst performance in real compensation growth based on purchasing power parities, with 0.3% per year; production workers' compensation fell 0.3% (*ibid.*, p. 365 and table 8.8). Chapter 12 (table 12.4) shows that the higher earnings, higher earnings growth, and greater earnings equality of our competitors in Europe did not make their economies less productive. By the mid-1990s several European countries, including France, Germany, the Netherlands, and Belgium, had matched or exceeded U.S. productivity levels, the value of goods and services produced on average in an hour of working (*ibid.*, table 8.3). Many others had narrowed the gap. In trends in labor productivity growth rates for 18 of our cases, 1979–96, only Switzerland was lower than the U.S.; the average annual increase was 1.9%, ours was 0.8%.

What all this says is that short of the radical wage compression of Sweden (chap. 2) neither raising the minimum pay of the working population nor decreasing wage inequality is a drag on the economy. The policy implication for the U.S.: Make work pay for the lowest fifth of the distribution. First make the minimum wage a living wage, which it was originally designed to be, and index it to the median wage of the labor force. The conservative opponents of the minimum wage should be grateful for this move; it would stop the periodic beating they take from the Democrats on the issue when it comes up in every Congress. On the merits, aside from arguments about fairness, dignity, family stability, and other values served by decent pay, aside from the contribution of a higher minimum wage to reducing poverty and the welfare mess, the findings regarding the employment and growth effects of such increases in U.S. studies confirm the cross-national findings. Because the beneficiaries among the working poor must spend what they get, they contribute to consumption-led growth (two-thirds of growth in the 1990s was attributed to consumption). More important, the employment effects are negligible.[8] When the U.S. finally approaches the minima of most rich democracies, it can follow their lead and make it more flexible by providing a training-wage exception to the minimum rate, thereby reducing business resistance.

The case for the second measure to reduce poverty among the working poor, who now comprise 27% of all poor families, is discussed in chapter 8 (pp. 323–324). The Earned Income Tax Credit (EITC) respects privacy, is invisible (a short tax form to the IRS), and is cheap to administer; its poverty-reducing effect is well established. Begun during the Reagan administration, at least until the mid-1990s it had bipartisan support, and at no time has it created a big political fuss.

These two policies, increases in both the minimum wage and the EITC, were important sources of the reduction in poverty of the working poor from 1996 to 1999. They have the merit of being at once politically feasible and effective.

- *A large-scale voluntary program of national civic and military service.* A greatly expanded AmeriCorps is the single policy shift that would do most to reduce mayhem, delinquency, and the balkanization of the United States. It should be seen as an alternative to military service. The aim of both is to harness the energy, enthusiasm, and idealism of youth and direct them toward solving pressing social problems or serving defense needs. If large enough, it would do much to reestablish the crucial link between public benefits and civic obligation, and thereby restore a sense of community. There are plenty of successful precedents: the New Deal's Civilian Conservation Corps and current programs such as the Peace Corps, Vista, the Job Corps, and President Clinton's most ardently pursued reform, AmeriCorps, launched September 1994 as a three-year $1.5 billion program. Center-left and center-right combined to authorize AmeriCorps. However, by October 1999 only 150,000 volunteers had been enrolled and Congress gave it a budget of $433.5 million, much less than the president requested and $15 million less than fiscal 1999. (For the rationale and detailed evaluation of such programs and their practical implementation see Moskos, 1988; Sagawa and Halperin, 1993; and Perry et al., 1999.)

The central exchange in an expanded AmeriCorps is this: young men and women agree to serve their community and nation for a fixed period in areas such as education (assist as tutors, mentors, child-care assistants, and coordinators of such services), health and human needs (help the elderly and frail to maintain their independence by home care and shopping assistance, assist in hospitals, mental institutions, church-based social services), the environment (conservation projects, park restoration), and public safety (enhance community policing, assist in rehabilitation projects). They serve at a quite low salary (the AmeriCorps started at $7500 a year plus free health care). In return, the participant receives education vouchers for college, vocational education, or to pay off a college loan (this started at $4,725 per year of work). For military service as a citizen-soldier—on average exposing oneself to greater risks—the college benefit would be substantially larger. If both military and civilian vouchers were as generous as, say, the GI bill, the participation rate would rise dramatically with the same benign effects.[9] On many projects the civilian service can be combined with formal and informal learning on the job.

Beyond the gain in raising the civic consciousness of each generation of young people, an expanded national service corps also trains and educates them for their role in a modern economy while it brings them into contact with culturally diverse groups. We do not need to look abroad for models; the American armed forces—combining social integration and meritocracy—have been enormously successful at both tasks.

- *Criminal and civil justice system reforms.* One in every 163 Americans is in jail or prison, a rate six times the average in Europe. The number locked up has tripled since 1980; something like a third of them are doing time for violating drug laws. Among scholars, hawks and doves alike now agree that incarceration of hundreds of thousands of nonviolent offenders (e.g., drug users) and violent criminals way past their prime is stupid and costly. Each 30-year-old given life imprisonment under the "three-strikes-and-you're-out" policy costs over one-half million dollars. That housing increasing portions of the population for longer and longer sentences has minimal deterrent effect is suggested by the fact that the prison boom coincided with the rise in crime rates (chap. 14). Surely at the level of imprisonment the U.S. achieved by 1990, further large increases in the prison population, like further large increases in the length of sentences, can produce only small reductions in crime rates (James Q. Wilson, 1994, pp. 38–39, explains those diminishing marginal returns).

We do not have to await major reductions in poverty and inequality or the salvation of the inner cities or the adoption of appropriate family and labor-market policies to take action to reverse this nonsense. We can divert some of the huge sums now supporting the burgeoning prison-industrial complex to prevention and rehabilitation. We can expand "drug courts" where people charged with possession or small dealing can opt to go through a supervised drug-treatment program at a fraction of the cost of trial and prison. We can mandate drug treatment for prisoners as well. We can strengthen probation and parole staffs and cut officer caseloads. Because 45% of state prisoners in the U.S. were on parole or probation when they committed their latest crime, we need tough, closely (e.g., electronically) monitored probation and parole combined with intensive supervision of offenders in community programs, including literacy and job training and the funding to back it up. (This ground is covered in chap. 14.) Some of this incarceration money could go to better training and supervision of the police and more community policing, more funding for defense attorneys, and more judges with restored discretion in sentencing. This would increase the moral authority and fairness of the criminal justice system, especially in poverty and/or minority-group neighborhoods where there is most intense distrust.

Another reform of the legal system that would not require a huge shift in the political landscape is tort reform. Chapter 12 (section on lawyers) discusses the costs of the explosion of civil litigation in all areas of American life. While this is often exaggerated, it is reasonable to reduce it. In view of the left love of class-action suits and trial lawyers' love of contingency fees, tort reform might require a Republican majority. However, safeguarding rights of the injured or aggrieved while reducing the load of lawsuits is essential. The spread of compulsory mediation and voluntary arbitration in many types of disputes has reduced the cost of dispute resolution. No-fault laws covering personal injury and accident filings have also helped.

Regarding the problem of Senate delays in confirmation of judicial nominees, to make it more orderly and less poisonous, as it was 15 years ago, would require substantial reduction in political polarization.

• *Gun control.* Opponents of stiff gun control offer one argument based on cross-national illustrations: low murder rates and minimal mayhem in Switzerland and Israel, both loaded with guns in the hands of citizens, both high in social cleavages, like the U.S. What they overlook is the multiple sources of social integration in these two exceptional cases. Most notably they are the only rich democracies with lengthy compulsory military service. The young men and women in these nations not only learn gun safety so accidental shootings are rare; they also experience the integrative effect of a national service that brings minorities and majorities together. Other democracies with low murder rates and a disarmed population also have many sources of social cohesion absent in the United States (chap. 14).

Gun control in a society as balkanized and fragmented as the U.S. is no panacea. Together with other criminal justice reforms, however, adopting the gun control advocates' agenda would decrease the likelihood that children and the mentally ill, and even a few violent criminals, would lay their hands on guns. It would reduce the chances that anyone would carry a concealed, unlicensed weapon while walking about town. Deaths from family violence and barroom brawls would also decline because kitchen knives, fists, and similar weapons are less effective than guns. Finally, gun control would reduce the deadliness of property crimes; a comparison of England and the U.S. shows that New York City has fewer thefts and burglaries than London, but much higher rates of death from these crimes because American thieves are armed (Zimring and Hawkins, 1997, pp. 44–47).

In sum: A feasible center-left agenda includes family policies, active-labor market policies, upgrading K–12 and making preschool universal, higher minimum pay and an expanded Earned Income Tax Credit, kiddiecare, a national service corps, improvements in the criminal justice system, and gun control. Because this agenda accents universal, categorical benefits and responsibilities crosscutting minorities and majorities, the affluent and the nonaffluent; because it is family- and work-oriented and reflects popular sentiments; because it substitutes simple income tests, where these are appropriate, for the divisive effects of means testing, *it constitutes an alternative to affirmative action based on descent (race, religion, ethnicity, skin color)*. That the American left has become mired in racial preferences as the road to reduced poverty and greater equality is a major barrier to the coalition politics essential for both party rebuilding and the policy shifts above. A brief statement of the egalitarian case for and against "racial" preferences might clarify the point.

"Affirmative Action" (AA) in essence is a government classification by descent and the allocation of rewards such as college admission, jobs, promotions, credit, and government contracts based on that classification. As it has been developed in the U.S. in the past 25 years it has taken the form of a complex system of racial and ethnic preferences, although the political debate often centers on blacks. The *moral* justification is that AA rectifies historical injustices done to minorities (e.g., slavery). The *practical political rationale* is that racial prejudice and discrimination are so firmly institutionalized in American society that a race-neutral policy accenting equality of opportunity will perpetuate inequality. If America really wants either social integration or real equality of opportunity, it must use racial preferences to level the playing field. The *efficiency* justification is that a full use of human resources is good for the economy. We should avoid a waste of talent by tapping the diverse talents of minority groups. The case against affirmative action as it is practiced in the U.S. is equally well known: If you start, as we have, with goals and timetables, you end up with group quotas. The result is reverse discrimination. Group preferences introduce new injustices as bad or worse than the injustices they aimed to right. The persons who lose from AA are innocent of historical wrongs. A quota for one minority is a quota against another; "underachieving" blacks displace "overachieving" Asians, Jews, and so on. Above all, minority-group preferences always assume uniform disadvantage within each group, which is patently and visibly wrong. The bloodline to which the applicant or employee belongs obscures what the group member has, in fact, suffered, endured, and triumphed over. Inevitably ordinary citizens will make the comparisons: an upper-middle-class black who sends his kids to private school vs. an ethnic white worker or a Latino from the barrio struggling to make ends meet whose kids are lucky to go to junior college; an Appalachian poor white vs. a black, both of whom worked their way through high school; a downsized white factory worker vs. a black or Latino in a secure Post Office job.

In my view, the unavoidable political consequences of all of this has become utterly clear and anyone interested in a center-left agenda should pay attention. Racial-ethnic-religious-linguistic criteria for state allocation of rewards in a society with hundreds of minority groups is subversive of the coalition politics necessary to reduce poverty and inequality and enhance family well-being. Such preferences provide abundant opportunities for racial-ethnic scapegoating, as we have seen in political campaigns that have mobilized backlash since the 1960s (chaps. 7, 8, 10, and 17). Three dimensions of minority preferences based on descent make this inevitable: the process of classification is intrusive and complex; descent awakens hideous historical memories; and such preferences can tear a society apart. Preferences by racial-ethnic descent are different from other criteria governments and industry use. As we have seen from our review of evidence on the structural and cultural integration of minority groups in chapter 1, rewards are everywhere distributed by seniority, age, gender, veterans status, student status, geography, union official status, physical or mental handicap. Academic institutions often favor nonacademic qualifications such as athletic prowess or musical talent. But nowhere do we find a voting population mobilized against the beneficiaries of these criteria. Even gender does not have much potential for virulent backlash; women are half the population and unlike members of different ethnic or racial groups they share ties of affection and family with the dominant group, men. Further, these criteria require rather clear and simple proofs, and there is generally consensus about favoring the individuals in the identified categories. Race and ethnic certifications, in contrast, are not only intrusive; they are also increasingly ambiguous and always more divisive. Walter Metzger (1980, p. 32) puts it best:

> Circular A-46 of the federal Office of Management and Budget prescribes that, to be a member of a minority group and thus entitled to minority benefits, one must have "at least one grandparent" who was "an American Indian, an Alaskan native, a person of Chinese, Japanese, Korean, Filipino, Mexican, Puerto Rican, or Cuban extraction, a person originally of Spanish culture or a person of black African descent"; all others, including the multitudinous European strains, are defined as ineligibly "white." In the wake of this kind of official pronouncement . . . come effects that give a pluralistic society cause to shudder: citizens pressed into inauthentic group commitments in order to gain access to public benefits; ethnic groups smoldering because they have been left out; government raising racial consciousness in a country where interracial tensions are never low.

With rates of intermarriage rising, even among the races, with the long-run structural and cultural integration of minorities proceeding, identity by descent becomes increasingly inventive (chap. 1).

Egalitarians should note the final flaw: the state that sorts its citizens by descent and treats them differently according to that scheme awakens hideous historical memories—memories of slavery and segregation, of tribal slaughter (blacks killing blacks), murderous ethnic struggles (Kosovo—white Christians slaughtering white Muslims—is one of a long line of them), outright genocide (the Holocaust), Kulturkampfs, apartheid, and the Nuremberg Laws, which specified that one grandfather with Jewish blood barred marriage to a pure Aryan (and ultimately proved fatal). As we have seen in chapter 1, 90 of the 120 shooting wars going on in the early 1990s were ethnic wars. State actions based on classifications by descent range from divisive to murderous.[10]

From a center-left egalitarian standpoint, racial-ethnic preferences are a major trap. They arouse justified anger among majorities of the electorate, who become easy targets for demagogues who play the race card. They foster a debilitating competition for the status of historically most victimized, setting one minority against another. They use up so much energy and passion among their defenders that there is little left for the promotion of a universalistic agenda and the coalition politics essential for its success. If we adopt substantial parts of the agenda above, divisive affirmative action would recede. Poverty and related mayhem would diminish.

How to Pay for It: Tax Balance and a Capital Budget Separate from Current Spending

The rich democracies that have successfully financed this center-left agenda have avoided heavy reliance on the most painfully visible taxes, property taxes on households and income taxes. By "painfully visible" I mean taxes taken in one or two big bites from taxpayers who believe that they will not receive direct benefits in line with contributions. (Social-security taxes are moderately visible, but most citizens connect the tax with specific future benefits.) As chapter 10 shows, these painfully visible taxes and sharp increases in them have triggered sustained tax-welfare backlash movements and parties that make it extremely difficult to pay for the social and labor-market policies demanded by large voting majorities. The Anglo-American democracies along with Denmark and Switzerland have specialized in these most unpopular taxes, with predictable political uproar.

Among the myths embraced by the American left, the most misleading is that the road to equality runs through progressive income taxes and taxes on business and property. Leaving aside the fact that evasion and avoidance (and the time and resources devoted to tax games) mean that income taxes in action are not highly progressive, ignoring the fact that corporate taxes and taxes on the rich cannot yield huge sums, the main mistake is to believe that by riveting one's attention on the tax side of the taxing/spending equation, one can achieve much of anything on the center-left agenda. In fact, the most egalitarian and civilized democracies have slightly regressive tax systems and highly progressive spending programs. They are well on the way to the tax balance that permits stable public finance with least political fuss—less than a third of total revenues in income taxes, a third in payroll taxes, almost a third in consumption taxes (e.g., VAT), approximating the German tax structure. They avoid heavy property taxes on households like the plague. They design the VAT so that it is proportional or only mildly regressive by exempting some items (e.g., home-consumed food).

If American progressives believe that taxes buy civilization; that public spending for health, education, and the general welfare produces a more humane, equitable, and just society; if they also believe that a strong government is needed to curb the power, venality, and greed of private groups, then they would be well advised to advocate a 15-year plan for incremental increases in social-security taxes on payroll and gradually phase in a European-style federal VAT (tax each business on the difference between sales to its customers and its purchases from other businesses). A responsible left would recognize that governments cannot persistently expand cash benefits and social services without increasing the tax take. It would accept the need for mass taxes and tax balance. My analysis (chap. 10) shows that nowhere since World War II has the introduction of or modest increases in payroll taxes or the VAT created tax-welfare backlash.

This talk about invisible taxes is anathema to economists and rational-choice theorists, who believe that all government actions, like all market transactions, should be transparent, and who see my argument as Machiavellian—a cynical program to manipulate citizens into painless payment of more taxes and transfers.[11] It is an attractive but wildly utopian idea that the average citizen can or should know everything about who pays what taxes (or their ultimate incidence) and, even more, what she or the larger community receives for each tax and thus the net benefit. If government were the local New England town meeting of old and the economy consisted of fully informed consumers in perfect markets, this argument for tax visibility would have more force. And its logical implication would be a shift from legislatures to the initiative and referendum for all tax legislation. Studies of the intentions of voters favoring California's Proposition 13, however, should give us pause: most of them believed that their taxes or rents would be cut, but they did not believe any government service, least of all schools, medical care, or the police, would be reduced (and the property tax at issue is the very model of a visible tax).

Whether or not we can revive a more responsible and responsive politics, it is misleading to invoke the public's "right to know" when it comes to the calculation of the net benefits of taxes. Realistically, what voters can know about the gains and costs of taxing and spending is whether the political economy close to home is performing well or poorly— their jobs unstable, their relatives and friends facing layoffs, prices going up faster than incomes, people in trouble being forced to the wall, and so on.

I have concentrated on the political costs of types of taxes and types of spending. Analysis in chapter 12 of the economic impact of consumption and payroll taxes, however, shows that they are good for economic performance as well as political legitimacy.

I have not said much about energy policy. If public finance must rely even modestly on gasoline taxes or any other energy tax, it is doomed. Although we have made some progress toward conservation and the development of alternative sources of energy, we continue to increase our dependence on automobiles and hence foreign oil. Successive presidents have tried to forge an energy policy to reduce this dependence, with little success. President Clinton's celebrated budget of 1993, passed by one vote, contained only a 4.3 cents/gallon tax increase which at this writing has barely survived. Energy taxes, especially gasoline taxes comparable to those of Europe and Japan, are the least likely source of revenue, whatever their merits as energy policy.

Finally, two shifts in budgeting process would help greatly to reduce deadlock on budgets and release political energy for investment in physical and human capital. First, simplify by making decisions less often. If Congress appropriated for two years or more, the daily routines of members would be a bit less frantic while agency executives could both plan better and spend more time delivering service rather than defending their budgets year-round. The second, bolder reform is to adopt a capital budget separate from current spending. It is another old-but-good idea, a practice of several modern democracies. In *Means to Prosperity,* a pamphlet published in 1933, Keynes urged that both government spending and the taxes to fund it should be divided into capital and income accounts. Like any prudently run corporation or household, the government would balance the budget for current consumption while borrowing on the capital account to finance investment in all the productivity-enhancing social and labor-market policies above. If the social rate of return on public investment described in this book is higher than the net cost of any borrowing used to finance it, then the ratio of debt to GNP will not rise.

CONCLUSION

Since pluralist democracies emerged there have been recurrent efforts to tame the market and make it serve human ends. Among the Anglo-American democracies these efforts at first took the form of stigmatized benefits targeted to the undeserving poor. In our time this tiny fraction of GDP and the escalating talk about the "safety net" has produced an elaborate welfare mess and a bundle of political trouble (chaps. 8 and 10). In view of the cultural ambivalence of voters in all rich democracies, their governments strike a balance between collective compassion and individual responsibility, between excessive generosity and immiseration of the poor, between long-term human capital investments and short-term fiscal constraints. All, sooner or later, make a choice between active labor-market policies, higher minimum pay, and family policies, on the one hand, and mandates for the poor to work at unstable, dead-end jobs for poverty wages, on the other. Plainly, the United States has moved to one side of this balance—to individual responsibility, immiseration, meager investment in human resources, low wages, and short-term taxing/spending constraints. Although the United States is not alone in cultivating the welfare mess, it is exceptional in the vigor of its means testing, the inadequacy and inefficiency of its programs, and the harassment of its welfare poor. This book shows unequivocally that community, equality, social cohesion, and even economic performance are undermined by a heavy accent on means testing and the related welfare mess.

Going beyond the welfare poor to the social rights enjoyed by the entire population, cross-national comparisons in chapters 12 and 5 show that there are no necessary trade-offs between the values of dignity, equality, security, family well-being, social integration, and political legitimacy protected by the welfare state, on the one hand, and good economic performance on the other. Nor is there necessarily a Phillips-curve trade-off between unemployment and inflation, a myth that has guided monetary policy in recent years (chap. 17). Nor is there any sharp contradiction between worker and union participation in workplace and community vs. capital investment and improved productivity (chaps. 1 and 2). Nor is there any long-term consistent relationship between the federal deficit and interest rates or between deficits and economic growth, although these two ideas are gospel among deficit hawks. Obviously, timely deficit spending in a recession is a contribution to quick recovery. Even the size of the national debt, like the amount of aggregate social spending, has no consistent relation to economic performance (chaps. 5 and 12). Debt used for long-term productive purposes (improving education, training, R&D, infrastructure, occupational health and safety) is a contribution to long-run economic growth and human welfare. And debt not officially used for productive purposes may or may not enhance economic performance. For instance, public pensions, which at first glance provide security and dignity and prevent poverty among the aged by placing a burden on the current economy, may in the long run be productive. As Bismarck foresaw, a generous pension at the end of a long working life would not only keep revolutionaries off the barricades but would also serve as a strong incentive for the entire adult population to keep working, even at unattractive jobs. Further, social security frees middle-aged, nonaffluent parents to invest in the productivity-enhancing college education of their children rather than shouldering the impossible burden of simultaneously supporting their aging parents. This leaves aside the fact that the recipients of pensions add to consumption-led economic growth.

These myths about deficits and debt have so permeated the verbal environment that they inspired President Clinton in his final year to boast that his budget strategy would bring us to the Promised Land, zero debt in 13 years. Central bankers, in their zeal to fight inflation at any cost, often embrace the same magic number, zero inflation. Unfortunately, empirical observation suggests that zero debt is a formula for political paralysis and the deterioration of public investment in human and physical capital, although in the short run a balanced budget helps to persuade monetarist ideologues to allow some growth and reduced unemployment. Equally unfortunate, zero inflation is achieved only on the way to a sharp recession.

We need to recognize the limits of our understanding of economic performance and resist the intellectual fads that inspire much of economic policy. An example is the distorted supply-side theory that guided the Reagan administration into adding $1.78 trillion to the national debt, a theory revived by Republican presidential candidate Bush in the 2000 election. Another is the budget deficit obsession that was nearly enshrined in the Constitution as the "Balanced Budget Amendment." Today that obsession, whose assumptions are contradicted by both cross-national comparisons and U.S. budgetary history, restrains serious congressional financing of those public policies that serve widely shared values. The center-left agenda I have outlined, much of it put into effect by most rich democracies, serves not only "The Market" but the values of work and family, dignity and equality, security and social justice, community and social integration.

NOTES

1. The Clinton plan and its close cousins comprise a heroic yearlong attempt to educate both Congress and the public on the tight interdependence of various dimensions of the uniquely fragmented and expensive health-care (non) system of the United States; touch one part and it creates problems in other parts (see chap. 16).

2. This New Deal for the big American investor is matched by IMF rescue packages which provide low-interest loans to debtor nations so they can sustain debt payments to private international creditors. This is a form of social insurance for creditors. It is financed by the taxes of IMF-member countries and by the suffering of citizens of less-developed countries who are the victims of IMF-imposed austerity measures—unemployment, cuts in social spending, chaos in their communities and families. (McCluskey, 2000.)

3. This section draws on my unpublished paper "What's Wrong With American Democracy?" presented at a workshop on American political institutions at the Institute of Governmental Studies, University of California at Berkeley, July 5–7, 1991.

4. David Mayhew (1991), in a systematic study of the frequency of investigations and legislation passed from 1946 to 1990, concludes that party-divided government does not make a difference. His analysis, however, is based on issues that rose to the top and were voted up or down; it ignores what did not happen—issues not addressed, and bills that were passed in a watered-down form inadequately addressing core issues. Further, when Mayhew makes a stab at qualitative differences, his analysis shows big differences. He identifies 19 "historic bills"—bills that fundamentally changed federal policy, altered the political landscape, and left a lasting legacy. Here unified periods produced historic laws at twice the yearly rate of divided periods (.61 to .31). Finally, other studies that give more attention to qualitative differences (e.g., new policy vs. modification of existing policy), issues that never make the agenda, and passage *rates* as opposed to absolute *number* of laws show that divided government accomplishes much less (e.g., Light, 1981/82, pp. 68, 73, 79; Peterson, 1990, pp. 210–212).

5. In 1980 a remarkable 1 in 20 workers who favored unions were fired. Freeman and Medoff (1984, pp. 232–233) estimate that this is about one case of NLRB-declared illegal discharge for every NLRB election. After President Reagan sent a signal by breaking the air traffic controllers PATCO strike in 1981, management militancy mounted. For example, the practice of breaking strikes and abandoning collective bargaining contracts by hiring permanent replacements accelerated after 1981 (LeRoy, 1995).

6. The Worker Representation and Participation Survey makes it clear that U.S. employees want more voice in the workplace (Freeman and Rogers, 1999, pp. 45, 69, 151, 156, 183). This 1994 survey was based on a national cross section of adults, age 18 or more, working in private companies or nonprofits with 25 or more employees ($N = 2,408$ plus 801 reinterviews). For all age, sex, race, occupation, education, and earnings groups, there is a large gap in the desire for participation and the current work situation. In nonunion companies 66% of nonmanagerial workers believe that management would oppose a union drive either through information campaigns or harassment and threats. Most of the total sample want cooperative joint committees with some independent standing inside their companies, and about half want a union or something very close to a union. Thirty-two percent of nonunion, nonmanagerial employees would vote union "if an election were held today." Among current union members, 90% would vote to keep their union if a new election were held today. Overall, 40% of respondents reported that they would vote union if a new election were held today. The "near-union" responses bring the figures to over 80%—adding those respondents who say that rather than a union they prefer cooperative programs including the right to elect representatives, access to company information, decisions by an outside arbitrator in cases of conflict, etc. These attitude surveys are validated by the growth of public-sector unionism. Where employees have a choice free of intimidation, where their preferences can be expressed in a legal context that constrains union-busting campaigns, they vote overwhelmingly for unions. (U.S. Commission on the Future of Worker-Management Relations, 1993, p. S.44)

7. The following is paraphrased from proposals by Ornstein et al. (1997); and the Free TV for Straight Talk Coalition (1997). Cantor, Rutkus, and Greely (1997) review the role of FCC, the history of congressional action, and legal and constitutional issues posed by these proposals; they conclude that there is no constitutional bar to their enactment.

8. The conviction that the minimum wage has negative employment effects is little affected by empirical research either by an older generation of labor economists (e.g., Richard Lester) or by more recent research. The legislated minimum wage was increased from $3.35 to $3.80 on April 1, 1990, to $4.25 in 1991, to $4.75 October 1, 1996, and to $5.15 October 1, 1997. The real legal minimum wage in 1998 dollars peaked at $7.50 in 1968 (Cashell, 1999, table 1). Some two dozen recent studies found that such moderate minimum wage hikes have had very small or no adverse effect on em-

ployment. The most systematic of these studies actually found a positive employment effect of an 80 cents increase in the minimum wage in New Jersey fast-food restaurants, comparing eastern Pennsylvania fast-food restaurants, where no increase occurred—and this during a recession (Card and Krueger, 1994, 1995). Following the last increase in the federal minimum wage and contrary to dire predictions from Congress and neoconservative think tanks, unemployment fell to its lowest level in 30 years. In each of the last two years the minimum was boosted, the job creation rate reached all-time highs (see chap. 13 for explanation of national differences). Opponents of the minimum wage say that it cuts jobs for teenagers, who do not need it anyway. In fact, in 1996, almost two-thirds of those who earned at or below the minimum wage were women; 40% of all minimum-wage employees are the sole earners in their households; and two-thirds of teenagers earning the minimum are in households with below-average incomes. With the last minimum-wage increase of 1997, even if we add the EITC and food stamps (on the shaky assumption that takeup rates are 100%) and deduct the increase in payroll taxes, a family of four with one full-time minimum-wage worker would still be $834 below the poverty line. In 1995, the year leading to the great debate about the harmful impact of an increase of 90 cents an hour for these workers, American chief executives' pay, including stock options, soared 31%, putting their median pay at $5 million (*New York Times*, March 31, 1996). For data on the trend toward wider inequality in earnings and wealth in the U.S. compared to other countries, see note 2, chapter 12.

9. A study of 1,000 men raised in poverty areas of Boston during the Great Depression found that military service was a turning point in their lives. Overseas duty, in-service schooling, and GI bill training and education at age 17 to 25 enhanced subsequent occupational achievement, job stability, and economic well-being independent of childhood differences and socioeconomic background. Benefits of the GI bill were even larger for veterans with a delinquent past. (Sampson and Laub, 1996.)

10. The "consociational democracies" that have more or less successfully managed systems of preferences based on religion, ethnicity, and language—the Netherlands, Belgium—have a combination of proportional representation, left and Catholic power, strong parties, and corporatist bargaining arrangements. Also because the warring groups are large, few, and geographically concentrated, the concept of "separate but equal" can be applied. As this book has shown, a centralized political economy can restrain minority-group conflict even if quota systems are used. The U.S. lacks any of these consensus-making structures. Canada, more like the U.S., has similar difficulty with legislated Francophone and tribal privileges, with similar political results. The case against minority-group preferences in the U.S. does not apply as forcefully to organizations whose main purpose is the representation of ethnic, religious, or racial groups as in competition for office within political parties or unions where "a balanced ticket" may be viewed as necessary for coalition building. But even in these cases, such preferences have torn democratic associations apart. An example is a union election where a black caucus squares off against an Asian or Latino caucus, while "whites," on a balanced slate built around a reform agenda, look on in dismay.

11. See my exchange with William Stubblebine, Ernest van den Haag, and George Gilder (Wilensky, 1979, pp. 7–12).

APPENDIX A
METHODS

The analysis is focused on subcategories of the 19 rich democracies—patterns of similarities and differences among nations with attention to deviant cases that suggest a reformulation of theory. Therefore I have used relatively simple methods of quantitative analysis rather than more complex methods which tend to obscure individual variation. I rely mainly on detailed cross-tabulations that permit me to examine a large number of variables at the same time and to demonstrate patterns of association while also identifying deviant or marginal cases and interaction effects.

These multivariate tables are supplemented by multiple regression techniques, which capture small differences between countries obscured by the dichotomies or trichotomies of the cross-tabulations, and permit tests of the significance and relative strength of causal variables. But because regression equations make rigorous assumptions about measurement on an interval scale as well as about linearity, I view them as complementary confirmation of the cross-tabulations. In fact, for almost all of the analysis reported here, the regression results show remarkable consistency with the tables. Together, regression analysis (including path diagrams) and the cross-tabulations give us more confidence in the conclusions than either method used alone.

With only at most 19 cases, there are not many degrees of freedom available to test the significance of effects in regression; I imposed a limit of three independent variables at a time in regression equations. When I test more than three independent variables, for example in the economic performance analysis, I examine sets of regressions using all possible combinations of the independent variables, taken three at a time. By seeing how each one behaves in combination with all others, we can uncover the variables that are both theoretically relevant and statistically robust. To provide a further check on these results, I compared them to the results of other quantitative analyses that use the same or similar variables, including others' studies using time series.

With such a small number of cases, I paid close attention to extreme cases which can distort the regression results, distinguishing between statistical outliers and deviant cases.

First, all statistical outliers are excluded from the regressions. These are cases with values more than three standard deviations away from the mean, for instance, Israel with very high inflation, or Italy with a very high strike rate. Second, other extreme or deviant cases are excluded when they distort the results. For instance, if we regress economic performance on corporate taxes, we find that they have a significant positive effect. But an examination of the scatter-plot of these two variables shows that this result is due to Japan, with high corporate taxes and excellent economic performance, while the plot shows no pattern of association for the rest of the cases. When we rerun the regression with Japan excluded, the effect of corporate taxes on economic performance is insignificant. Combining regression analysis with examination of the scatter-plots thus allows me to identify "exceptional" cases which require further exploration. For this I rely on case studies of these countries and my own interviews to highlight those historical and policy variations that explain this "exceptionalism." An example is the need to explain the very high scores of Belgium and France on family policy when theory says they should have only medium scores (see chap. 7, table 7.1).

For some purposes I have also used path diagrams, an adaptation of multiple regression analysis to causal models. For this analysis, I begin with a "saturated model," where each dependent variable is regressed on all independent or intervening variables which are causally prior to it (to its left in the path diagram). Then I eliminate those paths that are insignificant and theoretically uninteresting and rerun the analysis for the "unsaturated model." In a few cases (e.g., figure 14.2) insignificant paths from stage one were retained in stage two because of their special theoretical importance. Such exceptions are indicated by dashed lines and their p values are reported. The path coefficients are the estimated standardized regression coefficients in the appropriate equations. The residual effects (the downward arrows to all variables that are used as dependent variables in estimating the model) represent all other sources of variation in those variables which are not explicitly identified in the model. The coefficients on these arrows are the square roots of the residual variances, that is, the coefficient on each of these arrows = the square root of (1 minus R-squared), where R-squared is the unadjusted explained variance. Since the path analysis is essentially a form of regression analysis, I used the same procedures as discussed above for the regression analysis. For a good introduction to path analysis, see Otis Dudley Duncan, *Introduction to Structural Equation Models* (New York: Academic Press, 1975).

For the analysis of economic performance, I avoided a pooled time-series analysis, increasingly common in sociology and political science. This form of analysis increases the sample size by counting each combination of country and year as a case, but it does so at the cost of requiring a larger number of restrictive assumptions about the distributions of the variables and the forms of their relationships. To incorporate the variability of individual cases and the changes in the effects of some causal variables over time, a large number of dummy variables and interaction effects must be introduced. The large number of coefficients which must be estimated makes presentation of the results cumbersome. Furthermore, the coefficients of the dummy variables are difficult to interpret, as they may incorporate a number of different sources of variation between countries or time periods. When the independent variables are highly autocorrelated (correlated with themselves over time), as some of my variables are, the assumption of uncorrelated error terms is usually violated and the estimates of the standard errors may be biased. Assumptions about fixed vs. random effects and homoscedasticity vs. heteroscedasticity create still more complications. There are methods to test for and correct for some of these problems, but they make the results even more cumbersome to report and more difficult to interpret. For a good introduction to this method, which highlights these and other problems, see Lois W. Sayrs, *Pooled Time Series Analysis,* Sage University Paper series on Quantitative Applications in the Social Sciences No. 07–070 (Beverly Hills: Sage, 1989). In short, the use of this method takes the focus away from the substantive analysis of types of political economy and the individual cases and puts it on the technical details of the statistical method.

CONCEPTS AND MEASURES
OF LEFT AND
CATHOLIC PARTY POWER

Before asserting that left party power is a determinant of any outcome, one must develop clear concepts and sensitive measures of party power. No quantitative study to date is persuasive on this point. The most severe limitations include the measurement of party power in terms of popular vote (Peters, 1974) or representation in the legislature (Hewitt, 1977; Jackman, 1975). Because of vast national variations in political structure and electoral procedures, size of vote is a poor guide to power. Similarly, the use of legislative representation leads to an overestimate of left party power in Japan, Switzerland, and France (Hewitt, 1977, p. 459). In my view, considering the long-term ascendancy of the executive branch of government and the differences between presidential and parliamentary systems, the best single measure of party power is instead representation in the executive branch of government. Although Hibbs (1977, p. 1473) also applies this criterion, he fails to distinguish among degrees of strength, relying instead on "percentage of years Socialist-Labor parties in executive (1945–69)," thereby exaggerating the power of left parties in France and Italy.[1] In addition, Hibbs, Hewitt, and Jackman restrict their studies to socialist parties, thereby obscuring the essential similarities between them and the Democratic Party in the United States during the period studied—a likeness which they themselves recognize. Finally, all three authors ignore the Communist party, which for purposes of understanding macroeconomic domestic policy can be misleading, although maybe necessary for analysis of positions on participatory democracy and essential for positions on foreign policy and civil liberties.

To remedy these shortcomings and clarify this complex debate, we have developed a measure of left party power and, because of its obvious and enduring importance, a comparable measure of Catholic party power.

Details on measures and sources are in Wilensky (1981c). They are summarized below.

---

1. In his discussion, Hibbs does note that the representation of French and Italian socialists has been marginal, but in his code both score about one-third, much higher than West Germany (19%) and much closer to the United Kingdom (about 48%) than their executive power warrants.

Left Party Dominance. Defined in text. For 8 of our 19 nations and for the Weimar period of Germany we have used the classification scheme employed by De Swaan, *Coalition Theories and Cabinet Formations* (1973), with minor changes. For the other 11 we used monographic literature and sourcebooks (cited in Wilensky, 1981c, pp. 380–382).

The classification of center parties as left or nonleft is ambiguous in some cases, most notably those of the French Radicals and many Catholic parties. Because these parties are divided into highly diverse factions, some with a clearly leftist orientation, and because these factions shift in influence, it could be argued that we should ask which branches of which party are in the government at a given time. Thus, the Radicals in the French Cartel des Gauches in the early 1920s and the Belgian Social Christians in coalition with the Socialists after World War II could conceivably be classified as left. (For the Belgian case, see Henig, 1969, p. 83.) However, to classify the ideology of each faction each year is to incur high costs for small gains. Anyway, the research focus is left *party* power. Therefore, we coded center parties as nonleft, ignoring the leftist faction within them.

Amount of Left Power. From low to high we scored as follows:

0. A score of "0" is given for each year in which left parties did not meet the minimum criterion for left party power (see "1" below).

1. A score of "1" is assigned for each year that the left party has substantial, but not major or dominant power in the government.

2. A score of "2" is assigned for each year that a left party is the major party in government without being dominant.

3. A score of "3" is given to a left party for each year that it is either the sole member of a majority government or the dominant partner in a coalition government.

Figure 2B.1 summarizes this coding scheme.

Presidential Systems: For Finland, France, and the United States we modified our scoring system. In Finland, a left party receives a score of 1 for each year it holds the presidency. Then it receives an additional 1 point per year for being a minor partner in a coalition (see criterion 1 above); or an additional 2 points per year for being either the major or dominant partner in the coalition (see criteria 2 and 3 above). This makes for a possible score of 3 per year, as in parliamentary systems. For the United States we assign a score of 2 for each year the Democrats occupied the presidency and a score of 1 for each year the Democrats controlled both houses of Congress. For France, in the years prior to the Fifth Republic we use the normal scoring for nonpresidential systems; for Fifth Republic France, when the power of the presidency was enhanced, we would assign 2 points for every year that a left party holds the presidency and left parties would receive 1 point for each

Figure 2B.1   Coding scheme for Left and Catholic party dominance

Proportion of total seats in assembly held by the government									
Up to 1/2 (minority government)					*1/2 or more (majority government)*				
Proportion of government's seats in legislature occupied by Left party★					Proportion of government's seats in legislature occupied by Left party★				
0 up to 1/3	1/3 up to 1/2	1/2 up to 2/3		2/3–1	0 up to 1/3	1/3 up to 1/2		1/2 up to 2/3	2/3–1
No Left★ PM 0	Left PM 1	1	No Left PM 1	Left PM 2	2	No Left★ PM 0	Left PM 1	No Left PM 1	Left PM 2	2	3

★Substituting Catholic for Left reproduces the coding scheme for Catholic party dominance.

year they collectively hold a majority of seats in the legislature—a guide only to the future because neither left nor Catholic parties in fact received any score since de Gaulle took over in 1958 until 1976 when our code ends. Then there were intermittent periods of left power—Mitterand-Mauroy-Fabius, 1981–86; Mitterand-Rocard-Cresson-Bérégovoy, 1988–93; Jospin, 1997–now.

Thus, in both parliamentary and presidential systems there is a possible score of 3 points per year for left party power. Whenever possible, we dated the exact month of changes in government; in those few cases where we could not locate the precise date of cabinet change, we used the date of election, which in parliamentary systems usually corresponds closely to changes in government. To obtain a final score, we add up the yearly scores over the whole time period under consideration. (But to analyze the relative effects of amount of power, number of years in office, and frequency of interruptions, we keep these separate.)

Duration of Left Power. Number of months in office, excluding insignificant periods mentioned in Wilensky (1981c).

Number of Left Interruptions. Number of times a party with a power score of 1, 2, or 3 lost office for six months or more.

Measures of Catholic Party Power: Amount, Duration, and Number of Interruptions. We included among Catholic parties all those that fall under the definition given in the text. The scoring of Catholic party power was based on the same criteria as those used for the left parties.

Left Party Dominance, 1919–76. We then created an index for the whole period and one for the post–World War II period combining left party power and number of interruptions in order to single out those left parties that exercised "sufficient" power with few interruptions. For the period since 1919, sufficient power meant a score of 30 (West Germany) and above; low interruptions meant 2 or fewer. For the post–World War II period, sufficient power was defined as 21 (Australia) and above; low interruptions meant 1 or 0. For both periods, countries with sufficient power and low interruptions received a score of 1; all other countries received a score of 0. For the period since 1919, Sweden, New Zealand, Norway, the Netherlands, Israel, and Austria received a score of 1. For the post–World War II period, Sweden, West Germany, Israel, and Austria received scores of 1.

Catholic Party Dominance, 1919–76. We did not create a Catholic party dominance variable (that would combine amount of power and number of interruptions) for either the entire period or the post–World War II period because Catholic parties had significant power only in five countries, and their power was seldom interrupted. In place of quantitative analysis based on such a variable we have relied upon case-by-case examination.

Distribution of Interruptions to Party Power.

Left 1919–76. Belgium: 6; Denmark, West Germany, Finland, United Kingdom: 4.; USA, Australia, France: 3; Sweden, New Zealand, Norway, Netherlands: 2; Austria: 1; Switzerland, Canada, Israel, Italy, Japan, Ireland: 0.

Left 1946–76: Belgium, 4; Denmark, Finland: 3; USA, Australia, New Zealand, France, Norway, United Kingdom, Netherlands: 2; Austria: 1; Sweden, Switzerland, Canada, West Germany, Israel, Italy, Japan, Ireland: 0.

Catholic 1919–76: West Germany, Belgium: 2; France, Austria, Italy: 1.

Catholic 1946–76: Belgium: 2; West Germany, France, Austria: 1; Italy: 0.

All of the left and Catholic party variables together numbered 32. Because we would not use all of these in this analysis, we reduced them to 8 according to two criteria. First, if 2 variables were highly correlated we chose the one that made most theoretical sense. For example, power and duration for both left and Catholic parties were highly correlated. For left parties for the whole period, the correlation was .95; for Catholic parties, .98. In this case, we used the measure of amount of power, since it incorporated much more information. Second, we eliminated variables that were not conceptually independent of other variables. For example, interruptions of Catholic party rule is correlated .78 with Catholic party power because 13 countries never had significant Catholic party participation in government. Thus, their rule could not be interrupted—but this could hardly be considered an indicator of Catholic party dominance.

The correlations of several of these measures for each of two time periods appear in Wilensky 1981c in tables 10.5 – 10.8.

SOCIAL SPENDING, GNP, TAX EXPENDITURES, AND HOUSING EXPENDITURES

MEASURES OF AGGREGATE SOCIAL SPENDING

Students of the welfare state spend much time arguing about the comparability of the aggregate spending figures available. As note 5 of chapter 5 indicates, my conclusion from comparing alternative measures of social spending in the pre-1975 period (Wilensky, 1975, pp. 125–128), still stands: four different measures rooted in slightly different definitions—those by the International Labour Organization (ILO), by the Luxembourg Income Study (LIS), by the OECD data bank (which adds education expenditures), and by Flora et al., 1983 (which adds education and housing expenditures)—are highly correlated and yield a very similar country rank order (see Alestalo and Uusitalo, 1992, pp. 40–41). I use ILO data for 1950 to 1980 and the LIS for 1986; ILO data after 1980 are less reliable. "Welfare effort" is measured by social spending as a percentage of GNP or GDP. Spending per capita is best seen as a system output measure: cash and services delivered to each person.

Table 5C.1 illustrates the similarity in rank order of three of these measures of welfare effort. For instance for 1980, comparing my measure (SS/GNP at factor cost, column 1) and OECD's (SS/GDP, column 2), we see that of 18 countries, 14 have identical rank or only a one-rank difference, 3 have a two-rank difference. Comparing ours with LIS (SS/GDP, column 3), we see that of 18, 15 have identical or a one-rank difference. Three have a two-rank difference in 1980.

Each of these measures gives much the same results when we consider *trends* in spending. For instance, table 5C.1 compares welfare-state effort measured by social spending as a percentage of factor-cost GNP (based on ILO data supplemented by national sources used in my analysis) with social spending as a percentage of GDP at market prices (based on the LIS Aggregate Statistics file). The picture that emerges from either measure is the same.

GROSS NATIONAL PRODUCT AT FACTOR COST

This measure, rather than the more familiar GNP (or GDP) at market prices, is used as the denominator of all ratios requiring GNP in order to obtain a measure unbiased by the

TABLE 5C.1 Comparing levels and trends in social spending/GNP at factor cost and social spending/GDP 1950–86, in percent, nineteen rich democracies

	1950	1966		1971		1980			1986
	SS/GNP(f.c.)[a]	SS/GNP(f.c.)	SS/GDP[b]	SS/GNP(f.c.)	SS/GDP	SS/GNP(f.c.)	SS/GDP(OECD)[c]	SS/GDP	SS/GDP
W. Germany	17.0 (1)	19.6 (2)	17.2 (2)	19.7 (7)	17.5 (5)	27.0 (6)	26.6 (6)	24.0 (6)	23.4 (8)
Austria	14.3 (2)	20.8 (1)	18.1 (1)	22.3 (3)	18.7 (3)	26.3 (7)	26.0 (7)	22.5 (7)	25.2 (7)
France	13.2 (3)	18.3 (5)	15.9 (6)	17.5 (9)	15.3 (9)	30.4 (4)	30.9 (5)	26.3 (4)	28.5 (4)
Belgium	12.8 (4)	18.6 (3)	16.5 (5)	20.6 (4)	18.5 (4)	29.8 (5)	33.9 (2)	25.7 (5)	25.9 (6)
United Kingdom	10.9 (5)	13.3 (9)	12.4 (8)	14.4 (12)	13.9 (10)	17.3 (12)	20.0 (13)	18.0 (12)	20.1 (11)
New Zealand	10.4 (6)	12.0 (12)	11.5 (10)	10.5 (16)	10.6 (14)	16.1 (13)	22.4 (12)	17.7 (13)	18.0 (12)
Sweden	10.0 (7)	16.5 (7)	14.8 (7)	23.8 (1)	20.2 (1)	33.1 (1)	33.2 (3)	31.9 (1)	31.3 (1)
Italy	9.6 (8)	17.5 (6)	17.0 (3)	20.5 (5)	16.0 (8)	19.6 (11)	23.7 (10)	18.8 (10)	n.a.
Netherlands	9.1 (9)	18.3 (5)	16.9 (4)	23.6 (2)	20.0 (2)	31.3 (3)	31.8 (4)	28.3 (2)	28.6 (3)
Denmark	8.6 (10)	13.9 (8)	12.0 (9)	20.2 (6)	16.7 (7)	32.8 (2)	35.1 (1)	26.9 (3)	26.1 (5)
Ireland	8.0 (11)	11.2 (13)	10.1 (14)	12.7 (13)	11.0 (13)	23.3 (9)	23.8 (9)	20.1 (9)	23.2 (9)
Finland	7.7 (12)	13.1 (10)	11.3 (11)	16.3 (10)	13.6 (11)	21.1 (10)	22.9 (11)	18.0 (12)	22.8 (10)
Canada	6.8 (13)	9.4 (15)	10.4 (13)	15.8 (11)	12.0 (12)	15.1 (16)	19.5 (14)	13.9 (14)	15.2 (13)
Norway	6.7 (14)	12.6 (11)	11.2 (12)	19.6 (8)	16.7 (7)	23.3 (9)	24.2 (8)	20.2 (8)	29.8 (2)
Switzerland	6.3 (15)	9.5 (14)	8.8 (15)	11.4 (15)	10.3 (16)	16.0 (14)	19.1 (15)	13.7 (15)	14.7 (14)
Israel	5.6 (16)	6.8 (18)	n.a.	7.9 (18)	n.a.	7.0 (19)	n.a.	n.a.	n.a.
Australia	5.1 (17)	9.2 (16)	8.0 (16)	9.3 (17)	7.8 (17)	15.7 (15)	17.3 (17)	11.8 (17)	9.7 (17)
United States	4.6 (18)	7.9 (17)	7.2 (17)	11.7 (14)	10.3 (16)	14.6 (17)	18.0 (16)	12.3 (16)	12.5 (15)
Japan	3.8 (19)	5.1 (19)	5.5 (18)	5.5 (19)	5.8 (18)	11.0 (18)	16.1 (18)	11.2 (18)	12.2 (16)

[a]Sources for 1950–80: International Labour Office, *The Cost of Social Security* (Geneva, 1972, 1976, 1985). For definitions and discussion of comparability with EEC data and other sources, see Wilensky (1975, pp. 125–28).

[b]Source for 1966–86; Luxembourg Income Study (LIS) Aggregate Statistics File. LIS data for Italy for 1986 are excluded because they do not count expenditures for public employees benefits, the national health service, public assistance, and benefits for war victims.

[c]Source: European Centre for Social Welfare Policy and Research (1993, p. 91) based on OECD Social Data Bank. Includes education expenditures.

differing weights of indirect taxes in the tax systems of the countries studied and to make East-West comparisons in the larger study more valid (see Wilensky, 1975, pp. 131–132). Moreover, if we wish to predict welfare effort (e.g., SS/GNP) or output from reliance on indirect taxes and we use market price GNP, we introduce an element of tautology. Put in statistical terms, if higher indirect taxes lead to an inflation of market prices, then when we use reliance on indirect taxes to predict welfare effort (dividing social-security spending by a market price GNP which itself may include a share of indirect taxes), we introduce a spurious negative correlation between indirect taxes and the dependent variable. However, if indirect taxes do not inflate market prices, then the use of GNP at factor cost will produce a spurious positive correlation between indirect taxes and the dependent variable. Given the prevailing uncertainty regarding the inflationary impact of indirect taxes, we are unsure of the biases that may result from the treatment of indirect taxes in the measure of GNP. To protect against any biases that may result from our choice to measure GNP at factor cost, for this analysis of 19 rich democracies we ran all tables and all regressions containing GNP with both market-price GNP and factor-cost GNP where both were available. The correlation of the two measures for the 19 countries for 1971 is 0.996. Because substitution of market-price GNP or even GDP made only infinitesimal differences in all analysis, we report results in a few tables in chapters 5, 10, and 12 using only GNP at factor cost. However important theoretically, arguments about the use of either measure are empirically irrelevant. In most of the analysis we use GDP as specified.

TAX EXPENDITURES

In my analysis of social spending, I have not taken account of "tax expenditures"—revenues foregone because of tax breaks in the form of exemptions, allowances, credits, rate relief, and tax deferrals. No comparable data are available for our 19 countries. The OECD's recent study of this matter strongly advises against using the data for cross-national comparison and even cautions against aggregating various tax breaks within one country (OECD, 1996d). Problems include national variations in the treatment of the personal income tax unit and income tax allowances for marriage and children; different definitions and measures of "tax expenditures"; different benchmarks against which tax expenditures for pensions or depreciation allowances are measured; and substantial, unknown interactions between different tax breaks. If we had comparable data, my guess is that the rank order of welfare effort in table 5.1 would change very little.

HOUSING EXPENDITURES

Housing expenditures—housing allowances, rent rebates, producer subsidies, tax concessions (e.g., mortgage interest-rate deductions) and other subsidies—belong in any definition of aggregate welfare-state expenditures, but the data are thin. For discussion of the measurement problems, see Wilensky, 1975, pp. 8–9, where I point to indicators that suggest that government support of housing is moderately correlated with welfare effort and output. Since then several useful cross-national studies provide estimates we can use to further explore this relationship (e.g., Howenstine, 1986; McGuire, 1981; Headey, 1978; Heidenheimer, Heclo, and Adams, 1990, chap. 4). Table 5C.2 aligns an estimate in U.S. dollars of

TABLE 5C.2 Total housing subsidies circa 1980–81 compared to 1980 aggregate social spending for twelve rich democracies

	Housing subsidies per capita in US $	Housing subsidies as % GNP	Soc. spending per capita in US $[a]	Soc. spending as % GNP[a]
Sweden	586 H+	4.5 H+	4759 H+	33.1 H
Netherlands	199 H	2.4 HM	3386 H	31.3 H
Denmark	190 H	2.2 HM	3482 H	32.8 H
W. Germany	179 MH	1.9 M	3186 H	27.0 MH
United States	178 MH	1.5 M	1568 ML	14.6 L
Finland	165 M	1.8 M	1943 M	21.1 M
France	136 ML	1.6 M	3245 H	30.4 H
United Kingdom	130 ML	2.6 HM	1404 ML	17.3 L
Australia	66 L	0.7 L	1370 ML	15.7 L
Canada	48 L	0.4 L	1432 ML	15.1 L
Austria	44 L	0.7 L	2309 HM	26.3 MH
Belgium	43 L	0.4 L	3204 H	29.8 H

*Housing allowances, rent rebates, producer subsidies, tax concessions, and other subsidies. Total calculated from Howenstine, E. Jay, (1986) *Housing Vouchers: A Comparative International Analysis* (New Brunswick, NJ: Center for Urban Policy Research), table 11, pp. 110–111. Exchange rates from OECD, *Historical Statistics,* various years; population from UN, *Demographic Yearbook,* various years; GNP at factor cost calculated from OECD, *National Accounts Statistics,* various years. Housing data are for various years centered on 1981; exchange rates, population and GNP at factor cost used in calculating the figures in this table are for the appropriate year or period. Social spending from ILO, *The Cost of Social Security,* 1985. See footnotes to table 5C.1.

[a]High, medium, and low are ranked relative to all 19 countries, not the 12 countries here.

total housing subsidies per capita (circa 1980–81) and housing subsidies as a percentage of GNP and social spending per capita and as GNP share for the 12 countries Howenstine covers.

The correlation between per capita housing expenditures and per capita social expenditures is quite strong ($r = .68, p < .05$); the correlation between housing effort and welfare effort is weaker but positive ($r = .43, p = .16$). In housing subsidies per capita, Sweden by any measure is in a class by itself. Netherlands and Denmark are far above average; West Germany and the United States are above average; Finland is average; France and United Kingdom are below average, while Australia, Canada, Austria, and Belgium are far below average. Comparing the alignment between social spending and housing spending and subsidies per capita, only 1 country of the 12 is very far apart (Belgium ranks high on social spending and low on housing), while 3 evidence substantial disjunction: France is high in social spending, medium to medium-low in housing; Austria is medium in social spending, low in housing; United States is low in social spending, medium-high in housing. The rankings of the other 8 are quite close, confirming that housing effort and output go together with social security as a spending package. Because government expenditures for housing are so much smaller than the cost of core programs of the welfare state, if we had housing data on all 19 countries and added them to the rest of social spending, the rank order of welfare effort and output would not be changed. At most, the U.S. dollar figure for housing per capita is about one-tenth the figure for all other social spending per capita (for Sweden, 12.3%, United States, 11.4%, United Kingdom, 9.3%); typically it is much below that.

Examination of the rank order of owner-occupancy rates based on data from the LIS for 12 of our 19 rich democracies suggests that home ownership is unrelated to our types of political economy, or to aggregate social spending, or even to housing subsidies per capita (rent subsidies, for instance, would not boost home ownership). The only hint of any relationship is that three countries with the very highest owner-occupancy rates—Australia, Finland, and Israel with rates of 3 in 4 households to 9 in 10 households—all have below-average social spending/GNP. But there is no systematic pattern.

SECTOR SPENDING CORRELATIONS

TABLE 6D.I Correlations between sector spending variables, as a percentage of GNP, 1966, 1971, 1974, and 1980

	FAMILY	PENSION	HEALTH	WORK INJ	WAR VIC	PUB AS	EDUC	HI ED	SS/GNP
FAMILY ALLOWANCE	1.0								
PENSIONS	.59	1.0							
	.68								
	.68								
	.74								
HEALTH	.31	.32	1.0						
	.33	.36							
	.38	.50							
	.20	.34							
WORK INJURY	.68	.47	−.08	1.0					
	.57	.52	−.28						
	.60	.53	−.14						
	.70	.51	−.32						
WAR VICTIMS	.14	.18	−.37	.54	1.0				
	.27	.12	−.28	.39					
	.30	.20	−.25	.48					
	.02	−.05	−.53	.47					
PUBLIC ASSISTANCE	−.08	−.17	−.09	.12	−.13	1.0			
	−.23	−.31	−.12	.05	−.03				
	−.20	−.19	−.26	.09	−.03				
	−.11	−.28	−.39	−.06	−.04				
EDUCATION	−.08	−.16	.04	−.26	−.44	.53	1.0		
	−.05	−.05	.62	−.48	−.40	.30			
	−.11	−.12	.34	−.41	−.42	.25			
	.10	.01	.37	.04	−.12	−.07			
HIGHER EDUCATION	−.31	−.27	−.23	−.35	−.22	.50	.60	1.0	
	−.22	−.31	.18	−.42	−.24	.48	.69		
	−.17	−.33	−.09	−.28	−.16	.47	.74		
	−.17	−.36	−.20	−.07	.11	.56	.48		
SS/GNP	.75	.93	.52	.52	.19	−.20	−.14	−.34	1.0
	.68	.90	.68	.32	−.01	−.20	.30	−.10	
	.70	.90	.76	.35	.09	−.18	.18	−.18	
	.66	.88	.61	.31	−.26	−.21	.29	−.22	

Sources: ILO, *The Cost of Social Security* (Geneva, 1972, 1976, and 1977); education expenditures from *Educational Statistics in OECD Countries* (Paris, 1981), *Israeli Statistical Yearbook 1974*, and *UNESCO Statistical Yearbooks* 1977, 1978–79, and 1986.

TABLE 6D.2 Correlations between sector spending variables in dollars per capita, 1966, 1971, 1974, and 1980

	FAMILY	PENSION	HEALTH	WORK INJ	PUB AS	EDUC	HI ED	SS/CAP
FAMILY ALLOWANCE	1.0							
PENSIONS	.40	1.0						
	.59							
	.67							
	.80							
HEALTH	.45	.41	1.0					
	.43	.54						
	.51	.63						
	.50	.72						
WORK INJURY	.56	.37	.02	1.0				
	.35	.55	−.06					
	.54	.64	.02					
	.78	.60	.22					
PUBLIC ASSISTANCE	−.18	.07	−.11	.36	1.0			
	−.22	.13	.12	.38				
	−.14	.18	−.13	.35				
	−.03	−.15	−.20	.21				
EDUCATION	.19	.50	.62	.19	.42	1.0		
	.25	.56	.84	.05	.37			
	.33	.59	.79	.20	.18			
	.65	.79	.79	.65	.01			
HIGHER EDUCATION	−.17	.22	.29	.04	.47	.54	1.0	
	−.05	.19	.39	.05	.32	.48		
	.04	.29	.20	.30	.22	.47		
	.44	.36	.31	.55	.39	.62		
SS/CAP	.66	.83	.74	.44	.02	.63	.21	1.0
	.59	.85	.83	.31	.20	.83	.28	
	.74	.87	.86	.38	.05	.76	.18	
	.74	.90	.88	.49	−.06	.88	.40	

See table 6D.1 for sources.

FAMILY POLICY

TABLE 7E.1   Comparison of regression coefficients for family-policy index and its components[†]

Dependent Variables	Independent Variables		
	Corporatism	Female LF Part.	% of Pop. 65+
Family Policy Index	.51**	.38**	.43**
Parental Leave Policies	.37*	.29	.36
Child Care Policies	.55**	.31*	.31*
Flex. Retirement Policies	.42**	.41**	.45**

[†]Eighteen countries (Israel missing).
* $p < .10$.
*$p < .05$.
**$p < .01$.

ESTIMATING RELIANCE
ON MEANS TESTING

In cross-national studies of sector spending the least comparable of categories is what is called "public assistance" or "welfare" in the USA, "social assistance" in the UK or "social help" in Germany. After comparing ILO, OECD, and EEC data and discussing their methods of classification with some of the collectors of the data in Geneva, Paris, and Brussels in the mid-1970s and with students of the welfare state since, I decided to supplement ILO data with national statistical abstracts and monographic literature, checked by interviews.

Because our purpose was to analyze the structural and ideological roots of variation in public assistance spending and to uncover its political and economic effects, we tried to fit data to a "narrow" definition of public assistance: benefits targeted to what is widely viewed as the "undeserving poor"—a safety net of last resort mainly for the nonworking poor. Three criteria capture the idea: (1) noncategorical benefits are targeted to the poor via a stiff income and/or assets test; (2) applied by welfare administrators with substantial discretion; (3) with a high probability of stigma. Ideally we would have complete data for 19 countries on all programs where recipients must make heroic demonstrations of need, where administrators can say yes or no within broad guidelines, and where public opinion is hostile to the recipients.

A broad definition, in contrast, would include all income-tested benefits. In some countries (e.g., Scandinavian countries, Italy) many targeted benefits are triggered by simple declarations of income with little or no stigma; they also have clear eligibility rules that limit the discretionary power of caseworkers, or, if the rules are loose, they are administered with a presumption of eligibility and earned right with easy application and easy appeal (e.g., veterans' benefits in all countries). Such programs are not comparable to AFDC in the U.S.—a highly visible, discretionary, heavily stigmatized program.

To assess *targeting* to the poor, we looked for means tests or income tests that were tough and not simple. As a clue to *discretionary power* we eliminated most categorical benefits even though these might be targeted to the pretransfer poor (e.g., benefits for veterans, the unemployed, job trainees; universal, categorical pensions for the aged; home help services for the aged, disabled, and parents of young children; income-tested supplements for large or low-income families that are part of family allowance schemes. To infer *stigma* we looked for programs where the cutoff points are drawn low and where a significant percentage of those below the line do not apply for benefits; we assume that low takeup rates by people in need are a sign of stigma. We also examined public opinion data.

The rationale for specific inclusions and exclusions follows, along with compromises made necessary both by limitations of the data and the ambiguity of real life. Limitations of the data include insufficient evidence on eligibility rules and noncomparable methods of aggregation. Real life ambiguities include cross-national variations in styles of dealing with different categories of needy persons—for example, whether the disabled receive invalidity pensions or public assistance, whether the aged or unemployed must satisfy a means test to receive a pension or unemployment benefits, whether institutional care expenditures are part of a universal health system or selective public assistance.

We exclude unemployment insurance benefits because (1) they are highly sensitive to the business cycle and are for the most part determined by the country's economic performance, and (2) they are usually tied to earnings and are not as stigmatized as public assistance. But we include means-tested supplements that come into play when insurance is exhausted, sometimes labeled "unemployment assistance." For two of the countries in our sample (West Germany, Ireland) we could obtain figures for unemployment assistance. In other countries we could not obtain separate figures for unemployment assistance: the long-term unemployed either continue to receive benefits through the unemployment insurance scheme or else must fall back on general public assistance for needy persons. Australia and New Zealand present a special problem: for the periods in question (1966–74 and 1980) all unemployment benefits were means tested. We exclude these programs in Australia because by 1974, a clear majority of the unemployed received this benefit. We could not estimate the takeup rate for New Zealand, but the total expenditure figure for unemployment is low and its exclusion does not change the rank order for public assistance spending as a percentage of GNP.

We include expenditures for job training for public assistance recipients but exclude other manpower programs because it is impossible to consistently distinguish active policies that aid displaced or obsolescent workers from programs for hard-core "unemployables" such as the Job Corps in the United States. Veterans' benefits are also excluded because even though veterans may be overrepresented among the poor, they are everywhere viewed as deserving. When possible, housing assistance measures are excluded because we cannot obtain reliable data on these expenditures. Some expenditures for rent subsidies are included for the UK because they are part of the supplementary benefits scheme; some housing construction costs are included for Switzerland because we are unable to disaggregate these expenditures from the total public assistance expenditure figure.

Benefits for the disabled and expenditures for institutional care are included where they are tied to public assistance status. Benefits for the disabled are sometimes conditional upon a strict means test (Ireland) or sometimes require potential recipients to meet criteria similar or identical to those for other public assistance recipients (Canada, USA, UK, Israel). Similarly, we include public assistance measures for the disabled that provide a last resort for persons not eligible for other forms of social insurance (West Germany, Belgium, France) or provide special benefits (e.g., the hostel program for the handicapped in the Netherlands is funded through the National Assistance Act). Where the disabled receive benefits from public assistance programs they may share the stigma attached to such programs. Finally, some public expenditures for institutional care are included by Canada, Australia, Japan, Austria, West Germany, Italy, and the United States in their definition of public assistance expenditure.

Programs for the aged present special classification problems. On one hand, these benefits everywhere receive popular support (see text). On the other hand, in 12 of our 19 countries some benefits for the aged are conditional upon a means test. Therefore we include benefits for the aged poor where they are meshed with other types of aid to needy persons: such means-tested schemes make no administrative distinction between the aged poor and poor, and there is some evidence that public perception reflects administrative practice. The text elaborates and updates evidence on stigma. We exclude most pension supplement programs because these data are for the most part not separable from other forms of pensions benefits and in several countries they are triggered by a simple declaration of income (Denmark, Sweden, Norway, Finland, Italy). In Belgium and Switzerland, however, some supplementary benefits for the aged are included because they are part of public assistance schemes. This inclusion has little effect: the expenditures for special supplements are negligible as a percentage of total public assistance spending. Australia, New Zealand, and Ireland are anomalous cases: in Australia and New Zealand until 1974 all pension benefits were income tested. In Ireland in 1971, more than 80% of pensioners receive benefits from the noncontributory pension scheme, a "means-tested" program. We have excluded pension expenditures in these three countries because they are received by a majority of the eligible population and are therefore unlikely to be heavily stigmatized.

National statistical abstracts have been consulted for all 19 countries. Where data from the national sources tallied closely with ILO data we used ILO data because the ILO has made efforts to achieve cross-national comparability through the use of its standardized reporting system and because ILO data are readily accessible (U.S., Sweden, Switzerland, Australia, New Zealand,[1] Finland, the Netherlands, Israel, and Ireland). For Canada and the UK, we were unable to confirm the total expenditure figure but could confirm significant components of it (central government expenditures for public assistance in the UK, the Canadian Assistance Plan in Canada). For West Germany, Italy, Austria,[2] Denmark, and Japan we have taken the figures from the national statistical abstracts because of significant discrepancies between the figures from these sources and those from the ILO—interviews and readings suggest that the statistical abstracts were better for our purposes than the ILO. The Statistical Abstracts of Norway, Belgium, and France do not use classification methods similar to those of the ILO: for Norway, ILO figures were close to figures from the Nordic Union, *Social Tryghett i de Nordiske Lande 1974–5,* supplied by Gosta Esping-Andersen. For France we have relied on Pierre Laroque's work, *Social Institutions of France.* The 1971 French figure is an estimate but it tallies closely with the public assistance figures reported by INSEE in *Les Comtes de la Protection Sociale: Methodes et Series 1959–78,* Series

1. We have excluded New Zealand from the data series for 1980 because its method for reporting public assistance figures for 1980 is not comparable to earlier years.

2. The 1980 Austrian public assistance figure is from the ILO because 1980 data were not available from the national statistical abstract. The 1979 figures from these two sources were quite close (approximately 2% difference), so we have used 1980 ILO data.

C, No. 82, December 1978. Additional information on public assistance spending in Belgium was provided by Jan Vranken (University of Antwerp); in Israel by Abraham Doron (Hebrew University) and Mrs. Nira Shamai (Deputy Director General for Research and Planning, National Insurance Institute, Israel); for Finland by Hannu Uusitalo (Helsinki School of Economics); and for Italy by Pierpaolo Donati (University of Bologna). For the Scandinavian countries we compared 1974 ILO data with the Nordic Union source (above); the figures for the appropriate subcategories (the ILO's "assistance to needy persons" for Sweden and Finland, the Statistical Yearbook's figures for "other public assistance" for Denmark) were nearly identical to the figures from the Nordic Union source. Esping-Andersen's clarification of Danish social aid expenditures was very helpful.

General works recently used are cited in the text and bibliography. Among the earlier general works consulted are: P. R. Kaim-Caudle, *Comparative Social Policy and Social Security: A Ten Country Study.* London: Robertson, 1973. Eurostat, *Social Accounts: Accounts of Social Protection in the E.C.* Belgium: Eurostat, 1977. Organization for Economic Cooperation and Development, *Public Expenditure on Income Maintenance Programmes.* Paris: OECD, 1976.

Australia: Australian Bureau of Statistics, *Social Indicators, No. 2.* Canberra, 1978. Adam Graycar, *Social Policy: An Australian Introduction.* South Melbourne, Australia: MacMillan and Co. of Australia, 1977. R. B. Scotton and Helen Ferber, *Public Expenditure and Social Policy in Australia. Vol. I and II.* Melbourne: Longman Chesire, 1978 and 1980.

Austria: OECD, *Integrated Social Policy: A Review of the Austrian Experience.* Paris: OECD, 1981.

Belgium: David Lewis, "Guaranteed Income for the Aged." *Social Security Bulletin* 32, 9 (Sept. 1969): 30–32. Robert Lucas, "Improvements in Belgian Social Security." *Social Security Bulletin* 31, 12 (Dec. 1968): 35–38. Jan Vranken, "Anti-Poverty Policy in Belgium," in *Anti-Poverty Policy in the European Community,* ed. Joan C. Brown, pp. 72–92. London: Policy Studies Institute, 1984.

Canada: Consolidated Government Finance: Revenues and Expenditures and Assets and Liabilities of Federal, Provincial, and Local Governments, 1974. Canada Statistics, 1977.

Finland: Matti Alestalo and Hannu Uusitalo in *Growth to Limits. The Western Welfare States Since World War II, Vol. I: Sweden, Norway, Finland, Denmark,* ed. Peter Flora, pp. 197–292. New York: Aldine, 1986.

France: The Social Institutions of France, ed. Pierre Laroque. New York: Gordon and Breach Science Publishers, 1983. INSEE *Les Comptes de la Protection Sociale: Methodes et Series 1959–1978,* Series C, No. 82 (Dec. 1978).

Ireland: Irish Department of Social Welfare, *Summary of Social Insurance and Social Assistance Services.* Dublin, 1983.

Israel: Abraham Doron, "Public Assistance in Israel: Issues of Policy and Administration." *Journal of Social Policy* 7, 4 (1978): 441–460. Doris K. Lewis, "Poverty in Israel." *Social Security Bulletin* 32, 11 (Nov. 1969): 1–3. Itzhak Kanev and Arie Nizan, *Public Expenditure on Social Security and Social Services in*

Israel. Tel Aviv: The Social and Economic Research Institute and Research Department of Kupat-Holim, 1966. Ferenbach, J. and R. Steiner, *The Cost of Social Security in Israel in the Years 1950–76.* Jerusalem: National Insurance Institute of Israel, Bureau of Research and Planning, 1978.

Italy: Pierpaolo Donati, "Social Welfare and Social Services in Italy Since 1950." *Labor and Society* 7 (Jan.-March 1982): 23–33.

Netherlands: Dutch Ministry of Foreign Affairs, *The Kingdom of the Netherlands: Welfare Policy: Pamphlet No. 13.* The Hague: Government Printing Office, 1973/5. G. M. J.Veldkamp, "Social Security in the Netherlands." *International Social Security Review* 1970, pp. 1–61. Ministry of Social Affairs in the Netherlands, *Social Security in the Netherlands: A Short Survey.* The Hague, 1979.

New Zealand: Britan Easton, *Social Policy and the Welfare State in New Zealand.* Boston: George Allen and Unwin, 1980. New Zealand Department of Statistics, *Social Trends in New Zealand* (July, 1977). C. A. Oram, *Social Policy and Administration in New Zealand.* Wellington: New Zealand University Press, 1969.

United Kingdom: A. B. Atkinson, *Poverty in Great Britain and the Reform of Social Security.* Cambridge: University Press, 1969. National Consumer Council, *Means-Tested Benefits: A Discussion Paper.* London: National Consumer Council, 1976. Department of Health and Social Security, *Take-Up of Supplementary Benefits.* London: Supplementary Benefits Commission, SBA Paper No. 7, 1978. "Poverty: Facts and Figures," *Journal of the Child Poverty Action Group* 20–21 (Winter 1971): 1–27. R. J. Coleman, *Supplementary Benefits and the Administrative Review of Administrative Action.* Poverty Pamphlet Seven. London: Child Poverty Action Group [no date].

United States: Sar A. Levitan, "Job Corps Experience With Manpower Training." *Monthly Labor Review* 98 (Oct. 1975): 4. National Advisory Council on the Education of Disadvantaged Children, *Annual Report to the President and Congress.* Washington, D.C.: GPO, 1974 (p. 66) and 1975 (p. 143). Alfred M. Skolnick and Sophie R. Dales, "Social Welfare Expenditures, Fiscal Year 1974." *Social Security Bulletin* 38 (Jan. 1975): 7.

West Germany: The Federal Minister for Labor and Social Affairs, *Survey of Social Security in the Federal Republic of Germany.* Bonn: 1972. Stephen Leibfried, "The United States and West German Welfare Systems: A Comparative Analysis," *Cornell International Law Journal,* 12, 2 (Summer 1979): 175–198.

A recent comparison of means testing in France and Britain (Evans, Paugam, and Prélis, 1995) found that about 10% of the French population live in families that receive means-tested benefits 1989–93. The comparable British figure is about 20%, although there is now some convergence in process because of similar trends in family breakup and the labor market. My table 8.3 presents parallel findings for public assistance spending: the UK figure is roughly double that of France, whose welfare state relies more on universal, categorical benefits. Prominent economists in Britain who argue that the welfare state is an economic drag, call for more means testing, more privatization, more reliance on "the" market. In contrast, prominent economists in France such as Malinvaud call for a new social contract (*ibid.*, pp. 36–37), drawing on traditions of solidarity and Catholic communitarianism (Wilensky, 1981c).

MEASURES OF ECONOMIC
PERFORMANCE

REAL ECONOMIC GROWTH

Average annual growth of GDP per capita in constant purchasers' prices, 1950–74, 1965–74, 1974–79, 1980–84, 1985–88. Except for four countries the 1950–74 data are for the 24 years 1951–74. For Belgium and Japan the averages cover 1954–74. For New Zealand and Finland the averages cover 1955–74. Sources: UN *Yearbook of National Accounts Statistics* (New York), "International Tables," table 4a (various years), except for Australia and New Zealand, where data are from OECD, *National Accounts Statistics of OECD Countries* (Paris, various years).

In computation for 1950–74 and 1965–74, I used year-to-year discrete compounding instead of continuous compounding. This would make a difference only if there were large year-to-year fluctuations, but for GDP growth this is not the case. To cross-check sources that later became better I recalculated 1950–74 data on GDP per capita in constant purchasers' prices (which includes indirect taxes) using two additional sources and continuous compound interest. Sources: (1) World Bank, *World Tables,* 3rd edition, 1983; (2) OECD *National Accounts Statistics of OECD Countries 1950–1979,* Paris, 1981 and UN *Demographic Yearbook,* several issues. These different procedures, slightly different dates, and different sources made no important difference. For instance, the largest difference in growth 1950–74 between the three sources and two procedures is for Japan (the UN is 1.25% higher than the World Bank), but Japan always ranks #1 in growth anyway. In fact, in rank order only 5 of the 19 countries compared differ by more than one rank in the two sets of figures (UN vs. World Bank and OECD vs. OECD). Checking what we used for these five discrepant countries with OECD figures, the amounts are trivial and ranks are stable. I am grateful to Bent Hansen for advice and an independent check on growth data used in the tables and text.

For 1974–79, 1980–84, 1985–89, and 1990–92, in view of the greater annual fluctuations of growth rates in these periods, and the availability of "growth triangles" computed by OECD, we used average annual geometric growth rates expressed in percentages. These rates are calculated by OECD by fitting an exponential curve to the data by least squares. Sources: for 1974–79 and 1980–84, *National Accounts Statistics of OECD Countries 1960–84,*

(Paris, 1986), with Israel taken from *UN Yearbook of National Accounts Statistics 1980,* (New York, 1982) using a simple average of annual growth rates. For 1985–89, *National Accounts Statistics of OECD Countries, 1960–89* (Paris, 1991); for 1990–91, *National Accounts Statistics of OECD Countries, 1960–92* (Paris, 1994).

INFLATION

For 1950–74 and 1965–74, average year-to-year percentage increase in the GNP price deflator. Source: *UN Yearbook of National Accounts Statistics, 1979* (New York, 1980), Vol. 2, table 10a. For 1974–79, 1980–84, 1985–89, and 1990–96, we used the GDP implicit price deflator. The averages are geometric growth rates calculated as described above for growth; the sources for the last four periods are also the same as for growth.

UNEMPLOYMENT

For 1950–74 and 1965–74, we used three-year averages of unemployment centered on 1950, 1955, 1960, 1965, 1970, and 1973. For Australia, Canada, France, West Germany, Italy, Japan, Sweden, UK, and USA, the source is "Unemployment Rates adjusted to International Concepts, 1950–74, Nine Countries" (mimeo), provided by René Bertrand of OECD. For Belgium, Netherlands, and Norway, 1950, 1955, 1960, 1965, and 1970 figures are from *OECD Manpower Statistics 1950–62, OECD Labour Force Statistics 1956–66,* and *OECD Labour Force Statistics 1961–72.* Austria, Ireland, and Switzerland 1950 data are one-year rates for 1950 or 1951, from *OECD Manpower Statistics 1950–64.* Austria, Denmark, Finland, Ireland, and New Zealand 1960, 1965, and 1970 data are from *OECD Labour Force Statistics 1956–66, 1959–70,* and *1961–72.* 1973 data are from *OECD Labour Force Statistics 1962–73.* These sources were supplemented by *ILO Yearbook of Labour Statistics,* various years.

As standardized unemployment rates became available for later years, we used these when possible. For 1974–79 and 1980–84, the standardized rates are from *OECD Quarterly Labour Force Statistics,* 1989, No. 2; unstandardized rates for Switzerland, Denmark, New Zealand, Austria, and Ireland are from *OECD Labour Force Statistics 1968–79* and *1964–84;* and Israel is from *ILO Yearbook of Labour Force Statistics, 1982.* For 1985–89, the standardized rates are from *OECD Quarterly Labour Force Statistics,* 1991, No. 1; and unstandardized rates for Austria, Denmark, and Switzerland are from *OECD Labour Force Statistics 1968–88* and *OECD Economic Outlook #46,* Dec. 1989. For 1990–92 the standardized rates are from *OECD Quarterly Labour Force Statistics,* 1993, No. 4; unstandardized rates for Austria and Switzerland are from the same source; for Denmark from *OECD Main Economic Indicators* Dec. 1993.

ECONOMIC PERFORMANCE INDEX

This index weighs the three measures roughly equally. For 19 countries average annual real growth of GDP per capita, inflation, and unemployment are each given a score of 0 (low), 1 (medium), or 2 (high) based on averages for each period.

Rather than dividing the 19 countries arbitrarily by, say, quintiles (so that a one-tenth of 1% difference might separate high from medium), we used natural break points. We then added the three scores for a summary performance score ranging from 0 to 6 (poor to excellent). Thus for 1950−74 West Germany gets 1 for unemployment (medium), 2 for growth (high), and 2 for inflation (low) for a summary score of 5 (for this period and comparing all 19 countries, excellent). The United States gets 0 for unemployment (high), 0 for growth (low), and 2 for inflation (low) for a summary score of 2 (fair-to-poor). The same procedure is used for subsequent periods. This summary index avoids the assumption that high inflation is worse than high unemployment or high real growth is more important than avoiding high unemployment and/or inflation (a problem with commonly used "misery indexes"). The rationale is elaborated more fully in the text.

POST-OIL-SHOCK MEASURES OF ECONOMIC PERFORMANCE

These are dated from 1974 and 1980. Between 1973 and 1981−82 the nominal price of crude oil in OECD countries increased tenfold; in inflation-adjusted prices, fivefold. The first oil price explosion occurred from October 1973 to early 1974. The negative effects of the shock were evident in changes in economic performance from 1973 to 1974, continuing in 1975, with a comeback in 1976 for most of the 19 countries. The second oil shock occurred mainly in 1979. Spot prices had begun to move up in late 1978 because a strike of oil field workers shut down Iran's production; in December 1978 OPEC agreed to a schedule of price increases—roughly 15%—for early 1979 to begin January 1, 1979. In 1979, from a very high base, the price of oil doubled again (using constant 1973 dollars); prices also rose in 1980 but not nearly as much as in 1979. Sources: R. Stobaugh and D. Yergin, eds., *Energy Future,* New York, Random House, 1979, pp. 6, 28−29; *World Energy Outlook,* OECD, 1982, p. 65 and table 2.2; G. Koopman, M. Klaus, and B. Reszat, *Oil and the International Economy,* New Brunswick, NJ, Transaction Publishers, 1989, p. 26, table 1.1; P. Criqui and N. Kousnetzoff, *Énergie 1995: Après les Chocs,* Paris, Centre d'Études Prospectives et d'Information Internationale, p. 6 and graph 1.2, which plots the cost of oil from 1970−86 in current and constant 1973 dollars. This second shock was followed quickly by the Volker tight-money interest-rate shock (roughly Oct. 6, 1979 to Sept. 25, 1980)—an external shock for all countries except the United States, for which it was self-administered. Thus, in analyzing national differences in the capacity to adjust flexibly to external shocks we use year-to-year changes in economic growth 1973 to 1974 as the first postshock year after the first crisis and 1979 to 1980 as the first year after the second crisis. The relevant column heads are 1974−79, 1980−84. (The overlap of 1974 in the two periods 1950−74 and 1974−79 has no effect on the long-term averages for 1950−74 and 1965−74 reported in the text, so early analysis done with 1950−74 was not redone.)

The oil price shocks were roughly uniform among our importing rich democracies. The price differences across countries were either very minor (1979−80) or very short in duration. Source: J. M. Anderson, "Empirical Analysis of World Oil Trade, 1967−1984" in G. Horwich and D. L. Weimer, *Responding to International Oil Crises,* Washington, D.C.: American Enterprise Institute, 1988, p. 232.

By 1985, oil prices were down about 12% from their peak; they collapsed in 1986, washing out the price increases of 1979−86 (adjusted for inflation). Thus, economic performance 1985−89 should be much less affected by energy costs than the 1974−84 performance.

MEASURES OF VULNERABILITY TO EXTERNAL SHOCKS

In measuring national differences in vulnerability to external shocks I used three indicators—two measures of energy dependence which comprise an index of energy dependence in 1970 and 1978 and changes in the terms of trade 1973–74 and 1978–79 (tables 12.3 and 12.4). The idea is to measure big, sudden changes in economic resources beyond the reach of pubic policy. The two oil shocks clearly fit: what you have done or not done for many years to control inflation or improve productivity and trade balances cannot be changed overnight in the face of such energy price explosions. The same is true of sudden changes in the terms of trade—the ratio of export prices to import prices.

ENERGY DEPENDENCE INDEX

The two components of the index are (1) liquid fuels as a percentage of total energy consumption, and (2) energy production as a percentage of energy consumption 1970 and 1978. Source for 1978: United Nations, Department of Economic and Social Affairs, *World Energy Supplies: 1973—1978,* Statistical Papers, Vol. 22, 1979. For 1970 data see the same series Vol. 17, 1974. "Liquid Fuels" is mainly oil but also includes natural gas liquids (e.g., liquid hydrocarbon mixtures). "Energy production" includes solid fuels such as coal and lignite, liquid fuels such as oil and natural gas liquids, natural gas, and hydro-nuclear power.

The two measures of energy dependence are correlated in the right direction: $r = -.49^{\star}$ for 1970 and $r = -.64^{\star\star}$ for 1978. They are negative because both a *high* dependence on liquid fuels and a *low* level of production as a percentage of consumption means high energy dependence. Thus, liquid fuels as a percentage of consumption was scored 2 for high, 1 for medium, and 0 for low, and production as a percentage of consumption was scored 2 for low, 1 for medium, and 0 for high. The results for each component and the combined scores are in table 12G.13 below.

During the period 1973–78 many countries increased domestic energy production with the development of nuclear reactors, hydropower, and mines and wells. However, the ratio of produced to consumed energy changed significantly in only a few cases: in *Norway* in 1973 production equaled 58% of consumption, but in 1978—with the development of the North Sea oil fields—it skyrocketed to 228% of consumption; similarly, in 1973, energy production in the *United Kingdom* equaled about half of energy consumption, but in 1978, it had climbed to more than four-fifths. With the development of its natural gas fields, the ratio of production to consumption in the *Netherlands* rose from 74% in 1970 to 117% in 1973, increasing to 134% in 1978. On the other hand, in *Israel* the production/consumption ratio plunged from 109% in 1973 to 1.3% in 1978 following the return of the Abu Rudeis and Sudr oil fields in the Sinai to Egypt under the interim agreement. Except for these four countries there were no substantial changes in energy dependence between the two oil shocks.

It can be argued that countries that are least energy-dependent—that produce a big proportion of what they use and are low in oil dependence (like the United States and Canada)—are nevertheless exposed to price shocks because the price of oil and other fuels rises whether it is domestic or foreign. No doubt Eastern Canada and Northern and Northeastern United States do lose in the oil shock periods but these losses are offset by oil- and gas-producing regions that win—Western Canada and Southwest United States (Texas, etc.). In contrast, everyone is a loser in energy-dependent Japan. The index measures real differences in national vulnerability to energy price shocks.

CHANGES IN TERMS OF TRADE

An additional, broader measure of vulnerability to external shock is changes in the ratio of export prices to changes in import prices over a specified period. Some countries are in the unhappy position of buying dear and selling cheap. For instance, Japan and Italy were big importers of food, grain, energy, minerals, and lumber at the beginning of the oil shock period. Denmark was a big importer of grain, energy, and lumber. From 1973 to 1974 the prices of these imported commodities rose much more sharply than the prices of these countries' exports—the products they needed to sell to pay for their imports; their terms of trade quickly deteriorated (the figures in table 12.3 are .77 for Japan, .82 for Italy, and .87 for Denmark). Conversely, at the beginning of the oil shock Canada was a great exporter of grain, energy, minerals, lumber, and other commodities whose prices soared; its terms of trade improved (1.07). Source: *Yearbook of International Trade Statistics,* 1974 and 1977, Vol. 1, "Trade by Country," U.N. Statistical Office, New York, 1975 and 1978.

The story was repeated in 1978–79 when terms of trade deteriorated quite a lot for Japan (.84), West Germany (.95) and Denmark (.94) but improved for Norway (1.08), New Zealand (1.07), Canada (1.06) and the United Kingdom (1.04).

Thus, we can view changes in terms of trade from 1973 to 1974 and 1978 to 1979 as measures of external shocks. Because these shifts cover all export/import prices, they go far beyond the energy dependence index. They are statistically unrelated to that index for the first shock but are related for the second shock: the correlation between the energy dependence index 1970 and change in the terms of trade 1973–74 is −.05; the r with liquid fuels is −.16, and the r with energy production is .14. The correlation between the index 1978 and terms of trade 1978–79 is −.52*; the r with liquid fuels is −.52* and with production $r = .57$**. Both measures of vulnerability to external shocks are included in tables 12.3 and 12.4.

The formula for changes in terms of trade:

$$\text{ToT } 1973\text{–}74 \quad = \frac{(EXP74/EXP73)}{(IMP74/IMP73)}$$

where

ToT 1973–74	The unit value of exports in 1974—i.e., the price of exports with the units held constant
EXP73	The unit value of exports in 1973
IMP74	The unit value of imports in 1974
IMP73	The unit value of imports in 1973

Source: IMF, *International Financial Statistics Yearbook* 1984 (Washington, D.C., 1984).

It might be argued that these changes measure the failure or success of a country to adapt quickly to a shock rather than the shock itself. But nothing in the policy arsenal of a rich democracy can in one year have much of a benign effect on big one-year shifts in terms of trade. Incomes policy, union busting, cuts in government spending, tax changes, energy conservation—all take time. And a devaluation—very quick in its effects—if unaccompanied by other medium-term inflation-fighting measures will have disastrous effects (Letiche, 1977). In short, the one-year shifts in terms of trade used in this analysis are almost pure measures of vulnerability to external shock.

That these changes in terms of trade are unrelated to economic performance (in multiple regressions) in the subsequent five or six year period underscores the overwhelming importance of structures of bargaining and their policy consequences discussed in the text (corporatism as it relates to strikes, capital formation, tax structures, as well as social, industrial, and labor-market policies). See table 12.12. Tables 12G.13 and 12G.14 below report zero-order correlations for external shocks and subsequent economic performance, the index and its components.

GROSS FIXED CAPITAL FORMATION

The data on gross fixed capital formation for 1960–73, 1973–77, 1978–82, and 1983–87 come from *OECD Historical Statistics 1960–83,* OECD: Paris, 1985, table 6.8, p. 65. The 1983–87 data are from *OECD Historical Statistics 1960–87,* OECD: Paris, 1989, table 6.8, p. 65. OECD defines *gross fixed capital form* as "The outlays (purchases and own-account production) of industries, producers of government services and producers of private non-profit services to households, on additions of new durable goods to their stocks of fixed assets *less* their net sales of similar second-hand and scrapped goods." For details on exclusions see *National Accounts Statistics of OECD Countries, 1975–87* (Paris, 1989), p. 536, Vol. 2.

Net capital formation is defined as gross fixed capital formation plus increase in stocks minus consumption of fixed capital. Data from OECD *National Accounts Statistics of OECD Countries* (Paris, 1990). We used gross instead of net capital formation and averaged the yearly figures as a percentage of GDP for four periods: 1960–73, 1973–77, 1978–82, 1983–87. This avoids an understatement of U.S. investment performance. Net investment in the United States fell in the 1980s while gross investment was roughly steady. The reasons: Calculations of net investment subtract those allocations that replace worn out and obsolete capital on the assumption that only new investment beyond what is necessary to match genuine depreciation will contribute to productivity and growth. Thus the big increase in computers and other short-lived capital equipment is what prevented *gross* investment in the United States from falling in the 1980s; subtracting such replacement equipment shows that new capital formation declined.

I have used gross fixed capital investment so as not to bias the case in my favor and because some replacement equipment is for practical purposes truly new equipment. As Benjamin Friedman (1989, p. 202) suggests, when production technologies change, the replacement concept is slippery: "electronic programming takes the place of manual control, compact designs replace units that take up more space, better motors use energy more efficiently, and calibrations become finer. New buildings are not like old ones either." So my use of gross fixed capital formation overstates capital investment in the 1980s only in modest measure. Even using net investment as a percentage of GDP my analysis shows that American capital investment, like that of the UK, was anemic by comparative standards. In fact, for *both* measures the USA and UK rank among the bottom three of eighteen countries during all four periods 1960–73, 1973–77, 1978–82, 1983–87 (table not reported here).

STRIKES

The level of strike activity is defined as the average annual number of person-days lost to industrial disputes per 1,000 civilian, nonagricultural employees. Number of person-days lost comes from the *ILO Yearbook of Labour Force Statistics,* UN/ILO: Geneva, various years. The ILO tables are titled "Number of Working Days Lost in Industrial Disputes—All Divisions of Economic Activity."

ILO reports the total number of industrial disputes that resulted in a stoppage of work and the numbers of workers involved and working days lost. No consistent differentiation between lockouts and strikes is possible, but in a few cases the data cover strikes only. Disputes of small importance and political strikes are typically excluded. For most of our 19 countries some attempt is made to include workers indirectly affected (workers within the establishment directly affected by the stoppage, not parties to the dispute, but still thrown out of work). The data are reasonable approximations.

The basic source for civilian employment is the *OECD Labour Force Statistics,* OECD: Paris. Data for 1963–83 come from the 1983 volume (Table 2 for each country gives total civilian employment, and table 3 gives employment in "agriculture, hunting, forestry, and fishing," which was deducted to get non-agricultural civilian employment); data for 1960–62 are from the 1972 volume (table 5 and table 6, respectively]; and data for 1983–87 are from the 1987 volume (tables 5 and 7).

Missing data on civilian employment were filled in from the *ILO Yearbook.* All Israeli data come from this source (1970 and 1973 *Yearbooks,* table 3; and the 1983 *Yearbook,* table 3A). Also, New Zealand 1960–72 are from the 1970 *Yearbook* (table 3). Finally, for the Netherlands, 1960–71 data are from OECD, 1972; 1972–74 data are from ILO, 1975; and 1975–82 data are from OECD, 1983.

NOMINAL WAGE INCREASES

These are average annual changes in nominal wages in manufacturing (except Australia and New Zealand, which include all categories of economic activity, and Austria, which is for mining and manufacturing). The primary sources are *OECD Historical Statistics 1960–85* and *OECD Historical Statistics 1960–80.* Data not available in these sources were filled in with data from *OECD Main Economic Indicators—Historical Statistics 1964–83* and various earlier volumes. Data for Australia, 1979–84; New Zealand, 1984; and Austria, 1984 were filled in from *OECD Main Economic Indicators,* December 1982 and December 1985. OECD seems to use nominal hourly wages and nominal hourly earnings interchangeably, so I used nominal earnings where nominal wages were not reported. The one exception here is New Zealand, which gives weekly wage rates.

Since the two OECD sources (*Historical Statistics* and *Main Economic Indicators–Historical Statistics*) gave nominal wage data for different sets of countries, I compared the data from the two sources for consistency, on that set of six countries where data were given in both sources (Belgium, France, West Germany, Italy, Netherlands, and UK). The results were very close, except for UK. The *Main Economic Indicators* shows a break in its series in 1977, and the *Historical Statistics* adjusted for this, which would account for this discrepancy. This confirms that our use of *Historical Statistics* as the primary source and *Main Economic Indicators* as secondary is the appropriate strategy.

We made a further check of six countries (USA, Japan, W. Germany, France, UK, and Italy) where Wohlers and Weinert, *Employment Trends in the US, Japan, and the EC* (New Brunswick, NJ: Transaction Books, 1988), using different definitions, calculated nominal wages and real earnings. They show only small discrepancies with our data. We also checked Sweden's nominal wage data against three other sources: Karl-Olof Faxen, unpublished paper; Leon N. Lindberg, *The Politics of Inflation* (Washington, DC: Brookings, 1985); and Gosta Edgren, Karl-Olof Faxen and Clas-Erik Odhner, *Wage Formation and the Economy* (London: Allen and Unwin, 1973), again with trivial differences. While discrepancies between nominal wages and nominal earnings and real wages and real earnings for single years are sometimes notable, when averaged over the relevant periods the differences cancel out.

TAX DATA

The sources for all tax data as a percentage of GDP are *Revenue Statistics of OECD Member Countries 1965–1983,* OECD: Paris, 1984, and *Revenue Statistics of OECD Member Countries, 1965–1989,* OECD: Paris, 1991d. The total tax load measure used here is total tax revenues as a percentage of GDP. It includes taxes at every level of government.

Corporate taxes are total taxes on the income, profits, and capital gains of corporations (OECD category 1200). Social-security taxes includes contributions by employers and employees and payments by self-employed or nonemployed (OECD category 2000).

Property taxes are defined as all taxes on immovable property (OECD category 4100). For some countries, this category is broken down into taxes on households and taxes on others. According to OECD's description of this distinction (4110 vs. 4120), it

> is between households as consumers (i.e., excluding non-incorporated business) on the one hand and producers on the other hand. However, taxes on dwelling-houses occupied by households, whether paid by owner-occupiers, tenants or landlords, are classified under households. This follows the common distinction made between taxes on domestic property and taxes on business property. Some countries are not, however, in a position to make this distinction. (*Revenue Statistics 1965–83,* paragraph 26B, p. 42)

Ideally we would maintain this distinction for most purposes but it is available for only ten countries. For the backlash analysis we made adjustments described in footnotes to table 10.2; for the economic performance analyses we used the concept that fits immovable property taxes (4100), which includes both households and enterprises. Rationale described in text.

Consumption taxes include all sales taxes, value-added taxes, and multistage cumulative taxes "on the production, leasing, transfer, delivery or sales of a wide range of goods and/or the rendering of a wide range of services, irrespective of whether they are domestically produced or imported and irrespective of the stage of production or distribution at which they are levied." (*Revenue Statistics 1965–83*, p. 47). Import and export duties are excluded. This is OECD category 5110.

AGE STRUCTURE VARIABLES

The source for these data is *UN Demographic Yearbook,* UN: New York. The 1978 *Yearbook* is the source for 1970 and 1977 data. Various years, 1981–84, were used to attempt to get 1980 data for all countries. But for United States, Australia, New Zealand, and Belgium we had to use 1981 data. The 1985 *Yearbook* is the source for all 1985 data, but it gave 1985 data for only six countries (USA, SWED, CNDA, FRAN, NETH, and AUST). Data for the rest of the countries is from the following years: 1984 for DEN, NZ, WGER, NORW, FIN, UK, ISRL, JAPN, IRE; 1983 for ASTL; 1982 for SWIZ, BELG, ITAL.

EDUCATION VARIABLES

Educational expenditure variables and enrollment ratios for 1965, 1971, and 1974 are from *Educational Statistics in OECD Countries,* Paris, 1981, with missing data filled in from the *UNESCO Statistical Yearbook,* 1977 (Paris, 1978) and 1978–79 (Paris, 1980). The source for all 1980 and 1988 data is the *UNESCO Statistical Yearbook 1990,* Paris, 1990. The enrollment ratios are from table 3.2. The higher education expenditure data for 1988 are from table 4.4, which gives expenditures on the third level, where available. For USA, DEN, ASTL, and ISRL, these data are computed from table 4.3, which gives total education expenditure and the percent of the expenditure for the third level. All 1980 data are computed from table 4.3.

In addition, exchange rates used to calculate per person expenditures and GNP at factor cost, used to calculate expenditures as a percent of GNP, were taken from *National Accounts Statistics of OECD Countries 1960–89,* Paris, 1991, Volume I. For Israel, these data are from IMF, *International Financial Statistics Yearbook 1990,* New York, 1990. Population data used to calculate expenditures per person are from *UN Demographic Yearbook 1988* (New York, 1990).

TABLE 12G.1 Zero-order correlations among corporatist bargaining outcomes, taxing and spending policies, age structure, and economic performance, 1950–74

	Corpor. Score	Capital Formation 1960-73	Strikes 1960-72	Nom. Wage Increases 1965-73	SS/GNP 1950-74	Pub. Asst. as % GNP 1966,71	Total Tax Load 1965,71	Visible Taxes 1965,71	Corporate Taxes 1955-72	Soc. Sec. Taxes 1955-72	Consump. Taxes 1955-72	Pop. 15-19 1970	Pop. 65+ 1970
Cap. Form.	.38•	—											
Strikes	-.48*	-.58**	—										
Nom.Wage	.17	-.02	-.01	—									
SS/GNP	.51*	.23	-.47*	-.14	—								
PA/GNP	-.26	-.62**	.53*	-.27	-.26	—							
Total Tax	.68**	.18	-.29	-.02	.70**	-.17	—						
Vis. Tax	-.37•	-.03	.12	-.30	-.36•	-.03	-.00	—					
Corp. Tax	-.52*	-.43*	.31	-.15	-.63**	.27	-.51*	.29	—				
SS Tax	.55**	.04	-.41•	-.02	.69**	.16	.30	-.77**	-.39•	—			
Cons. Tax	.68**	.44*	-.29	-.10	.72**	-.18	.63**	-.56**	-.50*	.62**	—		
Pop. 15-19	-.22	-.25	.59**	.07	-.73**	.28	-.46*	.06	.59**	-.53*	-.26	—	
Pop. 65+	.45*	.15	-.40•	-.14	.85**	-.16	.80**	-.16	-.74**	.60**	.56*	-.84**	—

Correlations with Economic Performance

	Corpor. Score	Capital Formation 1960-73	Strikes 1960-72	Nom. Wage Increases 1965-73	SS/GNP 1950-74	Pub. Asst. as % GNP 1966,71	Total Tax Load 1965,71	Visible Taxes 1965,71	Corporate Taxes 1955-72	Soc. Sec. Taxes 1955-72	Consump. Taxes 1955-72	Pop. 15-19 1970	Pop. 65+ 1970
Index	.39*	.70**	-.83**	.02	.48*	-.59**	.21	-.11	-.23	.35•	.41*	-.57**	.35
Growth	.62**	.37•	-.34•	.43*	.45*	-.11	.43*	-.65**	-.62**	.71**	.70**	-.09	.22
Inflation	.25	.30	-.01	.62**	-.05	-.41*	.10	-.10	-.17	-.15	.08	.10	-.09
Unempl.	.01	-.61**	.58**	.06	-.27	.59**	-.01	-.22	-.00	.13	-.08	.50*	-.27

Note: all correlations for strikes exclude Italy; all correlations for capital formation and growth exclude Japan; all correlations for inflation exclude Israel.

TABLE 12G.2 Zero-order correlations among corporatist bargaining outcomes, taxing and spending policies, age structure, and economic performance, 1965–74

	Corpor. Score	Capital Formation 1960-73	Strikes 1960-72	Nom. Wage Increases 1965-73	SS/GNP 1966-72	Pub. Asst. as % GNP 1966,71	Total Tax Load 1965,71	Visible Taxes 1965,71	Corporate Taxes 1965-72	Soc. Sec. Taxes 1965-72	Consump. Taxes 1965-72	Pop. 15-19 1970	Pop. 65+ 1970
Cap. Form.	.38•	—											
Strikes	-.48*	-.58**	—										
Nom.Wage	.17	-.02	-.01	—									
SS/GNP	.67**	.22	-.43*	-.06	—								
PA/GNP	-.26	-.62**	.53*	-.27	-.24	—							
Total Tax	.68**	.18	-.29	-.02	.83**	-.17	—						
Vis. Tax	-.37•	-.03	.12	-.30	-.28	-.03	-.00	—					
Corp. Tax	-.55*	-.45*	.32	-.06	-.64**	.19	-.66**	.16	—				
SS Tax	.62**	.06	-.45*	-.02	.68**	.16	.39•	-.69**	-.38•	—			
Cons. Tax	.74***	.46*	-.27	-.01	.76**	-.26	.79**	-.37•	-.64**	.49*	—		
Pop. 15-19	-.22	-.25	.59**	.07	-.70**	.28	-.46*	.06	.66**	-.58**	-.26	—	
Pop. 65+	.45*	.15	-.40•	-.14	.85**	-.16	.80**	-.16	-.81**	.67**	.63**	-.84**	—

Correlations with Economic Performance

	Corpor. Score	Capital Formation 1960-73	Strikes 1960-72	Nom. Wage Increases 1965-73	SS/GNP 1966-72	Pub. Asst. as % GNP 1966,71	Total Tax Load 1965,71	Visible Taxes 1965,71	Corporate Taxes 1965-72	Soc. Sec. Taxes 1965-72	Consump. Taxes 1965-72	Pop. 15-19 1970	Pop. 65+ 1970
Index	.32•	.44*	-.51*	-.05	.40*	-.35•	.16	-.45*	-.03	.48*	.49*	-.26	.29
Growth	.57**	.35•	.04	.37**	.13	.00	.24	-.55**	-.22	.38•	.61**	.35•	-.18
Inflation	-.00	.07	.18	.71**	-.29	-.24	-.10	.13	-.06	-.47*	-.18	.26	-.31
Unempl.	-.13	-.59**	.86**	-.02	-.20	.67**	-.01	-.07	.10	-.07	-.07	.47*	-.21

Note: All correlations for strikes exclude Italy; all correlations for capital formation and growth exclude Japan; all correlations for inflation exclude Israel.

TABLE 12G.3 Zero-order correlations among corporatist bargaining outcomes, taxing and spending policies, age structure, and economic performance, 1974–79

	Corpor. Score	Capital Formation 1973-77	Strikes 1973-77	Nom. Wage Increases 1974-79	SS/GNP 1975-77	Pub. Asst. as % GNP 1974	Total Tax Load 1974	Visible Taxes 1974	Corporate Taxes 1973-77	Soc. Sec. Taxes 1974-78	Consump. Taxes 1974-78	Pop. 15-19 1977	Pop. 65+ 1977
Cap. Form.	.08	—											
Strikes	-.36•	-.12	—										
Nom.Wage	.09	-.01	.49*	—									
SS/GNP	.67**	-.28	-.37•	-.01	—								
PA/GNP	-.41*	-.46*	.26	-.12	-.20	—							
Total Tax	.60**	-.02	-.30	-.15	.74**	-.22	—						
Vis. Tax	-.32•	-.02	.32•	-.19	-.12	-.16	.19	—					
Corp. Tax	-.45*	.07	.23	-.13	-.65**	.36•	-.54*	.03	—				
SS Tax	.63**	-.12	-.69**	-.20	.65**	.09	.31	-.73**	-.27	—			
Cons. Tax	.77**	.14	-.18	.12	.80**	-.35•	.80**	-.19	-.71**	.44*	—		
Pop. 15-19	-.48*	-.22	.65**	.04	-.45*	.38•	-.32	.11	.38•	-.49*	-.27	—	
Pop. 65+	.45*	-.20	-.57**	-.17	.83**	-.13	.68**	-.06	-.77**	.68**	.64**	-.65**	—

Correlations with Economic Performance

	Corpor. Score	Capital Formation 1973-77	Strikes 1973-77	Nom. Wage Increases 1974-79	SS/GNP 1975-77	Pub. Asst. as % GNP 1974	Total Tax Load 1974	Visible Taxes 1974	Corporate Taxes 1973-77	Soc. Sec. Taxes 1974-78	Consump. Taxes 1974-78	Pop. 15-19 1977	Pop. 65+ 1977
Index	.19	.61**	-.68**	-.52*	.26	-.18	.25	-.24	-.04	.51*	.28	-.44*	.39•
Growth	.30	.43*	-.05	.24	.34•	-.01	.34•	-.38•	-.29	.37•	.55**	-.23	.30
Inflation	-.07	-.18	.58**	.92**	-.14	-.01	-.21	.04	-.02	-.36•	-.10	.16	-.27
Unempl.	-.01	-.50*	.67**	.47*	.08	.54**	-.07	-.19	.04	-.06	.07	.40•	-.20

Note: All correlations for strikes exclude Italy; all correlations for inflation exclude Israel.

TABLE 12G.4 Zero-order correlations among corporatist bargaining outcomes, taxing and spending policies, age structure, and economic performance, 1980–84

	Corpor. Score	Capital Formation 1978-82	Strikes 1978-82	Nom. Wage Increases 1980-84	SS/GNP 1980	Pub. Asst. as % GNP 1980	Total Tax Load 1980	Visible Taxes 1980	Corporate Taxes 1978-82	Soc. Sec. Taxes 1979-83	Consump. Taxes 1979-83	Pop. 15-19 1980	Pop. 65+ 1980
Cap. Form.	-.17	—											
Strikes	-.22	-.14	—										
Nom.Wage	.04	-.06	.75**	—									
SS/GNP	.59**	-.30	-.45*	-.07	—								
PA/GNP	-.51*	-.22	.09	-.19	-.21	—							
Total Tax	.72**	-.25	-.44*	-.17	.90**	-.30	—						
Vis. Tax	-.39•	-.26	.09	-.06	-.22	-.03	-.15	—					
Corp. Tax	-.14	.44*	.00	-.10	-.50*	.14	-.25	-.20	—				
SS Tax	.64**	-.13	-.31	-.15	.52*	-.08	.47*	-.78**	-.04	—			
Cons. Tax	.71**	-.17	-.24	.15	.87**	-.36•	.83**	-.24	-.43*	.36•	—		
Pop. 15-19	-.38•	-.16	.43*	.06	-.27	.51*	-.27	.33•	-.13	-.34•	-.16	—	
Pop. 65+	.38•	-.35•	-.44*	-.04	.70**	-.25	.69**	-.28	-.38•	.49*	.64**	-.49*	—
Correlations with Economic Performance													
Index	-.06	.40•	-.59**	-.57**	-.22	-.37•	-.14	.04	.19	.04	-.31	-.45*	.11
Growth	-.15	.59**	-.24	-.01	-.32	-.48*	-.22	.29	.29	-.43*	-.17	-.37•	-.17
Inflation	.11	-.17	.72**	.95**	.02	-.25	-.02	.07	-.13	-.17	.23	.15	.02
Unempl.	.02	-.38•	.53*	.35•	.21	.48*	.05	-.04	-.15	-.03	.21	.42*	-.18

TABLE 12G.5   Zero-order correlations among corporatist bargaining outcomes, taxing and spending policies, age structure, and economic performance, 1985–89

	Corpor. Score	Capital Formation 1983-87	Strikes 1983-87	Nom. Wage Increases 1980-84	SS/GNP 1980	Pub. Asst. as % GNP 1980	Total Tax Load 1988	Visible Taxes 1988	Corporate Taxes 1983-87	Soc. Sec. Taxes 1984-88	Consump. Taxes 1984-88	Pop. 15-19 1985	Pop. 65+ 1985
Cap. Form.	-.17	—											
Strikes	-.23	-.05	—										
Nom.Wage	.04	-.11	.63**	—									
SS/GNP	.59**	-.50*	-.31	-.07	—								
PA/GNP	-.51*	-.39•	.01	-.19	-.21	—							
Total Tax	.72**	-.35•	-.16	.03	.90**	-.38•	—						
Vis. Tax	-.41*	.05	.57*	.05	-.23	-.11	-.09	—					
Corp. Tax	.01	.42*	-.08	-.03	-.31	.00	-.06	-.23	—				
SS Tax	.62**	-.28	-.68**	-.24	.54*	-.01	.37•	-.86**	.02	—			
Cons. Tax	.64**	-.33•	.10	.22	.80**	-.32	.80**	-.12	-.25	.25	—		
Pop. 15-19	-.22	-.01	.32	.24	-.21	.12	-.13	.08	-.12	-.20	.11	—	
Pop. 65+	.37•	-.35•	-.32	-.08	.69**	-.26	.65**	-.17	-.01	.41*	.51*	-.46*	—
						Correlations with Economic Performance							
Index	-.15	.32•	-.62**	-.54*	-.17	-.07	-.26	-.31	.07	.27	-.34•	-.36•	.10
Growth	-.13	.02	.06	.26	-.25	.15	-.33•	-.36•	.05	.09	-.17	-.24	-.15
Inflation	-.19	.06	.72**	.57**	-.20	-.39•	-.04	.63**	-.15	-.62**	-.00	.27	-.11
Unempl.	-.01	-.55**	.37	.54*	.17	.35•	.06	-.15	-.19	.04	.26	.52*	-.31

TABLE 12G.6   Scores and ranks of corporatist bargaining outcomes, taxing and spending policies, age structure, and economic performance, 1950–74

Countries by Types of Political Econ.	Ec. Perf. Index 1950-74		Capital Formation 1960-73	Strikes 1960-72	Nom. Wage Increases 1965-73	SS/GNP 1950-74	Pub. Asst. as % GNP 1966,71	Total Tax Load 1965,71	Visible Taxes 1965,71	Corporate Taxes 1955-72	Soc. Sec. Taxes 1955-72	Consump Taxes 1955-72	Pop. 15-19 1970	Pop. 65+ 1970
Left Corporatist														
Sweden	4	G	23.3 (10)	17 (18)	9.4 (10)	15.5 (6)	0.2 (18)	38.3 (1)	45.0 (2)	2.4 (10)	3.2 (12)	2.6 (11)	6.9 (16)	13.7 (2)
Norway	4	G	28.3 (2)	62 (14)	9.5 (9)	12.3 (10)	0.2 (18)	37.9 (2)	30.7 (10)	1.9 (13)	4.1 (10)	7.3 (2)	7.8 (10)	13.1 (7)
Finland	4	G	26.4 (5)	288 (5)	11.7 (4)	11.8 (11)	0.4 (14)	31.2 (10)	35.6 (8)	2.4 (10)	1.8 (13)	5.8 (5)	9.1 (6)	9.3 (13)
Israel	2	FP	—	201 (8)	—	7.0 (18)	1.5 (4)	—	27.7 (13)	—	—	—	11.1 (1)	7.1 (18)
Denmark	3	F	23.8 (9)	131 (10)	12.6 (3)	13.8 (8)	0.3 (16)	36.7 (3)	46.0 (1)	1.2 (18)	1.4 (16)	2.6 (11)	7.6 (11)	12.4 (8)
Left-Cath. Corpor.														
Netherlands	4	G	25.0 (7)	23 (17)	10.4 (7)	15.5 (6)	1.0 (7)	36.3 (4)	29.8 (11)	3.0 (7)	9.1 (3)	4.7 (7)	—	—
Belgium	4	G	21.6 (13)	129 (11)	9.9 (8)	17.2 (4)	1.0 (7)	33.5 (7)	24.3 (16)	1.7 (16)	8.7 (5)	6.2 (4)	7.5 (12)	13.4 (4)
Austria	4	G	26.7 (4)	37 (15)	8.7 (13)	19.3 (1)	0.5 (13)	35.5 (5)	22.3 (17)	1.8 (15)	8.1 (6)	6.6 (3)	6.9 (16)	14.2 (1)
Catholic Corpor.														
Italy	3	F	21.2 (14)	1022 (1)	11.2 (5)	15.0 (7)	0.9 (10)	26.2 (14)	12.9 (18)	2.0 (11)	10.4 (2)	3.8 (9)	7.2 (14)	11.3 (10)
W. Germany	5	E	24.9 (8)	25 (16)	8.5 (14)	18.9 (2)	0.5 (13)	32.5 (9)	27.8 (12)	2.5 (8)	8.8 (4)	5.6 (6)	6.6 (18)	13.2 (6)
Corpor. w/o Labor														
France	3	F	22.8 (11)	174 (9)	10.4 (7)	17.4 (3)	0.9 (10)	34.5 (6)	10.9 (19)	1.9 (13)	12.6 (1)	8.7 (1)	8.3 (9)	13.4 (4)
Japan	4	G	32.8 (1)	113 (13)	15.8 (1)	5.1 (19)	0.7 (11)	19.2 (18)	26.6 (15)	4.3 (1)	3.4 (11)	0.0 (18)	8.8 (8)	7.1 (18)
Switzerland	4	G	28.0 (3)	3 (19)	6.6 (17)	11.6 (13)	1.0 (7)	22.1 (17)	37.4 (6)	1.5 (17)	4.8 (7)	2.0 (14)	7.3 (13)	11.4 (9)
Least Corporatist														
USA	2	FP	18.1 (18)	455 (4)	5.8 (18)	7.9 (17)	1.8 (3)	26.9 (13)	42.3 (3)	4.2 (2)	4.2 (9)	1.2 (17)	9.3 (4)	9.9 (12)
UK	2	FP	18.4 (17)	275 (6)	9.1 (12)	12.7 (9)	2.0 (1)	32.6 (8)	39.7 (5)	3.2 (6)	4.2 (9)	2.0 (14)	6.9 (16)	13.2 (6)
New Zealand	3	FP	21.0 (15)	121 (12)	9.2 (11)	11.7 (12)	0.1 (19)	26.1 (15)	35.8 (7)	4.1 (3)	0.0 (18)	2.1 (12)	9.3 (4)	8.5 (14)
Australia	3	F	25.6 (6)	271 (7)	7.5 (16)	8.6 (16)	0.3 (16)	24.0 (16)	41.5 (4)	3.8 (5)	0.0 (18)	2.0 (14)	8.9 (7)	8.3 (15)
Canada	2	FP	21.9 (12)	532 (3)	7.8 (15)	10.3 (15)	1.8 (3)	28.1 (12)	35.4 (9)	3.9 (4)	1.7 (14)	4.0 (8)	9.9 (2)	8.1 (16)
Ireland	1	PF	20.7 (16)	597 (2)	13.1 (2)	10.7 (14)	1.0 (7)	29.2 (11)	27.6 (14)	1.8 (15)	1.6 (15)	1.5 (16)	9.1 (6)	11.1 (11)

TABLE 12G.7 Scores and ranks of corporatist bargaining outcomes, taxing and spending policies, age structure, and economic performance 1965–74

Countries by Types of Political Econ.	Ec. Perf. Index 1965-74		Capital Formation 1960-73	Strikes 1960-72	Nom. Wage Increases 1965-73	SS/GNP 1966-72	Pub. Asst. as % GNP 1966,71	Total Tax Load 1965,71	Visible Taxes 1965,71	Corporate Taxes 1965-72	Soc. Sec. Taxes 1965-72	Consump Taxes 1965-72	Pop. 15-19 1970	Pop. 65+ 1970
Left Corporatist														
Sweden	3	F	23.3 (10)	17 (18)	9.4 (10)	20.5 (3)	0.2 (18)	38.3 (1)	45.0 (2)	1.9 (14)	5.5 (8)	4.9 (9)	6.9 (16)	13.7 (2)
Norway	3	F	28.3 (2)	62 (14)	9.5 (9)	16.4 (9)	0.2 (18)	37.9 (2)	30.7 (10)	1.2 (18)	6.1 (7)	8.6 (2)	7.8 (10)	13.1 (7)
Finland	3	F	26.4 (5)	288 (5)	11.7 (4)	15.1 (10)	0.4 (14)	31.2 (10)	35.6 (8)	2.0 (11)	1.6 (16)	6.3 (5)	9.1 (6)	9.3 (13)
Israel	2	FP	—	201 (8)	—	7.9 (18)	1.5 (4)	—	27.7 (13)	—	—	—	11.1 (1)	7.1 (18)
Denmark	2	FP	23.8 (9)	131 (10)	12.6 (3)	17.5 (8)	0.3 (16)	36.7 (3)	46.0 (1)	1.2 (18)	1.7 (15)	5.3 (8)	7.6 (11)	12.4 (8)
Left-Cath. Corpor.														
Netherlands	3	F	25.0 (7)	23 (17)	10.4 (7)	21.6 (2)	1.0 (7)	36.3 (4)	29.8 (11)	2.7 (6)	12.2 (2)	5.3 (8)	7.5 (12)	—
Belgium	5	E	21.6 (13)	129 (11)	9.9 (8)	20.1 (5)	1.0 (7)	33.5 (7)	24.3 (16)	2.3 (8)	10.8 (3)	6.8 (4)	7.5 (12)	13.4 (4)
Austria	6	E	26.7 (4)	37 (15)	8.7 (13)	21.9 (1)	0.5 (13)	35.5 (5)	22.3 (17)	1.7 (16)	9.0 (6)	6.8 (4)	6.9 (16)	14.2 (1)
Catholic Corpor.														
Italy	2	FP	21.2 (14)	1022 (1)	11.2 (5)	18.7 (7)	0.9 (10)	26.2 (14)	12.9 (18)	2.0 (11)	10.2 (4)	3.4 (11)	7.2 (14)	11.3 (10)
W. Germany	4	G	24.9 (8)	25 (16)	8.5 (14)	20.2 (4)	0.5 (13)	32.5 (9)	27.8 (12)	2.1 (9)	9.6 (5)	5.5 (6)	6.6 (18)	13.2 (6)
Corpor. w/o Labor														
France	5	E	22.8 (11)	174 (9)	10.4 (7)	18.8 (6)	0.9 (10)	34.5 (6)	10.9 (19)	1.9 (14)	12.6 (1)	8.7 (1)	8.3 (9)	13.4 (4)
Japan	4	G	32.8 (1)	113 (13)	15.8 (1)	5.3 (19)	0.7 (11)	19.2 (18)	26.6 (15)	4.4 (2)	4.4 (12)	0.0 (18)	8.8 (8)	7.1 (18)
Switzerland	3	F	28.0 (3)	3 (19)	6.6 (17)	10.5 (15)	1.0 (7)	22.1 (17)	37.4 (6)	1.7 (16)	5.1 (10)	2.0 (14)	7.3 (13)	11.4 (9)
Least Corporatist														
USA	2	FP	18.1 (18)	455 (4)	5.8 (18)	10.0 (16)	1.8 (3)	26.9 (13)	42.3 (3)	3.7 (5)	5.1 (10)	1.5 (17)	9.3 (4)	9.9 (12)
UK	1	PF	18.4 (17)	275 (6)	9.1 (12)	14.3 (11)	2.0 (1)	32.6 (8)	39.7 (5)	2.3 (8)	5.0 (11)	2.0 (14)	6.9 (16)	13.2 (6)
New Zealand	3	FP	21.0 (15)	121 (12)	9.2 (11)	11.5 (14)	0.1 (19)	26.1 (15)	35.8 (7)	4.4 (2)	0.0 (18)	2.0 (14)	9.3 (4)	8.5 (14)
Australia	3	F	25.6 (6)	271 (7)	7.5 (16)	9.3 (17)	0.3 (16)	24.0 (16)	41.5 (4)	3.8 (3)	0.0 (18)	1.8 (16)	8.9 (7)	8.3 (15)
Canada	3	F	21.9 (12)	532 (3)	7.8 (15)	13.1 (12)	1.8 (3)	28.1 (12)	35.4 (9)	3.7 (5)	2.2 (14)	4.8 (10)	9.9 (2)	8.1 (16)
Ireland	1	PF	20.7 (16)	597 (2)	13.1 (2)	11.8 (13)	1.0 (7)	29.2 (11)	27.6 (14)	2.0 (11)	2.2 (14)	3.0 (12)	9.1 (6)	11.1 (11)

TABLE 12G.8 Scores and ranks of corporatist bargaining outcomes, taxing and spending policies, age structure, and economic performance, 1974–79

Countries by Types of Political Econ.	Ec. Perf. Index 1974-79		Capital Formation 1973-77	Strikes 1973-77	Nom. Wage Increases 1974-79	SS/GNP 1975-77	Pub. Asst. as % GNP 1974	Total Tax Load 1974	Visible Taxes 1974	Corporate Taxes 1973-77	Soc. Sec. Taxes 1974-78	Consump Taxes 1974-78	Pop. 15-19 1977	Pop. 65+ 1977
Left Corporatist														
Sweden	3	F	21.3 (14)	29 (16)	11.1 (13)	30.6 (1)	0.3 (16)	42.8 (3)	45.5 (5)	1.7 (14)	10.9 (8)	6.0 (8)	6.5 (18)	15.4 (1)
Norway	6	E	33.5 (1)	66 (14)	13.0 (9)	21.9 (9)	0.2 (19)	44.8 (1)	39.4 (8)	1.6 (16)	10.9 (8)	9.4 (1)	7.6 (14)	14.1 (5)
Finland	2	FP	29.0 (3)	739 (3)	14.4 (6)	19.4 (11)	0.3 (16)	32.7 (11)	47.9 (4)	1.6 (16)	3.0 (15)	6.7 (6)	8.3 (7)	10.9 (12)
Israel	1	PF	—	251 (10)	—	9.7 (18)	0.6 (12)	—	20.2 (17)	—	—	—	9.0 (6)	8.2 (18)
Denmark	2	FP	23.0 (10)	430 (6)	14.2 (7)	25.0 (6)	0.3 (16)	44.2 (2)	60.8 (1)	1.4 (18)	0.6 (16)	7.8 (4)	7.3 (16)	13.6 (8)
Left-Cath. Corpor.														
Netherlands	4	G	21.2 (15)	40 (15)	9.5 (15)	30.1 (2)	1.6 (5)	42.3 (4)	29.3 (13)	3.0 (6)	16.5 (1)	6.6 (7)	—	—
Belgium	3	F	22.1 (12)	201 (12)	12.3 (10)	27.1 (4)	1.3 (6)	38.3 (5)	30.1 (12)	2.9 (7)	13.2 (3)	7.3 (5)	8.0 (9)	14.0 (6)
Austria	6	E	27.3 (4)	14 (18)	10.4 (14)	24.5 (7)	0.4 (13)	38.1 (6)	24.7 (16)	1.4 (18)	11.1 (6)	7.9 (3)	7.9 (10)	15.1 (2)
Catholic Corpor.														
Italy	1	PF	20.7 (16)	1381 (1)	22.2 (1)	22.7 (8)	0.6 (12)	25.7 (17)	16.0 (18)	1.9 (11)	12.4 (4)	4.6 (11)	7.5 (15)	12.5 (10)
W. Germany	5	E	21.3 (14)	19 (17)	7.3 (17)	26.2 (5)	0.9 (10)	36.5 (7)	33.2 (11)	1.8 (12)	12.3 (5)	5.3 (10)	7.8 (11)	15.0 (3)
Corpor. w/o Labor														
France	4	G	23.4 (8)	211 (11)	14.9 (4)	28.0 (3)	0.9 (10)	35.5 (8)	12.8 (19)	2.3 (9)	15.7 (2)	8.8 (2)	8.0 (9)	13.8 (7)
Japan	6	E	33.1 (2)	118 (13)	11.9 (11)	8.4 (19)	1.1 (8)	23.0 (18)	27.6 (15)	5.1 (1)	6.4 (11)	0.0 (18)	7.0 (17)	8.4 (17)
Switzerland	4	G	24.5 (7)	3 (19)	4.6 (18)	16.0 (12)	1.1 (8)	27.3 (15)	39.1 (9)	2.2 (10)	8.9 (9)	2.5 (15)	7.7 (12)	13.4 (9)
Least Corporatist														
USA	2	FP	18.0 (18)	429 (7)	8.6 (16)	14.8 (15)	2.6 (1)	29.2 (14)	43.0 (6)	3.2 (5)	7.2 (10)	2.0 (16)	9.8 (3)	10.9 (12)
UK	1	PF	19.8 (17)	345 (8)	16.7 (3)	15.8 (13)	2.4 (2)	35.0 (9)	39.9 (7)	2.5 (8)	6.3 (12)	3.1 (13)	7.6 (14)	14.2 (4)
New Zealand	2	FP	24.6 (5)	294 (9)	13.7 (8)	14.6 (16)	0.3 (16)	31.4 (13)	56.4 (2)	3.8 (3)	0.0 (18)	2.5 (15)	9.9 (2)	9.1 (15)
Australia	1	PF	22.9 (11)	655 (4)	14.6 (5)	14.3 (17)	0.3 (16)	27.1 (16)	47.9 (4)	3.7 (4)	0.0 (18)	1.9 (17)	9.1 (5)	9.1 (15)
Canada	2	FP	23.0 (10)	940 (2)	11.6 (12)	15.1 (14)	2.3 (3)	33.2 (10)	37.0 (10)	4.0 (2)	3.4 (14)	4.3 (12)	10.2 (1)	8.9 (16)
Ireland	2	FP	24.5 (7)	558 (5)	19.1 (2)	20.9 (10)	1.6 (5)	31.6 (12)	28.5 (14)	1.7 (14)	4.4 (13)	5.5 (9)	9.5 (4)	10.8 (13)

TABLE 12G.9   Scores and ranks of corporatist bargaining outcomes, taxing and spending policies, age structure, and economic performance, 1980–84

Countries by Types of Political Econ.	Ec. Perf. Index 1980-84	Capital Formation 1978-82	Strikes 1978-82	Nom. Wage Increases 1980-84	SS/GNP 1980	Pub. Asst. as % GNP 1980	Total Tax Load 1980	Visible Taxes 1980	Corporate Taxes 1978-82	Soc. Sec. Taxes 1979-83	Consump Taxes 1979-83	Pop. 15-19 1980	Pop. 65+ 1980
Left Corporatist													
Sweden	4 G	19.5 (14)	238 (10)	9.0 (9)	33.1 (1)	0.0 (18)	49.1 (1)	41.5 (6)	1.5 (16)	14.1 (4)	6.7 (8)	7.1 (18)	16.5 (1)
Norway	4 G	27.5 (3)	55 (14)	9.3 (8)	23.3 (9)	0.2 (17)	47.1 (2)	28.9 (13)	5.4 (2)	10.2 (8)	8.6 (3)	7.8 (17)	14.9 (4)
Finland	4 G	24.5 (5)	284 (9)	11.1 (5)	21.1 (10)	0.2 (17)	33.0 (12)	45.1 (4)	1.6 (15)	3.0 (15)	7.1 (6)	7.9 (15)	12.1 (11)
Israel	— —	—	744 (3)	—	7.0 (19)	0.5 (14)	—	52.8 (2)	—	—	—	8.7 (7)	8.6 (19)
Denmark	2 FP	18.6 (16)	119 (12)	8.4 (11)	32.8 (2)	0.9 (11)	45.5 (4)	—	1.3 (18)	1.1 (16)	10.0 (1)	7.9 (15)	14.5 (6)
Left-Cath. Corpor.													
Netherlands	2 FP	20.2 (12)	26 (16)	3.7 (18)	31.3 (3)	2.1 (4)	45.8 (3)	28.2 (14)	2.9 (7)	18.5 (1)	7.0 (7)	8.9 (5)	11.6 (12)
Belgium	3 F	19.9 (13)	170 (11)	7.3 (12)	29.8 (5)	0.9 (11)	43.5 (5)	36.0 (9)	2.7 (9)	13.8 (5)	7.7 (5)	8.1 (12)	14.3 (7)
Austria	5 E	24.9 (4)	2 (18)	6.1 (14)	26.3 (7)	0.8 (12)	41.2 (7)	24.1 (16)	1.4 (17)	13.1 (7)	8.4 (4)	8.6 (9)	15.5 (2)
Catholic Corpor.													
Italy	2 FP	19.3 (15)	956 (1)	17.9 (1)	19.6 (11)	0.3 (15)	30.2 (15)	23.4 (17)	2.9 (7)	14.5 (3)	5.2 (11)	8.1 (12)	13.4 (10)
W. Germany	4 G	21.6 (9)	42 (15)	4.4 (17)	27.0 (6)	1.1 (9)	38.0 (8)	30.6 (12)	2.1 (12)	13.2 (6)	6.2 (10)	8.6 (9)	14.8 (5)
Corpor. w/o Labor													
France	1 PF	21.3 (10)	117 (13)	12.8 (3)	30.4 (4)	1.4 (7)	41.7 (6)	14.7 (18)	2.1 (12)	18.4 (2)	9.0 (2)	7.9 (15)	13.5 (9)
Japan	6 E	31.2 (1)	18 (17)	5.3 (15)	11.0 (18)	1.5 (6)	25.5 (18)	27.7 (15)	5.4 (2)	7.9 (11)	0.0 (18)	7.0 (19)	9.3 (18)
Switzerland	5 E	22.8 (7)	1 (19)	5.1 (16)	16.0 (14)	1.1 (9)	30.8 (14)	39.6 (7)	1.9 (13)	9.6 (9)	2.8 (15)	8.1 (12)	13.9 (8)
Least Corporatist													
USA	4 G	18.4 (17)	342 (7)	6.6 (13)	14.6 (17)	2.9 (1)	29.5 (16)	41.7 (5)	2.9 (7)	8.1 (10)	2.0 (16)	9.0 (4)	11.4 (13)
UK	1 PF	17.7 (18)	501 (6)	12.0 (4)	17.3 (12)	2.8 (2)	35.4 (9)	34.8 (10)	3.0 (5)	6.3 (12)	4.7 (12)	8.3 (10)	15.1 (3)
New Zealand	3 F	20.3 (11)	300 (8)	10.3 (6)	16.1 (13)	—	33.1 (11)	65.7 (1)	2.6 (10)	0.0 (18)	3.5 (14)	9.7 (2)	10.0 (15)
Australia	3 F	23.1 (6)	543 (5)	10.1 (7)	15.7 (15)	0.5 (14)	28.6 (17)	46.7 (3)	3.3 (4)	0.0 (18)	1.9 (17)	8.8 (6)	9.7 (16)
Canada	1 PF	22.5 (8)	780 (2)	8.5 (10)	15.1 (16)	2.6 (3)	31.6 (13)	39.3 (8)	3.4 (3)	3.8 (14)	3.8 (13)	9.8 (1)	9.5 (17)
Ireland	1 PF	28.6 (2)	737 (4)	14.8 (2)	23.3 (9)	1.6 (5)	34.0 (10)	34.0 (11)	1.8 (14)	5.4 (13)	6.5 (9)	9.3 (3)	10.7 (14)

TABLE 12G.10   Scores and ranks of corporatist bargaining outcomes, taxing and spending policies, age structure, and economic performance, 1985–89

Countries by Types of Political Econ.	Ec. Perf. Index 1985-89		Capital Formation 1983-87	Strikes 1983-87	Nom. Wage Increases 1980-84	SS/GNP 1980	Pub. Asst. as % GNP 1980	Total Tax Load 1988	Visible Taxes 1988	Corporate Taxes 1983-87	Soc. Sec. Taxes 1984-88	Consump Taxes 1984-88	Pop. 15-19 1985	Pop. 65+ 1985
Left Corporatist														
Sweden	3	F	18.7 (14)	61 (11)	9.0 (9)	33.1 (1)	0.0 (17)	55.3 (1)	39.9 (6)	2.0 (14)	13.3 (6)	7.1 (9)	6.9 (18)	17.9 (1)
Norway	3	F	26.0 (2)	126 (9)	9.3 (8)	23.3 (9)	0.2 (16)	46.9 (4)	29.7 (13)	6.5 (1)	10.8 (8)	9.2 (2)	8.1 (9)	15.6 (2)
Finland	3	F	23.9 (4)	471 (2)	11.1 (5)	21.1 (10)	0.2 (16)	37.9 (10)	46.8 (4)	1.5 (16)	3.3 (15)	8.4 (5)	7.4 (16)	12.4 (11)
Denmark	2	FP	18.3 (15)	217 (7)	8.4 (11)	32.8 (2)	0.9 (11)	52.1 (2)	54.8 (1)	2.3 (10)	1.7 (16)	9.9 (1)	7.9 (12)	15.0 (3)
Left-Cath. Corpor.														
Netherlands	2	FP	19.3 (13)	12 (14)	3.7 (18)	31.3 (3)	2.1 (4)	48.2 (3)	22.3 (17)	3.1 (5)	20.1 (1)	7.6 (7)	8.5 (3)	12.0 (13)
Belgium	4	G	16.0 (18)	—	7.3 (12)	29.8 (5)	0.9 (11)	45.1 (5)	32.6 (10)	2.9 (6)	15.3 (3)	7.3 (8)	7.9 (12)	14.1 (7)
Austria	5	E	22.4 (7)	2 (16)	6.1 (14)	26.3 (7)	0.8 (12)	41.9 (7)	23.3 (16)	1.4 (17)	13.6 (5)	8.9 (3)	8.2 (8)	14.3 (6)
Catholic Corpor.														
Italy	2	FP	20.5 (8)	360 (4)	17.9 (1)	19.6 (11)	0.3 (14)	37.1 (13)	27.0 (15)	3.5 (4)	12.2 (7)	5.3 (12)	8.3 (6)	13.3 (9)
W. Germany	4	G	19.9 (11)	45 (12)	4.4 (17)	27.0 (6)	1.1 (9)	37.4 (11)	29.9 (12)	2.1 (12)	13.9 (4)	6.0 (10)	8.4 (5)	14.7 (5)
Corpor. w/o Labor														
France	2	FP	19.4 (12)	41 (13)	12.8 (3)	30.4 (4)	1.4 (7)	44.4 (6)	14.5 (18)	2.1 (12)	19.2 (2)	8.8 (4)	7.8 (14)	12.8 (10)
Japan	6	E	28.1 (1)	6 (15)	5.3 (15)	11.0 (18)	1.5 (6)	31.3 (16)	27.1 (14)	6.0 (2)	8.6 (11)	0.0 (18)	7.3 (17)	9.9 (18)
Switzerland	5	E	24.0 (3)	1 (17)	5.1 (16)	16.0 (14)	1.1 (9)	32.5 (15)	37.7 (8)	1.9 (15)	10.3 (9)	3.1 (15)	8.0 (10)	13.7 (8)
Least Corporatist														
USA	4	G	17.7 (16)	89 (10)	6.6 (13)	14.6 (17)	2.9 (1)	29.8 (18)	39.7 (7)	2.0 (14)	8.6 (11)	2.2 (17)	7.8 (14)	12.0 (13)
UK	2	FP	16.9 (17)	323 (5)	12.0 (4)	17.3 (12)	2.8 (2)	37.3 (12)	32.0 (11)	4.3 (3)	6.8 (12)	5.9 (11)	8.2 (8)	14.9 (4)
New Zealand	1	PF	23.7 (6)	488 (1)	10.3 (6)	16.1 (13)	—	37.9 (10)	54.6 (2)	2.7 (9)	0.0 (18)	5.0 (13)	9.2 (2)	10.1 (16)
Australia	2	FP	23.8 (5)	201 (8)	10.1 (7)	15.7 (15)	0.5 (13)	30.8 (17)	48.1 (3)	2.8 (8)	0.0 (18)	2.5 (16)	8.4 (5)	10.0 (17)
Canada	2	FP	20.1 (9)	373 (3)	8.5 (10)	15.1 (16)	2.6 (3)	34.0 (14)	41.6 (5)	2.8 (8)	4.5 (14)	4.7 (14)	7.8 (14)	10.4 (15)
Ireland	3	F	20.0 (10)	303 (6)	14.8 (2)	23.3 (9)	1.6 (5)	41.5 (8)	36.4 (9)	1.3 (18)	5.6 (13)	8.2 (6)	9.3 (1)	10.6 (14)

TABLE 12G.11   Zero-order correlations of inequality measures with corporatist bargaining outcomes and economic performance

Corporatist Bargaining Outcomes and Econ. Perf.	Equality Income Share to Lowest Quintile		Inequality Income Share to Highest Quintile		Inequality Ratio of Top to Bottom Quintiles	
Corporatism						
score	.41•	—	−.53*	—	−.54*	
Strikes						
1973-77	−.47	—	.15	—	.40•	—
1978-82	—	−.26	—	.24	—	.23
Capital Investment						
1973-77	.28	—	−.29	—	−.28	—
1978-82	—	.32	—	−.23	—	−.26
Nom. Wage Incr.						
1974-79	.04	—	−.09	—	−.10	—
1980-84	—	−.13	—	.15	—	.08
SS/GNP						
1975-77	.34•	—	−.42*	—	−.44*	—
1980	—	.32	—	−.46*	—	−.42*
Pub. Asst./GNP						
1974	−.10	—	.10	—	.11	—
1980	—	−.24	—	.27	—	.26
Total taxes						
1974	.15	—	−.56*	—	−.35•	—
1980	—	.29	—	−.56*	—	−.45*
Visible taxes						
1974	−.44*	—	.14	—	.42*	—
1980	—	−.48*	—	.35•	—	.52*
Corp. taxes						
1973-77	.04	—	.23	—	.16	—
1978-82	—	.20	—	−.20	—	−.16
SS taxes						
1974-78	.54*	—	−.34•	—	−.56*	—
1979-83	—	.57*	—	−.32	—	−.57*
Cons. taxes						
1974-78	.18	—	−.52*	—	−.40•	—
1979-83	—	.16	—	−.49*	—	−.38•
Pop. 15-19						
1977	−.64**	—	.53*	—	.66**	—
1980	—	−.63**	—	.55*	—	.62**
Pop. 65+						
1977	.25	—	−.34	—	−.35•	—
1980	—	.24	—	−.34•	—	−.34•
Econ. Perf. 1974-79						
Index	.50*	—	−.35•	—	−.47*	—
Growth	.40•	—	−.69**	—	−.54*	—
Inflation	−.11	—	.09	—	.08	—
Unempl.	−.13	—	−.16	—	.02	—
Econ. Perf. 1980-84						
Index	—	.28	—	−.09	—	−.14
Growth	—	.21	—	−.16	—	−.15
Inflation	—	−.28	—	.20	—	.19
Unempl.	—	−.12	—	−.15	—	.01

Note: Italy excluded from strike correlations for 1973–77; Israel excluded from inflation correlations for 1974–79.

TABLE 12G.12 Zero-order correlations of economic performance, five periods, with possible causes, including property taxes

Possible causes of economic performance	Property Taxes 1965–72	Property Taxes 1973–77	Property Taxes 1978–82	Property Taxes 1983–87	Economic Performance 1950–74	Economic Performance 1965–74	Economic Performance 1974–79	Economic Performance 1980–84	Economic Performance 1985–89
Property Taxes									
1965–72	—	—	—	—	−.87**	−.60**	—	—	—
1973–77	.99**	—	—	—	—	—	−.56**	—	—
1978–82	.92**	.96**	—	—	—	—	—	−.51*	—
1983–87	.89**	.94**	.99**	—	—	—	—	—	−.46*
Corporatism score	−.64**	−.64**	−.57**	−.53*	.39*	.32•	.19	−.06	−.15
Strikes									
1960–72	.79**	—	—	—	−.83**	−.51*	—	—	—
1973–77	—	.56*	—	—	—	—	−.68**	—	—
1978–82	—	—	.40•	—	—	—	—	−.59**	—
1983–87	—	—	—	.38	—	—	—	—	−.62**
Capital Investment									
1960–73	−.68**	—	—	—	.70**	.44*	—	—	—
1973–77	—	−.45*	—	—	—	—	.61**	—	—
1978–82	—	—	−.40*	—	—	—	—	.40•	—
1983–87	—	—	—	−.38•	—	—	—	—	.32•
Energy Dependence									
1970	−.64**	−.65**	−.62**	—	.42*	.11	.18	—	—
1978	—	—	—	−.64**	—	—	—	.34•	.36•
Real Growth SS/cap.									
1950–66	−.61**	—	—	—	.26	.10	—	—	—
1966–74	—	−.39•	—	—	—	—	.26	—	—
1974–80	—	—	−.25	−.28	—	—	—	.36•	.47*
Military Sp./cap.									
1966–71	.08	—	—	—	.09	−.07	—	—	—
1974	—	−.06	—	—	—	—	.06	—	—
1980	—	—	.07	—	—	—	—	−.21	—
1986	—	—	—	.13	—	—	—	—	−.14

TABLE 12G.12 (continued)

Possible causes of economic performance	Property Taxes 1965–72	Property Taxes 1973–77	Property Taxes 1978–82	Property Taxes 1983–87	Economic Performance 1950–74	Economic Performance 1965–74	Economic Performance 1974–79	Economic Performance 1980–84	Economic Performance 1985–89
Military Sp./GNP									
1966–71	.39•	—	—	—	−.22	—	—	—	—
1974	—	.44★	—	—	—	−.26	−.23	—	—
1980	—	—	.48★	—	—	—	—	−.31	—
1986	—	—	—	.58★★	—	—	—	—	−.17
Pop. age 0–14									
1960	.48★	—	—	—	−.54★★	−.35•	—	—	—
1977	—	.48★	—	—	—	—	−.42★	—	—
1980	—	—	.27	—	—	—	—	−.35•	—
1985	—	—	—	.24	—	—	—	—	−.29
Pub. Asst. /GNP									
1966–71	.61★★	—	—	—	−.59★★	−.35•	—	—	—
1974	—	.68★★	—	—	—	—	−.18	—	—
1980	—	—	.80★★	.79★★	—	—	—	−.37•	−.07
Pub. Asst./cap.									
1966–71	.61★★	—	—	—	−.45★	−.23	—	—	—
1974	—	.53★	—	—	—	—	−.07	—	—
1980	—	—	.70★★	.68★★	—	—	—	−.23	.01
Lawyers									
as % of LF 1982	.63★★	.63★★	.57★★	.57★★	−.53★	−.42★	−.61★★	−.10	−.24
growth 1970–79	.62★★	.62★★	.55★★	.53★	−.36•	−.46★	−.31•	−.23	−.04
Mobility									
in Higher Ed.	.15	.24	.35	.40•	−.06	−.21	−.37•	.12	.00
intergenerational	.78★★	.76★★	.77★★	.78★★	−.75★★	−.40•	−.57★	−.44•	−.46•
Min. Grp. Cleavages	.49★	.53★	.62★★	.62★★	−.33•	−.09	−.33•	−.16	−.08

Significance levels: • = p < .10, ★ = p < .05, ★★ = p < .01
Note: Italy excluded from strikes correlations for 1960–77; Israel excluded from all Mil/GNP correlations; Israel and USA excluded from all Mil/cap correlations.

TABLE 12G.13   Energy dependence among nineteen rich countries, 1970 and 1978, rank and score

	1970 Energy Dependence			1978 Energy Dependence		
	Oil as % of total energy consumption	Energy production as % of total energy consumption	Index Score and Rank	Oil as % of total energy consumption	Energy production as % of total energy consumption	Index Score and Rank
Sweden	83 (3)	10 (17)	4 H	78 (3)	18 (13)	3 MH
Switzerland	81 (4)	18 (15)	4 H	76 (4)	22 (11)	3 MH
Denmark	89 (2)	0 (19)	4 H	81 (2)	2 (18)	4 H
Finland	75 (6)	6 (18)	4 H	68 (8)	9 (16)	3 MH
Italy	75 (6)	18 (15)	4 H	71 (6)	14 (15)	3 MH
Japan	68 (7)	17 (16)	4 H	74 (5)	8 (17)	4 H
Belgium	50 (13)	19 (13)	3 MH	51 (12)	14 (15)	3 MH
New Zealand	57 (10)	43 (8)	2 M	51 (12)	58 (7)	2 M
West Germany	50 (13)	55 (7)	2 M	49 (15)	45 (8)	2 M
France	60 (8)	31 (11)	2 M	63 (9)	20 (12)	2 M
Norway	54 (11)	41 (10)	2 M	53 (10)	228 (1)	1 ML
Israel	98 (1)	83 (4)	2 M	99 (1)	1 (19)	4 H
Austria	50 (13)	42 (9)	2 M	51 (12)	34 (9)	2 M
Ireland	58 (9)	30 (12)	2 M	70 (7)	25 (10)	2 M
Canada	49 (15)	114 (1)	1 ML	49 (15)	113 (4)	1 ML
United Kingdom	43 (18)	55 (7)	1 ML	40 (18)	84 (5)	0 L
Netherlands	48 (16)	74 (5)	1 ML	38 (19)	133 (3)	0 L
United States	41 (19)	91 (3)	0 L	47 (16)	81 (6)	0 L
Australia	46 (17)	100 (2)	0 L	41 (17)	135 (2)	0 L

TABLE 12G.14   External shocks and subsequent economic performance, zero-order correlations, nineteen countries

	Economic Performance Index		Real Growth of GDP per capita		Inflation		Unemployment	
	1974-79	1980-84	1974-79	1980-84	1974-79	1980-84	1974-79	1980-84
Energy Dependence								
Oil/Cons.								
1970	−.16	—	−.30	—	.06	—	−.29	—
1978	—	.21	—	.40*	—	.18	—	−.31
Prod./Cons.								
1970	−.25	—	−.07	—	−.07	—	.34•	—
1978	—	−.11	—	−.15	—	.03	—	−.00
Index								
1970	.18	—	−.07	—	−.01	—	−.34•	—
1978	—	.34•	—	.52*	—	−.04	—	−.31
Change in Terms of Trade								
1973-74	.27	—	.34•	—	−.39•	—	.03	—
1978-79	—	−.42*	—	−.22	—	.45*	—	.12

Note: • =$p < .10$, *=$p < .05$, **=$p < .01$; Israel excluded from correlations with inflation 1974−79.

MEASURES OF
CENTRAL BANK AUTONOMY

The ranking of central bank independence in chapter 17 is based on empirical evidence and scorings in Cukierman (1992), Grilli, Masciandaro, and Tabellini (1991), Alesina (1988), Alesina and Summers (1993), Epstein and Shor (1986), Burdekin and Willett (1991), and Bade and Parkin (1987). All studies define independence or autonomy of the central bank as the ability of the central bank to pursue price stability free from the political pressure of the current government.

Formal central bank autonomy can be measured by examining the degree of independence conferred by law. All studies above except Cukierman use a legal definition. Cukierman supplements measures of legal independence with a questionnaire survey of qualified central bank officials, a subjective measure of what he calls "actual" independence plus a calculation of average turnover rates of central bank governors for over 50 countries for the 40 years ending 1989. Because turnover rates for our rich democracies fall in a narrow range, and because turnover is a dubious measure of autonomy, we ignore them. (The divergence between legal independence vs. independence measured by low turnover is substantial only for less developed countries.)

For my purposes Cukierman's questionnaire data can be viewed as validation of the formal-legal measures in table 17.4. If we array his scores based on survey data for the nine rich democracies he covers (ranging from 1.00 for the Bundesbank to .51 for Ireland's central bank) and translate them into four groups using natural cutting points (H, M, ML, L), we find only one clear difference. Our combined ranks for legal autonomy place Ireland medium-high; questionnaire data rank it low. Because Ireland's economic performance was poor, 1980–84, and average, 1985–89, changing its rank from medium-high to low would make only a slight difference in the negative correlation between bank independence and our economic performance index. As Cukierman (1992, p. 421) concludes from his statistical analysis, "legal independence is a reasonably good proxy for actual CB independence in developed but not in developing countries."

Two dimensions of legal independence are measured in table 17.4: "political" and "economic." Bade and Parkin and Alesina classify banks according to their degree of political independence. Higher scores for autonomy are given to banks that can set policy objectives free from government influence, that have few of their policymakers appointed by elected officials, and that have the objective of price stability written into their charters. Grilli, Masciandaro, and Tabellini and Cukierman use similar political measures but add economic independence measured by the central banks' ability to use monetary policy instruments at the banks' exclusive discretion. Scoring basically reflects whether the central bank is required to provide credit to finance government debt. Strict limitations on government borrowing from the central bank are an indicator of the economic independence of central banks.

For my 18-country analysis of CB autonomy and economic performance I used the four-point index developed by Bade and Parkin (1987) and extended by Alesina (1988) to include New Zealand. Austria (2 = medium) is scored by Burdekin and Willett (1991). I averaged these scores and the scores combining political and economic independence computed by Grilli et al. (1991). Ireland (2.5) and Finland (2.0) are added by translating Cukierman's unweighted index of overall legal independence (ranging from Switzerland's .68 to Norway's .14) into an equivalent metric (Cukierman, 1992, p. 382, table 19.4). The rationale for combining these somewhat different measures into a 4-point scale for 18 countries is that Cukierman is able to replicate fairly closely the results obtained by Alesina and Grilli et al. by comparing regressions of inflation on CBA using his scores for legal independence and the same subset of countries (Cukierman, 1992, p. 425). Any differences in Cukierman's results and the results from Alesina and Grilli et al. stem from the differences in samples, not from the measures of CBA. The correlation of the index used in table 17.4 and Cukierman's scale (with or without Ireland and Finland) is .81. Replicating our analysis of central bank autonomy and economic performance using his measure of legal independence yields almost identical results. In fact, the correlations of his measure and inflation are even weaker than ours for the same subset of countries and periods.

Various scholars disagree about Japan. Bade and Parkin rank the Bank of Japan high, Grilli et al. medium, Epstein and Schorr (1986) low. My judgment is that in relation to major ministries and the government, the autonomy of the Bank of Japan ranks low (1 − 1.5). See chapter 2 (on corporatism-without-labor).

MAYHEM INDEX,
MOBILITY-MERITOCRACY INDEX,
AND MINORITY-GROUP CLEAVAGES

MAYHEM INDEX

The Wilensky mayhem index is constructed from four components: death rates due to fire and to homicide, divorce rates, and unemployment rates. Its theoretical rationale is in the text. The distribution of values on each component is divided into high, medium, medium-low, and low values, based on natural cutting points. Each country receives a score of 3 for a high value on that component, 2 for a medium value, 1 for a medium-low value, and 0 for a low value. The scores on all four components are then summed for each country to create the mayhem index, which has a theoretical range from 0 to 12.

For 1970, the fire and homicide death rates per 100,000 inhabitants are from WHO, *World Health Statistics Annual,* 1972 and 1973 volumes (Geneva, 1973 and 1974, respectively). All rates are for 1973, except for Ireland and New Zealand for both measures and Belgium for homicide, where the data are for 1972. Divorce rates per 1,000 married couples for 1970 are taken from *UN Demographic Yearbook 1976* (New York, 1977), from the "Special Topic: Marriage and Divorce Statistics" section. The numbers of divorces used in calculating these rates are three-year averages centered on the census year closest to 1970, and the number of couples is for that census year. Netherlands is missing on this divorce rate, but it falls between France and Norway on divorce per 1,000 people for 1970, based on data from *UN Demographic Yearbook 1974* (New York, 1975). Since France is scored 0 (low) and Norway is scored 1 (medium) on divorce for purposes of creating the index, Netherlands was assigned a score of 0.5 on divorce in calculating its index score. The unemployment rates used are the average annual unemployment rates for the period 1960–75. See appendix G for details and sources.

For 1980, the fire and homicide death rates are taken from WHO, *World Health Statistics Annual,* 1982 volume (Geneva, 1983); except for France, New Zealand and Finland (the 1983 volume); and Canada, USA, Ireland, Italy and Belgium (the 1984 volume). All data are for 1980, except Finland and Belgium, where the data are for 1979. Divorce rates per 1,000 people for 1980 are from the *UN Demographic Yearbook 1982* (New York, 1984), table 33. Unemployment rates are average annual unemployment rates for the period 1975–84. Sources are described in appendix G.

TABLE 141.1 Mobility and meritocracy measures closely match residential mobility measures

| Country | Residential Mobility circa 1981[a] | | Occupational and Educational Mobility[b] | | |
	Long estimate, % population changing residence in 1 year	Long estimate, 5-year interval	Intergenerational occupational mobility	2-component mobility index	4-component mobility-meritocracy index
New Zealand	19.4 (1) H	45.3 (4)	na	na	na
Canada	18.0 (2) H	47.6 (1)	.184 (2) H	4 H	8 H
United States	17.5 (3) H	46.4 (3)	.114 (4) H	4 H	8 H
Australia	17.0 (4) H	47.1 (2)	.141 (3) H	4 H	6 H
Switzerland	13.7 (5) MH	36.0 (5)	na	2 MH	3 ML
Israel	11.3 (6) MH	29.8 (6)	.286 (1) H	4 H	6 H
United Kingdom	9.6 (7) ML	na	.102 (5) H	4 H	5 HM
Sweden	9.5 (9) ML	na	.045 (7) M	2 MH	4 M
Japan	9.5 (9) ML	22.6 (7)	-.048 (10) L	0 L	1 L
France	9.4 (10) ML	na	.056 (6) M	1 ML	2 LM
Netherlands	7.7 (11) L	na	.041 (8) M	1 ML	4 M
Austria	7.6 (12) L	20.1 (8)	na	0 L	0 L
Belgium	7.3 (13) L	na	-.033 (9) L	1 ML	3 ML
Ireland	6.1 (14) L	na	na	0 L	0 L

[a]Source: Long (1991), tables 1 and 2.

[b]Measures and index construction are described in appendix 1 and text for chapter 14 (mayhem). Numbers in parentheses indicate rank order from high to low. Read MH as a medium to high score; ML as a medium to low score.

For 1988, fire and homicide death rates per 100,000 are from WHO, *World Health Statistics Annual,* 1990 volume (Geneva, 1991), except for Sweden and Belgium (the 1989 volume). All data are for 1988, except Switzerland, West Germany, UK, Austria, and Japan (1989); Sweden, New Zealand, Israel, and Italy (1987); and Belgium (1986). Divorce rates per 1,000 people are from *UN Demographic Yearbook 1988* (New York, 1990). All data are for 1987, except USA and Denmark (1988); and Australia, Belgium, and Italy (1986). Average annual unemployment rates for the period 1985−88 are used for the unemployment component; see appendix G for sources.

MOBILITY-MERITOCRACY INDEX

The mobility-meritocracy index combines two mobility measures, an index of intergenerational occupational mobility and an index of educational mobility, and two meritocracy measures, enrollment in, and spending on, higher education. The occupational mobility index is from A. Tyree, M. Semyonov, and R. W. Hodge, "Gaps and Glissandos: Inequality, Economic Development, and Social Mobility in 24 Countries" *American Sociological Review* 44 (June 1979): 410−424, table 2, p. 416. They represent the relative levels of intergenerational mobility of sons from blue-collar origins into white-collar occupations, for each country. Since, on their index, negative values mean high mobility and positive values mean low mobility, we multiplied their index scores by minus 1 to create our mobility index. The educational mobility index is the percentage of students of working-class origins in higher education, for 1964 or the nearest year, from Conference on Policies for Educational Growth, *Group Disparities in Educational Participation and Achievement* Vol. IV (Paris: OECD, 1971), graph 21, p. 61. The other two meritocracy measures are the enrollment ratios in higher education and the expenditures on higher education per person in the total population averaged for 1965 and 1971. The details and sources for these measures appear in appendix G.

The construction of the mobility-meritocracy index is similar to that of the mayhem index. In this case, distributions were divided into high, medium, and low, countries were scored 2, 1, and 0, and the scores were summed over the four components, yielding an index with a theoretical range of 0 to 8. One modification was necessitated by missing data on the mobility components. Five countries (Austria, Finland, Ireland, New Zealand, and Switzerland) were missing on occupational mobility, and four (Australia, Israel, Japan, and New Zealand) were missing on educational mobility. Thus we had data on both mobility components for only 11 countries. Of these, five (high-ranking Canada, UK, USA; medium-ranking Sweden; and low-ranking West Germany) ranked the same on both measures, while six (Belgium, Denmark, France, Italy, Netherlands, and Norway) were medium on one component and low on the other. But two of these cases were borderline: Netherlands and Norway were just above the cutting point on one component and just below it on the other. Thus, for the 8 cases for which we had data on only one component, we assumed that it would rank the same (H, M, L) on the other component. This left only New Zealand, missing on both components, with a missing value for the index.

A partial validation of these early mobility measures—country rankings of structural variables that persist over long periods—comes from a study of residential mobility differences among developed countries by Larry Long (1991). We would expect some correlation between intergenerational occupational and educational mobility and residential mobility. Table 14I.1 aligns

TABLE 14I.2 Minority-group cleavages index

Country	Score	Country	Score
Canada	.71	France	.28
Israel	.58	Japan	.19
USA	.55	Austria	.17
Switzerland	.55	Finland	.12
UK	.47	Italy	.10
Australia	.44	Ireland	.08
New Zealand	.43	Denmark	.05
Netherlands	.37	Sweden	.04
Belgium	.34	Norway	.03
W. Germany	.28		

our crude intergenerational mobility rates (sons of blue-collar fathers who moved to white-collar jobs), our two-component index of mobility (intergenerational mobility and percentage of working-class sons and daughters in higher education), as well as the four-component mobility-meritocracy index (the two mobility measures above plus higher education enrollment ratios and per capita higher education expenditures) with two of Long's residential mobility measures: his estimate of the percentage of the population changing their usual residence in one year for 14 of our countries, circa 1981, and the percentage that moved in the preceding five years for 8 of our countries.

A glance at the table reveals a close match between residential and other mobility measures.

Only 1 case of our 18 countries ranked by mobility or meritocracy deviates substantially in residential mobility. Great Britain ranks high or medium-high on our mobility and meritocracy indexes but medium-low in residential mobility. Japan is a bit deviant; it ranks low on our mobility measures but is about average in the percentage of Japanese who have moved in the last year. Because of Japan's unusually swift growth in recent decades, however, its relative rank on our mobility measures has probably moved up to match its residential mobility rate.

Despite the well-known difficulties (Wilensky, 1966b), I read this table as an encouraging sign that the old intergenerational occupational mobility data we are using and the indexes that include them reflect reality and make sense.

MINORITY-GROUP CLEAVAGES

This is an average of the ethnolinguistic fractionalization index (measured for 1960–65), and the religious fractionalization index (measured for 1964), both from Charles L. Taylor and Michael C. Hudson, *World Handbook of Political and Social Indicators,* second edition (New Haven: Yale University Press, 1972), equally weighted. Linguistic cleavage scores range from .01 (Japan) to .75 (Canada); religious cleavage scores from .01 (Sweden) to .67 (Canada). From monographic literature, we infer that these rankings are both reasonable and stable, except for Israel. The Taylor-Hudson index captured only "Jewish vs. other religions," missing the strong divisions within the Jewish population between secular Jews and fundamentalist Jews, and to a lesser extent between Sephardic Jews ("Oriental," mainly Middle Eastern) and Ashkenazi Jews (mainly European or American), with more recent cleavages between Soviet immigrants and others, and Ethiopian Jews and others. An additional source of cleavage is the one-sixth of Israelis who are Arabs. We gave Israel a relatively high score of .58. The cleavage scores are shown in table 14I.2.

Although migration since the 1960s has increased and there has been some convergence in social heterogeneity (e.g., Sweden and Italy have perhaps moved up), the relative rankings are probably quite stable (see chap. 17 for a discussion of the amount of migration and its economic and political effects).

AFFLUENCE

This is measured by GNP per capita. The average of 1966 and 1971 figures for each country was used for this analysis. GNP at factor cost was calculated from data in *UN Yearbook of National Accounts Statistics 1973* (New York, 1975), using the formula GNP at factor cost = GNP at market prices minus indirect taxes net of subsidies. This was divided by total population, taken from *UN Demographic Yearbook,* 1970 and 1973 (New York, 1971 and 1974, respectively).

PUBLIC EMPLOYEES

Because cross-national figures on government employees generally include the armed forces, which are shaped mainly by war and alliance or pact position and fluctuate greatly over time, and because my interest is mainly in domestic policy and its impact, we aimed to estimate nonmilitary public employees as a percentage of the total civilian labor force. Several sources cover total public employees, military personnel, and the labor force. Data on total government are from OECD, *Employment in the Public Sector* (Paris: 1982), table A1, pp. 70–71. OECD's definition of general government includes "various departments and agencies at central, state, provincial, and local level which produce *non-market* goods and services" but excludes all "government-owned firms and public corporations which produce and sell goods and services in a market" (p. 9). Italian figures in this source exclude conscripts in the army, so we constructed estimates of these conscripts from two sources, OECD, Working Party No. 1 of the Economic Policy Committee, "The Role of the Public Sector," CPE/WP1(82)4, (Paris: OECD, 1982), and the Institute for Strategic Studies, *The Military Balance* series. For both Japan and Ireland for 1966, we calculated rates of growth in public employment, which we then used to extrapolate backwards from OECD data for later years. For Japan we used the *Japan Statistical Yearbook* series (Bureau of Statistics, Office of the Prime Minister); for Ireland both the *Census, 1966* (Central Statistics Office, Dublin, 1968) and the *Statistical Abstract of Ireland 1972–1973* (Central Statistics Office, Dublin, 1976). Figures for Israel's public employees are from the Statistical Abstract of Israel for 1967, 1972, 1975, and 1979. These figures already exclude the military.

Because the OECD figures include military forces, we used separate data on the size of the armed forces from the U.S. Arms Control and Disarmament Agency, *World Military Expenditures 1963–1973* (Washington, DC, no date). Table II provides data on the size of the armed forces for 1966 and 1971. In almost all cases these data were identical or nearly identical to those in the International Institute for Strategic Studies (until 1971, the Institute for Strategic Studies), *The Military Balance* (London), published annually. Our figures exclude military reserves but include conscripts, paramilitary border defense troops, and gendarmerie under the control of defense departments. We included gendarmerie when they are either under the control of the defense ministry or have military equipment (armored personnel carriers, artillery, tanks). The aim: to keep all data consistent with those of the ACDA, which include "active-duty military personnel, including paramilitary forces where those forces resemble regular units in their organization, equipment, training, or mission." Reserve forces are excluded (ACDA, *World Military Expenditures 1963–1973,* p. 10). In all cases these gendarmerie numbers were small enough so that including them does not affect the final public employee figures.

After subtracting the armed forces from the total government employees, we divided the result by the size of the civilian labor force. Labor-force figures for 1966, 1971, and 1974 were taken from the OECD, *Labor Force Statistics 1966–1977* (Paris: 1979), table II, with the exceptions of Israel, Czechoslovakia, the GDR, and the USSR, whose data were drawn from the International Labor Office (ILO), *Yearbook of Labor Statistics 1975* (Geneva: 1975), tables 3 and 10. The figures for Sweden, Switzerland, Norway, Austria, Japan, Czechoslovakia, the GDR, and the USSR originally included armed forces, so we subtracted the latter using figures from *The Military Balance,* cross-checked by the ACDA figures for 1966 and 1971. For 1978, labor force statistics come from the OECD, *Labor Force Statistics 1969–1980* (Paris, 1982), table 5, except for Israel, whose figures come from the ILO, *Yearbook for Labor Statistics* (Geneva, 1982), table 3A.

French figures presented several problems of changed definitions and comparability. Using the *Annuaire Statistique de la France* for 1984 and 1989 (Paris: INSEE) we adjusted French figures to include nondefense military employees and exclude hospital employees, doctors, and pharmacists (listed as public employees in 1980 but not after the mid-1980s). About two-thirds of all French physicians in the early 1970s, for example, were in private practice and the private medical sector has since grown (Hollingsworth et al., 1990, pp. 34–36). The net effect: civilian public employees are 11.8% of the 1980 civilian labor force, growing to 12.7% in 1986. If we counted all 620,858 doctors, pharmacists, and hospital employees as public employees, it would increase the percentage of civilian public employees by 2.7 percentage points, so the French figure in table 9.1 would be 14.5% for 1980 instead of 11.8%—on the high side of "low." Other minor adjustments make only trivial differences in the final figure.

For countries that provide unusually high subsidies for "private," "independent" "voluntary" associations such as churches—especially Holland and Italy—it can be argued that the employees of these quasi-public agencies should be counted as public employees, increasing the rank of these countries in table 9.1. Rein (1985, p. 112), for example, estimates that adding personnel in the nonprofit sector of the Netherlands would boost its percentage of public employees (11.3% in 1980) by half again as much. Because this is a gray area where data are not comparable and the blurring of lines between public and private is a general phenomenon, we have not attempted to adjust the figures for quasi-public employees any further than OECD has already done. OECD, in fact, tries to apply a strict definition that includes "nonprofit and non-market institutions serving households or business enterprises which are wholly or mainly financed *and* controlled by the public authorities" (Feys, 1994, p. 13). Thus our figures include employees in a few charitable associations but exclude employees in a great many autonomous but government-financed non-profits. These issues are discussed in chapter 2, in the section on the blurring of public and private divisions (pp. 95–99).

A study by Huber and Stephens (1996) covering 16 of our countries that came to my attention several years after I completed this analysis confirms chapter 9. Their measure in table 2 yields lower figures for public-employment ratios than those in my tables. But their rank order for 1975 is almost identical to my rank order for 1980 in table 7.2. There are only two notable discrepancies: Huber and Stephens rank France 6th, we rank it 13th (the explanation is above); and they rank Australia 3rd, we rank it 8th (a discrepancy everywhere in this literature, which I have been unable to resolve by consultation with OECD's experts). Eleven of their 16 are identical in rank or only one rank apart; one, Switzerland, is only two ranks apart (ours, 15th; theirs, 13th), Italy three (ours, 10th; theirs, 13th) and Belgium, four (ours, 7th; theirs, 11th). These minor discrepancies might be explained by the five-year difference in dates. In short, even quite different measures of public employment yield a similar picture.

Huber and Stephens (1996, p. 9), using different measures of both left power and public employment, add a finding regarding early and recent trends that is consistent with chapter 9: "Civilian government employment as a percentage of the working age population did not vary much among [16] countries in the 1960s. To the extent that there was variation, the Anglo-American countries tended to have the highest levels. All countries then expanded public employment until the mid-1970s. After that, public employment levels began to diverge sharply. Whereas they increased dramatically in the Scandinavian countries [from 1975 to 1980] they increased only marginally elsewhere, and in the United Kingdom they even declined."

BIBLIOGRAPHY

Aaron, Henry. "Social Security: International Comparisons." In *Studies in the Economics of Income Maintenance,* ed. Otto Eckstein, 13–48. Washington, DC: Brookings Institution, 1967.

Aaron, Henry J. *Who Pays the Property Tax? A New View.* Washington, DC: Brookings Institution, 1975.

Aaron, Henry J. *Politics and the Professors: The Great Society in Perspective.* Washington, DC: Brookings Institution, 1978.

Aaron, Henry J., ed. *The Value-Added Tax: Lessons from Europe.* Washington, DC: Brookings Institution, 1981.

Aaron, Henry J. "The Value-Added Tax: Sorting Through the Practical and Political Problems." *The Brookings Review* 6, 3 (1988): 10–16.

Aaron, Henry. "Thinking About Health Care Finance: Some Propositions." In *Health Care Reform: The Will to Change.* OECD Health Policy Studies No. 8: 47–57. Paris: OECD, 1996.

Aaron, Henry and William B. Schwartz. "Rationing Health Care: The Choice Before Us." *Science* 247 (1990): 418–422.

Aarts, Kees. "Intermediate Organizations and Interest Representation." In *Citizens and the State,* ed. Hans-Dieter Klingemann and Dieter Fuchs, 227–257. Oxford: Oxford University Press, 1995.

Aarts, Leo J. M., Richard Burkhauser, and Philip R. De Jong. *Curing the Dutch Disease.* Avebury, Aldershot, UK: 1995.

Aarts, Leo J. M. and Philip R. De Jong. *Economic Aspects of Disability Behavior.* Amsterdam: Elsevier Science Publishers, B.V., 1992.

Aarts, Leo J. M. and Philip R. De Jong. "Early Retirement of Older Male Workers under the Dutch Social Security Disability Insurance Programme." In *Age, Work, and Social Security,* ed. A. B. Atkinson and Martin Rein, 20–50. New York: St. Martin's Press, 1993.

Aarts, Leo J. M. and Philip De Jong. "European Experiences with Disability Policy." Revision of paper presented at the Workshop on Disability, Work, and Cash Benefits in Santa Monica, CA, 1995.

Aberbach, Joel D., Robert D. Putnam, and Bert A. Rockman. *Bureaucrats and Politicians in Western Democracies.* Cambridge, MA: Harvard University Press, 1981.

Aberbach, J. D. and B. A. Rockman. "On the Rise, Transformation, and Decline of Analysis in the U.S. Government." *Governance* 2 (1989): 293–314.

Abo, Tetsuo, ed. *Hybrid Factory: The Japanese Production System in the United States.* New York: Oxford University Press, 1994.

Abowd, John M. and Richard B. Freeman. "Introduction and Summary." In *Immigration, Trade and the Labor Market,* ed. John M. Abowd and Richard B. Freeman, 1–25. Chicago: University of Chicago Press, 1991a.

Abowd, John M. and Richard J. Freeman, eds. *Immigration, Trade and the Labor Market.* Chicago: University of Chicago Press, 1991b.

Abraham, David. *The Collapse of the Weimar Republic: Political Economy and Crisis.* Princeton: Princeton University Press, 1981.

Abraham, Steven E. and Paula B. Voos. "Changes in Canadian Labor Law and U.S. Labor Law Reform," 194–200. 48th Annual Proceedings, Industrial Relations Research Association, San Francisco, 1996.

Abramson, Paul R. "Developing Party Identification: A Further Examination of Life-Cycle, Generational, and Period Effects." *American Journal of Political Science* 23 (1979): 78–96.

Abramson, Paul R. *Political Attitudes in America: Formation and Change.* San Francisco: W. H. Freeman, 1983.

Abramson, Paul R., John H. Aldrich, Phil Paolino, and David W. Rhode. "Third-Party and Independent Candidates in American Politics: Wallace, Anderson, and Perot." *Political Science Quarterly* 110, 3 (1995): 349–368.

Abramson, Paul R., John H. Aldrich, and David W. Rohde. *Change and Continuity in the 1992 Elections.* Washington, DC: Congressional Quarterly Press, 1994.

Abramson, Paul R. and Ronald Inglehart. "Education, Security, and Postmaterialism: A Comment on Duch and Taylor's 'Postmaterialism and the Economic Condition.'" *American Journal of Political Science* 38, 3 (1994): 797–814.

Acs, Gregory. "Do Welfare Benefits Promote Out-of-Wedlock Childbearing?" In *Welfare Reform: An Analysis of the Issues,* ed. Isabel V. Sawhill, 51–54. Washington, DC: Urban Institute, 1995.

Adams, Carolyn and Kathryn Winston. *Mothers at Work: Public Policies in the United States, Sweden, and China.* New York: Longman, 1980.

Adams, F. Gerald and Lawrence R. Klein, ed. *Industrial Policies for Growth and Competitiveness.* Vol. 1. Lexington, MA: Lexington Books, D. C. Heath, 1983.

Adams, Orvill. "Understanding the Health Care System That Works." In *Looking North for Health: What We Can Learn from Canada's Health Care System,* ed. Arnold Bennett and Orville Adams, 113–141. San Francisco, CA: Jossey-Bass, 1993.

Adams, Roy J. "Industrial Relations in Europe and North America: Some Contemporary Themes." *European Journal of Industrial Relations* 1, 1 (1995): 47–62.

Adatto, Kiku. *Picture Perfect: The Art and Artifice of Public Image Making.* New York: Basic Books, 1993.

Adelman, Irma. *Income Distribution Policy in Developing Countries: A Case Study of Korea.* Stanford, CA: Stanford University Press for the World Bank, 1978.

Adler, Paul S. and Robert E. Cole. "Designed for Learning: A Tale of Two Auto Plants." *Sloan Management Review* (Spring 1993): 85–93.

Advisory Council on Social Security. *Report of the 1994–1996 Advisory Council on Social Security.* Volume 2. Advisory Council on Social Security, 1997.

Ajami, Riad A. and David A. Ricks. "Motives of Non-American Firms Investing in the United States." *Journal of International Business Studies* 12, 3 (1981): 25–34.

Alba, Richard D. *Ethnic Identity: The Transformation of White America.* New Haven: Yale University Press, 1990.

Alba, Richard D. "Assimilation's Quiet Tide." *The Public Interest* 119 (Spring 1995): 3–18.

Alber, Jens. "The Emergence of Welfare Classes in West Germany: Theoretical Perspectives and Empirical Evidence." Paper presented at the Tenth World Congress of Sociology, session on "Stratification, Politics, and Public Policy," Mexico City, August 16–21, 1982.

Bibliography

Alber, Jens. "Germany." In *Growth to Limits: The Western European Welfare States since World War II,* ed. Peter Flora, 4–154. Vol. 2. *Germany, United Kingdom, Ireland, Italy.* Berlin: Walter de Gruyter, 1986.

Alber, Jens. "Is There a Crisis of the Welfare State? Cross-national Evidence from Europe, North America, and Japan." *European Sociological Review* 4, 3 (1988): 181–207.

Alber, Jens. "Social Structure and Politics in the Federal Republic of Germany." Lecture presented at University of Wisconsin, Madison, April 3, 1989.

Alber, Jens. "Towards Explaining Anti-Foreign Violence in Germany." Unpublished lecture at the Center for European Studies, Harvard University, March 17, 1994.

Alber, Jens. "Selectivity, Universalism, and the Politics of Welfare Retrenchment in Germany and the United States." Paper presented at the 92nd Annual Meeting of the American Political Science Association, San Francisco, August 31, 1996.

Albrecht, James, Per-Anders Edin, Marianne Sundström, and Susan Vroman. "Parental Leave and Earnings Inequality: Estimates for Sweden." Paper presented at the Peder Sather Symposium, "Challenges to Labor," Center for Western European Studies, University of California at Berkeley, March 21–23, 1996.

Aldrich, John H. *Why Parties? The Origin and Transformation of Party Politics in America.* American Politics and Political Economy Series, ed. Benjamin I. Page. Chicago: University of Chicago Press, 1995.

Alesina, Alberto. "Macroeconomics and Politics." In *NBER Macroeconomic Annual 1988,* ed. Stanley Fischer, 13–51. Cambridge, MA: MIT Press, 1988.

Alesina, Alberto, Gerald Cohen, and Nouriel Roubini. *Macroeconomic Policy and Elections in OECD Democracies.* NBER Working Papers Series 3830. National Bureau of Economic Research, 1991.

Alesina, Alberto and Dani Rodrik. "Distribution, Political Conflict and Economic Growth: A Simple Theory and Some Empirical Evidence." In *Political Economy, Growth, and Business Cycles,* ed. Alex Cukierman, Zvi Hercowitz, and Leonardo Leiderman, 23–50. Cambridge, MA: MIT, 1992.

Alesina, Alberto and Nouriel Roubini. *Political Cycles in OECD Economies.* NBER Working Papers Series 3478. National Bureau of Economic Research, 1990.

Alesina, Alberto and Lawrence H. Summers. "Central Bank Independence and Macroeconomic Performance: Some Comparative Evidence." *Journal of Money, Credit, and Banking* 25, 2 (1993): 151–162.

Alestalo, Matti and Hannu Uusitalo. "Finland." In *Growth to Limits: The Western European Welfare States Since World War II,* ed. Peter Flora, Vol. 1, 200–292, 126–190. Berlin: Walter de Gruyter, 1986.

Alestalo, Matti and Hannu Uusitalo. "Social Expenditure: A Decompositional Approach." In *The Study of Welfare State Regimes,* ed. Jon Eivind Kolber, 37–68. London, England: M. E. Sharpe, 1992.

Allan, Emilie Andersen and Darrell J. Steffensmeier. "Youth, Underemployment, and Property Crime: Differential Effects of Job Availability and Job Quality on Juvenile and Young Adult Arrest Rates." *American Sociological Review* 54, 1 (1989): 107–123.

Allardt, Erik. *On the Relationship Between Objective and Subjective Predicaments.* University of Helsinki, 1977. Research Report of Research Group for Comparative Sociology 16.

Allardt, Erik. *Implications of the Ethnic Revival in Modern, Industrialized Society.* Helsinki-Helsingfors: Societas Scientiarum Fennica, 1979.

Allen, James P. and Eugene Turner. "Spatial Patterns of Immigrant Assimilation." *Professional Geographer* 48, 2 (1996): 140–155.

Alliance for Better Campaigns. "Money Shouldn't Be All That Talks: Five Minutes of Fresh Air." Washington, DC: Alliance for Better Campaigns, 1999.

Almond, Gabriel A. *A Discipline Divided: Schools and Sects in Political Science.* Newbury Park, CA: Sage, 1990.

Almond, Gabriel A. and Sidney Verba. *The Civic Culture.* Princeton, NJ: Princeton University Press, 1963.

Alonso, William and Mary C. Waters. "The Future Composition of the American Population: An Illustrative Projection." Fort Lauderdale, FL: American Statistical Association, 1993.

Alston, J. H. *A New Look at Infectious Diseases.* London: Pitman, 1967.

Alstott, Anne L. "The Earned Income Tax Credit and Some Fundamental Institutional Dilemmas of Tax-Transfer Integration." *National Tax Journal* 47, 3 (1994): 609–619.

Altmeyer, Arthur J. *The Formative Years of Social Security.* Madison: University of Wisconsin Press, 1968.

American Bar Foundation. *International Directory of Bar Associations.* 4th ed. Chicago: 1983.

Ames, Bruce N. and Lois Swirsky Gold. "The Causes and Prevention of Cancer." In *The True State of the Planet,* ed. Ronald Bailey, 141–175. New York: Free Press, 1995.

Ames, Bruce N., M. Profet, and Lois Swirsky Gold. "Dietary Pesticides (99.99% of All Natural)." *Proceedings of the National Academy of Sciences USA* 87 (1990): 7777–7781.

Ames, Walter L. *Police and Community in Japan.* Berkeley and Los Angeles: University of California Press, 1981.

Andersen, Jørgen Goul and Tor Bjørklund. "Structural Changes and Cleavages: the Progress Parties in Denmark and Norway." *Acta Sociologica* 33, 3 (1990): 195–217.

Anderson, Odin. *Health Care: Can There Be Equity? The United States, Sweden, and England.* New York: John Wiley, 1972.

Anderson, Odin W. *The Health Services Continuum in Democratic States.* Ann Arbor: Health Administration Press, 1989.

Ansolabehere, Stephen and Shanto Iyengar. *Going Negative: How Attack Ads Shrink and Polarize the Electorate.* New York: Free Press, 1995.

Ansolabehere, Stephen and Shanto Iyengar. "Winning, but Losing: How Negative Campaigns Shrink Electorate, Manipulate News Media." *Quill* 84, 4 (1996): 19–22.

Ansolabehere, Stephen, Shanto Iyengar, Adam Simon, and Nicholas Valentino. "Does Attack Advertising Demobilize the Electorate?" *American Political Science Review* 88, 4 (1994): 829–838.

Archambault, Edith. *The Nonprofit Sector in France.* Vol. 3. Johns Hopkins Nonprofit Sector Series. Manchester: Manchester University Press, 1997.

Archer, Dane and Rosemary Gartner. *Violence and Crime in Cross-National Perspective.* New Haven: Yale University Press, 1984.

Arendt, Hannah. *The Origins of Totalitarianism.* New York: Harcourt Brace, 1951.

Argyle, Michael and Maryanne Martin. "The Psychological Causes of Happiness." In *Subjective Well-Being: An Interdisciplinary Perspective,* ed. Fritz Strack, Michael Argyle, and Norbert Schwarz, 27–47. Oxford: Pergamon Press, 1991.

Aronson, J. Richard and John L. Hilley. *Financing State and Local Governments.* 4th ed. Washington, DC: Brookings Institution, 1986.

"A Survey of Multinationals." *The Economist* (March 27, 1993): 1–20.

Ascoli, Ugo. "Towards a Partnership between Statutory Sector and Voluntary Action: Italian Welfare Pluralism in the '90s." In *Government and Voluntary Organizations: A Relational Perspective,* ed. Stein Kuhnle and Per Selle, 136–156. Aldershot, England: Avebury, 1992.

Ashford, Douglas E. and E. W. Kelley, eds. *Nationalizing Social Security in Europe and America.* Greenwich, CT: JAI Press, 1986.

Ashton, Thomas S. "The Standard Life of the Workers in England, 1790–1830." In *Capitalism and the Historians,* ed. Friederich A. Hayek, 127–159. Chicago: University of Chicago Press, 1954.

Ashworth, Karl, Martha Hill, and Robert Walker. "Patterns of Childhood Poverty: New Challenges for Policy." *Journal of Policy Analysis and Management* 13, 4 (1994): 659–680.

Atkinson, A. B. "The Social Safety Net." Discussion Paper, WSP/66. Suntory-Toyota International Centre for Economics and Related Disciplines, London School of Economics, 1991.

Atkinson, A. B. "On Targeting Social Security: Theory and Western Experience with Family Benefits." Discussion Paper, WSP/99, London School of Economics, 1993.

Atkinson, A. B. "State Pensions for Today and Tomorrow." Discussion Paper, WSP/104, Suntory-Toyota International Centre for Economics and Related Disciplines, London School of Economics, 1994.

Atkinson, A. B. "The Welfare State and Economic Performance." Discussion Paper, WSP/109. Centre for Economics and Related Disciplines, London School of Economics, 1995.

Atkinson, A. B., Lee Rainwater, and Timothy Smeeding. "Income Distribution in Advanced Economies: Evidence from the Luxembourg Income Study." Working paper #120, Maxwell School of Citizenship and Public Affairs, Syracuse University, 1995.

Atkinson, A. B. *Poverty in Great Britain and the Reform of Social Security.* Cambridge: Cambridge University Press, 1969.

Atkinson, A. B. and Martin Rein, eds. *Age, Work, and Social Security.* New York: St. Martin's Press, 1993.

Atkinson, A. B. and H. Sutherland. "Two Nations in Early Retirement? The Case of Britain." In *Age, Work, and Social Security,* ed. A. B. Atkinson and Martin Rein, 132–160. New York: St. Martin's Press, 1993.

Austen, John, David Butler, and Austin Ranney. "Referendums, 1978–1986." *Electoral Studies* 6, 2 (1987): 139–147.

Babchuk, Nicholas and Alan Booth. "Voluntary Association Membership: A Longitudinal Analysis." *American Sociological Review* 34, 1 (1969): 31–45.

Babic, Anne L. "Flexible Retirement: An International Survey of Public Policies." *Aging and Work* 7, 1 (1984): 21–36.

Badaracco, Joseph L. *Loading the Dice: A Five-Country Study of Vinyl Chloride Regulation.* Boston: Harvard Business School Press: 1985.

Bade, Robin and Michael Parkin. "Central Bank Laws and Monetary Policy." (mimeo). University of Western Ontario, June 1987.

Badelt, Christoph. "Government versus Private Provision of Social Services: The Case of Austria." In *The Nonprofit Sector in International Perspective,* ed. Estelle James, 162–176. New York and Oxford: Oxford University Press, 1989.

Bagdikian, Ben H. *The Media Monopoly.* 5th ed. Boston: Beacon Press, 1997.

Bagehot, Walter. *The English Constitution.* London: Oxford University Press, 1928 [1867].

Bailey, Ronald, ed. *The True State of the Planet.* New York: Free Press, 1995.

Baldassare, Mark. "Abandoned Housing and Its People: The Case of New York City." *Urban Affairs Papers* 3 (1981a): 51–61.

Baldassare, Mark. *The Growth Dilemma: Residents' Views and Local Population Change in the United States.* Berkeley: University of California Press, 1981b.

Baldassare, Mark. "Introduction: Urban Change and Continuity." In *Cities and Urban Living,* ed. Mark Baldassare, 1–39. New York: Columbia University Press, 1983.

Baldwin, John, Timothy Dunne, and John Haltiwanger. *A Comparison of Job Creation and Job Destruction in Canada and the United States.* Working Paper No. 4726. Cambridge, MA: National Bureau of Economic Research, 1994.

Baldwin, J. Norman and Quinton A. Farley. "Comparing the Public and Private Sectors in the United States: A Review of the Empirical Research." In *Handbook of Comparative and Developmental Public Administration,* ed. Ali Farazmand, 27–39. New York: Marcel Dekker, 1991.

Baldwin, Peter. *The Politics of Solidarity: Class in the European Welfare State, 1875–1975.* Cambridge: Cambridge University Press, 1990.

Ball, Robert M., Edith U. Fierst, Gloria T. Johnson, Thomas W. Jones, George Kourpias, and Gerald M. Shea. *Social Security for the 21st Century: A Strategy to Maintain Benefits and Strengthen America's Family Protection Plan*. Advisory Council on Social Security, 1997.

Banducci, Susan. "Direct Legislation: When Is it Used and When Does It Pass?" In *Citizens as Legislators: Direct Democracy in the American States,* ed. Shaun Bowler, Todd Donovan, and Caroline Torbert. Columbus: Ohio State University Press, 1998.

Bane, Mary Jo. *Here to Stay: American Families in the Twentieth Century.* New York: Basic Books, 1976.

Bane, Mary Jo. "Welfare as We Might Know It." *The American Prospect* (January/February 1997): 47–53.

Bane, Mary Jo and David T. Ellwood. *Welfare Realities: From Rhetoric to Reform.* Cambridge, MA: Harvard University Press, 1994.

Bappas, G., S. Queen, W. Hadden, and G. Fisher. "The Increasing Disparity in Mortality between Socioeconomic Groups in the United States, 1960 and 1986." *New England Journal of Medicine* 329, 2 (1993): 103–109.

Barbier, J. C. and H. Nadel. "December 1995: The French Wage-Earners' Society in Crisis." Paper presented at 1996 France-Berkeley Seminar, UC Berkeley, February 23, 1996.

Bardach, Eugene. "Self-Regulation and Regulatory Paperwork." In *Social Regulation: Strategies for Reform,* ed. Eugene Bardach and Robert A. Kagan, 315–340. San Francisco, CA: Institute for Contemporary Studies, 1982.

Bardach, Eugene and Robert A. Kagan, ed. *Going by the Book: The Problem of Regulatory Unreasonableness.* Philadelphia, PA: Temple University Press, 1982.

Barer, Morris L. and Greg L. Stoddart. *Toward Integrated Medical Resource Policies for Canada: Canadian Medical Association Journal Series.* Health Policy Research Unit Discussion Paper Series HPRU 93:2R. Centre for Health Services and Policy Research, University of British Columbia, Vancouver, BC, 1993.

Barker, David J. P. *Fetal and Infant Origins of Adult Diseases.* London: BMJ, 1992.

Barnes, Samuel H., Max Kaase, et al. *Political Action: Mass Participation in Five Western Democracies.* London: Sage, 1979.

Barnett, Michael N., ed. *Israel in Comparative Perspective: Challenging the Conventional Wisdom.* Albany: State University of New York Press, 1996.

Baron, Larry and Murray A. Straus. *Four Theories of Rape in American Society: A State-Level Analysis.* New Haven, CT: Yale University Press, 1989.

Barro, Robert. "Economic Growth in a Cross-Section of Countries." *Quarterly Journal of Economics* 106 (1991): 407–433.

Bartik, Timothy J. *Who Benefits from State and Local Economic Development Policies.* Kalamazoo, MI: W.E. Upjohn Institute for Employment Research, 1991.

Bartolini, Stefano and Peter Mair. *Identity, Competition and Electoral Availability: The Stabilization of European Electorates, 1885–1985.* Cambridge: Cambridge University Press, 1990.

Baum, Matthew A. and Samuel Kernell. "Has Cable Ended the Golden Age of Presidential Television?" *American Political Science Review* 93, 1 (1999): 99–114.

Baumgartner, Frank R. and Jack L. Walker. "Survey Research and Membership in Voluntary Associations." *American Political Science Review* 32, 4 (November 1988): 908–928.

Baumol, William J. *Superfairness: Applications and Theory.* Cambridge, MA: MIT Press, 1986.

Bawden, D. Lee and John L. Palmer. "Social Policy: Challenging the Welfare State." In *The Reagan Record: An Assessment of America's Changing Domestic Priorities,* ed. John Palmer and Isabel V. Sawhill, 177–215. Cambridge, MA: Ballinger, 1984.

Baxter, Janeen. "Is Husband's Class Enough? Class Location and Class Identity in the United States, Sweden, Norway, and Australia." *American Sociological Review* 59 (April 1994): 220–235.

Bayley, David H. *Forces of Order: Police Behavior in Japan and the United States.* Berkeley, CA: University of California Press, 1976.

Bayley, David H. *Forces of Order: Policing Modern Japan.* Berkeley, CA: University of California Press, 1991.

Bean, C. R., P. R. G. Layard, and S. J. Nickell. "The Rise in Unemployment: A Multi-Country Study." *Economica* 53 (Supplement No. 210, 1986): S1–S22.

Beattie, Christopher. *Minority Men in a Majority Setting: Middle-level Francophones in the Canadian Public Service.* Toronto: McClelland and Stewart, 1975.

Beatty, Perrin. "A Comparison of Our Two Systems." In *Looking North for Health: What We Can Learn from Canada's Health Care System,* ed. Arnold Bennett and Orville Adams, 28–39. San Francisco, CA: Jossey-Bass, 1993.

Beaujot, R., K. G. Basavarajappa, and R. B. P. Verma. *Current Demographic Analysis: Income of Immigrants in Canada, a Census Data Analysis.* Ottawa: Statistics Canada, 1988.

Bechhofer, Frank and Brian Elliot. "Petty Property: The Survival of a Moral Economy." In *The Petite Bourgeoisie: Comparative Studies of the Uneasy Stratum,* ed. Frank Bechhofer and Brian Elliot. New York: St. Martin's Press, 1981.

Beck, Paul Allen. "The Dealignment Era in America." In *Electoral Change in Advanced Industrial Democracies,* ed. R. J. Dalton, S. C. Flanagan, and P. A. Beck, 240–266. Princeton, NJ: Princeton University Press, 1984.

Beck, Paul Allen, Lawrence Baum, Aage R. Clausen, and Charles E. Smith Jr. "Patterns and Sources of Ticket Splitting in Subpresidential Voting." *American Political Science Review* 86, 4 (1992): 916–928.

Beck, Paul Allen and Frank J. Sorauf. *Party Politics in America.* 7th ed. New York: HarperCollins, 1992.

Bedau, Hugo Adam and Michael L. Radelet. "Miscarriages of Justice in Potentially Capital Cases." *Stanford Law Review* 40, 1 (November 1987): 21–179.

Bell, Daniel. *The Coming of Post-Industrial Society: A Venture in Social Forecasting.* New York: Basic Books, 1973.

Bell, Daniel. *The Cultural Contradictions of Capitalism.* New York: Basic Books, 1976.

Bell, Wendell and M. Boat. "Urban Neighborhoods and Informal Social Relations." *American Journal of Sociology* 62 (January 1957): 391–398.

Bell, Winifred. *Aid to Dependent Children.* New York: Columbia University Press, 1965.

Belous, Richard S. *The Contingent Economy: The Growth of the Temporary, Part-Time, and Subcontracted Workforce.* Washington, DC: National Planning Association, 1989.

Bennefield, Robert L. "Who Loses Coverage and for How Long?" *Current Population Reports,* P70–64. Washington, DC: U.S. Census Bureau, August 1998.

Berelson, Bernard. "The Great Debate in Cultural Democracy." *Studies in Public Communication* 3 (Summer 1961): 3–14.

Berger, Suzanne. "Regime and Interest Representation: The French Traditional Middle Classes." In *Organizing Interests in Western Europe: Pluralism, Corporatism, and the Transformation of Politics,* ed. Suzanne Berger. Cambridge: Cambridge University Press, 1981a.

Berger, Suzanne. "The Uses of the Traditional Sector in Italy." In *The Petite Bourgeoisie: Comparative Studies of the Uneasy Stratum,* ed. Frank Bechhofer and Brian Elliot. New York: St. Martin's Press, 1981b.

Berger, Suzanne and Michael Piore. *Dualism and Discontinuity in Industrial Societies.* Cambridge: Cambridge University Press, 1980.

Berggren, Christian. *Alternatives to Lean Production: Work Organization in the Swedish Auto Industry.* Ithaca: ILR Press—an Imprint of Cornell University Press, 1992.

Berglund, Stan and Ulf Lindstrom. *The Scandinavian Party System(s): A Comparative Study.* Lund: Studentlitteratur, 1978.

Bergman, Abraham B. and Stanley J. Stamm. "The Morbidity of Cardiac Nondisease in Schoolchildren." *New England Journal of Medicine* 276 (1967): 1008–1013.

Bergmann, Barbara R. *The Economic Emergence of Women.* New York: Basic Books, 1986.

Berke, Richard L. "Politics: The Voters; Poll Shows Dole Slicing Away Lead Clinton Held." *New York Times,* August 20, 1996, late ed.

Berkman, Lisa F. "Physical Health and the Social Environment: A Social Epidemiological Perspective." In *The Relevance of Social Science for Medicine,* ed. Leon Eisenberg and Arthur Kleinman, 51–75. Boston: D. Reidel, 1981.

Berkman, Lisa F. and S. Leonard Syme. "Social Networks, Host Resistance, and Mortality: A nine-year followup study of Alameda County residents." *American Journal of Epidemiology* 109, 2 (1979): 186–204.

Berland, Theodore. *The Scientific Life.* New York: Coward-McCann, 1962.

Berliner, David C. "Mythology of the American System of Education." *Phi Delta Kappan* 74, 8 (1993): 632–640.

Berlow, Alan. "The Wrong Man." *Atlantic Monthly* 284, 5 (November 1999): 66–91.

Berry, Jeffrey M. "Citizen Groups and the Changing Nature of Interest Group Politics in America." *Annals, American Academy of Political and Social Science* 528 (1993): 30–41.

Besharov, Douglas J. "Fresh Start." *The New Republic,* June 14, 1993, 14–16.

Besharov, Douglas J. and Peter Germanis. "Welfare Reform—Four Years Later." *The Public Interest* 140 (Summer 2000): 17–35.

Besharov, Douglas J., Peter Germanis, and Peter H. Rossi. *Evaluating Welfare Reform: A Guide for Scholars and Practitioners.* College Park, MD: School of Public Affairs, The University of Maryland, 1997.

Bettelheim, Bruno and Morris Janowitz. *Social Change and Prejudice.* New York: Free Press of Glencoe, 1964.

Bianchi, Suzanne M. "America's Children: Mixed Prospects." *Population Bulletin* 45, 1 (1990): 1–43.

Birch, David L. "Who Creates Jobs?" *Public Interest* 65 (1981): 3–14.

Birch, David L. "The Contribution of Small Enterprise to Growth and Employment." In *New Opportunities for Entrepreneurship,* ed. Herbert Giersch, 1–17. Boulder, CO: Westview Press, 1987.

Bird, Edward J. "Repairing the Social Net: Is the EITC the Right Patch?" *Journal of Policy Analysis and Management* 15, 1 (1996): 1–31.

Birley, Sue. "The Role of New Firms: Births, Deaths, and Job Generation." *Strategic Management Journal* 7 (1986): 361–376.

Black Elected Officials: A National Roster. 21st ed. Washington, DC: Joint Center for Political and Economic Studies Press, 1993.

Blackburn, McKinley L. and David E. Bloom. *The Distribution of Family Income: Measuring and Explaining Changes in the 1980s for Canada and the United States.* NBER Working Paper #3659. National Bureau of Economic Research, 1991.

Blackman, W. *Swiss Banking in an International Context.* London: Macmillan Press Ltd., 1989.

Blanchflower, David G. and Richard B. Freeman. "Unionism in the United States and Other Advanced OECD Countries." *Industrial Relations* 31, 1 (1992): 56–79.

Blanchflower, David G. and Richard B. Freeman. "The Attitudinal Legacy of Communist Labor Relations." *Industrial and Labor Relations Review* 50, 3 (1997): 438–460.

Blank, Rebecca M. and Patricia Ruggles. *When Do Women Use AFDC and Food Stamps? The Dynamics of Eligibility vs. Participation.* NBER Working Paper Series 4429. National Bureau of Economic Research, 1993.

Blau, Francine D. "Trends in the Well-Being of American Women, 1970–1995." *Journal of Economic Literature* 36 (March 1998): 112–165.

Blau, Francine D. and Lawrence Kahn. "International Differences in Male Wage Inequality: Institutions vs. Market Forces." *Journal of Political Economy* 104, 4 (1996a): 791–837.

Blau, Francine D. and Lawrence M. Kahn. "Wage Structure and Gender Earnings Differentials: An International Comparison." *Economica* 63 (May 1996b): S29–S62.

Blau, Francine D. and Lawrence M. Kahn. "Swimming Upstream: Trends in the Gender Wage Differential in the 1980s." *Journal of Labor Economics* 15, 1 (1997): 1–42.

Blau, Judith R. and Peter M. Blau. "Cost of Inequality: Metropolitan Structure and Violent Crime." *American Sociological Review* 47 (1982): 114–129.

Blau, Peter M. "Social Mobility and Interpersonal Relations." *American Sociological Review* 21 (1956): 290–295.

Blau, Peter and Otis Dudley Duncan. *The American Occupational Structure.* New York: Wiley, 1967.

Blinder, Alan. "More Like Them?" *The American Prospect* No. 8 (1992): 51–62.

Blomquist, Ake. *The Health Care Business: Internal Evidence on Public Versus Private Health Care Systems.* Vancouver: Fraser Institute, 1979.

Blossfeld, Hans-Peter and Yossi Shavit. "Persisting Barriers: Changes in Educational Opportunities in Thirteen Countries." In *Persistent Inequality: Changing Educational Attainment in Thirteen Countries,* ed. Yossi Shavit and Hans-Peter Blossfeld, 1–23. Boulder, CO: Westview Press, 1993.

Bluestone, Barry and Bennett Harrison. *The Deindustrialization of America.* New York: Basic Books, 1982.

Bluestone, Barry and Bennett Harrison. *The Great American Job Machine: The Proliferation of Low-Wage Employment in the U.S. Economy.* Washington, DC: Joint Economic Committee of the U.S. Congress, 1986.

Blum, Alan. "Japan: Land of the Rise in Lung Cancer." *New York State Journal of Medicine* 85, 7 (1985): 425–427.

Blumenberg, Evelyn and Paul Ong. "Job Accessibility and Welfare Usage: Evidence from Los Angeles." *Journal of Public Policy Analysis and Management* 17, 4 (1998): 639–657.

Blumler, Jay G., ed. *Television and Public Interest: Vulnerable Values in Western European Broadcasting.* Newbury Park, CA: Sage, 1992.

Blumler, Jay G., Jack M. McLeod, and Karl Erik Rosengren, eds. *Comparatively Speaking: Communication and Culture Across Space and Time.* Newbury Park, CA: Sage, 1992.

Blumstein, James F. "The fraud and abuse statute in an evolving health care marketplace: life in the healthcare speakeasy." *American Journal of Law and Medicine* 22, 2–3 (1996): 205–231.

Bochenski, Joseph M. "The Poverty of Soviet Philosophy." In *Soviet Society,* ed. Alex Inkeles and Kent Geiger, 454–459. Boston: Houghton Mifflin, 1961.

Boden, Leslie I. "Creating Economic Incentives: Lessons from Workers' Compensation Systems." In *Proceedings of the 47th Annual Meeting, Industrial Relations Research Association,* 282–289. January 6–8, 1995.

Bodenhorn, Karen A. and Lee D. Kemper. *Spending for Health.* Living Well 3. California Center for Health Improvement, 1997.

Bogart, Leo. *The Age of Television.* New York: Frederick Ungar, 1958.

Bogdanor, Vernon. "Conclusion: Electoral Systems and Party Systems." In *Democracy and Elections: Electoral Systems and Their Political Consequences,* ed. Vernon Bogdanor and David Butler, 247–262. Cambridge: Cambridge University Press, 1983.

Bogdanor, Vernon and David E. Butler, eds. *Democracy and Elections: Electoral Systems and Their Political Consequences.* Cambridge: Cambridge University Press, 1983.

Bogue, Donald J. *Skid Row in American Cities*. Chicago: Chicago County and Family Study Center, University of Chicago, 1963.

Boisjoly, Johanne, Kathleen M. Harris, and Greg J. Duncan. "Trends, Events, and Duration of Initial Welfare Spells." *Social Service Review* December (1998): 466–492.

Bok, Derek C. "A Flawed System." *Harvard Magazine* 85, 5 (1983): 38–45, 70–71.

Borjas, George J. *Friends of Strangers: The Impact of Immigrants on the U.S. Economy*. New York: Basic Books, 1990.

Borjas, George J. "National Origin and Skills of Immigrants in the Postwar Period." In *Immigration and the Work Force: Economic Consequences for the United States and Source Areas*, ed. George J. Borjas and Richard B. Freeman, 17–47. Chicago: University of Chicago Press, 1992.

Borjas, George J. and Richard B. Freeman. "Introduction and Summary." In *Immigration and the Work Force: Economic Consequences for the United States and the Source Areas*, ed. George J. Borjas and Richard B. Freeman, 1–15. Chicago: University of Chicago Press, 1992.

Borjas, George J., Richard B. Freeman, and Lawrence F. Katz. "On the Labor Market Effects of Immigration and Trade." In *Immigration and the Work Force: Economic Consequences for the United States and Source Areas*, ed. George J. Borjas and Richard B. Freeman, 213–244. Chicago: University of Chicago Press, 1992.

Borjas, George J., Richard B. Freeman, and Kevin Lang. "Undocumented Mexican-born Workers in the United States: How Many, How Permanent?" In *Immigration, Trade and the Labor Market*, ed. John M. Abowd and Richard B. Freeman, 77–100. Chicago: University of Chicago Press, 1991.

Bornstein, Stephen and Pierre-Eric Tixier. "The Strikes of 1995: A Crisis of the French Model?" Paper presented at 1996 France-Berkeley Seminar, UC Berkeley, 19–23 February, 1996.

Borrel, Monique. *Conflits du travail et changement social et politique en France depuis 1950*. Paris: L'Harmattan, 1996.

Boston, Jonathan, John Martin, June Pallot, and Pat Walsh, eds. *Reshaping the State: New Zealand's Bureaucratic Revolution*. Aukland, New Zealand: Oxford University Press, 1991.

Bovenberg, A. Lans and Jocelyn P. Horne. "Taxes and Commodities: A Survey." In *Tax Harmonization in the European Community: Policy Issues and Analysis*, ed. George Kopits, 22–51. Washington, DC: International Monetary Fund, 1992.

Bowler, Shaun and David M. Farrell, eds. *Electoral Strategies and Political Marketing*. London: The Macmillan Press Ltd., 1992.

BPA, Presse und Informationsamt der Bundesregierung, ed. *Bericht der Bundesregierung über die Lage der Medien in der BRD*. Bonn: Drucksache 12/8587 des Deutschen Bundestags, 12. Wahlperiod vom 20, 1994.

Brace, Paul. *State Government and Economic Performance*. Baltimore and London: The Johns Hopkins University Press, 1993.

Bracey, Gerald D. "Why Can't They Be Like We Were?" *Phi Delta Kappan* 73, 2 (1991): 104–117.

Brants, Kees and Denis McQuail. "The Netherlands." In *The Media in Western Europe*, ed. Euromedia Research Group, 153–167. London: Sage, 1997.

Break, George F. "Professional Opinions about Tax Policy." *National Tax Journal* 48, 1 (1995): 155–158.

Breault, Kevin D. "Suicide in America: A Test of Durkheim's Theory of Religious and Family Integration, 1933–1980." *American Journal of Sociology* 92, 3 (1986): 628–656.

Brenner, Harvey. *Estimating the Social Costs of National Economic Policy: Implications for Mental and Physical Health, and Criminal Aggression*. Joint Economic Committee, U.S. Congress, 1976. Washington, DC: U.S. Government Printing Office.

Brenner, M. Harvey. *Mental Illness and the Economy*. Cambridge, MA: Harvard University Press, 1973.

Brenner, M. Harvey. "Importance of the Economy to the Nation's Health." In *The Relevance of Social Science for Medicine*, ed. Leon Eisenberg and Arthur Kleinman, 371–395. Boston: D. Reidel, 1981.

Brickman, Ronald, Sheila Jasanoff, and Thomas Ilgen. *Controlling Chemicals: The Politics of Regulation in Europe and the United States*. Ithaca, NY: Cornell University Press, 1985.

Briggs, Asa. "The Welfare State in Historical Perspective." *Archives in European Sociology* 11 (1961): 221–258.

Briggs, Asa. *The BBC: The First Fifty Years*. Oxford: Oxford University Press, 1985.

Brill, Steven. "Dan Rather on Fear, Money, and the News." *Brill's Content* 1, 3 (October 1998): 116–121.

Brint, Steven and Susan Kelley. "The Social Bases of Political Beliefs in the United States: Interests, Cultures, and Normative Pressures in Comparative Historical Context." *Research in Political Sociology* 6 (1993): 277–317.

Brittan, Samuel. "On the Economic Contradictions of Democracy." *British Journal of Political Science* 5 (1975): 129–159.

Brodkin, Evelyn Z. *The False Promise of Administrative Reform: Implementing Quality Control in Welfare*. Philadelphia: Temple University Press, 1986.

Brody, Richard A. "The Puzzle of Political Participation in America." In *The New American Political System*, ed. Anthony King, 287–324. Washington, DC: American Enterprise Institute, 1978.

Brody, Richard A. *Assessing the President: The Media, Elite Opinion, and Public Support*. Stanford, CA: Stanford University Press, 1991.

Brody, Richard A., David W. Brady, and Valerie Heitshusen. "Accounting for Divided Government: Generational Effects on Party and Split-Ticket Voting." In *Elections at Home and Abroad*, ed. M. Kent Jennings and Thomas E. Mann, 157–177. Ann Arbor: University of Michigan Press, 1994.

Brook, Robert H. et al. "Does Free Care Improve Adults' Health? Results from a Randomized Trial." *New England Journal of Medicine* 309, 23 (1983): 1426–1434.

Brooks, Joel E. "Abortion Policy in Western Democracies: A Cross-National Analysis." *Governance: An International Journal of Policy and Administration* 5, 3 (1992): 342–357.

Brown, Clair, Yoshifumi Nakata, Michael Reich, and Lloyd Ulman. *Work and Pay in the United States and Japan*. New York: Oxford University Press, 1997.

Brown, Henry Phelps. *The Origins of Trade Union Power*. Oxford: Clarendon Press, 1983.

Brown, Lawrence D. "Knowledge and Power: Health Services Research as a Political Resource." In *Health Services Research: Key to Health Policy*, ed. Eli Ginzberg, 20–45. Cambridge: Harvard University Press, 1991.

Brown, Lawrence D. "National Health Reform: An Idea Whose Time Has Come." *PS: Political Science and Politics* 27, 2 (1994): 198–201.

Brown, Michael K. "Remaking the Welfare State: A Comparative Perspective." In *Remaking the Welfare State: Retrenchment and Social Policy in America and Europe*, ed. M. K. Brown, 3–27. Philadelphia: Temple University Press, 1988.

Brubaker, Rogers. *Citizenship and Nationhood in France and Germany*. Cambridge, MA: Harvard University Press, 1992.

Bruce, Peter. "Political Parties and Labor Legislation in Canada in the United States." *Industrial Relations* 28, 2 (Spring 1989): 115–141.

Brulin, Göran and Tommy Nilsson. "Sweden: The Volvo and Saab Road beyond Lean Production." In *After Lean Production: Evolving Employment Practices in the World Auto Industry*, ed. Thomas A. Kochan, Russell D. Lansbury, and John Paul MacDuffie, 191–203. Ithaca: ILR Press—an Imprint of Cornell University Press, 1997.

Bruno, Michael and Jeffrey Sachs. *Economics of Worldwide Stagnation.* Cambridge, MA: Harvard University Press, 1985.

Bryner, Gary C. *Bureaucratic Discretion: Law and Policy in Federal Regulatory Agencies.* New York: Pergamon Press, 1987.

Buechtemann, Christoph F. "More Jobs through Less Employment Protection? Evidence for West Germany." *Labour* 3 (Winter 1989): 23 – 56.

Buechtemann, Christoph F. "Employment Security and Deregulation: The West German Experience." In *Employment Security and Labor Market Behavior,* ed. Christoph F. Buechtemann, 272 – 297. Ithaca, NY: ILR Press, 1993a.

Buechtemann, Christoph F. "Introduction: Employment Security and Labor Markets." In *Employment Security and Labor Market Behavior,* ed. Christoph F. Buechtemann, 3 – 69. Ithaca, NY: ILR Press, 1993b.

Buechtemann, Christoph F. and N. Meager. "Leaving Employment: Patterns in EC Countries." Discussion paper FSI-1991, Berlin, WZB, 1991.

Bumpass, L. and R. K. Raley. *Estimating Levels of Marital Disruption.* Working Paper 92 – 27. National Survey of Families and Households, 1992.

Bundesministerium für Gesundheit. *Statistiches Taschenbuch Gesundheit.* Bonn: Bundesministerium für Gesundheit, 1996.

Bunker, J. P., D. S. Gomby, and B. H. Kehrer. *Pathways to Health: The Role of Social Factors.* Menlo Park, CA: Henry J. Kaiser Family Foundation, 1989.

Burdekin, Richard C. K. and Thomas D. Willet. "Central Bank Reform: The Federal Reserve in International Perspective." *Public Budgeting and Financial Management* 3, 3 (1991): 619 – 649.

Burgess, Ernest Watson, ed. *The Urban Community: Selected Papers of the American Sociological Society, 1925.* Chicago: University of Chicago Press, 1926.

Burghardt, John, Ann Rangarajan, Anne Gordon, and Ellen Kisker. *Evaluation of the Minority Female Single Parent Demonstration.* Summary Report Volume 1. Princeton, NJ: Mathematica Policy Research, Inc., 1992.

Burke, Vincent J. and Vee Burke. *Nixon's Good Deed: Welfare Reform.* New York: Columbia University Press, 1974.

Burkhart, Ross E. and Michael S. Lewis-Beck. "Comparative Democracy: The Economic Development Thesis." *American Political Science Review* 88, 4 (1994): 903 – 910.

Burkitt, Denis P. "Epidemiology of Cancer of the Colon and Rectum." *Cancer* 28 (July 1971): 3 – 13.

Burstein, Paul. "Social Structure and Individual Political Participation in Five Countries." *American Sociological Review* 77, 6 (1972): 1087 – 1110.

Burtless, Gary. "Public Spending for the Poor: Trends, Prospects, and Economic Limits." In *Fighting Poverty: What Works and What Doesn't,* ed. Sheldon H. Danziger and Daniel H. Weinberg, 18 – 49. Cambridge, MA: Harvard University Press, 1986.

Burtless, Gary. "Employment Prospects of Welfare Recipients." In *The Work Alternative: Welfare Reform and the Realities of the Job Market,* ed. Demetra Smith Nightingale and Robert H. Haveman. Washington, DC: Urban Institute Press, 1995.

Butler, David E., Andrew Adonis, and Tony Travers. *Failure in British Government: The Politics of the Poll Tax.* Oxford: Oxford University Press, 1994.

Butler, David E. and Austin Ranney, eds. *Referendums Around the World: The Growing Use of Direct Democracy.* Washington, DC: AEI Press, 1994.

Butler, David E. and Donald E. Stokes. *Political Change in Britain.* London: Macmillan, 1974.

Butler, Robert N. "Dispelling Ageism: The Cross-Cutting Intervention." In *The Quality of Aging: Strategies for Interventions,* ed. M. W. Riley and J. W. Riley, 138 – 147. Newbury Park, CA: Sage, 1989.

Buttner, Thomas and Wolfgang Lutz. "Estimating Fertility Responses to Policy Measures in the German Democratic Republic." *Population and Development Review* 16 (1990): 539–555.

Cain, Bruce, John Ferejohn, and Morris Fiorina. *The Personal Vote: Constituency Service and Electoral Independence.* Cambridge: Harvard University Press, 1987.

Calder, Kent E. *Crisis and Compensation: Public Policy and Political Stability in Japan, 1949–1986.* Princeton, NJ: Princeton University Press, 1988.

Calderon, Desire. *La Droite Francaise. Formation et Projet.* Paris: Messidor/Editions Sociales, 1985.

California Constitution Revision Commission. *Final Report and Recommendations to the Governor and the Legislature.* Sacramento, CA: Forum on Government Reform, 1996.

California Cooperative Healthcare Reporting Initiative. *Report on Quality of Care Measures: Performance Results for 1995.* San Francisco: CCHI, 1996.

Callan, T., S. Adams, S. Dex, S. Gustafsson, J. Schupp, and N. Smith. *Gender Wage Differentials: New Cross-Country Evidence.* Working Paper 134. Luxembourg Income Study, Maxwell School of Citizenship and Public Affairs, Syracuse University, 1996.

Cameron, David R. "The Expansion of the Public Economy: A Comparative Analysis." *American Political Science Review* 72, 4 (1978): 1243–1261.

Cameron, David R. "On the Limits of the Public Economy." *The Annals* 459 (1982): 46–62.

Cameron, David R. "Social Democracy, Corporatism, Labour Quiescence and the Representation of Economic Interest in Advanced Capitalist Society." In *Order and Conflict in Contemporary Capitalism,* ed. John H. Goldthorpe, 143–178. Oxford: Oxford University Press, 1984.

Campbell, A., P. E. Converse, W. E. Miller, and D. E. Stokes. *The American Voter.* New York: John Wiley, 1960.

Campbell, A., P. Converse, and W. L. Rodgers. *The Quality of American Life: Perceptions, Evaluations, and Satisfactions.* New York: Russell Sage Foundation, 1976.

Campbell, John. "The Old People Boom and Japanese Policy Making." *Journal of Japanese Studies* 5 (1979): 321–357.

Campbell, John. *Collapse of an Industry: Nuclear Power and the Contradictions of U.S. Policy.* Ithaca, NY: Cornell University Press, 1988.

Campbell, Jennifer A. "Health Insurance Coverage." In *Current Population Reports,* 60–208. Washington, DC: U.S. Census Bureau, 1999.

Campbell, John Creighton. *How Policies Change: The Japanese Government and the Aging Society.* Princeton, NJ: Princeton University Press, 1992.

Campbell, Nigel. "The Decline of Employment Among Older People in Britain." Working Paper 19, ESRC Center for Analysis of Social Exclusion, London School of Economics, 1999.

Cantor, Joseph E., Denise S. Rutkus, and Kevin B. Greely. *Free and Reduced-Rate Television Time for Political Candidates.* Washington, DC, Library of Congress, Congressional Research Service, 1997. 97–680 GOV.

Cappella, Joseph N. and Kathleen Hall Jamieson. *Spiral of Cynicism: The Press and the Public Good.* New York: Oxford University Press, 1997.

Card, David and Alan B. Krueger. "Does School Quality Matter? Returns to Education and the Characteristics of Public Schools in the United States." *Journal of Political Economy* 100, 1 (Feb. 1992): 1–40.

Card, David and Alan B. Krueger. "Minimum Wages and Employment: A Case Study of the Fast-Food Industry in New Jersey and Pennsylvania." *American Economic Review* 84, 4 (1994): 487–496.

Card, David and Alan B. Krueger. *Myth and Measurement: The New Economics of the Minimum Wage.* Princeton: Princeton University Press, 1995.

Carlile, Lonny E. "Party Politics and the Japanese Labor Movement." *Asian Survey* 34, 7 (1994): 606–620.

Carlin, Wendy and David Soskice. *Macroeconomics and the Wage Bargain: A Modern Approach to Employment, Inflation, and the Exchange Rate.* Oxford: Oxford University Press, 1990.

Carlson, Rick. *The End of Medicine.* New York: Wiley Interscience, 1975.

Carson, Iain. "A Survey of the Dutch Economy." *The Economist* 304, 7515 (1987): 1–22.

Carstairs, Andrew McLaren. *A Short History of Electoral Systems in Western Europe.* London: George Allen & Unwin, 1980.

Carter, Luther J. *Nuclear Imperatives and Public Trust: Dealing with Radioactive Waste.* Washington, DC: Resources for the Future, 1987.

Casey, Bernard. "Early Retirement." *International Social Security Review* 40 (1987): 343–360.

Casey, Bernard and Gert Bruche. "Active Labor Market Policy: An International Overview." *Industrial Relations* 24 (1985): 37–61.

Cash, Wilbur Joseph. *The Mind of the South.* Garden City, NY: Doubleday, 1941.

Cashell, Brian W. *Inflation and the Real Minimum Wage: Fact Sheet.* Congressional Research Service Report for Congress. Washington, DC: Congressional Research Service, 1999.

Cassese, Sabino. *Il systema amministrativo italiano.* Bologna: il Mulino, 1983.

Castells, Manuel. *Towards the Informational City.* Working Paper 430. Institute of Urban and Regional Development, University of California, Berkeley, 1984.

Castells, Manuel and Yuko Aoyama. *Paths Towards the Information Society: A Comparative Analysis of the Transformation of Employment Structure in the G-7 Countries, 1920–2005.* Working Paper 62. Berkeley Roundtable on the International Economy, UC Berkeley, 1993.

Castells, Manuel and Yuko Aoyama. "Paths towards the Informational Society: Employment Structure in G-7 Countries, 1920–1990." *International Labour Review* 133, 1 (1994): 5–33.

Castles, Frank. *The Working Class and Welfare: Reflections on the Political Development of the Welfare State in Australia and New Zealand, 1890–1980.* London: Allen & Unwin, 1985.

Castles, Frances, Rolf Gerritsen, and Jack Vowles, eds. *The Great Experiment: Labour Parties and Public Transformation in Australia and New Zealand.* New South Wales, Australia: Allen Unwin, 1996.

Castles, Frances G. *The Social Democratic Image of Society: A Study of the Achievements and Origins of Scandinavian Social Democracy in Comparative Perspective.* London: Routledge and Kegan Paul, 1978.

Castles, Frances G. and Ian F. Shirley. "Labour and Social Policy: Gravediggers or Refurbishers of the Welfare State." In *The Great Experiment: Labour Parties and Public Policy Transformation in Australia and New Zealand,* ed. Frances Castles, Rolf Gerritsen, and Jack Vowles, 88–106. New South Wales, Australia: Allen Unwin, 1996.

Catalano, Ralph. "The Health Effects of Economic Insecurity." *American Journal of Public Health* 81, 9 (1991): 1148–1152.

Catterall, James S. Private School Participation and Public Policy. In *Comparing Public and Private Schools, Volume 1: Institutions and Organizations,* ed. Thomas James and Henry M. Levin, 46–66. New York: The Falmer Press, 1988.

Cebula, Richard J. "A Brief Empirical Note on the Impact of Welfare Benefit Levels on Property Crime in the United States." *Public Finance* 46 (1991): 512–516.

Center for Human Resource Research. *NLS Handbook 1999: The National Longitudinal Surveys.* Ohio State University, 1999.

Center for Political Studies. *American National Election Study, 1984: Pre-presidential Election Survey Interview Schedule and Post-presidential Election Survey Composite Interview Schedule.* Institute for Social Research, Ann Arbor, MI, 1984.

Center for the Study of Services. "Which HMO Is Best for You." *Bay Area Consumers Checkbook* 8, 2 (Winter/Spring 1998): 71–76.

Centers for Disease Control. *School Year Immunization Data 1980–1981, Special Tabulation.* 1980.

Central Statistics Office of the Irish Government. *Ireland: Statistical Abstract 1993.* Dublin: Stationery Office, 1993.

CETA. *Comprehensive Employment and Training Act (of 1973).* 1973.

Chambers, Clarke A. *Seedtime of Reform: American Social Service and Social Action 1918–1933.* Minneapolis: University of Minnesota Press, 1963.

Chandra, Ranjit Kumar. "Nutrition and Immunity: Lessons from the Past and New Insights into the Future." *American Journal of Clinical Nutrition* 53 (1991): 1087–1102.

Chang, Mariko. *The Evolution of Sex Segregation Regimes.* Harvard University, 1999.

Chapman, Roger. "A Political Culture Under Pressure: The Struggle to Preserve a Progressive Tax Base for Welfare and the Positive State." *Political Science* 44, 1 (1992): 1–27.

Charnovitz, Steve. "Worker Adjustment: The Missing Ingredient in Trade Policy." *California Management Review* 28 (Winter 1986): 156–173.

Chen, Xiangming and Xiaoyuan Gao. "China's Urban Housing Development in the Shift from Redistribution to Decentralization." *Social Problems* 40, 2 (1993): 266–283.

Chernick, Daniel, Louis Grothaus, and Edward H. Wagner. "The Effect of Office Visit Copayments on Preventive Care Services in an HMO." *Inquiries* 27 (Spring 1990): 24–38.

Chinoy, Ely. *Automobile Workers and the American Dream.* Garden City: Doubleday, 1955.

Chiricos, Theodore G. "Rates of Crime and Unemployment: An Analysis of Aggregate Research Evidence." *Social Problems* 34, 2 (1987): 187–212.

Christensen, Raymond V. "Electoral Reform in Japan." *Asian Survey* 34, 7 (1994): 589–605.

Chubb, John E. "U.S. Energy Policy: A Problem of Delegation." In *Can the Government Govern?,* ed. John E. Chubb and Paul E. Peterson, 47–99. Washington, DC: Brookings Institution, 1989.

Chubb, John E. and Terry M. Moe. *Politics, Markets, and America's Schools.* Washington, DC: Brookings Institution, 1990.

Church, Clive H. "The Swiss election of 1991: stability, not stasis." *Western European Politics* 15, 4 (1992): 184–188.

Cipolla, Carlo M. and Derek Birdsall. *The Technology of Man: A Visual History.* New York: Holt, Rinehart, 1980.

Citrin, Jack and Donald Philip Green. "Presidential Leadership and the Resurgence of Trust in Government." *British Journal of Political Science* 16 (1986): 431–453.

Clark, Burton R. *The Higher Education System: Academic Organization in Cross-National Perspective.* Berkeley: University of California Press, 1983.

Clark, Burton R. "Conclusions." In *The School and the University: An International Perspective,* ed. Burton R. Clark, 290–323. Berkeley: University of California Press, 1985a.

Clark, Burton R., ed. *The School and the University: An International Perspective.* Berkeley: University of California Press, 1985b.

Clark, David S. "Civil Litigation Trends in Europe and Latin America since 1945: The Advantage of Intra-country Comparisons." *Law and Society Review* 24 (1990): 549–569.

Clark, Rebecca L. and Jeffrey S. Passel. *How Much Do Immigrants Pay in Taxes? Evidence from Los Angeles County.* Program for Research on Immigration Policy, Washington, DC: Urban Institute, 1993.

Clark, Robert L. and Naohiro Ogawa. "Transitions from Career Jobs to Retirement in Japan." *Industrial Relations* 36, 2 (1997): 255–270.

Clarke, Harold D. and Nitish Dutt. "Measuring Value Change in Western Industrialized Societies: The Impact of Unemployment." *American Political Science Review* 85, 3 (1991): 905–920.

Clarke, Harold D. and Allan Kornberg. "Partisan Dealignment, Electoral Choice and Party-System Change in Canada." *Party Politics* 2 (1996): 455–478.

Clotfelter, Charles T., ed. *Who Benefits from the Nonprofit Sector?* Chicago: University of Chicago Press, 1992.

Cnossen, Sijbren. "Consumption Taxes and International Competitiveness: The OECD Experience." Statement before the Committee on Ways and Means, Hearings on Factors Affecting U.S. International Competitiveness, U.S. House of Representatives, Washington, DC, June 20, 1991.

Coale, Ansley J. and Susan Cotts Watkins, ed. *The Decline of Fertility in Europe: The Revised Proceedings of a Conference on the European Fertility Project.* Princeton, NJ: Princeton University Press, 1986.

Cochrane, A. L. *Effectiveness and Efficiency: Random Reflections on Health Services.* The Rock Carling Fellowship, London: Nuffield Provincial Hospitals Trust, 1972.

Cochrane, A. L., A. S. St. Leger, and F. Moore. "Health service 'input' and mortality 'output' in developed countries." *Journal of Epidemiology and Community Health* 32, 3 (1978): 200–205.

Coffin, T.E. "Television's Impact on Society." *The American Psychologist* 10 (October 1955): 630–641.

Coglianese, Cary. "Challenging the Rules: Litigation and Bargaining in the Administrative Process." Unpublished dissertation, University of Michigan, Ann Arbor, 1994.

Cohen, Akiba A. and Itzhak Roeh. "When Fiction and News Cross Over the Border." In *Mass Media Effects Across Cultures,* ed. Felipe Korzenny and Stella Ting-Toomey, 23–34. London: Sage, 1992.

Cohen, Joshua and Joel Rogers. "Secondary Associations and Democratic Governance." *Politics and Society* 20, 4 (1992): 393–472.

Cohen, Wilbur J. and Robert J. Lampman. "Introduction." In *The Development of the Social Security Act,* ed. Edwin E. Witte. Madison: University of Wisconsin Press, 1962.

Cole, Robert E. *Strategies for Living: Small-Group Activities in American, Japanese, and Swedish Industry.* Berkeley: University of California Press, 1989.

Cole, Robert E. "Issues in Skill Formation in Japanese Approaches to Automation." In *Technology and the Future of Work,* ed. Paul S. Adler, 187–209. New York: Oxford University Press, 1992.

Cole, Robert E. "Cross-National Perspectives on Work Organization: Sweden, Japan, and the U.S." Peder Sather Symposium III, University of California at Berkeley, 1996.

Coleman, James S., Elihu Katz, and Herbert Menzel. *Medical Innovation: A Diffusion Study.* Indianapolis and New York: Bobbs Merrill, 1966.

Collier, Ruth Berins and David Collier. *Shaping the Political Arena: Critical Junctures, the Labor Movement, and Regime Dynamics in Latin America.* Princeton, NJ: Princeton University Press, 1991.

Collins, Elizabeth and Rudolf Klein. "Self-Reported Morbidity, Socioeconomic Factors, and General Practitioners Consultation." Bath: Center for Social Policy Analysis, University of Bath, 1985.

Collinson, Sarah. *Europe and International Migration.* London and New York: Pinter Publishing, 1993.

Collver, Andrew and Eleanor Langlois. "The Female Labor Force in Metropolitan Areas: An International Comparison." *Economic Development and Cultural Change* X (1962): 367–385.

Commission of the European Communities. *The Perception of Poverty in Europe.* Brussels: EEC, 1977.

Commission of the European Communities. *Social Protection in Europe, 1993.* Luxembourg: Office for Official Publications of the European Communities, 1994.

Commission of the European Communities. *Social Protection in Europe.* Luxembourg: Office for Official Publications of the European Communities, 1995.

Comstock, George, Steven Chaffee, Nathan Katzman, Maxwell McCombs, and Donald Roberts. *Television and Human Behavior.* New York: Columbia University Press, 1978.

Comstock, George and Paik Haejung. *Television and the American Child.* San Diego: Academic Press, 1991.

Congressional Quarterly, Inc. *Congress and the Nation: A Review of Government and Politics, 1993–1996.* Vol. IX. Washington, DC: Congressional Quarterly, 1998.

Converse, Philip E. "The Nature of Belief Systems in Mass Publics." In *Ideology and Discontent,* ed. David E. Apter, 206–261. New York: Free Press, 1964.

Converse, Philip E. *The Dynamics of Party Support: Cohort-Analyzing Party Identification.* Beverly Hills, CA: Sage, 1976.

Converse, Philip E. "Rejoinder to Abramson." *American Journal of Political Science* 23 (1979): 97–100.

Converse, Philip E. and Richard Niemi. "Non-voting among Young Adults in the United States." In *Political Parties and Political Behavior,* ed. William J. Crotty, et al. 2nd ed. Boston: Allyn & Bacon, 1971.

Cook, Brian J., Jacque L. Emel, and Roger E. Kasperson. "Organizing and Managing Radioactive Waste Disposal as an Experiment." *Journal of Policy Analysis and Management* 9, 3 (1990): 339–366.

Cook, Brian J., Jacque L. Emel, and Roger E. Kasperson. "Problem of Politics or Technique? Insights from Waste-Management Strategies in Sweden and France." *Policy Studies Review* 10, 4 (1991/92): 103–113.

Cook, Fay Lomax and Edith J. Barrett. *Support for the American Welfare State: The Views of Congress and the Public.* New York: Columbia University, 1992.

Cook, Rhodes. "Actual District Votes Belie Ideal of Bipartisanship." *Congressional Quarterly* (April 12, 1997): 859–862.

Cook, T., H. Appleton, R. Conner, A. Shaffer, G. Tamkin, and S. Weber. *Sesame Street Revisited.* New York: Russell Sage Foundation, 1975.

Cooke, William N. and Deborah S. Noble. "Industrial Relations Systems and US Foreign Direct Investment Abroad." *British Journal of Industrial Relations* 36, 4 (1998): 581–609.

Cooley, Charles H. *Social Organization.* New York: Charles Scribner Sons, 1927.

Cooney, Rosemary Santana. "A Comparative Study of Work Opportunities for Women." *Industrial Relations* 17, 1 (1978): 64–74.

Cooper, Bruce S., ed. *Labor Relations in Education: An International Perspective.* Westport, CT: Greenwood Press, 1992.

Corbett, Thomas J. "Welfare Reform in Wisconsin: The Rhetoric and the Reality." In *The Politics of Welfare Reform,* ed. Lyke Thompson and Donald F. Norris, 19–54. Thousand Oaks, CA: Sage, 1995.

Cotrell, William Frederick. *Energy and Society: The Relation Between Energy, Social Change, and Economic Development.* New York: McGraw-Hill, 1955.

Cotter, Cornelius P. and John F. Bibby. "Institutional Development of Parties and the Thesis of Party Decline." *Political Science Quarterly* 95, 1 (1980): 1–27.

Couglin, Richard M. *Ideology, Public Opinion, and Welfare Policy: Attitudes Toward Taxes and Spending in Industrialized Societies.* Berkeley: Institute of International Studies, University of California Berkeley, Research Monograph Series, 42, 1980.

Coulton, Claudia J., Nandita Verma, and Shenyang Guo. *Time Limited Welfare and the Employment Prospects of AFDC Recipients in Cuyahoga County.* Center on Urban Poverty and Social Change, Mandel School of Applied Social Sciences, Case Western Reserve University, 1996.

Council on Graduate Medical Education. *Physician Distribution and Health Care Challenges in Rural and Inner City Areas,* 10. U.S. Department of Health and Human Services, 1998.

Coyle, Dennis J. and Aaron Wildavsky. "Requisites of Radical Reform: Income Maintenance versus Tax Preferences." *Journal of Policy Analysis and Management* 7, 1 (1987): 1–16.

Craig, Laurene A. *Health of Nations: An International Perspective on U.S. Health Care Reform.* Washington, DC: Wyatt, 1991.

Craig, Stephen C. *The Malevolent Leaders: Popular Discontent in America.* Boulder, CO: Westview Press, 1993.

Crewe, Ivor. "Electoral Participation." In *Democracy at the Polls: A Comparative Study of Competitive National Elections,* ed. David Butler, Howard R. Penniman, and Austin Ranney, 216–263. Washington, DC: American Enterprise Institute, 1981.

Criqui, Patrick and Nina Kousnetzoff. *Energie 1995: Aprés les Chocs.* Paris: Centre d'Etudes Prospectives et d'Information Internationale, 1987.

Crook, Sara Brandes and John R. Hibbing. "Congressional Reform and Party Discipline: The Effects of Changes in the Seniority System on Party Loyalty in the US House of Representatives." *British Journal of Political Science* 15, 2 (1985): 207–226.

Crotty, William. *American Politics in Decline.* 2nd ed. Boston: Little, Brown, 1984.

Crouch, Colin. "Conditions for Trade Union Wage Restraint." In *Politics of Inflation and Economic Stagnation,* ed. Leon N. Lindberg and Charles S. Maier, 105–139. Washington, DC: Brookings Institution, 1985.

Crouch, Colin and Ronald Dore. "Whatever Happened to Corporatism?" In *Corporatism and Accountability,* ed. Colin and Ronald Dore Crouch, 1–43. Oxford, England: Oxford University Press, 1990.

Crozier, Michel, Samuel P. Huntington, and Joji Watanuki. *The Crisis of Democracy: Report on the Governability of Democracies to the Trilateral Commission.* New York: New York University Press, 1975.

Cukierman, Alex. *Central Bank Strategy, Credibility, and Independence: Theory and Evidence.* Cambridge, MA: MIT Press, 1992.

Cukierman, Alex, Pantelis Kalaitzidakis, Lawrence H. Summers, and Steven B. Webb. *Central Bank Independence, Growth, Investment, and Real Rates.* Vol. 39. Carnegie-Rocheteer Conference Series on Public Policy, 1993.

Cummings, William K. *Education and Equality in Japan.* Princeton, NJ: Princeton University Press, 1980.

Currie, Elliott. *Confronting Crime.* New York: Pantheon Books, 1985.

Curtis, George B. "The Colonial County Court, Social Forum and Legislative Precedent, Accomack County, Virginia, 1633–1639." *Virginia Magazine of History and Biography* 85, 3 (1977): 274–288.

Curtis, James E., Edward Grabb, and Douglas Baer. "Voluntary Association Membership in Fifteen Countries: A Comparative Analysis." *American Sociological Review* 57 (April 1992): 139–152.

Curtis, Richard F. and Elton F. Jackson. *Inequality in American Communities.* New York: Academic Press, 1977.

Cutler, David M. and Lawrence F. Katz. *Rising Inequality? Changes in the Distribution of Income and Consumption in the 1980s.* NBER Working Paper 3964. National Bureau of Economic Research, 1992.

Cutright, Phillips. "Political Structure, Economic Development, and National Security Programs." *American Journal of Sociology* 70 (1965): 604–621.

D'Arcy, P. F. and J. P Griffin. *Iatrogenic Disease.* New York: Oxford University Press, 1972.

Daalder, Hans. "The Consociational Democracy Theme." *World Politics* 26, 4 (1974): 604–621.

Daalder, Hans, Galen A. Irwin, and Arend Lijphart. "From the Politics of Accommodation to Adversarial Politics in the Netherlands." *West European Politics* 12, 1 (Jan. 1989): 139–153.

Dahl, Robert A. "Some Explanations." In *Political Oppositions in Western Democracies,* ed. R. A. Dahl, 348–386. New Haven, CT: Yale University Press, 1966.

Dahl, Robert A. *Dilemmas of Pluralist Democracy: Autonomy vs. Control.* New Haven, CT: Yale University Press, 1982.

Dahl, Robert A. *Democracy and Its Critics.* New Haven, CT: Yale University Press, 1989.

Dahl, Robert A. *The New American Political (Dis)order.* Berkeley: University of California, Berkeley, Institute of Governmental Studies Press, 1994.

Dahl, Robert A. and Charles E. Lindblom. *Politics, Economics, and Welfare.* New York: Harper, 1953.

Dalton, Russell J. *Citizen Politics in Western Democracies.* Chatham: Chatham House, 1988.

Dalton, Russell J. *Politics in Germany.* 2nd ed. New York: HarperCollins College, 1993.

Danziger, Sheldon and Peter Gottschalk. "The Poverty of 'Losing Ground'." *Challenge* 28, 2 (1985): 32–38.

Danziger, Sheldon H., Robert H. Haveman, and Robert D. Plotnick. "Antipoverty Policy: Effects on the Poor and the Nonpoor." In *Fighting Poverty: What Works and What Doesn't,* ed. Sheldon H. Danziger and Daniel H. Weinberg, 50–77. Cambridge, MA: Harvard University Press, 1986.

Danziger, Sheldon and Jane Waldfogel, ed. *Securing the Future: Investing in Children from Birth to College.* New York: Russell Sage Foundation, 2000.

Daspin, Eileen. "Volunteering on the Run." *Wall Street Journal,* November 5, 1999, W1, W4.

Datta, Samar K. and Jeffrey B. Nugent. "Adversary Activities and Per Capita Income Growth." *World Development* 14, 12 (1986): 1457–1461.

Davidson, Alexander. *Two Models of Welfare: The Origins and Development of the Welfare State in Sweden and New Zealand, 1888–1988.* Uppsala: Upsaliensis Academiae, 1989.

Davidson, Carlos and Michael Reich. "Income Inequality: An Inter-Industry Analysis." *Industrial Relations* 27 (1988): 263–286.

Davidson, Roger H. "The New Centralization on Capital Hill." *Review of Politics* 50, 3 (1988): 345–364.

Davidson, William H. "The Location of Foreign Direct Investment Activity: Country Characteristics and Experience Effects." *Journal of International Business Studies* 11 (1980): 9–22.

Davies, Christie. "Crime, Bureaucracy, and Equality." *Policy Review* 23 (1983): 89–105.

Davis, Fred. *On Youth Subcultures: The Hippie Variant.* Morristown, NJ: General Learning Press, 1971.

Davis, James A. *Great Aspirations: The Graduate School Plans of America's College Seniors.* Chicago: Aldine, 1964.

Davis, James A. "Changeable Weather in a Cooling Climate Atop the Liberal Plateau: Conversion and Replacement in Forty-two General Social Survey Items, 1972–1989." *Public Opinion Quarterly* 56 (1992): 261–306.

Davis, James A. and Tom W. Smith. *General Social Surveys.* Chicago: National Opinion Research Center, 1989a.

Davis, James Allen and Tom W. Smith. *General Social Surveys, 1972–1989: Cumulative Codebook.* Chicago: National Opinion Research Center, 1989b.

Davis, Kingsley. "Wives and Work: The Sex Role Revolution and Its Consequences." *Population and Development Review* 10, 3 (1984): 397–417.

Davis, Natalie Z. "Poor Relief, Humanism, and Heresy: The Case of Lyon." *Studies in Medieval and Renaissance History* 5 (1968): 215–275.

Dawson, John E. and Peter J. E. Stan. *Public Expenditures in the United States: 1952–1993.* Santa Monica, CA: RAND, 1995.

Day, Christine L. *What Older Americans Think.* Princeton, NJ: Princeton University Press, 1990.

De Kock, M. H. *Central Banking.* 3rd ed. London: Staples Press, 1954.

De Leeuw, Frank, Michael Mohr, and Robert P. Parker. "Gross Product by Industry, 1977–1988: A Progress Report on Improving the Estimates." *Survey of Current Business* (U.S. Department of Commerce, Bureau of Economic Analysis) 71 (1991): 23–37.

De Schweinitz, Karl. *Industrialization and Democracy: Economic Necessities and Political Possibilities.* New York: Free Press of Glencoe, 1964.

De Swaan, Abram. *Coalition Theories and Cabinet Formations.* San Francisco: Jossey-Bass, 1973.

Deane, Marjorie and Robert Pringle. *The Central Banks.* London: Hamish Hamilton, 1994.

"Death Penalty." In *Issues and Controversies on File,* available at http://www.facts.com/cd/i00015.htm as of December 15, 1995 (hard copy on file with author), 1995.

DeGré, Gerard. "Freedom and Social Structure." *American Sociological Review* 11 (October 1946): 529–536.

Dekker, Paul and Peter Ester. *Social and Political Attitudes in Dutch Society: Theoretical Perspectives and Survey Evidence.* Social and Cultural Studies, 16, Rijswijk (Netherlands): Social and Cultural Planning Office, 1993.

Dekov, Eric. "Danish Labour Market Contributions are Contrary to Community Law." *International VAT Monitor* 11 (1993): 12–17.

Democratic Study Group, U.S. House of Representatives. "Myths of Reform, Sections I-IV." n.d.

Denison, Edward F. *Accounting for United States Economic Growth 1929–1960.* Washington, DC: Brookings Institution, 1974.

Denison, Edward F. *Accounting for Slower Economic Growth: The United States in the 1970s.* Washington, DC: Brookings Institution, 1979.

Denison, Edward F. *Trends in American Economic Growth, 1929–1982.* Washington, DC: Brookings Institution, 1985.

Denison, Edward F. with the assistance of Jean-Pierre Poullier. *Why Growth Rates Differ: Postwar Experience in Nine Western Countries.* Washington, DC: Brookings Institution, 1967.

DeParle, Jason. "Project to Rescue Needy Stumbles Against the Persistence of Poverty." *New York Times,* May 15, 1999, A1.

Derthick, Martha. *Policymaking for Social Security.* Washington, DC: Brookings Institution, 1979.

Derthick, Martha. *Agency Under Stress: The Social Security Administration in American Government.* Washington, DC: Brookings Institution, 1990.

DeSart, Jay A. "Information Processing and Partisan Neutrality: A Reexamination of the Party Decline Thesis." *Journal of Politics* 57, 3 (1995): 776–795.

deWitt, Thomas. "The Economics and Politics of Welfare in the Third Reich." *Central European History* 11, 3 (1978): 256–278.

Di Palma, Giuseppe. *To Craft Democracies: An Essay on Democratic Transitions.* Berkeley: University of California Press, 1990.

Diamandouros, P. Nikiforos and Richard Gunther. "Preface." In *The Politics of Democratic Consolidation: Southern Europe in Comparative Perspective,* ed. Richard Gunther, P. Nikiforos Diamandouros, and Hans-Jürgen Puhle, ix-xxx. Baltimore: Johns Hopkins University Press, 1995.

Diamond, Larry. "Economic Development and Democracy Reconsidered." *American Behavioral Scientist* 35, 4–5 (March–June 1992): 450–499.

Diamandouros, P. Nikiforos, Hans-Jürgen Puhle, and Richard Gunther. "Conclusion: The Consolidation of Democratic Regimes." In *The Politics of Democratic Consolidation: Southern Europe in Comparative Perspective,* ed. Richard Gunther, P. N. Diamandouros, and Hans-Jürgen Puhle, 389–413. Baltimore: Johns Hopkins University Press, 1995.

Diamond, Larry, Juan J. Linz, and Seymour M. Lipset, eds. *Democracy in Developing Countries.* Boulder, CO: Lynne Rienner, 1988–1990.

Dicken, Peter. *Global Shift: The Internationalization of Economic Activity.* 2nd ed. New York: Guilford Press, 1992.

Dickens, William T. and Jonathan Leonard. "Accounting for the Decline in Union Membership, 1950–1980." *Industrial and Labor Relations Review* 38, 3 (April 1985): 323–334.

Dickson, William J. *Management and the Worker.* Cambridge: Harvard University Press, 1939.

Dilulio, John J., Jr. "Defining Criminality Up." *Wall Street Journal,* July 3, 1996.

DiMaggio, Paul J. and Walter W. Powell. "Introduction." In *The New Institutionalism in Organizational Analysis,* ed. Paul J. DiMaggio and Walter W. Powell, 1–38. Chicago: University of Chicago Press, 1991.

Dixon, Jo and Alan J. Lizotte. "Gun Ownership and the 'Southern Subculture of Violence.'" *American Journal of Sociology* 93, 2 (1987): 383–405.

Dobbeck, Diane and Wendy Woods. "Mapping Industrial Activity." *OECD Observer* 188 (1994): 19–23.

Dogan, Mattei and John D. Kasarda. "Introduction: How Giant Cities Will Multiply and Grow." In *The Metropolis Era,* ed. Mattei Dogan and John D. Kasarda, 12–29. Vol. 1. Newbury Park, CA: Sage, 1988.

Döhler, Marian. "Policy Networks, Opportunity Structures and Neo-Conservative Reform Strategies in Health Policy." In *Policy Networks: Empirical Evidence and Theoretical Considerations,* ed. Bernd Marin and Renate Mayntz, 235–96. Frankfurt/Main: Campus Verlag, 1991.

Döhler, Marian. "The State as Architect of Political Order: Policy Dynamics in German Health Care." *Governance: An International Journal of Policy and Administration* 8, 3 (1995): 380–404.

Dominick, Joseph R. *The Dynamics of Mass Communication.* 2nd ed. New York: Random House, 1987.

Donovan, Marjorie. "And Let Who Must Achieve: High School Education and White Collar Work in Nineteenth Century America." Dissertation, University of California at Davis, 1977.

Donovan, Todd, Shaun Bowler, David McCuan, and Ken Fernandez. "Contending Players and Strategies: Opposition Advantages in Initiative Campaigns." In *Citizens as Legislators: Direct Democracy in the American States,* ed. Shaun Bowler, Todd Donovan, and Caroline Torbert, Chapter 4. Columbus: Ohio State University Press, 1998.

Dordick, Herbert S. and Georgette Wang. *The Information Society: A Retrospective View.* Newbury Park, CA: Sage, 1993.

Dore, Ronald. *Flexible Rigidities: Industrial Policy and Structural Adjustment in the Japanese Economy 1970–80.* London: Athlone, 1986.

Dore, Ronald. "Japan: A Nation Made for Corporatism?" In *Corporatism and Accountability,* ed. Colin Crouch and Ronald Dore, 45–62. Oxford, England: Oxford University Press, 1990.

Dore, Ronald. "Incurable Unemployment: A Progressive Disease of Modern Societies?" *Political Quarterly* 65, 3 (1994): 285–312.

Doron, Abraham. "Public Assistance in Israel: Issues of Policy and Administration." *Journal of Social Policy* 7, 4 (1978): 441–460.

Douglas, Mary and Aaron Wildavsky. *Risk and Culture: An Essay on the Selection of Technical and Environmental Dangers.* Berkeley: University of California Press, 1982.

Douglas, Paul H. and Aaron Director. *The Problem of Unemployment.* New York: Macmillan, 1931.

"Driving on." *The Economist* 321, 7730 (1991): 61–62.

DuBos, Rene. *The Mirage of Health: Utopian Progress and Biological Change.* New York: Anchor Books, 1959.

DuBos, Rene and Jean DuBos. *The White Plague: Tuberculosis, Man and Society.* Boston: Little, Brown, 1953.

Duch, Raymond M. and Michaell A. Taylor. "A Reply to Abramson and Inglehart's Education, Security, and Postmaterialism." *American Journal of Political Science* 38, no. 3 1994): 815–825.

Duleep, Harriet Orcutt. "Mortality and Income Inequality Among Economically Developed Countries." *Social Security Bulletin* 58, 2 (1995): 34–50.

Dulles, F. R. *America Learns to Play.* New York: Appleton-Century, 1940.

Duncan, Beverly and Otis Duncan. "Minorities and the Process of Stratification." *American Sociological Review* 33 (1968): 356–364.

Duncan, Greg J., Jeanne Brooks-Gunn, W. Jean Yeung, and Judith R. Smith. "How Much Does Childhood Poverty Affect the Life Chances of Children?" *American Sociological Review* 63 (June 1998): 406–423.

Duncan, Greg J., Björn Gustafsson, Richard Hauser, Günther Schmaus, et al. "Poverty Dynamics in 8 Countries." *Journal of Population Economics* 6 (1993): 215–234.

Duncan, Greg J., Björn Gustafsson, Richard Hauser, Günther Schmaus, et al. "Poverty and Social-Assistance Dynamics in the U.S., Canada, and Western Europe." In *Poverty, Inequality, and the Crisis of Social Policy,* ed. K. McFate. New York: Russell Sage Foundation, 1995.

Duncan, Greg J., Björn Gustafsson, Richard Hauser, Günther Schmaus, Stephen Jenkins, Hans Messinger, Ruud Muffels, Brian Nolan, Jean-Claude Ray, and Wolfgang Voges. *Poverty and Social-*

Assistance Dynamics in the United States, Canada, and Europe. Washington, DC: Joint Center for Political and Economic Studies, 1991.

Duncan, Greg J., Martha S. Hill, and Saul D. Hoffman. "Welfare Dependence Across the Generations." *Science* 239 (1988): 467–471.

Duncan, Greg J. and D. Saul Hoffman. "Welfare Benefits, Economic Opportunities, and Out-of-Wedlock Births Among Black Teenager Girls." *Demography* 27, 4 (1990): 519–536.

Duncan, Greg J. and Wolfgang Voges. "Do Generous Social-Assistance Programs Lead to Dependence? A Comparative Study of Lone-Parent Families in Germany and the U.S." University of Michigan Survey Research Center, 1994.

Duncan, Greg J. and Wei-Jun J. Yueng. "Extent and Consequences of Welfare Dependence Among America's Children." University of Michigan, Survey Research Center, 1994.

Duncan, Otis Dudley, David L. Featherman, and Beverly Duncan. *Socioeconomic Background and Achievement.* New York: Seminar Press, 1972.

Dunnell, Karen and Ann Cartwright. *Medical Takers, Prescribers and Hoarders.* London: Routledge, 1972.

Dunning, John H. "Trade, Location of Economic Activity, and the Multinational Enterprise: a Search for an Eclectic Paradigm." In *The International Allocation of Economic Activity,* ed. Bertil Ohlin, Per-Ove Hesselborn, and Per Magnus Wijkman. London: Macmillan, 1977.

Dunning, John H. "The Eclectic Paradigm of International Production: an Update and Some Possible Extensions." *Journal of International Business Studies* 19, 1 (1988): 1–32.

Dunning, John H., John A. Cantwell, and T. A. B. Corley. "The Theory of International Production: Some Historical Antecedents." In *Multinationals: Theory and History,* ed. Peter Hertner and Geoffrey Jones. Aldershot, UK: Gower, 1986.

Durkheim, Emile. *Suicide, a Study in Sociology.* Translated by John A. Spaulding and George Simpson. Edited by George Simpson. Glencoe, IL: Free Press, 1951 [1897].

Durkheim, Emile. "Preface to the Second Edition: Some Notes on Occupational Groups." In *The Division of Labor in Society,* 1–31. 2nd ed. Glencoe, IL: Free Press, 1960 [1893].

Dutton, D. B. "Social Class, Health, and Illness." In *Applications of Social Science to Clinical Medicine and Health Policy,* ed. L. H. Aiken and D. Mechanic. New Brunswick, NJ: Rutgers University Press, 1986.

Duval-Smith, Alexandra. "A Land Where Men (Sometimes) Are Left Holding the Baby." *Sweden Now* 120, 6 (1986): 27–28.

Dye, Richard F. and Therese J. McGuire. "Sorting Out State Expenditure Pressures." *National Tax Journal* 45, 3 (1992): 315–329.

Easton, Brian. "From Reaganomics to Rogernomics." In *The Influence of American Economics on New Zealand's Thinking and Policy: the Fulbright Anniversary Seminars,* ed. Allan Bollard, 42. Wellington, New Zealand: New Zealand—United States Educational Foundation, New Zealand Institute of Economic Research, 1988.

Eberle, Thomas Samuel. "Dislocation Policies in Western Europe: Past, Present, and Future." *The Annals of the American Academy of Political and Social Science* 544 (1996): 127–139.

Eberts, Randall W. and Timothy J. Gronberg. "Can Competition among Local Governments Constrain Government Spending?" *Economic Review* (Federal Reserve Bank of Cleveland) 24, 1 (1988): 2–9.

Edelstein, Michael. *Overseas Investment in the Age of High Imperialism: The United Kingdom, 1850–1914.* New York: Columbia University Press, 1982.

Edin, Kathryn and Laura Lein. *Making Ends Meet: How Single Mothers Survive Welfare and Low-Wage Work.* New York: Russell Sage Foundation, 1997a.

Edin, Kathryn and Laura Lein. "Work, Welfare, and Single Mothers' Survival Strategies." *American Sociological Review* 62, 2 (1997b): 253–266.

Edin, Per-Anders and Bertil Holmlund. "The Swedish Wage Structure: The Rise and Fall of Solidarity Wage Policy?" In *Differences and Changes in Wage Structures,* ed. Richard B. Freeman and Lawrence F. Katz, 307–343. Chicago: University of Chicago Press (for NBER), 1995.

Edsource. "School Finance: 1999–2000." *Reports* 11/99 (1999): 1–16.

Eduards, Maud. "The Swedish Woman in Political Life." *Current Sweden* 248, 7 (1980): 3–8.

Edwards, Paul K. and Richard Hyman. "Strikes and Industrial Conflict: Peace in Europe?" In *New Frontiers in European Industrial Relations,* ed. Richard Hyman and Anthony Ferner, 250–280. Oxford: Blackwell, 1994.

Egbuonu, Lisa and Barbara Starfield. "Congenital Hypothyroidism and Phenylketonuria." In *The Effectiveness of Medial Care: Validating Clinical Wisdom,* ed. Barbara Starfield, Lisa Egbuonu, Mark Farfel, Nancy Hutton, Alain Joffe, and Lawrence S. Wissow, 71–75. Baltimore: The Johns Hopkins University Press, 1985a.

Egbuonu, Lisa and Barbara Starfield. "Inadequate Immunization and the Prevention of Communicable Diseases." In *The Effectiveness of Medical Care: Validating Clinical Wisdom,* ed. Barbara Starfield, Lisa Egbuonu, Mark Farfel, Nancy Hutton, Alain Joffe, and Lawrence S. Wissow, 48–57. Baltimore: Johns Hopkins University Press, 1985b.

Ehrmann, Henry W. *Organized Business in France.* Princeton: Princeton University Press, 1957.

Ehrmann, Henry W. *Politics in France.* 3rd ed. Boston, MA: Little, Brown, 1976.

Eichengreen, Barry and Peter H. Lindhert, eds. *The International Debt Crisis in Historical Perspective.* Cambridge, MA: MIT Press, 1989.

Eisenberg, Leon and Arthur Kleinman. "Clinical Social Science." In *The Relevance of Social Science for Medicine,* ed. Leon Eisenberg and Arthur Kleinman, 1–23. Boston, MA: D. Reidel, 1981.

Ekert, Olivia. "Effets et Limites des Aides Financières au Familles: Une Experience at un Modèle." *Population* 41 (1986): 327–348.

Elder, Neil, Alastair H. Thomas, and David Arter. *The Consensual Democracies? The Government and Politics of the Scandinavian States.* Oxford: Martin Robertson, 1982.

Elley, Warwick B. *How in the World Do Students Read?* The Hague: The International Association for the Evaluation of Educational Achievement, 1992.

Ellwood, David T. and Mary Jo Bane. "The Impact of AFDC on Family Structure and Living Arrangements." In *Research in Labor Economics,* ed. Ronald G. Ehrenberg, 137–207. Vol. 7. Greenwich CT and London: JAI Press, 1985.

Elving, Ronald D. "Brighter Lights, Wider Windows: Presenting Congress in the 1990s." In *Congress, the Press, and the Public,* ed. Thomas E. Mann and Norman J. Ornstein, 171–204. Washington, DC: American Enterprise Institute and Brookings Institution, 1994.

Emerson, Michael. "Regulation or Deregulation of the Labour Market: Policy Regimes for the Recruitment and Dismissal of Employees in the Industrialized Countries." *European Economic Review* 32, 4 (1988): 775–817.

Encarnation, Dennis J. "A Common Evolution? A Comparison of United States and Japanese Transnational Corporations." *Transnational Corporations* 2, 1 (1993): 7–32.

Engel, George L. "Psychologic Factors in Instantaneous Cardiac Death." *New England Journal of Medicine* 294 (1976): 664–665.

Enloe, Cynthia H. *The Politics of Pollution in a Comparative Perspective: Ecology and Power in Four Nations.* New York: David McKay, 1975.

Enthoven, A. C. "The Rand Experiment and Economical Health Care." *New England Journal of Medicine* 310, 23 (1984): 1528–1530.

Epstein, Abraham. *Insecurity: A Challenge to America.* New York: Smith and Haas, 1933.

Epstein, Cynthia Fuchs. *Woman's Place: Options and Limits in Professional Careers.* Berkeley: University of California Press, 1970.

Epstein, Cynthia Fuchs. *Women in Law.* 2nd ed. Urbana and Chicago: University of Illinois Press, 1993.

Epstein, Gerald. "Political Economy and Comparative Central Banking." *Review of Radical Political Economics* 24 (1992): 1–30.

Epstein, Gerald and Juliet Schor. "The Political Economy of Central Banking." Discussion paper No. 1281. Harvard Institute of Economic Research, 1986.

Erikson, Robert and Jan O. Jonsson. "Introduction: Explaining Class Inequality in Education: The Swedish Test Case." In *Can Education Be Equalized? The Swedish Case in Comparative Perspective,* ed. Robert Erikson and Jan O. Jonsson, 1–63. Boulder, CO: Westview Press, 1996a.

Erikson, Robert and Jan O. Jonsson. "The Swedish Context: Educational Reform and Long-term Change in Educational Inequality." In *Can Education Be Equalized? The Swedish Case in Comparative Perspective,* ed. Robert Erikson and Jan O. Jonsson, 65–93. Boulder, CO: Westview Press, 1996b.

Esman, Milton J. "The Political Fallout of International Migration." *Diaspora* 2, 1 (1992): 3–41.

Espenshade, Thomas J. "Marriage Trends in America: Estimates, Implications, and Underlying Causes." *Population and Development Review* 11, 2 (1985): 193–245.

Esping-Andersen, Gosta. *Politics Against Markets.* Princeton: Princeton University Press, 1985.

Esping-Andersen, Gosta. *The Three Worlds of Welfare Capitalism.* Princeton: Princeton University Press, 1990.

Estes, Richard J. and Harold L. Wilensky. "Life Cycle Squeeze and the Morale Curve." *Social Problems* 25 (Feb. 1978): 277–292.

Ettner, Susan L. "Medicaid Participation Among the Eligible Elderly." *Journal of Policy Analysis and Management* 16, 2 (1997): 237–255.

Etzioni-Halevy, Eva. *National Broadcasting Under Siege: A Comparative Study of Australia, Britain, Israel, and West Germany.* New York: St. Martin's Press, 1987.

Eulau, Heinz and Michael S. Lewis-Beck, ed. *Economic Conditions and Electoral Outcomes: The United States and Western Europe.* New York: Agathon Press, 1985.

Euromedia Research Group. *The Media in Western Europe: The Euromedia Handbook,* ed. Bernt Stubbe Ostergaard. 2nd ed. London: Sage, 1997.

European Centre for Social Welfare Policy and Research. *Welfare in a Civil Society: Report for the Conference of European Ministers Responsible for Social Affairs.* Vienna: European Centre, 1993.

Eurostat. *Social Protection Expenditures and Receipts 1985–1988.* Luxembourg: Office of Official Publications for the European Communities, 1990.

Eurostat. *Social Protection Expenditure and Receipts 1980–1993.* Luxembourg: Office for Official Publications of the European Communities, 1995.

Evans, Martin. "Giving Credit Where It's Due? The Success of Family Credit Reassessed." Suntory and Toyota International Centres for Economics and Related Disciplines, London School of Economics and Political Science, 1996. Welfare State Programme WSP/121.

Evans, Martin, Serge Paugam, and Joseph Prélis. "Chunnel Vision: Poverty, social exclusion and the debate on social welfare in France and Britain." Discussion Paper, Suntory and Toyota International Centres for Economics and Related Disciplines, London School of Economics, 1995.

Evans, Martin, David Piachaud, and Holly Sutherland. "Designed for the Poor—Poorer by Design? The Effects of the 1986 Social Security Act on Family Incomes." Discussion Paper WSP/105, July, Welfare State Programme, London School of Economics, 1994.

Evans, Peter. *Dependent Development: The Alliance of Multinational, State and Local Capital in Brazil.* Princeton: Princeton University Press, 1979.

Evans, Robert G., Morris L. Barer, and Clyde Hertzman. "The 20-Year Experiment: Accounting For, Explaining, and Evaluating Health Care Cost Containment in Canada and the United States." *Annual Review of Public Health* 12 (1991): 481–518.

Evans, Robert G. and Gregory L. Stoddart. "Producing Health, Consuming Health Care." In *The Nation's Health,* ed. Philip R. Lee and Carroll L. Estes, 14–33. 4th ed. Boston and London: Jones and Bartlett, 1994.

Evans, Richard J. *The Feminists: Women's Emancipation Movements in Europe, America, and Australasia, 1840–1920.* New York: Barnes & Noble Books, 1977.

Evans, X. T. "Breast Cancer Symposium: Points in the Practical Management of Breast Cancer: Are Physical Methods of Diagnosis of Value?" *British Journal of Surgery* 56 (1969): 784–786.

Eyer, Joseph. "Hypertension as a Disease of Modern Society." *International Journal of Health Services* 5 (1975): 539–558.

Fairlie, Robert W. and Rebecca A. London. "The Effect of Incremental Benefit Levels on Births to AFDC Recipients." *Journal of Policy Analysis and Management* 16, 4 (1997): 575–597.

Fallows, James M. "Up Against the Wall Street Journal." *The American Prospect* No. 14 (1993): 21–27.

Fallows, James M. *Breaking the News: How the Media Undermine American Democracy.* New York: Pantheon Books, 1996.

Families USA Foundation. *Comparing Medicare HMOs: Do They Keep Their Members?* Washington, DC: Families USA Foundation, 1997.

Farley, Reynolds. "The New Census Question about Ancestry: What Did It Tell US?" *Demography* 28 (1991): 411–429.

Farley, Reynolds and William H. Frey. "Changes in the Segregation of Whites from Blacks during the 1980s: Small Steps toward a More Integrated Society." *American Sociological Review* 59 (1994): 23–45.

Farrell, David M. "Ireland." In *Party Organizations: A Data Handbook on Party Organizations in Western Democracies,* ed. Richard S. Katz and Peter Mair, 389–457. London: Sage, 1992.

Farrell, David M. "Campaign Professionalization and Political Parties." Paper presented at a workshop on "Change in the Relationship of Parties and Democracy," Texas A&M University, April 4–6, 1997.

Farrell, David M. and Paul Webb. "Political Parties as Campaign Organizations." In *Parties without Partisans,* ed. Russell Dalton and Martin Wattenberg. Oxford: Oxford University Press, 2001.

Farrell, Greg. "Lurching Into Reverse." *Brill's Content* 1, 1 (July 1998): 53–55.

Fassmann, Heinz and Rainer Münz. "European East-West Migration 1945–1992." *International Migration Review* 28 (1994): 520–538.

Featherman, David L. and Robert M. Hauser. *Opportunity and Change.* New York: Academic Press, 1978.

Federal Bureau of Investigation. *Uniform Crime Reports for the United States.* Washington, DC: U.S. Department of Justice, 1990.

Federal Office of Child Support Enforcement. *Twentieth Annual OCSE Report to Congress.* U.S. Department of Health and Human Services, Administration for Children, 1997.

Federal Register. Vol. 61, n. 43, 1996.

Feinstein, J. S. "The Relationship between Socioeconomic Status and Health: A Review of the Literature." *Milbank Quarterly* 71, 2 (1993): 279–322.

Ferguson, Charles H. "America's High-Tech Decline." *Foreign Policy* 74 (1989): 123–144.

Ferguson, Ronald F. "Paying for Public Education: New Evidence on How and Why Money Matters." *Harvard Journal on Legislation* 28 (1991): 465–498.

Ferner, Anthony. "The State as Employer." *New Frontiers in European Industrial Relations* (1994): 52–79.

Ferner, Anthony and Richard Hyman, ed. *Industrial Relations in the New Europe.* Oxford: Blackwell, 1992.

Ferrera, Maurizio. *EC Citizens and Social Protection: Main Results from a Eurobarometer Survey.* Brussels: Commission of the EC, Division V/E/2, 1993a.

Ferrera, Maurizio, ed. *Stato sociale e mercato mondiale.* Torino, Italy: Edizioni della Fondazione Giovanni Agnelli, 1993b.

Ferrera, Maurizio. "The Rise and Fall of Democratic Universalism: Health Care Reform in Italy, 1978–1994." Paper presented at workshop on "The State and the Health Care System," ECPR Joint Sessions of Workshops, Madrid, April 17–22, 1994.

Feys, Bernard. *Statistical Sources on Public Sector Employment.* Paris: Organization for Economic Cooperation and Development, 1994.

Finer, Herman. *Theory and Practice of Modern Government.* Westport, CT: Greenwood Press, 1970.

Fiorina, M. P. "The Decline of Collective Responsibility in American Politics." *Daedalus* 109 (1980): 25–45.

Firebaugh, Glenn. "Empirics of World Income Inequality." *American Journal of Sociology* 104, 6 (May 1999): 1597–1630.

Fischer, Claude S. *To Dwell among Friends: Personal Networks in Town and City.* Chicago: University of Chicago Press, 1982.

Fischer, Claude S. *The Urban Experience.* 2nd ed. New York: Harcourt Brace Jovanovich, 1984.

Fischer, Claude S. *America Calling: A Social History of the Telephone to 1940.* Berkeley: University of California Press, 1992.

Fisher, Paul. "The Social Security Crisis: An International Dilemma." *Aging and Work: Journal on Age, Work, and Retirement* 1, 1 (1978): 1–14.

Fitzgerald, Terry J. "Reducing Working Hours." *Economic Review* 32, 4 (1996): 13–22.

Fix, Michael and Jeffrey S. Passel. *Immigration and Immigrants: Setting the Record Straight.* Washington, DC: Urban Institute, 1994.

Flaherty, Sean. "Strike Activity and Productivity Change: The U.S. Auto Industry." *Industrial Relations* 26 (1987a): 174–185.

Flaherty, Sean. "Strike Activity, Worker Militancy, and Productivity Change in Manufacturing, 1961–1981." *Industrial and Labor Relations Review* 40 (1987b): 585–600.

Flanagan, Robert J., David W. Soskice, and Lloyd Ulman. *Unionism, Economic Stabilization, and Incomes Policies: European Experience.* Washington, DC: Brookings Institution, 1983.

Flora, Peter, ed. *Growth to Limits: The Western European Welfare States since World War II.* Berlin: Walter de Gruyter, 1986.

Flora, Peter and Jens Alber. "Modernization, Democratization, and the Development of Welfare States in Western Europe." In *The Development of Welfare States,* ed. Peter Flora and Arnold Heidenheimer, 37–80. New Brunswick, NJ: Transaction Books, 1981.

Flora, Peter, Jens Alber, Franz Kraus, and Winfried Pfennig. *State, Economy, and Society in Western Europe, 1815–1975.* Vol. 1. *The Growth of Mass Democracies and the Welfare States.* Frankfurt: Campus Verlag, 1983.

Flora, Peter and Arnold J. Heidenheimer, eds. *The Development of Welfare States in Europe and America.* New Brunswick, NJ: Transaction, 1981.

Flynn, James et al. *One Hundred Centuries of Solitude: Redirecting America's High-Level Nuclear Waste Policy.* Boulder, CO: Westview Press, 1995.

Fogarty, Michael Patrick. *Christian Democracy in Western Europe, 1820–1953.* London: Routledge and Paul: 1957.

Fogel, Robert W. "The Conquest of High Mortality and Hunger in Europe and America: Timing and Mechanisms." In *Favorites of Fortune: Technology, Growth, and Economic Development Since the Industrial Revolution,* ed. Patrice Higonnet, David S. Landes, and Henry Rosovsky, 33–71. Cambridge, MA: Harvard University Press, 1991.

Ford, L. "Advanced Nursing Practice." In *Charting Nursing's Future: Agenda for the 1990s,* ed. L. H. Aiken and C. M. Fagin, 287–299. Philadelphia: Lippencott, 1992.

Fox, Daniel M. "Health Policy and the Politics of Research in the United States." *Journal of Health Politics, Policy and Law* 15, 3 (1990): 481–499.

Frank, John W. "Why "Population Health"?" *Canadian Journal of Public Health* 86, 3 (May–June 1995): 162–164.

Frank, John W. and J. Fraser Mustard. "The Determinants of Health from a Historical Perspective." *Daedalus. Journal of the American Academy of Arts and Sciences* 123, 4 (1994): 1–17.

Frankenhauser, Marianne. "Coping with Job Stress: A Psychobiological Approach." In *Working Life: A Social Science Contribution to Work Reform,* ed. B. Gardell and G. Johanson, 213–233. 1981.

Franklin, Mark, Tom Mackie, and Henry Valen. *Electoral Change: Responses to Evolving Social and Attitudinal Structures in Western Countries.* Cambridge: Cambridge University Press, 1992.

Franklin, Mark N. and Wolfgang Rüdig. "On the Durability of Green Politics: Evidence From the 1989 European Election Study." *Comparative Political Studies* 28, 3 (1995): 409–439.

Frantzich, Stephen E. "Television and Congress: The Voyage to Public Understanding." Two Decades of House Television, for Better or Worse in Woodrow Wilson Center, 1999.

Fraschini, Angela. "La Spesa per il Personale." In *Il Deficit Pubblico: Origini e Problemi,* ed. E. Gerelli and A. Majocchi. Milan: Angeli, 1984.

Fratianni, Michele and Jürgen Von Hagen. *The European Monetary System and European Monetary Union.* Boulder, CO: Westview Press, 1992.

Frears, John. *Parties and Voters in France.* New York: St. Martin's Press, 1991.

Free, Lloyd A. and Hadley Cantril. *The Political Beliefs of Americans: A Study of Public Opinion.* New York: Simon & Schuster, 1967.

Free TV for Straight Talk Coalition. *Proposal for a National Time Bank.* Free TV for Straight Talk Coalition, 1997.

Freeman, Gary P. "Can Liberal States Control Unwanted Migration?" *Annals of the American Academy of Political and Social Science* 534 (1994): 17–30.

Freeman, Richard B. "Changes in the Labor Market for Black Americans, 1948–72." *Brookings Paper on Economic Activity* 3 (1973): 67–120.

Freeman, Richard B. "Create Jobs That Pay as Well as Crime." *New York Times,* July 20, 1986, Section 2, p. 3.

Freeman, Richard B. "Evaluating the European View That the United States Has No Unemployment Problem." *American Economic Review* 78, 2 (1988): 294–299.

Freeman, Richard B. and Harry J. Holzer, eds. *The Black Youth Employment Crisis.* Chicago: University of Chicago Press, 1986.

Freeman, Richard B. and James L. Medoff. *What Do Unions Do?* New York: Basic Books, 1984.

Freeman, Richard B. and Joel Rogers. *What Workers Want.* Ithaca: Cornell University Press and New York: Russell Sage Foundation, 1999.

Freidson, Eliot. *The Profession of Medicine: A Study of the Sociology of Applied Knowledge.* New York: Dodd, Mead, 1970.

Friedlander, Daniel and Gary Burtless. *Five Years After: The Long-Term Effects of Welfare-to-Work Programs.* New York: Russell Sage Foundation, 1995.

Friedlander, Daniel and Judith M. Gueron. "Are High-Cost Services More Effective than Low-Cost Services?" In *Evaluating Welfare and Training Programs,* ed. Charles F. Manski and Irwin Garfinkel, 143–198. Cambridge: Harvard University Press, 1992.

Friedman, Benjamin M. *Day of Reckoning: The Consequences of American Economic Policy.* New York: Vintage Books, 1989.

Friedman, Lawrence M. *Total Justice.* New York: Russell Sage, 1985.

Friedman, Meyer, and Ray H. Rosenman. *Type A Behavior and Your Heart.* New York: Knopf, 1974.

Fuchs, Victor R. *Who Shall Live? Health, Economics and Social Choice.* New York: Basic Books, 1974.

Fuchs, Victor R. "Economics, Values, and Health Care Reform." *The American Economic Review* 86, 1 (1986a): 1–24.

Fuchs, Victor R. *The Health Economy.* Cambridge, MA, and London: Harvard University Press, 1986b.

Fukai, Shigeko and Haruhiro Fukai. "Elite Recruitment and Political Leadership." *Political Science* 25, 1 (1992): 25–36.

Funkhauser, G. R. "Trends in Media Coverage of the Issues of the 1960s." *Journalism Quarterly* 50 (1973): 533–538.

Galanter, Marc. "Reading the Landscape of Disputes: What We Know and Don't Know (and Think We Know) about Our Allegedly Contentious and Litigious Society." *UCLA Law Review* 31, 1 (1983): 4–71.

Galbraith, James K. "Self-Fulfilling Prophets: Inflated Zeal at the Federal Reserve." *The American Prospect* 18 (Summer 1994): 31–39.

Galbraith, John K. *The New Industrial State.* Boston, MA: Houghton Mifflin, 1967.

Gallup Report. *Religion in America, 50 Years: 1935–1985.* Report #236, May 1985.

Gamson, William A. *Talking Politics.* Cambridge: Cambridge University Press, 1992.

Gans, Herbert J. *The Urban Villagers: Group and Class in the Life of Italian-Americans.* New York: Free Press, 1962.

Gans, Herbert J. *The Levittowners: Ways of Life and Politics in a New Suburban Community.* New York: Pantheon, 1967.

Gans, Herbert J. *Deciding What's News.* New York: Vintage Books, 1980.

Gardner, Margaret. "Labor Movements and Industrial Restructuring: Australia, New Zealand, and the United States." In *The Comparative Political Economy of Industrial Relations,* ed. Kirsten S. Wever and Lowell Turner, 33–69. Madison, WI: Industrial Relations Research Association, 1995.

Garfinkel, Irwin and Sara S. McLanahan. *Single Mothers and Their Children: A New American Dilemma.* Washington, DC: Urban Institute Press, 1986.

Garfinkel, Irwin, Sara S. McLanahan, Daniel Meyer, and Judith Seltzer, eds. *Fathers Under Fire: The Revolution in Child Support Enforcement.* New York: Russell Sage, 1998.

Garnham, Nicholas. "The Broadcasting Market and the Future of the BBC." *Political Quarterly* 65, 1 (1994): 11–19.

Garon, Sheldon. *The State and Labor in Modern Japan.* Berkeley: University of California Press, 1987.

Garrett, Geoffrey and Peter Lange. "Performance in a Hostile World: Economic Growth in Capitalist Democracies, 1974–1980." *World Politics* 38, 4 (1986): 517–545.

Gartner, Rosemary. "The Victims of Homicide—A Temporal and Cross-National Comparison." *American Sociological Review* 55, 1 (1990): 92–106.

Gastil, Raymond D. *Freedom in the World: Political Rights and Civil Liberties, 1988–1989.* New York: Freedom House, 1989.

Geddes, Barbara. "What Do We Know About Democratization After Twenty Years?" In *Annual Review of Political Science, Vol. 2,* ed. Nelson W. Polsby, 115–144. Palo Alto: Annual Reviews, 1999.

Geiger, Roger L. *Two Paths to Mass Higher Education: Issues and Outcomes in Belgium and France.* Yale Higher Education Research Group Working Paper, 1979. 4HERG-34.

George, Vic. "Social Security in the USSR." *International Social Security Review* 44, 4 (1991): 47–64.

Germani, Gino. "Social and Political Consequences of Mobility." In *Social Structure and Mobility in Economic Development,* ed. Neil J. Smelser and Seymour Martin Lipset, 364–394. Chicago: Aldine, 1966.

Gerschenkron, Alexander. *Economic Backwardness in Historical Perspective.* Cambridge, MA: Harvard University Press, 1962.

Gerson, Kathleen. *Hard Choices: How Women Decide about Work, Career, and Motherhood.* Berkeley: University of California Press, 1985.

Gerson, Kathleen. *No Man's Land: Men's Changing Commitments to Family and Work.* New York: Basic Books, 1993.

Giaimo, Susan. "Health Care Reform in Britain and Germany: Recasting the Political Bargain with the Medical Profession." *Governance: An International Journal of Policy and Administration* 8, 3 (1995): 354–379.

Gibson, James L., Cornelius P. Cotter, John F. Bibby, and Robert J. Huckshorn. "Whither Local Parties? A Cross-Sectional and Longitudinal Analysis of the Strength of Party Organizations." *American Journal of Political Science* 29, 1 (1985): 139–160.

Giglioli, Pier Paolo. Political Corruption and the Media: The Tangentopoli Affair." *International Social Science Journal* 48, 3 (Sept. 1996): 381–394.

Gilbert, Mark. "Warriors of the New Pontda: The Challenge of the Lega Nord to the Italian Party System." *Political Quarterly* 64, 1 (1993): 99–106.

Gilens, Martin. " "Race Coding" and White Opposition to Welfare." *American Political Science Review* 90, 3 (1996): 593–604.

Glaser, William A. *Health Insurance in Practice: International Variations in Financing, Benefits, and Problems.* San Francisco: Jossey-Bass, 1991.

Glendon, Mary Ann. *Abortion and Divorce in Western Law.* Cambridge, MA: Harvard University Press, 1987.

Glendon, Mary Ann. *The Transformation of Family Law.* Chicago: University of Chicago Press, 1989.

Glennerster, Howard. "United States Poverty Studies and Measurement: The Past 25 Years." CASE paper 42. London School of Economics, 2000.

Glennerster, Howard and Manos Matsaganis. *The English and Swedish Health Care Reforms.* Discussion Paper WSP/79. The Welfare State Program, London School of Economics, 1992.

Goddard, Maria and Peter Smith. *Equity of Access to Health Care.* Center for Health Economics, University of York, York, 1998.

Goddeeris, John H. and Burton A. Weisbrod. "Conversion from Non-profit to For-Profit Legal Status: Why does it happen and should we care?" *Journal of Policy Analysis and Management* 17, 2 (1998): 215–233.

Goklany, Indur M. "Richer Is Cleaner: Longer-Term Trends in Global Air Quality." In *The True State of the Planet,* ed. Ronald Bailey, 339–377. New York: Free Press, 1995.

Gold, David. "World Investment Report 1993: Transnational Corporations and Integrated International Production. An Executive Summary." *Transnational Corporations* 2, 2 (1993): 99–123.

Gold, Steven D., ed. *The Fiscal Crisis of the States: Lessons for the Future.* Washington, DC: Georgetown University Press, 1995a.

Gold, Steven D. "Lessons for the Future." In *The Fiscal Crisis of the States: Lessons for the Future,* ed. Steven D. Gold, 367–382. Washington, DC: Georgetown University Press, 1995b.

Gold, Steven D. "State Fiscal Problems and Policies." In *The Fiscal Crisis of the States: Lessons for the Future,* ed. Steven D. Gold, 6–40. Washington, DC: Georgetown University Press, 1995c.

Golden, Miriam, Peter Lange, and Michael Wallerstein. "Trends in Collective Bargaining and Industrial Relations in Non-Corporatist Countries: A Preliminary Report." Paper presented at American Political Science Association Annual Meeting, 1993.

Golden, Miriam A., Michael Wallerstein, and Peter Lange. "Postwar Trade-Union Organization and Industrial Relations in Twelve Countries." In *Continuity and Change in Contemporary Capitalism,* ed. Herbert Kitschelt, Peter Lange, Gary Marks, and John D. Stephens, 194–230. Cambridge, UK: Cambridge University Press, 1999.

Golden, Olivia. *Poor Children and Welfare Reform.* Westport, CT: Auburn House, 1992.

Goldey, David and Philip Williams. "France." In *Democracy and Elections: Electoral Systems and Their Political Consequences,* ed. Vernon Bogdanor and David Butler, 62–83. Cambridge: Cambridge University Press, 1983.

Goldin, Claudia. *Career and Family: College Women Look to the Past*. NBER Working Paper 5188. National Bureau of Economic Research, 1995.

Goldscheider, Frances K. and Linda J. Waite. *New Families, No Families? The Transformation of the American Home*. Berkeley: University of California Press, 1991.

Goldthorpe, John Ernest. *Family Life in Western Societies: A Historical Sociology of Family Relationships in Britain and North America*. Cambridge: Cambridge University Press, 1987.

Gönenç, Rauf. "A New Approach to Industrial Policy." *The OECD Observer* 187 (1994): 16–19.

Goode, William J. *World Revolution and Family Patterns*. New York: Free Press, 1963.

Goode, William J. *The Family*. 2nd ed. Englewood Cliffs, NJ: Prentice-Hall, 1982.

Goodhart, Charles. *The Evolution of Central Banks*. Cambridge, MA: MIT Press, 1988.

Goodman, Louis S. and Alfred Gilman. *The Pharmacological Basis of Therapeutics*. 4th ed. New York: Macmillan, 1970.

Gordon, Leon. "Indirect Taxes and Europe." *British Tax Review* 2 (1993): 164–171.

Gordon, Linda. *Pitied but Not Entitled*. New York: Free Press, 1994.

Gordon, Margaret S. *Social Security Policies in Industrial Countries*. Cambridge: Cambridge University Press, 1988.

Gornick, Janet C., Marcia K. Meyers, and Katherine E. Ross. "Supporting the Employment of Mothers: Policy Variation Across Fourteen Welfare States." *Journal of European Social Policy* 7, 1 (1997): 45–70.

Gosnell, Harold F. *Machine Politics: Chicago Model*. Chicago: University of Chicago Press, 1937.

Gottlieb, Robert. *Forcing the Spring: The Transformation of the American Environmental Movement*. Washington, DC: Island Press, 1993.

Gottschalk, Peter. "The Intergenerational Transmission of Welfare Participation; Facts and Possible Causes." *Journal of Policy Analysis and Management* 11, 2 (1992): 254–272.

Gottschalk, Peter, Sara McLanahan, and Gary Sandefur. "The Dynamics and Intergenerational Transmission of Poverty." In *Confronting Poverty: Prescriptions for Change,* ed. Sheldon H. Danziger, Gary D. Sandefur, and Daniel H. Weinberg, 85–108. Cambridge: Harvard University Press, 1994.

Gottschalk, Peter and Timothy M. Smeeding. "Empirical Evidence on Income Inequality in Industrialized Countries." Luxembourg Income Study Working Paper No. 154. Maxwell School of Citizenship and Public Affairs, Syracuse University, 1997.

Goudsblom, Johan. *Dutch Society*. New York: Random House, 1967.

Gourevitch, Peter. "The Second Image Reversed: The International Sources of Domestic Politics." *International Organization* 32 (Autumn 1978): 881–911.

Gourevitch, Peter. *Politics in Hard Times: Comparative Responses to International Economic Crises*. Ithaca, NY: Cornell University Press, 1986.

Governor's Budget Summary, 2000–01. Office of the Governor of the State of California, 1999b. Submitted by Gray Davis to the California Legislature 1999–2000 Regular Session.

Graham, Hugh Davis and Ted Robert Gurr, eds. *Violence in America*. London: Sage, 1979.

Graig, Laurene A. *Health of Nations: An International Perspective on U.S. Health Care Reform*. Washington, DC: The Wyatt Company, 1991.

Gramsci, Antonio. *Selections from the Prison Notebooks*. Translated by Quintin Hoare and Geoffrey Nowell Smith. New York: International Publishers, 1971.

Grant, Don Sherman, II, and Richard Hutchinson. "Global Smokestack Chasing: A Comparison of the State-Level Determinants of Foreign and Domestic Manufacturing Investment." *Social Problems* 43, 1 (1996): 21–38.

Greeley, Andrew M. *Ethnicity in the United States: A Preliminary Reconnaisance*. New York: Wiley, 1974.

Green, Donald. "Industrialization and the Engineering Ascendancy: A Comparative Study of American and Russian Engineering Elites, 1870–1920." Unpublished dissertation, Department of Economics, University of California at Berkeley, 1972.

Greenberg, David and Michael Wiseman. "What Did OBRA Programs Do?" In *Evaluating Welfare and Training Programs,* ed. Charles F. Manski and Irwin Garfinkel, 25–75. Cambridge: Harvard University, 1992a.

Greenberg, David and Michael Wiseman. *What did the Work-Welfare Demonstrations Do?* DP # 969–92. Institute for Research on Poverty, University of Wisconsin-Madison, 1992b.

Greenberg, Mark. *Beyond Stereotypes: What State AFDC Studies on Length of Stay Tell Us About Welfare as a "Way of Life."* Washington, DC: Center for Law and Social Policy, 1992.

Greenberg, Michael R., George W. Carey, and Frank J. Popper. "Violent Death, Violent States, and American Youth." *The Public Interest* 87 (1987): 38–48.

Greenberg, Stanley B. *The Road to Realignment: The Democrats and the Perot Voters.* Washington, DC: Democratic Leadership Council, 1993.

Greenberg, Stanley B. "After the Republican Surge." *The American Prospect* No. 23 (Fall 1995): 66–72.

Greenberg, Stanley B. "The Mythology of Centrism: Why Clinton and Blair Really Won." *The American Prospect* No. 34 (Sept./Oct. 1997): 42–44.

Greenstein, Robert. Executive Director of the Center on Budget and Policy Priorities, Testimony before the House Budget Committee, Washington, DC, March 7, 1996.

Greenstein, Robert, Richard Kogan, and Marion Nichols. "Bearing Most of the Burden: How Deficit Reduction During the 104th Congress Concentrated on Programs for the Poor." Washington, DC: Center on Budget and Policy Priorities, December 3, 1996.

Greenwald, Howard P. "HMO Membership, Copayment, and Initiation of Care for Cancer: A Study of Working Adults." *American Journal of Public Health* 77, 4 (1987): 461–466.

Greenwald, Howard P. and Curtis J. Hencke. "HMO Membership, Treatment, and Mortality Risk Among Prostatic Cancer Patients." *American Journal of Public Health* 82 (1992): 1099–1104.

Greenwood, Daphne T. "Age, Income, and Household Size: Their Relation to Wealth Distribution in the United States." In *International Comparisons of the Distribution of Household Wealth,* ed. Edward Wolff, 121–140. New York: Oxford University Press, 1987.

Greer, Scott. "Urbanism Reconsidered: A Comparative Study of Local Areas in a Metropolis." *American Sociological Review* 21 (Feb. 1956): 19–25.

Griliches, Zvi. "R & D and the Productivity Slowdown." *American Economic Review* 70, 2 (1980): 343–348.

Griliches, Zvi. "Productivity Puzzles and R&D: Another Nonexplanation." *Journal of Economic Perspectives* 2, 4 (1988): 9–21.

Grilli, Vittorio, Donato Masciandaro, and Guido Tabellini. "Political and Monetary Institutions and Public Financial Policies in the Industrial Countries." *Economic Policy* 13 (1991): 341–392.

Grofman, Bernard and Arend Lijphart, eds. *Electoral Laws and Their Political Consiquences.* New York: Agathon Press, 1986.

Gross, Edward. "Plus ça change . . . ? The Sexual Structure of Occupations over Time." *Social Problems* 16, 2 1968): 198–208.

Grush, J. E., K. L. McKeough, and R. G. Ahlering. "Extrapolating Laboratory Exposure Research to Actual Political Elections." *Journal of Personality and Social Psychology* 36 (1978): 257–270.

Gueron, Judith M. *Testimony of Judith M. Gueron, President Manpower Demonstration Research Corporation before the Senate Committee on Finance.* 1995.

Gueron, Judith M. and Edward Pauly. *From Welfare to Work.* New York: Russell Sage, 1991.

Gugelmann, Richard. "Personal Factors Influencing Child Survival in House Fires." Master's thesis, School of Public Health, University of North Carolina, Chapel Hill, NC, 1989.

Guillebaud, Claude. *The Social Policy of Nazi Germany.* New York: 1941.

Guillemard, Anne-Marie and Martin Rein. "Comparative Patterns of Retirement: Recent Trends in Developed Societies." *Annual Review of Sociology* 19 (1993): 469–503.

Guimezanes, Nicole. "What Laws for Naturalization?" *OECD Observer* 188 (1994): 24–26.

Gunlicks, Arthur B. *Local Government in the German Federal System.* Durham, NC: Duke University Press, 1986.

Gunter, Barrie. "The Question of Media Violence." In *Media Effects: Advances in Theory and Research,* ed. Jennings Bryant and Dalf Zillmann, 163–211. Hillsdale, NJ: Lawrence Erlbaum, 1994.

Gurr, Ted, ed. *Handbook of Political Conflict: Theory and Research.* New York: Free Press, 1980.

Gurr, Ted and Charles Ruttenberg. *Cross-National Studies of Civil Violence.* Washington, DC: American University, Center for Research in Social Systems, 1969.

Gurr, Ted Robert. "Crime Trends in Modern Democracies Since 1945." *International Annals of Criminology (or, Annals Internationales de Criminologie)* 16, 1 (1977): 41–85.

Gurr, Ted Robert. "On the History of Violent Crime in Europe and America." In *Violence in America,* ed. Hugh Davis Graham and Ted Robert Gurr, 353–374. London: Sage, 1979.

Gurr, Ted R. "Political Protest and Rebellion in the 1960s: The U.S. in World Perspective." In *Violence in America,* ed. Hugh Davis Graham and Ted Robert Gurr, 49–76. London: Sage, 1979a.

Gurr, Ted R. *Minorities at Risk: A Global View of Ethnopolitical Conflicts.* Washington, DC: U.S. Institute of Peace Press, 1993a.

Gurr, Ted R. "Why Minorities Rebel: A Global Analysis of Communal Mobilization and Conflict Since 1945." *International Political Science Review* 14, 2 (1993b): 161–201.

Gusfield, Joseph R. *The Culture of Public Problems: Drinking-Driving and the Symbolic Order.* Chicago: University of Chicago Press, 1981.

Gustaffson, Brent. "Church and People: A Contemporary Picture." In *Scandinavia Churches,* ed. L. S. Hunter. London: Faber and Faber, 1965.

Gustafsson, Siv. "Single Mothers in Sweden: Why Is Poverty Less Severe?" In *Poverty Inequality and the Future of Social Policy: Western States in the New World Order,* ed. Katherine McFate, Roger Lawson, and William Julius Wilson, 291–325. New York: Russell Sage Foundation, 1995.

Habakkuk, H. J. and M. Postan. *The Industrial Revolutions and After: Incomes, Population, and Technological Change.* Vol. 6, part 1. The Cambridge Economic History of Europe, Cambridge: Cambridge University Press, 1965.

Haber, Shraga and Bruno Lunenfeld. "Epidemiology, Health Policy, and Resource Allocation: The Israeli Perspective." *Public Health Reports* 99, 5 (1984): 455–460.

Habermas, Jürgen. *Legitimation Crisis.* Translated by Thomas McCarthy. Boston, MA: Beacon Press, 1975.

Habermas, Jürgen. "Problems of Legitimation in Late Capitalism." In *Critical Sociology,* ed. Paul Connerton, 363–387. New York: Penguin Books, 1976.

Hacker, Andrew. "Getting Rough on the Poor." *New York Review of Books* 35, 15 (1988): 12–17.

Hacker, Andrew. "Affirmative Action: A Negative Opinion." *New York Times Book Review,* July 1, 1990a, 1.

Hacker, Andrew. "Trans-National America." *New York Review of Books* 27, 18 (1990b): 19–24.

Hackney, Sheldon. "Southern Violence." *American Historical Review* 74, 3 (1969): 906–925.

Hadaway, C. Kirk, Penny Long Marler, and Mark Chaves. "Overreporting Church Attendance in America." *American Sociological Review* 63 (Feb. 1998): 122–130.

Hadley, Jack. *More Medical Care, Better Health?* Washington, DC: Urban Institute Press, 1982.

Hage, Jerald and Robert Hanneman. *The Growth of the Welfare State in Four Western European Societies: A Comparison of Three Paradigms.* Madison, WI: Institute for Research on Poverty, 1977.

Haggard, Stephan and Robert R. Kaufman. "Economic Adjustment in New Democracies." In *Fragile Coalitions: The Politics of Economic Adjustment,* ed. Joan M. Nelson, 57–77. Washington, DC: Overseas Development Council, 1989.

Hakovirta, Harto. "The Global Refugee Problem: A Model and Its Application." *International Political Science Review* 14 (1993): 35–57.

Halfmann, Jost. "Two Discourses of Citizenship in Germany: The Difference Between Public Debate and Administrative Practice." In *The Postwar Transformation of Germany: Democracy, Prosperity and Nationhood.* Center for German and European Studies, University of California, Berkeley, CA, 1995.

Hall, Peter A. *Governing the Economy: The Politics of State Intervention in Britain and France.* New York: Oxford University Press, 1986.

Hall, Peter A. "Central Bank Independence and Coordinated Wage Bargaining: Their Interaction in Germany and Europe." *German Politics and Society* 31 (Spring 1994): 1–23.

Hall, Peter A. and Robert J. Franzese. "Mixed Signals: Central Bank Independence, Coordinated Wage-Bargaining, and European Monetary Union." *International Organization* 52, 3 (1998): 505–536.

Hall, Robert E. and Dale W. Jorgenson. "Tax Policy and Investment Behavior." *American Economic Review* 57, 3 (1967): 391–414.

Hall, Robert E. and Richard A. Kasten. "The Relative Occupational Success of Blacks and Whites." *Brookings Papers on Economic Activity* 3 (1973): 781–798.

Haller, Max, Franz Höllinger, and Otto Raubal. "Leviathan or Welfare State? Attitudes Toward the Role of Government in Six Advanced Western Nations." In *Attitudes to Inequality and the Role of Government,* ed. Duane F. Alwin et al., 33–62. Rijswijk, Netherlands: Social and Cultural Planning Office, 1990.

Hamburger, Tom, Ted Marmor, and Jon Meacham. "What the Death of Health Reform Teaches Us about the Press." *Washington Monthly* 26, 11 (1994): 35–41.

Hamilton, Richard F. and James D. Wright. *The State of the Masses.* New York: Aldine de Gruyter, 1986.

Handler, Joel F. *The Poverty of Welfare Reform.* New Haven: Yale University Press, 1995.

Handler, Joel F. and Yeheskel Hasenfeld. *The Moral Construction of Poverty.* Newbury Park, CA: Sage, 1991.

Hardiman, Niamh. *Pay, Politics, and Economic Performance in Ireland, 1970–1987.* Oxford: Clarendon Press, 1988.

Harris, Jeffrey E. "Defensive Medicine: It Costs, But Does It Work?" *The Journal of the American Medical Association* 257, 20 (1987): 2801–2802.

Harris, Kathleen Mullan. "Teenage Mothers and Welfare Dependency: Working Off Welfare." *Journal of Family Issues* 12 (1991): 492–518.

Harris, Kathleen Mullan. "Work and Welfare among Single Mothers in Poverty." *American Journal of Sociology* 99 (1993): 317–352.

Harris, Kathleen Mullan. "Life After Welfare: Women, Work, and Repeat Dependency." *American Sociological Review* 61, 3 (1996): 407–426.

Harrison, Bennett. *Lean and Mean: The Changing Landscape of Corporate Power in the Age of Flexibility.* New York: Basic Books, 1994.

Harrison, Roderick and Claudette Bennett. "Racial and Ethnic Diversity." In *State of the Union: America in the 1990s,* ed. Reynolds Farely, 141–210. Vol. 2. *Social Trends.* New York: Russell Sage Foundation, 1995.

Hartley, James E., Steven M. Sheffrin, and J. David Vaché. "Reform During Crisis: the Transformation of California's Fiscal System During the Great Depression." *Journal of Economic History,* 56, 3 (Sept. 1996): 657–678.

Hartz, Louis. *The Liberal Tradition in America: An Interpretation of American Political Thought Since the Revolution.* New York: Harcourt, Brace, 1955.

Hauser, Richard. "Comparing the Influence of Social Security Systems on the Relative Economic Positions of Selected Groups in Six Major Industrialized Countries: The Case of One-Parent Families." *European Economic Review* 31 (1987): 192–201.

Haveman, Robert H. *Poverty Policy and Poverty Research: The Great Society and the Social Sciences.* Madison: University of Wisconsin Press, 1987.

Haveman, Robert H., Victor Halberstadt, and Richard Burkhauser, eds. *Public Policy Toward Disabled Workers: Cross-National Analyses of Economic Impacts.* Ithaca, NY: Cornell University Press, 1984.

Haveman, Robert H. and Daniel H. Saks. "Transatlantic Lessons for Employment and Training Policy." *Industrial Relations* 24 (1985): 20–36.

Haveman, Robert H. and John Karl Scholz. "Transfers, Taxes, and Welfare Reform." *National Tax Journal* 47, 2 (1994): 417–433.

Havrilesky, Thomas. "A Partisan Theory of Fiscal and Monetary Regimes." *Journal of Money, Credit and Banking* 19 (1987): 308–325.

Havrilesky, Thomas and James Granato. "Determinants of Inflationary Performance: Corporatist Structures vs. Central Bank Autonomy." *Public Choice* 76, 3 (1993): 249–261.

Headey, Bruce. *Housing Policy in the Developed Economy: The United Kingdom, Sweden, and the United States.* New York: St. Martin's Press, 1978.

Heady, Ferrel. *Public Administration: A Comparative Perspective.* 2nd ed. New York and Basel: Marcel Dekker, 1979.

Health Care Advisory Board. *Emerging from Shadow: Resurgence to Prosperity Under Managed Care.* 1995.

Heclo, Hugh. *Modern Social Politics in Britain and Sweden.* New Haven: Yale University Press, 1974.

Heclo, Hugh. "Issue Networks and the Executive Establishment." In *The New American Political System,* ed. Anthony King, 87–124. Washington, DC: American Enterprise Institute, 1978.

Heclo, Hugh and Henrik Madsen. *Policy and Politics in Sweden.* Philadelphia: Temple University Press, 1987.

Hedges, J. N. "Women Workers and Manpower Demands of the 1970s." *Monthly Labor Review* 93, 6 (1970): 19–29.

Hegre, Håvard, Tanja Ellingsen, Scott Gates, and Nils Petter Gleditsch. "Toward a Democratic Civil Peace? Democracy, Political Change and Civil War, 1816–1992." *American Political Science Review* 95 (March 2001): 33–48.

Heidenheimer, Arnold J. "Education and Social Security Entitlements in Europe and America." In *The Development of Welfare States in Europe and America,* ed. Peter Flora and Arnold J. Heidenheimer, 269–304. New Brunswick, NJ: Transaction, 1981.

Heidenheimer, Arnold J., Hugh Heclo, and Carolyn Teich Adams. *Comparative Public Policy: The Politics of Social Choice in America, Europe, and Japan.* 3rd ed. New York: St. Martin's Press, 1990.

Heidenheimer, Arnold J. and John Layson. "Social Policy Development in Europe and America: A Longer View on Selectivity and Income Testing." In *Income-Tested Transfer Programs: The Case For and Against,* ed. Irwin Garfinkel, 141–173. New York: Academic Press, 1982.

Heikkilä, Matti and Hannu Uusitalo. *The Cost of Cuts. Studies on cutbacks in social security and their effects in the Finland of the 1990s.* Helsinki: Gummerus Printing, 1997.

Heinz, John P., Edward O. Laumann, Robert L. Nelson, and Robert H. Salisbury. *The Hollow Core: Private Interests in National Policy Making.* Cambridge, MA: Harvard University Press, 1993.

Hellander, Ida, David U. Himmelstein, and Sidney M. Wolfe. "Administrative Waste in the U.S. Healthcare System in 1991: The Cost to the Nation, the States, and the District of Columbia." Cambridge, MA: Division of Social and Community Medicine, The Cambridge Hospital and Harvard Medical School, 1991.

Helms, L. Jay. "State and Local Taxes and Economic Growth." *Review of Economics and Statistics* 67 (1985): 574–582.

Henig, Stanley, ed. *European Political Parties.* New York: Praeger, 1969.

Henshaw, Stanley K. "Induced Abortion: A World Review, 1990." In *Abortion Factbook, 1992 Edition: Readings, Trends, and State and Local Data to 1988,* ed. Stanley K. Henshaw and Jennifer Van Vort, 13–26. New York: Alan Guttmacher Institute, 1992.

Hentschel,Volker. "Das System der sozialen Sicherung in historischer Sicht 1880 bis 1975." *Archiv fur Sozialgeschichte* 18 (1978): 307–352.

Hermens, Ferdinand A. *Democracy or Anarchy? A Study of Proportional Representation.* Notre Dame, Indiana: The Review of Politics, University of Notre Dame, 1941.

Hershey, Majorie Randon. "Citizens Groups and Political Parties in the United States." *Annals of the American Academy of Political and Social Science* 528 (1993): 142–156.

Hertner, Peter and Geoffrey Jones, eds. *Multi-nationals: Theory and History.* Aldershot, UK: Gower, 1986.

Hertzke, Allen D. "Religion and the Republican Congress." *Extensions: A Journal of the Carl Albert Congressional Research and Study Center* (Fall 1995): 7–10.

Hertzman, C. J. Frank and Robert G. Evans. "Heterogeneities in Health Status and the Determinants of Population Health." In *Why are Some People Healthy and Others Not?: The Determinants of Health of Populations,* ed. Robert G. Evans, Morris L. Barer, and Theodore R. Marmor, 67–92. New York: Aldine de Gruyter, 1994.

Hewitt, Christopher. "The Effect of Political Democracy and Social Democracy on Equality in Industrial Societies: A Cross-National Comparison." *American Sociological Review* 42 (1977): 450–464.

Heyde, Ludwig. *Abriss der Sozialpolitik.* Heidelberg: 1966.

Heyns, Barbara L. *Summer Learning and the Effects of Schooling.* New York: Academic Press, 1978.

Hibbing, John R. and Elizabeth Theiss-Morse. *Congress as Public Enemy.* Cambridge, UK: Cambridge University Press, 1996a.

Hibbing, John R. and Elizabeth Theiss-Morse. "The Media's Role in Fomenting Public Disgust with Congress." *Extensions* (Fall 1996b): 15–18.

Hibbing, John R. and Elizabeth Theiss-Morse. "The Media's Role in Public Negativity Toward Congress: Distinguishing Emotional Reactions and Cognitive Evaluations." *American Journal of Political Science* 42, 2 (1998): 475–498.

Hibbs, Douglas. "Political Parties and Macroeconomic Policy." *American Political Science Review* 71 (1977): 1467–1488.

Hibbs, Douglas. *The American Political Economy.* Cambridge, MA: Harvard University Press, 1987.

Hibbs, Douglas A., Jr. "On the Political Economy of Long-Run Trends in Strike Activity." *British Journal of Political Science* 8 (1978): 153–175.

Hibbs, Douglas A., Jr., and Håkan Locking. "Wage Dispersion and Productivity." *Journal of Labor Economics* 18 (October 2000): 755–782.

Hicks, Alexander and Joya Misra. "Political Resources and the Growth of Welfare in Affluent Capitalist Democracies, 1960–1982." *American Journal of Sociology* 99, 3 (1993): 668–710.

Hicks, Alexander, Joya Misra, and Tang Nah Ng. "The Programmatic Emergence of the Social Security State." *American Sociological Review* 60 (1995): 329–349.

Hilliard, Robert L. *The Federal Communications Commission: A Primer.* Boston: Focal Press, 1991.

Hills, John. "Thatcherism, New Labour and the Welfare State." CASE Paper 13, Centre for Analysis of Social Exclusion, London, August 1998.

Hills, John, Howard Glennerster, Julian Le Grand, and others. *Investigating Welfare: Final Report of the ESRC Welfare Research Programme.* London: The Welfare State Programme Suntory-Toyota International Centre for Economics and Related Disciplines, 1993.

Himmelweit, H. T., A. N. Oppenheim, and P. Vince. *Television and the Child.* New York: Oxford University Press, 1958.

Hinman, A. R. and S. R. Preblud. "Epidemic Potential of Measles and Rubella." *Journal of the American College Health Association* 29 (1980): 105–109.

Hirschi, Travis. "Crime and Family Policy." *Journal of Contemporary Studies* 6, no. 1 (1983): 3–16.

Hirst, Paul and Grahame Thompson. *Globalization in Question: The International Economy and Possibilities of Governance.* Cambridge: Polity Press, 1996.

Hobcraft, John and Kathleen Kiernan. *Becoming a Parent in Europe.* Discussion paper WSP#116. Welfare State Programme, The Toyota Centre, London School of Economics, 1995.

Hodgkinson, Virginia A. and Murray S. Weitzman. *Dimensions of the Independent Sector: A Statistical Profile.* Washington, DC: Independent Sector, 1984.

Hodson, Randy. "Individual Voice on the Shop Floor: The Role of Unions." *Social Forces* 74, 4 (June 1997): 1183–1212.

Hoechst Marion Roussel, Inc. *Managed Care Digest Series 1997: HMO-PPO/Medicare-Medicaid Digest.* Kansas City: Hoechst Marion Roussel, 1997.

Hoffman, Stanley, Charles P. Kindleberger, Laurence Wylie, Jesse R. Pitts, Jean-Baptiste Duroselle, and Francois Goguel. *In Search of France.* Cambridge, MA: Harvard University Press, 1963.

Hogben, Mathew. "Factors Moderating the Effect of Televised Aggression." *Communication Research* 25 (1998): 220–247.

Hoggart, Richard. *The Uses of Literacy.* London: Chatto and Windus, 1957.

Hollifield, James F. *Immigrants, Markets, and States: The Political Economy of Postwar Europe.* Cambridge, MA: Harvard University Press, 1992.

Hollingsworth, J. Rogers. *A Political Economy of Medicine: Great Britain and the United States.* Baltimore: Johns Hopkins University Press, 1986.

Hollingsworth, J. Rogers, Jerald Hage, and Robert A. Hanneman. *State Intervention in Medical Care: Consequences for Britain, France, Sweden, and the United States.* Ithaca, NY: Cornell University Press, 1990.

Hollingsworth, J. Rogers, Philippe C. Schmitter, and Wolfgang Streeck, eds. *Governing Capitalist Economies: Performance and Control of Economic Sectors.* New York: Oxford University Press, 1994.

Hollingsworth, J. Rogers and Wolfgang Streeck. "Countries and Sectors: Concluding Remarks on Performance, Convergence, and Competitiveness." In *Governing of Capitalist Economies: Performance and Control of Economic Sectors,* ed. J. Rogers Hollingsworth, Philippe C. Schmitter, and Wolfgang Streeck, 270–297. New York: Oxford University Press, 1994.

Hollingsworth, Rogers, Robert Hanneman, and Jerald Hage. "The Effect of Human Capital and State Intervention on the Performance of Medical Delivery Systems." Unpublished paper, University of Wisconsin, Madison, University of California, Riverside, and University of Maryland, College Park, 1992.

Holtfrerich, Carl-Ludwig and Ludger Lindlar. "Four Decades of German Export Expansion: an Enduring Success Story?" Paper presented at a conference on "The Postwar Transformation of Germany," Center for German and European Studies, UC Berkeley, Nov. 30–Dec. 2, 1995.

Holtz-Bacha, Christina and Lynda Lee Kaid. "A Comparative Perspective on Political Advertising: Media and Political System Characteristics." In *Political Advertising in Western Democracies: Parties and Candidates on Television,* ed. Lynda Lee Kaid and Christina Holtz-Bacha, 8–18. Thousand Oaks, CA: Sage, 1995.

Homans, George C. "Status Among Clerical Workers." *Human Organization* 12 (Spring 1953): 5–10.

Hoover, Herbert. *The Memoirs of Herbert Hoover. The Cabinet and the Presidency, 1920–1933.* New York: Macmillan, 1952.

Horowitz, Ruth. "The Dialogue on Violence." *Contemporary Sociology* 22, 3 (1993): 346–348.

Houska, Joseph J. *Influencing Mass Political Behavior: Elites and Political Subcultures in the Netherlands and Austria.* Research Series, Berkeley, CA: Institute of International Studies, University of California, 1985.

Hout, Michael and Joshua R. Goldstein. "How 4.5 Million Irish Immigrants Became 40 Million Irish Americans: Demographic and Subjective Aspects of the Ethnic Composition of White Americans." *American Sociological Review* 59 (1994): 64–84.

Hout, Michael and Andrew M. Greeley. "The Center Doesn't Hold: Church Attendance in the United States, 1940–1984." *American Sociological Review* 52, 3 (1987): 325–345.

Hout, Michael and David Knoke. "Change in Voting Turnout 1952–1972." *Public Opinion Quarterly* 39 (1975): 52–68.

Howe, Harold, II. "A Bumpy Ride on Four Trains." *Phi Delta Kappan* 73, 3 (1991): 192–204.

Howell, Chris. *Regulating Labor: The State and Industrial Relations Reform in Postwar France.* Princeton, NJ: Princeton University Press, 1992.

Howell, Joseph T. *Hard Living on Clay Street.* Garden City, New York: Anchor Books, 1973.

Howenstine, E. Jay. *Housing Vouchers: A Comparative International Analysis.* New Brunswick, NJ: Center for Urban Policy Research, 1986.

Hu, Arthur. "Us and Them." *New Republic,* June 1, 1992, 13–14.

Hubbard, Jeffrey C., Melvin L. DeFleur, and Lois B. DeFleur. "Mass Media Influences on Public Perceptions of Social Problems." *Social Problems* 23 (October 1975): 23–34.

Huber, Evelyne, Charles Ragin, and John D. Stephens. "Social Democracy, Christian Democracy, Constitutional Structure and the Welfare State." *American Journal of Sociology* 99, 3 (1993): 711–749.

Huber, Evelyne and John D. Stephens. "Internationalization and the Social Democratic Welfare State: Crisis and Future Prospects." Paper delivered at the Conference on Challenges to Labor: Integration, Employment and Bargaining in Scandinavia and the United States, Berkeley, CA, March 21–22, 1996.

Huber, Evelyne and John D. Stephens. "Internationalization and the Social Democratic Model." *Comparative Political Studies* 31, no. 3 (1998): 353–397.

Huber, Evelyne and John D. Stephens. "Welfare State and Production Regimes in the Era of Retrenchment." School of Social Sciences, Institute for Advanced Study, Occasional Paper 1 (1999): 1–29.

Huber, Peter W. *Liability: The Legal Revolution and Its Consequences.* New York: Basic Books, 1988.

Huddle, Donald. *The Costs of Immigration: Executive Summary.* Carrying Capacity Network, 1993.

Huessman, L. R. and L. D. Eron. *Television and the Aggressive Child: A Cross-National Comparison.* Hillsdale, NJ: Erlbaum, 1986.

Hughes, Christopher. *The Parliament of Switzerland.* London: Cassell, 1962.

Hughes, Everett C. *French Canada in Transition.* Chicago, IL: University of Chicago Press, 1943.

Humpage, Owen F. "An Introduction to the International Implications of U.S. Fiscal Policy." *Economic Review* [publication of the Federal Reserve Bank of Cleveland] 28, 3 (1992): 27–39.

Humphrey, Melvin. *Black Experiences Versus Black Expectations.* Equal Employment Opportunity Commisson, Research Report no. 53, 1977.

Humphries, Peter J. *Media and Media Policy in Germany: The Press and Broadcasting Since 1945.* Providence, RI: Berghan Books, 1994.

Humphries, Peter J. *Mass Media and Media Policy in Western Europe.* Manchester: Manchester University Press, 1996.

Hunt, Albert R. "This Republican Tax Cut Dog Won't Hunt." *Wall Street Journal,* June 26, 1997, A19.

Hunter, James Davidson. *American Evangelicalism.* New Brunswick, NJ: Rutgers University Press, 1983.

Huntington, Samuel P. "Post-Industrial Society: How Benign Will It Be?" *Comparative Politics* 6 (1974): 163–191.

Huntington, Samuel P. *The Third Wave: Democratization in the Late Twentieth Century.* Norman: University of Oklahoma Press, 1991.

Hutchinson, E. P. *Immigrants and their Children: 1850–1950.* New York: John Wiley and Sons, 1956.

Huttmann, Elizabeth D. and Terry Jones. "American Suburbs: Desegregation and Resegregation." In *Urban Housing Segregation of Minorities in Western Europe and the United States,* ed. Elizabeth D. Huttmann, Wim Blauw, and Juliet Saltman, 335–366. Durham, NC: Duke University Press, 1991.

Hutton, Nancy and Barbara Starfield. "Iron-Deficiency Anemia." In *The Effectiveness of Medical Care: Validating Clinical Wisdom,* ed. Barbara Starfield, Lisa Egbuonu, Mark Farfel, Nancy Hutton, Alain Joffe, and Lawrence S. Wissow, 87–94. Baltimore: The Johns Hopkins University Press, 1985.

Hyman, Richard. "Industrial Relations in Western Europe: An Era of Ambiguity?" *Industrial Relations, A Journal of Economy and Society* 33, 1 (1994): 1–12.

Hymer, Stephen. "The Multinational Corporation and the Law of Uneven Development." In *Economics and World Order,* ed. Jagdish N. Bhagwati. New York: Macmillan, 1972.

Illich, Ivan. *Medical Nemesis: The Expropriation of Health.* New York: Pantheon Books, 1976.

Immergut, Ellen M. *Health Politics: Interests and Institutions in Western Europe.* New York: Cambridge University Press, 1992.

Ingebritsen, Christine. "European Integration and Corporatist Bargaining in Norway." Paper presented at American Political Science Association Annual Meeting, 1996.

Ingham, Geoffrey K. *Strikes and Industrial Conflict; Britain and Scandinavia.* London: Macmillan, 1974.

Inglehart, Ronald. *The Silent Revolution: Changing Values and Political Styles Among Western Publics.* Princeton, NJ: Princeton University Press, 1977.

Inglehart, Ronald. *Culture Shift in Advanced Industrial Society.* Princeton, NJ: Princeton University Press, 1990.

Inglehart, Ronald. "Public Support for Environmental Protection: Objective Problems and Subjective Values in 43 Societies." *PS: Political Science and Politics* 28 (1995): 57–72.

Inglehart, Ronald and Paul R. Abramson. "Economic Security and Value Change." *American Political Science Review* 88, 2 (1994): 336–354.

Ingram, Helen and Steven Rathgeb Smith, ed. *Public Policy for Democracy.* Washington, DC: Brookings Institution, 1993.

Inkeles, Alex. "Industrial Man: The Relation of Status to Experience, Perception, and Value." *American Journal of Sociology* 66, 1 (1960): 1–31.

Inkeles, Alex. "Modernization and Family Patterns: A Test of Convergence Theory." In *Conspectus of History,* ed. Dwight W. Hoover and John T. A. Koumoulides, 31–62. London: Cambridge University Press, 1980.

Inkeles, Alex. "Convergence and Divergence in Industrial Societies." In *Directions of Change: Essays on Modernization Theory and Research,* ed. Z. and B. Holzner Suda, 3–39. Boulder, CO: Westview Press, 1981.

Inkeles, Alex. "The Responsiveness of Family Patterns to Economic Change in the United States." *The Tocqueville Review* 6, 1 (1984): 5–50.

Inkeles, Alex and Larry Sirowy. "Convergent and Divergent Trends in National Educational Systems." *Social Forces* 62, 2 (1983): 303–333.

International Institute of Strategic Studies. *The Military Balance.* London: International Institute of Strategic Studies, 1985.

International Labour Organization. "Protection of Working Mothers: An ILO Global Survey (1964–84)." *Women at Work* 2 (1984): 1–66.

International Labour Organization. *World Labour Report.* Geneva: International Labour Organization, 1992.

International Labour Organization. *World Employment 1995: An ILO Report.* International Labour Organization, 1995.

International Trade Administration, U.S. Dept. of Commerce. *U.S. Foreign Trade Highlights 1996.* Washington, DC: U.S. Dept. of Commerce, International Trade Administration, 1997.

Iversen, Torben. "Power, Flexibility, and the Breakdown of Centralized Wage Bargaining: Denmark and Sweden in Comparative Perspective." *Comparative Politics* 28, 4 (1996): 399–436.

Iyengar, Shanto and Donald Kinder. *News That Matters: Television and American Opinion.* Chicago: University of Chicago Press, 1987.

Jackman, Robert. *Politics and Social Equality: A Comparative Analysis.* New York: John Wiley, 1975.

Jackman, Robert. "Political Institutions and Voter Turnout in the Industrial Democracies." *American Political Science Review* 81 (1987): 405–423.

Jackman, Robert W. and Ross A. Miller. "Voter Turnout in the Industrial Democracies During the 1980s." *Comparative Political Studies* 27, 4 (1995): 467–492.

Jackman, Robert W. and Ross A. Miller. "A Renaissance of Political Culture?" *American Journal of Political Science* 40 (August 1996): 632–659.

Jackson, Peter and Keith Sisson. "Employers' Confederations in Sweden and the U.K. and the Significance of Industrial Infrastructure." *British Journal of Industrial Relations* 14, 3 (1976): 306–323.

Jacobs, David. "Dimensions of Inequality and Public Policy in the States." *Journal of Politics* 42, 1 (1980): 291–306.

Jacobs, Eva, ed. *Handbook of U.S. Labor Statistics. Employment, Earnings, Prices, Productivity, and other Labor Data.* Lanham, MD: Bennan Press, 1997.

Jacobs, Francis, ed. *Western European Political Parties: A Comprehensive Guide.* Essex, UK: Longman, 1989.

Jacobs, Lawrence R. "Politics of America's Supply State: Health Reform and Technology." *Health Affairs* (Summer 1995): 143–157.

Jacobson, Gary. "The Misallocation of Resources in House Campaigns." In *Congress Reconsidered,* ed. Lawrence C. Dodd and Bruce I. Oppenheimer, 115–140. 5th ed. Washington, DC: Congressional Quarterly Press, 1993.

Jacobson, Gary C. *The Electoral Origins of Divided Government: Competitions in U.S. House Elections, 1946–1988.* Boulder, CO: Westview Press, 1990.

Jacobson, Jodi L. "The Global Politics of Abortion." Paper 97. Washington, DC: The Worldwatch Institute, 1990.

Jacobson, Per. "Preface." In *Central Banking Legislation: A Collection of Central Bank, Monetary and Banking Laws,* ed. Hans Aufricht. Washington, DC: International Monetary Fund, 1961.

Jacoby, Sanford M. "Pacific Ties: Industrial Relations and Employment Systems in Japan and the United States Since 1900." In *Industrial Democracy in America: The Ambiguous Promise,* ed. Nelson Lichtenstein and Howell J. Harris, 206–248. Cambridge: Cambridge University Press, 1993.

Jacoby, William G. "Public Attitudes Toward Government Spending." *American Journal of Political Science* 38, 2 (1994): 336–361.

James, Estelle, ed. *The Nonprofit Sector in International Perspective.* New York and Oxford: Oxford University Press, 1989a.

James, Estelle. "The Private Provision of Public Services: A Comparison of Sweden and Holland." In *The Nonprofit Sector in International Perspective,* ed. James Estelle, 31–60. New York and Oxford: Oxford University Press, 1989b.

James, Estelle. "Averting the Old Age Crisis." Industrial Relations Research Association Proceedings of the 47th Annual Meeting, Washington, DC, pp. 64–75, January 6–8, 1995.

James, Thomas and Henry M. Levin, eds. *Volume 1: Institutions and Organizations.* Comparing Public and Private Schools. New York: The Falmer Press, 1988.

Jamieson, Kathleen Hall. *Dirty Politics.* New York: Oxford University Press, 1992.

Jamieson, Kathleen Hall. "Newspaper and Television Coverage of the Health Care Reform Debate, January 16-July 25, 1994." Annenberg Public Policy Center, 1994.

Jamieson, Kathleen Hall. "Assessing the Quality of Campaign Discourse—1960, 1980, 1988, and 1992." Annenberg Public Policy Center, 1996.

Jamieson, Kathleen Hall and Joseph N. Cappella. "Do Health Reform Polls Clarify or Confuse the Public?" *Journal of American Health Policy* 4, 3 (1994): 38–41.

Jankowski, J. E. *National Patterns of R&D Resources: 1990.* Final Report NSF 90–316. National Science Foundation, 1990.

Janoski, Thomas. *The Political Economy of Unemployment: Active Labor Market Policy in West Germany and the United States.* Berkeley: University of California Press, 1990.

Janowitz, Morris. *The Community Press in an Urban Setting.* Glencoe, IL: Free Press, 1952.

Janowitz, Morris. *The Professional Soldier: A Social and Political Portrait.* Glencoe, IL: Free Press, 1961.

Janowitz, Morris. "Sociological Models and Social Policy." In *Political Conflict: Essays in Political Sociology,* ed. Morris Janowitz, 243–259. Chicago: Quadrangle Books, 1970.

Jaschke, Hans-Gerd. *Die 'Republikaner': Profile einer Rechtsaussenpartei.* 2nd ed. Bonn: Dietz, 1993.

Jasper, James M. *Nuclear Politics: Energy and the State in the United States, Sweden, and France.* Princeton: Princeton University Press, 1990.

Jefferys, Steve. "European Industrial Relations and Welfare States." *European Journal of Industrial Relations* 1, 3 (1995): 317–340.

Jencks, Christopher. "Genes and Crime." *New York Review of Books,* February 12, 1987, 33–41.

Jencks, Christopher. "Deadly Neighborhoods." *New Republic* 198, 24 (1988): 23–32.

Jencks, Christopher. *Rethinking Social Policy: Race, Poverty, and the Underclass.* Cambridge: Harvard University Press, 1992a.

Jencks, Christopher. "Can We Put a Time Limit on Welfare?" *The American Prospect* No. 11 (1992b): 32–40.

Jencks, Christopher. *The Homeless.* Cambridge: Harvard University Press, 1994.

Jencks, Christopher and Kathryn Edin. "The Real Welfare Problem." *The American Prospect* No. 1 (1990): 30–50.

Jencks, Christopher and David Riesman. *The Academic Revolution.* Garden City, NY: Doubleday, 1968.

Jenkins, C. David. "Psychologic and Social Risk Factors for Coronary Disease." *New England Journal of Medicine* 294 (1976): 987–994, 1033–1038.

Jennett, Bryan. *High Technology Medicine: Benefits and Burdens.* New York: Oxford University Press, 1986.

Jennings, M. Kent. "Residues of a Movement: the Aging of the American Protest Generation." *American Political Science Review* 81, 2 (1987): 367–382.

Jennings, M. Kent et al. *Continuities in Political Action: A Longitudinal Study of Political Orientations in Three Western Democracies.* Berlin and New York: Walter de Gruyter, 1989.

Jennings, M. Kent and Richard G. Niemi. *The Political Character of Adolescence: The Influence of Families and Schools.* Princeton: Princeton University Press, 1974.

Jensen, Gail A., Michael A. Morrisey, Shannon Gaffney, and Derek K. Liston. "The New Dominance of Managed Care: Insurance Trends in the 1990s." *Health Affairs* 16, 1 (1997): 125–136.

Johnson, Chalmers. *MITI and the Japanese Miracle.* Stanford: Stanford University Press, 1982.

Johnson, Haynes and David Broder. *The System: The American Way of Politics at the Breaking Point.* Boston: Little, Brown, 1996.

Johnson, Norman. "The Changing Role of the Voluntary Sector in Britain from 1945 to the Present." In *Government and Voluntary Organizations: A Regional Perspective,* ed. Stein Kuhnle and Per Selle, 87–107. Aldershot, England: Avebury, 1992.

Johnston, Anne and Jacques Gerstlé. "The Role of Television Broadcasts in Promoting French Presidential Candidates." In *Political Advertising in Western Democracies: Parties and Candidates on Television,* ed. Lynda Lee Kaid and Christina Holtz-Bacha, 44–60. London: Sage, 1995.

Johnston, Richard, Andre Blais, Henry E. Brady and Jean Crete. *Letting the People Decide: Dynamics of a Canadian Election.* Stanford: Stanford University Press, 1992a.

Johnston, Richard. "Party Identification Measures in the Anglo-American Democracies: A National Survey Experiement." *American Journal of Political Science* 36, 2 (1992b): 542–559.

Jones, Derek C. and Takao Kato. "The Scope, Nature, and Effects of Employee Stock Ownership Plans in Japan." *Industrial and Labor Relations Review* 46, 2 (1993): 352–367.

Jones, Elise F., Jacqueline Darroch Forrest, Noreen Goldman, Stanley Henshaw, Richard Lincoln, Jeanie I. Rosoff, Charles F. Westoff, and Deirde Wulf. *Teenage Pregnancy in Industrialized Countries.* New Haven: Yale University Press, 1986.

Jönsson, Bengt and Agneta Paulsson. *Daghem och samhällsekonomi [Childcare Centers and the Nation's Economy].* Stockholm: Prisma, 1979.

Joppke, Christian. *Mobilizing Against Nuclear Energy: A Comparison of Germany and the United States.* Berkeley and Los Angeles: University of California Press, 1993.

Jorgenson, Dale W. and R. Landau, eds. *Technology and Capital Formation.* Cambridge, MA: MIT Press, 1988.

Jorgenson, Dale W. and Kun-Young Yun. "Tax Policy and Capital Allocation." *The Scandinavian Journal of Economics* 88, 2 (1986): 355–377.

Judis, John B. "The Bill." *The New Republic* 214, 23 (1996): 16–20.

Judt, Tony. "Austria and the Ghost of the New Europe." *The New York Review of Books* 43, no. 3 (1996): 22–25.

Jurgens, Ulrich, Larissa Klinzing, and Lowell Turner. "The Transformation of Industrial Relations in Eastern Germany." *Industrial and Labor Relations Review* 46, 2 (1993): 227–244.

Kaase, Max. "Is There Personalization in Politics? Candidates and Voting Behavior in Germany." *International Political Science Review* 15, 3 (1994): 211–230.

Kaelble, Hartmut. "Educational Opportunities and Government Policies in Europe in the Period of Industrialization." In *The Development of Welfare States in Europe and America,* ed. Peter Flora and Arnold J. Heidenheimer, 239–268. New Brunswick, NJ: Transaction, 1981.

Kagan, Robert A. "What Makes Sammy Sue?" *Law and Society Review* 21, 5 (1988): 717–742.

Kagan, Robert A. "Adversarial Legalism and American Government." *Journal of Policy Analysis and Management* 10, 3 (1991): 369–406.

Kagan, Robert A. and David Vogel. "The Politics of Smoking Regulation: Canada, France, the United States." *Smoking Policy: Law, Politics and Culture* (1993a): 22–48.

Kagan, Robert A. and David Vogel. "The Politics of Smoking Regulation in Comparative Perspective." Unpublished paper, Seminar in Smoking Policy, School of Law, University of California, Berkeley, 1993b.

Kahler, Miles. "International Financial Institutions and the Politics of Adjustment." In *Fragile Coalitions: The Politics of Economic Adjustment,* ed. Joan M. Nelson, 139–159. Washington, DC: Overseas Development Council, 1989.

Kahn, Alfred J. and Sheila B. Kamerman. *Income Transfers for Families with Children: An Eight-Country Study.* Philadelphia: Temple University Press, 1983.

Kahn, Alfred J., Sheila B. Kamerman, and Paul Kingston. *Maternity Policies and Working Women.* New York: Columbia University Press, 1983.

Kaid, Lynda Lee and Christina Holtz-Bacha, ed. *Political Advertising in Western Democracies: Parties and Candidates on Television.* Thousand Oaks, CA: Sage, 1995.

Kaldor, Mary, Margaree Sharp, and William Walker. "Industrial Competitiveness and Britain's Defense." *Lloyd's Bank Review* 162 (1986): 31–49.

Kalleberg, Arne L., David Knoke, Peter V. Marsden, and Joe L. Spaeth. *Organizations in America: Analyzing Their Structures and Human Resource Practices.* Thousand Oaks, CA: Sage, 1996.

Kamerman, Sheila B. *Maternity and Parental Benefits and Leaves: An International Review.* Impact on Policy Series, Monograph No. 1. New York: Columbia University, Center for the Social Sciences, 1980.

Kamerman, Sheila B. "Women, Children, and Poverty: Public Policies and Female-Headed Families in Industrialized Countries." *Signs* 10, 2 (1984): 249–271.

817

Kamerman, Sheila B. "Children and Their Families: The Impact of the Reagan Administration and the Choices for Social Work." In *Proceedings of the Werner and Bernice Boehm Distinguished Lectureship in Social Work.* New Brunswick, NJ: Rutgers, School of Social Work, 1985.

Kamerman, Sheila B. and Alfred J. Kahn, eds. *Family Policy: Government and Families in Fourteen Countries.* New York: Columbia University Press, 1978.

Kamerman, Sheila B. and Alfred J. Kahn. *Child Care, Family Benefits, and Working Parents: A Study in Comparative Policy.* New York: Columbia University Press, 1981.

Kamerman, Sheila B. and Alfred J. Kahn. "Government Expenditures for Children and Their Families in Advanced Industrialized Countries 1980–1985." UNICEF, International Child Development Centre, 1991a. Innocenti Occasional Papers, Economic Policy Series 20.

Kamerman, Sheila B. and Alfred J. Kahn, eds. *Child Care, Parental Leave, and the Under 3s: Policy Innovation in Europe.* New York: Auburn House, 1991b.

Kangas, Olli. "The Politics of Social Security: On Regressions, Qualitative Comparisons, and Cluster Analysis." In *The Comparative Political Economy of the Welfare State,* ed. Thomas Janoski and Alexander M. Hicks, 346–364. Cambridge: Cambridge University Press, 1994.

Karasek, Robert and Tores Theorell. *Health Work: Stress, Productivity, and the Reconstruction of Working Life.* New York: Basic Books, 1990.

Karier, Thomas. "U.S. Foreign Production and Unions." *Industrial Relations* 34, 1 (1995): 107–118.

Kato, Junko. *The Problem of Bureaucratic Rationality: Tax Politics in Japan.* Princeton: Princeton University Press, 1994.

Katz, Elihu. "Social Research on Broadcasting: Proposals For Further Development." A Report to the British Broadcasting Association. Publicity and Information Department, BBC, 1977.

Katz, Elihu and Paul Lazarsfeld. *Personal Influence.* Glencoe, IL: Free Press, 1955.

Katz, Lawrence F. and Ana L. Revenga. *Changes in the Structure of Wages: The U.S. versus Japan.* NBER Working Paper 3021. Cambridge, MA: National Bureau of Economic Research, 1989.

Katz, Richard S. and Peter Mair, eds. *Party Organizations: A Data Handbook on Party Organizations in Western Democracies, 1960–1990.* London: Sage, 1992.

Katzenstein, Peter J. *Corporatism and Change: Austria, Switzerland, and the Politics of Industry.* Ithaca, NY: Cornell University Press, 1984.

Katzenstein, Peter J. *Small States in World Markets: Industrial Policy in Europe.* New York: Cornell University Press, 1985a.

Katzenstein, Peter J. "Small Nations in an Open International Economy: The Converging Balance of State and Society in Switzerland and Austria." In *Bringing the State Back In,* ed. Peter B. Evans, Dietrich Rueschemeyer, and Theda Skocpol. Cambridge: Cambridge University Press, 1985b.

Kaus, Mickey. *The End of Equality.* New York: Basic Books, 1992.

Kawachi, Ichiro, Bruce P. Kennedy, Kimberly Lochner, and Deborah Prothrow-Stith. "Social Capital, Income Inequality, and Mortality." *American Journal of Public Health* 87, 9 (1997): 1491–1498.

Keeler, John. *The Politics of Neocorporatism in France: Farmers, the State and Agricultural Policy-making in the Fifth Republic.* New York: Oxford University Press, 1987.

Keenoy, Tom. "Review Article: European Industrial Relations in Global Perspective." *European Journal of Industrial Relations* 1, 1 (1995): 145–164.

Keith, Bruce E., David B. Magleby, Candice J. Nelson, Elizabeth Orr, Mark C. Westlye, and Raymond E. Wolfinger. "The Partisan Affinities of Independent 'Leaners'." *British Journal of Political Science* 16 (1986): 155–185.

Keith, Bruce E., David B. Magleby, Candice J. Nelson, Elizabeth Orr, Mark C. Westlye, and Raymond E. Wolfinger. *The Myth of the Independent Voter.* Berkeley: University of California Press, 1992.

Keizer, P. K. "A Critical Assessment of Recent Trends in Dutch Industrial Relations." Research Memorandum RM/96/012, University of Limburg, Maastricht, Faculty of Economics and Business Administration, 1996.

Kelley, Jonathan and M. D. R. Evans. "The Legitimation of Inequality: Occupational Earnings in Nine Nations." *American Journal of Sociology* 99, 1 (1993): 75–125.

Kelman, Steven J. *Regulating America, Regulating Sweden: A Comparative Study of Occupational Safety and Health Policy.* Cambridge, MA: MIT Press, 1981.

Kendrick, John W. "Productivity Trends in the United States." In *Lagging Productivity Growth: Causes and Remedies,* ed. Shlomo Maitel and Noah M. Meltz, 9–30. Cambridge, MA: Ballinger, 1980.

Kenworthy, Lane. "Labor Organization, Wage Restraint and Economic Performance." *Review of Radical Political Economics* 22, 4 (1990): 111–134.

Keohane, Robert O. and Joseph S. Nye. "Transnational Relations and World Politics: A Conclusion." *International Organization* 25, 3 (1971): 721–748.

Keohane, Robert O. and Joseph S. Nye. *Power and Interdependence: World Politics in Transition.* Boston: Little, Brown, 1977.

Kern, Horst and Charles F. Sabel. "Trade Unions and Decentralized Production: A Sketch of Strategic Problems in the West German Labor Movement." *Politics and Society* 19, 4 (1991): 373–402.

Kerr, Clark and Abraham Siegel. "The Interindustry Propensity to Strike—An International Comparison." In *Industrial Conflict,* ed. Arthur Kornhauser et al., 189–212. New York: McGraw-Hill, 1954.

Kessler, Ronald et al. "Lifetime and 12-Month Prevalence of DSM-III-R Psychiatric Disorders in the United States." *Archives of General Psychiatry* 51 (1994): 8–19.

Key, V. O., Jr. *Southern Politics in State and Nation.* New York: Knopf, 1949.

Keynes, John Maynard. *The Means to Prosperity.* London: Macmillan, 1933.

Kida, Hiroshi, Rentaro Ohno, Toshio Kanaya, Koji Kato, and Ryo Watanabe. "Japan." In *Schooling in East Asia: Forces of Change,* ed. R. Thomas Murray and T. Neville Postlethwaite, 51–85. Oxford, England: Pergamon Press, 1983.

Kiernan, Kathleen E. *Transition to Parenthood: Young Mothers, Young Fathers-Associated factors and later life experiences.* Welfare State Programme, Discussion Paper WSP/113. Suntory Toyota International Centre for Economics, London School of Economics, 1995.

Kim, Paul S. *Japan's Civil Service System: Its Structure, Personnel, and Politics.* New York: Greenwood Press, 1988.

Kimball, Penn. *Downsizing the News.* Washington, DC: Woodrow Wilson Center Press, 1994.

King, Anthony. *Running Scared: Why America's Politicians Campaign Too Much and Govern Too Little.* New York: Free Press, 1997.

King, Desmond S. and Bo Rothstein. "Institutional Choices and Labour Market Policy: A British-Swedish Comparison." Paper presented at the annual meeting of the American Political Science Association, August 29–Sept. 1, Washington, D.C., 1991.

King, Ronald. "On Particulars, Universals, and Neat Tricks." In *The Emergence of David Duke and the Politics of Race,* ed. Douglas Rose, 242–252. Chapel Hill: The University of North Carolina Press, 1992.

Kinmonth, Earl H. "Japanese Engineers and American Myth Makers." *Pacific Affairs* 64, 3 (1991): 328–350.

Kirk, Dudley. "The Influence of Business Cycles on Marriage and Birth Rates." In National Bureau of Economic Research, *Demographic and Economic Change in Developed Countries,* 241–257. Princeton, NJ: Princeton University Press, 1960.

Kirst, Michael W. and Carolyn Kelley. "Positive Impacts of Reform Efforts in the 1980s." In *Symposium on the 10th Anniversary of "A Nation at Risk," April 8, 1993 in University of California, Berkeley,* Consortium for the Study of Society and Education Year.

Kitschelt, Herbert. "Social Movements, Political Parties, and Democratic Theory." *Annals, American Academy of Political and Social Science* 528 (1993): 13–29.

Kitschelt, Herbert. *The Transformation of European Social Democracy.* Cambridge: Cambridge University Press, 1994.

Kitschelt, Herbert, in collaboration with Anthony J. McGann. *The Radical Right in Western Europe: A Comparative Analysis.* Ann Arbor: University of Michigan Press, 1995.

Klapper, Joseph T. *The Effects of Mass Communication.* Glencoe, IL: Free Press, 1960.

Klein, Rudolph. "National Health Service: After Reorganization." *The Political Quarterly* 44 (July–Sept. 1973): 316–328.

Klein, Rudolf. *The New Politics of the National Health Service.* 3rd ed. London: Longman, 1995.

Klein, Rudolf and Michael O'Higgins. "Introduction: Old Myths-New Challenges." In *The Future of Welfare,* ed. Rudolf Klein and Michael O'Higgins, 1–7. Oxford: Basil Blackwell, 1985.

Kleppner, Paul and Nikolas Theodore. *Work after Welfare: Is the Midwest's Booming Economy Creating Enough Jobs?* Midwest Job Gap Project, 1997.

Klöti, Ulrich. "Small States in an Interdependent World." Paper presented at the World Congress of the International Political Science Association, Buenos Aires, July 21–25, 1991.

Klotz, Robert. "Positive Spin: Senate Campaigning on the Web." *PS* 30, 3 (1997): 482–486.

Kobach, Kris W. "Switzerland." In *Referendums Around the World: The Growing Use of Direct Democracy,* ed. David Butler and Austin Ranney, 98–153. Washington, DC: AEI Press, 1994.

Kochan, Thomas A., Russell D. Lansbury, and John Paul MacDuffie, eds. *After Lean Production: Evolving Employment Practices in the World Auto Industry.* Ithaca, NY: ILR Press—an Imprint of Cornell University Press, 1997a.

Kochan, Thomas A., Russell D. Lansbury, and John Paul MacDuffie. "Conclusion: After Lean Production?" In *After Lean Production: Evolving Employment Practices in the World Auto Industry,* ed. Thomas A. Kochan, Russell D. Lansbury, and John Paul MacDuffie, 303–324. Ithaca, NY: ILR Press—an Imprint of Cornell University Press, 1997b.

Kochan, Thomas A., Michal Smith, John C. Wells, and James B. Rebitzer. "Human Resource Strategies and Contingent Workers: The Case of Safety and Health in the Petrochemical Industry." *Human Resource Management* 33, 1 (1994): 55–77.

Koh, Byung Chul. *Japan's Administrative Elite.* Berkeley: University of California Press, 1989.

Kohli, Martin. "Labor Market Perspectives and Activity Patterns of the Elderly in an Aging Society." In *Opportunities and Challenges in an Aging Society,* ed. W. van den Heuvel, R. Illsley, A. Jamieson, and K. Knipscheer. Amsterdam: Elsevier, 1991.

Kohli, Martin. *Public Solidarity Between Generations: Historical and Comparative Elements.* Research Report 39. Research Group on Aging and the Life Course, Free University of Berlin, 1993.

Kohli, Martin and Martin Rein. "The Changing Balance of Work and Retirement." In *Time for Retirement: Comparative Studies of Early Exit from the Labor Force,* ed. Martin Kohli, Martin Rein, Anne-Marie Guillemard, and Herman van Gunsteren, 1–35. Cambridge: Cambridge University Press, 1991.

Kommers, Donald P. "The Federal Constitutional Court in the German Political System." *Comparative Political Studies* 26, 4 (1994): 470–491.

Kone, Susan L. and Richard F. Winters. "Taxes and Voting: Electoral Retribution in the American States." *The Journal of Politics* 55, 1 (1993): 22–40.

Konig, David Thomas. *Law and Society in Puritan Massachusetts: Essex County, 1629–1692.* Chapel Hill: University of North Carolina Press, 1979.

Koop, C. Everett. "The Interface of Health Care Reform and Telemedicine." *Bulletin, The American Academy of Arts and Sciences* 49, 1 (October 1995): 36–51.

Koopman, Georg, Klaus Matthies, and Beate Reszat. *Oil and the International Economy: Lessons from Two Price Shocks.* New Brunswick, NJ: Transaction, 1989.

Koopmans, Ruud and Hanspeter Kriesi. "Institutional Structures and Prevailing Strategies." In *New Social Movements in Western Europe: A Comparative Analysis,* ed. Hanspeter Kriesi, Ruud Koopmans, Jan Willem Duyvendak, and Marco G. Giugni, 26–52. Minneapolis: University of Minnesota Press, 1995.

Kopits, George. "Overview." In *Tax Harmonization in the European Community: Policy Issues and Analysis,* ed. George Kopits, 1–21. Washington, DC: International Monetary Fund, 1992.

Kornhauser, William. *The Politics of Mass Society.* Glencoe, IL: Free Press, 1959.

Korpi, Walter. *The Working Class in Welfare Capitalism.* London: Routledge & Kegan Paul, 1978.

Kraft, Philip and Jorgen Bansler. "Mandatory Voluntarism: Negotiating Technology in Denmark." *Industrial Relations* 32 (1993): 329–343.

Kramer, Ralph. *Voluntary Agencies in the Welfare State.* Berkeley: University of California Press, 1981.

Kramer, Ralph M. "The Use of Government Funds by Voluntary Social Service Agencies in Four Welfare States." In *The Nonprofit Sector in International Perspective,* ed. James Estelle, 217–244. New York and Oxford: Oxford University Press, 1989.

Kramer, Ralph M. "The Roles of Voluntary Social Service Organizations in Four European States: Policies and Trends in England, The Netherlands, Italy, and Norway." In *Government and Voluntary Organizations: A Relational Perspective,* ed. Stein Kuhnle and Per Selle, 34–52. Aldershot, England: Avebury, 1992.

Krauft, Robert, Michael Patterson, Vicki Lundmark, Sara Kiesler, Tridas Mukopadhayay, and William Scherlis. "Internet Paradox: A Social Technology That Reduces Social Involvement and Psychological Well-Being?" *American Psychologist* 53, 9 (1998): 1017–1032.

Kravis, Irving B. and Robert E. Lipsey. *The Location of Overseas Production and Production for Export by U.S. Multinational Firms.* NBER Working Paper 482. National Bureau of Economic Research, 1980.

Kreile, Michael. "West Germany: The Dynamics of Expansion." In *Between Power and Plenty,* ed. Peter Katzenstein, 191–224. Madison: University of Wisconsin Press, 1978.

Krieger, Joel. *Reagan, Thatcher, and the Politics of Decline.* New York: Oxford University Press, 1986.

Kriesi, Hanspeter. "The Structure of the Swiss Political System." In *Trends Towards Corporatist Intermediation,* ed. Gerhard Lehmbruch and Philippe C. Schmitter, 133–161. Beverly Hills: Sage, 1982.

Kriesi, Hanspeter. *Political Mobilization and Social Change: The Dutch Case in Comparative Perspective.* Brookfield, VT: Avebury, 1993.

Kriesi, Hanspeter, Ruud Koopmans, Jan Willem Duyvendak, and Marco G. Ciugni, eds. *New Social Movements in Western Europe: A Comparative Analysis.* Minneapolis: University of Minnesota Press, 1995.

Krist, Michael W. and Carolyn Kelley. "Postitive Impacts of Reform Efforts in the 1980s." Paper prepared for University of California Symposium on the 10th anniversary of *A Nation at Risk.* Consortium for the Study of Society and Education, Berkeley, CA, April 8, 1993.

Krueger, Alan B. "Skill Intensity and Industrial Price Growth." In *Proceedings of the 48th Annual Industrial Relations Research Association,* ed. Paula B. Voos, 11–18. San Francisco: IRRA, 1996.

Kudrle, Robert T. and Theodore R. Marmor. "The Development of the Welfare State in North America." In *The Development of Welfare States in Europe and America,* ed. Peter Flora and Arnold J. Heidenheimer, 81–121. New Brunswick, NJ: Transaction Books, 1981.

Kuhn, Raymond and Mark Wheeler. "The Future of the BBC Revisited." *Political Quarterly* 65, 4 (1994): 432–440.

Kuhnle, Stein. "European Integration and the National Welfare State." Paper presented at the Peder Sather symposium on "Challenges to Labor: Integration, Employment, and Bargaining in Scandinavia and the U.S.," Center for Western European Studies, University of California, Berkeley, March 21–22, 1996.

Kuhnle, Stein and Per Selle, eds. *Government and Voluntary Organizations: A Relational Perspective.* Aldershot, England: Avebury, 1992a.

Kuhnle, Stein and Per Selle. "Governmental Understanding of Voluntary Organizations: Policy Implications of Conceptual Change in Post-War Norway." In *Government and Voluntary Organizations: A Relational Perspective,* ed. Stein Kuhnle and Per Selle, 157–184. Aldershot, England: Avebury, 1992b.

Kuklinski, James H. and Lee Sigelman. "When Objectivity Is Not Objective: Network Television Coverage of U.S. Senators and the 'Paradox of Objectivity'." *Journal of Politics* 54, 3 (August 1992): 810–833.

Kume, Ikuo. *Disparaged Success: Labor Politics in Postwar Japan.* Ithaca, NY: Cornell University Press, 1998.

Kurth, James R. "The Political Consequences of the Product Cycle: Industrial History and Political Outcomes." *International Organization* 33, 1 (1979): 1–34.

Kurzer, Paulette. *Business and Banking: Political Change and Economic Integration in Western Europe.* Ithaca, NY: Cornell University Press, 1993.

Kurzer, Paulette. "European Integration and Corporatist Bargaining: Sweden." Peder Sather Symposium, University of California, Berkeley, CA, March, 1996.

Kuttner, Robert. "Only Connect." *The American Prospect* 17 (1994): 6–10.

Kuznets, Simon S. "Economic Growth and Income Inequality." *American Economic Review* 54 (1955): 1–28.

Ladd, Carll Everett. "The 1992 Vote for President Clinton: Another Brittle Mandate?" *Political Science Quarterly* 108, 1 (1993): 1–26.

Ladd, Everett Carll. *Where Have All the Voters Gone?* 2nd ed. New York: W. W. Norton, 1982.

Ladinsky, Jack. "Careers of Lawyers, Law Practice and Legal Institutions." *American Sociological Review* 28 (February 1963a): 47–54.

Ladinsky, Jack. "The Impact of Social Backgrounds of Lawyers on Law Practice and the Law." *Journal of Legal Education* 16 (1963b): 127–144.

Lafferty, William M. *Economic Development and the Response of Labor in Scandinavia: A Multi-Level Analysis.* Oslo: Universitetsforlaget, 1971.

Lancaster, H. O. *Expectations of Life: A Study in the Demography, Statistics, and History of World Mortality.* New York: Springer Verlag, 1990.

Land, Kenneth C., Patricia L. McCall, and Lawrence E. Cohen. "Structural Covariates of Homicide Rates—Are There any Invariances Across Time and Social Space?" *American Journal of Sociology* 95, 4 (1990): 922–963.

Landes, David. "Rich Country, Poor Country." *New Republic* 201, 21 (1989): 23–27.

Lane, Robert E. "Does Money Buy Happiness?" *The Public Interest* 113 (1993): 56–65.

Langbein, John H. "The German Advantage in Civil Procedure." *The University of Chicago Law Review* 52, 4 (1985): 823–866.

Lange, Peter. "The Politics of the Social Dimension." In *Euro-Politics: Institutions and Policymaking in the European Community,* ed. Alberta M. Sbragia, 225–256. Washington, DC: Brookings Institution, 1992.

Lange, Peter and Geoffrey Garrett. "The Politics of Growth: Strategic Interaction and Economic Performance in the Advanced Industrial Democracies, 1974–1980." *Journal of Politics* 47 (1985): 792–827.

Lange, Peter, Michael Wallerstein, and Miriam Golden. "The End of Corporatism? Wage Setting in the Nordic and Germanic Countries." In *The Workers of Nations: Industrial Relations in a Global Economy,* ed. Sanford M. Jacoby, 76–100. New York: Oxford University Press, 1995.

Laroque, Pierre. *Social Welfare in France.* Translated by Philip Gaunt and Noel Lindsay. Paris: Documentation française, 1966.

Laslett, Peter with the assistance of Richard Wall. *Household and Family in Past Time*. New York: Cambridge University Press, 1972.

Lauber, Volkmar, ed. *Contemporary Austrian Politics*. Boulder, CO: Westview Press, 1996.

Lawson, Kay. "How State Laws Undermine Parties." In *Elections American Style*, ed. A. James Reichley, 240–260. Washington, DC: Brookings Institution, 1987.

Lazar, Irving et al. *Lasting Effects After Pre-school: A Summary Report*. Washington, DC: HEW Consortium for Longitudinal Studies, 1979.

Lazarsfeld, Paul F., Bernard Berelson, and Hazel Gaudet. *The People's Choice*. New York: Columbia University Press, 1948.

Lazarsfeld, Paul F. and Robert K. Merton. "Mass Communication, Popular Taste, and Organized Social Action." In *The Process and Effects of Mass Communication*, ed. W. Schramm and D. F. Roberts, 554–578. Rev. ed. Urbana: University of Illinois Press, 1971.

Lederer, Emil. *State of the Masses*. New York: W. W. Norton, 1940.

Lee, Barrett A., R. S. Oropesa, Barbara J. Metch, and Avery M. Guest. "Testing the Decline-of-Community Thesis: Neigborhood Organizations in Seattle, 1929 and 1979." *American Journal of Sociology* 89, 5 (1984): 1161–1188.

Lee, Philip R. and Carroll L. Estes, eds. *The Nation's Health*. 4th ed. Boston/London: Jones and Bartlett, 1994.

Lehmbruch, Gerhard. "Corporatism, Labour, and Public Policy." Unpublished paper presented at the Ninth World Congress of Sociology, Uppsala, August, 1978.

Lehmbruch, Gerhard. "Liberal Corporatism and Party Government." In *Trends Toward Corporatist Intermediation*, ed. Philippe C. Schmitter and Gerhard Lehmbruch, 147–184. Beverly Hills: Sage, 1979.

Lehmbruch, Gerhard. "Consociational Democracy and Corporatism in Switzerland." *Publius: The Journal of Federalism* 23, 2 (1993): 43–60.

Lehmbruch, Gerhard. "The Organization of Society, Administrative Strategies, and Policy Networks." In *Political Choice: Institutions, Rules, and the Limits of Rationality*, ed. Roland M. Czada, Adrienne Windhoff-Heriter, and Hans Keman, 61–84. Amsterdam: Vu University Press, 1998.

Leibfried, Stephan. "The United States and West German Welfare Systems: A Comparative Analysis." *Cornell International Law Journal* 12, 2 (1979): 175–198.

Leichsenring, Kai. *Social Protection for Pensioners and Frail Older Persons in Austria*. European Centre for Social Welfare Policy and Research, Vienna, Austria, 1997.

Leigh, Duane E. *Assisting Workers Displaced by Structural Change: An International Perspective*. Kalamazoo, MI: W.E. Upjohn Institute for Employment Research, 1995.

Leithner, Chris and Jack Vowles. "Back to Instability? The Rise and Decline of Party Loyalty in the New Zealand Electorate, 1905–1993." Paper presented at the American Political Science Association, Annual Meeting in San Francisco, CA, Aug. 29–Sept. 1, 1996.

Leman, Christopher. *The Collapse of Welfare Reform: Political Institutions, Policy, and the Poor in Canada and the United States*. Cambridge, MA: MIT University Press, 1980.

Lembruch, G. "The Organization of Society, Administrative Strategies, and Policy Networks." In *Political Choice*, ed. R. Czada and A. Windhoff-Héritier, 121–158. Boulder: Westview Press, 1991.

Lenski, Gerhard. "Status Crystallization: A Non-Vertical Dimension of Social Status." *American Sociological Review* 19 (August 1954): 405–413.

Leonard, Jonathan S. "In the Wrong Place at the Wrong Time: The Extent of Frictional and Structural Unemployment." In *Unemployment and the Structure of Labor Markets*, ed. Lang Kevin and Jonathan S. Leonard, 141–163. New York: Basil Blackwell, 1982.

Leonard, Jonathan S. "Unions and Employment Growth." *Industrial Relations* 31, 1 (1992): 80–94.

Leonesio, Michael V. "Social Security and Older Workers." *Social Security Bulletin* 56, 2 (1993): 47–57.

LeRoy, Michael H. "The Changing Character of Strikes Involving Permanent Striker Replacements, 1935–1990." *Journal of Labor Research* 16, 4 (1995): 423–438

Lesser, G. *Children and Television: Lessons from Sesame Street.* New York: Random House, 1974.

Lester, Richard A. *Manpower in a Free Society.* Princeton, NJ: Princeton University Press, 1966.

Lesthaeghe, Ron and Chris Wilson. "Modes of Production, Secularization, and the Pace of the Fertility Decline in Western Europe, 1870–1930." In *The Decline of Fertility in Europe: The Revised Proceedings of a Conference on the European Fertility Project,* ed. Ansley J. Coale and Susan Cotts Watkins, 261–292. Princeton, NJ: Princeton University Press, 1986.

Letiche, John M. "Lessons of the Oil Crisis." *Lloyds Bank Review* 124 (April 1977): 31–43.

Levin, Henry M. "Educational Vouchers: Effectiveness, Choice, and Costs." *Journal of Policy Analysis and Management* 17, 3 (1998): 373–392.

Levin, Martin A. and Barbara Ferman. "Youth Employment Program Successes: A Cautionary Tale." *Journal of Contemporary Studies* 4 (1981): 53–69.

Levine, Robert A., Marian A. Solomon, Gerd-Michael Hellstern, and Hellmut Wollman, eds. *Evaluation Research and Practice: Comparative and International Perspectives.* Beverly Hills and London: Sage, 1981.

Levine, Solomon B. "Japanese Industrial Relations: What Can We Import?" In *Thirty-sixth Annual National Conference on Labor,* Chapter 2. New York: Bender & Co., 1983.

Levy, B., F. Wilkinson, and W. Marine. "Reducing Neonatal Mortality Rate with Nurse-Midwives." *American Journal of Obstetrics and Gynecology* 109 (1971): 50–58.

Levy, Frank. *Dollars and Dreams: The Changing American Income Distribution.* New York: Russell Sage Foundation, 1987.

Levy, Frank and Richard J. Murnane. "U.S. Earnings Levels and Earnings Inequality: A Review of Recent Trends and Proposed Explanations." *Journal of Economic Literature* 30, 3 (1992): 1333–1381.

Levy, Marion J. *The Family Revolution in Modern China.* Cambridge, MA: Harvard University Press, 1949.

Levy, Marion J. "Some Sources of the Vulnerability of the Structures of Relatively Nonindustrialized Societies to Those of Highly Industrialized Societies." In *The Progress of Underdeveloped Areas,* ed. Bert F. Hoselitz, 113–125. Chicago: University of Chicago Press, 1952.

Levy, Marion J. *Modernization and the Structure of Societies: A Setting for International Affairs.* Princeton, NJ: Princeton University Press, 1972.

Levy, Marion J. "Confucianism and Modernization." *Current* 345 (1992): 26–29.

Lewis, Paul M. "Family, Economy, and Polity: A Case Study of Japan's Public Pension Policy." Ph.D. dissertation, Department of Sociology, University of California at Berkeley, 1980.

Lichtenberg, Frank R. *Crowding Out: The Impact of the Strategic Defense Initiative on U.S. Civilian R&D Investment and Industrial Competitiveness.* First Boston Working Paper Series, 1988. FB-88–19.

Lichter, S. Robert and Daniel R. Amundson. "Less News Is Worse News: Television News Coverage of Congress, 1972–92." In *Congress, the Press, and the Public,* ed. Thomas E. Mann and Norman J. Ornstein, 131–140. Washington, DC: American Enterprise Institute and Brookings Institution, 1994.

Lichter, S. Robert and Ted Smith. "Bad News Bears." *Forbes Media Critic* 1 (1993): 36–39.

Lieberson, Stanley. *A Piece of the Pie: Blacks and White Immigrants Since 1880.* Berkeley: University of California Press, 1980.

Lieberson, Stanley and Mary C. Waters. *From Many Strands: Ethnic and Racial Groups in Contemporary America.* New York: Russell Sage Foundation, 1988.

Liebow, Elliott. *Tally's Corner: A Study of Negro Streetcorner Men.* Boston: Little, Brown, 1967.

Light, Ivan H. *Ethnic Enterprise in America: Business and Welfare among Chinese, Japanese, and Blacks.* Berkeley: University of California Press, 1972.

Light, Ivan and Stavros Karageorgis. "Economic Saturation and Immigrant Entrepreneurship." In *Immigrant Entrepreneurs and Immigrant Absorption in the United States and Israel,* ed. Ivan Light and Richard E. Isralowitz, 1–17. Brookfield, VT: Ashgate Publishing, 1997.

Light, Ivan, Georges Sabagh, Mehdi Bozorgmehr, and Claudia Der-Martirosian. "Beyond the Ethnic Enclave Economy." *Social Problems* 41, 1 (1994): 65–80.

Light, Paul C. "Passing Nonincremental Policy: Presidential Influence in Congress, Kennedy to Carter." *Congress and the Presidency* 9, 1 (1981/1982): 61–82.

Lijphart, Arend. *The Politics of Accommodation: Pluralism and Democracy in Divided Societies.* Berkeley: University of California Press, 1968.

Lijphart, Arend. *Democracies: Patterns of Majoritarian and Consensus Government in Twenty-One Countries.* New Haven: Yale University Press, 1984.

Lijphart, Arend. "The Political Consequences of Electoral Laws 1945–85." *American Political Science Review* 84, 2 (1990): 481–496.

Lijphart, Arend. "Constitutional Choices for New Democracies." *Journal of Democracy* 2, 1 (Winter 1991): 70–84.

Lijphart, Arend. *Electoral Systems and Party Systems: A Study of Twenty-seven Democracies, 1945–1990.* Oxford: Oxford University Press, 1994.

Lin, Ching-Jiang. "The Republic of China (Taiwan)." In *Schooling in East Asia: Forces of Change,* ed. R. Murray Thomas and T. Neville Postlethwaite, 104–135. New York: Pergamon Press, 1983.

Lincoln, James R., Harold R. Kerbo, and Elke Wittenhagen. "Japanese Companies in Germany: A Case Study in Cross-Cultural Management." *Industrial Relations: A Journal of Economy and Society* 34, 3 (1995): 417–440.

Lindbeck, Assar, Per Molander, Torsten Persson, Olof Petersson, Agnar Sandmo, Birgitta Swedenborg, and Niels Thygesen. *Turning Sweden Around.* Cambridge: MIT Press, 1994.

Lindblom, Charles E. *Politics and Markets: The World's Political-Economic Systems.* New York: Basic Books, 1977.

Lindert, Peter H. "The Rise of Social Spending, 1880–1930." Working Paper Series No. 68, Agricultural History Center, University of California, Davis, May 1992.

Lindert, Peter H. "What Limits Social Spending?" *Explorations in Economic History* 33 (1996a): 1–34.

Lindert, Peter H. "Social Spending: What Happened to Growth Effects?" Paper presented at Allied Social Sciences Association, Jan. 7, 1996b.

Linton, Ralph. *The Study of Man.* New York: Appleton-Century, 1936.

Linz, Juan. "Totalitarian and Authoritarian Regimes." In *Handbook of Political Science,* ed. N. Polsby and F. Greenstein, 175–411. Vol. 3. Reading, MA: Addison Wesley, 1975.

Linz, Juan J. and Alfred Stepan. *Problems of Democratic Transition and Consolidation: Southern Europe, South America and Post-Communist Europe.* Baltimore: Johns Hopkins University Press, 1996.

Lipset, Seymour Martin. *Agrarian Socialism: The Cooperative Commonwealth Federation in Saskatchewan, a Study in Political Sociology.* Berkeley: University of California Press, 1950.

Lipset, Seymour Martin. *Political Man: The Social Bases of Politics.* New York: Doubleday, 1960.

Lipset, Seymour Martin. *Continental Divide: The Values and Institutions of the United States and Canada.* New York: Routledge, 1990.

Lipset, Seymour Martin. "The Social Requisites of Democracy Revisited [1993 Presidential Address]." *American Sociological Review* 59 (1994): 1–22.

Lipset, Seymour Martin. *American Exceptionalism: A Double-Edged Sword.* New York: W. W. Norton, 1996.

Lipset, Seymour Martin "American Union Density in Comparative Perspective." *Contemporary Sociology* 27, 2 (1998): 123–125.

Lipset, Seymour Martin and Stein Rokkan. "Cleavage Structures, Party Systems, and Voter Alignments: An Introduction." In *Party Systems and Voter Alignments: Cross-National Perspectives,* ed. Seymour Martin Lipset and Stein Rokkan, 1 – 64. New York: Free Press, 1967.

Lipset, Seymour Martin and William Schneider. *The Confidence Gap: Business, Labor, and Government in the Public Mind.* New York: Free Press, 1983.

Litwak, Eugene. "Occupational Mobility and Extended Family Cohesion." *American Sociological Review* 25, 1 (1960a): 9 – 21.

Litwak, Eugene. "Geographic Mobility and Extended Family Cohesion." *American Sociological Review* 25, 3 (1960b): 385 – 394.

Liu, Korbin, Marilyn Moon, Margaret Sulvetta, and Juhi Chawla. "International infant mortality rankings: A look behind the numbers." *Health Care Financing Review* 13, 4 (Summer 1992): 105 – 118.

Livi-Bacci, Massimo. "Social-Group Forerunners of Fertility Control in Europe." In *The Decline of Fertility in Europe: The Revised Proceedings of a Conference on the European Fertility Project,* ed. Ansley J. Coale and Susan Cotts Watkins, 182 – 200. Princeton, NJ: Princeton University Press, 1986.

Livi-Bacci, Massimo. "South-North Migration: A Comparative Approach to North American and European Experiences." In *The Changing Course of International Migration,* 37 – 46. Paris: OECD, 1993.

Long, Clarence D. *The Labor Force under Changing Income and Employment.* Princeton, NJ: Princeton University Press, 1958.

Long, David A., Charles D. Mallar, and Craig V. D. Thornton. "Evaluating the Benefits and Costs of the Job Corps." *Journal of Policy Analysis and Management* 1 (1981): 55 – 76.

Long, Larry. "Residential Mobility Differences Among Developed Countries." *International Regional Science Review* 12, 2 (1991): 133 – 147.

Lorwin, Val. "Segmented Pluralism: Ideological Cleavages and Political Cohesion in the Smaller European Democracies." *Comparative Politics* 3 (1971): 141 – 175.

Lowrey, George H. "The Problem of Hospital Accidents to Children." *Pediatrics* 32, 12 (1963): 1064 – 1068.

Lublin, Joann S. "Pay for No Performance." *Wall Street Journal Report* Executive Pay (1998): R1, R4.

Lubove, Roy. *The Struggle for Social Security 1900–1935.* Cambridge: Harvard University Press, 1968.

Lucas, Robert E., Jr. "On the Mechanics of Economic Development." *Journal of Monetary Economics* 22 (1988): 3 – 42.

Lundqvist, Lennart J. *The Hare and the Tortoise: Clean Air Policies in the United States and Sweden.* Ann Arbor: University of Michigan Press, 1980.

Lynn, Leonard H. and Timothy J. McKeown. *Organizing Business: Trade Associations in America and Japan.* Washington, DC: American Enterprise Institute, 1988.

Lyons, Gene and Editors of Harper's Magazine. *Fools for Scandal: How the Media Invented Whitewater.* New York: Franklin Square Press, 1996.

Lyttleton, Adrian. "Italy: The Triumph of TV." *The New York Review of Books* 1 (August 11, 1994): 25 – 29.

MacCoun, Robert J. "Drugs and the Law: A Psychological Analysis of Drug Prohibition." *Psychological Bulletin* 113 (1993): 497 – 512.

MacDuffie, John Paul and Thomas A. Kochan. "Do U.S. Firms Invest Less in Human Resources? Training in the World Auto Industry." *Industrial Relations* 34, 2 (April 1995): 147 – 168.

MacDuffie, John Paul and Frits K. Pil. "Changes in Auto Industry Employment Practices: An International Overview." In *After Lean Production: Evolving Employment Practices in the World Auto Industry,* ed. Thomas A. Kochan, Russell D. Lansbury, and John Paul MacDuffie, 9 – 42. Ithaca: ILR Press—an Imprint of Cornell University Press, 1997.

MacFarlan, Maitland and Howard Oxley. "Reforming Social Transfers." *OECD Observer* No. 199 (April/May 1996): 28–31.

Mackie, Thomas T. and Richard Rose. *The International Almanac of Electoral History.* Washington, DC: Congressional Quarterly, 1991.

MacKuen, M. B. "Social Communication and the Mass Policy Agenda." In *More Than News: Media Power in Public Affairs,* ed. M. B. MacKuen and S. L. Coombs, 19–144. Beverly Hills: Sage, 1981.

MacManus, Susan. "Taxing and Spending Politics: A Generational Perspective." *Journal of Politics* 57, 3 (1995): 607–630.

MacShane, Denis. "Do Europeans Do It Better?" *The American Prospect* 1993, 14 (1993): 88–95.

Maddison, Angus. *Phases of Capitalist Development.* Oxford: Oxford University Press, 1982.

Magleby, David B. "Direct Legislation in the American State." In *Referendums Around the World: The Growing Use of Direct Democracy,* ed. David Butler and Austin Ranney, 218–257. Washington, DC: AEI Press, 1994.

Maier, Charles S. "Preconditions for Corporatism." In *Order and Conflict in Contemporary Capitalism,* ed. John H. Goldthorpe, 39–59. Oxford: Clarendon Press, 1984.

Mair, Peter. "The Electoral Universe of Small Parties in Postwar Western Europe." In *Small Parties in Western Europe,* ed. Ferdinand Müller-Rommel and Geoffrey Pridham, 41–70. London: Sage, 1991.

Mallar, Charles D. et al. *The Lasting Impacts of Job Corps Participation.* Princeton, NJ: Mathematica, 1980.

Mallar, Charles, Stuart Kerachsky, Craig Thornton, and David Long. *An Evaluation of the Economic Impact of the Job Corps Program: Third Follow-up Report.* Princeton, NJ: Mathematica Policy Research, 1982.

Mann, Thomas E. and Norman J. Ornstein. "Introduction." In *Congress, the Press, and the Public,* ed. Thomas E. Mann and Norman J. Ornstein, 1–13. Washington, DC: American Enterprise Institute and Brookings Institution, 1994.

Mannheim, Karl. "The Problem of Generations." In *Essays on the Sociology of Knowledge,* ed. Paul Kecskemeti, 276–320. London: Routledge & Kegan Paul, 1952 [1928].

Mannheim, Karl. *Man and Society in an Age of Reconstruction.* London: Routledge and Kegan Paul, 1940.

Manning, Willard G. et al. "A Controlled Trial of the Effect of a Prepaid Group Practice on Use of Services." *New England Journal of Medicine* 310, 23 (1986): 1505–1510.

Mansbridge, Jane. "A Deliberate Perspective on Neocorporatism." *Politics and Society* 20, 4 (1992): 493–505.

Marcus, Robert D. *Grand Old Party: Political Structure in the Gilded Age 1880–1896.* New York: Oxford University Press, 1971.

Marie, Claude-Valentin. "From the Campaign Against Illegal Migration to the Campaign Against Illegal Work." *Annals of the American Academy of Political and Social Science* 534 (1994): 118–132.

Marmor, Theodore R. "Japan: A Sobering Lesson." *Health Management Quarterly* 14, 3 (1992): 10–14.

Marmor, Theodore R. *Understanding Health Care Reform.* New Haven: Yale University Press, 1994.

Marmor, Theodore R., Morris L. Barer, and Robert G. Evans. "The Determinants of a Population's Health: What Can Be Done to Improve a Democratic Nation's Health Status?" In *Why Are Some People Healthy and Others Not? The Determinants of the Health of Populations,* ed. R. G. Evans, M. L. Barer, and T. R. Marmor. New York: Aldine de Gruyler, 1994.

Marmor, Theodore R. and Jerry L. Mashaw, eds. *Social Security: Beyond the Rhetoric of Crisis.* Princeton, NJ: Princeton University Press, 1988.

Marmor, Theodore R., Timothy M. Smeeding, and Vernon L. Greene. *Economic Security and Intergenerational Justice: A Look at North America.* Washington, DC: Urban Institute Press, 1994.

Marmot, Michael G. "Social Inequalities in Mortality: The Social Environment in Class and Health." In *Class and Health,* ed. Richard G. Wilkinson, 21–34. London: Tavistock, 1986.

Marmot, Michael G., George Davey-Smith, and Stephen Stansfeld, et al. "Health Inequalities Among British Civil Servants: The Whitehall II Study." *Lancet* 1 (1991): 1387–1393.

Marmot, Michael G., George Davey-Smith, Stephen Stansfield, Chandra Patel, Fiona North, Jenny Head, Ian White, Eric Brunner, and Amanda Feeney. "Health Inequalities and Social Class." In *The Nation's Health,* ed. Philip R. Lee and Carroll L. Estes, 34–39. Boston and London: Jones and Bartlett, 1994.

Marsden, Peter V., Cynthia R. Cook, and David Knoke. "American Organizations and Their Environments." In *Organizations in America: Analyzing Their Structures and Human Resource Practices,* ed. Arne Kalleberg, David Knoke, Peter V. Marsden, and Joe L. Spaeth, 45–66. Thousand Oaks: Sage, 1996.

Marsh, Alan and Max Kaase. "Background of Political Action." In *Political Action: Mass Participation in Five Western Democracies,* ed. Samuel Barnes and Max Kaase, 97–136. London: Sage, 1979.

Marshall, Ray. "Foreword." In *Competitive Manufacturing: New Strategies for Regional Development,* ed. Stuart A. Rosenfeld, xiii–xvi. New Brunswick, NJ: Center for Urban Policy Research, 1992.

Marshall, T. H. (Thomas Humphrey). *Class, Citizenship, and Social Development.* Garden City, NJ: Doubleday, 1964.

Martin, Andrew. *Macroeconomic Policy, Politics, and the Demise of Central Wage Negotiations in Sweden.* Harvard Center for European Studies, 1996.

Martin, Andrew and George Ross. "European Integration and the Europeanization of Labor." In *Transnational Cooperation Among Labor Unions,* ed. Michael E. Gordon and Lowell Turner, 120–149. Ithaca: ILR Press/Cornell University Press, 2000.

Martin, Philip L. "The Migration Issue." *Migration World* 20, no. 5 (1992): 10–15.

Martin, Philip L. "Immigration and Integration: Challenges for the 1990s." Unpublished paper, 1993.

Martin, Philip and Elizabeth Midgley. "Immigration to the United States: Journey to an Uncertain Destination." *Population Bulletin* 49, 2 (1994): 1–47.

Martinez, Ramiro, Jr. "Latinos and Lethal Violence: The Impact of Poverty and Inequality." *Social Problems* 43, 2 (1996): 131–146.

Marvin, Carolyn. *When Old Technologies Were New: Thinking About Electric Communication in the Late Nineteenth Century.* New York: Oxford University Press, 1988.

Marwell, Gerald, Michael T. Aiken, and N. J. Demerath III. "The Persistance of Political Attitudes Among 1960s Civil Rights Activists." *Public Opinion Quarterly* 51, 3 (1987): 359–375.

Mashaw, Jerry L. *Bureaucratic Justice: Managing Social Security Disability Claims.* New Haven, CT: Yale University Press, 1983.

Mashaw, Jerry L. "Disability Insurance in an Age of Retrenchment: The Politics of Implementing Rights." In *Social Security: Beyond the Rhetoric of Crisis,* ed. Theodore M. Marmor and Jerry L. Mashaw, 151–175. Princeton, NJ: Princeton University Press, 1988.

Mason, Karen O., John L. Czajka, and Sara Arber. "Change in U.S. Women's Sex-Role Attributes, 1964–74." *American Sociological Review* 4 (1976): 573–596.

Mason, Timothy. *Arbeiterklasse und Volksgemeinschaft.* Opladen: Westdeutscher Verlag, 1976.

Massey, Douglas S. "Hispanic Residential Segregation: A Comparison of Mexicans, Cubans, and Puerto Ricans." *Sociology and Social Research* 65 (1981): 311–322.

Massey, Douglas S. and Nancy A. Denton. "Trends in the Residential Segregation of Blacks, Hispanics, and Asians: 1970–1980." *American Sociological Review* 52 (1987): 802–825.

Massey, Douglas S. and Nancy A. Denton. "Residential Segregation of Asian-Origin Groups in U.S. Metropolitan Areas." *Sociology and Social Research* 76, 4 (1992): 170–177.

Massey, Douglas S. and Nancy A. Denton. *American Apartheid: Segregation and the Making of the Underclass.* Cambridge: Harvard University Press, 1993.

Massey, Douglas S., Andrew B. Gross, and Kumiko Shibuya. "Migration, Segregation, and the Concentration of Poverty." *American Sociological Review* 59 (1994): 425–445.

Masters, Marick and John D. Robertson. "Class Compromises in Industrial Democracies." *American Political Science Review* 82 (1988): 1183–1202.

Matthews, Trevor. "Interest Group Politics: Corporatism without Business." In *Australia Compared: People, Policies and Politics,* ed. Francis G. Castles, 191–218. North Sydney: Allen & Unwin, 1991.

Mauer, Marc. "Americans Behind Bars: A Comparison of International Rates of Incarceration." The Sentencing Project, Washington, DC, 1991.

Mauldon, Jane and Kristin Luker. "Does Liberalism Cause Sex?" *The American Prospect* 24 (Winter 1996): 80–85.

Maxfield, Sylvia. *The International Political Economy of Central Banking in Developing Countries.* Princeton: Princeton University Press, 1997.

Maxwell, Robert. *Health and Wealth: An International Study of Health Care Spending.* Lexington, MA: Lexington Books, 1981.

Maybury-Lewis, David. "A New World Dilemma: The Indian Question in the Americas." *Bulletins* 46, 7 (1993): 57–59.

Mayer, Nonna and Pascal Perrineau, eds. *Le Front National à découvert.* Paris: Presses de la Fondation nationale des sciences politiques, 1989.

Mayer, Susan E. and Christopher Jencks. "Poverty and the Distribution of Material Hardship." *The Journal of Human Resources* 24, 1 (1989): 88–113.

Mayer, William G. *The Changing American Mind: How and Why American Public Opinion Changed between 1960 and 1988.* Ann Arbor: University of Michigan Press, 1992.

Mayhew, David R. *Divided We Govern: Party Control, Lawmaking, and Investigations, 1946–1990.* New Haven, CT: Yale University Press, 1991.

Mayhew, Leon. "Ascription in Modern Societies." *Sociological Inquiry* 38, 2 (1968): 105–120.

Maynard, Rebecca A. "Subsidized Employment and Non-Labor Market Alternatives for Welfare Recipients." In *The Work Alternative: Welfare Reform and the Realities of the Job Market,* ed. Demetra Smith Nightingale and Robert H. Haveman, 109–136. Washington, DC: Urban Institute Press, 1995.

Mayo. *The Human Problems of an Industrial Civilization.* Cambridge: Harvard University Press, 1933.

Mayo, Elton. *The Social Problems of an Industrial Civilization.* Cambridge: Harvard University Press, 1945.

McArthur, Andrew A. and Alan McGregor. "Training and Economic Development: National Versus Local Perspectives." *Political Quarterly* 57, 3 (1986): 246–255.

McCallum, Bennett. "The Political Business Cycle: An Emprirical Test." *Southern Economic Journal* 44 (1978): 504–515.

McClintick, David. "Towncrier for the New Age." *Brill's Content* 1, 4 (November 1998): 113–127.

McClosky, Herbert and Alida Brill. *Dimensions of Tolerance: What Americans Believe about Civil Liberties.* New York: Russell Sage Foundation, 1983.

McCluskey, Martha T. "Whose Risk, Whose Security?" *The American Prospect* 11, 6 (January 2000): 38–42.

McCormick, Richard L. *The Party Period and Public Policy: American Politics from the Age of Jackson to the Progressive Era.* New York: Oxford University Press, 1986.

McGuire, Chester C. *International Housing Policies: A Comparative Analysis.* Lexington, MA: Lexington Books, 1981.

McKean, Margaret A. *Environmental Protest and Citizen Politics in Japan.* Berkeley: University of California Press, 1980.

McKeown, Thomas. *The Role of Medicine: Dream, Mirage, or Nemesis.* Princeton, NJ: Princeton University Press, 1979.

McKeown, Thomas. "Determinants of Health." In *The Nation's Health,* ed. Philip R. Lee, Carroll L. Estes, and Liz Close, 9–17. 5th ed. Sudbury, MA: Jones and Bartlett, 1997.

McKeown, Thomas and Gordon McLachlan, eds. *Medical History and Medical Care: A Symposium of Perspectives.* New York: Oxford University Press, 1971.

McKinlay, John B. and Sonja M. McKinlay. "The Questionable Contribution of Medicine Measures to the Decline of Mortality in the United States in the Twentieth Century." *Milbank Memorial Fund Quarterly* 55 (Summer 1977): 405–428.

McKinlay, John B., Sonja M. McKinlay, and Robert Beaglehole. "A Review of the Evidence Concerning the Impact of Medical Measures on Recent Mortality and Morbidity in the United States." *International Journal of Health Services* 19, 2 (1989): 181–208.

McKinnon, N. E. "The Effects of Control Programs on Cancer Mortality." *Canadian Medical Association Journal* 82 (1960): 1308–1312.

McKinsey Global Institute. *Employment Performance.* Washington, DC: McKinsey and Co., Section 2, 1994.

McLamb, J. T. and R. R. Huntley. "The Hazards of Hospitalization." *Southern Medical Journal* 60 (1967): 469–472.

McLaughlin, Eugene. "Ireland: Catholic Corporatism." In *Comparing Welfare States: Britain in International Context,* ed. Allan Cochrane and John Clarke, 205–237. Newbury Park, CA: Sage, 1993.

McManus, Susan. "Taxing and Spending Politics: A Generational Perspective." *Journal of Politics* 57, 3 (1995): 607–629.

McQuail, Denis. "The Netherlands: Safeguarding Freedom and Diversity under Multichannel Conditions." In *Television and the Public Interest: Vulnerable Values in West European Broadcasting,* ed. Jay G. Blumler, 96–111. London: Sage, 1992.

Meador, Clifton. "The Art and Science of Nondisease." *New England Journal of Medicine* 272 (1965): 92–95.

Meager, Nigel. "Self-Employment Schemes for the Unemployed in the European Community: The Emergence of a New Institutions, and Its Evaluation." In *Labor Market Institutions in Europe: A Socioeconomic Evaluation of Performance,* ed. Günther Schmid, 183–242. Armonk, NY: M. E. Sharpe, 1994.

Mechanic, David. "Professional Judgement and the Rationing of Medical Care." *University of Pennsylvania Law Review* 140, 5 (May 1992): 1713–1754.

Mechanic, David. "America's Health Care System and Its Future." *Medical Care Review* 50, 1 (1993): 7–48.

Mechanic, David. *Inescapable Decisions: the Imperatives of Health Reform.* New Brunswick, NJ: Transaction, 1994.

Mechanic, David. "Dilemmas in Rationing Health Care Services: The Case for Implicit Rationing." *British Medical Journal* 310 (June 1995): 1655–1659.

Mechanic, David. "Reconciling the Demand and Provision of Health Services." In *The State, Politics, and Health: Essays for Rudolf Klein,* ed. P. Day, D. M. Fox, R. Maxwell, and E. Scrivens, 145–164. Oxford: Blackwell, 1996.

Mechanic, David and David A. Rochefort. "Comparative Medical Systems." *Annual Review of Sociology* 22, 2 (1996): 239–270.

Medoff, James L. *Smart Stimulus: More Good Jobs.* Washington, DC: Center for National Policy Review, 1993.

Melaville, Atelia I., Martin J. Blank, and Gelareh Asayesh. *Together We Can: A Guide for Crafting a Profamily System of Education and Human Services.* U.S. Dept. of Education, Office of Educational Research and Improvement; U.S. Dept. of Health and Human Services, Office of the Assistant Secretary for Planning and Evaluation, 1993.

Mellanby, Keith. *Pesticides and Pollution.* New York: Collins, 1967.

Mellor, Earl F. "Shift Work and Flexitime: How Prevalent are They?" *Monthly Labor Review* 109, 11 (1986): 14–21.

Melnick, R. Shep. *Between the Lines: Interpreting Welfare Rights.* Washington, DC: Brookings Institution, 1994.

Meltz, Noah. "Interstate and Inter-province Differences in Union Density." *Industrial Relations* 28, 2 (Spring 1989): 142–158.

Merton, Robert K. "Social Structure and Anomie." In *Social Theory and Social Structure,* 131–160. Glencoe, IL: Free Press, 1957.

Messner, Steven F. "Income Inequality and Murder Rates: Some Cross-National Findings." *Comparative Social Research* 3 (1980): 185–198.

Messner, Steven F. "Societal Development, Social Equality and Homicide: A Cross-National Test of a Durkheimian Model." *Social Forces* (1982): 225–240.

Messner, Steven F. "Economic Discrimination and Societal Homicide Rates: Further Evidence on the Cost of Inequality." *American Sociological Review* 54 (1989): 597–611.

Metzger, Walter P. "The Advantages of Disadvantage." *Academe* 66, 1 (1980): 28–34.

Meyerson, Harold. "Dead Center." *The American Prospect* (January–February 1997): 60–67.

Millar, Jane. "The 'Feminisation of Poverty': Lone Mothers and Their Children." Centre for European Policy Studies Conference, "Demographic Change in Europe and Its Socio-Economic Consequences," Belgium, 1987.

Miller, A. H., T. A. Brown, and A. S. Raine. "Social Conflict and Political Estrangement 1958–1972." Paper presented at the annual meeting of the Midwest Political Science Association, Chicago, IL, 1973.

Miller, Cynthia, Virginia Knox, Patricia Auspos, Jo Anna Hunter-Manns, and Alan Orenstein. *Making Welfare Work and Work Pay: Implementation and 18-Month Impacts of the Minnesota Family Investment Program.* Manpower Demonstration Research Corporation, State of Minnesota, Department of Human Services, 1997.

Miller, C. Arden. *Maternal Health and Infant Survival.* National Center for Clinical Infant Programs, 1991.

Miller, Daniel and Guy E. Swanson. *The Changing American Parent.* New York: John Wiley, 1958.

Miller, Mark J. *Employer Sanctions in Western European Countries.* Staten Island, NY: Center for Migration Studies, 1987.

Miller, Mark J. "Preface." *Annals of the American Academy of Political and Social Science* 534 (1994): 8–16.

Miller, Raymond and Helen Catt. *Season of Discontent—By-elections and the Bolger Government.* Palmerston North: Dunmore Press, 1993.

Miller, Robert H. and Harold S. Luft. "Managed Care Plan Performance Since 1980: A Literature Analysis." *The Journal of the American Medical Association* 271, 19 (1994): 1512–1519.

Miller, S. M. "Faith, Hope, and Charity—the Public Relations of Charity." *Contemporary Sociology* 14, 6 (November 1985): 684–687.

Miller, Warren E. "Party Identification, Realignment, and Party Voting: Back to the Basics." *American Political Science Review* 85 (1991): 557–567.

Miller, Warren E. and J. Merrill Shanks. *The New American Voter.* Cambridge, MA: Harvard University Press, 1996.

Mills, C. Wright. *White Collar.* New York: Oxford University Press, 1956.

Milward, H. Brinton and Keith G. Provan. "The Hollow State: Private Provision of Public Services." In *In Public Policy for Democracy,* ed. Helen Ingram and Steven Rathgeb Smith, 222–237. Washington, DC: Brookings Institution, 1993.

Mincer, Jacob. *Schooling, Experience, and Earnings.* New York: National Bureau of Economic Research, 1974.

Minkler, Meredith. "'Generational Equity' and the New Victim Blaming: An Emerging Public Policy." *International Journal of Health Services* 16, 4 (1986): 539–551.

Minow, Newton and Craig L. LaMay. *Abandoned in the Wasteland: Children, Television, and the First Amendment.* New York: Hill & Wang, 1995.

Mintz, Alex and Chi Huang. "Guns versus Butter: The Indirect Link." *American Journal of Political Science* 35 (1991): 738–757.

Mishel, Lawrence and Jared Bernstein. "Did Technology's Impact Accelerate in the 1980s?" In *Proceedings of the 48th Annual Meeting of the Industrial Relations Research Association,* ed. Paula B. Voos, 19–27. San Francisco: 1996.

Mishel, Lawrence, Jared Bernstein, and John Schmitt. *The State of Working America: 1998–99.* Ithaca, NY: ILR Press, an imprint of Cornell University Press, 1999.

Mitchell, B. R. *European Historical Statistics, 1750–1975.* 2nd revised ed. New York: Facts on File, 1981.

Mitchell, B. R. *International Historical Statistics: The Americas and Australasia.* Detroit: Gale Research, 1983.

Mitchell, B. R. *International Historical Statistics: Europe, 1750–1988.* 3rd ed. New York: Stockton Press, 1992.

Mitchell, B. R. *International Historical Statistics: The Americas, 1750–1988.* 2nd ed. New York: Stockton Press, 1993.

Mitra, Subtra. "The National Front in France. A Single Issue Movement?" *West European Politics* 11, 2 (1988): 47–64.

Mjøset, Lars. *The Irish Economy in a Comparative Institutional Perspective.* Dublin: National Economic and Social Council, 1992.

Moch, Leslie Page. *Moving Europeans: Migration in Western Europe Since 1650.* Bloomington: Indiana University Press, 1992.

Moffitt, Robert. "An Economic Model of Welfare Stigma." *American Economist Review* 73, 5 (1983): 1023–1035.

Monks, James and Steven D. Pizer. "Trends in Voluntary and Involuntary Job Turnover." *Industrial Relations* 37, 4 (1998): 440–458.

Moore, Barrington, Jr. *Social Origins of Dictatorship and Democracy.* Cambridge: Harvard University Press, 1966a.

Moore, Barrington, Jr. *Terror and Progress—USSR. Some Sources of Change and Stability in the Soviet Dictatorship.* Cambridge: Harvard University Press, 1966b.

Moore, David W. "Desire for Health Care Reform Remains Strong." *The Gallup Poll Monthly* 343 (1994a): 7–10.

Moore, David W. "Public Firm on Health Reform." *The Gallup Poll Monthly* 346 (1994b): 12–16.

Moore, David W. "Polling on Health Care and Medicare: Continuity in Public Opinion." *The Public Perspective* 6, 6 (1995): 13–15.

Moore, Wilbert E. *Industrialization and Labor: Social Aspects of Economic Development.* New York: Cornell University Press, 1951.

Morales, Laura. "Changing Patterns of Political Membership in Western Countries: the Spanish Case." Paper presented at the annual conference of the International Sociological Association, Montreal, Canada, 1998.

Moreddu, Catherine. "Farm Household Incomes." *The OECD Observer* 194 (June/July 1995): 21–23.

Morgan, James N. "Equity Considerations and Means-Tested Benefits." *Journal of Policy Analysis and Management* 12, 4 (Fall 1993): 773–778.

Morgan, J. N., K. Dickinson, J. Dickinson, J. Benus, and G. Duncan. *Five Thousand American Families: Patterns of Economic Progress.* Vol. 1. Ann Arbor: Institute of Social Research, University of Michigan, 1974.

Morio, Shinsuke. "Quantitative Relationship Between Infant Mortality and Social Factors." *Yonago Acta Medica* 28, 1 (1985): 8–37.

Moritz, Charles. *Current Bibliography Yearbook, 1969.* New York: H. W. Wilson, 1970.

Morone, James A. *The Democratic Wish: Popular Participation and the Limits of American Government.* New York: Basic Books, 1990.

Morone, James A. "Hidden Complications: Why Health Care Competition Needs Regulation." *The American Prospect* No. 10 (1992): 40–48.

Mosel, James. "Communications Patterns and Political Socialization in Transitional Thailand." In *Communications and Political Development,* ed. Lucien W. Pye, 184–228. Princeton: Princeton University Press, 1963.

Moser, Robert H. *The Disease of Medical Progress: A Study of Iatrogenic Disease.* 3rd ed. Springfield, IL: Charles C Thomas, 1969.

Moskos, Charles C. "Racial Integration in the Armed Forces." *American Journal of Sociology* 72, 2 (1966): 132–148.

Moskos, Charles C. *A Call to Civic Service: National Service for Country and Community.* New York: Free Press, 1988.

Moynihan, Daniel Patrick. *Maximum Feasible Misunderstanding: Community Action in the War on Poverty.* New York: Free Press, 1970.

Moynihan, Daniel P. *The Politics of a Guaranteed Income: The Nixon Administration and the Family Assistance Plan.* New York: Random House, 1973.

Mudd, John. *Neighborhood Services.* New Haven, CT: Yale University Press, 1984.

Mueller, C. B. "Surgery for Breast Cancer: Less May Be as Good as More." *New England Journal of Medicine* 312 (1985): 712–713.

Muller, Thomas. *Immigrants and the American City.* New York: New York University Press, 1993.

Müller, Wolfgang C. "Political Institutions." In *Contemporary Austrian Politics,* ed. Volkmar Lauber, 59–102. Boulder, CO: Westview Press, 1996.

Müller-Rommel, Ferdinand. "Small Parties in Comparative Perspective: the State of the Art." In *Small Parties in Western Europe,* ed. Ferdinand Müller-Rommel and Geoffrey Pridham, 1–22. London: Sage, 1991.

Müller-Rommel, Ferdinand. "Ethno-regional Parties in Western Europe." In *Non-State Wide Parties in Europe,* ed. Lieven de Winter. Barcelona: Institut de Ciències Politiques i Socials, 1994.

Munnell, Alicia H. "Reforming Social Security and Privatization: The Case Against Individual Accounts." *National Tax Journal* 52, 4 (Dec. 1999): 803–817.

Muramatsu, Michio and Masaru Mabuchi. "Introducing a New Tax in Japan." In *Parallel Politics,* ed. Samuel Kernell, 184–207. Washington, DC: Brookings Institution, 1991.

Murayama, Masayuki. "Japanese City Police: A Study of Social Structure and Legal Conduct." LL.M. dissertation, School of Law, University of California at Berkeley, 1980.

Murayama, Masayuki. "Patrol Activities in Changing Urban Conditions: The Case of the Tokyo Police." Paper presented at the meeting of the International Sociological Association Research Committee on the Sociology of Law, Bologna, Italy, 1989.

Murnane, Richard J. and Frank Levy. "Comment: Stimulating Employer-Provided General Training." *Journal of Policy Analysis and Management* 13, 1 (1994): 75–81.

Murray, Charles A. *Losing Ground: American Social Policy, 1950–1980.* New York: Basic Books, 1984.

Murray, Charles A. "Welfare and the Family: The U.S. Experience." *Journal of Labor Economics* 11, 1 (1993): S224–S262.

Murray, Charles A. and Louis A. Cox, Jr. *Beyond Probation: Juvenile Corrections and the Chronic Delinquent.* Beverly Hills, CA: Sage, 1979.

Myers, Dowell. "Upward Mobility in Space and Time: Lessons from Immigration." In *America's Demographic Tapestry: Baseline for the New Millennium,* ed. James Hughes and Joseph Seneca, 135 – 157. New Brunswick, NJ: Rutgers University Press, 1999.

Myles, John. *Old Age in the Welfare State: The Political Economy of Public Pensions.* Lawrence: University Press of Kansas, 1989 (1984).

Myles, John. "Post-Industrialism and Alternative Futures." In *In the New Era of Global Competition: State Policy and Markets,* ed. D. and M. S. Gertzler Drache, 351 – 366. Montreal and Kingston: McGill-Queens University Press, 1991.

Myles, John. "Strutture sociali e politiche di welfare: prospettive per il Canada e gli Stati Uniti." In *Stato sociale e mercato mondiale,* ed. Maurizio Ferrera, 99 – 126. Torino, Italy: Edizioni della Fondazione Giovanni Agnelli, 1993.

Myles, John and Jill Quadagno. "The Politics of Income Security for the Elderly in Canada and the United States: Explaining the Difference." In *Economic Security for the Elderly: North American Perspectives,* ed. Theordore R. Marmor and Timothy M. Smeeding, 61 – 85. Washington: Urban Institute, 1994.

Myles, John and Jill Quadagno. "Recent Trends in Public Pension Reform: A Comparative View." Conference on Reform of the Retirement Income System, Queen's University, February 1 – 2, 1996.

Myrdal, Gunnar. *Beyond the Welfare State.* New Haven, CT: Yale University Press, 1960.

Myrdal, Hans-Goran. "The hard way from a centralized to a decentralized industrial relations system: The case of Sweden and SAF." In *Employers' Associations in Europe: Policy and Organization,* ed. Otto Jacobi and Dieter Sadowski. Baden-Baden: Nomos Verlag, 1991.

Nachmias, D. "The Role of Evaluation in Public Policy." *Policy Studies Journal* 8 (1980): 1163 – 1169.

National Center for State Courts. *State Court Caseload Statistics: Annual Report 1984.* Williamsburg, VA: National Center for State Courts, Court Statistics and Information Management Project, 1986.

National Commission on Excellence in Education. *A Nation at Risk: The Imperative for Educational Reform: A Report to the Nation and the Secretary of Education, United States Department of Education.* Washington, DC: The Commission [The Superintendent of Documents, U.S. Government Printing Office, distributor], 1983.

National Science Board. *Science and Engineering Indicators—1989.* Washington, DC: U.S. Government Printing Office, 1989.

National Science Foundation. *National Patterns of R & D Resources: 1989.* Final Report NSF 89 – 308. National Science Foundation, 1989.

National Science Foundation. *National Patterns of R&D Resources: 1990.* Final Report by J. E. Jankowski, NSF 90-316. Washington, DC, 1990.

Nee, Victor, Jimy M. Sanders, and Scott Sernau. "Job Transitions in an Immigrant Metropolis: Ethnic Boundaries and the Mixed Economy." *American Sociological Review* 59 (1994): 849 – 872.

Neely, Paul. "The Threats to Liberal Arts Colleges." *Daedalus* 128, 1 (Winter 1999): 27 – 45.

Nelson, Joan M. *Fragile Coalitions: The Politics of Economic Adjustment.* Washington, DC: Overseas Development Council, 1989a.

Nelson, Joan M. "Summaries of Chapter Recommendations." In *Fragile Coalitions: The Politics of Economic Adjustment,* ed. Joan M. Nelson, 27 – 36. Washington, DC: Overseas Development Council, 1989b.

Netzer, Dick. *Economics of the Property Tax.* Washington, DC: Brookings Institution, 1966.

Neuman, W. Russell. *The Future of the Mass Audience.* Cambridge: Cambridge University Press, 1991.

Neuman, W. Russell, Marion J. Just, and Ann N. Crigler. *Common Knowledge: News and the Construction of Meaning.* Chicago: University of Chicago Press, 1992.

Neumann, Franz L. *Behemoth: The Structure and Practice of National Socialism.* New York: Oxford University Press, 1942.

Nevitte, Neil, Richard Johnston, André Blais, Henry Brady, and Elisabeth Gidengil. "Electoral Discontinuity: The 1993 Canadian Federal Election." *International Social Science Journal* 47, 4 (1995): 583–600.

Newman, Katherine S. "Jobs for Welfare Moms?" *New York Times,* May 20, 1995.

Nick, Rainer and Anton Pelinka. *Österreichs politische Landschaft.* Innsbruck: Haymon Verlag, 1993.

Nie, Norman, Sidney Verba, and Jae-On Kim. "Participation and the Life-cycle." *Comparative Politics* 6, 3 (1974): 319–340.

Niemelä, Heikki and Kari Salminen. "State or Corporations: Trends of Pension Policy in Scandanavia." *Politiikka* 35, 4 (January 1994).

Niemelä, Heikki, Kari Salminen, and Jussi Vanamo. "Pensionssystemen i Norden—totalreform eller stegvis förnyelse." Helsinki: Pensionsskyddscentralen, 1993.

Niemelä, Heikki, Kari Salminen, and Jussi Venamo. "Converging Social Security Models? The Making of Social Security in Denmark, France, and the Netherlands." Social Security and Health Reports 10, The Social Insurance Institution, Helsinki, Finland, 1996.

Niemi, Richard G., Harold W. Stanley, and Ronald J. Vogel. "State Economies and State Taxes: Do Voters Hold Governors Accountable?" *American Journal of Political Science* 39, 4 (1995): 936–958.

Nightingale, Demetra Smith and Robert H. Haveman, eds. *The Work Alternative: Welfare Reform and the Realities of the Job Market.* Washington, DC: Urban Institute, 1995.

Nisbet, Robert A. *The Quest for Community.* New York: Oxford University Press, 1953.

Nishiguchi, Toshihiro. *Strategic Industrial Sourcing: The Japanese Advantage.* New York: Oxford University Press, 1994.

Noam, Eli. *Television in Europe.* Oxford: Oxford University Press, 1991.

Noiriel, Gérard. "Difficulties in French Historical Research on Immigration." In *Immigrants in Two Democracies: French and American Experience,* ed. Donald L. Horowitz and Gérard Noiriel, 66–79. New York: New York University Press, 1992.

Nolan, Brian and Christopher T. Whelan. *Resources, Deprivation, and Poverty.* Oxford: Clarendon Press, 1996.

Nonet, Philippe. *Administrative Justice: Advocacy and Change in a Government Agency.* New York: Russell Sage Foundation, 1969.

Nordhaus, William D. "Alternative Approaches to the Political Business Cycle." *Brookings Papers on Economic Activity* 2 (1989): 1–49.

Nørregaard, John and Jeffrey Owens. "Taxing Profits in a Global Economy." *The OECD Observer* 175 (1992): 35–38.

Norris, Donald F. and Lyke Thompson. "Findings and Lessons from the Politics of Welfare Reform." In *The Politics of Welfare Reform,* ed. Lyke Thompson and Donald F. Norris, 215–238. Thousand Oaks, CA: Sage, 1995.

Norsworthy, J. R., Michael J. Harper, and Kent Kunze. "The Slowdown in Productivity Growth: Analysis of Some Contributing Factors." *Brookings Papers on Economic Activity* 2 (1979): 387–421.

Norsworthy, J. R. and Craig A. Zabala. "Worker Attitudes, Worker Behavior, and Productivity in the U.S. Automobile Industry, 1959–1976." *Industrial and Labor Relations Review* 38 (1985): 544–557.

O'Connor, James. *The Fiscal Crisis of the State.* New York: St. Martin's Press, 1973.

O'Donnell, Guillermo and Philippe C. Schmitter. *Transitions from Authoritarian Rule: Tentative Conclusions about Uncertain Democracies.* Baltimore: Johns Hopkins University Press, 1986.

O'Donnell, Guillermo, Phillipe C. Schmitter, and Laurence Whitehead, eds. *Transitions from Authoritarian Rule: Comparative Perspectives.* Baltimore: Johns Hopkins University Press, 1986.

O'Hagan, John W. and Kevin M. Carey. "The Proposal for Upward Alignment of Tobacco Taxes in the European Community: A Critique." *British Tax Review* 8 (Aug. 1988): 329–348.

O'Sullivan, Arthur, Terri A. Sexton, and Steven M. Sheffrin. *The Future of Proposition 13 in California.* Berkeley: California Policy Seminar, University of California, 1993.

O'Sullivan, Arthur, Terri A. Sexton, and Steven M. Sheffrin. "Differential Burdens from the Assessment Provisions of Proposition 13." *National Tax Journal* 47, 4 (1994): 721–729.

Oberlander, Jonathan. "Remaking Medicare: the Voucher Myth." *International Journal of Health Services* 28, 1 (1998): 29–46.

OECD. *Revenue Statistics of OECD Member Countries 1965–1971.* Paris: OECD, 1973.

OECD. *Main Aggregates.* Vol. 1. National Accounts of OECD Countries, Paris: OECD, 1974.

OECD. *The Adjustment of Personal Income Tax Systems for Inflation.* Paris: OECD, 1976.

OECD. *Labor Force Statistics 1976–1977.* Paris: OECD, 1979.

OECD. *Measuring Health Care, 1960–1983: Expenditure, Costs and Performance.* Paris: OECD, 1985a.

OECD. *Social Expenditure 1960–1990: Problems of Growth and Control.* Paris: OECD, 1985b.

OECD. *Living Conditions in OECD Countries: A Compendium of Social Indicators.* Vol. OECD Social Policy Studies #3. Paris: OECD, 1986a.

OECD. *Personal Income Tax Systems Under Changing Economic Conditions.* Paris: OECD, 1986b.

OECD. *Employment Outlook.* Paris: OECD, 1987a.

OECD. *Financing and Delivering Health Care: A Comparative Analysis of OECD Countries.* Paris: OECD, 1987b.

OECD. *Economic Outlook.* Vol. 43. Paris: OECD, 1988a.

OECD. *Employment Outlook.* Vol. 43. Paris: OECD, 1988b.

OECD. *Education in OECD Countries 1986–1987: A Compendium of Statistical Information.* Paris: OECD, 1989a.

OECD. *Main Economic Indicators.* Paris: OECD, 1989b.

OECD. *Labour Market Flexibility: Trends in Enterprises.* Paris: OECD, 1989c.

OECD. *Health and Pension Reform in Japan.* Labour Market and Social Policy Occasional Papers. No. 2. Paris: OECD, 1990a.

OECD. *Education in OECD Countries 1987–88: A Compendium of Statistical Information.* Paris: OECD, 1990b.

OECD. *Main Economic Indicators.* Paris: OECD, 1990c.

OECD. *Netherlands: Reviews of National Policies for Education.* Paris: OECD, 1991a.

OECD. *The State of the Environment.* Paris: OECD, 1991b.

OECD. *Switzerland: Reviews of National Policies for Education.* Paris: OECD, 1991c.

OECD. *Revenue Statistics of OECD Member Countries 1965–1989.* Paris: OECD, 1991d.

OECD. *Agricultural Policies, Markets and Trade: Monitoring and Outlook 1992.* Paris: OECD, 1992a.

OECD. *Detailed Tables.* Vol. 2. National Accounts 1978–1990, Paris: OECD, 1992b.

OECD. *Main Economic Indicators.* Paris: OECD, 1992c.

OECD. *Economic Surveys: Ireland 1992–1993.* Paris: OECD, 1993a.

OECD. *Labour Force Statistics, 1971–1991.* Paris: OECD, 1993b.

OECD. *National Accounts Statistics of OECD Countries 1960–62, Volume 1: Main Aggregates.* Paris: OECD, 1993c.

OECD. *National Accounts, Volume 1: Main Aggregates, 1960–1991.* Paris: OECD, 1993d.

OECD. *OECD Economic Surveys 1992–1993: New Zealand.* Paris: OECD, 1993e.

OECD. *OECD Health Systems, Volume 1: Facts and Trends 1960–1991.* Health Policy Studies. No. 3. Paris: OECD, 1993f.

OECD. *The Reform of Health Care Systems: A Review of Seventeen OECD Countries.* Health Policy Studies. No. 5. Paris: OECD, 1994a.

OECD. *Main Aggregates 1960–1992.* Vol. 4. National Accounts, Paris: OECD, 1994b.

OECD. *Revenue Statistics of OECD Member Countries: A Standardized Classification, 1965–1993.* Paris: OECD, 1994c.

OECD. *Trends in Public Sector Pay: A Studey of Nine OECD Countries 1985–1990.* Public Management Occasional Papers, Series no. 1, Paris: OECD, 1994d.

OECD. *Employment Outlook.* Paris: OECD, 1994e.

OECD. *Revenue Statistics of OECD Member Countries: 1965–1994.* Paris: OECD, 1995.

OECD. *Employment Outlook.* July ed. Paris: OECD, 1996a.

OECD. *Health Care Reform: The Will to Change.* Vol. 8. Health Policy Studies, Paris: OECD, 1996b.

OECD. *OECD Economic Surveys: Canada 1995–96.* Paris: OECD, 1996c.

OECD. *Tax Expenditures: Recent Experiences.* Paris: OECD, 1996d.

OECD. *OECD in Figures: Statistics on the Member Countries.* Supplement to the *OECD Observer* 212 (June/July 1998).

OECD. *Agricultural Policies in OECD Countries: Monitoring and Evaluation.* Paris: OECD, 1999.

OECD. *Historical Statistics.* Paris: OECD, Various years.

Oeser, H. *Krebsbekaempfung: Hoffnung und Realitaet.* Stuttgart: Thieme, 1974.

Offe, Claus. *Strukturprobleme des kapitalistischen Staates.* Frankfurt am Main: Suhrkamp, 1972a.

Offe, Claus. "Political Authority and Class Structures: An Analysis of Late Capitalist Societies." *International Journal of Sociology* 2 (1972b): 73–108.

Offe, Claus. "The German Welfare State: Principles, Performances, and Prospects after Unification." Paper presented at a conference on "The Postwar Transformation of Germany," Center for German and European Studies, University of California, Berkeley, Nov. 30–Dec. 2, 1995.

Offe, Claus and Volker Ronge. "Theses on the Theory of the State." *New German Critique* 6 (1975): 137–147.

Ogburn, William F. and Meyer F. Nimkoff. *Technology and the Changing Family.* Boston, MA: Houghton Mifflin, 1955.

Okun, Arthur M. *Equality and Efficiency: The Big Trade-Off.* Washington, DC: Brookings Institution, 1975.

Oliver, Thomas R. "Analysis, Advice, and Congressional Leadership: The Physician Payment Review Commission and the Politics of Medicare." *Journal of Health Politics, Policy, and Law* 18, 1 (Spring 1993): 113–174.

Oliver, W. Hugh. "The Labour Caucus and Economic Policy Formation, 1981–1984." In *The Making of Rogernomics,* ed. Brian Easton, 11–52. Auckland: Auckland University Press, 1989.

Olsen, Gregg M. "Re-modeling Sweden: The Rise and Demise of the Compromise in a Global Economy." *Social Problems* 43, 1 (February 1996): 1–20.

Olsen, Marvin E. "Social Participation and Voting Turnout: A Multivariate Analysis." *American Sociological Review* 37 (June 1972): 317–333.

Olsen, Marvin E. "Interest Association Participation and Political Activity in the United States and Sweden." *Journal of Voluntary Action Research* 3, 3–4 (1974): 17–33.

Olson, Walter K. *The Litigation Explosion: What Happens When America Unleashed the Lawsuit.* New York: Truman Talley, 1991.

Olsson, Sven E. *Social Policy and Welfare State in Sweden.* Lund, Sweden: Arkiv, 1990.

"On Trial: The Legal Profession. A Survey." *The Economist,* July 18, 1992, 1–18.

Oppenheimer, Valerie Kincaide. *The Female Labor Force in the United States: Demographic and Economic Factors Governing Its Growth and Changing Composition.* UC-Berkeley Institute for International Studies, 1970.

Oppenheimer, Valerie Kincaide. "The Life-cycle Squeeze: The Interaction of Men's Occupational and Family Life Cycles." *Demography* 11 (1974): 227–246.

Orloff, Ann Shola and Theda Skocpol. " 'Why not Equal Protection?' Explaining the Politics of Public Spending in Britain, 1900–1911, and the United States, 1880s–1920." *American Sociological Review* 49, 6 (Dec. 1984): 726–750.

Ornstein, Norman. "Money in Politics: Campaign Finance Reform." *Current,* October 1992, 10–14.

Ornstein, Norman J. "Less Seems More: What to Do About Contemporary Political Corruption." *The Responsive Community* 4, 1 (1993/94): 7–22.

Ornstein, Norman J., Thomas E. Mann, Paul Taylor, Michael J. Malbin, and Anthony Corrado, Jr. "Five Ideas for Practical Campaign Reform." League of Women Voters Education Fund, July 21, 1997.

Ory, Marci G., Ronald P. Abeles, and Paula D. Lipman, ed. *Aging, Health, and Behavior.* London: Sage Publications, 1992.

Osterman, Paul. "Welfare Participation in a Full Employment Economy: The Impact of Neighborhood." *Social Problems* 38 (Nov. 1991): 475–491.

Osterman, Paul and Rosemary Batt. "Employer-Centered Training for International Competitiveness: Lessons from the State Programs." *Journal of Policy Analysis and Management* 12, 3 (1993): 456–477.

Overbye, Einar. "Convergence in Policy Outcomes: Social Security Systems in Perspective." *Journal of Public Policy* 14, 2 (1994): 147–174.

Overbye, Einar. "Explaining Welfare Spending." *Public Choice* 83 (1995): 313–335.

Overbye, Einar. "The New Zealand Pension System in an International Context: An Outsider's View." *Social Policy Journal of New Zealand* No. 6 (1996): 23–42.

Owens, John and Larry L. Wade. "Campaign Spending on California Ballot Propositions, 1924–1984: Trends and Voting Effects." *Western Political Quarterly* 39, 4 (1986): 675–689.

Page, Benjamin I. and Robert Y. Shapiro. *The Rational Public: Fifty Years of Trends in Americans' Policy Preferences.* Chicago: The University of Chicago Press, 1992.

Page, Benjamine I., Robert Y. Shapiro, and Glenn R. Dempsey. "What Makes Public Opinion?" *American Political Science Review* 81, 1 (1987): 23–43.

Paik, Haejung and George Comstock. "The Effects of Television Violence in Antisocial Behavior." *Communication Research* 21 (1994): 516–546.

Paldam, Martin. "Is There an Electional Cycle? A Comparative Study of National Accounts." *Scandinavian Journal of Economics* 81, 2 (1979): 323–342.

Palme, Joakim. *Pension Rights in Welfare Capitalism: The Development of Old-Age Pensions in 18 OECD Countries 1930 to 1985.* Report #14. Stockholm: Swedish Institute for Social Research, 1990.

Palme, Joakim and Irene Wennemo. *Swedish Social Security in the 1990s: Reform and Retrenchment.* Stockholm: Valfardsprojektat, Cabinet Office and Ministries, 1998.

Palmer, Gladys L. and Ann Miller. "The Occupational and Industrial Distribution of Employment, 1910–1950." In *Manpower in the United States,* ed. William Haber et al., 83–92. New York: Harper, 1954.

Pampel, Fred C. and John B. Williamson. *Age, Class, Politics, and the Welfare State.* ASA Rose Monograph Series, Cambridge, England: Cambridge University Press, 1992.

Papadopoulos, George. "Radical Reform for Swedish Education." *The OECD Observer* 181 (1993): 23–26.

Parai, Louis. *The Economic Impact of Immigration.* Ottawa: Department of Manpower and Immigration, Canadian Immigration and Population Study, 1974.

Parish, Henry J. *A History of Immunization.* Edinburgh: Livingstone, 1965.

Parisotto, Aurelio. "Direct Employment in Multi-national Enterprises in Industrialized and Developing Countries in the 1980s: Main Characteristics and Recent Trends." In *Multinationals and Employment: The Global Economy of the 1990s,* ed. Paul Bailey, Aurelio Parisotto, and Geoffrey Renshaw, 33 – 68. Geneva: International Labour Organization, 1993.

Park, Robert E., Ernest W. Burgess, Roderick D. McKenzie, and with bibliography by Lewis Wirth. *The City.* Chicago: Chicago University Press, 1925.

Parker, Kimberly Coursen. "How the Press Views Congress." In *Congress, the Press, and the Public,* ed. Thomas E. Mann and Norman J. Ornstein, 157 – 170. Washington, DC: American Enterprise Institute and Brookings Institution, 1994.

Parkinson, C. Northcote. *Parkinson's Law and Other Studies in Administration.* Boston, MA: Riverside Press, 1957.

Parsons, Talcott. *Essays in Sociological Theory Pure and Applied.* Glencoe, IL: Free Press, 1949.

Parsons, Talcott. *The Social System.* New York: Free Press, 1951.

Pascal, Anthony and Mark David Menchik. "Fiscal Containment: Who Gains? Who Loses?" In *Policy Studies Review Annual,* ed. Bertram H. Rauen, 292 – 302. Beverly Hills: Sage, 1980.

Passel, Jeffrey S. *Immigrants and Taxes: A Reappraisal of Huddle's "The Cost of Immigrants."* Program for Research on Immigration Policy, Washington, DC: Urban Institute, 1994.

Patrick, Donald L. and Pennifer Erickson. *Health Status and Health Policy: Quality of Life in Health Care Evaluation and Resource Allocation.* New York: Oxford University Press, 1993.

Patterson, Thomas E. *The Mass Media Election: How Americans Choose Their President.* New York: Praeger, 1980.

Patterson, Thomas E. *Out of Order.* New York: Vintage, 1993a.

Patterson, Thomas E. "Trust Politicians, Not the Media." *New York Times,* Dec. 15, 1993b, A19, Op-ed page.

Patterson, Thomas E. "Bad News, Period." *Political Science and Politics* 29, 1 (1996): 17 – 20.

Patterson, Thomas E. "Time and News: The Media's Limitations as an Instrument of Democracy." *International Political Science Review* 19, 1 (1998): 55 – 67.

Payer, Lynn. *Medicine and Culture: Varieties of Treatment in the United States, England, West Germany, and France.* New York: Henry Holt, 1988.

Pearce, Neil. "Traditional Epidemiology, Modern Epidemiology, and Public Health." *American Journal of Public Health* 86, 5 (1996): 678 – 683.

Pechman, Joseph A., ed. *Comparative Tax Systems: Europe, Canada, and Japan.* Arlington, VA: Tax Analysts, 1987.

Pedersen, Mogens N. "Dynamics of European Party Systems: Changing Patterns of Electoral Volatility." *European Journal of Political Research* 7, 1 (1979): 1 – 26.

Pempel, T. J. "Bureaucracy in Japan." *PS* 25, 1 (1992): 19 – 24.

Pempel, T. J. and K. Tsunekawa. "Corporatism Without Labor?" In *Trends Toward Corporatist Intermediation,* ed. Gerhard Lehmbruch and Philippe C. Schmitter, 231 – 270. Beverly Hills, CA: Sage, 1979.

Perlmann, Joel and Roger Waldinger. "Second Generation Decline? Children of Immigrants, Past and Present—A Reconsideration." *International Migration Review* 31, 4 (Winter 1997): 893 – 922.

Perrow, Charles. *Normal Accidents.* New York: Basic Books, 1984.

Perry, James L., Ann Marie Thomson, Mary Tschirrhart, Debra Mesch, and Geunjoo Lee. "Inside a Swiss Army Knife: An Assessment of AmeriCorps." *Journal of Public Administration Research and Theory* 9, 2 (April 1999): 225 – 250.

Persson, Torsten and Guido Tabellini. *Is Inequality Harmful for Growth? Theory and Evidence.* Working Paper 91 – 155. IBER, University of California, Berkeley, 1991.

Persson, Torsten and Guido Tabellini. "Growth, Distribution and Politics." In *Political Economy, Growth, and Business Cycles,* ed. Alex Cukierman, Zvi Hercowitz, and Leonardo Leiderman, 3–22. Cambridge, MA: MIT Press, 1992.

Pestoff, Victor A. *Voluntary Associations and Nordic Party Systems: A Study of Overlapping Memberships and Cross-Pressures in Finland, Norway, and Sweden.* University of Stockholm, Department of Political Science, 1977.

Peters, B. Guy. "Economic and Political Effects on the Development of Social Expenditures in France, Sweden, and the United Kingdom." *Midwest Journal of Political Science* 16 (1972): 225–238.

Peters, B. Guy. "Income Redistribution: A Longitudinal Analysis of France, Sweden, and the United Kingdom." *Political Studies* 22 (1974): 311–323.

Peters, B. Guy. *The Politics of Taxation: A Comparative Perspective.* Cambridge, MA: B. Blackwell, 1991.

Peterson, George E. "The Property Tax and Low-Income Housing Markets." In *Property Tax Reform,* ed. George E. Peterson, 107–124. Washington, DC: Urban Institute, 1973.

Peterson, Mark A. *Legislating Together: The White House and Capitol Hill from Eisenhower to Reagan.* Cambridge, MA: Harvard University Press, 1990.

Peterson, Mark A. "How Health Policy Information is Used in Congress." In *Intensive Care: How Congress Shapes Health Policy,* ed. Thomas E. Mann and Norman J. Ornstein, 79–125. Washington, DC: American Enterprise Institute and Brookings Institution, 1995.

Peterson, Paul E. and Mark C. Rom. *Welfare Magnets: A New Case for National Standards.* Washington, DC: Brookings Institution, 1990.

Petersson, Olof. "Democracy and Power in Sweden." *Scandinavian Political Studies* 14 (1991): 173–191.

Pettersen, Per Arnt. "Comparing Non-voters in the USA and Norway: Permanence Versus Transience." *European Journal of Political Research* 4, 17 (1989): 351–359.

Phaff, Martin and Walter Huber. "Disability Policy in the Federal Republic of Germany." In *Public Policy Toward Disabled Workers: Cross-National Analyses of Economic Impacts,* ed. Robert H. Haveman, Victor Halberstadt, and Richard V. Burkhauser, 193–239. Ithaca, NY: Cornell University Press, 1984.

Phillips, Roderick. *Putting Asunder: A History of Divorce in Western Society.* Cambridge: Cambridge University Press, 1988.

Pierson, Paul. *Dismantling the Welfare State? Reagan, Thatcher and the Politics of Retrenchment.* Cambridge: Cambridge University Press, 1994.

Pierson, Paul E. and Mark C. Rom. *Welfare Magnets: A New Case for a National Standard.* Washington, DC: Brookings Institution, 1990.

Pil, Frits K. and John Paul MacDuffie. "Japanese and Local Influences on the Transfer of Work Practices at Japanese Transplants." Paper presented at the 48th Annual Meeting of the Industrial Relations Research Association in San Francisco, January 5–7, 1996.

Piore, Michael J. and Charles F. Sabel. *The Second Industrial Divide: Possibilities for Prosperity.* New York: Basic Books, 1984.

Platt, Tony. "U.S. Criminal Justice in the Reagan Era: An Assessment." *Crime and Social Justice* 29 (1987): 58–69.

Pleck, Joseph H. *Working Wives/Working Husbands.* Beverly Hills, CA: Sage Publications, 1985.

Pollack, Ron. "Eleven Lessons from Canada's Health Care System." In *Looking North for Health: What We Can Learn from Canada's Health Care System,* ed. Arnold Bennet and Orville Adams, 142–176. San Francisco, CA: Jossey-Bass, 1993.

Polsby, Nelson W. *Consequences of Party Reform.* New York: Oxford University Press, 1983.

Polsby, Nelson W. *Political Innovation in America: The Politics of Policy Initiation.* New Haven, CT: Yale University Press, 1984.

Polsby, Nelson W. and Aaron Wildavsky. *Presidential Elections: Strategies and Structures in American Politics.* 9th ed. Chatham, NJ: Chatham House, 1996.

Pontusson, Jonas and Peter Swenson. "Labor Markets, Production Strategies, and Wage Bargaining Institutions: The Swedish Employer Offensive in Comparative Perspective." *Comparative Political Studies* 29 (April 1996): 223–250.

Popenoe, David. "Beyond the Nuclear Family: A Statistical Portrait of the Changing Family in Sweden." *Journal of Marriage and the Family* 49 (1987): 173–183.

Popenoe, David. "American Family Decline 1960–1990: A Review and Appraisal." *Journal of Marriage and the Family* 55 (1993): 527–555.

Popkin, Samuel. "When the People Decline to be Spun." *New York Times,* November 10, 1998, A31.

Portes, Alejandro and Leif Jensen. "Disproving the Enclave Hypothesis." *American Sociological Review* 57 (June 1992): 418–420.

Portes, Alejandro and Richard Schauffler. "Language Acquisition and Loss Among Children of Immigrants." In *Origins and Destinies: Immigration, Race and Ethnicity in America,* ed. Silvia Pedraza and Ruben G. Rumbaut, 432–443. Belmont, CA: Wadsworth, 1996.

Posen, Adam S. *Restoring Japan's Economic Growth.* Washington, DC: Institute for International Economics, 1998.

Postlethwaite, T. Neville, and R. Murray Thomas. "Country Comparisons and Future Prospects." In *Schooling in East Asia: Forces of Change,* ed. R. Murray Thomas and T. Neville Postlethwaite, 308–342. Oxford: Pergamon Press, 1983.

Potter, Joseph E. "Explanation of Fertility Decline in Latin America." *Items* 40, 2 (1986): 31–36.

Poullier, Jean-Pierre. "Administrative Costs in Selected Industrialized Countries." *Health Care Financing Review* 13, 4 (1992): 167–172.

Powell, G. Bingham, Jr. "Voting Turnout in Thirty Democracies: Partisan, Legal, and Socio-Economic Influences." In *Electoral Participation: A Comparative Analysis,* ed. Richard Rose, 5–34. Beverly Hills, CA: Sage, 1980.

Powell, Lawrence N. "Slouching Toward Baton Rouge: The 1989 Legislative Election of David Duke." In *The Emergence of David Duke and the Politics of Race,* ed. Douglas Rose, 12–40. Chapel Hill: The University of North Carolina Press, 1992.

Powell, Margaret and Masahira Anesaki. *Health Care in Japan.* London and New York: Routledge, 1990.

Powell, Walter W. and Paul J. DiMaggio. "Introduction." In *The New Institutionalism in Organizational Analysis,* ed. Walter W. Powell and Paul J. DiMaggio, 1–38. Chicago: University of Chicago Press, 1991.

Powles, John. "On the Limitations of Modern Medicine." *Science, Medicine and Man* 1, 1 (1973): 1–30.

Presser, Harriet B. "Job, Family, and Gender: Determinants of Nonstandard Work Schedules Among Employed Americans in 1991." *Demography* 32, 4 (1995): 577–598.

Presser, Harriet B. "Toward a 24-Hour Economy." *Science* 284 (1999): 1778–1779.

Presser, Harriet B. and Amy G. Cox. "The Work Schedules of Low-Educated American Women and Welfare Reform." *Monthly Labor Review* 120 (April 1997): 25–34.

Presser, Stanley and Linda Stinson. "Data Collection Mode and Social Desirability Bias in Self-Reported Religions Attendance." *American Sociological Review* 63 (Feb. 1998): 137–145.

Price, Daniel O. *Changing Characteristics of the Negro Population.* U.S. Census, 1969. A 1960 Census Monograph.

Prime Minister's Office, Tokyo, Japan. *The U.N. Decade for Women and the Women of Japan.* Prime Minister's Office, 1985.

Protess, David L., Fay Lomax Cook, Jack C. Doppelt, James S. Ettema, and Margaret T. Gordon. *The Journalism of Outrage: Investigative Reporting and Agenda Building in America.* New York: Guilford, 1991.

Pryor, Frederick. *Public Expenditure in Capitalist and Communist Nations.* Homewood, IL: Richard D. Irwin, 1968.

Przeworski, Adam. *Democracy and the Market: Political and Economic Reforms in Eastern Europe and Latin America.* Cambridge: Cambridge University Press, 1991.

Purcell, John. "The End of Institutional Industrial Relations." *Political Quarterly* 64, 1 (1993): 6–23.

Putnam, Robert D. "The Strange Disappearance of Civic America." *The American Prospect* No. 24 (1996): 34–48.

Putnam, Robert D. "Tuning In, Tuning Out: The Strange Disappearance of Social Capital in America." *PS: Political Science and Politics* 28, 4 (1995a): 664–683.

Putnam, Robert D. "Bowling Alone, Revisited." *The Responsive Community* 5, 2 (1995b): 18–33.

Putnam, Robert D. "Bowling Alone: America's Declining Social Capital." *Journal of Democracy* 6, 1 (1995c): 65–78.

Putnam, Robert D. with Robert Leonardi and Raffaella Y. Nanetti. "Institutional Performance and Political Culture: Some Puzzles about the Power of the Past." *Governance* 1 (1988): 221–242.

Putnam, Robert D. with Robert Leonardi and Raffaella Y. Nanetti. *Making Democracy Work: Civic Traditions in Modern Italy.* Princeton, NJ: Princeton University Press, 1993.

Questiaux, Nicole and Jacques Fournier. "France." In *Family Policy: Government and Families in Fourteen Countries,* ed. Sheila B. Kamerman and Alfred J. Kahn, 117–182. New York: Columbia University Press, 1978.

Quillian, Lincoln. "Prejudice as a Response to Perceived Group Threat: Population Composition and Anti-Immigrant and Racial Prejudice in Europe." *American Sociological Review* 60 (1995): 586–611.

Rabin, Robert and Stephen Sugarman, eds. *Smoking Policy: Law, Politics and Culture.* New York: Oxford University Press, 1993.

Rae, Douglas. *Equalities.* Cambridge, MA: Harvard University Press, 1981.

Raffle, P. A. B., P. H. Adams, P. J. Baxter, and W. R. Lee. *Hunter's Diseases of Occupations.* London: Edward Arnold Publishers, 1994.

Rainwater, Lee. Table 5, "Living Levels of Children in 2-Parent Families," and Table 6, "Living Levels of Children Under 18 in Solo Mother Families." Luxembourg Income Study, 1994. Unpublished Tabulations.

Rainwater, Lee and Martin Rein. "The Economic Well-Being of Older Men in Six Countries." In *Age, Work, and Social Security,* ed. A. B Atkinson and Martin Rein, 115–131. New York: St. Martin's Press, 1993.

Rainwater, Lee, Martin Rein, and Joseph Schwartz. *Income Packaging in the Welfare State: A Comparative Study of Family Income.* Oxford: Clarendon Press, 1986.

Rassmussen, David W. and Bruce L. Benson. *The Economic Anatomy of a Drug War: Justice in the Commons.* Lanham, MD: Rowman and Littlefield, 1994.

Reder, Melvin and Lloyd Ulman. "Unionism and Unification." In *Labor and an Integrated Europe,* ed. Lloyd Ulman, Barry Eichengreen, and William T. Dickens, 13–44. Washington, DC: Brookings Institution, 1993.

Regalia, Ida, Marino Regini, and Emilio Reyneri. "Labour Conflicts and Industrial Relations in Italy." In *The Resurgence of Class Conflict in Western Europe Since 1968, Volume I,* ed. Colin Crouch and Alessandro Pizzorno, 101–158. 1. London: Macmillan, 1978.

Regini, Marino. "Labour Unions, Industrial Actions and Politics." *West European Politics* 2. 3 (1979): 49–66.

Regini, Marino. "Changing Relationships between Labour and the State in Italy: Towards a Neo-Corporatist System?" In *Patterns of Corporatist Policy-Making,* ed. Gerhard Lehmbruch and Philippe Schmitter, 109–132. London: Sage, 1982.

Regini, Marino. "The Conditions for Political Exchange: How Concertation Emerged and Collapsed in Italy and Great Britain." In *Order and Conflict in Contemporary Capitalism,* ed. John Goldthorpe, 124–142. Oxford, England: Oxford University Press, 1984.

Regini, Marino. "Political Bargaining in Western Europe during the Economic Crisis of the 1980s." In *Economic Crisis, Trade Unions and the State,* ed. O. Jacobi, B. Jessop, H. Kanstendiek, and M. Regini, 61–76. London: Croom Helm, 1986.

Regini, Marino. "Industrial Relations in the Phase of "Flexibility"." *International Journal of Political Economy* 17, 3 (1987a): 88–107.

Regini, Marino. "Social Pacts in Italy." In *Political Stability and Neo-Corporatism,* ed. Ilja Scholten, 195–215. London: Sage, 1987b.

Regini, Marino. "Employer's Reactions to the Productivity Drive: The Search for Labour Consensus." *Labour* 6, 2 (1992): 31–47.

Regini, Marino. "Firms and Institutions: The Demand for Skills and Their Social Production in Europe." *European Journal of Industrial Relations* 1, 2 (1995): 191–202.

Regini, Marino. "Still Engaging in Corporatism? Recent Italian Experience in Comparative Perspective." *European Journal of Industrial Relations* 3, 3 (1997): 259–278.

Regini, Marino and Gosta Esping-Anderson. "Trade Union Strategies and Social Policy in Italy and Sweden." *West European Politics* 3, 1 (1980): 107–123.

Reichly, James A. *Religion in American Public Life.* Washington, DC: Brookings Institution, 1985.

Rein, Martin. "Social Class and the Utilization of Medical Care Service." *Journal of American Hospital Association* 3 (July 1969): 43–54.

Rein, Martin, ed. *The Social Welfare Labour Market.* The Welfare State and Its Aftermath. London: Croom Helm in association with the Jerusalem Institute for Israel Studies, 1985.

Reinhardt, Uwe E. "Can America Afford Its Elderly Citizens? Thoughts on the Political Economy of Sharing." In *Policy Options for Reforming the Medicare Program,* ed. Stuart H. Altman, Uwe E. Reinhardt, and David Shactman, 171–199. Princeton, NJ: Robert Wood Johnson Foundation,1997.

Reiss, Albert J., Jr. "Rural-Urban and Status Difference in Interpersonal Contacts." *American Journal of Sociology* 65, 2 (1959): 182–195.

Reiss, Albert J., Jr., and Jeffrey A. Roth, eds. *Understanding and Preventing Violence.* Washington, DC: National Academy Press, 1993.

Reiter, Howard L. "Party Decline in the West: A Skeptic's View." *Journal of Theoretical Politics* 1, 3 (1989): 325–348.

Relman, Arnold S. "What Market Values Are Doing to Medicine." *The Atlantic Monthly* 269, 3 (1992): 99–106.

Relman, Arnold S. "Dr. Business." *The American Prospect* No. 34 (1997): 91–95.

Reubens, Beatrice. *The Hard to Employ: European Programs.* New York: Columbia University Press, 1970.

Ribicoff, Abe. "He Left at Half-Time." *New Republic* 168, 17 (February 1973): 22–26.

Riccio, James, Daniel Friedlander, and Stephen Freedman. *GAIN: Benefits, Costs, and Three-Year Impacts of a Welfare-to-Work Program: California's Greater Avenues for Independence Program.* Manpower Demonstration Research Corporation, 1994.

Richardson, J. J. "Programme Evaluation in Britain and Sweden." *Parliamentary Affairs* 35 (1982): 160–180.

Ridley, Frederick and Jean Blondel. *Public Administration in France.* 2nd ed. London: Routledge & Kegan Paul, 1969.

Riesman, David in collaboration with Reuel Denney and Nathan Glazer. *The Lonely Crowd: A Study of the Changing American Character.* New Haven, CT: Yale University Press, 1950.

Riesman, David, Joseph Gusfield, and Zelda Gamson. *Academic Values and Mass Education: The Early Years at Oakland and Monteith.* Garden City, NY: Anchor Books, 1971.

Riggs, Fred W. "Ethnonational Rebellions and Viable Constitutionalism." *International Political Science Review* 16, 4 (1995): 375–404.

Riley, Margaret and Anne Foner. *Aging and Society*. Vol. 1. *An Inventory of Research Findings*. New York: Russell Sage Foundation, 1968.

Rimlinger, G. *Welfare Policy and Industrialization in Europe, America, and Russia*. New York: Wiley, 1971.

Rix, Sara E. and Paul Fisher. *Retirement Age Policy: An International Perspective*. New York: Pergamon Press, 1982.

Roberts, Donald F. and Nathan Maccoby. "Effects of Mass Communication." In *The Handbook of Social Psychology*, ed. Gardner Lindzey and Elliot Aronson, 539–598. New York: Random House, 1985.

Roberts, Michael, Peggy Hite, and Cassie Bradley. "Understanding Attitudes Toward Progressive Taxation." *Public Opinion Quarterly* 58, 2 (1994): 165–190.

Robillard, Serge. *Television in Europe: Regulatory Bodies, Status, Functions, and Powers in 35 European Countries*. London: European Institute for the Media, 1995.

Robinson, James C. "Payment Mechanisms, Nonprice Incentives, and Organizational Innovation in Health Care." *Inquiry* 30, 3 (1993): 328–333.

Robinson, James C. "Consolidation of Medical Groups into Physician Practice Management Organizations." *Journal of the American Medical Association* 279, 2 (January 1998): 144–149.

Robinson, James C. and Lawrence P. Casalino. "Vertical Integration and Organizational Networks in Health Care." *Health Affairs* 15, 1 (1996): 205–219.

Robinson, John P. *How Americans Use Time*. New York: Praeger, 1977.

Robinson, John P. "The Changing Reading Habits of the American Public." *Journal of Communication* 30, 1 (1980): 141–152.

Robinson, John P. and Edward L. Fink. "Beyond Mass Culture and Class Culture: Subcultural Differences in the Structure of Music Preferences." In *Media, Audience, and Social Structure*, ed. Sandra Ball-Rokeach and Muriel G. Cantor, 226–239. Newbury Park, CA: Sage, 1986.

Robinson, Michael J. "Public Affairs Television and the Growth of Political Malaise: the case of the selling of the Pentagon." *American Political Science Review* 702. (1976): 409–432.

Robinson, Michael J. "Television and American Politics: 1956–76." *Public Interest* 48 (Summer 1977): 3–39.

Roche, Bill. "Social Partnership and Political Control: State Strategy and Industrial Relations in Ireland." In *Power, Conflict and Inequality*, ed. Mary Kelly, Liam O'Dowd, and James Wickham, 44–67. Dublin: Turoe Press, 1982.

Rochlin, Gene. *Trapped in the Net: The Unanticipated Consequences of Computerization*. Princeton, NJ: Princeton University Press, 1997.

Roemer, John E. "Political Cycles." *Economics and Politics* 7, 1 (1995): 1–20.

Roemer, Milton and Max Shain. *Hospital Utilization Under Insurance*. Vol. 6. Hospital Monograph Series. Chicago: American Hospital Association, 1959.

Roemer, Milton I. *National Health Systems of the World*. Vols. 1, 2. New York: Oxford University Press, 1991.

Roemer, Ruth. *Legislative Action to Combat the World Tobacco Epidemic*. 2nd ed. Geneva: World Health Organization, 1993.

Roethlisberger, Fritz J. and William J. Dickson. *Management and Worker*. Cambridge: Harvard University Press, 1939.

Rogers, David. "The Automobile Dealer: A Study of the Status and Ideology of the Small Businessman." Ph.D. dissertation, Harvard University, 1960.

Rogers, David L., Gordon L. Bultena, and Ken H. Barb. "Voluntary Association Membership and Political Participation: An Exploration of the Mobilization Hypothesis." *The Sociological Quarterly* 16 (Summer 1975): 305–318.

Rogers, Joel. "Divide and Conquer: Further Reflections on the Distictive Character of American Labor Laws." *Wisconsin Law Review* 1990, 1 (1990): 1–147.

Rogoff, Natalie. *Recent Trends in Social Mobility.* Glencoe, IL: Free Press, 1953.

Rohde, David W. *Parties and Leaders in the Postreform House.* Chicago: University of Chicago Press, 1991.

Rohlen, Thomas P. *Japan's High Schools.* Berkeley: University of California Press, 1983.

Rohlen, Thomas P. "Japanese Education: If They Can Do It, Should We?" *The American Scholar* 55 (1985/86): 29–43.

Rohrschneider, Robert. "Impact of Social Movements on European Party Systems." *Annals, American Academy of Political and Social Science* 528 (1993a): 157–170.

Rohrschneider, Robert. "New Party versus Old Left Realignments: Environmental Attitudes, Party Policies, and Partisan Affiliations in Four West European Countries." *Journal of Politics* 55, 3 (1993b): 682–701.

Rokkan, Stein. *Citizens, Elections, Parties.* Oslo: Universitetsforlaget, 1970.

Rokkan, Stein and Angus Campbell. "Citizen Participation in Political Life: Norway and the United States." *International Social Science Journal* 12, 1 (1960): 69–99.

Rollén, Berit. "Gently Towards Equality." *Working Life [Swedish Information Service, New York, NY]* 5 (1978): 1–4.

Romer, Christina D. and David H. Romer. "Does Monetary Policy Matter? A New Test in the Spirit of Friedman and Schwartz." *NBER Macroeconomics Annual 1989* (1989): 121–170.

Romer, Christina D. and David H. Romer. "What Ends Recessions?" *NBER Macroeconomics Annual* 9 (1994): 13–57.

Romer, Paul M. "Increasing Returns and Long-Run Growth." *Journal of Political Economy* 94 (1986): 1002–1037.

Room, Graham. "Towards a European Welfare State?" In *Towards a European Welfare State?,* ed. Graham Room, 1–14. Bristol, England: School for Advanced Urban Studies, 1991.

Rose, Douglas D. and Gary Esolen. "DuKKKe for Governor: 'Vote for the Crook. It's Important.' " In *The Emergence of David Duke and the Politics of Race,* ed. Douglas Rose, 197–241. Chapel Hill: University of North Carolina Press, 1992.

Rose, Richard, ed. *Electoral Participation: A Comparative Analysis.* Beverly Hills, CA: Sage, 1980.

Rose, Richard. *Understanding Big Government: The Program Approach.* London: Sage, 1984.

Rose, Richard and Guy Peters. *Can Government Go Bankrupt?* New York: Basic Books, 1978.

Rose, Richard D., ed. *Public Employment in Western Nations.* Cambridge: Cambridge University Press, 1985a.

Rose, Richard D. "The Significance of Public Employment." In *Public Employment in Western Nations,* ed. Richard D. Rose, 1–53. Cambridge: Cambridge University Press, 1985b.

Rosenberg, Charles E. *The Cholera Years: The United States in 1832, 1849 and 1866.* Chicago: University of Chicago Press, 1962.

Rosenberg, Nathan and L. E. Birdzell, Jr. *How the West Grew Rich.* New York: Basic Books, 1986.

Rosenfeld, Stuart A. *Competitive Manufacturing: New Strategies for Regional Development.* New Brunswick, NJ: Center for Urban Policy Research, 1992.

Rosenheim, Margaret K. "Teenage Parenthood: Policies and and Perspectives." In *Early Parenthood and Coming of Age in the 1990s,* ed. Margaret K. Rosenheim and Mark F. Testa, 200–226. New Brunswick: Rutgers University Press, 1992.

Rosenstone, Steven J. and John Mark Hansen. *Mobilization, Participation, and Democracy in America.* New York: Macmillan, 1993.

Rosenthal, Andrew. "Foes Accuse Bush Campaign of Inflaming Racial Tension." *New York Times,* October 24, 1988, A1, column 1; B5, column 1.

Rosenthal, Marilynn and Marcell Frenkel, eds. *Health Care Systems and Their Patients.* Boulder, CO: Westview Press, 1992.

Rossi, Peter Henry. *Down and Out in America: The Origins of Homelessness.* Chicago: Chicago University Press, 1989.

Rossi, Peter H., James D. Wright, Eleanor Weber-Burdin, and Joseph Pereira. *Victims of the Environment: Loss from Natural Hazards in the United States, 1970–1980.* New York: Plenum Press, 1983.

Rovati, Giancarlo. "Political Localism and National Identity in Italy: The Case of Regional Leagues." *Innovation* 5, 2 (1992): 69–76.

Roy, Donald. "Quota Restriction and Goldbricking in a Machine Shop." *American Journal of Sociology* 57 (March 1952): 427–442.

Rubinow, Isaac Max. *Social Insurance with Special Reference to American Conditions.* New York: Holt, 1913.

Rubinow, Isaac Max. *Standards of Health Insurance.* New York: Holt, 1916.

Rubinow, Isaac Max. *The Quest for Social Security.* New York: Holt, 1934.

Rüegg, Bernard. "La politique de choix des fonctionnaires en Suisse." In *La fonction publique en Europe: la politique de choix des fonctionnaires dans les pays européens,* ed. Charles Debbasch, 257–267. Paris: CNRS, 1981.

Rueschemeyer, Dietrich, Evelyne Huber Stephens, and John D. Stephens. *Capitalist Development and Democracy.* Chicago: University of Chicago Press, 1992.

Ruffieux, Roland. "The Political Influence of Senior Civil Servants in Switzerland." In *The Manderins of Western Europe: The Political Role of Top Civil Servants,* ed. Mattei Dogan, 238–251. New York: Sage, 1975.

Ruggie, Mary. "The Paradox of Liberal Intervention: Health Policy and the American Welfare State." *American Journal of Sociology* 97, 4 (1992): 919–944.

Rule, Wilma. "Electoral Systems, Contextual Factors, and Women's Opportunity for Election to Parliament in Twenty-Three Democracies." *Western Political Quarterly* 40 (September 1987): 477–498.

"Ruling Coalition Wins National Vote." *Facts on File* 55 (2865 1995b): 804–805.

Rumbaut, Ruben G. "Ties That Bind: Immigration and Immigrant Families in the United States." In *Immigration and the Family: Research and Policy on U.S. Immigrants,* ed. Alan Booth, Ann C. Crouter, and Nancy Landale, 3–46. Mahwah, NJ: Erlbaum, 1997.

Russell, Louise B. *Is Prevention Better Than Cure?* Washington, DC: Brookings Institution, 1986.

Russell, Louise, B. *Educated Guesses: Making Policy About Medical Screening Tests.* Berkeley: University of California Press, 1994.

Rydell, C. Peter and Susan S. Everingham. *Controlling Cocaine: Supply vs. Demand Programs.* Santa Monica: RAND, 1994.

Ryder, Norman B. "What Is Going to Happen to American Fertility?" *Population and Development Review* 16, 3 (1990): 433–454.

Sabato, Larry. *Feeding Frenzy: How Attack Journalism Has Transformed American Politics.* New York: Free Press, 1991.

Saffran, William. *The French Polity.* 2nd ed. New York and London: Longman, 1985.

Sagawa, Shirley and Samuel Halperin, eds. *Visions of Service: The Future of the National and Community Service Act.* Washington, DC: National Women's Law Center and American Youth Policy Forum, 1993.

Sah-Myung, Hong. "The Republic of Korea (South Korea)." In *Schooling in East Asia: Forces of Change,* ed. R. Murray Thomas and T. Neville Postlethwaite, 205–235. Oxford, England: Pergamon Press, 1983.

Sahr, Robert. "Credentialing Experts: The Climate of Opinion and Journalist Selection of Sources in Domestic and Foreign Policy." In *Media and Public Policy,* ed. Robert J. Spitzer, 153–169. Westport: Praeger, 1993.

Salamon, Lester M. *Partners in Public Service: Government-Nonprofit Relations in the Modern Welfare State.* Baltimore: Johns Hopkins University Press, 1995.

Salamon, Lester M. *America's Nonprofit Sector: A Primer.* 2nd ed. N.p.: The Foundation Center, 1999a.

Salamon, Lester M. "Government-Nonprofit Relations in International Perspective." In *Nonprofits and Government: Collaboration and Conflict,* ed. Elizabeth T. Boris and C. Eugene Steuerle, 329–367. Washington, DC: Urban Institute Press, 1999b.

Salminen, Kari. *Pension Schemes in the Making: A Comparative Study of the Scandinavian Countries.* Helsinki: Central Pension Security Institute, 1993.

Sampson, Robert J. and John H. Laub. *Crime in the Making: Pathways and Turning Points through Life.* Cambridge, MA: Harvard University Press, 1993.

Sampson, Robert J. and John H. Laub. "Socioeconomic Achievement in the Life Course of Disadvantaged Men: Military Service as a Turning Point, Circa 1940–1965." *American Sociological Review* 61 (June 1996): 347–367.

Sandefur, Gary and Tom Wells. *Trends in AFDC Participation Rates: The Implications for Welfare Reform.* Discussion Paper No. 1116–96. Institute for Research on Poverty, University of Wisconsin, Madison, 1996.

Sander, Richard H. and E. Douglass Williams. "Why Are There So Many Lawyers? Perspectives on a Turbulent Market." *Law and Social Inquiry* 14, no. 3 (1989): 431–479.

Sanders, Arthur. "Rationality, Self-Interest, and Public Attitudes on Public Spending Issues." *Social Science Quarterly* 69 (1988): 311–324.

Sanders, Joseph. "The Meaning of the Law Explosion: on Friedman's *Total Justice*." *American Bar Foundation Research Journal* 2, 3 (1987): 601–615.

Saraceno, Chiara and Nicola Negri. "The Changing Italian Welfare State." *Journal of European Social Policy* 4, 1 (1994): 19–34.

Sassen, Saskia. *The Mobility of Capital and Labor: A Study in International Investment and Labor Flow.* Cambridge: Cambridge University Press, 1988.

Saunders, Peter. "Rising on the Tasman Tide: Income Inequality in the 1980s." Discussion Paper #49, Social Policy Research Centre, the University of New South Wales, June 1994.

Saunders, Peter, Timothy J. Smeeding, et al. "Noncash Income, Living Standards and Inequality: Evidence from the Luxembourg Income Study." Final version for publication in IEA Proceedings Volume: November 1992, International Economics Association, Moscow, Russia, CIS, 1992.

Sauvant, Karl P., Padma Mallampally, and Persephone Economou. "Foreign Direct Investment and International Migration." *Transnational Corporations* 2, 1 (1993): 33–69.

Sawhill, Isabel V., ed. *Welfare Reform: An Analysis of the Issues.* Washington, DC: Urban Institute, 1995.

Scarr, Sandra. "Child Care Research, Social Values, and Public Policy." *Bulletin of the American Academy of Arts and Sciences* 50, 1 (1996): 28–45.

Schafer, Byron, ed. *Is America Different? A New Look at American Exceptionalism.* Oxford: Clarendon Press, 1991.

Schandl, Franz and Gerhard Schattauer. *Die Grünen in Österreich: Entwicklung und Konsolidierung einer politischen Kraft.* Vienna: Pro-Media, 1996.

Scharpf, Fritz W. "Economic and Institutional Constraints of Full-Employment Strategies: Sweden, Austria, and Western Germany, 1973–1982." In *Order and Conflict in Contemporary Capitalism,* ed. John H. Goldthorpe, 257–290. Oxford: Clarendon Press, 1984.

Scharpf, Fritz W. "A Game-Theoretical Interpretation of Inflation and Unemployment in Western Europe." *Journal of Public Policy* 7, 3 (1987): 227–257.

Scheuch, Erwin K. and Ute Scheuch. "Abkehr von den Parteien? Dimensionen des Parteiverdrusses." In *Krise der Institutionen,* ed. Eduard J. M. Kroker and Bruno Dechamps, 63–81. Frankfurt: Frankfurt Allgemeine, 1997.

Schieber, George J., Jean-Pierre Poullier, and Leslie M. Greenwald. "U.S. Health Expenditure Performance: An International Comparison and Data Update." *Health Care Financing Review* 13, 4 (1992): 1–87.

Schmid, Günther. "Equality and Efficiency in the Labour Market: Towards a Socio-Economic Theory of Cooperation in the Context of a Globalizing Economy." Discussion Paper FS I 92–1.Wissenschaftszentrum Berlin für Sozialforschung (WZB); Research Area Labour Market and Employment, 1992.

Schmid, Günther, ed. *Labor Market Institutions in Europe: A Socioeconomic Evaluation of Performance.* Armonk, NY: M. E. Sharpe, 1994.

Schmid, Günther, Bernd Reissert, and Gert Bruche. *Unemployment Insurance and Active Labor Market Policy: An International Comparison of Financing Systems.* Detroit, MI: Wayne State University Press, 1992.

Schmid, Günther and Klaus Schomann. "Institutional Choice and Flexible Coordination: A Socioeconomic Evaluation of Labor Market Policy in Europe." In *Labor Market Institutions in Europe: A Socioeconomic Evaluation of Performance,* ed. Günther Schmid, 9–58. Armonk, NY: M. E. Sharpe, 1994.

Schmidt, Manfred G. "Does Corporatism Matter? Economic Crisis, Politics and Rates of Unemployment in Capitalist Democracies in the 1970s." In *Patterns of Corporatist Policy-Making,* ed. Gerhard Lehmbruch and Phillipe C. Schmitter, 237–258. Beverly Hills: Sage, 1982.

Schmitter, Philippe. "Still the Century of Corporatism?" In *The New Corporatism: Social-Political Structures in the Iberian World,* ed. F. B. and T. Stritch Pike, 85–131. Notre Dame, IN: University of Notre Dame Press, 1974.

Schmitter, Philippe. "Interest Intermediation and Regime Governability in Contemporary Western Europe and North America." In *Organizing Interests in Western Europe: Pluralism, Corporatism, and the Transformation of Politics,* ed. Suzanne Berger, 287–327. Cambridge: Cambridge University Press, 1981.

Scholz, John Karl. "The Earned Income Tax Credit: Participation, Compliance, and Antipoverty Effectiveness." *National Tax Journal* 47, 1 (1994): 63–87.

Schor, Juliet B. *The Overworked American: The Unexpected Decline of Leisure.* New York: Basic Books, 1991.

Schrag, Peter. "The Populist Road to Hell: Term Limits in California." *The American Prospect* No. 24 (1996): 24–30.

Schulten, Thorsten. "European Works Councils: Prospects for a New System of European Industrial Relations." *European Journal of Industrial Relations* 2, 3 (1996): 303–324.

Schultz, Theodore W. *Investment in Human Capital: The Role of Education and of Research.* New York: Free Press, 1971.

Schultze, Charles L. "Of Wolves, Termites, and Pussycats: or, Why We Should Worry about the Budget Deficit." *Brookings Review* 7, 3 (1989): 26–33.

Schuman, Howard and Cheryl Rieger. "Historical Analogies, Generational Effects, and Attitudes Toward War." *American Sociological Review* 57 (1992): 315–326.

Schumpeter, Joseph A. *Capitalism, Socialism, and Democracy.* New York: Harper and Brothers, 1942.

Schumpeter, Joseph A. "The Crisis of the Tax State." *International Economic Papers* No. 4 (1954 [1918]): 5–38.

Schweinhart, L. J. and D. P. Weikart. *Young Children Grow Up: The Effects of the Perry Preschool Program on Youths Through Age 15.* Ypsilanti, MI: The High/Scope Press, 1980.

Schweizerische Nationalbank. *Das Schweizerische Bankwesen im Jahre 1992.* Vol. 77. Zürich, Switzerland: Schweizerische Nationalbank, 1993.

Scitovsky, Tibor. *The Joyless Economy: The Psychology of Human Satisfaction.* Revised ed. New York: Oxford University Press, 1992.

Scott, Franklin D. *Sweden: The Nation's History.* Carbondale: Southern Illinois Press, 1988.

Scott, Joan W. and Louise A. Tilly. "Women's Work and the Family in Nineteenth-Century Europe." *Comparative Studies in Society and History* 17 (1975): 36–64.

Sears, David O. and Jack Citrin. *Tax Revolt: Something for Nothing in California.* Cambridge, MA: Harvard University Press, 1985.

Sears, David O. and Rick Kosterman. "Mass Media and Political Persuasion." In *Psychology of Persuasion,* ed. T. C. Brock and S. Shavitt, 251–278. New York: W. H. Freeman, 1987.

Seaton, Jean. "Broadcasting in the Age of Market Ideology: Is It Possible to Underestimate the Public Taste?" *Political Quarterly* 65, 1 (1994): 29–38.

Seeman, Teresa. George A. Kaplan, Lisa Knudsen, Richard Cohen, and Jack Guralnik. "Social Network Ties and Mortality Among the Elderly in the Alameda County Study." *American Journal of Epidemiology* 126, 4 (1987): 714–723.

Seibel, Wolfgang. "Government-Nonprofit Relationship: Styles and Linkage Patterns in France and Germany." In *Government and Voluntary Organizations: A Relational Perspective,* ed. Stein Kuhnle and Per Selle, 53–70. Aldershot, England: Avebury, 1992.

Seisel, Hans. *The Limits of Law Enforcement.* Chicago: University of Chicago Press, 1983.

Sekulic, Dusko, Garth Massey, and Randy Hodson. "Who Were the Yugoslavs? Failed Sources of a Common Identity in the Former Yugoslavia." *American Sociological Review* 59 (1994): 83–97.

Selle, Per and Lars Svåsand. "Membership in Party Organizations and the Problem of Decline of Parties." *Comparative Political Studies* 23, 4 (1991): 459–477.

Seltzer, Richard A., Jody Newman, and Melissa Voorhees Leighton. *Sex as a Political Variable: Women as Candidates and Voters in U.S. Elections.* Boulder, CO: Lynne Rienner, 1997.

Selznick, Philip. "Institutional Vulnerability in Mass Society." *American Journal of Sociology* 56 (1951): 320–331.

Sen, Amartya. *Levels of Poverty: Policy and Change: A Background Study.* World Bank Staff Working Paper, Washington, DC: World Bank, 1980.

Sen, Amartya. "The Economics of Life and Death." *Scientific American* (May 1993): 40–47.

Sengenberger, Werner. "Protection, Participation, Promotion: The Systematic Nature and Effects of Labour Standards." In *Creating Economic Opportunities: The Role of Labour Standards in Industrial Restructuring,* ed. Werner Sengenberger and Duncan Campbell, 45–60. Geneva: International Institute for Labour Studies, 1994.

Shabecoff, Philip. *A Fierce Green Fire: The American Environemental Movement.* New York: Hill & Wang, 1993.

Shafer, Byron E., ed. *Is America Different?* Oxford: Clarendon Press, 1991.

Shafer, Byron E. "American Exceptionalism." *Annual Review of Political Science* 2 (1999): 445–463.

Shalev, Michael. *Labour and the Political Economy in Israel.* Oxford: Oxford University Press, 1992.

Shanker, Albert. "United States of America." In *Labor Relations in Education: An International Perspective,* ed. Bruce S. Cooper, 273–298. Westport, CT: Greenwood Press, 1982.

Shanker, Albert and Bella Rosenberg. "Do Private Schools Outperform Public Schools?" In *The Choice Controversy,* ed. Peter W. Cookson, 128–145. Newbury Park, CA: Corwin Press, 1992.

Shanks, J. Merrill and Warren E. Miller. "Partisanship, Policy and Performance: The Reagan Legacy in the 1988 Election." *British Journal of Political Science* 21, 2 (1991): 129–197.

Shannon, Elaine. "A Losing Battle." *Time* 136, 24 (1990): 44–48.

Shapiro, Martin. *Who Guards the Guardians? Judicial Control of the Administration.* Athens, Georgia: University of Georgia Press, 1988.

Shapiro, Martin and Alec Stone. "The New Constitutional Politics of Europe." *Comparative Political Studies* 26, 4 (1994): 397–420.

Shapiro, Robert Y. and John T. Turner. "Public Opinion and the Welfare State: The United States in Comparative Perspective." *Political Science Quarterly* 104, 1 (1989): 59–89.

Sharkansky, Ira. *Whither the State? Politics and Public Enterprise in Three Countries.* Chatham, NJ: Chatham House, 1979.

Shaw, David. "A Negative Spin on the News." *Los Angeles Times,* April 17, 1996, A1–A6.

Shaw, David. "Revolution in Cyberspace; Digital Age Poses the Riddle of Dividing or Uniting Society." *Los Angeles Times,* June 15, 1997, A26.

Shefter, Martin. *Political Parties and the State: The American Historical Experience.* Princeton: Princeton University Press, 1994.

Shils, Edward A. "Mass Society and Its Culture." *Daedalus* 89, 2 (1960): 288–314.

Shiratori, Rei. "The Experience of the Welfare State in Japan and Its Problems." In *The Welfare State and Its Aftermath,* ed. S. N. Eisenstadt and Ora Ahimeir, 200–223. London: Croom Helm in association with the Jerusalem Institute for Israel Studies, 1985.

Shiratori, Rei. "Japan and European Welfare State. Convergence or Conflict?" Conference on Globalization and Systems of Welfare, Turin, 1990.

Shonfield, Andrew. *Modern Capitalism: The Changing Balance of Public and Private Power.* New York: Oxford University Press, 1965.

Shorrocks, Anthony F. "UK Wealth Distribution: Current Evidence and Future Prospects." In *International Comparisons of the Distribution of Household Wealth,* ed. Edward N. Wolff, 29–50. Oxford: Claredon Press, 1987.

Siaroff, Alan. "Work, Welfare, and Gender Equality." In *Gendering Welfare States,* ed. Diane Sainsbury, 82–100. Thousand Oaks, CA: Sage, 1994.

Siegler, Mark and Mark Sheldon. "Paying the Price of Medical Progress: Causation, Responsibility, and Liability for Bad Outcomes after Innovative Medical Care." In *Medical Innovation and Bad Outcomes: Legal, Social and Ethical Responses,* ed. Mark Siegler, Stephen Toulmin, Franklin E. Zimring, and Kenneth F. Schaffner. Ann Arbor, MI: Health Administration Press, 1987.

Sills, David L. *The Volunteers: Means and Ends in a National Organization.* Glencoe, IL: Free Press, 1957.

Simon, David. *Homicide: A Year on the Killing Streets.* Boston: Houghton Mifflin, 1991.

Simonnot, Philippe. *Les Nucleocrates.* Grenoble: Presses Universitaires de Grenoble, 1978.

Sinclair, Barbara. *Legislators, Leaders, and Lawmaking: The U.S. House of Representatives in the Postreform Era.* Baltimore: Johns Hopkins University Press, 1995.

Singelmann, Joachim. *From Agriculture to Services: The Transformation of Industrial Employment.* Beverly Hills, CA: Sage, 1978.

Singleton, Gwynneth. *The Accord and the Australian Labour Movement.* Carlton, Victoria: Melbourne University Press, 1990.

Siu, Albert L. et al. "Inappropriate Use of Hospitals in a Randomized Trial of Health Insurance Plans." *New England Journal of Medicine* 315, 20 (1991): 1259–1266.

Siune, Karen and Wolfgang Truetzchler, eds. *Dynamics of Media Politics: Broadcast and Electronic Media in Western Europe.* Newbury Park, CA: Sage, 1992.

Skolnick, Jerome H. "Making Sense of the Crime Decline." *Newsday,* February 2, 1997, G8, G15.

Sloan, Frank A. "Commercialism in Nonprofit Hospitals." *Journal of Policy Analysis and Management* 17, 2 (1998): 234–252.

Smeeding, Timothy M. "Cross-National Patterns of Retirement and Poverty among Men and Women in the 1980s: Full Stop or Gradual Withdrawal?" In *Age, Work, and Social Security,* ed. A. B. Atkinson and Martin Rein, 91–114. New York: St. Martin's Press, 1993.

Smeeding, Timothy M., Peter Saunders, John Coder, Stephen Jenkins, Johan Fritzell, Aldi J. M. Hagenaars, Richard Hauser, and Michael Wolfson. "Poverty, Inequality, and Family Living Standards Impacts across Seven Nations: The Effect of Noncash Subsidies for Health, Education, and Housing." *Review of Income and Wealth* 39, 3 (1993): 229–256.

Smelser, Neil. *Social Change in the Industrial Revolution.* Chicago: University of Chicago Press, 1959.

Smelser, Neil J. and Seymour Martin Lipset, ed. *Social Structure and Mobility in Economic Development.* Chicago: Aldine, 1966a.

Smelser, Neil J. and Seymour Martin Lipset. "Social Structure, Mobility and Development." In *Social Structure and Mobility in Economic Development,* ed. Neil J. Smelser and Seymour Martin Lipset, 1–50. Chicago: Aldine, 1966b.

Smelser, Ronald. *Robert Ley: Hitler's Labor Front Leader.* Oxford: Berg, 1988.

Smith, Anthony. *Goodbye Gutenberg: The Newspaper Revolution of the 1980s.* New York: Oxford University Press, 1980.

Smith, Anthony. "Mass Communications." In *Democracy at the Polls: A Comparative Study of Competitve National Elections,* ed. David Butler, Howard R. Penniman, and Austin Ranney, 173–195. Washington, DC: American Enterprise Institute for Public Policy Research, 1981.

Smith, Bruce L. R. "The U.S. Higher Civil Service in Comparative Perspective." In *The Higher Civil Service in Europe and Canada: Lessons for the United States,* ed. Bruce L. R. Smith, 1–19. Washington, DC: Brookings Institution, 1984.

Smith, J., W. H. Form, and G. P. Stone. "Local Intimacy in a Middle-Sized City." *American Journal of Sociology* 60 (Nov. 1954): 276–284.

Smith, James P. *Unequal Wealth and Incentives to Save.* RAND, 1995. Documented Briefing.

Smith, James P. and Barry Edmonston, eds. *The New Americans: Economic, Demographic, and Fiscal Effects of Immigration.* Washington, DC: National Academy Press, 1997.

Smith, Michael R. *Power, Norms, and Inflation: A Skeptical Treatment.* New York: Adline de Gruyter, 1992.

Smith, Steven Rathgeb and Michael Lipsky. *Nonprofits for Hire: The Welfare State in the Age of Contracting.* Cambridge, MA: Harvard University Press, 1993.

Smith, Tom W. "Inequality and Welfare." In *British Social Attitudes: Special International Report,* ed. Roger Jowell, Sharon Witherspoon, and Lindsay Brook, 59–77. Brookfield, VT and Hants, England: Gower, 1989.

Smith, Tom W. "Social Inequality in Cross-National Perspective." In *Attitudes to Inequality and the Role of Government,* ed. Duane F. Alwin et al., 21–31. Rijswijk, Netherlands: Social and Cultural Planning Office, 1990.

Smith, Tom W. "A Review of Church Attendance Measures." *American Sociological Review* 63 (Feb. 1998): 131–136.

Smolensky, Eugene, Eirik Evenhouse, and Siobhan Reilly. *Welfare Reform in California.* Berkeley: Institute of Governmental Studies, 1992.

Smolensky, Eugene, Eirik Evenhouse, and Siobhan Reilly. *Welfare Reform: A Primer in 12 Questions.* Public Policy Institute of California, San Francisco CA, 1997.

Solow, Robert M. "A Contribution to the Theory of Economic Growth." *Quarterly Journal of Economics* 17 (1956): 65–94.

Solow, Robert M. "Technical Change and the Aggregate Production Function." *Review of Economics and Statistics* 39 (1957): 312–320.

Solow, Robert M. "Growth Theory and After." *American Economic Review* 78, 3 (1988): 307–317.

Sombart, Werner. *Why Is There No Socialism in America?* Trans. By Patricia M. Hocking and C. T. Husbands. London: Macmillan, 1976 [1906].

SOPEMI. *Trends in International Migration.* Paris: OECD, 1992.

Soskice, David. "Reinterpreting Corporatism and Explaining Unemployment: Co-ordinated and Non-co-ordinated Market Economies." In *Labour Relations and Economic Performance,* ed. Ranato Brunetta and Carlo Dell'Aringa, 170–211. New York: New York University Press, 1990a.

Soskice, David. "Wage Determination: The Changing Role of Institutions in Advanced Industrial Societies." *Oxford Review of Economic Policy* 6 (1990b): 36–61.

Soskice, David. "Divergent Production Regimes: Coordinated and Uncoordinated Market Economies in the 1980s and 1990s." In *Continuity and Change in Contemporary Capitalism,* ed. Herbert Kitschelt, Peter Lange, Gary Marks, and John D. Stephens, 101–134. New York: Cambridge University Press, 1999.

Soskice, David and Ronald Schettkat. "West German Labor Market Institutions and East German Transformation." In *Labor and an Integrated Europe,* ed. Lloyd Ulman, Barry Eichengreen, and William T. Dickens, 102–127. Washington, DC: Brookings Institution, 1993.

Sowell, Thomas. "Three Black Histories." In *Essays and Data on American Ethnic Groups,* ed. Thomas Sowell, 7–49. Washington, DC: Urban Institute, 1978.

Sowell, Thomas. *Migration and Cultures: A World View.* New York: Basic Books, 1996.

Spain, David M. *The Complications of Modern Medical Practices.* New York: Grune & Stratton, 1963.

Sparks, Jo. "Schools, Education and Social Exclusion." Case Paper 29, Center for Analysis and Social Exclusion, London School of Economics, 1999.

Sparrow, Malcolm K., Mark H. Moore, and David M. Kennedy. *Beyond 911: A New Era for Policing.* Glencoe, IL: Basic Books, 1990.

Spitzer, Robert J. "Presidential Policy Determinism: How Policies Frame Congressional Responses to the President's Legislative Program." *Presidential Studies Quarterly* 12, 4 (1983): 556–574.

Spitzer, Robert J. *Media and Public Policy.* Westport: Praeger, 1993.

Staber, Udo. "The Organizational Properties of Trade Associations." Unpublished Ph.D. dissertation, Cornell University, 1982.

Staber, Udo and Howard Aldrich. "Trade Association Stability and Public Policy." Unpublished paper, 1982.

Stanley, Harold W. "Southern Partisan Changes: Dealignment, Realignment or Both?" *Journal of Politics* 50, 1 (1988): 64–88.

Starfield, Barbara. *Primary Care: Concept, Evaluation, and Policy.* New York: Oxford University Press, 1992.

Starfield, Barbara, Lisa Egbuonu, Mark Farfel, Alain Joffe, and Lawrence S. Wissow. *The Effectiveness of Medical Care: Validating Clinical Wisdom.* Baltimore: Johns Hopkins University Press, 1985.

Starr, Paul. *The Social Transformation of American Medicine.* New York: Basic Books, 1982.

Stein, Herbert. "Professor Knight's Law of Talk." *Wall Street Journal,* October 14, 1981, 28, column 4.

Stein, H. *Presidential Economics.* New York: Simon & Schuster, 1985.

Steinberg, Laurence, with B. Bradford Brown, and Sanford M. Dornbusch. *Beyond the Classroom: Why School Reform Has Failed and What Parents Need to Do.* New York: Simon & Schuster, 1996.

Steinberg, Laurence, Sanford M. Dornbusch, and B. Bradford Brown. "Ethnic Differences in Adolescent Achievement: An Ecological Perspective." *American Psychologist* 47, 6 (June 1992a): 723–729.

Steinberg, Laurence, Susie D. Lamborn, Sanford M. Dornbusch, and Nancy Darling. "Impact of Parenting Practices on Adolescent Achievement: Authoritative Parenting, School Involvement, and Encouragement to Succeed." *Child Development* 63, 2 (Oct. 1992b): 1266–1281.

Steiner, Gary A. *The People Look at Televison.* New York: Alfred Knopf, 1963.

Steiner, Gilbert Y. *The State of Welfare.* Washington, DC: Brookings Institution, 1971.

Steiner, Jörg. *Amicable Agreement Versus Majority Rule.* Chapel Hill: University of North Carolina Press, 1974.

Steinmetz, George and Erik Olin Wright. "The Fall and Rise of the Petty Bourgeoisie: Changing Patterns of Self-Employment in the Postwar United States." *American Journal of Sociology* 94 (March 1989): 973–1018.

Stephens, Evelyne Huber and John D. Stephens. "The Labor Movement, Political Power, and Workers' Participation in Western Europe." *Political Power and Social Theory* 3 (1982): 215–249.

Stephens, John D. "Democratic Transition and Breakdown in Western Europe, 1870–1939: A Test of the Moore Thesis." *American Journal of Sociology* 94, 5 (1989): 1019–1077.

Stephens, Robert. "Radical Tax Reform in New Zealand." *Fiscal Studies* 14, 3 (1993): 45–63.

Steslicke, William E. "The Japanese State of Health: A Political-Economic Perspective." In *Health Illness and Medical Care in Japan: Cultural and Social Dimensions,* ed. Edward Norbeck and Margaret Lock, 24–65. Honolulu: University of Hawaii Press, 1987.

Steuerle, C. Eugene and Virginia A. Hodgkinson. "Meeting Social Needs: Comparing the Resources of the Independent Sector and Government." In *Nonprofits and Government: Collaboration and Conflict,* ed. Elizabeth T. Boris and Eugene C. Steuerle, 71–98. Washington, DC: The Urban Institute Press, 1999.

Stevens, Candice. "The Knowledge-Driven Economy." *The OECD Observer* No. 200 (June/July 1996): 6–15.

Stevens, Elizabeth L. "Mouse.Ke.Fear." *Brill's Content* 1, 5 (1998): 94–103.

Stevenson, Harold W. and James W. Stigler. *The Learning Gap: Why Our Schools Are Failing and What We Can Learn from Japanese and Chinese Education.* New York: Summit Books, 1992.

Stilwell, Frank. *The Accord . . . and Beyond.* Sydney and London: Pluto Press, 1986.

Stinchcombe, Arthur L. "Bureaucratic and Craft Administration of Production: A Comparative Study." *Administrative Science Quarterly* 4, 2 (1959): 168–187.

Stone, Deborah A. *The Disabled State.* London: Macmillan, 1985.

Stopford, John and John H. Dunning. *Multinationals: Company Performance and Global Trends.* London: Macmillan, 1983.

Straubhaar, Thomas. *On the Economics of International Labor Migration.* Bern: Paul Haupt, 1988.

Strauss, George. "Notes on Power Equalization." In *The Social Science of Organization,* ed. Harold Leavitt, 41–84. Englewood Cliffs, NJ: Prentice Hall, 1963.

Strauss, George and Leonard Sayles. *Personnel: The Human Problems of Management.* 2nd ed. Englewood Cliffs, NJ: Prentice Hall, 1967.

Streeck, Wolfgang. "Organizational Consequences of Corporatist Cooperation in West German Labor Unions: A Case Study." Discussion paper, International Institute of Management, 1978.

Streeck, Wolfgang. "Between Pluralism and Corporatism: German Business Associations and the State." *Journal of Public Policy* 3 (August 1983): 265–283.

Streeck, Wolfgang. "Interest Heterogeneity and Organizing Capacity: Two Class Logics of Collective Action?" In *Political Choice: Institutions, Rules, and the Limits of Rationality,* ed. Roland M. Czada and Adrienne Windhoff-Heritier, 161–198. Boulder, CO: Westview Press, 1991a.

Streeck, Wolfgang. "More Uncertainties: German Unions Facing 1992." *Industrial Relations* 30, 3 (1991b): 317–347.

Streeck, Wolfgang. "Inclusion and Secession: Questions on the Boundaries of Associative Democracy." *Politics and Society* 20, 4 (1992): 513–520.

Streeck, Wolfgang. "Works Councils in Western Europe: From Consultation to Participation." In *Works Councils: Consultation, Representation, and Cooperation in Industrial Relations,* ed. Joel Rogers and Wolfgang Streeck, 313–348. Chicago: University of Chicago Press, 1995.

Streeck, Wolfgang and Philippe C. Schmitter, eds. *Private Interest Government: Beyond Market and State.* London: Sage, 1985.

Strodtbeck, Fred L. "Family Interaction, Values, and Achievement." In *Talent and Society: New Perspectives in the Identification of Talent,* ed. David C. McClelland, Alfred L. Baldwin, Urie Bronfenbrenner, and Fred L. Strodtbeck, 135–194. Princeton, NJ: Van Nostrand, 1958.

Suleiman, Ezra N. *Politics, Power, and Bureaucracy in France: An Administrative Elite.* Princeton, NJ: Princeton University Press, 1974.

Suleiman, Ezra N. "From Right to Left: Bureaucracy and Politics in France." In *Bureaucrats and Policy Making: A Comparative Overview*, ed. Ezra N. Suleiman, 107–135. New York and London: Holmes & Meier, 1984.

Sullivan, Mercer L. *Getting Paid: Youth Crime and Work in the Inner City*. Ithaca, NY: Cornell University Press, 1989.

Summers, Robert, Alan Heston, Bettina Aten, and Daniel Nuxoll. *Penn World Table (PWT) Mark 5.6a Data (MRDF)*. Center for International Comparisons, University of Pennsylvania, 1994.

Super, David A., Sharon Parrott, Susan Steinmetz, and Cindy Mann. *The New Welfare Law*. Center on Budget and Policy Priorities, Washington, DC, 1996.

Susser, Mervyn and Ezra Susser. "Choosing a Future for Epidemiology: Eras and Paradigms (Part 1)." *American Journal of Public Health* 86, 5 (1996): 668–673.

Sussman, Marvin B. "The Help Pattern in the Middle Class Family." *American Sociological Review* 18 (February 1953): 22–28.

Suttles, Gerald D. *The Social Order of the Slum: Ethnicity and Territory in the Inner City*. Chicago: University of Chicago Press, 1970.

Svallfors, Stefan, ed. *In the Eye of the Beholder: Opinions on Welfare and Justice in Comparative Perspective*. Bank of Sweden Tercentenary Foundation with Impello Säljsupport AB, 1995.

Swedish Institute. "Fact Sheets on Sweden: Childcare in Sweden." Stockholm, April 1987.

Swenson, Peter. "Bringing Capital Back In, or Social Democracy Reconsidered: Employer Power, Cross-Class Alliances, and Centralization of Industrial Relations in Denmark and Sweden." *World Politics* 43, 4 (1991): 513–544.

Syme, S. Leonard. "Social Determinants of Health and Disease." In *Maxcy-Rosenau-Last Public Health and Preventive Medicine*, ed. John M. Last, 953–970. 12th ed. Norwalk, Conn: Appleton-Century-Crofts, 1986.

Syrup, Friedrich. *Hundert Jahre Staatliche Sozialpolitik 1839–1939*. Stuttgart: 1957.

Szalai, Alexander. *The Uses of Time*. The Hague: Mouton, 1972.

Taira, Koji and Solomon B. Levine. "Japan's Industrial Relations: A Social Compact Emerges." In *Industrial Relations in a Decade of Economic Change*, ed. Hervey Juris, Mark Thompson, and Wilbur Daniels, 247–300. Madison, WI: Industrial Relations Research Association, 1985.

Tanzi, Vito. "Review of *Tax Policy in OECD Countries: Choices and Conflicts* by Ken Messere." *National Tax Journal* 47, 2 (1994): 447–450.

Tarrow, Sidney. "Mass Mobilization and Regime Change: Pacts, Reform, and Popular Power in Italy (1918–1922) and Spain (1975–1978)." In *The Politics of Democratic Consolidation: Southern Europe in Comparative Perspective*, ed. Richard Gunther, P. Nikifornos Diamandouros, and Hans-Jürgen Puhle, 204–230. Baltimore: Johns Hopkins University Press, 1995.

Taxation in the Single Market. Vol. 6. European Documentation Series, Luxembourg: Office for Official Publications of the European Community, 1990.

Taylor, Humphrey. "Testimony." In *Hearing Before the Select Committee on Aging, House of Representatives, 99th Congress, Second Session, April 8, 1986*, 13–15. Committee Publication No. 99–570. Washington, DC: U.S. Government Printing Office, 1986.

Taylor, Malcolm G. *Health Insurance and Canadian Public Policy: The Seven Decisions that Created the Canadian Health Insurance System*. Montreal: McGill-Queen's University Press, 1978.

Taylor, Malcolm G. *Insuring National Health Care: The Canadian Experience*. Chapel Hill: University of North Carolina Press, 1990.

Taylor-Gooby, Peter. "The Role of the State." In *British Social Attitudes: Special International Report*, ed. Roger Jowell, Sharon Witherspoon, and Lindsay Brook, 35–58. Brookfield, VT and Hants, England: Gower, 1989.

Teixeira, Ruy A. and Joel Rogers. "Who Deserted the Democrats in 1994?" *The American Prospect* No. 23 (Fall 1995): 73–77.

Teppe, Karl. "Zur Sozialpolitik des Dritten Reiches am Beispiel der Sozialversicherung." *Archiv fuer Sozialgeschichte* 17 (1977): 195–250.

Tetswaart, Heleen. "The International Comparison of Court Caseloads: The Experience of the European Working Group." *Law and Society Review* 24 (1990): 571–593.

"The Challenge to Public Broadcasting." *Transatlantic Perspectives* 16 (Autumn 1987): 10–12.

"The Overselling of Candidates on Television." *Transatlantic Perspectives* 11 (April 1984): 3–6.

"The Public Decides on Health Care Reform: A Polling Review of the Great Debate." *The Public Perspective* 5, 6 (1994): 23–28.

Thelen, Kathleen A. *Union of Parts: Labor Politics in Postwar Germany.* Ithaca, NY: Cornell University Press, 1992.

Thernstrom, Abigail. "Guinier Miss." *The New Republic,* June 14, 1993, 16, 18–19.

Thernstrom, Stephan and Abigail Thernstrom. *America in Black and White: One Nation, Indivisible.* New York: Simon & Schuster, 1997.

Thomas, R. Murray. "Part I: The Case of Japan—A Prologue." In *Schooling in East Asia: Forces of Change,* ed. R. Murray Thomas and T. Neville Postlethwaite, 37–50. Oxford, England: Pergamon Press, 1983.

Thomas, R. Murray and T. Neville Postlethwaite, eds. *Schooling in East Asia: Forces of Change.* Oxford, England: Pergamon Press, 1983.

Thompson, Lyke and Donald F. Norris, eds. *The Politics of Welfare Reform.* Thousand Oaks, CA: Sage, 1995.

Thrasher, Frederic Milton. *The Gang: A Study of 1,313 Gangs in Chicago.* Chicago: University of Chicago Press, 1936.

Tietz, Michael. *Small Business and Employment Growth in California.* Berkeley: Institute of Urban and Regional Development, University of California, 1981.

Tilly, Charles. *The Formation of National States in Western Europe.* Princeton, NJ: Princeton University Press, 1975.

Tilly, Charles, Rudolph Andorka, and David Levine. "Review Symposium." *Population and Development Review* 12, 2 (June 1986): 323–340.

Timmersfeld, Andrea. "Chancen und Perspektiven europäischer Kollektivverhandlungen." Dissertation, Trier, 1992.

Titmuss, Richard M. *Essays on 'The Welfare State'.* London: Allen & Unwin, 1958.

Tocqueville, Alexis de. *Democracy in America.* The Henry Reeve text as revised by Francis Bowen now further corrected and edited with introduction, editorial notes, and bibliographies by Phillips Bradley. ed., Vol. 1. New York: Knopf, 1963 [1835].

Tracy, Martin. "Trends in Retirement." *International Social Security Review* 32, 3 (1979a): 131–159.

Tracy, Martin. *Retirement Age Practices in Ten Industrial Societies, 1960–76.* Geneva: International Social Security Administration, 1979b.

Travers, P. "Deprivation Among Low Income DSS Australian Families: Results from a Pilot Study." In *Mortgaging Our Future? Families and Young People in Australia,* ed. Róisín Thanki and Cathy Thomson, 27–45. New South Wales: Social Policy Research Centre, University of New South Wales, 1996.

Traxler, Franz. "Farewell to Labour Market Associations: Organized versus Disorganized Decentralization as a Map For Industrial Relations." In *Organized Industrial Relations in Europe: What Future?,* ed. Colin Crouch and Franz Traxler, 3–19. Aldershot, UK and Brookfield, VT: Avebury, Ashgate Publishing, 1995.

Traxler, Franz and Brigitte Unger. "Industry or Infrastructure? A Cross-National Comparison of Governance: Its Determinants and Economic Consequences in the Dairy Sector." In *Governing Capitalist Economies,* ed. J. Rogers Hollingsworth, Phillippe C. Schmitter, and Wolfgang Streeck, 183–214. New York: Oxford University Press, 1994.

Treppe, Karl. "Zur Socialpolitik des Dritten Reiches am Beispiel der Sozialversicherung." *Archiv fur Sozialgeschichte* 17 (1977): 195–250.

Trow, Martin. "Small Businessmen, Political Tolerance, and Support for McCarthy." *American Journal of Sociology* 64 (1958): 270–281.

Trow, Martin. *The Expansion and Transformation of Higher Education.* Morristown, NJ: General Learning Press, 1972.

Trow, Martin. "Problems in the Transition from Elite to Mass Education." In *Politics for Higher Education: General Report,* 51–101. Paris: OECD, 1974.

Trow, Martin. "American Higher Education: Past, Present, and Future." *Educational Researcher* 17, 3 (1988): 13–23.

Trow, Martin. "American Higher Education: Exceptional or Just Different?" In *Is America Different: A New Look at American Exceptionalism,* ed. Byron E. Shafer, 138–186. Oxford: Clarendon Press, 1991a.

Trow, Martin. "The Exceptionalism of American Higher Education." In *University and Society: Essays on the Social Role of Research and Higher Education,* ed. Martin Trow and Thorsten Nybom, 156–172. London: Jessica Kingsley, 1991b.

Trow, Martin. "California After Racial Preferences." *The Public Interest* 135 (Spring 1999): 64–85.

Trump, Thomas M. "Value Formation and Postmaterialism: Inglehart's Theory of Value Change Reconsidered." *Comparative Political Studies* 24, 3 (1991): 365–390.

Tsai, Y. M. and L. Sigelman. "The Community Question: A Perspective from National Survey Data—the Case of the USA." *British Journal of Sociology* 33 (1982): 579–588.

Tucker, M. Belinda and Claudia Mitchell-Kernan. "New Trends in Black American Interracial Marriage: The Social Structural Context." *Journal of Marriage and the Family* 52 (February 1990): 209–218.

Tuckman, Howard P. "Competition, Commercialization, and the Evolution of Nonprofit Organizational Structures." *Journal of Policy Analysis and Management* 17, 2 (1998): 175–194.

Tunstall, Jeremy. *The Media Are American.* New York: Columbia University Press, 1977.

Tunstall, Jeremy. "The United Kingdom." *The Media in Western Europe* (1997): 244–259.

Tuohy, Carolyn J. *Policy and Politics in Canada: Institutionalized Ambivalence.* Philadelphia: Temple University Press, 1992.

Turner, Lowell. *Democracy at Work: Changing World Markets and the Future of Labor Unions.* Ithaca, NY: Cornell University Press, 1991.

Turner, Lowell. "Prospects for Worker Participation in Management." In *Labor and an Integrated Europe,* ed. Lloyd Ulman, Barry Eichengreen, and William T. Dickens. Washington, DC: Brookings Institution, 1993a.

Turner, Lowell. "Beyond National Unionism? Cross-National Labor Collaboration in the European Community." Paper presented at the American Political Science Association Annual Meeting, Washington, DC, September 2–5, 1993b.

Turner, Lowell. "The Europeanization of Labor: Structure Before Action." *European Journal of Industrial Relations* 2, 3 (Nov. 1996): 325–344.

Turner, Lowell. *Fighting for Partnership: Labor and Politics in Unified Germany.* Ithaca: Cornell University Press, 1998.

Turner, Ralph H. "The Real Self: From Institution to Impulse." *American Journal of Sociology* 81 (1976): 989–1016.

Tusa, John. "Implications of Recent Changes at the BBC." *Political Quarterly* 65, 1 (1994): 6–10.

U.S. Bureau of Labor Statistics. *Contingent and Alternative Employment Arrangements.* Bureau of Labor Statistics, 1995. Report 900.

U.S. Bureau of the Census. *Historical Statistics of the United States, Colonial Times to 1970.* Vol. 1. Washington, DC: U.S. Government Printing Office, 1975.

U.S. Bureau of the Census. *Statistical Abstract of the United States.* 98th ed. Washington, DC: U.S. Government Printing Office, 1977.

U.S. Bureau of the Census. *Who's Minding the Kids?* Statistical Brief, Series SB-2 – 87. Washington, DC: U.S. Government Printing Office, 1987.

U.S. Bureau of the Census. *Fertility of American Women: June 1988.* Current Population Reports, Series P-20, No. 436. Washington, DC: U.S. Government Printing Office, 1988.

U.S. Bureau of the Census. *Statistical Abstract of the United States: 1991.* 111th ed., Washington, DC: U.S. Bureau of Census, 1991.

U.S. Bureau of the Census. *Black Americans: A Profile.* Bureau of the Census, 1993a. Statistical Brief SB 93 – 2.

U.S. Bureau of the Census. *Money Income of Households, Families and Persons in the U.S.: 1992.* Housing and Household Economic Statistics Division, Bureau of the Census, 1993b. Current Population Reports, Series P-60 184.

U.S. Bureau of the Census. *Statistical Abstract of the United States: 1998.* 118th ed., Washington, DC: U.S. Bureau of the Census, 1998.

U.S. Bureau of the Census. "Voting and Registration in the Election of November 1996." *Currrent Population Survey,* P20-504, 1998a.

U.S. Bureau of the Census. *Annual Demographic Survey.* Detailed Poverty Survey, no. P-60. March Supplement, Washington, DC: U.S. Census Bureau, 1999a.

U.S. Bureau of the Census. *Statistical Abstract of the United States 1999.* Washington DC: U.S. Census Bureau, 1999b.

U.S. Commission on the Future of Worker-Management Relations. *Fact Finding Report* (The Dunlop Report). The Bureau of National Affairs, 1993.

U.S. Commission on the Future of Worker-Mangement Relations. *Report and Recommendations.* Washington, DC: U.S. Dept. of Labor and U.S. Dept. of Commerce, 1994.

U.S. Commission on the Future of Worker-Management Relations. *Report and Recommendations.* Washington, DC: The Bureau of National Affairs, Jan. 9, 1995.

U.S. Court Statistics Project. *State Court Caseload Statistics: Annual Report 1989.* Williamsburg, VA: National Center for State Courts in cooperation with the Conference of State Court Administrators, 1991.

U.S. Department of Commerce. *United States Trade Performance in 1988.* Washington, DC: U.S. Government Printing Office, 1989.

U.S. Department of Commerce. "Economics and Statistics Administration." In *Statistical Abstract of the United States, 1991,* Bureau of the Census. 111th ed., The National Data Book, 1991.

U.S. Department of Commerce, International Trade Administration. *U.S. Foreign Trade Highlights 1996.* Washington, DC, August 1997.

U.S. Department of Education, National Center for Education Statistics. NCES 1999 – 036. *Digest of Education Statistics, 1998.* Washington, DC: U.S. Department of Education, 1999.

U.S. Department of Education, Office of Educational Research and Improvement, National Center for Education Statistics. *Digest of Education Statistics, 1980.* Washington, DC: NCES, 1980.

U.S. Department of Education, Office of Educational Research and Improvement, National Center for Education Statistics. *Digest of Education Statistics, 1992.* Washington, DC: NCES, 1992.

U.S. Department of Labor, Bureau of Labor Statistics. *Educational Attainment of Workers.* Special Labor Force Report 186, Washington, DC: U.S. Government Printing Office, 1975a.

U.S. Department of Labor, Bureau of Labor Statistics. *Jobseeking Methods Used by American Workers.* Washington, DC: U.S. Government Printing Office, 1975b.

U.S. Department of Labor, Bureau of Labor Statistics. *Employment and Earnings.* Vol. 31, 1 (January). Employment and Earnings, 1984.

U.S. Department of Labor, Bureau of Labor Statistics. "Press Release of November 6, 1989: Multiple Jobholding Reached Record High in May 1989." Washington, DC: U.S. Government Printing Office/USDL 89–529, 1989.

U.S. Department of Labor, Bureau of Labor Statistics. *Employment and Earnings.* Vol. 39, 1 (January), 1992.

U.S. Department of Labor. *Contingent and Alternative Employment Arrangements.* Report 900. U.S. Labor Department, 1995.

U.S. Department of Labor, Bureau of Labor Statistics. *Employment and Earnings.* Vol. 42. Washington, DC: U.S. Department of Labor, 1995.

U.S. Department of Labor, Bureau of Labor Statistics. *Employment and Earnings.* Vol. 45, 1 (January): 1998.

U.S. Department of Labor, Employment Standards Administration. "Family and Medical Leave Act Final Regulations Take Effect Today." Press release, April 6, 1995.

U.S. General Accounting Office. *Occupational Safety and Health: Differences Between Programs in the United States and Canada.* Fact Sheet for the Chairman, Committee on Education and Labor, U.S. House of Representatives, U.S. Congress, 1993.

U.S. House of Representatives, Committee on Ways and Means. *Green Book: Background Material and Data on Programs within the Jurisdiction of the Committee on Ways and Means.* Washington, DC: U.S. Government Printing Office, 1994, 1996.

U.S. Office of Management and Budget. *Budget of the United States Government, Fiscal Year 1993.* 1992.

U.S. Office of Management and Budget. *Budget of the United States Government, Fiscal Year 1996.* Washington, DC: Office of Management and Budget, 1996a.

U.S. Office of Management and Budget. *Budget of the United States Government, Fiscal Year 1996. Historical Tables.* Washington, DC: Office of Management and Budget, 1996b.

UNESCO. *Statistical Yearbook, 1986.* Belgium: UNESCO, 1986.

United Nations. *Demographic Yearbook.* New York: United Nations, various years.

United Nations. *Demographic Yearbook 1989.* New York: United Nations Statistical Office, 1991.

United Nations Department of International and Social Affairs. *Adolescent Reproductive Behavior: Evidence from Developed Countries, Volume 1.* United Nations, 1988. Population Studies 109.

United States Conference of Mayors. *A Status Report on Hunger and Homelessness in America's Cities 1999.* United States Conference of Mayors,

University of California. *2000/01 Budget for Current Operations.* Office of the President, October, 1999.

Uusitalo, Hannu. *Income Distribution in Finland: The Effects of the Welfare State and Structural Changes in Society on Income Distribution in Finland in 1966–1985.* Helsinki: Central Statistical Office of Finland, 1989.

Valen, Henry and Bernt Aardal. "The Norwegian Programme of Electoral Research." *European Journal of Political Research* 25 (1994): 287–309.

Van Amersfoort, Hans and Rinus Penninx. "Regulating Migration in Europe: The Dutch Experience." *Annals of the American Academy of Political and Social Science* 534 (1994): 133–146.

van Haitsma, Martha. "Attitudes, Social Context and Labor Force Attachment: Blacks and Immigrant Mexicans in Chicago Poverty Areas." Paper presented at Chicago Urban Poverty and Family Life Conference, 1991.

van Oorschot, Wim. "Non-Take-Up of Social Security Benefits in Europe." *Journal of European Social Policy* 1, 1 (1991): 15–30.

van Oorschot, Wim. *Realizing Rights: A Multi-Level Approach to Non-Take-up of Means-tested Benefits.* Aldershot, UK, Brookfield, VT: Aldershot, 1995.

Van Zijl, W. J. "Studies on Diarrheal Disease in Seven Countries." *Bulletin of the World Health Organization* 35 (1966): 249–261.

Vanek, Joann. "Keeping Busy: Time Spent in Housework, United States, 1920–1970." Ph.D. dissertation, University of Michigan, 1973.

Veblen, Thorstein. *The Engineers and the Price System.* New York: Viking Press, 1921.

Veblen, Thorstein. *The Theory of the Leisure Class: An Economic Study in the Evolution of Institutions.* New York: The Modern Library, 1934 [1899].

Veenhoven, Ruut and Willem E. Saris. "Satisfaction in 10 Countries: A Summary of Findings." In *A Comparative Study of Satisfaction in Europe,* ed. Willem E. Saris, Ruut Veenhoven, Annette Scherpenzeel, and Brendan Bunting, Chap. 15. Budapest: Eotvos University Press, 1996.

Verba, Sidney and Norman H. Nie. *Participation in America: Political Democracy and Social Equity.* New York: Harper & Row, 1972.

Verba, Sidney, Norman H. Nie, and Jae-on Kim. *Participation and Political Equality: A Seven-Nation Comparison.* Chicago: University of Chicago Press, 1978.

Verba, Sidney, Kay Lehman Schlozman, and Henry E. Brady. *Voice and Equality: Civic Voluntarism in American Politics.* Cambridge, MA: Harvard University Press, 1995.

Veroff, Joseph, Elizabeth Douvan, and Richard A. Kulka. *The Inner American: A Self-Portrait from 1957 to 1976.* New York: Basic Books, 1981.

Vickery, Graham and Gregory Wurzburg. "Flexible Firms, Skills and Employment." *The OECD Observer* No. 202 (Oct./Nov. 1996): 17–21.

Visser, Jelle. "The Strength of Union Movements in Advanced Capitalist Democracies: Social and Organizational Variations." In *The Future of Labour Movements,* ed. Marino Regini, 17–52. Newbury Park, CA: Sage, 1992.

Visser, Jelle and Anton Hemerijck. *"A Dutch Miracle": Job Growth, Welfare Reform and Corporatism in the Netherlands.* Amsterdam: Amsterdam University Press, 1997.

Vogel, David. *National Styles of Regulation: Environmental Policy in Great Britain and the United States.* Ithaca, NY: Cornell University Press, Cornell Studies in Political Economy, 1986.

Vogel, David, Robert A. Kagan, and Timothy Kessler. "Political Culture and Tobacco Control: An International Comparison." *Tobacco Control* 2, 4 (1993): 317–326.

Vogel, David with the assistance of Veronica Kun. "The Comparative Study of Environmental Policy: A Review of the Literature." In *Comparative Policy Research: Learning From Experience,* ed. Meinholf Dierkes, Hans Weiler, and Ariane B. Antal, 99–170. Aldershot: Gower, 1986.

Vogel, Steven K. *Freer Markets, More Rules: Regulatory Reform in Advanced Industrial Countries.* Ithaca, NY: Cornell University Press, 1996.

Von Hagen, Jürgen. *Budgeting Procedures and Fiscal Performance in the European Communities.* University of California at Berkeley Center for German and European Studies, 1992. Political Economy of European Integration Research Group, Working Paper 1.9.

Vowles, Jack. "Dealignment and Demobilization: Nonvoting in New Zealand, 1938–1990." *Australian Journal of Political Science* 28, 1 (1994): 96–114.

Vowles, Jack. "Evaluating Electoral System Changes: The Case of New Zealand." Paper presented at the 28th World Congress of the International Political Science Association, Quebec City, August 1–5, 2000.

Vowles, Jack and Peter Aimer. *Voter's Vengeance: The 1990 Election in New Zealand and the Fate of the Fourth Labour Government.* Auckland: Auckland University Press, 1993.

Vowles, Jack and Ian McAllister. "Electoral Foundations and Electoral Consequences: From Convergence to Divergence." In *The Great Experiment: Labour Parties and Public Transformation in Aus-*

tralia and New Zealand, ed. Rolf Gerritsen, Francis Castles and Jack Vowles, 192–210. Sydney: Allen & Unwin, 1996.

Wachter, Michael L. "Cyclical Variation in the Interindustry Wage Structure." *American Economic Review* 60, 1 (1970): 75–84.

Wacquant, Loic J. D. and William J. Wilson. "Poverty, Joblessness and the Social Transformation of the Inner City." In *Welfare Policy for the 1990s,* ed. P. Cottingham and D. Ellwood, 70–102. Cambridge, MA: Harvard University Press, 1989.

Wadensjö, Eskil. "Disability Policy in Sweden." In *Public Policy Toward Disabled Workers: Cross-National Analyses of Economic Impacts,* ed. Robert H. Haveman, Victor Halberstadt, and Richard Burkhauser, 444–516. Ithaca, NY: Cornell University Press, 1984.

Waitzkin, Howard. "A Marxist Analysis of the Health Care Systems of Advanced Capitalist Societies." In *The Relevance of Social Science for Medicine,* ed. Leon Eisenberg and Arthur Kleinman, 333–369. Boston: D. Reidel, 1981.

Waldfogel, Jane. *What Do We Expect Lone Mothers to Do? Competing Agendas for Welfare Reform in the United States.* WSP 124. Suntory-Toyota International Centre for Economics and Related Disciplines, London School of Economics, 1996.

Waldmann, D. A. and B. J. Avolio. "A Meta-Analysis of Age Differences in Job Performance." *Journal of Applied Psychology* 71 (1986): 33–38.

Walker, Charles R. and Robert H. Guest. *The Man on the Assembly Line.* Cambridge: Harvard University Press, 1952.

Walker, Jack L. *Mobilizing Interest Groups in America: Patrons, Professions, and Social Movements.* Ann Arbor: University of Michigan Press, 1991.

Wallerstein, Immanuel. *The Modern World System: Capitalist Agriculture and the Origins of the World Economy in the Sixteenth Century.* New York and London: Academic Press, 1974.

Wallerstein, Michael. "Union Organization in Advanced Industrial Democracies." *American Political Science Review* 83, 2 (1989): 481–501.

Wallerstein, Michael and Miriam Golden. "The Fragmentation of the Bargaining Society: Wage-Setting in the Nordic Countries, 1950–1992." *Comparative Political Studies* 30, 6 (Dec. 1997): 699–731.

Wallis, John, Arthur Grinath, and Richard Sylla. "Debt, Default, and Revenue Structure: The Debt Crisis and American State Governments in the 1840s." Paper presented at the Conference on "Fiscal Crises in Historical Perspective," University of California, Berkeley, April 8–10, 1994.

Ward, Michael D. and David R. Davis. "Sizing Up the Peace Dividend: Economic Growth and Military Spending in the United States, 1948–1996." *American Political Science Review* 86, 3 (1992): 748–755.

Ware, Alan. *Between Profit and State: Intermediate Organizations in Britain and the United States.* Princeton: Princeton University Press, 1989.

Ware, Alan. "The Funding of Political Parties in North America: The Early Years." In *Funding Democratization: Parties and Money in the New Democracies,* ed. Peter Burnell and Alan Ware. Manchester: Manchester University Press, 1996.

Ware, John E., Jr., et al. "Comparisons of Health Outcomes at a Health Maintenance Organization With Those of Fee-for-Service Care." *The Lancet* (May 3, 1986): 1017–1022.

Ware, John E., Jr., Martha S. Bayliss, William H. Rogers, Mark Kosinski, and Alvin R. Tarlov. "Differences in 4-Year Health Outcomes for Elderly and Poor, Chronically Ill Patients Treated in HMO and Fee-for-Service Systems: Results from the Medical Outcomes Study." *Journal of the American Medical Association* 276, 13 (1996): 1039–1047.

Wasylenko, Michael and Theresa McGuire. "Jobs and Taxes: The Effect of Business Climate on States' Employment Growth Rates." *National Tax Journal* 38 (1985): 497–511.

Waters, Mary C. *Ethnic Options: Choosing Identities in America.* Berkeley, CA: University of California Press, 1990.

Waters, Mary C. "Comparing Old and New Immigrants: Historical Conditions and Prospects for Assimilation." Paper presented at a Conference on Social Fragmentation in America, American Jewish Committee and Princeton University, 1996.

Waters, Mary C. "Multiple Ethnicities and Identity Choices: Some Implications for Race and Ethnic Relations in the United States." In *We Are a People: Narrative and Multiplicity in the Construction of Ethnic Identity,* ed. Jeff Burroughs and Paul Spickard, 23–40. Philadelphia: Temple University Press, 2000.

Waters, Mary C., John Mollenkopf, and Philip Kasinitz. "The Second Generation in New York City: A Demographic Overview." Paper presented at the Population Association of America Annual Meeting, New York City, 1999.

Wattenberg, Martin P. *The Decline of American Political Parties 1952–1988.* Enlarged ed. Cambridge, MA: Harvard University Press, 1990.

Weber, Nathan. *Product Liability: The Corporate Response.* Conference Board Report 893. The Conference Board, Inc., 1987.

Wegener, Bernd. "Relative Deprivation and Social Mobility: Structural Constraints on Distributive Justice Judgments." *European Sociological Review* 7, 1 (1991): 3–18.

Weil, Frederick D. "Will Democracy Survive Unification in Germany? Extremism, Protest, and Legitimation Three Years after the Fall of the Berlin Wall." Paper presented at the American Sociological Association Annual Meeting, Miami Beach, Florida, 1993.

Weil, Frederick D. "Cohorts and the Transition to Democracy in Germany after 1945 and 1989." In *Solidarity of Generations? Demographic, Economic and Social Change, and its Consequences,* ed. Hank A. Becker and Piet L. J. Hermkens, 385–423. Amsterdam: Thesis Publishers, 1994.

Weiner, Jonathan P. "Primary Care Delivery in the United States and Four Northwest European Countries: Comparing the 'Corporatized' with the 'Socialized.' " *The Millbank Quarterly* 65, 3 (1987): 426–461.

Weintraub, Robert E. "Congressional Supervision of Monetary Policy." *Journal of Monetary Economics* 4 (1978): 341–362.

Weisbrod, Burton A. "The Future of the Nonprofit Sector: Its Entwining with Private Enterprise and Government." *Journal of Policy Analysis and Management* 16, 4 (1997): 541–555.

Weiss, Andrew. *Efficiency Wages: Models of Unemployment, Layoffs, and Wage Dispersion.* Princeton, NJ: Princeton University Press, 1990.

Weiss, Carol H. "Research for Policy's Sake: The Enlightenment Function of Social Science Research." *Policy Analysis* 3, 4 (1977): 531–545.

Weiss, Carol H. "Evaluation for Decision: Is Anybody There? Does Anybody Care?" *Evaluation Practice* 9 (1988): 5–20.

Weiss, Carol H. and Michael J. Bucuvalas. *Social Science Research and Decision-Making.* New York: Columbia University Press, 1980.

Wennemo, Irene. *Sharing the Costs of Children: Studies on the Development of Family Support in the OECD Countries.* Dissertation Series #25. Swedish Institute for Social Research, Stockholm, 1994.

West, D. J. and David P. Farrington. *The Delinquent Way of Life.* London: Heinemann, 1977.

West, Darrell M. *Air Wars: Television Advertising in Election Campaigns, 1952–1992.* Washington, DC: Congressional Quarterly Press, 1993.

Western, Bruce. "Postwar Unionization in Eighteen Advanced Capitalist Countries." *American Sociological Review* 58 (April 1993): 266–282.

Western, Bruce. "A Comparative Study of Working-Class Disorganization: Union Decline in Eighteen Advanced Capitalist Countries." *American Sociological Review* 60 (1995): 179–201.

Western, Bruce and Katherine Beckett. "How Unregulated Is the U.S. Labor Market?" *American Journal of Sociology* 104, 4 (1999): 1030–1060.

Wheldon, Huw. "Lecture Broadcast on BBC1." London: British Broadcasting Corporation, 1976.

White, Joseph. "Health Care Here and There: An International Perspective on American Reform." *Domestic Affairs* No. 2 (1993/94): 195–243.

White, Joseph. *Competing Solutions: American Health Care Proposals and International Experience.* Washington, DC: Brookings Institution, 1994.

White, Joseph. "Medical Savings Accounts: Fact versus Fiction." Brookings Occasional Papers. Washington, DC: Governmental Studies Program, Brookings Institution, 1995.

Whyte, William Foote. *Street Corner Society: The Social Structure of an Italian Slum.* Chicago: University of Chicago Press, 1943.

Whyte, William Foote, ed. *Industry and Society.* New York: McGraw-Hill, 1946.

Wildavsky, Aaron. "Doing Better and Feeling Worse: The Political Pathology of Health Policy." *Daedalus* 106 (Winter 1977): 105–123.

Wildavsky, Aaron. *Searching for Safety.* ed. Ellen Frankel Paul. Bowling Green: Social Philosophy and Policy Center, 1988.

Wildavsky, Aaron. "Is Culture the Culprit?" *The Public Interest* No. 113 (1993): 110–118.

Wildavsky, Aaron. *But Is It True? A Citizen's Guide to Environmental Health and Safety Issues.* Cambridge, MA: Harvard University Press, 1995.

Wilensky, Harold L. *Industrial Relations: A Guide to Reading and Research.* Chicago: University of Chicago Press, Syllabus Division, 1954.

Wilensky, Harold L. "The Labor Vote: A Local Union's Impact on the Political Conduct of Its Members." *Social Forces* 35 (1956a): 111–120.

Wilensky, Harold L. *Intellectuals in Labor Unions: Organizational Pressures on Professional Roles.* Glencoe, IL: Free Press, 1956b.

Wilensky, Harold L. "Human Relations in the Workplace: An Appraisal of Some Recent Research." In *Research in Industrial Human Relations,* ed. Arensberg et al., 25–54. New York: Harper and Bros., 1957.

Wilensky, Harold L. "Work, Careers, and Social Integration." *International Social Science Journal* 12 (1960): 543–560.

Wilensky, Harold L. "Orderly Careers and Social Participation: The Impact of Work History on Social Integration in the Middle Mass." *American Sociological Review* 26, 4 (1961a): 521–539.

Wilensky, Harold L. "Life Cycle, Work Situation, and Participation in Formal Associations." In *Aging and Leisure: Research Perspectives on the Meaningful Use of Time,* ed. R. W. Kleemeier, 213–242. New York: Oxford University Press, 1961b.

Wilensky, Harold L. "The Uneven Distribution of Leisure: The Impact of Economic Growth on "Free Time"." *Social Problems* 9, 1 (1961c): 32–56.

Wilensky, Harold L. "Social Structure, Popular Culture and Mass Behavior." *Studies in Public Communication* No. 3 (1961d): 15–22.

Wilensky, Harold L. "The Moonlighter: A Product of Relative Deprivation." *Industrial Relations* 3 (October 1963): 105–124.

Wilensky, Harold L. "Mass Society and Mass Culture: Interdependence or Independence?" *American Sociological Review* 29 (1964a): 173–197.

Wilensky, Harold L. "The Professionalization of Everyone?" *American Journal of Sociology* 70 (1964b): 137–158.

Wilensky, Harold L. "Varieties of Work Experience." In *Man in a World at Work,* ed. H. Borow, 125–154. Boston: Houghton Mifflin, 1964c.

Wilensky, Harold L. "The Problems and Prospects of the Welfare State." In *Industrial Society and Social Welfare* by Harold L. Wilensky and Charles N. Lebeaux, v–lii. Enlarged Edition. New York: Free Press-Macmillan, 1965.

Wilensky, Harold L. "Class, Class Consciousness, and American Workers." In *Labor in a Changing America,* ed. William Haber, 12–44. New York: Basic Books, 1966a.

Wilensky, Harold L. "Measures and Effects of Social Mobility." In *Social Structure, Social Mobility and Economic Development,* ed. Neil J. Smelser and Seymour M. Lipset, 98–140. Chicago, IL: Aldine Press, 1966b.

Wilensky, Harold L. "Work as a Social Problem." In *Social Problems,* ed. Howard S. Becker, 117–166. New York: John Wiley, 1966c.

Wilensky, Harold L. *Organizational Intelligence: Knowledge and Policy in Government and Industry.* New York: Basic Books, 1967a.

Wilensky, Harold L. "Careers, Counseling, and the Curriculum." *The Journal of Human Resources* 2 (1967b): 19–40.

Wilensky, Harold L. "Women's Work: Economic Growth, Ideology, and Social Structure." *Industrial Relations: A Journal of Economy and Society* 7 (1968): 235–248.

Wilensky, Harold L. *The Welfare State and Equality: Structural and Ideological Roots of Public Expenditures.* Berkeley: University of California Press, 1975.

Wilensky, Harold L. *The 'New Corporatism,' Centralization and the Welfare State.* London and Beverly Hills: Sage, 1976a.

Wilensky, Harold L. "The Welfare Mess: Is It American, Who Needs It, Will It Last?" *Society* 13 (May–June 1976b): 12–16, 64.

Wilensky, Harold L. "The Political Economy of Income Distribution: Issues in the Analysis of Government Approaches to the Reduction of Inequality." In *Major Social Issues: A Multi-disciplinary View,* ed. Milton J. Yinger and S. J. Cutler, 87–108. New York: Free Press, 1978.

Wilensky, Harold L. "Taxing, Spending, and Backlash: An American Peculiarity?" *Taxing and Spending* 2, 3 (July 1979): 6–12; and subsequent exchange between Stubblebine, van den Haag, Gilder, and Wilensky in *Taxing and Spending* 2, 4 (1979): 7–12.

Wilensky, Harold L. "Foreword" to *Ideology, Public Opinion, and Welfare Policy: Attitudes Toward Taxes and Spending in Industrialized Societies,* by Richard M. Couglin, xi–xiv. Berkeley: Institute of International Studies, 1980.

Wilensky, Harold L. "Democratic Corporatism, Consensus, and Social Policy: Reflections on Changing Values and the 'Crisis' of the Welfare State." In *The Welfare State in Crisis: An Account of the Conference on Social Policies in the 1980's,* 185–195. Paris: OECD, 1981a.

Wilensky, Harold L. "Family Life Cycle, Work, and the Quality of Life: Reflections on the Roots of Happiness, Despair and Indifference in Modern Society." In *Working Life: A Social Science Contribution to Work Reform,* ed. Bertil B. Gardell and Gunn Johansson, 235–265. London: John Wiley, 1981b.

Wilensky, Harold L. "Leftism, Catholicism, and Democratic Corporatism: The Role of Political Parties in Welfare State Development." In *The Development of Welfare States in Europe and America,* ed. Peter Flora and Arnold J. Heidenheimer, 345–382. New Brunswick, NJ: Transaction Books, 1981c.

Wilensky, Harold L. "Foreword" to *Voluntary Agencies in the Welfare State,* Ralph Kramer, xiv–xxvii. Berkeley: University of California Press, 1981d.

Wilensky, Harold L. "Ideology, Education, and Social Security." In *Income-Tested Transfer Programs: The Case for and Against,* ed. Irwin Garfinkel, 166–173. New York: Academic Press, 1982.

Wilensky, Harold L. "Political Legitimacy and Consensus: Missing Variables in the Assessment of Social Policy." In *Evaluating the Welfare State: Social and Political Perspectives,* ed. S. E. Spiro and E. Yuchtman-Yaar, 51–74. New York: Academic Press, 1983.

Wilensky, Harold L. "Preface to the Japanese edition" of *The Welfare State and Equality,* 2–14. Tokyo: Bokutakusha Publishing Company, 1984.

Wilensky, Harold L. "Nothing Fails Like Success: The Evaluation-Research Industry and Labor-Market Policy." *Industrial Relations: A Journal of Economy and Society* 24, 1 (1985): 1–19.

Wilensky, Harold L. "Common Problems, Divergent Policies: An 18-Nation Study of Family Policy." *Public Affairs Report* 31: 1–3. Institute of Governmental Studies, University of California, 1990.

Wilensky, Harold L. "What's Wrong With American Democracy?" Unpublished paper, Institute of Governmental Studies, University of California at Berkeley, July 5, 1991.

Wilensky, Harold L. "Active Labor-Market Policy: Its Content, Effectiveness, and Odd Relation to Evaluation Research." In *Social Research and Social Reform,* ed. Colin Crouch and Anthony Heath, 315–350. Oxford: Oxford University Press, 1992a.

Wilensky, Harold L. "The Great American Job Creation Machine in Comparative Perspective." *Industrial Relations: A Journal of Economy and Society* 31, 3 (1992b): 473–488.

Wilensky, Harold L. "The Nation-State, Social Policy, and Economic Performance." In *Globalizzazione e sistemi di welfare,* ed. M. Ferrara, 41–63. Torino, Italy: Edzioni della Fondazione G. Agnelli, 1993.

Wilensky, Harold L. "Social Science and the Public Agenda: Reflections on the Relation of Knowledge to Policy in the United States and Abroad." *Journal of Health Politics, Policy and Law* 22, 5 (1997): 1241–1265.

Wilensky, Harold L. and Hugh Edwards. "The Skidder: Ideological Adjustments of Downwardly Mobile Workers." *American Sociological Review* 24, 2 (1959): 215–231.

Wilensky, Harold L. and Jack Ladinsky. "From Religious Community to Occupational Group: Structural Assimilation among Professors, Lawyers, and Engineers." *American Sociological Review* 32 (1967): 541–561.

Wilensky, Harold L. and Anne T. Lawrence. "Job Assignment in Modern Societies: A Re-examination of the Ascription-Achievement Hypothesis." In *Societal Growth: Processes and Implications,* ed. Amos H. Hawley, 202–248. New York: Free Press-Macmillan, 1979.

Wilensky, Harold L. and Charles N. Lebeaux. *Industrial Society and Social Welfare: The Impact of Industrialization on the Supply and Organization of Social Welfare Services in the United States.* New York: Russell Sage Foundation, 1958.

Wilensky, Harold L., Gregory M. Luebbert, Susan R. Hahn, and Adrienne M. Jamieson. *Comparative Social Policy: Theories, Methods, Findings.* Research Monograph Series #62, Berkeley, CA: Institute of International Studies, University of California, Berkeley, 1985.

Wilensky, Harold L. and Lowell Turner. *Democratic Corporatism and Policy Linkages: The Interdependence of Industrial, Labor-Market, Incomes and Social Policies in Eight Countries.* Research Monograph Series #69, Berkeley, CA: Institute of International Studies, University of California, Berkeley, 1987.

Wilkinson, Richard G. "National Mortality Rates: The Impact of Inequality." *American Journal of Public Health* 82 (1992): 1082–1086.

Williams, Bret C. and C. Arden Miller. *Preventive Health Care for Young Children: Findings from a 10-Country Study and Directions for United States Policy.* National Center for Clinical Infant Programs, 1991.

Williams, Gregory. "A Research Note on Trends in Occupational Differentiation by Sex." *Social Problems* 22 (1975): 543–547.

Williams, Lucy. "The Ideology of Division: Behavior Modification Welfare Reform Proposals." *Yale Law Journal* 102 (1992): 719–746.

Williams, T. M. *The Impact of Television: A Natural Experiment in Three Communities.* Orlando, FL: Academic Press, 1986.

Williamson, John B. and Fred C. Pampel. *Old-Age Security in Comparative Perspective.* New York: Oxford University Press, 1993.

Wilson, Graham K. "Why Is There No Corporatism in the United States?" In *Patterns of Corporatist Policy-Making,* ed. Gerhard Lehmbruch and Philippe Schmitter, 219–236. Beverly Hills, CA: Sage, 1982.

Wilson, Graham K. *Interest Groups.* Oxford: Basil Blackwell, 1990.

Wilson, James Q. Book Review of Sparrow et al. *Beyond 911: A New Era for Policing. Washington Monthly* 22, 9 (1990): 58–60.

Wilson, James Q. "Prisons in a Free Society." *The Public Interest* No. 117 (1994): 37–48.

Wilson, James Q. and Richard J. Herrnstein. *Crime and Human Nature.* New York: Simon & Schuster, 1985.

Wilson, James Q. and George L. Kelling. "Making Neighborhoods Safe." *The Atlantic Monthly* 263, 2 (1989): 46–52.

Wilson, William J. *The Declining Significance of Race: Blacks and Changing American Institutions.* Chicago: The University of Chicago Press, 1978.

Wilson, William J. *The Truly Disadvantaged: The Inner City, The Underclass, and Public Policy.* Chicago: University of Chicago Press, 1987.

Wilson, William J. "Poverty, Joblessness, and Family Structure in the Inner City: A Comparative Perspective." Chicago Urban Poverty and Family Life Conference in Chicago, IL, 1991a.

Wilson, William J. "The Truly Disadvantaged Revisited: A Response to Hochschild and Boxill." *Ethics* 101, 3 (1991b): 593–609.

Wilson, William J. *When Work Disappears: The World of the New Urban Poor.* New York City: Knopf, 1996.

Winch, Robert F. and Scott A. Greer. "Urbanism, Ethnicity, and Extended Familialism." *Journal of Marriage and the Family* 30 (February 1968): 40–45.

Wingard, Deborah L., Lisa F. Berkman, and Richard J. Brand. "A Multivariate Analysis of Health-Related Practices: A Nine-Year Mortality Follow-Up of the Alameda County Study." *American Journal of Epidemiology* 116, 5 (1982): 765–775.

Winnick, Louis. "Is Reinventing Government Enough?" *City Journal* 3, 3 (1993): 18–29.

Winock, Michel. *Nationalisme, antisémitisme et fascisme en France.* Paris: Seuil, 1990.

Winstrand, Birgitta. *Swedish Women on the Move.* Translated and edited by Jeanne Rosen. Stockholm: Swedish Insitute, 1981.

Wirth, Louis. *The Ghetto.* Chicago: University of Chicago Press, 1928.

Wirtz, Willard W. *The Older American Worker: Age Discrimination in Employment.* U.S. Government Printing Office, 1965. A report of the Secretary of Labor to the Congress under Section 715 of the Civil Rights Act of 1964.

Wissow, Lawrence S. and Barbara Starfield. "Asthma." In *The Effectiveness of Medical Care: Validating Clinical Wisdom,* ed. Barbara Starfield, Lisa Egbuonu, Mark Farfel, Nancy Hutton, Alan Joffe, and Lawrence S. Wissow, 130–135. Baltimore: Johns Hopkins University Press, 1985a.

Wissow, Lawrence S. and Barbara Starfield. "Child Battering (abuse)." In *The Effectiveness of Medical Care: Validating Clinical Wisdom,* ed. Barbara Starfield, Lisa Egbuonu, Mark Farfel, Nancy Hutton, Alain Joffe, and Lawrence S. Wissow, 63–68. Baltimore: Johns Hopkins University Press, 1985b.

Wolff, Edward N., ed. *International Comparisons of the Distribution of Household Wealth.* Oxford: Clarendon Press, 1987.

Wolff, Edward N. *Top Heavy: A Study of the Increasing Inequality of Wealth in America.* Twentieth Century Fund Report. New York: The Twentieth Century Fund Press, 1995.

Wolff, Edward N. "Recent Trends in Asset Ownership." In *Assets and the Disadvantaged,* ed. Thomas M. Shapiro and Edward N. Wolff. New York: Russell Sage, forthcoming.

Wolfgang, Marvin E., Robert Figlio, and Thorsten Sellin. *Delinquency in a Birth Cohort.* Chicago: University of Chicago Press, 1972.

Wolfinger, Raymond E. "Why Political Machines Have Not Withered Away and Other Revisionist Thoughts." *The Journal of Politics* 34 (1972): 365–398.

Wolfinger, Raymond E., David P. Glass, and Peverill Squire. "Predictors of Electoral Turnout: An International Comparison." *Policy Studies Review* 9, 3 (1990): 551–574.

Wolfinger, Raymond E. and Benjamin Highton. "Can More Efficient Purging Boost Turnout?" Paper presented at Annual Meeting of the American Political Science Association, New York City, September 1–4, 1994.

Wolfinger, Raymond E. and Steven J. Rosenstone. *Who Votes?* New Haven: Yale University Press, 1980.

Wolfsfeld, Gadi. "The Politics of Provocation Revisited: Participation and Protest in Israel." In *Israeli Democracy Under Stress,* ed. Ehud Sprinzak and Larry Diamond, 199–220. Boulder, CO, and London: Lynne Rienner, 1993.

Wolinetz, Steven B. "Wage Regulation in the Netherlands: The Rise and Fall of the Postwar Social Contract." Paper presented at the Council for European Studies, 4th Annual Conference of Europeanists, Washington, DC, October 1985.

Wolinetz, Steven B. "Socio-economic Bargaining in the Netherlands: Redefining the Post-War Policy Coalition." *West European Politics* 12, 1 (1989): 79–98.

Wolinetz, Steven B. "A Quarter Century of Dutch Politics: A Changing Political System or le plus que change . . . ?" *Acta Politica* 25 (1990): 403–431.

Wolinetz, Steven B. "Is There Life After Corporatism? Tripartite Encounters in the Netherlands in the 1980s and Beyond." Unpublished manuscript, Memorial University of Newfoundland, St. Johns Newfoundland, Canada, 1993.

Wolinetz, Steven B. "Modell Nederland: Social Partnership and Competitive Corporatism in the Netherlands." In *Unemployment in the New Europe,* ed. Nancy Bermeo. Cambridge: Cambridge University Press, 2001.

Wolton, Dominique. "Values and Normative Choices in French Television." In *Television and the Public Interest: Vulnerable Values in West European Broadcasting,* ed. Jay G. Blumler. London: Sage (in association with the Broadcasting Standards Council), 1992.

Womack, James D., Daniel T. Jones, and Daniel Roos. *The Machine That Changed the World.* New York: Rawson, 1990.

Woods, Dwayne. "The Crisis of Center-Periphery Integration in Italy and the Rise of Regional Populism." *Comparative Politics* 27, 2 (1995): 187–203.

Woodward, Douglas P. and Norman J. Glickman. "Regional and Local Determinants of Foreign Firm Location in the United States." In *Industry, Location and Public Policy,* ed. Henry W. Herzog, Jr., and Alan M. Schlottmann, 190–217. Knoxville: University of Tennessee, 1991.

Woolhandler, Steffie and David Himmelstein. "The Deteriorating Administrative Efficiency of the U.S. Health Care System." *New England Journal of Medicine* 324, 18 (May 1991): 1253–1258.

Woolley, John T. *Monetary Politics.* Cambridge, UK: Cambridge University Press, 1984.

World Almanac and Book of Facts 1999. Mahway, NJ: World Almanac Books, 1998.

World Bank. *World Tables.* 1988–1989 ed. Baltimore: Johns Hopkins University Press, 1989.

World Bank. *World Development Report 1990.* New York: Oxford University Press, 1990.

World Bank. *World Development Report 1993: Investing in Health.* New York: Oxford University Press, 1993.

World Health Organization. *World Health Statistics Annual 1988.* Geneva: World Health Organization, 1988.

World Health Organization. *Health Statistics Annual 1993.* Geneva: World Health Organization, 1994.

Wright, Charles R. and Herbert H. Hyman. "Voluntary Association Memberships of American Adults: Evidence from National Sample Surveys." *American Sociological Review* 23 (June 1958): 284–294.

Wright, Erik Olin, Janeen Baxter, and Gunn Elisabeth with Birkelund. "The Gender Gap in Workplace Authority: A Cross-National Study." *American Sociological Review* 60 (1995): 407–435.

Wright, Erik Olin and Donmoon Cho. "The Relative Permeability of Class Boundaries to Cross-Class Friendships: A Comparative Study of the United States, Canada, Sweden, and Norway." *American Sociological Review* 57, 1 (Feb. 1992): 85–103.

Wright, John C. and Aletha C. Huston. "Effects of Educational TV Viewing of Lower Income Preschoolers on Academic Skills, School Readiness, and School Adjustment One to Three Years Later." Report to Children's Television Workshop, Center for Research on the Influences of Television on Children. The University of Kansas, Lawrence, KS, 1995.

Wu, Lawrence, L. "Effects of Family Structure and Income on Risks of Premarital Birth." *American Sociological Review* 61, 3 (1996): 386–406.

Wuthnow, Robert. *Sharing the Journey: Support Groups and America's New Quest for Community.* New York: Free Press, 1994.

Wyn, Grant. "Is Agricultural Policy Still Exceptional?" *The Political Quarterly* 66, 3 (1995): 156–169.

Yamagishi, Toshio, Karen S. Cook, and Motoki Watabe. "Uncertainty, Trust, and Commitment Formation in the United States and Japan." *American Journal of Sociology* 104, 1 (1998): 165–194.

Yankelovich, Daniel. "How Changes in the Economy Are Reshaping American Values." In *Values and Public Policy,* ed. Henry J. Aaron, Thomas E. Mann, and Timothy Taylor, 16–53. Washington, DC: Brookings Institution, 1994.

Zaller, John and Mark Hunt. "The Rise and Fall of Candidate Perot: Unmediated Versus Mediated Politics—Part I." *Political Communication* 11, 4 (1994): 357–390.

Zaller, John and Mark Hunt. "The Rise and Fall of Candidate Perot: The Outsider Versus the Political System—Part II." *Political Communication* 12, 1 (1995): 97–123.

Zaller, John R. *The Nature and Origin of Mass Opinion.* New York: Cambridge University Press, 1992.

Zhou, Min. "Growing Up American: The Challenge Confronting Immigrant Children and Children of Immigrants." *Annual Review of Sociology* 23 (1997): 63–95.

Zimring, Franklin E. and Gordon Hawkins. *Crime Is Not the Problem: Lethal Violence in America.* New York: Oxford University Press, 1997.

Zincone, Giovanna. "The Political Rights of Immigrants in Italy." *New Community* 20, 1 (1993): 131–145.

Zincone, Giovanna. "Immigration to Italy: Data and Policies." In *Migration Policies—A Comparative Perspective,* ed. M. F. Heckmann and W. Bosswick. Bamberg: 1994.

Zolberg, Aristide R., Astri Suhrke, and Sergio Aguayo. *Escape from Violence: Conflict and the Refugee Crisis in the Developing World.* New York: Oxford University Press, 1989.

Zysman, John. *Governments, Markets, and Growth: Finance and the Politics of Industrial Change.* Ithaca, NY: Cornell University Press, 1983

INDEX

Page numbers in italics refer to tables and figures

Text: 10/13 Bembo
Display: Bembo
Compositor: Impressions Book and Journal Services, Inc.
Printer: Sheridan Books, Inc.